The Cambridge Handbook of Violent Behavior and Aggression

Second Edition

The Cambridge Handbook of Violent Behavior and Aggression presents the current state of knowledge related to the study of violent behaviors and aggression. An important extension of the first Handbook published ten years ago, the second edition maintains a distinctly cross-disciplinary focus by representing the newest scholarship and insights from behavior genetics, cross-cultural comparative psychology/criminology, evolutionary psychology, criminal justice, criminology, human development, molecular genetics, neurosciences, psychology, prevention and intervention sciences, psychiatry, psychopharmacology, public health, and sociology. The Handbook is divided into introductory and overview chapters on the study of violent behavior and aggression, followed by chapters on biosocial bases, individual and interpersonal factors, contextual factors, and prevention and intervention work and policy implications. It is an essential resource for researchers, scholars, and graduate students across social and behavioral science disciplines interested in the etiology, intervention, and prevention of violent behavior and aggression.

ALEXANDER T. VAZSONYI is the John I. and Patricia J. Buster Endowed Professor of Family Sciences, Professor of Psychology, and Professor of Sociology at the University of Kentucky. He is recognized as a leading scholar in criminology and in cross-cultural comparative research on adolescent development and has published more than 100 peer-reviewed papers. He was a Fulbright fellow in Slovenia (2004) and the Fulbright-Masaryk University Distinguished Chair in Social Studies (2010) in the Czech Republic. He is editor-in-chief of the *Journal of Early Adolescence* and the editor of the five-volume *Adolescence* (2015).

DANIEL J. FLANNERY is the Dr. Semi J. and Ruth W. Begun Professor and Director of the Begun Center for Violence Prevention Research and Education at Case Western Reserve University. He served as founding director of the Institute for the Study and Prevention of Violence at Kent State University. He is the author of *Wanted on Warrants: The Fugitive Safe Surrender Program* (2013) and *Violence and Mental Health in Everyday Life* (2006). He has more than 100 peer-reviewed publications and has advised the Institute of Medicine, the US Departments of Justice and Education, the Centers for Disease Control and Prevention, the National Crime Prevention Council, and the National Resource Center for Safe Schools.

MATT DELISI is Professor and Coordinator of Criminal Justice Studies and Affiliate with the Center for the Study of Violence at Iowa State University. He is the author of over 350 scholarly publications, mostly in the areas of pathological criminality, psychopathy, and self-control. A fellow of the Academy of Criminal Justice Sciences, he has consulted on capital murder and multiple-homicide offender cases in numerous federal and state jurisdictions, provided testimony to the United States Senate Judiciary Committee, and consulted on criminal justice policy to a variety of federal stakeholders including the United States Attorney General, United States Probation and Pretrial Services, and the Federal Bureau of Investigation.

The Cambridge Handbook of Violent Behavior and Aggression

Second Edition

Edited by

Alexander T. Vazsonyi
University of Kentucky

Daniel J. Flannery
Case Western Reserve University

Matt DeLisi
Iowa State University

CAMBRIDGE
UNIVERSITY PRESS

University Printing House, Cambridge CB2 8BS, United Kingdom

One Liberty Plaza, 20th Floor, New York, NY 10006, USA

477 Williamstown Road, Port Melbourne, VIC 3207, Australia

314-321, 3rd Floor, Plot 3, Splendor Forum, Jasola District Centre, New Delhi – 110025, India

79 Anson Road, #06-04/06, Singapore 079906

Cambridge University Press is part of the University of Cambridge.

It furthers the University's mission by disseminating knowledge in the pursuit of education, learning, and research at the highest international levels of excellence.

www.cambridge.org
Information on this title: www.cambridge.org/9781316632215
DOI: 10.1017/9781316847992

First and Second editions © Cambridge University Press 2007, 2018

This publication is in copyright. Subject to statutory exception and to the provisions of relevant collective licensing agreements, no reproduction of any part may take place without the written permission of Cambridge University Press.

First published 2007

Second edition 2018

Printed and bound in Great Britain by Clays Ltd, Elcograf S.p.A.

A catalogue record for this publication is available from the British Library.

Library of Congress Cataloging-in-Publication Data
Names: Vazsonyi, Alexander T., 1964– editor. | Flannery, Daniel J., 1962– editor. | DeLisi, Matt, editor.
Title: The Cambridge handbook of violent behavior and aggression / edited by Alexander T. Vazsonyi, University of Kentucky, Daniel J. Flannery, Case Western Reserve University, Ohio, Matt DeLisi, Iowa State University.
Description: Second edition. | Cambridge, United Kingdom; New York, NY: Cambridge University Press, 2018. | Includes bibliographical references and index.
Identifiers: LCCN 2017053514 | ISBN 9781107180437 (hardback) | ISBN 9781316632215 (paperback)
Subjects: LCSH: Violence. | Aggressiveness. | Deviant behavior. | Antisocial personality disorders.
Classification: LCC HM1116 .C36 2018 | DDC 303.6–dc23
LC record available at https://lccn.loc.gov/2017053514

ISBN 978-1-107-18043-7 Hardback
ISBN 978-1-316-63221-5 Paperback

Cambridge University Press has no responsibility for the persistence or accuracy of URLs for external or third-party internet websites referred to in this publication and does not guarantee that any content on such websites is, or will remain, accurate or appropriate.

We dedicate this book to our children Alexander, Philip, Marc, and Katarina (AV); Joseph, Patrick, Ellen, and Katie (DF); Jamison, Landon, and Finley (MD)

Each of you continues to both test and surprise us!

Contents

List of Contributors *page* xi

Introduction: The Cambridge Handbook of Violent Behavior and Aggression xv
ALEXANDER T. VAZSONYI, DANIEL J. FLANNERY, AND MATT DELISI

Part I Introduction and Overview

1 Origins of Violent Behavior over the Life Span 3
DAVID P. FARRINGTON

2 Longitudinal Study of Personality and Social Development: Insights about Aggression after Five Decades 31
LEA PULKKINEN

3 A Life-Course Model for the Development of Intimate Partner Violence 52
J. MARK EDDY, JEAN SCHUMER, JOANN WU SHORTT,
DEBORAH M. CAPALDI, STACEY S. TIBERIO, AND SABINA LOW

4 The Dark Violence Hybrid: The Cross-Cultural Validation of an Integrative Model 65
AURELIO JOSÉ FIGUEREDO, EMILY ANNE PATCH,
MARISOL PEREZ-RAMOS, AND GABRIELA JACQUELINE CRUZ

Part II Biosocial Foundations of Violence and Aggression

5 The Behavioral Genetics of Aggression and Violent Behavior 83
J. C. BARNES AND JORIM TIELBEEK

6 Neuroimaging Evidence of Violence and Aggression 106
HEATHER MCLERNON, JEREMY FEIGER, AND ROBERT SCHUG

7 Biosocial Bases of Aggression and Antisocial Behavior 125
JILL PORTNOY

8 The Neuropsychology of Violence 136
JEAN R. SÉGUIN, LINDA BOOIJ, AND SCOTT O. LILIENFELD

9	The Interaction of Nature and Nurture in Antisocial Behavior MATT DELISI	159
10	The Neurobiology of Bullying Victimization TRACY VAILLANCOURT	175
11	Molecular Genetics of Aggression and Violent Crime CASHEN M. BOCCIO, MARIANNA MCBRIDE, AND KEVIN M. BEAVER	187
12	Biosocial Foundations of Drug Abuse and Violent Delinquency MICHAEL G. VAUGHN, CHRISTOPHER P. SALAS-WRIGHT, AND JENNIFER M. REINGLE-GONZALEZ	206
13	Personality and Aggression: A General Trait Perspective COURTLAND S. HYATT, CHELSEA E. SLEEP, BRANDON M. WEISS, AND JOSHUA D. MILLER	221

Part III Individual and Interpersonal Factors for Violence and Aggression

14	Applying Empirically Based Trait Models to an Understanding of Personality and Violence DANIEL M. BLONIGEN AND CHRISTOPHER J. PATRICK	241
15	Social-Cognitive Processes in the Development of Antisocial and Violent Behavior BRIAN ENJAIAN, SARAH BETH BELL, ZACHARY WHITT, AND C. NATHAN DEWALL	259
16	Violent Juvenile Offenders: A Psychiatric and Mental Health Perspective MARCEL AEBI AND HANS-CHRISTOPH STEINHAUSEN	278
17	Self-Control Theory and Criminal Violence MICHAEL R. GOTTFREDSON	301
18	Peers and Aggression: From Description to Prevention FRANK VITARO, MARA BRENDGEN, AND MICHEL BOIVIN	324
19	Developmental Processes of Resilience and Risk for Aggression and Conduct Problems J. J. CUTULI, JORGE M. CARVALHO PEREIRA, SARAH C. VRABIC, AND JANETTE E. HERBERS	345
20	Child Abuse and Neglect TAMARA DEL VECCHIO, RICHARD E. HEYMAN, AMY M. SMITH SLEP, AND HEATHER M. FORAN	366
21	The Role of Gender in Violent and Aggressive Behaviors JAMIE M. OSTROV AND KRISTIN J. PERRY	382

22 Lessons Learned: Serial Sex Offenders Identified from Backlogged
    Sexual Assault Kits (SAKs) — 399
    RACHEL LOVELL, DANIEL J. FLANNERY, AND MISTY LUMINAIS

23 Research on Social Structure and Cross-National Homicide Rates — 418
    MEGHAN L. ROGERS AND WILLIAM ALEX PRIDEMORE

24 Preventing Violent Crimes by Reducing Wrongful Convictions — 438
    BRIAN FORST AND C. RONALD HUFF

25 Strain Theory and Violent Behavior — 453
    ROBERT AGNEW AND BYONGOOK MOON

26 On Cumulative Childhood Traumatic Exposure and Violence/
    Aggression: The Implications of Adverse Childhood Experiences (ACE) — 467
    MICHAEL T. BAGLIVIO

Part IV Contextual Factors for Violence and Aggression

27 Youth Gangs and Violent Behavior — 491
    VICTOR MORA AND SCOTT H. DECKER

28 Social Networks and Violence — 513
    MARK S. FLEISHER AND CHRISTOPHER C. MCCARTY

29 The Contagion of Violence — 527
    L. ROWELL HUESMANN

30 School Violence — 557
    GARY D. GOTTFREDSON AND DENISE C. GOTTFREDSON

31 Violence and Culture in the United States — 575
    MARK WARR

32 Violence Prevention in a Global Context: Progress and
    Priorities for Moving Forward — 589
    LINDA L. DAHLBERG, ALEXANDER BUTCHART, AND
    CHRISTOPHER MIKTON

33 Terrorism as a Form of Violence — 626
    KEVIN R. CARRIERE, GEORGIA GARNEY, AND
    FATHALI M. MOGHADDAM

34 Psychopharmacology of Violence — 645
    JAN VOLAVKA AND LESLIE CITROME

35 Individual, Family, Neighborhood, and Regional Poverty/
    Socioeconomic Status and Exposure to Violence in the Lives of
    Children and Adolescents: Considering the Global North and South — 654
    HOLLY FOSTER AND JEANNE BROOKS-GUNN

36 Firearms and Violence   687
    BRANDON TURCHAN AND ANTHONY A. BRAGA

Part V Looking Toward the Future

37 The Interrelationship of Self-Control and Violent
    Behavior: Pathways and Policies   711
    BRIE DIAMOND, JENNIFER R. GONZALEZ, WESLEY JENNINGS, AND
    ALEX R. PIQUERO

38 The New Frontier: Leveraging Innovative Technologies
    to Prevent Bullying   724
    CATHERINE P. BRADSHAW, LINDSEY M. O'BRENNAN,
    TRACY E. WAASDORP, ELISE PAS, JULIA BLUMENSTYK,
    DANIELLE BARTOLO, AND STEPHEN S. LEFF

39 Neural Substrates of Youth and Adult Antisocial Behavior   736
    REBECCA WALLER, HAILEY L. DOTTERER, LAURA MURRAY,
    AND LUKE W. HYDE

40 Research Designs and Methods for Evaluating and Refining
    Interventions for Youth Violence Prevention   756
    ALBERT D. FARRELL AND KRISTA R. MEHARI

41 New Directions in Research on Violence: Bridging Science,
    Practice, and Policy   777
    ALEXANDER T. VAZSONYI, DANIEL J. FLANNERY, AND MATT DELISI

    Index   791

Contributors

Marcel Aebi
University of Zurich

Robert Agnew
Emory University

Michael T. Baglivio
TrueCore Behavioral Solutions

J. C. Barnes
University of Cincinnati

Danielle Bartolo
Ad Council

Kevin M. Beaver
Florida State University

Sarah Beth Bell
University of Kentucky

Daniel M. Blonigen
Palo Alto University

Julia Blumenstyk
Ad Council

Cashen M. Boccio
Florida State University

Michel Boivin
Université Laval

Linda Booij
Concordia University

Catherine P. Bradshaw
University of Virginia

Anthony A. Braga
Northeastern University

Mara Brendgen
University of Quebec at Montreal

Jeanne Brooks-Gunn
Columbia University

Alexander Butchart
World Health Organization

Deborah M. Capaldi
Oregon Social Learning Center

Kevin R. Carriere
Georgetown University

Jorge M. Carvalho Pereira
University of Utah

Leslie Citrome
New York Medical College

Gabriela Jacqueline Cruz
Metropolitan Autonomous University Campus Iztapalapa (UAM-I), Mexico City, Mexico

J. J. Cutuli
Rutgers University–Camden

Linda L. Dahlberg
Center for Disease Control and Prevention

Scott H. Decker
Arizona State University

Tamara Del Vecchio
St. John's University

Matt DeLisi
Iowa State University

C. Nathan DeWall
University of Kentucky

Brie Diamond
Texas Christian University

Contributors

Hailey L. Dotterer
University of Michigan

J. Mark Eddy
New York University

Brian Enjaian
University of Kentucky

Albert D. Farrell
Virginia Commonwealth University

David P. Farrington
Cambridge University

Jeremy Feiger
Cal State University, Long Beach

Aurelio José Figueredo
The University of Arizona

Daniel J. Flannery
Case Western Reserve University

Mark S. Fleisher
Case Western Reserve University

Heather M. Foran
Alpen-Adria-Universität Klagenfurt

Holly Foster
Texas A&M University

Brian Forst
American University

Georgia Garney
Georgetown University

Jennifer R. Gonzalez
University of Texas Southwestern Medical Center

Denise C. Gottfredson
University of Maryland

Gary D. Gottfredson
University of Maryland

Michael R. Gottfredson
UC Irvine

Janette E. Herbers
Villanova University

Richard E. Heyman
New York University

L. Rowell Huesmann
University of Michigan

C. Ronald Huff
UC Irvine

Courtland S. Hyatt
University of Georgia

Luke W. Hyde
University of Michigan

Wesley Jennings
University of South Florida

Stephen S. Leff
Children's Hospital of Philadelphia

Scott O. Lilienfeld
Emory University

Rachel Lovell
Case Western Reserve University

Sabina Low
Arizona State University

Misty Luminais
Case Western Reserve University

Marianna McBride
Florida State University

Christopher C. McCarty
University of Florida

Heather McLernon
California State University, Long Beach

Krista R. Mehari
University of South Alabama

Christopher Mikton
World Health Organization

Joshua D. Miller
University of Georgia

Fathali M. Moghaddam
Georgetown University

Byongook Moon
University of Texas San Antonio

Victor Mora
World Health Organization

Laura Murray
University of Michigan

Lindsey M. O'Brennan
University of South Florida

Jamie M. Ostrov
University of Buffalo

Elise Pas
Johns Hopkins University

Emily Anne Patch
University of Arizona

Christopher J. Patrick
Florida State University

Marisol Perez-Ramos
Metropolitan Autonomous University Campus Iztapalapa (UAM-I), Mexico City, Mexico

Kristin J. Perry
University of Buffalo

Alex R. Piquero
University of Texas at Dallas

Jill Portnoy
University of Pennsylvania

William Alex Pridemore
University at Albany-SUNY

Lea Pulkkinen
University of Jyväskylä

Jennifer M. Reingle-Gonzalez
University of Texas Southwestern Medical Center

Meghan L. Rogers
University at Albany–SUNY

Christopher P. Salas-Wright
Boston University

Robert Schug
California State University, Long Beach

Jean Schumer
Oregon State University

Jean R. Séguin
University of Montreal

Chelsea E. Sleep
University of Georgia

Amy M. Smith Slep
New York University

Hans-Christoph Steinhausen
University of Basel

Stacey S. Tiberio
Oregon Social Learning Center

Jorim Tielbeek
VU University Medical Center
Vrije Universiteit Amsterdam

Brandon Turchan
Rutgers, The State University of New Jersey

Tracy Vaillancourt
University of Ottawa

Michael G. Vaughn
Saint Louis University

Alexander T. Vazsonyi
University of Kentucky

Frank Vitaro
University of Montreal

Jan Volavka
New York University School of Medicine

Sarah C. Vrabic
Villanova University

Rebecca Waller
University of Michigan

Mark Warr
University of Texas at Austin

Tracy E. Waasdorp
Johns Hopkins University

Brandon M. Weiss
University of Georgia

Zachary Whitt
University of Kentucky

Joann Wu Shortt
Oregon Social Learning Center

Introduction: The Cambridge Handbook of Violent Behavior and Aggression

Alexander T. Vazsonyi, Daniel J. Flannery, and Matt DeLisi

The second edition of *The Cambridge Handbook of Violent Behavior and Aggression* represents an important extension of the first Handbook, published ten years ago. We believe we have been able to compile the current state of the art and state of our knowledge related to the study of violent behavior and aggression. As we did with the first edition, we maintain the distinctly cross-disciplinary focus, represented by the newest scholarship and insights from behavior genetics, cross-cultural comparative psychology/criminology, evolutionary psychology, criminal justice, criminology, human development, molecular genetics, neurosciences, psychology, prevention and intervention sciences, psychiatry, psychopharmacology, public health, and sociology. We find that this feature is paramount as our understanding of violent behavior and aggression is informed by a multitude of efforts originating from across all these areas of study and disciplines.

Each editor brought to this Handbook different and unique strengths, experiences, and networks of colleagues, which proved critical to being able to successfully recruit the current panel of expert contributors. We were quite fortunate to be able to add Matt DeLisi to our editorial team – he was essential in making the Handbook what it is, in so many different ways. We maintained a similar structure of the Handbook, which is divided into (1) introductory and overview chapters on the study of violent behavior and aggression; (2) chapters focused on biosocial bases; (3) individual and interpersonal factors; (4) contextual factors; and finally, (5) a section on "looking toward the future" that includes four content chapters in addition to a conclusion by the editors, which examines prevention work, intervention efforts, and policy implications moving forward. We omitted a section we had included in the first edition focused on research methodology for studying violent behavior in favor of adding new content, in particular the research on biological bases of violence that has emerged over the past decade, but also with insights looking to the future, related to prevention and intervention efforts. In addition to an entirely new chapter content in a number of contributions, including the editors' conclusion chapter, new chapters were included on the molecular genetics of aggression and violent crime, on lessons learned from serial sex offenders based on a backlog of sexual assault kits, and on insights about the development of aggression and violence over the life-course, based on long-term longitudinal work from Finland. Each of these contributions, from an internationally renowned panel of experts in their respective fields, contains important new information.

We believe that the current Handbook continues to differentiate itself from other related work in the published literature and to occupy a unique position in scholarship focused on violent behavior and aggression, by its particular cross-disciplinary focus, by both an in-depth and focused treatment of the study of violent behavior and aggression, and by considering these behaviors across the lifespan of human development, rather than focusing on particular developmental periods. In this sense, the current Cambridge Handbook represents a unique resource for researchers and scholars, but also for graduate students across social and behavioral science disciplines interested in the study and etiology of violent behavior and aggression.

Acknowledgments

We would like to thank Cambridge University Press for the opportunity to publish the second edition of the Handbook, in particular Janka Romero, for her encouragement and steadfast support throughout the process. Thank you also to Gabriela Ksinan Jiskrova, a doctoral student at the University of Kentucky, for her tireless assistance with managing the submissions, as well as Matthew K. Weiland at Case Western Reserve University, for his work on the index.

The cover of the Handbook is Franz Marc's "Fighting Forms" (1914), inspired by the artist's experiences related to World War I, which would also ultimately lead to his demise, in 1916 near Verdun, France.

PART I

Introduction and Overview

1 Origins of Violent Behavior over the Life Span

David P. Farrington

Introduction

The most basic definition of violence is behavior that is intended to cause, and that actually causes, physical or psychological injury. The most important violent offenses defined by the criminal law are homicide, assault, robbery, and rape. This chapter has three main sections. The first section briefly reviews basic knowledge about violence over the life span: measurement and prevalence, continuity from childhood to adulthood, specialization or versatility, and changes with age. The second section reviews individual and family risk factors for violence. The third section reviews methods of preventing violence by targeting key individual and family risk factors. There is not space to review immediate situational influences on violence, or theories of violence, in this chapter. Sex offending is also excluded.

Risk factors for violence are defined as variables that predict a high probability of violence. Usually, risk factors are dichotomized. This makes it easy to study interaction effects, to identify persons with multiple risk factors, to specify how outcomes vary with the number of risk factors, and to communicate results to policy-makers and practitioners as well as to researchers (Farrington & Loeber, 2000). In order to determine whether a risk factor is a predictor or possible cause of violence, the risk factor needs to be measured before the violence occurs. It is important to examine and establish which risk factors cause violence. To the extent that a risk factor causes violence, interventions could be designed to reduce its impact and, in turn, reduce violence. However, it is extremely difficult to establish causal influences in nonexperimental research. It is widely accepted that the main criteria for establishing that X causes Y is: (1) X is correlated with Y, (2) X can change or be changed within individuals, (3) X precedes Y, and (4) X predicts Y after controlling for confounding variables (Murray, Farrington, & Eisner, 2009).

In trying to draw conclusions about whether any factors might have a causal influence on offending, this chapter will focus especially on knowledge gained in major prospective longitudinal studies of offending, and especially on longitudinal studies of large community samples of several hundred persons containing information from several data sources (to maximize validity). This chapter focuses on the most important results obtained in such studies (for a review, see Farrington, 2015b). The best prospective surveys include interview as well as record data and span a follow-up period of at least five years. Such surveys are surprisingly rare. For example, Mossman (1994) reviewed 44 studies of the prediction of violence, and only two (Farrington, 1989a; Kandel, Brennan, Mednick, & Michelson, 1989) met these criteria.

The main emphasis here is on results obtained in the United Kingdom and the United States and on stranger or street violence rather than dating or within-family violence (e.g., Theobald, Farrington, Ttofi, & Crago, 2016). Most research focuses on male offenders and on the most common offenses of assault and robbery. There are few prospective longitudinal studies of homicide (but see Loeber & Farrington, 2011). Within a single chapter, it is impossible to review everything that is known about violence; for more extensive information, see Riedel and Welsh (2015) and DeLisi and Conis (2017).

This chapter will first report some relevant results obtained in classic longitudinal studies of violence, and it will then report more recent results, especially those obtained in the Cambridge Study in Delinquent Development (CSDD; see Farrington et al., 2006; Farrington, Piquero, & Jennings, 2013) and the Pittsburgh Youth Study (PYS; see Jennings, Loeber, Pardini, Piquero, & Farrington, 2016; Loeber, Ahonen, Stallings, & Farrington, 2017). The next section provides short descriptions of the CSDD and the PYS.

The CSDD and the PYS

The CSDD is a prospective longitudinal survey of 411 London males. These males are now called Generation 2 (G2). Their parents are Generation 1 (G1) and their children are Generation 3 (G3). The G2 males were originally assessed in 1961–62, when they were in six state primary schools in a lower-class urban area and were aged 8–9 years (West & Farrington, 1973). Therefore, the most common year of birth of the males is 1953. The G2 males are not a sample drawn systematically from a population, but rather the complete population of boys of that age in those schools at that time. The vast majority of boys were living in two-parent families, had fathers in manual jobs, and were White and of British origin.

The G2 males have been interviewed and assessed nine times between age 8 and age 48. Attrition has been very low; for example, 95% of those still alive were interviewed at age 18, 94% at age 32, and 93% at age 48 (for information about how the males were traced, see Farrington, Gallagher, Morley, St. Ledger, & West, 1990). The assessments in schools measured such factors as intelligence, personality, and impulsiveness, while information was collected in the interviews about such topics as living circumstances, employment histories, relationships with females, leisure activities such as drinking, drug use and fighting, and of course self-reported offending behavior.

The G1 parents were also interviewed about once a year from when the G2 males were aged 8 until when they were aged 15 and in most cases leaving school. The G1 parents provided details about such matters as family income, family composition, their employment histories, their child-rearing practices (including discipline and supervision) and the boy's temporary or permanent separations from them. Also, the boys' teachers completed questionnaires when the boys were aged about 8, 10, 12, and 14. These furnished information about such topics as their restlessness or poor concentration, truancy, school attainment, and disruptive behavior in class.

Between 2004 and 2013, 551 G3 children aged at least 18 (84%) were interviewed at the average age of 25 (Farrington, Ttofi, Crago, & Coid, 2015). These interviews covered many of the same topics that the G1 males were asked about, and they included retrospective questions to the G3 children about their school behavior in childhood (before age 12) and the child-rearing that they had experienced from their parents. In addition, criminal records were searched for the G1 parents up to the average age of 70, for the G2 males up to age 56, and for the G3 children at the median age of 30.

The PYS is a prospective longitudinal study of three cohorts of Pittsburgh boys, totaling 1,517 boys, originally in the first, fourth, and seventh grades of public schools in 1987–88. The youngest cohort was assessed yearly from age 7 to age 19, while the oldest cohort was assessed yearly from age 13 to age 25. The middle cohort was only assessed from age 10 to age 13 and finally at age 24, so most of the analyses have been based on the youngest and oldest cohorts. A wide range of risk factors, including self-reported offending, was measured at all ages, and criminal records were searched up to age 32 to 38 (Loeber, Farrington, Stouthamer-Loeber, & White, 2008).

Violence over the Life Span

Measurement and Prevalence

The most common ways of identifying violent offenders are by using police or court records or self-reports of offending. For example, Elliott (1994) in the US National Youth Survey enquired about aggravated assault (attacking someone with the idea of seriously hurting or killing that person), being involved in a gang fight, and robbery (using force or strongarm methods to get money or things from people). Prevalences were surprisingly high. In the first wave of the survey (age 11 to 17 in 1976), 31% of African-American boys and 22% of White boys admitted a felony assault in the previous year (aggravated assault, gang fight, or sexual assault). At the same time, 13% of African-American boys and 6% of White boys admitted robbery (of teachers, students, or others) in the previous year.

The comparison between self-reports and official records gives some indication of the probability of a violent offender being caught and convicted. In the CSDD, 45% of boys admitted starting a physical fight or using a weapon in a fight between ages 15 and 18, but only 3% were convicted of assault between these ages (Farrington, 1989b). Self-reported violence had predictive validity: 10% of those who admitted assault up to age 18 were subsequently convicted of assault, compared with 5% of the remainder.

More recently, Farrington, Auty, Coid, and Turner (2013) studied self-reported and official offending in the CSDD from age 10 to age 56. The number of convictions for violent offenses (robbery, assault, threatening behavior, possessing weapons) increased to a peak at age 16 to 20 (43 convictions for just over 400 G2 males at risk), but there were still 42 convictions for violence after age 40. Self-reported assaults increased to a peak at age 15 to 18 (62% prevalence) and then decreased. The ratio of self-reported to official assault offenders decreased steadily with age from age 10 to 14 (52) to age 42 to 47 (8). Similarly, the ratio of self-reported to official assault offenses decreased with age, from age 10 to 14 (366) to age 42 to 47 (16).

In the PYS, the annual prevalence of reported serious violence (robbery, rape, attacking to hurt) increased to a peak (11%) at age 18 to 19 for the oldest cohort and then decreased up to age 25 (Loeber et al., 2008). The annual prevalence of arrests for serious violence also increased to a peak (10%) at age 18 to 19 and then decreased up to age 25. Theobald, Farrington, Loeber, Pardini, and Piquero (2014) found that there were seventeen self-reported serious violent offenses for every conviction on average, although 66% of self-reported serious violent offenders were convicted at some stage between the ages of 13 and 24. African-American boys were more likely than White boys to be convicted for serious violence, but this was partly because African-American boys self-reported more serious violent offenses and partly because they tended to live in worse neighborhoods.

Continuity

In the CSDD, 74 of the G2 males (18%) were convicted for a total of 168 violent offenses between the ages of 10 and 56; 44 (11%) were convicted for violence between the ages of 10 and 21, and 49 (12%) were convicted for violence between the ages of 22 and 56. Of those who had youthful convictions for violence, 44% also had adult convictions for violence, compared with only 8% of the remainder (odds ratio or OR = 8.52, $p < 0.05$; one-tailed tests used in light of directional predictions). There was also continuity in self-reported violence; 29% of youthful (age 15 to 18) violent offenders were also adult (age 27 to 32) violent offenders, compared with 12% of nonviolent youth (OR = 3.0, $p < 0.05$). While it is possible that part of the continuity in officially recorded violence may be attributable to continuity in police targeting, the continuity in self-reported violence indicates that there is real continuity in violent behavior.

Generally, violent males have an early age of onset of offending of all types (Farrington, 1991). Both in official records and self-reports, an early age of onset of violent offending predicts a relatively large number of violent offenses, as in the US National Youth Survey (Elliott, 1994). Moffitt (1993) suggested that the "life-course-persistent" offenders who started early (around the age of 10) and had long criminal careers were fundamentally different from the "adolescence-limited" offenders who started later (around the age of 14) and had short criminal careers lasting no longer than 5–6 years.

Childhood aggression predicts later violence. For example, in the Orebro (Sweden) longitudinal study (Stattin & Magnusson, 1989), two-thirds of boys who were officially recorded for violence up to the age of 26 had high aggressiveness scores at ages 10 and 13 (rated by teachers), compared with 30% of all boys. Also, in the Woodlawn (Chicago) follow-up study of African-American children, teacher ratings of aggressiveness at age 6 predicted arrests for violent crimes up to age 32 (McCord & Ensminger, 1997); Ttofi, Farrington, and Lösel (2012) completed a systematic review showing that school bullying predicted later violence.

One likely explanation of the continuity in violence over time is that there are persisting individual differences in an underlying potential to commit aggressive or violent behavior. In any cohort, the people who are relatively more aggressive at one age also tend to be relatively more aggressive at later ages, even though absolute levels of aggressive behavior and behavioral manifestations of violence are different at different ages (Piquero, Carriaga, Diamond, Kazemian, & Farrington, 2012).

Specialization or Versatility

Generally, violent offenders tend to be versatile rather than specialized. They tend to commit many different types of crimes and also show other problems such as heavy drinking, drug use, an unstable job record, and sexual promiscuity (West & Farrington, 1977). However, there is often a small degree of specialization in violence superimposed on this versatility (e.g., Brennan, Mednick, & John, 1989). There is also versatility in types of violence. For example, males who assault their female partners are significantly likely to have convictions for other types of violent offenses (Farrington, 1994; Piquero, Theobald, & Farrington, 2014).

As an indication of their versatility, violent people typically commit more nonviolent offenses than violent offenses. In the CSDD, the convicted violent delinquents up to age 21 had nearly three times as many convictions for nonviolent offenses as for violent offenses (Farrington, 1978). Similarly, in the Oregon Youth Study, the boys arrested for violence had an average of 6.6 arrests of all kinds (Capaldi & Patterson, 1996). These results suggest that the continuity in violence from childhood to adulthood may largely reflect continuity in general antisocial behavior.

In the CSDD, the probability of committing a violent offense increased steadily with the number of offenses committed (Farrington, 1991). Indeed, it was not possible to disprove the hypothesis that violent offenses were committed at random in criminal careers. In the present analysis, 177 (43%) G2 males were convicted at some time between the ages of 10 and 56 and, as mentioned, 74 (42% of the offenders) were convicted for a violent offense. The probability of a violence conviction increased from those with one offense (10%) to those with two or three offenses (37%), four to ten offenses (63%), and more than ten offenses (78%). To a considerable extent, violent offenders are frequent offenders.

Risk Factors for Violence

In the interests of throwing light on possible causes of violence and implications for prevention methods, the emphasis in this chapter is on psychosocial risk factors (individual and family factors) that can change over time. Thus, gender, race, and genetic factors that are fixed at birth, such as the XYY chromosome abnormality, are not discussed, and neither are biological factors that can change, such as resting heart rate (e.g., Jennings, Piquero, & Farrington, 2013; Portnoy & Farrington, 2015). Where results differ by gender or race, this will be noted. There is not space to review peer, neighborhood, or community risk factors, but socioeconomic factors will be reviewed with family factors. The main focus is on individual-level as opposed to aggregate-level studies (e.g., rates of violence in different areas), and on violent offenders rather than victims of violence. However, it should be noted that victims of violence overlap significantly with violent offenders (e.g., Jennings, Piquero, & Reingle, 2012; Rivara, Shepherd, Farrington, Richmond, & Cannon, 1995).

Lipsey and Derzon (1998) reviewed the predictors at age 6 to 11 of serious or violent offending at age 15 to 25. The best explanatory predictors (i.e., predictors not measuring some aspect of the child's antisocial behavior) were antisocial parents, male gender, low socioeconomic status of the family, and psychological factors (daring, impulsiveness, poor concentration, etc.). Other moderately strong predictors were minority race, poor parent–child relations (poor supervision, discipline, low parental involvement, low parental warmth), other family characteristics (parental stress, family size, parental discord), antisocial peers, low intelligence, and low school achievement. In contrast, abusive parents and broken homes were relatively weak predictors. It is clear that some individual and family factors are at least as important in the prediction of offending as are gender and race. Risk factors for crime and violence have also been reviewed by Farrington, Loeber, & Ttofi (2012) and Farrington, Gaffney, & Ttofi (2017).

Table 1.1 shows the childhood risk factors for youthful and adult violence for G2 males, while Table 1.2 shows the childhood risk factors for youthful violence (age 10 to 21) for G3 males. These tables are based on convictions; for childhood predictors of youthful and adult self-reported violence, see Farrington (2007); for other reviews of predictors of violence in the CSDD, see Farrington (2000, 2001, 2012). Some of the G3 risk factors were truly predictive, because they were measured in interview of the G2 males at age 32, while others were measured retrospectively in the G3 interview. Over 90% of G3 males were searched in criminal records up to at least age 21; 37 out of 343 (11%) G3 males were convicted between the ages of 10 and 21, for a total of 63 violent offenses. The prevalence for G3 males was the same as for G2 males (see above), although for most property offenses the prevalence was lower for G3 males (Farrington, Ttofi, & Crago, 2017). As expected, earlier measures of antisocial behavior in the CSDD (troublesomeness and dishonesty in G2, and suspended/expelled and frequent truancy in G3) significantly predicted later violence. In the PYS, running away and high truancy significantly predicted later violence (Loeber et al., 2008).

Risk factors for offending are generally replicable over time and place (e.g., Farrington, 2015a). For example, Farrington and Loeber (1999) compared the childhood predictors of juvenile offending in the CSDD and the PYS. Fifteen out of 21 risk factors yielded similar results in the two countries, even though they were measured in the early 1960s in London and in the late 1980s in Pittsburgh. Similarly, risk factors for offending are generally replicable between generations. In the CSDD, the strength of 20 risk factors for G2 offending up to age 21 correlated 0.80 with the strength of the same 20 risk factors for G3 offending up to age 21 (see Farrington et al., 2015 for information about how the risk factors were measured).

Individual Factors

Among the most important personality dimensions that predict violence are hyperactivity, impulsiveness, poor behavioral control, and attention problems. For example, in the Dunedin (New Zealand) follow-up, ratings of poor behavioral control (e.g., impulsiveness, lack of persistence) at age 3–5 significantly differentiated boys convicted of violence up to age 18, compared to those with no convictions or with nonviolent convictions (Henry, Caspi, Moffitt, & Silva, 1996). In the

Table 1.1 *Childhood Risk Factors for Violence for Generation 2 Males*

Childhood Risk Factors	% Violent 10–21 NR	R	OR	% Violent 22–56 NR	R	OR
Individual						
High troublesomeness	7.0	24.4	4.29*	10.3	20.0	2.18*
High dishonesty	8.8	17.0	2.13*	7.8	23.3	3.59*
High daring	6.4	21.7	4.04*	9.0	20.7	2.63*
High hyperactivity	9.0	18.5	2.30*	10.2	21.3	2.39*
Low nonverbal IQ	8.3	18.6	2.54*	9.8	20.0	2.30*
Low verbal IQ	8.7	16.8	2.13*	9.2	22.0	2.78*
Low attainment	7.9	20.0	2.90*	10.2	16.1	1.69
Parental						
Convicted G1 father	7.7	23.5	3.65*	8.9	25.9	3.59*
Convicted G1 mother	9.4	30.0	4.15*	11.7	20.0	1.88
Young G1 father	10.8	11.8	1.11	11.4	15.8	1.46
Young G1 mother	10.1	12.8	1.31	11.4	13.8	1.24
Family						
Harsh discipline	6.3	21.4	4.09*	9.0	20.2	2.57*
Poor supervision	7.6	22.2	3.49*	9.0	24.3	3.23*
Parental conflict	7.6	20.5	3.15*	9.2	18.6	2.26*
Disrupted family	8.3	20.0	2.77*	9.5	22.2	2.73*
Socioeconomic						
Low family income	7.7	21.5	3.28*	9.8	20.9	2.42*
Poor housing	8.7	14.7	1.81*	10.5	15.5	1.57
Low SES	9.5	16.5	1.87*	10.1	21.8	2.49*
Large family size	8.2	19.4	2.70*	10.0	19.8	2.22*

Notes: G1 = Generation 1, SES = socioeconomic status, NR = nonrisk category, R = risk category, OR = odds ratio, *p < 0.05, one-tailed.

Based on Cambridge Study in Delinquent Development data.

same study, the personality dimensions of low constraint (e.g., low cautiousness, seeking excitement) and high negative emotionality (e.g., nervousness, alienation) at age 18 were significantly correlated with convictions for violence (Caspi et al., 1994).

Many other studies show linkages between impulsiveness and violence. In the Seattle Social Development Project, hyperactivity and risk taking in adolescence predicted violence in young adulthood (Herrenkohl et al., 2000). In the Copenhagen perinatal project, hyperactivity (restlessness and poor concentration) at age 11 to 13 significantly predicted arrests for violence up to age 22, especially among boys experiencing delivery complications (Brennan, Mednick, & Mednick, 1993). More than half of those

Table 1.2 *Childhood Risk Factors for Violence for Generation 3 Males*

	% Violent 10–21		
Childhood Risk Factors	NR	R	OR
Individual			
Suspended/expelled G3	7.0	19.7	3.27*
Frequent truant G3	8.0	18.8	2.65*
High risk taking G3	6.7	19.8	3.45*
Poor attention G3	10.5	10.8	1.04
Early school leaving G3	6.3	37.8	9.05*
Parental			
Convicted G2 father 32	5.7	18.6	3.75*
Convicted G2 mother 32	10.0	22.2	2.58
Young G2 father	10.4	10.9	1.06
Young G2 mother	11.4	6.1	0.51
Family			
Physical punishment G3	6.7	18.9	3.26*
Poor supervision G3	5.6	15.7	3.11*
Poor supervision 32	7.2	19.3	3.07*
Parental conflict 32	8.4	13.3	1.67
Disrupted family 32	9.5	14.9	1.66
Socioeconomic			
Low take-home pay 32	8.0	15.9	2.19
Poor housing 32	8.5	17.7	2.31*
Low SES 32	9.1	16.7	1.99
Large family size 32	8.5	16.7	2.16*

Notes: G2 = Generation 2, G3 = measured in Generation 3 interview, 32 = measured in G2 interview at age 32, SES = socioeconomic status, NR = nonrisk category, R = risk category, OR = odds ratio, *p < 0.05, one-tailed.

Based on Cambridge Study in Delinquent Development data.

with both hyperactivity and high delivery complications were arrested for violence, compared to less than 10% of the remainder. Similarly, in the Orebro longitudinal study in Sweden, hyperactivity at age 13 predicted police-recorded violence up to age 26. The highest rate of violence was among males with both motor restlessness and concentration difficulties (15%), compared to 3% of the remainder (Klinteberg, Andersson, Magnusson, & Stattin, 1993).

Similar results were obtained in the CSDD and PYS (Farrington, 1998). Tables 1.1 and 1.2 show that high daring (risk taking) and high hyperactivity (restlessness in class) significantly predicted violence for G2 males in the CSDD, while high risk taking (but not poor attention) significantly predicted violence for G3 males. Also, a systematic review by Jolliffe and Farrington (2009) showed that early measures of impulsiveness (especially daring and risk taking) predicted later measures of violence.

The most extensive research on different measures of impulsiveness was carried out in the PYS by White et al. (1994). The measures that were most strongly related to self-reported delinquency at ages 10 and 13 were teacher-rated impulsiveness, self-reported impulsiveness, self-reported under-control, motor restlessness, and psychomotor impulsiveness on the Trail Making Test. Interestingly, attention deficit hyperactivity disorder (ADHD) seemed to be more of a protective factor than a risk factor for violence in the PYS (Loeber et al., 2008). Also in the PYS, Defoe, Farrington, and Loeber (2013) concluded that hyperactivity caused low school attainment, which in turn caused offending.

The other main group of individual factors that predict violence comprise low intelligence and low school attainment. For example, in the Philadelphia perinatal cohort (Denno, 1990), low verbal and performance IQ at ages 4 and 7, and low scores on the California Achievement Test at age 13 to 14 (vocabulary, comprehension, maths, language, spelling), all predicted arrests for violence up to age 22. In the Woodlawn study in Chicago, low IQ at age 6 predicted arrests for violent crimes up to age 32 (McCord & Ensminger, 1997). In the US National Longitudinal Study of Adolescent Health, repeating a grade was reported to be a risk factor for youth violence, whereas grade point average was reported to be a protective factor (Resnick, Ireland, & Borowsky, 2004). These conclusions about risk and protective factors were based on positive as opposed to negative relationships with youth violence (see later).

Similar results were obtained in the CSDD and PYS (Farrington, 1998). Table 1.1 shows that low verbal IQ, low nonverbal IQ, and low school attainment predicted later violence for G2 males in the CSDD, while Table 1.2 shows that early school leaving (the only comparable risk factor, although it was measured later) was significantly associated with violence for G3 males. In the PYS, low academic achievement and repeating a grade significantly predicted later violence (Loeber et al., 2008).

Low IQ may lead to delinquency through the intervening factor of school failure. The association between school failure and delinquency has been demonstrated repeatedly in longitudinal surveys (e.g., Maguin & Loeber, 1996). In the PYS, Lynam, Moffitt, and Stouthamer-Loeber (1993) concluded that low verbal IQ led to school failure and subsequently to self-reported delinquency, but only for African-American boys. An alternative theory is that the link between low IQ and delinquency is mediated by disinhibition (impulsiveness, ADHD, low guilt, low empathy), and this was also tested in the PYS (Koolhof, Loeber, Wei, Pardini, & D'Escury, 2007). Ttofi et al. (2016) reviewed research on IQ as a protective factor against offending.

Parental Factors

Numerous parental and family factors predict violence. Derzon (2009) carried out a meta-analysis of parental and family factors as predictors of criminal and violent behavior (as well as aggressive and problem behavior). The meta-analysis was based on longitudinal studies, but many predictions were over short time periods (less than four years in 55% of cases), many outcome variables were measured at relatively young ages (up to 15 in 40% of cases), and many studies were relatively small (less than 200 participants in 43% of cases). The strongest predictors of criminal or violent behavior were parental education (r = 0.30 for criminal behavior), parental supervision (r = 0.29 for violent behavior), child-rearing skills (r = 0.26 for criminal behavior), parental discord (r = 0.26 for criminal behavior), and family size (r = 0.24 for violent behavior). Notably weak predictors were young parents, broken homes, and socio-economic status.

Table 1.1 shows that a convicted G1 father and mother significantly predicted later violence by G2 males in the CSDD. Table 1.2 shows that a convicted G2 father (up to age 32, when the G3 males were under age 10) significantly predicted later violence by G3 males. In the case of a convicted G3 mother, the relationship was quite strong (OR = 2.58) but not significant because of small numbers of convicted G2 mothers. Many other researchers have also found that antisocial parents tend to have aggressive children (e.g., Johnson, Smailes, Cohen, Kasen, & Brook, 2004).

In the CSDD, the concentration of offending in a small number of families was remarkable. Less than 6% of the original G1–G2 families were responsible for half of the criminal convictions of all members (fathers, mothers, sons, and daughters) of all 400 families. Similarly, 9% of the next generation of G2–G3 families accounted for half of all convictions of these family members (Farrington & Crago, 2016).

Having a convicted mother or father significantly predicted the convictions of both G2 and G3 boys (Farrington et al., 2015). Furthermore, a convicted parent predicted self-reported as well as official violence (Farrington, 2007). Therefore, there is clear intergenerational continuity in offending.

Farrington, Jolliffe, Loeber, Stouthamer-Loeber, and Kalb (2001) reported on the extent to which arrested parents predicted arrests of sons in the PYS, and the extent to which arrests were concentrated in PYS families. They reviewed six possible explanations for why antisocial behavior was concentrated in families and transmitted from one generation to the next. First, there may be intergenerational continuities in exposure to multiple risk factors such as poverty, disrupted families, and living in deprived neighborhoods. Second, assortative mating (the tendency of antisocial females to choose antisocial males as partners) facilitates the intergenerational transmission of antisocial behavior. Third, family members may influence each other (e.g., older siblings may encourage younger ones to be antisocial). Fourth, the effect of an antisocial parent on a child's antisocial behavior may be mediated by environmental mechanisms such as poor parental supervision and inconsistent discipline. Fifth, intergenerational transmission may be mediated by genetic mechanisms. Sixth, there may be labeling and police bias against known criminal families.

Young mothers (mothers who had their first child at an early age, typically as a teenager) also tend to have violent sons, as Morash and Rucker (1989) demonstrated in the prediction of self-reported violence in the CSDD at age 16. Interestingly, the relationship between a young mother and a convicted son in this study disappeared after controlling for other variables, notably large family size, a convicted parent, and a broken family (Nagin, Pogarsky, & Farrington, 1997). However, Tables 1.1 and 1.2 show that a young mother and young father did not significantly predict violence in the CSDD. An older mother seemed to act as a protective factor against violence in the PYS (Loeber et al., 2008). In the Dunedin study, Jaffee, Caspi, Moffitt, Belsky, and Silva (2001) concluded that the link between teenage mothers and violent children was mediated by maternal characteristics (e.g., intelligence, criminality) and family factors (e.g., harsh discipline, family size, disrupted families).

Family Factors

In her classic follow-up of 250 Boston boys in the Cambridge-Somerville Youth Study, McCord (1979) found that the strongest predictors at age 10 of later convictions for violence (up to age 45) were poor parental supervision, parental aggression (including harsh, punitive discipline), and parental conflict. An absent father was almost significant as a predictor, but a mother's lack of affection was not significant. McCord (1977) also demonstrated that fathers who were convicted for violence tended to have sons who were convicted for violence. In her later analyses, McCord (1996) showed that violent offenders were less likely than nonviolent offenders to have experienced parental affection and good discipline and supervision, but equally likely to have experienced parental conflict.

Similar results have been obtained in other longitudinal studies. In the Chicago Youth Development Study, poor parental monitoring and low family cohesion predicted self-reported violent offending (Gorman-Smith, Tolan, Zelli, & Huesmann, 1996). Also, poor parental monitoring and low attachment to parents predicted self-reported violence in the Rochester Youth Development Study (Thornberry, Huizinga, & Loeber, 1995). In the Seattle Social Development Project, poor family management (poor supervision, inconsistent rules, and harsh discipline) in adolescence predicted violence in young adulthood (Herrenkohl et al., 2000).

Harsh physical punishment by parents, and child physical abuse, typically predict violent offending by sons (Malinosky-Rummell & Hansen, 1993). In the Columbia County Study, Eron, Huesmann, and Zelli (1991) reported that parental punishment at age 8 predicted not only arrests for violence up to age 30, but also the severity of the man's punishment of his child at age 30 and also his history of spouse assault.

In the PYS, harsh physical punishment predicted violence for White boys but not for African-Americans (Farrington, Loeber, & Stouthamer-Loeber, 2003). It has been suggested (e.g., by Deater-Deckard, Dodge, Bates, & Pettit, 1996; Kelley, Power, & Wimbush, 1992) that this is because physical discipline is associated with neglect and coldness in White families but with concern and warmth in African-American families. In the Cambridge-Somerville Youth Study, McCord (1997) found that physical punishment predicted convictions for violence especially when it was combined with low parental warmth and affection.

Broken families between birth and age 10 predicted convictions for violence up to age 21 in the British National Survey (Wadsworth, 1978), and single-parent status at age 13 predicted convictions for violence up to age 18 in the Dunedin study

(Henry et al., 1996). Parental conflict and a broken family predicted official violence in the CSDD and PYS, and coming from a single-parent female-headed household predicted official and reported violence in the PYS (Farrington, 1998). This may be because the conflict in G2 families (when divorce was rare and warring parents tended to stay together) was greater than the conflict in G3 families (when divorce was more common). In the PYS, having one or no biological parents present in the house significantly predicted violence (Loeber et al., 2008).

Few longitudinal studies of offending have begun before age 7 or 8. However, in the British Cohort Study of children born in 1970, Murray, Irving, Farrington, Colman, and Bloxsom (2010) investigated the extent to which very early risk factors (measured up to age 5) predicted self-reported convictions at ages 30 and 34. Murray and his colleagues found that the strongest early predictors were a single mother, a teenage mother, maternal smoking during pregnancy, loss of a biological parent, and family deprivation (low social class, low parental education, poverty, and household overcrowding). The likelihood of a conviction increased with the early risk score, from 17% to 44% for boys and from 3% to 11% for girls.

Socioeconomic Factors

In general, coming from a family of low socioeconomic status (SES) predicts violence. For example, in the US National Youth Survey, the prevalences of self-reported felony assault and robbery were about twice as high for lower-class youth as for middle-class ones (Elliott, Huizinga, & Menard, 1989). Similar results were obtained for official violence in the Dunedin Study in New Zealand (Henry et al., 1996). The strongest predictor of official violence in the PYS was family dependence on welfare benefits (Farrington, 1998). Low SES predicted violence more strongly for White boys than for African-Americans in this project (Farrington et al., 2003). Table 1.1 shows that, in the CSDD, low family income, poor housing, and low SES of the G1 family predicted violence for G2 males. Similarly, low take-home pay, poor housing, and low SES of the G2 male at age 32 predicted violence for G3 males (Table 1.2).

It was interesting that the peak age of offending in the CSDD, at 17 to 18, coincided with the peak age of affluence for many convicted males. In the CSDD, convicted males tended to come from low-income families at age 8 and later tended to have low incomes themselves at age 32. However, at age 18, they were relatively well paid in comparison with nondelinquents (West & Farrington, 1977). Whereas convicted delinquents might be working as unskilled laborers on building sites and getting the full adult wage for this job, nondelinquents might be in poorly paid jobs with prospects, such as bank clerks, or might still be students. These results show that the link between income and offending is quite complex.

Several researchers have suggested that the link between a low-SES family and antisocial behavior is mediated by family socialization practices. For example, Larzelere and Patterson (1990) in the Oregon Youth Study concluded that the effect of SES on delinquency was entirely mediated by parental management skills. In other words, low SES predicted delinquency because low-SES families used poor child-rearing practices. In the Christchurch Health and Development Study, Fergusson, Swain-Campbell, and

Horwood (2004) reported that living in a low-SES family between birth and age 6 predicted self-reported and official delinquency between the ages of 15 and 21. However, this association disappeared after controlling for family factors (physical punishment, maternal care, and parental changes), conduct problems, truancy, and deviant peers, suggesting that these may have been mediating factors.

Large family size (a large number of children in the family) predicted violence in both the CSDD and PYS (Farrington, 1998). In the Oregon Youth Study, large family size at age 10 predicted self-reported violence at age 13 to 17 (Capaldi & Patterson, 1996). There are many possible reasons why a large number of siblings might increase the risk of a child's delinquency (Brownfield & Sorenson, 1994). Generally, as the number of children in a family increases, the amount of parental attention that can be given to each child decreases. Also, as the number of children increases, the household tends to become more overcrowded, possibly leading to increases in frustration, irritation, and conflict. In the CSDD, large family size did not predict delinquency for boys living in the least crowded conditions, with two or more rooms more than there were children (West & Farrington, 1973, p. 33). This suggests that household overcrowding might be an important factor mediating the association between large family size and offending.

Risk Mechanisms

It is important to investigate mechanisms linking risk factors and antisocial behavior. As an example, Juby and Farrington (2001) tested different explanations of the relationship between disrupted families and delinquency in the CSDD. Trauma theories suggest that the loss of a parent has a damaging effect on a child, most commonly because of the effect on attachment to the parent. Life-course theories focus on separation as a sequence of stressful experiences, and on the effects of multiple stressors such as parental conflict, parental loss, reduced economic circumstances, changes in parent figures, and poor child-rearing methods. Selection theories argue that disrupted families produce delinquent children because of pre-existing differences from other families in risk factors such as parental conflict, criminal or antisocial parents, low family income or poor child-rearing methods.

It was concluded that the results favored life-course theories rather than trauma or selection theories. While boys from broken homes (permanently disrupted families) were more delinquent than boys from intact homes, they were not more delinquent than boys from intact high-conflict families. These results were later replicated in Switzerland (Haas, Farrington, Killias, & Sattar, 2004). Generally, broken homes caused by disharmony were more damaging than those caused by death. Overall, the most important factor was the post-disruption trajectory. Boys who remained with their mother after the separation had the same delinquency rate as boys from intact low-conflict families. Boys who remained with their father, with relatives, or with others (e.g., foster parents) had high delinquency rates. The results were similar whether convictions or self-reported delinquency were studied.

A later analysis of mediators between childhood broken homes and later convictions for violence was carried out by

Theobald, Farrington, and Piquero (2013). They concluded that broken homes led to hyperactivity and self-reported violence at age 14 and then to convictions for violence between ages 15 and 50. They also found that the most important moderator of the broken home-violence relationship was harsh parental discipline. In the absence of harsh discipline, broken homes did not predict violence (13% violent in both no broken home and broken home categories). In the presence of harsh discipline, broken homes did predict violence (20% violent when there was no broken home, 52% violent in broken homes).

Effects of Life Events

It is also important to investigate the effects of life events on the course of development of antisocial behavior. In the CSDD, going to a high-delinquency-rate school at age 11 did not seem to amplify the risk of offending, since badly behaved boys tended to go to high-delinquency-rate schools (Farrington, 1972). However, getting convicted did lead to an increase in offending, according to the boys' self-reports, and a plausible intervening mechanism was increased hostility to the police (Farrington, 1977). Unemployment also caused an increase in offending, but only for crimes leading to financial gain, such as theft, burglary, robbery, and fraud. There was no effect of unemployment on other offenses such as violence, vandalism, or drug use, suggesting that the link between unemployment and offending was mediated by lack of money rather than boredom (Farrington, Gallagher, Morley, St. Ledger, & West, 1986).

It is often believed that marriage to a good woman is one of the most effective treatments for male offending, and indeed Farrington and West (1995) found that getting married led to a decrease in offending compared with staying single. Also, later separation from a wife led to an increase in offending compared with staying married, and the separated men were particularly likely to be violent. The effects of getting married, and of marital breakdown, were confirmed in later analyses by Theobald and Farrington (2009, 2013). Another protective life event was moving out of London, which led to a decrease in self-reported violence (Osborn, 1980). This was probably because of the effect of the move in breaking up delinquent groups.

Studies of the effects of life events on the course of development usually involve within-individual analyses. A major problem with most research on violence is that knowledge about risk factors is based on between-individual differences. For example, it is demonstrated that children who receive poor parental supervision are more likely to offend than other children who receive good parental supervision, after controlling for other between-individual factors that influence both parental supervision and offending. However, within-individual variations are more relevant to the concept of cause, as well as to prevention or intervention research (which requires within-individual change). For example, if it was demonstrated that children were more likely to offend during time periods when they were receiving poor parental supervision than during time periods when they were receiving good parental supervision, this would be more compelling evidence that poor parental supervision caused offending.

In the PYS, peer delinquency was the strongest correlate and predictor of a boy's delinquency (between individuals) but it did not predict within individuals (Farrington, Loeber, Yin, & Anderson, 2002). In other words, changes in peer delinquency from one wave to the next did not predict changes in delinquency (for the same individual) from one wave to the next. In contrast, parental factors such as poor parental supervision and low involvement of the boy in family activities predicted the boy's delinquency both between and within individuals. Because the concept of a cause requires that a change in a factor within individuals predicts a change in delinquency within individuals, it was concluded that parental factors might be causes of delinquency but peer delinquency was not. Because most offenses by young people are committed with other young people (Reiss & Farrington, 1991), peer delinquency is probably an indicator rather than a cause of delinquency.

Protective Factors

Most research on violence seeks to identify risk factors: variables that predict an increased probability of violence. It is also important to identify protective factors: variables that predict a decreased probability of violence. Protective factors may have more implications than risk factors for prevention and treatment. However, there are at least four separate meanings of protective factors.

The first suggests that a protective factor is merely the opposite end of the scale (or the other side of the coin) to a risk factor. For example, if low intelligence is a risk factor, high intelligence could be regarded as a protective factor. The value of this depends, however, on whether there is a linear relationship between the variable and violence. To the extent that the relationship is linear, little is gained by identifying the protective factor of high intelligence as well as the risk factor of low intelligence.

The second definition specifies protective factors that are free-standing, with no corresponding, symmetrically opposite, risk factor. Loeber et al. (2008) proposed that a variable that predicted a low probability of offending should be termed a "promotive factor." In order to investigate risk and promotive factors separately in the PYS, they trichotomized explanatory variables into the "worst" quarter (e.g., low school achievement), the middle half, and the "best" quarter (e.g., high school achievement). They studied risk factors by comparing the probability of offending in the worst quarter vs. the middle half, and they studied promotive factors by comparing the probability of offending in the middle half vs. the best quarter. If a predictor is linearly related to delinquency, so that the percent delinquent is low in the best quarter and high in the worst quarter, that variable could be regarded as both a risk factor and a promotive factor. However, if the percent delinquent is high in the worst quarter but not low in the best quarter, that variable could be regarded only as a risk factor. Conversely, if the percent delinquent is low in the best quarter but not high in the worst quarter, that variable could be regarded only as a promotive factor.

Loeber et al. (2008) systematically investigated relationships between predictor variables and violence, and found many examples of pure risk factors and pure promotive factors. The most important pure promotive factors were high academic achievement, an older mother, low ADHD, low physical punishment, and good parental supervision. For example, in predicting violence in early adulthood (age 20 to 25) by variables measured in early adolescence (age 13 to 15), school achievement was clearly a pure promotive factor. The percentage of boys who were violent was 8% (high achievement), 21% (medium achievement), and 21% (low achievement).

The third definition of a protective factor is a variable that interacts with a risk factor to nullify or buffer its effect, while the fourth definition identifies a variable that predicts a low probability of violence among a group at risk. Farrington, Ttofi, and Piquero (2016) termed the former "an interactive protective factor" and the latter "a risk-based protective factor." There have been fewer studies of interaction effects than of protective effects in a high-risk group. An interactive protective factor is defined as follows: When the protective factor is present, the probability of violence does not increase in the presence of the risk factor; when the protective factor is absent, the probability of violence does increase in the presence of the risk factor.

Farrington and Ttofi (2011) investigated protective factors that predicted a low percentage of conviction among G2 males who had the risk factor of poor housing, and found that the most important were good child-rearing and small family size. The percentage of conviction (between ages 10 and 50) was 66% for males in poor housing with poor child-rearing, 33% for males in poor housing with good child-rearing, and 31% for males in good housing. Therefore, the interactive protective factor of good child-rearing nullified the risk factor of poor housing.

Jolliffe, Farrington, Loeber, and Pardini (2016) investigated promotive factors and risk-based protective factors for violence in the PYS. They confirmed that important promotive factors were high academic achievement, low hyperactivity, good parental supervision, and an older mother. They also studied protective factors that predicted a low probability of violence in risk categories. For example, for boys living in deprived neighborhoods, the most important risk-based protective factors were high achievement, low hyperactivity, and an older mother. Remarkably, for boys in deprived neighborhoods, only 3% of those with high achievement were violent, compared with 35% of those who did not have high achievement.

More research is needed on protective factors. It is particularly important to identify risk-based and interactive protective factors, because they can help to specify what factors to target for people in specific risky situations. Lösel and Farrington (2012) reviewed knowledge about promotive (termed direct protective) factors and buffering protective factors for youth violence.

Risk-Focused Prevention

The most effective intervention programs target risk factors for offending. It is rare for evaluations to report effects on violence specifically, but it is likely that interventions that succeed in reducing offending will also succeed in reducing violence. The basic idea of developmental or risk-focused prevention is very simple: Identify the key risk factors for offending and implement prevention techniques designed to counteract them. There is often a related attempt to identify key protective factors against offending and to implement prevention techniques designed to enhance or strengthen them (see Farrington, 2015c; Farrington, Gaffney, Lösel, & Ttofi, 2017).

The best evidence about the effectiveness of intervention programs has been obtained in randomized experiments, especially those that have included a cost-benefit analysis. A randomized experiment ensures that those who are treated are equivalent before the intervention to those who are not treated, on all possible measured and unmeasured variables. Therefore, it is possible to disentangle the effects of the treatment from pre-existing differences and the influence of all other variables. The focus here is especially on programs that have been evaluated in randomized experiments with reasonably large samples, since the effect of any intervention on delinquency can be demonstrated most convincingly in such experiments (Farrington & Welsh, 2006). The best randomized experiments have long-term follow-ups, which make it possible to determine if effects persist or wear off (Farrington & Welsh, 2013).

Skills Training Programs

The most important individually based prevention techniques are cognitive-behavioral skills training programs and preschool programs. The most important prevention techniques that target the risk factors of high impulsiveness and low empathy are cognitive-behavioral skills training programs, which have been reviewed by Zara and Farrington (2014). The "Stop Now and Plan" (SNAP) program is one of the most important skills training programs for children aged 6 to 11. It was developed in Toronto by Augimeri, Walsh, Liddon, and Dassinger (2011). Children referred by the police for problematic behavior are taught to calm down, take deep breaths, and count to ten when they are angry. They are also taught coping statements and effective solutions to interpersonal problems. Small-scale experiments showed that SNAP was effective in reducing delinquency and aggression, and this was confirmed by large-scale independent evaluations (e.g., Burke & Loeber, 2015).

The Montreal Longitudinal-Experimental Study combined child skills training and parent training. Tremblay, Pagani-Kurtz, Masse, Vitaro, and Pihl (1995) identified disruptive (aggressive or hyperactive) boys at age 6, and randomly allocated over 300 of these to experimental or control conditions. Between the ages of 7 and 9, the experimental group received training designed to foster social skills and self-control. Coaching, peer modeling, role playing, and reinforcement contingencies were used in small group sessions on such topics as "how to help," "what to do when you are angry," and "how to react to teasing."

This prevention program was successful. By age 12, the experimental boys committed less burglary and theft, were less likely to get drunk, and were less likely to be involved in fights than the controls (according to self-reports). Also, the experimental boys had higher school achievement. At every age from 10 to 15, the experimental boys had lower self-reported delinquency scores than the control boys. Interestingly, the differences in antisocial behavior between experimental and control boys increased as the follow-up progressed. Later follow-ups showed that fewer experimental boys had a criminal record by age 24 (Boisjoli, Vitaro, Lacourse, Barker, & Tremblay, 2007), and that the experimental boys self-reported less property crime at age 28 (Vitaro, Brendgen, Giguere, & Tremblay, 2013).

Preschool Programs

If low intelligence and school failure are causes of offending, then any program that leads to an increase in school success should lead to a decrease in offending. One of the most successful delinquency prevention programs was the Perry preschool project, carried out in Michigan by Schweinhart and Weikart (1980). This was essentially a "Head Start" program targeted on disadvantaged African-American children. A small sample of 123 children was allocated (approximately at random) to experimental and control groups. The experimental children attended a daily pre-school program, backed up by weekly home visits, usually lasting two years (covering ages 3 to 4). The aim of the "plan-do-review" program was to provide intellectual stimulation, to increase thinking and reasoning abilities, and to increase later school achievement.

This program had long-term benefits. At age 19, the experimental group was more likely to be employed, more likely to have graduated from high school, more likely to have received college or vocational training, and less likely to have been arrested (Berrueta-Clement, Schweinhart, Barnett, Epstein, & Weikart, 1984). By age 27, the experimental group had accumulated only half as many arrests on average as the controls (Schweinhart, Barnes, & Weikart, 1993). Also, they had significantly higher earnings and were more likely to be home-owners. More of the experimental women were married, and fewer of their children were born to unmarried mothers.

The most recent follow-up of this program at age 40 found that it continued to make an important difference in the lives of the participants (Schweinhart et al., 2005). Compared to the control group, those who received the program had significantly fewer life-time arrests for violent crimes (32% vs. 48%), property crimes (36% vs. 56%), and drug crimes (14% vs. 34%), and they were significantly less likely to be arrested five or more times (36% vs. 55%). Improvements were also recorded in many other important life-course outcomes. For example, significantly higher levels of schooling (77% vs. 60% graduating from high school), better records of employment (76% vs. 62%), and higher annual incomes were reported by the program group compared to the controls.

Home-Visiting Programs

Family programs are usually targeted on risk factors such as poor parental supervision and inconsistent discipline. Among the most important types of family-based programs are home-visiting programs, parent training programs, and multiple-component programs.

In the most famous intensive home-visiting program, Olds, Henderson, Chamberlin, and Tatelbaum (1986) in Elmira (New York) randomly allocated 400 mothers either to receive home visits from nurses during pregnancy, or to receive visits both during pregnancy and during the first two years of life, or to a control group who received no visits. Each visit lasted about one-and-a-quarter hours, and the mothers were visited on average every two weeks. The home visitors gave advice about prenatal and postnatal care of the child, about infant development, and about the importance of proper nutrition and avoiding smoking and drinking during pregnancy. Therefore, this was a general parent education program.

In a 15-year follow-up, the effects on delinquency of this Nurse Family

Partnership (NFP) program were evaluated. Among lower-class unmarried mothers, those who received prenatal and postnatal home visits had fewer arrests than those who received prenatal visits or no visits (Olds et al., 1997). Also, children of these mothers who received prenatal and/or postnatal home visits had less than half as many arrests as children of mothers who received no visits (Olds et al., 1998). Up to age 19, 25% of the treated children had been arrested, compared with 37% of the controls (Eckenrode et al., 2010).

Parent Training Programs

One of the most famous parent training programs, the Triple-P Parenting program, was developed by Sanders, Markie-Dadds, Tully, and Bor (2000) in Brisbane, Australia. The Triple-P program can either be delivered to the whole community in primary prevention using the mass media or can be used in secondary prevention with high-risk or clinic samples. The success of Triple-P was evaluated with over 300 high-risk children aged 3 by randomly allocating them either to receive Triple-P or to be in a control group. The Triple-P program involves teaching parents 17 child management strategies, including talking with children, giving physical affection, praising, giving attention, setting a good example, setting rules, giving clear instructions, and using appropriate penalties for misbehavior ("time-out," or sending the child to his or her room). The evaluation showed that Triple-P was successful in reducing children's antisocial behavior. The effectiveness of Triple-P has been confirmed in meta-analyses (e.g., Sanders, Kirby, Tellegen, & Day, 2014).

Multiple-Component Programs

Multisystemic Therapy (MST) is an important multiple-component family preservation program that was developed by Henggeler, Schoenwald, Borduin, Rowland, and Cunningham (2009) in South Carolina. The particular type of treatment is chosen according to the particular needs of the youth. Therefore, the nature of the treatment is different for each person. MST is delivered in the youth's home, school, and community settings. The treatment typically includes family intervention to promote the parent's ability to monitor and discipline the adolescent, peer intervention to encourage the choice of prosocial friends, and school intervention to enhance competence and school achievement.

In an evaluation in Missouri, Borduin et al. (1995) randomly assigned 176 juvenile offenders (with an average age of 14) either to MST or to individual therapy focusing on personal, family, and academic issues. Four years later, only 26% of the MST offenders had been rearrested, compared with 71% of the individual therapy group. Later follow-ups to ages 29 and 37 (Sawyer & Borduin, 2011) demonstrated the cumulative benefits of MST. The effectiveness of MST was confirmed in a meta-analysis by Curtis, Ronan, and Borduin (2004).

Conclusion

The major long-term psychosocial risk factors for violence are individual (high impulsiveness and low intelligence), parental (convicted parents and young parents), family (poor supervision, harsh discipline, parental conflict, a broken family), and socioeconomic (low family income, low socioeconomic status, poor housing, large family size). These conclusions may be useful in developing risk assessment instruments. More research is needed specifically in searching for protective factors against violence, for example, by investigating why some aggressive children do not become violent adults. The discovery of protective factors could have important policy implications, especially for interventions for children in specific types of risky environments.

In order to investigate development and risk factors for violence and the effects of life events, longitudinal studies are needed. Such studies should include multiple cohorts, in order to draw conclusions about different age groups from birth to the mid-20s. They should include both males and females and the major racial/ethnic groups, so that results can be compared for different subgroups. Research on risk factors for violence by females is especially needed. Previous research suggests that males and females, and African-Americans and Whites, differ in their number of risk factors more than in their relationships between risk factors and violence (Farrington et al., 2003; Moffitt, Caspi, Rutter, & Silva, 2001), but this needs to be investigated further. Longitudinal studies should measure a wide range of risk and especially protective factors, and seek to discover interaction effects. They should be based on large, high-risk samples, especially in inner-city areas, incorporating screening methods to maximize the yield of violent offenders while simultaneously making it possible to draw conclusions about the total population. They should include long-term follow-ups to permit conclusions about developmental pathways.

Violence-reduction programs should be based on knowledge about risk factors (Farrington, & Welsh, 2007). More systematic reviews and meta-analyses of risk factors and prevention programs are needed. High-quality evaluation research shows that many types of programs are effective, and that in many cases their financial benefits outweigh their financial costs (Welsh, Farrington, & Raffan Gowar, 2015). The best programs include preschool intellectual enrichment programs, child skills training, general parental education in home visiting, and parental management training. Risk-focused prevention can not only reduce crime and violence but also improve mental and physical health and life success in areas such as education, employment, relationships, housing, and child-rearing.

The most pressing problem is to advance knowledge about causes of violence. More tests of alternative causal mechanisms that may intervene between risk factors and violence are needed, and especially more within-individual analyses should be carried out. Virtually all knowledge about risk factors is based on between-individual analyses, but variables that are related to violence between individuals may not be related within individuals. Longitudinal studies with frequent data collection are needed for within-individual analyses. Such analyses may radically alter our conclusions about the causes of violent behavior over the life span. This is the new frontier.

References

Augimeri, L. K., Walsh, M. M., Liddon, A. D., & Dassinger, C. R. (2011). From risk identification to risk management: A comprehensive strategy for young children engaged in antisocial behaviour. In D. W. Springer & A. Roberts (Eds), *Juvenile justice and delinquency* (pp. 117–140). Sudbury, MA: Jones and Bartlett.

Berrueta-Clement, J. R., Schweinhart, L. J., Barnett, W. S., Epstein, A. S., & Weikart, D. P. (1984). *Changed lives: The effects of the Perry Preschool Program on youths through age 19.* Ypsilanti, MI: High/Scope Press.

Boisjoli, R., Vitaro, F., Lacourse, E., Barker, E. D., & Tremblay, R. E. (2007). Impact and clinical significance of a preventive intervention for disruptive boys. *British Journal of Psychiatry*, 191, 415–419.

Borduin, C. M., Mann, B. J., Cone, L. T., Henggeler, S. W., Fucci, B. R., Blaske, D. M., & Williams, R. A. (1995). Multisystemic treatment of serious juvenile offenders: Long-term prevention of criminality and violence. *Journal of Consulting and Clinical Psychology*, 63, 569–587.

Brennan, P. A., Mednick, S. A., & John, R. (1989). Specialization in violence: Evidence of a criminal subgroup. *Criminology*, 27, 437–453.

Brennan, P. A., Mednick, B. R., & Mednick, S. A. (1993). Parental psychopathology, congenital factors, and violence. In S. Hodgins (Ed.), *Mental disorder and crime* (pp. 244–261). Newbury Park, CA: Sage.

Brownfield, D. & Sorenson, A. M. (1994). Sibship size and sibling delinquency. *Deviant Behavior*, 15, 45–61.

Burke, J. D. & Loeber, R. (2015). The effectiveness of the Stop Now And Plan (SNAP) Program for boys at risk for violence and delinquency. *Prevention Science*, 16, 242–253.

Capaldi, D. M. & Patterson, G. R. (1996). Can violent offenders be distinguished from frequent offenders? Prediction from childhood to adolescence. *Journal of Research in Crime and Delinquency*, 33, 206–231.

Caspi, A., Moffitt, T. E., Silva, P. A., Stouthamer-Loeber, M., Krueger, R. F., & Schmutte, P. S. (1994). Are some people crime-prone? Replications of the personality-crime relationship across countries, genders, races, and methods. *Criminology*, 32, 163–195.

Curtis, N. M., Ronan, K. R., & Borduin, C. M. (2004). Multisystemic treatment: A meta-analysis of outcome studies. *Journal of Family Psychology*, 18, 411–419.

Deater-Deckard, K., Dodge, K. A., Bates, J. E., & Pettit, G. S. (1996). Physical discipline among African American and European American mothers: Links to children's externalizing behaviors. *Developmental Psychology*, 32, 1065–1072.

Defoe, I. N., Farrington, D. P., & Loeber, R. (2013). Disentangling the relationship between delinquency and hyperactivity, low achievement, depression, and low socio-economic status: Analysis of repeated longitudinal data. *Journal of Criminal Justice*, 41, 100–107.

DeLisi, M., & Conis, P. J. (Eds) (2017). *Violent offenders: Theory, research, policy, and practice* (3rd ed.). Burlington, MA: Jones and Bartlett.

Denno, D. W. (1990). *Biology and violence: From birth to adulthood.* Cambridge: Cambridge University Press.

Derzon, J. H. (2009). The correspondence of family features with problem, aggressive, criminal, and violent behavior: A meta-analysis. *Journal of Experimental Criminology*, 6, 263–292.

Eckenrode, J., Campa, M., Luckey, D. W., Henderson, C. R., Cole, R., Kitzman, H., ... & Olds, D. (2010). Long-term effects of prenatal and infancy nurse home visitation on the life course of youths: 19-year follow-up of a randomized trial. *Archives of Pediatrics and Adolescent Medicine*, 164, 9–15.

Elliott, D. S. (1994). Serious violent offenders: Onset, developmental course, and termination. *Criminology*, 32, 1–21.

Elliott, D. S., Huizinga, D., & Menard, S. (1989). *Multiple problem youth: Delinquency, substance use, and mental health problems.* New York: Springer-Verlag.

Eron, L. D., Huesmann, L. R., & Zelli, A. (1991). The role of parental variables in the learning of aggression. In D. J. Pepler & K. J. Rubin (Eds), *The development and treatment of childhood aggression* (pp. 169–188). Hillsdale, NJ: Lawrence Erlbaum.

Farrington, D. P. (1972). Delinquency begins at home. *New Society*, 21, 495–497.

Farrington, D. P. (1977). The effects of public labelling. *British Journal of Criminology*, 17, 112–125.

Farrington, D. P. (1978). The family backgrounds of aggressive youths. In L. Hersov, M. Berger, & D. Shaffer (Eds), *Aggression and antisocial behavior in childhood and adolescence* (pp. 73–93). Oxford, England: Pergamon.

Farrington, D. P. (1989a). Early predictors of adolescent aggression and adult violence. *Violence and Victims*, 4, 79–100.

Farrington, D. P. (1989b). Self-reported and official offending from adolescence to adulthood. In M. W. Klein (Ed.), *Cross-national research in self-reported crime and delinquency* (pp. 399–423). Dordrecht, Netherlands: Kluwer.

Farrington, D. P. (1991). Childhood aggression and adult violence: Early precursors and later life outcomes. In D. J. Pepler & K. H. Rubin (Eds), *The development and treatment of childhood aggression* (pp. 5–29). Hillsdale, NJ: Lawrence Erlbaum.

Farrington, D. P. (1994). Childhood, adolescent, and adult features of violent males. In L. R. Huesmann (Ed.), *Aggressive behavior: Current perspectives* (pp. 215–240). New York: Plenum.

Farrington, D. P. (1998). Predictors, causes, and correlates of youth violence. In M. Tonry & M. H. Moore (Eds), *Youth violence* (pp. 421–475). Chicago: University of Chicago Press.

Farrington, D. P. (2000). Adolescent violence: Findings and implications from the Cambridge Study. In G. Boswell (Ed.), *Violent children and adolescents: Asking the question why* (pp. 19–35). London: Whurr.

Farrington, D. P. (2001). Predicting adult official and self-reported violence. In G.-F. Pinard & L. Pagani (Eds), *Clinical assessment of dangerousness: Empirical contributions* (pp. 66–88). Cambridge: Cambridge University Press.

Farrington, D. P. (2007) Origins of violent behavior over the life span. In D. J. Flannery, A. T. Vazsonyi, & I. D. Waldman (Eds), *The Cambridge handbook of violent behavior and aggression.* (pp. 19–48). New York: Cambridge University Press.

Farrington, D. P. (2012). Predictors of violent young offenders. In B. C. Feld & D. M. Bishop (Eds), *The Oxford handbook on juvenile crime and juvenile justice* (pp. 146–171). Oxford, UK: Oxford University Press.

Farrington, D. P. (2015a). Cross-national comparative research on criminal careers, risk factors, crime, and punishment. *European Journal of Criminology*, 12, 386–399.

Farrington, D. P. (2015b). Prospective longitudinal research on the development of offending. *Australian and New Zealand Journal of Criminology*, 48, 314–335.

Farrington, D. P. (2015c). The developmental evidence base: Prevention. In D. A. Crighton & G. J. Towl (Eds), *Forensic psychology* (2nd ed., pp. 141–159). Chichester, UK: Wiley.

Farrington, D. P., Auty, K. M., Coid, J. W., & Turner, R. E. (2013). Self-reported and official offending from age 10 to age 56. *European Journal of Criminal Policy and Research*, 19, 135–151.

Farrington, D. P., Coid, J. W., Harnett, L., Jolliffe, D., Soteriou, N., Turner, R., & West, D. J. (2006). *Criminal careers up to age 50 and life success up to age 48: New findings from the Cambridge Study in Delinquent Development.* London: Home Office (Research Study No. 299).

Farrington, D. P. & Crago, R.V. (2016). The concentration of convictions in two generations of families. In A. Kapardis & D. P. Farrington (Eds), *The psychology of crime, policing and courts* (pp. 7–23). Abingdon, UK: Routledge.

Farrington, D. P., Gaffney, H., Lösel, F., & Ttofi, M. M. (2017). Systematic reviews of the effectiveness of developmental prevention programs in reducing delinquency, aggression, and bullying. *Aggression and Violent Behavior*, 33, 91–106.

Farrington, D. P., Gaffney, H., & Ttofi, M. M. (2017). Systematic reviews of explanatory risk actors for violence, offending, and delinquency. *Aggression and Violent Behavior*, 33, 24–36.

Farrington, D. P., Gallagher, B., Morley, L., St. Ledger, R. J., & West, D. J. (1986). Unemployment, school leaving, and crime. *British Journal of Criminology*, 26, 335–356.

Farrington, D. P., Gallagher, B., Morley, L., St. Ledger, R. J., & West, D. J. (1990). Minimizing attrition in longitudinal research: Methods of tracing and securing cooperation in a 24-year follow-up. In D. Magnusson & L. Bergman (Eds), *Data quality in longitudinal research* (pp. 122–147). Cambridge: Cambridge University Press.

Farrington, D. P., Jolliffe, D., Loeber, R., Stouthamer-Loeber, M., & Kalb, L. M. (2001). The concentration of offenders in families, and family criminality in the prediction of boys' delinquency. *Journal of Adolescence*, 24, 579–596.

Farrington, D. P., & Loeber, R. (1999). Transatlantic replicability of risk factors in the development of delinquency. In P. Cohen, C. Slomkowski, & L. N. Robins (Eds), *Historical and geographical influences on psychopathology* (pp. 299–329). Mahwah, NJ: Lawrence Erlbaum.

Farrington, D. P. & Loeber, R. (2000). Some benefits of dichotomization in psychiatric and criminological research. *Criminal Behavior and Mental Health*, 10, 100–122.

Farrington, D. P., Loeber, R., & Stouthamer-Loeber, M. (2003). How can the relationship between race and violence be explained? In D. F. Hawkins (Ed.), *Violent crime: Assessing race and ethnic differences* (pp. 213–237). Cambridge: Cambridge University Press.

Farrington, D. P., Loeber, R., & Ttofi, M. M. (2012). Risk and protective factors for offending. In B. C. Welsh & D. P. Farrington (Eds), *The Oxford handbook of crime prevention* (pp. 46–69). Oxford, UK: Oxford University Press.

Farrington, D. P., Loeber, R., Yin, Y., & Anderson, S. J. (2002). Are within-individual causes of delinquency the same as between-individual causes? *Criminal Behaviour and Mental Health*, 12, 53–68.

Farrington, D. P., Piquero, A. R., & Jennings, W. G. (2013). *Offending from childhood to late middle age: Recent results from the Cambridge Study in Delinquent Development*. New York: Springer.

Farrington, D. P., & Ttofi, M. M. (2011) Protective and promotive factors in the development of offending. In T. Bliesener, A. Beelman, & M. Stemmler (Eds), *Antisocial behavior and crime: Contributions of developmental and evaluation research to prevention and intervention* (pp. 71–88). Cambridge, MA: Hogrefe.

Farrington, D. P., Ttofi, M. M., & Crago, R. V. (2017). Intergenerational transmission of convictions for different types of offenses. *Victims and Offenders*, 12, 1–20.

Farrington, D. P., Ttofi, M. M., Crago, R. V., & Coid, J. W. (2015). Intergenerational similarities in risk factors for offending. *Journal of Developmental and Life-Course Criminology*, 1, 48–62.

Farrington, D. P., Ttofi, M. M., & Piquero, A. R. (2016). Risk, promotive, and protective factors in youth offending: Results from the Cambridge Study in Delinquent Development. *Journal of Criminal Justice*, 45, 63–70.

Farrington, D. P. & Welsh, B. C. (2006). A half-century of randomized experiments on crime and justice. In M. Tonry (Ed.), *Crime and justice* (vol. 34, pp. 55–132). Chicago: University of Chicago Press.

Farrington, D. P. & Welsh, B. C. (2007). *Saving children from a life of crime: Early risk factors and effective interventions.* Oxford, UK: Oxford University Press.

Farrington, D. P. & Welsh, B. C. (2013). Randomized experiments in criminology: What has been learned from long-term follow-ups? In B. C. Welsh, A. A. Braga, & G. J. N. Bruinsma (Eds), *Experimental criminology: Prospects for advancing science and public policy* (pp. 111–140). New York: Cambridge University Press.

Farrington, D. P. & West, D. J. (1995). Effects of marriage, separation and children on offending by adult males. In J. Hagan (Ed.), *Current perspectives on aging and the life cycle. Vol. 4: Delinquency and disrepute in the life course* (pp. 249–281). Greenwich, CT: JAI Press.

Fergusson, D., Swain-Campbell, N., & Horwood, J. (2004). How does childhood economic disadvantage lead to crime? *Journal of Child Psychology and Psychiatry*, 45, 956–966.

Gorman-Smith, D., Tolan, P. H., Zelli, A., & Huesmann, L. R. (1996). The relation of family functioning to violence among inner-city minority youths. *Journal of Family Psychology*, 10, 115–129.

Haas, H., Farrington, D. P., Killias, M., & Sattar, G. (2004). The impact of different family configurations on delinquency. *British Journal of Criminology*, 44, 520–532.

Henggeler, S. W., Schoenwald, S. K., Borduin, C. M., Rowland, M. D., & Cunningham, P. B. (2009). *Multisystemic therapy for antisocial behavior in children and adolescents* (2nd ed.). New York: Guilford.

Henry, B., Caspi, A., Moffitt, T. E., & Silva, P. A. (1996). Temperamental and familial predictors of violent and nonviolent criminal convictions: Age 3 to age 18. *Developmental Psychology*, 32, 614–623.

Herrenkohl, T. I., Maguin, E., Hill, K. G., Hawkins, J. D., Abbott, R. D., & Catalano, R. F. (2000). Developmental risk factors for youth violence. *Journal of Adolescent Health*, 26, 176–186.

Jaffee, S., Caspi, A., Moffitt, T. E., Belsky, J., & Silva, P. A. (2001). Why are children born to teen mothers at risk for adverse outcomes in young adulthood? Results from a 20-year longitudinal study. *Development and Psychopathology*, 13, 377–397.

Jennings, W. G., Loeber, R., Pardini, D. A., Piquero, A. R., & Farrington, D. P. (2016). *Offending from childhood to young adulthood: Recent results from the Pittsburgh Youth Study*. New York: Springer.

Jennings, W. G., Piquero, A. R., & Farrington, D. P. (2013). Does resting heart rate at age 18 distinguish general and violent offending up to age 50? Findings from the Cambridge Study in Delinquent Development. *Journal of Criminal Justice*, 41, 213–219.

Jennings, W. G., Piquero, A. R., & Reingle, J. M. (2012). On the overlap between victimization and offending: A review of the literature. *Aggression and Violent Behavior*, 17, 16–26.

Johnson, J. G., Smailes, E., Cohen, P., Kasen, S., & Brook, J. S. (2004). Antisocial parental behavior, problematic parenting, and aggressive offspring behavior during adulthood. *British Journal of Criminology*, 44, 915–930.

Jolliffe, D. & Farrington, D. P. (2009). A systematic review of the relationship between childhood impulsiveness and later violence. In M. McMurran & R. Howard (Eds), *Personality, personality disorder, and risk of violence* (pp. 41–61). Chichester, UK: Wiley.

Jolliffe, D., Farrington, D. P., Loeber, R., & Pardini, D. (2016). Protective factors for violence: Results from the Pittsburgh Youth Study. *Journal of Criminal Justice*, 45, 32–40.

Juby, H. & Farrington, D. P. (2001). Disentangling the link between disrupted families and delinquency. *British Journal of Criminology*, 41, 22–40.

Kandel, E., Brennan, P. A., Mednick, S. A., & Michelson, N. M. (1989). Minor physical anomalies and recidivistic adult violent criminal behavior. *Acta Psychiatrica Scandinavica*, 79, 103–107.

Kelley, M. L., Power, T. G., & Wimbush, D. D. (1992). Determinants of disciplinary practices in low-income black mothers. *Child Development*, 63, 573–582.

Klinteberg, B. A., Andersson, T., Magnusson, D., & Stattin, H. (1993). Hyperactive behavior in childhood as related to subsequent alcohol problems and violent offending: A longitudinal study of male subjects. *Personality and Individual Differences*, 15, 381–388.

Koolhof, R., Loeber, R., Wei, E. H., Pardini, D., & D'Escury, A. C. (2007). Inhibition deficits of serious delinquent boys of low intelligence. *Criminal Behaviour and Mental Health*, 17, 274–292.

Larzelere, R. E. & Patterson, G. R. (1990). Parental management: Mediator of the effect of socioeconomic status on early delinquency. *Criminology*, 28, 301–324.

Lipsey, M. W. & Derzon, J. H. (1998). Predictors of violent or serious delinquency in adolescence and early adulthood: A synthesis of longitudinal research. In R. Loeber & D. P. Farrington (Eds), *Serious and violent juvenile offenders: Risk factors and successful interventions* (pp. 86–105). Thousand Oaks, CA: Sage.

Loeber, R., Ahonen, L., Stallings, R., & Farrington, D. P. (2017). Violence demystified: Findings on violence by young males in the Pittsburgh Youth Study. *Canadian Psychology*, in press.

Loeber, R. & Farrington, D. P. (Eds) (1998). *Serious and violent juvenile offenders: Risk factors and successful interventions*. Thousand Oaks, CA: Sage.

Loeber, R. & Farrington, D. P. (2011). *Young homicide offenders and victims: Risk factors, prediction, and prevention from childhood*. New York: Springer.

Loeber, R., Farrington, D. P., Stouthamer-Loeber, M., & White, H. R. (2008). *Violence and serious theft: Development and prediction from childhood to adulthood*. New York: Routledge.

Lösel, F. & Farrington, D. P. (2012). Direct protective and buffering protective factors in the development of youth violence. *American Journal of Preventive Medicine*, 43 (2S1), S8–S23.

Lynam, D., Moffitt, T. E., & Stouthamer-Loeber, M. (1993). Explaining the relation between IQ and delinquency: Class, race, test motivation, school failure or self-control? *Journal of Abnormal Psychology*, 102, 187–196.

McCord, J. (1977). A comparative study of two generations of native Americans. In R. F. Meier (Ed.), *Theory in criminology* (pp. 83–92). Beverly Hills, CA: Sage.

McCord, J. (1979). Some child-rearing antecedents of criminal behavior in adult men. *Journal of Personality and Social Psychology*, 37, 1477–1486.

McCord, J. (1996). Family as crucible for violence: Comment on Gorman-Smith et al. (1996). *Journal of Family Psychology*, 10, 147–152.

McCord, J. (1997). On discipline. *Psychological Inquiry*, 8, 215–217.

McCord, J. & Ensminger, M. E. (1997). Multiple risks and comorbidity in an African-American population. *Criminal Behavior and Mental Health*, 7, 339–352.

Maguin, E. & Loeber, R. (1996). Academic performance and delinquency. In M. Tonry (Ed.), *Crime and justice*, vol. 20 (pp. 145–264). Chicago: University of Chicago Press.

Malinosky-Rummell, R. & Hansen, D. J. (1993). Long-term consequences of childhood physical abuse. *Psychological Bulletin*, 114, 68–79.

Moffitt, T. E. (1993). Adolescence-limited and life-course-persistent antisocial behavior: A developmental taxonomy. *Psychological Review*, 100, 674–701.

Moffitt, T. E., Caspi, A., Rutter, M., & Silva, P. A. (2001). *Sex differences in antisocial behavior*. Cambridge: Cambridge University Press.

Morash, M. & Rucker, L. (1989). An exploratory study of the connection of mother's age at childbearing to her children's delinquency in four data sets. *Crime and Delinquency*, 35, 45–93.

Mossman, D. (1994). Assessing predictions of violence: Being accurate about accuracy. *Journal of Consulting and Clinical Psychology*, 62, 783–792.

Murray, J., Farrington, D. P., & Eisner, M. P. (2009). Drawing conclusions about causes from systematic reviews of risk factors: The Cambridge Quality Checklists. *Journal of Experimental Criminology*, 5, 1–23.

Murray, J., Irving, B., Farrington, D. P., Colman, I., & Bloxsom, C. A. J. (2010). Very early predictors of conduct problems and crime: Results from a national cohort study. *Journal of Child Psychology and Psychiatry*, 51, 1198–1207.

Nagin, D. S., Pogarsky, G., & Farrington, D. P. (1997). Adolescent mothers and the criminal behavior of their children. *Law and Society Review*, 31, 137–162.

Olds, D. L., Eckenrode, J., Henderson, C. R., Kitzman, H., Powers, J., Cole, R., ... & Luckey, D. (1997). Long-term effects of home visitation on maternal life course and child abuse and neglect: Fifteen-year follow-up of a randomized trial. *Journal of the American Medical Association*, 278, 637–643.

Olds, D. L., Henderson, C. R., Chamberlin, R., & Tatelbaum, R. (1986). Preventing child abuse and neglect: A randomized trial of nurse home visitation. *Pediatrics*, 78, 65–78.

Olds, D. L., Henderson, C. R., Cole, R., Eckenrode, J., Kitzman, H., Luckey, D., ... & Powers, J. (1998). Long-term effects of nurse home visitation on children's criminal and antisocial behavior: 15-year follow-up of a randomized controlled trial. *Journal of the American Medical Association*, 280, 1238–1244.

Osborn, S. G. (1980). Moving home, leaving London, and delinquent trends. *British Journal of Criminology*, 20, 54–61.

Piquero, A. R., Carriaga, M., Diamond, B., Kazemian, L., & Farrington, D. P. (2012). Stability in aggression revisited. *Aggression and Violent Behavior*, 17, 365–372.

Piquero, A., Theobald, D., & Farrington, D. P. (2014). The overlap between offending trajectories, criminal violence, and intimate partner violence. *International Journal of Offender Therapy and Comparative Criminology*, 58, 286–302.

Portnoy, J. & Farrington, D. P. (2015). Resting heart rate and antisocial behavior: An updated systematic review and meta-analysis. *Aggression and Violent Behaviour*, 22, 33–45.

Reiss, A. J. & Farrington, D. P. (1991). Advancing knowledge about co-offending: Results from a prospective longitudinal survey of London males. *Journal of Criminal Law and Criminology*, 82, 360–395.

Resnick, M. D., Ireland, M., & Borowsky, I. (2004). Youth violence perpetration: What protects? What predicts? Findings from the National Longitudinal Study of Adolescent Health. *Journal of Adolescent Health*, 35, 424e1–424e10.

Riedel, M. & Welsh, W. (2015). *Criminal violence: Patterns, causes, and prevention* (4th ed.). New York: Oxford University Press.

Rivara, F. P., Shepherd, J. P., Farrington, D. P., Richmond, P. W., & Cannon, P. (1995). Victim as offender in youth violence. *Annals of Emergency Medicine*, 26, 609–614.

Sanders, M. R., Kirby, J. N., Tellegen, C. L., & Day, J. J. (2014). The Triple-P Positive Parenting program: A systematic review and meta-analysis of a multi-level system of parenting support. *Clinical Psychology Review*, 34, 337–357.

Sanders, M. R., Markie-Dadds, C., Tully, L. A., & Bor, W. (2000). The Triple P-Positive Parenting Program: A comparison of enhanced, standard and self-directed behavioral family intervention for parents of children with early onset conduct problems. *Journal of Consulting and Clinical Psychology*, 68, 624–640.

Sawyer, A. M. & Borduin, C. M. (2011). Effects of multisystemic therapy through midlife: A 21.9-year follow-up to a randomized clinical trial with serious and violent juvenile offenders. *Journal of Consulting and Clinical Psychology*, 79, 643–652.

Schweinhart, L. J., Barnes, H. V., & Weikart, D. P. (1993). *Significant benefits: The High/Scope Perry Preschool Study through age 27*. Ypsilanti, MI: High/Scope Press.

Schweinhart, L. J. & Weikart, D. P. (1980) *Young children grow up: The effects of the Perry Preschool Program on youths through age 15*. Ypsilanti, MI: High/Scope Press.

Schweinhart, L. J., Montie, J., Zongping, X., Barnett, W. S., Belfield, C. R., & Nores, M. (2005). *Lifetime effects: The High/Scope Perry Preschool Study through age 40*. Ypsilanti, MI: High/Scope Press.

Stattin, H. & Magnusson, D. (1989). The role of early aggressive behavior in the frequency, seriousness, and types of later crime. *Journal of Consulting and Clinical Psychology*, 57, 710–718.

Theobald, D. & Farrington, D. P. (2009). Effects of getting married on offending: Results from a prospective longitudinal survey of males. *European Journal of Criminology*, 6, 496–516.

Theobald, D. & Farrington, D. P. (2013). The effects of marital breakdown on offending: Results from a prospective longitudinal survey of males. *Psychology, Crime and Law*, 19, 391–408.

Theobald, D., Farrington, D. P., Loeber, R., Pardini, D. A., & Piquero, A. R. (2014). Scaling up from convictions to self-reported offending. *Criminal Behaviour and Mental Health*, 24, 65–276.

Theobald, D., Farrington, D. P., & Piquero, A. R. (2013). Childhood broken homes and adult iolence: An analysis of moderators and mediators. *Journal of Criminal Justice*, 41, 44–52.

Theobald, D., Farrington, D. P., Ttofi, M. M., & Crago, R. V. (2016). Risk factors for dating violence versus cohabiting violence: Results from the third generation of the Cambridge Study in delinquent Development. *Criminal Behaviour and Mental Health*, 26, 229–239.

Thornberry, T. P., Huizinga, D., & Loeber, R. (1995). The prevention of serious delinquency and violence: Implications from the program of research on the causes and correlates of delinquency. In J. C. Howell, B. Krisberg, J. D. Hawkins, & J. J. Wilson (Eds), *Sourcebook on serious, violent and chronic juvenile offenders* (pp. 213–237). Thousand Oaks, CA: Sage.

Tremblay, R. E., Pagani-Kurtz, L., Masse, L. C., Vitaro, F., & Pihl, R. O. (1995). A bimodal preventive intervention for disruptive kindergarten boys: Its impact through mid-adolescence. *Journal of Consulting and Clinical Psychology*, 63, 560–568.

Ttofi, M. M., Farrington, D. P., & Lösel, F. (2012). School bullying as a predictor of violence later in life: A systematic review and meta-analysis of prospective longitudinal studies. *Aggression and Violent Behavior*, 17, 405–418.

Ttofi, M. M., Farrington, D. P., Piquero, A. R., Losel, F., DeLisi, M., & Murray, J. (2016). Intelligence as a protective factor against offending: A meta-analytic review of prospective longitudinal studies. *Journal of Criminal Justice*, 45, 4–18.

Vitaro, F., Brendgen, M., Giguere, C. E., & Tremblay, R. E. (2013). Early prevention of life-course personal and property violence: A 19-year follow-up of the Montreal Longitudinal-Experimental Study (MLES). *Journal of Experimental Criminology*, 9, 411–427.

Wadsworth, M. E. J. (1978). Delinquency prediction and its uses: The experience of a 21-year follow-up study. *International Journal of Mental Health*, 7, 43–62.

Welsh, B. C., Farrington, D. P., & Raffan Gowar, B. (2015). Benefit-cost analysis of crime prevention programs. In M. Tonry (Ed.), *Crime and Justice*, vol. 44 (pp. 447–516). Chicago: University of Chicago Press.

West, D. J. & Farrington, D. P. (1973). *Who becomes delinquent?* London: Heinemann.

West, D. J. & Farrington, D. P. (1977). *The delinquent way of life.* London: Heinemann.

White, J. L., Moffitt, T. E., Caspi, A., Bartusch, D. J., Needles, D. J., & Stouthamer-Loeber, M. (1994). Measuring impulsivity and examining its relationship to delinquency. *Journal of Abnormal Psychology*, 103, 192–205.

Zara, G. & Farrington, D. P. (2014). Cognitive-behavioral skills training in preventing offending and reducing recidivism. In E. M. Jiminez Gonzalez & J. L. Alba Robles (Eds), *Criminology and forensic psychology* (pp. 55–102). Charleston, SC: Criminology and Justice Publisher.

2 Longitudinal Study of Personality and Social Development: Insights about Aggression after Five Decades

Lea Pulkkinen

Introduction

My insights about aggression after five decades of study are presented below from three perspectives: description of aggression, continuity of aggression, and developmental processes associated with aggressive behavior. I focus on two studies: a Kindergarten Study that I (then: Pitkänen) conducted in the middle of the 1960s, and its successor, the Jyväskylä Longitudinal Study of Personality and Social Development (JYLS), the baseline study of which was the second part of my doctoral dissertation (Pitkänen, 1969). The description of the JYLS from its inception and the synthesis of its results are presented in a book by Pulkkinen (2017). Below I discuss 28 insights about aggression.

During the first half of the 1960s, I was working as a research assistant at a university and my task was to collect data with children on three needs within the taxonomy of 20 needs by Murray (1938): the needs of Achievement, Affiliation, and Aggression. A need was a construct that organizes perception and action to transform an unsatisfying situation. It was seen as being sometimes provoked by internal processes, but more frequently by environmental pressures. I became skeptical about a need being a unitary construct when I discovered that different measurement techniques produced different results. I wanted to more closely study the variety of expressions of a need, such as aggression that was defined as "To overcome opposition forcefully. To fight. To revenge an injury. To attack, injure, or kill another. To oppose forcefully or punish another" (Hall & Lindzey, 1957, p. 173). I found that Goodenough (1931) had investigated children aged 7 months to 8 years and listed nearly 2,000 different outbursts of anger based on the recordings of mothers. Mandel (1959), in turn, had listed 2,205 different aggressive responses while observing the behavior of 9–16-year-old boys in a boarding school. He classified them into seven categories, from which five categories belonged to serious behavior (three subcategories for more reactive and two subcategories for more spontaneous aggression). The second category included behaviors in which serious aggression was questionable, and the third category included playful behaviors. Based on factor analysis, he extracted three factors: Hostility comprising severe spontaneous and reactive aggression; body contact including playful aggression; and inhibition or control of aggression.

Other distinctions had been made between, for instance, physical and verbal aggression (Jersild & Markey, 1935); indirect, provoked, and unprovoked aggression (Lesser, 1959); competitiveness and dominance (Kagan & Moss, 1962); and active and passive quality of aggression (Buss, 1961). McNeil (1962), who had studied interrelationships between different expressions of aggression, concluded that "future investigations of aggression ought to exercise some caution about viewing expressions of hostility as a unitary phenomenon that can be captured by means of a single global estimate of aggressiveness" (p. 75).

I found several definitions of aggression in the literature, and preferred the simplest definition by Buss (1961, p. 1): Aggression is "a response that delivers noxious stimuli to another person." A dominant theoretical approach to aggression was the frustration-aggression theory (Dollard, Doob, Miller, Mowrer, & Sears, 1939). According to it, aggression was always a reaction to a frustration. I was critical of it because it neglected proactive aggression. Based on modification of the S-R theory by Spence (1956), I thought that an individual may learn to anticipate secondary reinforcements of aggressive behavior. He or she may learn to use the delivery of noxious stimuli instrumentally, as a tool for aiming at one's goals, such as gaining more power. It would explain proactive aggression (Pitkänen, 1966, 1969, pp. 36–39).

I made an attempt to construct a descriptive model of aggressive behavior by outlining dimensions that would explain individual differences in aggression and be closely based on theoretical interpretations of human learning of aggressive behavior. The descriptive model (Figure 2.1) focuses on the observable characteristics of aggressive acts. Behavior that does not have the characteristics of observable aggressive acts, such as aggressive autonomic responses and aggression in fantasy, were not included in the model.

The first dimension in the descriptive model of aggression, called *the intensity of aggressive behavior*, can be defined by the quantity of noxious stimuli delivered by the act in question. The second dimension of the model describes the *motivational sequence of an aggressive act*: either the initiation of an aggressive act (offensive, henceforth: proactive aggression), including, for instance, attacking others for no apparent reason and teasing others, or a response to an aggressive act (defensive, henceforth: reactive aggression). The third dimension describes the direct/indirect *direction of aggression*. A person may target aggression directly at another person (e.g., by hitting) or express aggression indirectly via mediating events or persons, for instance, by gossiping about another person. There are also different *modes of aggression*, such as physical, verbal, and facial expressions of aggression. The qualitative characteristics can be combined into four categories: proactive–direct, proactive–indirect, reactive–direct, and reactive–indirect aggression; each category can be displayed physically, verbally, and facially, and used for the analysis of an aggressive act. For example, a push may be reactive or proactive depending on the sequence of events. It displays aggression directly and physically, and it may be mild or stronger depending on the consequences of the push.

I formulated 32 observable aggressive acts to represent different combinations of the dimensions (Pitkänen, 1966, 1969: Appendix A). Kindergarten teachers (26) observed these expressions of aggression in 216 boys' behaviors during a one-month period and rated them on how often they noted these behaviors in each child; who had been the

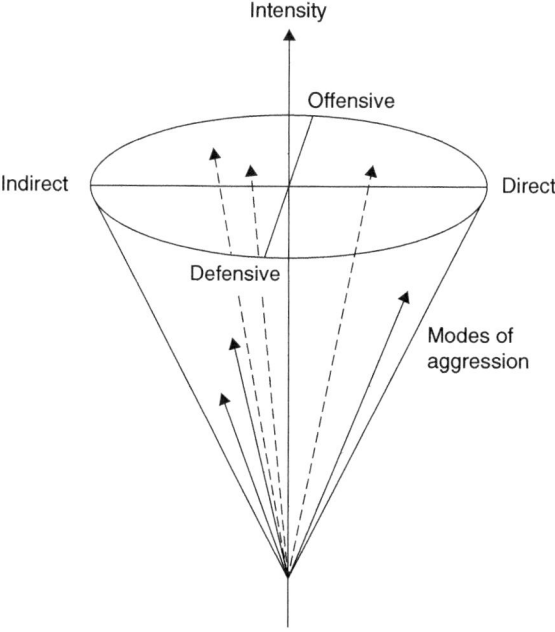

Figure 2.1 *A descriptive model of aggression.*
(Source: Pitkänen [1969, Figure 1, p. 29]. Reproduced with permission.)

target of aggression; and in what kind of context did the aggressive behavior occur. The average age of the boys was 6.1 years (children start school at the age of 7 in Finland). This study resulted in several insights about aggression.

Insight 1 is that *the dimensions presented in the descriptive model of aggressive acts are relevant for individual differences.* Aggressive acts could be described in terms of the intensity, direction (direct vs. indirect), and sequence (reactive vs. proactive) of aggression (Pitkänen, 1969, pp. 52–55). Three main factors were obtained: reactive aggression without proactive aggression; indirect aggression involving both reactive and proactive aggression; and proactive aggression with intensive reactive aggression. The commonly used distinction between physical and verbal aggression did not appear as major differentiating aspects of aggression. Those who express their aggression physically also express it verbally (Knight, Fabes, & Higgins, 1996).

Insight 2 is that *the most differentiating quality of boys' aggressive behavior is proactive aggression.* Proactively aggressive children were rated as most aggressive, and they generally defended themselves if attacked.

Insight 3 is that *reactive aggression may appear in children without proactive aggression.* Reactive aggression for self-defense is to some extent acceptable assertive behavior, if its intensity fits the intensity of the attack.

The person-situation controversy was raised in the literature by Mischel (1968) when he criticized the trait concept as a stable and enduring characteristic of individuals and argued that individual behavior is relatively situation-specific.

Insight 4 is that *aggressive behavior is situation-specific.* Situation-specificity of aggression was investigated in the Kindergarten Study (Pitkänen, 1966), and it indicated that aggression displayed in either a proactive or reactive manner was most commonly directed at a boy of the same size in free-play periods, both indoors and outdoors. Aggression towards a teacher was rare and indirect, and it was displayed during teacher-directed activity (Pitkänen, 1969, Part I).

Further support to *Insight 4* was received in the JYLS, where the targets of aggression were studied with two sets of Question Series administered to a sample of 8-year-old boys (Pitkänen, 1969, Part II). The Question Series for *reactive aggression* included questions of direct physical (hurts), verbal (says naughty things), and facial (makes faces), as well as indirect physical (takes another's possession) and verbal (tells stories) aggression. For instance: "You certainly know what it is like when somebody hurts you, say, by hitting, pushing or throwing something. What would you do if one of the boys in your class, who is of the same size as you, would hurt you?" The opponent was varied: a boy of the same size, a taller boy, a smaller boy, a girl, a teacher, and parents. In the Question Series for *proactive aggression,* the question took on the following form: "Do you attack a boy of your size or try to hurt him in any way, even if he had done you no harm, just to tease him?" The types of aggression and opponents varied in the same way as for reactive aggression.

As in the Kindergarten Study, the most common target of reactive, direct, physical aggression was a boy of the same size, followed by a smaller boy, a girl, and a taller boy (Pitkänen, 1969, p. 161). Parents were rarely targets, teachers never. Differences between the targets were smaller in reactive verbal and facial aggression. In direct proactive aggression, the frequency of the targets corresponded to that found in reactive physical aggression. Differences were smaller in indirect than in direct aggression.

Reactive physical aggression, the nonverbal type, was more closely studied at the age of 9 with an *Aggression Machine* (PAM), which I developed (Pitkänen, 1973a,b). In the PAM, the inclining side of the apparatus had two parallel rows: one consisting of lamps for stimulus presentation, the other consisting of buttons for participants to press. The lights were programmed by means of a built-in program disc. Each stimulus was recorded on the recording tape along with the pressing of the button. Aggressive attacks/responses were illustrated by pictures and words on a scale of the intensity (doing nothing, pushing a little, pinching, slapping, knocking down, pulling hair, hitting with a stick, and punching). The attacker (a boy of the same size, taller boy, smaller boy, girl, father, female teacher) was depicted by a picture on the top of the apparatus. The participant was asked to press the button as a response to an attack. The results confirmed the situation-specificity of aggressive responses.

Insight 5 is that *the concurrent validity of the measure of aggression depends on the context of aggression in which it occurs.* The PAM study indicated that when the attacker was a boy of the same size, the intensity of reactive aggression correlated significantly with teacher ratings of children's general aggressiveness and low self-control (Pitkänen, 1973b). Aggressive responses to other targets did not correlate with teacher-ratings of aggressiveness.

This is consistent with Mischel's (1968, p. 36) statement that "behaviors sampled in closely similar situations yield the best correlations." Aggressive behavior most often takes place between same-sized, same-sex peers.

The PAM was later computerized (Juujärvi, 2003; Juujärvi, Kooistra, Kaartinen, & Pulkkinen, 2001) and used with both male and female offspring of the JYLS original participants. Results added new insights about situation-specificity of aggression.

Insight 6 is that *situation-specificity of aggression is similar by sex*. The highest intensity was found in responses to the attacks of the same-sized, same-sex peers in boys and girls. Same-sized peers (of the same sex and of the opposite sex), and also taller peers, evoked less situational control in aggressive reactions than a smaller peer or the parent.

Insight 7 is that *reactions to mild provocations differentiate between aggressive and nonaggressive individuals*. It was found that differences between aggressive and nonaggressive children as rated by their teachers occurred particularly when the attacks were mild: more aggressive children reacted to mild attacks more intensively than less aggressive children.

Insight 8 is that *the predictive validity of the aggression measure depends on the type and context of aggression*. It was found that proactive aggression of any type and reactive physical aggression to attacks of the same-sized, same-sex peer predicted adult aggression ten years later. This conclusion was based on the predictive validity of the Question Series (Pitkänen-Pulkkinen, 1981) and the PAM (Pitkänen-Pulkkinen, 1980).

Insight 9 is that *the delay of aggressive response indicates self-control*. It was found with the PAM that a longer reaction time to aggression was associated with higher self-control ten years later (Pitkänen-Pulkkinen, 1980).

Insight 10 is that *most valid information is received from children's aggressive behavior when tests or observations concern (1) proactive behavior of any type and reactive direct physical aggression, (2) aggression towards a same-sex peer of the same-size, and (3) reactions to mild provocations.*

Continuity of Aggression from Childhood to Middle Age: The Jyväskylä Longitudinal Study of Personality and Social Development

The Kindergarten Study revealed that only a small percentage of boys were often aggressive in their social interactions. It raised a question of how children handle social conflicts in nonaggressive ways. In a search of the literature in the middle of the 1960s, I found only a few analyses of positive responses (Pitkänen, 1969). The study of prosocial behavior was only started in the late 1970s (e.g., Mussen & Eisenberg-Berg, 1977), and the movement of positive psychology at the beginning of this millennium (Seligman & Csikszentmihalyi, 2000).

While thinking of behavioral alternatives in threatening or conflicting situations, I got an idea that was an extension from an approach/avoidance behavior. From animal experiments, I had learned about fight/flight behavior. I thought, however, that children at a rather young age are cognitively more capable than animals and able to self-reflect about their behaviors, intentions, and emotions, and exercise control over how these are expressed. Inspired by the work of Schachter and Singer (1962) on the interface between emotion and cognition, I concluded that it is a human being's capacity for cognitive control over his or her emotional behavior that makes him or her able to decide between alternative behaviors. With this, I anticipated the role of executive control of the forebrain in human emotional behaviour, which was not yet known at that time.

I described aggressive and nonaggressive behavior with a two-dimensional impulse control model (Pitkänen, 1969, p. 102). One dimension depicted expression vs. inhibition of behavior, and the other dimension depicted cognitive control of behavior (Figure 2.2). Aggressive behavior was characterized by uncontrolled expression of impulses and the three different ways of how nonaggressive behaviors were depicted by other combinations of these dimensions.

To test the model, data were collected with 8-year-old children (N = 369, 53% males). The sample included 12 school classes that had been randomly drawn from the schools of a town with about 60,000 inhabitants. It was an industrialized university town with a similar social structure as found in Finland in general at that time. This cross-sectional study transitioned to be a longitudinal study when the same individuals were studied again at ages 14, 20, 27, 36, 42, and 50 years of age. It is called the Jyväskylä Longitudinal Study of Personality and Social Development (JYLS).

I chose *peer nominations* and *teacher ratings* at ages 8 and 14 for the assessment of socioemotional behavior, including aggression. At age 8, the items for aggression (12) covered direct and indirect reactive aggression, and direct and indirect proactive aggression, expressed physically, verbally, and facially (see Pitkänen, 1969; Pulkkinen, 1987, 2017). At age 14, aggression was assessed with the item "Who attacks without reason, teases others, says naughty things" representing proactive aggression. It was combined on the basis of findings on the relationships between single items at age 8 (Pitkänen,

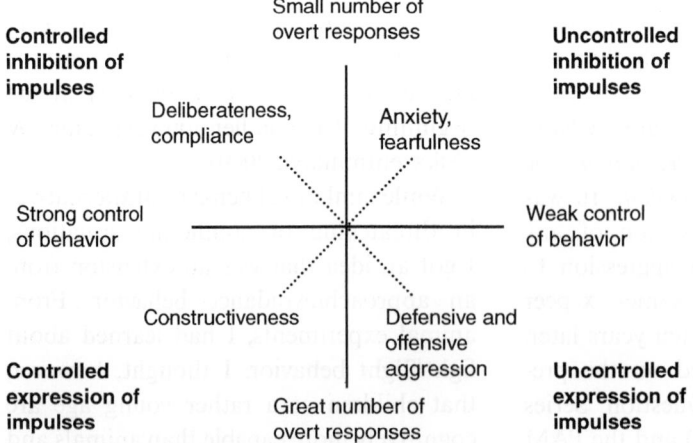

Figure 2.2 *A two-dimensional impulse control model.*
(Source: Pitkänen [1969, Figures 3 and 4, pp. 102 and 107 combined]. Reproduced with permission.)

1969). In addition, reactive aggression was assessed by "Who defends oneself if teased, but does not attack without reason?" Three names were requested as a response, when possible.

The same items were used in teacher ratings formulated as statements, e.g., "May hurt another child…" At age 8, the ratings were made on a scale from 0 (the teacher has never observed the characteristic in question in the pupil) to 3 (the characteristic is very prominent in the pupil). At age 14, the teachers were asked to think of 100 same-sex peers, because the participants were spread from 12 school classes (at age 8) to 78 classes (at age 14), and teachers were often asked to rate only one student in a class.

It was found that reactive aggression (without proactive aggression) correlated with constructive (prosocial) behavior positively (r = 0.61), whereas proactive aggression correlated negatively (r = −0.26, p < 0.001 for each; Pulkkinen, 1987). Therefore, the item for proactive aggression was used to indicate aggressive behavior at age 14.

Peer nominations and teacher ratings of aggression correlated highly (0.73) at age 8 for boys, but less so for girls (0.39). At age 14, the sex difference in the agreement was smaller than at age 8 (r = 0.49 for boys and 0.41 for girls). It was at the level (0.44) reported by Achenbach, McConaughy, and Howell (1987) in their meta-analysis on cross-informant agreement. Peers and teachers make their observations in the same context, whereas parents see children in a different context (r = 0.27).

A *Self-report Scale* on aggression was built for assessing aggression at age 26/27 (Pulkkinen & Pitkänen, 1993; Tuuli is my daughter and had followed her mother's longitudinal research since childhood).

The scale was based on the self-rating item of "I get angry often and I become easily involved in quarrels and fights," responses to nine questions such as: "Do you hit another person," and "Do you argue with people." At ages 36, 42, and 50, two inventories were used. One of them, the *Aggression Questionnaire,* included eight items (Kokko & Pulkkinen, 2005). Five items were drawn from the Aggression Questionnaire by Buss and Perry (1992), for instance, "Given enough provocation, I may hit another person." Three items were formulated for the study, for instance, for proactive aggression, "I sometimes feel the desire to tease, to annoy or to attack another person without reason." The other inventory was included in the *Karolinska Scales of Personality* (KSP; Schalling, 1986), which consist of 15 scales. The scales for verbal aggression, indirect aggression, irritability, suspicion, and guilt were combined into a scale for KSP Aggression (Pulkkinen, Feldt, & Kokko, 2005).

Boys were rated by teachers as more aggressive than girls both at ages 8 and 14 (p < 0.001 for each), as also found in many other studies. The difference was more than half a standard deviation (d = 0.67 for age 8 and 0.64 for age 14) (Pulkkinen & Pitkänen, 1993). Peer nomination of aggression in which the participants were asked to nominate only same-sex classmates did not reveal sex differences. In adulthood, sex differences did not exist in aggression, assessed with the self-report scale on aggression at age 26/27 (Pulkkinen & Pitkänen, 1993); the KSP sum scale for Aggression at ages 36 and 42 (Pulkkinen et al., 2005); and the Aggression Questionnaire (Kokko & Pulkkinen, 2005).

It has been argued by some researchers (e.g., Lagerspetz, Björkqvist, & Peltonen, 1988) that girls display indirect aggression more than boys, but this difference has not been consistently shown. In the JYLS, boys were more aggressive than girls both in direct and indirect aggression at age 8, as rated by teachers. A recent meta-analysis by Hyde (2014) also shows that boys are capable of relational (indirect) aggression, not only of direct aggression. In a Finnish twin study with 12-year-old twins, boys scored higher than girls on direct aggression both in teacher and parental ratings, but there was no significant sex difference on indirect aggression in either rating (Vierikko, Pulkkinen, Kaprio, Viken, & Rose, 2003). This suggests that since girls are generally perceived as less aggressive than boys, the *relative* meaning of equally high indirect aggression in girls' behavior may make indirect aggression more characteristic of girls than of boys.

Continuity of aggression was studied in the JYLS by comparing the means of aggression scores across ages (mean-level continuity), if possible, and by studying the relative stability of individuals' aggression scores across ages (differential continuity). The latter shows the stability of the order of individuals. The analyses resulted in several insights.

Insight 11 is that *the level of aggression is very stable in adulthood*. Aggression assessed with the KSP remained the same for men from age 36 to 50 (Pulkkinen, 2017). Also, for women, aggression remained the same from age 36 to 42, but diminished from age 42 to 50. It was due to a decrease in indirect aggression and irritability. The stability of mean scores from age 8 to 14 and then to adulthood could not been studied in the JYLS, because the items and measures were different across ages.

Insight 12 is that *the relative stability of aggression is high in adulthood*. The scores of the KSP Aggression at ages 36 and 42 were highly correlated (r = 0.82 for males and 0.67 for females) as well as scores at ages 42 and 50 (r = 0.78 for both sexes). The relative stability of the scores in the Aggression Questionnaire was of the same size (Pulkkinen et al., 2005).

It is commonly argued, with a reference to Olweus (1979), who conducted a meta-analysis of longitudinal studies on male aggression, available in the 1970s, that there is continuity of aggression from childhood to adulthood. A series of studies with the JYLS data has shown that there are age, methodological, sex, and cultural limitations to this argument.

Insight 13 is that *childhood aggression does not significantly correlate with self-reported adult aggression in Finland*. Correlations between age 8 peer nominations and teacher ratings on aggression with self-reported aggression at age 26/27 were not significant (Pulkkinen & Pitkänen, 1993). This finding was confirmed by a comparative study with two US samples. The comparison was started between the JYLS and the Columbia County Longitudinal Study, CCLS (Kokko, Pulkkinen, Huesmann, Dubow, & Boxer, 2009). There were several identical items on peer-nominated aggression at age 8 in these studies, because I had formulated items for the JYLS in 1968 to match with those used in previous studies, when possible. Items common with the study by Walder, Abelson, Eron, Banta, & Laulicht (1961) made it possible to carry out a comparative study on aggression 40 years later when the participants of both studies had reached middle age (48 years in the CCLS and 42 in the JYLS). The comparison indicated a higher continuity of physical aggression in the USA than in Finland from childhood to adolescence, and to adulthood. The model explained 49% of adult male physical aggression in the US sample (24% of female aggression), but only 12% of male (8% of female) aggression in the Finnish sample. The path coefficients between the adolescence and adulthood were in the JYLS half of those in the CCLS (0.67 for males and 0.53 for females in the CCLS, and 0.33 and 0.29 in the JYLS, respectively).

For the re-examination of the country differences in continuity of physical aggression, corresponding items and measurement points were carefully chosen. Adolescent aggression was omitted, because the continuity from childhood to adolescence and from adolescence to adulthood might explain the continuity between childhood and adulthood. Furthermore, another US sample (Child Development Project, CDP; Dodge, Bates, & Pettit, 1990) was added to the comparison (Kokko, Simonton, Dubow et al., 2014). In childhood, the intensity of overall aggression was assessed using peer nominations, and in adulthood the measures of actual physical aggression committed by the participant were used. Adult measures were from age 26/27 for the JYLS and from age 30 for the CCLS; for the CDP, from age 21 to 26. The results showed that there was no significant continuity of aggression from age 8 to adulthood in the Finnish sample, but there was continuity in the US samples. The analyses were continued by analyzing continuity of aggression with different socioeconomic backgrounds.

Insight 14 is that *a lack of continuity of physical aggression from childhood to adulthood is independent of socioeconomic background in Finland but dependent on socioeconomic background in the USA*. It was found for the US samples that when the socioeconomic status of the participants' parents was considered, continuity of aggression existed in males and females with nonprofessional backgrounds, but not in participants with professional backgrounds. This difference was not found in the Finnish sample. The similarity of the findings between the two US samples was notable, because the participants represented different age cohorts (born in the 1950s, CCLS, and in the 1980s, CDP), were located in different parts of the country, and had been assessed with different methods by different research teams. Explanations for country differences were sought from higher equality of income, schools, and opportunities for education in Finland as compared to the USA. Income inequality is associated with social problems (Wilkinson, 2011).

Continuity of aggression from childhood to adolescence and from adolescence to adulthood was studied with several models in which the amount of shared variance varied.

Insight 15 is that *there is a successive continuity of aggression from childhood to adolescence and from adolescence to adulthood independent of the method of assessment in males, but with methodological limitations in females*. It was found in the study by Pulkkinen and Pitkänen (1993) for both males and females that aggression assessed at age 8 with peer nomination correlated significantly with peer-nominated aggression at age 14, which, in turn, correlated with self-reported aggression at age 26/27. In contrast, this chain was significant only for boys in teacher ratings. Teacher ratings of girls' aggression did not show continuity.

Successive continuity in aggression from childhood through adolescence to adulthood was confirmed with a LISREL model by Kokko and Pulkkinen (2005). In this study, peer-nominated items and teacher-rated items at age 8 were separately standardized over the entire sample and then averaged across methods. Adult aggression was assessed at ages 36 and 42 with the Aggression Questionnaire. Earlier aggression explained 15% of the variance of adult aggression for males and 4% for females. Aggression at age 8 was associated with aggression at age 14, and age-14 aggression was linked to a latent variable for aggression in adulthood, covering the ages of 36 and 42. It was notable that male aggression at age 8 also directly contributed to adult aggression, not only via age 14. Further analyses revealed continuity of aggression from age 8 to adulthood only in those males who were high in aggression at ages 8 and 14.

Insight 16 is that *continuity of male general aggressiveness from childhood to adulthood is only found in men who are very aggressive both in childhood and adolescence.* Analyses with the standardized averaged scores (Kokko & Pulkkinen, 2005) indicated for males (but not for females) that the participants who were above the 75th percentile in aggression at ages 8 and 14 were higher in adult (age 36) aggression than the participants who were below the 75th percentile in aggression at both ages. Being above the 75th percentile in aggression at age 8, but below it at age 14, did not predict adult aggression.

Insight 17 is that *the increase of shared variance of aggression in childhood and adolescence by using several methods of assessment and measurement points increases the predictability of adult aggression on the basis of youth aggression.* In the study by Kokko and Pulkkinen (2005), a latent variable was formed to capture the shared variance of two measures and measurement points (peer nominations and teacher ratings of aggression at ages 8 and 14). This latent variable was a significant stability estimate with the latent variable for adult (ages 36 and 42) aggression in a LISREL analysis.

Developmental Processes Associated with Aggressive Behavior

Continuity from one point of time to another in phenotypically similar behaviors such as aggression was described above. This kind of continuity is called homotypic continuity by Kagan (1980). He distinguishes it from heterotypic continuity, which means continuity between phenotypically different behaviors. In order to interpret the connection between phenotypically different behaviors as continuity, the behaviors must be theoretically related. Gottfredson and Hirschi (1990) argue in their general theory of crime that individuals possessing high self-control prior to the age of responsibility for crime would be less likely to engage in criminal acts than individuals who lack self-control indicated by being impulsive, short-sighted, and by taking risks. In my theoretical framework (e.g., Pitkänen, 1969; Pulkkinen, 1982, 1995, 2017), aggression is an indicator of low self-control. When I started to study connections between aggression and criminal behavior, I assumed that aggression and criminal behavior share low self-control and that there is continuity between them. Several analyses focused on this were completed with the JYLS data. The results have shown continuity from aggression to crime, but only for the most aggressive individuals and for the most serious crimes.

Information about criminal records (both from the government register for convicted crime and local police records including also petty offences and arrests for which the person was not necessarily prosecuted) were examined at age 20. The criminal age of responsibility, that is, the age at which individuals can be accused of crimes, is 15 years in Finland. The government register was searched every five years up to age 46, because only certain offenses remain permanently on the register. Half of the convicted men had committed their first offence before the age of 21. Criminal behavior was highly concentrated in the same individuals (Pulkkinen, 1988): half of all criminal offenses for men up to age 20 were committed by 4.1% of males (eight men out of the whole male sample, n = 196) in Finland (5.5% of males in England). For convicted crime by age 32, the concentration of crime was even higher (Hämäläinen & Pulkkinen, 1995).

Insight 18 is that *childhood aggression correlates with male criminality, but reactive aggression without proactive aggression does not predict criminal offenses.* Peer-nominated aggression at age 8 correlated with the total number of arrests up to age 26 at r = 0.33 for males and r = 0.12 for females, and peer-nominated aggression at age 14 at r = 0.35 for males and r = 0.10 for females (Pulkkinen & Pitkänen, 1993). Different types of offenses were most highly predicted by physical, indirect, and proactive aggression in childhood, such as teasing others. Reactive aggression without proactive aggression at age 14 did not correlate with arrests up to age 20 (Pulkkinen, 1983, 1987).

Insight 19 is that *the correlation between childhood aggression and crime is explained by highly aggressive individuals. If they are removed, the longitudinal relationship between aggression and criminality completely disappears.* A correlation coefficient does not disclose the linearity of the relationship between aggression and crime. The nonlinearity of the relationship was demonstrated by Pulkkinen and Pitkänen (1993) by comparing low-, medium-, and high-aggressive groups formed at age 8, in the number of their arrests up to age 26. The high-aggressive group had more arrests than the medium- and low-aggressive groups, which did not differ from each other. This finding also applied to problem drinking. In terms of correlation coefficients, the significant correlation between aggression at age 8 and the number of arrests up to age 26 dropped to zero (0.03) when the most aggressive men (above the 75th percentile) were removed (Pulkkinen, 1998). Magnusson and Bergman (1988) had also found that the connection between childhood aggression and crime disappeared when highly aggressive men were removed from the sample.

Insight 20 is that *high aggression in childhood predicts multitype and serious offenses.* Eight men had committed three types (alcohol, violence, theft) of offenses by age 20; they had been rated as much more aggressive at age 8 than the rest of them (Pulkkinen, 1983). The seriousness of criminality was indicated by the legal consequences of a crime: convicted (n = 32), arrested (n = 62), and noncriminals (n = 102) in the study by Hämäläinen and Pulkkinen (1995). The men, who had committed crimes of which they were convicted by age 32, had the highest scores in different types of aggression at age 8 and in proactive aggression at age 14. The most prominent characteristic of the convicted men was indirect aggression indicated by teasing smaller peers and venting one's anger by kicking objects. This was consistent with the finding by Megargee (1966) that the assaultive characteristic in criminals is connected with inhibitions of overt aggression. For women, a grouping was made into noncriminals (n = 145) and criminals (comprising 22 arrested and 6 convicted women). The criminal women had also received higher scores than noncriminals in aggression at age 14, both in teacher ratings and peer nominations, and in indirect aggression as rated by teachers at age 8.

Insight 21 is that *high aggression in childhood is associated with committing offenses in early adolescence and persistent offending in males.* This conclusion was based on two studies. First, the following "onset groups" of convicted crime were formed for males in the study by Hämäläinen and Pulkkinen (1995): age 15 to 16; age 17 to 20; and age 21 to 32. The men who had committed the first recorded crime during middle adolescence scored higher on aggression at age 8 than the men who had committed their first recorded crime later. Furthermore, peers had rated the recidivists as more aggressive at age 8 than the occasional criminals.

In the second study, four male groups were formed at age 42 (Pulkkinen, Lyyra, & Kokko, 2009): (1) adolescent-limited offenders (offences existed only in youth, from age 15 to 20); (2) persistent offenders (offences had been committed in youth and adulthood); (3) adult-onset offenders (offenses only in adulthood), and (4) nonoffenders. The persistent and adult-onset offenders had been more aggressive at ages 8 and 14 than the nonoffenders and the adolescent-limited offenders. The persistent and adult-onset offenders did not differ from each other in teacher-rated aggressive behaviors at ages 8 and 14, neither did the nonoffenders and the adolescent-limited offenders in childhood aggression or in adult social functioning. The adolescent-limited offenders were better adjusted to adult life than the other offender groups, with lower drinking and lower disinhibition scores and with higher self-worth and contentment with their achievements (Pulkkinen et al., 2009). Heavy drinking, which was also predicted by aggressive behavior (Pitkänen, Kokko, Lyyra, & Pulkkinen, 2008), was associated with persistent and adult-onset offending. Aggressive behavior in childhood predicted heavy drinking via problem behaviors in adolescence (Kokko & Pulkkinen, 2000; Pulkkinen & Pitkänen, 1994).

A Person-Oriented Approach to the Predictors of Crime

Predicting of adult outcomes on the basis of childhood behavior is expected to be more valid when the effects of several variables are simultaneously considered compared to the effects of a single variable, such as aggression. Magnusson (2014, p. 328), who has advocated a holistic view of human development, has demonstrated with his research team that "partialing out the effect of other frequently used person variables in the prediction of adult problems documented in official registers, not one of the single variables demonstrated a unique prediction coefficient above 0.10." The unique contribution of single variables such as aggression to the total variance of criminality was less than 1 percent. A person-oriented approach made it possible to consider several relevant predictors simultaneously.

Insight 22 is that *childhood aggression is the predictor of crime in the interaction with poor school success in adolescence*. A logit analysis was performed to assess the independence of the effect of aggressiveness on later offences (Hämäläinen & Pulkkinen, 1996). It was found that if childhood aggression leads to poor school success in adolescence, the risk of crime increases. Childhood aggression had no independent effect on crime; the effect was in interaction with poor school success.

Insight 23 is that *norm-breaking behavior independent of aggression is more predictive of crime than aggression with poor school success*. This result was obtained in the logit analysis by Hämäläinen and Pulkkinen (1996). Norm-breaking behavior indicated by disobedience at age 8, and truancy, sanctions at school, and substance use at age 14 had a stronger main effect on arrests than aggression in interaction with poor school success.

Insight 24 is that *low self-regulation without aggression predicts criminality*. This conclusion was based on several findings: first, the effect of norm-breaking on arrests mentioned above. Second, a cluster without aggression (inattentiveness, non-prosociality, and hyperactivity-impulsivity) at age 8 was scored as high in the arrest rate, both up to age 20 and 26 as the multiproblem cluster (Pulkkinen & Tremblay, 1992). Third, the arrest rate in a cluster for poor school motivation, low school success, and lack of concentration (without aggression) was the same (33%) as the arrest rate in a mild multiproblem cluster (29%) including aggression (Pulkkinen, 1992). For females, the highest arrest rate (40%) was found in a cluster for lack of concentration and poor school motivation and success, which did not include aggression (Pulkkinen, 1992).

A fourth study was an unpublished study by Kooistra, Tolvanen, Mäkiaho, and Pulkkinen (2001). The results obtained with latent growth curve modelling showed that low self-control (moody, poor concentration) and poor (and worsening) school success explained 53% of the variance of criminal convictions in men. Criminal convictions in women were mainly predicted by low self-control; the model explained 44% of the variance. These results indicate that low self-regulation, not including aggression, is also predictive of criminal behavior. These findings are in concordance with the general theory of crime by Gottfredson and Hirschi (1990).

Insight 25 is that *low constructive behavior in childhood has an independent effect on criminality*. Constructive behavior (also called prosociality) that indicates strong control of behavior in the Impulse Control Model (Figure 2.2), was assessed in the JYLS by teacher ratings on items for active coping with a problem ("Tries to act reasonably even in an annoying situation"), positive thinking and active confrontation ("Thinks that if one negotiates, everything will be better"), and consideration of others with helpfulness and empathy ("Sides with smaller and weaker peers") (Pulkkinen, 2017, p. 24). Evidence comes from three studies. First, non-prosociality was a common element in the male cluster for Inattentiveness, where aggression was low, and in the cluster for Multiproblem behavior, where aggression was high; both clusters had later higher arrest rates than the other clusters (Pulkkinen & Tremblay, 1993). Second, constructive behavior (and high self-regulation more generally) correlated negatively with the number of arrests up to age 26 in men and women (Pulkkinen & Hämäläinen, 1995). Third, in the logit analysis by Hämäläinen and

Pulkkinen (1996), low prosociality at age 8 had an independent effect on arrests at age 27 besides the effects of norm-breaking behavior and aggression with poor school success. The result confirms the argument by Gottfredson and Hirschi (1990) on the protective effect of self-control on crime; constructive behavior indicates high self-control. Furthermore, it has been shown by Kokko and Pulkkinen (2000) that high constructive behavior is a protective factor against long-term unemployment. In this study, prosociality (containing constructive behavior, stability of mood, lack of disobedience towards the teacher) protected highly aggressive participants from becoming unemployed long-term up until the age 36. Other results on the positive role of childhood self-control (Pulkkinen, 2014) and constructive behavior (Pulkkinen, 2017) in adult social functioning are summarized elsewhere.

Insight 26 is that *a severe multiproblem pattern including high aggression predicts arrests for criminal offences*. This conclusion was based on two comparative studies. First, patterns of social adjustment were studied with the JYLS and a Canadian sample of 6–10-year-old boys (Pulkkinen & Tremblay, 1992). Aggressive behavior assessed with teacher rating divided into three clusters: (1) Multiproblem (formed by aggression, inattention, restlessness, and non-prosociality); (2) Bully; and (3) Uncontrolled behavior. The multiproblem boys of the JYLS scored highest on the arrest rate up to age 26: 33% of the multiproblem boys had been arrested, 18% of the Uncontrolled, and 8% of the Bullies.

The second comparison was made with seven clusters extracted in the Swedish study by Magnusson and Bergman (1988) by using similar clustering variables in the JYLS (Pulkkinen, 1992). In both samples of males, aggressiveness at age 8 appeared in four clusters: restlessness at age 8 (Cluster 3); poor concentration at age 14 (Cluster 5); restlessness, poor concentration, poor school motivation, and poor success at age 14 (Cluster 6, called mild multiproblem); and all of these plus poor peer relations (Cluster 7, called severe multiproblem). The highest arrest rate up to age 26 was found in the severe multiproblem cluster; almost half (45%) of the men were arrested. About 30% had been arrested in Clusters 6 and 5, and 24% in Cluster 3. The inclusion of adolescent school variables in this clustering improved the prediction of the arrest rate compared to the study by Pulkkinen and Tremblay (1992). In general, the more elements of low self-control with high intensity (such as aggression, lack of concentration, lack of prosociality, poor school attendance) were included in the cluster, the more likely the membership in the cluster was associated with criminal offending in adulthood.

Insight 27 is that *aggression may be associated with an educational career in women*. Five clusters were extracted for females from the same clustering variables as for males in the JYLS (Pulkkinen, 1992). Aggressiveness (at age 8) only appeared in one specific cluster where other problems did not appear. The Aggressiveness cluster did not predict a high arrest rate (13%) up to age 26, but it did predict educational career; 39% of the women in this cluster had an educational career (26% on the average). An educational career meant that at least half of the last seven-year period was spent for education. It turned out that there were two different routes to studying between ages 20 and 26. One group was formed by women who had been successful at school and attended higher education. They had been rated verbally as more aggressive than girls on average at age 8. Teachers had also rated them socially active and energetic at age 14. The other group was formed by physically aggressive girls who were less motivated towards school attendance, and the youngest mothers were found among them. There were, however, women among them who began their occupational training at a later age, and therefore they were on an educational career.

Aggression in the Framework of Socioemotional Development

In the 1960s, when the baseline data of the JYLS were collected, I described aggression and nonaggression with the two-dimensional impulse control model (cf. Figure 2.2). During five decades, results have confirmed that the individual differences in socioemotional behavior that the model depicted formed a basis for their differences in further development. The model has been updated during the course of the longitudinal study theoretically and by including different developmental paths to the model (Pulkkinen, 2017: Figure 4.1, p. 50). In the revised model, entitled the Model for the Unfolding of Socioemotional Behavior, self-regulation has two components: behavior regulation and emotion regulation. Low behavior regulation is seen in the Undercontrolled style of life, which ignores social norms, whereas high behavior regulation is seen in the Overcontrolled style of life. High emotion regulation characterized by the anticipatory appraisal of a situation and behavior is seen in the Resilient style of life, whereas low emotion regulation characterized by reactions to unwanted emotions aroused by a situation is seen in the Brittle style of life.

Different types of aggression are located in the two-dimensional framework of socioemotional development in Figure 2.3. It means that individuals characterized by different lifestyles are likely to express reactive aggression in different ways: First, direct reactive aggression is most likely associated with impulsive, undercontrolled behavior. Second, reactive aggression may be displayed in a controlled way, associated with high emotion regulation in conditions where constructive behavior is not effective and self-defense is deemed necessary (Pulkkinen, 1996). Third, reactive aggression may also be associated with low emotion regulation of Brittle individuals when emotional arousal exists but behavior is inhibited. Negative emotions may be expressed to another person in indirect ways, such as by damaging property. Proactive aggression involves low behavior regulation, seen in an individual's low socialization to social norms, and low emotion regulation, seen in a low understanding of another person's suffering while aiming at one's own goals, for instance by bullying. The combination of low behavior regulation and low emotion regulation also increases the likelihood of intensive reactive aggression with negative emotions (anger). Proactively aggressive individuals generally defend themselves intensively. Most nonaggressive, overcontrolled individuals with inhibited behavior may react aggressively to aggression tests, which lower their inhibitory control of behavior. Their responses to projective tests may be unrealistic in respect to overt behavior (Olweus, 1969; Pitkänen, 1969) without indicating inhibited emotions.

Aggressive behavior in childhood tends to be patterned with other problems in

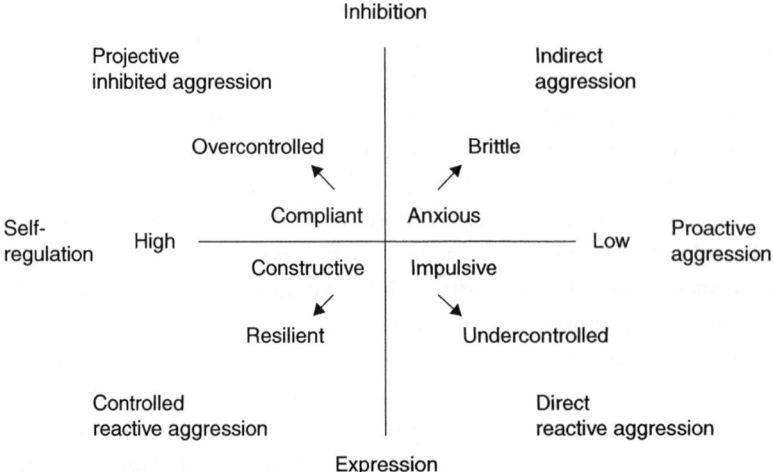

Figure 2.3 *Different types of aggression in the framework of socioemotional behavior.*

adolescence, which leads to the accumulation of problems in social functioning, such as an unstable career line, heavy drinking, financial problems, and poor relations (Rönkä & Pulkkinen, 1995). Aggression affects an individual's social functioning in various spheres of life, not only in antisocial behavior. In a marital relationship, aggressiveness is a risk factor for a divorce (Kinnunen & Pulkkinen, 2003). In the work domain, aggression is a risk factor for long-term unemployment (Kokko & Pulkkinen, 2000). In general, the JYLS findings have shown that children with aggressive behavior were at a heightened risk of having a relatively higher orientation to peers than to parents; problems in adjustment to school; early onset of substance use; and norm-breaking behaviors. It tended to lead to the style of life called Undercontrolled (Pulkkinen, 1982, 2017). The Undercontrolled style of life was a risk for criminal offences, heavy substance use, and other problems in social functioning. These risks were also found in individuals with the Brittle style of life, particularly in women.

Insight 28 is that *aggressive behavior in childhood increases an individual's risk for following a path to the Undercontrolled style of life in adulthood, and this development is associated with parenting.* A parent-centered parenting style tended to cause problems with the development of self-regulation, as seen in the Undercontrolled and Brittle styles of life (Pulkkinen, 1982, 2012, 2017). It included, for instance, the parents' lack of knowledge of the child's whereabouts, low interest in his/her school and other activities, conflicts in relationships, physical punishment, little support and empathy for the child, and inconsistent and unjust sanctions in child-rearing. A lower socioeconomic status was associated with the Brittle lifestyle. Also, unsteady living conditions were found as a background to the Brittle lifestyle. Proactive and indirect aggression was most highly associated with criminal behavior; offenders had more difficult living conditions than nonoffenders (Pulkkinen, 1983, 2012). The opposite styles of life entitled Overcontrolled and Resilient had been promoted by child-centered parenting, which involves mentalizing, that is, an individual's ability to contemplate his or her own and another person's perspective and experience; see Bateman & Fonagy (2012). It encouraged the development of high self-regulation. Higher socioeconomic status of the family of origin was associated with the development of the Resilient lifestyle.

Conclusion

Aggression can be displayed in numerous ways. The sampling of aggressive acts for the measures of aggression may be random if certain empirical facts about individual differences in aggression are not considered. My insights about aggression presented above concerned, first, the observable aspects of aggressive behavior, and they can be applied to the analysis of the construct validity of a measure of aggression. The analysis of the aspects of aggression revealed qualitative dimensions that are significant for individual differences besides the quantity (intensity) of aggression. They are proactive and reactive sequences of aggression and direct and indirect ways of displaying aggression. Aggressive behavior is situation-specific, which means that individuals choose their responses considering the status of the partner. Aggressive acts are most often displayed towards a partner who is of the same sex as the actor and of the same age, and in situations where the external control of behavior is low. Proactive aggression, such as teasing others, and particularly physically aggressive reactions to mild provocations affect other people's perceptions of a person's general level of aggressiveness. Most valid information (concurrently and predictively) is received with a measurement technique that captures these aspects and considers the target of aggression having the same status as the actor, such as the same sex and size among children.

The second set of insights concerned the continuity of aggression across time. The commonly known argument that childhood aggression predicts adult aggression is valid only with strict limitations: the intensity of childhood aggression predicts physical aggression among individuals with lower social class background in conditions where social inequality is high. Continuity is not found in the conditions of high social equality and among individuals with higher social class background. Generally, continuity of aggression is successive: from childhood to adolescence, and from adolescence to adulthood, but with methodological limitations for females. Significant predictability of aggression across ages is based on the stability of very high aggression (above the 75th percentile): individuals who remain very high in aggression across two time points tend to be very aggressive also in the next time point. High childhood aggression that does not continue to adolescence does not predict adult aggression. The increase of shared variance by forming a latent variable for aggression from several measurement techniques and measurement points increases the stability of aggression from youth to adulthood.

The third set of insights concerned aggression as a predictor of criminal behavior. Childhood aggression correlates positively with criminal arrests in males, but the correlation is formed by very aggressive males: only aggression above the 75th percentile predicts arrests, convictions, and multitype offending. Aggression does not have an independent effect on criminal behavior; the effect is formed by the interaction of high aggression and poor school motivation and achievements. High aggression tends to be associated with other problem behaviors that, together, are highly predictive of criminal behavior, but aggression is not necessary in this pattern. Norm-breaking behavior in adolescence without aggression accounts for criminal behavior. Also, low self-regulation indicated by lack of concentration and low constructive behavior (non-prosociality) account for criminal behavior. These results support the view that high self-regulation protects an individual against antisocial development.

When I started the study of aggression I was skeptical about interpreting aggression as a need. I extend this skepticism also to the interpretation of aggression as a personality trait. My view is that aggression is a vulnerability trait that causes risks for social and personality adjustment if it exceeds a critical threshold. Aggression primarily is a natural self-defensive reaction, but human beings can learn to regulate self-defensive behavior and avoid the expression of aggression. In unfortunate living conditions (sometimes also for neurological and temperament reasons), this learning process may remain poor or external pressures may become overwhelming, which may cause an excessive use of aggression for self-defense, and additionally for other purposes such as gaining power over other people.

References

Achenbach, T. M., McGonaughy, S. H., & Howell, C. T. (1987). Child/adolescent behavioral and emotional problems: Implications of cross-informant correlations of situational specificity. *Psychological Bulletin*, 101, 213–232.

Buss, A. H. (1961). *The psychology of aggression.* New York: Wiley.

Buss, A. H. & Perry, M. (1992). The aggression questionnaire. *Journal of Personality and Social Psychology*, 63, 452–459.

Dodge, K. A., Bates, J. E., & Pettit, G. S. (1990). Mechanisms in the cycle of violence. *Science*, 250, 1678–1683.

Dollard, J., Doob, L. W., Miller, N. E., Mowrer, O. H., & Sears, R. R. (1939). *Frustration and aggression.* New Haven, CT: Yale University Press.

Bateman, A. W. & Fonagy, P. (2012). *Handbook of mentalizing in mental health practice.* Washington, DC: American Psychiatric Publishing.

Goodenough, F. (1931). *Anger in young children.* Minneapolis: University of Minnesota Press.

Gottfredson, M. R. & Hirschi, T. (1990). *A general theory of crime.* Standford, CA: Stanford University Press.

Hall, C. S. & Lindzey, G. (1957). *Theories of personality.* New York: Wiley.

Hämäläinen, M. & Pulkkinen, L. (1995). Aggressive and non-prosocial behaviour as precursors of criminality. *Studies on Crime and Crime Prevention*, 4, 6–21.

Hämäläinen, M. & Pulkkinen, L. (1996). Problem behavior as a precursor of male criminality. *Development and Psychopathology*, 8, 443–455.

Hyde, J. S. (2014). Gender similarities and differences. *Annual Review of Psychology*, 65, 373–398.

Jersild, A. & Markey, F. (1935). Conflicts between preschool children. *Child Development Monographs*, Nr. 21.

Juujärvi, P. (2003). *A three-level analysis of reactive aggression among children* (Jyväskylä Studies in Education, Psychology and Social Research, No 229). Jyväskylä, Finland: Jyväskylä University Printing House.

Juujärvi, P., Kooistra, L., Kaartinen, J., & Pulkkinen, L. (2001). An aggression machine. Determinants in reactive aggression revisited. *Aggressive Behavior*, 27, 430–445.

Kagan, J. (1980). Perspectives on continuity. In O. G. Brim Jr. & J. Kagan (Eds), *Constancy and change in human development* (pp. 26–74). Cambridge, MA: Harvard University Press.

Kagan, J. & Moss, H. A. (1962). *Birth to maturity*. New York: Wiley.

Kinnunen, U. & Pulkkinen, L. (2003). Childhood socioemotional characteristics as antecedents of marital stability and quality. *European Psychologist*, 8, 223–237.

Knight, G. P., Fabes, R. A., & Higgins, D. A. (1996). Concerns about drawing causal inferences from meta-analyses: An example in the study of gender differences in aggression. *Psychological Bulletin*, 119, 410–421.

Kokko, K. & Pulkkinen, L. (2000). Aggression in childhood and long-term unemployment in adulthood: A cycle of maladaptation and some protective factors. *Developmental Psychology*, 36, 463–472.

Kokko, K. & Pulkkinen, L. (2005). Stability of aggressive behavior from childhood to middle age in women and men. *Aggressive Behavior*, 31, 485–497.

Kokko, K., Pulkkinen, L., Huesmann, L. R., Dubow, E. F., & Boxer, P. (2009). Intensity of aggression in childhood as a predictor of different forms of adult aggression: A two-country (Finland and United States) analysis. *Journal of Research on Adolescence*, 19, 9–34.

Kokko, K., Simonton, S., Dubow, E., Lansford, J. E., Olson, S. L., Huesmann, L. R., ... & Pettit, G. S. (2014). Country, sex, and parent occupational status: Moderators of the continuity of aggression from childhood to adulthood. *Aggressive Behavior*, 40, 553–567.

Kooistra, L., Tolvanen, A., Mäkiaho, A., & Pulkkinen, L. (2001). Criminal offence and mental health problems in adulthood: Modelling the predictive relationship with inattentiveness. Unpublished manuscript.

Lagerspetz, K. M. J., Björkqvist, K., & Peltonen, T. (1988). Is indirect aggression typical of females? Gender differences in aggressiveness in 11- to 12-year-old children. *Aggressive Behavior*, 14, 403–414.

Lesser, G. S. (1959). The relationships between various forms of aggression and popularity among lower-class children. *Journal of Educational Psychology*, 50, 20–25.

Magnusson, D. (2014). Individual development – a transformation process. In R. M. Lerner, A. C. Petersen, R. K. Silbereisen, & J. Brooks-Gunn (Eds), *The developmental science of adolescence: History through autobiography* (pp. 318–331). New York: Psychology Press Taylor & Francis Group.

Magnusson, D. & Bergman, L. R. (1988). Individual and variable-based approaches to longitudinal research on early risk factors. In M. Rutter (Ed.), *Studies of psychosocial risk: The power of longitudinal data* (pp. 45–61). New York: Cambridge University Press.

Mandel, R. (1959). *Die Aggressivität bei Schülern*. Bern, Switzerland: Huber.

McNeil, E. B. (1962). Patterns of aggression. *Journal of Child Psychology and Psychiatry*, 3, 65–77.

Megargee, E. I. (1966). Undercontrolled and overcontrolled personality types in extreme antisocial aggression. *Psychological Monographs*, 30, Whole No. 611.

Mischel, W. (1968). *Personality and assessment*. New York: Wiley.

Murray, H. A. (1938). *Explorations in personality*. New York: Oxford University Press.

Mussen, P. H. & Eisenberg-Berg, N. (1977). *Roots of caring, sharing, and helping: The development of prosocial behavior in children*. San Francisco, CA: Freeman, 1977.

Olweus, D. (1969). *Prediction of aggression. (On the basis of a projective test.)* Stockholm: Scandinavian Test Corporation.

Olweus, D. (1979). Stability of aggressive reaction patterns in males: a review. *Psychological Bulletin*, 86, 852–875.

Pitkänen, L. (1966). *Havaittavan aggression monidimensionaalisuudesta* [Multidimensionality of observable aggression.] (Licentiate thesis, Department of Psychology). Jyväskylä, Finland: University of Jyväskylä.

Pitkänen, L. (1969). *A descriptive model of aggression and nonaggression with applications to children's behaviour.* (Jyväskylä Studies in Education, Psychology and Social Research, No. 19). Jyväskylä, Finland: University of Jyväskylä. Available at: http://users.jyu.fi/~leapulkk/dissertation.html.

Pitkänen, L. (1973a). An aggression machine: I. The intensity of aggressive defence aroused by aggressive offence. *Scandinavian Journal of Psychology,* 14, 56–64.

Pitkänen, L. (1973b). An aggression machine: II. Interindividual differences in the aggressive defence responses aroused by varying stimulus conditions. *Scandinavian Journal of Psychology,* 14, 65–74.

Pitkänen, T., Kokko, K., Lyyra, A.-L., & Pulkkinen, L. (2008). A developmental approach to alcohol drinking behaviour in adulthood: A follow-up study from age 8 to age 42. *Addiction,* 103 (Suppl. 1), 48–68.

Pitkänen-Pulkkinen, L. (1980). An aggression machine. IV. Concurrent and predictive validity over ten years. *Scandinavian Journal of Psychology,* 21, 275–281.

Pitkänen-Pulkkinen, L. (1981). Concurrent and predictive validity of self-reported aggressiveness. *Aggressive Behavior,* 7, 97–110.

Pulkkinen, L. (1982). Self-control and continuity from childhood to adolescence. In B. P. Baltes & O. G. Brim, Jr. (Eds), *Life-span development and behavior* (Vol 4, pp. 63–105). New York: Academic Press.

Pulkkinen, L. (1983). The search for alternatives to aggression. In A. P. Goldstein & M. Segall (Eds), *Aggression in global perspective* (pp. 104–144). New York: Pergamon Press.

Pulkkinen, L. (1987). Offensive and defensive aggression in humans: A longitudinal perspective. *Aggressive Behavior,* 13, 197–212.

Pulkkinen, L. (1988). Delinquent development: theoretical and empirical considerations. In M. Rutter (Ed.), *The power of longitudinal data: Studies of risk and protective factors for psychosocial disorders* (pp. 184–199). Cambridge: Cambridge University Press.

Pulkkinen, L. (1992). The path to adulthood for aggressively inclined girls. In K. Björkqvist & P. Niemelä (Eds), *Of mice and women: Aspects of female aggression* (pp. 113–121). San Diego, CA: Academic Press.

Pulkkinen, L. (1996). Proactive and reactive aggression in early adolescence as precursors to anti- and prosocial behavior in young adults. *Aggressive Behavior,* 22, 241–257.

Pulkkinen, L. (1998). Levels of longitudinal data differing in complexity and the study of continuity in personality characteristics. In R. B. Cairns, L. R. Bergman, & J. Kagan (Eds), *Methods and models for studying the individual* (pp. 161–184). Beverly Hills, CA: Sage.

Pulkkinen, L. (2012). Family factors in the development of antisocial behavior. In T. Bliesener, A. Beelman, & M. Stemmler (Eds), *Antisocial behavior and crime: Contributions of developmental and evaluation research to prevention and intervention* (pp. 89–108). Göttingen, Germany: Hogrefe.

Pulkkinen, L. (2014b). Self-control at the heart of successful development. In R. M. Lerner, A. C. Petersen, R. K. Silbereisen, & J. Brooks-Gunn (Eds), *The developmental science of adolescence: History through autobiography* (pp. 373–385). New York: Psychology Press Taylor & Francis Group.

Pulkkinen, L. (2017). *Human Development from middle childhood to middle age: Growing up to be middle-aged* (in collaboration with Katja Kokko). London: Routledge.

Pulkkinen, L., Feldt, T., & Kokko, K. (2005). Personality in young adulthood and functioning in middle age. In S. Willis & M. Martin (Eds), *Middle Adulthood: A lifespan perspective* (pp. 99–141). Thousand Oaks, CA: Sage.

Pulkkinen, L. & Hämäläinen, M. (1995). Low self-control as a precursor to crime and accidents in a Finnish longitudinal study. *Criminal Behaviour and Mental Health*, 5, 424–438.

Pulkkinen, L., Lyyra, A.-L., & Kokko, K. (2009). Life success of males on nonoffender, adolescence-limited, persistent and adult-onset antisocial pathways: Follow-up from age 8 to 42. *Aggressive Behavior*, 35, 117–135.

Pulkkinen, L. & Pitkänen, T. (1993). Continuities in aggressive behavior from childhood to adulthood. *Aggressive Behavior*, 19, 249–263.

Pulkkinen, L. & Pitkänen, T. (1994). A prospective study of the precursors to problem drinking in young adulthood. *Journal of Studies on Alcohol*, 55, 578–587.

Pulkkinen, L. & Tremblay, R. E. (1992). Patterns of boys' social adjustment in two cultures and at different ages: A longitudinal perspective. *International Journal of Behavioural Development*, 15, 527–553.

Schachter, S. & Singer, J. E. (1962). Cognitive, social, and psychological determinants of emotional state. *Psychological Review*, 69, 379–399.

Schalling, D. (1986). The development of the KSP inventory. In B. af Klinteberg, D. Schalling, and D. Magnusson (Eds), *Self-report assessment of personality traits.* (Reports from the Project Individual Development and Adjustment, No 64, pp. 1–8.) Department of Psychology, University of Stockholm, Sweden.

Seligman, M. E. P. & Csikszentmihalyi, M. (2000). Positive psychology: An introduction. *American Psychologist*, 55, 5–14.

Spence, K. (1956). *Behavior theory and conditioning.* New Haven, CT: Yale University Press.

Vierikko, E., Pulkkinen, L., Kaprio, J., Viken, R., & Rose, R. J. (2003). Sex differences in genetic and environmental effects on aggression. *Aggressive Behavior*, 29, 55–68.

Walder, L., Abelson, R., Eron, L., Banta, T., & Laulicht, J. (1961). Development of a peer-rating measure of aggression. *Psychological Report*, 9, 497–556.

Wilkinson, R. (2011). Inequality and the wellbeing of adults and childhood in rich countries. In C. Clouder, B. Heys, M. Matthes, & P. Sullivan (Eds), *Improving the quality of childhood in Europe 2011* (Vol. 2, pp. 62–79). Forest Row: ECSWE.

3 A Life-Course Model for the Development of Intimate Partner Violence

J. Mark Eddy, Jean Schumer, Joann Wu Shortt,
Deborah M. Capaldi, Stacey S. Tiberio, and Sabina Low

Violence within the USA is often framed within public discourse as an "always on the rise" phenomenon that is perpetrated by "others" who look, think, and act in qualitatively different ways than the rest of us. Thus, violence is viewed as pathological, and that pathology is thought to reside either in the individual or within a group of individuals. In terms of the individual, the other may be given a label or diagnosis that sets them apart as deviant. In terms of groups, these others are often defined by some combination of nationality, race and/or ethnicity, and cultural practices and beliefs. Typically, the solution to dealing with the other, and thus "solving" the problem of violence, is twofold: remove them from the general population (e.g., increase incarceration) and don't allow new others into our midst (e.g., decrease immigration).

A common extension of this argument is that violence is most often committed by "strangers" – by people who are unknown to us. This conception does not square with the data. It has long been known that much of the violence experienced by people within the United States, and particularly deadly violence, is perpetrated not by strangers, but by someone known to the victim. For example, between 1993 and 2010, from 73% to 79% of homicides where the victim-offender relationship was known were committed by offenders who were either an intimate partner, relative, friend, neighbor, or acquaintance (Harrell, 2012). During this same period of time, the rate of nonfatal violent victimization committed by offenders known to the victim dropped from 39.4 to 10.5 per 1,000 people and by strangers from 37.7 to 7.1 per 1,000 people. While these statistics are at odds with popular conceptions – regarding not only the trend for violence across time but also the social context within which most violence occurs – concerns about the overall level of violence within our society are well placed. Violence is one of the top public health problems in the United States, and this is true across most of the life span. For example, intentional injury due to assault is one of the top ten leading causes of injury for people for each (5 to 10-year) age group from 10 to 64 years (CDC, 2014a), and homicide is one of the top ten leading causes of death for people, again within age groups, from birth to 64 years (CDC, 2014b).

While stranger violence has most often been studied from a cross-sectional perspective, violence that occurs within existing social or intimate relationships, and most notably within romantic relationships, has frequently been studied from a life-course developmental perspective (Capaldi, Knoble, Shortt, & Kim, 2012). Over the past four decades in particular, a number of studies have been conducted that have centered specifically on predictors of intimate partner violence (IPV), including several longitudinal studies that have followed cohorts of children as they grew into adolescence, young adulthood, and beyond. In this chapter, we focus on what is known about how IPV develops using a dynamic developmental systems approach (DDS; Capaldi & Clark, 1998; Capaldi, Kim, & Shortt, 2004; Capaldi, Shortt, & Kim, 2005; Capaldi & Wiesner, 2009; Kim, Shortt, Tiberio, & Capaldi, 2016), a life-course developmental framework that built on a program of research from the Oregon Social Learning Center (Patterson, Reid, & Eddy, 2002) and arose specifically from the findings of the longitudinal Oregon Youth Study (OYS; Patterson & Capaldi, 1991). We review recent IPV findings applying a DDS model to longitudinal data from the Linking the Interests of Families and Teachers Study (LIFT; Reid, Eddy, Fetrow, & Stoolmiller, 1999; Eddy, Reid, & Fetrow, 2000), which was conducted in the same community as the OYS but initiated a decade later. We discuss the implications of the DDS model for the prevention of IPV and place it within the context of the broader discourse surrounding violence.

Intimate Partner Violence

IPV is typically defined as physical, sexual, or psychological violence toward a romantic partner of the same or opposite sex (e.g., Capaldi et al., 2012). Physical violence is defined as unwanted forceful physical contact, and may vary, for example, from a push, to a slap, to a beating, to murder. Sexual violence is defined as physical behavior of a sexual nature that is conducted without the consent of the partner. Psychological violence (sometimes labeled "emotional" violence) is defined as acting in an otherwise unwanted offensive manner toward a partner, and may range from behaviors such as withdrawal and withholding affection, to behaviors such as ridiculing, making threats, or attempting to restrict various aspects of the life of their partner, such as contact with others or access to financial resources.

IPV within couples in the United States is a common phenomenon, occurring within 17% to 39% of adult couples in a given year (e.g., Plichta, 1996; Schafer, Caetano, & Clark, 1998). For example, in recent rigorous reviews of studies on physical IPV, an average of 23% of women and 19% of men report being victims of physical IPV (Desmarais, Reeves, Nicholls, Telford, & Fiebert, 2012a), with an overall lifetime prevalence of 34% and a past-year prevalence of 19%. In contrast, an average of 28% of women and 22% of men report being perpetrators of physical IPV (Desmarais, Reeves, Nicholls, Telford, & Fiebert, 2012b), with an overall lifetime prevalence of 24% and a past-year prevalence of 23%. Considering each of the various types of physical IPV, the majority (i.e., 58%) were reported to be *bidirectional* (e.g., from man to woman and woman to man; Langhinrichsen-Rohling, Misra, Selwyn, & Rohling, 2012), a finding that is consistent with prior rigorous reviews (e.g., Archer, 2000). Unsurprisingly, bidirectional IPV is associated with an increased likelihood of IPV-related injuries caused both by men and by women (Capaldi & Owen, 2001; Whitaker, Haileyesys, Swahn, & Saltzman, 2007).

While bidirectional IPV is the most common type, it does vary across samples (e.g., bidirectional IPV is reported less in female-oriented, nonmilitary treatment-seeking samples and higher in male-oriented, military legal/justice samples). Further, the predominance of bidirectional IPV does not mean that IPV has symmetrical impacts on men and women (Langhinrichsen-Rohling et al., 2012). It does not. Based on crime survey data, between 2002 and 2011, a greater percentage of IPV victimizations against women than men resulted in serious injury, such as broken bones, internal injury, or unconsciousness (i.e., 13% vs. 5%; Catalano, 2013). During this same time period, more women than men that were victimized (i.e., 18% vs. 11%) were medically treated for IPV-related injuries. Across a different set of studies, Archer (2000) found that 62% of those injured by partners were women. Given these findings, it is not surprising that in recent years the homicide rate due to intimate partners for women has been twice the rate for men (1.07 vs. 0.47 per 100,000), and that 70% of all victims killed by an intimate partner were women (e.g., Catalano, Smith, Snyder, & Rand, 2009). Importantly, most injuries occur in the context of bi-directional violence, which is often in opposition to public perceptions. In short, IPV is relatively common and often bidirectional within US couples, and while injury may be more common in the context of mutual aggression, regardless of the pattern of IPV (e.g., uni- or bidirectional), women are disproportionately affected in terms of serious injury and death.

Dynamic Developmental Systems Model

While IPV is a concerning aspect of adulthood for many men and women, what is often not discussed is that the majority of victims of IPV experience violence within a relationship for the first time during their emerging adulthood years, before they are 25 years of age (71% for women, 58% for men; Breiding, 2014). Between the ages of 18 and 27 years, 50% of women and 43% of men report that some form of IPV is occurring within their relationships, and further, that most of such violence is bidirectional (Renner & Whitney, 2012). Once violence becomes a part of the repertoire of behaviors practiced within a couple relationship, it can be quite difficult to eradicate (Ehrensaft et al., 2003; Shortt et al., 2012). Further, partners who learn social interactional patterns that include IPV to resolve conflicts with a romantic partner may be at increased risk to use IPV again when they enter a new relationship. Clearly, understanding what leads to the initiation of IPV in young couple relationships is vital to the development of effective prevention programs.

A promising model in this regard is the DDS model. The DDS model was developed within the context of a longitudinal study, the OYS, that began in early 1983 with 206 boys attending public elementary schools located in neighborhoods with a higher-than-usual incidence of delinquency for the local moderately sized metropolitan area (i.e., Eugene-Springfield, OR). All fourth-grade boys in selected schools were invited to participate, and 74% of families accepted. Like the population in the neighborhoods from which it was drawn, the sample was 90% European-American and 75% lower and working class. At the start of the study, the local area was in the midst of a severe economic recession, a situation that was slow to lift. Since that time, the boys have been followed as they grew into adulthood, and additional related studies have been launched focusing on their romantic relationships and on their children.

Within the DDS model, IPV is viewed as a behavior that is influenced not only by the social interactional history of a given couple, but also by the developmentally based characteristics and behaviors that each partner brings to the relationship and the current contextual factors within which their relationship is embedded. Biological, psychological, and social systems, and the interactions between and among these systems over time, are all posited to have a role in the genesis and maintenance of IPV. Multiple layers of influence from both the past and the present are related to whether or not IPV occurs within a relationship.

The model begins with a consideration of the histories and characteristics of each partner at the very beginning of their relationship. Each person grew up within a family, and their family-of-origin context generated some degree of risk or protection against the display of IPV as they entered a couple relationship. A particularly risky situation in this regard is the one described for youth on a pathway to antisocial behavior and delinquency within Patterson's Coercion Theory (Patterson, 1982; Patterson, Reid & Dishion, 1992; Dishion & Snyder, 2016), which forms the base for the DDS model. In Coercion Theory, a child enters the world with a set of biologically based response tendencies, often referred to as "temperament." Of particular note within parent–child interactions is how irritable, fussy, and soothable a baby tends to be. Parents, as well, vary in such tendencies, and their responses to their child are influenced not only by such but also by a host of other factors, including, but not limited to, their developed "personality," their current relationships, and the contexts within which they live their daily lives.

In parent–child relationships where factors such as these lead to one or both people engaging in frequent aversive behaviors (e.g., nattering, arguing, yelling) in the presence of each other, both positive and negative reinforcement contingencies coalesce around those behaviors that are likely to lead to increases in aversive behaviors not only by the parent and the child, but also by other family members (Patterson, 2016). In turn, this social interactional context increases the likelihood that aversive behaviors by parent, child, siblings, and other caregivers will be accompanied by periodic "outbursts" of intense negative emotion. In essence, family members inadvertently learn to "turn off" the aversive behavior of each other by being even more aversive, and every time this "works," this "coercive process" is insidiously reinforced to happen again. Along the way, children not only participate in this process, but observe others participating. At times, this may include being the victim of, or observing others be the victim of, violence (e.g., parent IPV, child abuse). This conception does not imply that this developmental process is the only route to domestic violence within a family, but hypothesizes that it may be one route.

Children who receive this type of "basic training" in the use of coercive social interaction within their family are primed to employ such in other relationships as well, whether with peers and caregivers in daycare, or fellow students and teachers in kindergarten and beyond. Sadly, "coercion is the antithesis of processes that bring about changes in social skill, affection, or happiness" (p. 11; Patterson, 2016). Children who use coercion tend to be rejected by others, and often end up with few, if any, friendships. With no other choices available to them, they may gravitate to other children in similar circumstances, and this connection forms the beginning of a deviant peer group. As happened with their family interactions, delinquent peer groups use positive and negative reinforcement to train each other in ways to be even more antisocial, aggressive, and delinquent. This, in turn, leads to further failure in conventional areas of achievement, such as academics, youth groups, and sports; increasing conflict and estrangement from family; and increasing contact with authority figures, including the police and members of the juvenile justice system.

When these children eventually become interested in romantic relationships, their partner choices are limited, at least to some degree, to the youth with whom they frequently interact – those who are connected to or a part of their delinquent peer group. The result is that assortative partnering is more likely – youth with difficult social interactional histories, including experience with coercive processes, are more likely to develop intimate partner relationships with youth with similar histories (Kim & Capaldi, 2004; Yamaguchi & Kandel, 1993). Once two people come together and form a couple, their behaviors with each other are influenced not only by their histories of interacting with family members and friends, but also by their individual characteristics (e.g., personality, developmental stage) and contexts (e.g., peers and peer groups, substance use), and the context that surrounds the new couple (e.g., economic circumstances, connection to family). These factors influence the social interactions that they engage in together, and the patterns of interacting that become a part of their coupleness, including unidirectional and, in the majority of couples, bidirectional IPV.

Review of Risk Factors

The DDS model postulates that a variety of risk factors, acting alone and interacting together, influence whether or not IPV is part of a couple's interactional repertoire. Capaldi, Knoble, Shortt, and Kim (2012) conducted a rigorous literature review of the IPV literature and examined the broader evidence base for risk factors called out in the DDS model. Building on earlier reviews by Schumacher, Feldbau-Kohn, Slep, and Heyman (2001), Foran and O'Leary (2008), Stith, Green, Smith, and Ward (2008), and Stith et al. (2000), Capaldi et al. (2012) identified over 17,000 abstracts of potentially relevant articles, chapters, and books, and, after inspection, 228 reports (170 on adult couples, 58 on adolescent couples), representing 95 independent samples, were selected for inclusion in the review. One such sample was the OYS, and ten reports on that sample were included (less than 5% of the total).

Evidence on the predictors of IPV were examined within three key domains of the DDS model: contextual characteristics, developmental characteristics and behavior of partners, and relationship characteristics and interactions. In terms of contextual characteristics, the most consistent risk factors included low income and unemployment, stress (often related to financial problems), minority-group status, and age, with IPV more likely to be experienced during adolescence and young adulthood. In terms of developmental characteristics and behaviors of partners, the strongest predictors found were antisocial behavior and conduct problems, and association with deviant peers. However, family-of-origin experiences, such as exposure to IPV between parent figures and being a victim of child abuse or neglect, were also found to be risk factors, as were current individual-level problems, such as substance use, depression, and a lack of support (e.g., from other adults, from parents). In terms of relationship characteristics and interactions, low relationship satisfaction and high discord and conflict were found to be risk factors for IPV, as was not being in a committed relationship, with the risk for separated women particularly high.

Across the reports reviewed, Capaldi et al. (2012) concluded that the risk factors for IPV are similar to risk factors identified for a variety of other problems during adolescence and adulthood, including delinquency and crime, substance use and abuse, and high-risk sexual behaviors (e.g., Lipsey & Derzon, 1998). Further, these risk factors tend to be associated with each other, and to interact together in various ways. For example, many of the relations between two risk factors were found to be modified by associations with other variables. Finally, there appeared to be more similarities than differences between men and women in terms of the importance of various risk factors to later IPV. These findings suggested that the DDS model highlights important factors in the development of IPV and provides a promising heuristic for additional studies.

Examination in an Independent Longitudinal Study

Over the past few years, we examined various aspects of the DDS model in a new longitudinal sample, drawn from the LIFT Study of 671 boys and girls. LIFT began ten years after OYS, and was also conducted in the Eugene-Springfield, Oregon metropolitan area. A similar process to that which was used in OYS was utilized to identify the public elementary schools that were in the neighborhoods with the highest rates of juvenile delinquency, and an attempt was made to recruit either the entire first or the entire fifth-grade class of students and their families. Approximately 85% of students and their families agreed to participate. As in OYS, most participants were European-American and members of lower- and working-class families. In the first year of the study, LIFT participants were randomly assigned by school to either receive a short-term evidence-informed, multi-modal prevention program designed to reduce child aggressive and other antisocial behaviors or to services as usual. Participants were interviewed yearly across a 15-year period, with the first interviews beginning in 1991 and the last ending in 2009, at which point the local economy was once again experiencing a severe economic recession.

When LIFT participants reached young adulthood, 323 (60%; 182 women; average age 21 years) participated with a romantic partner or spouse (146 women; average age 22 years) in a couple assessment that included interviews and questionnaires, including IPV measures administered separately to participant and partner and observed dyadic interaction. Both members of participating couples tended to be European-American (88% of participants and 83% of partners) and of lower income (76% of participants and 62% of partners earned under $25,000). No minimum length of relationship was required for participation. Couples defined their relationship status as follows: 41% were dating (5% engaged),

43% cohabitating (12% engaged), and 16% married. To date, a variety of analyses have been conducted relevant to the DDS model in this sample, and the results are overviewed in the following sections.

High prevalence of bidirectional IPV. Based on self and partner reports on the Revised Conflict Tactics Scale (Straus, Hamby, Boney-McCoy, & Sugarman, 1996), couples' IPV prevalence rates were high, with 92% of couples reporting psychological IPV, 40% physical IPV, and 55% sexual IPV, as well as 13% reporting IPV-related injuries. For the couples with IPV in their relationships, 91% participated in bidirectional psychological IPV, 71% bidirectional physical IPV, 66% bidirectional sexual IPV, and 27% experienced bidirectional IPV-related injuries. Thus, the majority of IPV occurred as dyadic and bidirectional behavior, with men and women reporting that they both perpetrated and experienced IPV in their relationships. These bidirectional IPV prevalence rates were in the range, or higher, of those found in the Langhinrichsen-Rohling et al. (2012) review of the literature.

Family-of-origin risk factors predict IPV. The prospective longitudinal design in LIFT was employed to examine the predictive power of unskilled parenting and interparent IPV in family-of-origin to IPV involvement in young adulthood (Shortt, Capaldi, Eddy, Owen, Tiberio, Low, Kim, & Jordan, 2016; Low, Tiberio, Shortt, Capaldi, Eddy, & Mulford, 2016). Family-of-origin risk factors had only small direct effects on later IPV involvement, but heightened the risk for later IPV indirectly by increasing the likelihood of problematic development. Basically, antisocial behavior and association with antisocial peers mediated the impacts of these risk factors on later IPV.

Sex differences in mediational effects on IPV. A moderation of mediation effects was found by sex, with findings suggesting that the transmission of IPV may operate somewhat differently for men and women. Antisocial behavior, in light of exposure to interparent IPV and unskilled parenting, was found to be a developmental pathway to later IPV involvement for men. In one set of analyses, mediation was found for women, but differences were uncovered in terms of the time for "windows" of risk. For men, greater conveyance of risk occurred earlier in development; for women, risk magnified later in development for those who demonstrated antisocial behaviors during adolescence. Some of these differences may be related to differences in the course and prevalence rate of antisocial behavior for girls compared to boys (e.g., Maughan, Rowe, Messer, Goodman, & Meltzer, 2004).

Peer risk factors predict IPV. Despite the compelling evidence of peer influences on various types of aggression (Espelage & Holt, 2007; Werner, & Crick, 2004), as well as other antisocial behaviors (Dishion & Patterson, 2006; Snyder, Bank, & Burraston, 2005), the role of peers in the development of IPV has been less examined. Using the LIFT prospective longitudinal design, delinquent peer association in adolescence was found to be a mediator between early risk (indicated by aggression in childhood) and later IPV perpetration and victimization during young adulthood (Tiberio, Shortt, Low, Capaldi, & Eddy, 2016). Peer factors in childhood and adolescence did not increase risk for young adult IPV beyond what could be explained by young adult delinquent peer association. Thus, evidence was found for engagement with antisocial peers as an important developmental step related to later involvement with IPV.

Proximal partner influences on IPV. In analyses of LIFT data, concurrent partner antisocial behavior and delinquent peer association was found to attenuate mediated effects from childhood risk factors to IPV in young adulthood. These findings suggest that it is not only family and developmental experiences that partners bring to their relationships that are relevant to IPV. Rather, partner influences and relationship factors also contribute to IPV. Lower levels of concurrent relationship satisfaction were related to higher levels of physical and psychological IPV victimization in young adulthood. Regarding partner substance-use influences on IPV, women's alcohol and marijuana use was associated with partner (men's) physical IPV and men's alcohol and marijuana use was associated with partners (women's) sexual IPV perpetration (Low, Tiberio, Shortt, Capaldi, & Eddy, 2016).

LIFT program effects on IPV. The overlap in risk factors for IPV and risk factors relevant to conduct disorder (Reid, Patterson, Snyder, 2002) suggested the possibility that the LIFT program might reduce the likelihood of IPV. In prior analyses, the three-month-long LIFT program, which included parenting training, child social and problem-solving skills training, a behavior management program in effect during school recesses, and enhanced parent-teacher communication, was found to have immediate impacts on strengthening social and problem-solving skills (Reid, Eddy, Fetrow, & Stoolmiller, 1999) and reducing physical aggression on the playground (Stoolmiller, Eddy, & Reid, 2000), as well as having long-term impacts on reducing conduct problems, substance use, and related outcomes during adolescence (Reid & Eddy, 2002; Eddy, Reid, Stoolmiller, & Fetrow, 2003; DeGarmo, Eddy, Reid, & Fetrow, 2009; Eddy, Barkan, & Lanham, 2016; Eddy, Feldman, & Martinez, 2016). However, these intervention effects did not carry over into the prevention of either physical, psychological, or sexual IPV perpetration or victimization during young adulthood.

Closing Thoughts

As articulated in the opening of the chapter, because we, as a society, pathologize violent acts, it is often too easy to construe violence as a "victim vs. perpetrator" duality. However, while this frame does describe some relationships marked by violence, developmental findings over the last two decades suggest this may not be an appropriate, let alone useful, framework to consider all acts of violence. Rather, intimate partner violence can also be described as a family system problem that requires attention at the level of the couple (Straus, 2016), and this frame may apply to a much larger group of couples than a pathological frame. The developmental findings from the OYS that led to the DDS model, and subsequent findings from rigorous literature reviews and analyses of LIFT longitudinal data, all support this conclusion. In short, within the general population at large, IPV is often bidirectional, and rates of IPV are similar for men and for women. Within some couples, acts of IPV will lead to serious injury and even death. Sometimes this may happen within a relationship where serious levels of abuse have been ongoing, and the psychological issues of one or both partners are pathological in nature. Regardless of the specifics of a given couple, a key question is how to prevent acts of violence from occurring in the first place within any intimate partner relationship.

Given that the majority of adults who experience IPV do so for the first time during their emerging adulthood years, prevention programs need to start early – before youth begin to engage in intimate relationships of any type. Evidence-informed prevention programs are needed for boys and girls and for men and women that recognize that both unidirectional and bidirectional IPV occurs, and that bidirectional IPV is actually more common. Given this, it is clear that both partners in a relationship need the cognitive, emotional, and behavioral skills to stop the occurrence of IPV, and to know how to leave a relationship if that is what it takes to stay safe and sound.

One promising route to the prevention of IPV may be through programs that target, more generally, the development of antisocial behavior. Given the strong relations between antisocial behavior and subsequent (and concurrent) delinquent peer affiliation, and between each of these problems and IPV, programs during middle childhood that target the prevention of antisocial behavior and delinquent peer affiliation have the potential to impact both the development and the elaboration of partner violence over the life span. However, as was found with the LIFT multimodal preventive intervention, a single exposure to such a program is no panacea. Rather, a lifespan approach to the prevention of antisocial behavior and related problems seems indicated (see Eddy, Feldman, & Martinez, 2016). Tailored booster sessions, or additional programs with new and specific targets, such as dating violence, are likely to be necessary at key points in time to extend and expand initial gains, and, ultimately, to reduce the likelihood of IPV in adolescence and adulthood. In short, given the multitude of potential determinants of IPV, multiple evidence-informed approaches, over time, seem warranted. Such efforts have the potential not only to reduce the psychological and physical trauma, disability, and mortality related to IPV for adult men and women, but also for their children.

References

Archer, J. (2000). Sex differences in aggression between heterosexual partners: A meta-analytic review. *Psychological Bulletin*, 126 (5), 651–680.

Breiding, M. J. (2014). Prevalence and characteristics of sexual violence, stalking, and intimate partner violence victimization – National Intimate Partner and Sexual Violence Survey, United States, 2011. *Morbidity and Mortality Weekly Report. Surveillance summaries* (Washington, DC: 2002), 63(8), 1–18.

Capaldi, D. M. & Clark, S. (1998). Prospective family predictors of aggression toward female partners for at-risk young men. *Developmental Psychology*, 34 (6), 1175–1188.

Capaldi, D. M., Kim, H. K., & Shortt, J. W. (2004). Women's involvement in aggression in young adult romantic relationships: A developmental systems model. In M. Putallez & K. L. Bierman (Eds), *Aggression, antisocial behavior, and violence among girls: A developmental perspective* (pp. 223–241). New York: Guilford Press.

Capaldi, D. M. & Owen, L. D. (2001). Physical aggression in a community sample of at-risk young couples: Gender comparisons for high frequency, injury, and fear. *Journal of Family Psychology*, 15, 425–440. doi: 10.1037/0893-3200.15.3.425.

Capaldi, D. M., Shortt, J. W., & Kim, H. K. (2005). A life span developmental systems perspective on aggression toward a partner. In W. M. Pinsof & J. L. Lebow (Eds), *Family psychology: The art of the science* (pp. 141–167). New York: Oxford University Press.

Capaldi, D. M., Knoble, N. B., Shortt, J. W., & Kim, H. K. (2012). A systematic review of risk factors for intimate partner violence. *Partner Abuse*, 3 (2), 231–280.

Capaldi, D. M. & Wiesner, M. (2009). A dynamic developmental systems approach to understanding offending in early adulthood. In J. Savage (Ed.), *The development of persistent criminality* (pp. 374–388). New York: Oxford University Press.

Catalano, S. (2013). *Intimate partner violence: Attributes of victimization, 1993–2011*. U.S. Department of Justice, Office of Justice Programs, Bureau of Justice Statistics, NCJ, 243300.

Catalano, S., Smith, E., Snyder, H., & Rand, M. (2009). *Female victims of violence*. US Department of Justice, Office of Justice Programs, Bureau of Justice Statistics, NCJ, 228356.

Centers for Disease Control (2014b). *Ten leading causes of death by age group, United States – 2014*. National Center for Injury Prevention and Control, CDC.

Centers for Disease Control (2014a). *Ten leading causes of nonfatal injury, United States, 2014*. National Center of Injury Prevention and Control, CDC.

DeGarmo, D. S., Eddy, J. M., Reid, J. B., & Fetrow, B. (2009). Evaluating mediators of the impact of the linking the interests of families and teachers (LIFT) multimodal preventive intervention on substance use initiation and growth across adolescence. *Prevention Science*, 10, 208–220. doi: 10.1007/s11121-009-0126-0.

Desmarais, S. L., Reeves, K. A., Nicholls, T. L., Telford, R. P., & Fiebert, M. S. (2012a). Prevalence of physical violence in intimate relationships, part I: Rates of male and female victimization. *Partner Abuse*, 3(2), 140–169.

Desmarais, S. L., Reeves, K. A., Nicholls, T. L., Telford, R. P., & Fiebert, M. S. (2012b). Prevalence of physical violence in intimate relationships, part II: Rates of male and female perpetration. *Partner Abuse*, 3(2), 170–198.

Dishion, T. J. & Patterson, G. R. (2006). The development and ecology of antisocial behavior in children and adolescents. In D. Cicchetti & D. J. Cohen (Eds), *Developmental psychopathology: Risk, disorder, and adaptation* (Vol. 3, pp. 503–541). New York: Wiley.

Dishion, T. J. & Snyder, J. (Eds) (2016). *The Oxford handbook of coercive relationship dynamics*. New York: Oxford University Press.

Eddy, J. M., Barkan, S. E., & Lanham L. (2016). Universal multimodal preventive intervention to reduce youth conduct problems and substance use. In L. M. Scheier (Ed.), *Handbook of adolescent drug use prevention: Research, intervention strategies, and practice*. Washington, DC: American Psychological Association.

Eddy, J. M., Feldman, B., & Martinez, C. R., Jr. (2016). Short- and long-term impacts of a Coercion Theory-based intervention on aggression on the school playground. In Dishion, T. J. & Snyder, J. (Eds), *The Oxford handbook of coercive relationship dynamics* (pp. 286–299). New York: Oxford University Press.

Eddy, J. M., Reid, J. B., & Fetrow, R. A. (2000). An elementary school-based prevention program targeting modifiable antecedents of youth delinquency and violence: Linking the Interests of Families and Teachers (LIFT). *Journal of Emotional and Behavioral Disorders*, 8(3), 165–176.

Ehrensaft, M. K., Cohen, P., Brown, J., Smailes, E., Chen, H., & Johnson, J. G.

(2003). Intergenerational transmissions of partner violence: A 20-year prospective study. *Journal of Consulting and Clinical Psychology*, 71 (4), 741–753.

Espelage, D. L. & Holt, M. K. (2007). Dating violence and sexual harassment across the bully-victim continuum among middle and high school students. *Journal of Youth and Adolescence*, 36, 799–811. doi: 10.1007/s10964-006-9109-7.

Foran, H. M. & O'Leary, K. D. (2008). Alcohol and intimate partner violence: A meta-analytic review. *Clinical Psychology Review*, 28(7), 1222–1234.

Harrell, E. (2012). Violent victimization committed by strangers, 1993–2010. US DOJ, Office of Justice Programs, Bureau of Justice Statistics. NCJ239424.

Kim, H. K. & Capaldi, D. M. (2004). The association of antisocial behavior and depressive symptoms between partners and risk for aggression in romantic relationships. *Journal of Family Psychology*, 18(1), 82–96.

Kim, H. K., Shortt, J. Wu., Tiberio, S., & Capaldi, D. M. (2016). Aggression and coercive behaviors in early adult relationships: Findings from the Oregon Youth Study-Couples Study. In T. J. Dishion & J. Snyder (Eds), *Handbook of Coercive Relationship Dynamics* (pp. 169–181). New York: Oxford University.

Langhinrichsen-Rohling, J., Misra, T. A., Selwyn, C., & Rohling, M. L. (2012). Rates of bidirectional versus unidirectional intimate partner violence across samples, sexual orientations, and race/ethnicities: A comprehensive review. *Partner Abuse*, 3(2), 199–230.

Lipsey, M. W. & Derzon, J. H. (1998). Predictors of violent or serious delinquency in adolescence and early adulthood: A synthesis of longitudinal research. In R. Loeber & D. P. Farrington (Eds), *Serious and violent juvenile offenders: Risk factors and successful interventions* (pp. 86–105). Thousand Oaks, CA: Sage.

Low, S., Tiberio, S. S., Shortt, J. W., Capaldi, D. M., & Eddy, J. M. (2016). Associations of couples' intimate partner violence in young adulthood and substance use: A dyadic approach. *Psychology of Violence, Advance online publication.* doi: 10.1037/vio0000038.

Low, S., Tiberio, S. S., Shortt, J. W., Capaldi, D. M., Eddy, J. M., & Mulford, C. (2016). *Childhood exposure to interparent violence and young adult intimate partner violence.* Manuscript submitted for publication.

Maughan, B., Rowe, R., Messer, J., Goodman, R., & Meltzer, H. (2004). Conduct disorder and oppositional defiant disorder in a national sample: Developmental epidemiology. *Journal of Child Psychology and Psychiatry*, 45, 609–621. doi: 10.1111/j.1469-7610.2004.00250.x.

Patterson, G. R. (1982). *A social learning approach: Vol. 3: Coercive family process.* Eugene, OR: Castalia.

Patterson, G. R. (2016). Coercion theory: The study of change. In Dishion, T. J. & Snyder, J. (Eds), *The Oxford handbook of coercive relationship dynamics* (pp. 7–22). New York: Oxford University Press.

Patterson, G. R. & Capaldi, D. M. (1991). Antisocial parents: Unskilled and vulnerable. In P. A. Cowen & E. M. Heatherington (Eds), *Family transitions* (pp. 195–218). Hillsdale, NJ: Lawrence Erlbaum.

Patterson, G. R., Reid, J. B., & Dishion, T. J. (1992). *A social interactional approach: Vol. 4: Antisocial boys.* Eugene, OR: Castalia.

Patterson, G. R., Reid, J. B., & Eddy, J. M. (2002). A brief history of the Oregon model. In J. B. Reid, G. R. Patterson, & J. Snyder (Eds), *Antisocial behavior in children and adolescents: A developmental analysis and model for intervention* (pp. 3–24). Washington, DC: American Psychological Association.

Plichta, S. B. (1996). Violence and abuse: Implications for women's health. In M. M. Falik & K. S. Collins (Eds), *Women's health: The Commonwealth Fund Study* (pp. 237–272). Baltimore, MD: Johns Hopkins University Press.

Reid, J. B. & Eddy, J. M. (2002). Preventive efforts during the elementary school years: The Linking the Interests of Families and Teachers project. In Reid, J. B., Patterson, G. R., Snyder, J. (Eds), *Antisocial behavior in children and adolescents: A developmental analysis and model for intervention* (pp. 219–234). Washington, DC: American Psychological Association.

Reid, J. B., Eddy, J. M., Fetrow, R. A., & Stoolmiller, M. (1999). Description and immediate impacts of a preventive intervention for conduct problems. *American Journal of Community Psychology*, 24(4), 483–517.

Reid, J. B., Patterson, G. R., Snyder, J. (Eds) (2002). *Antisocial behavior in children and adolescents: A developmental analysis and model for intervention*. Washington, DC: American Psychological Association.

Renner, L. M. & Whitney, S. D. (2012). Risk factors for unidirectional and bidirectional intimate partner violence among young adults. *Child Abuse and Neglect*, 36, 40–52.

Schafer, J., Caetano, R., & Clark, C. (1998). Rates of intimate partner violence in the United States. *American Journal of Public Health*, 88 (11), 1702–1704.

Schumacher, J. A., Feldbau-Kohn, S., Slep, A. M., & Heyman, R. E. (2001). Risk factors for male-to-female partner physical abuse. *Aggression and Violent Behavior*, 2(2–3), 281–352.

Shortt, J. Wu., Capaldi, D. M., Kim, H. K., Kerr, D. C. R., Owen, L. D., & Feingold, A. (2012). Stability of intimate partner violence by men across 12 years in young adulthood: Effects of relationship transitions. *Prevention Science*, 13, 360–369.

Shortt, J. W., Capaldi, D. M., Eddy, J. M., Owen, L. D., Tiberio, S. S., Low, S., … & Jordan, K. (2016). *Prospective family predictors of intimate partner violence for young men and women*. Manuscript submitted for publication.

Snyder, J., Bank, L., & Burraston, B. (2005). The consequences of antisocial behavior in older male siblings for younger brother and sisters. *Journal of Family Psychology*, 19, 643–653. doi: 10.1037/0893-3200.19.4.643.

Stoolmiller, M., Eddy, J. M., & Reid, J. B. (2000). Detecting and describing preventative intervention effects in a universally school-based randomized trail targeting delinquent and violent behavior. *Journal of Consulting and Clinical Psychology*, 68, 296–306. doi: 10.1037/0022-006X.68.2.296.

Stith, S. M., Green, N. M., Smith, D. B., & Ward, D. B. (2008). Marital satisfaction and marital discord at risk markers for intimate partner violence: A meta-analytic review. *Journal of Family Violence*, 23(3), 149–160.

Stith, S. M., Rosen, K. H., Middleton, K. A., Busch, A. L., Lundeberg, K., & Carlton, R. P. (2000). The intergenerational transmission of spouse abuse: A meta-analysis. *Journal of Marriage & the Family*, 62(3), 640–654.

Straus, M. A. (2016). Gender-violence, dyadic-violence, and dyadic concordance types: A conceptual and methodological alternative to Hamby (2016) that incorporates both the gendered and dyadic interaction aspects of violence to enhance research and the safety of women. *Psychology of Violence*, 6, 336–346.

Straus, M. A., Hamby, S. L., Boney-McCoy, S., & Sugarman, D. B. (1996). The revised conflict tactics scales (CTS2): Development and preliminary psychometric data. *Journal of Family Issues*, 17, 283–316. doi: 10.1177/019251396017003001.

Tiberio, S. S., Shortt, J. W., Low, S., Capaldi, D. M., & Eddy, J. M. (2016). *Longitudinal associations between childhood aggression, adolescent delinquent peer affiliation, and young adult intimate partner violence*. Manuscript submitted for publication.

Werner, N. E. & Crick, N. R. (2004). Peer relationship influences on the development of relational and physical aggression during middle childhood: The roles of peer rejection and association with aggressive friends. *Social Development*, 13, 495–513.

Whitaker, D. J., Haileyesus, T., Swahn, M., & Saltzman, L. S. (2007). Differences in frequency of violence and reported injury between relationships with reciprocal and nonreciprocal intimate partner violence. *American Journal of Public Health*, 97, 941–947. doi: 10.2105/AJPH.2005/079020.

Yamaguchi, K. & Kandel, D. (1993). Marital homophily on illicit drug use among young adults: Assortative mating or marital influence? *Social Forces*, 72 (2), 505–528.

4 The Dark Violence Hybrid: The Cross-Cultural Validation of an Integrative Model

Aurelio José Figueredo, Emily Anne Patch, Marisol Perez-Ramos, and Gabriela Jacqueline Cruz

Introduction

Viewing behavior through an evolutionary lens allows researchers to identify both adaptive and maladaptive proximate responses to certain contexts in relation to their ultimate consequences. The purpose of this paper is to follow a theoretically predicted cascade of consequences starting from the life history strategies of individuals, through the development of various cognitive social schemata, to their effects on behavioral self-regulation and rule governance, to their ultimate *sequelae* in enacting various forms of interpersonal aggression. In so doing, we also hoped to provide some support for the criterion validation of a recently introduced, mostly attitudinal measure called the Dark Inventory (DI) (Patch, 2014) with respect to self-reported interpersonal aggression.

Life History (LH) *theory* is a seminal theory derived from evolutionary biology that describes how and why individual organisms allocate varying amounts of bioenergetic resources towards different components of fitness, whereas the different resource allocation profiles that may evolve and develop as a result of varying selective pressures are called LH *strategies*. Allocations towards different components of fitness include those dedicated to growth and maintenance of the body as well as those dedicated to producing offspring (Figueredo, Patch, & Goméz-Ceballos, 2015); these two disparate resource expenditures are denoted *somatic effort* and *reproductive effort*, respectively. Within the domain of reproductive effort, there are two subordinate domains of resource allocation: *mating effort* and *parental effort* (Ellis et al., 2009; Figueredo & Jacobs, 2010). Mating effort consists of expending time and energy acquiring and retaining sexual partners while parental effort refers to expending energy contributing to the development and survival of an organism's offspring and other genetic kin.

LH theory predicts that organisms will allocate more resources towards somatic than reproductive effort if their environments are stable and predictable, resulting in a *slow* LH strategy; for instance, the organism has the time to devote developmental resources to growing long bones or developing a larger brain. Conversely, an individual would instead devote more resources to early sexual maturation and reproduction if the environment is harsh or unpredictable. In a harsh or unpredictable environment, uncontrollable or *extrinsic* mortality is high. It therefore becomes adaptive to develop and reproduce quickly, enhancing the probability that an organism's genes will be passed on prior to being overtaken by any unavoidable cause of premature death.

LH theory makes predictions related to observable, biodemographic outcomes such as parental effort, inception of puberty, age of first sexual activity, or age of first birth (MacArthur & Wilson, 1967; Pianka, 1970). Fast LH strategists evolve traits that facilitate reproduction: (1) earlier pubertal timing; (2) higher number of mating partners; (3) earlier first parturition; (4) higher number of offspring; or (5) lower levels of parental care, as compared with their slower counterparts. Slower LH strategists first expend resources in promoting their own growth and preservation and only then in producing offspring, thus evolving: (1) later first parturition; (2) fewer offspring; (3) high parental investment; and (4) extended lifespan.

In addition to these biodemographic outcomes, LH theory makes predictions about psychological traits (Figueredo et al., 2014). Fast-LH individuals display a constellation of psychosocial characteristics selected to increase their proximate expenditure of mating effort, with the ultimate function of achieving a higher fertility. They maintain positive attitudes toward promiscuity and risk-taking behavior, are more impulsive, maintain suspicious attitudes towards others, and are less governed by social norms (Figueredo et al., 2015; Olderbak & Figueredo, 2010).

Figueredo and Jacobs (2010), as well as Patch, Figueredo, Garcia, and Kavanagh (in prep.), have proposed that faster-LH strategists are likely to evolve and develop antagonistic social schemata, thus increasing the likelihood of developing Dark Triad (DT) traits, such as *psychopathy,* *narcissism,* and *machiavellianism.* New research supports the prediction that harsh or unpredictable early childhood environments may result in elevated DT characteristics (Jonason, Icho, & Ireland, 2016). LH theory (and evolutionary theory more broadly) might be particularly important when examining behavior that may appear deviant or maladaptive, such as the DT traits, especially when they continue to persist in the general population despite our efforts to suppress them. The three DT personalities have many seemingly maladaptive characteristics. High-DT individuals are callous (Jonason et al., 2009; Jones & Figueredo, 2013; Paulhus & Williams, 2002), have a grandiose sense of self (Patch et al., in prep.), are highly suspicious and coercive (Jones & Paulhus, 2010), and rarely conform to societal rules (Figueredo et al., 2015), very much akin to the constellation of traits associated with faster-LH individuals.

In addition to LH speed and DT personalities, executive functioning is believed to be another important determinant of aggressive behavior. Individuals with a high degree of executive functioning abilities demonstrate superior cognitive flexibility in domains ranging from future planning to inhibiting or delaying responding. They plan and prioritize actions in a streamlined manner (Lezak, Howieson, & Loring, 2004). Importantly, individuals with good executive functioning are able to suppress their impulses.

Executive functions have been shown to function at low levels in DT personalities (Patch et al., in prep.). A fast-LH individual with low executive function and high DT traits would have little concern for following the rules of society and exhibit a high degree of interpersonal aggression (Figueredo et al., 2015). It is probably for this reason that, while psychopaths make up less than 3% of the male population, they make up 20% of the prison population (Tuvblad et al., 2014).

Based on prior research, the present study tests a structural model for the prediction of interpersonal aggression, using two very disparate samples. One sample represents an undergraduate college student population from the State of Arizona and the other represents a population of married homemakers, each with at least one adolescent child, residing in the Mexican Municipality of Ixtapaluca. We compared the second sample to the first for the purpose of trying to offset for any biases that might arise when relying exclusively upon student samples.

Ixtapaluca is a municipality that comprises part of the State of Mexico, located 23 kilometers east of Mexico City. The Secretariado Ejecutivo del Sistema Nacional de Seguridad Pablica (2012) places Ixtapaluca as having the tenth-highest crime rate among the 125 municipalities that constitute the State of México (SESNSP, 2012). The most common crime is common robbery, followed by injuries, burglaries, sexual assaults, homicides, and kidnappings. As might be imagined, the problem of criminality exists not only at the level of the Municipality but also at the level of the State. As recently as only two years ago, the Mexican Federal Government issued a *gender alarm* in response to the very high rates of femicides in the State of Mexico, and the Municipality of Ixtapaluca was once again found to have one of the top ten rates of femicide within the State of Mexico.

Within this context of criminality, one of the most common manifestations of violence within the Ixtapaluca community is domestic (or "intimate partner") violence, meaning those acts of aggression that are restricted to interactions within private contexts. Violence may be present among couples that are currently dating or in a sexual relationship, whether or not they are living together under the same roof, or between former sexual partners. Another modality of family violence extends itself to children and to elders. This makes it especially important to validate better measures of the DT personality factors as possible risk factors for violent behavior in one sample derived from a context of violence in comparison with another sample seemingly without presenting these same levels of aggression. Such comparisons would empirically support the validity of the hypothesized measurement and structural models predicting interpersonal aggression.

Another aim of this study was to examine the mediating role of the DT personalities, and specifically the construct of an *antagonistic social schema*, hypothesized to account for much of the observed association between LH strategy and interpersonal aggression (Figueredo, Gladden, & Beck, 2012; Figueredo, Gladden, & Hohman, 2012). Previous research had examined Culture of Honor "Revenge" Ideology (see Figueredo et al., 2004) in the mediating role; however, as might be evident from much of the foregoing, DT personalities may be more causally influential.

Method

Participants

Sample 1 consisted of 121 participants that were recruited from a southwestern US university undergraduate psychology subject pool. The sample was 72% female with a mean age of 19.33 years (SD = 1.72, range

18–31). Ethnicity distribution was 55% White, 18% Hispanic, 9% Asian, 5% other, and 7% mixed race. Three participants identified as Native American, one as African-American, and one declined to identify their ethnicity.

Sample 2 consisted of 100 Mexicans from the city of Ixtapaluca in Mexico. The sample was 91% female, with a median age of 38.53 years. While the entire sample reported they were Mexican nationals, 51% identified as indigenous Mexicans, while 31% reported they were Mestizo.

Procedure

Sample 1 participants completed a set of self-report measures online to ensure anonymity and confidentiality. All participants gave informed consent and were debriefed in person. The data were collected using Qualtrics data collection software.

Sample 2 parents were contacted through a high school located in the "El Molino" neighborhood of Ixtapaluca. They were initially contacted by telephone to invite them to participate in the study and to set a time and date for meeting. Data were collected by face-to-face interviews, during school hours. Data collection took approximately 24 months to complete.

Measures

Higher-Order LH (Super-K)

LH strategy. The Mini-K Short Form (Figueredo et al., 2006) measures slow LH strategy. The Mini-K consists of 20 items and is a short form of the Arizona Life History Battery (Figueredo, 2007). The Mini-K measures a variety of LH indicators such as familial closeness and risk avoidance rated on a 7-point Likert scale (-3 = *strongly disagree*; $+3$ = *strongly agree*). Slower LH strategies were also measured using the High-K Strategy Scale (HKSS; Giosan, 2006). The scale consists of 26 items rated on a 5-point Likert scale (-2 = *strongly disagree*; $+2$ = *strongly agree*). It contains items that are indicators of health, "upward mobility," and extended family; all are attempting to measure the larger latent life history factor.

Covitality. Current levels of mental and physical functioning were measured using the Rand 36 Item Health Survey: Version 1 (Ware & Sherbourne, 1992). The Rand 36 Short Form correlates with the Mini-K as a measure of slow LH strategy. The measure consists of 36 items assessing emotional and physical well-being.

Personality. The General Factor of Personality was measured using an aggregate of the *Ten-Item Personality Inventory* (TIPI; Gosling et al., 2003). The TIPI consists of ten items, measured using a 7-point Likert scale (-3 = *disagree strongly*; $+3$ = *agree strongly*). The TIPI measures the Big 5 personality dimensions.

Dark Triad Personalities

The Dark Inventory (DI; Patch et al., in prep.). The DI is a measure of DT characteristics that does not classify the three personalities into separate traits, but rather groups them according to dissimilar cognitive social schemata: antagonistic and mutualistic. In addition, a third cluster of the scale, lability, measures impulsive attitudes, boredom, and ability to remain calm under stressful circumstances. The Antagonistic Social Schema (ASS) cluster consists of: (1) deception; (2) grandiosity; (3) external blame; (4) suspicion of others and their motives; and (5) social nonconformity. The Mutualistic Social Schema (MSS) consists of: (1) emotional empathy; (2) emotional attachment; and (3) affiliative dominance. Lability consists of: (1) impulsivity; and (2) stress reactivity. Participants rate how much they agree or disagree with each item on a 7-point Likert scale (−3 = *strongly disagree*; +3 = *strongly agree*). Each of these scales is estimated as the mean of each cluster with certain items reversed. When constructing the general DI factor, the entire MSS cluster is reversed.

Behavioral self-regulation (BRIEF; Gioia et al., 2002). The Behavioral Regulation Scales of the Brief Ratings Inventory of Executive Function (BRIEF) measured behavioral and cognitive inhibition, as well as self-regulation, all as indicators of executive functioning. The Behavioral Regulation Scales of the BRIEF contains 30 items within four subscales, each rated on a 7-point scale (0 = *never*; 6 = *almost always*).

Rule Governance (RG)

The Rule Governance Scale (Garcia, Gladden, Figueredo, & Jacobs, in preparation) consists of two subscales: Rule Governance Good (RGG) and Rule Governance Lawful (RGL). RGG measures altruistic behaviors (i.e., generosity toward strangers). RGL measures one's concern for following societal laws (i.e., respecting the authority of a police officer). A sample RGG item was "Would you donate time and money to improve the local community?" Typically, two of the response options would result in a positive score (+1) on the respective component, such as: "Yes, the needs of the community are a top priority to me" and "Yes, I would donate as much as I can once my own needs are met." A sample RGL item was "I would obey the authorities in the community," with the two positive response options: "Almost Always" and "Sometimes."

Same-Sex and Opposite-Sex Interpersonal Aggression

The 94-item Interpersonal Relations Rating Scale (IRRS; Figueredo et al., 2010) was used to measure psychological and physical aggression towards any and all members of their same sex and with any and all members of the opposite sex (whether or not they were romantic partners) with which participants had interacted. Participants rated how often each action had occurred in the past 12 months on a 6-point scale (0 = *never*; 5 = *daily*). The scale contains 47 parallel items for same-sex victims of interpersonal aggression, aggregated into a scale called the IRRS-S, and 47 parallel items for opposite-sex victims of interpersonal aggression, aggregated into a scale called the IRRS-O. These items were constructed to be otherwise equivalent in form and content to the items of the Relationship Behavior Rating Scale – Revised (RBRS-R), except that they asked participants to report their perpetration rather than their victimization, and that the questions were not limited to interactions with romantic partners. The IRRS-S scale includes items such as "I put down a member of my same sex" and "I threw objects at a member of my same sex." The IRRS-O scale includes items such as "I put down a member of the opposite sex" and "I threw objects at a member of the opposite sex." A total of five subscales were constructed for each IRRS perpetration scale, equivalent to those of the RBRS-R victimization scale.

Statistical Analyses

The measurement models. A hierarchical analytical strategy was employed to construct the measurement models, using SAS 9.1.3 (SAS Institute, 2004). Using PROC STANDARD and DATA, unit-weighted composite scores were estimated by computing: (1) the means of the standardized scores for all nonmissing items on each subscale; (2) the means of the standardized scores for all nonmissing subscales on each scale; and (3) the means of the standardized scores for all nonmissing scales on each factor (Figueredo, McKnight, McKnight, & Sidani, 2000). The Cronbach's alphas and the part-whole correlations of the scales with the unit-weighted factor scales were computed using PROC CORR. The hierarchical regressions within the sequential cascade model were estimated using the UniMult 2 software (UM2; Gorsuch, 2016) package.

The structural models. The structural models for combining the results of Study 1 and Study 2 were structured as a system of hierarchical multiple regressions referred to as a *cascade model* in cognitive psychology (Demetriou, Christou, Spanoudis, & Platsidou, 2002; Mouyi, 2006). This procedure is conceptually equivalent to a sequential canonical analysis (Figueredo & Gorsuch, 2007), which controls statistically for any indirect effects of the predictors through the causally prior criterion variables.

In a cascade model, a series of hierarchical multiple regressions is performed in which the multiple criterion variables are analyzed sequentially according to a hypothesized causal order. Because these criterion variables are expected to causally influence each other, they are entered sequentially into a system of multiple regression equations with each hierarchically prior criterion variable entered as the first predictor for the next. Thus, each successive criterion variable is predicted from an initial predictor variable, each time entering the immediately preceding criterion variable hierarchically as the first predictor, then entering all the ordered predictors from the previous regression equation. Thus, each successive regression enters all of the preceding criterion variables in reverse causal order, to statistically control for any indirect effects that might be transmitted through them. Within this analytical scheme, the estimated effect of each predictor is limited to its direct effect on each of the successive criterion variables. As the present study entails a constructive replication, a binary (1,0) "dummy variable" was also created for performing formal cross-sample comparisons of parameter estimates (Cohen & Cohen, 1983). The interaction of each successive variable in the cascade was used in the prediction of the next, as well as all that follow.

Cascade models were preferable because they allowed for the collinearities among our dependent criterion variables to be examined and sequentially statistically controlled. In the model presented here, Super-K, a latent common factor measuring LH strategy, is used to predict MSS in the first equation. In the second equation, the contribution of MSS to the prediction ASS is statistically controlled prior to estimating that of the Super-K Factor, which was the only predictor in the first equation. In each equation, any significant predictor of the dependent criterion variable thus represents the direct contribution of that predictor after having already statistically controlled for any indirect effects that might have been transmitted through the prior ones.

The ordering of variables is of paramount importance in a cascade model and each must be entered sequentially as specified by theory. In our model, MSS is hypothesized to be directly influenced by Super-K, as a slower LH speed is theorized to give rise to an individual who is more empathic and cooperative. ASS is the second criterion variable in the model, as those low on mutualism will likely lack empathy, be highly suspicious of others, use deception frequently, and blame others for their transgressions and devious actions. These traits are highly indicative of DT personalities, which are associated with low anxiety and high impulsivity, so we hypothesize that Affective and Cognitive Lability can be predicted from antagonism. Faster-LH individuals are high on DT traits but have disparate executive functioning abilities. While they are high on some aspects of executive functioning, like the ability to shift from one task to another with ease, they are low on behavioral and emotional regulation (Mittal, Griskevicius, Simpson, Sung, & Young, 2015). Executive function is therefore the next criterion variable in the model, following Affective and Cognitive Lability. A deficit in executive functioning then predicts a lack of rule governance; an individual may be unable to control their impulses or regulate their behavior well enough to properly adhere to societal and cultural norms. Ultimately, we hypothesize that this inability and failure to follow rules leads to a high degree of interpersonal aggression.

Results

Measurement Models

The first major psychometric question to address is whether the basic measurement models for the DI were replicated across the Arizona and Ixtapaluca samples, as the validity of the results of the structural model is critically dependent upon that fundamental premise. The following set of tables display those results in parallel for the two cross-cultural samples.

Table 4.1 displays the unit-weighted factor structures of the Mutualistic Social Schema (MSS) Factor with respect to its three indicators. We observe that the factor loadings were literally identical.

Table 4.2 displays the unit-weighted factor structures of the Antagonistic Social Schema (ASS) Factor with respect to its five indicators. We observe that the factor loadings were nearly identical, with the exception of two corresponding pairs of factor loadings differing by 0.01.

Table 4.3 displays the unit-weighted factor structures of the Affective and Cognitive Lability (ACL) Factor with respect to its two indicators. We observe that the factor loadings were, once again, literally identical.

We conclude that the results of these comparisons indicate an acceptable degree of measurement invariance.

Structural Models

The second major theoretical question to address is whether the basic structural model for predicting interpersonal aggression from the DI, through our theoretically specified order of hypothesized mediators, was replicated across the Arizona and Ixtapaluca samples. Table 4.4 displays those results in parallel for the two cross-cultural samples.

Mutualistic Social Schema. We see from this first regression equation that slow life history strategy, as operationalized by the Super-K Factor, significantly and positively predicted the Mutualistic Social Schema Factor, as expected by theory.

Table 4.1 *Mutualistic Social Schema*

Mutualistic Social Schema	Arizona Factor Loading	Arizona p(H₀)	Ixtapaluca Factor Loading	Ixtapaluca p(H₀)
Affiliative dominance	0.70*	< 0.0001	0.70*	< 0.0001
Emotional attachment	0.75*	< 0.0001	0.75*	< 0.0001
Emotional empathy	0.63*	< 0.0001	0.63*	< 0.0001

Note: *$p < 0.05$.

Table 4.2 *Antagonistic Social Schema*

Antagonistic Social Schema	Arizona Factor Loading	Arizona p(H₀)	Ixtapaluca Factor Loading	Ixtapaluca p(H₀)
Distrust	0.83*	< 0.0001	0.82*	< 0.0001
Deception	0.78*	< 0.0001	0.78*	< 0.0001
External blame	0.78*	< 0.0001	0.77*	< 0.0001
Grandiosity	0.80*	< 0.0001	0.79*	< 0.0001
Social nonconformity	0.58*	< 0.0001	0.58*	< 0.0001

Note: *$p < 0.05$.

Table 4.3 *Affective and Cognitive Lability*

Affective and Cognitive Lability	Arizona Factor Loading	Arizona p(H₀)	Ixtapaluca Factor Loading	Ixtapaluca p(H₀)
Impulsivity	0.77*	< 0.0001	0.77*	< 0.0001
Stress reactivity	0.77*	< 0.0001	0.77*	< 0.0001

Note: *$p < 0.05$.

Further, we see that there was no significant parametric difference in the size of this effect between the Arizona and Ixtapaluca samples, as operationalized by the interaction of our binary dummy variable for Sample with the Super-K Factor.

Antagonistic Social Schema. We see from this second regression equation that the Mutualistic Social Schema Factor significantly and negatively predicted the Antagonistic Social Schema Factor, as expected by theory. Further, we see that there was no significant parametric difference in the size of this effect between the Arizona and Ixtapaluca samples.

In addition, we see that the Super-K Factor had no significant main effect upon the Antagonistic Social Schema Factor, but that the interaction of the Super-K Factor with our binary dummy variable for Sample did significantly and negatively

Table 4.4 *Sequential Canonical "Cascade" Model*

Criterion Variables	Prior Criterion Variables	Predictor Variables	DF	Semipartial Correlations	$p(H_0)$
Mutualistic Social Schema		Super-K	1,209	0.18*	0.009
		Super-K *sample	1,209	0.09	0.20
Mutualistic R^2			2,209	0.20*	0.01
Antagonistic	Mutualistic		1,207	−0.39*	< 0.0001
	Mutualistic *sample		1,207	0.07	0.29
		Super-K	1,207	−0.08	0.19
		Super-K *sample	1,207	−0.17*	0.007
Antagonistic R^2			4,207	0.44*	< 0.0001
Affective and Cognitive Lability	Antagonistic		1,205	0.49*	< 0.0001
	Antagonistic *sample		1,205	0.04	0.44
	Mutualistic		1,205	−0.29*	< 0.0001
	Mutualistic *sample		1,205	0.15*	0.01
		Super-K	1,205	−0.05	0.38
		Super-K *sample	1,205	−0.05	0.38
Lability R^2			6,205	0.60*	< 0.0001
Executive Functions	Lability		1,203	−0.39*	< 0.0001
	Lability *sample		1,203	0.20*	0.0005
	Antagonistic		1,203	−0.30*	< 0.0001
	Antagonistic *sample		1,203	0.02	0.76
	Mutualistic		1,203	0.04	0.45
	Mutualistic *sample		1,203	−0.01	0.90
		Super-K	1,203	0.10	0.10
		Super-K *sample	1,203	0.20*	0.0004
Executive R^2			8,203	0.58*	< 0.0001

(*continued*)

Table 4.4 *(cont.)*

Criterion Variables	Prior Criterion Variables	Predictor Variables	DF	Semipartial Correlations	p(H₀)
Rule Governance	Executive		1,201	0.24*	0.0004
	Executive *sample		1,201	−0.09	0.16
	Lability		1,201	−0.04	0.57
	Lability *sample		1,201	−0.07	0.30
	Antagonistic		1,201	−0.13*	0.05
	Antagonistic *sample		1,201	0.13*	0.05
	Mutualistic		1,201	−0.01	0.83
	Mutualistic *sample		1,201	0.05	0.45
		Super-K	1,201	0.05	0.44
		Super-K *sample	1,201	0.08	0.24
Governance R²			10,201	0.34*	0.004
Interpersonal Aggression	Governance		1,199	−0.21*	0.0009
	Governance *sample		1,199	0.14*	0.03
	Executive		1,199	−0.40*	< 0.0001
	Executive *sample		1,199	−0.13*	0.03
	Lability		1,199	0.04	0.47
	Lability *sample		1,199	−0.04	0.49
	Antagonistic		1,199	0.11	0.08
	Antagonistic *sample		1,199	−0.05	0.44
	Mutualistic		1,199	−0.06	0.29
	Mutualistic *sample		1,199	0.08	0.20
		Super-K	1,199	−0.01	0.83
		Super-K *sample	1,199	−0.04	0.46
Aggression R²			12,199	0.52*	< 0.0001

Note: *p < 0.05.

predict the Antagonistic Social Schema Factor. This indicated that there was a significant parametric difference in the size of this effect between the Arizona and Ixtapaluca samples, where the effect only reached acceptable levels of statistical significance in the latter and not the former.

Affective and Cognitive Lability. We see from this third regression equation that Antagonistic Social Schema Factor significantly and positively predicted the Affective and Cognitive Lability Factor, as expected by theory. Further, we see that there was no significant parametric difference in the size of this effect between the Arizona and Ixtapaluca samples.

We also see that Mutualistic Social Schema Factor significantly and negatively predicted the Affective and Cognitive Lability Factor, again as expected by theory. Further, the interaction of the Mutualistic Social Schema Factor with our binary dummy variable for Sample did significantly and positively predict the Affective and Cognitive Lability Factor. This indicated that there was a significant parametric difference in the size of this effect between the Arizona and Ixtapaluca samples, where this effect in the Ixtapaluca sample was reduced to about half of its negative magnitude in the Arizona sample, without reversing its direction. Finally, we see that the Super-K Factor had no significant main effect or interaction with Sample upon the Affective and Cognitive Lability Factor, once statistically controlled for those of the Antagonistic and Mutualistic Social Schemata.

Executive Functions. We see from this fourth regression equation that the Affective and Cognitive Lability Factor significantly and negatively predicted the Executive Functions Factor, as expected by theory. Further, we see that there was no significant parametric difference in the size of this effect between the Arizona and Ixtapaluca samples. Further, the interaction of Affective and Cognitive Lability with our binary dummy variable for Sample also significantly and positively predicted the Executive Functions Factor. This indicated that there was a significant parametric difference in the size of this effect between the Arizona and Ixtapaluca samples, where this effect in the Ixtapaluca sample was once again reduced to about half of its negative magnitude in the Arizona sample, without reversing its direction.

We also see that the Antagonistic Social Schema Factor significantly and negatively predicted the Executive Functions Factor, again as expected by theory. Further, we see that there was no significant parametric difference in the size of this effect between the Arizona and Ixtapaluca samples.

Finally, we see that neither the Mutualistic Social Schema Factor nor the Super-K Factor had any significant main effects or interactions with Sample upon the Executive Functions Factor, once statistically controlled for those of Affective and Cognitive Lability as well as Antagonistic and Mutualistic Social Schemata.

Rule Governance. We see from this fifth regression equation that the Executive Functions Factor significantly and positively predicted the Rule Governance Factor, as expected by theory. Further, we see that there was no significant parametric difference in the size of this effect between the Arizona and Ixtapaluca samples.

We also see that the Antagonistic Social Schema Factor significantly and negatively predicted the Rule Governance Factor, again as expected by theory. Further, we see that there was a significant parametric difference in the size of this effect between the Arizona and Ixtapaluca samples, with the interaction effect completely cancelling out the main effect such that the effect is virtually abolished in Ixtapaluca.

Finally, we see that neither the Affective and Cognitive Lability, the Mutualistic Social Schema Factor, nor the Super-K Factor had any significant main effects or interactions with Sample upon the Executive Functions Factor, once statistically controlled for the prior criterion variables.

Interpersonal Aggression. We see from this sixth and final regression equation that the Rule Governance Factor significantly and negatively predicted the Interpersonal Aggression Factor, again as expected by theory. Further, we see that there was a significant parametric difference in the size of this effect between the Arizona and Ixtapaluca samples, with the interaction effect reducing the main effect by nearly three-quarters of its magnitude in Ixtapaluca, without reversing its direction.

We also see that the Executive Functions Factor significantly and negatively predicted the Rule Governance Factor, as expected by theory. Further, we see that there was a significant parametric difference in the size of this effect between the Arizona and Ixtapaluca samples, with the interaction effect augmenting the magnitude of the main effect such that the effect is larger by over one-third in Ixtapaluca, and of course in the same direction.

Finally, we see that the neither the Affective and Cognitive Lability Factor, the Antagonistic Social Schema Factor, the Mutualistic Social Schema Factor, nor the Super-K Factor had any significant main effects or interactions with Sample upon the Executive Functions Factor, once statistically controlled for the prior criterion variables.

Discussion

We have presented the results of a theoretically specified sequential cascade model, following the consequences of the varying life history strategies of individuals, through the development of various social cognitive schemata (as measured by the DI), their influences upon behavioral self-regulation and rule governance, to the behavioral expression of various forms of interpersonal aggression. We have reported that, with just a few statistically significant parametric differences, in no case reversing the direction of any effects, the hybrid "Dark Violence" model cross-validated reasonably well across two independent and highly discrepant populations, a low-risk University of Arizona undergraduate student convenience sample and a high-risk adult non-student Ixtapaluca community sample collected by the Universidad Autónoma Metropolitana-Iztapalapa.

To summarize, we were not at all surprised that the DT family of personality traits measured by the DI was predictive of interpersonal aggression, although it is always scientifically satisfying to be able to predict behavioral self-reports from attitudinal ones. What these results might imply about the composition of the DI, which was designed to partition the variance among DT traits in a more theoretically motivated manner, were the main foci of our interest. The ASS cluster of the DI represented the critical unique component of the DT in predicting interpersonal aggression, as expected by theory (Patch, 2014; Jones & Figueredo, 2013); ASS was formerly implicit in the latent common factor underlying the DT, but not discriminable as such (Jonason et al., 2009). The ACL cluster of the DI represented another implicit DT common factor component that was fully mediated by its effects upon executive functions; this enhanced the effect of executive functions upon interpersonal aggression once the ACL component was extracted. The MSS cluster of the DI had no significant direct effects on either executive functions or interpersonal aggression after those of the other two DI factors had been statistically controlled; MSS was not formerly implicit in the DT common factor except as a presumed deficit.

Despite the fact that both populations sampled showed quite similar results psychometrically, the structural differences found might be explained from varying perspectives given that interpersonal violence is a multifactorial phenomenon. Using the nonstudent populations as our focus, one might start by considering the fact that all participants from Ixtapaluca had high school as their maximum level of formal schooling, generally having discontinued their education between the ages of 14 and 15, and consequently may not have achieved their optimal levels of development in certain domains of cognitive ability such as memory, attention, and mathematical processing (e.g., Welsh, Nix, Blair, Bierman, & Nelson, 2010); further, it is reasonable to suppose that the decisions they might subsequently take as adults, and the types of short- and long-term plans that they construct, might be affected by these circumstances, as situated with the context of poverty (Lacour & Tissington, 2011).

Given the context of daily violence in which they live, the following of certain deviant social norms that might develop are likely to promote values such as distrust and lack of cooperation among groups (Wagner & Christ, 2007); such social norms include the "law of the strongest," in which it is better to abuse than be the "fool" who is abused, and in which it is better to attack before being attacked. Further, exposure to constant violence in daily life generates very high levels of tolerance towards aggression, favoring its short- and long-term perpetuation both in the private and public sectors of the community. The violent cycle that follows starts within parental behaviors in the home and is maintained beyond the home throughout adulthood. It was found that 60% of those interviewed in a study parallel to this one (Perez-Ramos, Pérez-Vargas, & Apolinar, 2016), with adult participants having the same sociodemographic characteristics as described here, reported having been the victim of some type of mistreatment by their parents; it was further discovered that their levels of anxiety and uncontrolled anger were directly proportional to the levels of abuse received during childhood. These same adults showed difficulties in discriminating emotions such as anger, surprise, worry, or disgust, which reduced their efficiency in interpersonal relations through a diminished capacity to empathize with the emotions of others (Pérez-Ramos, Pérez-Vargas, & Hurtado, in press); recall that emotional empathy was one of the principal indicators assessed in the present study and these differentials were among the major motivations for comparing high- and low-risk populations so as to better understand the psychometric performance of the DI under varying conditions.

Nevertheless, we conclude that even these striking differences between populations had very minor effects upon our results, and although we give due consideration to the importance of environmental context in the development of "malicious" attitudes and behaviors, it is also evident that our results showed that the DT components assessed by the DI were manifestly present in both groups.

References

Cohen, J. & Cohen, P. (1983). *Applied multiple regression/ correlation analysis for the behavioral sciences* (2nd ed.). Hillsdale, NJ: Erlbaum.

Demetriou, A., Christou, C., Spanoudis, G., & Platsidou, M. (2002). The development of mental processing: Efficiency, working memory, and thinking. *Monographs of the Society of Research in Child Development,* 67, 1–154.

Ellis, B. J., Figueredo, A. J., Brumbach, B. H., & Schlomer, G. L. (2009). Fundamental dimensions of environmental risk: The impact of harsh versus unpredictable environments on the evolution and development of life history strategies. *Human Nature,* 20, 204–268.

Figueredo, A. J. (2007). *The Arizona Life History Battery* [Electronic Version]. www.u.arizona.edu/~ajf/alhb.html.

Figueredo, A. J. & Gorsuch, R. (2007). Assortative mating in the Jewel wasp: 2. Sequential canonical analysis as an exploratory form of path analysis. *Journal of the Arizona Nevada Academy of Science,* 39(2), 59–64.

Figueredo, A. J. & Jacobs, W. J. (2010). Aggression, risk-taking, and alternative life history strategies: The behavioral ecology of social deviance. In M. Frias-Armenta & V. Corral-Verdugo (Eds), *Bio-psychosocial perspectives on interpersonal violence* (pp. 3–28). Hauppauge, NY: NOVA Science Publishers.

Figueredo, A. J., Cabeza de Baca, T., Black, C. J., García, R. A., Fernandes, H. B., Wolf, P. S. A., et al. (2014). Methodologically sound: Evaluating the psychometric approach to the assessment of human life history [reply to Copping, Campbell, & Muncer, 2014]. *Evolutionary Psychology: An International Journal of Evolutionary Approaches to Psychology and Behavior,* 13(2), 299–338.

Figueredo, A. J., Gladden, P. R., & Beck, C. J. A. (2012). Intimate partner violence and life history strategy. In A. Goetz & T. Shackelford (Eds), *The Oxford handbook of sexual conflict in humans* (pp. 72–99, chapter 5). New York: Oxford University Press.

Figueredo, A. J., Gladden, P. R., & Hohman, Z. (2012). The evolutionary psychology of criminal behavior. In S. C. Roberts (Ed.), *Applied evolutionary psychology* (pp. 201–221, chapter 13). New York: Oxford University Press.

Figueredo, A. J., Gladden, P. R., Sisco, M. M., Patch, E. A., & Jones, D. N. (2015). The unholy trinity: The Dark Triad, sexual coercion, and Brunswik-Symmetry. *Evolutionary Psychology,* 13(2), 435–454.

Figueredo, A. J., McKnight, P. E., McKnight, K. M., & Sidani, S. (2000). Multivariate modeling of missing data within and across assessment waves. *Addiction,* 95 (Suppl. 3), S361–S380.

Figueredo, A. J., Patch, E. A., & Gómez Ceballos, C. E. (2015). A life history approach to the dynamics of social selection. In V. Zeigler-Hill, L. L. M. Welling, & T. K. Shackelford (Eds), *Evolutionary perspectives on social psychology* (pp. 363–372, chapter 29). New York: Springer.

Figueredo, A. J., Patch, E. A., & Ceballos, C. E. G. (2015). A life history approach to the dynamics of social selection. In V. Zeigler-Hill et al. (Eds), *Evolutionary perspectives on social psychology* (pp. 363–372). New York: Springer International Publishing.

Figueredo, A. J., Tal, I. R., McNeill, P., & Guillén, A (2004). Farmers, herders, and fishers: The ecology of revenge. *Evolution and Human Behavior*, 25(5), 336–353.

Figueredo, A. J., Vásquez, G., Brumbach, B. H., Schneider, S. M., Sefcek, J. A., Tal, I. R., et al. (2006). Consilience and life history theory: From genes to brain to reproductive strategy. *Developmental Review*, 26(2), 243–275.

Figueredo, A. J., Wolf, P. S. A., Olderbak, S. G., Gladden, P. R., Fernandes, H. B. F., Wenner, C., Hill, D., et al. (2014). The psychometric assessment of human life history strategy: A meta-analytic construct validation. *Evolutionary Behavioral Sciences*, 8(3), 148–185.

Garcia, R. A., Gladden, P. R., Figueredo, A. J., & Jacobs, W. J. (in preparation). *Aligning one's self within the group: Development of a prospective rule governance scale.* Manuscript in preparation.

Gioia, G. A., Isquith, P. K., Retzlaff, P. D., & Espy, K. A. (2002). Confirmatory factor analysis of the Behavior Rating Inventory of EF (BRIEF) in a clinical sample. *Child Neuropsychology*, 8, 249–257.

Giosan, C. (2006). High-K Strategy Scale: A measure of the High-K independent criterion of fitness. *Evolutionary Psychology*, 4, 394–405.

Gorsuch, R. L. (2016). *UniMult for uni- and multi-variate data analysis*. Altadena, CA: UniMult. www.unimult.com/index.php.

Gosling, S. D., Rentfrow, P. J., & Swann, W. B. (2003). A very brief measure of the Big-Five personality domains. Journal of Research in Personality, 37, 504–528.

Jonason, P. K., Icho, A., & Ireland, K. (2016). Resources, harshness, and unpredictability: The socioeconomic conditions associated with the Dark Triad traits. *Evolutionary Psychology*, 14, 1–11.

Jonason, P. K., Li, N. P., Webster, G. D., & Schmitt, D. P. (2009). The dark triad: Facilitating a short-term mating strategy in men. *European Journal of Personality*, 23(1), 5–18.

Jones, D. N. & Figueredo, A. J. (2013). The core of darkness: Uncovering the heart of the Dark Triad. *European Journal of Personality*, 27(6), 521–531.

Jones, D. N. & Paulhus, D. L. (2011). Differentiating the dark triad within the interpersonal circumplex. In Horowitz, L., Strack, S. (Eds), *Handbook of interpersonal psychology: Theory, research, assessment, and therapeutic interventions* (pp. 249-267). Hoboken, NJ: John Wiley.

Jones, D. N., Olderbak, S. G., & Figueredo, A. J. (2010). Intentions toward infidelity. In Fisher, T. D., Davis, C. M., Yarber, W. L., & Davis, S. L., (Eds), *Handbook of Sexuality-Related Measures* (3rd ed., pp. 251–253). New York, Routledge.

Lacour, M. & Tissington, L. D. (2011). The effects of poverty on academic achievement. *Educational Research and Reviews*, 6(7), 522–527.

Lezak, M. D., Loring, D. W., & Howieson, D. B. (Eds) (2004). *Neuropsychological assessment* (4th ed.). Oxford: Oxford University Press.

MacArthur, R. H. & Wilson, E. O. (1967). *The theory of island biogeography*. Princeton, NJ: Princeton University Press.

Mittal, C., Griskevicius, V., Simpson, J. A., Sung, S., & Young, E. S. (2015). Cognitive adaptations to stressful environments: When childhood adversity enhances adult executive function. Journal of Personality and Social Psychology, 109, 604-621.

Mouyi, A. (2006). *Untangling the cognitive processes web. Paper. Seventh Annual Conference of the International Society for Intelligence Research.* San Francisco, CA.

Olderbak, S. G. & Figueredo, A. J. (2010). Life history strategy as a longitudinal predictor of relationship satisfaction and dissolution. *Personality and Individual Differences*, 49, 234–239.

Patch, E. A. (2014). The Dark Inventory Validation Study. Unpublished Masters Thesis, Department of Psychology, University of Arizona.

Patch, E. A., Garcia, R. A., Figueredo, A. J., & Kavanagh, P. (Submitted). Social Deviance in Dark Personalities.

Paulhus, D. L. & Williams, K. M. (2002). The Dark Triad of personality: Narcissism, Machiavellianism, and psychopathy. *Journal of Research in Personality*, 36, 556–563.

Pérez-Ramos, M., Pérez-Vargas, C., & Hurtado, J. C. (press). Identificación emocional en adultos con y sin maltrato en la infancia. Manuscript in press.

Pérez-Ramos, M., Pérez-Vargas, C., & Apolinar, H. E. (2016). Consecuencias emocionales en adultos que sufrieron maltrato en la infancia. *Aportaciones Actuales de la Psicología Social*, 3, 764–769.

Pianka, E. R. (1961). *Theoretical ecology: Principles and applications* (2nd ed.). Oxford: Blackwell Science.

Pianka, E. R. (1970). On r and K selection. *American Naturalist, 104*, 592–597.

SAS Institute Inc. (2004). *SAS/STAT ® 9.1 User's Guide*. Cary, NC: SAS Institute Inc.

Secretariado Ejecutivo del Sistema Nacional de Seguridad Pública (2012). Estadísticas delictivas por Estados y Municipios. Retrieved October 13, 2012 from www.estadisticadelictiva.secretariadoejecutivo.gob.mx/mondrian/testpage.jsp.

Tuvblad, C., Bezdjian, S., Raine, A., & Baker, L. A. (2014). The heritability of psychopathic personality in 14 to 15-year-old twins: A multirater, multimeasure approach. *Psychological Assessment*, 26, 704.

Wagner, U. & Christ, O. (2007). Intergroup aggression and emotions: A framework and first data. In G. Steffgen & M. Gollwitzer (Eds), *Emotions and aggressive behavior* (pp. 133–148). Ashland, OH: Hogrefe & Huber

Ware, J. E. & Sherbourne, C. D. (1992). The MOS 36-Item Short-Form Health Care Survey (SF-36): I. Conceptual Framework and Item Selection. *Medical Care*, 30, 473–483.

Welsh, J. A., Nix, R. L., Blair, C., Bierman, K. L., & Nelson, K. E. (2010). The development of cognitive skills and gains in academic school readiness for children from low-income families. *Journal of Educational Psychology*, 102(1), 43.

PART II

Biosocial Foundations of Violence and Aggression

5 The Behavioral Genetics of Aggression and Violent Behavior

J. C. Barnes and Jorim Tielbeek

Introduction

Behavioral genetics (BG) is an area of study that has, in a relatively short period of time, evolved from a promising but unproven perspective to one that is now forming the foundation for many studies of human behavior. We are now at a point where BG evidence can be summarized into "10 replicated findings" (Plomin, DeFries, Knopik, & Neiderhiser, 2016), where one of the largest meta-analyses ever conducted summarizes BG estimates (Polderman et al., 2015), and where there are not only "laws" of BG (Turkheimer, 2000), but there is even talk of expanding those laws (Chabris, Lee, Cesarini, Benjamin, & Laibson, 2015). This is all to say the BG perspective has grown at a rapid clip and is now recognized as one of the most instructive ways to study human development.

Against this backdrop, the current chapter has three primary objectives. First, we will offer a brief overview of the BG perspective as it applies to the study of human aggression and violent behavior. As we see it, BG research can be divided into two broad approaches: (1) methods that seek to estimate the degree to which genetic and environmental influences affect the development of a phenotype; and (2) methods that seek to identify which genes/environments influence the phenotype. This leads to our second objective, which is to provide an overview of both of the above-mentioned areas of BG research. Finally, our third objective is to explain how these two areas of BG research have been used to develop a more holistic understanding of the etiology of human aggression and violent behavior.

The Foundation of Behavioral Genetics

Behavioral genetics (BG) developed out of the quantitative genetics paradigm. Space provisions do not allow a full review of either of these perspectives. But, briefly, one can think of quantitative genetics as the area of study that integrates molecular principles learned from biology and genomics to the study of phenotypic scores and variation (see, generally, Falconer & Mackay, 1996). Quantitative geneticists can be credited with a simple, yet revelatory, proposal about the sources influence on a phenotype (note that *phenotype* is the term applied to any trait or outcome that varies in a population): a phenotype is made up of genetic and environmental components, such that:

$P = G + E$

where P is the phenotypic score for an individual, G is that person's genotypic score, and E is that person's environmental score plus noise/error.

This deceptively simple equation conceals many important philosophical and mathematical points. First, note that the G is listed before the E. Although the left-hand side of the equation is identical regardless of whether G or E is listed first, there is a great philosophical divide that can be identified here. Specifically, BG researchers and quantitative geneticists are trained to see the world such that G affects P and any influence of E can be thought of as noise. E, in this framework, becomes a nuisance parameter; something that must be accounted for but is not necessarily of primary interest.

Sociologically oriented researchers are often trained to see the world such that $P = E + G$. Here, the environment E is the primary influence of phenotypic scores and genetic influences G are the noise that must be controlled/accounted for (see, generally, Rafter, Posick, & Rocque, 2016).

This is, of course, a gross oversimplification. But it is important to differentiate these perspectives because most phenotypes are not defined in a simple linear way, meaning it will not be possible to view one element of the equation as more important than the other. Instead, most phenotypes – including those related to aggression and violent behavior – arise due to a complicated causal process that involves G, E, their covariance (rGE), and their interaction (G × E). In other words, our simple equation must be expanded:

$$P = G + E + rGE + G \times E$$

Because genetic and environmental influences are likely to covary and interact with one another, the researcher cannot ignore one to focus on the other. As Burt (2016, p. 114) recently noted, "Indeed, one important, and often overlooked, consideration in studies of environmental influences is that the 'environment' may not be genetically independent of the outcome variable..." This quote serves to remind us that rGE and G × E make it so that we cannot accurately estimate the impact of E on P unless we have made an effort to account for the influence of G.

The remaining sections of this chapter will, therefore, be built around a central theme: research into the etiology of human aggression and violence is complicated due to the covariance and interaction of G and E. But this is not to say that research endeavors are doomed due to irreducible complexity. On the contrary, advances have been and will continue to be made as we (scientists) incrementally work our way to a more holistic understanding of what makes humans harm one another. Below, we consider the two main streams of research that have both (1) recognized the complexity discussed above and (2) attempted to further our understanding of the causes of violence and aggression by studying G and E.

Two Modern Approaches

Generally speaking, there are two types of BG analyses. The first is what we will call *variance decomposition* research. This approach seeks to estimate the degree to which variance in a phenotype P can be attributed to genetic influences G and environmental influences E. The second type of BG analysis is what we will call *gene finding* research. Gene finding studies often begin by referencing the results from variance decomposition research. For example, imagine a variance decomposition analysis revealed some phenotype P

was largely influenced by genetic influences G. But, as we will explain momentarily, variance decomposition only tells us how much G matters, not which genes matter. The latter issue is what the gene finding study would seek to address.

Variance Decomposition Methods

Variance decomposition models are a broad class of analytic strategies that primarily – although not exclusively – seek to estimate the impact of genetic G and environmental E influences on variance in the phenotype P. Obviously, the emphasis here is on variance in P, which redirects our focus away from any specific predicted value of P and instead forces us to think about what might cause P to exhibit variation in a population/sample. With these points in mind, variance decomposition methods deal with a slightly different version of the equations outlined above. Specifically, the focus now is on whether and how much variance in G and E contribute to variance in P:

$$V_P = V_G + V_E + 2\operatorname{cov}(V_G, V_E) + V_{G \times E}$$

where V stands for variance and the other subscripts are consistent with their previous definitions.

In addition to redirecting our focus to variance in P (i.e., V_P), variance decomposition models can also be credited with highlighting an important point about the environmental component that has been expressed, to this point, as E in our mathematical models. Specifically, when variance decomposition models were being developed, it became apparent that more than one environmental parameter was needed to account for all of the observed variance in P. Thus, scholars who were at the forefront of model development proposed that the E component be separated into two parts: one for the "common" environment C that could account for between-family variation and one for the within-family variation.

The reason C stands for the common environment is worth attention. Early model development was carried out by studying twins and the sources of variance that caused two twins from the same family to develop similarly. Of course, it is obvious that any environment shared between two twins should make them more similar to one another. This influence, therefore, is captured by the common environment C. But observation tells us that twins do not always develop identically (Bouchard et al., 1990). Even though this point was obvious, it was not obvious how this could happen if the environment had a single effect captured by C. Thus, as these models were being developed, the source of variance that led to differences between twins was captured by an extra environmental component (it may have even been considered "error") and was labeled E. It was not until sometime later that this component was coined the "nonshared" environment (though the E label stuck).

Because twins were – and often remain – the focus, it was also obvious that variance decomposition models would need to account for heritable variation. Indeed, this was the focus for much of the early research that used these techniques. But the variance in P that is due to genetic factors – like its environmental counterpart(s) – comes in more than one version. Broadly, we can speak about the heritable variation in P, which is akin to calculating:

$$\text{broad-sense } H^2 = \frac{V_G}{V_P}$$

The calculation above reveals that if one were to estimate a simple ratio of the variance in P that were due to variance in G, one would actually be calculating what has come to be known as *broad-sense heritability* (H^2). This estimate is referred to as *broad-sense* because it is now well understood that G actually captures the influence of at least three forms of genetic influence (ignoring, for the time being, G × E and rGE):

$$V_G = V_A + V_D + V_I$$

where G still refers to the genetic influence, A identifies the additive genetic influence, D refers to the dominance genetic influence, and I captures epistatic genetic influence. Page limitations do not allow us to outline the differences between these various types of genetic influence so interested readers are directed to Falconer and Mackay (1996) and Plomin, DeFries, Knopik, and Neiderhiser (2013). For a host of various reasons (Hill, Goddard, & Visscher, 2008; Zuk, Hechter, Sunyaev, & Lander, 2012), much of the variance decomposition focus has been given to the genetic influences captured by A, such that estimates of h^2 in most variance decomposition models captures what is known as *narrow-sense* h^2:

$$\text{narrow-sense } h^2 = \frac{V_A}{V_P}$$

Relevant Findings

So what has more than half-a-century of research using variance decomposition models shown us? This was precisely the question that a recent meta-analysis conducted by Polderman and colleagues (2015) sought to address. As you might imagine, this was a massive undertaking.

More than 2,700 studies were included in the review, leading to a grand total of 17,804 phenotypes being analyzed among more than 14.5 million twin pairs. Across all these traits, the mean h^2 estimate was 0.49, leaving 0.51 attributable to the environment. Given the above discussion about the distinction between broad-sense H^2 and narrow-sense h^2, it is important to note that Polderman and colleagues (2015) reported that a majority of the studies included in the meta-analysis found evidence to support the simpler, additive version of genetic influence (i.e., narrow-sense h^2).

A mean h^2 estimate of roughly 0.50, as it turns out, was not all that surprising. Indeed, Turkheimer's (2000) three laws of BG had anticipated this finding 15 years earlier. Polderman and colleagues' (2015) study, thus, did researchers a huge service by putting this prediction to the test. Also, the authors did not simply describe the mean h^2 across all those 17,000+ phenotypes; rather, they provide h^2 estimates for different domains of phenotypes. Some of the major domains are discussed in their paper, but others – especially those that were too nuanced to single out in the publication – are posted to the MaTCH website that was created to accompany the study (see http://match.ctglab.nl/#/home). Exploration of the MaTCH webtool reveals that *conduct disorders* was the phenotype classification that most closely resembled the traits of focus here (i.e., aggression and violence). Indeed, "aggressive behavior" was one of the most frequently used terms in the papers that were classified as having analyzed conduct disorders (see the word cloud function at http://match.ctglab.nl/#/specific/cloud). Estimates gleaned from nearly 300,000 pairs of twins revealed that this phenotype (i.e., conduct disorder) has a mean h^2 estimate of approximately 0.486.

A h^2 estimate of 0.486 is right in line with previous meta-analyses and systematic reviews (Mason & Frick, 1994; Rhee & Waldman, 2002). For example, the meta-analysis of aggression performed by Burt (2009) suggested h^2 for aggressive forms of rule-breaking was 0.65, while the systematic review performed by Raine (1993) concluded the h^2 estimate for various forms of delinquency and criminal behavior was probably in the small (e.g., perhaps around 0.20) to moderate (e.g., around 0.50) range. In all, research using variance decomposition methods to study the elements that contribute to variation in aggression and violent behavior has converged on a key conclusion: about 50% of the variation in these behaviors is due to heritable factors and the remaining portion is due to environmental factors.

Limitations

As can be deduced from the discussion above, there has been a lot of empirical attention paid to the h^2 of aggressive, violent, and antisocial behavior (cf., Barnes, Boutwell, & Beaver, 2016; Veroude et al., 2016; Waltes, Chiocchetti, & Freitag, 2016). But a fair amount criticism has be leveled against these studies (Wright et al., 2015). Although critics have invoked a number of arguments and highlighted several limitations, two concerns are commonly raised. The first is that variance decomposition methods often rely on twin pairs, leaving open the possibility that the results from these studies do not generalize to the singleton (i.e., non-twin) population. This concern was assessed by Barnes and Boutwell (2013), who tested whether twins systematically differed from non-twin subjects on a range of phenotypes that are typically of interest to scholars studying aggressive and violent behavior. Specifically, Barnes and Boutwell (2013) analyzed whether twins differed from their non-twin counterparts on 27 phenotypes, which included an index of delinquent behavior, victimization experiences, levels of self-control, drug-using behaviors, and the respondent's level of involvement with delinquent peers. The findings from this analysis, although nuanced in places, are easy to summarize: twins and non-twins do not differ on most traits. Thus, there is little reason to worry that results from, say, the Polderman et al. (2015) study will fail to generalize to the broader population of singletons.

The second concern involves something known as the equal environments assumption (EEA). Briefly, the EEA states that identical twins (i.e., monozygotic [MZ]) share the same amount of their environment as nonidentical (i.e., dizygotic [DZ]) twins. Put differently, the degree to which twins share their environment is assumed to be uncorrelated with their level of genetic overlap (i.e., whether they are MZ or DZ). Critics argue that the assumption is only rarely met, drawing into question the inferences that can be taken from variance decomposition research. Luckily, there are now dozes of studies that have analyzed the degree to which the EEA is violated in behavioral genetic research. The results of these studies were summarized by Barnes and colleagues (2014) and the conclusions were clear: the EEA is a robust assumption that, even if it is violated, is unlikely to lead to large biases in BG research.

Beyond the two criticisms covered above, there are other concerns with variance decomposition models that – while not reaching the level of a flaw or even a limitation *per se* – *do* restrict their utility. Two broad points stand most prominent. First, variance decomposition models "lump together" the genetic influences such that one does not know which, or even how many, genes contribute to the h^2 estimate (and the same goes for the environmental estimates). Thus, the h^2 estimate can be thought of as a global average estimate that sums over the influence of an unknown number of genes with unknown effect sizes. This raises one's attention to the importance of the BG strategies discussed in the next section; those that seek to find the genes that influence variation in P. The second concern to be aware of is that variance decomposition models often are unable to model the effects of rGE and G × E. Although various modeling strategies are available to tease apart these influences (Purcell, 2002; Turkheimer & Harden, 2014), most variance decomposition studies do not utilize them. Thus, a large portion of the evidence base assumes that narrow-sense h^2 is not only an appropriate proxy for broad-sense h^2 (see above), but also that it is not confounded with rGE and G × E. To the extent that these latter assumptions are violated, estimates gleaned from variance decomposition models will be affected in predictable ways. Readers interested in learning more about the impact of omitting rGE and G × E are encouraged to see Purcell (2002) and the methodological discussion offered by Turkheimer and Harden (2014).

Gene Finding Methods

Although variance decomposition methods are extremely useful, they do not allow one to identify which genes play a role in the etiology of the phenotype P. This, therefore, has become the focus of what we will call *gene finding* techniques. In an effort to provide a meaningful, yet tractable, discussion of this approach to BG research, we have chosen to highlight two broad classes of gene finding strategies: (1) candidate gene studies and (2) genome-wide association (GWA) studies.

Both of these approaches rest on the same foundation of principles and aims. Specifically, they both seek to identify the specific genes that make up the G component of our $P = G + E$ equation. Placed in the context of the variance decomposition models from above, recall that h^2 is an estimate of the degree to which the variation in P is attributable to variation in (additive) G. Gene finding studies can be thought of as a tool that can help the researcher parse out the various genes that go into that h^2 estimate.

So how do we go about finding the genes that are cloaked by the h^2 estimate? First, we have to recast the $P = G + E$ equation. Let us express the variance of P as a function of the variance in the genes plus variance in the environment, assuming no rGE and no G × E:

$$V_P = V_G + V_E = V_{g1} + \ldots + V_{gk} + V_E$$
$$= \sum V_g + V_E$$

which simply shows that the variance in P that is attributable to G can be expressed as the summed influence of all the individual genes g that make up G.

If we assume the genetic influence captured by any specific gene is not affected by rGE or G × E, then we can seek to pull apart the h^2 estimate one gene at a time:

$$V_P = V_{gk} + V_r$$

where V_r captures the collective influence of the omitted genes and the environmental influences E.

So how does one go about searching for the individual genetic components that might play a role in the etiology of P? One might address the issue by drawing on previous literature to develop a hypothesis about the potential relationship between a specific genetic variant and P. We call this *hypothesis-driven* research and will, broadly speaking, align it with the candidate gene literature. A second strategy is to take a hypothesis-free approach and simply search the entire genome for any associations between all known genetic variants and P. We call this *hypothesis-free* research and align our discussion here with the development of GWA methods that have recently become the go-to approach for scholars studying the etiology of human complex traits like aggression (Pappa et al., 2016) and antisocial behavior (Tielbeek et al., 2017).

Hypothesis-Driven: Candidate Genes

Some of the first gene finding studies were conducted on animals. As such, gene finding research in humans is often guided by animal models, thus providing researchers studying human behavior the opportunity to develop *a priori* hypotheses about which genes might paly a role in the etiology of specific behaviors.

The molecular underpinnings of aggression have been explored among a range of subjects such as flies, zebra fish, rodents, monkeys, and other nonhuman primates (Olivier & Young, 2002). Studies in *Drosophila*, using a forward genetic approach by selecting aggressive lines of flies, have indicated molecular targets such as octopamine, the insect equivalent of norepinephrine, and serotonin to be associated with fly aggression (Dierick & Greenspan, 2007, 2006; Zhou et al., 2008). Rodent studies have implicated brain circuits relevant to the etiology of aggression. For instance, a study utilizing an optogenetic design demonstrated that the stimulation of neurons in the mouse hypothalamus led to an increase of offensive aggression in male mice (Lin et al., 2011). Studies in rats have implicated the role of serotonin and dopamine in the regulation of aggression: with increased dopamine levels in the nucleus accumbens and decreased serotonin in the medial prefrontal cortex after the triggering of aggressive acts (van Erp & Miczek, 2000). Early studies in monkeys reported lower levels of serotonin metabolite in the cerebrospinal fluid of high-ranked aggressive monkeys, compared to low-ranked monkeys (Higley et al., 1992).

Although the use of such experimental designs in animal studies have a clear benefit, these controlled settings also eliminate potential relevant environmental factors that could have had crucial effects in a natural setting. Moreover, widely studied animal paradigms such as territorial or maternal aggression assess the more reactive type of aggression in which most individuals would fight, whereas pathological aggression can occur in situations where almost no one would fight (Nelson & Trainor, 2007). The ecological validity is an important limitation hindering the translation of animal models to human models, which is not necessarily straightforward. For instance, the anatomical distribution of dopamine input and the expression of different dopamine receptor subtypes differ between rodents and primates (Berger, Gasper, & Verney, 1991). Moreover, there has been a long debate within the field of translational neuroscience regarding the existence of the rodent prefrontal cortex and several scholars have questioned the homology between specific prefrontal regions in the rodent and human brain (Preuss, 1995; Uylings, Groenewegen, & Kolb, 2003; Wise, 2008). Despite its limitations, animal studies have been extremely informative by indicating plausible biological pathways and candidate genes, thereby fueling the search for molecular targets in human aggression.

RELEVANT FINDINGS There has been an explosion of research activity surrounding candidate genes over the past 20 years or so (Dick et al., 2015). Research into the etiology of aggression and violence is no different. Building on the animal model results discussed above, as well as some of the earliest gene finding studies (see Brunner, Nelen, Breakefield, Ropers, & van Oost, 1993), one of the first reports of a link between a candidate gene and antisocial behavior was published by Caspi and colleagues (2002). These researchers, drawing on a sample of New Zealanders, found evidence of a link between a specific gene on the X chromosome, the *MAOA* gene, and antisocial behavior. Certain variants of this gene were shown to have an association with antisocial outcomes for respondents who had reported being maltreated as a child. In other words, the "risk" alleles of the *MAOA* gene had an impact on aggression and violence if environmental risk was also present. Not only was this some of the first evidence to show a link between a candidate gene and human antisocial behavior, it was one of the first studies to report evidence of a G × E. Since Caspi and colleagues' (2002) landmark study was published, others have sought to replicate the results. Some studies have were successful, while others have failed to replicate (Tilihonen et al., 2015; Vassos, Collier, & Fazel, 2014).

Other candidate genes, too, have been studied. For example, Beaver and colleagues (2008) analyzed the association between *DRD2*, *DRD4*, *5HTT*, *DAT1*, *MAOA*, and desistance from delinquent/ criminal behavior. Their results revealed that all but the *5HTT* gene had a unique influence on desistance. Similar findings have been reported in various other studies, suggesting that there is robust evidence that these genes have important influences on the etiology of human antisocial behavior. But such research findings have, in recent years, raised at least as many question as have they answered (Charney, 2012; Charney & English, 2012). We consider a few of the most important questions generated by candidate gene research in the next subsection.

LIMITATIONS There is now a relatively large body of evidence pointing to a handful of candidate genes and their relationship(s) with various forms of human antisocial behavior (see, generally, Charney & English, 2012; Dick et al., 2015; Tielbeek et al., 2016). But, as with many new advancements, the proliferation of findings has outpaced methodological discussion about the limitations of this line of work. Dick and her colleagues (2015), therefore, recently set out to rectify this concern by outlining some of the most important limitations of the candidate gene literature. At the same time, they set forth a number of recommendations for how candidate gene research can continue to develop in a way that will promote confidence in the literature base.

Confidence in a literautre base is important to consider because some areas of work have recently fallen into a crisis of confidence. The crisis began when Ioannidis (2005) noted there is a very real chance the majority of published research findings are false-positives. This possibility is, at the very least, a realistic concern for the candidate gene literature. Some have even argued this possibility is heightened in the candidate gene literature due to the way in which scholars in the area have conducted these studies (Duncan & Keller, 2011). Some of the concerns surrounding candidate gene research can be traced to the very issues highlighted by Ioannidis (2005). Others are linked to the modern practice of statistical analysis, one that may be biased by multiple testing effects or, at a minimum, is biased by what Gelman and Loken (2014) called the "garden of forking paths" that emerge during the course of any statistical analysis. A key concern is that scholars may have approached many candidate gene studies as an exploratory exercise, overlooking the importance of *a priori* hypothesis development.

Recognizing these points, Dick and colleagues (2015) set forth a "recipe" for candidate gene researchers to follow, especially those interested in studying G × Es. Rather than restating or briefly summarizing their points, we strongly encourage readers to consider the recommendations made by Dick et al. (2015) for themselves.

Hypothesis-free: Genome-wide Association (GWA)

The newest wave of gene finding research is known as genome-wide association (GWA). Although the technical details of a GWA are beyond the scope of this chapter, it is important that we give some indication of how GWA studies are conducted. Plomin and colleagues (2013, p. 143) define a GWA as "An association study that assesses DNA variation throughout the genome." In other words, GWA searches the entire genome for any association between known genetic variants and the phenotype of focus. The process is carried out by running hundreds of thousands (sometimes even millions) of association tests and by correcting *P*-values for the multiple testing bias that is expected. In the end, corrected *P*-values are referenced to try and identify which genetic variants *may* have an influence on phenotypic development.

This task of GWA is easier to envision if one imagines a researcher has genetic information on a sample of respondents. Imagine also that the researcher has phenotypic data on those same respondents. For example, perhaps the researcher collected information about whether the participant had ever been diagnosed with antisocial personality disorder (ASPD). Given the abovementioned concerns stemming from candidate gene research, this researcher decides a hypothesis-free design is most appropriate for his/her study that seeks to identify whether any common genetic variants are linked to ASPD. At this point, the researcher has several ways s/he could move forward. Perhaps s/he could simply analyze the association between ASPD diagnosis and every single nucleotide polymorphism (SNP) that was tagged. This would remove the need to hypothesize about the influence of any one gene (or SNP). But a key issue would emerge: specifically, the biasing effects that would accompany *that many* analyses. To be sure, modern genetic technologies often identify upwards of 1,000,000 individual SNPs. If the researcher were to run 1,000,000 logistic regression models with a standard α-level of 0.05, then s/he could expect to receive back roughly 50,000 statistically significant results even if none of the SNPs had an effect on the phenotype. Thus, one of the key problems facing gene finding research is that the risk for Type I error is too high and must be controlled. And this is exactly what GWA does. To be specific, GWA results must reach genome-wide significance values of $P < 5 \times 10^{-8}$ (or $P < 0.00000005$).

Risch and Merikangas (1996) are sometimes credited as being the first to reveal the power of GWA for modern BG research (Jorgenson & Witte, 2006). Risch and Merikangas (1996) showed that association studies have more statistical power than linkage analyses, the latter of which were a popular research approach for early BG scholars interested in gene finding techniques. But modern GWA has also had to face issues surrounding statistical power. As we will discuss in the *Limitations* section below, statistical power is often quite low for any given GWA, which has led researchers to the realization that sample sizes of a magnitude never seen in the social sciences are necessary to reliably detect the signals in the genome. It has also led to other unique challenges that are currently facing the big data era (see, for a discussion, Liu & Guo, 2016).

RELEVANT FINDINGS GWA is still, relatively speaking, a new technology that is just beginning to come of age. Only in the past ten years or so has GWA become available to researchers interested in studying human behavioral phenotypes. The vast majority of early GWAs were conducted in the medical sciences by researchers interested in understanding disease traits. As prices for the technology necessary to conduct a GWA came down, more and more studies were carried out on a range of human behavioral outcomes. There are now seven GWA studies on human aggressive behavior (or some closely related phenotype such as violence or antisocial behavior) (Brevik et al., 2016; Dick et al., 2011; Pappa et al., 2016; Rautiainen et al., 2016; Salvatore et al., 2015; Tielbeek et al., 2012, 2017). The first ever GWA conducted on a form of antisocial behavior was reported by Dick and colleagues (2011). Their GWA study was performed on a sample of children ($n = 3,963$) and the phenotypic outcome was conduct disorder. Four genetic loci reached genome-wide significance and were pointed to as potential markers for future research to study in a candidate gene approach.

The first GWA study performed on adult antisocial behavior was reported by Tielbeek and colleagues (2012). Analyzing data from nearly 5,000 respondents did not produce any genome-wide statistically significant loci. But there were a few loci that were strongly associated and at least suggestive of an association. One of the most recent GWA studies was conducted by Rautiainen et al. (2016) and the phenotypic outcome was antisocial personality disorder. Results identified several loci that might be associated with the phenotype.

A recent review summarizing previous candidate gene and GWA studies on aggression and closely related phenotypes found 156 genes to be nominally ($P < 0.05$) associated (Fernàndez-Castillo & Cormand, 2016). These genetic loci are predominantly involved in dopaminergic and serotonergic neurotransmission and in hormone regulation. Moreover, that same study found certain biological pathways were overrepresented across the six GWA studies, revealing significant enrichment in axon guidance, estrogen receptor signaling, neurodevelopmental processes, and synaptic plasticity pathways. Nonetheless, the authors stress that well-powered replication designs utilizing standardized measurements and more homogenous subtypes of aggression are needed to reliably identify pathways affecting aggressive behavior.

LIMITATIONS Although GWA studies help to address some of the well-known concerns with candidate gene research, they are not without their own limitations. A number of studies have raised awareness of perhaps the most important issue surrounding GWA research: the influence of underpowered study designs in biomedical and psychological research (see, generally, Button et al., 2013; Ioannidis, 2005; Sham & Purcell, 2014; Simmons, Nelson, & Simonsohn, 2011).

Three key problems can arise when a study suffers from low statistical power: (1) type II error increases to unacceptable levels (i.e., there are too many false-negative findings); (2) false-positive rates increase to an unacceptable level; and (3) reported effect sizes are likely to be inflated due to the "winner's curse." There is reason to believe that these issues have affected genetic association studies of all sorts, even those published in journals with a high impact factor (Munafo, Stothart, & Flint, 2009).

Genetic epidemiological studies often lack sufficient statistical power, which then leads to low replication rates (Ioannidis, 2003; Sullivan, 2007). As discussed earlier, candidate gene research proposed a number of genes or genetic variants as predictors of variation in aggression and violence. These candidate gene studies were meta-analyzed by Vassos and colleagues (2014) who found no evidence of a significant association, despite prior replication efforts. These findings indicate that either previous candidate gene results were false positives or that the previous effect size estimates were highly exaggerated (i.e., the winner's curse). In light of these findings, it has become increasingly clear that antisocial behavior is a highly complex trait, with a large number of genetic influences, each of which only contributes a small amount of variance to the phenotype. Thus, scholars should seek to perform statistical power calculations prior to beginning a novel GWA study.

Such power calculations, however, require prior knowledge of the expected effect size of the tested genetic association. Power analyses could, therefore, be aided by effect size estimates of genetic variants derived from studies on other complex traits yielding a comparable heritability. Well-powered study designs of consortia, such as the Social Science Genetic Association Consortium (SSGAC), can anchor power analyses in other studies by taking the effect sizes of their most significant associations as an upper limit for the effect sizes in genetically similar traits. The SSGAC GWA on educational attainment reported an estimated R^2 of 0.02% for all their genome-wide significant genetic variants (Okbay et al., 2016). These estimates are uncorrected for inflation due to the winner's curse and therefore might still overestimate the magnitude of their effects (Pereira & Ioannidis, 2011). Thus, in GWA, the effect sizes are likely to be very small.

Power analyses can be performed via the user-friendly "pwr" package in the freely available statistical software R. This package contains functions for basic

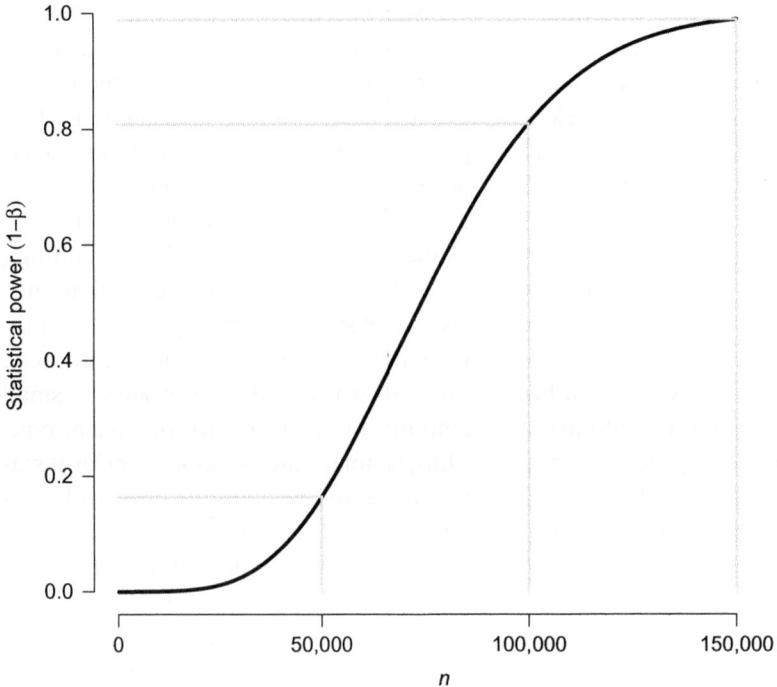

Figure 5.1 *Statistical power at various sample sizes when r = 0.02.*

power calculations using effect sizes and notations from Cohen (1988):

pwr.r.test(r=<correlation coefficient>, n=<sample size>, power=<0.8>, alternative="two.sided", sig. level=<EWAS=1E-7, GWAS=5E-8>)

If we assume that each of the genetic variants has an effect size roughly equal to $r = 0.02$, we can calculate that in order to achieve 80% power to identify genetic variants associated with antisocial traits, a sample size of about 100,000 individuals is required. These power calculations reveal that, in hindsight, early GWA studies on antisocial behavior were underpowered. Figure 5.1 displays a statistical power curve for various sample sizes assuming an effect size of $r = 0.02$.

Although GWA studies have been successful in detecting disease loci for outcomes such as Crohn's disease, type 2 diabetes, and schizophrenia (see Figure 5.2; Franke et al., 2010; Schizophrenia Working Group of the Psychiatric Genomics Consortium, 2014; Scott et al., 2007), the limitation of conventional single-marker association analyses focusing on complex outcomes, such as aggression, is that they have often been underpowered. The general conclusion that can be drawn from large-scale GWA studies is that aggression, violence, and antisocial behavior is likely to be influenced by many common causal genetic variants each conferring only a small effect (Chabris et al., 2015; Tielbeek et al., 2012; Tielbeek et al., 2017). Moreover, given the substantial polygenic component of antisocial behavior, it is likely that the genetic variants involved are not distributed randomly across the genome, but are distributed in ways that allow them to share a common biological

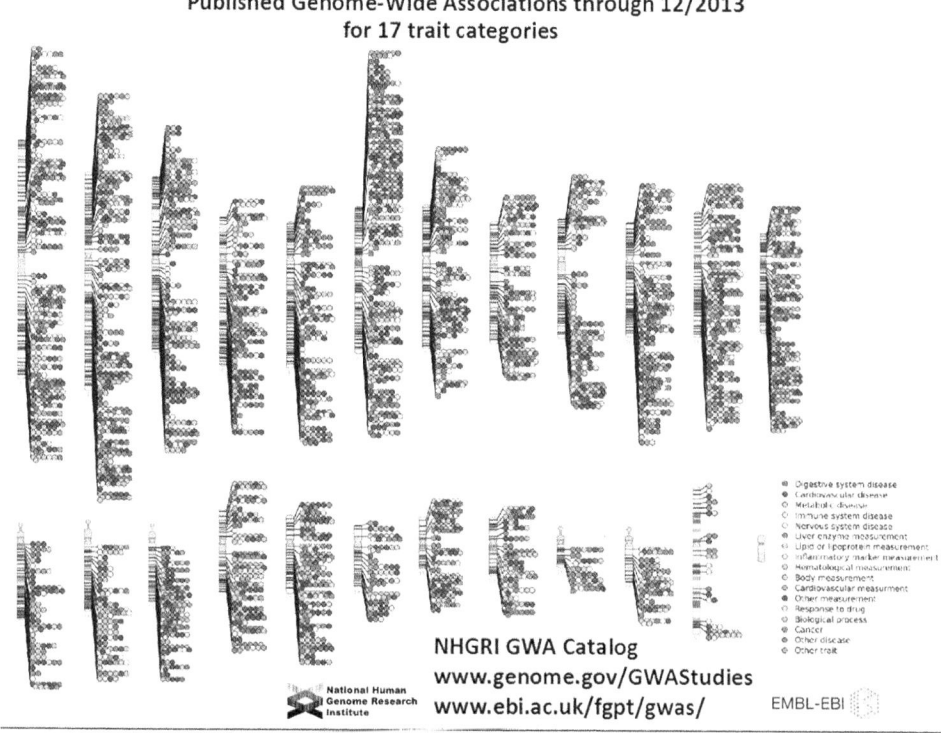

Figure 5.2 *Genome-wide association results as of 2013 (Hindorff et al., n.d.).*

function or pathway (Khatri, Sirota, & Butte, 2012; Lips et al., 2012). To partly overcome this issue, gene-based and pathways-based association analyses must begin to utilize prior biological knowledge on genes and pathways, yielding a more powerful analysis of GWA data (Wang, Li, & Hakonarson, 2010).

DEALING WITH LOW STATISTICAL POWER: GENE-SET ANALYSES Gene-based association analyses, rather than single-marker analyses, take into account all markers within a gene, thus examining the combined effect of all SNPs on the phenotype of interest. The advantage of a gene-based test is that it reduces the burden of multiple testing (to ≈ 21,000 tests, compared to millions of tests in GWA) and facilitates a more immediate gene-level interpretation. Moreover, because it aggregates multiple weak associations while accounting for linkage disequilibrium between the SNPs, it increases power and accounts better for heterogeneity in a gene (Liu, Wang, & Wong, 2010).

Gene-set analyses (GSA), which are adopted from gene expression methods (Mootha et al., 2003), are now commonly used in GWA studies. Strikingly, de Leeuw, Neale, Heskes, and Posthuma (2016), reviewing the statistical structure of GSA, found that as the heritability of a phenotype increased, the statistical power decreased. Moreover, larger sample sizes only modestly increased statistical power, with even less improvement for more strongly heritable phenotypes (de Leeuw et al., 2016). Also, most of the current GSA tools do not sufficiently address bias due to gene size and linkage disequilibrium as well as the major limitation of confounding among gene sets, which could lead to false conclusions if not taken into account. In sum, gene-based and gene-set analyses offer a powerful tool in analyzing and interpreting genetic data, but some issues are still present, meaning further development of novel techniques should remain a priority.

DEALING WITH LOW STATISTICAL POWER: COLLABORATION/CONSORTIA As we have shown above, issues surrounding low statistical power have recently occupied the minds of GWA analysts. Although there are several ways one can increase the statistical power of any given study (see above and, generally, Cohen, 1988), the most common way to induce higher power in GWA is to increase sample sizes. But the increases we are talking about are well beyond the level that could be expected by any one researcher or even a research team. For example, as was shown in Figure 5.1, a sample size of 100,000 is necessary to identify an effect size of $r = 0.02$; an effect size that is realistic and expected for a complex trait like aggression or violent behavior. As a result, GWA analysts have begun to form consortia so that they can combine their data in an effort to increase statistical power.

BG researchers' willingness to form consortia represents a great example of a scientific community remaining critical of its own research and taking action to address known limitations. Of course, one's scientific career is often judged by his/her unique contribution to the literature (see, generally, Merton, 1957). Consortia are decidedly collaborative projects that often force a scientist to forgo his/her own unique interests in order to better the group's collective efforts. While this may not be the best way forward for all research questions/areas, we see it as an extremely positive and commendable approach to addressing the problems facing the GWA community of scholars. With that said, one of us (JT) has established a consortium, known as the Broad Antisocial Behavior Consortium (BroadABC), for studying human antisocial behavior. The BroadABC is a collaborative research initiative to conduct genetic analyses at a large scale. Information about the BroadABC can be found here: http://broadabc.ctglab.nl.

The Future of BG Research into Human Aggression and Violence

In this final section of our chapter, we offer a brief discussion of five approaches that are sure to represent the next generation of BG research. Of course, a few sentences on any of these analytic techniques or broader perspectives does not even come close to doing justice to the true complexity that it entails. Thus, readers should not take these summaries as anything more than a cursory overview of what we believe will be the next wave of BG research.

Genome-Wide Complex Trait Analysis (GTCA)

Aggression and violent behaviors can be considered complex traits and, despite their considerable heritability ($h^2 \approx 0.50$), associated SNPs identified through GWA studies typically explain a fraction of estimated familial clustering. This considerable gap between twin-based heritability estimates and the tiny proportion of phenotypic variation explained by GWA has been generally referred to as the "missing heritability" problem (Eichler et al., 2010; Manolio et al., 2009). Mixed-model techniques such as the genome-wide complex trait analysis (GCTA) software were introduced to partly overcome the missing heritability problem by testing the aggregate effect of all SNPs available on the GWA chips simultaneously on trait variance (Yang, Lee, Goddard, & Visscher, 2011). The mixed-model technique and various extensions of it have been successful in characterizing the missing heritability of many complex traits (Lee, Wray, Goddard, & Visscher, 2011; Yang et al., 2015, 2010). When applied to children's aggressive behavior, the proportion of the heritability estimated through GCTA software ranged from 0.10 to 0.54 in the different cohorts included in the EAGLE consortium (Pappa et al., 2016). Since GCTA requires raw genotype data, its use remains mainly restricted to individual cohorts (unless raw data is being merged), thus yielding a limited sample size and estimates with wide confidence intervals. For example, when applied to adult antisocial behavior in an Australian study (Tielbeek et al., 2012), the proportion of the variance explained by common SNPs was 0.55; however, the standard error was high (0.41) and the estimate non-significant ($P = 0.07$).

Linkage Disequilibrium Score Regression

Recently, the linkage disequilibrium (LD) score regression method was introduced to decompose the inflated test statistics of GWA into true polygenic signal and confounding bias due to population stratification. The advantage of this ground-breaking tool is that it can use summary statistics, such as large meta-analyzed GWA datasets, to estimate SNP heritability in a fast and efficient manner (Bulik-Sullivan et al., 2015). This means that LD regression can be performed by scholars who may not otherwise have access to genome-wide analytic resources. Indeed, we can confirm that LD regression can be estimated on many (if not most) modern personal computers. Also, the lab responsible for developing and maintaining the program has a very useful and information-rich webpage that indexes GWA results and LD regression output for hundreds of human phenotypes (http://ldsc.broadinstitute.org).

Polygenic Risk Scoring

SNP heritability estimates, if unbiased, can be helpful in determining the upper boundaries of genetic risk-prediction models, yet its clinical use is limited as it cannot serve as a guide for risk stratification (Chatterjee, Shi, & García-Closas, 2016). To construct risk-prediction models, a selection of markers highly associated with a trait are combined into a single polygenic risk score (PRS). First, a GWA is conducted in an initial, large training sample. Second, the SNPs are ranked based on their strength of association. Finally, polygenic scores are computed based on the weighted sum of the alleles associated with the trait in an independent replication sample (Dudbridge, 2013).

An example of such a training sample for antisocial behavior is the BroadABC, which was introduced above. The BroadABC recently performed such PRS analysis in an at-risk Finnish forensic replication sample by testing whether an antisocial genetic risk score – based on a broad conceptualization of ASB – could significantly discriminate between prisoners and matched controls (Tielbeek et al., 2017). The software package PRSice (Euesden, Lewis, & O'Reilly, 2016) was employed to estimate the best-fit PRS at a broad range of P-value thresholds. Their analyses showed that case-control status of antisocial personality disorder in the Finnish prisoners sample was significantly predicted by antisocial genetic risk scores of the BroadABC, although the effect size was very small. The small effect size indicates the limited prediction accuracy and clinical utility for the current GWA outcomes. Nevertheless, this study demonstrated that population-based genetic association studies can be informative for samples that are at-risk. Therefore, large, high-quality epidemiological studies should inform and help build risk prediction models for aggression and violent behavior that incorporate both polygenic risk scores and environmental risk factors, along with their interaction (see Wertz et al., 2017).

Analyzing Endophenotypes with Neuroimaging

Clinical populations are likely to contain an admixture of etiologically different disorders (Bearden & Freimer, 2006). Therefore, intermediate phenotypes, also referred to as endophenotypes, have been proposed as a less heterogeneous outcome that may help overcome some of the difficulties that arise when GWA is conducted on a complex phenotype. Endophenotypes are defined as "measurable components unseen by the unaided eye along the pathway between disease and distal genotype" and have become an important concept in psychiatry (Gottesman & Gould, 2003, p. 636). In other words, the use of endophenotypes in genetic epidemiology seems promising since they are thought to be more proximal to the primary biological defects and are therefore hypothesized to be more sensitive to genetic signals than broad and heterogenic clinical phenotypes (Kendler & Neale, 2010).

In this respect, brain imaging offers a promising endophenotype-based approach by parsing the complexity of phenotypes into objectively measurable components. Converging evidence has emerged regarding promising brain endophenotypes for a range of antisocial phenotypes. For example, a meta-analysis conducted by Yang and Raine (2009) found significantly reduced prefrontal grey matter in antisocial individuals. Likewise, a study in psychopathic individuals reported significant bilateral volume reductions in the amygdala in these individuals compared with controls (Yang, Raine, Narr, Colletti, & Toga, 2009). Moreover, Motzkin and colleagues (2011) showed that diminished neural connectivity in certain regions of the brain is a robust neural correlate of psychopathy. Another study found reduced amygdala–orbitofrontal connectivity during moral judgments in youth with disruptive behavior disorders and psychopathic traits (Marsh et al., 2011). As such, these studies demonstrate that structural volume, structural connectivity and functional connectivity (e.g., during resting state) measures can potentially serve as putative brain endophenotypes of antisocial behavior.

Along these lines, Buckholtz and colleagues (2008) showed that genetic variation in the *MAOA* gene modulates ventromedial prefrontal circuitries, which in turn contribute to individual differences in human personality. Another study examining the impact of *MAOA* on brain structure and function found that the low-expression allele (*MAOA-L*) was linked to limbic volume reductions, amygdala hyper-responsiveness, and blunted reactivity of the prefrontal cortex (Meyer-Lindenberg et al., 2006).

Last, it is important to point out that neuroimaging studies – like their GWA counterparts – have begun to recognize and appreciate the importance of consortia in the creation of new knowledge. One of the – if not *the* – largest such consortium is the ENIGMA Consortium. ENIGMA is a large-scale collaborative analysis of neuroimaging and genetic data with the stated mission to explore the shared genetic etiology between various traits and phenotypes. Interested readers can find more information on ENIGMA here: http://enigma.ini.usc.edu.

Epigenetics

We would be remiss if we did not mention the vast potential surrounding epigenetics research. Around the time the human genome was mapped in the early 2000s, researchers began to confront the startling reality that there simply were not enough genes to go around. In other words, the human genome does not contain enough unique information to code for all the complexity and variation that we observe among human outcomes. Thus, it must be that genes interact with other genes, with environments, and perhaps even with some other "higher-order" property in the cell. That higher-order property has come to be known as the epigenome and scholars are now beginning to understand that mechanism. Briefly, the epigenome is responsible for turning genes "on" and turning them "off." As you might imagine, the biological processes can be complex, but the short of it is this: the epigenome controls which genes are expressed, thereby allowing them to have an influence (or not) on protein production.

But these points are not sufficient to explain why epigenetics has become, as some have put it, "the currently fashionable response to any question to which you do not know the answer." (Smith, 2011, p. 539). Social scientists' enthusiasm for epigenetics seems to be grounded in the possibility that it could reinvigorate research into environmental influences. But note that the environment captures everything that is not the genome. This might include biological factors such as prenatal environments and larger, social environments like neighborhood conditions. Because of the vast complexity involved, we encourage caution when conducting and interpreting epigenetics results.

Conclusion

The development of BG modeling has been a boon to the study of human variation across a wide range of phenotypes. Studies of human aggression and violence are no different. There is now a large body of evidence revealing that genetic and environmental influences play a role in the etiology of these phenotypes. Thus, the goal of this chapter was to introduce the reader to the two major strands of research that have, to date, delineated this body of evidence. As can be seen, the two approaches to BG modeling differ in their goals: variance decomposition models typically focus on estimating the degree to which variation in P is attributable to G and E, while gene finding models seek to identify the specific genetic variants that may underlie that variation in *P*.

But the BG literature is not nearly as bifurcated as our review may seem to indicate. Indeed, we presented the material in this chapter in a way that we thought would make it more tractable. This should not be taken as an indication that BG researchers who estimate variance decomposition models are at odds with those who estimate gene finding models. On the contrary, BG scholars are notable for their versatility and for their interests in finding the best way to estimate the impact of the various contributing factors to variance in *P*. The challenges to doing so, however, are formidable. Variance decomposition models are not without their limitations. Gene findings strategies, too, have come under fire for a host of substantive and statistical shortcomings. We have highlighted a few of the most important limitations and areas in need of improvement for both approaches. There is still much work to be done.

References

Barnes, J. C. & Boutwell, B. B. (2013). A demonstration of the generalizability of twin-based research on antisocial behavior. *Behavior Genetics*, 43, 120–131.

Barnes, J. C., Boutwell, B. B., & Beaver K. M. (2016). Contemporary biosocial criminology: A systematic review of the literature, 2000–2012. In A. R. Piquero (Ed.), *The handbook of criminological theory*. New York: Wiley-Blackwell.

Barnes, J. C., Wright, J. P., Boutwell, B. B., Schwartz, J. A., Connolly, E. J., Nedelec, J. L., & Beaver, K. M. (2014). Demonstrating the validity of twin research in criminology. *Criminology*, 52, 588–626.

Bearden, C. E. & Freimer, N. B. (2006). Endophenotypes for psychiatric disorders: ready for primetime? *Trends in Genetics*, 22, 306–313.

Beaver, K. M., Wright, J. P., DeLisi, M., & Vaughn, M. G. (2008). Desistance from delinquency: The marriage effect revisited and extended. *Social Science Research*, 37, 736–752.

Berger, B., Gaspar, P., & Verney, C. (1991). Dopaminergic innervation of the cerebral cortex: unexpected differences between rodents and primates. *Trends in Neuroscience*, 14, 21–27.

Bouchard, T. J., Lykken, D. T., McGue, M., Segal, N. L., & Tellegen, A. (1990). Sources of human psychological differences: The Minnesota Study of Twins Reared Apart. *Science*, 250, 223–228.

Brevik, E. J., van Donkelaar, M. M., Weber, H., Sánchez-Mora, C. Jacobs, C., Rivero, O., ... & Cormand, B. (2016). Genome-wide analyses of aggressiveness in attention-deficit hyperactivity disorder. *American Journal of Medical Genetics Part B*, 171:B, 733–747.

Brunner, H. G., Nelen, M., Breakefield, X. O., Ropers, H. H., & van Oost, B. A. (1993). Abnormal behavior associated with a point mutation in the structural gene for monoamine oxidase A. *Science*, 262, 578–580.

Buckholtz, J. W., Callicott, J. H., Kolachana, B., Hariri, A. R., Goldberg, T. E., Genderson, M., ... & Meyer-Lindenberg, A. (2008). Genetic variation in MAOA modulates ventromedial prefrontal circuitry mediating individual differences in human personality. *Molecular Psychiatry*, 13, 313–324.

Bulik-Sullivan, B. K., Loh, P.-R., Finucane, H. K., Ripke, S., Yang, J., Patterson, N., ... & Consortium, S.W.G. of the P.G. (2015). LD Score regression distinguishes confounding from polygenicity in genome-wide association studies. *Nature Genetics*, 47, 291–295.

Burt, S. A. (2009). Are there meaningful etiological differences within antisocial behavior? Results of a meta-analysis. *Clinical Psychology Review*, 29, 163–178.

Burt, S. A. (2016). Editorial: Chickens and eggs – how should we interpret environment-behavior associations? *Journal of Child Psychology and Psychiatry*, 57, 113–115.

Button, K. S., Ioannidis, J. P., Mokrysz, C., Nosek, B. A., Flint, J., Robinson, E. S., & Munafò, M. R. (2013). Power failure: Why small sample size undermines the reliability of neuroscience. *Nature Reviews Neuroscience*, 14, 365–376.

Caspi, A., McClay, J., Moffitt, T. E., Mill, J., Martin, J., Craig, I. W., ... & Poulton, R. (2002). Role of genotype in the cycle of violence in maltreated children. *Science*, 297, 851–854.

Chabris, C. F., Lee, J. J., Cesarini, D., Benjamin, D. J., & Laibson, D. I. (2015). The fourth law of behavior genetics. *Current Directions in Psychological Science* 24, 304–312.

Charney, E. (2012). Behavior genetics and postgenomics. *Behavioral and Brain Sciences*, 35, 331–410.

Charney, E. & English, W. (2012). Candidate genes and political behavior. *American Political Science Review*, 106, 1–34.

Chatterjee, N., Shi, J., & García-Closas, M. (2016). Developing and evaluating polygenic risk prediction models for stratified disease prevention. *Nature Reviews Genetics*, 17, 392–406.

Cohen, J. (1988). *Statistical power analysis for the behavioral sciences* (2nd ed.). Hillsdale, NJ: Lawrence Erlbaum.

De Leeuw, C. A., Neale, B. M., Heskes, T., & Posthuma, D. (2016). The statistical properties of gene-set analysis. *Nature Reviews Genetics*, 17, 353–364.

Dick, D., Agrawal, A., Keller, M. C., Adkins, A., Aliev, F., Monroe, S., ... & Sher, K. J. (2015). Candidate gene-environment interaction research: Reflections and recommendations. *Perspectives on Psychological Sciences*, 10, 37–59.

Dick, D. M., Krueger, R. F., Edwards, A., Agrawal, A., Lynskey, M., Lin, P., ... & Almasy, L. (2011). Genome-wide association study of conduct disorder symptomatology. *Molecular Psychiatry*, 16, 800–808.

Dierick, H. A. & Greenspan, R. J. (2006). Molecular analysis of flies selected for aggressive behavior. *Nature Genetics*, 38, 1023–1031.

Dierick, H. A. & Greenspan, R. J. (2007). Serotonin and neuropeptide F have opposite modulatory effects on fly aggression. *Nature Genetics*, 39, 678–682.

Dudbridge, F. (2013). Power and predictive accuracy of polygenic risk scores. *PLoS Genetics*, 9, e1003348.

Duncan, L. E. & Keller, M. C. (2011). A critical review of the first 10 years of candidate gene-by-environment interaction research in psychiatry. *American Journal of Psychiatry*, 168, 1041–1049.

Eichler, E. E., Flint, J., Gibson, G., Kong, A., Leal, S. M., Moore, J. H., & Nadeau, J. H. (2010). Missing heritability and strategies for finding the underlying causes of complex disease. *Nature Reviews Genetics*, 11, 446–450.

Euesden, J., Lewis, C. M., & O'Reilly, P. F. (2016). PRSice: Polygenic risk score software. http://PRSice.info.

Falconer, D. S. & Mackay, T. F. C. (1996). *Introduction to quantitative genetics* (4th ed.). New York: Pearson.

Fernàndez-Castillo, N. & Cormand, B. (2016). Aggressive behavior in humans: Genes and pathways identified through association studies. *American Journal of Medical Genetics Part B: Neuropsychiatric Genetics*, 1–21.

Franke, A., McGovern, D. P., Barrett, J. C., Wang, K., Radford-Smith, G. L., Ahmad, T., ... & Anderson, C. A. (2010). Genome-wide meta-analysis increases to 71 the number of confirmed Crohn's disease susceptibility loci. *Nature Genetics*, 42, 1118–1125.

Gelman, A. & Loken, E. (2014). The statistical crisis in science. *American Scientist*, 102, 460–465.

Gottesman, I. I. & Gould, T. D. (2003). The endophenotype concept in psychiatry: Etymology and strategic intentions. *American Journal of Psychiatry*, 160, 636–645.

Higley, J., Mehlman, P. T., Taub, D. M., Higley, S. B., Suomi, S. J., Linnoila, M., & Vickers,

J. H. (1992). Cerebrospinal fluid monoamine and adrenal correlates of aggression in free-ranging rhesus monkeys. *Archives of General Psychiatry*, 49, 436–441.

Hill, W. G., Goddard, M. E., & Visscher, P. M. (2008) Data and theory point to mainly additive genetic variance for complex traits. *PLoS Genetics*, 4, e1000008.

Hindorff, L. A., MacArthur, J., Morales, J., Junkins, H. A., Hall, P. N., Klemm, A. K., & Manolio, T. A. *A Catalog of Published Genome-Wide Association Studies*. Available at: www.genome.gov/gwastudies. Accessed November 1, 2017.

Ioannidis, J. P. (2003). Genetic associations: False or true? *Trends in Molecular Medicine*, 9, 135–138.

Ioannidis, J. P. (2005). Why most published research findings are false. *PLoS Medicine*, 2, e124.

Jorgenson, E. & Witte, J. S. (2006). A gene-centric approach to genome-wide association studies. *Nature Reviews Genetics*, 7, 885–891.

Kendler, K. S. & Neale, M. C. (2010). Endophenotype: A conceptual analysis. *Molecular Psychiatry*, 15, 789–797.

Khatri, P., Sirota, M., & Butte, A. J. (2012). Ten years of pathway analysis: Current approaches and outstanding challenges. *PLoS Computational Biology* 8, e1002375.

Lee, S. H., Wray, N. R., Goddard, M. E., & Visscher, P. M. (2011). Estimating missing heritability for disease from genome-wide association studies. *American Journal of Human Genetics*, 88, 294–305.

Lin, D., Boyle, M. P., Dollar, P., Lee, H., Perona, P., Lein, E. S., & Anderson, D. J. (2011). Functional identification of an aggression locus in the mouse hypothalamus. *Nature*, 470, 221–226.

Lips, E. S., Cornelisse, L. N., Toonen, R. F., Min, J. L., Hultman, C. M., International Schizophrenia Consortium, ... & Posthuma, D. (2012). Functional gene group analysis identifies synaptic gene groups as risk factor for schizophrenia. *Molecular Psychiatry*, 17, 996–1006.

Liu, G., Wang, Y., & Wong, L. (2010). FastTagger: An efficient algorithm for genome-wide tag SNP selection using multi-marker linkage disequilibrium. *BMC Bioinformatics*, 11, 66.

Liu, H. & Guo, G. (2016). Opportunities and challenges of big data for the social sciences: The case of genomic data. *Social Science Research*, 59, 13–22.

Manolio, T. A., Collins, F. S., Cox, N. J., Goldstein, D. B., Hindorff, L. A., Hunter, D. J., ... & Chakravarti, A. (2009). Finding the missing heritability of complex diseases. *Nature*, 461, 747–753.

Marsh, A. A., Finger, E. C., Fowler, K. A., Jurkowitz, I. T. N., Schechter, J. C., Yu, H. H., ... & Blair, R. J. R. (2011). Reduced amygdala-orbitofrontal connectivity during moral judgments in youths with disruptive behavior disorders and psychopathic traits. *Psychiatry Research: Neuroimaging*, 194, 279–286.

Mason, D. A. & Frick, P. J. (1994). The heritability of antisocial behavior: A meta-analysis of twin and adoption studies. *Journal of Psychopathology and Behavioral Assessment*, 16, 301–323.

Merton, R. K. (1957). Priorities in scientific discovery: A chapter in the sociology of science. *American Sociological Review*, 22, 635–659.

Meyer-Lindenberg, A., Buckholtz, J. W., Kolachana, B., Hariri, A. R., Pezawas, L., Blasi, G., ... & Egan, M., (2006). Neural mechanisms of genetic risk for impulsivity and violence in humans. *Proceedings of the National Academy of Sciences*, 103, 6269–6274.

Mootha, V. K., Lindgren, C. M., Eriksson, K. F., Subramanian, A., Sihag, S., Lehar, J., ... & Houstis, N. (2003). PGC-1α-responsive genes involved in oxidative phosphorylation are coordinately downregulated in human diabetes. *Nature Genetics*, 34, 267–273.

Motzkin, J. C., Newman, J. P., Kiehl, K. A., & Koenigs, M. (2011). Reduced prefrontal connectivity in psychopathy. *The Journal of Neuroscience*, 31(48), 17348–17357.

Munafo, M. R., Stothart, G., & Flint, J. (2009). Bias in genetic association studies and impact factor. *Molecular Psychiatry*, 14, 119–120.

Nelson, R. J. & Trainor, B. C. (2007). Neural mechanisms of aggression. *Nature Reviews Neuroscience*, 8, 536–546.

Okbay, A., Beauchamp, J. P., Fontana, M. A., Lee, J. J., Pers, T. H., Rietveld, C. A., ... & Oskarsson, S. (2016). Genome-wide association study identifies 74 loci associated with educational attainment. *Nature*, 533(7604), 539–542.

Olivier, B. & Young, L. J. (2002). Animal models of aggression. *Neuropsychopharmacology: The Fifth Generation of Progress*, 118, 1699–1708.

Pappa, I., St Pourcain, B., Benke, K., Cavadino, A., Hakulinen, C., Nivard, M. G., ... & Evans, D. M. (2016). A genome-wide approach to children's aggressive behavior: The EAGLE consortium. *American Journal of Medical Genetics Part B: Neuropsychiatric Genetics*, 171, 562–572.

Pereira, T. V. & Ioannidis, J. P. (2011). Statistically significant meta-analyses of clinical trials have modest credibility and inflated effects. *Journal of Clinical Epidemiology*, 64, 1060–1069.

Plomin, R., DeFries, J. C., Knopik, V. S., & Neiderhiser, J. M. (2016). Top 10 replicated findings from behavioral genetics. *Perspectives on Psychological Science* 11, 3–23.

Plomin, R., DeFries, J. C., Knopik, V. S., & Neiderhiser, J. M. (2013). *Behavioral genetics* (6th ed.). New York: Worth.

Polderman, T. J. C., Benyamin, B., de Leeuw, C. A., Sullivan, P. F., van Bochoven, A., Visscher, P. M., & Posthuma, D. (2015). Meta-analysis of the heritability of human traits based on fifty years of twin studies. *Nature Genetics*, 47, 702–709.

Preuss, T. M. (1995). Do rats have prefrontal cortex? The Rose-Woolsey-Akert program reconsidered. *Journal of Cognitive Neuroscience*, 7, 1–24.

Purcell, S. (2002). Variance components models for gene-environment interaction in twin analysis. *Twin Research*, 5, 554–571.

Raine, A. (1993). *The psychopathology of crime: Criminal behavior as a clinical disorder*. San Diego, CA: Academic Press.

Rafter, N., Posick, C., & Rocque, M. (2016). *The criminal brain: Understanding biological theories of crime*. New York: New York University Press.

Rautiainen, M. R., Paunio, T., Repo-Tiihonen, E., Virkkunen, M., Ollila, H. M., Sulkava, S., ... & Tiihonen, J. (2016). Genome-wide association study of antisocial personality disorder. *Translational Psychiatry*, 6, e883.

Rhee, S. H. & Waldman, I. D. (2002). Genetic and environmental influences on antisocial behavior: A meta-analysis of twin and adoption studies. *Psychological Bulletin*, 128, 490–529.

Risch, N. & Merikangas, K. (1996). The future of genetic studies of complex human diseases. *Science*, 273, 1516–1517.

Salvatore, J. E., Edwards, A. C., McClintick, J. N., Bigdeli, T. B., Adkins, A., Aliev, F., ... & Nurnberger, J. I. (2015). Genome-wide association data suggest ABCB1 and immune-related gene sets may be involved in adult antisocial behavior. *Translational Psychiatry*, 5, e558.

Schizophrenia Working Group of the Psychiatric Genomics Consortium, 2014. Biological insights from 108 schizophrenia-associated genetic loci. *Nature*, 511, 421–427.

Scott, L. J., Mohlke, K. L., Bonnycastle, L. L., Willer, C. J., Li, Y., Duren, W. L., ... & Prokunina-Olsson, L. (2007). A genome-wide association study of type 2 diabetes in Finns detects multiple susceptibility variants. *Science*, 316 (5829), 1341–1345.

Sham, P. C. & Purcell, S. M. (2014). Statistical power and significance testing in large-scale genetic studies. *Nature Reviews Genetics*, 15(5), 335–346.

Simmons, J. P., Nelson, L. D., & Simonsohn, U. (2011). False-positive psychology: Undisclosed flexibility in data collection and analysis allows presenting anything as significant. *Psychological Science*, 22, 1359–1366.

Smith, G. D. (2011). Epidemiology, epigenetics and the "gloomy prospect": Embracing randomness in population health research and practice. *International Journal of Epidemiology*, 40, 537–562.

Sullivan, P. F. (2007). Spurious genetic associations. *Biological Psychiatry*, 61, 1121–1126.

Tielbeek, J. J., Johansson, A., Polderman, T. J. C., Rautiainen M. R., Jansen, P., Taylor, M., ... & Posthuma, D. (2017). Genome-wide association studies of a broad spectrum of antisocial behavior. *JAMA Psychiatry*, 74, 1242-1250.

TiChabelbeek, J. J., Medland, S. E., Benyamin, B., Byrne, E. M., Heath, A. C., Madden, P. A. F., ... & Verweij, K. J. H. (2012). Unraveling the genetic etiology of adult antisocial behavior: A genome-wide association study. *PLoS ONE, 7, e45086.*

Tielbeek, J. J., Linnér, R. K., Beers, K., Posthuma, D., Popma, A., & Polderman, T. J. C. (2016). Meta-analysis of the serotonin transporter promoter variant (*5-HTTLPR*) in relation to adverse environment and antisocial behavior. *American Journal of Medical Genetics Part B*, 171:B, 748–760.

Tilihonen, J., Rautiainen, M.-R., Ollila, H. M., Repo-Tilihonen, E., Virkkunen, M., Palotie, A., ... & Paunio, T. (2015). Genetic background of extreme violent behavior. *Molecular Psychiatry*, 20, 786–792.

Turkheimer, E. (2000). Three laws of behavior genetics and what they mean. *Current Directions in Psychological Science*, 9, 160–164.

Turkheimer, E. & Harden, K. P. (2014). Behavior genetic research methods: Testing quasi-causal hypotheses using multivariate twin data. In H. T. Reis & C. M. Jude (Eds), *Handbook of research methods in social and personality psychology* (2nd ed.). New York: Cambridge University Press.

van Erp, A. M. M. & Miczek, K. A. (2000). Aggressive behavior, increased accumbal dopamine, and decreased cortical serotonin in rats. *The Journal of Neuroscience*, 20, 9320–9325.

Vassos, E., Collier, D. A., & Fazel, S. (2014). Systematic meta-analyses and field synopsis of genetic association studies of violence and aggression. *Molecular Psychiatry*, 19, 471–477.

Veroude, K., Zhang-James, Y., Fernàndez-Castillo, N., Bakker, M. J., Cormand, B., & Faraone, S. V. (2016). Genetics of aggressive behavior: An overview. *American Journal of Medical Genetics Part B*, 171, 3–43.

Uylings, H. B., Groenewegen, H. J., & Kolb, B. (2003). Do rats have a prefrontal cortex? *Behavioural Brain Research*, 146, 3–17.

Waltes, R., Chiocchetti, A. G., & Freitag, C. M. (2016). The neurobiological basis of human aggression: A review on genetic and epigenetic mechanisms. *American Journal of Medical Genetics Part B*, 171, 650–675.

Wang, K., Li, M., & Hakonarson, H. (2010). Analysing biological pathways in genome-wide association studies. *Nature Reviews Genetics*, 11, 843–854.

Wertz, J., Caspi, A., Belsky, D. W., Beckley, A. L., Arseneault, L., Barnes, J. C., Corcoran, D. L., Hogan, S., Houts, R., Morgan, N., Odgers, C., Prinz, J., Sugden, K., Williams, B., Poulton, R., & Moffitt, T. E. (2017). Genetics and crime: Integrating new genomic discoveries into psychological research about antisocial behavior. *Psychological Science*, forthcoming.

Wise, S. P. (2008). Forward frontal fields: Phylogeny and fundamental function. *Trends in Neuroscience*, 31, 599–608.

Wright, J. P., Barnes, J. C., Boutwell, B. B., Schwartz, J. A., Connolly, J. A., Nedelec, J. L., & Beaver, K. M. (2015). Mathematical proof is not minutiae and irreducible complexity is not a theory: A final response to Burt and Simons and a call to criminologists. *Criminology*, 53, 113–120.

Yang, J., Bakshi, A., Zhu, Z., Hemani, G., Vinkhuyzen, A. A., Lee, S. H., ... & van Vliet-Ostaptchouk, J. V. (2015). Genetic variance estimation with imputed variants finds negligible missing heritability for human height and body mass index. *Nature Genetics*, 47, 1114–1120.

Yang, J., Benyamin, B., McEvoy, B. P., Gordon, S., Henders, A. K., Nyholt, D. R., ... & Visscher, P. M. (2010). Common SNPs explain a large proportion of the heritability for human height. *Nature Genetics*, 42, 565–569.

Yang, J., Lee, S. H., Goddard, M. E., & Visscher, P. M. (2011). GCTA: A tool for genome-wide complex trait analysis. *American Journal of Human Genetics*, 88, 76–82.

Yang, Y. & Raine, A. (2009). Prefrontal structural and functional brain imaging findings in antisocial, violent, and psychopathic individuals: A meta-analysis. *Psychiatry Research: Neuroimaging*, 174, 81–88.

Yang, Y., Raine, A., Narr, K. L., Colletti, P., & Toga, A. W. (2009). Localization of deformations within the amygdala in individuals with psychopathy. *Archives of General Psychiatry*, 66, 986–994.

Zhou, C., Rao, Y., & Rao, Y. (2008). A subset of octopaminergic neurons are important for Drosophila aggression. *Nature Neuroscience*, 11, 1059–1067.

Zuk, O, Hechter, E., Sunyaev, S. R., & Lander, E. S. (2012). The mystery of missing heritability: Genetic interactions create phantom heritability. *Proceedings of the National Academy of Sciences*, 109, 1193–1198.

6 Neuroimaging Evidence of Violence and Aggression

Heather McLernon, Jeremy Feiger, and Robert Schug

Introduction

Imaging techniques have consistently been used to demonstrate abnormalities of the brain in antisocial, aggressive, and violent individuals. These irregularities occur in several regions of the brain. Deficiencies begin in the prefrontal cortices, traverse back to the cingulate cortex, and to the temporal lobe, including the limbic system (i.e., amygdala and hippocampus). Not only do these abnormalities span various structures, but they manifest in various respects, including structural abnormalities (e.g., decreased tissue volumes), functional abnormalities (e.g., decreased neuronal activations), and even neurotransmitter performance (e.g., decreased serotonin functionality).

Researchers use different imaging techniques for measuring structural and functional characteristics of the brain. Structural studies most commonly use magnetic resonance imaging (MRI). As the name suggests, this technique uses a large magnet and the electrical current of the spinning protons in the brain to generate an anatomical image of regional or whole-brain tissue volume. Functional studies that measure brain activity most often use functional magnetic resonance imaging (fMRI), positron-emission tomography (PET), or single-photon emission computerized tomography (SPECT). fMRI scans utilize a large magnet and can produce an image of activity in the brain by measuring the changes in blood oxygen levels. Both PET and SPECT scans use radioactive tracers that are injected into the blood stream in material such as glucose. When the glucose is metabolized by active brain tissue, the scanner detects the nuclear material and creates an image of active and inactive brain regions. Functional imaging techniques are also used to measure neurotransmitter activity by looking at activity at the receptor sites and the changes in activity following administration of neurotransmitter manipulating drugs.

Researchers use these various brain imaging techniques to study participants who are at rest, performing a particular task, or even responding to a particular stimulus. Researchers conduct imaging studies on various populations as well, including not only healthy controls, but also other community samples, offender populations, and even psychiatric populations. The differences between groups presented speak to the deficits that characterize antisocial and aggressive populations.

Here, we describe the structural, functional, and neurochemical qualities of antisocial and aggressive individuals in the areas of the brain that show marked deficits: the frontal and prefrontal regions, the cingulate cortex, and the limbic system – namely, the amygdala and hippocampus. The majority of research focuses on finding significant differences in various imaging techniques between assorted violent and nonviolent groups. The results of these brain imaging studies have contributed greatly to the understanding of antisocial, aggressive, and violent behavior.

The Frontal Lobe and Prefrontal Cortex

The frontal lobe is a region of the brain consisting of a large amount of brain tissue anterior to the large brain fissure known as the central sulcus. The frontal lobe can be divided into sub regions, primarily the motor cortex, which controls movements, and the prefrontal cortex, which controls cognitive processes or what has been termed executive functioning. The prefrontal cortex can then be divided into smaller sub-regions, including the dorsolateral prefrontal cortex (DLPFC) and the orbitofrontal cortex (OFC; Kolb & Whishaw, 2009). Neuroimaging research has widely focused on the structural, functional, and neurochemical characteristics of the frontal lobes and their association to violence, aggression, and antisocial behavior.

Structural

The most common method of imaging brain structure is magnetic resonance imaging (MRI) and has been used by researchers to examine tissue volume in different areas of the brain. While some MRI studies did not find any significant differences in the frontal lobe volume of violent offenders diagnosed with a mental illness compared to controls (Barkataki, Kumari, Das, Taylor, & Sherma, 2006; Dolan, Deakin, Roberts, & Anderson, 2002), many studies using MRI techniques have shown volumetric differences in the frontal lobe tissue of violent offenders and antisocial, psychopathic, and aggressive individuals compared to controls – particularly regarding cortical thinning and gray matter reduction in the prefrontal cortex (Calzada-Reyes et al., 2015; Narayan et al., 2007; Raine, Lencz, Bihrle, La Casse, & Colletti, 2000; Raine, Yang, Narr, & Toga, 2009; Tiihonen et al., 2008).

A subgroup of particularly violent offenders was individuals diagnosed with psychopathy. Psychopaths are characterized by both affective and behavioral symptoms including lack of empathy or guilt and impulsivity, which may contribute to their high rates of violent recidivism (Hare, Mcpherson, Forth, & Kazdin, 1998; Harris, Rice, & Cormier, 1991; Kiehl, Kiehl, & Hoffman, 1991). Yang et al. (2005) used MRI scans of participants who were rated as high in psychopathy to look at any structural differences compared with non-psychopaths. The psychopath group was divided into those that had been caught for their crimes (the unsuccessful psychopaths) and those that had not been caught (the successful psychopaths). Results indicated that those who were high in psychopathy were characterized by reduced gray matter volume in the prefrontal region. Furthermore, while unsuccessful psychopaths had even lower prefrontal gray matter volume compared to both controls and successful psychopaths, the successful psychopaths did not differ from controls. These structural imaging findings suggest that prefrontal deficits may lead to poor decision making.

In a later study, Howner et al. (2012) used MRI to compare the cortical thickness in the frontal lobes of psychopathic offenders, offenders with antisocial personality disorder (ASPD) and nonoffender healthy controls. ASPD is characterized by a pattern of neglect for others' rights, and often includes impulsive and aggressive behavior. While researchers did not find any significant difference in the cortical thickness of the frontal lobes between the ASPD offenders and psychopathic offenders, they did report a tendency towards a thinner frontal cortex in psychopaths when compared to healthy controls. In another study that compared both violent and nonviolent offenders to controls, Calzada-Reyes et al. (2015) found no differences in frontal lobe volume within the violent groups comparing psychopaths to non-psychopaths; however, when compared to controls, the violent groups showed reduced gray matter in the orbitofrontal gyrus region of the prefrontal cortex. Violent psychopaths had reduced gray matter volume in the right superior orbitofrontal gyrus and violent non-psychopaths had reduced gray matter in the left middle frontal gyrus when compared to controls. This indicates that violent behavior exhibits a specific manifestation in the frontal regions, Furthermore, psychopathy compared to ASPD presents differently in frontal lobe structures.

Neuroimaging literature has also associated antisocial and aggressive behavior to structural deficits in regions of the prefrontal cortex, including the OFC (Antonucci et al., 2006; Gansler et al., 2009; Raine, Yang, Narr, & Toga, 2009; Tiihonen et al., 2008,), and DLPFC (Hirono, Mega, Dinov, Mishkin, & Cummings, 2000; Kola et al., 2015; Kumari et al., 2006; Tiihonen et al., 2008). Studies that examined the relationship between structural deficits in the OFC have produced mixed results. Antonucci et al., (2006) conducted a study using MRI to detect structural differences in relation to aggression and impulsivity of non-psychotic psychiatric patients. Results demonstrated a relationship between asymmetrical volume of the OFC and aggressive behavior, such that the greater the right OFC volume compared to the left, the greater the lifetime history of aggressive behavior. Motor impulsivity, a factor in aggressive behaviors, was also found to be significantly positively correlated with bilateral OFC volume. Gansler et al., (2009) in another MRI study, however, found no relationship between aggression and right OFC, but did find a significant negative relationship between left OFC volume and aggression in psychiatric patients but not healthy controls. Still another MRI study of violent offenders at a forensic hospital found violent offenders to have reduced gray matter volume bilaterally in the OFC as well as the frontopolar cortex (Tiihonen et al., 2008). In a longitudinal study, Trazepacz et al. (2013) was able to use MRI scanning to measure the effects of brain atrophy over time and its effect on aggression. They found that atrophy of the OFC and DLPFC overtime was associated with increases in aggression and agitation in Alzheimer's and dementia patients with a history of aggressive behavior. These mixed results may demonstrate that structural abnormalities may be contingent on not only aggression and violence, but also mental status (psychotic versus non-psychotic populations).

Functional

In addition to structural studies, a variety of brain imaging techniques have been used by researchers to study the functionality of frontal and prefrontal cortices in violent and antisocial individuals. Studies have reported functional deficits at rest in the frontal lobes of antisocial individuals (Goyer et al., 1994; Juhasz, Behen, Muzik, Chugani, & Chugani, 2001; Soderstorm, Tulberg, Wikkelso, & Forman, 2000). For example, Liu, Liao, Jiang, and Wang (2014) conducted a resting-state fMRI comparing brain activity of patients diagnosed with ASPD compared to healthy controls. They found decreased frontal cortex activity in the ASPD group. These results support earlier findings by Volkow et al. (1995), who used PET scans of at-rest violent psychiatric patients with a history of intermittent explosive behavior or ASPD. The results of this study indicated significantly lower prefrontal glucose metabolism in the violent patients compared to controls.

Other functional studies have found mixed results characterizing frontal lobe deficits. Amen, Stubblefield, Carmichael, and Thisted (1996) compared aggressive psychiatric patients to nonaggressive patients using SPECT. Results showed decreased prefrontal cortex activity, but also increased activity in the anteromedial prefrontal cortex. A later PET study of aggressive dementia patients found that, at rest, aggressive patients did not differ from nonaggressive patients in OFC functioning but did show reduced bilateral dorsolateral frontal cortex functioning (Hirono, Mega, Dinov, Mishkin, & Cummings, 2000). Functional MRI has also been used to evaluate the connectivity between the frontal lobe and other areas of the brain. Phillipi and colleagues (2015) used resting-state fMRI to assess the functional connectivity of three primary cortical networks in psychopathic and non-psychopathic adult prison inmates. They found that higher psychopathy scores were associated with lower functional connectivity between the frontal and parietal lobes.

While many functional brain imaging procedures are conducted while participants are at rest, several researchers utilize various tasks during imaging to measure traits characteristics and investigate impairments in the frontal lobe of aggressive individuals (Intrator et al., 1997; Joyal et al., 2007; Raine et al., 1998; Schiffer et al., 2014). Deficits in inhibitory control of impulses have been linked to impulsive violence. Reduced prefrontal activity in impulsive violent offenders has been theorized to explain poor cognitive inhibition of affective impulses (Raine et al., 1998). An externalizing mental disorder that is characterized by highly impulsive aggressive and violent behavior is intermittent explosive disorder (IED; Coccaro, 2012). In order to better understand the neural mechanisms involved in the disinhibition component of IED, Moeller et al. (2014) conducted an experiment using fMRI to scan the brains of individuals diagnosed with IED and healthy controls. The scans were taken during a Stroop color-naming task, which required the participant to name the color ink that a color word is printed in, with some of the color words being printed in a noncongruent color. This requires the participant to inhibit the impulse to say the word instead of the color of the ink. Results showed greater activity in the left DLPFC of the IED group compared to controls during errors on the Stroop task. Furthermore, the greater the outward expression of anger, the greater the activity in the left DLPFC during error processing. These results could indicate that left DLPFC hyperactivity could be a biological marker for impulsive aggression and related to inhibitory control. In another study that used a task to engage inhibitory processes while conducting an fMRI scan, patients diagnosed with ASPD performed a go/no-go task. This task requires the participant to engage in a behavior in response to certain stimuli and to stop that behavior when other stimuli are present. Results of this study found that healthy controls showed activation during response inhibition primarily in the right DLPFC and the left OFC, while ASPD individuals showed activation in the medial, superior, and inferior frontal gyri. These findings support neural inhibitory response pattern abnormalities in individuals with externalizing disorders (Völlum et al., 2004).

Contrasting results were reported in Schiffer et al. (2014), who conducted an fMRI study with violent offenders and nonoffenders while engaging in the Stroop color-naming task. These researchers found that violent offenders displayed reduced DLPFC activation during error processing compared with controls. Similar results showed reduced activation in the left DLPFC during a go/no-go task (Völlum et al., 2010). In this study, ASPD individuals were characterized by decreased glucose metabolism during a PET scan compared with controls. While the present literature does demonstrate abnormality in prefrontal cortex functioning in relation to impulsive violence, results differ in the nature and direction of this relationship, highlighting the need for further research in this area and again indicating differences due to variable mental statuses (IED versus ASPD).

Differences in functional activity in the frontal and prefrontal regions may be closely related to emotionality and the differences in emotional regulation seen in varying mental disorders. Neuroimaging research has demonstrated impaired or dysfunctional emotional (Decety, Michalska, Aitsuki, & Lahey, 2009; Prehn et al., 2013) and cognitive (Joyal et al., 2007; Schiffer et al., 2014) processes and the combination of deficits in these areas can contribute to antisocial behavior and violence (Birbaumer, 2005; Sterzer, Stadler, Krebs, Kleinschmid, & Poustka, 2005). In a study to investigate the neural abnormalities in criminal psychopaths, a population characterized by affective deficits, Müller et al. (2003) conducted a study showing criminal psychopaths and healthy volunteers pictures with both positive and negative affective content while recording fMRI data. A differential pattern of activation emerged between the two groups in frontal lobe regions. During the viewing of negative emotional content, psychopaths showed increased activation of the right prefrontal areas among other limbic structures; however, when psychopaths viewed positive emotional content, reduced activation was seen in the right medial frontal gyrus when compared with controls. Neuroimaging research has also been extended to abnormalities in adolescents. Decety et al. (2009) presented images to adolescents diagnosed with aggressive conduct disorder (CD). Conduct disorder is a childhood or adolescent disorder that is marked by a pattern of antisocial behavior that often includes aggression. Participants were shown people in pain or not in pain, and pain caused on purpose or by accident, during fMRI procedure. Again, a differential pattern of activation was found between the aggressive conduct disorder group and controls. When watching pain inflicted intentionally versus by accident, controls showed activation in the lateral OFC, and the superior frontal and medial prefrontal gyrus. The CD group showed only activation in the medial OFC in frontal cortex regions. Together these studies demonstrate that even beginning in adolescence, emotionality and its specific relationship to mental disorder may explain some of the irregularities in neurofunctionality for antisocial and aggressive individuals.

In addition to emotional deficits, cognitive deficits have been expressed via frontal lobe impairment in violent offenders. This was demonstrated in a series of classic early PET studies. Raine, Buchsbaum, and Lacasse (1997) conducted PET scans of offenders while they were performing a continuous performance task that had been established to activate the frontal lobes. These offenders had been tried for murder and had pleaded not guilty by reason of insanity. Violent offenders showed reduced glucose metabolism in multiple areas of the prefrontal cortex, including the right OFC, when compared to controls. In a subsequent study, Raine et al. (1998) separated the murderers into those that had experienced a significant level of psychosocial deprivation and those that had not. They found that only murderers without psychosocial deprivation showed reduced glucose metabolism in the prefrontal cortex compared to murderers with significant psychosocial deprivation. In a third follow-up study, Raine et al. (1998) divided the same murderers into predatory and affective murderers. These results found that affective murderers showed both reduced prefrontal glucose metabolism and increased subcortical metabolism compared with controls. Predatory murderers did not differ from controls in prefrontal glucose metabolism but showed a similar increase in subcortical metabolism as the affective murderers. The results highlight the high emotional reactivity with poor cognitive control seen in impulsive violent offenders.

Functional neuroimaging has been used to study frontal lobe activity when aggression is experimentally provoked in violent individuals diagnosed with a mental disorder. Using PET imaging during induced autobiographical memories, Spoont, Kuskowski, and Pardo (2010) compared violent offenders diagnosed with a personality disorder or IED to healthy controls. In results that suggested violent individuals have deficient cognitive control of impulsive aggression, the violent group showed lower frontal activity during angry memories versus neutral memories compared to controls. The violent group also had overall lower frontal activity during both types of memory. These results are supported by an earlier study using a computer task to provoke aggression. Reported results found individuals diagnosed with bipolar disorder or IED showed decreased activation of the OFC during neutral conditions and increased OFC activity during the provoked condition compared with controls (New et al., 2009).

Neurotransmitters

Neurotransmitters are the chemicals used by the brain to function. These chemicals pass from one brain cell to another signaling a particular response. Recent studies have used functional neuroimaging to report the involvement of neurotransmitters serotonin and dopamine in aggression and violence (Kunz et al., 1995; Virkkunen & Linnoila, 1993; Schlüter et al., 2016; Tiihonen et al., 2015). New et al. (2002)

investigated the role of frontal cortex serotonin in impulsive aggression by using PET scans of patients with impulsive aggression following the administration of a serotonergic stimulus or a placebo. The aggressive patients showed reduced activation in the right lateral OFC as well as the left medial OFC compared with controls when receiving the serotonergic stimulus. These results suggest that impulsively aggressive individuals may have a deficient inhibitory response process to serotonin in frontal lobe regions. In a follow-up study, New et al. (2004) injected fluoxetine, which increases the amount of serotonin being used by blocking its reuptake into the cells, into impulsive aggressive patients who met the criteria for a borderline personality diagnosis. PET scans before and after the injections showed an increase of metabolic activity in the OFC, which in their previous study was hypoactive in aggressive individuals.

Additional evidence of the role of neurotransmitters comes from brain imaging studies that examine monoamine oxidase A (MAO-A), an enzyme in the brain that breaks down serotonin and dopamine, among other neurotransmitters (Bortolato et al., 2011). A recent pair of studies examined the role of MAO-A in impulsive violence (Kolla et al., 2015; Kolla et al., 2016). Kolla et al. (2015) administered a task that measures impulsivity to males with ASPD and a history of violence. A tracer that selectively marks MAO-A was used with PET scans to determine levels of MAO-A active in frontal cortex regions. The investigators reported that significantly lower MAO-A was found in ASPD males compared to controls in several prefrontal cortex regions including the OFC and DLPFC, as well as in the ventrolateral PFC and medial PFC.

The role of the frontal lobe structures in violence, aggression, and antisocial behavior has been widely studied using various neuroimaging techniques. MRI scans have shown structural deficits in antisocial individuals, while fMRI, PET, and SPECT studies indicate functional abnormalities and neurotransmitter deficits in violent individuals as well. Results of these studies have come to varying conclusions. While some of the results are mixed, this may be explained by emotionality and varying mental disorders. Varying mental status may be deemed antisocial, aggressive, and violent (e.g., IED, ASPD, psychopathy); however, the role that emotion plays in these disorders vary, and the disparate neuroimaging results may reflect this difference. Despite these varying results, however, the neuroimaging data compiled lays a solid ground work for future brain imaging studies of antisocial behavior and violence.

The Cingulate Cortex

Like the OFC, DLPFC, and other frontal and prefrontal regions, the cingulate cortex is a brain region often implicated in various executive functioning roles that are associated with aggressive and violent behavior. More specifically, the cingulate cortex has continuously been related to decision making, affective regulation, and impulsivity. Various studies have demonstrated structural, functional, and other abnormalities specific to the cingulate cortex as it relates to antisocial behavior, aggression, and violence. These studies have demonstrated robust findings spreading across both healthy and clinical samples, adolescents and adults, as well as males and females.

Structural

As found in the frontal and prefrontal cortices, structural abnormalities including reduced gray matter and decreased cortical thickness have been observed in the cingulate cortex in antisocial and violent populations. Similar to studies that implicate prefrontal cortices in antisocial behavior and specifically psychopathy, Yang et al. (2009) performed MRIs on psychopaths and healthy controls to determine differences in gray matter. This study found reduced gray matter in the posterior cingulate gyrus among other areas in psychopaths compared to healthy controls. Using fMRI to measure, Ly et al. (2012) separated adult male offenders into psychopathic and non-psychopathic groups. Offenders with increased psychopathic traits had significant cortical thinning in the anterior cingulate cortex. Jiang et al. (2015) found similar results in adolescent participants aged 14 to 16. This study included both male and female participants with adolescent-onset CD. It was found that the CD group showed decreased cortical thickness in the posterior cingulate cortex. Additionally, a reduced amount of cortical folding was found in the anterior cingulate cortex. Increased cortical folding has often been associated with increased intelligence (due to the increased amount of surface area). Together, these studies implicate structural abnormalities in the cingulate cortex in antisocial behavior not only for adult males, but also for adolescents, as well as for female participants, who are often overlooked in antisocial research.

Research has also expanded literature on antisocial individuals who are comorbid with other disorders, namely borderline personality disorder (Bertsch et al., 2013) and schizophrenia (Kumari et al., 2014). Bertsch et al. (2013) conducted MRIs on adult male offenders convicted for capital violent crimes. The offenders were separated into those with borderline personality disorder traits and those with psychopathic traits. Results found that increased psychopathic traits were associated with reduced gray matter in the posterior cingulate cortex. Interestingly, these significant reductions were not as marked in those with borderline personality disorder traits. Similarly, Kumari et al. (2014) separated participants with diagnoses of ASPD or schizophrenia with serious violence, or schizophrenia without serious violence. Reduced gray matter in the anterior cingulate was found for both the ASPD disorder group and the violent schizophrenia group compared to healthy controls. This marked decrease was not found in the schizophrenia without serious violence group.

Akin to the structural neuroimaging results of prefrontal and frontal regions, disparate findings (i.e., reduced gray matter) may be contingent on violent status (violent versus nonviolent) and mental status (psychopathy versus borderline personality disorder).

Functional

In addition to structural deficiencies, functional abnormalities present in the cingulate cortex are also related to antisocial, aggressive, and violent behavior. Similar to studies regarding the frontal and prefrontal cortices, functional studies implicating the cingulate cortex demonstrate decreased neuronal activity. Like the structural deficits found in the cingulate cortex, the functional discrepancies are found in adolescents and adults, as well as clinical and healthy control samples.

Research continues to find relationships between decreased neuronal activity as it relates to psychopathy and emotionality in particular. Kiehl et al. (2001) separated offenders into psychopathic and non-psychopathic groups. Psychopathic offenders showed decreased emotional-related activity in the anterior and posterior cingulate gyrus, among other areas. Furthermore, these results are not limited to adult populations. Adolescent male participants aged from 9 to 15 who met DSM criteria for CD demonstrated a marked deactivation in the anterior cingulate cortex compared to healthy controls via an fMRI after viewing negative-affective pictures (Sterzer et al., 2005).

Similar to the functional connectivity deficiencies found in the frontal lobes (Philippi et al., 2016), functional deficiencies in antisocial and aggressive individuals are not limited to a single area of the brain, but also manifest as connectivity deficits between the cingulate cortex and other brain regions. Ly et al. (2012) found that psychopathic offenders demonstrated reduced functional connectivity between the insula and the anterior cingulate cortex relative to their non-psychopathic counterparts. Analogous results demonstrated that increased psychopathic traits were associated with decreased connectivity between the intraparietal sulcus and the anterior cingulate cortex (Philippi et al., 2016).

Studies have also indicated that it is not just psychopathy as a whole that relates to decreased functional activity in the cingulate cortex. Researchers continue to find that reduced neuronal activity is specifically related to the emotional blunting associated with psychopathy (Prehn et al., 2013; Searo-Cardoso et al., 2015). Prehn et al., 2013 separated a group of violent criminal offenders into those with emotional hyporeactivity or those with emotional hyperreactivity. While all the offenders met the DSM criteria for ASPD, only those with below-average emotional reactivity – or hyporeactivity – showed decreased activity in the anterior cingulate cortex. This same pattern is seen in nonoffender populations. Seara-Cardoso et al. (2015) measured psychopathic traits in a healthy sample of adult males with no history of mental illness. MRI results demonstrated that those with increased affective-interpersonal psychopathic traits demonstrated decreased neural responses in the cingulate cortex after seeing others pain. Interestingly, those with increased lifestyle-antisocial psychopathic traits showed increased responses in the cingulate cortex. These disparate findings indicate that the emotional component of antisociality is particularly related to decreased activity in the cingulate cortex. This specificity could possibly explain studies that have shown no differences between psychopathic and nonpsychopathic individuals as related to cingulate cortex abnormalities (Dvorak-Bertsch et al., 2007).

Neurotransmitters

Like the research that has used functional neuroimaging in the frontal and prefrontal cortices to implicate neurotransmitters in matters of antisociality and aggression, studies have found similar results in the cingulate cortex. In a sample of adult male and female participants who met criteria for IED, PET scans demonstrated that those with IED showed decreased serotonin transporters in the anterior cingulate cortex compared to healthy controls (Frankle et al., 2005). Völlum et al. (2010) found that in both healthy and ASPD patients, activation of the cingulate cortex was increased during an inhibition task after a serotonin receptor agonist was administered. Parallel to neurotransmitter behavior in the frontal and prefrontal cortex, these results indicate that deficient serotonin processing in the cingulate cortex is associated with antisocial and aggressive behavior.

Limbic System

Like the cingulate cortex, the limbic system, a medial part of the temporal lobe, is consistently implicated in antisocial, aggressive, and violent behavior, especially as it relates to emotional regulation. The amygdala and the hippocampus are two structures in the limbic system that are particularly implicated in antisocial behavior. The amygdala is often related to the processing of emotion from sensory stimuli. The amygdala is strongly and bidirectionally connected to the hippocampus, which is implicated in memory. Together, these structures are responsible for fear conditioning, threat response, and other emotionally modulated memory processes.

Akin to imaging studies of the prefrontal, frontal, and cingulate cortex, imaging studies of the limbic system also demonstrate robust findings of structural, functional, as well as neurochemical abnormalities in antisocial, aggressive, and violent individuals. Additionally, affective contributions influence how these abnormalities manifest in antisociality.

Structural

Imaging studies consistently demonstrate structural abnormalities in the limbic system for antisocial, aggressive, and violent individuals, but disparate from the prefrontal, frontal, and cingulate cortex findings, structural abnormalities of the limbic system are not limited to reduced gray matter and decreased cortical thickness. Antisociality is also characterized by aberrant morphology or shape in limbic structures, namely the hippocampus and amygdala.

Several studies have indicated that increased psychopathy is associated with abnormal gray matter in limbic structures (Boccardi et al., 2011; Ermer et al., 2012); however, results are mixed. Parallel to volumetric decreases in other brain structures, Ermer et al. (2012) used MRI to measure gray matter in adult male offenders. Results demonstrated that as psychopathy scores increased, gray matter volume and tissue density decreased in the amygdala and hippocampus. In contrast, Boccardi et al. (2011) found increased amygdala volume in psychopathic violent offenders; however, this study was cautious to remove any offenders with schizophrenia spectrum disorders, including schizotypal personality disorder. Barkataki et al. (2006) may shed light on these disparate findings. In this study, participants were separated into ASPD, violent schizophrenia, nonviolent schizophrenia, and healthy control groups. Participants underwent MRI procedures and results indicated that the ASPD and the violent schizophrenia group demonstrated reduced brain volume overall compared to healthy control. Furthermore, the violent schizophrenia group had decreased hippocampal volumes compared to ASPD and control groups. Together, these results indicate that schizophrenia spectrum disorders can differentially impact structural abnormalities in antisocial individuals.

Pardini et al. (2014) used longitudinal methodologies to expand on volumetric disparities of the limbic system in antisociality, aggression, and violence. In this study, men who had been followed since childhood underwent MRI procedures as adults. Decreased amygdala volume was found in men who had demonstrated aggressive and psychopathic traits since childhood and adolescence. This study also indicated that decreased amygdala volume is a risk factor for future aggressive and violent behavior. These results show robust evidence for structural deficits in antisocial individuals even beginning in adolescence.

As mentioned, imaging studies have found not only volumetric disparities, but also morphologic abnormalities in limbic structures (Boccardi et al., 2010; Coccaro et al., 2015). In one such study, violent offenders and healthy controls underwent MRI to measure volumetric differences. While volumes did not significantly differ between groups, structurally the surface shape of the hippocampus differed between violent offenders and healthy controls. Coccaro et al. (2015) found similar results, such that participants with IED demonstrated significantly different surface shape deformations in the hippocampus and the amygdala compared to their healthy counterparts.

Functional

Similar to structural imaging studies, research has continued to find functional abnormality in the limbic system. Additionally, similar to results found in the cingulate cortex, many of the anomalies are modulated by affective or emotional involvement. Hypoactivity or hyperactivity of limbic structures, mainly the amygdala, is contingent on differences in affective manifestations of various antisocial disorders.

Similar to studies that measure functional deficiencies in the frontal, prefrontal, and cingulate cortex, fMRI studies have found decreased functionality in the limbic system in those who exhibit antisocial behavior. Kiehl et al. (2001) separated offenders into psychopathic and non-psychopathic groups. Psychopathic offenders showed decreased emotional-related activity in the amygdala and hippocampus. Fairchild et al. (2014) found similar results in adolescent females. Adolescent females with CD and healthy controls underwent similar procedures of viewing facial expressions during fMRI. CD was significantly correlated to amygdala activation, such that as CD increased, amygdala activation decreased.

While many studies demonstrate this decreased activity in the amygdala, these results are strongly contingent on the emotional characteristics related to different types of antisociality. Studies have also found increased activity in the limbic system in response to negative emotions (Hyde et al., 2014; McCloskey et al., 2016; Osumi et al., 2012). These conflicting results demonstrate that antisocial behavior, aggression, and violence can be correlated to hypoactivity or hyperactivity dependent on the type of antisociality.

Hyde et al. (2014) demonstrated how limbic activity can increase or decrease dependent on the type of antisocial disorder (e.g., ASPD or psychopathy). Hyde et al. (2014) conducted fMRI procedure on a community sample of both male and female adults. ASPD traits were positively related to amygdala reactivity, whereas psychopathic traits were negatively related to amygdala reactivity. This study found that negative emotion is what separates the difference between ASPD and psychopathy such that the increased negative emotionality (present in ASPD, but not psychopathy) is responsible for amygdala activation. Osumi et al. (2012) found similar results in healthy male undergraduate students such that increased psychopathic traits correlated to decreased activity in the amygdala following a frustrating task. The authors suggest that this may indicate that psychopaths have decreased neural response to reactive aggression.

Another study that demonstrated the differences in antisociality both in behavior and in neural activity of the limbic system was conducted by McCloskey et al. (2016). In this study, participants were patients meeting DSM criteria for intermittent explosive disorder and healthy controls. Participants were shown human facial expressions during the fMRI procedure. Results showed that the intermittent explosive disorder group showed increased amygdala activation in response to angry faces compared to healthy controls; however, this difference did not occur after being shown happy faces. Together, these studies indicate that manifestations of antisocial behavior are different behaviorally and neurologically and that these disparities are due to how negative emotions are processed. Psychopathic characteristics demonstrate decreased emotionality and this is expressed by decreased activity in the limbic structures. In contrast, other disorders, including ASPD and intermittent explosive disorder, show increased emotionality and this corresponds to increased activity in the limbic structures.

Neurotransmitters

Similar to studies that used functional neuroimaging in other regions of the brain to associate neurotransmitters to matters of antisocial behavior, research has found similar results in the limbic system. Osumi et al. (2012) found that psychopathic traits were related to decreased dopaminergic functionality between the amygdala and another area of the brain – namely the striatum. Kolla et al. (2016) found similar results in the hippocampus for a group of ASPD participants who had a history of violence. ASPD participants demonstrated decreased MAO-A functionality in the hippocampus, again indicating deficiencies in dopaminergic functioning.

The limbic structures, like other regions of the brain, also show marked abnormalities, and, like other areas of the brain, these abnormalities manifest in various ways dependent on mental status and emotionality. It is important for researchers to consider how different disorders process emotions in order to relate this back to the disparate findings in the structural and functional processes of various brain regions. Neuroimaging data continues to play an integral role in understanding antisociality, aggression, and violence. Neuroimaging allows researchers to better understand behavioral manifestations of aggression via the structural and functional deficiencies that are apparent throughout various regions of the brain, including frontal and prefrontal cortices, the cingulate cortex, and even the temporal lobes, namely the limbic system. This data also allows researchers to expand research to implications for the law and policy, for prevention efforts of future aggression, and for interventions for mental disorders marked by antisocial and aggressive behavior.

Policy, Prevention, and Intervention

There are significant implications for the law as well as for prevention and interventions for aggressive and violent behavior. The legal system has used imaging techniques not only as evidence during court proceedings but also in various briefing documents (Yang, Glenn, & Raine, 2008). Oftentimes, brain imaging results are presented as evidence for mitigating circumstances. Several court cases have pointed to structural or functional deficits as rationalizations for antisocial and aggressive behavior (e.g., John Hinckley, Jr.'s structural deficiencies). In Baird and Fugelsang (2004), researchers use brain imaging studies to weigh in on development and mental culpability as it relates to age. While it is important to consider empirical evidence within the legal system, it is also important to remember that, as evidenced throughout the literature, there are mixed results. These mixed results are continually linked to the different manifestations of emotionality in various mental disorders. When considering policy or legal consequences, one must take into account that antisocial behavior is not a single and invariable concept. While many disorders are characterized by antisocial behavior, as well as aggressive and violent behavior, neuroimaging studies continue to show that these antisocial and aggressive disorders do not manifest in the same way, both cognitively and behaviorally. This is also important to consider in respect to prevention and intervention for antisociality and aggression.

Brain imaging research lays solid groundwork for prevention efforts and intervention methods to reduce aggression and violence. This is evident especially as related to the functional imaging studies that implicate neurotransmitters in antisociality. As indicated throughout the literature, there are various anomalies in serotonin and dopaminergic functionality. This may imply that neurochemical interventions may ameliorate aggressive and violent behavior. Research has already found that using neurochemical intervention can impact impulsively aggressive populations (New et al., 2004).

In light of research that indicates brain abnormalities in children and adolescents, research has also advocated for proactive and early intervention to prevent future aggressive and violent behavior (Anderson & Kiehl, 2014). These early interventions can include cognitive behavioral methods as well as enhancing internal motivations to combat treatment resistance (Bayliss, Miller, & Henderson, 2010). Early interventions are especially important when considering that, as a whole, interventions for psychopathy in adults only show modest success (Anderson & Kiehl, 2014). When considering neuroplasticity of children and adolescents, it very important to target those at risk for aggression and violence as early as possible to allow increased functionality in the brain (Anderson & Kiehl, 2014).

Affective factors, especially emotional regulation, are key components related to brain abnormalities and antisociality. Research has indicated that various intervention methods can enhance emotional regulation. In addition to cognitive behavioral therapies, integrative methods that include body-mind training (body relaxation, mental imagery, mindfulness) have shown positive results for emotional regulation (Tang et al., 2012). Another study found that biofeedback interventions have shown positive results in antisociality (Howard, Schellhorn, & Lumsden, 2013). The patient in this study demonstrated a history of impulsivity, hostility, and aggression and, after several weeks of biofeedback intervention, the patient had positive results in self-regulating his emotions.

Neuroimaging provides a biological understanding of antisocial, aggressive, and violent behavior. Various imaging techniques allow researchers to consider both structural and functional manifestations of antisociality and aggression in several structures of the brain. An important implication of neuroimaging evidence is that antisocial, aggressive, and violent individuals are characterized by abnormalities in the brain. Furthermore, many of these deficiencies are linked to emotionality, and while several mental disorders are distinguished by antisocial behavior, they demonstrate differences in emotional processing, which may lead to variable manifestations of aggressive and violent behavior. Neuroimaging research also lays a basis for implications related to policy and legal standards, prevention, and intervention for antisocial individuals who are characterized by aggression and violence.

References

Amen, D. G., Stubblefield, M., Carmichael, B., & Thisted, R. (1996). Brain SPECT findings and aggressiveness. *Annals of Clinical Psychiatry*, 8(3), 129–137.

Antonucci, A. S., Gansler, D. A., Tan, S., Bhadelia, R., Patz, S., & Fulwiler, C. (2006). Orbitofrontal correlates of aggression and impulsivity in psychiatric patients. *Psychiatry Research: Neuroimaging*, 147(2–3), 213–220.

Anderson, N. E. & Kiehl, K. A. (2014). Psychopathy: Developmental perspectives and their implications for treatment. *Restorative Neurology and Neuroscience*, 32(1), 103–117.

Baird A. & Fugelsang J. A. (2004). The emergence of consequential thought: evidence from neuroscience, *Philosophical Transactions of the Royal Society of London B*, 359, 1797–1804.

Barkataki, I., Kumari, V., Das, M., Taylor, P., & Sharma, T. (2006). Volumetric structural brain abnormalities in men with schizophrenia or antisocial personality disorder. *Behavioural Brain Research*, 169(2), 239–247.

Bayliss, C. M., Miller, A. K., & Henderson, C. E. (2010). Psychopathy development and implications for early intervention. *Journal of Cognitive Psychotherapy*, 24(2), 71–80.

Bertsch, K., Grothe, M., Prehn, K., Vohs, K., Berger, C., Hauenstein, K., Keiper, P., Domes, G., Teipel, S., & Herpertz, S. C. (2013). Brain volumes differ between diagnostic groups of violent criminal offenders. *European Archives of Psychiatry and Clinical Neuroscience*, 263(7), 593–606.

Birbaumer, N., Veit, R., Lotze, M., Erb, M., Hermann, C., Grodd, W., & Flor, H. (2005). Deficient Fear Conditioning in Psychopathy: A Functional Magnetic Resonance Imaging Study. *Archives of General Psychiatry*, 62(7), 799–805.

Boccardi, M., Frisoni, G. B., Hare, R. D., Cavedo, E., Najt, P., Pievani, M., Rasser, P. E., Laakso, M. P., Aronen, H. J., Repo-Tiihonen, E., Vaurio, O., Thompson, P. M., & Tiihonen, J. (2011). Cortex and amygdala morphology in psychopathy. *Psychiatry Research: Neuroimaging*, 193(2), 85–92.

Boccardi, M., Ganzola, R., Rossi, R., Sabattoli, F., Laakso, M. P., Repo-Tiihonen, E., Vaurio, O., Könönen, M., Aronen, H. J., Thompson, P. M., Frisoni, G. B., & Tiihonen, J. (2010). Abnormal hippocampal shape in offenders with psychopathy. *Human Brain Mapping*, 31(3), 438–447.

Bortolato, M., Chen, K., Godar, S., Chen, G., Wu, W. et al. (2011). Social deficits and perseverative behaviors, but not overt aggression, in MAOA hypomorphic mice. *Neuropsychopharmacology*, 36(13), 2674–2678.

Calzada-Reyes, A., Alvarez-Amador, A., Galán-García, L., Valdés-Sosa, M., Melie-García, L., Alemán-Gómez, Y., & del Carmen Iglesias-Alonso, J. (2015). MRI study in psychopath and non-psychopath offenders. In M. Fitzgerald (ed.), *Psychopathy: Risk factors, behavioral symptoms and treatment options* (pp. 41–59). Hauppauge, NY: Nova Science Publishers.

Coccaro, E. F., Lee, R., McCloskey, M., Csernansky, J. G., & Wang, L. (2015). Morphometric analysis of amygdla and hippocampus shape in impulsively aggressive and healthy control subjects. *Journal of Psychiatric Research*, 69, 80–86.

Coccaro, E. (2012). Intermittent explosive disorder as a disorder of impulsive aggression for dsm-5. *American Journal of Psychiatry*, 169(6), 577

Decety, J., Michalska, K. J., Akitsuki, Y., & Lahey, B. B. (2009). Atypical empathic responses in adolescents with aggressive conduct disorder: A functional MRI investigation. *Biological Psychology*, 80(2), 203–211.

Dolan, M. C., Deakin, J. W., Roberts, N., & Anderson, I. M. (2002). Quantitative frontal and temporal structural MRI studies in personality-disordered offenders and control subjects. *Psychiatry Research: Neuroimaging*, 116(3), 133–149.

Dvorak-Bertsch, J. D., Sadeh, N., Glass, S. J., Thornton, D., & Newman, J. P. (2007). Stroop tasks associated with differential activation of anterior cingulate do not differentiate psychopathic and non-psychopathic offenders. *Personality and Individual Differences*, 42(3), 585–595.

Ermer, E., Cope, L. M., Nyalakanti, P. K., Calhoun, V. D., & Kiehl, K. A. (2012). Aberrant paralimbic gray matter in criminal psychopathy. *Journal of Abnormal Psychology*, 121(3), 649–658.

Fairchild, G., Hagan, C. C., Passamonti, L., Walsh, N. D., Goodyer, I. M., & Calder, A. J. (2014). Atypical neural responses during face processing in female adolescents with conduct disorder. *Journal of the American Academy Of Child & Adolescent Psychiatry*, 53(6), 677–687.

Frankle, W. G., Lombardo, I., New, A. S., Goodman, M., Talbot, P. S., Huang, Y., Hwang, D. R., Slifstein, M., Curry, S., Abi-Dargham, A., Laruelle, M., & Siever, L. J. (2005). Brain Serotonin Transporter Distribution in Subjects With Impulsive Aggressivity: A Positron Emission Study With [^{11}C]McN 5652. *American Journal of Psychiatry*, 162(5), 915–923.

Gansler, D. A., McLaughlin, N. R., Iguchi, L., Jerram, M., Moore, D. W., Bhadelia, R., & Fulwiler, C. (2009). A multivariate approach to aggression and the orbital frontal cortex in psychiatric patients. *Psychiatry Research: Neuroimaging*, 171(3), 145–154.

Gordon, H. L., Baird, A. A., & End, A. (2004). Functional differences among those high and low on a trait measure of psychopathy. *Biological Psychiatry*, 56(7), 516–521.

Goyer, P. F., Andreason, P. J., Semple, W. E., Clayton, A. H., King, A. C., Compton-Toth, B. A., Schulz, S. C., & Cohen, R. M. (1994). Positron-emission tomography and personality disorders. *Neuropsychopharmacology*, 10(1), 21–28.

Hare, R., Mcpherson, L., Forth, A., & Kazdin, A. (1998) Male Psychopaths and Their Criminal Careers. *Journal of Consulting and Clinical Psychology*, 56(5), 710–714.

Harris, G., Rice, M., & Cormier, C. (1991). Psychopathy and violent recidivism. *Law and Human Behavior*, 15(6), 625–637.

Hirono, N., Mega, M. S., Dinov, I. D., Mishkin, F., & Cummings, J. L. (2000). Left frontotemporal hypoperfusion in associated with aggression in patients with dementia. *Archives of Neurology*, 57(6), 861–866.

Howard, R., Schellhorn, K., & Lumsden, J. (2013). Complex case: A biofeedback intervention to control impulsiveness in a severely personality disordered forensic patient.

Personality and Mental Health, 7(2), 168–173. doi: 10.1002/pmh.1231.

Howner, K., Eskildsen, S., Fischer, H., Dierks, T., Wahlund, L., et al. (2012). Thinner cortex in the frontal lobes in mentally disordered offenders. *Psychiatry Research*, 203, 126–131.

Hyde, L. W., Byrd, A. L., Votruba-Drzal, E., Hariri, A. R., & Manuck, S. B. (2014). Amygdala reactivity and negative emotionality: Divergent correlates of antisocial personality and psychopathy traits in a community sample. *Journal of Abnormal Psychology*, 123(1), 214–224.

Intrator, J., Hare, R., Stritzke, P., Brichtswein, K., Dorfman, D., Harpur, T., Bernstein, D., Handelsman, L., Schaefer, C., Keilp, J., Rosen, J., & Machac, J. (1997). A brain imaging (single photon emission computerized tomography) study of semantic and affective processing in psychopaths. *Biological Psychiatry*, 42(2), 96–103.

Jiang, Y., Guo, X., Zhang, J., Gao, J., Wang, X., Situ, W., Yi, J., Zhang, X., Zhu, X., Yao, S., & Huang, B. (2015). Abnormalities of cortical structures in adolescent-onset conduct disorder. *Psychological Medicine*, 45(16), 3467–3479.

Joyal, C. C., Putkonen, A., Mancini-Marïe, A., Hodgins, S., Kononen, M., Boulay, L., Pihlajamaki, M., Soininen, H., Stip, E., Tiihonen, J., & Aronen, H. J. (2007). Violent persons with schizophrenia and comorbid disorders: A functional magnetic resonance imaging study. *Schizophrenia Research*, 91(1–3), 97–102.

Juhász, C., Behen, M. E., Muzik, O., Chugani, D. C., & Chugani, H. T. (2001). Bilateral medial prefrontal and temporal neocortical hypometabolism in children with epilepsy and aggression. *Epilepsia*, 42(8), 991–1001.

Kiehl, K., Kiehl, A., & Hoffman, M. (1991). The Criminal Psychopath: History, Neuroscience, Treatment, and Economics. *Jurimetrics Journal of Law, Science and Technology*, 51.4, 355.

Kiehl, K. A., Smith, A. M., Hare, R. D., Mendrek, A., Forster, B. B., Brink, J., & Liddle, P. F. (2001). Limbic abnormalities in affective processing by criminal psychopaths as revealed by functional magnetic resonance imaging. *Biological Psychiatry*, 50(9), 677–684.

Kolb, B. & Whishaw, I. Q. (2009). *Fundamentals of Human Neuropsychology.* New York: Worth Publishers.

Kolla, N., Matthews, B., Wilson, A., Houle, S., Michael Bagby, R., et al. (2015). Lower monoamine oxidase-a total distribution volume in impulsive and violent male offenders with antisocial personality disorder and high psychopathic traits: An [11c] harmine positron emission tomography study. *Neuropsychopharmacology*, 40(11), 2596–2603.

Kolla, N. J., Dunlop, K., Downar, J., Links, P., Bagby, R. M., Wilson, A. A., Houle, S., Rasquinha, F., Simpson, A. I., & Meyer, J. H. (2016). Association of ventral striatum monoamine oxidase-a binding and functional connectivity in antisocial personality disorder with high impulsivity: A positron emission tomography and functional magnetic resonance imaging study. *European Neuropsychopharmacology*, 26(4), 777–786.

Kumari, V., Aasen, I., Taylor, P., Ffytche, D. H., Das, M., Barkataki, I., Goswami, S., O'Connell, P., Howlett, M., Williams, S. C., & Sharma, T. (2006). Neural dysfunction and violence in schizophrenia: An fMRI investigation. *Schizophrenia Research*, 84(1), 144–164.

Kumari, V., Uddin, S., Premkumar, P., Young, S., Gudjonsson, G. H., Raghuvanshi, S., Barkataki, I., Sumich, A., Taylor, P., & Das, M. (2014). Lower anterior cingulate volume in seriously violent men with antisocial personality disorder or schizophrenia and a history of childhood abuse. *Australian and New Zealand Journal of Psychiatry*, 48(2), 153–161.

Kunz, M., Sikora, J., Krakowski, M., Convit, A., Cooper, T., et al. (1995). Serotonin in violent patients with schizophrenia. *Psychiatry Research*, 59(1), 161–163.

Liu, H., Liao, J., Jiang, W., & Wang, W. (2014). Changes in low-frequency fluctuations in patients with antisocial personality disorder revealed by resting-state functional MRI. *PLoS ONE*, 9(3): e89790.

Ly, M., Motzkin, J. C., Philippi, C. L., Kirk, G. R., Newman, J. P., Kiehl, K. A., & Koenigs, M. (2012). Cortical thinning in psychopathy. *American Journal of Psychiatry*, 169(7), 743–749.

McCloskey, M. S., Phan, K. L., Angstadt, M., Fettich, K. C., Keedy, S., & Coccaro, E. F. (2016). Amygdala hyperactivation to angry faces in intermittent explosive disorder. *Journal of Psychiatric Research*, 7934–7941.

Moeller, S. J., Froböse, M. I., Konova, A. B., Misyrlis, M., Parvaz, M. A., Goldstein, R. Z., & Alia-Klein, N. (2014). Common and distinct neural correlates of inhibitory dysregulation: Stroop fMRI study of cocaine addiction and intermittent explosive disorder. *Journal of Psychiatric Research*, 5855–5862.

Müller, J. L., Sommer, M., Wagner, V., Lange, K., Taschler, H., Röder, C. H., Schuierer, G., Klein, H. E., & Hajak, G. (2003). Abnormalities in emotion processing within cortical and subcortical regions in criminal psychopaths: Evidence from a functional magnetic resonance imaging study using pictures with emotional content. *Biological Psychiatry* 54(2), 152–162.

Narayan, V. M., Narr, K. L., Kumari, V., Woods, R. P., Thompson, P. M., Toga, A. W., & Sharma, T. (2007). Regional cortical thinning in subjects with violent antisocial personality disorder or schizophrenia. *American Journal of Psychiatry*, 164(9), 1418–1427.

New, A. S., Hazlett, E. A., Buchsbaum, M. S., Goodman, M., Reynolds, D., Mitropoulou, V., Sprung, L., Shaw, R. B., Jr., Koenigsberg, H., Platholi, J., Silverman, J., & Siever, L. J. (2002). Blunted prefrontal cortical[18] fluorodeoxyglucose positron emission tomography response to meta-chlorophenylpiperazine in impulsive aggression. *Archives of General Psychiatry*, 59(7), 621–629.

New, A. S., Buchsbaum, M. S., Hazlett, E. A., Goodman, M., Koenigsberg, H. W., Lo, J., Iskander, L., Newmark, R., Brand, J., O'Flynn, K., & Siever, L. J. (2004). Fluoxetine increases relative metabolic rate in prefrontal cortex in impulsive aggression. *Psychopharmacology*, 176(3–4), 451–458.

New, A. S., Hazlett, E. A., Newmark, R. E., Zhang, J., Triebwasser, J., Meyerson, D., Lazarus, S., Trisdorfer, R., Goldstein, K. E., Goodman, M., Koenigsberg, H. W., Flory, J. D., Siever, L. J., & Buchsbaum, M. S. (2009). Laboratory induced aggression: A positron emission tomography study of aggressive individuals with borderline personality disorder. *Biological Psychiatry*, 66(12), 1107–1114.

Osumi, T., Nakao, T., Kasuya, Y., Shinoda, J., Yamada, J., & Ohira, H. (2012). Amygdala dysfunction attenuates frustration-induced aggression in psychopathic individuals in a non-criminal population. *Journal of Affective Disorders*, 142(1–3), 331–338.

Pardini, D. A., Raine, A., Erickson, K., & Loeber, R. (2014). Lower amygdala volume in men is associated with childhood aggression, early psychopathic traits, and future violence. *Biological Psychiatry*, 75(1), 73–80.

Philippi, C. L., Pujara, M. S., Motzkin, J. C., Newman, J., Kiehl, K. A., & Koenigs, M. (2015). Altered resting-state functional connectivity in cortical networks in psychopathy. *The Journal of Neuroscience*, 35(15), 6068–6078.

Prehn, K., Schlagenhauf, F., Schulze, L., Berger, C., Vohs, K., Fleischer, M., Hauenstein, K., Keiper, P., Domes, G., & Herpertz, S. C. (2013). Neural correlates of risk taking in violent criminal offenders characterized by emotional hypo- and hyper-reactivity. *Social Neuroscience*, 8(2), 136–147.

Raine, A., Buchsbaum, M., & LaCasse, L. (1997). Brain abnormalities in murderers indicated by positron emission tomography. *Biological Psychiatry*, 42(6), 495–508.

Raine, A., Stoddard, J., Bihrle, S., & Buchsbaum, M. (1998). Prefrontal glucose deficits in murderers lacking psychosocial deprivation. *Neuropsychiatry, Neuropsychology, & Behavioral Neurology*, 11(1), 1–7.

Raine, A., Meloy, J. R., Bihrle, S., Stoddard, J., LaCasse, L., & Buchsbaum, M. S. (1998). Reduced prefrontal and increased subcortical brain functioning assessed using positron emission tomography in predatory and affective murderers. *Behavioral Sciences and the Law*, 16(3), 319–332.

Raine, A., Lencz, T., Bihrle, S., LaCasse, L., & Colletti, P. (2000). Reduced prefrontal gray matter volume and reduced autonomic activity in antisocial personality disorder. *Archives of General Psychiatry*, 57(2), 119–127.

Raine, A., Yang, Y., Narr, K., & Toga, A. (2009). Sex differences in orbitofrontal gray as a partial explanation for sex differences in antisocial personality. *Molecular Psychiatry*, 16(2), 227.

Seara-Cardoso, A., Viding, E., Lickley, R. A., & Sebastian, C. L. (2015). Neural responses to others' pain vary with psychopathic traits in healthy adult males. *Cognitive, Affective & Behavioral Neuroscience*, 15(3), 578–588.

Schiffer, B., Pawliczek, C., Müller, B., Forsting, M., Gizewski, E., Leygraf, N., & Hodgins, S. (2014). Neural mechanisms underlying cognitive control of men with lifelong antisocial behavior. *Psychiatry Research: Neuroimaging*, 222(1–2), 43–51.

Schlüter, T., Winz, O., Henkel, K., Eggermann, T., Mohammadkhani-Shali, S., Dietrich, C., Heinzel, A., Decker, M., Cumming, P., Zerres, K., Piel, M., Mottaghy, F. M., & Vernaleken, I. (2016). MAOA-VNTR polymorphism modulates context-dependent dopamine release and aggressive behavior in males. *Neuroimage*, 125378–125385.

Soderstrom, H., Tullberg, M., Wikkelsö, C., Ekholm, S., & Forsman, A. (2000). Reduced regional cerebral blood flow in non-psychotic violent offenders. *Psychiatry Research: Neuroimaging*, 98(1), 29–41.

Spoont, M. R., Kuskowski, M., & Pardo, J. V. (2010). Autobiographical memories of anger in violent and non-violent individuals: A script-driven imagery study. *Psychiatry Research: Neuroimaging*, 183(3), 225–229.

Sterzer, P., Stadler, C., Krebs, A., Kleinschmidt, A., & Poustka, F. (2005). Abnormal Neural Responses to Emotional Visual Stimuli in Adolescents with Conduct Disorder. *Biological Psychiatry*, 57(1), 7–15.

Tang, Y., Yang, L., Leve, L. D., & Harold, G. T. (2012). Improving executive function and its neurobiological mechanisms through a mindfulness-based intervention: Advances within the field of developmental neuroscience. *Child Development Perspectives*, 6(4), 361–366.

Tiihonen, J., Rossi, R., Laakso, M. P., Hodgins, S., Testa, C., Perez, J., & Frisoni, G. B. (2008). Brain anatomy of persistent violent offenders: More rather than less. *Psychiatry Research: Neuroimaging*, 163(3), 201–212.

Tiihonen, J., Rautiainen, M., Ollila, H. M., Repo-Tiihonen, E., Virkkunen, M., Palotie, A., Pietiläinen, O., Kristiansson, K., Joukamaa, M., Lauerma, H., Saarela, J., Tyni, S., Vartiainen, H., Paananen, J., Goldman, D., & Paunio, T. (2015). Genetic background of extreme violent behavior. *Molecular Psychiatry*, 20(6), 786–792.

Trzepacz, P. T., Yu, P., Bhamidipati, P. K., Willis, B., Forrester, T., Tabas, L., Schwarz, A. J., Saykin, A. J.; Alzheimer's Disease Neuroimaging Initiative & Saykin, A. J. (2013). Frontolimbic atrophy is associated with agitation and aggression in mild cognitive impairment and Alzheimer's disease. *Alzheimer's & Dementia*, 9(5), S95–S104.

Virkkunen, M. & Linnoila, M. (1993). Brain serotonin, type II alcoholism and impulsive violence. *Journal of Studies on Alcohol*, 54, 163–165.

Volkow, N. D., Tancredi, L. R., Grant, C., Gillespie, H., Valentine, A., Mullani, N., Wang, G.-J., & Hollister, L. (1995). Brain glucose metabolism in violent psychiatric patients: A preliminary study. *Psychiatry Research: Neuroimaging*, 61(4), 243–253.

Völlum, B., Richarson, P., Stirling, J., Elliott, R., Dolan, M., Chaudhry, I., & Del Ben, C., McKie, S., Anderson, I., & Deakin, B. (2004). Neurobiological substrates of antisocial and borderline personality disorder: preliminary results of a functional fMRI study. *Criminal Behaviour and Mental Health*, 14(1), 39–54.

Völlum, B., Richardson, P., McKie, S., Reniers, R., Elliott, R., Anderson, I. M., Williams, S., Dolan, M., & Deakin, B. (2010). Neuronal correlates and serotonergic modulation of behavioural inhibition and reward in healthy and antisocial individuals. *Journal of Psychiatric Research*, 44(3), 123–131.

Yang, Y., Glenn, A. L., & Raine, A. (2008). Brain abnormalities in antisocial individuals: Implications for the law. *Behavioral Sciences and the Law*, 26(1), 65–83.

Yang, Y., Raine, A., Colletti, P., Toga, A. W., & Narr, K. L. (2009). Abnormal temporal and prefrontal cortical gray matter thinning in psychopaths. *Molecular Psychiatry*, 14(6), 561–562.

Yang, Y., Raine, A., Lencz, T., Bihrle, S., LaCasse, L., & Colletti, P. (2005). Volume Reduction in Prefrontal Gray Matter in Unsuccessful Criminal Psychopaths. *Biological Psychiatry*, 57(10), 1103–1108.

7 Biosocial Bases of Aggression and Antisocial Behavior

Jill Portnoy

Introduction

There is growing evidence that the development of aggression is a multilevel process that cannot be entirely explained by either biological or social factors alone. Instead, biological and social factors likely contribute both independently and in interaction with one another in the development of aggression and antisocial behavior (Raine, 2002b, 2013). Biological domains contributing to antisocial behavior include genetics, neuropsychology, and psychophysiology. Research in these areas has demonstrated the presence of biosocial interactions, whereby biological factors interact with social factors to predict antisocial behavior (Raine, 2002b, 2013). Several theoretical models have been proposed to explain the pattern of biosocial interactions observed in criminological research; these include the dual-risk model, the social push perspective, the biological protective factors approach, mediation models, and the differential susceptibility theory.

Here, I review research examining the biological basis of aggression and antisocial behavior. This chapter primarily focuses on biosocial research involving psychophysiological risk factors. Psychophysiological risk factors are relatively easy and less costly to measure than other biological risk factors (Gao et al., 2012), and therefore may be of particular interest to socially oriented researchers who would like to incorporate biological measures into their research. This chapter begins with a review of research involving psychophysiological risk factors for aggression and antisocial behavior. This chapter then discusses psychophysiological research in the context of the dual-risk, social push, protective factors, differential susceptibility, and mediation models of biosocial interactions. I conclude with a discussion of how biosocial interactions could contribute in the future to improving interventions for aggression and antisocial behavior.

Psychophysiological Risk Factors for Antisocial Behavior

Psychophysiology is the study of cognition, behavior, and emotions as revealed through bodily states (Hugdahl, 2001). Psychophysiological indices are non-invasive to record and capture nearly immediate physiological changes. Psychophysiological measures are often recorded at rest, but may also be recorded in response to experimental stimuli, such as fear conditioning tasks or stress tasks. Heart rate and skin conductance are two of the best-studied psychophysiological risk factors for aggression.

Heart Rate

Heart rate is controlled by the sympathetic and parasympathetic branches of the autonomic nervous system. Low resting heart rate has been suggested as the "best-replicated biological correlate of antisocial behavior in child and adolescent populations" (Ortiz & Raine, 2004, p. 159). A recent meta-analysis of 114 reports and 115 independent effect sizes yielded of random effects summary effect size of $d = -0.20$ ($SE = 0.04$, $p < 0.001$) for the relationship between resting heart rate and antisocial behavior (Portnoy & Farrington, 2015). Under the random effects model, the summary effect size was unmoderated by sex, type of antisocial behavior (including violence and aggression), age group, or recruitment (clinical/institutional vs. community). The effect size was also unmoderated by study design (prospective vs. concurrent). This suggests that a low heart rate could *precede* the onset of antisocial behavior, rather than *result* from antisocial behavior. Consistent with this, an analysis of 411 males participating in the Cambridge Study in Delinquent Development found that resting heart rate at age 18 predicted convictions for violence up to age 50 (Jennings, Piquero, & Farrington, 2013). Results were largely unchanged after controlling for numerous covariates, including sports participation, impulsivity, binge drinking, and body mass index. These results suggest that the relationship between resting heart rate and antisocial behavior is unlikely to be the result of confounding variables.

This raises the important question of why low resting heart rate is associated with higher levels of antisocial behavior and aggression. Although the mechanism underlying the low resting heart rate–antisocial behavior relationship is not yet fully understood, low resting heart rate is hypothesized to be associated with increased levels of antisocial behavior, because low autonomic nervous system arousal may reflect a relative lack of fear, which could facilitate antisocial behavior by impeding early fear conditioning to socializing punishments and reducing fear of the negative consequences of the antisocial act (Raine, 2002a, 2013). Alternatively, reduced autonomic nervous system arousal could be an unpleasant physiological state, leading those with low resting heart rates to engage in stimulating behaviors, including antisocial behaviors, in order to increase their level of arousal to a more optimal level (Quay, 1965; Raine, 2002a, 2013). Recent studies have provided support for a sensation-seeking explanation of the low heart rate–antisocial behavior relationship. A study of 335 adolescent boys participating in the Pittsburgh Youth Study found that sensation-seeking but not fearlessness mediated the relationship between heart rate and aggression (Portnoy et al., 2014). Sijtsema et al. (2010) found that sensation-seeking at ages 13.5 and 16 partially mediated the relationship between heart rate at age 11 and rule-breaking at age 16 in boys. Despite these findings, which suggest that sensation-seeking may underlie the heart rate–antisocial behavior relationship, the lack of experimental evidence leaves our current understanding of this mechanism inconclusive.

In addition to heart rate at rest, researchers are also interested in heart rate reactivity to experimental conditions, including stressors tasks. A meta-analysis of child and adolescent studies reported that reduced heart rate during a stressor task was associated with increased levels of antisocial behavior ($d = -0.76$, $p < 0.0001$; Ortiz & Raine, 2004). Reduced heart rate reactivity during a laboratory stressor may reflect an impairment in fear or stress processing, which as discussed above could predispose some individuals to engage in antisocial behavior.

As mentioned earlier, heart rate is controlled by the parasympathetic and sympathetic branches of the autonomic nervous system. The parasympathetic nervous system slows down heart rate, while the sympathetic nervous system increases heart rate. Some researchers have attempted to determine whether the relationship between heart rate and antisocial behavior is driven by increased parasympathetic activation or alternatively decreased sympathetic activation. Vagal tone is an index of parasympathetic regulation of the heart that is often estimated using respiratory sinus arrhythmia (RSA) or high-frequency heart rate variability (HRV). Because RSA is an index of parasympathetic nervous system activity, high RSA is associated with a low heart rate. Increased RSA at baseline is thought to index appropriate emotional regulation and engagement with the environment (Beauchaine, 2001). Consistent with this interpretation, several studies have found that low RSA serves as a risk factor for aggression (Beauchaine, Hong, & Marsh, 2008) and antisocial behavior more generally (Mezzaccapa et al., 1997; de Wied, van Boxtel, Posthumus, Goudena, & Matthys, 2009). On the other hand, some authors noted that findings have been inconsistent (Pang & Beauchaine, 2013). In particular, a number of studies observed *increased*, rather than decreased, RSA in antisocial individuals (Dietrich et al., 2007; Scarpa, Fikretoglu, & Luscher, 2000; Scarpa, Haden, & Tanaka, 2010; Slobodskaya, Roifman, & Krivoschekov, 1999). These inconsistencies in findings may be due to the importance of the social environment in moderating the effects of RSA on antisocial behavior, as will be discussed later in this chapter.

Skin Conductance

Unlike heart rate – which is controlled by both the sympathetic and parasympathetic branches of the autonomic nervous system – skin conductance is controlled exclusively by the sympathetic branch of the autonomic nervous system. Poor skin conductance fear conditioning (also referred to as electrodermal fear conditioning) is associated with higher levels of aggression (Gao, Raine, Venables, Dawson, & Mednick, 2010a) and general antisocial behavior in children and adolescents (Fairchild, van Goozen, Stollery, & Goodyer, 2008). Poor fear conditioning has also been found to prospectively predict future antisocial behavior. In a sample of 1,795 children from Mauritius, poor electrodermal fear conditioning at age 3 predicted criminal offending at age 23 (Gao, Raine, Venables, Dawson, & Mednick, 2010b). Electrodermal fear conditioning in a laboratory setting is thought to reflect conditioning to socializing punishments in childhood. In turn, fear conditioning to socializing punishments in childhood is thought to be central to socialization and conscience development, making the failure to condition a factor that could predispose some individuals to commit aggressive and antisocial behavior (Eysenck, 1977).

In general, results of psychophysiological studies suggest that antisocial and aggressive individuals display reduced levels of autonomic activity at rest and in stress conditions. This could reflect a relative lack of fear in antisocial individuals or may be driven by a desire for sensation-seeking among those with low arousal. However, some results are inconsistent. It is possible that this inconsistency is due to the failure of some studies to take into account the influence of social variables. The following section will discuss psychophysiological studies that have incorporated a biosocial perspective.

Biosocial Models of Antisocial Behavior

The Dual-Risk Model and Social Push Perspective

In a seminal work, Raine (2002b) reviewed biosocial research that had been conducted to date. He argued that the limited research available at the time provided support for two main models of biosocial interactions: the dual-risk model and the social push perspective. According to the dual-risk model, the presence of both a biological and social risk factor increases the likelihood of antisocial behavior. The risk of aggression is lowered in individuals with only biological *or* social risk. Unlike the dual-risk model – which considers antisocial behavior as the outcome variable – in the social push perspective, the biological factor is the outcome variable. The social push perspective argues that the relationship between biological factors and antisocial behavior is strongest in those from benign social backgrounds. In other words, in those from disadvantaged backgrounds, biology is less likely to play a role in the development of antisocial behavior; instead, social factors are more likely to be implicated.

A number of psychophysiological studies have provided support for the dual-risk model. Farrington (1997), for instance, found that the relationship between heart rate at age 18 and convictions for violence at age 18 to 40 was stronger in those with a poor relationship with a parent at age 18 or a large family size at age 10. More recently, in a study of 8–10-year-old children, Gao, Huang, and Li (2016) found that prenatal maternal stress was only associated with dimensions of psychopathy in children who also had low resting heart rate or high RSA.

There is also support in the psychophysiological literature for the social push perspective. Raine and Venables (1984), for instance, found that the relationship between low heart rate and antisocial behavior was confined to those children from higher social classes. As predicted by the social push perspective, heart rate did not predict antisocial behavior in lower-class boys.

Biological Protective Factors

Since the publication of Raine (2002b), there has been a vast increase in the number of researchers investigating biosocial interactions. This new research has broadened our understanding of biosocial interaction and spurred the development of new models to explain these interactions. One such model is the biological protective factors model. While most researchers study risk factors – which increase the likelihood of antisocial behavior – researchers have also begun to emphasize protective factors in antisocial behavior research (Cicchetti, 2010; Rutter, 2012). Buffering protective factors buffer or reduce the effects of a risk factor (Lösel & Farrington, 2012). In other words, even if a risk factor is present, the simultaneous presence of a protective factor reduces the probability of antisocial behavior. Protective factors are also thought to promote desistance from antisocial behavior in otherwise high-risk individuals. The biosocial protective factors model argues that biological factors may actually reduce the harmful effects of social risk factors for antisocial behavior (Farrington, 1997; Farrington & Lösel, 2012; Portnoy, Chen, & Raine, 2013). Biological factors could also promote desistance from antisocial behavior and violence.

A small, but growing body of psychophysiological research is consistent with the biological protective factors model. For instance, some evidence suggests that a *high* heart rate may act as a protective factor for antisocial behavior. Using data from the Cambridge Study in Delinquent Development, Farrington (1997) found that amongst subjects with high heart rates at age 18, large family size – which was normally a risk factor for violence – was no longer associated with violent convictions. High resting heart rate has also been examined as a possible predictor of desistance. One study showed that antisocial adolescents who desisted from offending by adulthood had higher resting heart rates than antisocial adolescents who later became criminal by age 29 (Raine, Venables, & Williams, 1995). In another study using this same sample, Raine, Venables, and Williams (1996) found that antisocial adolescents who desisted from adult crime had significantly better skin conductance conditioning at age 15 than persisters, who were criminal at age 29, and tended to display better conditioning than normal controls ($p < 0.053$). On the other hand, De Vries-Bouw et al. (2011) found that resting heart rate did not predict desistance from offending. Though high resting heart rate and enhanced skin conductance fear conditioning appear to be candidates as protective factors, in light of these mixed findings, more research is needed before firm conclusions can be drawn.

Differential Susceptibility Theory

The differential susceptibility theory recognizes that children raised in the same social environment may develop quite differently. This theory argues that some children may be more receptive to environmental influences – either positive or negative – than others (Belsky, 2005; Belsky, Bakermans-Kranenberg, & van Ijzendoorn, 2007). In particular, high biological stress reactivity may be either adaptive or maladaptive, depending on the child's social context (Ellis, Boyce, Belsky, Bakermans-Kranenburg, & van Ijzendoorn, 2011). The theory predicts that a highly reactive child who grows up in an adverse social environment will be negatively affected by that environment. On the other hand, a highly reactive child who grows up in an especially enriching environment will be positively affected by that environment. A child with low stress reactivity will be little affected by the social environment – either positive or negative. This contrasts with the dual-risk hypothesis, which makes the implicit assumption that neutral and especially enriching environments interact similarly with biological reactivity (Ellis et al., 2011).

There is some evidence that lower physiological activity may be beneficial to children living in adverse social environments.

High baseline RSA has been found to buffer children against antisocial behavior problems associated with higher levels of parental marital conflict (El-Sheikh, Harger, & Whitson, 2001), though at least one study failed to find this effect (Leary & Katz, 2004). High RSA has also been shown to protect against the harmful effects of parental problem drinking (El-Sheikh, 2005a) and maltreatment amongst boys (Gordis, Feres, Olezeski, Rabkin, & Trickett, 2010). Research has also shown that increased reactivity could be harmful when combined with an adverse social environment; several studies found that high skin conductance was actually a risk factor for antisocial behavior amongst children at high social risk (Cummings, El-Sheikh, Kouros, & Keller, 2007; El-Sheikh, 2005b). This is in contrast to the studies mentioned earlier, which found that high skin conductance was a possible protective factor for antisocial behavior in high-risk individuals (Raine et al., 1996).

More research is needed to reconcile the competing claims of the dual-risk and differential susceptibility theories as they relate to biological stress reactivity. Additionally, while researchers often examine children living in adverse social environments, little research has examined whether children from especially enriching environments *benefit* from high autonomic reactivity, as predicted by the differential susceptibility theory. More research is needed that examines children across a wide range of social contexts – both positive and negative.

Biosocial Mediation Models

Most biosocial models consider how biological and social factors interact with one another. However, there is also substantial evidence that social factors could actually *affect* biological and psychophysiological functioning. Chronic stress, for instance, is thought to affect the body's biological stress response. Specifically, chronic stress is hypothesized to result in the downregulation of the body's stress response system as a way for individuals to cope with chronically threatening environments without constantly evoking hormonal and cardiovascular stress responses (Susman, 2006). As discussed earlier, reduced autonomic stress responses are also associated with higher levels of antisocial behavior. In response to this, Choy, Farrington, and Raine (2015) argued that autonomic arousal may act as a mechanism linking social adversity and antisocial behavior. In other words, autonomic arousal may mediate the well-documented relationship between an adverse social environment and antisocial behavior.

Although very little empirical research has tested biosocial mediation models of antisocial behavior, there has been some preliminary research in this area. In a community sample of 454 children living in Philadelphia, early childhood social adversity – as measured by items such as parental education, parental employment, teenage pregnancy, living accommodation status, family size and structure, and parental supervision – was associated with reduced heart rate during stress (Choy et al., 2015). In turn, low heart rate during stress was associated with increased levels of antisocial behavior. Consistent with the biosocial mediation model, low heart rate during stress partially mediated the observed relationship between social adversity and both general antisocial behavior and aggressive symptoms of conduct disorder. These results suggest that low heart rate during stress may partly explain why social adversity is associated with higher levels of antisocial behavior and aggression. Research in this area, however, remains very preliminary and it is not yet possible to draw firm conclusions.

Implications for Prevention

There is increasing support for the possibility that biosocial research could help to inform efforts to prevent and treat antisocial and aggressive behavior (Rocque, Welsh, & Raine, 2012; Vaske, Galyean, & Cullen, 2011). Cornet, de Kogel, Nijman, Raine, and van der Laan (2014) reviewed studies that examined whether neurobiological factors – including psychophysiological factors – predicted cognitive behavioral therapy treatment outcomes in individuals with antisocial behavior. They concluded that, in general, lower levels of arousal – as indicated by psychophysiological factors, including lower skin conductance, lower resting heart rate, and higher levels of HRV, predicted more favorable outcomes in cognitive-behavioral treatment studies of antisocial behavior. This suggests that psychophysiological factors could help to explain observed heterogeneity in responses to more traditional psychological treatments; this in turn could help researchers to develop more targeted treatments for individuals with antisocial behavior.

More recent findings have not provided support for this conclusion. Cornet, van der Laan, Nijman, Tollenaar, and de Kogel (2015) examined 121 convicted adult offenders detained in prisons in the Netherlands who took part in a cognitive skills training program. They found that heart rate and RSA stress reactivity did not predict treatment outcomes. On the other hand, poor concentration, a neurocognitive measure, did predict dropout of the treatment. In general, more research is needed in order to better understand how psychophysiological measures and biological factors more generally could help to predict who benefits most from treatment for antisocial behavior. Additionally, little is known about how biological factors predict treatment outcomes in studies of aggression and violence specifically, rather than antisocial behavior more generally.

Conclusion

This chapter reviewed research into the psychophysiology of antisocial behavior and aggression. In general, studies find that reduced autonomic activity is associated with higher levels of aggression and antisocial behavior. This is evidenced by the reduced heart rate and skin conductance observed in antisocial individuals. Despite the growing acceptance of a biological basis of antisocial behavior, there is also unmistakable evidence that the development of aggression is a multilevel process that cannot be entirely explained by either biological or social factors alone. Several models have been used to explain biosocial interactions; these include the dual-risk hypothesis, social push perspective, biological mediation model, biological protective factors approach, and differential susceptibility theory.

To date, research testing the claims of the biological mediation model, biological protective factors approach, and differential susceptibility theory is limited. More research is needed to determine how well these models explain the interplay between biological and social factors in predicting antisocial behavior. This research could have important implications for the prevention of aggression and antisocial behavior. If researchers are able to identify biological factors that predict treatment outcomes, interventions could be better targeted at those who will most benefit from treatment. Additionally, a better understanding of the social contexts under which biological factors either confer risk or protection could help to improve risk assessment and prediction for aggression and antisocial behavior. Because psychophysiological factors are more easily and inexpensively measured than other biological measures (Gao et al., 2012), they may be especially beneficial in informing the future treatment and prevention of aggression and antisocial behavior.

References

Beauchaine, T. (2001). Vagal tone, development, and Gray's motivational theory: Toward an integrated model of autonomic nervous system functioning in psychopathology. *Development and Psychopathology*, 13, 183–214.

Beauchaine, T. P., Hong, J., & Marsh, P. (2008). Sex differences in autonomic correlates of conduct problems and aggression. *Journal of the American Academy of Child and Adolescent Psychiatry*, 47, 788–796.

Belsky, J. (2005). Differential susceptibility to rearing influence: An evolutionary hypothesis and some evidence. In B. Ellis & D. Bjorklund (Eds), *Origins of the social mind: Evolutionary psychology and child development* (pp. 139–163). New York: Guilford.

Belsky, J., Bakermans-Kranenburg, M. J., & van Ijzendoorn, M. H. (2007). For better and for worse: Differential susceptibility to environmental influences. *Association for Psychological Science*, 16, 300–304.

Choy, O., Raine, A., Portnoy, J., Rudo-Hutt, A., Gao, Y., & Soyfer, L. (2015). The mediating role of heart rate on the social adversity-antisocial behavior relationship: A social neurocriminology perspective. *Journal of Research in Crime and Delinquency*, 52, 303–341.

Choy, O., Farrington, D. P., & Raine, A. (2015). The need to incorporate autonomic arousal in developmental and life-course research and theories. *Journal of Developmental and Life-Course Criminology*, 1, 189–207.

Cicchetti, D. (2010). Resilience under conditions of extreme stress: A multilevel perspective. *World Psychiatry*, 9, 145–154.

Cornet, L. J., de Kogel, C. H., Nijman, H. L., Raine, A., & van der Laan, P. H. (2014). Neurobiological factors as predictors of cognitive-behavioral therapy outcome in individuals with antisocial behavior: A review of the literature. *International Journal of Offender Therapy and Comparative Health*, 58, 1279–1296.

Cornet, L. J. M., van der Laan, P. H., Nijman, H. L. I., Tollenaar, N., & de Kogel, C. H. (2015). Neurobiological factors as predictors of prisoners' response to a cognitive skills training. *Journal of Criminal Justice*, 43, 122–132.

Cummings, E. M., El-Sheikh, M., Kouros, C. D., & Keller, P. S. (2007). Children's skin conductance reactivity as a mechanism of risk in the context of parental depressive symptoms. *Journal of Child Psychology and Psychiatry*, 48, 436–445.

De Vries-Bouw, M., Popma, A., Vermeiren, R., Doreleijers, T. A., Van De Ven, P. M., & Jansen, L. M. (2011). The predictive value of low heart rate and heart rate variability during stress for reoffending in delinquent male adolescents. *Psychophysiology*, 48, 1597–1604.

de Wied, M., Boxtel, A. V., Posthumus, J. A., Goudena, P. P., & Matthys, W. (2009). Facial EMG and heart rate responses to emotion-inducing film clips in boys with disruptive behavior disorders. *Psychophysiology*, 46, 996–1004.

Dietrich, A., Riese, H., Sondeijker, F. E., Greaves-Lord, K., van Roon, A. M., Ormel, J., ... & Rosmalen, J. G. (2007). Externalizing and internalizing problems in relation to autonomic function: a population-based study in preadolescents. *Journal of the American Academy of Child and Adolescent Psychiatry*, 46, 378–386.

El-Sheikh, M. (2005a). Does poor vagal tone exacerbate child maladjustment in the context of parental problem drinking? A longitudinal examination. *Journal of Abnormal Psychology*, 114, 735–741.

El-Sheikh, M. (2005b). The role of emotional responses and physiological reactivity in the marital conflict-child functioning link. *Journal of Child Psychology and Psychiatry*, 46, 1191–1199.

El-Sheikh, M., Harger, J., & Whitson, S. M. (2001). Exposure to interpersonal conflict and children's adjustment and physical health: The moderating role of vagal tone. *Child Development*, 72, 1617–1636.

Ellis, B. J., Boyce, W. T., Belsky, J., Bakermans-Kranenburg, M. J., & van Ijzendoorn, M. H. (2011). Differential susceptibility to the environment: an evolutionary-neurodevelopmental theory. *Development and Psychopathology*, 23, 7–28.

Eysenck, H. J. (1977). *Crime and personality*. London: Routledge & Kegan Paul Ltd.

Fairchild, G., Van Goozen, S. H., Stollery, S. J., & Goodyer, I. M. (2008). Fear conditioning and affective modulation of the startle reflex in male adolescents with early-onset or adolescence-onset conduct disorder and healthy control subjects. *Biological Psychiatry*, 63, 279–285.

Farrington, D. P. (1997). The relationship between low resting heart rate and violence. In A. Raine, P. A. Brennan, D. P. Farrington & S. A. Mednick (Eds), *Biosocial bases of violence* (pp. 89–105). New York: Plenum Press.

Gao, Y., Glenn, A. L., Peskin, M., Rudo-Hutt, A., Schug, R. A., Yang, Y., & Raine, A. (2012). Neurocriminological approaches. In D. Gadd, S. Karstedt, & S. F. Messner (Eds), *Handbook of criminological research methods* (pp. 63–75). Los Angeles: SAGE.

Gao, Y., Raine, A., Venables, P. H., Dawson, M. E., & Mednick, S. A. (2010a). Reduced electrodermal fear conditioning from ages 3 to 8 years is associated with aggressive behavior at age 8 years. *Journal of Child Psychology and Psychiatry*, 51, 550–558.

Gao, Y., Raine, A., Venables, P. H., Dawson, M. E., & Mednick, S. A. (2010b). Association of poor childhood fear conditioning and adult crime. *American Journal of Psychiatry*, 167, 56–60.

Gao, Y., Huang, Y., & Li, X. (2016). Interaction between prenatal maternal stress and autonomic arousal in predicting conduct problems and psychopathic traits in children. *Journal of Psychopathology and Behavioral Assessment*. doi: 10.1007/s10862-016-9556-8.

Gordis, E. B., Feres, N., Olezeski, C. L., Rabkin, A. N., & Trickett, P. K. (2010). Skin conductance reactivity and respiratory sinus arrhythmia among maltreated and comparison youth: relations with aggressive behavior. *Journal of Pediatric Psychology*, 35, 547–558.

Hugdahl, K. (2001). *Psychophysiology*. Cambridge, MA: Harvard University Press.

Jennings, W. G., Piquero, A. R., & Farrington, D. P. (2013). Does resting heart rate at age 18 distinguish general and violent offending up to age 50? Findings from the Cambridge Study in Delinquent Development. *Journal of Criminal Justice*, 41, 213–219.

Leary, A. & Katz, L. F. (2004). Coparenting, family-level processes, and peer outcomes: The moderating role of vagal tone. *Development and Psychopathology*, 16, 593–608.

Lösel, F. & Farrington, D. P. (2012). Direct protective and buffering protective factors in the development of youth violence. *American Journal of Preventive Medicine*, 43(2 Suppl. 1), S8–S23.

Mezzacappa, E., Tremblay, R. E., Kindlon, D., Saul, J. P., Arseneault, L., Seguin, J., ... & Earls, F. (1997). Anxiety, antisocial behavior, and heart rate regulation in adolescent males. *Journal of Child Psychology and Psychiatry*, 38, 457–469.

Ortiz, J. & Raine, A. (2004). Heart rate level and antisocial behavior in children and adolescents: A meta-analysis. *Journal of the American Academy of Child and Adolescent Psychiatry*, 43, 154–162.

Pang, K. C. & Beauchaine, T. P. (2013). Longitudinal patterns of autonomic nervous system responding to emotion evocation among children with conduct problems and/or depression. *Developmental Psychobiology*, 55, 698–706.

Portnoy, J., Chen, F. R., & Raine, A. (2013). Biological protective factors for antisocial and criminal behavior. *Journal of Criminal Justice*, 41, 292–299.

Portnoy, J. & Farrington, D. P. (2015). Resting heart rate and antisocial behavior: An updated systematic review and meta-analysis. *Aggression and Violent Behavior*, 22, 33–45.

Portnoy, J., Raine, A., Chen, F. R., Pardini, D., Loeber, R., & Jennings, J. R. (2014). Heart rate and antisocial behavior: The mediating role of impulsive sensation seeking. *Criminology*, 52, 292–311.

Quay, H. C. (1965). Psychopathic personality as pathological stimulation-seeking. *American Journal of Psychiatry*, 122, 180–183.

Raine, A. (2002a). Annotation: The role of prefrontal deficits, low autonomic arousal, and early health factors in the development of antisocial and aggressive behavior in children. *Journal of Child Psychology and Psychiatry*, 43, 417–434.

Raine, A. (2002b). Biosocial studies of antisocial and violent behavior in children and adults: A review. *Journal of Abnormal Child Psychology*, 30, 311–326.

Raine, A., Venables, P. H., & Williams, M. (1996). Better autonomic conditioning and faster electrodermal half-recovery time at age 15 years as possible protective factors against crime at age 29 years. *Developmental Psychology*, 32, 624–630.

Raine, A., Venables, P. H., & Williams, M. (1995). High autonomic arousal and electrodermal orienting at age 15 years as protective factors against criminal behavior at age 29 years. *American Journal of Psychiatry*, 152, 1595–1600.

Raine, A. (2013). *The anatomy of violence*. New York: Pantheon Books.

Raine, A. & Venables, P. H. (1984). Tonic heart rate level, social class and antisocial behaviour in adolescents. *Biological Psychology*, 18, 123–132.

Rocque, M., Welsh, B. C., & Raine, A. (2012). Biosocial criminology and modern crime prevention. *Journal of Criminal Justice*, 40, 306–312.

Rutter, M. (2012). Resilience as a dynamic concept. *Development and Psychopathology*, 24, 335–344.

Scarpa, A., Fikretoglu, D., & Luscher, K. (2000). Community violence exposure in a young adult sample: II. Psychophysiology and aggressive behavior. *Journal of Community Psychology*, 28, 417–425.

Scarpa, A., Haden, S. C., & Tanaka, A. (2010). Being hot-tempered: Autonomic, emotional, and behavioral distinctions between childhood reactive and proactive aggression. *Biological Psychology*, 84, 488–496.

Sijtsema, J. J., Veenstra, R., Lindenberg, S., van Roon, A. M., Verhulst, F. C., Ormel, J., & Riese, H. (2010). Mediation of sensation seeking and behavioral inhibition on the relationship between heart rate and antisocial behavior: The TRAILS study. *Journal of the American Academy of Child and Adolescent Psychiatry*, 49, 493–502.

Slobodskaya, H. R., Roifman, M. D., & Krivoschekov, S. G. (1999). Psychological health, physical development and autonomic nervous system (ANS) activity in Siberian adolescents. *International Journal of Circumpolar Health*, 58, 176–187.

Susman, E. J. (2006). Psychobiology of persistent antisocial behavior: stress, early vulnerabilities and the attenuation hypothesis. *Neuroscience and Biobehavioral Reviews*, 30, 376–389.

Vaske, J., Galyean, K., & Cullen, F. T. (2011). Toward a biosocial theory of offender rehabilitation: Why does cognitive-behavioral therapy work? *Journal of Criminal Justice*, 39, 90–102.

8 The Neuropsychology of Violence

Jean R. Séguin, Linda Booij, and Scott O. Lilienfeld[1]

Introduction

Neuropsychology has long sought to assess the often-subtle, yet dramatic, effects of brain lesions on information processing and behavior. Following certain brain lesions, a previously well-adapted individual can become irritable, impulsive, incapable of sustaining concentration, and neglectful of social rules. In such cases, the individual's ability to process information in a socially adaptive way becomes severely impaired. The observation of these profound changes prompted the development of neuropsychological accounts for the deficits, seen in a broad range of behavior problems, including violent behavior.

Here, we update our original review of the neuropsychological approach to violent behavior published in an earlier edition of the handbook (Séguin, Sylvers, & Lilienfeld, 2007). In Section I we examine issues pertaining to the assessment of neuropsychological function and the assessment of clinical syndromes, including delinquency and criminality, associated with violence. In Section II, we review developmental issues affecting brain maturation and behavioral regulation. We integrate the aforementioned issues in Section III, where we review studies that help us understand violence from a neuropsychological perspective. As we note, because a key method in neuropsychology has been the use of lesion analyses, we examine the extent to which brain lesions contribute to violence. We then turn to the few neuropsychological studies of violence, and examine the larger body of literature on clinical syndromes associated with violence. There, we examine the extent to which neuropsychological problems have been identified in violence-prone individuals. Finally, we integrate the key observations derived from this review, address limitations in the extant research, and offer suggestions for further research on this important and still-growing area.

Section I: Assessment

Classic neuropsychological testing involves the administration of a battery of tests. These tests are designed to assess a variety of brain functions, ranging from basic perception to more complex neocortical problem-solving, and require either verbal or motor responses. The stimuli may be visual or auditory. Visual stimuli include pictures, abstract designs,

---

1 We would like to thank Patrick Sylvers, who co-authored the previous installment of this chapter with J. R. S and S. O. L and whose input at the time served to flesh out the current structure of the chapter.

and combinations of these stimuli, such as those found in various puzzles, mazes, assortments of objects, pictorial depictions of story lines, printed colors, words, and numbers. Auditory stimuli may involve spoken words, numbers, problems, or stories. Computerized batteries are usually limited to motor responses performed through the click of a mouse or by means of a touch-screen interface, although voice onset recording, eye tracking devices, electrophysiology, and functional brain imaging are increasingly used. Many of these tests qualify as neuropsychological because they were developed to test theories of brain function and were typically validated with lesion analysis studies, brain electrophysiological studies, or functional brain imaging studies. In other words, individuals with relatively well-circumscribed brain lesions performed poorly on such tests, or these tests were found to engage specific brain regions. Thus, these batteries provide a profile of strengths and weaknesses that presumably vary as a function of location and extent of lesions. Findings from these assessments can further help tailor intervention or prevention (Séguin & Pilon, 2013).

Neuropsychological lesions can result from pregnancy or birth complications, various illnesses, aging, head injury, intracranial tumors, cerebrovascular disorders, exposure to toxic substances, or corrective surgical procedures. The extent to which these events lead to neuropsychological lesions may in turn depend on a variety of moderators, such as the developmental timing of lesions, genetic make-up, and socioeconomic factors. They can also be temporary and reversible, such as those observed under the acute effects of drugs and alcohol or of certain illnesses.

Finally, the results of neuropsychological tests are often assumed to reflect the competence of the individual. Nevertheless, there may be a sizable gap between competence and performance. Thus, interpretation of test results should take into account the individual's test motivation, affect (e.g., mood, anxiety), attention, capacity to remember the sometimes complex rules required for optimal performance, language of administration, and cultural background. We refer the reader to more specialized sources for additional information (Goldstein & McNeil, 2012; Lezak, Howieson, Bigler, & Tranel, 2012).

Finally, and to build on the important role of motivation, the more explicit integration of cognitive and affective neuroscience in the past two decades has contributed to more systematic consideration of both "cool" and rational versus "hot" and affective neuropsychological assessment (Castellanos, Sonuga-Barke, Milham, & Tannock, 2006). Whereas "cool" tasks are designed to be more emotionally neutral, tasks can also vary in the degree to which they are administered in an emotionally arousing and "hot" context (Séguin, Arseneault, & Tremblay, 2007). Whereas the former tasks involve more "top-down" integrative regulation (e.g., dorsolateral frontal cortex), the latter tasks involve more "bottom-up" processing (e.g., ventromedial/orbital frontal cortex), such as those more generally described by Stuss (2011). Although the "cool – hot" distinction has considerable face validity and seems to be taken for granted by many, it is much harder to define operationally as it may not be as categorical as the language we use to describe it implies (Welsh & Peterson, 2014).

Clinical Syndromes Associated with Violence

Although physical violence is relatively easy to identify because of its overt nature, there is a paucity of studies examining the neuropsychology of violence. Much of what we know in this domain derives from research on conditions that are associated with violence rather than violence *per se*. Thus, to appreciate the strengths and limitations of this body of literature, we first discuss clinical syndromes most commonly associated with violence.

Violence research is conducted within two broad and overlapping nomenclatures: legal/judicial and clinical. In the legal/judicial areas, researchers have studied delinquency and criminal behavior. In the clinical arena, physical violence or aggression as a feature, and sometimes as a diagnostic criterion, can be found in a variety of disorders of the *Diagnostic and Statistical Manual of Mental Disorders* (DSM-5) (American Psychiatric Association, 2013) and *the International Classification of Diseases – Mental and Behavioral Disorders* (ICD-10CM) (World Health Organization [WHO], 1992). Accordingly, an approach linking neuropsychological function to violence as manifested in clinical disorders fits well within the objectives of the Research Domain Criteria project recently launched by the National Institute of Mental Health (www.nimh.nih.gov/research-priorities/rdoc/index.shtml). Specifically, physical aggression or violence may be found among disorders that are listed under disruptive, impulse-control, neurodevelopmental, and neurocognitive disorders, including Intermittent Explosive Disorder, other Specified Disruptive Impulse-Control and Conduct Disorder, Unspecified Disruptive Impulse-Control and Conduct Disorder, and Antisocial Personality Disorder (ASPD). Physical violence can also occur as a symptom of the Personality Change due to a General Medical Condition, Aggressive Type; Trauma or Stressor-Related Disorders, and in the newly added DSM-5 Disruptive Mood Dysregulation disorder. It is not a formal feature of, but is a potential consequence of, Delusional Disorder – persecutory type, Schizophrenia, Sleep-Wake Disorders, Bipolar Disorder, several Substance-Related and Addictive Disorders, and relational problems including Spouse or Partner Violence. Nevertheless, for none of these disorders is violence a necessary or sufficient criterion.

Psychopathy has not been listed as a separate disease category in DSM-5 or its predecessors. Nevertheless, although DSM-IV-TR regarded ASPD as essentially synonymous with psychopathy, in DSM-5, psychopathy has been added as a specifier to the ASPD category in Section III (but not to the main text) – the section of the manual devoted to newly emerging models and measures. Psychopathic traits are also listed in the Conduct Disorder (CD) category using the specifier "with limited prosocial emotions," which captures children and adolescents with pronounced callous-unemotional (CU) traits. Indeed, research has shown that children with CD and marked CU traits are distinct from children with CD without these traits in etiology, risk for ASPD later in life (Frick, Ray, Thornton, & Kahn, 2014), and neurocognitive functioning (Blair, Leibenluft, & Pine, 2014).

Physical violence has also been studied developmentally. However, in most developmental studies, aggression scales often neglect to distinguish physical from other forms of aggression. For example, the Child Behavior Checklist (CBCL,

Achenbach, Edelbrock, & Howell, 1987) yields an aggression scale that comprises 23 items, only three of which refer explicitly to physical aggression. Physical aggression in these scales can be defined as hitting, kicking, biting, use of a weapon, and getting into fights. In some cases, this definition is broadened to include bullying and threats of violence.

Given these limitations, it is possible for neuropsychological studies in the antisocial behavior literature to include nonphysically violent forms of CD, ASPD, psychopathy, or aggression. Further, the clinical syndromes in which physical violence is present are often comorbid with other conditions characterized by impulsivity, drug and alcohol abuse, Attention Deficit Hyperactivity Disorder (ADHD), and Oppositional Defiant Disorder (ODD). Although there is merit to examining how components shared across such externalizing problems (if not across all disorders) relate to neuropsychological function (Castellanos-Ryan et al., 2016), such an approach is also complemented by studies of specificity.

Section II: Developmental Issues

A developmental approach allows the identification of children for whom problems may be chronic as opposed to acute or transient. Accordingly, longitudinal studies in community samples have provided insight into trajectories of antisocial behaviors throughout development. A recent review of this literature indicates that antisocial behaviors tend to display different developmental trajectories, that they have shared but also unique risk factors, that the trajectories associated with violence generally emerge in the preschool years, and, although some trajectories remain high for a small proportion of children as they enter adulthood, antisocial behaviors tend to decline across adulthood – but are nonetheless accompanied by adaptational problems later in life (Séguin & Tremblay, 2013). The bulk of that research has been on males; so much more needs to be done to study females.

On the basis of early prospective longitudinal studies, Moffitt (1993) noted that adolescents with a form of early-onset/persistent antisocial behavior, which includes aggression and hyperactivity, showed poorer neuropsychological test performance in early adolescence than did those with a later onset. This finding has been supported by several studies (e.g., Johnson, Kemp, Heard, Lennings, & Hickie, 2015; Fairchild et al., 2009), although brain-imaging studies have not fully supported this distinction (e.g., Fairchild et al., 2011; Jiang et al., 2015). These findings underscore a key methodological point, namely, that comparing groups of adolescents or adults without knowledge of their natural developmental history can be fraught with problems. Nevertheless, the developmental sequence is often assumed to be from neuropsychological function to behavior but little research has been conducted to verify that assumption. Hence, developmental studies need to use a more fully longitudinal approach that permits the examination of reciprocal transactions between neuropsychological function and behavior (Pinsonneault, Parent, Castellanos-Ryan, & Séguin, 2015).

Risk Factors that May Affect Brain Development

As developmental patterns have been studied with longitudinal designs, there has been increasing interest in conditions that can contribute both to those patterns *and* to poor neuropsychological function, such as a history of exposure during or after pregnancy to brain-altering psychopharmacological agents (e.g., cigarette smoke, alcohol, drugs), perinatal or birth complications, nutrition, traumatic experiences (e.g., abuse), chronic stress, or behavior problems that heighten the risk of head trauma through accidents or fights (e.g., ADHD, ODD). For example, cigarettes may exert early effects in the intrauterine environment and later in the home environment. For example, a review of 20 published articles on the association between tobacco smoke exposure in utero and cognition found robust associations for lower academic achievement and intellectual functioning after controlling for other variables (Clifford, Lang, & Chen, 2012). Nevertheless, genetically informed designs raise the possibility that at least some of this linkage may be genetic (e.g., D'Onofrio, Van Hulle, Goodnight, Rathouz, & Lahey, 2012).

The mechanisms through which in-utero or early-life adverse exposures affect brain development and violence risk are unclear, but an emerging overarching hypothesis is that early-life adversity produces long-lasting epigenetic alterations that influence gene expression profiles in key biological systems, such as the hypothalamic–pituitary–adrenal axis, the immune system, as well as neurotransmitters, such as serotonin (Booij et al., 2010; Wang et al., 2012), which, in turn, alter the ability to learn to inhibit physical aggression. Genetic factors probably moderate these effects of early-life stress on the epigenome and influence the risk for, or resilience to, developing violent behaviors (Provençal, Booij, & Tremblay, 2015). Furthermore, there could be an assumption that neurocognitive problems lead to behavior problems. This would not be surprising given that this literature developed out of lesion research and that remedial interventions often target cognitive abilities to change behavior. However, this assumption is rarely tested as it is equally possible for transactions to change direction across developmental stages. Consequently, children who show behavior problems could eventually get more or less support and exposure to alternative problem-solving approaches through social moderators, which would enhance or diminish their repertoire of cognitive and self-regulatory skills (see Pinsonneault et al., 2015). Finally, substance use during adolescence, such as smoking (Lydon, Wilson, Child, & Geier, 2014) or cannabis use (Castellanos-Ryan et al., 2017), probably also affects the developmental course of brain cognitive and motivational systems.

Section III: The Effects of Brain Lesions on the Risk for Violence

Given the background considerations reviewed thus far, we now address two complementary questions: (1) "Do some brain lesions dependably increase the risk for violent behavior?" and (2) "Do violence-prone individuals exhibit specific neuropsychological deficits?"

Interest in the cognitive and emotional regulation aspects of the brain-violence relation has centered largely on the role of the frontal lobe because of its centrality to the regulation of social behavior. Frontal patients have difficulty organizing and regulating their behavior in response to external stimuli. The more cognitive functions of the frontal lobe, often referred to as the executive functions, include working memory, which involves the online maintenance of information and the active processing of that information as an individual engages in action, interference control (attention and inhibition), and cognitive flexibility (Diamond, 2013). The emotional regulation function was supported by a study of individuals with lesions comprising the orbitofrontal cortex, who tend to be disinhibited, socially inappropriate, susceptible to misinterpreting others' moods, impulsive, unconcerned with the consequences of their actions, irresponsible in everyday life, lacking in insight into the seriousness of their condition, and prone to weak initiative (Fazel, Philipson, Gardiner, Merritt, & Grann, 2009). The main consequence of such lesions has been linked with impaired performance on a wide variety of neuropsychological tests measuring reward and punishment sensitivity, decision making, and processing of social cues (Jonker, Jonker, Scheltens, & Scherder, 2015). In many imaging studies, differences in brain function or structure were independent of performance deficits, and therefore require additional neuropsychological testing to be evaluated. Many of these neuropsychological deficits reflect malfunction of limbic brain regions, such as the amygdala, cingulate, and/or striatum.

The ensuing syndrome from orbitofrontal lesions was historically labeled acquired sociopathy (Damasio, 2000), acquired ASPD (Meyers, Berman, Scheibel, & Hayman, 1992), or pseudopsychopathy. Because these lesions appear to lead to certain psychopathic-like behaviors, they were often thought to underlie physical violence. Nevertheless, there is limited support for this hypothesis. Studies of war veterans, for example, revealed that although veterans with prefrontal lesions exhibit more positive implicit attitudes towards violence compared with veterans without lesions, they do not differ on explicit measures of aggression. Thus, although prefrontal lesions may impact inhibition over automatic (implicit) aggressive reactions to perceived provocation (Cristofori et al., 2016), physical violence directly resulting from lesions is rare in acquired forms of antisocial behavior. This finding may in part be due to the fact that individuals with acquired brain lesions do not necessarily possess the many pre-morbid risk factors associated with physical violence. In fact, aggression (including physical aggression) appears to be more likely to be associated with acquired frontal lesions only when there is a premorbid history of psychopathology (Fazel et al., 2009). Otherwise, normative behavior may be the result of interactions among these dynamically related frontal systems (Verbruggen, 2016).

Other cortical abnormalities associated with aggressive outbursts include acute episodes of temporal lobe (temporolimbic) epilepsy (also known as interictal violence), which is similar in manifestation to IED. Nevertheless, violence in epilepsy seems to be lower than in the general population (Fazel et al., 2009). Taken together, these findings suggest that brain lesions are rarely sufficient causes of violence. At the same time, they may lead to violence in the context of other risk factors.

Neuropsychological Studies of Physically Violent Behavior

The other main approach to the neuropsychology of violence is to study physically violent individuals. We begin with the most severe form of violence, murder, and move on to less severe forms of physical aggression. We then follow with disorders and antisocial behavior problems in which physical violence is sometimes present.

Murderers

Several studies of murderers have shown reduced activity in frontal brain regions, which is consistent with the dysfunctional frontal lobe hypothesis, a theory postulated for the first time more than two decades ago during the early years of brain imaging research. In one of the first studies, "frontal dysfunctions" were found in 65% of murderers (Blake, Pincus, & Buckner, 1995). In a more recent study, among incarcerated youth, homicide offenders (80% self-reported) showed structural differences in the temporal lobes, hippocampus, and posterior insula (Cope et al., 2014). Further, when these homicide offenders were compared to typically developing youth in a recent meta-analysis, they appeared to show consistently larger effect sizes across several structures (Rogers & De Brito, 2016).

Few studies have examined neuropsychological performance in murderers. The neuropsychological performance in murderers seems to depend on subtype; affective/impulsive murderers tend to display poorer neuropsychological performance than predatory/instrumental murderers, especially on measures of intelligence, memory, attention, and executive functions (Hanlon, Brook, Stratton, Jensen, & Rubin, 2013). These differences appear to be consistent with differences in brain activation (Raine et al., 1998).

Although the frontal lobe has been implicated in these and other studies, they almost surely account for only one portion of the explanation. Indeed, in addition to frontal hypoactivation, many imaging studies found increases in the activity of subcortical areas, which is consistent with neural models of aggression, postulating that aggression results from deficits in cortical top-down control and/or facilitation of bottom-up signaling triggered from subcortical limbic circuits (Davidson, Putnam, & Larson, 2000). Importantly, frontal lobe hypofunction is not specific to murderers (e.g., Siever, 2008). The lack of specificity indicates that other factors like genetic make-up, early development, and other factors reviewed in this book may play an important role in the risk for committing homicide.

Physical Aggression

Although murder is the most severe form of violence, investigators have also examined whether neuropsychological problems are evident in milder forms of violence, such as in physical aggression as observed in community samples. There are surprisingly few neuropsychological studies of physical aggression *per se*.

Séguin et al. (1995) sought to develop a neuropsychological test battery on the basis of (a) the frontal lobe and memory work of Petrides and Milner (1985) and (b) reviews of the neuropsychology of delinquency and conduct disorder, such as Moffitt's (1990), which identified deficits in language abilities, executive function, and cerebral dominance. Using that approach, we first found that working memory, a basic ability involved in executive function, was poorest in boys from a community sample with a history of physical aggression even after controlling for nonexecutive abilities (Séguin, Pihl, Harden, Tremblay, & Boulerice, 1995). In follow-up, we controlled statistically for ADHD or teacher-rated hyperactivity and still found working memory impairments even after controlling for IQ (Séguin, Boulerice, Harden, Tremblay, & Pihl, 1999). In a third study, we selected young adult males not only on the basis of a physically aggressive history (teacher-rated from kindergarten to age 15), but also of hyperactivity (without a focus on inattention or impulsivity) (Séguin, Nagin, Assaad, & Tremblay, 2004). We found no statistical interaction, but we did find clear additive effects, even after controlling for test motivation. In other words, both physical aggression and hyperactivity exhibited significant independent and additive associations with neuropsychological function.

In sum, poor neuropsychological function is often found in adolescents and young adults from the community with a history of physical aggression. These deficits appear to be independent from other externalizing behavior problems. Developmentally, these associations and specificity to physical aggression or hyperactivity can be detected as early as the preschool years (Séguin, Parent, Tremblay, & Zelazo, 2009).

Neuropsychological Studies of Antisocial Disorders in Which Physical Violence May Be Present

The bulk of research on the neuropsychology of violence derives from clinically oriented studies of disorders and antisocial behavior problems that may include physical violence.

Antisocial Behaviors

Several of the behavioral problems listed here have been grouped under the global label of "antisocial behaviors." These behaviors, among others, were examined in meta-analyses of studies of executive function by Morgan and Lilienfeld (2000) and more recently updated and expanded by Ogilvie et al. (2011). The first meta-analysis by Morgan and Lilienfeld (2000) comprised 39 studies, yielding 4,589 participants total. To be included in the meta-analysis, tests of executive functioning must have attempted to measure volition, planning, purposive action, or effective performance, and either differentiated patients with frontal lesions from other patients or preferentially activated the frontal cortex in previous studies. To investigate whether antisocial behavior was related to executive functioning deficits *per se* rather than neuropsychological deficits in general, three neuropsychological tests that do not rely heavily on executive functioning were analyzed as "control" measures. The antisocial behavior groups used in the meta-analysis included individuals meeting criteria for one or more of the following antisocial behavior problems: ASPD, CD, psychopathic personality disorder, criminality, or delinquency.

The results indicated that the antisocial behavior groups performed significantly worse than comparison groups, with a combined and weighted effect size (Cohen's d [Cohen, 1992] of 0.62 standard deviations). Two of the three non-executive functioning neuropsychological tests also produced significant, albeit weaker, differences between groups, with the antisocial behavior groups performing significantly worse with effect sizes of $d = 0.34$ and $d = 0.39$ standard deviations. However, tests revealed significant heterogeneity of effect sizes, pointing to the possibility of moderators. When considering the type of antisocial grouping used in the studies, the heterogeneity of effect sizes was reduced within each group and all group effect sizes remained significantly different than zero. Moreover, criminality ($d = 1.09$, weighted $d = 0.94$) and delinquency ($d = 0.86$, weighted $d = 0.78$) were most strongly associated with executive functioning deficits. Potential moderators including age, sex, ethnicity, and IQ were not associated with the magnitude of the observed effect sizes, although scores on some of these moderators (e.g., sex, ethnicity) were not reported in all studies.

The second meta-analysis by Ogilvie, Stewart, Chan, and Shum (2011), built on the Morgan and Lilienfeld (2000) meta-analysis, brought up the total number of studies to 126, involving 14,786 participants. This meta-analysis added more recent studies published since the original meta-analysis as well as a wider range of EF and non-EF tasks. It corroborated the results of the initial meta-analysis by showing an overall association between executive functioning and antisocial behaviors ($d = 0.44$), but also heterogeneity of effect sizes across definitions of antisocial behavior. This heterogeneity may in part have stemmed from the fact that studies used to estimate effect size could be considered under more than one antisocial behavior category. Nonetheless, and as in the initial meta-analysis, the largest effect size was found for criminality ($d = 0.61$). Other reported effect sizes were ODD/CD ($d = 0.54$), psychopathy ($d = 0.42$), delinquency ($d = 0.41$), physical aggression ($d = 0.41$), and ASPD ($d = 0.19$).

Although the effect sizes across meta-analyses were mostly similar, Ogilvie et al. (2011) suggested that some of the differences may have been due to the inclusion of a wider range of EF and non-EF tasks as well as measures and operationalization of antisocial behaviors that have become more specific and sensitive over the years. Some of our work can serve to illustrate this issue. For example, when forming groups on the basis of a history of physical aggression, the effect sizes of neuropsychological tests in a study using developmental trajectory methodology (empirically based) as was used in a later study (Séguin et al., 2004) were much larger than those found when using arbitrary thresholds (theoretically based) in an earlier study (Séguin et al., 1995).

By the time of the later meta-analysis (Ogilvie et al., 2011), there was then also a sufficient number of studies to examine the potential additive role of ADHD. The studies that included participants with comorbid ADHD diagnoses showed the largest effect sizes. The mechanisms through which ADHD adds these other antisocial behavior problems in their association with neurocognitive functioning remain to be better studied (see also hypotheses proposed by Sonuga-Barke, Cortese, Fairchild, & Stringaris, 2016). This finding supports the need for careful selection of study participants in future studies when studying specific relationships between executive functioning and antisocial behaviors.

Both meta-analyses identified several limitations in this body of research, including small sample sizes, poor comparison group selection, and minimal control over potentially confounding factors such as psychiatric comorbidity. Furthermore, Morgan and Lilienfeld (2000) pointed out that the finding that criminality and delinquency were associated with more pronounced executive functioning deficits than the other groups is difficult to interpret given the differences in comparison groups used across studies. For example, executive functioning studies frequently compared criminals or delinquents with normal or unselected samples, whereas psychopaths were frequently compared with nonpsychopathic criminals. These concerns were supported empirically (Ogilvie et al., 2011).

Psychopathy

Psychopaths are generally more violent than other criminals (Hare, 1999) and consequently have received considerable research attention in the past three decades. Reports of neuropsychological performance among psychopathic participants, especially executive functioning, have been mixed. The two meta-analyses examining PCL-R and non-PCL-R-defined psychopathy indicate that the average effect sizes of neuropsychological (executive functioning) deficits were small to medium ($d = 0.29$ in Morgan and Lilienfeld [2000] and $d = 0.42$ in Ogilvie et al. [2011]).

Possible explanations for the high levels of variability across studies are differences in the operationalization of psychopathy as well as the existence of potential psychopathy subtypes. For instance, a number of studies have shown that low-anxious psychopaths show impaired functioning on neuropsychological tasks that rely primarily on frontal lobe function, such as executive functioning (Smith, Arnett, & Newman, 1992), cued attention (Zeier, Maxwell, & Newman, 2009), as well as economic decision making (Koenigs, Kruepke, & Newman, 2010). In addition, successful psychopaths (defined by being nonconvicted) showed better performance on an executive functioning task than unsuccessful (convicted) psychopaths (Ishikawa, Raine, Lencz, Bihrle, & LaCasse, 2001). It is unclear, however, whether this lattermost difference is independent of possible between-group differences in general intelligence.

Beyond studies using more classic neuropsychological tests, psychopaths appear to experience greater difficulty in shifting a dominant behavior when contingencies are changed and reversed. Newman and colleagues have proposed two pathways to account for that impairment: (1) a difficulty in regulation of affect and (2) a more fundamental information-processing deficit related to attention, i.e., a difficulty in shifting attention to peripheral but potentially meaningful information from the environment (Newman & Lorenz, 2003). This so-called response modulation theory is one of the most widely studied cognitive models of psychopathy. After its initial formulation more than three decades ago (Gorenstein & Newman, 1980), the theory has been refined over the years, taking into account new research. A recent meta-analysis (Smith & Lilienfeld, 2015), including 94 studies involving 7340 participants, found a small to medium effect size ($d = 0.41$) for the association between response modulation deficits and psychopathy, which is within the same range as those found with other psychological theories of psychopathy (Lilienfeld, Smith, & Watts, 2016). Nevertheless, the several clinical, demographic and methodological variables (e.g., anxiety levels, ethnicity, measures used) that were found to moderate the strength of the relationship, as well as the several methodological shortcomings of studies (e.g. publication bias), raise questions regarding the comprehensiveness of the theory in explaining psychopathy.

A number of other cognitive theories preceded and followed the response modulation theory. Recently, the impaired integration theory has been proposed to integrate cognitive and affective models of psychopathy with neurobiological data (Hamilton, Racer, & Newman, 2015). This theory postulates that psychopathy results from an impaired ability to rapidly integrate sensory information into a unified percept. This deficit in turn leads to unelaborated mental representations and an underdevelopment of associative neural networks. Underdeveloped connectivity in specific brain networks ostensibly underlies the psychopathy profile. For instance, decreased connectivity in networks involved in affective processing underlie the callous emotional traits present in psychopathy, whereas decreased connectivity in attentional networks leads to poor integration of different types of information (e.g., cognitive-affective, perceptual-motor). Although more research is needed to support this promising theory, such an integrative approach dovetails with developments in cognitive neuroscience, modeling behavioral and cognitive processes as dynamic large-scale neural networks, rather than as isolated, static brain regions.

Criminality and Delinquency

Some of the important theoretical work of Moffitt (1993) initially centered on delinquency. In one study, early-onset/persistent delinquents performed more poorly than did "late-onset" delinquents on IQ and other neuropsychological tests (Taylor, Iacono, & McGue, 2000), as predicted by Moffitt's (1993) developmental theory of antisocial behavior. In this study, however, IQ was not used as a covariate, rendering conclusions regarding the specificity of cognitive deficits unclear. Furthermore, the use of global scales of delinquency or criminality may obscure key relations between specific behaviors and neuropsychological function. For example, one study revealed that, among juvenile delinquents, IQ was positively related to theft, but negatively related to violence (Walsh, 1987). Presumably, this finding reflects the requirement for planning for theft, but an impulsive problem-solving style for violence. Intrigued by this isolated report, we analyzed data from the Rutgers longitudinal study (White, Bates, & Buyske, 2001). In that study, theft and violence were initially combined within a global index of delinquency. Neuropsychological function had failed to separate persistent from adolescence-limited delinquents. Following our own work with physical aggression and hyperactivity (Séguin et al., 2004), we identified trajectories for theft and for physical violence. Using the same tests as used by White et al. (2001), we replicated Walsh's (1987) finding and found the poorest neuropsychological function in highly violent individuals who were low on theft (Barker et al., 2007). In another follow-up to the Séguin et al. (2004) study, we found that verbal abilities were negatively related to trajectories of physical aggression but positively associated with theft (Barker et al., 2011). In that study, lower levels of inductive reasoning were associated with increases in theft across adolescence. Interestingly, symptoms of ADHD accounted for part of the neurocognitive test links with physical aggression, but did not account for the associations with theft. Together, these studies highlight the need for a finer parsing of the relation between neuropsychological function and global indices of antisocial behavior.

One category of delinquency that is receiving increasing attention is sexual offending. A meta-analysis, involving 23 studies and a total of 1,756 participants, on neuropsychological performance in sex offenders confirmed that adult sex offenders performed worse on neuropsychological tasks than did members of the general population ($d = 0.59$), but also showed that sex-offending is highly heterogeneous (Joyal, Beaulieu-Plante, & de Chantérac, 2014). Subgroup analyses showed that sex offenders against children tended to perform lower on so-called higher-order executive functioning tasks compared to sex offenders against adults (albeit with small effect size, $d = 0.23$), whereas sex offenders against adults were similar to nonsex offenders, with lower scores in verbal fluency and inhibition. The meta-analysis highlights the need for studies in specific subgroups. Few studies have focused on adolescent sex offenders. One study examined a sample of 127 adolescent sex offenders and 56 adolescents convicted of nonsexual offenses (Morais, Joyal, Alexander, Fix, & Burkhart, 2016). In contrast to studies conducted in adults, adolescent sex offenders who had victimized children obtained significantly higher scores on measures of complex executive functioning tasks than both adolescent offenders with peer-aged or older victims and adolescent nonsex offenders. Taken together, these findings suggest possible complex interactions involving developmental age of the offender and victim. Longitudinal studies following adolescent offenders over time are needed to understand the relevance of neuropsychological performance for recidivism and recovery.

Many of the findings related to the neuropsychology of violence may bear implications for the justice system. Although neuroscientific evidence on altered frontal-limbic brain function in relation to violence in adults appears to be increasingly being used in the courtroom (see Klaming & Koops (2012) and Steinberg (2013) for reviews of the literature and case examples), decisions for trying adolescents who committed violent crimes in adult courts hinge on research on brain development and maturation. From a brain maturation perspective, some claim that adolescent brains are not sufficiently mature to justify trying violent adolescents in adult courts. Nevertheless, the overwhelming majority of adolescents are not violent, raising the question of why legal decision making should use age *per se* as a criterion (Satel & Lilienfeld, 2013). Moreover, neuropsychological function and brain maturation may account only for a relatively small amount of variance in physical violence. Thus, the sensitive issue of trying violent adolescents in adult courts should probably rest on broader grounds and evidence reviewed herein to inform the legal decision making system should be used with caution.

Intermittent Explosive Disorder

DSM-5 (American Psychiatric Association, 2013) places intermittent explosive disorder (IED) under the category of Disruptive Impulse-Control and Conduct Disorders. The primary feature of IED is the frequent experience of short and discrete episodes of aggressive behavior of rapid onset resulting in personal injuries or property damage. The course, onset, and prevalence of IED are poorly understood, although this condition appears to be more common in males than females. Not surprisingly, there is a dearth of studies on the neuropsychological correlates of IED, although its neurobiology is better understood (Coccaro, 2012). In one controlled study, Best, Williams, and Coccaro (2002) showed that IED participants performed poorly on the Iowa Gambling Task compared with healthy controls. Nevertheless, there were no group differences on the Self-Ordered Pointing test, a working memory test most sensitive to physical aggression (Séguin et al., 2004). This finding is consistent with the idea that IED may be neurocognitively distinctive from other, more common forms of violence, suggesting an IED profile with predominantly affective and social rather than cognitive deficits (Lee et al., 2016). More research is needed to further understand whether impaired neuropsychological functioning in IED is distinct from other impulse-control disorders. Such research should be embedded in a developmental framework capturing the age of onset (Coccaro, 2012).

Conduct Disorder

When Morgan and Lilienfeld (2000) reviewed the CD literature they found a medium effect size of $d = 0.4$ (weighted $d = 0.36$) for poor performance on executive functioning tasks. The meta-analysis by Ogilvie et al. (2011), which mixed both ODD and CD but separated ADHD, reported a slightly higher effect size ($d = 0.54$).

Combining CD and ODD in analyses may be justified when addressing certain research questions, especially those aimed at understanding what is common among externalizing problems, if not across psychopathologies (Castellanos-Ryan et al., 2016). At the same time, this approach is problematic when trying to examine specificity to violence, because neither ODD nor CD necessarily encompass physical aggression. We first provide an example to illustrate the potential importance of accounting for the CD symptom of physical aggression in studies of the neuropsychology of antisocial behavior. In one study that focused on physical aggression and hyperactivity, 67% of boys classified as CD and 72% of boys classified as ADHD between the ages of 14 and 16 were in the high physical aggression and high hyperactivity trajectories, respectively, on the basis of teacher ratings from age 6 to 15 (Séguin et al., 2004). Nevertheless, across the entire sample only 5% and 6.7% of boys met criteria for CD or ADHD, respectively. This finding suggests that if one is high in physical aggression (or hyperactivity), one is more likely to meet criteria for CD (or ADHD). But that study was different from the typical ones selecting for CD and ADHD in that it selected children on the basis of physical aggression and hyperactivity instead. A selection based on CD and ADHD may not necessarily have included either physical aggression or hyperactivity, or these specific behaviors may have contributed only a low weight to the diagnoses. Thus, a focus on physical aggression and hyperactivity yielded a greater number of study participants, most of whom did not meet criteria for CD or ADHD, and those more specific behaviors were sensitive to neuropsychological function (Séguin et al., 2004).

Second, in addition to the comorbidity of other externalizing problems with CD, we have already highlighted the problem of heterogeneity of mechanisms correlated with two of the four key symptoms of CD – physical aggression and theft. There is now a growing number of studies examining subtypes of CD symptoms that supports the replicability of the negative association between physical aggression and neurocognitive dysfunction, but that finds links between such dysfunction and theft or other nonaggressive conduct problems to be either essentially nonexistent (Barker et al., 2007; Hancock, Tapscott, & Hoaken, 2010) or positive (Barker et al., 2011; Walsh, 1987). Thus, from a neuropsychological perspective, the conflation of symptoms within CD may mask otherwise-important heterogeneity (Burt, 2009, 2013).

Antisocial Personality Disorder

In DSM-5, ASPD is diagnosed only in individuals over the age of 18 with evidence of CD. As we mentioned earlier, psychopathy is often found among individuals with ASPD. We also note that PCL-R scores > 20 but < 30 (the standard PCL-R cut-off for psychopathy) may also reflect ASPD, and that many ASPD individuals will have a criminal record. Compared with other categories in which antisocial behavior plays a role, there are relatively few neuropsychological studies of ASPD. The most recent meta-analysis included 11 studies and found that ASPD's associations with executive dysfunction are weak (effect size $d = 0.19$), (Ogilvie et al., 2011). One study found poorer executive function (working memory, cognitive flexibility, and inhibitory control) in ASPD relative to nonoffenders, regardless of the presence or absence of co-occurring psychopathy (De Brito, Viding, Kumari, Blackwood, & Hodgins, 2013).

Other Disorders Where Violence May Be Present

Although violence is likely to be found in the more explicitly antisocial disorders already reviewed, violence is often associated with alcohol- and substance-use disorders, schizophrenia, and bipolar disorder. Hence, we briefly review their relation to neuropsychological function.

Alcohol and Substance Use

A considerable limitation to the literature investigating neuropsychological function in violent problem behaviors and associated disorders is a potential confound with alcohol and substance abuse. In fact, most violent acts may occur under the influence of substances (Murdoch, Pihl, & Ross, 1990; Room, Babor, & Rehm, 2005). Although the culture of illegal drugs is also associated with violence, this is not dispositive evidence for the violence potential of the drugs themselves. The other key issue to consider is developmental transactions between substance use and neuropsychological function. Although several studies note cross-sectional correlations between substance use and neuropsychological function in acute states, few have examined whether the association found before the onset of substance use was changed afterwards or if use was related to developmental change in neuropsychological function. Building on a series of longitudinal studies on the neuropsychology of physical aggression (Séguin et al., 1995; Séguin, Arseneault, Boulerice, Harden, & Tremblay, 2002; Séguin et al., 2004), we have recently reported that early onset of cannabis use was predicted by pre-use IQ and poor short-term and working memory (Castellanos-Ryan et al., 2017). Nevertheless, we also showed that, by age 20, changes only in verbal IQ (accounted for by poor high-school graduation), trial-and-error learning, and reward-processing were linked to onset and frequency of use in adolescence, even after controlling for CD, ADHD, and concurrent cannabis or alcohol use. Although such studies do not demonstrate causality, the developmental transactions observed need to be taken into account in studying the neuropsychology of violence.

Our central question concerns the role of neuropsychological factors in this equation. Most research on this topic has focused on executive function. The role of executive function in alcohol-associated aggression has been illustrated well by the work of Giancola (2004), who showed that aggression in reaction to provocation (using a shock paradigm) was possibly more a function of executive function than of alcohol. Nevertheless, synergistic mechanisms may be at play, as alcohol preferentially increased aggression in men with lower levels of executive function. Alcohol may also moderate the quality of executive function on a state (temporary) basis, mostly on the descending limb of the blood-alcohol curve (Pihl, Paylan, Gentes-Hawn, & Hoaken, 2004). Finally, recent models have attempted to integrate cognitive theories of alcohol-induced aggression with neurobiological theories of aggression. For example, Heinz, Beck, Meyer-Lindenberg, Sterzer, and Heinz (2011) proposed that the presence of certain risk genotypes/alleles in combination with adverse environmental factors (e.g., early-life stress) affect the functioning of key neurotransmitter systems (e.g., serotonin, GABA). This outcome in turn would lead to an increased activation in subcortical (bottom-up) limbic circuits and impaired (top-down) prefrontal function, which may place individuals at risk for both increased alcohol intake and impulsive aggression. Acute or chronic alcohol intake, in turn, can further inhibit executive control and facilitate aggressive behavior.

Schizophrenia

Although the prevalence of violence in schizophrenia and other disorders where psychosis is present is about 10% across several studies, its relative prevalence as opposed to the general population is highly variable, with odds ratios varying from 1 to 7 for men, to 4–29 for women (Fazel, Gulati, Linsell, Geddes, & Grann, 2009). In that meta-analytic study, the risk of violent behavior seemed to be highest when there was comorbid substance use, but the rate of violence did not differ between individuals with schizophrenia and with non-schizophrenia-related psychosis. One meta-analysis, investigating risk factors for violence in (primarily) schizophrenia, found that, among several clinical and demographic factors, substance misuse and particularly factors related to violent and nonviolent criminal history (e.g., history of assault, history of imprisonment for any offense, history of recent arrest for any offense, history of conviction for a violent offense) were the strongest predictors of risk of violent behavior (Witt, van Dorn, & Fazel, 2013).

Another meta-analysis (Schug & Raine, 2009) compared neuropsychological performance in individuals with (a) schizophrenia and antisocial behavior, (b) schizophrenia without antisocial behaviors, and (c) antisocial behaviors without schizophrenia. The authors found that individuals with schizophrenia and antisocial behaviors showed widespread cognitive impairments (IQ, attention, executive function, and memory) relative to individuals with antisocial behaviors without schizophrenia, and exhibited reduced general intellectual functioning and memory dysfunction, relative to individuals with schizophrenia without antisocial behaviors. These associations were characterized by small effect sizes ($d = 0.2$–0.3 range), but may suggest that schizophrenia with antisocial behaviors may be a subcategory of schizophrenia, a finding supported by electrophysiological and imaging studies (Schug & Raine, 2009). The authors explicitly chose liberal, though arguably valid, approaches to classifying antisociality and schizophrenia. Accordingly, they noted considerable heterogeneity of effect sizes. Because of this they also highlight the need to further clarify neuropsychological differences between violent versus nonviolent forms of antisocial problems within studies of schizophrenia. This is also important because the stigma against schizophrenia stems mostly from the minority of patients that show violence. Thus, interventions could be tailored to a better understanding of these subtypes.

Mood Disorders

Bipolar disorder is associated with several reckless behaviors characterized by impulsivity, as well as poor judgment and planning (Moeller, Barratt, Dougherty, Schmitz, & Swann, 2001). Bipolar disorder may be associated with violence when it co-exists with substance abuse (OR: 6.4), but markedly less so when substance is absent (OR: 1.3) (Fazel, Lichtenstein, Grann, Goodwin, & Langstrom, 2010). Bipolar disorder has been characterized by overall impairments in neuropsychological functioning, including impairments in intelligence, attention, verbal learning and memory, executive functioning, response inhibition, working memory, set shifting, and processing speed. Some of these impairments, such as those in attention, processing speed, verbal learning/memory, and verbal fluency, have, albeit to a lesser extent, also been observed in healthy first-degree relatives, suggesting a potential trait marker for bipolar disorder (Cardenas, Kassem, Brotman, Leibenluft, & McMahon, 2016). Whether violent bipolar patients are cognitively distinct from nonviolent patients is unknown.

The two core symptoms of the new DSM-5 Disruptive Mood Dysregulation Disorder are (a) recurrent severe temper outbursts that are out of proportion to the situation and inconsistent with the developmental stage and (b) high levels of irritability and anger for most of the day, nearly every day. Despite a conceptual and face-value relevance of this disorder to the study of violence (Mayes, Waxmonsky, Calhoun, & Bixler, 2016) there have yet to be studies of its cognitive neuropsychology.

Conclusion

The neuropsychology of antisocial behavior has a rich history, dating back at least to the mid-nineteenth century. As our review shows, however, not as much can be said about the neuropsychology of physical violence. The main problem is that the specificity of neuropsychological deficits to physically violent behavior has been difficult to establish. The bulk of our knowledge derives from studies of clinical syndromes in which the presence of violence is plausible, but rarely confirmed. Global measures of antisocial, disruptive, externalizing, delinquent, or criminal behavior are also often used. This state of affairs reflects the heterogeneity of processes underlying those conditions.

Nonetheless, as this book shows, violence is a common outcome of a wide variety of heterogeneous conditions. Violence is present in many disorders for which there may be a partial neuropsychological basis, although that neuropsychological basis may not necessarily be for violence per se. To advance a research agenda in the study of the neuropsychology of violence, we recommend testing for the specificity of behavior problems, such as identifying physical aggression and isolating it from other co-occurring behavior problems. More explicit assessment of violence or physical aggression is needed with key contrasts to such disorders as ADHD, substance use, and to nonviolent forms of antisocial behavior. Although this approach should reduce the heterogeneity in the behavior of interest, it may not reduce the heterogeneity of underlying processes as much as one hopes; subtypes of physical violence will also need to be addressed. A well-documented history of behavior problems should also help to reduce heterogeneity. The study of the process of desistance from violence would be informative in this regard.

Our review shows that neuropsychological impairments, even in executive function, are not necessarily specific to physical aggression. We first observed that lesions among frontal lobe patients, despite their poor executive function, rarely lead to physical violence, though these lesions may lead to explicit forms of violence in the context of other risk factors. Further, there is considerable literature on other problems, such as ADHD, and their relation to executive function. Nevertheless, we noted that studies of ADHD have rarely controlled for co-occurring physical aggression. Further, neuropsychological variables tend to explain at most 8–10% of the variance in measures of violence. Therefore, studies need to examine potential moderators that may increase our ability to predict the risk of violence from neuropsychological dysfunction. Such factors could include a history of abuse or neglect, malnutrition, abilities to process and regulate emotions (including autonomic arousal), capacities to cope with stress and perceived provocation, perinatal factors, and genetic and epigenetic factors (e.g., Provençal et al., 2015). Although many of these variables have been widely studied, few have been examined in conjunction with neuropsychological function.

Furthermore, whereas neuroscience research up to the first decade of this century focused primarily on how cognitive deficits are linked to alterations in the function or structure of one or more single brain areas, cognitive theories have increasingly attempted to explain antisocial behavior-associated cognitive deficits as an alteration within a larger neural dynamic network. Greater application of advanced brain-imaging methodologies such as dynamic functional connectivity and multimodal imaging would help us in understanding the complex dynamic interplay between brain regions; for example, in how an alteration in one region could impact the function of others, and its possible consequences for violence. Neuropsychological function almost certainly comprises one element of an exceedingly complex model of violent behavior. As this chapter illustrates, however, it may provide one essential piece of a still-unsolved puzzle.

References

Achenbach, T. M., Edelbrock, C. S., & Howell, C. T. (1987). Empirically based assessment of the behavioral/emotional problems of 2- and 3- year-old children. *Journal of Abnormal Child Psychology*, 15, 629–650.

American Psychiatric Association. (2013). *Diagnostic and statistical manual of mental disorders – Fifth Edition*. Arlington, VA: American Psychiatric Press.

Barker, E. D., Séguin, J. R., White, H. R., Bates, M. E., Lacourse, É., Carbonneau, R., et al. (2007). Developmental trajectories of physical violence and theft: Relation to neurocognitive performance. *Archives of General Psychiatry*, 64, 592–599.

Barker, E. D., Tremblay, R. E., van Lier, P. A. C., Vitaro, F., Nagin, D. S., Assaad, J. M., et al. (2011). The neurocognition of conduct disorder behaviors: Specificity to physical aggression and theft after controlling for ADHD symptoms. *Aggressive Behavior*, 37, 63–72.

Best, M., Williams, J. M., & Coccaro, E. F. (2002). Evidence for a dysfunctional prefrontal circuit in patients with an impulsive aggressive disorder. *Proceedings of the National Academy of Sciences*, 99, 8448–8453.

Blair, R. J. R., Leibenluft, E., & Pine, D. S. (2014). Conduct disorder and callous-unemotional traits in youth. *New England Journal of Medicine*, 371(23), 2207–2216.

Blake, P. Y., Pincus, J. H., & Buckner, C. (1995). Neurologic abnormalities in murderers. *Neurology*, 45, 1641–1647.

Booij, L., Tremblay, R. E., Leyton, M., Séguin, J. R., Vitaro, F., Gravel, P., et al. (2010). Brain serotonin synthesis in adult males characterized by physical aggression during childhood: A 21-year longitudinal study. *PLoS ONE*, 5, e11255.

Burt, S. A. (2009). Are there meaningful etiological differences within antisocial behavior? Results of a meta-analysis. *Clinical Psychology Review*, 29, 163–178.

Burt, S. A. (2013). Do etiological influences on aggression overlap with those on rule breaking? A meta-analysis. *Psychological Medicine*, 43(9), 1801–1812.

Cardenas, S. A., Kassem, L., Brotman, M. A., Leibenluft, E., & McMahon, F. J. (2016). Neurocognitive functioning in euthymic patients with bipolar disorder and unaffected relatives: A review of the literature. *Neuroscience and Biobehavioral Reviews*, 69, 193–215.

Castellanos, F. X., Sonuga-Barke, E. J. S., Milham, M. P., & Tannock, R. (2006). Characterizing cognition in ADHD: Beyond executive dysfunction. *Trends in Cognitive Sciences*, 10, 117–123.

Castellanos-Ryan, N., Pingault, J. B., Parent, S., Vitaro, F., Tremblay, R. E., & Séguin, J. R. (2017). Adolescent cannabis use, change in neurocognitive function, and high-school graduation: A longitudinal study from early adolescence to young adulthood. *Development and Psychopathology*, 29(4), 1253–1266.

Castellanos-Ryan, N., Brière, F. N., O'Leary-Barrett, M., Banaschewski, T., Bokde, A., Bromberg, U., et al. (2016). The structure of psychopathology in adolescence and its common personality and cognitive correlates. *Journal of Abnormal Psychology*, 125 (8), 1039–1052.

Clifford, A., Lang, L. D., & Chen, R. L. (2012). Effects of maternal cigarette smoking during pregnancy on cognitive parameters of children and young adults: A literature review. *Neurotoxicology and Teratology*, 34(6), 560–570.

Coccaro, E. F. (2012). Intermittent explosive disorder as a disorder of impulsive aggression for DSM-5. *American Journal of Psychiatry*, 169(6), 577–588.

Cohen, J. (1992). A power primer. *Psychological Bulletin*, 112, 155–159.

Cope, L. M., Ermer, E., Gaudet, L. M., Steele, V. R., Eckhardt, A. L., Arbabshirani, M. R., et al. (2014). Abnormal brain structure in youth who commit homicide. *Neuroimage-Clinical*, 4, 800–807.

Cristofori, I., Zhong, W. T., Mandoske, V., Chau, A., Krueger, F., Strenziok, M., et al. (2016). Brain regions influencing implicit violent attitudes: A lesion-mapping study. *Journal of Neuroscience*, 36(9), 2757–2768.

D'Onofrio, B. M., Van Hulle, C. A., Goodnight, J. A., Rathouz, P. J., & Lahey, B. B. (2012). Is maternal smoking during pregnancy a causal environmental risk factor for adolescent antisocial behavior? Testing etiological theories and assumptions. *Psychological Medicine*, 42(7), 1535–1545.

Damasio, A. R. (2000). A neural basis for sociopathy. *Archives of General Psychiatry*, 57, 128–129.

Davidson, R. J., Putnam, K. M., & Larson, C. L. (2000). Dysfunction in the neural circuitry of emotion regulation: A possible prelude to violence. *Science*, 289, 591–594.

De Brito, S. A., Viding, E., Kumari, V., Blackwood, N., & Hodgins, S. (2013). Cool and hot executive function impairments in violent offenders with antisocial personality disorder with and without psychopathy. *PLoS ONE*, 8(6), e65566.

Diamond, A. (2013). Executive functions. *Annual Review of Psychology*, 64, 135–168.

Fairchild, G., Passamonti, L., Hurford, G., Hagan, C. C., von dem Hagen, E. A. H., van Goozen, S. H. M., et al. (2011). Brain structure abnormalities in early-onset and adolescent-onset conduct disorder. *American Journal of Psychiatry*, 168 (6), 624–633.

Fairchild, G., van Goozen, S. H. M., Stollery, S. J., Aitken, M. R. F., Savage, J., Moore, S. C., et al. (2009). Decision making and executive function in male adolescents with early-onset or adolescence-onset Conduct Disorder and control subjects. *Biological Psychiatry*, 66(2), 162–168.

Fazel, S., Gulati, G., Linsell, L., Geddes, J. R., & Grann, M. (2009). Schizophrenia and violence: Systematic review and meta-analysis. *Plos Medicine*, 6(8), e1000120.

Fazel, S., Philipson, J., Gardiner, L., Merritt, R., & Grann, M. (2009). Neurological disorders and violence: A systematic review and meta-analysis with a focus on epilepsy and traumatic brain injury. *Journal of Neurology*, 256(10), 1591–1602.

Fazel, S., Lichtenstein, P., Grann, M., Goodwin, G. M., & Langstrom, N. (2010). Bipolar disorder and violent crime: New evidence from population-based longitudinal studies and systematic review. *Archives of General Psychiatry*, 67, 931–938.

Frick, P. J., Ray, J. V., Thornton, L. C., & Kahn, R. E. (2014). Can callous-unemotional traits enhance the understanding, diagnosis, and treatment of serious conduct problems in children and adolescents? A comprehensive review. *Psychological Bulletin*, 140(1), 1–57.

Giancola, P. R. (2004). Executive functioning and alcohol-related aggression. *Journal of Abnormal Psychology*, 113, 541–555.

Goldstein, L. H. & McNeil, J. E. (2012). *Clinical neuropsychology: A practical guide to assessment and management for clinicians* (2nd ed.). Hoboken, NJ: Wiley-Blackwell.

Gorenstein, E. E. & Newman, J. P. (1980). Disinhibitory psychopathology: A new perspective and a model for research. *Psychological Review*, 87, 301–315.

Hamilton, R. K. B., Racer, K. H., & Newman, J. P. (2015). Impaired integration in psychopathy: a unified theory of psychopathic dysfunction. *Psychological Review*, 122(4), 770–791.

Hancock, M., Tapscott, J. L., & Hoaken, P. N. S. (2010). Role of executive dysfunction in predicting frequency and severity of violence. *Aggressive Behavior*, 36(5), 338–349.

Hanlon, R. E., Brook, M., Stratton, J., Jensen, M., & Rubin, L. H. (2013). Neuropsychological and intellectual differences between types of murderers: Affective/impulsive versus predatory/instrumental (premeditated) homicide. *Criminal Justice And Behavior*, 40(8), 933–948.

Hare, R. D. (1999). Psychopathy as a risk factor for violence. *Psychiatric Quarterly*, 70, 181–197.

Heinz, A. J., Beck, A., Meyer-Lindenberg, A., Sterzer, P., & Heinz, A. (2011). Cognitive and neurobiological mechanisms of alcohol-related aggression. *Nature Reviews Neuroscience*, 12(7), 400–413.

Ishikawa, S. S., Raine, A., Lencz, T., Bihrle, S., & LaCasse, L. (2001). Autonomic stress reactivity and executive function in successful and unsuccessful criminal psychopaths from the community. *Journal of Abnormal Psychology*, 110, 423–432.

Jiang, Y., Guo, X., Zhang, J., Gao, J., Wang, X., Situ, W., et al. (2015). Abnormalities of cortical structures in adolescent-onset conduct disorder. *Psychological Medicine*, 45(16), 3467–3479.

Johnson, V. A., Kemp, A. H., Heard, R., Lennings, C. J., & Hickie, I. B. (2015). Childhood- versus adolescent-onset antisocial youth with conduct disorder: Psychiatric illness, neuropsychological and psychosocial function. *PLoS ONE*, 10(4).

Jonker, F. A., Jonker, C., Scheltens, P., & Scherder, E. J. A. (2015). The role of the orbitofrontal cortex in cognition and behavior. *Reviews in the Neurosciences*, 26(1), 1–11.

Joyal, C. C., Beaulieu-Plante, J., & de Chantérac, A. (2014). The neuropsychology of sex offenders. *Sexual Abuse*, 26(2), 149–177.

Klaming, L. & Koops, B. J. (2012). Neuroscientific evidence and criminal responsibility in the Netherlands. In T. M. Spranger (Ed.), *International neurolaw: A comparative analysis* (pp. 227–256). Heidelberg: Springer.

Koenigs, M., Kruepke, M., & Newman, J. P. (2010). Economic decision-making in psychopathy: A comparison with ventromedial prefrontal lesion patients. *Neuropsychologia*, 48(7), 2198–2204.

Lee, R., Arfanakis, K., Evia, A. M., Fanning, J., Keedy, S., & Coccaro, E. F. (2016). White matter integrity reductions in intermittent explosive disorder. *Neuropsychopharmacology*, 41(11), 2697–2703.

Lezak, M. D., Howieson, D. B., Bigler, E. D., & Tranel, D. T. (2012). *Neuropsychological assessment*. New York: Oxford University Press.

Lilienfeld, S. O., Smith, S. F., & Watts, A. L. (2016). The perils of unitary models of the etiology of mental disorders-the response modulation hypothesis of psychopathy as a case example: Rejoinder to Newman and Baskin-Sommers (2016) reply. *Psychological Bulletin*, 142(12), 1394–1403.

Lydon, D. M., Wilson, S. J., Child, A., & Geier, C. F. (2014). Adolescent brain maturation and smoking: What we know and where we're headed. *Neuroscience and Biobehavioral Reviews*, 45, 323–342.

Mayes, S. D., Waxmonsky, J. D., Calhoun, S. L., & Bixler, E. O. (2016). Disruptive mood dysregulation disorder symptoms and association with oppositional defiant and other disorders in a general population child sample. *Journal of Child and Adolescent Psychopharmacology*, 26(2), 101–106.

Meyers, C. A., Berman, S. A., Scheibel, R. S., & Hayman, A. (1992). Case report: Acquired antisocial personality disorder associated with unilateral left orbital frontal lobe damage. *Journal of Psychiatry and Neuroscience*, 17, 121–125.

Milner, B., Petrides, M., & Smith, M. L. (1985). Frontal lobes and the temporal organization of memory. *Human Neurobiology*, 4, 137–142.

Moeller, F. G., Barratt, E. S., Dougherty, D. M., Schmitz, J. M., & Swann, A. C. (2001). Psychiatric aspects of impulsivity. *American Journal of Psychiatry*, 158, 1783–1793.

Moffitt, T. E. (1990). The neuropsychology of juvenile delinquency: A critical review. In M. Tonry & N. Morris (Eds), *Crime and justice: A review of research* (12th ed., pp. 99–169). Chicago: University of Chicago Press.

Moffitt, T. E. (1993). Adolescence-limited and life-course-persistent antisocial behavior: A developmental taxonomy. *Psychological Review*, 100, 674–701.

Morais, H. B., Joyal, C. C., Alexander, A. A., Fix, R. L., & Burkhart, B. R. (2016). The Neuropsychology of adolescent sexual offending: Testing an executive dysfunction hypothesis. *Sexual Abuse-A Journal of Research and Treatment*, 28(6), 741–754.

Morgan, A. B. & Lilienfeld, S. O. (2000). A meta-analytic review of the relation between antisocial behavior and neuropsychological measures of executive function. *Clinical Psychology Review*, 20(1), 113–136.

Murdoch, D. D., Pihl, R. O., & Ross, D. F. (1990). Alcohol and crimes of violence: Present issues. *The International Journal of the Addictions*, 25, 1065–1081.

Newman, J. P. & Lorenz, A. R. (2003). Response modulation and emotion processing: Implications for psychopathy and other dysregulatory psychopathology. In R. J. Davidson, K. Scherer, & H. H. Goldsmith (Eds), *Handbook of affective sciences* (pp. 904–929). New York: Oxford University Press.

Ogilvie, J. M., Stewart, A. L., Chan, R. C. K., & Shum, D. (2011). Neuropsychological measures of executive function and antisocial behavior: A meta-analysis. *Criminology*, 49, 1063–1107.

Pihl, R. O., Paylan, S. S., Gentes-Hawn, A., & Hoaken, P. N. S. (2004). Alcohol affects executive cognitive functioning differentially on the ascending versus descending limb of the blood alcohol concentration Curve. *Alcoholism: Clinical and Experimental Research*, 27, 773–779.

Pinsonneault, M., Parent, S., Castellanos-Ryan, N., & Séguin, J. R. (2015). Low intelligence and poor executive function as risk factors for externalizing spectrum disorders. In T. P. Beauchaine & S. P. Hinshaw (Eds), *The oxford handbook of externalizing spectrum disorders.* (pp. 375–400). New York: Oxford University Press.

Provençal, N., Booij, L., & Tremblay, R. E. (2015). The developmental origins of chronic physical aggression: Biological pathways triggered by early life adversity. *Journal of Experimental Biology*, 218(1), 123–133.

Raine, A., Meloy, J. R., Bihrle, S., Stoddard, J., LaCasse, L., & Buchsbaum, M. S. (1998). Reduced prefrontal and increased subcortical brain functioning assessed using positron emission tomography in predatory and affective murderers. *Behavioral Sciences & the Law*, 16(3), 319–332.

Rogers, J. C. & De Brito, S. A. (2016). Cortical and subcortical gray matter volume in youths with conduct problems: A meta-analysis. *JAMA Psychiatry*, 73(1), 64–72.

Room, R., Babor, T., & Rehm, J. (2005). Alcohol and public health. *The Lancet*, 365, 519–530.

Satel, S. & Lilienfeld, S. O. (2013). *Brainwashed: The seductive appeal of mindless neuroscience*. New York: Basic books.

Schug, R. A. & Raine, A. (2009). Comparative meta-analyses of neuropsychological functioning in antisocial schizophrenic persons. *Clinical Psychology Review*, 29, 230–242.

Séguin, J. R., Arseneault, L., Boulerice, B., Harden, P. W., & Tremblay, R. E. (2002). Response perseveration in adolescent boys with stable and unstable histories of physical aggression: The role of underlying processes. *Journal of Child Psychology and Psychiatry*, 43, 481–494.

Séguin, J. R., Arseneault, L., & Tremblay, R. E. (2007). The contribution of "Cool" and "Hot" components of executive function to problem solving in adolescence: Implications for developmental psychopathology. *Cognitive Development*, 22, 530–543.

Séguin, J. R., Boulerice, B., Harden, P., Tremblay, R. E., & Pihl, R. O. (1999). Executive functions and physical aggression after controlling for attention deficit hyperactivity disorder, general memory, and IQ. *Journal of Child Psychology and Psychiatry*, 40, 1197–1208.

Séguin, J. R., Nagin, D. S., Assaad, J. M., & Tremblay, R. E. (2004). Cognitive-neuropsychological function in chronic physical aggression and hyperactivity. *Journal of Abnormal Psychology*, 113, 603–613.

Séguin, J. R., Parent, S., Tremblay, R. E., & Zelazo, P. D. (2009). Different neurocognitive functions regulate physical aggression and hyperactivity in early childhood. *Journal of Child Psychology and Psychiatry*, 50, 679–687.

Séguin, J. R., Pihl, R. O., Harden, P. W., Tremblay, R. E., & Boulerice, B. (1995). Cognitive and neuropsychological characteristics of physically aggressive boys. *Journal of Abnormal Psychology*, 104, 614–624.

Séguin, J. R. & Pilon, M. (2013). Integration of neuropsychological assessment and clinical intervention for youth with conduct and oppositional defiant disorders. In L. A. Reddy, J. B. Hale, & A. S. Weissman (Eds), *Neuropsychological assessment and intervention for emotional and behavior disordered youth: An integrated step-by-step evidence-based approach* (pp. 177–199). Washington, DC: American Psychological Association.

Séguin, J. R., Sylvers, P., & Lilienfeld, S. O. (2007). The neuropsychology of violence. In I. D. Waldman, D. J. Flannery, & A. T. Vazsonyi (Eds), *The Cambridge handbook of violent behavior and aggression* (pp. 187–214). New York: Cambridge University Press.

Séguin, J. R. & Tremblay, R. E. (2013). Aggression and anti-social behavior: A developmental perspective. In P. D. Zelazo (Ed.), *Oxford handbook of developmental psychology, Vol. 2: Self and other* (pp. 507–526). Oxford Library of Psychology. New York: Oxford University Press.

Siever, L. J. (2008). Neurobiology of aggression and violence. *American Journal of Psychiatry*, 165, 429–442.

Smith, S. F. & Lilienfeld, S. O. (2015). The response modulation hypothesis of psychopathy: A meta-analytic and narrative analysis. *Psychological Bulletin*, 141 (6), 1145–1177.

Smith, S. S., Arnett, P. A., & Newman, J. P. (1992). Neuropsychological differentiation of psychopathic and nonpsychopathic criminal offenders. *Personality and Individual Differences*, 13, 1233–1243.

Sonuga-Barke, E. J. S., Cortese, S., Fairchild, G., & Stringaris, A. (2016). Annual research review: Transdiagnostic neuroscience of child and adolescent mental disorders – differentiating decision making in attention-deficit/hyperactivity disorder, conduct disorder, depression, and anxiety. *Journal of Child Psychology and Psychiatry*, 57(3), 321–349.

Steinberg, L. (2013, print). The influence of neuroscience on US Supreme Court decisions about adolescents' criminal culpability. *Nature Reviews Neuroscience*, 14(7), 513–518.

Stuss, D. T. (2011). Functions of the frontal lobes: Relation to executive functions. *Journal of the International Neuropsychological Society*, 17, 759–765.

Taylor, J., Iacono, W. G., & McGue, M. (2000). Evidence for a genetic etiology of early-onset delinquency. *Journal of Abnormal Psychology*, 109, 634–643.

Verbruggen, F. (2016). Executive control of actions across time and space. *Current Directions in Psychological Science*, 25(6), 399–404.

Walsh, A. (1987). Cognitive functioning and delinquency: Property versus violent offenses. *International Journal Of Offender Therapy And Comparative Criminology*, 31, 285–289.

Wang, D. S., Szyf, M., Benkelfat, C., Provençal, N., Turecki, G., Caramaschi, D., et al. (2012). Peripheral SLC6A4 DNA methylation is associated with in vivo measures of human brain serotonin synthesis and childhood physical aggression. *PLoS ONE*, 7, e39501.

Welsh, M. & Peterson, E. (2014). Issues in the conceptualization and assessment of hot executive functions in childhood. *Journal of the International Neuropsychological Society*, 20(2), 152–156.

White, H. R., Bates, M. E., & Buyske, S. (2001). Adolescence-limited versus persistent delinquency: Extending Moffitt's hypothesis into adulthood. *Journal of Abnormal Psychology*, 110, 600–609.

Witt, K., van Dorn, R., & Fazel, S. (2013). Risk factors for violence in psychosis: Systematic review and meta-regression analysis of 110 studies. *PLoS ONE*, 8(2), e55942.

World Health Organization (WHO) (1992). *International statistical classification of diseases and related health problems, Tenth Revision.* Geneva: retrieved from http://apps.who.int/classifications/apps/icd/icd10online/.

Zeier, J. D., Maxwell, J. S., & Newman, J. P. (2009). Attention moderates the processing of inhibitory information in primary psychopathy. *Journal of Abnormal Psychology*, 118(3), 554–563.

9 The Interaction of Nature and Nurture in Antisocial Behavior

Matt DeLisi

Introduction

After decades of rigid adherence to nature *or* nurture perspectives on human behavior, both conventional and antisocial, the contemporary scene is one where the interaction of nature *and* nurture is assumed and increasingly the object of scientific inquiry (DeLisi & Vaughn, 2015; Rutter, 1997; Moffitt, 2005). One consequence of this newer paradigm is the blending of constructs where the relative effects of biological and social phenomena have been shown to be dynamic, fluid, and interactive. A recent study is illustrative of this trend. Using data from 1,037 birth cohort participants in the Dunedin (New Zealand) Multidisciplinary Health and Development Study, Israel et al. (2014) examined how human capital as measured by one's credit score is associated with cardiovascular health, socioeconomic achievement, and self-control. Their findings were fascinating. Cognitive ability, self-control, and educational attainment were positively predictive of credit score and negatively predictive of cardiovascular disease, and these human capital factors accounted for nearly half of the correlation between credit score and cardiovascular disease. Although all cohort members were 38 years old at the time of the study, their heart age varied tremendously. The mean heart age was 38.5 years, which is roughly equivalent to their chronological age, but the variance in heart age was 22 to 85 years. In addition, a 100-point increase in credit score (which ranged from 12 to 961 and had a mean of 675.2) was associated with a 13-month difference in heart age. The differences in heart age, heart health, wealth, and self-control among participants were evident in the first years of life. Childhood human capital competencies in the first decade accounted for 22% of the link between credit score and cardiovascular disease at midlife.

In a related study using the same data, strong associations were found between childhood self-control and lifelong problem behaviors. For instance, about 45% of those with low childhood self-control had an adult criminal conviction. Among those with high childhood self-control, approximately 10% had an adult criminal conviction (Moffitt et al., 2011) – a nearly fivefold difference. Those with lower self-control during childhood also had worse physical health, greater depression, higher likelihood of drug dependence, lower socioeconomic status, lower income, greater likelihood of single-parenthood, worse financial planning, and more financial struggles at midlife.

Self-control is clearly implicated in a variety of biologically related outcomes (e.g., cardiovascular disease, heart health, mental health, and physical health) and environmentally related outcomes (e.g., socioeconomic achievement, credit score, family relationships, and crime) to such a degree that self-control – as a powerful engine of antisocial behavior – itself seems a blend of biological and social factors. It is. In their influential general theory of crime, Gottfredson and Hirschi (1990) theorized that inadequate parenting practices (e.g., weak bonds to one's child, low monitoring of a child's activity, low oversight of a child's activities and peers, inconsistent and/or low response to child deviance, inconsistent punishment, and others) failed to inculcate self-control (or, put another way, produced low self-control), which was characterized by low gratification delay, low tenacity, risk taking, self-centeredness, and a poor temper. These traits are associated with a broad swath of imprudent and antisocial behaviors including delinquency, crime, and violence. A large literature has supported the proposed theoretical links between parenting deficits, low self-control, and antisocial conduct (Botchkovar, Marshall, Rocque, & Posick, 2015; Finkenauer, Engels, & Baumeister, 2005; Vazsonyi & Huang, 2010; Vazsonyi, Jiskrova, Ksinan, & Blatný, 2016; Vazsonyi, Mikuška, & Kelley, 2017; Vazsonyi, Roberts, & Huang, 2015) such that better parenting correlates with better child self-control and worse parenting correlates with child behavioral problems.

However, studies using biosocial designs have also shown that socialization is far from the only source of self-control. Using data from the Early Childhood Longitudinal Study, Kindergarten Class of 1998–1999 (ECLS-K), Wright and Beaver (2005) conducted two sets of analyses: first, where the genetic relatedness of respondents was not considered, and thus parental socialization was the focus, and second, those where genetic relatedness was controlled. In seven of the eight models where the outcome variable was child self-control in kindergarten or first grade, the number of significant parenting parameters declined. In seven of the models, the number of statistically significant parenting parameters decreased from three to either one or zero. Overall, their study demonstrated that parenting effects become much weaker, and even insignificant, once genetic factors were considered (Beaver, Connolly, Schwartz, Al-Ghamdi, & Kobeisy, 2013; Beaver, Wright, & DeLisi, 2007; Boisvert, Wright, Knopik, & Vaske, 2012; Hay & Meldrum, 2015). Similarly, Wright, Beaver, DeLisi, and Vaughn (2008) found that parenting factors accounted for negligible variance in self-control – sometimes just 0–1% – and that genetic factors and nonshared environmental factors (those that make siblings different) accounted for the remaining variance.

In other words, forces of nature and nurture create deficits in self-control that facilitate criminal conduct across life. The current chapter highlights the interaction of nature and nurture in the etiology, maintenance, and reduction of antisocial behavior. Although self-control is a prominent area of biosocial inquiry, it is just one of many exciting and vibrant areas of the social sciences that reveal the sublime intricacy of criminal conduct.

Mechanisms of Nature–Nurture Interaction and Antisocial Behavior

Nature and nurture interact in a variety of ways or mechanisms to increase the likelihood of specific behavioral outcomes.

In some cases, the forces of nurture are so noxious or constitute such an environmental pathogen that the biological functioning of an individual is altered to tremendous extent. The textbook example of this is Phineas Gage, who, in 1848, was injured in a railroad accident when a tamping iron blasted through his face and exited his head. Despite losing consciousness and suffering heavy bleeding, Gage miraculously not only survived the blast, but appeared to recover quickly. Unfortunately, the accident caused a dramatic personality transformation of Gage from a hard-working, responsible, intelligent, prudent, and socially well-adjusted person to an irreverent, impulsive, capricious, rowdy, irresponsible person whose life devolved into that of a drifter. As a result of the accident, Gage morphed from a conventionally behaved, upstanding citizen to deviant. Subsequent research of Gage's skull revealed that his injuries were consistent with persons with similar injuries who display similar impairments in rational decision making, self-control, and emotional processing (Damasio, Grabowski, Frank, Galaburda, & Damasio, 1994; Van Horn et al., 2012).

Although the Gage example is dramatic, the broader effect of a traumatic brain injury on behavioral functioning reveals how environmental trauma can damage the brain and subsequently increase conduct problems. Behnken, DeLisi, Trulson, and Vaughn (2015) compared 132 serious delinquents who had lost consciousness due to a head injury to 588 delinquents who had not. The differences were striking. Those with prior head injury had significantly worse delinquent careers, had lower self-control, were more psychopathic, and had greater likelihood of ADHD. In addition, head injury was a significant predictor of career criminality and withstood controls for neurological medical condition, self-control, ADHD, psychopathy, age, sex, and race. Their findings were not unique; meta-analytic studies indicate that traumatic brain injury is several times more prevalent in antisocial or juvenile justice system-involved samples than the general population (Farrer, Frost, & Hedges, 2012, 2013; Farrer & Hedges, 2011; Shiroma, Ferguson, & Pickelsimer, 2010).

Why are head injuries so deleterious? One answer is that neuropsychological functioning is commonly reduced after sustaining a head trauma, particularly when there is also a loss of consciousness. Neuropsychological deficits figure prominently in general conceptual models of antisocial behavior (e.g., DeLisi & Vaughn, 2014; Moffitt, 1993) and numerous studies have shown that the most severe, pathological offenders tend to have the most neuropsychological deficits. In a study of serious offenders in the Pittsburgh Youth Study, Raine et al. (2005) found that males on the life-course-persistent pathway had significantly greater neuropsychological deficits compared to behaviorally less severe comparison groups. Specifically, life-course-persistent offenders scored significantly worse on four measures of intelligence, two measures of spatial memory, and one measure of executive functioning. The life-course-persistent group also had a higher prevalence of ADHD diagnosis, higher child abuse victimization, higher child neglect victimization, more extreme family poverty, and had a greater number of head injuries that resulted in unconsciousness.

In a latent class analysis of data from the Early Childhood Longitudinal Survey-Kindergarten Class, Vaughn, DeLisi, Beaver, and Wright (2009) found that 9.3% of kindergarteners comprised a severe impairment group characterized by deficits in verbal skills and attendant problems with higher impulsivity, higher externalizing behaviors, reduced self-regulation, reduced cognitive abilities, and greater classroom difficulties. Drawing on data from the Early Childhood Longitudinal Study: Birth Chort (ECLS-B), Jackson and Newsome (2016) recently found that infant neuropsychological deficits predicted antisocial behavior among males; however, the effects were only found for those who also had neonatal health risks. In short, injuries to the brain have the potential to reduce neuropsychological functioning and increase behavioral pathology.

Another source of environmental trauma occurs prenatally in the case of drugs, toxins, substances, or other teratogens that damage the developing embryo (for a review, see Graham, Glass, & Mattson, 2016). Unfortunately, these teratogens are readily present in the environment. In a landmark study, Wright et al. (2008) illustrated the effects of prenatal lead exposure by taking multiple measures of child lead concentrations among 250 persons recruited at birth between 1979 and 1984. The participants lived in impoverished neighborhoods in Cincinnati, characterized by a high concentration of older, lead-contaminated buildings. Those individuals with higher levels of lead in their blood as children were significantly more likely to be arrested and to be arrested for violent crimes later in life. Lead not only increased the incidence and severity of criminal behavior, but also psychopathic personality traits. Using data from the Cincinnati Lead Study, Wright, Boisvert, and Vaske (2009) reported a significant association between blood lead concentrations at age 78 months or age 6.5 years and *adult* psychopathic personality features. These effects persisted despite controls for gender, race, mother's IQ, child's intellectual achievement, and quality of the home environment (an essential nurture variable).

Prenatal exposure to firsthand and secondhand cigarette smoke is another example of an environmental context that disrupts biological development and contributes to behavioral problems. In a recent study using data from the US Study of Early Child Care and Youth Development, Meldrum and Barnes (2016) found that prenatal exposure to secondhand smoke was negatively associated with self-control from ages 54 months to 15 years. Moreover, the enduring damaging effects of this prenatal exposure withstood confounding effects including maternal self-control, maternal intelligence, maternal education, and maternal depression symptoms. Prenatal smoke exposure has also been linked to psychopathic personality traits (Beaver, DeLisi, & Vaughn, 2010), to neuropsychological deficits (Beaver, Vaughn, DeLisi, & Higgins, 2010) to Conduct Disorder and related externalizing behaviors (Wakschlag, Pickett, Cook, Benowitz, & Leventhal, 2002; Wakschlag, Leventhal, Pine, Pickett, & Carter, 2006), and to the emergence of the criminal career (Gibson, Piquero, & Tibbetts, 2000).

A general rule is that individuals who have a biological (or genetic) risk for some outcome (or phenotype) are more likely than individuals without the biological risk factor to present with the particular phenotype. In similar fashion, individuals who have exposure to an environmental risk factor for a phenotype are more likely to display a phenotype than individuals who do not have the exposure to the environmental risk factor. It is also true that individuals with biological or genetic risks for a specific phenotype are more sensitive to the stressors of environmental risk factors – this is known as the diathesis-stress model.

In recent years, researchers have shown that individuals with putative biological risk factors can surmount their biological/genetic risks when exposed to positive and nurturing environments. In other words, biological factors and environmental factors exist on a continuum ranging from negative to positive and, depending on the type of interaction, differential behavioral outcomes can ensue. This more dynamic conceptualization is known as the differential susceptibility model (Belsky, Bakermans-Kranenburg, & van IJzendoorn, 2007; Belsky & Pluess, 2009, 2013; Pluess & Belsky, 2011). In this model, biological/genetic risk factors are referred to as plasticity genes because their effects are variable depending on their environmental context.

Psychology and behavioral genetics have provided additional concepts that are critical for understanding the nature and nurture interplay that produces behavior. One is gene–environment correlation, where the influences of genes and environments are inextricably linked (Plomin, DeFries, & Loehlin, 1977; Rutter et al., 1997; Scarr & McCartney, 1983). There are three types of gene–environment correlations, commonly abbreviated as rGE. Passive gene–environment correlations (passive rGEs) reveal that children receive both their genes (half from each parent) and their early-life environments from their parents. Since children resemble their parents in terms of their antisocial traits and behaviors, it is difficult to ascertain whether genetic risk factors explain a youth's delinquency, whether the antisocial household environment is responsible, or some mixture of the two. The way to resolve this is to use an adoption study where the parents are not biologically related to the child and thus environmental effects can be accessed without being correlated to the child's genes.

Evocative gene–environment correlations (evocative rGEs) indicate that people differentially elicit responses from the environment based upon their temperament and personality traits that are themselves heritable, or of a genetic etiology. Evocative gene–environment correlations explain why antisocial or aggressive children elicit or evoke negative and punitive reactions from care-givers just as obedient and good-natured children evoke positive and nurturing reactions from care-givers. In families with multiple children, the child who has the most disagreeable traits and the worst self-regulation is usually targeted by his parents for more severe discipline and other negative parenting behaviors. This likely is due to genetic factors that evoke the negative responses. Active gene–environment correlations are where individuals self-select environments, peers, and situations that are compatible with their own personality, temperament, and behaviors, all of which are heritable.

Active gene–environment correlations (active rGEs) are sometimes referred to as niche-picking because of the tendency for people to gravitate to others like themselves and to gravitate toward situations that are congruent with their interests. Consider the case of delinquent or antisocial peers. Highly prosocial youth are unlikely to have antisocial peers because their attitudes, beliefs, and behaviors conflict. What is acceptable or "cool" to a delinquent youth is anathema to what is acceptable or "cool" to conventional youth. Moreover, they seem like fundamentally different people and the awkwardness that antisocial and prosocial youth would hold toward one another is largely mutual. However, the dynamics of peer relations are not simply the outcome of environmental or social factors; genetic factors also play an important role. For instance, nearly two-thirds of the variance in delinquent peer association has been shown to be accounted for by genetic factors (Cleveland, Wiebe, & Rowe, 2005) and criminologists have shown that the dopamine transporter gene (DAT1) and brain-derive neurotropic factor (BDNF) are two of the genes implicated in delinquent peer association (Beaver, Wright, & DeLisi, 2008; Kretschmer, Vitaro, & Barker, 2014). These examples illustrate the interplay of active rGEs.

Another concept that reveals nature–nurture interaction is gene x environment (G x E, sometimes referred to as molecular genetic association, or candidate gene x environment, or cG x E) studies, where measured genes and measured environmental conditions are included in the same statistical models. Gene x environment studies are among the most scientifically exciting studies because they provide estimates of the ways that nature and nurture interact to produce or insulate from antisocial behavior. Due to space constraints, this review of gene–environment studies does not purport to be exhaustive. Readers are encouraged to read a meta-analysis of the serotonin transporter gene and antisocial conduct (Tielbeek et al., 2016), a meta-analysis of the dopamine receptor D4 gene and externalizing behavior (Pappa, Mileva-Seitz, Bakermans-Kranenburg, Tiemeier, & van IJzendoorn, 2015), a chapter on MAOA and antisocial conduct in males (Holland & DeLisi, 2015), a systematic review of genetic association studies of aggression (Fernandez-Castillo & Cormand, 2016; Veroude et al., 2016), and systematic reviews of the effects of MAOA, DRD2, DRD4, DAT1, 5HTTLPR, and COMT and externalizing behaviors (Samek et al., 2016; Weeland, Overbeek, Orobio de Castro, & Matthys, 2015) for greater coverage. Some of these studies are reviewed next.

Gene x Environment Studies of Antisocial Behavior

Environmental Moderators Predicting Antisocial Behavior

Diathesis-stress and differential susceptibility models posit that individuals with biological or genetic risks and with environmental risks are most likely to engage in diverse forms of antisocial conduct. The seminal work by Caspi et al. (2002) was the first criminological G x E study to model genetic and environmental conditions in the creation of antisocial behavior. Using the Dunedin birth cohort data, Caspi and colleagues examined the moderation of childhood maltreatment by variants in the MAOA gene. Among their participants between the ages of 3 and 11, 8% had been severely maltreated, 28% experienced probable maltreatment, and 64% experienced no maltreatment. Dramatic interactive effects were found between low MAOA activity and maltreatment in the prediction of Conduct Disorder, violent convictions, violent disposition, and symptoms of Antisocial Personality Disorder. For example, 80% of youth with MAOA risk (low-activity) alleles and severe maltreatment had Conduct Disorder and 30% were convicted of a violent crime. Comparatively, among those at genetic risk with no maltreatment, 20% had Conduct Disorder and 5% were convicted of a violent crime. About 85% of males with both genetic and environmental risk factors displayed some form of antisocial behavior.

Several independent research teams using their own genetically sensitive data largely replicated the MAOA-maltreatment-crime sequela (Byrd & Manuck, 2014; Choe, Shaw, Hyde, & Forbes, 2014; Taylor & Kim-Cohen, 2007; Thibodeau, Cicchetti, & Rogosch, 2015). In a longitudinal study of nearly 400 male participants from the Christchurch (New Zealand) Health and Development Study followed through age 30, Fergusson, Boden, Horwood, Miller, and Kennedy (2011, 2012) linked MAOA and childhood exposure to sexual and physical abuse to hostility, conduct problems, property offending, and violent offending. Relying on data from the Minnesota Twin Family Study, Derringer, Krueger, Irons, and Iacono (2010) found that persons who had experienced childhood sexual assault victimization and had low-activity alleles of MAOA displayed more antisocial behaviors and evinced more symptoms of Conduct Disorder than peers with other MAOA variants. Based on data from the Virginia Twin Study for Adolescent Behavioral Development, Foley, Eaves, Wormley, Silberg, Maes, et al. (2004) demonstrated an MAOA-childhood adversity defined by interparental violence, parental neglect, and inconsistent discipline interaction in the prediction of Conduct Disorder. Among boys with low-activity MAOA alleles with the highest childhood adversity exposure, 100% had Conduct Disorder. Among those at genetic risk with the lowest level of environmental exposure, only about 5% had Conduct Disorder.

Drawing on data from the Environmental Risk (E-Risk) Longitudinal Twin Study, Kim-Cohen et al. (2006) compared the interaction between MAOA genotype, early-life exposure to physical abuse, and various pediatric mental health and behavioral outcomes. On every measure, low-activity MAOA genotype among abused children was associated with significantly worse outcomes, and the effect sizes were large. Children had more mental health problems, more antisocial behaviors, more ADHD symptoms, and more emotional problems.

To date, a variety of environmental conditions have been shown to interact with or moderate genetic factors in producing antisocial conduct. Although the 7R allele of DRD4 is commonly the risk allele of the dopamine receptor D4 gene, other alleles have also been shown to be predictive of conduct problems. Drawing on data from the Tracking Adolescents' Individual Lives Survey from the Netherlands, Kretschmer, Dijkstra, Ormel, Verhulst, and Veenstra (2013) found that those with the 4R allele who had lower social well-being and greater peer victimization were more likely to engage in later delinquency compared to those with the 7R allele. Using data from the Avon Longitudinal Study of Parents and Children, Kretschmer, Vitaro, and Barker (2014) found that carriers of the BDNF Met-Met variant who affiliated with aggressive peers at age 10 were more likely to be aggressively delinquent at age 15 compared to those with the BDNF val-val allele.

In addition to genetic factors predicting antisocial conduct, there is also evidence that genetic factors can significantly increase the likelihood that an individual will experience assorted forms of abuse, neglect, and victimization. Using the Add Health data, Beaver et al. (2007) reported that delinquent peers and DRD2 interacted to increase the criminal victimization among adolescents. Linkages have also been shown between DAT1 polymorphisms and childhood sexual abuse victimization among men and DAT1 and childhood emotional abuse and women (Rehan et al., 2016). In other words, environmental moderation of genetic factors can increase the likelihood of both offending and victimization, often in the same individual.

Environmental Buffers against Antisocial Behavior

A variety of molecular genetic association studies have also modeled ways that genetic variants or polymorphisms interact with environmental conditions to insulate individuals from conduct problems even when the individual has genetic vulnerability. Attachment to parents has been shown to be strongly associated with antisocial development. Kochanska, Philibert, and Barry (2009) examined the polymorphic serotonin transporter gene (5HTTLPR) and its interaction with a child's maternal attachment to study self-regulation among youth at ages 15 months, 25 months, 38 months, and 52 months. Children with short alleles of 5HTTLPR have higher and more unstable levels of synaptic serotonin. Among those who were insecurely attached to their mother, there were self-regulation problems. Among those who were securely attached, there were no self-regulation problems. In their study using data from a Swedish population-based cohort, Tuvblad et al. (2016) found that homozygous Val allele carriers of the COMT gene had lower levels of physical aggression when they were exposed to violence and when they experienced a positive relationship with their parents compared to carriers of the Met allele of COMT. In this case, the parental relationship trumped the noxious effects of violence exposure to reduce aggressive conduct. Using data from the National Longitudinal Study of Adolescent to Adult Health, Roettger, Boardman, Harris, and Guo (2016) reported that the 2R allele of the MAOA gene was directly associated with delinquency. However, those with the 2R allele who had high closeness to their father were less likely to be delinquent (interestingly, no buffer effect was found for those who were close to their mother).

Environmental protective factors are also helpful for understanding sex differences in antisocial conduct vis-à-vis their genetic underpinnings. Drawing on data from adolescents in Russia, Dmitrieva, Chen, Greenberger, Ogunseitan, and Ding (2011) found that males with the 7R allele of DRD4 had greater involvement in delinquency and more antisocial personality features, including short temper and thrill-seeking. Females with genetic risks did not have these behaviors, in part because they had greater parental monitoring and lower exposure to violence. Once parental monitoring and violence exposure were controlled, the sex differences in delinquency were no longer significant.

Other research reveals targets for interventions that can reduce problem behaviors in children who evince genetic risks for antisocial conduct. For instance, Jackson and Beaver (2015) found that meal deprivation was associated with verbal deficits and psychopathic personality traits and poor nutrition quality was linked to verbal deficits among youth in the National Longitudinal Study of Adolescent to Adult Health. Gene–environment interactions between MAOA and measures of food quality were detected. Their findings readily show that interventions that increase the amount and quality of nutrition that children receive can improve their verbal/cognitive ability and render their personality less antisocial. The findings put the simplicity of donating food to a food bank in a new context when one considers the downstream behavioral benefits.

Direct Genetic Effects on Antisocial Behavior

Although nature–nurture interplay is the norm in contemporary studies of antisocial conduct, it is also important to observe that genetic effects often have direct effects on antisocial phenotypes, albeit the effects usually have a small effect size – known as the fourth law of behavior genetics (Chabris, Lee, Cesarini, Benjamin, & Laibson, 2015). There are several examples of these direct effects. Caspi et al. (2008) examined the association between the COMT Val^{158}Met and antisocial behavior among three samples of children with ADHD. The samples included the Cardiff ADHD Genetic Study, which is a sample of 376 white British children selected from child psychiatry and pediatric clinics in England and Wales between 1997 and 2003. The second sample was the Environmental Risk (E-Risk) Study, which is a birth cohort of 2,232 British children drawn from the 1994 to 1995 birth registry in England and Wales, and the third sample was the Dunedin Longitudinal Study described at the outset of this chapter. Caspi and his colleagues (2008) found across the three samples that children with the Valine/Valine (Val/Val) homozygotes had more symptoms of Conduct Disorder, were more aggressive, and were more likely to be convicted of crimes than Methionine carriers (Met/Met or Val/Met). Barkley, Smith, Fischer, and Navia (2006) found that the homozygous DBH Taq1 A2 allele and the dopamine transporter gene (DAT1) were associated with greater hyperactivity during childhood and pervasive behavioral problems during adolescence among respondents from a Milwaukee longitudinal study of hyperactive and normal-activity children.

Myriad direct genetic effects have been shown for other forms of antisocial behavior. These include polymorphisms in the vasopressin 1B receptor gene (AVP1B), aggression, and conduct problems among clinically referred children (Luppino, Moul, Hawes, Brennan, & Dadds, 2014), the rs1465108 polymorphism in the MAOA gene, aggression, and negative urgency (Chester et al., 2015), low-activity alleles of MAOA and violent crime (Stetler et al., 2014), and several serotonergic genes and aggressive behavior (Chen et al., 2015). Finally, most molecular genetic association studies include aggression or other moderately serious forms of antisocial conduct as outcome variables of phenotypes. However, research has also shown direct genetic effects for more extreme forms of antisocial behavior. A study of prisoners in Finland found that low-activity variants of the MAOA gene were associated with being in the 90th percentile on a violent offending distribution, which equates to at least ten convictions for serious criminal violence. The 78 offenders who met this threshold committed 1,154 murders, attempted murders, and aggravated assaults (Tiihonen et al., 2015).

The takeaway point from molecular genetic research is that investigators have come a long way from philosophical debates about the relative merits of nature and nurture to highly sophisticated quantitative estimates of the precise effects of genetic variants, including particular alleles and the environmental contexts in which these genetic vulnerabilities are enflamed into antisocial conduct or suppressed into normative behavior.

Discussion

The nature–nurture interplay in the creation of antisocial conduct is intellectually exciting and scientifically impressive, but what is the practical utility in terms of behavioral interventions and policy? Although the nature–nurture or biosocial vernacular was not originally part of most primary, secondary, and tertiary prevention programs, most have nevertheless included targets that fit well within a nature–nurture understanding of the development of antisocial conduct. Indeed, in their biosocial reinterpretation of cognitive behavioral therapy, Vaske, Galyean, and Cullen (2011, p. 90), observed that programs that target "social skills, coping skills, and problem-solving skills are consistently associated with activation in the medial prefrontal cortex, dorsolateral prefrontal cortex, dorsomedial prefrontal cortex, ventromedial prefrontal cortex, orbitofrontal cortex, cingulate cortex, insula, and temporo-parietal junction." In other words, treatment and correctional interventions that attempt to reduce delinquency and conduct problems might seem like social/environmental endeavors, but they also explicitly target the brain to improve neuropsychological and, hence, behavioral functioning.

This is seen especially in programs that seek to improve executive functioning. The basic logic of targeting neuropsychological deficits relating to self-control is at the core of the Promoting Alternative THinking Strategies (PATHS) Curriculum. Designed for school entry through fifth grade, PATHS is a comprehensive educational program taught three times per week for a minimum of 20 minutes per day. Among its targets are instruction on delaying gratification, controlling impulses, self-talk, self-awareness, reading and interpreting social cues and the needs/perspective of others, verbal skills, nonverbal communication, problem solving, and decision making. Improvements in these target areas contribute to an assortment of positive program outcomes, including improved self-control, reduced conduct problems, reduced anxiety/depression symptoms, and reduced aggression, and PATHS is hailed as a model prevention program (Greenberg, Kusche, & Mihalic, 2006).

Relatedly, Castellanos-Ryan, Séguin, Vitaro, Parent, and Tremblay (2013) conducted a randomized controlled trial for behaviorally disordered kindergarten boys using data from the Montreal Longitudinal and Experimental Study. The two-year intervention targeted social and problem-solving skills among the boys and training on effective child-rearing for their parents. Eight years after the program, boys in the experimental condition had fewer drug-related delinquency problems and a main reason was due to reductions in impulsivity. Other researchers have shown a gene x intervention interaction where variants of the brain-derived neurotrophic factor (BDNF) gene interacted with an impulsivity school-based program to produce reductions in aggression among youth (Musci et al., 2014). Originally used to study antisocial conduct, genetically informed research findings are now being incorporated into prevention programs (Gajos, Fagan, & Beaver, 2016).

To conclude, the notion of nature–nurture interplay has existed for decades in psychiatry, genetics, and psychology and has more recently diffused to criminology, criminal justice, and even sociology. Environmental and biological factors are not independent silos, but instead exert independent, interactive, and reciprocal effects, particularly when the phenotype of interest is antisocial behavior. The last decade or so has witnessed a flurry of studies identifying numerous candidate genes for antisocial behavior. The next steps are replication of these early findings so that behavioral and pharmaceutical interventions can be devised to reduce the incidence and severity of crime.

References

Barkley, R. A., Smith, K. M., Fischer, M., & Navia, B. (2006). An examination of the behavioral and neuropsychological correlates of three ADHD candidate gene polymorphisms (DRD4 7+, DBH Taq1 A2, and DAT1 40 bp VNTR) in hyperactive and normal children followed to adulthood. *American Journal of Medical Genetics B Neuropsychiatric Genetics*, 141, 487–498.

Beaver, K. M., Connolly, E. J., Schwartz, J. A., Al-Ghamdi, M. S., & Kobeisy, A. N. (2013). Genetic and environmental contributions to stability and change in levels of self-control. *Journal of Criminal Justice*, 41(5), 300–308.

Beaver, K. M., DeLisi, M., & Vaughn, M. G. (2010). A biosocial interaction between prenatal exposure to cigarette smoke and family structure in the prediction of psychopathy in adolescence. *Psychiatric Quarterly*, 81(4), 325–334.

Beaver, K. M., Vaughn, M. G., DeLisi, M., & Higgins, G. E. (2010). The biosocial correlates of neuropsychological deficits: Results from the National Longitudinal Study of Adolescent Health. *International Journal of Offender Therapy and Comparative Criminology*, 54(6), 878–894.

Beaver, K. M., Wright, J. P., & DeLisi, M. (2007). Self-control as an executive function: Reformulating Gottfredson and Hirschi's parental socialization thesis. *Criminal Justice and Behavior*, 34(10), 1345–1361.

Beaver, K. M., Wright, J. P., & DeLisi, M. (2008). Delinquent peer group formation: Evidence of a gene X environment correlation. *Journal of Genetic Psychology*, 169(3), 227–244.

Beaver, K. M., Wright, J. P., DeLisi, M., Daigle, L. E., Swatt, M. L., & Gibson, C. L. (2007). Evidence of a gene x environment interaction in the creation of victimization results from a longitudinal sample of adolescents. *International Journal of Offender Therapy and Comparative Criminology*, 51(6), 620–645.

Behnken, M. P., DeLisi, M., Trulson, C. R., & Vaughn, M. G. (2015). The traumatic brain injury association with career criminality withstands powerful confounds. In M. DeLisi & M. G. Vaughn (Eds), *The Routledge International Handbook of Biosocial Criminology* (pp. 418–424). New York: Routledge.

Belsky, J., Bakermans-Kranenburg, M. J., & Van IJzendoorn, M. H. (2007). For better and for worse differential susceptibility to environmental influences. *Current Directions in Psychological Science*, 16(6), 300–304.

Belsky, J. & Pluess, M. (2009). Beyond diathesis stress: differential susceptibility to environmental influences. *Psychological Bulletin*, 135(6), 885–908.

Belsky, J. & Pluess, M. (2013). Beyond risk, resilience, and dysregulation: Phenotypic plasticity and human development. *Development and Psychopathology*, 25(4), 1243–1261.

Boisvert, D., Wright, J. P., Knopik, V., & Vaske, J. (2012). Genetic and environmental overlap between low self-control and delinquency. *Journal of Quantitative Criminology*, 28(3), 477–507.

Botchkovar, E., Marshall, I. H., Rocque, M., & Posick, C. (2015). The importance of parenting in the development of self-control in boys and girls: Results from a multinational study of youth. *Journal of Criminal Justice*, 43(2), 133–141.

Byrd, A. L. & Manuck, S. B. (2014). MAOA, childhood maltreatment, and antisocial behavior: Meta-analysis of a gene-environment interaction. *Biological Psychiatry*, 75(1), 9–17.

Caspi, A., Langley, K., Milne, B., Moffitt, T. E., O'Donovan, M., Owen, M. J., ... & Williams, B. (2008). A replicated molecular genetic basis for subtyping antisocial behavior in children with attention-deficit/hyperactivity disorder. *Archives of General Psychiatry*, 65(2), 203–210.

Caspi, A., McCray, J., Moffitt, T. E., Mill, J., Martin, J., Craig, I. W. ... & Poulton, R. (2002) Role of genotype in the cycle of violence in maltreated children. *Science*, 297(5582), 851–854.

Castellanos-Ryan, N., Séguin, J. R., Vitaro, F., Parent, S., & Tremblay, R. E. (2013). Impact of a 2-year multimodal intervention for disruptive 6-year-olds on substance use in adolescence: Randomised controlled trial. *The British Journal of Psychiatry*, 203(3), 188–195.

Chabris, C. F., Lee, J. J., Cesarini, D., Benjamin, D. J., & Laibson, D. I. (2015). The fourth law of behavior genetics. *Current Directions in Psychological Science*, 24(4), 304–312.

Chen, C., Liu, C., Chen, C., Moyzis, R., Chen, W., & Dong, Q. (2015). Genetic variations in the serotoninergic system and environmental factors contribute to aggressive behavior in Chinese adolescents. *Physiology & Behavior*, 138, 62–68.

Chester, D. S., DeWall, C. N., Derefinko, K. J., Estus, S., Peters, J. R., Lynam, D. R., & Jiang, Y. (2015). Monoamine oxidase A (MAOA) genotype predicts greater aggression through impulsive reactivity to negative affect. *Behavioural Brain Research*, 283, 97–101.

Choe, D. E., Shaw, D. S., Hyde, L. W., & Forbes, E. E. (2014). Interactions between monoamine oxidase A and punitive discipline in African American and Caucasian men's antisocial behavior. *Clinical Psychological Science*, 2(5), 591–601.

Cleveland, H. H., Wiebe, R., & Rowe, D. C. (2005). Genetic influences on associations with substance using peers. *Journal of Genetic Psychology*, 166, 153–169.

Damasio, H., Grabowski, T., Frank, R., Galaburda, A. M., & Damasio, A. R. (1994). The return of Phineas Gage: Clues about the brain from the skull of a famous patient. *Science*, 264, 1102–1105.

DeLisi, M. & Vaughn, M. G. (2014). Foundation for a temperament-based theory of antisocial behavior and criminal justice system involvement. *Journal of Criminal Justice*, 42(1), 10–25.

DeLisi, M., & Vaughn, M. G. (Eds) (2015). *The Routledge international handbook of biosocial criminology*. New York: Routledge.

Derringer, J., Krueger, R. F., Irons, D. E., & Iacono, W. G. (2010). Harsh discipline, childhood sexual assault, and MAOA genotype: an investigation of main and interactive effects on diverse clinical externalizing outcomes. *Behavior Genetics*, 40(5), 639–648.

Dmitrieva, J., Chen, C., Greenberger, E., Ogunseitan, O., & Ding, Y. C. (2011). Gender-specific expression of the DRD4 gene on adolescent delinquency, anger and thrill seeking. *Social Cognitive and Affective Neuroscience*, 6(1), 82–89.

Farrer, T. J., Frost, R. B., & Hedges, D. W. (2012). Prevalence of traumatic brain injury in intimate partner violence offenders compared to the general population: A meta-analysis. *Trauma, Violence, & Abuse*, 13(2), 77–82.

Farrer, T. J., Frost, R. B., & Hedges, D. W. (2013). Prevalence of traumatic brain injury in juvenile offenders: A meta-analysis. *Child Neuropsychology*, 19(3), 225–234.

Farrer, T. J. & Hedges, D. W. (2011). Prevalence of traumatic brain injury in incarcerated groups compared to the general population: A meta-analysis. *Progress in Neuro-Psychopharmacology and Biological Psychiatry*, 35(2), 390–394.

Fergusson, D. M., Boden, J. M., Horwood, L. J., Miller, A. L., & Kennedy, M. A. (2011). MAOA, abuse exposure and antisocial behaviour: 30-year longitudinal study. *The British Journal of Psychiatry*, 198(6), 457–463.

Fergusson, D. M., Boden, J. M., Horwood, L. J., Miller, A., & Kennedy, M. A. (2012). Moderating role of the MAOA genotype in antisocial behaviour. *The British Journal of Psychiatry*, 200(2), 116–123.

Fernàndez-Castillo, N. & Cormand, B. (2016). Aggressive behavior in humans: Genes and pathways identified through association studies. *American Journal of Medical Genetics Part B: Neuropsychiatric Genetics*, 171B, 676–696.

Finkenauer, C., Engels, R. C., & Baumeister, R. F. (2005). Parenting behaviour and adolescent behavioural and emotional problems: The role of self-control. *International Journal of Behavioral Development*, 29(1), 58–69.

Foley, D. L., Eaves, L. J., Wormley, B., Silberg, J. L., Maes, H. H., Kuhn, J., & Riley, B. (2004). Childhood adversity, monoamine oxidase a genotype, and risk for conduct disorder. *Archives of General Psychiatry*, 61(7), 738–744.

Gajos, J. M., Fagan, A. A., & Beaver, K. M. (2016). Use of genetically informed evidence-based prevention science to understand and prevent crime and related behavioral disorders. *Criminology & Public Policy*, 15(3), 683–701.

Gibson, C. L., Piquero, A. R., & Tibbetts, S. G. (2000). Assessing the relationship between maternal cigarette smoking during pregnancy and age at first police contact. *Justice Quarterly*, 17(3), 519–542.

Gottfredson, M. R. & Hirschi, T. (1990). *A general theory of crime*. Stanford, CA: Stanford University Press.

Graham, D. M., Glass, L., & Mattson, S. N. (2016). Teratogen exposure and externalizing behavior. In T. P. Beauchaine & S. P. Hinshaw (Eds), *The Oxford handbook of externalizing spectrum disorders* (pp. 416–439). New York: Oxford University Press.

Greenberg, M. T., Kusche, C., & Mihalic, S. F. (2006). *Promoting alternative thin strategies (PATHS): Blueprints for violence prevention, Book Ten*. Boulder, CO: Center for the Study and Prevention of Violence.

Hay, C. & Meldrum, R. (2015). *Self-control and crime over the life course*. Thousand Oaks, CA: SAGE.

Holland, N. R. & DeLisi, M. (2015). The warrior gene: MAOA genotype and antisocial behavior in males. In M. DeLisi & M. G. Vaughn (Eds), *The Routledge international handbook of biosocial criminology* (pp. 179–189). New York: Routledge.

Israel, S., Caspi, A., Belsky, D. W., Harrington, H., Hogan, S., Houts, R., Ramrakha, S., Sanders, S., Poulton, R., & Moffitt, T. E. (2014). Credit scores, cardiovascular disease risk, and human capital. *Proceedings of the National Academy of Sciences*, 111(48), 17087–17092.

Jackson, D. B. & Beaver, K. M. (2015). The influence of nutritional factors on verbal deficits and psychopathic personality traits: Evidence of the moderating role of the MAOA genotype. *International Journal of Environmental Research and Public Health*, 12(12), 15739–15755.

Jackson, D. B. & Newsome, J. (2016). The link between infant neuropsychological risk and childhood antisocial behavior among males: The moderating role of neonatal health risk. *Journal of Criminal Justice*, 47, 32–40.

Kochanska, G., Philibert, R. A., & Barry, R. A. (2009). Interplay of genes and early mother-child relationship in the development of self-regulation from toddler to preschool age. *Journal of Child Psychology and Psychiatry*, 50, 1331–1338.

Kim-Cohen, J., Caspi, A., Taylor, A., Williams, B., Newcombe, R., Craig, I. W., & Moffitt,

T. E. (2006). MAOA, maltreatment, and gene–environment interaction predicting children's mental health: new evidence and a meta-analysis. *Molecular Psychiatry*, 11(10), 903–913.

Kretschmer, T., Dijkstra, J. K., Ormel, J., Verhulst, F. C., & Veenstra, R. (2013). Dopamine receptor D4 gene moderates the effect of positive and negative peer experiences on later delinquency: The Tracking Adolescents' Individual Lives Survey study. *Development and Psychopathology*, 25(4), 1107–1117.

Kretschmer, T., Vitaro, F., & Barker, E. D. (2014). The association between peer and own aggression is moderated by the BDNF Val-Met polymorphism. *Journal of Research on Adolescence*, 24(1), 177–185.

Luppino, D., Moul, C., Hawes, D. J., Brennan, J., & Dadds, M. R. (2014). Association between a polymorphism of the vasopressin 1B receptor gene and aggression in children. *Psychiatric Genetics*, 24(5), 185–190.

Meldrum, R. C. & Barnes, J. C. (2016). Prenatal exposure to secondhand smoke and the development of self-control. *Journal of Developmental and Life Course Criminology*, doi: 10.1007/s40865-016-0038-1.

Moffitt, T. E. (1993). Adolescence-limited and life-course-persistent antisocial behavior: A developmental taxonomy. *Psychological Review*, 100(4), 674–701.

Moffitt, T. E. (2005). The new look of behavioral genetics in developmental psychopathology: gene-environment interplay in antisocial behaviors. *Psychological Bulletin*, 131(4), 533–554.

Moffitt, T. E., Arseneault, L., Belsky, D., Dickson, N., Hancox, R. J., Harrington, H., ... & Caspi, A. (2011). A gradient of childhood self-control predicts health, wealth, and public safety. *Proceedings of the National Academy of Sciences*, 108(7), 2693–2698.

Musci, R. J., Bradshaw, C. P., Maher, B., Uhl, G. R., Kellam, S. G., & Ialongo, N. S. (2014). Reducing aggression and impulsivity through school-based prevention programs: A gene by intervention interaction. *Prevention Science*, 15(6), 831–840.

Pappa, I., Mileva-Seitz, V. R., Bakermans-Kranenburg, M. J., Tiemeier, H., & van IJzendoorn, M. H. (2015). The magnificent seven: A quantitative review of dopamine receptor d4 and its association with child behavior. *Neuroscience & Biobehavioral Reviews*, 57, 175–186.

Plomin, R., DeFries, J. C., & Loehlin, J. C. (1977). Genotype-environment interaction and correlation in the analysis of human behavior. *Psychological Bulletin*, 84(2), 309–322.

Pluess, M. & Belsky, J. (2011). Prenatal programming of postnatal plasticity? *Development and Psychopathology*, 23(1), 29–38.

Raine, A., Moffitt, T. E., Caspi, A., Loeber, R., Stouthamer-Loeber, M., & Lynam, D. (2005). Neurocognitive impairments in boys on the life-course persistent antisocial path. *Journal of Abnormal Psychology*, 114, 38–49.

Rehan, W., Antfolk, J., Johansson, A., Aminoff, M., Sandnabba, N. K., Westberg, L., & Santtila, P. (2016). Gene–environment correlation between the dopamine transporter gene (DAT1) polymorphism and childhood experiences of abuse. *Journal of Interpersonal Violence*. doi: 10.1177/0886260515622299.

Roettger, M. E., Boardman, J. D., Harris, K. M., & Guo, G. (2016). The association between the MAOA 2R genotype and delinquency over time among men: The interactive role of parental closeness and parental incarceration. *Criminal Justice and Behavior*, 43(8), 1076–1094.

Rutter, M. L. (1997). Nature–nurture integration: the example of antisocial behavior. *American Psychologist*, 52(4), 390–398.

Rutter, M., Dunn, J., Plomin, R., Simonoff, E., Pickles, A., Maughan, B., Ormel, J., Meyer, J., & Eaves, L. (1997). Integrating nature and nurture: Implications of person–environment correlations and interactions for developmental psychopathology. *Development and Psychopathology*, 9(2), 335–364.

Samek, D. R., Bailey, J., Hill, K. G., Wilson, S., Lee, S., Keyes, M. A., ... & McGue, M. (2016). A test-replicate approach to candidate gene research on addiction and externalizing disorders: A collaboration across five longitudinal studies. *Behavior Genetics*, 46(5), 608–626.

Scarr, S. & McCartney, K. (1983). How people make their own environments: A theory of genotype→environment effects. *Child Development*, 54, 424–435.

Shiroma, E. J., Ferguson, P. L., & Pickelsimer, E. E. (2010). Prevalence of traumatic brain injury in an offender population: a meta-analysis. *Journal of Correctional Health Care*, 16(2), 147–159.

Stetler, D. A., Davis, C., Leavitt, K., Schriger, I., Benson, K., Bhakta, S., ... & Bortolato, M. (2014). Association of low-activity MAOA allelic variants with violent crime in incarcerated offenders. *Journal of Psychiatric Research*, 58, 69–75.

Taylor, A. & Kim-Cohen, J. (2007). Meta-analysis of gene–environment interactions in developmental psychopathology. *Development and Psychopathology*, 19(4), 1029–1037.

Thibodeau, E. L., Cicchetti, D., & Rogosch, F. A. (2015). Child maltreatment, impulsivity, and antisocial behavior in African American children: Moderation effects from a cumulative dopaminergic gene index. *Development and Psychopathology*, 27(4), 1621–1636.

Tielbeek, J. J., Karlsson Linnér, R., Beers, K., Posthuma, D., Popma, A., & Polderman, T. J. (2016). Meta-analysis of the serotonin transporter promoter variant (5-HTTLPR) in relation to adverse environment and antisocial behavior. *American Journal of Medical Genetics Part B: Neuropsychiatric Genetics*, 171(5), 748–760.

Tiihonen, J., Rautiainen, M. R., Ollila, H. M., Repo-Tiihonen, E., Virkkunen, M., Palotie, A., ... & Paunio, T. (2015). Genetic background of extreme violent behavior. *Molecular Psychiatry*, 20(6), 786–792.

Tuvblad, C., Narusyte, J., Comasco, E., Andershed, H., Andershed, A. K., Colins, O. F., Fanti, K. A., & Nilsson, K. W. (2016). Physical and verbal aggressive behavior and COMT genotype: Sensitivity to the Environment. *American Journal of Medical Genetics Part B: Neuropsychiatric Genetics*, 171B, 708–718.

Van Horn, J. D., Irimia, A., Torgerson, C. M., Chambers, M. C., Kikinis, R., & Toga, A. W. (2012). Mapping connectivity damage in the case of Phineas Gage. *PLoS ONE*, 7(5), e37454.

Vaske, J., Galyean, K., & Cullen, F. T. (2011). Toward a biosocial theory of offender rehabilitation: Why does cognitive-behavioral therapy work? *Journal of Criminal Justice*, 39(1), 90–102.

Vaughn, M. G., DeLisi, M., Beaver, K. M., & Wright, J. P. (2009). Identifying latent classes of behavioral risk based on early childhood manifestations of self-control. *Youth Violence and Juvenile Justice*, 7, 16–31.

Vazsonyi, A. T. & Huang, L. (2010). Where self-control comes from: on the development of self-control and its relationship to deviance over time. *Developmental Psychology*, 46(1), 245–257.

Vazsonyi, A. T., Jiskrova, G. K., Ksinan, A. J., & Blatný, M. (2016). An empirical test of self- control theory in Roma adolescents. *Journal of Criminal Justice*, 44, 66–76.

Vazsonyi, A. T., Mikuška, J., & Kelley, E. L. (2017). It's time: A meta-analysis on the self-control-deviance link. *Journal of Criminal Justice*, 48, 48-63.

Vazsonyi, A. T., Roberts, J. W., & Huang, L. (2015). Why focusing on nurture made and still makes sense: The biosocial development of self-control. In M. DeLisi & M. G. Vaughn (Eds), *The Routledge international handbook of biosocial criminology* (pp. 263–279). New York: Routledge.

Veroude, K., Zhang-James, Y., Fernàndez-Castillo, N., Bakker, M. J., Cormand, B., & Faraone, S. V. (2016). Genetics of aggressive behavior: An overview. *American Journal of Medical Genetics Part B: Neuropsychiatric Genetics*, 171(1), 3–43.

Wakschlag, L. S., Leventhal, B. L., Pine, D. S., Pickett, K. E., & Carter, A. S. (2006).

Elucidating early mechanisms of developmental psychopathology: The case of prenatal smoking and disruptive behavior. *Child Development*, 77(4), 893–906.

Wakschlag, L. S., Pickett, K. E., Cook, E., Jr., Benowitz, N. L., & Leventhal, B. L. (2002). Maternal smoking during pregnancy and severe antisocial behavior in offspring: A review. *American Journal of Public Health*, 92(6), 966–974.

Weeland, J., Overbeek, G., de Castro, B. O., & Matthys, W. (2015). Underlying mechanisms of gene–environment interactions in externalizing behavior: A systematic review and search for theoretical mechanisms. *Clinical Child and Family Psychology Review*, 18(4), 413–442.

Wright, J. P. & Beaver, K. M. (2005). Do parents matter in creating self-control in their children? A genetically informed test of Gottfredson and Hirschi's theory of low self-control. *Criminology*, 43, 1169–1198.

Wright, J. P., Beaver, K. M., DeLisi, M., & Vaughn, M. G. (2008). Evidence of negligible parenting influences on self-control, delinquent peers, and delinquency in a sample of twins. *Justice Quarterly*, 25, 544–569.

Wright, J. P., Boisvert, D., & Vaske, J. (2009). Blood lead levels in early childhood predict adulthood psychopathy. *Youth Violence and Juvenile Justice*, 7(3), 208–222.

Wright, J. P., Dietrich, K. N., Ris, M. D., Hornung, R. W., Wessel, S. D., Lanphear, B. P., ... & Rae, M. N. (2008). Association of prenatal and childhood blood lead concentrations with criminal arrests in early adulthood. *PLoS Medicine*, 5(5), e101.

10 The Neurobiology of Bullying Victimization

Tracy Vaillancourt

Introduction

Bullying is a subtype of aggression that is characterized by intentionality, repetition, and an imbalance of power (Olweus, 1999). Bullying takes many forms including verbal, physical, relational (i.e., traditional bullying), and cyber. Most population-based studies indicate that bullying affects about 30% of children and youth worldwide (Nansel et al., 2001; National Academies of Sciences, Engineering, and Medicine, 2016; UNICEF, 2013; Vaillancourt et al., 2010a), making it the most prevalent form of aggression youth are exposed to. Being the target of bullying is associated with significant mental health issues, which persist long after the bullying has stopped (Lereya, Copeland, Costello, & Wolke, 2015; Takizawa, Maughan, & Arseneault, 2014; see review by McDougall & Vaillancourt, 2015). There is also evidence that being the target of peer bullying in childhood has a more pronounced negative impact on adult mental health than being exposed to childhood maltreatment (Lereya et al., 2015).

Research on perpetrators of bullying suggests different outcomes than that of targets. Whereas targets of bullying tend to be marginalized, rejected, and lonely (Knack, Tsar, Vaillancourt, Hymel, & McDougall, 2012; Nansel et al., 2001), several studies have shown that perpetrators of bullying often wield considerable power and influence in their peer groups and that many are the most popular children and adolescents in their schools (Faris & Felmlee, 2011; Farmer, Estell, Bishop, O'Neal, & Cairns, 2003; Vaillancourt, Hymel, & McDougall, 2003). Longitudinal studies of perpetrators point to a problematic developmental trajectory punctuated by problems with later offending (Ttofi, Farrington, Lösel, & Loeber, 2011) and substance abuse (Ttofi, Farrington, Lösel, Crago, & Theodorakis, 2016). However, when controlling for family hardship and childhood psychiatric disorders, known predictors of aggression, the negative impact of bullying perpetration on adult health, wealth, crime, and social outcomes is not found (Wolke, Copeland, Angold, & Costello, 2013), nor is it found for most adult psychiatric outcomes (Copeland, Wolke, Angold, & Costello, 2013). Vaillancourt, Clinton, McDougall, Schmidt, and Hymel (2010b) have argued that such discrepancies in outcomes should be expected because there are in fact two general types of bullies – high-status perpetrators and low-status perpetrators. High-status bullies have assets and competencies that the peer group values, such as being good athletes and being attractive (Vaillancourt et al., 2003). These perpetrators engage in a mélange of prosocial and antisocial behavior (i.e., they are Machiavellian) and the aggression they direct at peers is instrumental insofar as it is used to achieve and maintain hegemony. Most perpetrators of bullying are high-status (Vaillancourt et al., 2003). Low-status bullies tend to have few assets and competencies that the peer group value (Vaillancourt et al., 2003), they are more reactive in their use of aggression, they tend to have problems with emotional self-regulation, and they are oftentimes life-course persistent in their use of aggression. Many low-status perpetrators are also victims of bullying (Vaillancourt et al., 2010b).

When targets and perpetrators are compared on different outcomes, victims invariably fare worse than bullies (Copeland et al., 2013; Wolke et al., 2013), and are thus the focus of this chapter. This discrepancy in outcomes is likely due to the fact that being the victim of bullying interferes with the fundamental need to belong (Baumeister & Leary, 1995), whereas being the perpetrator of bullying does not. For example, Nansel et al. (2001) reported in their large population-based study of American youth that the ability to make friends was negatively associated with being the victim of bullying, but positively associated with being the perpetrator of bullying.

In addition to the robust literature documenting the negative effects of bullying victimization on mental health, there is also a growing literature suggesting that the effects of bullying are more pernicious than previously thought. Specifically, recent studies have shown that bullying can "get under the skin" and cause biological changes that increase the risk of poorer outcomes (see Vaillancourt et al., 2010b; Vaillancourt, Hymel, & McDougall, 2013; Vaillancourt, Sanderson, Arnold, & McDougall, 2017 for reviews). Specifically, converging evidence suggests that early-life adversity, which includes being the target of bullying, "programs physiology and behavior" (Shalev & Belsky, 2016, p. 41). The focus of this chapter is on reviewing the current state of knowledge about the neurobiological effects of bullying victimization and its links to mental health.

Stress-Response System

It is well-established in animal and human studies that early adversity is associated with changes to the neuroendocrine stress-response system and that these changes are in turn linked to disease (Lupien, McEwen, Gunna, & Heim, 2009; Miller, Chen, & Parker, 2011). The most widely studied stress-response system is the hypothalamic–pituitary–adrenal (HPA) axis. The HPA axis helps the organism adapt to stressors, thus supporting homeostasis and promoting health (McEwen, 2004).

When a person is exposed to psychological or physical stressors, a biological cascade is initiated that begins with an increased production and secretion of corticotropin-releasing hormone (CRH) released from the paraventricular nucleus of the hypothalamus. CRH travels through the hypophyseal portal circulation and stimulates the anterior pituitary gland to release adrenocorticotropic hormone (ACTH). ACTH is carried through the peripheral circulation to the adrenal cortex where it triggers the production and release of cortisol, a glucocorticoid with widespread regulatory influence that helps mobilize energy needed to meet the demands of a stressor. Following activation of this system, cortisol acts on the pituitary gland, the hypothalamus, and the hippocampus as a negative-feedback inhibition, suppressing this hormonal pathway, and thus protecting the individual against the damaging effects of chronic activation of the HPA axis (Jacobson & Sapolsky, 1991; Sapolsky, Krey, & McEwen, 1986).

Several psychiatric disorders have been implicated in the dysfunction of the HPA axis, and, in particular, its end product cortisol (Ehlert, 2013). Specifically, researchers have focused on the dysregulation of cortisol, including its hyper-secretion or hypo-secretion, and its pattern across the day and after exposure to an acute stressor. For example, although cortisol typically follows a diurnal pattern, peaking 20–30 minutes after awakening and gradually dropping throughout the day (i.e., cortisol awakening response), in some individuals, cortisol levels are consistently high throughout the day. Moreover, in other individuals, exposure to a stressor is associated with an increase in cortisol that does not abate as would be expected. Cortisol dysregulation may result because of a failure to "(a) habituate to recurring stress, (b) inhibit allostatic processes following termination of stress, or (c) mount an adaptive response in some systems that can lead to the hyperactivation of others" (Morris, Compas, & Garber, 2012, p. 303).

Although elevated cortisol levels are viewed as adaptive when faced with a stressor, extended activation of the HPA axis has been shown to have adverse effects, termed allostatic load (McEwen, 1998). The hyper-secretion of cortisol is often associated with the pathogenesis of major depression (Stetler & Miller, 2011) and is presumed to be due to an insensitive negative glucocorticoid feedback of the HPA axis loop (Ehlert, 2013, p. 1852). Exposure to prolonged and/or severe stress may also lead to a different type of "adaptive" change, which alters the response of the HPA axis in a different direction (Tyrka, Ridout, & Parade, 2016 for review). Specifically, constant activation of the HPA axis in response to stress can cause a counter-regulatory state leading to the hypo-secretion of cortisol (Tyrka et al., 2016). The hypo-secretion of cortisol is often linked to stress-related disorders like post-traumatic stress disorder (PTSD; Morris et al., 2012) and is presumed to be due to "a negative feedback hypersensitivity of glucocorticoids associated with an up-regulated leukocyte glucocorticoid receptor (GR) number and sensitivity" (Ehlert, 2013, p. 1852). Glucocorticoids are a class of steroid hormones known as corticosteroids that bind with the glucocorticoid receptor. They are implicated in the immune system as part of a feedback mechanism that is associated with the reduction of functions like inflammation.

Although exposure to adversity can be associated with an exaggerated or blunted neuroendocrine response to stress, much of the variability in HPA axis activity has been shown to be attributable to the features of the stressor and the person. For example, results of Miller, Chen, and Zhou's (2007) meta-analysis indicated that cortisol tended to be high at stressor onset and attenuated over time. Stressors that were extreme in nature such as those involving trauma or threatening physical integrity tended to elicit a high, flat diurnal cortisol pattern. This was also true of uncontrollable stressors. Although subjective distress elicited heightened cortisol, in individuals with PTSD, cortisol levels were lower. Low cortisol has been linked to extreme traumas that are associated with the development of PTSD such as exposure to early sexual abuse (King et al., 2001) and being a survivor of the Holocaust (Yehuda et al., 1995). Being the target of peer bullying is also linked to PTSD symptoms (Idsoe, Dyregrov, & Idsoe, 2012; Litman et al., 2015), and consistent with the notion that bullying is a form of trauma (Mishna, 2007), to a *blunted* cortisol response in children (Carney, Hazler, Oh, Hibel, & Granger, 2010; Kliewer, 2006; Kliewer, 2016; Ouellet-Morin et al., 2011a; Ouellet-Morin et al., 2011b; Ouellet-Morin et al., 2013; Vaillancourt et al., 2008) and adults (Hansen et al., 2006; Hansen, Hogh, & Persson, 2011). This blunted response to stress among bullied youth has been linked to the development of social and behavioral problems (Ouellet-Morin et al., 2011b).

Bullying victimization is also associated with an atypical cortisol awakening response and an atypical response to acute stress. For example, Knack, Jensen-Campbell, and Baum (2011) found that while the diurnal pattern for nonbullied adolescents was characteristic (i.e., cortisol levels peaking 30 minutes after waking and then decreasing across the day), for bullied adolescents, an atypical pattern was found. Bullied adolescents had lower levels of cortisol 30 minutes after waking and 30 minutes before bed than their nonbullied peers. Knack et al. also found that exposure to an acute stressor (i.e., Trier Social Stress Test) in nonbullied adolescents resulted in a peak in cortisol 30 minutes after delivering the speech that was sustained 30 minutes post-speech, but in bullied adolescents, a significant drop in cortisol was found 30 minutes following the speech delivery. This fall in cortisol in bullied youth was associated with more frequent visits to the doctor. Although the drop in cortisol post-stressor among bullied youth was unexpected it was notably similar to the pattern reported by Ouellet-Morin et al. (2011b), who found that nonabused children showed elevated cortisol levels post-stress delivery (adapted Trier Social Stress Test), while maltreated/bullied children showed decreasing levels in cortisol post-stress delivery. In another study involving monozygotic twins discordant on bullying victimization, Ouellet-Morin et al. (2011a) found that bullied twins showed a decrease in cortisol post-stress delivery, while nonbullied twins showed an increase in cortisol post-stress delivery. These differences between twins were not due to genetics, familial environment, or individual factors. Nor were they due to the perception of stress or the emotional response associated with the stressor. Rather, the results provided "support for a causal effect of adverse childhood experiences on the neuroendocrine response to stress" (p. 2011).

Atypical diurnal patterns have also been noted in bullied youth. González-Cabrera, Calvete, León-Mejía, Pérez-Sancho, and Peinado (2017) found that cortisol concentrations across the day were flatter for adolescent victims of severe cyberbullying. Being the victim of cyberbullying was also linked with a larger area under the curve (i.e., total cortisol output over the day), which, in turn, was associated with higher perceived stress and anxiety. Brendgen, Ouellet-Morin, Lupien, Vitaro, Dionne, and Boivin (2017) found that controlling for awakening levels of cortisol, twins who were more victimized by their peers than their co-twin demonstrated a steeper decline of cortisol until bedtime. The results of these studies are consistent with the idea that exposure to stressors that are extreme and/or prolonged in nature are associated with a down-regulation of the stress response system (Miller et al., 2007).

Finally, there is evidence that the hyper-secretion of cortisol is linked to peer victimization via depression. Depression is reliably linked to higher cortisol levels (Stetler & Miller, 2011). Vaillancourt et al. (2011) examined adolescents every six months on four occasions and found that being the target of bullying in childhood was related to increases in depression symptoms, which, in turn, was related to increases in basal cortisol. Notably, increased cortisol was related with impaired memory associated with areas of the brain that are rich in glucocorticoid receptor sites – the hippocampus and the prefrontal cortex (Lupien et al., 2005). Cortisol binds to the glucocorticoid receptor and, in doing so, regulates gene transcription, which is the first step in the expression of a gene. This finding is in keeping with a well-replicated literature involving animals and humans demonstrating that high levels of cortisol are bad for the brain. Specifically, high exposure to glucocorticoids is associated with memory impairment and even atrophy of the hippocampus (e.g., Lupien et al., 1998).

Taken together, studies examining the relation between being bullied and the stress-response system suggest a cortisol profile that is similar to what is seen among survivors of extreme trauma that often go on to receive a diagnosis of PTSD. Perhaps not surprising is the strong link between bullying victimization and PTSD (Idsoe et al., 2012; Litman et al., 2015). For example, Idsoe et al. (2012) reported that 27.6% of boys and 40.5% of girls in their large study of Norwegian adolescents scored within the clinical range on PTSD symptoms.

Inflammation

Exposure to psychosocial stressors like childhood trauma has also been shown to influence circulating inflammatory markers such as C-reactive protein, interleukin-6, and tumor necrosis factor-α (Baumeister, Akhtar, Ciufolini, Pariante, & Mondelli, 2016). This relation is distinguished because inflammation has been shown to play a vital role in mental disorders (Baumeister, Russell, Pariante, & Mondelli, 2014). For example, peripheral inflammation as indexed by plasma C-reactive protein has been linked to the development of PTSD (Eraly, Nievergelt, & Maihofer, 2014).

Considering that bullying victimization is a form of trauma (Mishna, 2007), it is not surprising that recent studies have shown longitudinal links between bullying in childhood and inflammation in adulthood. For example, Copeland et al. (2014) found in their longitudinal population-based study that, when compared with those not involved in bullying, being the target of bullying in childhood predicted greater C-reactive protein levels in adulthood, while being the perpetrator of bullying in childhood predicted lower C-reactive protein levels in adulthood. Moreover, cumulative experiences with bullying victimization predicted increases in C-reactive protein levels even when controlling for relevant covariates that have been shown to be associated with C-reactive protein levels *and* involvement with bullying. In another population-based study of individuals followed prospectively for 50 years, Takizawa, Danese, Maughan, and Arsenault (2015) found that being the target of frequent bullying in childhood was associated with increased levels of C-reactive protein in mid-life. And in a recent study of adolescents,

Arana et al. (in press) reported that relational peer victimization (e.g., rumour spreading, peer group exclusion) was associated with higher levels of depression, somatic complaints, and inflammation. Specifically, relational peer victimization indirectly influenced interleukin-6 through depression and C-reactive protein through depression and interleukin-6.

The results of these studies are interesting because there is evidence for a bidirectional association between the inflammatory system and other related systems concerned with the pathogenesis of mental disorders, such as the HPA axis (Baumeister et al., 2014; Miller, Maletic, & Raison, 2009). In particular, cortisol has been shown to have an anti-inflammatory effect (Straub, Buttgereit, & Cutolo, 2011), such that lower cortisol levels are associated with higher levels of inflammation and higher cortisol levels are associated with lower levels of inflammation. As mentioned, researchers have typically reported an association between blunted cortisol and bullying victimization (Carney et al., 2010; Hansen et al., 2006; Hansen et al., 2011; Kliewer, 2006; Kliewer, 2016; Ouellet-Morin et al., 2011a; Ouellet-Morin et al., 2011b; Ouellet-Morin et al., 2013; Vaillancourt et al., 2008), which is consistent with studies on childhood adversity (Lin, Neylan, Epel, & O'Donovan, 2016), including bullying (Arana et al., in press; Copeland et al., 2014; Takizawa et al., 2015), being linked to higher levels of inflammation.

Genetic Factors

In addition to its relation to HPA dysregulation and inflammation, childhood trauma has been shown to be associated with epigenetic alterations such as DNA methylation (see Szyf & Bick, 2013 for review). DNA methylation is type of epigenetic mechanism that "maintains gene activity or changes gene expression by activating or silencing the gene, resulting in the development of phenotypes that are time-dependent and are not determined by the DNA sequence at that locus" (Vaillancourt et al., 2013, p. 243–244). Simply stated, while experiences cannot alter the nucleotide acid sequence of DNA (i.e., do not alter the genetic code); they can alter the epigenome that tells the genome what to do. DNA methylation is thought to be the most stable type of epigenetic alteration and it is presumed to be a mechanism by which early-life adversity has long-term effects on the developing person (Tyrka et al., 2016).

Besides studies showing that early negative life experiences are associated with DNA methylation (Szyf & Bick, 2013), there is also one study showing that being bullied by peers was associated with epigenetic alterations. Specifically, Ouellet-Morin et al. (2013) found that bullying victimization influenced DNA methylation of the serotonin transporter gene (5-HTT). Bullied twins had higher 5-HTT DNA methylation than nonbullied twins and increases in DNA methylation were associated with a blunted cortisol response to stress. These results suggest that biological modifications (i.e., DNA methylation) and HPA functioning may be functionally associated. According to Tyrka et al. (2016) this is indeed the case. Childhood adversity is linked to altered methylation patterns, which are implicated in the stress-response system.

The 5-HTT gene has been connected in the development of many psychiatric conditions, especially in the context of environmental adversity (Uher & McGuffin, 2008). In particular, a functional polymorphism (i.e., genetic variation) in the promoter region of the serotonin transporter gene (5-HTTLPR) has been linked to depression in the context of trauma. For example, Caspi et al. (2003) found that individuals maltreated in childhood were far more likely to be depressed in adulthood if they had two copies of the short allele (SS) in the 5-HTTLPR and less likely to be depressed if they had at least one copy of the long allele (L). The short allele is considered a risk variant of the 5-HTT because it has been shown to have lower transcriptional efficiency of the promoter than the long allele (Caspi et al., 2003; Lesch et al., 1996).

Several researchers have replicated Caspi et al.'s (2003) finding with regard to bullied youth. Sugden et al. (2010) found that bullied children who carried the SS genotype were at greater risk for developing emotional problems than bullied children with the SL or LL genotype. Benjet, Thompson, and Gotlib (2010) reported that relationally bullied girls were far more likely to be elevated on symptoms of depression if they carried the SS genotype than if they were homozygous for the long allele or heterozygous for the short and long alleles. Other researchers have also shown that 5-HTTLPR moderates the relation between health problems and peer victimization (Banny, Cicchetti, Rogosch, Oshri, & Crick, 2013; Iyer, Dougall, & Jensen-Campbell, 2013). Although these results are intriguing, it is worthy to note that there is a lot of controversy associated with candidate gene by environment interactions because of their low replicability and their high rates of false discoveries (Duncan, Pollastri, & Smoller, 2014). Still, the genetics research suggests at least two simple pathways to consider. Candidate gene by environment interaction studies support that biological risk can interact with trauma to produce mental health problems (i.e., biological risk + exposure to bullying → poor mental health) and epigenetic studies support that exposure to trauma is associated with biological alterations, which, in turn, are associated with mental health problems (i.e., exposure to bullying → biological changes → poor mental health). What has not been considered to date is how these two pathways interact over time in the context of being bullied to confer a risk for poorer mental health outcomes.

Conclusion

The research reviewed in this chapter suggests that experience of being bullied is not inconsequential. Rather, being subjected to repeated, intentional humiliation and oppression by peers seems to become biologically embedded. Furthermore, the neurobiological changes associated with this trauma appear to presage psychobiological sequela that undermine victims' ability to cope with subsequent psychosocial stressors and confer a risk for poorer outcomes, like the mental health difficulties linked to this prevalent problem.

References

Arana, A. A., Boyd, E. Q., Guarneri-White, M., Iyer-Eimerbrink, P., Liegey Dougall, A., & Jensen-Campbell, L. (in press). The impact of social and physical peer victimization on systemic inflammation in adolescence. *Merrill-Palmer Quarterly*.

Banny, A. M., Cicchetti, D., Rogosch, F. A., Oshri, A., & Crick, N. R. (2013). Vulnerability to depression: A moderated mediation model of the roles of child maltreatment, peer victimization, and serotonin transporter linked polymorphic region genetic variation among children from low socioeconomic status backgrounds. *Development and Psychopathology*, 25, 599–614.

Baumeister, D., Akhtar, R., Ciufolini, S., Pariante, C. M., & Mondelli, V. (2016). Childhood trauma and adulthood inflammation: a meta-analysis of peripheral C-reactive protein, interleukin-6 and tumour necrosis factor-α. *Molecular Psychiatry*, 21, 642–649.

Baumeister, D., Russell, A., Pariante, C. M., & Mondelli, V. (2014). Inflammatory biomarker profiles of mental disorders and their relation to clinical, social and lifestyle factors. *Social Psychiatry and Psychiatric Epidemiology*, 49, 841–849. doi: 10.1007/s00127-014-0887-z.

Baumeister, R. F. & Leary, M. R. (1995). The need to belong: Desire for interpersonal attachments as a fundamental human motivation. *Psychological Bulletin*, 117, 497–529.

Benjet, C., Thompson, R. J., & Gotlib, I. H. (2010). 5-HTTLPR moderates the effect of relational peer victimization on depressive symptoms in adolescent girls. *Journal of Child Psychology and Psychiatry*, 51, 173–179. doi: 10.1111/j.1469-7610.2009.02149.x.

Brendgen, M., Ouellet-Morin, I., Lupien, S. J., Vitaro, F., Dionne, G., & Boivin, M. (2017). Environmental influence of problematic social relationships on adolescents' daily cortisol secretion: a monozygotic twin-difference study. *Psychological Medicine*, 47, 460–470.

Carney, J. V., Hazler, R. J., Oh, I., Hibel, L. C., & Granger, D. A. (2010). The relations between bullying exposures in middle childhood, anxiety, and adrenocortical activity. *Journal of School Violence*, 9, 194–211. doi: 10.1080/15388220903479602.

Caspi, A., Sugden, K., Moffitt, T. E., Taylor, A., Craig, I. W., Harrington, H., ... & Poulton, R. (2003). Influence of life stress on depression: Moderation by a polymorphism in the 5-HTT gene. *Science*, 301, 386–389.

Copeland, W. E., Wolke, D., Angold, A., & Costello, E. J. (2013). Adult psychiatric outcomes of bullying and being bullied by peers in childhood and adolescence. *JAMA Psychiatry*, 70, 419–426.

Copeland, W. E., Wolke, D., Lereya, S. T., Shanahan, L., Worthman, C., & Costello, E. J. (2014). Childhood bullying involvement predicts low-grade systemic inflammation into adulthood. *Proceedings of the National Academy of Sciences*, 111, 7570–7575.

Duncan, L. E., Pollastri, A. R., & Smoller, J. W. (2014). Mind the gap: Why many geneticists and psychological scientists have discrepant views about gene-environment interaction (G×E) research. *American Psychologist*, 69, 249–268.

Ehlert, U. (2013). Enduring psychobiological effects of childhood adversity. *Psychoneuroendocrinology*, 38(9), 1850–1857.

Eraly, S. A., Nievergelt, C. M., & Maihofer, A. X. (2014). Assessment of Plasma C-Reactive Protein as a Biomarker of Posttraumatic Stress Disorder Risk. *JAMA Psychiatry*, 71, 423–431. doi: 10.1001/jamapsychiatry.2013.4374.

Faris, R. & Felmlee, D. (2011). Status struggles: Network centrality and gender segregation in same- and cross-gender aggression. *American Sociological Review*, 76, 48–73.

Farmer, T. W., Estell, D. B., Bishop, J. L., O'Neal, K. K., & Cairns, B. D. (2003). Rejected bullies or popular leaders? The social relations of aggressive subtypes of rural African American early adolescents. *Developmental Psychology*, 39, 992–1004.

González-Cabrera, J., Calvete, E., León-Mejía, A., Pérez-Sancho, C., & Peinado, J. M. (2017). Relationship between cyberbullying roles, cortisol secretion and psychological stress. *Computers in Human Behavior*, 70, 153–160.

Hansen, Å. M., Hogh, A., & Persson, R. (2011). Frequency of bullying at work, physiological response, and mental health. *Journal of Psychosomatic Research*, 70, 19–27. doi: 10.1016/j.jpsychores.2010.05.010.

Hansen, Å. M., Hogh, A., Persson, R., Karlson, B., Garde, A. H., & Ørbæk, P. (2006). Bullying at work, health outcomes, and physiological stress response. *Journal of Psychosomatic Research*, 60, 63–72.

Idsoe, T., Dyregrov, A., & Idsoe, E. C. (2012). Bullying and PTSD symptoms. *Journal of Abnormal Child Psychology*, 40, 901–911.

Iyer, P. A., Dougall, A. L., & Jensen-Campbell, L. A. (2013). Are some adolescents differentially susceptible to the influence of bullying on depression? *Journal of Research in Personality*, 47, 272–281.

Jacobson, L. & Sapolsky, R. (1991). The role of the hippocampus in feedback regulation of the hypothalamic–pituitary–adrenocortical axis. *Endocrine Reviews*, 12, 118–134.

King, R. A., Schwab-Stone, M., Flisher, A. J., Greenwald, S., Kramer, R. A., Goodman, S. H., & Gould, M. S. (2001). Psychosocial and risk behavior correlates of youth suicide attempts and suicidal ideation. *Journal of the American Academy of Child & Adolescent Psychiatry*, 40, 837–846. doi: 10.1097/00004583-200107000-00019.

Kliewer, W. (2006). Violence exposure and cortisol responses in urban youth. *International Journal of Behavioral Medicine*, 13, 109–120.

Kliewer, W. (2016). Victimization and biological stress responses in urban adolescents: emotion regulation as a moderator. *Journal of Youth and Adolescence*, 45, 1812–1823.

Knack, J. M., Jensen-Campbell, L. A., & Baum, A. (2011). Worse than sticks and stones? Bullying is associated with altered HPA axis functioning and poorer health. *Brain and cognition*, 77, 183–190.

Knack, J. M., Tsar, V., Vaillancourt, T., Hymel, S., & McDougall, P. (2012). What protects rejected adolescents from also being bullied by their peers? The moderating role of peer-valued characteristics. *Journal of Research on Adolescence*, 22, 467–479.

Lereya, S. T., Copeland, W. E., Costello, E. J., & Wolke, D. (2015). Adult mental health consequences of peer bullying and maltreatment in childhood: Two cohorts in two countries. *The Lancet Psychiatry*, 2, 524–531.

Lesch, K.-P., Bengel, D., Heilis, A., Sabol, S. Z., Greenberg, B. D., Petri, S., ... & Murphy, D. L. (1996). Association of anxiety-related traits with a polymorphism in the serotonin transporter gene regulatory region. *Science*, 274, 1527–1531.

Lin, J. E., Neylan, T. C., Epel, E., & O'Donovan, A. (2016). Associations of childhood adversity and adulthood trauma with C-reactive protein: A cross-sectional population-based study. *Brain, Behavior, and Immunity*, 53, 105–112.

Litman, L., Costantino, G., Waxman, R., Sanabria-Velez, C., Rodriguez-Guzman, V. M., Lampon-Velez, A., ... & Cruz, T. (2015). Relationship between peer victimization and posttraumatic stress among primary school children. *Journal of Traumatic Stress*, 28, 348–354.

Lupien, S. J., Fiocco, A., Wan, N., Maheu, F., Lord, C., Schramek, T., & Tu, M. T. (2005). Stress hormones and human memory function across the lifespan. *Psychoneuroendocrinology*, 30(3), 225–242. doi: 10.1016/j.psyneuen.2004.08.003.

Lupien, S. J., DeLeon, M., DeSanti, S., Convit, A., Tarshish, C., Nair, N. P. V., ... & Meaney, M.J. (1998). Longitudinal increase in cortisol during human aging predicts hippocampal atrophy and memory deficits. *Nature Neuroscience*, 1, 69–73. doi: 10.1038/271.

Lupien, S. J., McEwen, B. S., Gunnar, M. R., & Heim, C. (2009). Effects of stress throughout the lifespan on the brain, behaviour and cognition. *Nature Reviews Neuroscience*, 10, 434–445.

McDougall, P. & Vaillancourt, T. (2015). Long-term adult outcomes of peer victimization in childhood and adolescence: Pathways to adjustment and maladjustment. *American Psychologist*, 70, 300–310.

McEwen, B. S. (1998). Stress, adaptation, and disease: Allostasis and allostatic load. *Annals of the New York Academy of Sciences*, 840, 33–44.

McEwen, B. S. (2004). Protection and damage from acute and chronic stress: Allostasis and allostatic overload and relevance to the pathophysiology of psychiatric disorders. *Annals of the New York Academy of Sciences*, 1032, 1–7.

Miller, A. H., Maletic, V., & Raison, C. L. (2009). Inflammation and its discontents: The role of cytokines in the pathophysiology of major depression. *Biological Psychiatry*, 65, 732–741. doi: 10.1016/j.biopsych.2008.11.029.

Miller, G. E., Chen, E., & Parker, K. J. (2011). Psychological stress in childhood and susceptibility to the chronic diseases of aging: Moving toward a model of behavioral and biological mechanisms. *Psychological Bulletin*, 137, 959–997.

Miller, G. E., Chen, E., & Zhou, E. S. (2007). If it goes up, must it come down? Chronic stress and the hypothalamic-pituitary-adrenocortical axis in humans. *Psychological Bulletin*, 133, 25–45.

Mishna, F. (2007). Bullying and victimization: Transforming trauma through empowerment. In M. Bussey & J. Bula Wise (Eds), *Trauma transformed: An empowerment response* (pp. 124–141). New York: Columbia University Press.

Morris, M. C., Compas, B. E., & Garber, J. (2012). Relations among posttraumatic stress disorder, comorbid major depression, and HPA function: A systematic review and meta-analysis. *Clinical Psychology Review*, 32, 301–315.

Nansel, T. R., Overpeck, M., Pilla, R. S., Ruan, W. J., Simons-Morton, B., & Scheidt, P. (2001). Bullying behaviors among US youth: Prevalence and association with psychosocial adjustment. *JAMA*, 285, 2094–2100.

National Academies of Sciences, Engineering, and Medicine (2016). *Preventing Bullying Through Science, Policy, and Practice*. Washington, DC: The National Academies Press.

Olweus, D. (1999). Sweden. In P. K. Smith, Y. Morita, J. Junger-Tas, D. Olweus, R. Catalano, & P. Slee (Eds), *The nature of school bullying: A cross-national perspective* (pp. 7–27). London; New York: Routledge.

Ouellet-Morin, I., Danese, A., Bowes, L., Shakoor, S., Ambler, A., Pariante, C. M., … & Arseneault, L. (2011a). A discordant monozygotic twin design shows blunted cortisol reactivity among bullied children. *Journal of the American Academy of Child & Adolescent Psychiatry*, 50, 574–582.

Ouellet-Morin, I., Odgers, C. L., Danese, A., Bowes, L., Shakoor, S., Papadopoulos, A. S., … & Arseneault, L. (2011b). Blunted cortisol responses to stress signal social and behavioral problems among maltreated/bullied 12-year-old children. *Biological Psychiatry*, 70, 1016–1023.

Ouellet-Morin, I., Wong, C. C. Y., Danese, A., Pariante, C. M., Papadopoulos, A. S., Mill, J., & Arseneault, L. (2013). Increased serotonin transporter gene (SERT) DNA methylation is associated with bullying victimization and blunted cortisol response to stress in childhood: a longitudinal study of discordant monozygotic twins. *Psychological Medicine*, 43, 1813–1823.

Sapolsky, R. M., Krey, L. C., & McEwen, B. S. (1986). The neuroendocrinology of stress and aging: The glucocorticoid cascade hypothesis. *Endocrine Reviews*, 7, 284–301.

Shalev, I. & Belsky, J. (2016). Early-life stress and reproductive cost: A two-hit developmental model of accelerated aging? *Medical Hypotheses*, 90, 41–47. doi: 10.1016/j.mehy.2016.03.002.

Stetler, C. & Miller, G. E. (2011). Depression and hypothalamic-pituitary-adrenal activation: A quantitative summary of four decades of research. *Psychosomatic Medicine*, 73, 114–126.

Straub, R., Buttgereit, F., & Cutolo, M. (2011). Alterations of the hypothalamic-pituitary-adrenal axis in systemic immune diseases – a role for misguided energy regulation. *Clinical and Experimental Rheumatology*, 29(5 Suppl. 68), S23–S31.

Sugden, K., Arseneault, L., Harrington, H., Moffitt, T. E., Williams, B., & Caspi, A. (2010). Serotonin transporter gene moderates the development of emotional problems among children following bullying victimization. *Journal of the American Academy of Child and Adolescent Psychiatry*, 49, 830–840.

Szyf, M. & Bick, J. (2013). DNA methylation: A mechanism for embedding early life experiences in the genome. *Child Development*, 84, 49–57. doi: 10.1111/j.1467-8624.2012.01793.x.

Takizawa, R., Danese, A., Maughan, B., & Arseneault, L. (2015). Bullying victimization in childhood predicts inflammation and obesity at mid-life: a five-decade birth cohort study. *Psychological Medicine*, 45, 2705–2715.

Takizawa, R., Maughan, B., & Arseneault, L. (2014). Adult health outcomes of childhood bullying victimization: Evidence from a five-decade longitudinal British birth cohort. *American Journal of Psychiatry*, 171, 777–784.

Ttofi, M. M., Farrington, D. P., Lösel, F., & Loeber, R. (2011). The predictive efficiency of school bullying versus later offending: A systematic/meta-analytic review of longitudinal studies. *Criminal Behaviour and Mental Health*, 21, 80–89.

Ttofi, M. M., Farrington, D. P., Lösel, F., Crago, R. V., & Theodorakis, N. (2016). School bullying and drug use later in life: A meta-analytic investigation. *School Psychology Quarterly*, 31, 8–27.

Tyrka, A. R., Ridout, K. K., & Parade, S. H. (2016). Childhood adversity and epigenetic regulation of glucocorticoid signaling genes: Associations in children and adults. *Development and Psychopathology*, 28, 1319–1331.

Uher, R. & McGuffin, P. (2008). The moderation by the serotonin transporter gene of environmental adversity in the aetiology of mental illness: Review and methodological analysis. *Molecular Psychiatry*, 13, 131–146.

UNICEF Office of Research (2013). Child Well-being in Rich Countries: A comparative overview, Innocenti Report Card 11, UNICEF Office of Research, Florence. Retrieved from www.unicef-irc.org/publications/pdf/rc11_eng.pdf.

Vaillancourt, T., Brittain, H., Bennett, L., Arnocky, S., McDougall, P., Hymel, S., ... & Cunningham, L. (2010a). Places to avoid: Population-based study of student reports of unsafe and high bullying areas at school. *Canadian Journal of School Psychology*, 25, 40–54.

Vaillancourt, T., Clinton, J., McDougall, P., Schmidt, L., & Hymel, S. (2010b). The neurobiology of peer victimization and rejection. In S. R. Jimerson, S. M. Swearer, & D. L. Espelage (Eds), *The handbook of bullying in schools: An international perspective* (pp. 293–327). New York: Routledge.

Vaillancourt, T., Duku, E., Becker, S., Schmidt, L., Nicol, J., Muir, C., & MacMillian, H. (2011). Peer victimization, depressive symptoms, and high salivary cortisol predict poor memory in children. *Brain and Cognition*, 77, 191–199.

Vaillancourt, T., Duku, E., Decatanzaro, D., MacMillan, H., Muir, C., & Schmidt, L. A. (2008). Variation in hypothalamic–pituitary–adrenal axis activity among bullied and non-bullied children. *Aggressive Behavior*, 34, 294–305.

Vaillancourt, T., Hymel, S., & McDougall, P. (2003). Bullying is power: Implications for school-based intervention strategies. *Journal of Applied School Psychology*, 19, 157–176.

Vaillancourt, T., Hymel, S., & McDougall, P. (2013). The biological underpinnings of peer victimization: Understanding why and how the effects of bullying can last a lifetime. *Theory into Practice*, 52, 241–248.

Vaillancourt, T., Sanderson, C., Arnold, P., & McDougall, P. (2017). The neurobiology of peer victimization: Longitudinal links to health, genetic risk, and epigenetic mechanisms. In C. P. Bradshaw (Ed.), *Handbook of bullying prevention: The life course perspective* (pp. 35–47). National Association of Social Workers Press.

Wolke, D., Copeland, W. E., Angold, A., & Costello, E. J. (2013). Impact of bullying in childhood on adult health, wealth, crime, and social outcomes. *Psychological Science*, 24, 1958–1970.

Yehuda, R., Kahana, B., Binder-Brynes, K., Southwick, S. M., Mason, J. W., & Giller, E. L. (1995). Low urinary cortisol excretion in holocaust survivors with posttraumatic stress disorder. *American Journal of Psychiatry*, 152, 982–986. doi: 10.1176/ajp.152.7.982.

11 Molecular Genetics of Aggression and Violent Crime

Cashen M. Boccio, Marianna McBride, and Kevin M. Beaver

Introduction

Aggression and violent behavior represent serious threats to public safety. In the United States alone, approximately 5.4 million people were the victims of violent crimes in 2014 (Truman & Langton, 2015). To put this number in perspective, the most recent estimates from the National Crime Victimization Survey data suggest that approximately 20.1 out of every 1,000 Americans were victims of violent crime in 2014 (Truman & Langton, 2015). In addition, the Federal Bureau of Investigation's most recent Uniform Crime Report data indicate that more than 1,100,000 violent crimes were reported to the police in 2013 (US Department of Justice, Federal Bureau of Investigation, 2014). Consistently high rates of violent crime highlight the need for research examining the etiology of aggressive and violent behavior. In conjunction with this research, innovative policy changes are also needed to address the primary sources of violence in order to reduce the threat to public safety.

Criminological theory and research has traditionally examined environmental explanations for aggression and violent behavior. Mainstream criminological theories, for instance, generally locate the source of antisocial behavior in neighborhoods, peer associations, or parenting practices. Recently, however, there has been a shift in the field with increased interest on exploring the possibility that genetic factors may influence aggression and violent behavior.

The aim of this chapter is to provide an overview of the connection between molecular genetics and aggression and violent crime. In order to do so, we will first briefly discuss findings from behavioral genetics studies. Second, we will briefly discuss the structure of DNA and how genes influence variation in behavioral phenotypes. Third, we will present the current research on candidate genes studies and genome-wide association studies (GWAS) in relation to aggressive and violent behavior. Fourth, we will outline the extant research on gene–environment interactions. Finally, we will discuss the implications of molecular genetics studies for policies, interventions, and possible preventative treatments for aggression and violent behavior.

Behavioral Genetics

Behavioral genetic research typically involves estimating the influence of genetic and environmental influences on variation in human behavior. To do this, researchers utilize quantitative genetics methodologies that are capable of disentangling the proportion of phenotypic variance that is attributable to genetic and environmental factors. The environmental component of the variance is further divided into shared and nonshared environmental factors. Shared environments are environmental components that influence children in the same household to develop similarly to one another. In contrast, nonshared environments are environmental components that influence children who grow up in the same household to develop differently from one another. Common methodologies used by behavioral geneticists include twin studies and adoption studies (Plomin, DeFries, Knopik, & Neiderhiser, 2013).

In twin studies, researchers compare the behavior of twins living in the same household to obtain heritability estimates (Plomin et al., 2013). By incorporating twins with different levels of genetic relatedness, behavioral geneticists are able to calculate estimates of the influence of genetic and environmental factors on variance in human behavioral outcomes. For example, dizygotic (DZ) twins share approximately 50% of their genetic material, whereas monozygotic (MZ) twins share around 100% of their genetic material. As a result, researchers can use correlations between MZ and DZ twins to determine which portions of the variance of behavioral phenotypes are the result of genetic and environmental factors. According to these estimates, if the assumptions of twin-based methodologies are met – and mathematical simulations indicate that they are (Barnes et al., 2014) – MZ twins will be more phenotypically similar to each other than DZ twins if the traits in question are heritable.

Behavioral geneticists are also able to estimate the influence of genetic and environmental factors by examining adoptees. Adoption studies measure the influence of genetic and environmental factors on human behavior by taking into account the genes the adopted child inherited from their biological parents, as well as the environment provided by their adoptive parents (Beaver, 2008). Phenotypic similarities between adoptees and their biological parents would suggest that the phenotype was more influenced by genetics than by the environment (Beaver, 2011). Likewise, if a child resembles their adoptive parents more so than their biological parents on several phenotypes, it would serve as evidence that those particular phenotypes were influenced more by the environment than by biology.

In general, findings from twin and adoption studies reveal that approximately 50% of the variance in behavioral phenotypes is attributable to genetic factors. This estimate has been supported by a recent meta-analysis conducted by Polderman and colleagues (2015) that examined twin studies published in the last half-century. Polderman et al.'s (2015) analysis of more than 2,700 studies examining nearly 17,800 traits in more than 14,500 twin pairs, revealed that approximately 49% of the variance of human phenotypes is the result of genetic factors. Related studies have also revealed that approximately 50% of the variance in antisocial phenotypes, including aggression and violent behavior, is attributable to genetic factors (Ferguson, 2010; Mason & Frick, 1994; Miles & Carey, 1997; Rhee & Waldman, 2002). The remaining half of the variance of these phenotypes is attributed to environmental influences, with the majority of this variance being explained by environmental factors that are not shared between twins. As a whole, behavioral genetics studies suggest that aggressive and violent behavior are due, at least in part, to the influence of genetics.

Molecular Genetics

The methodologies and analytical approaches used in behavioral genetic research are valuable for identifying the proportion of variance that is due to genetic and environmental factors, but these methodologies do not provide information on the specific genes involved in creating phenotypic variance. Molecular genetics studies, however, can be used to identify specific genes that are implicated in the development of human phenotypes. Molecular genetic studies are able to pinpoint specific genes involved in phenotypic outcomes by testing for associations between possessing particular genetic markers and behavioral outcomes. Using molecular genetics methodologies, a number of genes have been linked with the development of antisocial phenotypes including aggressive and violent behavior (Caspi et al., 2002; Guo, Roettger, & Shih, 2007). Before discussing specific genes that are involved in the development of aggression and violent behavior, we will briefly outline the structure of DNA and explain how specific genes can influence variation in phenotypes.

Genes are housed on deoxyribonucleic acid (DNA), which resides in the nucleus of all cells (expect for red blood cells). The genetic code is written in nucleotide bases, which, along with a sugar phosphate backbone, make up the structure of the DNA molecule. There are four nucleotide bases in DNA – Adenine (A), Thymine (T), Guanine (G), and Cytosine (C). Each of these bases is able to bond with one, and only one, of the other three bases. To illustrate, A bonds with T and G bonds with C. As a result of these pair-specific bonds between nucleotide bases, the DNA strands in the double helix are complementary to one another.

Genes are composed of contiguous nucleotide base pairs that work together and contain the information required for the production and structure of proteins. Proteins are complex organic molecules that are necessary for the development, structure, and function of organisms. For example, proteins compose the structure of cells, transport nutrients throughout the body, and are responsible the transportation of information between neurons. Proteins are composed of amino acids that are linked together in a particular order. The specific configuration of amino acids in proteins is specified by sequences of nucleotide bases present in genes. In order to create proteins, the DNA code is first transcribed into ribonucleic acid (RNA) and then translated into the corresponding sequence of amino acids. The nucleotide bases in the subsequent RNA are complementary to the DNA sequence, however, in RNA molecules "U" is substituted in place of "T." Importantly, the reading frame for translating the genetic code to amino acids is three nucleotide bases – referred to as codons. Each codon corresponds to an individual amino acid and, therefore, the order of nucleotide bases and codons in a gene is responsible for the sequence of amino acids that are joined together to form a protein. If there are errors in the order of nucleotide bases in a gene, then this can lead to changes in the structure of the protein that can result in compromised protein functionality.

Most of the genes in the human genome have only one version. However, a small subset of genes, referred to as polymorphisms, have more than one version present in the population (Mielke, Konigsberg, & Relethford, 2006). The different versions of genes available within the population are called alleles. The presence of different alleles within a population accounts for the variation in physical and behavioral phenotypes observed between people. For instance, hair texture may be determined by a polymorphic gene that has one allele that codes for curly hair and another allele that codes for straight hair.

Most of the polymorphisms present in the population do not appear to cause visible or functional differences in phenotypes because the differences between the available alleles do not lead to changes in protein structure. That is, many polymorphisms do not lead to functional differences because the different alleles still code for the same protein. There are, however, some polymorphisms in the population that correspond to functional differences that lead to the production of different phenotypes. Polymorphisms can lead to the development of different phenotypes when the differences between the available alleles leads to different amino acids being substituted into proteins that may then affect the protein's structure and function. For instance, a polymorphism that codes for a neurotransmitter may have two alleles where version A functions efficiently, but version B may code for a different amino acid leading the subsequent neurotransmitter to be less efficient. As a result, individuals who have version B of the gene may exhibit a different behavioral phenotype than individuals with version A (e.g., temper, impulsivity).

In general, there are two main kinds of polymorphisms that can lead to differences in phenotypes. The first type of polymorphism involves the substitution of single nucleotides within genes, while the second type of polymorphism involves sections of repeating sequences of nucleotides – referred to as variable-number tandem repeats (VNTRs). VNTRs are further broken down into microsatellite and minisatellite polymorphisms based on the number of nucleotides involved in the repeated sections.

The first type of polymorphism, single-nucleotide polymorphisms (SNPs), are the result of the substitution of one nucleotide in a gene. Changing a single nucleotide within a codon can lead to the substitution of a different amino acid in the resulting protein, leading to structural and functional differences. To illustrate, a transcribed gene may have one copy that reads AUACUUCA<u>U</u>UAG, and another copy that reads AUACUUCA<u>G</u>UAG. In this case, substituting a G in place of the U in the second allele leads to the substitution of a glutamine amino acid in place of histidine. The substitution of a single amino acid within a protein can lead to changes in the structure and function of the protein that can lead to phenotypic changes. Notably, SNPs are the most common type of polymorphisms and are believed to be responsible for the majority of human genetic diseases (Plomin, DeFries, Craig, & McGuffin, 2001).

VNTRs are polymorphisms that are characterized by repeating sections of nucleotides within genes. There are two main types of VNTRs, microsatellites and minisatellites, which differ according to the number of nucleotides involved in the repeating sections. In both of these types of VNTRs, the differences between alleles are due to differences in the length of the gene. That is, some alleles, with more repeated sections, are longer than others.

The first type of VNTRS, microsatellites, are polymorphisms where a small set of nucleotide bases (usually less than six bases) repeat for a variable number of times. Minisatellites, on the other hand, are VNTR polymorphisms that have a larger number of repeated bases (usually greater than ten) than in microsatellites. VNTRs have been implicated in a number of human genetic diseases. For example, Huntington's disease has been found to be the result of a microsatellite polymorphism where a three-nucleotide segment (CAG) of the huntingtin gene can repeat a variable number of times. Alleles that have between 6 and 35 CAG repeats usually result in properly functioning huntingtin proteins, whereas huntingtin genes that have 36 or more CAG repeats tend to result in a protein mutation that leads to the development of Huntington's disease (Budworth & McMurray, 2013).

The types of polymorphisms we have discussed can influence phenotypes in several ways. The most straightforward way polymorphisms can affect phenotypes is through monogenic effects. Monogenic effects refer to phenotypes that are the result of a single gene. In monogenic effects, only one gene is responsible for the development of a phenotype, and the presence or absence of an allele can be used to predict whether an individual will exhibit a specific phenotype. Several human diseases are the result of monogenic effects, including polycystic kidney disease and Tay-Sachs disease.

A second way that polymorphisms can influence phenotypes is through polygenic effects. Polygenic effects involve a process through which multiple genes work together to influence an individual's phenotype. In polygenic effects, genes work together probabilistically. In these cases, the effect of each individual gene is small, but the genes function together to increase the likelihood of developing certain phenotypes. In other words, individuals who carry more alleles that predispose them to developing a certain phenotype will be more likely to the exhibit the phenotype in question than individuals who carry fewer of these specific alleles. Human behavioral outcomes such as aggression and violent behavior are likely the result of polygenic effects where multiple genes work together to increase the risk of developing aggressive behavioral outcomes.

A final way polymorphisms can influence phenotypes is through pleiotropic effects. Pleotropic effects occur when a single gene influences multiple phenotypes. For example, cystic fibrosis is a genetic disease that arises from a single gene mutation that affects the function of multiple organs including the lungs, pancreas, liver, and kidneys. In relation to aggression and violent behavior, a number of genes associated with neurotransmission have been shown to influence multiple behavioral outcomes associated with antisocial behavior (Beaver, DeLisi, Wright, & Vaughn, 2009; Beaver, Wright, & Walsh, 2008; Gill, Daly, Heron, Hawi, & Fitzgerald, 1997; Rowe et al., 1998).

Candidate Genes for Aggression and Violent Behavior

Molecular genetic studies are designed to pinpoint genetic polymorphisms that are involved in the development of phenotypic variance, including variation in aggressive and violent phenotypes. In general, candidate gene studies are largely "theory-driven" and are aimed at identifying specific genes associated with certain phenotypes. The targets of candidate gene studies are generally selected in accordance with neurobiological theories of behavior. Accordingly, most of the genes implicated as candidate genes for aggressive and violent phenotypes are related to neurotransmission. To date, candidate gene studies have identified several genes involved in the development of ADHD, alcoholism, aggression, and violence (Caspi et al., 2002; Dick & Faroud, 2003; Guo et al., 2007; Li, Sham, Owen, & He, 2006; Rujescu, Giegling, Gietl, Hartman, & Moller, 2003). Many of the genes identified as contributing to these antisocial phenotypes, including aggression and violence, code for proteins involved in the transportation, reception, and breakdown of neurotransmitters.

Neurotransmitters are proteins that deliver chemical messages from one cell to another in the nervous system. In general, neurotransmitters deliver a message from one cell to another by first being released by the presynaptic neuron and then traversing the synapse (space between neurons) to receptors on the postsynaptic neuron. Once the neurotransmitters have delivered the message to the postsynaptic neuron they are removed from the synapse through one of two mechanisms. In the first mechanism, referred to as reuptake, neurotransmitters are removed from the synapse and delivered back to the presynaptic neuron by transporter proteins. In the second mechanism, neurotransmitters that still remain in the synapse are metabolized (chemically broken down) by enzymes. If the transporter proteins or the enzymes responsible for metabolizing neurotransmitters have structural abnormalities, they may not function efficiently, which may cause neurotransmitter levels to fluctuate, leading to disturbances in mood and behavior.

Candidate gene studies have focused on genes related to the transportation and reception of neurotransmitters along with genes that code for enzymes that breakdown neurotransmitters in the synapse. To date, researchers have identified genes related to three classes of neurotransmitters that appear to be associated with aggression and violent behavior. Specifically, researchers have identified genes involved in the transportation and reception of dopamine, serotonin, and GABA that are associated with antisocial outcomes. In addition, researchers have identified genes coding for two enzymes (MAOA, COMT) that are involved in the breakdown of neurotransmitters that are linked with aggression and violent behavior. In the following section, we discuss the extant research pertaining to genes related to the transportation of neurotransmitters and enzymes that have been associated with aggression and violent behavior.

Genes Related to the Transportation, Reception, and Breakdown of Neurotransmitters

There are three types of neurotransmitters that have been linked with aggression and violent behavior. First, we will discuss the role of dopamine levels and dopaminergic genes in aggression and violent behavior. Second, we will discuss the role of serotonin levels and serotonergic polymorphisms in antisocial outcomes. Finally, we will discuss GABA levels and GABAergic genes associated with aggression and violent behavior.

Dopamine is an excitatory neurotransmitter that is involved in the reward system of the brain. There is a considerable amount of variation in baseline dopamine levels between different people and dopamine levels can change in response to environmental factors. High levels of dopamine have been shown to be associated with increased involvement in impulsive and violent behavior (Niehoff, 1999). However, there is also evidence linking low levels of dopamine to involvement in aggressive behavior (Raine, 1993). As a result, the relationship between dopamine levels and aggressive behavior may be nonlinear such that high and low levels of dopamine are both associated with aggressive conduct. Molecular genetic studies have revealed that many of the genes involved in the transportation of dopamine are polymorphic, including DAT1, DRD2, DRD3, DRD4, and DRD5.

A number of polymorphisms that influence the transportation of dopamine have been associated with aggressive and violent behavior. For instance, DAT1, a dopamine transporter gene, is a polymorphism with a minisatellite that repeats up to 11 times, where the 10-repeat allele has been linked with violent delinquency and violent behavior in adulthood (Guo et al., 2007). Empirical studies have also revealed that several dopamine receptor genes are associated with antisocial outcomes. For example, DRD2, a dopamine receptor gene that codes for D2 dopamine receptors, is a polymorphism with a SNP that has two alleles present in the population – A1 and A2. Empirical research has demonstrated that the A1 allele is associated with involvement in violent delinquency (Guo et al., 2007). The association between the A1 allele and aggressive behavior may be explained by inefficient dopamine reception in carriers of the A1 allele. Not surprisingly, studies have revealed that individuals who carry the A1 allele tend to have fewer D2 dopamine receptors, which may result in poorer regulation of dopamine levels (Pohjalainen et al., 1998).

Serotonin is an inhibitory neurotransmitter that is involved with the regulation of behavior and impulse control. A significant body of research demonstrates that low levels of serotonin are associated with aggressive and violent behavior. The first studies examining serotonin levels and aggression, used a cerebrospinal fluid (CSF) measures of the main metabolite of serotonin, 5-hydroxyindoleactic acid (5-HIAA), and found that serotonin levels accounted for more than 60% of the variation in aggression in subjects with personality disorders (Brown et al., 1979). This finding led to a flurry of research on the association between serotonin levels and aggression. Subsequent studies examining this association have revealed mixed results. In general, however, previous studies have found evidence of an inverse association between serotonin levels and violent offending, childhood disruptive behavior, and arson (Kruesi et al., 1990; Limson et al., 1991; Virkkunen et al., 1994). To date, three meta-analyses have been conducted on studies that have examined the relationship between serotonin and aggressive and violent behavior and they have revealed some evidence for a significant inverse relationship between serotonin and aggressive/violent behavior (Balaban, Alper, & Kasamon, 1996; Duke, Begue, Bell, & Eisenlohr-Moul, 2013; Moore, Scarpa, & Raine, 2002; Raine, 1993). Molecular genetics studies have revealed that several of the genes involved in the transportation and breakdown of serotonin appear to be involved in the development of aggressive and violent phenotypes.

For instance, 5HTTLPR, a serotonin transporter gene, is polymorphic with a minisatellite that results in two different alleles. One of the alleles (S) is significantly shorter than the other allele (L). The S allele of 5HTTLPR has been identified as conferring increased risk for the development of antisocial phenotypes, including ADHD (Cadoret et al., 2003), heavy drinking (Herman, Smolen, & Hewitt, 2003), and violent aggression (Haberstick, Smolen, & Hewitt, 2006; Liao, Hong, Shih, & Tsai, 2004; Retz, Retz-Junginger, Supprian, Thome, & Rösler, 2004). Moreover, at least one study has demonstrated that the S allele of 5HTTLPR is significantly more prevalent in violent offenders than in nonviolent offenders (Retz et al., 2004). There is some reason to believe that the association between 5HTTLPR and antisocial behavior can be explained by the S allele coding for transporter proteins with reduced serotonin reuptake abilities (Lesch et al., 1996). Several serotonin receptor genes have also been linked with the development of aggressive and violent phenotypes. For instance, HTR1B, a gene that codes for the serotonin 1B receptor, is a polymorphism with several different alleles, where some alleles code for higher or lower HTR1B gene expression. The low-expression alleles have been linked with greater levels of anger, hostility, and aggression (Conner et al., 2010; Jensen et al., 2009).

GABA is another inhibitory neurotransmitter that has been associated with aggression and antisocial behavior. In general, previous research has revealed that low levels of GABA are linked with aggressive behavior in humans and nonhumans (Bjork et al., 2001). These findings, along with findings from studies that indicate that GABA levels are under the influence of genetic factors (Petty et al., 1999), suggest that genes related to regulating GABA levels may be associated with aggression and violent behavior. For instance, several studies have indicated that GABRA2, a GABA A receptor gene with several SNPs, is linked with increased risk of externalizing behavior, conduct disorder, and antisocial personality disorder (Dick et al., 2006a; Dick et al., 2006b; Dick et al., 2009). In addition, there is some evidence that GABBR2, a GABA B receptor gene, is associated with antisocial behavior (Terranova et al., 2013).

Along with genes involved in the transportation and reception of neurotransmitters, genes that code for enzymes that breakdown neurotransmitters have also been associated with aggression and violent behavior. Specifically, genes related to two enzymes (MAOA, COMT) have been implicated in developing aggressive behavior. The MAOA gene codes for the production of the monoamine oxidase A (MAOA) enzyme, which breaks down monoamine neurotransmitters such as serotonin and dopamine. The MAOA gene contains a minisatellite that repeats between two and five times. The alleles for MAOA are generally considered to consist of two groups, one group of high-activity MAOA alleles (4R, 3.5R) and a group of low-activity MAOA alleles (2R, 3R). The low-activity MAOA alleles are less efficient at breaking down neurotransmitters and, as a result, carriers of the low-activity MAOA alleles may have fluctuations in their neurotransmitter levels. Low-activity MAOA alleles have been associated with involvement in aggressive and antisocial behavior in males (Ficks & Waldman, 2014). The empirical research surrounding this association, however, is inconclusive, with some studies suggesting a positive association between the low-activity

MAOA alleles and aggression, and some studies suggesting a negative association (Manuck, Flory, Ferrell, Mann, & Muldoon, 2000), or no direct association at all (Caspi et al., 2002; Verhoeven et al., 2012). A recent meta-analysis examining the main effect of MAOA on behavioral outcomes revealed a significant positive relationship between the low–activity MAOA alleles and increased involvement in aggressive and antisocial behavior (Ficks & Waldman, 2014). The inconsistent findings regarding the relationship between MAOA and antisocial behavior are likely explained by the effects of environmental factors moderating the influence of MAOA on behavioral outcomes. For instance, several studies have documented that the low-functioning alleles of MAOA interact with childhood maltreatment to predict antisocial behavior (Caspi et al., 2002) and conduct disorder (Foley et al., 2004).

COMT is a gene that codes for the production of the catechol-O-methyltransferase (COMT) enzyme, which breaks down catecholamines such as dopamine and epinephrine. The COMT gene contains a SNP with two alleles. One of the alleles codes for the amino acid Methionine (Met) while the other codes for the amino acid Valine (Val). Individuals who carry the Met allele have been shown to have reduced COMT activity, which is associated with increased levels of catecholamines. The Met allele has also been identified as conferring increased risk for the development of antisocial phenotypes. Specifically, the Met allele has been shown to be associated with involvement in aggressive and violent behavior (Hirata, Zai, Nowrouzi, Beitchman, & Kennedy, 2013; Jones et al., 2001; Volavka, Bilder, & Nolan, 2004).

Genome-Wide Association Studies (GWAS)

Genome-wide association studies (GWAS) test for associations between common genetic variants and variation in phenotypes. Unlike candidate gene studies, GWAS are data-driven and examine the entire genome of participants and test to see if there is an association between the frequency of common allelic variants and the development of certain phenotypes. As a result, GWAS are able to identify novel genes associated with particular phenotypes that might not be predicted by any existing theory of the etiology of particular phenotypes. GWAS generally focus on associations between SNPs and diseases or behavioral phenotypes. Previous GWAS that have investigated behavioral phenotypes have revealed several polymorphisms that are associated with conduct disorder (Dick et al., 2011), anger-proneness (Mick et al., 2014), and hostility (Merjonen et al., 2011).

GWAS have only recently been applied to investigating aggression and violent behavior. One of the first GWAS to examine the etiology of antisocial behavior did not find any genetic polymorphisms that reached the level of genome-wide significance; however, the authors did identify one gene (DYRK1A) that appeared to be nearing significance (Tielbeek et al., 2012). A second GWAS by Salvatore and colleagues (2015) was also not able to identify any polymorphisms that reached genome-wide significance; however, they were able to identify several SNPs that were nearing significance for adult antisocial behavior. A third study by Pappa and colleagues (2015) was able to identify one gene on chromosome 2 that neared genome-wide significance for predicting childhood aggression. In addition, they were able to identify several other polymorphisms that may be related to childhood aggression (Pappa et al., 2015). While these studies suggest several genes that may be involved in the development of aggressive and violent behavior, the inability of these studies to detect genes that reach the level of statistical significance highlights several concerns with GWAS.

One major concern for GWAS is that genes associated with phenotypes may only explain a very small portion (< 1%) of the variance in the particular trait. As a result, large sample sizes are needed in order to detect these associations. Further exacerbating the problem, the analytic strategy employed in GWAS necessitates a very conservative estimate of statistical significance ($p < 5.0 \times 10^{-8}$), making it difficult to find polymorphisms that reach the level of genome-wide significance.

The findings of GWAS also raise concerns about what researchers have termed as "missing heritability." Missing heritability refers to the gap between the heritability estimates of twin studies and heritability as estimated by associations identified in GWAS. Unfortunately, SNPs (as detected by GWAS) only appear to account for approximately 10% of phenotypic outcomes, and 5% or less of the variance in behavioral phenotypic outcomes (Plomin, 2013). Therefore, these findings contrast research from behavioral genetic studies that imply that approximately 50% of the variance of human phenotypes is attributable to genetic factors. One explanation for missing heritability is that GWAS are only able to identify the additive genetic effects of common SNPs, and, therefore, they miss heritability that is due to rare gene variants and genes that may be involved in gene–environment interactions (Manolio et al., 2009; Manuck & McCaffery, 2014). That is, while associated polymorphisms may only have a small effect on their own, polymorphisms may interact with specific environments to have larger effects on particular phenotypes. As a result, GWAS may miss associated genes that do not appear to significantly influence aggression on their own, but may be involved in gene–environment interactions for the prediction of aggression and violent behavior.

Gene–Environment Interactions

The previous sections have discussed individual genes that have been identified as influencing the development of aggressive and violent behavior, however, genetic factors do not work independently to influence the formation of antisocial phenotypes. Frequently, instead, genetic factors work interactively with the environment to produce behavioral phenotypes. To illustrate, alleles that confer increased risk for developing antisocial behavior may have a more pronounced influence on the development of aggressive and violent behavior when paired with adverse environments compared to more favorable environments. In this way, the influence of an allele may be dependent on the environment. This dependent relationship between genotype and environmental factors is referred to as a gene–environment interaction.

Gene–environment interactions capture the complex relationships between genotypes and environmental factors. The logic of gene–environment interactions is based on individuals each having unique genotypes that confer different genetic predispositions and different susceptibilities to the influence of environmental factors. As a result of these genetic differences, some individuals may be more affected by certain environmental factors than others. Therefore, gene–environment interactions are able to explain why different people may react to the same environment in different ways. To illustrate, individuals with a genetic propensity toward aggressive behavior may be more susceptible to respond to environmental factors, such as maltreatment, with aggressive behavior than individuals without the genetic predisposition toward aggression. In this way, behavioral phenotypes are the product of an interaction of both genetic propensities and environmental factors.

For example, one of the earliest studies to explore gene–environment interactions revealed that carriers of low-functioning MAOA alleles were more likely to develop antisocial behavior in response to childhood maltreatment than carriers of the high-functioning alleles (Caspi et al., 2002). To illustrate, only 12% of the study's participants were both carriers of the low-functioning MAOA alleles and exposed to maltreatment, yet they comprised 44% of the serious convictions of all the participants in the study. Importantly, individuals who were exposed to only one of the risk factors (genetic or environmental) were significantly less likely to develop antisocial phenotypes than individuals exposed to both risk factors. The gene–environment interaction between low-functioning MAOA alleles and childhood maltreatment has also been demonstrated to predict conduct disorder (Foley et al., 2004) and mental health problems (Kim-Cohen et al., 2006). In addition, a recent meta-analysis by Byrd and Manuck (2014) revealed consistent support for the interaction between the low-functioning MAOA alleles and childhood maltreatment for the prediction of developing an antisocial phenotype.

Several other gene–environment interactions have also been implicated in the development of aggressive and violent phenotypes. For instance, several genes related to dopamine function have been documented to interact with environmental risk factors. For example, empirical studies have indicated that DRD2 interacts with having a criminal father to influence involvement in violent delinquency (DeLisi, Beaver, Vaughn, & Wright, 2009) and DAT1 interacts with delinquent peers to predict violent behavior (Vaughn, DeLisi, Beaver, & Wright, 2009). DRD2 and DRD4 have also been shown to interact with neighborhood characteristics to predict involvement in violent delinquency (Beaver, Gibson, DeLisi, Vaughn, & Wright, 2012). Similarly, dopamine risk, as conferred by possessing the risk alleles of DRD2, DRD4, and DAT1, has been shown to interact with neighborhood characteristics to predict increased involvement in violent behavior (Barnes & Jacobs, 2013). Furthermore, there is some evidence that the serotonin transporter gene 5HTTLPR interacts with socioeconomic status to predict psychopathic traits (Sadeh et al., 2010) and childhood maltreatment to predict the development of antisocial personality disorder (Douglas et al., 2011).

Further complicating the relationship between genes and the environment, gene–environment interactions appear to have a number of different forms. The most common form of gene–environment interaction is where risk alleles interact with environmental risk factors to produce antisocial behavior. In this case, the environmental risk factors can be seen as "triggering" the effects of an individual's genetic propensity towards antisocial behavior. This form of gene–environment interaction is referred to as the "diathesis-stress" model. The diathesis-stress model of gene–environment interactions has received the most empirical attention and support (Manuck & McCaffery, 2014). For example, the diathesis stress model is indicated in the MAOA-childhood maltreatment interaction mentioned above.

While gene–environment interaction research frequently indicates that risk alleles will have their greatest effects on behavioral outcomes when paired with adverse environments, this is not always the case. For instance, DRD2 has been shown to interact with delinquent peers to predict victimization for individuals who appear to have a low level of environmental risk. To illustrate, in a study by Beaver and colleagues (2007), the A1 risk allele appeared to have a more pronounced effect on victimization for males with a low number of delinquent peers compared to males with a high number of delinquent peers. This kind relationship can be explained by the "social push hypothesis," where individuals will be most susceptible to their genetic predispositions in good environments, whereas, in adverse environments, environmental factors may have more of an influence over the development of behavioral phenotypes that genetic predispositions.

A third model for gene–environment interactions, referred to as the "differential susceptibility model," has been posed by Belsky and colleagues (Belsky & Pluess, 2009). According to this model, alleles should be considered to be "plasticity alleles." Plasticity alleles determine how malleable an individual is to environmental influences. In this case, someone who has a high number of plasticity alleles would be more influenced by environmental factors for the development of behavioral phenotypes. For instance, an individual with a high degree of plasticity would be more likely to develop aggressive and violent behavior in a criminogenic environment. Conversely, this same individual would also be more likely to be affected by the influences of a prosocial environment. Empirical studies that have examined the differential-susceptibility hypothesis have revealed some support for this model (Manuck & McCaffery, 2014). For example, the S allele of 5HTTLPR appears to operate as a plasticity allele that interacts with parenting practices to predict the presentation of positive affect or depressive symptoms, when compared to behavioral outcomes of individuals with the L allele (Taylor et al., 2006).

Policy Implications, Prevention Efforts, and Interventions

New advancements in the study of the genetic contributors to crime open opportunities for new policies that can attempt to prevent and intervene in the development of aggression and violent behavior. Previous research demonstrates that individuals' responses to treatment, intervention, and preventive programs are affected by individual characteristics. For instance, males and high-rate offenders may be more responsive to particular treatment programs than females and low-rate offenders. The new knowledge obtained through molecular genetic research may be able to be used to tailor preventative and intervention programs to individuals' genotypes. For example,

Gajos, Fagan, and Beaver (2016) recently outlined how genetic research can be used to inform policies pertaining to prevention programs. Specifically, Gajos and colleagues suggest that gene–environment interactions (especially as related to the differential susceptibility model) are a key area of research for genetically informed preventative research and policies.

Similarly, our overview of the existing molecular genetic research suggests that gene–environment interactions may be the most promising area of research for exploring both preventative and intervening practices. Of particular importance, gene–environment interactions can be used to explain why two different individuals respond to the same environment in different ways. As a result, findings from this area of research may be able to distinguish between certain genotypes that may make individuals more or less amenable to preventative practices and intervention policies. Therefore, findings from this area of research may be able to be used to design targeted treatment strategies for individuals who have different genotypes.

Recent studies have attempted to examine whether genotype can be incorporated into creating targeted intervention strategies. For instance, a study examining the influence of parental training on parental discipline practices and childhood externalizing behaviors found that changes in parental discipline practices were more effective in reducing childhood externalizing behavior in children who possessed the seven-repeat allele of DRD4 (Bakermans-Kranenburg, van Ijzendoorn, Pijlman, Mesman, & Juffer, 2008). In addition, the ten-repeat allele of DAT1 has been associated with increased responsivity to family-based intervention strategies designed to decrease the presentation of ADHD symptoms and behavioral problems (van den Hoofdakker et al., 2012). While these studies do not directly address aggression and violent behavior it is reasonable to suggest that findings implicating gene-moderated responses to intervention programs may be generalizable to other behavioral phenotypes.

Findings from molecular genetics studies can also be used to inform preventative strategies by helping to identify which individuals may be the most at risk for developing aggressive or violent behavior in response to certain environmental stresses. For instance, knowledge of an individual's genotype can be used to identify if the individual is at "high risk" for developing aggressive or violent behavior in response to adverse environments. As a result, this knowledge could be used to target preventative programs to those individuals deemed the highest risk for developing aggression. Two studies that have been conducted by Brody and colleagues using this line of thinking have found that genetically informed preventative programs can be used to decrease involvement in risky behavior in teenagers. In the first study, Brody, Beach, Philibert, Chen, and Murry (2009) found that parenting interventions affected the association between 5HTTLPR genotype and engagement in risky behavior in adolescents. In the second study, Brody and colleagues (2014) found that parenting interventions moderated the relationship between DRD4 genotype and substance use in male adolescents. While these findings are promising, to date, very little research has attempted to alter environmental factors in such a way to ameliorate individual's genetic risk of developing aggressive or violent behavior. Therefore, preventative strategies based on the logic of gene–environment interactions for preventing aggression and violence are currently situated in the theoretical realm. Further research will have to be conducted in order to determine if the moderating effects of prevention efforts on genetic risk for substance use and risky behavior carry over to aggressive and violent behavior.

Conclusion

Molecular genetics research is rapidly increasing knowledge pertaining to the development of aggression and violent behavior. Over the past two-and-a-half decades molecular genetics research has identified several candidate genes for aggression and violent behavior in humans. In addition, research exploring gene–environment interactions moves the field closer to being able to understand why some individuals may develop aggressive and/or violent behavior in response to certain environments while others do not develop these behaviors. More recently, GWAS have been employed to attempt to identify genes involved in the etiology of violence and aggression; however, this line of research is only in its infancy. Together these new avenues of research are useful in both the exploration of causes of aggressive and violent behavior and introducing possible new directions for preventative and intervention programs.

References

Bakermans-Kranenburg, M. J., Van Ijzendoorn, M. H., Pijlman, F. T. A., Mesman, J., & Juffer, F. (2008). Experimental evidence for differential susceptibility: Dopamine D4 receptor polymorphism (DRD4 VNTR) moderates intervention effects on toddlers' externalizing behavior in a randomized controlled trial. *Developmental Psychology*, 44, 293–300.

Balaban, E., Alper, J. S., & Kasamon, Y. L., (1996). Review mean genes and the biology of aggression: A critical review of recent animal and human research. Journal of Neurogenetics, 11, 1–43.

Barnes, J. C. & Jacobs, B. A. (2013). Genetic risk for violent behavior and environmental exposure to disadvantage and violent crime: The case for gene-environment interaction. *Journal of Interpersonal Violence*, 18, 92–120.

Barnes, J. C., Wright, J. P., Boutwell, B. B., Schwartz, J. A., Connolly, E. J., Nedelec, J. L., & Beaver, K. M. (2014). Demonstrating the validity of twin research in criminology. *Criminology*, 52, 588–626.

Beaver, K. M. (2011). Genetic influences on being processed through the criminal justice system: Results from a sample of adoptees. *Biological Psychiatry*, 69, 282–87.

Beaver, K. M., DeLisi, M., Wright, J. P., & Vaughn, M. G. (2009). Gene-environment interplay and delinquency involvement: Evidence of direct, indirect, and interactive effects. *Journal of Adolescent Research*, 24, 147–168.

Beaver, K. M., Gibson, C. L., DeLisi, M., Vaughn, M. G., & Wright, J. P. (2012). The interaction between neighborhood disadvantage and genetic factors in the prediction of antisocial outcomes. *Youth Violence and Juvenile Justice*, 10, 25–40.

Beaver, K. M., Wright, J. P., DeLisi, M., Daigle, L. E., Swatt, M. L., & Gibson, C. L. (2007). Evidence of a gene X environment interaction in the creation of victimization: Results from a longitudinal sample of adolescents. *International Journal of Offender Therapy and Comparative Criminology*, 51, 620–645.

Beaver, K. M., Wright, J. P., & Walsh, A. (2008). A gene-based evolutionary explanation for the association between criminal involvement and number of sex partners. *Biodemography and Social Biology*, 54, 47–55.

Belsky, J. & Pluess, M. (2009). Beyond diathesis stress: Differential susceptibility to environmental influences. *Psychological Bulletin*, 135, 885–908.

Bjork, J. M., Moeller, F. G., Kramer, G. L., Kram, M., Suris, A., Rush, A. J., & Petty, F. (2001). Plasma GABA levels correlate with aggressiveness in relatives of patients with unipolar depressive disorder. *Psychiatry Research*, 101, 131–136.

Brody, G. H., Beach, S. R. H., Philibert, R. A., Chen, Y.-F., & Murry, V. M. (2009). Preventative effects moderate the association of 5-HTTLPR and youth risk behavior initiation: Gene x environment hypotheses tested via a randomized prevention design. *Child Development*, 80, 645–661.

Brody, G. H., Chen, Y. F., Beach, S. R., Kogan, S. M., Yu, T., DiClemente, R. J., Wingwood, G. M., Windle, M., & Philibert, R. A. (2014). Differential sensitivity to prevention programming: A dopaminergic polymorphism-enhanced prevention effect on protective parenting and adolescent substance use. *Health Psychology*, 33, 182–191.

Brown, G. L., Goodwin, F. K., Ballenger, J. C., Goyer, P. F., & Major, L. F. (1979). Aggression in humans correlated with cerebrospinal fluid amine metabolites. *Psychiatry Research*, 1, 131–139.

Budworth, H. & McMurray, C. T. (2013). A brief history of triplet repeat diseases. *Methods in Molecular Biology*, 1010, 3–17.

Byrd, A. L. & Manuck, S. B. (2014). MAOA, childhood maltreatment, and antisocial behavior: A meta-analysis of gene-environment interaction. *Biological Psychiatry*, 75, 9–17.

Cadoret, R. J., Langebehn, D., Caspers, K., Troughton, E. P., Yucuis, R., Sandhu, H. K., & Philibert, R. (2003). Associations of the serotonin transporter promoter polymorphism with aggressivity, attention deficit, and conduct disorder in an adoptee population. *Comprehensive Psychiatry*, 44, 88–101.

Caspi, A., McClay, J., Moffitt, T. E., Mill, J., Martin, J., Craig, I. W., Taylor, A., & Poulton, R. (2002). Role of genotype in the cycle of violence in maltreated children. *Science*, 297, 851–854.

Conner, T. S., Jensen, K. P., Tennen, H., Furneaux, H. M., Kranzler, H. R., & Covault, J. (2010). Functional polymorphisms in the serotonin 1B receptor gene (HTR1B) predict self-reported anger and hostility among young men. *American Journal of Medical Genetics, Part B*, 153, 67–78.

DeLisi, M., Beaver, K. M., Vaughn, M. G., & Wright, J. P. (2009). All in the family: Gene x environmental interaction between DRD2 and criminal father is associated with five antisocial phenotypes. *Criminal Justice and Behavior*, 36, 1187–1197.

Dick, D. M., Agrawal, A., Schuckit, M. A., Bierut, L., Hinrichs, A., Fox, L., ... & Begleiter, H. (2006a). Marital status, alcohol dependence, and GABRA2: Evidence for gene-environment correlation and interaction. *Journal of Studies on Alcohol*, 67, 185–194.

Dick, D. M., Beirut, L., Hinrichs, A., Fox, L., Bucholz, K. K., Kramer, J., ... & Foroud, T. (2006b). The role of GABRA2 in risk for conduct disorder and alcohol and drug dependence across developmental stages. *Behavior Genetics*, 36, 577–590.

Dick, D. M., Latendresse, S. J., Lansford, J. E., Budde, J. P., Goate, A., Dodge, K. A., ... & Bates, J. E. (2009). Role of GABRA2 in trajectories of externalizing behavior across development and evidence of moderation by parental monitoring. *Archives of General Psychiatry*, 66, 649–657.

Dick, D. M., Aliev, F., Krueger, R. F., Edwards, A., Agrawal, A., Lynskey, M., Lin, P., Schuckit, M., Hesselbrock, V., Nurnberger, J., Almasy, L., Porjesz, B., Edenberg, H. J., Bucholz, K., Kramer, J., Kuperman, S., & Bierut, L. (2011). Genome-wide association study of conduct disorder symptomatology. *Molecular Psychiatry*, 16, 800–808.

Dick, D. M. & Foroud, T. (2003). Candidate genes for alcohol dependence: A review of genetic evidence form human studies. *Alcoholism: Clinical and Experimental Research*, 27, 868–879.

Douglas, K., Chan, G., Gelernter, J., Arias, A. J., Anton, R. F., Poling, J., ... & Kranzler, H. R. (2011). 5-HTTLPR as a potential moderator of the effects of adverse childhood experiences on risk of antisocial personality disorder. *Psychiatric Genetics*, 21, 240–248.

Duke, A. A., Begue, L., Bell, R., & Eisenlohr-Moul, T. (2013). Revisiting the serotonin-aggression relation in humans: A meta-analysis. *Psychological Bulletin*, 139, 1148–1172.

Ferguson, C. J. (2010). Genetic contributions to antisocial personality and behavior: A meta-analytic review from an evolutionary perspective. *Journal of Social Psychology*, 150, 1–21.

Ficks, C. A. & Waldman, I. D. (2014). Candidate genes for aggression and antisocial behavior: A meta-analysis of association studies of the 5HTTLPR and MAOA-uVNTR. *Behavior Genetics*, 44, 427–444.

Foley, D. L., Eaves, L. J., Wormley, B., Silberg, J. L., Maes, H. H., Kuhn, J., & Riley, B. (2004). Childhood adversity, monoamine oxidase A genotype, and risk for conduct disorder. *Archives of General Psychiatry*, 61, 738–744.

Gajos, J. M., Fagan, A. A., & Beaver, K. M. (2016). Use of genetically informed evidence-based prevention science to understand and prevent crime and related behavioral disorders. *Criminology & Public Policy*, 15, 1–19. doi: 10.1111/1745-9133.12214.

Gill, M., Daly, G., Heron, S., Hawi, Z., & Fitzgerald, M. (1997). Confirmation of association between attention deficit hyperactivity disorder and a dopamine transporter polymorphism. *Molecular Psychiatry*, 2, 311–313.

Guo, G., Roettger, M. E., & Shih, J. C. (2007). Contributions of the DAT1 and DRD2 genes to serious and violent delinquency among adolescents and young adults. *Human Genetics*, 121, 125–136.

Haberstick, B. C., Smolen, A., & Hewitt, J. K. (2006). Family-based association test of the 5HTTLPR and aggressive behavior in a general population sample of children. *Biological Psychiatry*, 59, 836–843.

Herman, A. I., Philbeck, J. W., Vasilopoulos, N. L., & Depetrillo, P. B., (2003). Serotonin transporter promoter polymorphism and differences in alcohol consumption behavior in a college student population. *Alcohol and Alcoholism*, 38, 446–449.

Hirata, Y., Zai, C. C., Nowrouzi, B., Beitchman, J. H., & Kennedy, J. L. (2013). Study of the catechol-O-methyltransferase (COMT) gene with high aggression in children. *Aggressive Behavior*, 39, 45–51.

Jensen, K. P., Covailt, J., Conner, T. S., Tennen, H., Kranzler, H. R., & Furneaux, H. M. (2009). A common polymorphism in serotonin receptor 1B mRNA moderates regulation by miR-96 and associates with aggressive behavior in humans. *Molecular Psychiatry*, 14, 381–389.

Jones, G., Zammit, S., Norton, N., Hamshere, M. L., Jones, S. J., Milham, C., ... & Owen, M. J. (2001). Aggressive behavior in patients with schizophrenia is associated with catechol-O-methyltransferase genotype. *British Journal of Psychiatry*, 179, 351–355.

Kim-Cohen, J., Caspi, A., Taylor, A., Williams, B., Newcombe, R., Craig, I. W., & Moffitt, T. E. (2006). MAOA, maltreatment, and gene-environment interaction predicting children's mental health: New evidence and a meta-analysis. *Molecular Psychiatry*, 11, 903–913.

Kruesi, M. J. P., Rapoport, J. L., Hamburger, S., Hibbs, E., Potter, W. Z., Lenane, M., & Brown, G. L. (1990). Cerebrospinal fluid monoamine metabolites, aggression, and impulsivity in disruptive behavior disorders of children and adolescents. *Archives of General Psychiatry*, 47, 419–426.

Lesch, K. P., Bengel, D., Heils, A., Sabol, S. Z., Greenberg, B. D., Petri, S., ... & Murphy, D. I. (1996). Association of anxiety-related traits with a polymorphism in the serotonin transporter gene regulatory region. *Science*, 274, 1527–1531.

Li, D., Sham, P. S., Owen, M. L., & He, L. (2006). Meta-analysis shows significant association between dopamine system genes and attention deficit hyperactivity disorder (ADHD). *Human Molecular Genetics*, 15, 2276–2284.

Liao, D. L., Hong, C. G., Shih, H. L., & Tsai, S. J. (2004). Possible association between serotonin transporter promoter region polymorphism and extremely violent crime in Chinese males. *Neuropsychobiology*, 50, 284–287.

Limson, R., Goldman, D., Roy, A., Lamparski, D., Ravitz, D., Adinoff, B., & Linnoila, M. (1991). Personality and cerebrospinal fluid monoamine metabolites in alcoholics and controls. *Archives of General Psychiatry*, 48, 37–441.

Manolio, T. A., Collins, F. S., Cox, N. J., Goldstein, D. B., Hindorff, L. A., Hunter, D. J., ... & Visscher, P. M. (2009). Finding the missing heritability of complex diseases. *Nature*, 461, 747–753.

Manuck, S. B., Flory, J. D., Ferrell, R. E., Mann, J. J., & Muldoon, M. F. (2000). A regulatory polymorphism of the monoamine oxidase-A gene may be associated with variability in aggression, impulsivity, and central nervous system serotonergic responsivity. *Psychiatry Research*, 95, 9–23.

Manuck, S. B., & McCaffery, J. M. (2014). Gene-environment interaction. *Annual Review of Psychology*, 65, 41–70.

Mason, D. A. & Frick, P. J. (1994). The heritability of antisocial behavior: A meta-analysis of twin and adoption studies. *Journal of Psychopathology and Behavioral Assessment*, 16, 301–323.

Merjonen, P. Keltikangas-Järvinen, L., Jokela, M., Seppälä, I, Lyytikäinen, L. P., Pulkki-Råback, L., ... & Lehtimäki, T. (2011). Hostility in adolescents and adults: a genome-wide association study of the young Finns. *Translational Psychiatry*, 1, e11.

Mick, E., McGough, J., Deutsch, C. K., Frazier, J. A., Kennedy, D., & Goldberg, R. J. (2014). Genome-wise association study of proneness to anger. *PLoS ONE*, 9, e87257.

Mielke, J. H., Konigsberg, L. W., & Relethford, J. H. (2006). *Human biological variation*. New York: Oxford University Press.

Miles, D. R. & Carey, G. (1997). Genetic and environmental architecture in human aggression. *Journal of Personality and Social Psychology*, 72, 207–217.

Moore, T. M., Scarpa, A., & Raine, A. (2002) A meta-analysis of serotonin metabolite 5-HIAA and antisocial behavior. *Aggressive Behavior*, 28, 299–316.

Niehoff, D. (1999). *The biology of violence: How understanding the brain, behavior, and environment can break the vicious cycle of aggression*. New York: The Free Press.

Pappa, I., St Pourcain, B., Benke, K., Cavadino, A., Hakulinen, C., Nivard, M. G., ... & Tiemeier, H. (2015). A genome-wide approach to children's aggressive behavior: The EAGLE consortium. *American Journal of Medical Genetics Part B*, 9999, 1–11.

Petty, F., Fulton, M., Kramer, G. L., Kram, M., Davis, L. L., & Rush, A. J. (1999). Evidence for the segregation of a major gene for human plasma GABA levels. *Molecular Psychiatry*, 4, 587–589.

Plomin, R., DeFries, J., Craig, I., & McGuffin, P. (2001). *Behavioral genetics* (4th ed.). New York: Worth Publishers.

Plomin, R., DeFries, J. C., Knopik, V. S., & Neiderhiser, J. M. (2013). *Behavioral genetics* (6th ed.). New York: Worth Publishers.

Plomin, R. (2013). Child development and molecular genetics: 14 years later. *Child Development*, 84, 104–120.

Pohjalainen, T., Rinne, J. O., Någren, K., Lehikoinen, O., Anttila, K., Syvalahti, E. K. G., & Hietala, J. (1998). The A1 allele of the human D_2 dopamine receptor gene predicts low D_2 receptor availability in healthy volunteers. *Molecular Psychiatry*, 3, 256–260.

Polderman, T. J. C., Benyamin, B., de Leeuw, C. A., Sullivan, P. F., van Bochoven, A.,

Visscher, P. M., & Posthuma, D. (2015). Meta-analysis of the heritability of human traits based on fifty years of twin studies. *Nature Genetics, 47*, 702–709.

Raine, A. (1993). *The psychopathology of crime: Criminal behavior as a clinical disorder.* San Diego, CA: Academic Press.

Retz, W., Retz-Junginger, P., Supprian, T., Thome, J., & Rösler, M. (2004). Association of serotonin transporter promoter gene polymorphism with violence: Relation with personality disorders, impulsivity, and childhood ADHD psychopathology. *Behavioral Sciences & the Law, 22*, 415–425.

Rhee, S. H. & Waldman, I. D. (2002). Genetic and environmental influences on antisocial behavior: A meta-analysis of twin and adoption studies. *Psychological Bulletin, 128*, 490–529.

Rowe, D. C., Stever, C., Gard, J. M. C., Cleveland, H. H., Sanders, M. L., Abramowitz, A., ... & Waldman, I. D. (1998). The relation of the dopamine transporter gene (DAT1) to symptoms of internalizing disorders in children. *Behavioral Genetics, 28*, 215–225.

Rujescu, D., Giegling, I., Gietl, A., Hartman, A. M., & Moller, H. J. (2003). A functional single nucleotide polymorphism (V158M) in the COMT gene is associated with aggressive personality traits. *Biological Psychiatry, 54*, 34–39.

Sadeh, N., Javdani, S., Jackson, J. J., Reynolds, E. K., Potenza, M. N., Gelernter, J., ... & Verona, E. (2010). Serotnin transporter gene associations with psychopathic traits in youth vary as a function of socioeconomic resources. *Journal of Abnormal Psychology, 119*, 604–609.

Salvatore, J. E., Edwards, A. C., McClintick, J. N., Bigdeli, T. B., Adkins, A., Aliev, F., ... & Dick, D. M. (2015). Genome-wide association data suggest ABCB1 and immune-related gene sets may be involved in adult antisocial behavior. *Translational Psychiatry, 5*, e558.

Taylor, S. E., Way, B. M., Welch, W. T., Hilmert, C. J., Lehman, B. J., & Eisenberger, N. I. (2006). Early family environment, current adversity, the serotonin transporter promoter polymorphism, and depressive symptomatology. *Biological Psychiatry, 60*, 671–676.

Terranova, C., Tucci, M., Sartore, D., Cavarzeran, F., Pietra, L., Barzon, L., ... & Ferrara, S. D. (2013). GABA receptors, alcohol dependence and criminal behavior. *Journal of Forensic Sciences, 58*, 1227–1232.

Tielbeek, J. J., Medland, S. E., Benyamin, B., Byrne, E. M., Heath, A. C., Madden, P. A., ... & Verweij, K. J. H. (2012). Unraveling the genetic etiology of adult antisocial behavior: A genome-wide association study. *PLoS ONE, 7*, e45086.

Truman, J. L. & Langton, L. (2015). *Criminal victimization, 2014.* Washington, DC: US Department of Justice, Office of Justice Programs, Bureau of Justice Statistics.

US Department of Justice, Federal Bureau of Investigation. (2014). *Crime in the United States in 2013.* Retrieved on July 5, 2016 from www.fbi.gov/about-us/cjis/ucr/crime-in-the-u.s/2013/crime-in-the-u.s.-2013/violent-crime/violent-crime-topic-page/violentcrimemain_final.

Van den Hoofdakker, B. J., Nauta, M. H., Dijck-Brouwer, D. A. J., van der Veen-Mulders, L., Sytema, S., & Emmelkamp, P. M. G. (2012). Dopamine transporter gene moderate response to behavioral parent training in children with ADHD: A pilot study. *Developmental Psychology, 48*, 567–574.

Vaughn, M. G., DeLisi, M., Beaver, K. M., Wright, J. P. (2009). DAT1 and 5HTT are associated with pathological criminal behavior in a nationally representative sample of youth. *Criminal Justice and Behavior, 36*, 1113–1124.

Verhoeven, F. E., Booij, L., Kruijt, A. W., Cerit, H., Antypa, N., Does, W. (2012). The effects of MAOA genotype, childhood trauma, and sex on trait and state-dependent aggression. *Brain and Behavior*, 2, 806–813.

Virkkunen, M., Rawlings, R. R., Tokola, R., Poland, R. E., Guidotti, A., Nemeroff, C., ... & Linoila, M. (1994). CSF biochemistries, glucose metabolism, and diurnal activity rhythms in alcoholic, violent offenders, fire setters, and healthy volunteers. *Archives of General Psychiatry*, 51, 20–27.

Volavka, J., Bilder, R., & Nolan, K. (2004). Catecholamines and aggression: The role of COMT and MAO polymorphisms. *Annals of the New York Academy of Sciences*, 1036, 393–398.

12 Biosocial Foundations of Drug Abuse and Violent Delinquency

Michael G. Vaughn, Christopher P. Salas-Wright, and Jennifer M. Reingle-Gonzalez

Introduction

Throughout history, the intersection between the ingestion of psychoactive intoxicants and aberrant and violent behavior has garnered significant and inglorious attention. Nations have struggled with how best to effectively and humanely handle drug experimentation and abuse and its links to violence. This may be particularly difficult with respect to young people, where, at least in Western nations, experimentation with drug use begins. Our approach to these vexing issues is to enact policies based upon scientific findings. We realize there is often a substantial lag time between the accumulation of research and its dissemination and absorption by the general population. There are signs, however, that this does indeed eventually occur.

We consider the co-occurrence of drug abuse and violence in adolescence to be a *generalized neuro-dysregulation syndrome of altered behavior that is genetically and developmentally sensitive and socially and culturally contingent over time*. With respect to addiction, we focus more on the concept of drug abuse because children and adolescents are less likely to experience the full bloom of the addiction career and also to demarcate from behavioral addictions such as gambling, compulsive sex, internet use, or exercise dependence.

Here, we provide readers a grasp of the inherent multilevel dynamism of drug abuse and violent delinquency across the biosocial spectrum. Specifically, we address the genetic and neurobiological landscape linking the research currents to those found in the corpus of literature on the life-course. We then draw connections to policy, prevention, and treatment implications of our approach.

The Genetic Architecture of Drug Abuse and Addiction

It appears that some youth are more prone to drug abuse than other youth. We direct attention now to examining the genetic architecture of the addiction-crime phenomenon. Interestingly, violence researchers are only beginning to recognize the value of genetics as related to aggression, but addiction scientists have been busy studying the genetic underpinnings of substance-use disorders for decades. Both violence and addiction researchers largely accept that drug abuse and offending runs in families; however, they often disagree about whether biology or environment is the driver. We, like many others, recognize that both biological factors and environmental drivers are significant causes of violence and addiction.

Much like violence, addiction is not a single gene or Mendelian disorder. There is no single addiction gene. Addictive behaviors are polygenic (i.e., caused by many genes). Addiction, like antisocial behavior, is a complex multifactorial behavioral phenotype. The level of complexity researchers are confronting is aptly stated by Volkow and Muenke (2012, p. 773):

> In the case of substance use disorders, the powerful modulatory role played by complex environmental factors on brain processes which further muddle the picture, is particularly relevant. This is because, in the absence of drug exposure, itself an environmental factor, the specific addiction phenotype would remain hidden, even in the presence of an overwhelming genetic load. On the other hand, brain development and architecture, which are partly determined by genetic factors, can be affected by exposure to drugs. These two way interactions highlight the importance of genes involved in human brain development and function in the subsequent emergence of personality styles and emotional behavior reactivities.

Despite the challenges of uncovering the genetic architecture of addiction liability, there has been an increase in knowledge on this topic.

Similar to many, if not most, traits and behavioral phenotypes, investigations into the heritability of addiction using twin samples indicate that approximately 50% of the variance is due to genetic factors (Demers, Bogdan, & Agrawal, 2014). One might wonder whether the substance of abuse matters with regard to these heritability estimates. The answer is not really. Regardless of whether the substance is alcohol, nicotine, marijuana, or cocaine, the results are relatively invariant. Results do change, however, depending on the developmental period at hand. Studies on the developmental sensitivity of heritability estimates suggest that genetic factors actually increase from early adolescence to adulthood (Kendler, Schmitt, Aggen, & Prescott, 2008). While heritability studies do indeed possess utility when beginning to study a phenomenon, it is now more important to study the many genes that place children and adolescents vulnerable to drug abuse and dependence at risk, and to study these genes in conjunction with modifiable environment risk factors.

Although there is no specific gene that is responsible for addiction vulnerability, the assumption underlying the investigation into specific genes is that there are important genes that underlie key neural systems in the brain that are in turn linked to both addiction and violence-proneness. As such, they serve as biomarkers. Many of these genes are found in key neurotransmitter systems such as the dopaminergic, serotonergic, or many other such systems. It is important to point out that these genes are polymorphic, meaning that they occur in more than one form. A number of genes have been implicated in drug abuse and addiction. Importantly, many of these genes overlap with externalizing and antisocial behavior as well, suggesting their role in both violence and drug abuse liability. GABRA2 is one such gene. This particular gene, expressed more strongly in men, codes for proteins in a major inhibitory neurotransmitter region, and is associated with alcohol dependence (Edenberg et al., 2004) and general externalizing behavior (Dick et al., 2009). Low-activity alleles of the monoamine oxidase A (MAOA) have been found to be associated with a wide swath of antisocial behaviors, including addiction (Guo, Wilhelmsen, & Hamilton, 2007), and occur at a significantly higher level among persons who suffer from alcohol dependency or antisocial personality (Samochowiec et al., 1999). Using the Add Health data, Beaver and colleagues (2010) found that adolescents possessing the low-activity MAOA alleles were more likely to join a gang and, while in the gang, more likely to fight and use weapons. Other genes involved in neurotransmission (chemicals that transmit signals that allow for communication between neurons in the brain) include those in the dopaminergic and serotonergic systems.

Dopamine in normal amounts is released when we eat, drink, and engage in sex. In contrast, super-normal amounts of dopamine are released with the use of amphetamines, cocaine, opiates, nicotine, alcohol, and cannabis – greatly stimulating the reward pathway. Dopamine receptor genes (i.e., DRD2) have been associated with heightened risk for addiction (Noble, 2000). Another dopamine gene, DRD4, has been explored due to its linkage with this system and its association with novelty seeking. Research on serotonin, an important regulator of mood, has found that decreases in serotonin are associated with alcohol abuse and aggression (Nelson & Chiavegatto, 2001). One genetic polymorphism in the serotonergic region that has garnered heightened interest is the low-activity short allele (5-HTTLPR). A bevy of studies has produced interaction effects with this gene, suggesting it may be particularly sensitive to environmental stressors such as childhood maltreatment or witnessing or experiencing other traumatic events.

Researchers have been keen to study how genes interact with environments because these types of studies illuminate ways in which a modifiable environmental factor moderates genetic risk. Hicks and colleagues (2009) found that several environmental risk factors (i.e., academic achievement, peer affiliations, familial relationship problems and other stressful life events) each interacted with genetic vulnerability to produce combined antisocial behavior and substance use. However, the literature on gene–environment interaction studies is notably inconsistent and findings cannot always be replicated in different samples. To illustrate the magnitude of this problem, Weeland and colleagues (2015) conducted a systematic review of 53 published gene–environment interaction studies of externalizing behavior that focused on major candidate genes such as MAOA, DRD2, DRD4, DAT1, 5-HTTLR, and COMT and identified mixed results across samples. The environmental factor assessed in most of these interaction studies was some form of family conflict or adversity. So much about the intertwined nature of genes and environment is unknown. There are likely numerous environmental factors that are understudied and gene–environment interactions can occur throughout the life-course even in gestation and infancy.

Let's now turn to what is perhaps the most interesting and important concept involving genes and environment: the concept of gene–environment correlation. Traditional thinking on drug abuse and violence among juveniles tends to regard the environment as actively bathed over us as individuals who are passive recipients. From the standpoint of gene–environment correlation, however, things are quite different; indeed, it is posited that an individual's genetic makeup largely activates or influences the surrounding environment. The three types of gene–environment correlation interactions include active, evocative, and passive typologies. All three are likely important with regard to the etiology of drug abuse and violence. Active gene–environment correlation interactions occur when an individual seeks out environmental niches that reinforce their genetic proclivities. So, adolescents seeking out risky environments or friends who are more likely to experiment with substances is one avenue by which active gene–environment correlation works. In the evocative form of gene–environment correlation, the genetic-based attributes set in motion environmental responses. For instance, challenging adolescents who possess difficult temperaments or personalities provoke behavioral responses from others (harsh parenting or rejection) in the environment that might lead to further rebellious or self-medicating behavior. Passive gene–environment correlations occur when the environment is selected for by parents who share the same genes with the child. If the parent has had a history of drug abuse, they may expose the child to social environments that facilitate experimentation or regular use. As you might conclude, genes alone are just one part of the hypothetical recipe. Now, we turn to upstream neurobiological factors and take a look at what is going on "under the hood," so to speak.

Neurobiology: What's Going on Under the Hood?

It seems at times that we are awash in neuroscientific findings. Fields outside of neuroscience are linking their theories to what is being learned about the brain. While some may lament these developments as neurocentrism, a more positive spin on this trend is that the brain, as the seat of thought and behavior, is so fundamental to so many areas that it is becoming hard to avoid and this knowledge can be harnessed for the greater good. A growing number of violence researchers have recognized these developments and begun to incorporate neuroscience theories and research into their work. The problem of addiction and violence needs robust research from neuroscience to shed new light not only on the causal origins of problem behavior but also to inform prevention and policy.

The human brain is not only comparatively larger than that of other mammals but it also features substantial frontal regions (neocortex) that facilitate executive functioning and higher-level cognitive tasks. For adolescents, the basic functions of reward, motivation, emotion, and behavior inhibition are still developing, but substantial variation can also be observed. For example, some adolescents are more prone to anger and negative emotionality than others. These executive functions are important for a wide swath of human behavior including, of course, addiction and antisocial behavior (Berkman, Falk, & Lieberman, 2011). An abundance of research has shown that frontal regions are impaired in antisocial and risky behavior phenotypes (Brower & Price, 2001). Because there are an enormous amount of new connections being rapidly formed early in the life-course (and even through adulthood), plasticity to environmental stimuli is the rule rather than the exception. Several well-designed studies have shown that early problems (as early as age 3) in executive function are tied to a host of problem behaviors later in life, including addiction and offending (Fergusson, Horwood, & Ridder, 2007; Moffitt et al., 2011; Tarter, Kirisci, Habeych, Reynolds, & Vanyukov, 2003). However, there is ample room for change and these links are not inevitable but probabilistic.

It is generally well accepted in addiction science that the key to understanding addictive processes lies in what is known as the brain's reward pathway, or, more technically, the mesolimbic reward pathway. The mesolimbic reward pathway is made up of the ventral tegmental area (VTA), the amygdala, and the nucleus accumbens (NAc). The VTA is the front door of the reward pathway and is located beneath a substantial number of the brain's opiate receptors. When stimulated, the VTA releases a flood of dopamine that streams to the amygdala. Being the command center of the fight/flight response that is crucial for detecting and evaluating threat, the amygdala passes information on to executive centers of the brain for processing. The NAc is the final destination for dopamine levels and levels of this pleasurable chemical are recorded, thereby representing a drug-using memory. The reward pathway, also known as the mesolimbic reward system, is essential for survival. This system evolved to provide the positive reinforcement for eating, drinking, sex, and other life-preserving functions. As a consequence, feel-good chemicals in the form of dopamine are released when we engage in eating, drinking, and sex. When we ingest psychoactive drugs, supernormal amounts of dopamine are released, resulting in what addiction researchers have commonly termed "hijacking" of this key neural circuit. For those who are especially vulnerable or susceptible, compulsive drug-seeking follows, representing one pathway to crime.

This drive for repeated reinforcement of rewarding behavior is moderated by one's ability to self-regulate. Childress (2006) has suggested that this "stop" (behavior inhibition) and "go" (drive) analogy provides a simple way for understanding the interchange between the reward pathway and executive governance. Although much more complex, adolescents who are high on "go" and low on "stop" are obviously the most at risk. Some drugs of abuse such as heroin or amphetamines may overwhelm the ability to exercise self-control. This is complicated by the phenomenon known as tolerance, where stronger or larger doses of the drug are needed to achieve the desired effect. Even more deleterious, larger amounts of the drug are sometimes needed to just feel normal. This is due to the NAc being hyper-stimulated. Moreover, developmental periods such as adolescence, where episodic use of drugs or minor engagement in delinquent acts is often considered normative (especially for males) (Moffitt, 1993), are also time periods when executive functions are not fully developed. Steinberg (2007) regards this basic relationship between reward and behavior inhibition a central feature of adolescent risk.

So what are the avenues by which addiction and violence among adolescents are closely linked? One influential framework for approaching this question is Goldstein's (1985) tripartite explanation of the drugs-crime nexus in which he articulated three forms of drug-related violence: systemic, psychopharmacological, and economic-compulsive. However, it is clear that this conceptualization is biosocial in nature. Although one could readily subscribe to the view that systemic violence is largely social, that view would only be partially correct as there is likely a mix of genes, brain, and environmental reasons as to why those in the drug trade are more violent than others.

Outside of violence stemming from turf disputes and interpersonal conflict associated with the drug trade, there are two major pathways to violence for adolescents that are directly linked to neural substrates of addiction. One of these pathways involves violence that is a direct cause of the drug use; the second is violence as a consequence of compulsive drug-seeking. In the former case, the causal effect is difficult to measure as it can be confounded by the individuals' previous tendency toward using violence. For example, a meta-analysis of 13 imaging studies involving youth (age 12 to 17) with conduct problems found gray matter deficits in frontal regions and emotional processing areas prior to being classified as drug-dependent (Rogers & De Brito, 2016). However, one could see this as an enhancement effect where drugs amplify the pre-existing tendency toward violence or via the drug's ability to lower neural inhibitions and thereby removing any barriers to the use of violence. We know some drugs of abuse are better at this than others. For example, alcohol is likely to have a greater enhancement effect than cannabis. Compulsive drug-seeking occurs when adolescents steal or rob others to obtain money to buy drugs; this behavior is closely coupled with drug-selling. Although we often think of systemic violence around the drug trade, many adolescents sell drugs within a network or keep the drugs for themselves. For instance, in a study of adolescent offenders who sold drugs, approximately 70% kept more than half of the drugs for themselves (Shook, Vaughn, Goodkind, & Johnson, 2011). These low-level dealings, however, can escalate into physical altercations or bad feelings that erupt into aggressive acts in future interpersonal encounters.

Findings on the neural substrates of addiction and of violence are common. Although the reward pathway is considered key, other areas of the brain are involved. According to Volkow (2003, p. 3): "We are beginning to understand that drugs exert persistent neurobiological effects that extend beyond the midbrain centers of pleasure and reward to disrupt the brain's frontal cortex – the thinking region of the brain, where risks and benefits are weighed and decisions made." Given that the adolescent (and even young adult) brain is still undergoing tremendous development, poor decisions and behavior dysregulation are unsurprising among adolescents who abuse drugs. This observation not only has broad implications for prevention and policy but also highlights the importance of unraveling the developmental origins of addiction and violence.

Childhood Precursors

It is critical that a biosocial approach to understanding drug abuse and violence be situated within the broader framework of a developmental, life-course perspective. This is due to the fact that, invariably, salient biological and socioenvironmental factors change and evolve as we age and develop across the spectrum of childhood, adolescence, and beyond. One clear example of this is the human brain. We have made the case that neuroscience plays an essential role in understanding both drug abuse and violence; however, it is now very well established that the brain is not hardwired or static across the life-course, but rather it looks and functions differently as we grow and are shaped by our experiences and the social environment. Along the same lines, our childhood, adolescent, and adult experiences are not independent of one another, but rather what we experience as children is profoundly related to our growth and development during later life stages. Indeed, drawing from the work of Glen Elder (1974) and others (Hser, Longshore, & Anglin, 2007; Piquero, Jennings, & Barnes, 2012), we can see that a life-course perspective provides a critical foundation for understanding, preventing, and potentially interrupting long-term trajectories of drug abuse and violence.

One important developmental, life-course insight is that problem behavior can be observed across nearly the full spectrum of childhood. How early can we meaningfully identify problem behaviors among children? Arguably, quite early. Researchers have noted that there is substantial variation in the degree to which one-year-old infants exhibit noncompliance, throw temper tantrums, and exercise physical aggression (van Zeijl et al., 2006; Carter, Briggs-Gowan, Jones, & Little, 2003). We would argue that caution should be exercised in making too much of infant "externalizing," but such behavior becomes more and more meaningful as we get further into the toddlerhood stage. Indeed, substantial research has accrued examining the trajectories of behavior problems across toddlerhood (age 1 to 3) and the preschool years (age 3 to 5; Campbell, 2006). The bulk of these studies point to two core insights. First, problem behavior, including physical aggression, is quite common during early childhood. Indeed, it has been observed that the pinnacle in the prevalence physical aggression among humans is between the ages of 2 and 4 (Tremblay, 2015). Second, while the vast majority of children exhibit some degree of aggression during toddlerhood and the preschool years, these behaviors tend to dissipate as children move further and further away from their third and fourth birthdays. By the time children reach middle childhood (age 6 to 12), most have developed the cognitive, emotional, and social skills needed to deal with conflict such that physical aggression and other impulse-related outbursts are simply less common than among younger children.

What relevance does child problem behavior have when it comes to a broader, biosocial understanding of drug abuse and antisocial behavior across the life-course? Regretfully, child externalizing seems to very often set the stage for later behavior problems. Indeed, multiple longitudinal studies have found that young people who consistently exhibit elevated levels of aggression and/or other forms of problem behavior across early and middle childhood are far more likely than their peers to persist in this behavior into adolescence and, frequently, well into adulthood (Aguilar et al., 2000; Broidy et al., 2003; Campbell et al., 2006; Farrington, Lambert, & West, 1998; Moffitt, 1993; Piquero, Jennings, & Barnes, 2012; Roisman et al., 2010; Sampson & Laub, 2003). Along the same lines, a number of studies have also found that early and persistent behavior problems during childhood often portent of issues with alcohol and drug abuse at later developmental stages (Englund et al., 2008; Moffitt et al., 2002). Of course, we should be very clear in stating that not all children who exhibit problem behaviors during childhood persist in such behavior in later development stages. However, evidence clearly indicates that an important subset of individuals (roughly 3–6%) exhibit serious behavior problems early on in life and, regretfully, often continue to struggle for decades.

What predicts early and persistent behavior problems among children?

A review of the extant literature suggests that the answer is – perhaps unsurprisingly – both biological and social. One biologically based factor that is often examined is temperament. Temperament is a largely innate and stable characteristic that is moderately heritable (Tuvblad et al., 2010) and can be measured in children as young as 3 to 6 months of age (Gartstein & Rothbart, 2003). Fundamentally, temperament refers to the ways in which individuals experience and, in turn, regulate their responses to the world around them (Rothbart, 2011). Evidence indicates that children with "difficult" temperaments (i.e., those who are highly active, difficult to soothe, and easily distressed) at 6 months of age are far more likely to exhibit physical aggression as toddlers and during the early preschool years (Naerde et al., 2014). Moreover, other studies suggest that a temperamental "lack of control" at age 3 to 5 is robustly predictive of externalizing behavior further down the road (Althoff, Verhulst, Rettew, Hudziak, & Vander Ende, 2010; Caspi et al., 1995; Fearon et al., 2014). Simply put, temperament is a salient example of how our biological makeup relates to the risk of behavior problems during childhood as well as drug abuse and violence later on in life.

Of course, social and contextual factors also play a very important role in the etiology of behavior problems during childhood and beyond. Our assessment is that biological factors, such as temperament, are clearly part of the puzzle, but by no means the sole driver of behavior problems. Indeed, substantial research points to the importance of social factors such as parenting practices, family stress, home environment, and community violence exposure as central in understanding behavior problems across the life-course.

In fact, findings from a variety of prospective studies suggest that a "difficult temperament" may be most troublesome when combined with exposure to environmental adversities such as harsh parenting and family stress. In other words, the etiology of child behavior problems is likely more a function of *bio* × *social* interactions, rather than independent biological and/or social risk factors.

Adolescent Expressions

As noted above, a full account of the etiology of drug abuse and antisocial behavior is not complete without giving careful consideration to the childhood years. However, adolescence – typically understood as beginning around the time of puberty and stretching into the early 20s – is a critically important time in which the full flowering of problem behaviors often begins to take place. Moreover, in keeping with a life-course perspective, adolescent trajectories related to drug abuse and antisocial behavior are most fully understood when situated within a broader understanding of the intrapersonal, contextual, and behavioral factors that precede – and, indeed, follow – such behavior. Below, we delve into two issues that are situated in the framework and logic of a developmental, life-course perspective and of direct relevance to adolescent drug abuse and violence.

One important issue relates to "child-persistent" versus "adolescent-onset" behavior problems. Above, we noted that a minority of individuals begin to exhibit serious behavior problems early in life and that, for some, such behaviors persist into the adolescent years and beyond. This is certainly the case, but many of us know from our own experience that there is a degree to which taking part in risky behavior – including alcohol and drug use and delinquency – is somewhat normative. As argued by Terrie Moffitt (1993), a bit of teenage experimentation with substance use and relatively minor property crimes, status offenses, and skirmishes is certainly disconcerting but not unexpected. Moffitt theorized that adolescent-onset problem behaviors were primarily rooted in a gap between biological and social maturity such that young people act out and imitate antisocial peers in an effort to be viewed as full-fledged adults. Whereas child-persistent behavior problems are understood to be rooted primarily in biosocial risk (e.g., genetic susceptibility, neurological impairment, elevated social adversity), adolescent-onset problem behavior is viewed more in normative developmental terms. We are of the mind that a bit of (short-lived) risky behavior is, indeed, normative. That being said, let's be unequivocal in stating that growing evidence from a variety of studies indicates quite clearly that it is *not* developmentally normative for youth to begin to frequently take part in serious antisocial behaviors during adolescence. More precisely, whether it begins during childhood or around the onset of puberty, research has repeatedly shown that the lives of individuals who exhibit serious behavior problems during adolescence are often marked by early childhood issues (e.g., difficult temperament, lower cognitive functioning) and long-term difficulties (e.g., mental health and substance abuse problems) that are anything but the norm.

In reference to children, we discussed early-onset behavior problems, such as physical aggression, and their implications for long-term development; however, up to this point, we have not discussed early- versus later-onset substance use. This is partially the case because, by and large, substance use among children prior to puberty is relatively uncommon. However, by the time early adolescence rolls around, we begin to see an important minority of young people taking part in alcohol and other drug use. Research suggests that the age at which young people begin initiating substance use seems to matter. Indeed, studies have repeatedly found alcohol and drug use during the first few years of adolescence – typically operationalized as either age 11/12 to 14 or prior to age 15 – to be linked with academic and mental health issues, later substance use and delinquency, and the diagnosis of substance use disorders during adulthood (Anthony & Petronis, 1995; Chen, Storr, & Anthony, 2009; DeWit, Aldaf, Offord, & Ogborne, 2000; Ellickson, Tucker, & Klein, 2003; Meier et al., 2016; Odgers et al., 2008). Importantly, while results are not entirely uniform, it should be noted that even studies that have accounted for genetic factors (i.e., the same genes that predict early alcohol/drug use may predict later substance abuse and behavioral problems) suggest that early substance use initiation seems to have long-term developmental implications.

Overall, we can say with confidence that biosocial factors are related to both the onset of antisocial behavior and drug use during adolescence. Whereas early theorizing was rooted in the understanding that adolescent-onset antisocial behavior was best understood as primarily a socially influenced phenomenon, a mounting body of evidence indicates that there is, in part, a genetic basis to the emergence of serious conduct problems during the teenage years. Similarly, evidence certainly seems to indicate that the prevention of alcohol and drug use initiation during adolescence is important with respect to the development of later behavior problems, including adult drug abuse, addiction, and criminal offending. Importantly, however, research also seems to indicate that alcohol and other drug use at an early age may be best understood not as a cause of addiction in adulthood, but rather as a reflection of underlying genetic risk related to both early-onset use and addiction. Similarly, evidence also suggests that drug abuse and other high-risk and delinquent behaviors may be related to overlapping genetic and neurological vulnerabilities related to risk-taking and externalizing in general.

Prevention and Treatment Efforts

As discussed in this chapter, violent behavior and its genetic and neurobiological underpinnings are highly dependent and must be viewed through a social, economic, and environmental lens. Targeting a single dimension, such as a school environment, is commonly less effective than those programs that target multiple dimensions (such as the school environment and students within the school) in preventing the onset of violence or problem behavior. As a result, some of the most effective prevention programs target multiple layers of influence to maximally optimize protective factors and reduce (or mitigate) risk. This framework upon which many intervention and prevention programs today are built is known as the social ecological model (also referred to more generally as ecological models). The individual (or micro) level is the most common prevention target, including demographic factors, personality and attitudes. This level would include modifiable (e.g., amenable to prevention or intervention) biological targets. Among adolescents, life skills training and educational programs targeting individual-level risk and protective factors are common.

Few interventions or prevention programs inherently target gene–environment interactions for various reasons. First, an array of ethical issues present when considering genetic testing for violence or problem behavior predisposition among youth. Second, these genetic influences are less modifiable than the environment and are therefore less amenable to intervention. However, interventions might be most cost-effective if targeted towards youth predisposed (with biological and environmental susceptibility) to violent behavior. Because the research on many of these gene–environment interactions remains inconclusive, it is important to consider the mechanisms of action to move this field of research beyond exploration and towards causational modeling. For example, are deviant peers directly related to antisocial behavior? Or, is this relationship, which is particularly strong among males, driven by testosterone? These are important considerations for future research to continue considering the effect of biological, in addition to psychosocial, effects on addiction that are useful implications for prevention science.

Noticeably absent from this chapter is a discussion of how biosocial theory fits into current prevention (and intervention) programs. A long-lasting criticism of biosocial theories of crime relates to its implications, as if "bad apple" youth would be identified and assigned a scarlet letter to follow them through life. This premonition could not be further from the intent of biosocial theories, which are derived from sound clinical research and applied to social science in an effort to *improve,* not detract from, population health. The role of biosocial theory in prevention remains unclear, and the undeniable biological underpinnings of deviant behavior have not yet been optimally incorporated into our evidence-based programs. However, there is little doubt that innovators in prevention science will integrate fundamental biologic elements, including susceptibility, into indicated (or targeted) substance use prevention programs.

Let's consider this analogy in the domain of medical screening (e.g., the genetic testing for Huntington's, which has no cure). This test was highly controversial given its implications – the patient testing positive will have a high likelihood of developing a debilitating chronic disease, which will result in premature mortality and severe morbidity. Considering these circumstances, why would someone get this test? Although the prognosis is poor, Huntington's may be prevented through use of creatine (Science Daily, 2014), healthy behaviors, exercise, and diligently following a restrictive diet. Or, a person might wish to cognitively prepare for the development of symptoms. If a susceptibility test for addiction or criminality were created, results might be sought by diligent parents who wish to gain training to ensure all protective measures are optimized in their home. A positive test does not indicate that a child will become addicted; instead, it is a call to maximize all possible protective factors and minimize risks. The conversation must be shifted away from labeling youth and towards expanding our capacity for prevention, acknowledging the strong evidence in support of biological roots for problem behavior.

Policy Implications

Violent behavior is just beginning to be viewed as a public health problem. This movement shifts the attention away from the criminal justice system (e.g., tertiary prevention and treatment, which is costly) and toward health behavior, risk reduction, and policy (e.g., primary and secondary prevention, which is less costly). To this end, a recent APHA (2013) policy statement, entitled "Defining and Implementing a Public Health Response to Drug Use and Misuse," identified the movement to shift away from the criminalization of drug possession and use as a core component of a public health approach. Specifically, the APHA statement highlights how the mass incarceration of drug users in the criminal justice system has made treatment more difficult, created other public health problems, and – not inconsequentially – contributed to the problem of mass incarceration in the United States. Because the majority of persons housed in United States jails and prisons are incarcerated for drug-related offenses (Carson & Golinelli, 2012), even a small dent in the rate of substance use at the population level will result in great cost savings in criminal justice.

Understanding violence and antisocial behavior and how it fits within the framework of public health allows us to leverage the strengths of epidemiology and public health practice and policy to address the challenges associated with these problem behaviors. Because violence and antisocial behavior are so closely coupled with mental health problems and substance use disorders, healthcare resources must be dedicated to address the root of these problems rather than a behavioral manifestation (e.g., violence that is due to untreated mental health conditions may be resolved through medication management). In this way, application of a public health approach to violence opens up exciting possibilities with respect to large-scale health-promotion efforts designed to prevent violence (and its known causes) before they begin, increase treatment access for sufficient causes, and reduce drug-related health consequences among those in the criminal justice system.

Conclusion

The struggle to develop effective policies and treatments for drug abuse and violence among young people in a free society is a consistent theme. However, there is growing awareness that a science of addiction and human violence have much to offer. As previously mentioned, there is typically a substantial time lag between the accumulation of research findings and their adoption by practitioners and policy-makers. In this chapter we considered the underlying genetic, neuro-scientific, and socio-developmental foundations of the co-occurrence of drug abuse and violence that have a direct bearing on policy and treatment. Consistent with our holistic definition of a *generalized neuro-dysregulation syndrome of altered behavior that is genetically and developmentally sensitive and socially and culturally contingent over time,* each domain along the biosocial continuum is a necessary component. We encourage research and prevention that embraces this inherent dynamism.

References

Aguilar, B., Sroufe, L. A., Egeland, B., & Carlson, E. (2000). Distinguishing the early-onset/persistent and adolescence-onset antisocial behavior types: From birth to 16 years. *Development and Psychopathology*, 12(2), 109–132.

Althoff, R. R., Verhulst, F. C., Rettew, D. C., Hudziak, J. J., & van der Ende, J. (2010). Adult outcomes of childhood dysregulation: a 14-year follow-up study. *Journal of the American Academy of Child & Adolescent Psychiatry*, 49(11), 1105–1116.

American Public Health Association (2013). Defining and Implementing a Public Health Response to Drug Use and Misuse. Retrieved on June 10, 2016 from www.apha.org/policies-and-advocacy/public-health-policy-statements/policy-database/2014/07/08/08/04/defining-and-implementing-a-public-health-response-to-drug-use-and-misuse.

Anthony, J. C. & Petronis, K. R. (1995). Early-onset drug use and risk of later drug problems. *Drug and Alcohol Dependence*, 40(1), 9–15.

Beaver, K. M., DeLisi, M., Vaughn, M. G., & Barnes, J. C. (2010). MAOA genotype is associated with gang membership and weapon use, *Comprehensive Psychiatry*, 51, 130–134.

Berkman, E. T., Falk, E. B., & Lieberman, M. D. (2011). In the trenches of real-world self-control: Neural correlates and breaking the link between craving and smoking. *Psychological Science*, 22, 498–506.

Broidy, L. M., Nagin, D. S., Tremblay, R. E., Bates, J. E., Brame, B., Dodge, K. A., ... & Lynam, D. R. (2003). Developmental trajectories of childhood disruptive behaviors and adolescent delinquency: a six-site, cross-national study. *Developmental Psychology*, 39(2), 222–245.

Brower, M. C. & Price, B. H. (2001). Neuropsychiatry of frontal lobe dysfunction in violent and criminal behaviour: a critical review. *Journal of Neurology, Neurosurgery, and Psychiatry*, 71, 720–726.

Campbell, S. B., Spieker, S., Burchinal, M., & Poe, M. D. (2006). Trajectories of aggression from toddlerhood to age 9 predict academic and social functioning through age 12.

Journal of Child Psychology and Psychiatry, 47(8), 791–800.

Campbell, S. B. (2006). *Behavior problems in preschool children: Clinical and developmental issues.* New York: Guilford Press.

Carson E. A. & Golinelli, D. (2013). Prisoners in 2012: Trends in Admissions and Releases, 1991–2012. Washington, DC: Bureau of Justice Statistics.

Carter, A. S., Briggs-Gowan, M. J., Jones, S. M., & Little, T. D. (2003). The infant–toddler social and emotional assessment (ITSEA): Factor structure, reliability, and validity. *Journal of Abnormal Child Psychology,* 31(5), 495–514.

Caspi, A., Henry, B., McGee, R. O., Moffitt, T. E., & Silva, P. A. (1995). Temperamental origins of child and adolescent behavior problems: From age three to age fifteen. *Child Development,* 66(1), 55–68.

Chen, C. Y., Storr, C. L., & Anthony, J. C. (2009). Early-onset drug use and risk for drug dependence problems. *Addictive Behaviors,* 34(3), 319–322.

Childress, A. R. (2006). What can human brain imaging tell us about vulnerability to addiction and to relapse? In W. R. Miller & K. M. Carroll (Eds), *Rethinking substance abuse: what the science shows, and what we should do about it* (46–60). New York: Guilford Press.

Demers, C. H., Bogdan, R., & Agrawal, A. (2014). The Genetics, Neurogenetics and Pharmacogenetics of Addiction. *Current Behavioral Neuroscience Reports,* 1(1), 33–44.

DeWit, D. J., Adlaf, E. M., Offord, D. R., & Ogborne, A. C. (2000). Age at first alcohol use: a risk factor for the development of alcohol disorders. *American Journal of Psychiatry,* 157(5), 745–750.

Dick, D. M., Latendresse, S. J., Lansford, J. E., Budde, J. P., Goate, A., Dodge, K. A., ... & Bates, J. E. (2009). Role of GABRA2 in trajectories of externalizing behavior across development and evidence of moderation by parental monitoring. *Archives of General Psychiatry,* 66, 649–657.

Edenberg, H. J., Dick, D. M, Xuei, X., Tian, H., Almasy, L., Bauer, L. O., ... & Begleiter, H. (2004). Variations in GABRA2, encoding the alpha 2 subunit of the GABA(A) receptor, are associated with alcohol dependence and with brain oscillations. *American Journal of Human Genetics,* 74, 705–714.

Elder, G. H. (1974). *Children of the Great Depression: Social change in life experience.* Chicago: University of Chicago Press.

Ellickson, P. L., Tucker, J. S., & Klein, D. J. (2003). Ten-year prospective study of public health problems associated with early drinking. *Pediatrics,* 11(5), 949–955.

Englund, M. M., Egeland, B., Oliva, E. M., & Collins, W. A. (2008). Childhood and adolescent predictors of heavy drinking and alcohol use disorders in early adulthood: a longitudinal developmental analysis. *Addiction,* 103(s1), 23–35.

Farrington, D. P., Lambert, S., & West, D. J. (1998). Criminal careers of two generations of family members in the Cambridge Study in Delinquent Development. *Studies on Crime and Crime Prevention,* 7, 85–106.

Fearon, R. M., Reiss, D., Leve, L. D., Shaw, D. S., Scaramella, L. V., Ganiban, J. M., & Neiderhiser, J. M. (2014). Child-evoked maternal negativity from 9 to 27 months: Evidence of gene–environment correlation and its moderation by marital distress. *Development and Psychopathology,* 27(4pt1), 1251–1265.

Fergusson, D. M., Horwood, L. J., & Ridder, E. M., (2007). Conduct and attentional problems in childhood and adolescence and later substance use, abuse and dependence: results of a 25 year longitudinal study. *Drug and Alcohol Dependence,* 88S, S14–S26.

Gartstein, M. A. & Rothbart, M. K. (2003). Studying infant temperament via the revised infant behavior questionnaire. *Infant Behavior and Development,* 26(1), 64–86.

Goldstein, P. J. (1985). The drugs/violence nexus: A tripartite conceptual framework. *Journal of Drug Issues,* 15, 493–506.

Guo, G., Wilhelmsen, K., & Hamilton, N. (2007). Gene-lifecourse interaction for alcohol consumption in adolescence and young adulthood: Five monoamine genes. *American Journal of Medical Genetics Part B (Neuropsychiatric Genetics)*, 144B, 417–423.

Hicks, B. M., South, S. C., DiRago, A. C., Iacono, W. G., & McGue, M. (2009). Environmental adversity and increasing genetic risk for externalizing disorders. *Archives of General Psychiatry*, 66, 640–648.

Hser, Y. I., Longshore, D., & Anglin, M. D. (2007). The life course perspective on drug use: A conceptual framework for understanding drug use trajectories. *Evaluation Review*, 31(6), 515–547.

Kendler K. S., Schmitt E., Aggen, S. H., & Prescott, C. A. (2008). Genetic and environmental influences on alcohol, caffeine, cannabis, and nicotine use from early adolescence to middle adulthood. *Archives of General Psychiatry*, 65: 674–682.

Meier, M. H., Hall, W., Caspi, A., Belsky, D. W., Cerdá, M., Harrington, H. L., ... & Moffitt, T. E. (2016). Which adolescents develop persistent substance dependence in adulthood? Using population-representative longitudinal data to inform universal risk assessment. *Psychological Medicine*, 46(4), 877–889.

Moffitt, T. E. (1993). "Life-course persistent" and "adolescence-limited" antisocial behavior: A developmental taxonomy. *Psychological Review*, 100, 674–701.

Moffitt, T. E., Arseneault, L., Belsky, D., Dickson, N., Hancox, R. J., Harrington, H., Caspi, A. (2011). A gradient of childhood self-control predicts health, wealth, and public safety. *Proceedings of the National Academy of Sciences, U.S.A.*, 108, 2693–2698.

Moffitt, T. E., Caspi, A., Harrington, H., & Milne, B. J. (2002). Males on the life-course-persistent and adolescence-limited antisocial pathways: Follow-up at age 26 years. *Development and Psychopathology*, 14(1), 179–207.

Nærde, A., Ogden, T., Janson, H., & Zachrisson, H. D. (2014). Normative development of physical aggression from 8 to 26 months. *Developmental Psychology*, 50(6), 1710–1720.

Nelson, R. J. & Chiavegatto, S. (2001). Molecular basis of aggression. *Trends in Neuroscience*, 24, 713–719.

Noble, E. P. (2000). Addiction and its reward process through polymorphisms of the D2 dopamine receptor gene: A review. *European Psychiatry*, 15, 7–89.

Odgers, C. L., Caspi, A., Nagin, D. S., Piquero, A. R., Slutske, W. S., Milne, B. J., ... & Moffitt, T. E. (2008). Is it important to prevent early exposure to drugs and alcohol among adolescents? *Psychological Science*, 19(10), 1037–1044.

Piquero, A. R., Jennings, W. G. & Barnes, J. C. (2012). Violence in criminal careers: A review of the literature from a developmental life-course perspective. *Aggression and Violent Behavior*, 17(3), 171–179.

Rogers, J. C. & De Brito, S. A. (2016). Cortical and subcortical gray matter volume in youths with conduct problems: A meta-analysis. *JAMA Psychiatry*, 73, 64–72.

Roisman, G. I., Monahan, K. C., Campbell, S. B., Steinberg, L., & Cauffman, E. (2010). Is adolescence-onset antisocial behavior developmentally normative? *Development and Psychopathology*, 22(2), 295–311.

Rothbart, M. K. (2011). *Becoming who we are: Temperament and personality in development.* New York: Guilford Press.

Samochowiec, J., Lesch, K. P., Rottman, M., Smolka, M., Syagailo, Y. V., Okladnova, O., ... & Sander, T. (1999). Association of a regulatory polymorphism in the promoter region of the MAOA gene with antisocial alcoholism. *Psychiatry Research*, 86, 67–72.

Sampson, R. J. & Laub, J. H. (2003). Life-course desisters? Trajectories of crime among delinquent boys followed to age 70. *Criminology*, 41(3), 555–592.

Science Daily. (2014). Huntington disease prevention trial shows creatine safe, slows progression. Retrieved from www.sciencedaily.com/releases/2014/02/140208080705.htm. Acessed November 1, 2017.

Shook, J. J., Vaughn, M. G., Goodkind, S., & Johnson, H. (2011). An empirical portrait of youthful offenders who sell drugs. *Journal of Criminal Justice*, 39, 224–231.

Steinberg, L. (2007). Risk-taking in adolescence: New perspectives from brain and behavioral science. *Current Directions in Psychological Science*, 16, 55–59.

Tarter, R. E., Kirisci, L., Habeych, M., Reynolds, M., & Vanyukov, M. (2003). Neurobehavior disinhibition in childhood predisposes boys to substance use disorder by young adulthood: direct and mediated etiologic pathways. *American Journal of Psychiatry*, 160, 1078–1085.

Tremblay, R. E. (2015). Antisocial behavior before the age–crime curve: Can developmental criminology continue to ignore developmental origins? In J. Morizot & L. Kazemian (Eds), *The development of criminal and antisocial behavior* (pp. 39–49). Cham, Switzerland: Springer International Publishing.

Tuvblad, C., Isen, J., Baker, L. A., Raine, A., Lozano, D. I., & Jacobson, K. C. (2010). The genetic and environmental etiology of sympathetic and parasympathetic activity in children. *Behavior Genetics*, 40(4), 452–466.

Van Zeijl, J., Mesman, J., Stolk, M. N., Alink, L. R., Van Ijzendoorn, M. H., Bakermans-Kranenburg, M. J., ... & Koot, H. M. (2006). Terrible ones? Assessment of externalizing behaviors in infancy with the Child Behavior Checklist. *Journal of Child Psychology and Psychiatry*, 47(8), 801–810.

Volkow, N. D. (2003). The addicted brain: Why such poor decisions? *NIDA Notes*, 18, 1–15.

Volkow, N. D. & Muenke, M. (2012). The genetics of addiction. *Human Genetics*, 131, 773–777.

Weeland, J., Overbeek, G., Orobio de Castro, B., & Matthys, W. (2015). Underlying mechanisms of gene–environment interactions in externalizing behavior: A systematic review and search for theoretical mechanisms. *Clinical Child and Family Psychology Review*, 18, 413–442.

13 Personality and Aggression: A General Trait Perspective

Courtland S. Hyatt, Chelsea E. Sleep,
Brandon M. Weiss, and Joshua D. Miller

Introduction

Typically defined as the intentional harming of an individual who is motivated to avoid such treatment (Anderson & Bushman, 2002), aggression is a construct of substantial interest to public health broadly. In its most serious instantiations, aggression in the form of violent crime (e.g., murder, aggravated assault) can constitute a direct threat to human life, while other forms of aggression may function in more subversive, yet potent, ways (e.g., domestic violence, bullying). Aggression can also manifest subtly in the form of exclusionary social practices. Noting how this heterogeneity in behavioral content is belied by homogeneity of harmful intent, personality theorists have attempted to identify a coherent set of traits that is helpful in explaining meaningful patterns of this behavior. To the extent that a trait model such as the Big Five (John & Srivastava, 1999) or Five-Factor Model (FFM; McCrae & John, 1992) has the capacity to account for variation in individuals' tendencies to act aggressively toward another, it must be seriously considered as an important theoretical account of aggression. For the purposes of this review, we focus our attention on how one of the most extensively researched structural models of personality, the FFM, contributes to our understanding of aggressive behavior. Additionally, we review several other well-researched personality configurations (e.g., Dark Triad) that have been linked to aggression, and conclude that key common traits underlie these various instantiations.

FFM Background

The Big Five/FFM has enjoyed a rich developmental history (for a review see Digman, 1990). Henceforth we use "FFM" to refer to the Big Five and Five-Factor Models of personality, given their substantial theoretical and empirical overlap. This model is rooted in the lexical hypothesis, which has two key premises: (1) differences that are most socially relevant in people's lives will become symbolically represented in language, and (2) the more important a difference, the more likely it is to be delineated from other words and expressed as an independent term (e.g., Ashton & Lee, 2005). Put differently, this hypothesis purports that the aspects of human personality most important to differentiate have become the most robustly encoded into language, and these differences can be quantified. Once distilled, these traits can be conceived of as enduring patterns of behavior, cognition, and emotion.

One widely used operationalization of the FFM (e.g., NEO PI-R, Costa & McCrae, 1992) consists of a hierarchical structure that includes *Neuroticism* (i.e., a tendency to experience strong negative emotions such as anger, sadness, vulnerability), *Extraversion* (i.e., an approach orientation, or a tendency to seek out social interaction, exciting activities, and positive emotions), *Openness to experience* (i.e., willingness to consider different values, ideas, experiences, and tastes), *Agreeableness* (i.e., a tendency to be gentle with and trusting of others, and motivation toward social harmony and cooperation), and *Conscientiousness* (i.e., a driven, organized approach to work and the ability to delay gratification and act nonimpulsively). This model also posits the existence of six narrower, more specific facets that comprise each domain, although other faceted models of the FFM exist as well (e.g., DeYoung, Quilty, & Peterson, 2007). The FFM is arguably the predominant model of general and pathological personality (e.g., Samuel & Widiger, 2008; APA, 2013) and, as such, benefits from a large empirical literature. It enjoys considerable convergent and divergent validity across raters and cultures (Carlson, Vazire, & Oltmanns, 2013; McCrae, Costa, Del Pilar, Rolland, & Parker, 1998), presence in childhood (John, Caspi, Robins, Moffitt, & Stouthamer-Loeber, 1994), temporal stability across the lifespan (Blonigen, 2010), and support from behavioral genetics research (Yamagata et al., 2006). More importantly for our purposes, it has been linked to a wide variety of important outcomes such as happiness, relationship satisfaction, and job performance (Ozer & Benet-Martinez, 2006).

FFM and Aggression

The most recent meta-analytic review of the relations between FFM personality and aggression included aggregated data from over 30 studies published since 2000 with over 10,000 participants. As expected, the authors found evidence that Agreeableness, Conscientiousness, and Neuroticism were the most consistent correlates of aggression. For instance, Agreeableness was negatively associated with elevated levels of aggression (effect size [ES, r]: −0.33; Jones, Miller, & Lynam, 2011). It is notable that this moderate relationship was consistent across population (e.g., community vs. prison, student vs. community) and method of assessment (self-report vs. laboratory paradigms). Next, Conscientiousness also evinced a significant negative effect size (ES) on aggression (ES: −0.18). In contrast, Neuroticism evinced a small, but positive relationship with aggression (ES: 0.17). Though moderation analyses suggested that these effect sizes varied slightly by sample characteristics (e.g., gender), all effects were in the expected direction (Table 13.1).

A second meta-analysis, consisting of studies published before 2001, corroborates these findings, indicating that low Agreeableness and Conscientiousness are the primary FFM traits associated with antisocial behavior (ASB; Miller & Lynam, 2001). Although ASB is not synonymous with aggression, virtually all operationalizations of ASB include aggressive behavior, and both constructs are subsumed under a latent "externalizing" factor of psychopathology (Krueger, Caspi, Moffitt, & Silva, 1998). Additionally, numerous studies have confirmed the relations between low Agreeableness and Conscientiousness and a range of ASBs, including aggression, substance use, and risky sex (e.g., Miller, Lynam, & Jones, 2008). A third

Table 13.1 *Effect Sizes of FFM and Aggression/ASB*

	Aggression	Proactive Aggression	Reactive Aggression	
Five-Factor Model				
Neuroticism	0.17[a]	0.07[b]	0.42[b]	
Angry hostility	0.22[a]	0.34[b]	0.59[b]	
Extraversion	−0.03[a]	−0.07[b]	−0.18[b]	
Warmth	−0.23[a]	−0.30[b]	−0.29[b]	
Openness	−0.10[a]	−0.13[b]	−0.07[b]	
Agreeableness	−0.33[a]	−0.49[b]	−0.50[b]	
Straightforwardness	−0.25[a]	−0.38[b]	−0.29[b]	
Altruism	−0.26[a]	−0.39[b]	−0.39[b]	
Compliance	−0.26[a]	−0.44[b]	−0.58[b]	
Conscientiousness	−0.18[a]	−0.12[b]	−0.15[b]	
Dark Triad				
Psychopathy	0.44[c]	0.36[d]	0.35[d]	
Self-centered impulsivity	0.42[i]			
Fearless dominance	−0.04[i]			
Narcissism	0.23[c]	0.11[e]	0.53[e]	
Machiavellianism	0.39[c]	0.33[f]	0.32[f]	
Psychopathy	Violent Offending			Violent Recidivism
Factor 1	0.40[g]			0.16[h]
Interpersonal		0.44[d]	0.42[d]	
Affective		0.38[d]	0.31[d]	
Factor 2	0.57[g]			0.24[h]
Lifestyle		0.41[d]	0.49[d]	
Antisocial		0.28[d]	0.30[d]	

Note: FFM facets are reported only if their effect sizes are |0.20|.
[a] Jones, Miller, & Lynam (2011); [b] Miller & Lynam (2006); [c] Vize, Lynam, Collison, & Miller (2018); [d] Blais, Solodukhin, & Forth (2014); [e] Bettencourt, Talley, Benjamin, & Valentine (2006); [f] Jonason, Duineveld, & Middleton (2015); [g] Lestico, Salekin, DeCoster, & Rogers (2008); [h] Walters (2003); [i] Miller & Lynam (2012).

meta-analysis found that psychoticism (as operationalized by Eysenck's three-factor model; e.g., Eysenck & Eysenck, 1985), a trait that blends low Agreeableness and low Conscientiousness, was a robust correlate of ASB (Cale, 2006; $r = 0.39$).

In addition to these findings at the broader domain level, Jones et al. (2011) also meta-analyzed the relations between FFM and aggression at the narrower, facet level. Importantly, the pattern in the facet analyses closely mirrored the findings from the domain level. For the sake of parsimony, we report only those with effect sizes ≥ |0.20|. Using this criterion, three facets of Agreeableness (Straightforwardness [ES: 0.25]; Altruism [ES: −0.26]; Compliance [ES: −0.26]), one facet of Neuroticism (Angry-Hostility [ES: 0.21]), and one facet of Extraversion (Warmth [ES: −0.23]) were the most notable correlates, although several other expected facets neared this arbitrary cut-off (e.g., Trust, Modesty, and Tenderminded facets of Agreeableness; Deliberation facet of Conscientiousness).

FFM and Proactive/Reactive Aggression

A classic (albeit controversial, see Bushman & Anderson, 2001) distinction in the aggression literature is made between proactive (PA) and reactive (RA) forms of aggression. Describing the former, Albert Bandura (1983, p. 57) noted, "A great deal of aggression is prompted by its anticipated benefits ... the instigator is the pull of expected success, rather than the push of aversive treatment." This description emphasizes that aggression can have an instrumental function and can be used to bring about some desired end (e.g., intimidation, retribution, monetary reward, etc.). Alternately, RA can be understood in terms of the frustration-aggression model (e.g., Dollard, Miller, Doob, Mowrer, & Sears, 1939), in which aggression is understood as a response to an obstacle to goal attainment, and in light of its instigating precursors, such as an influx of anger. RA can be thought of as a "hot-headed," angry, impulsive response to provocation, and PA is thought to be "cold-blooded," premeditated, and deliberate, although Bushman and Anderson note that these characteristics can describe both forms of aggression. There is also research suggesting these variants are underscored by different cognitive processes (e.g., Brugman et al., 2015; Dodge & Coie, 1987). It is worth noting, however, that self-reported RA and PA tend to be substantially correlated, suggesting that individuals who engage in one form are likely to engage in the other as well (Miller & Lynam, 2006).

Though the literature on personality differences that underlie PA and RA is small, a study by Miller and Lynam (2006) revealed an interesting distinction consistent with theoretical characterizations. First, both constructs were significantly correlated with Agreeableness (PA, $r = -0.49$; RA, $r = -0.50$) and its underlying facets. The correlations with the Conscientiousness domain were also similar (PA, $r = -0.15$; RA, $r = -0.12$). However, while RA displayed a medium-to-large correlation with Neuroticism ($r = 0.42$), PA did not show a significant correlation ($r = 0.07$). It is also of note that while PA did evince significant relationships with the Neuroticism facets Angry Hostility (PA, $r = 0.34$; RA, $r = 0.59$) and Impulsiveness (PA, $r = 0.22$; RA, $r = 0.36$), RA was more strongly correlated to every Neuroticism facet. This is consistent with the conception of RA as a relatively more emotion (i.e., anger, frustration)-driven response, though it is notable that this data suggests that PA is also characterized to some degree by this description. In line with the previously discussed meta-analytic findings, neither PA nor RA were significantly correlated with the Extraversion domain, but both were significantly negatively correlated with the Warmth facet (PA, $r = -0.30$; RA, $r = -0.29$) and the Positive Emotions facet

(PA, $r = -0.23$; RA, $r = -0.35$). Neither PA nor RA were significantly correlated with the Openness domain, and there were only minor facet-level differences.

Despite these differences, it must be emphasized that overall, PA and RA displayed relatively similar correlations with the FFM. In fact, Miller and Lynam (2006) reported that PA and RA themselves displayed a large correlation ($r = 0.54$), and an even higher similarity index across the 30 FFM facets ($r_{ICC} = 0.79$), which takes into account the absolute similarity (i.e., convergence in shape and magnitude) of two sets of correlations. Thus, regardless of the distinct theoretical underpinnings of PA and RA, their trait profiles are quite similar. Although some scholars have gone as far as to suggest that it is "time to pull the life-support plug" on the distinction between PA and RA (Bushman & Anderson, 2001), we are more cautious and suggest that these small, yet detectable FFM profile differences warrant further investigation. For example, extant neurobiological research suggests that men who scored highly on a measure of RA exhibit structural differences in the amygdala compared to a nonaggressive group and to a primarily PA group (Rosell & Siever, 2015), suggesting that different neural underpinnings may, in part, underlie these processes. Particular attention should be paid to the role of negative emotional reactivity as both theory and the reported FFM findings suggest this is critical to possible differences in these forms of aggression.

FFM and Relational Aggression

Relational aggression is a relatively new, but increasingly popular focus among aggression researchers, who have recognized that deliberate harm can also take the form of damage to another's social status and interpersonal relationships (Archer & Coyne, 2005). This form of aggression may be a particularly worthwhile focus of research given the increasing opportunities for its manifestation through social media outlets. Though research on this type of aggression's relation to personality is nascent compared to the general aggression literature, initial studies suggest that it shares many of the same correlates as other forms. For instance, a study by Tackett, Daoud, De Bolle, and Burt (2013) on children and adolescents found that a general aggression measure (Agg) and a relational aggression (RAgg) measure were both significantly negatively correlated with trait Agreeableness (Agg $r = -0.65$; RAgg $= -0.32$), as well as Conscientiousness (Agg $r = -0.37$; RAgg $r = -0.18$). Both general ($r = 0.62$) and relational aggression ($r = 0.33$) were also positively related to Neuroticism. Relatively similar patterns of findings have also been reported in young adult samples (e.g., Miller, Zeichner, & Wilson, 2012). Thus, while further research is encouraged, current findings suggest that like other types of aggression, similar personality traits underlie this form.

Pathological Personality Traits and Aggression

Over the past 20 to 30 years, greater interest has been shown in developing comprehensive, dimensional trait models of personality pathology that capture more extreme, more impairing, and/or more distressing traits (e.g., Livesley, Schroeder, Jackson, & Jang, 1994; Widiger, 1993). Research into these dimensional models of personality pathology/personality disorder (PD) came about as a result of a variety of theoretical and empirical critiques (e.g., Clark, 2007; Widiger & Trull, 2007) of the categorical diagnostic models within the American Psychiatric Association's Diagnostic and Statistical Manual of Mental Disorders (DSM). The wealth of data supporting the benefits of a dimensional, trait approach to the conceptualization, assessment, and diagnosis of PDs led to the inclusion of a trait-based "Alternative Model" in the fifth edition of the DSM (DSM-5; American Psychiatric Association, 2013). This model emphasizes that the core of personality disturbance is impairment in personality functioning (Criterion A) coupled with evidence of maladaptive elevations in dimensional traits (Criterion B; APA, 2013). The inclusion of these traits was designed to allow for elaboration of individual differences in personality psychopathology, especially given the evidence that dimensional personality traits can reproduce the nomological networks of the traditional DSM PD constructs (see Miller, 2012 for a review).

This research culminated in the publication of the Personality Inventory for DSM-5 (PID-5; Krueger et al., 2012), a 220-item self-report measure developed to assess the five pathological traits detailed by the Alternative Model (Negative Affect, Detachment, Psychoticism, Antagonism, Disinhibition). Although similar to the FFM in structure and content, the Alternative Model was explicitly developed as a pathological model of personality psychopathology to be used in clinical and research settings. PID-5 and NEO PI-R domains consistently evidence moderate to strong convergence, with the exception of mixed findings in regard to the relation between Openness and Psychoticism (e.g., Few et al., 2013; c.f. Gore & Widiger, 2013).

Most extant literature to date on the relation of the DSM-5 pathological traits to aggression involves the constructs of Antagonism and Disinhibition, which parallel the FFM domains Agreeableness and Conscientiousness (Gore & Widiger, 2013) – the two strongest personality correlates of aggression and antisocial behavior. Initial studies support moderate to large correlations between these DSM-5 personality domains and behavior dysfunction and aggression (Anderson et al., 2015). However, empirical examinations of the DSM-5 traits in relation to behavioral or functional outcomes are sparse (Al-Dajani, Gralnick, & Bagby, 2016). Though findings have been reported supporting the role of Antagonism in aggressive driving violations (Beanland, Sellbom, & Johnson, 2014), studies assessing a range of aggressive behavior are lacking.

Specific Personality Profiles

In addition to the examination of these general and pathological traits' relations to aggression and antisocial behavior, there is much interest in specific, multi-trait configurations that are linked both conceptually and empirically with aggression. In the following section, we focus on a set of related constructs – psychopathy, narcissism, and Machiavellianism – that are often studied together as part of the Dark Triad (Paulhus & Williams, 2002), as well as diagnostic profiles described in DSM-5.

Psychopathy

Psychopathy is a personality profile that is characterized by traits such as egocentricity, callousness, superficial charm, and recklessness/disinhibition and is associated with persistent, pervasive antisociality. Research suggests that psychopathy, like other PDs, can be conceptualized as a configuration of general personality traits (e.g., Miller, Lynam, Widiger, & Leukefeld, 2001; Miller & Lynam, 2003) with a large emphasis on Agreeableness/Antagonism and Conscientiousness/Disinhibition.

In general, psychopathy manifests a robust correlation with aggression. A recent meta-analytic review of psychopathy's relation with aggression as part of the Dark Triad reported an effect size (r) of 0.44 (Vize, Lynam, Collison, & Miller, 2018). Generally, these findings have been unequivocal across forensic, community adult, youth, and psychiatric samples (e.g., Blais, Solodukhin, & Forth, 2014; Leistico, Salekin, DeCoster, & Roger, 2008; Miller, Rausher, Hyatt, Maples, & Zeichner, 2014). Of note, psychopathy has been extensively studied in forensic populations, where it is vastly overrepresented (~ 15–30% of forensic populations vs. 0.2–3.3% 12-month community prevalence rate; Cale & Lilienfeld, 2006; APA, 2013). Thus, it is unsurprising that psychopathy has been linked to violent criminal offending, as well rates of violent recidivism (Lestico, Salekin, DeCoster, & Rogers, 2008; Walters, 2003).

However, there are substantial, ongoing debates about the structure of psychopathy and which components are more or less relevant and important to the construct (e.g., Lilienfeld et al., 2012; Miller & Lynam, 2012). These debates are especially important in this context, as these components manifest differential relations with outcomes like aggression. These debates are too substantial to delve into in detail in the current chapter, but surround the importance/centrality of a set of traits deemed fearless dominance (Lilienfeld & Widows, 2005), boldness (Patrick, Fowles, & Krueger, 2009) and emotional stability (Few, Miller, & Lynam, 2013). This configuration of traits involves resilience to stress and decreased susceptibility to negative emotions along with an assertive interpersonal approach. Although these traits can be found in historical accounts of psychopathy, including Cleckley's (Crego & Widiger, 2016) and several existing measures (Lilienfeld, Watts, Francis Smith, Berg, & Latzman, 2015), concerns have been raised that these traits demonstrate an almost entirely adaptive nomological network, including mostly null correlations with externalizing-related outcomes like aggression (see Miller & Lynam, 2012 for a meta-analytic review) that most consider critical to psychopathy. Conversely, the more consensual traits – callousness, lack of remorse, egocentricity, impulsivity, irresponsibility – demonstrate reliably moderate to strong correlations with externalizing problems such as aggression (meta-analytic $r = 0.42$; Miller & Lynam, 2012). Although there has been some suggestion that certain aspects of psychopathy are primarily related to proactive but not reactive aggression (Reidy, Shelley-Tremblay, & Lilienfeld, 2011), this is inconsistent with meta-analytic evidence that demonstrates a comparable link between psychopathy and both reactive and proactive aggression (Blais et al., 2014).

Narcissism

Narcissism is another personality/PD construct with a long theoretical history (e.g., Freud; Foss, 2014) that is of substantial interest to researchers from a wide array of behavioral science domains (e.g., Campbell & Miller, 2011). Despite extant controversies regarding the nature of narcissism as a construct (Miller, Lynam, Hyatt, & Campbell, in press), academics, clinicians, and lay-persons alike agree that this profile is typically characterized by traits such as grandiosity, callousness, entitlement, exploitativeness, and noncompliance (Miller, Lynam, Siedor, Crowe, & Campbell, 2016; Thomas, Wright, Lukowitsky, Donnellan, & Hopwood, 2012).

Vize and colleagues' recent meta-analytic review reported a small to moderate effect size for narcissism's relation to aggression ($r = 0.23$). Whether this relation is contingent upon the presence of provocation is less clear. Bettencourt, Talley, Benjamin, and Valentine (2006) conducted a meta-analysis examining the relationship between personality traits and aggressive behavior under "provoked" vs. "neutral" conditions, and results suggested that trait narcissism was only related to aggressive behavior *after* provocation. This is consistent with findings from the seminal study by Bushman and Baumeister (1998; see also Twenge & Campbell, 2003) that posited the "ego-threat" hypothesis, which suggests that narcissistic individuals will react particularly aggressively when faced with an insult to their status, potentially as a method of conserving their inflated self-perception.

However, several recent publications have identified links between narcissism and aggression even in the absence of an explicit ego-threat (e.g., Lobbestael, Baumeister, Fiebig, & Eckel, 2014; Reidy, Foster, & Zeichner, 2010), which suggests that while an ego-threat may potentiate elevated levels of aggression in narcissistic individuals, it might not be necessary. Thus, it remains unclear whether aggression is rooted in an emotional response (e.g., anger) coupled with an appetite for retaliation, as suggested by the narcissistic rage hypothesis, a separate process arising from an interest in demonstrating social dominance (Kohut, 1972; Krizan & Johar, 2015), or is simply the manifestation of a general behavioral pattern for narcissistic individuals to aggress more often due to interests in dominance paired with low levels of empathy and compliance. From a general trait perspective, narcissism is characterized by low Agreeableness (Miller et al., in press), suggesting that narcissistic individuals may be globally prone to being aggressive.

Machiavellianism

Similar to its Dark Triad counterparts, Machiavellianism exhibits a strong association with aggression (meta-analytic $r = 0.39$; Vize et al., 2018). It is characterized by a cynical, dog-eat-dog world view, a dispositional tendency to manipulate others, as well as strategic, nonimpulsive thinking (Jones & Paulhus, 2011). It is moderately to largely associated with self-reported reactive and proactive aggression (Jonason, Duineveld, & Middleton, 2015), physical aggression, verbal aggression, anger, and hostility (Jones & Neria, 2015; Stead & Fekken, 2014).

The association between Machiavellianism and aggression is difficult to interpret, however, in light of recent work that suggests that, as measured, Machiavellianism may simply be a proxy for psychopathy (McHoskey, Worzel, & Szyarto, 1998; Miller, Hyatt, Maples-Keller, Carter, & Lynam, in press). As measured, Machiavellianism's trait profile is nearly indistinguishable from psychopathy (Miller et al., in press; O'Boyle et al., 2015), and characterized by interpersonal antagonism, disinhibition, and anger – traits known to be substantially correlated with aggression (e.g., Jones et al., 2011). This similarity is problematic due to the inclusion of disinhibition (e.g., impulsivity; failure to delay gratification; low ambitiousness), which is counter to theoretical descriptions of the construct and experts' conceptualizations (Miller, Hyatt, et al., in press). As such, the relation between Machiavellianism and aggression can be difficult to interpret, as it includes disinhibitory content that should be excluded from measures of Machiavellianism. In fact, when one removes the variance shared by measures of psychopathy and Machiavellianism, the latter no longer demonstrates substantial correlations with externalizing outcomes (Sleep, Lynam, Hyatt, & Miller, 2016).

Borderline Personality Disorder

Borderline personality disorder (BPD) is characterized by a pervasive pattern of instability in interpersonal relationships, emotion regulation, self-image, and impulse control (Skodol et al., 2002). Despite its heterogeneous nature, aggression and emotional dysregulation are considered to be core features (Mancke, Herpertz, & Bertsch, 2015), and expert ratings and meta-analytic review suggest that aggression-relevant traits are central to the construct (e.g., angry/hostility, noncompliance, deceitfulness; Samuel & Widiger, 2008). Indeed, empirical work has linked BPD to elevated aggression across methodology (Dougherty, Bjork, Huckabee, Moeller, & Swann, 1999; Russel, Moskowitz, Zuroff, Sookman, &

Paris, 2007). Longitudinal findings suggest that over the course of a year, 73% of individuals with BPD engaged in violent behavior, although this relation is diminished once BPD's shared variance with psychopathy is removed (Newhill, Eack, & Mulvey, 2009).

BPD has primarily exhibited relations to reactive forms of aggression (Berenson, Downey, Rafaeli, Coifman, & Leventhal-Paquin, 2011; Gardner, Archer, & Jackson, 2012), although links to both reactive and proactive aggression have been reported (Lobbestael, Cima, & Lemmens, 2015). Indirect evidence for a link between BPD symptoms and aggressive, antisocial behaviors comes from the degree to which BPD appears to be over-represented in prison settings, particularly among female offenders (Sansone & Sansone, 2009). Indeed, 30% of aggression-prone populations (e.g., prison inmates) exhibit borderline features (Black et al., 2007). Recently, Jackson, Sippel, Mota, Whalen, and Schumacher (2015) reviewed BPD's relation to interpersonal violence (IPV), and found that individuals with BPD were more likely to perpetrate IPV against a partner. Separate findings indicate that BPD is associated with verbal aggression (South, Turkheimer, & Oltmanns, 2008), minor to severe physical violence (Whisman & Schronbrun, 2009), and spousal homicide (e.g., 1/3 of men incarcerated for spousal homicide; Dixon, Hamilton-Giachritsis, & Browne, 2008).

Personality Traits and Aggression: Conclusions and Mechanisms

In sum, a robust body of literature supports the importance of certain personality traits in the prediction of aggression. The evidence is resoundingly clear that the FFM domains low Agreeableness/Antagonism and low Conscientiousness/Disinhibition are among the most robust individual difference correlates of aggression. Though high Neuroticism/Negative Affect has also been linked to aggression, a meta-analytic examination of the facet-level data suggests much of this relation is driven by traits related to anger/hostility. Interestingly, this trait has sometimes been considered to be "interstitial" in nature, in that it seems to be an admixture of negative emotionality and antagonism. Thus, scales of this trait tend to load on both domains in structural analyses. It is significant to note that the contributing roles of these traits are consistent across the aforementioned models, as well across populations, assessment method, and the lifespan.

Although these relations are well-established, questions as to how these traits manifest "in the moment" to lead to aggressive responding requires further investigation. In other words, the proximal mechanisms by which low trait Agreeableness (i.e., Antagonism) and Conscientiousness (i.e., Disinhibition) function to precipitate aggressive behavior are still largely under investigation. However, advances in this area have emerged. For example, Bresin and Robinson (2015) found that participants who were low in trait Agreeableness displayed a relatively exaggerated tendency to view negative images (e.g., a snarling dog) for a longer period of time than positive images, in line with previous research suggesting that similar individuals also have a difficult time disengaging from antisocial stimuli (Wilkowski, Robinson, & Meier, 2006).

Complementary research has also found that low Agreeableness is related to a particular tendency to interpret ambiguous social behavior as hostile, and also an increased likelihood of responding to these cues with aggression (Miller, Lynam, & Jones, 2008). This is consistent with other findings that suggest that low Agreeableness is associated with the tendency to view power assertion as an appropriate conflict resolution strategy (Graziano, Jensen-Campbell, & Hair, 1996). Furthermore, individuals low in Agreeableness appear to be more susceptible to aggressing after exposure to violent priming, which may be due to their relative inability to activate prosocial thoughts when primed with antisocial stimuli (Meier, Robinson, & Wilkowski, 2006).

Implications for Intervention

In contrast to the large body of research on FFM personality and aggression, very little research has been conducted into personality *per se* as the target of intervention. This dearth of study in this area is likely related to the impressive temporal stability of traits (test-retest coefficients from childhood to older adulthood = 0.31–0.74; Blonigen, 2010), as well as the contested subject of personality change as a result of therapeutic intervention (e.g., Rogers, 2007; c.f. Samstag, 2007). However, Hopwood et al. (2013) reported that symptoms of personality pathology are significantly less stable than personality traits, suggesting that pathological manifestations of traits may be more dynamic and susceptible to environmental dynamics. Thus, instead of specifically addressing trait-level change, it is likely that interventions focusing on individually relevant, practical change will proffer the most benefit. It is in these efforts that the research on mechanisms of antagonism will be able to speak most loudly.

For example, understanding that individuals low in Agreeableness are prone to misinterpreting ambiguous situations as hostile should inform intervention efforts that are aimed at addressing this distorted, deleterious cognitive pattern. In this way, micro-level modifications to individual tendencies may summate to meaningful change. This approach is represented by the Fast Track program, which has demonstrated modest but meaningful efficacy in decreasing aggression and increasing prosocial behavior, in part by teaching social skills and conflict resolution (Bierman et al., 2010). On the other hand, intensive interventions efforts that involve significant environmental changes (e.g., daily in-home consultations with an interventionist), such as Multisystemic Therapy, have shown to be successful in reducing arrest rates and aggression in peer relationships (Henggeler, Melton, & Smith, 1992). Thus, while few interventions have purported to directly target personality as the dependent variable in a treatment outcome study, researchers have made strides in reducing aggression by directing efforts at 1) mechanisms by which antagonistic tendencies lead to aggressive behavior and 2) the environmental contingencies that contribute to aggression. In sum, while personality is a multifactorially determined construct involving the intersection of biology and environment, there is cause for tentative optimism in treatments that aim to reduce aggressive behavior.

Conclusion

In this chapter, we have reviewed the evidence for the importance of personality in understanding aggression using a basic, general trait perspective to guide our review. A rich literature, including numerous meta-analyses, strongly supports the importance of several key traits: low Agreeableness (Antagonism) and low Conscientiousness (Disinhibition). Although anger/hostility (Neuroticism) and (lack of) warmth (Extraversion) seem to be important facets from other domains, Antagonism and Disinhibition are most central to FFM accounts of aggression.

In addition to general and pathologically oriented trait models, we also reviewed several frequently studied personality profiles that have been of interest to clinical practitioners, criminologists, and social-personality psychologists alike. Antagonism and Disinhibition appear to generally underlie the majority of the multidimensional configurations psychopathy, narcissism, and Machiavellianism (e.g., Paulhus & Williams, 2002). As such, investigations into the underlying mechanisms by which antagonistic and disinhibited traits lead to aggress against others in different contexts and manner will also inform our understanding of how these broader constructs exert their effects on relevant outcomes like aggression. It is also hoped these investigations will prove useful in the development of interventions aimed at reducing aggressive behavior.

To this end, we encourage further investigation into the role of personality in aggression, and suggest collaboration across disciplines, including (but not limited to) clinical psychology, social-personality psychology, criminology, educational psychology, developmental psychopathology, neuroscience, and genetics. In conjunction, we encourage the burgeoning research on the mechanisms that underlie the relations between personality and aggression, especially since their bivariate relations are no longer in question. These types of mechanistic approaches are more likely to yield information that may be germane to the development of prevention and intervention approaches.

References

Al-Dajani, N., Gralnick, T. M., & Bagby, R. M. (2016). A psychometric review of the Personality Inventory for DSM-5 (PID-5): Current status and future directions. *Journal of Personality Assessment*, 98, 62–81.

American Psychiatric Association. (2013). *Diagnostic and statistical manual of mental disorders* (5th ed.). Arlington, VA: Author.

Anderson, C. A. & Bushman, B. J. (2002). Human aggression. *Annual Review of Psychology*, 53, 27–51.

Anderson, J. L., Sellbom, M., Ayearst, L., Quilty, L. C., Chmielewski, M., & Bagby, R. M. (2015). Associations between DSM-5 section III personality traits and the Minnesota Multiphasic Personality Inventory 2-Restructured Form (MMPI-2-RF) scales in a psychiatric patient sample. *Psychological Assessment*, 27, 801–815.

Archer, J. & Coyne, S. M. (2005). An integrated review of indirect, relational, and social aggression. *Personality and Social Psychology Review*, 9, 212–230.

Ashton, M. C. & Lee, K. (2005). A defence of the lexical approach to the study of personality structure. *European Journal of Personality*, 19, 5–24.

Bandura, A. (1973). *Aggression: A social learning analysis*. Englewood Cliff, NJ: Prentice-Hall.

Beanland, V., Sellbom, M., & Johnson, A. K. (2014). Personality domains and traits that predict self-reported aberrant driving behaviours in a southeastern US university sample. *Accident Analysis and Prevention*, 72, 184–192.

Berenson, K. R., Downey, G., Rafaeli, E., Coifman, K. G., & Leventhal-Paquin, N. (2011). The rejection-rage contingency in borderline personality disorder. *Journal of Abnormal Psychology*, 120, 681–690.

Bettencourt, B., Talley, A., Benjamin, A. J., & Valentine, J. (2006). Personality and aggressive behavior under provoking and neutral conditions: A meta-analytic review. *Psychological Bulletin*, 132, 751–777.

Bierman, K. L., Coie, J. D., Dodge, K. A., Greenberg, M. T., Lochman, J. E., McMahon, R. J., & Pinderhughes, E. (2010). The effects of a multiyear universal social–emotional learning program: The role of student and school characteristics. *Journal of Consulting and Clinical Psychology*, 78, 156–168.

Black, D. W., Gunter, T., Allen, J., Blum, N., Arndt, S., Wenman, G., & Sieleni, B. (2007). Borderline personality disorder in male and female offenders newly committed to prison. *Comprehensive Psychiatry*, 48, 400–405.

Blais, J., Solodukhin, E., & Forth, A. E. (2014). A meta-analysis exploring the relationship between psychopathy and instrumental versus reactive violence. *Criminal Justice and Behavior*, 41, 797–821.

Blonigen, D. M. (2010). Explaining the relationship between age and crime: Contributions from the developmental literature on personality. *Clinical Psychology Review*, 30, 89–100.

Bresin, K. & Robinson, M. D. (2015). You are what you see and choose: Agreeableness and situation selection. *Journal of Personality*, 83, 452–463.

Brugman, S., Lobbestael, J., Arntz, A., Cima, M., Schuhmann, T., Dambacher, F., & Sack, A. T. (2015). Identifying cognitive predictors of reactive and proactive aggression. *Aggressive Behavior*, 41, 51–64.

Bushman, B. J. & Anderson, C. A. (2001). Is it time to pull the plug on hostile versus instrumental aggression dichotomy? *Psychological Review*, 108, 273–279.

Bushman B. J. & Baumeister R. F. (1998). Threatened egotism, narcissism, self-esteem, and direct and displaced aggression: Does self-love or self-hate lead to violence? *Journal of Personality and Social Psychology*, 75, 219–229.

Cale, E. M. (2006). A quantitative review of the relations between the "Big 3" higher order personality dimensions and antisocial behavior. *Journal of Research in Personality*, 40, 250–284.

Cale, E. M. & Lilienfeld, S. O. (2002). Sex differences in psychopathy and antisocial personality disorder. A review and integration. *Clinical Psychology Review*, 22(8), 1179–1207.

Campbell, W. K. & Miller, J. D. (2011). *The handbook of narcissism and narcissistic personality disorder*. Hoboken, NJ: John Wiley & Sons.

Carlson, E. N., Vazire, S., & Oltmanns, T. F. (2013). Self-other knowledge asymmetries in personality pathology. *Journal of Personality*, 81, 155–170.

Clark, L. A. (2007). Assessment and diagnosis of personality disorder: Perennial issues and an emerging reconceptualization. *Annual Review of Psychology*, 58, 227–257.

Crego, C. & Widiger, T. A. (2016). Cleckley's psychopaths: Revisited. *Journal of Abnormal Psychology*, 125, 75–87.

Costa, P. T. & McCrae, R. R. (1992). Normal personality assessment in clinical practice: The NEO Personality Inventory. *Psychological Assessment*, 4, 5–13.

DeYoung, C. G., Quilty, L. C., & Peterson, J. B. (2007). Between facets and domains: 10 aspects of the Big Five. *Journal of Personality and Social Psychology*, 93, 880–896.

Digman, J. M. (1990). Personality structure: Emergence of the five-factor model. *Annual Review of Psychology*, 41, 417–440.

Dixon, L., Hamilton-Giachritsis, C., & Browne, K. (2008). Classifying partner femicide. *Journal of Interpersonal Violence*, 23, 74–93.

Dodge, K. A. & Coie, J. D. (1987). Social-information-processing factors in reactive and proactive aggression in children's peer groups. *Journal of Personality and Social Psychology*, 53, 1146–1158.

Dollard, J., Miller, N. E., Doob, L. W., Mowrer, O. H., & Sears, R. R. (1939). *Frustration and Aggression*. New Haven, CT: Yale University Press.

Dougherty, D. M., Bjork, J. M., Huckabee, H. C., Moeller, F. G., & Swann, A. C. (1999). Laboratory measures of aggression and impulsivity in women with borderline personality disorder. *Psychiatry Research*, 85, 315–326.

Eysenck, H. J. & Eysenck, M. W. (1985). *Personality and individual differences: A natural science approach*. New York: Plenum.

Few, L. R., Miller, J. D., Rothbaum, A. O., Meller, S., Maples, J., Terry, D. P., ... & MacKillop, J. (2013). Examination of the Section III DSM-5 diagnostic system for personality disorders in an outpatient clinical sample. *Journal of Abnormal Psychology*, 122, 1057–1069.

Few, L. R., Miller, J. D., & Lynam, D. R. (2013). An examination of the factor structure of the Elemental Psychopathy Assessment. *Personality Disorders: Theory, Research, and Treatment*, 4, 247–253.

Foss, T. (2014). Freud 100 years ago: On narcissism: An introduction (1914a); On the history of the psychoanalytic movement (1914b); Preface to the 3rd edition of Three essays on the theory of sexuality (1914c). *The Scandinavian Psychoanalytic Review*, 37, 80–84.

Gardner, K. J., Archer, J., & Jackson, S. (2012). Does maladaptive coping mediate the relationship between borderline personality traits and reactive and proactive aggression? *Aggressive Behavior*, 38, 403–413.

Gore, W. L. & Widiger, T. A. (2013). The DSM-5 dimensional trait model and five-factor models of general personality. *Journal of Abnormal Psychology*, 122, 816–821.

Graziano, W. G., Jensen-Campbell, L. A., & Hair, E. C. (1996). Perceiving interpersonal conflict and reacting to it: the case for agreeableness. *Journal of Personality and Social Psychology*, 70, 820–835.

Henggeler, S. W., Melton, G. B., & Smith, L. A. (1992). Family preservation using multisystemic therapy: an effective alternative to incarcerating serious juvenile offenders. *Journal of Consulting and Clinical Psychology*, 60(6), 953.

Hopwood, C. J., Morey, L. C., Donnellan, M. B., Samuel, D. B., Grilo, C. M., McGlashan, T. H., ... & Skodol, A. E. (2013). Ten-year rank-order stability of personality traits and disorders in a clinical sample. *Journal of Personality*, 81(3), 335–344.

Jackson, M. A., Sippel, L. M., Mota, N., Whalen, D., & Schumacher, J. A. (2015). Borderline personality disorder and related constructs as risk factors for intimate partner violence perpetration. *Aggression and Violent Behavior*, 24, 95–106.

John, O. P., Caspi, A., Robins, R. W., Moffitt, T. E., & Stouthamer-Loeber, M. (1994). The "little five": Exploring the nomological network of the five-factor model of personality in adolescent boys. *Child Development*, 160–178.

John, O. P. & Srivastava, S. (1999). The Big Five trait taxonomy: History, measurement, and theoretical perspectives. *Handbook of personality: Theory and research*, 2(1999), 102–138.

Jonason, P. K., Duineveld, J. J., & Middleton, J. P. (2015). Pathology, pseudopathology, and the Dark Triad of personality. *Personality and Individual Differences*, 78, 43–47.

Jones, S. E., Miller, J. D., & Lynam, D. R. (2011). Personality, antisocial behavior, and aggression: A meta-analytic review. *Journal of Criminal Justice*, 39, 329–337.

Jones, D. N. & Neria, A. L. (2015). The Dark Triad and dispositional aggression. *Personality and Individual Differences*, 86, 360–364.

Jones, D. N. & Paulhus, D. L. (2011). The role of impulsivity in the Dark Triad of personality. *Personality and Individual Differences*, 51, 670–682.

Kohut, H. (1972). Thoughts on narcissism and narcissistic rage. In R. S. Eissler, A. Freud, M. Kris, & A. J. Solnit (Eds), The psychoanalytic study of the child (Vol. 27, pp. 360–400). New York: Quadrangle Books.

Krizan, Z. & Johar, O. (2015). Narcissistic rage revisited. *Journal of Personality And Social Psychology*, 108(5), 784–801.

Krueger, R. F., Caspi, A., Moffitt, T. E., & Silva, P. A. (1998). The structure and stability of common mental disorders (DSM-III-R): A longitudinal-epidemiological study. *Journal of Abnormal Psychology*, 107(2), 216.

Krueger, R. F., Derringer, J., Markon, K. E., Watson, D., & Skodol, A. E. (2012). Initial construction of a maladaptive personality trait model and inventory for DSM-5. *Psychological Medicine*, 42, 1879–1890.

Leistico, A. M. R., Salekin, R. T., DeCoster, J., & Rogers, R. (2008). A large-scale meta-analysis relating the hare measures of psychopathy to antisocial conduct. *Law and Human Behavior*, 32, 28–45.

Lilienfeld, S. O., Patrick, C. J., Benning, S. D., Berg, J., Sellbom, M., & Edens, J. F. (2012). The role of fearless dominance in psychopathy: Confusions, controversies, and clarifications. *Personality Disorders: Theory, Research, And Treatment*, 3(3), 327–340.

Lilienfeld, S. O., Watts, A. L., Francis Smith, S., Berg, J. M., & Latzman, R. D. (2015). Psychopathy deconstructed and reconstructed: Identifying and assembling the Personality building blocks of Cleckley's chimera. *Journal of Personality*, 83(6), 593–610.

Lilienfeld, S. O. & Widows, M. R. (2005). *PPI-R: Psychopathic personality inventory revised: Professional Manual*. Lutz, FL: Psychological Assessment Resources, Incorporated.

Livesley, W. J., Schroeder, M. L., Jackson, D. N., & Jang, K. L. (1994). Categorical distinctions in the study of personality disorder: Implications for classification. *Journal of Abnormal Psychology*, 103(1), 6–17.

Lobbestael, J., Baumeister, R. F., Fiebig, T., & Eckel, L. A. (2014). The role of grandiose and vulnerable narcissism in self-reported and laboratory aggression and testosterone reactivity. *Personality and Individual Differences*, 69, 22–27.

Lobbestael, J., Cima, M., & Lemmens, A. (2015). The relationship between personality disorder traits and reactive versus proactive motivation for aggression. *Psychiatry Research*, 229, 155–160.

Mancke, F., Herpertz, S. C., & Bertsch, K. (2015). Aggression in borderline personality disorder: A multidimensional model. *Personality Disorders: Theory, Research, and Treatment*, 6, 278–291.

McCrae, R. R. & John, O. P. (1992). An introduction to the five-factor model and its applications. *Journal of Personality*, 60, 175–215.

McCrae, R. R., Costa, P. T., Del Pilar, G. H., Rolland, J. P., & Parker, W. D. (1998). Cross-cultural assessment of the five-factor model the revised NEO personality inventory. *Journal of Cross-Cultural Psychology*, 29, 171–188.

McHoskey, J. W., Worzel, W., & Szyarto, C. (1998). Machiavellianism and psychopathy. *Journal of Personality and Social psychology*, 74, 192–210.

Meier, B. P., Robinson, M. D., & Wilkowski, B. M. (2006). Turning the Other Cheek: Agreeableness and the Regulation of Aggression-Related Primes. *Psychological Science*, 17, 136–142.

Miller, J. D. (2012). Five-factor model personality disorder prototypes: A review of their development, validity, and comparison to alternative approaches. *Journal of Personality*, 80, 1565–1591.

Miller, J. D., Hyatt, C. S., Maples-Keller, J. L., Carter, N. T., & Lynam, D. R. (2017). Psychopathy and Machiavellianism: A distinction without a difference?. *Journal of Personality*, 85, 439–453.

Miller, J. D. & Lynam, D. R. (2001). Structural models of personality and their relation to antisocial behavior: a meta-analytic review. *Criminology*, 39, 765–798.

Miller, J. D. & Lynam, D. R. (2003). Psychopathy and the five-factor model of personality: A replication and extension. *Journal of Personality Assessment*, 81, 168–178.

Miller, J. D. & Lynam, D. R. (2006). Reactive and proactive aggression: Similarities and differences. *Personality and Individual Differences*, 41, 1469–1480.

Miller, J. D. & Lynam, D. R. (2012). An examination of the Psychopathic Personality Inventory's nomological network: a meta-analytic review. *Personality Disorders: Theory, Research, and Treatment*, 3, 305–326.

Miller, J. D., Lynam, D. R., Hyatt, C. S., & Campbell, W. K. (in press). Controversies in narcissism. *Annual Review of Clinical Psychology*.

Miller, J. D., Lynam, D. R., & Jones, S. E. (2008). Externalizing behavior through the lens of the Five Factor Model: A focus on agreeableness and conscientiousness. *Journal of Personality Assessment*, 90, 158–164.

Miller, J. D., Lyman, D. R., Widiger, T. A., & Leukefeld, C. (2001). Personality disorders as extreme variants of common personality dimensions: can the five factor model adequately represent psychopathy?. *Journal of Personality*, 69, 253–276.

Miller, J. D., Lynam, D. R., Siedor, L., Crowe, M., Campbell, W. K. (2016) Consensual lay profiles of narcissism and their connection to existing assessment measures. Manuscript under review.

Miller, J. D., Rausher, S., Hyatt, C. S., Maples, J., & Zeichner, A. (2014). Examining the relations among pain tolerance, psychopathic traits, and violent and nonviolent antisocial behavior. *Journal of Abnormal Psychology*, 123, 205.

Miller, J. D., Zeichner, A., & Wilson, L. F. (2012). Personality correlates of aggression: Evidence from measures of the Five-Factor Model, UPPS Model of Impulsivity, and BIS/BAS. *Journal of Interpersonal Violence*, 27, 2903–2919.

Newhill, C. E., Eack, S. M., & Mulvey, E. P. (2009). Violent behavior in borderline personality. *Journal of Personality Disorders*, 23, 541–554.

O'Boyle, E. H., Forsyth, D. R., Banks, G. C., Story, P. A., & White, C. D. (2015). A meta-analytic test of redundancy and relative importance of the dark triad and five-factor model of personality. *Journal of Personality*, 83, 644–664.

Ozer, D. J. & Benet-Martinez, V. (2006). Personality and the prediction of consequential outcomes. Annual Review of Psychology, 57, 401–421.

Patrick, C. J., Fowles, D. C., & Krueger, R. F. (2009). Triarchic conceptualization of psychopathy: Developmental origins of disinhibition, boldness, and meanness. *Developmental Psychopathology*, 21, 913–938.

Paulhus, D. L. & Williams, K. M. (2002). The dark triad of personality: Narcissism, Machiavellianism, and psychopathy. *Journal of Research in Personality*, 36, 556–563.

Reidy, D. E., Foster, J. D., & Zeichner, A. (2010). Narcissism and unprovoked aggression. *Aggressive Behavior*, 36, 414–422.

Reidy, D. E., Shelley-Tremblay, J. F., & Lilienfeld, S. O. (2011). Psychopathy, reactive aggression, and precarious proclamations: A review of behavioral, cognitive, and biological research. *Aggression and Violent Behavior*, 16, 512–524.

Rogers, C. R. (2007). The necessary and sufficient conditions of therapeutic personality change. *Psychotherapy: Theory, Research, Practice, Training*, 44(3), 240–248.

Rosell, D. R. & Siever, L. J. (2015) The neurobiology of aggression and violence. *CNS Spectrums*, 20, 254–279.

Russel, J. J., Moskowitz, D. S., Zuroff, D. C., Sookman, D., & Paris, J. (2007). Stability and variability of affective experience and interpersonal behavior in borderline personality disorder. *Journal of Abnormal Psychology*, 116, 578–588.

Samstag, L. W. (2007). The necessary and sufficient conditions of therapeutic personality change: Reactions to Rogers' 1957 article. *Psychotherapy: Theory, Research, Practice, Training*, 44(3), 295–299.

Samuel, D. B. & Widiger, T. A. (2008). A meta-analytic review of the relationships between the five-factor model and DSM-IV-TR personality disorders: A facet level analysis. *Clinical Psychology Review*, 28, 1326–1342.

Sansone, R. A. & Sansone, L. A. (2009). Borderline personality and criminality. *Psychiatry*, 6, 16–20.

Sleep, C. E., Lynam, D. R., Hyatt, C. S., & Miller, J. D. (2016). Perils of partialling Redux: The case of the dark triad. Manuscript in preparation.

Skodol, A. E., Gunderson, J. G., Pfohl, B., Widiger, T. A., Livesley, W. J., & Siever, L. J. (2002). The borderline diagnosis I: Psychopathology, comorbidity, and personality structure. *Biological Psychiatry*, 51, 936–950.

South, S. C., Turkheimer, E., & Oltmanns, T. F. (2008). Personality disorder symptoms and marital functioning. *Journal of Consulting and Clinical Psychology*, 76, 769–780.

Stead, R. & Fekken, G. C. (2014). Agreeableness at the core of the dark triad of personality. *Individual Differences Research*, 12, 131–141.

Tackett, J. L., Daoud, S. L., De Bolle, M., & Burt, S. A. (2013). Is relational aggression part of the externalizing spectrum? A bifactor model of youth antisocial behavior. *Aggressive Behavior*, 39, 149–159.

Thomas, K. M., Wright A. G. C., Lukowitsky M. R., Donnellan M. B., & Hopwood C. J. (2012) Evidence for the criterion validity and clinical utility of the Pathological Narcissism Inventory. *Assessment*, 19, 135–145.

Twenge, J. M. & Campbell, W. K. (2003). 'Isn't it fun to get the respect that we're going to deserve?' Narcissism, social rejection, and aggression. *Personality and Social Psychology Bulletin*, 29, 261–272.

Vize, C. E., Lynam, D. R., Collison, K. L., & Miller, J. D. (2018). Differences among dark triad components: A meta-analytic investigation. *Personality Disorders: Theory, Research, and Treatment*, 9(2), 101–111.

Walters, G. D. (2003). Predicting institutional adjustment and recidivism with the psychopathy checklist factor scores: A meta-analysis. *Law and Human Behavior*, 27, 541–558.

Whisman, M. A. & Schonbrun, Y. C. (2009). Social consequences of borderline personality disorder symptoms in a population-based survey: Marital distress, marital violence, and marital disruption. *Journal of Personality Disorders*, 23, 410–415.

Widiger, T. A. (1993). The DSM-III-R categorical personality disorder diagnoses: A critique and an alternative. *Psychological Inquiry*, 4, 75–90.

Widiger, T. A. & Trull, T. J. (2007). Plate tectonics in the classification of personality disorder: Shifting to a dimensional model. *American Psychologist*, 62, 71–83.

Wilkowski, B. M., Robinson, M. D., & Meier, B. P. (2006). Agreeableness and the prolonged spatial processing of antisocial and prosocial information. *Journal of Research in Personality*, 40, 1152–1168.

Yamagata, S., Suzuki, A., Ando, J., One, Y., Kijima, N., Yoshimura, K. ... & Livesly, W. J. (2006). Is the genetic structure of human personality universal? A cross-cultural twin study from North America, Europe, and Asia. *Journal of Personality and Social Psychology*, 90, 987–998.

PART III

Individual and Interpersonal Factors for Violence and Aggression

14 Applying Empirically Based Trait Models to an Understanding of Personality and Violence

Daniel M. Blonigen and Christopher J. Patrick

Introduction

The link between personality and violence has traditionally been viewed from a categorical, disorder-centric lens, as instantiated in the *Diagnostic and Statistical Manual of Mental Disorders* (DSM). In our previous chapter (Blonigen & Krueger, 2007), we highlighted the limitations of this categorical model relative to a dimensional model of personality and argued for an analysis of the personality-violence link using an empirically based model of *traits*, with a focus on structural models of normal-range personality. The fifth edition of the DSM (DSM-5; American Psychiatric Association, 2013) has ushered in the first empirically based model of maladaptive traits – Section III Personality Trait Model (Krueger & Markon, 2014). This landmark development in the classification of personality pathology will serve as our framework for analyzing the relationship of personality and violence in this chapter and for offering directions for future research in this area.

Here, we review the empirical literature on personality and violence since the previous version of this chapter. We target relevant research from the adult literature with a primary focus on empirically based models of maladaptive traits, which have emerged in recent years and gained greater acceptance vis-à-vis the establishment of Section III of DSM-5. We begin by reviewing the most recent research on personality and violence from the standpoint of DSM-defined personality disorders, and structural models of normal-range personality. From there, we review DSM-5's alternative models of personality disorders, particularly the Section III personality trait system and complementary models of maladaptive traits that have emerged since the previous version of this chapter (e.g., Externalizing Spectrum Model; Triarchic Model of Psychopathy), and discuss how these alternative models may be used to conceptualize specific personality disorders and the link between those disorders and violent behavior. Finally, we discuss the implications and utility of this research for driving policy and prevention and intervention efforts to reduce risk of violent behavior among adults.

Personality and Violence from a Categorical Perspective

Historically, the role of personality in relation to violence and aggression has been examined from the perspective of the DSM's categorical model of personality disorders. In past versions of the DSM and in Section II of DSM-5, personality disorders are organized into ten categories, organized into three clusters: Cluster A (*Odd or Eccentric*) includes paranoid, schizoid, and schizotypal personality disorders; Cluster B (*Dramatic, Emotional, or Erratic*) includes antisocial, borderline, histrionic, and narcissistic personality disorders; and Cluster C (*Anxious or Fearful*) includes avoidant, dependent, and obsessive-compulsive personality disorders. Importantly, neither the ten-category model, nor the three-cluster system under which these diagnoses are organized, were derived empirically, and it is widely agreed that this classification system lacks validity (Watson, Clark, & Chmielewski, 2008).

From this categorical perspective, a number of studies have demonstrated that a personality disorder diagnosis is associated with elevated risk for engaging in violent and aggressive behavior in both clinical-forensic (Egan et al., 2003; Yarvis, 1990) and community-epidemiological samples (Berman, Fallon, & Coccaro, 1998; Johnson et al., 2000). This association remains after controlling for comorbid mental health conditions that are also associated with violence (Berman et al., 1998; Johnson et al., 2000). More recent large-scale studies affirm the personality disorder-violence link. Among a nationally representative sample of 3,929 college students, Schwartz, Beaver, and Barnes (2015) reported that a personality disorder diagnosis was associated with a larger increase in odds of violent behavior than other common mental disorders (e.g., mood, anxiety, and substance use disorder diagnoses). Among the eight personality disorders assessed, the adjusted odds ratio for antisocial personality disorder (APD) was highest (see also a meta-analysis by Yu et al., 2012).

Although it has been consistently observed that personality disorders are robust predictors of violent behavior, given that the diagnostic criteria of several of these disorders include patterns of aggressive actions, the finding of an association between personality disorders and violence is potentially tautological. However, the predictive value of this literature is demonstrated by research on multidimensional models of personality disorders. For example, Nestor (2002) posited that personality dimensions of *impulse control, affect regulation, threatened egotism,* and a *paranoid cognitive personality style* underlie associations between certain forms of mental illness and violence. Specifically, Nestor (2002) argued that impairments in impulse control and affect regulation contribute to increased risk for violence across virtually all psychiatric conditions (particularly Cluster B personality disorders and substance use disorders), whereas threatened egotism may account for unique variance in the relationship between personality disorders and violence (see Bushman & Baumeister, 1998; Lambe, Hamilton-Giachritsis, Garner, & Walker, 2016). Nestor (2002) also posited that a paranoid cognitive personality style accounts uniquely for the association between psychotic-spectrum disorders and violence (see Arsenault et al., 2000). However, other studies have demonstrated that symptoms of paranoid personality disorder are predictive of violent behavior even after controlling for comorbid psychosis (Berman et al., 1998; Johnson et al., 2000). A multidimensional model of aggression in borderline personality disorder was also proposed by Mancke et al. (2015). Similar to Nestor (2002), this biobehavioral model theorizes that dimensions of affective dysregulation, impulsivity, and threatened hypersensitivity comprise distinct pathways to violence among borderline patients.

Collectively, this research suggests that different processes underlie observed relations between personality disorders and violence. Nevertheless, many of the existing models of the intersection between the two describe the personality disorder-violence link from a categorical perspective rather than a dimensional, trait-based perspective. Widiger and Costa (1994) and others (see Howard, 2015) have raised this issue and argued that examining the personality disorder-violence relationship through the lens of a structural model of traits is necessary due to limited validity for the categorical model of personality disorders, and to the need to ground the literature in a nomological network to guide hypothesis testing and theory development.

Personality and Violence from a Trait-Based Perspective: Structural Models of Normal-Range Personality

Structural models of normal-range personality focus on traits as their unit of analysis and conceptualize these constructs as internal dispositions and tendencies to behave, think, and feel in consistent ways across time and across situations (Kenrick & Funder, 1988). Further, traits are not simply descriptive but explanatory such that they represent fundamental (latent) causal processes, which explain systematic covariation among observed behaviors and provide surplus meaning through prediction of behaviors above and beyond the inferred structure of the trait itself.

Relative to the DSM's categorical model of personality disorders, structural models of personality traits have a number of advantages. First, central to the interpretation of traits is the notion that traits are organized in a hierarchical fashion. That is, latent traits, inferred from systematic covariation among a set of observed measures, co-vary with similar traits to form higher-order (global) trait factors. By providing both breadth of coverage at a higher-order level and more detailed coverage at a lower-order level of the trait hierarchy, structural models allow for the examination of personality in relation to behavioral phenomena at broad *and* fine-grained levels of analysis. Another advantage of structural models is that they are grounded in dimensional constructs that span both normal and abnormal personality domains and thus make them conducive to research in community-epidemiological populations. By contrast, the categorical, pathological perspective of personality has tended to emphasize examination of clinical and/or forensic populations, which have a high prevalence of DSM-based personality disorder diagnoses. Finally, structural models of personality are grounded in rich nomological networks, which help to organize, interpret, and integrate disparate findings from a given literature. That is, structural models of personality traits aid in the translation of findings across studies and ultimately help to guide theory development and hypothesis testing to explicate the relationship between personality and violence more generally. For example, the Externalizing Spectrum Model (ESM; Krueger et al., 2007) was developed within a trait-based framework and has explicit ties to structural models of personality. The past decade has seen notable advancements in the etiology and neurobiology of the ESM (Venables & Patrick, 2014; Patrick, 2015), which provides a framework for hypothesis testing and interpretation of research findings in the personality-violence literature.

Although several structural models have been proposed in the personality literature, the Big 5 and Big 3 models represent the most common and well-validated. The Big 5 model was derived from a lexical approach to the examination of personality structure (Goldberg, 1993). In this model, which is operationalized by self-report measures such as the NEO Personality Inventory (NEO PI) and its variants, lower-order traits (or facets) cohere into higher-order domains of Extraversion, Neuroticism, Openness to Experience, Agreeableness, and Conscientiousness. Various Big 3 models have been proposed in the literature (Eysenck & Eysenck, 1975; Cloninger, Svrakic, & Przybeck, 1993). Tellegen's (2000) model, operationalized via the Multidimensional Personality Questionnaire (MPQ), comprises 11 lower-order, primary traits, which cohere into higher-order factors of Positive Emotionality (PEM), Negative Emotionality (NEM), and Constraint (CON). Elevations on PEM and NEM reflect dispositional tendencies to experience a range of positive and aversive emotional states, respectively. Elevations on CON reflect a disposition to be cautious and restrained in one's behavior, such as the avoidance of dangerous activities and adherence to social norms.

Much of the prior research on links between violence and traits from normal-range personality models has targeted the higher-order domains in the Big 5 and Big 3 trait hierarchies. For example, in the Big 5 literature, a recent meta-analysis on trait correlates of aggression and indicators of antisocial behavior indicated that lower Agreeableness (higher Antagonism) and Conscientiousness (higher Disinhibition), and, to a lesser extent, elevations on Neuroticism have the strongest and most consistent associations with aggression and other indicators of antisocial behavior (Jones, Miller, & Lynam, 2011). From a Big 3 perspective, higher NEM and lower CON have been identified as the most robust personality correlates of a host of problematic behaviors including violence (Caspi et al., 1997; Elkins, Iacono, Doyle, & McGue, 1997).

At this point, the links between violent behavior and aggression and broad domains of personality from structural models are well known and converge on a personality profile marked by heightened sensitivity to a range of negative emotional states, higher interpersonal antagonism, and general deficits in impulse control and response inhibition. However, it is important to note that these trait constructs are not unique to violence *per se* but rather operate as indicators of a spectrum of disinhibitory problems including antisocial behavior and alcohol and drug abuse – an idea formalized in the ESM (Krueger et al., 2007).

Personality and Violence from the Perspectives of Integrative Models of Externalizing Psychopathology and Psychopathic Personality

Externalizing Spectrum Model

While the focus of this chapter is on violence and aggression, we suggest that these behavioral tendencies can best be understood by conceptualizing them as part of a broader spectrum of personality traits and clinical problems. The *externalizing spectrum model* (ESM) posits that antisocial behavior (including both aggressive and non-aggressive criminal acts), alcohol and drug use problems, and traits related to impulsivity and aggression co-occur at higher-than-chance rates and form a coherent spectrum of disinhibitory tendencies (Krueger et al., 2002, 2007). Similar to structural models of personality, the ESM is a quantitative, empirically based model derived from analysis of patterns of relations among common mental disorders as defined in the DSM nosology.

A foundation and impetus for the ESM was factor-analytic work by Krueger (1999) and others (e.g., Achenbach & Edelbrock, 1984) showing that unipolar depression and anxiety disorders covary systematically around a broad psychopathological dimension of "internalizing." Impulse-control disorders such as alcohol and drug use disorders and child and adult antisocial behavior, on the other hand, were shown to load together on a common "externalizing" factor – correlated with but distinct from the internalizing dimension – and associated with low scores on the Big 3 dimension of CON along with elevations on NEM (Krueger et al., 2002). Notably, findings from genetically informed studies indicate that the externalizing factor underlying these latter disorders is appreciably heritable in nature, consistent with the idea that it reflects a general liability towards a variety of disinhibitory problems (Hicks, Krueger, Iacono, McGue, & Patrick, 2004; Krueger et al., 2002).

While the concept of an externalizing spectrum originally emerged out of factor analyses of clinical disorders, subsequent research demonstrated that the model encompasses disinhibitory personality traits along with psychopathological conditions. This was suggested by the fact that the personality correlates of antisocial behavior and substance use disorders are highly similar (e.g., Sher & Trull, 1994). Specifically, both are marked by elevated levels of traits from the domains of impulsiveness (i.e., low Conscientiousness from the Big 5; low CON from the MPQ) and negative affectivity (i.e., low agreeableness [or high antagonism] from the Big 5, and high aggression and alienation from the MPQ). Building on this work, Krueger et al. (2007) formulated a more comprehensive, construct-oriented model of the externalizing domain in the form of a self-report instrument, the Externalizing Spectrum Inventory (ESI). These investigators mapped out expressions of externalizing proneness in terms of 23 facet scales, each assessing a distinct manifestation of disinhibitory tendencies through a set of relevant items. Using scores on the ESI's facet scales as indicators, Krueger and colleagues modeled the externalizing spectrum as operationalized by this instrument, and showed that all 23 scales loaded together on a common factor, labeled externalizing proneness (or general disinhibition; Patrick et al., 2013). In addition, residual variances from certain scales covaried together to form subfactors, one labeled callous-aggression and the other substance abuse. The callous-aggression subfactor was defined by residual variances from facet scales assessing empathy and variants of aggressive behavior (i.e., relational aggression most strongly, followed by destructive and physical aggression). The implication is that scores on the aggression-related scales of the ESI are indicative of two distinguishable tendencies, one involving poor emotion regulation and weak behavioral restraint (i.e., externalizing proneness) and the other entailing a lack of sensitivity to the feelings and welfare of others (i.e., callous-exploitativeness).

Triarchic Model of Psychopathy

The distinction in the ESM between a general externalizing propensity and a residual factor reflecting tendencies towards callous-aggressive behavior is echoed in contemporary theories of psychopathic personality ("psychopathy"). Historically, accounts of the clinical condition known as psychopathy have highlighted the occurrence of impulsive-externalizing behavior in the absence of anxious-depressive ("neurotic") symptoms. From the standpoint of current nosologies, psychopathy is most closely linked to the DSM-based diagnosis of antisocial personality disorder (APD); however, it has been widely noted that the diagnostic criteria for this personality disorder diverge substantially from early conceptions of psychopathy, which predated the diagnosis of APD. Most notable among these is Hervey Cleckley's seminal book, titled *The Mask of Sanity* (1941/1976), in which he described psychopathy as an unusual clinical condition involving an outward appearance of normalcy that conceals a deep-rooted emotional disturbance, displayed in terms of chronically deviant and antisocial behavior.

Notably, Cleckley did not characterize psychopathic patients as inherently predatory or cruel. Instead, he considered the harm they caused others to be an unintended consequence of their general lack of emotional sensitivity and social connectedness. As such, along with case descriptions of career criminals, Cleckley included examples of "successful psychopaths," such as businessmen, scholars, and physicians, who displayed many of the same core traits as chronically antisocial individuals, but without engagement in aggressive criminal acts. In contrast, experts working with psychopathic criminal offenders placed greater emphasis on more uniformly pathological features such as viciousness, exploitativeness, and coldness in their definitions of psychopathy. For example, McCord & McCord (1964) identified "lovelessness" and "guiltlessness" as the core deficits underlying psychopathy. Thus, historic conceptions differ in their relative emphasis on positive adjustment features vs. callous and antagonistic features in defining the interpersonal characteristics of psychopathy.

Contemporary research on psychopathy has converged on the idea that psychopathy is dimensional in nature rather than typological (i.e., occurs in gradations, rather than being "all or none") and includes distinguishable symptom subdimensions or facets (Skeem, Polaschek, Patrick, & Lilienfeld, 2011). For example, the most widely used instrument for assessing psychopathy in clinical-forensic populations, Hare's (2003) Psychopathy Checklist-Revised (PCL-R), contains two types of items: items that index interpersonal and affective tendencies (e.g., superficial charm, grandiosity, deceitfulness, lack of remorse, callousness) and items that index impulsive-antisocial tendencies (e.g., boredom proneness, impulsivity, irresponsibility, temper/aggressiveness, criminal versatility). A counterpart instrument for assessing psychopathic tendencies in clinic-referred youth, the Antisocial Process Screening Device (APSD; Frick & Hare, 2001), contains subsets of items indexing callous-unemotional traits and impulsive conduct problems. The best-validated self-report measure for this domain, the Psychopathic Personality Inventory-Revised (PPI-R; Lilienfeld & Widows, 2005), assesses psychopathy through sets of scales that index fearless-dominant and impulsive/self-centered tendencies. The PPI-R also includes a separate scale that indexes callous tendencies, labeled Coldheartedness.

The triarchic model of psychopathy (Patrick, Fowles, & Krueger, 2009) was advanced as a framework for integrating alternative historic accounts of psychopathy and clarifying what different assessment instruments for psychopathy measure. Drawing from research on the externalizing domain as well as the literature on psychopathy, the triarchic model characterizes psychopathy as encompassing three distinct symptomatic (phenotypic) constructs: disinhibition, meanness, and boldness. *Disinhibition* entails impulsiveness, weak behavioral restraint, and difficulties in regulating emotion – and corresponds to the general externalizing factor of the ESM. This subdimension of psychopathy is indexed by the PCL-R's impulsive-irresponsible facet, the APSD's impulsive/conduct problems factor, and the PPI-R's self-centered impulsivity factor. *Meanness* entails deficient empathy, lack of affiliative capacity, contempt toward others, and predatory exploitativeness – and corresponds to the callous-aggression subfactor of the ESM. This subdimension of psychopathy is indexed by the PCL-R's affective symptom facet, the APSD's callous-unemotional traits factor, and the PPI-R's Coldheartedness scale. *Boldness* encompasses tendencies toward confidence and social assertiveness, emotional resiliency, and venturesomeness. This subdimension of psychopathy is indexed by the PCL-R's interpersonal facet, and by the PPI-R's Fearless Dominance factor.

Conceptual and Empirical Links to Aggressive Behavior

ESM subfactors and aggression. Consistent with the notion that trait liabilities contribute importantly to the occurrence of aggressive behavior, population-based research has provided compelling evidence for the long-held notion that violent offending runs in families. Frisell, Lichtenstein, and Långström (2011) utilized registry records for the total population of Sweden (over 12.5 million persons) to examine nearly all violent criminal convictions occurring in the country between 1973 and 2004. Through identification of full familial pedigrees within the sample, evidence was found for concordance of violent tendencies between biologically related individuals, with degree of biological relatedness and familial proximity both contributing to the degree of observed concordance.

What dispositional characteristics underlie the family transmission of violent behavior? Hicks et al. (2004) addressed this question through a focus on disinhibitory problems including conduct disorder and adult antisocial behavior along with alcohol and other drug dependence in parents and their biological twin offspring assessed for these disorders. Consistent with prior work (e.g., Krueger et al., 2002), the covariance among these disorders in the twin offspring was found to be substantially heritable, confirming the contribution of a common externalizing factor underlying these disorders. The authors modeled this externalizing factor in the parents of the twins and found that variations in this general propensity accounted almost entirely for parent-to-child transmission of individual externalizing disorders. That is, results demonstrated that family resemblance for problems of these differing types was attributable more to the transmission of a general disinhibitory propensity than to the transmission of separate liabilities. When considered in relation to the findings of Frisell et al. (2011), the results reported by Hicks et al. (2004) for child and adult components of APD (which include prominent aggressive features) strongly suggest some role for heritable disinhibitory tendencies in the transmission of violent tendencies within families.

Further clarification regarding the nature of transmitted liabilities for violent behavior comes from research demonstrating separate sources of genetic influence contributing to aggressive vs. non-aggressive (rule-breaking) subdimensions of antisocial behavior. A twin study by Kendler, Aggen, and Patrick (2013) focusing on the adult symptom criteria for APD reported evidence for aggressive and non-aggressive subfactors underlying this set of symptoms, with distinguishable genetic sources of influence contributing preferentially to each. Irritability/aggressiveness and disregard for safety of self/others emerged as prominent selective indicators of the aggressive factor, whereas irresponsibility and impulsivity/failure to plan emerged as dominant indicators of the non-aggressive factor. These two adult APD factors resemble the separable callous-aggression and general disinhibitory factors of the ESM, as described above, which correspond to the meanness and disinhibition constructs of the triarchic model (Patrick et al., 2009).

In sum, findings from the ESM work and results from studies of the structure and etiology of antisocial symptoms in adulthood suggest two distinct sources of genetic influence contributing to violent/aggressive behavior and its transmission within families – one consisting of a general disinhibitory propensity (cf. Hicks et al., 2004), and the other a more specific disposition involving lack of social connectedness and exploitative reward-seeking (Venables & Patrick, 2014).

Psychopathy facets and aggression. The features that distinguish psychopathy from APD have important implications for understanding violence and aggression. Whereas APD is defined primarily in terms of impulsive, reckless, and illicit behaviors, psychopathy is defined by impulsive-antisocial behavior in the context of distinctive affective-interpersonal features entailing a dominant and forceful social style, manipulativeness, callousness, and deficient emotional sensitivity. Scores on these two symptomatic components of psychopathy correlate in different ways with clinical criterion variables. Scores on the affective-interpersonal (Factor 1) component are inversely associated with negative affective tendencies such as trait anxiety, depression, and suicide risk, whereas scores on the impulsive-antisocial (Factor 2) component are associated positively with such variables (Hicks & Patrick, 2006). Factor 1 scores are also associated with high Machiavellianism and narcissism (Harpur, Hare, & Hakstian, 1989), low empathic tendencies (Hare, 2003), and proneness to proactive or instrumental aggressive acts (Patrick & Zempolich, 1998). Scores on Factor 2, on the other hand, show substantially stronger associations with symptoms of APD and extent of offense history (Hare, 2003), substance-related problems

(Reardon, Lang, & Patrick, 2002), and reactive or angry aggression (Patrick & Zempolich, 1998).

Factor analytic research indicates that the impulsive-antisocial features of psychopathy reflect externalizing proneness (Patrick, Hicks, Krueger, & Lang, 2005), and account for its robust associations with APD, whereas variance unique to the affective-interpersonal features reflects tendencies distinct from these DSM-defined antisocial conditions, and externalizing psychopathology more broadly. As noted earlier, the triarchic model views impulsive-antisocial features of psychopathy as a combination of disinhibitory tendencies and callous-aggression (meanness), and affective-interpersonal features as a combination of boldness and meanness. Viewed this way, a key question is whether observed predictive associations for PCL-R psychopathy with violent offending and criminal recidivism are accounted for by the externalizing component it has in common with APD, or by the affective-interpersonal features that distinguish it from this condition.

As reviewed by Kennealy, Skeem, Walters, and Camp (2010), PCL-R psychopathy is predictive of violent behavior largely as a function of the impulsive-antisocial features encompassed by Factor 2. Using a meta-analytic, regression-based approach in which scores on the two PCL-R factors were evaluated as concurrent predictors, these authors found that the antisocial deviance features associated with PCL-R Factor 2 were substantially predictive of violence (effect size $d = 0.40$), whereas the affective-interpersonal features associated with Factor 1 were only mildly predictive ($d = 0.11$). Further analyses were undertaken to examine whether Factor 1 and Factor 2 features might interact to predict elevated risk for violence in a non-additive fashion. Results indicated that these two components of PCL-R psychopathy do not contribute interactively to violence prediction.

In sum, the findings of Kennealy et al. (2010) indicate that Factor 2 of the PCL-R is markedly predictive of violent behavior, whereas the affective-interpersonal features contribute little beyond this to the prediction of violence (see also Camp et al., 2013). The obvious question raised by these results is why this factor of the PCL-R in particular seems to be predictive of violent behavior. One explanation is that the close relationship of PCL-R Factor 2 to the externalizing liability construct (cf. Patrick et al., 2005) accounts for its robust prediction relationship with aggressive outcomes. Notably, the variance in Factor 2 that overlaps with Factor 1 appears to reflect callous-aggression or meanness, and this may (per earlier discussion of the role of callous-aggressive tendencies in the transmission of violence) account in part for the PCL-R's predictive validity with respect to violence.

Synopsis and implications. The ESM and TriPM are useful integrative frameworks in that they highlight the existence of two related, yet distinct, trait-based processes that can contribute to violent behavior and aggression among individuals – one process is a general propensity to be disinhibited, break rules, and misuse alcohol and drugs; the other process is a more specific tendency to be cruel and malicious and to have impairments in the ability to empathize with others. In other words, structural models of personality traits suggest that these two processes should be the focus of any efforts to understand vulnerability towards and the etiology and development of violent and aggressive behavior.

Interface Between Broad Trait-Based Liabilities and Specific Violence-Promoting Processes

In addition to providing a connection to the nomological networks of the ESM and psychopathy, studying the link between violence and personality within the framework of a structural model of traits is advantageous in that the hierarchical nature of these models allow for examination of lower-order traits and associated psychological processes that may provide a unique pathway to violence and aggression separate from broader trait liabilities. That is, violent behavior may be associated with distinct cognitive-affective processes that liabilities such as disinhibition and callousness-meanness contribute to but are not synonymous with.

Within a Big 3 framework, research on NEM and the lower-order indicators of this dimension are illustrative of this issue. Elevations on NEM demonstrate the strongest association with violence *per se*, as opposed to externalizing behavior in general, which is more consistently linked with lower CON. For example, in testing whether the personality correlates of domestic violence can be differentiated from those of crime in general, Moffitt, Krueger, Caspi, and Fagan (2000) found that higher scores on NEM at age 18 among participants from the Dunedin Multidisciplinary Health and Development Study predicted an increased likelihood of both domestic violence and criminal behavior in general, whereas CON traits only predicted increased likelihood of general crime. A similar pattern of findings was reported by Verona, Patrick, and Lang (2002) as part of a laboratory threat-based paradigm to examine the impact of individual differences in negative affect on aggression.

In terms of the lower-order traits of NEM, various lines of research point towards the Alienation (or "Mistrust" in Big 5 terms) as a specific process that may underlie the observed associations between NEM and violence. As operationalized by the MPQ, Alienation is a dimension marked (at the high end) by tendencies to be suspicious of others' motives and to feel that they are often treated unfairly. Caspi and colleagues (1997) examined the personality correlates of a range of health-risk behaviors among participants from the Dunedin study. Higher scores on the NEM subfacets of Alienation and Aggression exhibited the strongest associations with perpetration of violent crime. However, in contrast to Aggression, which predicted all health-risk behaviors, Alienation was related selectively to the outcome of violent crime and had a negligible association with other health-risk behaviors. In addition, Jockin, Arvey, and McGue (2001) observed that associations between a number of established risk factors of violence (e.g., past antisocial behavior, alcohol abuse, and personality markers of low agreeableness and high neuroticism) and workplace aggression were significantly greater among those high on MPQ Alienation (see also Arsenault et al., 2000). These early studies of associations between trait Alienation and violence from a Big 3 model is further supported by more recent studies of the Big 5 trait of Mistrust. For example, Sanz et al. (2010) found that, within the Agreeableness domain, Mistrust accounted for significant variance in self-reported anger and hostility (see also the meta-analysis by Jones et al., 2011).

Collectively, both early and contemporary research has identified Alienation/Mistrust as a specific violence-promoting process that may serve as an independent pathway to violence and aggression. These empirical findings, based on structural models of personality, align with findings from the personality disorder literature in terms of links between paranoid personality disorder and violence (Berman et al., 1998; Johnson et al., 2000), as well as with various conceptual models of violence and aggression. Most notably, Nestor's (2002) theorized that a paranoid cognitive style increases risk of violence among those with psychotic-spectrum disorders, and Dodge and colleagues (1995) theorized that a hostile attribution bias regarding the intentions of others is a developmental marker of aggression in childhood and adolescence. However, in contrast to Nestor's (2002) theory, the impact of Alienation/Mistrust on risk for violence is not limited to those with psychotic disorders. Further, the risk for violence conferred by more proximal violence-promoting processes such as Alienation/Mistrust is independent from any risk conferred via one's general externalizing liability. To this point, it is notable that in the development of the ESM, Krueger et al. (2007) found that the Alienation subscale of their model had the second-lowest loading on the general factor of disinhibition, and no substantive loadings on either the callous-aggression or substance abuse sub-factors, and, consequently, had the largest residual variance in the hierarchical model. This lends support to the notion of Alienation/Mistrust as a specific violence-promoting process that is distinct from broader trait-based liabilities of disinhibition and callousness-exploitativeness.

Empirically-Based Models of Maladaptive Personality Traits: DSM-5 Section III

Since our previous version of this chapter, one of the more significant developments in the personality literature is the trait-based model of personality pathology included in Section III ("Emerging Measures and Models") of DSM-5. Consistent with structural models of personality described above, the DSM trait model is a landmark development in the classification of personality and psychopathology as it represents the first formal effort by the DSM to move from a categorical, disorder-centric model to a dimensional model of pathological personality. While the categorical approach to personality disorder diagnosis in DSM-IV was retained in Section II of DSM-5 ("Diagnostic Criteria and Codes"), an alternative dimensional-trait system was introduced in Section III, based on the recommendations of the DSM-5 Personality and Personality Disorders (PPD) Workgroup.

The Section III model was born largely out of efforts to develop dimensional alternatives to the DSM-IV categorical model of personality disorders. In developing this new model, a key goal was to not rely exclusively (or even primarily) on clinical experience to determine the structure of personality pathology, but instead to use empirical data to resolve such issues and create a formal nosology for this domain of mental illness. Further, the PPD Workgroup compiled a wide range of constructs from the normal and abnormal personality literatures and operationalized them with the goal of using data to discern how those constructs were organized empirically (Krueger & Markon, 2014).

The resulting trait system includes five broad domains of personality: Negative Affectivity (vs. Emotional Stability), Detachment (vs. Extraversion), Antagonism (vs. Agreeableness), Disinhibition (vs. Conscientiousness), and Psychoticism (vs. Lucidity). The Personality Inventory for the DSM-5 (PID-5; Krueger et al., 2012), which is publicly available on the APA website, provides a psychometrically effective means for operationalizing the traits of this new system in the domain of self-report. An iterative process of data collection and scale refinement was used to develop this 220-item self-report measure, which assesses 25 maladaptive personality traits organized under the five domains identified by the PPD Workgroup. Notably, the five-factor structure of this trait system resembles the dimensional model of personality pathology described by Widiger and Simonsen (2005), which represents maladaptive extremes of the Big 5 model of personality. It is also notable that the structure of the PID-5 aligns with other work demonstrating that variation in normal and abnormal personality traits can be viewed within a single hierarchical framework (Markon, Krueger, & Watson, 2005).

Research to date on the criterion-related validity of the PID-5 is promising in that scores on its facet-level trait scales capture substantial variance in DSM-IV personality disorder diagnoses (Few et al., 2013). In terms of links between PID-5 constructs and violence, a number of facet-level traits have clear links to risk for violence (e.g., hostility; callousness). Others that have less-direct links to violence are nonetheless variants of traits that have been identified in the literature as correlating reliably with violent behavior (e.g., impulsivity; suspiciousness). At the broader dispositional level, the PID-5 domains of Antagonism and Disinhibition have the strongest conceptual overlap with violence and aggression, and as noted earlier are two broad personality domains that connect both with the ESM and the triarchic model of psychopathy. A study by Dowgwillo, Menard, Krueger, and Pincus (2016) found that these two broad domains were linked to interpersonal violence (IPV), though the relationship differed across genders, with Antagonism significantly predicting IPV perpetration for women and Disinhibition significantly predicting IPV perpetration for men.

Other research focusing directly on psychopathy as defined by the triarchic model provides further perspective on the utility of the Section III model for articulating links between this personality disorder and violence. For example, Strickland et al. (2013) reported that the PID-5 provides effective coverage of the two psychopathy subdimensions that are most closely linked to violence (i.e., disinhibition and callousness). By explicitly operationalizing and differentiating these two trait liabilities (Disinhibition and Antagonism), the Section III model provides a clearer and more nuanced interface with research on violence and psychopathy than the Section II diagnosis of APD.

In sum, the Section III trait system and its corresponding measurement via the PID-5 integrates concepts from the abnormal and normal-range personality literatures and provides a formal means for indexing major trait constructs that appear to underlie established links between personality disorders and violence. Although we note above that the structure of normal and abnormal personality can be viewed within a single structural framework, the Section III trait model and the PID-5 operationalization of this model differ in important ways from models of normal personality that may have implications for studying links with violence. For example, from an item-response theory framework, many of the item-indicators of personality disorder dimensions are likely to be more extreme (or "difficult"), thus reflecting not just trait dispositional tendencies but also more symptomatic or pathologic tendencies. In this sense, because of the more extreme or pathological content in the Section III trait system and PID-5, it is conceivable that dimensions of disinhibition and callousness contain items that are indicative of distinct violence-promoting processes than measures of normal-range personality and therefore may have predict violent outcomes more strongly.

Policy Implications: Risk Management and the Research Domain Criteria (RDoC) Initiative

At this point, the basic science literature is clear regarding the importance of empirically based trait models in understanding pathways to violent and aggressive behavior. Less clear, however, are the practical implications of this research for informing policies and other preventative or intervention efforts to reduce violence and aggression. In this last section, we briefly review two specific ways in which the extant findings from the personality-violence literature can inform these practical issues.

One practical issue is the implications of the personality-violence literature for policies and clinical practice related to risk management of criminal offenders. As noted at the outset of this chapter, the association between personality and violence has traditionally been viewed from a categorical, disorder-centric lens. In the forensic arena, the personality disorder most commonly linked with violence is psychopathy, in particular its operationalization via the PCL-R. Though not one formally listed in diagnostic systems such as the DSM, psychopathy, when viewed from a categorical perspective, may lead to an inappropriate one-size-fits-all approach to risk assessment and offender rehabilitation policies. By contrast, a trait-based viewed of psychopathy can help to hone in on the components of this disorder that are most predictive of violence and aggression, some of which are not unique to psychopathy *per se* (e.g., general disinhibition). That is, a high score on a psychopathy measure such as the PCL-R represents a constellation of multiple traits, including general liabilities of disinhibition and callousness/meanness, as well as a fearless (boldness) liability that does not significantly predict violence. Measures that do not distinguish between these distinct trait liabilities may inappropriately apply a one-size-fits-all approach to risk management of offenders with psychopathic tendencies.

The importance of focusing on trait liabilities is further demonstrated in other work by Skeem et al. (2014) in that traits related to an antisocial personality pattern predict risk for violent criminal recidivism just as well among offenders with serious mental illness (SMI) as among those without SMI. The clear policy and practical implication of this work is the importance of explicitly targeting and measuring trait liabilities such as disinhibition and callousness in risk management of all offenders rather than focusing on an ostensible categorical diagnosis of psychopathy. This approach is consistent with the Risk-Need-Responsivity (RNR) model of offender rehabilitation, in which antisocial traits (vs. psychopathy, or any other mental health diagnosis for that matter) are included among the Central Eight criminogenic needs to be targeted in risk assessment and treatment planning. This well-validated model suggests that regardless of an individual's designation as being a "psychopath" or an "SMI" patient, it is the presence of certain trait liabilities, particularly those encompassed in the ESM, that establish an individual's risk for violence and that measurement of those traits should be the focus of risk-management efforts.

A second implication of the personality-violence literature is the extent to which conceptual models that are consistent with a trait-liability framework are formalized and prioritized by national funding agencies. The National Institute of Mental Health's (NIMH) Research Domain Criteria (RDoC) initiative is an example of such a funding priority. The mission of NIMH is to transform the understanding and treatment of mental illnesses through basic and clinical research in order to progress toward improved methods of prevention and treatment. To this end, in 2012 the NIMH formally introduced the RDoC research matrix (Kozak & Cuthbert, 2016), which calls for a focus on transdiagnostic biobehavioral processes and varied measurement methods in studies of mental health problems, in order to reshape existing conceptions of such problems and methods for addressing them.

A number of biobehavioral process constructs within the RDoC research matrix have clear relevance to the study of violent behavior in terms of personality dispositions highlighted in the current review. Two of these are: response inhibition and affiliation. In trait-dispositional terms, the ability to inhibit and regulate responses corresponds to restraint vs. impulsiveness, and relates to constructs of general externalizing and disinhibition in the ESM and triarchic models, respectively. The capacity to affiliate with and care for others corresponds to social connectedness vs. detachment, and relates to constructs of callous-aggression and meanness in the ESM and triarchic models, respectively. A major avenue for innovation in the use of constructs such as these in studies of mental health problems including aggression is the potential to move toward multi-method or cross-domain operationalizations of these constructs. For example, as knowledge increases regarding brain correlates of the construct of response inhibition conceptualized as externalizing proneness or disinhibition, it becomes feasible to quantify individual differences in disinhibition using brain-response indicators along with self-report scales (see Yancey et al., 2013). In addition to serving as improved targets for subject selection in studies investigating brain bases of dispositional liability factors, cross-domain composites of this can also serve as points of reference for reshaping trait constructs in a neurobehavioral direction (Patrick, Durbin, & Moser, 2012).

Conclusion

In closing, the years since our prior chapter on personality and violence have seen significant advancements in empirically based trait models. The introduction of a trait system to DSM-5 represents the first effort to incorporate a structural model of traits into a psychiatric classification system, and provides a formal means for indexing broad trait liabilities of general disinhibition and callousness that underlie established links between personality disorders and violence. These trait liabilities have direct ties to key constructs from contemporary research on externalizing psychopathology and psychopathic personality. Combined with specific violence-promoting processes such as Alienation/Mistrust, these trait liabilities map onto core bio-biobehavioral constructs from the RDoC matrix and can serve to anchor research on the etiology and neurobiology and violent behavior and aggression going forward.

References

Achenbach, T. M. & Edelbrock, C. S. (1984). Psychopathology of childhood. *Annual Review of Psychology*, 35, 227–256.

American Psychiatric Association (2013). *Diagnostic and statistical manual of mental disorders, fifth edition*. Arlington, VA: American Psychiatric Association.

Arsenault, L., Moffitt, T. E., Caspi, A., Taylor, P. J., & Silva, P. A. (2000). Mental disorders and violence in a total birth cohort: Results from the Dunedin study. *Archives of General Psychiatry*, 57, 979–986.

Berman, M. E., Fallon, A. E., & Coccaro, E. F. (1998). The relationship between personality psychopathology and aggressive behavior in research volunteers. *Journal of Abnormal Psychology*, 107, 651–658.

Blonigen, D. M. & Krueger, R. F. (2007). Personality & violence: The unifying role of structural models of personality. In D. J. Flannery, A. T. Vazsonyi, & I. D. Waldman (Eds), *The Cambridge handbook of violent behavior* (pp. 288–305). New York: Cambridge University Press.

Bushman, B. J. & Baumeister, R. F. (1998). Threatened egotism, narcissism, self-esteem, and direct and displaced aggression: does self-love or self-hate lead to violence? *Journal of Personality and Social Psychology*, 75(1), 219–229.

Camp, J. P., Skeem, J. L., Barchard, K., Lilienfeld, S. O., & Poythress, N. G. (2013). Psychopathic predators? Getting specific about the relation between psychopathy and violence. *Journal of Consulting and Clinical Psychology*, 81(3), 467–480.

Caspi, A., Begg, D., Dickson, N., Harrington, H., Langley, J., Moffitt, T. E., et al. (1997). Personality differences predict health-risk behaviors in young adulthood: Evidence from a longitudinal study. *Journal of Personality and Social Psychology*, 73, 1052–1063.

Cleckley, H. (1976). *The mask of sanity* (5th ed.). St. Louis, MO: Mosby (Original edition published in 1941).

Cloninger, C. R., Svrakic, D. M., & Przybeck, T. R. (1993). A psychobiological model of temperament and character. *Archives of General Psychiatry*, 50, 975–990.

Dodge, K. A., Pettit, G. S., Bates, J. E., & Valente, E. (1995). Social-information processing patterns partially mediate the effect of early physical abuse on later conduct problems. *Journal of Abnormal Psychology*, 104(4), 632–643.

Dowgwillo, E. A., Menard, K. S., Krueger, R. F., & Pincus, A. L. (2016). DSM-5 pathological personality traits and intimate partner violence among male and female college students. *Violence and Victims*, 31(3), 416–437.

Egan, V., Austin, E., Elliot, D., Patel, D., & Charlesworth, P. (2003). Personality traits, personality disorders and sensational interests in mentally disordered offenders. *Legal and Criminological Psychology*, 8(1), 51–62.

Elkins, I. J., Iacono, W. G., Doyle, A. E., & McGue, M. (1997). Characteristics associated with the persistence of antisocial behavior: Results from recent longitudinal research. *Aggression and Violent Behavior*, 2, 101–124.

Eysenck, H. J. & Eysenck, S. B. G. (1975). *Manual of the Eysenck Personality Questionnaire*. London: Hodder & Stoughton.

Few, L. R., Miller, J. D., Rothbaum, A., Meller, S., Maples, J., et al. (2013). Examination of Section III DSM-5 diagnostic system for personality disorders in an outpatient clinical sample. *Journal of Abnormal Psychology*, 122, 1057–1069.

Frick, P. J. & Hare, R. D. (2001). *Antisocial process screening device*. Toronto: Multi Health Systems.

Frisell, T., Lichtenstein, P., & Långström, N. (2011). Violent crime runs in families: A total population study of 12.5 million individuals. *Psychological Medicine*, 41(1), 97–105.

Goldberg, L. R. (1993). The structure of phenotypic personality traits. *American Psychologist*, 48, 26–34.

Hare, R. D. (2003). *The Hare psychopathy checklist – revised* (2nd ed.). Toronto: Multi-Health Systems.

Harpur, T. J., Hare, R. D., & Hakstian, R. (1989). A two-factor conceptualization of psychopathy: Construct validity and implications for assessment. *Psychological Assessment: A Journal of Consulting and Clinical Psychology*, 1, 6–17.

Hicks, B. M., Krueger, R. F., Iacono, W. G., McGue, M., & Patrick, C. J. (2004). Family transmission and heritability of externalizing disorders: A twin-family study. *Archives of General Psychiatry*, 61(9), 922–928.

Hicks, B. M. & Patrick, C. J. (2006). Psychopathy and negative affectivity: Analyses of suppressor effects reveal distinct relations with trait anxiety, depression, fearfulness, and anger-hostility. *Journal of Abnormal Psychology*, 115, 276–287.

Howard, R. (2015). Personality disorders and violence: What is the link? *Borderline Personality Disorder and Emotion Regulation*, 2(12). doi: 10.1186/s40479-015-0033-x.

Jockin, V., Arvey, R. D., & McGue, M. (2001). Perceived victimization moderates self-reports of workplace aggression and conflict. *Journal of Applied Psychology*, 86(6), 1262–1269.

Johnson, J. G., Cohen, P., Smailes, E., Kasen, S., Oldham, J. M., Skodol, A. E., et al. (2000). Adolescent personality disorders associated with violence and criminal behavior during adolescence and early adulthood. *American Journal of Psychiatry*, 157, 1406–1412.

Jones, S. E., Miller, J. D., & Lynam, D. R. (2011). Personality, antisocial behavior, and aggression: A meta-analytic review. *Journal of Criminal Justice*, 39, 329–337.

Kendler, K. S., Aggen, S. H., & Patrick, C. J. (2013). Familial influences on conduct disorder reflect 2 genetic factors and 1 shared environmental factor. *JAMA Psychiatry*, 70, 78–86.

Kennealy, P. J., Skeem, J. L., Walters, G. D., & Camp, J. (2010). Do core interpersonal and affective traits of PCL-R psychopathy interact with antisocial behavior and disinhibition to predict violence? *Psychological Assessment*, 22, 569–580.

Kenrick, D. T. & Funder, D. C. (1988). Profiting from controversy: Lessons from the personality-situation debate. *American Psychologist*, 43(1), 23–34.

Kozak, M. J. & Cuthbert, B. N. (2016). The NIMH Research Domain Criteria Initiative: Background, issues, and pragmatics. *Psychophysiology*, 53, 286–297.

Krueger, R. F. (1999). The structure of common mental disorders. *Archives of General Psychiatry*, 56, 921–926.

Krueger, R. F, Derringer, J., Markon, K. E., Watson, D., & Skodol, A. E. (2012). Initial construction of a maladaptive personality trait model and inventory for DSM-5. *Psychological Medicine*, 42(9), 1879–1890.

Krueger, R. F., Hicks, B., Patrick, C. J., Carlson, S., Iacono, W. G., & McGue, M. (2002). Etiologic connections among substance dependence, antisocial behavior, and personality: Modeling the externalizing spectrum. *Journal of Abnormal Psychology,* 111, 411–424.

Krueger, R. F & Markon, K. E. (2014). The role of the DSM-5 personality trait model in moving toward a quantitative and empirically-based approach to classifying personality and psychopathology. *Annual Review of Clinical Psychology,* 10, 477–501.

Krueger, R. F., Markon, K. E., Patrick, C. J., Benning, S. D., & Kramer, M. (2007). Linking antisocial behavior, substance use, and personality: An integrative quantitative model of the adult externalizing spectrum. *Journal of Abnormal Psychology,* 116, 645–666.

Lambe, S., Hamilton-Giachritsis, C., Garner, E., & Walker, J. (2016). The role of narcissism in aggression and violence: A systematic review. *Trauma Violence and Abuse.*

Lilienfeld, S. O. & Widows, M. R. (2005). *Psychopathic personality inventory – revised professional manual.* Odessa: Psychological Assessment Resources.

McCord, W. & McCord, J. (1964). *The psychopath: An essay on the criminal mind.* Princeton: Van Nostrand.

Mancke, F., Herpertz, S. C., & Bertsch, K. (2015). Aggression in borderline personality disorder: A multidimensional model. *Personality Disorders: Theory, Research, and Treatment,* 6(3), 278–291.

Markon, K. E., Krueger, R. F., & Watson, D. (2005). Delineating the structure of normal and abnormal personality: An integrative hierarchical approach. *Journal of Personality and Social Psychology,* 88, 139–157.

Moffitt, T. E., Krueger, R. F., Caspi, A., & Fagan, J. (2000). Partner abuse and general crime: How are they the same? How are they different? *Criminology,* 38(1), 199–232.

Nestor, P. G. (2002). Mental disorder and violence: Personality dimensions and clinical features. *American Journal of Psychiatry,* 159(12), 1973–1978.

Patrick, C. P. (2015). Physiological correlates of psychopathy, antisocial personality disorder, habitual aggression, and violence. *Current Topics in Behavioral Neuroscience,* 21, 197–227.

Patrick, C. J., Durbin, C. E., & Moser, J. S. (2012). Conceptualizing proneness to antisocial deviance in neurobehavioral terms. *Developmental Psychopathology,* 24, 1047–1071.

Patrick, C. J., Fowles, D. C., & Krueger, R. F. (2009). Triarchic conceptualization of psychopathy: developmental origins of disinhibition, boldness, and meanness. *Developmental Psychopathology,* 21(3), 913–938.

Patrick, C. J., Hicks, B. M., Krueger, R. F., & Lang, A. R. (2005). Relations between psychopathy facets and externalizing in a criminal offender sample. *Journal of Personality Disorders,* 19, 339–356.

Patrick, C. J., Kramer, M. D., Krueger, R. F., & Markon, K. E. (2013). Optimizing efficiency of psychopathology assessment through quantitative modeling: Development of a brief form of the externalizing spectrum inventory. *Psychological Assessment,* 25, 1332–1348.

Patrick, C. J. & Zempolich, K. A. (1998). Emotion and aggression in the psychopathic personality. *Aggression and Violent Behavior,* 3, 303–338.

Reardon, M. L., Lang, A. R., & Patrick, C. J. (2002). Antisociality and alcohol problems: An evaluation of subtypes, drinking motives, and family history in incarcerated men. *Alcoholism: Clinical and Experimental Research,* 26, 1188–1197.

Sanz, J., Garcia-Vera, M. P., & Magan, I. (2010). Anger and hostility from the perspective of the Big Five personality model. *Scandinavian Journal of Psychology,* 51(3), 262–270.

Schwartz, J. A., Beaver, K. M., & Barnes, J. C. (2015). The association between mental health and violence among a nationally representative sample of college students from the United States. *PLoS ONE,* 10(10): e0138914.

Sher, K. J. & Trull, T. J. (1994). Personality and disinhibitory psychopathology: Alcoholism and antisocial personality disorder. *Journal of Abnormal Psychology,* 103, 92–102.

Skeem, J. L., Polaschek, D. L., Patrick, C. J., & Lilienfeld, S. O. (2011). Psychopathic personality: Bridging the gap between scientific evidence and public policy. *Psychological Science in the Public Interest*, 12(3), 95–162.

Strickland, C. M., Drislane, L. E., Lucy, M. D., Krueger, R. F., & Patrick, C. J. (2013). Representing psychopathy using DSM-5 personality disorder traits. *Assessment*, 20(3), 327–338.

Tellegen, A. (2000). *Manual of the Multidimensional Personality Questionnaire*. Minneapolis: University of Minnesota Press.

Venables, N. C. & Patrick, C. J. (2014). P3 brain response amplitude in criminal psychopathy: Distinct relations with impulsive-antisocial vs. affective-interpersonal features. *Psychophysiology*, 51, 427–436.

Verona, E., Patrick, C. J., & Lang, A. R. (2002). A direct assessment of the role of state and trait negative emotion in aggressive behavior. *Journal of Abnormal Psychology*, 111, 249–258.

Watson, D., Clark, L. A., & Chmielewski, M. (2008). Structures of personality and their relevance to psychopathology: II. Further articulation of a comprehensive unified trait structure. *Journal of Personality*, 76(6), 1545–1586.

Widiger, T. A. & Costa, P. T. (1994). Personality and personality disorders. *Journal of Abnormal Psychology*, 103, 78–91.

Widiger, T. A. & Simonsen, E. (2005). Alternative dimensional models of personality disorder: Finding a common ground. *Journal of Personality Disorders*, 19(2), 110–130

Yancey, J. R., Venables, N. C., Hicks, B. M., & Patrick, C. J. (2013). Evidence for a heritable brain basis to deviance-promoting deficits in self-control. *Journal of Criminal Justice*, 41, 309–317.

Yarvis, R. M. (1990). Axis I and Axis II diagnostic parameters of homicide. *Bulletin of the American Academy of Psychiatry and Law*, 18, 249–269.

Yu, R., Geddes, J. R., & Fazel, S. (2012). Personality disorders, violence, and antisocial behavior: A systematic review and meta-regression analysis. *Journal of Personality Disorders*, 26, 775–792.

15 Social-Cognitive Processes in the Development of Antisocial and Violent Behavior

Brian Enjaian, Sarah Beth Bell, Zachary Whitt, and C. Nathan DeWall

Introduction

Everyday most of us get up in the morning and make our morning commute. Some days it is as boring as sitting in a waiting room with no magazines. Other days things can take a turn for the worst. Have you ever had one of those days where you are sitting in a traffic jam, waiting to arrive at work, only to be rear-ended? Though frustrating, you think this will be a civil exchange of insurances and other information so you can be on your way. But once you get out of the car, instead of using your name, the other driver refers to you as every "colorful" name you can imagine. Things escalate, and next thing you know the other driver is pushing you to the ground, screaming that it is your fault, and threatening to kill you.

Is that an extreme reaction to a fender bender? Perhaps. Yet, there are countless cases of road rage ending in violence. Take, for example, a case in Albuquerque, New Mexico. After being cutoff in traffic a driver open fired on a vehicle, killing the driver's 4-year-old daughter (Martinez, Cabrera, Weisfeldt, & Criss, 2015). While we live in the most peaceful of times, some people are still willing to push, punch, kick, and yell at others on a daily basis.

You may notice differences in your own behavior. The day before you may have been honking your horn because you were running late to a meeting. However, today you were early and let a couple people merge in front of you. What leads us to behave aggressively or antisocially in some cases and not in others? Or why are some people willing to get into fights while others avoid aggression like the plague?

Here, we'll address both of those questions. By adopting a multidisciplinary perspective, this chapter will examine how aggressive tendencies and antisocial behavior develop based on social and cognitive perspectives. This chapter will also address how responses to perceptions or situations can vary greatly amongst individuals. To address these topics, the chapter will be broken into five main sections. First, we review of major theories about aggressive and antisocial behavior. Second, we discuss various individual differences and situations that increase the likelihood of aggressive and antisocial responses. Third, we review evidence explaining why people follow through with aggressive behaviors. Fourth, we show the consequences of aggressive behavior. Finally, the fifth section discusses aggression-reducing interventions, policies, and future directions in aggression research.

Definitions of Aggression and Antisocial Behavior

The term aggression is used constantly throughout society. The definition, however, differs for laypeople and researchers. For example, an athlete that attacks each play rather than playing defensively may be deemed aggressive. Social psychologists define aggression as any behavior that harms another that does not want to be harmed (Baron & Richardson, 1994; Bushman & Huesmann, 2010). This includes hitting, stabbing, kicking, or yelling at someone. By this definition, the athlete is not aggressive because they do not wish harm on other players. They are just playing to win.

It is important to note the key features of the definition. First, aggression is defined as a behavior. Thus, it is something that can be seen. Aggression is not an emotion, like anger. Everyone knows someone they consider a "hothead." Though that person gets angry over seemingly nothing, as long as they do not act on that anger the hothead is not behaving aggressively. Similarly, aggression is not a thought, such as planning a murder. Only by doing something can a person behave aggressively.

It is also important to note that aggression is a behavior meant to intentionally cause harm. While people get hurt in car accidents, if there was no intent then the crash is not considered aggressive. Similarly, doctors attempting to diagnose pain may push on a sore spot causing you to scream in agony. Even though it hurts, the intent is to help rather than harm the patient. Lastly, the victim must be motivated to avoid the intended harm. Professional fighters who willingly fight for money are not aggressive because they knowingly place themselves in harms way.

Laypeople often use the term violence synonymously with aggression. However, violence is defined as any behavior that intends to cause extreme physical harm, whether it is injury or death. The United States Federal Bureau of Investigation (FBI) classifies four crimes as "violent:" aggravated assault, robbery, homicide, and forcible rape. Thus, violent behaviors are aggressive, but aggressive behaviors are not necessarily violent (Bushman & Huesmann, 2010). For example, pushing someone who cut in front of you is aggressive. Pushing someone down a flight of stairs is violent.

Antisocial behavior generally refers to behavior that is culturally undesirable or damages social relationships. Aggression is often considered an antisocial behavior (e.g., American Psychiatric Association, 2000). For example, in the US we have numerous laws forbidding aggressive behaviors, including aggravated assault, robbery, rape, murder, etc. Nonaggressive antisocial behaviors include cheating, stealing, and lying. Aggression can be expressed in a variety of different forms including physical, verbal, and relational aggression (Bushman & Huesmann, 2010). Physical aggression involves physically harming another individual. This includes pushing, hitting, stabbing, or shooting. While sticks and stones may break bones, words can also hurt. Verbal aggression involves using words to harm others. Yelling every curse word at someone who cut you off in traffic is an example of verbal aggression. Lastly, relational aggression is defined as harming another's social relationships (e.g., Crick & Grotpeter, 1995). Despite relational aggression being completely social, recent research shows that social pain is perceived to be as painful as physical pain (Eisenberger, 2012).

Aggression is not constrained to the proximity of the target. Rather, aggression can occur directly or indirectly towards a target (Lagerspetz, Bjorkqvist, & Peltonen, 1988). Direct aggression occurs when the target is present. Indirect aggression refers to instances when the victim is absent. Physical aggression can occur directly (e.g., hitting someone in the face) or indirectly (e.g., keying a person's car while they are at work). Similarly, verbal and relational aggression can also be direct (e.g., cursing at someone or ignoring them, respectively) or indirect (e.g., calling someone names or spreading rumors, respectively).

While the victim does not always have to be present, sometimes the victim is not the intended target. A substitute target for the aggressive behavior is called displaced aggression (Marcus-Newhall, Pedersen, Carlson, & Miller, 2000). For example, a person gets pulled over for speeding and receives a ticket. Upon returning home, the driver yells at their dog. Triggered displaced aggression occurs when the victim is not completely innocent, but commits a minor offense (Pedersen, Gonzales, & Miller, 2000).

There are two main reasons people displace aggression. First, aggressing against the target is not feasible either because the target is unavailable (e.g., the target left the area) or because it is a nontangible entity (e.g., hot temperature). Second, people refrain from directly aggressing in fears of punishment or retaliation. For example, the person who received a speeding ticket does not aggress in fears of being arrested. No matter how, when, or who the victim of aggression is, there are ways to understand what led to those aggressive situations.

Major Theories of Aggressive Behavior

General Aggression Model

In order to understand aggressive behavior, the General Aggression Model (GAM; Anderson & Bushman, 2002; DeWall, Anderson, & Bushman, 2011) simultaneously incorporates biological (e.g., genetics, neurological), personality, social processes, basic cognitive processes (e.g., priming, perception), short- and long-term processes, and decision processes. By incorporating a variety of factors, the GAM explains that neither single situation nor an emotion directly results in an aggressive act. Rather, it is the combination of multiple interacting factors that results in aggressive behaviors.

GAM has three main stages in understanding a single aggressive event: (1) person and situation inputs, (2) present internal states (i.e., arousal, affect, brain activity), and (3) decision-making processes and outcomes of appraisal. For example, an individual may not be chosen for a game of basketball with their friends (i.e., social and person inputs). Thus, the situation is telling the individual they are being excluded. This may then lead to an increase in negative affect and an increase in the sensation of pain (i.e., present internal states). The interaction between situation and internal states all lead to impulsively punching one of their friends in order to alleviate the pain of rejection (i.e., decision-making processes).

I³ Theory

I³ theory is a meta-theory of aggression consisting of three processes (Slotter

& Finkel, 2011). Similar to the GAM, I³ theory suggests aggression is not the result of a single instance in a situation, but rather an interaction of effects. The processes in the model are instigation, impellance, and inhibition.

Instigation refers to the effect a target object or behavior may have on an individual depending on the context. Different contexts will lead to various outcomes, despite having the same target object/behavior. For example, imagine you are with your friend and someone at the other side of the room calls you a moron. In this case, the target object is the insult of intelligence. Your response to the insult, however, depends on the context. If the insult occurred in a bar, you may step outside with the insulter and settle the dispute yourself. If this occurred in a meeting with top executives, you may choose to ignore the insult and continue with the meeting. Thus, the normative behaviors within each context help guide responses to target objects.

Impellance refers to factors that are likely to increase the chances of aggressive behavior or intensify aggression. For example, the prior insult was in a bar that has no A/C. The overbearing heat made you irritable, increasing the odds of an aggressive reaction. Not all impellance factors need to be situational or occur in the moment. For instance, children who experience their parent going through an aggressive divorce may grow up being more aggressive themselves (Amato, 2001). The upbringing of the child is an impeller because an aggressive environment increased the chances of the child growing up and becoming aggressive.

Finally, inhibition refers to factors that increase the likelihood of overriding the effects of instigation and impellance. These factors allow us to ignore situations of instigation and override factors that increase the chances of aggression. For example, a good night's rest can help reduce irritability so we can ignore any forms of instigation. Behaving aggressively is not dependent on just one of these factors. Rather, it is the interaction between all three factors that determines aggressive behavior. According to perfect storm theory, the most aggressive behavior occurs when instigation and impellance are high and inhibition is low (Finkel, 2014). For example, imagine being insulted by numerous people in an overheated bar after not being able to sleep the night before. The interaction between the insults, heat, and lack of sleep determine what the response will be to the insults.

Hostile Attribution Bias

Hostile attribution bias takes a cognitive approach to explain aggressive behavior. The hostile attribution bias involves misplaced attributions of others' hostile intent. That is, individuals perceive hostile intent in ambiguous situations in which there may have been no hostility. For example, children who get bumped in the hallway may view an innocent bump as a hostile threat. Consequently, they retaliate against their supposed provocateur (Dodge et al., 2015).

Growing accustomed to feelings of social devaluation and an increased vigilance towards others leads individuals to make more hostile attributions (Davis & Reyna, 2015). This places those who are low in socioeconomic status at a higher risk for misperceived hostility. Over time, such attributions become routine, steadily escalating in levels of hostility and eventually generating serious problems with aggressive behavior (Dodge, 1980). Hostile attribution bias has been shown to predict above-average aggressive behavior in children (Yaros, Lochman, Rosenbaum, & Jimenez-Camargo, 2014). Similarly, hostility in early to middle childhood predicts similar problems with aggression later in life (Nelson & Perry, 2015). Hostile attribution bias seems to be particularly relevant in certain ecological contexts, such as the American South "Culture of Honor" and among groups where maintaining a level of respect from one's peers is considered necessary for survival (Dodge et al., 2015).

Situational and Personal Inputs

Situational Inputs

Aggression in Children. As parents soon discover, there is a reason it is called the "terrible twos." Across a lifetime, humans are the most aggressive between the ages of 1 and 3 (e.g., Cote, Vaillancourt, LeBlanc, Nagin, & Tremblay, 2006; Tremblay et al., 2004). Despite the high rates of aggression, the harm that a 1- to 3-year-old can inflict is far less than that of a criminal. For most, aggression decreases as they age, while only a small subset of the population continues to exhibit elevated aggressive behavior. One predictor of adult aggression is the lasting aggressive tendencies of children. Aggressive children tend to become aggressive adolescents, then transitioning into aggressive adults (see Bushman & Huesmann, 2010, for a review).

Family structure, economic status, and stress are all contributors to aggressive and antisocial behaviors in children (Amato, 2001; Elder, Eccles, Ardelt, & Lord, 1995). For example, children raised in single-parent homes tend to have poor monitoring, lack of warmth from the parent, and increased stress, leading to increases in aggression and delinquent behavior (Loeber & Stouthamer-Loeber, 1986). Similarly, children behave more aggressively when their parents are highly stressed and fighting while going through a divorce (Amato, 2001). Social support, financial security, and positive contact from the parents can help negate these aggressive and antisocial tendencies (Amato & Dorius, 2010). However, in some cases, parents teach their children to adopt aggressive tendencies.

Culture of Honor. In general, aggression is considered an antisocial behavior. However, in some cultures, aggression is viewed as a necessity. These cultures are called cultures of honor. Cultures of honor have heightened concerns surrounding reputation and social standing (Barnes, Brown, & Osterman, 2012). Specifically, individuals in a culture of honor focus on family, male reputation, female fidelity, and property. In the United States, these qualities are predominately found in Southern and, slightly less so, Western states (Nisbett & Cohen, 1996, p. 4).

Due to the emphasis on reputation and status in a culture of honor, threats are often met with aggression. It is seen as a man's duty to respond to threats with strength and aggression (Nisbett & Cohen, 1996, p. 4). Threats can come in a variety of forms including vandalizing property, insulting one's family, or flirting with one's spouse. A simple bump in the hallway is enough of an insult to one's honor to evoke an aggressive response (Cohen, Nisbett, Bowdle, & Schwarz, 1996). In this study, participants were asked to walk down a hallway and were bumped into by a confederate. On the way back down the hallway, a 250-pound football player was asked to play "chicken" with the participant walking toward them and to not get out of the way until the last second. Participants from the South who were bumped the first time through the hall on average refused to give way in the hallway to others, and even gave more aggressive handshakes following the interaction.

Cultures of honor and aggressive retaliation thrive in environments in which law enforcement are low (Nowak, Gelfand, Borkowski, Cohen, & Hernandez, 2015). By modeling behaviors in society, one finds that as law enforcement decreases, aggressive individuals increase. In response to an increase in threats, cultures of honor appear. That is, when law enforcement is unreliable and there are threats to one's self and family, men are expected to take matters in their own hands. In a culture of honor, reputation and status speak louder than sheer strength (Nowak, Gelfand, Borkowski, Cohen, & Hernandez, 2015).

While the men are expected to protect the family, women socialize the next generation of boys to become protectors (Nisbett & Cohen, 1996, p. 86). From a very young age, boys are taught by their mothers to never back down from a fight and to protect their family. For example, Andrew Jackson's mother told him: "Never tell a lie, nor take what is not your own, nor sue anybody for slander or assault and battery. Always settle them cases yourself!" (McWhiney, 1988, pp. 169–170). Similarly, Sam Houston was taught: "Never disgrace it; for remember, I had rather all my sons should fill one honorable grave, than that one of them should turn his back to save his life" (Wyatt-Brown, 1982, p. 138).

Social Influences/Media. Each day American adults spend over ten hours consuming media (Nielsen, 2016). How might exposure to certain types of media influence aggression? Nearly 50 years of research has led to a consistent answer: Exposure to violent media has a causal relationship to greater aggression, lower empathy, and lower prosocial behavior (Anderson et al., 2010; Bushman & Anderson, 2015). Critics argue that these experiments offer inconsistent evidence, small effect sizes, do not relate to real-world aggression, and note that the rise of various forms of media violence has accompanied the decline of violent crime (Elson & Ferguson, 2014; Ferguson, 2015). Future research will continue to search for evidence that supports or contradicts that the hypothesis that exposure to media violence increases aggression.

Provocation. Provocation refers to any action that causes another person to feel annoyed or angry. Sometimes we provoke others intentionally, as when we insult someone who offended us. Other times we use provocation inadvertently, such as when we carry on conversations on an early airplane flight when nearby passengers crave quiet. Regardless of our intentions, provocation is the most reliable predictor of aggression (Anderson & Bushman, 2002). In one classic study, participants wrote an essay on a contentious topic and then swapped it with a partner's essay (Bushman & Baumeister, 1998). In reality, the partner's essay was composed by the experimenter before the testing session. By random assignment, half of the participants received positive feedback ("No comments, great essay!"). The other half of the participants experienced provocation. They received negative numerical ratings on their essay and an insulting handwritten comment, "This is one of the worst essays I've read!" Next, participants could behave aggressively toward their partner. Provoked participants behaved more aggressively than did nonprovoked participants.

Cognitive. Situations alone may not be enough to evoke an aggressive response. Rather, aggression can also arise depending on the perception of the situation. How individuals perceive a situation can lead to emotional responses, such as anger. Anger arises as a result of perceived hostility from others. When individuals are not capable of controlling angry impulses, anger can lead to aggressive behaviors (Wilkowski & Robinson, 2010). Aggressive responses due to anger also depend on the intensity of anger and the tendency of the individual to mull over their anger for a period of time. The more intense and the longer individuals ruminate on their anger, the more aggressive their responses are likely to be.

Despite the tendency to increase aggression, aggressive behaviors can be thwarted if the individual is able to control their angry impulses (Eisenlohr-Moul, Peters, Pond, & DeWall, 2016). An individual's ability to control their anger can be diminished by a cognitive load. For example, having too much information on their mind can hamper their ability to control angry emotions, leading to aggressive reactions (Vasquez & Howard-Field, 2016; DeWall, Baumeister, Stillman, & Gailliot, 2007).

Personal Inputs

Individual Differences. Situations and perception are not enough to elicit aggressive responses. Our own personalities and feelings of self-worth also influence our behavior. For example, narcissism and psychopathy are linked with aggressive behaviors. Narcissism, a personality trait characterized by a grandiose level of self-esteem, is a reliable predictor of aggression (Chester & DeWall, 2016). Social threat is a common provocation for narcissists. In this case, narcissists use aggression to preserve their own unrealistic self-views that have come under threat (Baumeister, Smart, & Boden, 1996; Chester & DeWall, 2016).

Psychopathy also correlates highly with aggression (Long, Felton, Lilienfeld, & Lejuez, 2014). Psychopaths have been shown to pursue reactive aggressive behaviors. Reactive aggression is considered a "hot" or impulsive aggressive behavior motivated to harm someone in the moment. For example, a husband stabbing his wife and her lover upon finding them together is not a planned behavior. Instead, the husband probably found the closest object and used that to harm them. Not only do psychopaths respond impulsively, they have the capacity for "cold" and calculated aggression, also known as proactive aggression. This form of aggression involves premeditation and is motivated by a goal (Buss, 1962). A husband planning on shooting his wife's lover at work in a month is an example of proactive aggression.

Basing self-worth in certain areas of one's life, called contingent self-esteem, has been linked to aggressive behavior (Turner & White, 2015). Failure in the domains on which individuals base their self-worth leads to an increase in anger rumination, consequently leading to more aggressive behavior. Similarly, people who are more sensitive towards feelings of rejection tend to act aggressively towards others. This is especially true in romantic relationships (Croft & Zimmer-Gembeck, 2014). Aggression in those who are sensitive to rejection is used as a way of sparing themselves from the pain of the perceived inevitable rejection (Zimmer-Gembeck & Nesdale, 2013).

Similarly, in both romantic and platonic relationships, people who are more sensitive towards feelings of rejection tend to act aggressively towards others (Croft & Zimmer-Gembeck, 2014). Aggression is used as a preemptive means of sparing themselves from the emotional pain of – in their minds, inevitable – rejection (Zimmer-Gembeck & Nesdale, 2013).

Biological. Like personality, biology also predisposes people toward different behaviors. Certain genes, brain structures, and hormones all contribute to an increased likelihood of violent behavior. It is important to note that biology does not guarantee aggressive behavior but rather increases the odds of behaving aggressively.

The MAOA genetic polymorphism is one genetic structure that is associated with aggressive behavior (Caspi, 2002; McDermott et al., 2009). This gene metabolizes neurotransmitters that influence mood (e.g., dopamine, norepinephrine, serotonin; Cases et al., 1995). Some people have a low-expression form of MAOA, while others have the high-expression form (L-MAOA and H-MAOA, respectively). People with L-MAOA have more activity in the area of the brain associated with social pain after they are rejected. It is the increase in social pain following rejection that is associated with aggressive behaviors (Chester et al., 2015; Eisenberger et al., 2007)

Activity in various brain structures also predicts aggressive behavior. Without considering MAOA, constant activations in the part of the brain associated with social pain leads individuals to react with aggression (Chester et al., 2014; Denson et al., 2009). The part of the brain associated with fears and instincts is also related to aggressive behavior. For example, that part of the brain has been shown to be more active in people with intermittent explosive disorder. Constant experiences of fear then lead these individuals to react aggressively (Coccaro et al., 2007). On the other hand, impairments in the fear part of the brain are associated with aggression (Miczek et al., 2007). In this case, people may not fear the consequences of lashing out as much as others. The reward centers of the brain are also associated with aggression. When feelings of reward or pleasure were blocked or dampened in rats, they behaved less aggressively (Aragona et al., 2006; Couppis & Kennedy, 2008).

Like brain structures, hormonal activity also predicts aggression. Increases in adrenaline prepare people for aggression by mobilizing energy, increasing vigilance, and decreasing pain perception (Haller, Makara, & Kruk, 1997). Testosterone is notoriously linked to aggression by reducing an individual's ability to control their impulses (Mehta & Beer, 2010). By examining testosterone in young men, those who committed crimes had higher levels than those who avoided delinquent behavior (Mattsson et al., 1980; Olweus et al., 1988). Cortisol moderates the link between testosterone and aggression. Low cortisol levels and normal testosterone levels are associated with more aggression (Terburg et al., 2009). This may be because high cortisol is associated with more inhibition (Goldsmith & Lemery, 2000; Kagan et al., 1988).

Internal States

Lost Honor

The primary purpose of behaving aggressively in a culture of honor is to restore or enhance reputation (Nisbett & Cohen, 1996). Reputation acts as a deterrent from future threats. Being known as weak and not willing to stand up for one's self and family opens you up to being robbed and taken advantage of. In order to gain reputation, people must stand up for themselves, and men must retaliate aggressively. Win or lose, the outcome of the fight is not important. Rather, the act of standing up for oneself or one's family is enough for a boost in reputation (Nowak, Gelfand, Borkowski, Cohen, & Hernandez, 2015). In fact, challenging someone to a fight that you are guaranteed to lose builds reputation faster than only fighting when you are guaranteed to win. It is considered braver and shows more courage to stand up to a bigger foe, win or lose, than only challenging the weak.

Attempts to restore reputation have been linked to school shootings from 1988 to 2008. School shootings are twice as likely to occur in culture-of-honor states (Brown, Osterman, & Barnes, 2009). School shootings can be linked to retaliation due to bullying and threatening self-worth. Often, the shooter was attempting to restore lost honor due to bullying. In Pakistan, family members of newlyweds killed the couple because the marriage went against the wishes of the family (Erdman, 2014). Restoring reputation and honor was more important than the love of their family members who threatened their families' honor.

Lack of Impulse Control

A simple lack of impulse control is one cause of aggressive behavior (DeWall, Baumeister, Stillman, & Gailliot, 2007). People fail to reign in their impulses because they lack defined personal standards, fail to monitor their behavior, or are not strong enough to monitor their behavior (Baumeister & Heatherton, 1996). These problems all fall under the umbrella of a failure in self-regulation. A failure of self-regulation is the struggle to avoid instant gratification in favor of delayed but greater rewards (Baumeister, Schmeichel, Vohs, & Petrocelli, 2007).

Besides failure due to behavioral reasons, genetic predispositions can also increase impulsivity. While individuals with a low expression of the MAOA gene are more aggressive, the MAOA gene is also linked to impulsive behavior. Outside of high and low expression, the MAOA gene can be divided into four separate subcategories. One of these subgroups of MAOA is associated with impulsive behavior and aggression due to influencing positive mood (Manuck, Flory, Ferrell, Mann, & Muldoon, 2000). For example, individuals with this subgroup may not receive desired pleasure from a situation, leading to aggressive or antisocial behavior.

Serotonin levels influence levels of impulsivity related to aggression. This link has been studied in nonhuman primates. Rhesus monkeys with lower levels of serotonin have been found to be both more aggressive and more impulsive (Mehlman et al., 1994). Low serotonin levels in psychiatric patients correlate with impulsivity and violence potential (Apter et al., 1990). Additionally, developing young men who have personality traits that are associated with aggression and impulsivity have also been shown to be correlated with low levels of serotonin (Manuck et al., 2000). With less serotonin people may act more impulsively, with less strength to control aggressive behavior.

Positive Affect

Aggression can be used as a way of making people feel better. For example, social rejection hurts. In fact, our brains perceive social pain the same as physical pain (Eisenberger & Lieberman, 2004). When people are rejected, areas of the brain linked to physical pain become active (Kross et al., 2011). The anterior cingulate cortex, another pain region, also becomes active after social rejection. Prior to feeling hurt, however, we can sense feelings of rejection beforehand. We become informed that rejection may occur, making us feel distressed by the situation prior to feeling pain (Eisenberger, Lieberman, & Williams, 2003).

After feeling rejected people begin to cope with the situation immediately (DeWall & Bushman, 2011). For example, positive emotions become more easily accessible to rejected people. Rejected people also sometimes turn to religion to cope. When unable to cope with the situation, the pleasure of revenge proves tempting (DeWall & Bushman, 2011).

Through the use of brain scanning technology, harming others who harmed you was discovered to be rewarding (Chester & DeWall, 2015). In this study participants were told to play an online ball-tossing game with two other players. During the game half of the participants were left to watch their partners throw the ball back and forth without them (i.e., they were excluded from the game). Participants were then given the opportunity to lash out against one of their partners by giving them a loud and unpleasant blast of noise. Those who were rejected gave louder noise blasts. The act of blasting their partner led the reward center of the brain to become more active. Harming their partner following rejection made the participant feel rewarded. Receiving pleasure from harming others has also been linked to more aggression in society (Chester & DeWall, 2015).

Consequences of Aggressive Behavior

Guilt and Shame

For most people, engaging in aggressive or antisocial behaviors leads to feelings of guilt and/or shame. Feeling guilty about antisocial behavior is a natural response and an important adaptation in human social interactions. Feelings of guilt have been demonstrated to work as a protection against such behavior by mediating the relationship between social dysfunction and acts of aggression (Colasante, Zuffianò, & Malti, 2016; Onishi, Kawabata, Kurokawa, & Yoshida, 2012). This is due to guilt being closely intertwined with empathy and understanding of others. Guilt produces a negative emotional state, motivating people to avoid those behaviors. For example, if you punch your friend for lying, you may feel extremely guilty. Guilt then makes you feel horrible for punching your friend, deterring future instances of fighting.

Shame, on the other hand, is a much less helpful emotion. Where guilt has been shown to reduce aggressive behavior, shame increases aggression (Peters & Geiger, 2016; Velotti, Elison, & Garofalo,

2014). Shame operates in the same manner as social devaluation or rejection. Feelings of shame also cause feelings of pain similar to guilt (Macdonald & Leary, 2005). However, people who feel guilty blame themselves for the rejection. Those who feel shame attribute the rejection to other individuals. This misattribution leads individuals to retaliate, hoping to alleviate their pain (Peters & Geiger, 2016; Velotti, Elison, & Garofalo, 2014).

Policies and Law

Situation factors, personal factors, and an interaction of the two can influence aggressive behavior. Some of the influences on aggressive behavior can be avoided or reduced (e.g., avoiding situations of rejection). On the other hand, some inputs cannot be avoided (e.g., the MAOA-L gene). The judicial system has adopted some of this research to explain aggressive behavior. For example, in 2007 Abdelmalek Bayout admitted to stabbing and killing a man in Italy. At the time of sentencing he only received nine years in prison. However, in 2009, Abdelmalek's sentence was reduced by another year due to evidence showing the presence of the MAOA-L gene (Feresin, 2009).

To examine the affects that situational and biological explanations have on sentencing, 181 judges were given a fictional scenario (Aspinwall, Brown, & Tabery, 2012). The scenario was based on the case involving Stephen Mobley, who robbed and killed a pizza store manager. In the fictional scenario the man was found guilty of a similar crime, although the victim was not killed. Rather, the victim was left with permanent brain damage. Without any information about personality or biological influences, the judges sentenced the man to around nine years in prison. Once the judges were told the man was diagnosed as an untreatable psychopath, the judges increased their sentencing to an average of 14 years. Upon hearing evidence for a genetic mutation causing the psychopathic behavior the sentences were lowered to, on average, 13 years.

Recidivism

Laws are made to help prevent aggressive behavior. While factors such as personality can influence sentences, society demands aggression and violence to be met with consequences. This is due to aggression and violence being antisocial behaviors (e.g., American Psychiatric Association, 2000). When the criminal justice system becomes involved, the offender can face many consequences that can range from community service, a fine, or imprisonment. Each decision can have trickle-down effect. While in jail, the person loses wages and often their job, which can lead to a loss of a home. With so many negative consequences this punishment would ideally reduce re-offenses. However, the prison experience is a risk factor for more aggressive behavior. When comparing people who committed the same crimes, those who went to prison were more likely to recidivate than those who received parole (Cullen, Jonson, & Nagin, 2011).

This cycle is due to prisoners spending time in a micro-society with other criminals (see Sykes, 2007). Essentially, prisoners become isolated from their loved ones, left only to associate with other prisoners. In these ways, prison can actually have an adverse effect (Cullen et al., 2011). The only source of information and social contact is linked to antisocial values, thoughts, and behaviors. Being engulfed in this type of environment leads prisoners to recommit crimes, ending with more imprisonment (Gendreau, Little, & Goggin, 1996).

Interventions

Not all aggression leads to a vicious cycle involving imprisonment to prevent aggression. Psychological researchers and clinicians have worked for years to understand the mechanisms that underlie aggressive and antisocial behavior in order to better devise treatments to reduce its prevalence. As a result, a number of different treatment strategies have been proposed. With varying degrees of efficacy, the most successful treatments focus on emotional and cognitive states of individuals. It is impossible to control everything in the environment (e.g., you cannot turn on the world's A/C). What you can do, however, is control internal states in the situation, which in turn change the outcome (Velotti, Elison, & Garofalo, 2014; Brown, 2004).

Dialectical behavioral therapy has shown promising results in reducing aggressive behavior, particularly among those with borderline personality disorder. The therapy works by stressing the "opposite action" to people. People are taught to identify which emotions they are experiencing in the moment, observe the urges caused by the emotions, and choose to respond with an action opposite of that urge (Rizvi & Linehan, 2005). For example, a rejected individual may be angry and feel like stabbing someone. In the moment, they person should recognize their desire to stab someone, and do something they feel is in the opposite direction. In this case, the person may feel shaking their rejecter's hand is acceptable. In this manner, clients develop a response strategy that is more adaptive to social interactions than their customary aggression.

Furthermore, in dialectical behavioral therapy, people learn to examine and identify their own feelings. This is an important step because most aggression is an impulsive response to a negative emotional state (Velotti, Elison, & Garofalo, 2014). Properly identifying the emotion and slowing down the situation is a first step in affect regulation. This "opposite action" strategy works especially well because it represents a positive treatment option (teaching clients something to *do*). Positive options have been shown to be significantly more effective at reducing further antisocial behavior than negative treatments (telling clients what *not* to do; Brown, 2004).

Cognitive behavioral therapy (CBT) involves confronting specific patterns of thought that are associated with aggression and antisocial behavior. For example, forming hostile attributions in ambiguous situations can lead to aggressive responses, a problem for narcissists. Narcissists will view some situations as threats against their ego, despite it being an innocent social interaction (Baumeister, Smart, & Boden, 1996). CBT confronts these and other erroneous beliefs that cause people to behave aggressively, and encourages clients to adopt more realistic views of themselves and others (Walker & Bright, 2009). Another type of therapy, which takes the CBT approach one step further, is "forgiveness therapy." This approach teaches individual to be less sensitive to their self-image and embraces the positive-treatment approach. Individuals are encouraged to avoid the impulse to be aggressive or antisocial and replace it with forgiveness (real or imagined; Day, Gerace, Wilson, & Howells, 2008).

A possible shift in aggression therapy may include drug therapy. Naltrexone is a drug that works by binding to opioid receptors, reducing reward sensation (Krystal et al., 2001). In humans, it has been used to reduce alcohol overconsumption by reducing the pleasurable effects of alcohol (King et al., 1997; Volpicelli et al., 1995). However, since we know vengeful acts can be pleasurable, perhaps naltrexone could help people who seriously struggle with anger management aggress less.

Future Research

Despite what we know, researchers still do not fully understand aggression. Inputs from each individual can make us predisposed to aggressive tendencies. Situations can elicit these behaviors. And an interaction between the two can increase the probability of an individual acting aggressively. But much more is to be discovered. For example, sadism has been shown to be correlated with aggressive thoughts and self-report aggression (Reidy, Zeichner, & Seibert, 2011). However, no work has examined if sadists actually behave aggressively. In a six-study package, sadism has been shown to predict aggressive behavior, above and beyond other personality traits (e.g., psychopathy, neuroticism; Chester, DeWall, & Enjaian, 2017). These results open the door to other person inputs that influence aggression.

Future research should continue to examine situation inputs as well. For example, cultures of honor have been shown to be more aggressive than non-cultures of honor (Nisbett & Cohen, 1996). Recent models of human interactions suggest that the primary purpose of cultures of honor is protection (Nowak, Gelfand, Borkowski, Cohen, & Hernandez, 2015). Through simulations, you find that as the number of aggressive individuals in society increase, cultures of honor start to form. Cultures of honor continue to grow as the number of aggressive individuals dissipate. Once aggressive individuals are reduced, cultures of honor start to dissipate. Future research should examine whether individuals within cultures of honor are specifically aggressive, or if they are more protective. That is, are they only aggressive when provoked? Are they more aggressive when protecting family compared to themselves? Also, how far does the protection go?

Cocaine, alcohol, caffeine, and nicotine are all addictive. When ingesting these drugs, our body receives pleasure from the sensation, followed by an increase in guilt and negative affect (Baker, Piper, McCarthy, Majeskie, & Fiore, 2004). To remove these negative feelings, individuals must continue to use the drug or complete the behavior. Sometimes, in order to receive the same positive boost, individuals must increase the dosage. Could aggression be viewed the same way? People receive pleasure from watching others get hurt, or behaving aggressively (Chester & DeWall, 2015). Like an addiction, though, the immediate pleasure is followed by an increase in negative affect, thus resulting in the need to harm another individual to feel better again. This pattern would suggest an addiction to behaving aggressively.

Conclusion

Whether it is someone honking their horn at us, cursing our names, or throwing punches at a bar, aggression and antisocial behavior are part of our society. For over a century psychologists have sought to understand why people behave aggressively. By examining the development of aggression, identifying situational and personal risk factors, and contemplating the role of internal states, including cognition and arousal, interventions and policies were created to reduce aggressive tendencies. This chapter reviewed classic and contemporary theories of aggression along with the research used to help understand aggressive behavior. It is only with a better understanding of aggression that we as a society can begin to prevent aggression.

References

Amato, P. R. (2001). Children of divorce in the 1990s: An update of the Amato and Keith (1991) meta-analysis. *Journal of Family Psychology*, 15, 355–370.

Amato, P. R. & Dorius, C. (2010) Fathers, children, and divorce. In M. Lamb (Ed.), *The role of the father in child development* (5th ed., pp. 177–200) Hoboken, NJ: Wiley.

American Psychiatric Association. (2000). *Diagnostic and statistical manual of mental disorders* (4th ed.). Washington, DC: Author.

Anderson, C. A. & Bushman, B. J. (2002). Human aggression. *Annual Review of Psychology*, 53, 27–51.

Anderson, C. A., Shibuya, A., Ihori, N., Swing, E. L., Bushman, B. J., Sakamoto, A., ... & Saleem, M. (2010). Violent video game effects on aggression, empathy, and prosocial behavior in Eastern and Western countries: a meta-analytic review. *Psychological Bulletin*, 136, 151–173.

Apter, A., van Praag, H. M., Plutchik, R., Sevy, S., Korn, M., & Brown, S. L. (1990). Interrelationships among anxiety, aggression, impulsivity, and mood: A serotonergically linked cluster? *Psychiatry Research*, 32, 191–199.

Aragona, B. J., Liu, Y., Yu, Y. J., Curtis, J. T., Detwiler, J. M., Insel, T. R., & Wang, Z. (2006). Nucleus accumbens dopamine differentially mediates the formation and maintenance of monogamous pair bonds. *Nature Neuroscience*, 9, 133–139.

Aspinwall, L. G., Brown, T. R., & Tabery, J. (2012). The double-edged sword: Does biomechanism increase or decrease judges' sentencing of psychopaths? *Science*, 337, 846–849.

Baker, T. B., Piper, M. E., McCarthy, D. E., Majeskie, M. R., & Fiore, M. C. (2004). Addiction motivation reformulated: An affective processing model of negative reinforcement. *Psychological Review*, 111, 33–51.

Barnes, C. D., Brown, R. P., & Osterman, L. L. (2012). Don't tread on me masculine honor ideology in the US and militant responses to terrorism. *Personality and Social Psychology Bulletin*, 38, 1018–1029.

Baron, R. A. & Richardson, D. R. (1994). *Human aggression* (2nd ed.). New York: Plenum.

Baumeister, R. F. & Heatherton, T. F. (1996). Self-regulation failure: An overview. *Psychological Inquiry*, 7, 1–15.

Baumeister, R. F., Schmeichel, B. J., Vohs, K. D., & Petrocelli, J. V. (2007). Self-regulation and the executive function: The self as controlling agent. *Social Psychology: Handbook of Basic Principles*, 148, 775–777.

Baumeister, R. F., Smart, L., & Boden, J. M. (1996). Relation of threatened egotism to violence and aggression: The dark side of high self-esteem. *Psychological Review*, 103, 5–33.

Brown, J. (2004). Shame and domestic violence: Treatment perspectives for perpetrators from self-psychology and affect theory. *Sexual and Relationship Therapy*, 19, 39–56.

Brown, R. P., Osterman, L. L., & Barnes, C. D. (2009). School violence and the culture of honor. *Psychological Science*, 20, 1400–1405.

Bushman, B. J. & Anderson, C. A. (2015). Understanding causality in the effects of media violence. *American Behavioral Scientist*, 59, 1807–1821.

Bushman, B. J. & Baumeister, R. F. (1998). Threatened egotism, narcissism, self-esteem, and direct and displaced aggression: Does self-love or self-hate lead to violence? *Journal of Personality and Social Psychology*, 75, 219–229.

Bushman, B. J. & Huesmann, L. R. (2010). Aggression. In S. T. Fiske, D. T. Gilbert, and G. Lindzey (Eds), *Handbook of social psychology* (Vol. 2). Hoboken, NJ: John Wiley & Sons.

Buss, A. H. (1962). The psychology of aggression. *The Journal of Nervous and Mental Disease*, 135, 180–181.

Cases, O., Seif, I., Grimsby, J., Gaspar, P., Chen, K., Pournin, S., … & Shih, J. C. (1995). Aggressive behavior and altered amounts of brain serotonin and norepinephrine in mice lacking MAOA. *Science*, 268, 1763–1766.

Caspi, A. (2002). Role of genotype in the cycle of violence in maltreated children. *Science*, 297, 851–854.

Chester, D. S. & DeWall, C. N. (2015). The pleasure of revenge: Retaliatory aggression arises from a neural imbalance toward reward. *Social Cognitive and Affective Neuroscience*, 11, 1173–1182.

Chester, D. S. & DeWall, C. N. (2016). Sound the alarm: The effect of narcissism on retaliatory aggression is moderated by dACC reactivity to rejection. *Journal of Personality*, 84, 361–368.

Chester, D. S., DeWall, C. N., Derefinko, K. J., Estus, S., Peters, J. R., Lynam, D. R., & Jiang, Y. (2015). Monoamine oxidase A (MAOA) genotype predicts greater aggression through impulsive reactivity to negative affect. *Behavioural Brain Research*, 283, 97–101.

Chester, D. S., DeWall, C. N., & Enjaian, B. (2017). Sadism and aggressive behavior: Inflicting pain to feel pleasure. Manuscript submitted for publication.

Chester, D. S., Eisenberger, N. I., Pond, R. S., Richman, S. B., Bushman, B. J., & Dewall, C. N. (2014). The interactive effect of social pain and executive functioning on aggression: An fMRI experiment. *Social Cognitive and Affective Neuroscience*, 9, 699–704.

Coccaro, E. F., McCloskey, M. S., Fitzgerald, D. A., & Phan, K. L. (2007). Amygdala and orbitofrontal reactivity to social threat in individuals with impulsive aggression. *Biological Psychiatry*, 62, 168–178.

Cohen, D., Nisbett, R. E., Bowdle, B. F., & Schwarz, N. (1996). Insult, aggression, and the southern culture of honor: An "experimental ethnography." *Journal of Personality and Social Psychology*, 70, 945–960.

Colasante, T., Zuffianò, A., & Malti, T. (2016). Daily deviations in anger, guilt, and sympathy: A developmental diary study of aggression. *Journal of Abnormal Child Psychology*, 1–12.

Cote, S., Vaillancourt, T., LeBlanc, J., Nagin, D. W., & Tremblay, R. E. (2006). The development of physical aggression from toddlerhood to pre-adolescence: A nationwide longitudinal study of Canadian children. *Journal of Abnormal Child Psychology*, 34, 71–85.

Couppis, M. H. & Kennedy, C. H. (2008). The rewarding effect of aggression is reduced by nucleus accumbens dopamine receptor antagonism in mice. *Psychopharmacology*, 197, 449–456.

Crick, N. R. & Grotpeter, J. K. (1995). Relational aggression, gender, and social-psychological adjustment. *Child Development*, 66, 710–722.

Croft, C. D. & Zimmer-Gembeck, M. J. (2014). Friendship conflict, conflict responses, and instability: Unique links to anxious and angry forms of rejection sensitivity. *The Journal of Early Adolescence*, 34, 1094–1119.

Cullen, F. T., Jonson, C. L., & Nagin, D. S. (2011). Prisons do not reduce recidivism: The high cost of ignoring science. *The Prison Journal*, 91, 48S–65S.

Davis, J. R. & Reyna, C (2015). Seeing red: How perceptions of social status and worth influence hostile attributions and endorsement of aggression. *British Journal of Social Psychology*, 54, 728–747.

Day, A., Gerace, A., Wilson, C., & Howells, K. (2008). Promoting forgiveness in violent offenders: A more positive approach to offender rehabilitation. *Aggression and Violent Behavior*, 13, 195–200.

Denson, T. F., Pedersen, W. C., Ronquillo, J., & Nandy, A. S. (2009). The angry brain: Neural correlates of anger, angry rumination, and aggressive personality. *Journal of Cognitive Neuroscience*, 21, 734–744.

DeWall, C. N., Anderson, C. A., & Bushman, B. J. (2011). The general aggression model: Theoretical extensions to violence. *Psychology of Violence*, 1, 245–258.

DeWall, C. N., Baumeister, R. F., Stillman, T., & Gailliot, M. T. (2007). Violence restrained: Effects of self-regulation and its depletion on aggression. *Journal of Experimental Social Psychology*, 43, 62–76.

DeWall, C. N. & Bushman, B. J. (2011). Social acceptance and rejection: The sweet and the bitter. *Current Directions in Psychological Science*, 20, 256–260.

Dodge, K. A., Malone, P. S., Lansford, J. E., Sorbring, E., Skinner, A. T., Tapanya, S., & Pastorelli, C. (2015). Hostile attributional bias and aggressive behavior in global context. *Proceedings of the National Academy of Sciences of the United States of America*, 112, 9310–9315.

Dodge, K. A. (1980) Social cognition and children's aggressive behavior. *Child Development*, 51, 162–170.

Eisenberger, N. I. (2012). Broken hearts and broken bones: A neural perspective on the similarities between social and physical pain. *Psychological Science*, 21, 42–47.

Eisenberger, N. I. & Lieberman, M. D. (2004). Why rejection hurts: A common neural alarm system for physical and social pain. *Trends in Cognitive Sciences*, 8, 294–300.

Eisenberger, N. I., Lieberman, M. D., & Williams, K. D. (2003). Does rejection hurt? An fMRI study of social exclusion. *Science*, 302, 290–292.

Eisenberger, N. I., Way, B. M., Taylor, S. E., Welch, W. T., & Lieberman, M. D. (2007). Understanding genetic risk for aggression: Clues from the brain's response to social exclusion. *Biological Psychiatry*, 61, 1100–1108.

Eisenlohr-Moul, T. A., Peters, J. R., Pond, R. J., & DeWall, C. N. (2016). Both trait and state mindfulness predict lower aggressiveness via anger rumination: A multilevel mediation analysis. *Mindfulness*, 7, 713–726.

Elder, G. H., Eccles, J. S., Ardelt, M., & Lord, S. (1995). Inner-city parents under economic pressure: Perspective on the strategies of parenting. *Journal of Marriage and the Family*, 57, 771–784.

Elson, M. & Ferguson, C. J. (2014). Twenty-five years of research on violence in digital games and aggression: Empirical evidence, perspectives, and a debate gone astray. *European Psychologist*, 19, 33–46.

Erdman, S. L. (2014, June 29). Pakistani newlyweds decapitated by bride's family in honor killing. Retrieved August 15, 2016, from: www.cnn.com/2014/06/28/world/asia/pakistan-honor-murders/.

Feresin, E. (2009, October 30). Lighter sentence for murderer with "bad genes." Retrieved August 15, 2016, from: www.nature.com/news/2009/091030/full/news.2009.1050.html.-analysis.

Ferguson, C. J. (2015). Do angry birds make for angry children? A meta-analysis of video game influences on children's and adolescents' aggression, mental health, prosocial behavior and academic performance. *Perspectives on Psychological Science*, 10, 646–666.

Finkel, E. J. (2014). The I3 model: Metatheory, theory, and evidence. *Advances in Experimental Social Psychology*, 49, 1–104.

Gendreau, P., Little, T., & Goggin, C. (1996). Of adult offender recidivism. *Criminology*, 34, 575–607.

Goldsmith, H. H. & Lemery, K. S. (2000). Linking temperamental fearfulness and anxiety symptoms: A behavior-genetic perspective. *Biological Psychiatry*, 48, 1199–1209.

Haller, J., Makara, G. B., & Kruk, M. R. (1997). Catecholaminergic involvement in the control of aggression: Hormones, the peripheral sympathetic, and central noradrenergic systems. *Neuroscience & Biobehavioral Review, 22,* 85–97.

Kagan, J., Reznick, J. S., Snidman, N., Gibbons, J., & Johnson, M. O. (1988). Childhood derivatives of inhibition and lack of inhibition to the unfamiliar. *Child Development, 59,* 1580–1589.

King, A. C., Volpicelli, J. R., Frazer, A., & O'Brien, C. P. (1997). Effect of naltrexone on subjective alcohol response in subjects at high and low risk for future alcohol dependence. *Psychopharmacology, 129,* 15–22.

Kross, E., Berman, M. G., Mischel, W., Smith, E. E., & Wager, T. D. (2011). Social rejection shares somatosensory representations with physical pain. *Proceedings of the National Academy of Sciences of the United States of America, 108,* 6270–6275.

Krystal, J. H., Cramer, J. A., Krol, W. F., Kirk, G. F., & Rosenheck, R. A. (2001). Naltrexone in the treatment of alcohol dependence. *New England Journal of Medicine, 345,* 1734–1739.

Lagerspetz, K. M., Bjorkqvist, K., & Peltonen, T. (1988). Is indirect aggression typical of females? Gender differences in aggressiveness in 11- to 12-year old children. *Aggressive Behavior, 14,* 403–414.

Loeber, R. & Stouthamer-Loeber, M. (1986). Family factors as correlates as predictors of juvenile conduct problems and delinquency. In M. Tonry (Ed.), *Crime and justice: An annual review of research* (Vol. 7, pp. 29–150), Chicago, IL: University of Chicago Press.

Long, K., Felton, J. W., Lilienfeld, S. O., & Lejuez, C. W. (2014). The role of emotion regulation in the relations between psychopathy factors and impulsive and premeditated aggression. *Personality Disorders: Theory, Research, And Treatment, 5,* 390–396.

MacDonald, G. & Leary, M. R. (2005). Why does social exclusion hurt? The relationship between social and physical pain. *Psychological Bulletin, 131,* 202–223.

Manuck, S. B., Flory, J. D., Ferrell, R. E., Mann, J. J., & Muldoon, M. F. (2000). A regulatory polymorphism of the monoamine oxidase-A gene may be associated with variability in aggression, impulsivity, and central nervous system serotonergic responsivity. *Psychiatry Research, 95,* 9–23.

Marcus-Newhall, A., Pedersen, W. C., Carlson, M., & Miller, N. (2000). Displaced aggression is alive and well: A meta-analytic review. *Journal of Personality and Social Psychology, 78,* 670–689.

Martinez, M., Cabrera, A., Weisfeldt, S., & Criss, D. (2015, October 21). Albuquerque road rage: Man in custody after 4-year-old shot, killed. Retrieved August 15, 2016, from: www.cnn.com/2015/10/21/us/child-road-rage-death/index.html.

Mattsson, Å., Schalling, D., Olweus, D., Löw, H., & Svensson, J. (1980). Plasma testosterone, aggressive behavior, and personality dimensions in young male delinquents. *Journal of the American Academy of Child Psychiatry, 19,* 476–490.

McDermott, R., Tingley, D., Cowden, J., Frazzetto, G., & Johnson, D. D. P. (2009). Monoamine oxidase A gene (MAOA) predicts behavioral aggression following provocation. *Proceedings of the National Academy of Sciences of the United States of America, 106,* 2118–2123.

McWhiney, G. (1988). *Cracker culture: Celtic ways in the Old South.* Tuscaloosa: University of Alabama Press.

Mehlman, P. T., Higley, J. D., Faucher, I., Lilly, A. A., Taub, D. M., Vickers, J., ... & Linnoila, M. (1994). Low CSF 5-HIAA concentrations and severe aggression and impaired impulse control in nonhuman primates. *American Journal of Psychiatry, 151,* 1485–1491.

Mehta, P. H. & Beer, J. (2010). Neural mechanisms of the testosterone-aggression relation: The role of orbitofrontal cortex. *Journal of Cognitive Neuroscience, 22,* 2357–2368.

Miczek, K. A., de Almeida, R. M., Kravitz, E. A., Rissman, E. F., de Boer, S. F., &

Raine, A. (2007). Neurobiology of escalated aggression and violence. *The Journal of Neuroscience*, 27, 11803–11806.

Nelson, J. A. & Perry, N. B. (2015). Emotional reactivity, self-control and children's hostile attributions over middle childhood. *Cognition and Emotion*, 29, 592–603.

Nielsen (2016, June 27). The total audience report: Q1 2016. Retrieved August 15, 2016, from: www.nielsen.com/us/en/insights/reports/2016/the-total-audience-report-q1-2016.html.

Nisbett, R. E. & Cohen, D. (1996). *Culture of honor: The psychology of violence in the south*. Boulder, CO: Westview Press.

Nowak, A., Gelfand, M. J., Borkowski, W., Cohen, D., & Hernandez, I. (2015). The evolutionary basis of honor cultures. *Psychological Science*, 27, 12–24.

Olweus, D., Mattsson, A., Schalling, D., & Löw, H. (1988). Circulating testosterone levels and aggression in adolescent males: A causal analysis. *Psychosomatic Medicine*, 50, 261–272.

Onishi, A., Kawabata, Y., Kurokawa, M., & Yoshida, T. (2012). A mediated model of relational aggression, narcissistic orientations, guilt feelings, and perceived classroom norms. *School Psychology International*, 33, 367–390.

Pederson, W. C., Gonzales, C., & Miller, N. (2000). The moderating effect of trivial triggering provocation on displaced aggression. *Journal of Personality and Social Psychology*, 78, 913–927.

Peters, J. R. & Geiger, P. J. (2016). Borderline personality disorder and self-conscious affect: Too much shame but not enough guilt? *Personality Disorders: Theory, Research, and Treatment*, 7, 303–308.

Reidy, D. E., Zeichner, A., & Seibert, L. A. (2011). Unprovoked aggression: Effects of psychopathic traits and sadism. *Journal of Personality*, 79, 75–100.

Rizvi, S. L. & Linehan, M. M. (2005). The treatment of maladaptive shame in borderline personality disorder: A pilot study of "opposite action." *Cognitive and Behavioral Practice*, 12, 437–447.

Slotter, E. B. & Finkel, E. J. (2011). I³ theory: Instigating, impelling, and inhibiting factors in aggression. In M. Mikulincer & P. R. Shaver (Eds), *Human aggression and violence: Causes, manifestations, and consequences* (pp. 35–52). Washington, DC: American Psychological Association.

Sykes, G. M. (2007). *The society of captives: A study of a maximum security prison*. Princeton, NJ: Princeton University Press.

Terburg, D., Morgan, B., & van Honk, J. (2009). The testosterone-cortisol ratio: A hormonal marker for proneness to social aggression. *International Journal of Law and Psychiatry*, 32, 216–223.

Tremblay, R. E., Nagin, D. S., Seguin, J. R., Zoccolillo, M., Zelazo, P., Boivin, M., & Japel, C. (2004). Physical aggression during early childhood: Trajectories and predictors. *Pediatrics*, 114, e43–e50.

Turner, K. A. & White, B. A. (2015). Contingent on contingencies: Connections between anger rumination, self-esteem, and aggression. *Personality and Individual Differences*, 82, 199–202.

Vasquez, E. A. & Howard-Field, J. (2016). Too (mentally) busy to chill: Cognitive load and inhibitory cues interact to moderate triggered displaced aggression. *Aggressive Behavior*, 42(6), 598-604.

Velotti, P., Elison, J., & Garofalo, C. (2014). Shame and aggression: Different trajectories and implications. *Aggression and Violent Behavior*, 19, 454–461.

Volpicelli, J. R., Watson, N. T., King, A. C., Sherman, C. E., & O'Brien, C. P. (1995). Effect of naltrexone on alcohol "high" in alcoholics. *American Journal of Psychiatry*, 152, 613–615.

Walker, J. S. & Bright, J. A. (2009). Cognitive therapy for violence: Reaching the parts that nager management doesn't reach. *Journal of Forensic Psychiatry & Psychology*, 20, 174–201.

Wilkowski, B. M. & Robinson, M. D. (2010). The anatomy of anger: An integrative cognitive model of trait anger and reactive aggression. *Journal of Personality*, 78, 9–38.

Wyatt-Brown, B. (1982). *Southern honor: Ethics and behavior in the Old South*. New York: Oxford University Press.

Yaros, A., Lochman, J. E., Rosenbaum, J., & Jimenez-Camargo, L. A. (2014). Real-time hostile attribution measurement and aggression in children. *Aggressive Behavior*, 40, 409–420.

Zimmer-Gembeck, M. J. & Nesdale, D. (2013). Anxious and angry rejection sensitivity, social withdrawal, and retribution in high and low ambiguous situations. *Journal of Personality*, 81, 29–38.

16 Violent Juvenile Offenders: A Psychiatric and Mental Health Perspective

Marcel Aebi and Hans-Christoph Steinhausen

Introduction

Finding a mental health perspective on aggression and violence is important for several reasons. Firstly, the association of these phenomena with mental disorders may shed light on the origins of aggression and violence on theoretical grounds. Secondly, this etiological perspective is also of clinical importance, as it can supplement assisting individuals with these problems by providing proper assessment and treatment for their problems and potentially underlying mental disorders. Closely linked to this perspective, there is the third task of assisting the criminal justice system by offering specific forensic services in order to provide expert knowledge for the evaluation and treatment of individuals who, due to violation of the law, are facing court examinations and potential incarceration. These activities rest on both clinical experience in the mental health domain and an extensive amount of studies based on community, clinical, and forensic samples of youth indicating that the presence of one or more mental disorders increases the risk of various forms of violent behaviors in adolescence and later adulthood (Arseneault, Moffitt, Caspi, Taylor, & Silva, 2000; Benedek, Ash, & Scott, 2010; Copeland, Miller-Johnson, Keeler, Angold, & Costello, 2007).

Here, violence is defined as any behavior that is directed against other people and causes harm to them (e.g., direct forms such as physical attacks/bodily harm, but also indirect forms such as verbal aggression, bullying, and property crimes). The differentiation of two different forms of physical violence is useful for clinical purposes (Blair, Leibenluft, & Pine, 2015; Dooley, Anderson, Hemphill, & Ohan, 2008; Steiner et al., 2011): (1) proactive or instrumental aggression as a goal-directed behavior (2) reactive aggression that is performed in response to provocation/frustration. These two types of violence have different neuronal correlates and, therefore, may be associated with different mental disorders (Blair et al., 2015). For example, there is evidence that reactive aggression is related to both emotional and brain trauma and affective disorders, whereas instrumental and goal-directed aggression may be grounded in antisocial and psychopathic traits (Blair et al., 2015; Dooley et al., 2008; Steiner et al., 2011). However, no moderator effect of this subtyping of aggression on treatment outcome has been found (Smeets et al., 2015).

According to the prevailing medical model in the understanding of mental disorders, most studies of associations of violence and aggression follow the categorical model, with distinct diagnostic entities as reflected in the major classification system, the International Classification of Diseases (ICD) and the US Diagnostic and Statistical Manual (DSM). The relation between psychiatric disorders and violence is complicated by the fact that the definitions of various ICD-10 (World Health Organization, 1992) or DSM-5 (American Psychiatric Association, 2013) mental disorders may, amongst others, relate to aspects of violence. For example, irritability is a criterion of depression that is also associated with temper tantrums and aggression. Conduct disorders describe a 6-to-12-month persistent pattern of rule-breaking behaviors that encompasses several aspects of violent behaviors against other persons. Substance abuse and dependency is directly related to drug-related crimes, including illegal and violent procurements. Thus, if the relation between psychopathology and violence is not merely circular, it needs a more specific focus on the etiology of the disorders and its neural and psychological mechanisms, its assessment, and specific treatment implications.

We provide an overview of the most frequent child and adolescent mental disorders and their associations with violent behaviors. In particular, we address brain disorders, substance use disorders, schizophrenia, affective disorders, anxiety disorders, trauma-related disorders, attention-deficit-hyperactivity disorder, and disruptive behavior disorders, and the association of these disorders with violent behaviors. For each of these disorders, the description will include the various specific associations with aggression and violence, their forensic aspects in the presentation, and a brief sketch of specific interventions.

Brain Disorders

Although all mental disorders are brain-related, there is a group of disorders that are due to a noxious agent or a neurobiological deficit leading to neurological alterations of brain functions and structures. These disorders comprise traumatic brain injury (TBI), infectious brain disorder, epilepsy, and brain tumor. Only TBI and epilepsy will be considered here as potentially affecting child and adolescent mental health, including the development of aggression. In addition, the noxious brain effects of prenatal alcohol exposure as manifested in Fetal Alcohol Spectrum Disorders (FASD) with the potential development of serious delinquent and violent behavior have to be addressed.

All brain disorders are characterized by a wide range of functional sequelae on various levels, including neuropsychiatric, neurologic, endocrine, neurocognitive, educational, and psychosocial effects. The clinical manifestations vary widely depending on the type, cause, and severity of the noxious agent and individual preconditions, including pre-morbid functioning, developmental age, and various personal and environmental characteristics (Steinhausen & Gillberg, 2006). Among the multifold aspects of this varying clinical picture, features of aggression and violence may play a role.

According to a global review, the worldwide incidence of hospital-treated TBI is estimated at 100 to 300 per 100,000, but a true population prevalence in excess of 600 per 100,000 has been assumed and the vulnerability for TBI is highest among young men (Cassidy et al., 2004). A recent Australian study in adolescents (Moore, Indig, & Haysom, 2014) provided evidence that the rates of TBI were excessively high among incarcerated youth. Young people who reported a history of TBI were significantly more likely to be diagnosed with a mental health disorder. This included problematic substance use, participation in fights, and offending behaviors. Another large study, based on Australian registry data on N = 7694 individuals with the first hospital-recorded TBI at age 10.6 in males and 6.9 in females, found that, relative to general population controls, TBI was associated with an increased risk of any conviction and violent convictions, in particular at a mean follow-up of age 12.5 (males) and 16.5 (females). After comprehensive adjustment for confounding, the study concluded that there was a modest causal link between TBI and criminality, and that reducing the rate of TBI might result in a reduction of crime (Schofield et al., 2015).

Systematic observations in clinical samples have documented that aggressive behavior increased from pre-injury to post-injury after one year in individuals with severe pediatric TBI, and that children with greater disability after injury were also at greater risk for aggressive behaviors (Cole et al., 2008). However, another clinical study revealed that measures of global psychopathology as represented in common behavioral questionnaires do not permit detailed examination of specific behavior problems such as aggression. In contrast, the distinction between reactive and proactive aggression provided greater insight into post-TBI aggression by showing that reactive disorders, in terms of emotional lability, increased levels of anger, feelings of emotional release, and an inability to tolerate frustration, were more common in individuals who had had TBI compared to controls (Dooley et al., 2008)

Interventions for the various sequelae of TBI, including aggression, have profited most strongly from a behavioral approach. Although most of the research on behavioral treatment after TBI has involved clinical case studies or studies employing single-subject experimental designs across a series of cases, there is sufficient support of the effectiveness of these interventions across ages, injury severities, and stages of recovery after TBI. For these interventions the following guidelines for behavior management were recommended: direct behavioral observations, systematic assessment of environmental and within-patient variables associated with aberrant behavior, antecedent management to minimize the probability of aberrant behavior, provision of functionally equivalent alternative means of controlling the environment, and differential reinforcement to shape positive behavior and coping strategies, while not inadvertently shaping emergent, disruptive sequelae (Slifer & Amari, 2009).

Another large group of brain-disordered individuals of all ages is affected by *epilepsy*. The disorder comprises various types of partial, generalized, and unclassified seizures. By age 20, a total of 5% of all children and adolescents will have experienced a seizure but fewer than one in five will develop epilepsy, and, within five years of seizure onset, 80% of all children and adolescents will be expected to be seizure-free. There is a heightened vulnerability for various types of psychopathology in children with epilepsy (Davies, Heyman, & Goodman, 2003). Furthermore, aggression is only seen in a minority of people with epilepsy. It is rarely seizure-related, sometimes occurring as part of complex psychiatric and behavioral comorbidities, and it is sometimes associated with certain anti-epileptic drugs.

The literature on the association of epilepsy and aggression is mostly based on observations in adult patients (Brodie et al., 2016). Likewise, a recent Swedish population-based patient registry study had a mean age of 19.8 years at first diagnosis and so only part of the sample was comprised of children and adolescents. This study found a rate of 4.2% of violent offense after diagnosis, which was significantly higher than the 2.5% rate in the population controls. However, this association disappeared when individuals with epilepsy were compared with their unaffected siblings. After adjustment for familial confounding, epilepsy was not associated with increased risk of violent crime, questioning previous suggestions of a causal relation. The rate for violent crime was significantly lower in those first diagnosed before age 16 than in those first diagnosed at age 16 or older. In addition, subtypes of epilepsy involving loss of consciousness (complex partial seizures and generalized epilepsy) were associated with lower rates of violent crime (Fazel, Lichtenstein, Grann, & Langstrom, 2011).

The devastating effects of *prenatal alcohol exposure* had been first described by the term Fetal Alcohol Syndrome (FAS) comprising the main features of pre- and postnatal growth deficiency, developmental delay, and mental disability due to prenatal damage, and characteristic craniofacial dysmorphic features. Taking various degrees of severity into account, FAS has later been extended to Fetal Alcohol Spectrum Disorders (FASD) or Neurobehavioral Disorder with Prenatal Alcohol Exposure (ND-PAE) as a condition for further study in the current DSM-5 classification.

Besides neurocognitive impairments, there are varying impairments in self-regulation, including impairments in mood and behavior regulation (e.g., frequent behavioral outburst), attention deficits, and impulse control deficits. According to a recent systematic review and meta-analysis, conduct disorders expressed as a disorder of conduct, behavioral problems, disruptive disorders, or impulsivity in the original studies was the second-most frequently diagnosed comorbid disorder in FASD studies, with a pooled prevalence of 90.7 (CI 77.9–97.4)% (Popova et al., 2016). In addition to the long-lasting deleterious effects on development and mental and psychosocial functioning (Steinhausen, Willms, & Spohr, 1993), the large Seattle Secondary Disability Study on the long-term development of FASD individuals revealed that 60% had had conflicts with the law. The study demonstrated an incarceration rate of 35% in such individuals, in addition to psychiatric hospitalizations in 23% of the subjects (Streissguth, Barr, Kogan, & Bookstein, 1996). Due to their disability resulting from brain damage, individuals with FASD may not only be victimized, but also may be accused of criminal activities in the justice system (Fast & Conry, 2009).

Treatment approaches of children and adolescents with brain disorders vary according to the type of the disorder. Furthermore, they often include various medical interventions in the acute phase, and a multidisciplinary approach for the often-chronic conditions reflected by different courses of the illness with varying patterns of recovery or incomplete remission. Long-term rehabilitation approaches are often needed (for a more detailed description see Steinhausen & Gillberg, 2006).

Substance Use Disorders

Clinically, the pathological use of substances represents conditions of acute intoxications, withdrawal states, psychotic disorders, and amnestic disorders and the primary diagnoses are *mental and behavioural disorders due to psychoactive substance use* according to ICD-10 or *substance use disorder* according to DSM-5. Substance use disorders (SUD) are defined for alcohol, amphetamines, caffeine, cannabis, cocaine, hallucinogens, inhalants, nicotine, opioids, phencyclidine, and sedatives or anxiolytics. With an onset most frequently in adolescence or young adulthood, the lifetime prevalence of illicit drug use shows marked international differences, with the highest rates in the USA and Australia (> 40%), followed by Canada (> 35%), and lower rates in Europe (20–25 %). For all substances, males abuse more than females, although the gender gap seems to have narrowed during the last decades (Bukstein, 2006). In US community adolescents, the prevalence of alcohol and illicit drug use disorders is around 8% and 2–3%, respectively (Swendsen et al., 2012). However, in detained samples, SUD are more prevalent, with rates of 26.2% for alcohol, 39.2% for cannabis, and 6.4% for other drug disorders (Colins et al., 2010). It has also been shown recently that substance use was related to current violent criminal offenses with odd ratios of 2.91 for alcohol, 2.62 for cannabis, and 2.7 for other drug-related disorders (Elkington et al., 2015).

Disruptive behavior disorders are the most common mental disorders diagnosed in adolescents with SUD, and conduct disorder (CD) including the component of aggression is manifested in 50–80% of clinical populations with SUD. Usually CD precedes and coexists with SUD and an early onset of CD, often comorbid with attention-deficit-hyperactivity disorder (ADHD), increases the risk of later SUD. Direct drug effects resulting in aggression may be exacerbated further by pre-existing psychopathology, simultaneous use of multiple substances, and the frequent, relative inexperience of the adolescent. Among the various individual, biological, and environmental risk factors, early aggressive and disruptive disorders stand out as particularly strong elements in the development of SUD in adolescents (Bukstein, 2006).

A Swiss longitudinal community study differentiated between various manifestations of alcohol use by studying the validity of a typology that considers empirically defined adolescent groups of abstainers, social drinkers, heavy drinkers, and problem drinkers. It was shown that, in particular, problem drinkers showed a highly abnormal behavioral and psychosocial profile, including the highest scores in the domains of delinquent and aggressive behaviors according to their self-reports (Steinhausen & Winkler Metzke, 2003). In the same study, problematic substance use (PSU) in young adulthood was most strongly predicted by preceding PSU, externalizing problem behavior, and male sex (Steinhausen, Eschmann, & Winkler Metzke, 2007). Furthermore, in this study, PSU as represented in a developmental trajectory model from adolescence to young adulthood was second best predicted by a self-report of externalizing behavior in early adolescence (Eschmann, Zimprich, Winkler, Metzke, & Steinhausen, 2011).

Furthermore, various community-based studies reported that early drug use, including alcohol use, was related to later criminal outcomes (Aebi, Giger, Plattner,

Metzke, & Steinhausen, 2014; Brook, Zhang, & Brook, 2011; Copeland et al., 2007; Hodgins, Larm, Molero-Samuleson, Tengstrom, & Larsson, 2009; Stouthamer-Loeber, Wei, Loeber, & Masten, 2004). It also demonstrated that the consumption of so-called *hard* drugs predicted persistent criminal offending behaviors, even when controlling for other forms of conduct problems (Copeland et al., 2007; Stouthamer-Loeber et al., 2004). Problematic alcohol use during adolescence tripled the risk of committing any adult crime, suggesting that it may well play a pivotal role in the development of later criminal outcomes in various ways (Aebi et al., 2014). First, alcohol may serve as a starter drug for the consumption of further illegal substances (Kandel, 1982). Second, the disinhibitory effects of alcohol may lower the thresholds for criminal behaviors (Leigh, 1999; Martin, 2001). Third, alcohol use may reflect an inadequate coping strategy, which increases the possibility of delinquent behaviors (Baer, Garmezy, McLaughlin, Pokorny, & Wernick, 1987). In detained adolescent offenders, drug use disorders (other than alcohol and cannabis) were the exclusive predictor of violent recidivism in adolescent boys, and cannabis use disorder was the exclusive predictor of violent recidivism in adolescent girls (Elkington et al., 2015). In sum, the existing body of literature convincingly shows that SUDs are crucial for the explanation of concurrent and future violent behaviors in a substantial proportion of youth and young adults.

The clinical management of SUD is guided by the primary goal of achieving and maintaining abstinence and harm reduction within a broad concept of rehabilitation. This includes dealing concurrently with comorbid physical and mental disorders and problems, functioning within the family, among peers and in other interpersonal relationships, and academic/vocational functioning. The success of any intervention in adolescents is most dependent on family interventions aimed at reducing conflicts between parents and adolescents, and at increasing parental effectiveness. Various forms of family therapy have been shown to be effective (Bukstein, 2006).

Schizophrenic Disorders

The manifestation of delusions, hallucinations, disorganized thinking, grossly disorganized motor behavior (e.g., catatonia), and negative symptoms, such as diminished emotional expression or a decrease of self-initiated purposeful activities, are central to the clinical manifestation of schizophrenic disorders. It is internationally well established that around 1% of the adult population suffer from schizophrenic disorders (American Psychiatric Association, 2013). Typically, these disorders manifest for the first time in the early 20s, whereas an early onset in adolescence or a very early onset in childhood is rare (American Psychiatric Association, 2013). However, psychotic symptoms may occur in childhood and adolescence without the full clinical picture of schizophrenia. For example, a review of population studies demonstrated that symptoms of delusions, hallucinations, and thought disorders were reported in 7.5% of adolescents (Kelleher et al., 2012). In forensic youth samples, psychotic symptoms have been assessed more frequently, with reported rates of 66 to 78% (Colins et al., 2009; Vreugdenhil, Vermeiren, Wouters, Doreleijers, & van den Brink, 2004) and even a full manifestation of psychotic disorders have been observed in 1.35% (Colins et al., 2010).

There is evidence that adult patients diagnosed with schizophrenia or psychotic disorder have higher rates of criminal convictions than the general population (Fazel, Gulati, Linsell, Geddes, & Grann, 2009), and that schizophrenia is a serious risk factor for violent behaviors in young adults (Arseneault et al., 2000). Due to the low prevalence of schizophrenic disorders in youth and the lack of specific studies, a potential relationship between schizophrenia and violence in youth remains unclear. A study based on youth in detention centers in Flandern (Belgium) found that the presence of psychotic symptoms did not increase the risk of violent reoffending after release from detention. Male youth with paranoid delusions and threat/control override delusions were found to have low risk for violent re-offending even when comorbid substance use disorders were present (Colins, Vermeiren, Noom, & Broekaert, 2013). From the limited empirical evidence one may tentatively conclude that schizophrenic disorders without further comorbidity do not play a substantial role in the manifestation of violence in adolescent populations.

Schizophrenic disorders often are not fully remitting, so that long-term rehabilitation efforts are needed. Very frequently, medication is the backbone of these interventions in both adolescents and adults. Antipsychotic medication has been found to be helpful in decreasing psychotic symptoms and preventing violent crimes in adults (Fazel, Zetterqvist, Larsson, Langstrom, & Lichtenstein, 2014). With the additional use of CBT a patient may learn to challenge the habitation patterns of thinking and to examine the evidence of the pros and cons of distressful beliefs in order to develop more rational and personally acceptable alternative explanations (Jones, Hacker, Cormac, Meaden, & Irving, 2012).

Affective Disorders

Major Depression

Major depression is characterized by the core symptoms of depressed mood (feelings of sadness, emptiness, and hopelessness) and a loss of interest (diminished pleasure and inactivity) that are present almost every day for a period of two weeks. Children and adolescents may show feelings of irritability instead of depressed mood. Further symptoms of major depression include significant weight loss or failure of weight gain, insomnia, psychomotor agitation or retardation, lack of energy, feelings of worthlessness, diminished ability to concentrate, and recurrent thoughts of death or suicide. The worldwide prevalence of major depression has been estimated at 1.3% in youth (Polanczyk, Salum, Sugaya, Caye, & Rohde, 2015), with an increase up to 7.5% in adolescence (Avenevoli, Swendsen, He, Burstein, & Merikangas, 2015). Adolescents with major depression have a fourfold increased risk for additional disruptive behavior disorders (Avenevoli et al., 2015). Compared to adolescents in the community higher rates were reported for major depression in juvenile delinquents, with prevalence rates of 12.0% (Colins et al., 2010).

At first glance, there seems to be little resemblance between the presence of depression and the emergence of violent behaviors. Symptoms of decreased energy, gloomy mood, and loss of interest lead to limited social interactions, and this therefore may decrease rather than increase aggression in adolescents (Dutton & Karakanta, 2013). Furthermore, attributional biases of aggressive and depressed individuals seem contradictory. Depressed individuals attribute negative events to internal causes, whereas aggressive individuals make other people responsible for their situation. However, the attribution of negative events is less stable in adolescents compared to adults, as the development of the personality is still ongoing. Feelings of irritability and angry rumination may elevate the risk for impulsive aggression after frustration in adolescents (Roland, 2002; Weiss & Catron, 1994). However, unlike other mental disorders the presence of a major depression was not specifically related to serious violent crimes (e.g., crimes with weapons) in detained adolescents (Elkington et al., 2015). Nevertheless, depression and violence may share common risk factors (e.g., genetics, personality, and insecure attachment to primary caregivers; Dutton & Karakanta, 2013).

Adults with an outpatient diagnosis of depression were found to have increased odds of being convicted for violent offenses in the following three years, compared to matched controls from the community, as well as compared to unaffected siblings (Fazel et al., 2015). In contrast, studies with children and adolescents did not support the finding that depression is a risk factor to predict later violent offenses when comorbid drug disorders were controlled for (e.g., Aebi et al., 2014; Copeland et al., 2007). Some findings suggest an indirect link between depression and later violent behaviors (Dutton & Karakanta, 2013). For example, depressed youth show elevated levels of alcohol and drug consumption, more social isolation, and a lack of social support, which contribute to the emergence of future violent behaviors.

Treatment of depression aims to induce remission of symptoms and achieve a full return to the baseline level of functioning. Medication should not be the first choice for treating depression in youth because of its limited efficacy and tolerability in this subgroup (Cipriani et al., 2016). Family therapy, cognitive behavioral therapy (CBT), and inter-personnel therapies are most often provided to adolescents with depressive disorders (Nolen-Hoeksema & Hilt, 2009) and should include psychoeducation, activity training, problem solving training, and cognitive restructuring (e.g., change of attribution biases, enhancing of mindfulness for positive events). CBT and inter-personnel therapy were found to reduce symptoms of depression (Nolen-Hoeksema & Hilt, 2009). Skills training and problem solving may not only reduce feelings of sadness and lack of energy, but also increase interpersonal skills and reduce social conflicts that may otherwise trigger aggressive behaviors.

Bipolar Disorders

Adolescents with bipolar disorders show periods of depression and periods of mania (or hypomania) with an elevated, expansive, or irritable mood. Periods of mania include symptoms of inflated self-esteem and grandiosity, a decreased need for sleep, garrulity, racing thoughts, distractibility, increased psychomotor agitation, and excessive involvement in activities. A prevalence rate of bipolar disorders was estimated at 2.5% in US adolescents (Merikangas & He, 2014). Among detained US-adolescent offenders quite similar rates of 2.0% in males and 1.2% in females for mania periods were reported (Teplin, Abram, McClelland, Dulcan, & Mericle, 2002).

Violent behaviors and criminal acts are typically related to the manic phases of bipolar disorder (Quanbeck et al., 2005). These phases are often associated with megalomaniac ideas and feelings of omnipotence that could lead to public order offenses or police arrests (Christopher, McCabe, & Fisher, 2012). Manic symptoms of bipolar disorder may also present a risk of judicial complication, as behavioral and sexual disinhibition may lead to problematic sexual behaviors. However, most studies on bipolar disorders and violence perpetration were based on adult samples. One study among juvenile detainees found the presence of mania or hypomania to be associated with contemporaneous violent crimes (before detention), but the presence of bipolar disorder did not predict later violent crimes after release from detention (Elkington et al., 2015). The treatment of bipolar disorders largely relies on various forms of medication (e.g., mood stabilizers, antidepressants) in the acute phase of the disorder (Kowatch et al., 2005). Additional family-based therapy may decrease the number and duration of manic phases in the subsequent years (Miklowitz et al., 2014).

Disruptive Mood Dysregulation Disorders

Recently introduced in the DSM-5, children and adolescents with persistent forms of irritability can be diagnosed with disruptive mood dysregulation disorder (DMDD). Symptoms of DMDD include severe recurrent temper outbursts that manifest verbally or physically (aggression toward people or property) several times a week (an average of three or more times) in different settings (home, school, or peers), and starts before age 10. Prevalence rates of DMDD were 0.8% to 1.1% among 9–17-years-olds in US community samples and DMDD was highly comorbid with depressive disorders (OR [odds ratio] 16.3–23.5), oppositional defiant disorder (ODD; OR 61.0–103.0) and conduct disorder (CD: OR 1.4–11.9) in late childhood and adolescence (Copeland, Angold, Costello, & Egger, 2013). No study has yet examined DMDD in forensic samples of adolescents. Youth with DMDD were found to be different from youth with other bipolar disorders (Leibenluft, 2011) and typically presented with impulsive and reactive aggressions. Adolescents with DMDD had higher rates of contact with police in young adulthood than youths without DMDD (Copeland, Shanahan, Egger, Angold, & Costello, 2014). Currently there are no established guidelines or thorough reviews summarizing the treatment of DMDD. Treatment options of both aggression and chronic irritability include behavior therapy, parenting training, and medication.

Anxiety Disorders and Obsessive-Compulsive Disorders

Anxiety disorders and obsessive-compulsive disorders are frequent disorders in youth, and often begin in childhood or adolescence. Anxiety disorders encompass various specific disorders including separation anxiety disorder (distress and extensive anxiety from separation to attachment figures), selective mutism (lack of speech in social situations), specific phobia (anxiety in the presence of a particular situation or object; e.g., animals, blood, etc.), social anxiety disorder (intensive fear of social situations), panic disorder (abrupt surge of intense fear), agoraphobia (fear in situations of public transport, open/closed rooms, being in a crowd), and generalized anxiety disorders.

Obsessive-compulsive disorders have previously been considered as a subtype of anxiety disorders, but are now addressed in a separate chapter of DSM-5. They include a symptom pattern of repetitive and persistent thoughts (e.g., contamination), images (violent scenes), or urges (e.g., to stab someone), and/or repetitive compulsive behaviors (e.g., to controlling behaviors, washing hands, etc.). In children and adolescents the prevalence rate of anxiety disorders including obsessive-compulsive disorders is 6.5% (Polanczyk et al., 2015). In samples of detained adolescents 16.5% of youth were found to have an anxiety disorder or an obsessive-compulsive disorder (Colins et al., 2010).

Although aggression and anxiety may co-occur in children and adolescents, and may even affect each other over time (Bubier & Drabick, 2009), only few studies have addressed how anxiety disorders may increase the risk for violent behaviors. Findings from community samples studies failed to find a relationship between adolescent anxiety and adult crime when controlling for externalizing disorders (Sourander et al., 2006). However, some studies reported that anxiety disorders increase the risk for violent behaviors when comorbid conduct problems or substance use problem exist (Copeland et al., 2007; Hoeve, McReynolds, & Wasserman, 2014).

In terms of intervention, cognitive behavioral therapy (CBT) is highly effective in treating anxiety disorders (James, James, Cowdrey, Soler, & Choke, 2015) and obsessive-compulsive disorders (Franklin et al., 2015) in adolescents. Behavioral therapy involves relaxation and guided confrontation with fearful stimuli to reduce symptoms of anxiety (Ollendick & Seligman, 2006; Silverman, Pina, & Viswesvaran, 2008). However, so far no study has addressed how treatment of anxiety disorders is related to co-existing aggression problems in children and adolescents.

Posttraumatic Stress Disorder

Posttraumatic Stress disorder (PTSD) has been conceptualized as a disorder that occurs after direct or indirect exposure to threatening death, serious injury or sexual violence with symptoms of intrusion (symptom cluster B), persistence avoidance of trauma-related stimuli (symptom cluster C), negative alternations in cognitions and mood (symptom cluster D), and marked alternations in arousal and reactivity (symptom cluster E). Prevalence rates for PTSD of 3.7–6.3% of community adolescents (Kilpatrick et al., 2003) and of 9.6% for PTSD (Colins et al., 2010) have been reported. PTSD and symptom domains were found to partly mediate the relation between trauma exposure and violent offending (Aebi, Mohler-Kuo, et al., 2016; Ruchkin, Henrich, Jones, Vermeiren, & Schwab-Stone, 2007). The risk of violent behaviors may not only relate to PTSD as a diagnostic entity, but may also depend on individual symptom profiles: symptoms of avoidance and anxiety decrease the risk of violence, whereas symptoms of dysphoric arousal increase the risk of violence (Aebi, Mohler-Kuo, et al., 2016; Allwood & Bell, 2008).

Furthermore, emotional numbing and acquired callousness were PTSD-related symptoms (Allwood, Bell, & Horan, 2011; Kerig, Bennett, Thompson, & Becker, 2012). Emotional numbing represents a state when an individual is not emotionally present and operates merely at an intellectual level, displaying no emotional connection with others. The inability to display empathy increases the probability of violence by lowering their threshold to committing violent behaviors. Finally, youth exposed to violence may acquire and maintain dysfunctional aggressive schemata and may have difficulties in social bonding or in building trusting relationships with other people (Dodge, Bates, & Pettit, 1990).

Longitudinal studies have consistently revealed that maltreated and traumatized youth have an increased risk of becoming violent offenders (Maas, Fleming, Herrenkohl, & Catalano, 2010; Wilson, Stover, & Berkowitz, 2009). According to a study by Maxfield and Widom (1996) based on 900 children, those who had been physically abused or neglected before the age of 11 were twice as likely to be arrested for juvenile violence than those who had not been exposed to abuse and neglect. However, it is important to recognize that only a small minority of maltreated and abused adolescents will display delinquent and violent behaviors in their later lives, whereas the majority do not show serious violent behaviors.

Various effective treatment approaches for PTSD have been developed, such as trauma-focused cognitive behavioral therapy with children and adolescents and eye movement desensitization and reprocessing therapy (EMDR) (Smith et al., 2013). Both these treatments focus on a cognitive reorganization of the traumatic memory using structured and psychologically guided exposure techniques. Further interventions to improve emotion regulation skills may be useful (e.g., Trauma Affect Regulation: Guide for Education and Therapy; TARGET; Ford, Elhai, Connor, & Frueh, 2010). More recently, more specific interventions for juvenile violent offenders with trauma history have been introduced that not only reduce trauma-related symptoms, but have also been shown to be promising in reducing violent behaviors. For example, multisystemic therapy (Swenson, Schaeffer, Henggeler, Faldowski, & Mayhew, 2010) or narrative exposure therapy for forensic offender rehabilitation (Hecker, Hermenau, Crombach, & Elbert, 2015) were found to be effective in the prevention of violent behaviors.

Attention-Deficit-Hyperactivity Disorder

Attention-deficit-hyperactivity disorder (ADHD) is a common neurodevelopmental disorder characterized by inattention or hyperactivity-impulsivity or both, with a worldwide prevalence of 5.3% (Polanczyk, de Lima, Horta, Biederman, & Rohde, 2007). In samples of adolescent detainees, the prevalence of ADHD amounts to 13.5% (Colins et al., 2010). Only a small proportion of clinic-referred children present with pure ADHD, whereas the majority show a pattern of multiple problems. Amongst the latter, disruptive behaviors including violent and aggressive behaviors leading to the diagnosis of comorbid conduct disorder (CD) represent one of the most frequent associations (Bauermeister et al., 2007; Elia et al., 2009; Freitag et al., 2012; Ghanizadeh, 2009; Jensen, Martin, & Cantwell, 1997; Kadesjo &

Gillberg, 2001; Kraut et al., 2013; Larson, Russ, Kahn, & Halfon, 2011; Levy, Hay, Bennett, & McStephen, 2005; Wichstrom et al., 2012). In a recent large register-based study in Denmark that identified the full range of mental disorders comorbid to ADHD in youth aged 4 to 17 over the period from 1995 to 2020, the comorbidity rate for CD amounted to 16.5% of all individuals diagnosed with ADHD (C. M. Jensen & Steinhausen, 2015). Given the size, the time frame, and the representativeness of the sample, this figure may be the best current account available of the coexistence of the two disorders.

In terms of its etiology, ADHD arises from several genetic and environmental risk factors that each have a small individual effect and act together to increase susceptibility, with no single risk factor being necessary or sufficient to cause ADHD (Faraone et al., 2015). A multitude of risk factors on the individual, family, and societal levels also contribute to the development of CD, as outlined in several chapters of the present handbook. For the understanding of the association of ADHD and CD, the finding of a recent genetic study may be of specific interest and pave the way for further research. It suggested that a polygenic score considering common genetic variants en masse was significantly higher in ADHD case subjects with conduct disorder relative to ADHD case subjects without conduct disorder. The ADHD polygenic score showed significant association with comorbid conduct disorder symptoms, and the relationship was explained by the aggression items. According to these findings, aggression in ADHD indexes both genetic and clinical severity (Hamshere et al., 2013).

Among the most serious consequences of ADHD there is a disproportionately high number of individuals with ADHD involved with the Criminal Justice System. Studies among offenders in the UK have indicated that around 45% of youths and 24% of male adults screen positive for a childhood history of ADHD, 14% of whom have persisting symptoms in adulthood. Those with persisting symptoms have a significantly younger onset of offending and a higher rate of recidivism. ADHD was the most powerful predictor of violent offending, even above substance misuse. Those with ADHD accounted for eight times more institutional aggressive behavioral disturbances (critical incidents) than other non-ADHD prisoners (Young & Thome, 2011).

A recent meta-analysis of the world literature (Mohr-Jensen & Steinhausen, 2016) found that ADHD was significantly associated with adolescent and adulthood arrests, convictions, and incarcerations. Individuals with ADHD had a younger age at onset of antisocial involvement and an increased risk of criminal recidivism. Early antisocial behavior problems, childhood maltreatment, sex, and IQ were identified as potentially relevant predictors for antisocial outcomes. The most frequently committed criminal offenses were theft, assault, and drug- and weapon-related crimes. Based on qualitative analyses it was concluded that comorbid antisocial disorders represent the most frequently identified predictor of long-term crime outcomes. However, it remains unclear as to how much antisocial behavior unfolds an independent effect on crime outcomes, and as to how much they act in combination or interaction with other risk factors, e.g., with low SES, which is frequently associated with CD. Furthermore, it needs to be emphasized that while antisocial behavior problems in general do carry some risk, not all antisocial symptoms or diagnoses will lead to adult delinquency, and some childhood symptoms may be more specific than other symptoms. The findings of this meta-analysis also support the conclusion that despite the predictive effect of antisocial behaviors childhood ADHD carries a risk by itself.

The findings of this meta-analysis were confirmed in a recent large nationwide register study in Denmark showing that children and adolescents with ADHD had a significantly increased risk of conviction compared to a matched control group of individuals without ADHD. The same study, which was based on a large sample of clinic-referred subjects, showed that comorbid ODD/CD before the age of 15 was a significant predictor of later conviction. Anti-social involvement of parents, placements outside the home, low family income, and coming from broken or single-parent households proved to be equally strong predictors for later conviction, indicating that multiple risk factors besides the disruptive behavior of the child and adolescent were responsible for the delinquent outcome (Mohr-Jensen & Steinhausen, 2016).

Clearly, coexistent aggressive and antisocial behaviors represent a major challenge to effective intervention. Pharmacological treatments and behavioral interventions are the main avenues of clinical management of ADHD. A recent Canadian guideline was based on a systematic review of medications studied in placebo-controlled trials for treating disruptive and aggressive behavior in children and adolescents with ADHD, ODD, or CD (Gorman et al., 2015). The consensus group of authors found that for children and adolescents with disruptive or aggressive behavior associated with ADHD, psychostimulants were most strongly recommended for use, while the drugs atomoxetine, clonidine, and guanfacine received only a conditional recommendation for use. Furthermore, the authors concluded that risperidone has the most evidence for use for patients who do poorly with other ADHD medications. Risperidone also has the most evidence for treating disruptive or aggressive behavior in the absence of ADHD. However, given risperidone's major adverse effects, it received only a conditional recommendation in favor of use in the guidelines.

Behavioral interventions for children and adolescents with ADHD rest on programs that had originally been developed for treating conduct problems. Their rationale is that challenging childhood behavior develops due to coercive interactional cycles that co-reinforce noncompliant and oppositional behaviors in the child, and negative and inappropriate responses from the parent and, in some cases, also teachers and other caregivers (Granic & Patterson, 2006). The main principle of the intervention is to teach behavior modification techniques so that appropriate behaviors are reinforced and inappropriate child behaviors are discouraged, and effective and enjoyable adult–child interactions are enhanced (Kazdin, 1997). As a result, negative interaction cycles should be transformed into more positive ones. A recent meta-analysis of randomized controlled trials across multiple outcome domains of these behavioral interventions in ADHD (Daley et al., 2014) found that for assessments made by individuals closest to the treatment setting (usually unblinded), there were significant improvements in parenting quality, parenting self-concept, and child ADHD, conduct problems, social skills, and academic performance. With blinded assessments, significant effects persisted for parenting and conduct problems. Thus, in contrast to the lack of blinded evidence of ADHD symptom decrease, behavioral interventions have positive effects, particularly on parenting and decrease childhood conduct problems.

Disruptive Behavior Disorders

Oppositional Defiant Disorders

Oppositional defiant disorder (ODD) encompasses a persistent pattern of irritable, defiant, and rebellious behaviors against parents or other authority figures. As ODD was originally designed as a diagnosis for younger children, and was seen as a precursor of the more severe conduct disorder (CD), ICD-10 did not allow ODD and CD to be diagnosed together. More recent research has confirmed that ODD is a distinct disorder that may persist into adolescence independent of CD (Maughan, Rowe, Messer, Goodman, & Meltzer, 2004) and leads to specific functional impairments (Burke, Rowe, & Boylan, 2014). In the current version of the DSM-5, ODD can be diagnosed independently of CD in children, adolescents, and adults. A worldwide prevalence rate of 3.6% for ODD in children and adolescents has been established (Polanczyk et al., 2015). In detained adolescent offenders, the prevalence rate of ODD amounted to 19.8% (Colins et al., 2010). Research findings confirmed two related symptom dimensions of ODD among community and forensic youth (e.g., Aebi, Barra, et al., 2016; Burke, 2012), namely, a behavioral dimension with defiant and spiteful/vindictive behaviors, and an affective dimension with irritable mood symptoms.

The latter dimension may largely overlap with symptoms of disruptive mood dysregulation disorder (see above).

Symptoms of ODD such as temper tantrums and irritability include milder forms of violent behaviors against other people and property damage that are associated with low levels of frustration and an impaired behavioral control. These forms of aggressions are more frequent in younger children and decrease during development from childhood to adolescence (Tremblay, 2012). However, within a small group these problems persist into adolescence (Maughan et al., 2004). Few studies have analyzed ODD and its relation to serious violence and further criminal behaviors in older adolescents. In community samples of children and adolescents, the behavioral dimension of ODD and in particular symptoms of spiteful and vindictive behaviors are found to predict later violence (Aebi, Plattner, Winkler Metzke, Bessler, & Steinhausen, 2013; Kolko & Pardini, 2010). Further studies confirmed the relevance of ODD and irritable behaviors in adolescent detainees for predicting criminal violent recidivism (Aebi, Barra, et al., 2016; Plattner et al., 2012).

Treatment of ODD usually consists of parent management training to break up negative parent-child interactions (see ADHD treatment above). Additionally, youth may profit from general social skills training, as well as anger management and relaxation techniques. Youth with spiteful and vindictive behaviors may show limited treatment responses to social skills and parent training (Kolko & Pardini, 2010).

Conduct Disorder

Conduct disorder (CD) is defined as repetitive and persistent patterns of behavior that seriously violate the right of others or violate age-appropriate social norms and rules. Symptoms of CD fall into four main categories: (1) physical aggression towards people and animals, (2) destruction of property, (3) deceitfulness or theft, and (4) serious violations of rules. Many symptoms of CD relate to criminal behaviors that are punishable by law. Other symptoms, such as "lying to obtain goods and/or to avoid obligations" or "staying out late despite parental prohibitions," relate to rule-braking behaviors without juridical consequences. In the community, 2.1% of children and adolescents meet the criteria for CD (Polanczyk et al., 2015). In adolescent detainees, the presence of CD goes up to 46.4% (Colins et al., 2010). One might expect that all youth in the criminal system will meet the criteria for CD, but some youth only have committed isolated delinquent acts and do not show a persistent pattern of delinquency. In fact, the criminal behaviors of some youth are limited to their unfavorable interactions within (delinquent) peer groups.

Findings from longitudinal studies on criminal behaviors in youth suggest the existence of two different *subgroups according to the onset and chronicity of conduct problems* (Moffitt, 1993). Besides an early starter group with a childhood onset and severe course of delinquent behaviors, adolescents demonstrate less severe symptomatology and less functional impairments, but a higher association to delinquent peers (Moffitt, 1993; Moffitt, Caspi, Harrington, & Milne, 2002). These two types have different etiologies (see chapter by Moffitt) and have been reflected both in the DSM-5 and the ICD-10 classification. Another subtyping of CD according to the presence of "limited prosocial emotions" was introduced in DSM-5. Persons who meet criteria for CD and additionally show two of the following symptoms during the past 12 months in multiple settings and relationships can be labeled with a specifier of limited prosocial emotions: (1) a lack of remorse or guilt, (2) callousness/a lack of empathy, (3) shallow or deficient affect, and (4) a lack of concern about performance.

In previous studies these symptoms have been labeled as the affective dimensions of psychopathy or as *callous-unemotional traits* (CU traits). Findings from these studies show that youth who met criteria for CD and CU traits showed a more stable course and more serious antisocial behaviors than those with CD only (Frick, Ray, Thornton, & Kahn, 2014). Furthermore, a CD and CU group displayed rather proactive and instrumental forms of aggression compared to other youth with severe conduct problems (Frick et al., 2014). In addition, youth with CD and CU traits had a number of specific neurocognitive dysfunctions in affect perception and processing, lowered threat sensitivity, and deficient social decision making and related abnormalities in correlated brain areas (Blair et al., 2015). For example, Viding et al. (2012) reported that amygdala responses to fearful faces were weaker in boys who showed CD and elevated CU traits compared to other boys with CD only and controls. Regarding treatment, adolescents with CD and CU traits were found to show limited responses (Frick et al., 2014).

There is a strong clinical consensus that conduct disorder belongs to a group of the most difficult to treat disorders, although various interventions have been suggested that combine behavior therapy, cognitive therapy, and family-based interventions. One of the most promising approaches is multisystemic therapy (MST) that conceptualizes the adolescent's problem behavior as being linked with the various aspects of the multiple systems in which the adolescent is embedded. MST interventions were designed to promote disengagement from deviant peers, build stronger bonds to the family and school, enhance family skills, such as monitoring and discipline, and develop greater social and academic competence in the adolescent (Henggeler & Schaeffer, 2016). Although some studies found MST to be effective in reducing CD symptoms and future criminal behaviors even in the long run, treatment effects differed across countries and settings and MST was more effective with younger adolescents below age 15 than older youth (van der Stouwe, Asscher, Stams, Dekovic, & van der Laan, 2014).

In many countries, adolescents with serious and persistent antisocial behaviors are sent to correctional facilities and do not receive psychiatric treatment. Given the different subtypes of youth with CD, more specific treatment approaches have to be developed. Adolescents without CU traits may profit from more specific interventions that may reduce responses to affective stimuli and deficits in cognitive information processing. In contrast, interventions with adolescents who show CD and CU traits should provide techniques to enhance emotional activation and eye contact in social interactions (Blair et al., 2015; Dadds et al., 2014).

Conclusion

This overview has shown that various mental disorders may contribute to aggression and violence and that there is no single psychiatric disorder that explains why a juvenile begins to perpetrate violence. In fact, many of the juveniles who commit serious offenses have experienced several adversities in childhood, and meet criteria for multiple psychiatric disorders simultaneously. Comorbidity of mental disorders is a highly relevant predictor of violent outcomes in adulthood, with the most impaired youth having the highest risk for persistent criminal behaviors.

The psychiatric and mental health perspective on aggression and violence provides important clues to the understanding of these widespread individual and societal problems. With its roots both in medicine and various psychosocial disciplines, child and adolescent psychiatry may provide a theoretical framework that focuses on the causes in terms of the etiology of aggressive behaviors by relating it to psychopathologies frequently seen in patients referred for mental health services. Furthermore, the differentiated nosology of developmental psychopathology shows that the various paths of aggression in association with different disorder entities require both highly specific assessment and intervention strategies by mental health professionals.

Thus, there is ample room for the inclusion of these professionals into the multidisciplinary approach of helping aggressive youth in the task of overcoming their problematic behaviors. These efforts may start early when first signs of aggressive behavior become apparent so that the development of more serious life trajectories may be prevented. But in the more advanced delinquent careers there is still the important task for forensic adolescent psychiatry of consulting with the criminal justice system so that the needs of both the delinquent adolescent and society are well covered.

References

Aebi, M., Barra, S., Bessler, C., Steinhausen, H. C., Walitza, S., & Plattner, B. (2016). Oppositional defiant disorder dimensions and subtypes among detained male adolescent offenders. *Journal of Child Psychology and Psychiatry*, 57, 729–736.

Aebi, M., Giger, J., Plattner, B., Metzke, C. W., & Steinhausen, H. C. (2014). Problem coping skills, psychosocial adversities and mental health problems in children and adolescents as predictors of criminal outcomes in young adulthood. *European Child Adolescent Psychiatry*, 23, 283–293.

Aebi, M., Mohler-Kuo, M., Barra, S., Schnyder, U., Maier, T., & Landolt, M. A. (2016). Posttraumatic stress and youth violence perpetration: A population-based cross-sectional study. *European Psychiatry*.

Aebi, M., Plattner, B., Winkler Metzke, C., Bessler, C., & Steinhausen, H. C. (2013). Parent-and self-reported dimensions of oppositionality in youth: Construct validity, comorbidity and criminal outcomes in adulthood. *Journal of Child Psychology and Psychiatry*, 54, 941–949.

Allwood, M. A. & Bell, D. J. (2008). A preliminary examination of emotional and cognitive mediators in the relations between violence exposure and violent behaviors in youth. *Journal of Community Psychology*, 36, 989–1007.

Allwood, M. A., Bell, D. J., & Horan, J. (2011). Posttrauma numbing of fear, detachment, and arousal predict delinquent behaviors in early adolescence. *Journal of Clinical Child Adolescent Psychology*, 40, 659–667.

American Psychiatric Association. (2013). *Diagnostic and statistical manual of mental disorders* (5th ed.). Arlington, VA: APA.

Arseneault, L., Moffitt, T. E., Caspi, A., Taylor, P. J., & Silva, P. A. (2000). Mental disorders and violence in a total birth cohort: results from the Dunedin Study. *Archives of General Psychiatry*, 57, 979–986.

Avenevoli, S., Swendsen, J., He, J. P., Burstein, M., & Merikangas, K. R. (2015). Major depression in the national comorbidity survey-adolescent supplement: prevalence, correlates, and treatment. *Journal of the American Academy of Child Adolescent Psychiatry*, 54, 37–44, e32.

Baer, P. E., Garmezy, L. B., McLaughlin, R. J., Pokorny, A. D., & Wernick, M. J. (1987). Stress, coping, family conflict, and adolescent alcohol use. *Journal of Behavioral Medicine*, 10, 449–466.

Bauermeister, J. J., Shrout, P. E., Ramirez, R., Bravo, M., Alegria, M., Martinez-Taboas, A., ... & Canino, G. (2007). ADHD correlates, comorbidity, and impairment in community and treated samples of children and adolescents. *Journal of Abnormal Child Psychology*, 35, 883–898.

Benedek, E. P., Ash, P., & Scott, C. L. (2010). *Principles and Practice of Child and Adolescent Forensic Mental Health*. Arlington, VA: American Psychiatric Publishing.

Blair, R. J., Leibenluft, E., & Pine, D. S. (2015). Conduct disorder and callous-unemotional traits in youth. *New England Journal of Medicine*, 372, 784.

Brodie, M. J., Besag, F., Ettinger, A. B., Mula, M., Gobbi, G., Comai, S., ... & Steinhoff, B. J. (2016). Epilepsy, Antiepileptic Drugs, and Aggression: An Evidence-Based Review. *Pharmacology Review*, 68, 563–602.

Brook, J. S., Zhang, C., & Brook, D. W. (2011). Antisocial behavior at age 37: Developmental trajectories of marijuana use extending from adolescence to adulthood. *American Journal of Addiction*, 20, 509–515.

Bubier, J. L. & Drabick, D. A. (2009). Co-occurring anxiety and disruptive behavior disorders: the roles of anxious symptoms, reactive aggression, and shared risk processes. *Clinical Psychology Review*, 29, 658–669.

Bukstein, O. G. (2006). Substance use disorders. In C. Gillberg, R. Harrington, & H.-C. Steinhausen (Eds), *A clinician's handbook of child and adolescent psychiatry*. Cambridge: Cambridge University Press

Burke, J. D. (2012). An affective dimension within oppositional defiant disorder symptoms among boys: personality and psychopathology outcomes into early adulthood. *Journal of Child Psychology and Psychiatry,* 53, 1176–1183.

Burke, J. D., Rowe, R., & Boylan, K. (2014). Functional outcomes of child and adolescent oppositional defiant disorder symptoms in young adult men. *Journal of Child Psychology and Psychiatry,* 55, 264–272.

Cassidy, J. D., Carroll, L. J., Peloso, P. M., Borg, J., von Holst, H., Holm, L., ... & Corondo, V. G. (2004). Incidence, risk factors and prevention of mild traumatic brain injury: results of the WHO Collaborating Centre Task Force on Mild Traumatic Brain Injury. *Journal of Rehabilative Medicine,* Suppl. 43: 28–60.

Christopher, P. P., McCabe, P. J., & Fisher, W. H. (2012). Prevalence of involvement in the criminal justice system during severe mania and associated symptomatology. *Psychiatric Services,* 63, 33–39.

Cipriani, A., Zhou, X., Del Giovane, C., Hetrick, S. E., Qin, B., Whittington, C., ... & Xie, P. (2016). Comparative efficacy and tolerability of antidepressants for major depressive disorder in children and adolescents: a network meta-analysis. *Lancet,* 388, 881-890.

Cole, W. R., Gerring, J. P., Gray, R. M., Vasa, R. A., Salorio, C. F., Grados, M., ... & Slomine, B. S. (2008). Prevalence of aggressive behaviour after severe paediatric traumatic brain injury. *Brain Injury,* 22, 932–939.

Colins, O. F., Vermeiren, R. R., Noom, M., & Broekaert, E. (2013). Psychotic-like symptoms as a risk factor of violent recidivism in detained male adolescents. *Journal of Nervous and Mental Disease,* 201, 478–483.

Colins, O. F., Vermeiren, R. R., Vreugdenhil, C., Schuyten, G., Broekaert, E., & Krabbendam, A. (2009). Are psychotic experiences among detained juvenile offenders explained by trauma and substance use? *Drug Alcohol Dependence,* 100, 39–46.

Colins, O. F., Vermeiren, R. R., Vreugdenhil, C., van den Brink, W., Doreleijers, T., & Broekaert, E. (2010). Psychiatric disorders in detained male adolescents: a systematic literature review. *Canadian Journal of Psychiatry,* 55, 255–263.

Copeland, W. E., Angold, A., Costello, E. J., & Egger, H. (2013). Prevalence, comorbidity, and correlates of DSM-5 proposed disruptive mood dysregulation disorder. *American Journal of Psychiatry,* 170, 173–179.

Copeland, W. E., Miller-Johnson, S., Keeler, G., Angold, A., & Costello, E. J. (2007). Childhood psychiatric disorders and young adult crime: a prospective, population-based study. *American Journal of Psychiatry,* 164, 1668–1675.

Copeland, W. E., Shanahan, L., Egger, H., Angold, A., & Costello, E. J. (2014). Adult diagnostic and functional outcomes of DSM-5 disruptive mood dysregulation disorder. *American Journal of Psychiatry,* 171, 668–674.

Dadds, M. R., Allen, J. L., McGregor, K., Woolgar, M., Viding, E., & Scott, S. (2014). Callous-unemotional traits in children and mechanisms of impaired eye contact during expressions of love: a treatment target? *Journal of Child Psychology and Psychiatry,* 55, 771–780.

Daley, D., van der Oord, S., Ferrin, M., Danckaerts, M., Doepfner, M., Cortese, S., ... & European, A. G. G. (2014). Behavioral interventions in attention-deficit/hyperactivity disorder: a meta-analysis of randomized controlled trials across multiple outcome domains. *Journal of the American Academy of Child Adolescent Psychiatry,* 53, 835–847, 847, e831–835.

Davies, S., Heyman, I., & Goodman, R. (2003). A population survey of mental health problems in children with epilepsy. *Developmental Medicine Child Neurology,* 45, 292–295.

Dodge, K. A., Bates, J. E., & Pettit, G. S. (1990). Mechanisms in the cycle of violence. *Science,* 250, 1678–1683.

Dooley, J. J., Anderson, V., Hemphill, S. A., & Ohan, J. (2008). Aggression after paediatric traumatic brain injury: a theoretical approach. *Brain Injury,* 22, 836–846.

Dutton, G. D. & Karakanta, C. (2013). Depression as a risk marker for aggression: A critical review. *Aggression and Violent Behavior*, 18, 310–319.

Elia, J., Arcos-Burgos, M., Bolton, K. L., Ambrosini, P. J., Berrettini, W., & Muenke, M. (2009). ADHD latent class clusters: DSM-IV subtypes and comorbidity. *Psychiatry Research*, 170, 192–198.

Elkington, K. S., Teplin, L. A., Abram, K. M., Jakubowski, J. A., Dulcan, M. K., & Welty, L. J. (2015). Psychiatric disorders and violence: a study of delinquent youth after detention. *Journal of the American Academy of Child and Adolescent Psychiatry*, 54, 302–312, e305.

Eschmann, S., Zimprich, D., Winkler Metzke, C., & Steinhausen, H. C. (2011). A developmental trajectory model of problematic substance use and psychosocial correlates from late adolescence to young adulthood. *Journal of Substance Use*, 16, 295–312.

Faraone, S. V., Asherson, P., Banaschewski, T., Biederman, J., Buitelaar, J. K., Ramos-Quiroga, J. A., ... & Franke, B. (2015). Attention-deficit/hyperactivity disorder. *Nature Reviews Disease Primers*, 1, 15020.

Fast, D. K. & Conry, J. (2009). Fetal alcohol spectrum disorders and the criminal justice system. *Developmental Disability Research Reviews*, 15, 250–257.

Fazel, S., Gulati, G., Linsell, L., Geddes, J. R., & Grann, M. (2009). Schizophrenia and violence: systematic review and meta-analysis. *PLoS Medicine*, 6, e1000120.

Fazel, S., Lichtenstein, P., Grann, M., & Langstrom, N. (2011). Risk of violent crime in individuals with epilepsy and traumatic brain injury: a 35-year Swedish population study. *PLoS Medicine*, 8, e1001150.

Fazel, S., Wolf, A., Chang, Z., Larsson, H., Goodwin, G. M., & Lichtenstein, P. (2015). Depression and violence: a Swedish population study. *Lancet Psychiatry*, 2, 224–232.

Fazel, S., Zetterqvist, J., Larsson, H., Langstrom, N., & Lichtenstein, P. (2014). Antipsychotics, mood stabilisers, and risk of violent crime. *Lancet*, 384, 1206–1214.

Ford, J. D., Elhai, J. D., Connor, D. F., & Frueh, B. C. (2010). Poly-victimization and risk of posttraumatic, depressive, and substance use disorders and involvement in delinquency in a national sample of adolescents. *Journal of Adolescent Health*, 46, 545–552.

Franklin, M. E., Kratz, H. E., Freeman, J. B., Ivarsson, T., Heyman, I., Sookman, D., ... & Accreditation Task Force of The Canadian Institute for Obsessive Compulsive, D. (2015). Cognitive-behavioral therapy for pediatric obsessive-compulsive disorder: Empirical review and clinical recommendations. *Psychiatry Research*, 227, 78–92.

Freitag, C. M., Hanig, S., Schneider, A., Seitz, C., Palmason, H., Retz, W., & Meyer, J. (2012). Biological and psychosocial environmental risk factors influence symptom severity and psychiatric comorbidity in children with ADHD. *Journal of Neural Transmission*, 119, 81–94.

Frick, P. J., Ray, J. V., Thornton, L. C., & Kahn, R. E. (2014). Can callous-unemotional traits enhance the understanding, diagnosis, and treatment of serious conduct problems in children and adolescents? A comprehensive review. *Psychological Bulletin*, 140, 1–57.

Ghanizadeh, A. (2009). Psychiatric comorbidity differences in clinic-referred children and adolescents with ADHD according to the subtypes and gender. *Journal of Child Neurology*, 24, 679–684.

Gorman, D. A., Gardner, D. M., Murphy, A. L., Feldman, M., Belanger, S. A., Steele, M. M., ... & Pringsheim, T. (2015). Canadian guidelines on pharmacotherapy for disruptive and aggressive behaviour in children and adolescents with attention-deficit hyperactivity disorder, oppositional defiant disorder, or conduct disorder. *Canadian Journal of Psychiatry*, 60, 62–76.

Granic, I. & Patterson, G. R. (2006). Toward a comprehensive model of antisocial development: a dynamic systems approach. *Psychological Review*, 113, 101–131.

Hamshere, M. L., Langley, K., Martin, J., Agha, S. S., Stergiakouli, E., Anney, R. J.,

... & Thapar, A. (2013). High loading of polygenic risk for ADHD in children with comorbid aggression. *American Journal of Psychiatry*, 170, 909–916.

Hecker, T., Hermenau, K., Crombach, A., & Elbert, T. (2015). Treating traumatized offenders and veterans by means of narrative exposure therapy. *Frontiers in Psychiatry*, 6, 80.

Henggeler, S. W. & Schaeffer, C. M. (2016). Multisystemic therapy(R): Clinical overview, outcomes, and implementation research. *Family Process*, 55(3), 514–528.

Hodgins, S., Larm, P., Molero-Samuleson, Y., Tengstrom, A., & Larsson, A. (2009). Multiple adverse outcomes over 30 years following adolescent substance misuse treatment. *Acta Psychiatry Scandanvica*, 119, 484–493.

Hoeve, M., McReynolds, L. S., & Wasserman, G. A. (2014). Service referral for juvenile justice youths: associations with psychiatric disorder and recidivism. *Administration and Policy in Mental Health and Mental Health Services Research*, 41, 379–389.

James, A. C., James, G., Cowdrey, F. A., Soler, A., & Choke, A. (2015). Cognitive behavioural therapy for anxiety disorders in children and adolescents. *Cochrane Database Systematic Reviews*, CD004690.

Jensen, C. M. & Steinhausen, H. C. (2015). Comorbid mental disorders in children and adolescents with attention-deficit-hyperactivity disorder in a large nationwide study. *ADHD*, 7, 27–38.

Jensen, P. S., Martin, D., & Cantwell, D. P. (1997). Comorbidity in ADHD: implications for research, practice, and DSM-V. *Journal of the American Academy Child Adolescent Psychiatry*, 36, 1065–1079.

Jones, C., Hacker, D., Cormac, I., Meaden, A., & Irving, C. B. (2012). Cognitive behavior therapy versus other psychosocial treatments for schizophrenia. *Schizophrenia Bulletin*, 38, 908–910.

Kadesjo, B. & Gillberg, C. (2001). The comorbidity of ADHD in the general population of Swedish school-age children. *Journal of Child Psychology and Psychiatry*, 42, 487–492.

Kandel, D. B. (1982). Epidemiological and psychosocial perspectives on adolescent drug use. *Journal of American Academy Child Adolescent Psychiatry*, 21, 328–347.

Kazdin, A. E. (1997). Parent management training: evidence, outcomes, and issues. *Journal of American Academy of Child Adolescent Psychiatry*, 36, 1349–1356.

Kelleher, I., Connor, D., Clarke, M. C., Devlin, N., Harley, M., & Cannon, M. (2012). Prevalence of psychotic symptoms in childhood and adolescence: a systematic review and meta-analysis of population-based studies. *Psychological Medicine*, 42, 1857–1863.

Kerig, P. K., Bennett, D. C., Thompson, M., & Becker, S. P. (2012). "Nothing really matters": emotional numbing as a link between trauma exposure and callousness in delinquent youth. *Journal of Trauma Stress*, 25, 272–279.

Kilpatrick, D. G., Ruggiero, K. J., Acierno, R., Saunders, B. E., Resnick, H. S., & Best, C. L. (2003). Violence and risk of PTSD, major depression, substance abuse/dependence, and comorbidity: results from the National Survey of Adolescents. *Journal of Consulting and Clinical Psychology*, 71, 692–700.

Kolko, D. J. & Pardini, D. A. (2010). ODD dimensions, ADHD, and callous-unemotional traits as predictors of treatment response in children with disruptive behavior disorders. *Journal of Abnormal Psychology*, 119, 713–725.

Kowatch, R. A., Fristad, M., Birmaher, B., Wagner, K. D., Findling, R. L., Hellander, M., & Child Psychiatric Workgroup on Bipolar, D. (2005). Treatment guidelines for children and adolescents with bipolar disorder. *Journal of the American Academy Child Adolescent Psychiatry*, 44, 213–235.

Kraut, A. A., Langner, I., Lindemann, C., Banaschewski, T., Petermann, U., Petermann, F., ... & Garbe, E. (2013).

Comorbidities in ADHD children treated with methylphenidate: a database study. *BMC Psychiatry*, 13, 11.

Larson, K., Russ, S. A., Kahn, R. S., & Halfon, N. (2011). Patterns of comorbidity, functioning, and service use for US children with ADHD, 2007. *Pediatrics*, 127, 462–470.

Leibenluft, E. (2011). Severe mood dysregulation, irritability, and the diagnostic boundaries of bipolar disorder in youths. *American Journal of Psychiatry*, 168, 129–142.

Leigh, B. C. (1999). Peril, chance, adventure: Concepts of risk, alcohol use and risky behavior in young adults. *Addiction*, 94, 371–383.

Levy, F., Hay, D. A., Bennett, K. S., & McStephen, M. (2005). Gender differences in ADHD subtype comorbidity. *Journal of the American Academy Child Adolescent Psychiatry*, 44, 368–376.

Maas, C. D., Fleming, C. B., Herrenkohl, T. I., & Catalano, R. F. (2010). Childhood predictors of teen dating violence victimization. *Violence & Victims*, 25, 131–149.

Martin, S. E. (2001). The links between alcohol, crime and the criminal justice system: Explanations, evidence and interventions. *Amrican Journal of Addictions*, 10, 136–158.

Maughan, B., Rowe, R., Messer, J., Goodman, R., & Meltzer, H. (2004). Conduct disorder and oppositional defiant disorder in a national sample: developmental epidemiology. *Journal of Child Psychology and Psychiatry*, 45, 609–621.

Maxfield, M. G. & Widom, C. S. (1996). The cycle of violence. Revisited 6 years later. *Archives of Pediatrics & Adolescent Medicine*, 150, 390–395.

Merikangas, K. R. & He, J. P. (2014). Epidemiology of mental disorders in children and adolescents. In J.-P. Raynaud, M. Hodes, & S. Shur-Fen Gau (Eds), *From Research to Practice in Child and Adolescent Mental Health*. Lanham, ML: Rowman & Littelfield.

Miklowitz, D. J., Schneck, C. D., George, E. L., Taylor, D. O., Sugar, C. A., Birmaher, B., ... & Axelson, D. A. (2014). Pharmacotherapy and family-focused treatment for adolescents with bipolar I and II disorders: a 2-year randomized trial. *American Journal of Psychiatry*, 171, 658–667.

Moffitt, T. E. (1993). Adolescence-limited and life-course-persistent antisocial behavior: a developmental taxonomy. *Psychological Review*, 100, 674–701.

Moffitt, T. E., Caspi, A., Harrington, H., & Milne, B. J. (2002). Males on the life-course-persistent and adolescence-limited antisocial pathways: follow-up at age 26 years. *Development and Psychopathology*, 14, 179–207.

Mohr-Jensen, C., & Steinhausen, H. C. (2016). A meta-analysis and systematic review of the risks associated with childhood attention-deficit hyperactivity disorder on long-term outcome of arrests, convictions, and incarcerations. *Clinical Psychology Review*, 48, 32–42.

Moore, E., Indig, D., & Haysom, L. (2014). Traumatic brain injury, mental health, substance use, and offending among incarcerated young people. *Journal of Head Trauma Rehabilitation*, 29, 239–247.

Nolen-Hoeksema, S. & Hilt, L. M. (2009). *Handbook of Depression in Adolescents*. New York: Taylor & Francis Group.

Ollendick, T. H. & Seligman, L. D. (2006). Anxiety Disorders. In C. Gillberg, R. Harrington, & H. C. Steinhausen (Eds), *A clinician's handbook of child and adolescent psychiatry*. Cambridge: Cambridge University Press.

Plattner, B., Giger, J., Bachmann, F., Bruhwiler, K., Steiner, H., Steinhausen, H. C., ... & Aebi, M. (2012). Psychopathology and offense types in detained male juveniles. *Psychiatry Research*, 198, 285–290.

Polanczyk, G. V., de Lima, M. S., Horta, B. L., Biederman, J., & Rohde, L. A. (2007). The worldwide prevalence of ADHD: A systematic review and metaregression analysis. *Amrican Journal of Psychiatry*, 164, 942–948.

Polanczyk, G. V., Salum, G. A., Sugaya, L. S., Caye, A., & Rohde, L. A. (2015). Annual research review: A meta-analysis of the worldwide prevalence of mental disorders in children and adolescents. *Journal of Child Psychology and Psychiatry*, 56, 345–365.

Popova, S., Lange, S., Shield, K., Mihic, A., Chudley, A. E., Mukherjee, R. A., ... & Rehm, J. (2016). Comorbidity of fetal alcohol spectrum disorder: a systematic review and meta-analysis. *Lancet*, 387, 978–987.

Quanbeck, C. D., Stone, D. C., McDermott, B. E., Boone, K., Scott, C. L., & Frye, M. A. (2005). Relationship between criminal arrest and community treatment history among patients with bipolar disorder. *Psychiatric Services*, 56, 847–852.

Roland, E. (2002). Aggression, depression and bullying others. *Aggressive Behavior*, 27, 198–206.

Ruchkin, V., Henrich, C. C., Jones, S. M., Vermeiren, R., & Schwab-Stone, M. (2007). Violence exposure and psychopathology in urban youth: the mediating role of post-traumatic stress. *Journal of Abnormal Child Psychology*, 35, 578–593.

Schofield, P. W., Malacova, E., Preen, D. B., D'Este, C., Tate, R., Reekie, J., ... & Butler, T. (2015). Does Traumatic Brain Injury Lead to Criminality? A Whole-Population Retrospective Cohort Study Using Linked Data. *PLoS ONE*, 10, e0132558.

Silverman, W. K., Pina, A. A., & Viswesvaran, C. (2008). Evidence-based psychosocial treatments for phobic and anxiety disorders in children and adolescents. *Journal of Clinical Child Adolescent Psychology*, 37, 105–130.

Slifer, K. J. & Amari, A. (2009). Behavior management for children and adolescents with acquired brain injury. *Developmental Disability Research Review*, 15, 144–151.

Smeets, K. C., Leeijen, A. A., van der Molen, M. J., Scheepers, F. E., Buitelaar, J. K., & Rommelse, N. N. (2015). Treatment moderators of cognitive behavior therapy to reduce aggressive behavior: a meta-analysis. *European Child Adolescent Psychiatry*, 24, 255–264.

Smith, P., Perrin, S., Dalgleish, T., Meiser-Stedman, R., Clark, D. M., & Yule, W. (2013). Treatment of posttraumatic stress disorder in children and adolescents. *Current Opinion in Psychiatry*, 26, 66–72.

Sourander, A., Elonheimo, H., Niemelä, S., Nuutila, A.-M., Helenius, H., Sillanmäki, L., ... & Almqvist, F. (2006). Childhood predictors of male criminality: A prospective population – based follow – up study from age 8 to late adolescence. *Journal of the American Academy of Child Adolescent Psychiatry*, 45, 578–586.

Spohr, H. L., Willms, J., & Steinhausen, H. C. (1993). Prenatal alcohol exposure and long-term developmental consequences. *Lancet*, 341, 907–910.

Steiner, H., Silverman, M., Karnik, N. S., Huemer, J., Plattner, B., Clark, C. E., ... & Haapanen, R. (2011). Psychopathology, trauma and delinquency: subtypes of aggression and their relevance for understanding young offenders. *Child Adolesc Psychiatry Mental Health*, 5, 21.

Steinhausen, H.-C., Eschmann, S., & Winkler Metzke, C. (2007). Continuity, psychosocial correlates, and outcome of problematic substance use from adolescence to young adulthood in a community sample. *Child Adolescent Psychiatry Mental Health*, 1, 12.

Steinhausen, H.-C. & Gillberg, C. (2006). Brain disorders. In C. Gillberg, R. Harrington, & H.-C. Steinhausen (Eds), *A clinician's handbook of child and adolescent psychiatry*. Cambridge: Cambridge University Press.

Steinhausen, H.-C., Willms, J., & Spohr, H. L. (1993). Long-term psychopathological and cognitive outcome of children with fetal alcohol syndrome. *Journal of the American Academy of Child Adolescent Psychiatry*, 32, 990–994.

Steinhausen, H.-C. & Winkler Metzke, C. (2003). The validity of adolescent types of alcohol use. *Journal of Child Psychology and Psychiatry*, 44, 677–686.

Stouthamer-Loeber, M., Wei, E., Loeber, R., & Masten, A. S. (2004). Desistance from persistent serious delinquency in the transition to adulthood. *Development and Psychopathology*, 16, 897–918.

Streissguth, A. P., Barr, H. M., Kogan, J., & Bookstein, F. L. (1996). *Understanding th occurrence of secondary disabilities in clients with fetal alcohol syndrome (FAS) and fetal alcohol effects (FAE)*. Seattle: University of Washington, Fetal Alcohol and Drug Unit, Tech. Rep. No. 96-06.

Swendsen, J., Burstein, M., Case, B., Conway, K. P., Dierker, L., He, J., & Merikangas, K. R. (2012). Use and abuse of alcohol and illicit drugs in US adolescents: results of the National Comorbidity Survey-Adolescent Supplement. *Archives of General Psychiatry*, 69, 390–398.

Swenson, C. C., Schaeffer, C. M., Henggeler, S. W., Faldowski, R., & Mayhew, A. M. (2010). Multisystemic Therapy for Child Abuse and Neglect: a randomized effectiveness trial. *Journal of Family Psychology*, 24, 497–507.

Teplin, L. A., Abram, K. M., McClelland, G. M., Dulcan, M. K., & Mericle, A. A. (2002). Psychiatric disorders in youth in juvenile detention. *Archives of General Psychiatry*, 59, 1133–1143.

Tremblay, R. E. (2012). The Development of Physical Aggression. *Encyclopedia of early child development*. Retrieved August 28, 2016, from www.child-encyclopedia.com/.

van der Stouwe, T., Asscher, J. J., Stams, G. J., Dekovic, M., & van der Laan, P. H. (2014). The effectiveness of Multisystemic Therapy (MST): a meta-analysis. *Clinical Psychology Review*, 34, 468–481.

Viding, E., Sebastian, C. L., Dadds, M. R., Lockwood, P. L., Cecil, C. A., De Brito, S. A., & McCrory, E. J. (2012). Amygdala response to preattentive masked fear in children with conduct problems: the role of callous-unemotional traits. *American Journal of Psychiatry*, 169, 1109–1116.

Vreugdenhil, C., Vermeiren, R., Wouters, L. F., Doreleijers, T. A., & van den Brink, W. (2004). Psychotic symptoms among male adolescent detainees in The Netherlands. *Schizophrenia Bulletin*, 30, 73–86.

Weiss, B. & Catron, T. (1994). Specificity of the comorbidity of aggression and depression in children. *Journal of Abnormal Child Psychology*, 22, 389–401.

Wichstrom, L., Berg-Nielsen, T. S., Angold, A., Egger, H. L., Solheim, E., & Sveen, T. H. (2012). Prevalence of psychiatric disorders in preschoolers. *Journal of Child Psychology and Psychiatry*, 53, 695–705.

Wilson, H. W., Stover, C. S., & Berkowitz, S. J. (2009). Research review: the relationship between childhood violence exposure and juvenile antisocial behavior: a meta-analytic review. *Journal of Child Psychology and Psychiatry*, 50, 769–779.

World Health Organization. (1992). *The International Classification of Diseases and Related Health Problems, 10th Revision (ICD-10)* Geneva, Switzerland: World Health Organization.

Young, S. & Thome, J. (2011). ADHD and offenders. *World Journal of Biological Psychiatry*, 12(Suppl. 1), 124–128.

17 Self-Control Theory and Criminal Violence

Michael R. Gottfredson

Introduction

Self-control theory is a perspective in criminology that attempts to explain the distribution of crime and delinquency, including interpersonal violence among individuals, groups, and societies. As proposed in *A General Theory of Crime* (Gottfredson & Hirschi, 1990), self-control theory belongs to a family of theories in criminology that includes social control theory (Hirschi, 1969) as well as other criminological theories that emphasize individual differences in attention to the costs and benefits of various behavioral choices (Gottfredson, 2006; 2011a). A distinguishing characteristic of control theory is the assumption that conforming behavior, rather than deviant behavior, is what needs to be explained. Control theorists thus seek to understand the forces that compel most people, most of the time, to behave nonviolently and noncriminally. Control theories in criminology begin by assuming that the motives for crime and violence are similar to the motives for all other behavior. Rather than focusing on motives for violence, they focus on the constellation of restraints against violent acts. Self-control theory predicts that variation in personal tendencies to consider the negative consequences of acts and the ability to consider long-term consequences of behavior are among the most significant restraints, or controls, against interpersonal violence.

Since it was proposed in 1990, both the concept of self-control and the general theory that incorporates it as a principal cause of crime and interpersonal violence have received substantial research attention. The theory has been referred to as "arguably one of the most prominent theories in criminology" (Vazsonyi et al., 2017) and as "one of the most prominent and most researched theories of crime causation in international contemporary criminology" (Hirtenlehner & Kunz, 2017, p. 37). Self-control has been shown to be one of the most robust correlates of a wide variety of measures of crime, deviance, and violent behavior. According to Hirtenlehner and Kunz (2017, p. 37), "In the empirical literature, low self-control has been established as one of the best predictors of deviant and criminal activity." They cite studies finding that measures of low self-control increase offending for criminal and analogous behaviors, for different demographic groups, in different countries, with both attitudinal and behavioral measures, and that the relationship holds even when concepts from other social theories are controlled. As Moffitt (2011), and colleagues recently (p. 2693) put it, "Impaired childhood self-control is highly important as it is associated with an abundance of negative life experiences, such as substance use, criminal offending, school dropout, or unplanned teenage pregnancies, and with negative long term health and financial outcomes."

Self-control theory locates the most important basis for conforming behavior in the attachments formed early in life between parents or other care-givers and their children. These attachments, or social bonds, develop into the tendency to regulate individual conduct by attending to consequences of actions (Hirschi, 1969; Gottfredson & Hirschi, 1990). Differences in parenting and other early childhood experiences create differences in the ability to delay the gratification of near-term desires and needs in favor of avoiding negative consequences both short and long term. These negative consequences can include the rather immediate negative costs of physical and interpersonal harm, but also include losing the respect and affection of others, and risking success in school and employment and actions of the justice system. Self-control theory has connections to theories of self-regulation (e.g., Baumeister & Heatherton, 1996; Hirschi, 2004) and impulsiveness in psychology, to the concept of time discounting in economics, and to the idea of problem behaviors in sociology (e.g., Donovan, Jessor, & Costa, 1991). In fact, the concept of self-control has been shown to help explain lifelong differences found in longitudinal and experimental research for a variety of outcomes, ranging from educational and employment success to better health and fewer involvements with the criminal justice system (Heckman, 2006, 2007; Moffitt et al., 2011, 2013).

Self-control theory places much, but not all (as described below), violent behavior into the class of acts the theory was designed to explain. As such, self-control theory is also a theory of interpersonal violence. The theory owes much of its development to the cumulative advances in scientific studies of crime and delinquency. From the beginning, self-control theory was designed to account for the major facts about individual differences in crime and delinquency as revealed in the empirical literature (Gottfredson, 2006). Since an appreciation of these facts is critical to an appreciation of the theory, before describing the theory further, some of the established correlates of violence central to the development of self-control theory will be outlined briefly. Precisely what forms of violent behavior are included in the definition of violence specified by control theory will be addressed, followed by a discussion of the contemporary research bearing on the validity of self-control theory.

Key Facts About Criminal Violence

Behavioral scientists interested in explaining violent behavior have at their disposal a considerable body of high-quality research studies that have produced a set of correlates of criminal violence that are impressively robust with respect to time and method of measurement. These correlates – or key facts about violence – are so strongly documented, that explanatory schemes not attending to them, or inconsistent with any of them, cannot be said to be valid according to the best empirical science available. There are, to be sure, important uncertainties and arguments in the literature about some correlates of violent behavior and there are many more arguments about the meaning of those correlates that are agreed upon, but the foundational facts of a behavioral science of criminal violence surely must at least include the following consistently found findings about interpersonal violence.

First, there is a robust and substantial correlation between misconduct early in life and violence during adolescence and adulthood. The correlation between early childhood problem behaviors and crime (including violent behavior) later in life is one of the longest-standing findings from systematic delinquency research (see, e.g., Glueck & Glueck, 1940; 1950; McCord & McCord, 1959; Robbins, 1966). This relationship is reported regularly in studies from a variety of disciplines (for summaries, see Gottfredson & Hirschi, 1990; Hirschi, 1969; Loeber & Stouthamer-Loeber, 1986; Loeber & Dishion, 1983; Olweus, 1979; Farrington, 2003). Studies documenting this effect are found in psychological research (e.g., Mischel et al. 1988; Tangney et al., 2004), in criminology (e.g., Hirschi, 1969; West & Farrington, 1973) in recidivism studies (e.g., McCord & McCord, 1959), and longitudinal research (Glueck & Glueck, 1950; Robbins, 1966; Farrington, 2003; Moffitt et al., 2011; Moffitt et al., 2013).

Second, there is a characteristic distribution of violent behavior over the life-course, such that incidents of violence increase in frequency with age up to late adolescence or early adulthood and then rapidly and continuously decline throughout life (Hirschi & Gottfredson, 1983). This general "age/crime" curve has been studied for well over a century and, with few exceptions, is applicable also to interpersonal violence. The peak age for some forms of criminal violence seems to be modestly older than for some forms of property offenses, but by and large the distributions are remarkably the same whatever the type of crime studied (Gottfredson & Hirschi, 2016).

The general distribution between age and criminal violence is illustrated in Figures 17.1 and 17.2, which depict age-standardized offending rates from California for homicide and for robbery (the forcible taking of property from another), two prominent forms of criminal violence. For comparison purposes, Figure 17.3 shows the age-standardized rates for alcohol-impaired motor vehicle accidents and motor vehicle theft, offenses not generally considered falling within the concept of violence, but which have virtually identical relationships with age over the life-course. Although the figures show modest differences in the peak age and very modest differences in the rate of decline from the peak, their overall similarity is striking.

The theoretical and practical importance of that fundamental relationship is considerable (Hirschi & Gottfredson, 1983; Gottfredson & Hirschi, 1990). Violent behavior, like most problem behaviors, is very disproportionately adolescent and young adult behavior. As illustrated by the data in Figures 17.1–17.3, rates of offending rise very sharply during the pre-teen years and decline rapidly after adolescence and continuously throughout life, whatever the initial level of violence (Hirschi & Gottfredson, 1983; 2016).

Researchers have long sought subgroups or "types" of offenders with substantially different age-crime offense rates as a function of age, but only modest variation in the relationship has been documented – variation that has been reported tends to be from samples highly restricted on age, or from offenses that include some age restriction as part of the definition of the acts studied (e.g., crime among executives or "assaults" among very young children). A number of researchers have deployed

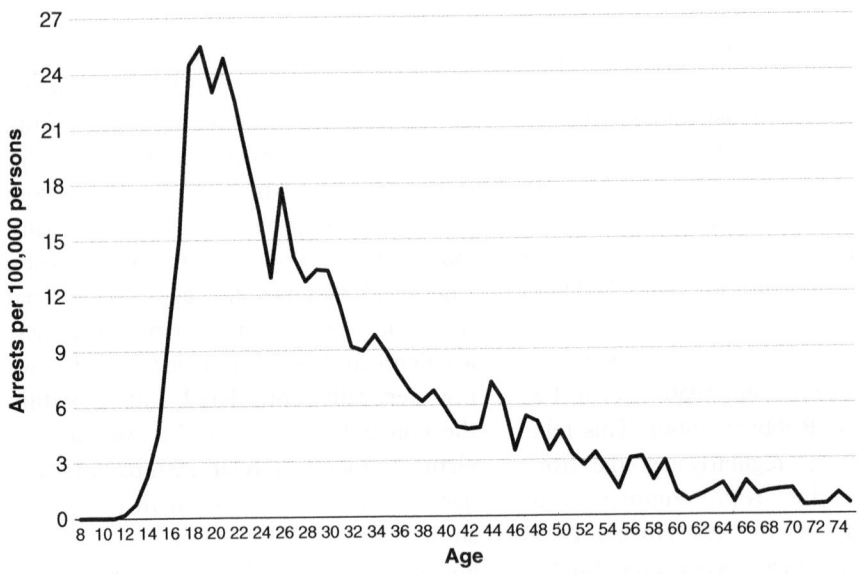

Figure 17.1 *Arrest rates by age, murder, and non-negligent manslaughter, USA (2010). (Source: age data from State of California Department of Finance, California State Data Center; Arrest data from United States Department of Justice. Federal Bureau of Investigation. Uniform Crime Reporting: National Incident-Based Reporting System, 2010. ICPSR33530-v1. Ann Arbor, MI: Inter-university Consortium for Political and Social Research (distributor), June 22, 2012.)*

statistical "trajectory modelling" in search of subgroups that maintain high rates of offending even into older age groups, often in search of "career criminals" who might be targets for enhanced criminal justice interventions (see Gottfredson & Hirschi, 2016, for a critique of these efforts) but convincing studies that reliably discover such trajectory groups are lacking, as are examples of replication among trajectory studies. Independent reviews have concluded that the evidence supports the ideas that offense rates decline substantially and rapidly after early adulthood for all groups (see reviews and analysis in Gottfredson & Hirschi, 2016; Erosheva et al., 2014; Skardhamar, 2009; Macmillan, 2008).

Because the form of the age/violence relationship is so ubiquitous, the initial level of activity in childhood and the teen years substantially predicts differences in the overall level of violence throughout life – i.e., individuals with relatively high rates in childhood have relatively high rates as teens and as adults, even though their rates tend to decline as they age past adolescence. Individuals with relatively low rates in childhood and the teen years tend to have relatively low rates throughout life. Of course the distributions of levels of violence at each age are continua, not discreet groups. Although it is possible to arbitrarily create categories or types from the continuous distributions, such classifications likely obscure what might be common causes or correlates of violence across individuals. The ubiquity of the age distribution itself accounts for the

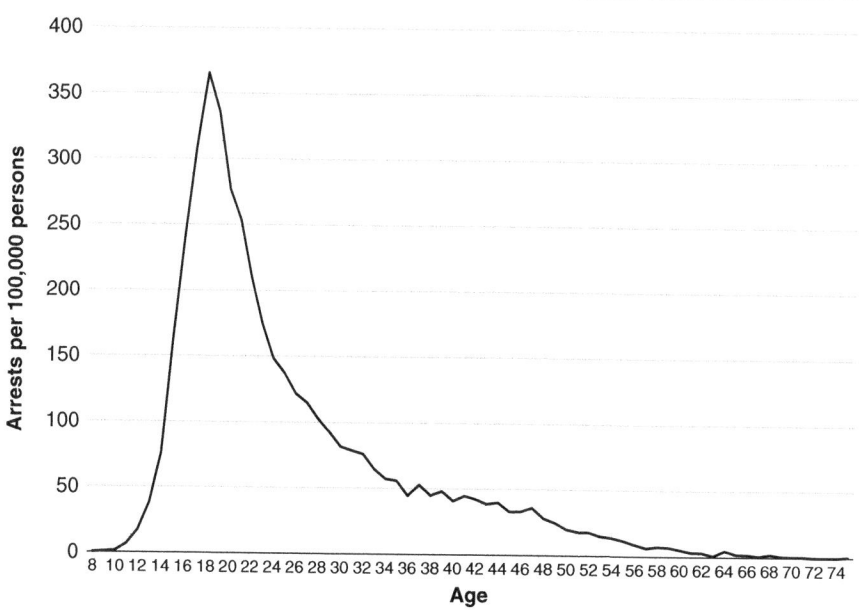

Figure 17.2 *Arrest rates by age, robbery, USA (2010).*
(Source: age data from State of California Department of Finance, California State Data Center; Arrest data from United States Department of Justice. Federal Bureau of Investigation. Uniform Crime Reporting: National Incident-Based Reporting System, 2010. ICPSR33530-v1. Ann Arbor, MI: Inter-university Consortium for Political and Social Research (distributor), June 22, 2012.)

apparent "predictability" of "early onset" for higher rates of crime and violence throughout the life-course (i.e., it is a statistical necessity that "early onset" results in "later desistence," but the terms are somewhat misleading, given the common form of the distribution for all groups). Rather, two very important conclusions are supported by the data about age and interpersonal violence: even the most active offenders will tend to engage in fewer acts as they age into and through adulthood; and violence, like other problem behaviors, must have important causes in earliest years of life. If teenage and adult violence are substantially "predicted" by levels of childhood problem behavior, then the causes of teenage and adult violence must include factors from the pre-teen years.

A third established fact is that there are substantial and persistent correlations between various aspects of the family during childhood and violence later in life. For example, there is a substantial correlation between the amount of problem behaviors of parents and the level of violence of their children. Furthermore, there are strong correlations between the strength of attachment between children and their parents and level of crime and violence. The effect of family on crime and violence has been a staple of empirical criminology for decades and remains so in contemporary research (Gottfredson & Hirschi, 1990; Glueck & Glueck, 1950; Loeber & Dishion, 1983; Loeber & Stouthamer-Loeber, 1986; Hirschi, 1969; McCord & McCord, 1959;

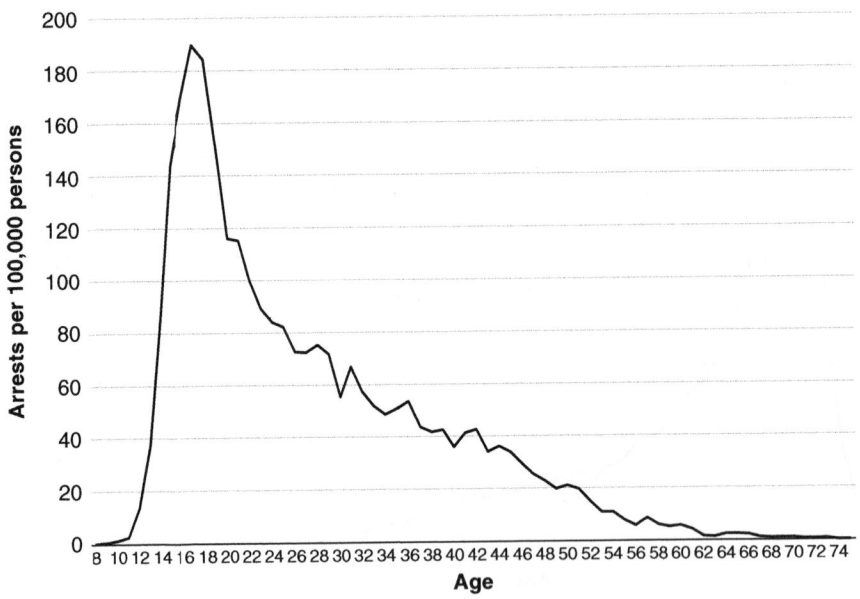

Figure 17.3 *Arrest rates by age, motor vehicle theft, USA (2010).*
(Source: age data from State of California Department of Finance, California State Data Center, Arrest data from United States Department of Justice. Federal Bureau of Investigation. Uniform Crime Reporting: National Incident-Based Reporting System, 2010. ICPSR33530-v1. Ann Arbor, MI: Inter-university Consortium for Political and Social Research (distributor), June 22, 2012.)

Maxfield & Widom, 1996; Brannigan et al., 2002; Hirschi & Gottfredson, 2003; Vazsonyi & Belliston, 2007; Vazsonyi & Huang, 2010).

Fourth, research also documents substantial correlations for individuals between levels of violent behavior and levels of other forms of delinquent and criminal behavior. There are also substantial correlations between violent behavior and other non-crime problem behaviors, such as drug use, accidents, illnesses, poor school performance, and employment problems. Criminologists refer to this inter-relationship among problem behaviors as the "versatility" or "generality" effect (Gottfredson & Hirschi, 1990; 1991). This means that offenders by and large do not specialize in violent or in nonviolent behavior, a fact validated in both self-report and in official statistics (Britt, 1994; DeLisi, 2005; DeLisi & Piquero, 2011; Gottfredson & Hirschi, 1990, 1994, 2016; Hindelang et al., 1981; Junger & Tremblay, 1999; Junger et al., 2001; Osgood et al., 1988; Wolfgang et al., 1972). This "generality" fact presents special problems for explanations of interpersonal violence that are designed to be specific to violence rather than to a general cluster of problem behaviors (as, for example, many explanations that focus on specific motivations or on specific learning for violent acts). Rather, across individuals, violent acts tend to go together with other forms of problem behaviors (theft and substance abuse, for example) and many of these behaviors do not correspond well to specific motives or learning for violent acts.

A fifth fact with considerable practical consequence is that there is significant, but only low-level, predictability for individuals for specific acts of violence. Such acts tend to be statistically rare events and efforts to predict violence for individuals are fraught with over-prediction problems (Gottfredson & Gottfredson, 1994). A related fact is that general measures of crime and delinquency, which include violence, are more reliable and have greater discriminant validity than do specific measures of crime and delinquency (Hindelang et al., 1981). The fact that prediction of violence at the individual level is problematic and that violence cannot be predicted as well as can crime, suggests that violent or aggressive behavior belongs to the larger construct of problem behavior (Gottfredson & Hirschi, 1994).

Finally, studies of criminal violence suggest strongly that most interpersonal violent behavior is better characterized as rather mundane, short-sighted, and adventitious rather than as original, well-planned, or deliberate. It typically produces little gain and engenders considerable long-term negative consequences for the actor, even as it often results in great harm to the victims. Violent acts tend not to be planned long in advance, but rather often seem nearly spontaneous (and, in hindsight, even to the offender to be unaccountable). Quite frequently, alcohol or other drugs are involved (Boyum & Kleiman, 1995). In result, it can hardly be said to be utilitarian. There are, of course, exceptions (which often attract much public attention), but studies of homicide, robbery, assault, family violence, gang assaultive behavior, and other forms of interpersonal violence depict the nature of the acts as frequently unplanned, alcohol-involved, and without long-term gain to the offender (Gottfredson & Hirschi, 1990). Putting an end to an argument, showing off, bullying for momentary advantage, threatening victims to accomplish a theft and small conflicts that escalate on impulse are characteristic of interpersonal violence. All are examples of momentary gain or satisfaction, with potential longer-term substantial costs that are ignored.

Control Theory Definition of Violence

The definition of crime, and by extension the definition of interpersonal violence, incorporated in self-control theory departs substantially from the legal definition often used by criminologists to explain crime and also from the concept of aggression as it is frequently used by psychologists (see Gottfredson & Hirschi, 1993; Gottfredson, 2011b). Quite obviously, not all violent behavior, even all criminal violence, fits the description of crime provided above or the self-control theory definition of crime: "acts of force, fraud or mood enhancement for short-term gain with longer term negative consequences." The intentional infliction of bodily harm, without excuse and not in defense of self or others, is the standard definition of criminal violence. In most instances of criminal violence, the violence permits the offender some momentary personal gain – the theft of property, the end of an argument, or even a sense of personal status. On the other hand, some criminal violence, such as some terrorist acts, is designed, at least in part, to satisfy collective rather than individual interests and long-term rather than short-term objectives. And there certainly is violent or aggressive behavior that is neither criminal nor within the scope of the definition of violence used by self-control theory.

Should a behavioral theory of violence attempt to explain in the same way the wide variety of violent conduct, from school-yard bullying, to homicides, to robberies, to spousal assaults, to terrorism? Is criminal violence a category of conduct suitable for scientific explanation? Should we seek one causal explanation for violent crime and another for theft crimes, or one for domestic assault and a different one for street robbery? Should noncriminal violence be included or excluded? Certainly not all types of violent behavior are technically criminal; some "accidents" cause considerable damage to others and there is much violent conduct in some sports. The threshold problem for the science of violent conduct is thus the problem of scope or definition.

Confronted with these issues (as all theories of violence should be) control theorists reject a legal definition of violence and instead incorporate into the theory only those behaviors characterized as providing short-term benefit to the actor without regard to negative longer-term consequences (Gottfredson & Hirschi, 1993, p. 40):

> violent and assaultive acts that produce immediate benefit at the same time they produce long term social costs are of interest to students of crime and deviance. Indeed, to the extent that aggressive acts share these defining characteristics of most forms of crime and deviance, they will easily fall within the scope of ... control theory ... many violent acts can be understood in precisely this way ... much homicide, child abuse, spouse abuse, and violent robbery is undertaken to gain some momentary advantage without regard to long term social consequences. When a husband strikes his wife repeatedly as a way to end an argument; when a father physically assaults a child to end an annoyance of the moment; or, when a robber shoots a clerk because he is nervous about his escape, the advantage of the moment has outweighed consideration of distant costs.

Thus, a definition of violence for a theory of criminal violence does not include all conduct ordinarily classified as violence – not even by the criminal law. Many terrorist acts, involving homicide and assault, would not fall into the definition for control theory since these acts may be undertaken precisely with the long-term in view, just as many violent acts are in defense of self or others (such as in combat). Many are even very highly planned and difficult to execute. The individuals involved do not have extensive involvement with other problem behaviors; indeed some may be highly disciplined in other ways, leading to higher education and substantial employment. Even though the legal system includes them as crimes, these acts are, in some ways, very different from the kinds of acts that characterize ordinary crimes.

Other behavior that could be classified as violent, but not criminal, also does not belong in the definition used by control theorists. Some sports certainly involve aggression and interpersonal violence; violent behavior in military settings usually has long-term goals and, indeed, requires the subordination of individual self-interest to the collective interest. Sometimes, however, violence in military settings seems well within the intended scope of the theory, such as prisoner abuse or crimes during occupations. So too may many acts be classified as terrorism, when such acts fall substantially within the scope of other problem behaviors and the terrorism label is conferred to describe an otherwise "inexplicable" act.

Self-Control Theory

The general correlates of crime and violence, and the nature of violence that they presume, helped shape the theory of self-control (Gottfredson & Hirschi, 1990, 1991; Hirschi & Gottfredson, 1994, 1995). Control theorists assume that all people are motivated to pursue self-interest and that individual behavior is motivated by the pursuit of pleasure and the avoidance of pain. There are, to be sure, countless constellations of pleasures and pains, from the physical to the emotional, from short-term to long-term. The unrestrained pursuit of these wants in everyday life will inevitably lead to conflict with the wants and rights of others. Aggressive, bullying, and assaultive acts can lead to the immediate satisfaction of wants, but only if the longer-term costs are disregarded. Consequently, controls are established by social groups (including parents, communities, and states) to channel the pursuit of these wants in ways that minimize harm to others (Gottfredson, 2011a).

Sociologists have identified several forms of controls for violent behavior. Of course, deterrence from the legal system is the formal method, seeking to control crime and violence through fear of legal punishments. But many nonlegal mechanisms also help control unwanted behavior, such as the approval, respect, and affection of family, teachers, and friends. Because these controls are exerted, or not, in the social environment, and because individuals experience different environments related to these controls, the extent to which individuals are "free to deviate" varies. When these controls need to be present in the environment to be effective, they are often referred to as external or social controls. When the process of socialization during the early years of life establishes a tendency to be concerned about others and about the costs of behaviors, they are referred to as self-control. Self and social controls are, of course, closely related concepts and work to the same general effects (Hirschi, 2004; Gottfredson, 2006, 2011a). Self-control theory postulates important variation among people in their tendencies to subordinate momentary or immediate pleasure or satisfactions in light of their negative consequences or costs, as well as the ability to attend to longer-term goals and objectives; tendencies that, once established, have substantial and continuing effects on well-being throughout life (Gottfredson & Hirschi, 1990; Moffitt et al., 2011; Heckman, 2007).

Put another way, self-control is the tendency to delay short-term personal gain for long-term personal and collective interests. Crime and delinquency can provide satisfaction of universal human wants and desires, but only by risking longer-term goals (the avoidance of punishment, the ability to achieve conventional accomplishments like education and employment, interpersonal relationships). Thus, those with lower levels of self-control are, all things equal, more likely than those with higher levels of self-control to behave violently, to commit crime, or to engage in delinquent acts. Those with higher levels of self-control tend to have relatively high rates of school and employment success, many better health outcomes, fewer juvenile and criminal justice involvements, and more lasting interpersonal relationships (Moffitt et al., 2011, 2013; Heckman, 2006;

Hirschi & Gottfredson, 1994). Self-control is not, of course, a discrete characteristic but rather a continuously distributed one (a point often misunderstood in criminological statements of the theory). Although for communication purposes individuals are sometimes described as having "low self-control" or "high self-control," such conventions are not meant to imply discrete types.

As distributed, self-control has important correlations, but by no means perfect relationships, with a very wide array of life outcome variables. Gottfredson and Hirschi's general theory of crime is stated in probabilistic terms. They are clear about the notion that self-control theory does not imply that low self-control requires crime or that the concept is inconsistent with the notion of agency (Gottfredson & Hirschi, 1990; Gottfredson, 2011a) The opposite is central to the meaning of self-control. The concept of a *general cause* can be misunderstood to imply deterministic or mandatory causation, an idea foreign to modern notions of causation (see, e.g., Hirschi & Selvin, 1967). Although Gottfredson and Hirschi (1990) argue that self-control is the most important individual-level concept for crime and delinquency, they clearly do not argue that self-control is the sole cause of crime.

Self-control helps to account for the fact that many delinquencies, crimes, and other problem behaviors seem to "go together," i.e., that interpersonal violence, stealing, drug use, accidents, and school misbehavior are commonly found in association. The acts associated with these problems all provide some immediate benefit for the actor (money, pleasure, the end of a troubling dispute). But each also carries with it the possibility of harmful consequences to the actor or to others. What differentiates people is not that such acts may provide benefits, but that some individuals routinely ignore the potential costs and do them anyway. Thus, self-control theory is sometimes called "restraint theory," a theory that focuses on why people don't engage in crime and delinquency rather than why they do (Hirschi, 1969; Gottfredson, 2011a).

Self-control theory locates the most important basis for conforming behavior in the attachments formed early in life between parents or other care-givers and their children. These attachments, when accompanied by other elements of child socialization, develop within the child the tendency to regulate individual conduct by attending to consequences of actions (Hirschi, 1969; Gottfredson & Hirschi, 1990). Differences in parenting and other early childhood experiences create differences in the ability to delay the gratification of short-term desires and needs in favor of avoiding negative consequences, both short- and long-term. These negative consequences can include the rather immediate negative costs of physical and interpersonal harm, but also include losing the respect and affection of others and risking success in school and employment.

Self-control theory is influenced by the observation that differences among people in the tendency to ignore long-term costs appear to be established in childhood and, once established, tend to persist throughout life. Control theory assumes that human nature includes the general tendency to pursue satisfaction of individual needs and desires. Left unregulated, the pursuit of this nature causes inevitable conflict with others and, because of that, potentially harmful consequences to the actor. As a result, those who care about the long-term interests of the child seek to train the child to restrict the pursuit of self-interest by attending to the needs and wants of others. For self-control theory, this process is what socialization entails. As the child develops, care-givers (parents, other relatives, friends and neighbors, and schools) sanction selfish behavior. Children are taught to pay attention to the longer-term consequences of their actions. When a caring adult is present in the developing child's environment and takes an active role in socialization, high levels of self-control are readily produced and appear to become a stable characteristic of the individual (Gottfredson & Hirschi, 1990). But sometimes such early care giving is not present in the child's environment. Furthermore, there are differences among groups and cultures in the level and duration of this socialization process. These differences are thought to produce the differences in levels of crime, violence, and other problem behaviors among individuals, communities, and in different time periods.

How socialization of young people generates self-control is described by Gottfredson and Hirschi (Gottfredson & Hirschi, 1990; Hirschi & Gottfredson, 2003): (1) parental affection for the child establishes a long-term interest in the success of the child; (2) which enables a parenting style characterized by positive efforts to monitor conduct and appropriately sanction deviance; (3) which creates self-control; (4) which is expressed by affection from the child to the parent and, by logical extension, to other socializing institutions like schools and friends. This model implies that the social bonds among parents and children and self-control in the child will be very difficult to discriminate empirically and, under some circumstances, amount to the same thing.

It is important to stress that in the creation of self-control, affection for the child is the key:

> A major premise of the model outlined is that the parent, caretaker, or guardian must care enough about the child or the child's behavior to devote the immense amounts of time and energy monitoring and discipline require ... Interest in the outcome, whatever its source, tends to assure monitoring and discipline. It also severely limits the range of usable or acceptable sanctions. (Hirschi & Gottfredson, 2003, pp. 156–157)

Gibbs et al. (2003, p. 443) describe the theory well:

> For their children to develop high levels of self-control, parents must regularly monitor them, recognize deviant behavior when it occurs, and punish the behavior by non-corporal means. Self-control is associated with the consistent application of these principles during the early development of the child. Investment in the child, which often takes the form of an emotional attachment, is pivotal. It is a necessary but insufficient condition for the implementation of child rearing practices that enhance self-control.

Control theories place considerable emphasis on the development of affectionate bonds between children and parents in the creation of self-control (Hirschi & Gottfredson, 2003). Both overly harsh (including physically abusive) and overly neglectful parenting are associated with later problem behavior in children (Hirschi & Gottfredson, 2003). For example, Maxfield and Widom (1996) report that both abuse and neglect in early childhood correlate with later delinquency. Similar results are reported by Eckenrode et al., "Most of the maltreatment experienced by children in our study was neglect, and neglected children showed as many EO [early-onset problem behaviors] as children experiencing physical or sexual abuse" (2001, p. 877).

Considerable evidence suggests that parents or other early care-givers are crucial to the development of self-control (Gottfredson & Hirschi, 1990, ch. 5; Hirschi & Gottfredson, 2003). Wright and Cullen (2001; see also Burton et al., 1995) studied the connection between parenting behaviors and self-reported delinquency in the National Youth Survey data, documenting important effects for parenting:

> From these data, it appears that parents who are nurturing, reliable, and closely attached to their youths and who provide guidance in the form of rules and supervision reduce the delinquency of their adolescents, even when the effects of delinquent peers and sources of parental heterogeneity are controlled ... Our empirical analysis found that delinquency was reduced by child-parent attachment, household rules, and parental supervision ... Our research both reinforces and specifies the contention that control is central to the etiology of delinquent involvement. (2001, 693, 695; see also Feldman and Weinberger [1994]). Parenting effects need not operate entirely through self-control, since supervision itself restricts the opportunity for some delinquency.

Although Gottfredson and Hirschi (1990) argue that variation in childhood socialization is the principal cause of the individual differences in self-control observed in childhood, they do not rule out other causes of self-control. They argue that, in modern society, the school can play a significant role and that, perhaps, biological differences in the ease of socialization may be important. It is sometimes wrongly argued that Gottfredson and Hirschi claim biological causes of self-control are not possible. Rather, they argue against "biological positivism" (just as they argue against psychological and sociological positivism) as a misguided methodology to study crime, delinquency and violence (1990, ch. 3; Gottfredson & Hirschi, 1990a), and they critique existing adoption studies purporting to show heritable effects on *crime* (not studies of the biological causes of self-control). In discussing biological research in criminology, they do not rule out individual differences appearing prior to efforts at early socialization:

> There is good evidence that some of the traits predicting subsequent involvement in crime appear as early as they can be reliably measured, including low intelligence, high activity level, physical strength, and adventuresomeness (Glueck & Glueck 1950; West & Farrington 1973) ... The evidence suggests that the connection between these traits and commission of criminal acts ranges from weak to moderate. Obviously, we do not suggest that people are born criminals, inherit a gene for criminality, or anything of the sort. In fact, we explicitly deny such notions ... What we do suggest is that individual differences may have an impact on the prospects for effective socialization (or adequate control). Effective socialization is, however, always possible whatever the configuration of individual traits (1990, p. 96).

It remains to be seen whether modern research on *self-control* and violence can avoid the problems of past biological positivism and produce replicable and replicated, consistent heritability estimates for plausible concepts that meet the standards of science and meet the criticisms of biological positivism. Such research will also need to confront the increasingly strong experimental evidence (discussed below) apparently showing effects of family and early environmental factors (including schooling) on subsequent measures of self-control and certainly will need to abandon the deterministic claims characteristic of biological (as well as psychological and sociological) positivism of the past.

Research on the Validity of Self-Control Theory

Summarizing the research on the validity of self-control theory is not an easy task. There are several kinds of studies relevant to the question of the validity of self-control theory. The first pertains to the accuracy of the factual portrait of violence depicted earlier – especially research addressing the age, stability, and generality postulates of the theory. A second body of work seeks to operationalize the concepts from the theory, especially "self-control," and studies the relationship between the concept and crime or violence in a sample representative of a particular population. A third area of validity studies is planned interventions, sometimes experimental, often quasi-experimental, that manipulate either family factors or the creation of self-control and determines whether there are subsequent differences on crime or violence. A fourth branch of research seeks to summarize the results of studies on some aspect of the theory and to estimate areas of strength or weakness of predictions from the theory systematically, especially via meta-analysis. Given the interest that the theory has generated from the research community, there is now a very large empirical literature bearing on the question of validity.

Research on the "foundational facts" continues to support the claim that early childhood socialization practices, particularly parenting effects, are important determinants of the level of aggressive or violent behavior (Brannigan et al., 2002; DeLi, 2004; Eckenrode et al., 2001; Farrington, 2003; Gibbs et al., 1998; Maxfield & Widom, 1996; Olds et al., 1998; Perrone et al., 2004). Also, it is clear that there is very considerable stability in individual differences in the tendency to engage in crime, violence, and other problem behaviors over the life course, and correlations between measures of self-control during childhood and adult problem behaviors (Baumeister & Heatherton, 1996; Farrington, 2003; Heckman, 2006, 2007; Laub & Sampson, 2004; Moffitt et al., 2011; Tangney et al., 2004; Zhang et al., 2002). The general age-violence distribution is replicated consistently (Erosheva et al., 2014; Gottfredson & Hirschi, 2016; Laub & Sampson, 2004; Vold et al., 2002). The versatility effect, which implicates violent behavior in a complex of problem behaviors and which questions strongly explanations for violence that take violence as a special or specific topic for study, continue to be reported (Junger et al., 2001; Moffitt et al., 2011; Heckman, 2007); the overall finding is still well described in Farrington's summary (2003, p. 224): "Offenders tend to be versatile not only in committing several types of crimes but also in committing several types of antisocial behavior." With respect to crime, generally, DeLisi (2005, p. 40) provides a useful summary of the evidence:

> To be sure, scholars have found modest statistical evidence of offenders who recurrently engaged in similar types of offending, such as auto theft, armed robbery, and narrow clusters of violent or property crime. However, affirmative evidence of specialization is heavily statistical in nature, and its substantive meaning is often unclear ... Overwhelmingly, researchers have found that criminals are generalists who commit an array of offenses, not specialists who fixate on one type of crime.

With respect to the concept of self-control, a considerable body of individual studies has found strong support for the validity of self-control theory (see, e.g., Pratt & Cullen, 2000; Tittle et al., 2003; Vold et al., 2002; Vazsonyi et al., 2004; Lanier & Henry, 2004; Tittle et al., 2004; DeLisi, 2005; Vazsonyi et al., 2017; Hirtenlehner & Kunz, 2017; Heckman, 2007). Studies have found self-control effects for violence for males and females, for a variety of age groups, for offender samples, for several ethnicities, and in several countries (Vazsonyi et al., 2017; Vazsonyi et al., 2001; Vazsonyi and Belleston, 2007; DeLisi, 2001a; b; Ribeaud & Eisner, 2010; Kobayashi et al., 2010). Baron (2003) found self-control effects in homeless youth for property crime, drug use, and violent crime. Studies have found that self-control predicts serious delinquency (Junger & Tremblay, 1999), intimate violence (Sellers, 1999), crime (Brownfield & Sorenson, 1993; Gibbs et al., 1998), a wide variety of delinquent acts and drug use in French-speaking Canadian samples (LeBlanc & Girard, 1997), drinking among adolescents (Baker, 2010), adolescent substance abuse (Chapple et al., 2005), and general delinquency in a national probability sample of adolescents (De Li, 2004). The list of empirical demonstrations of self-control effects in Tittle et al. (2004, p. 144) includes:

> A relationship between low self-control and criminal or analogous behaviors has been documented for non-student adults [all citations omitted] ... college students; youth; males as well as females; those with and without official criminal backgrounds; and among people in various countries and place. In addition, many types of measures of self-control predict a variety of acts. At least some measures of self-control predict some misbehavior for cross-sectional and longitudinal samples as well as for experimental subjects.

The connection between self-control and wide variety of acts analogous to violence is documented by Perrone et al. (2004) in a list that includes cheating, drugs, accidents, and traffic risks; accidents by Keane et al. (1993); accidents and crime by Junger and Tremblay (1999) and Junger et al., (2001); drinking, drug use, and delinquency among adolescents by Zhang et al. (2002); aggression in adolescents (Ribeaud & Eisner, 2010); attention-deficit hyperactivity disorder and bullying by Unnever and Cornell (2003); gang and dating violence (Chapple & Hope, 2003). In summary, according to DeLisi (2005, p. 91):

> Empirically, the relationship between low self-control and various antisocial outcomes has been nothing short of spectacular. Dozens of studies have explicitly tested the theory and found that low self-control was predictive of failure in family relationships, dating, attachment to church, educational attainment, and occupational status; risky traffic behavior; work-related deviance; having criminal associates and values; residing in a neighborhood perceived to be disorderly; and noncompliance with criminal justice system statuses. Moreover, persons with low self-control are significantly more likely to engage in drinking alcohol; substance abuse; smoking; gambling; violent, property, white-collar, and nuisance offending, and they are more likely to be victimized.

Meta-analyses and General Reviews of Self-Control Research

A number of meta-analyses and general reviews of the research literature have been undertaken specifically focused on the relationship between self-control as described by Gottfredson and Hirschi and a dependent variable of delinquency or crime (Pratt & Cullen, 2000; Engel, 2012; Vazsonyi et al., 2017; see also the general review by Schulz, 2006; a related meta-analysis of self-control and a broad range of outcome variables by de Ridder et al., 2012; and the narrative reviews by DeLisi, 2005 and Gottfredson, 2006). Each of these studies found consistent evidence that self-control is associated substantially with delinquency, crime, and other problem behaviors. Pratt and Cullen's (2000) widely cited study examined research selected for rigor published between 1993 and 1999 included 21 studies and 49,727 individual cases. The strength and consistency of the self-control/crime relationship led them to conclude the research "would rank self-control as one of the strongest known correlates of crime," and that "future research omitting self-control from its empirical analyses risks being misspecified" (2000, p. 952).

Vazsonyi et al. (2017) updated both the methods and the research in the Pratt and Cullen study, and included a larger number of qualified studies, all published between 2000 and 2010. A total of 99 studies with over 200,000 subjects were included. They found random effects mean correlation between self-control and crime and deviance of 0.415 for cross-sectional studies and 0.345 for longitudinal studies (design difference was not significant). The strongest effects of low self-control in their study were discovered for "general deviance" (r = 0.56) and for physical violence (r = 0.46). They conclude their study of some of the best available research,

> provided strong and convincing evidence, based on about 100 cross-sectional and longitudinal studies, that a strong link between low self-control and deviance or crime exists and that it does not greatly vary across modes of assessment, across study designs (cross-sectional versus longitudinal), across measures of deviance, across different populations within the United States, but also across samples across cultures (Vazsonyi et al., 2017, p. 30).

Thus, with respect to reviews of some of the most rigorous research, reviewers consistently report strong validity for self-control theory from several disciplines and methodologies. In fact, reviews place the empirical support for the theory as among the strongest known to criminology.

Evidence from Planned Interventions

Experimental evidence from planned interventions in parenting is consistent with the expectations of self-control theory and thus provides yet another body of research support for the theory. Clarke and Campbell's (1998) review concludes that "[i]t is increasingly clear that the most effective approach to the prevention of chronic problem behaviors requires early intervention before these behaviors emerge in late childhood and early adolescence [citations omitted]" (1998, p. 319). Eckenrode et al. (2001, pp. 876, 886) report that "[t]here are many forms of family support and parent education programs aimed at reducing child abuse and neglect, but the interventions that have received the greatest attention in recent years have involved home visitation services to new parents [citations omitted]" and "[t]hese findings seem highly consistent with research suggesting that neglected children are as likely to be involved with antisocial behavior, even violent offenses, as are physically abused children [citations omitted]." Olds et al. (1998, pp. 73–74) argue that parenting differences may account for the prevention effect discovered in their famous nurse visitation experiments.

A burgeoning research literature based on relatively strong research designs now clearly supports the idea that substantial and lasting prevention effects can be achieved by affecting early childhood experiences in ways designed to enhance socialization and monitoring. Greenwood's review (2006) provides a classification of six types of effective programs, ranging from home visits by nurses to parent training (see also Eckenrode et al., 2001; Olds et al., 1998). Piquero and colleagues (2009, 2016) performed meta-analyses of studies of parenting undertaken with children under the age of 5. In the 78 studies meeting their criteria for inclusion, and using self-report criteria for delinquency, they report a mean effect size of 0.37. In a companion review, Piquero et al. (2010) focused on self-control training in random design studies (n = 34) that sought self-control improvement among young children. They conclude that not only was it possible to systematically alter self-control, but that these interventions reduced delinquency. Similarly, Heckman (2006) finds an array of early-childhood education research to bolster his argument that family environments variously foster skills essential to crime and health, as well as school and work-place success. An economist, he argues strongly that the financial returns to society from early intervention greatly exceed those from later interventions, such as those available to the criminal justice system.

Gottfredson (2006) argued that these early-intervention studies that experimentally produce variation in socialization and monitoring experiences coupled with good follow-up measures are, in fact, properly seen as validity studies for self-control theories. These studies manipulate levels of self-control in experimental groups and contrast the outcomes with nonintervention groups that were selected at random. They show an effect on delinquency for the self-control changes, supporting the theory and its emphasis on early family relationships.

The experimental studies from education, psychology, and criminology are critically important for yet another reason: they lend support to the policy implications of self-control theory. As described by Gottfredson and Hirschi (1990, 1995, 2016) the theory makes strong predictions about the potential effectiveness of long-removed sanctions, such as those possible in the criminal justice system and about the likelihood of greater crime control and violence prevention by a focus on enhancements in early childhood designed to affect self-control. The general inability to document consistent effects from the criminal justice system for enhanced severity of punishments, such a through incarceration, coupled with these promising findings from early intervention support the prevention implications of self-control theory (for a contrast with a focus on criminal justice as a means for reducing crime and violence, see Gottfredson & Hirschi, 2016).

Self-Control and a General Theory of Crime: Some Research Issues

In self-control theory, individual differences in self-control are seen to be a general cause of crime and violence, but certainly not the only cause. Given the early appearance of self-control differences in childhood and the sizable impact of self-control on a variety of problem behaviors, the impact of self-control on other putative causes is presumably substantial. The effect of self-control on participation in or association with many of the institutions plausibly related to delinquency and crime (schools, families, communities, jobs, peer groups, marriages, and other measures of interpersonal relations) makes clear inferences about these other potential causes problematic. However, according to Gottfredson and Hirschi (1990) not all family, school, or individual effects are accounted for by the theory. In addition to the direct effect of age, Gottfredson and Hirschi (1990) considered individual differences including physic, strength, cognitive abilities, as individual-level causes not in the scope of the theory and situational causes of specific crimes as causes apart from self-control differences. Both the school and the family are considered to be social structures with influence on crime in addition to their influence due to self-control differences. Teasing the effects of these and other structural variables, such as community effects, from the effects of self-control is, of course, a difficult task in what is essentially observational research, a task not made much easier with the common method of passive observational longitudinal research. Creative conceptual and measurement work is needed to help with these tasks.

Although opportunity is a cause of crime in the theory, opportunity differences are extremely difficult to sort out from differences in self-control, since where people go, with whom, at what times, and for what purposes are, to some extent, correlated with self-control. Self-control theory was influenced by developments in opportunity or routine activity theories, which themselves focused attention on situational elements of crime as it typically occurs (Hindelang, Gottfredson, & Garofalo, 1978; Cohen & Felson, 1979). Self-control theory assumes that differences among people in self-control are also associated with the distribution of people in settings that vary in the opportunities for crime and delinquency. Thus, being among adolescent males in unsupervised settings, especially at night and in the presence of readily available drugs or alcohol enhances opportunity for delinquency and is also a function of self-control. Similarly, persistence in school and in the work force are associated with those with higher levels of self-control and also with reduced opportunities for crime and violence. Throughout the life-course, differences among people in self-control influence friend and family associations, employment patterns, and many other life experiences that in turn affect the opportunities for violence (Moffitt et al., 2011; Tangney et al., 2004). How self-control effects can be estimated apart from the effects of institutional and opportunity causes remains an important and problematic area in research on the causation of violence (see, e.g., Gottfredson, 2006). Research on situational crime prevention establishes the importance of opportunity variables as causes of crime (Clarke, 1995). How self-control differences are implicated in placing people in high opportunity settings, and the differences among people in recognizing or reacting to such opportunities is likely an important focus for continued research.

Measurement issues surround the concepts in self-control theory and should be at the heart of future research (Marcus, 2003, 2004). For example, age-appropriate measures of self-control are lacking, making the study of how self-control differences may change with age often confounded completely with potential measurement error (e.g., the indicator "childhood tantrums" becomes a less compelling measure after the earliest years). Such measures are likely best constructed relying on counts of behavioral indicators, provided by others in addition to self-reports, given confounds between self-reports of problem behaviors and self-control. Attention to measurement issues, such as the reliability of instruments, will likely help situate studies that report short-term instability in their measures of self-control (likely influenced by unreliability) from substantive changes in self-control itself and the apparent lack of discrimination in attitudinal measures except for the tails of the self-control distribution (see Burt, Simons, & Simons, 2006 for examples of both problems).

Self-control measures that rely on counts of instances of problem behaviors – taking full advantage of the versatility effect – also seem likely to enhance predictability of violence and other problem behavior. For example, it seems likely that school data about truancy or school absence would have higher validity than questions asked of pre-adolescents about liking school, for the purpose of predictions of subsequent crime and violence. In any event, the research accumulated so far amply justifies a strong focus on the concept of self-control and its measurement in the future, and less reliance on commonly used self-report scales, as a means of progress in testing the theory.

Conclusion

According to self-control theory, caring and attentive parents or other care-givers create the tendency in their children to subordinate their immediate desires to long-term interests. Self-control in children is created by establishing a reciprocal bond between parent and child. This bond inhibits the pursuit of short-term objectives unfettered by longer-term concerns, such as parental and peer respect, interpersonal relations, and the development of social capital. Much violent criminal behavior jeopardizes these long-term interests and is thus generally prevented by high levels of self-control. The general characteristics of acts inhibited by high levels of self-control suggest a cause for the versatility effect routinely found in the literature and the early development of self-control in childhood suggests a reason for the stability of individual differences in the tendency for problem behaviors that persists over the life-course. Much behavioral research is consistent with the theory and the assumptions on which it is based and supports the general statement by Moffitt et al. (2011, p. 2693) that "[t]he need to delay gratification, control impulses, and modulate emotional expression is the earliest and most ubiquitous demand that societies place on their children, and success at many life tasks depends critically on children's mastery of such self-control."

References

Baron, S. (2003). Self-control, social consequences and criminal behavior: Street youth and the general theory of crime. *Journal of Research in Crime and Delinquency*, 40, 403–425.

Baumeister, R. & Heatherton, T. (1996). Self-regulation failure: An overview. *Psychological Inquiry*, 7, 1–15.

Boyum, D. & Kleiman, M. (1995). Alcohol and other drugs. In J. Wilson & J. Petersilia (Eds), *Crime*. San Francisco: ICS Press.

Brannigan, A., Gemmell, W., Pevalin, D., & Wade, T. (2002). Self-control and social control in childhood misconduct and aggression: The role of family structure, hyperactivity, and hostile parenting. *Canadian Journal of Criminology*, 9, 142–160.

Britt, C. (1994). Versatility. In T. Hirschi & M. Gottfredson (Eds), *The Generality of Deviance*. New Brunswick, NJ: Transaction.

Brownfield, D. & Sorenson, S. (1993). Self-control and juvenile delinquency: Theoretical issues and empirical assessment of selected elements of *A General Theory of Crime*. *Deviant Behavior*, 14, 243–264.

Burt, C., Simons, R., & Simons, L. G. (2006). A longitudinal test of the effects of parenting and the stability of self-control: Negative evidence for the general theory of crime. *Criminology*, 44, 353–396.

Burton, V., Evans, T. D., Cullen, F., Olivares, K., & Dunaway, R. (1995). Age, self-control, and adults' offending behaviors: A research note assessing *A General Theory of Crime*. *Journal of Criminal Justice*, 27(1), 45–54.

Chapple, C., Hope, T., & Whiteford, S. (2005). The direct and indirect effects of parental bonds, parental drug use, and self-control on adolescent substance use. *Journal of Child and Adolescent Substance Abuse*, 14, 17–38.

Chapple, C. & Hope, T. (2003). An analysis of the self-control and criminal versatility of gang and dating violence offenders. *Violence and Victims*, 18, 671–690.

Clarke, R. V. (1995). Situational crime prevention. In M. Tonry & D. P. Farrington (Eds), *Crime and justice: A review of research: Vol. 19*. Chicago, IL: University of Chicago Press.

Clarke, S. & Campbell, F. (1998). Can intervention early prevent crime later? The abecedarian project compared with other programs. *Early Childhood Research Quarterly*, 13(2), 319–343.

Costello, B. & Dunaway, R. (2003). Egotism and delinquent behavior. *Journal of Interpersonal Violence*, 18, 572–590.

Cohen, L. & Felson, M. (1979). Social change and crime rate trends: A routine activities approach. *American Sociological Review*, 44, 588–608.

De Li, S. (2004). The impacts of self-control and social bonds on juvenile delinquency in a national sample of mid-adolescents. *Deviant Behavior*, 2, 351–373.

DeLisi, M. (2001a). Designed to fail: Self-control and involvement in the criminal justice system. *American Journal of Criminal Justice*, 26(1), 131–148.

DeLisi, M. (2001b). It's all in the record: assessing self-control theory with an offender sample. *Criminal Justice Review*, 26, 1–16.

DeLisi, M. (2005). *Career criminals in society*. Thousand Oaks, CA: Sage.

DeLisi, M. & Piquero, A. R. (2011). New frontiers in criminal careers research, 2000–2011: A state-of-the-art review. *Journal of Criminal Justice*, 39, 289–301.

de Ridder, D., Lensvelt-Mulders, G., Finkenauer, C., Stok, F., & Baumeister, R. (2012). Taking stock of self-control: a meta-analysis of how trait self-control relates to a wide range of behaviors. *Personality and Social Psychology Review*, 16, 76–99.

Donovan, J., Jessor, R., & Costa, F. (1991). Adolescent health behavior and conventionality-unconventionality: An extension of problem-behavior theory. *Health Psychology*, 10(1), 52–61.

Duckworth, A. (2011). The significance of self-control. *Proceedings of the National Academy of Sciences*, 108, 2639–40.

Eckenrode, J., Zielinske, D., Smith, E., Marcynyszyn, L., Henderson, C. Jr., Kitzman, H., ... & Olds, D. (2001). Child maltreatment and the early onset of problem behaviors: Can a program of nurse home visitation break the link? *Development and Psychopathology*, 13, 873–890.

Engel, C. (2012). *Low self control as a source of crime: a meta-study*. Bonn: Max Planck Institute for Research on Collective Goods.

Erosheva, E., Matsueda, R., & Telesca, D. (2014). Breaking bad: Two decades of life-course data analysis in criminology, developmental psychology, and beyond. *Annual Review of Statistics and Applications,* 1, 301–332.

Farrington, D. (2003). Developmental and life-course criminology: Key theoretical and empirical issues. The 2002 Sutherland Award Address. *Criminology,* 41, 221–255.

Gibbs, J., Giever, D., & Higgins, G. (2003). A test of Gottfredson and Hirschi's general theory using structural equation modeling. *Journal of Research in Crime and Delinquency,* 35(4), 441–458.

Gibbs, J., Giever, D., & Martin, J. (1998). Parental-management and self-control: An empirical test of Gottfredson and Hirschi's general theory. *Journal of Research in Crime and Delinquency,* 35, 42–72.

Glueck, S. & Glueck, E. (1950). *Unraveling juvenile delinquency.* Cambridge, MA: Harvard University Press.

Gottfredson, M. (2013). A note on the role of basic theory in thinking about crime prevention. *European Journal of Criminal Policy and Research,* 19, 91–97.

Gottfredson, M. (2011a). Sanctions, situations, and agency in control theories of crime. *European Journal of Criminology,* 8, 129 143.

Gottfredson, M. (2011b). Some advantages of a crime-free criminology. In M. Bosworth & C. Hoyle (Eds), *What is criminology?* (p. 35–48). Oxford: Oxford University Press.

Gottfredson, M. (2006). The empirical status of control theories in criminology. In F. Cullen et al. (Eds), *Taking Stock: The Empirical Status of Theory in Criminology.* New Brunswick: Transaction.

Gottfredson, S. & Gottfredson, D. (1994). Behavioral prediction and the problem of incapacitation. *Criminology,* 32, 441–474.

Gottfredson, M. & Hirschi, T. (2016). The criminal career perspective as an explanation of crime and a guide to crime control policy: The view from general theories of crime. *Journal of Research in Crime and Delinquency,* 53, 406–419.

Gottfredson, M. & Hirschi, T. (1995). National crime control policies. *Society,* 32(2), 30–36.

Gottfredson, M. & Hirschi, T. (1994). *The Generalilty of Deviance.* New Brunswick, NJ: Transaction.

Gottfredson, M. & Hirschi, T. (1993). A control theory interpretation of psychological research on aggression. In R. Felson & J. Tedeschi (Eds), *Aggression and Violence.* Washington, DC: American Psychological Association.

Gottfredson, M. & Hirschi, T. (1991). Three facts and their implications for research on crime. In G. Albrecht & H. Otto (Eds), *Social Prevention and the Social Sciences* (pp. 525–537). New York: de Gruyter.

Gottfredson, M. R. & Hirschi, T. (1990). *A general theory of crime.* Stanford, CA: Stanford University Press.

Gottfredson, M. R. & Hirschi, T. (1990a). Substantive positivism and the idea of crime. *Rationality and Society,* 2, 412–428.

Greenwood, P. (2006). *Changing lives: Delinquency prevention as crime control policy.* Chicago: University of Chicago Press.

Heckman, J. (2006). Skill formation and the economics of investing in disadvantaged children. *Science,* 312, 1900–1902.

Heckman, J. (2007). The economics, technology, and neuroscience of human capability formation. *Proceedings of the National Academy of Sciences,* 104(33), 13250–13255.

Hindelang, M., Gottfredson, M., & Garofalo, J. (1978). *Victims of personal crime: An empirical foundation for a theory of personal victimization.* Cambridge, MA: Ballinger.

Hindelang, M., Hirschi, T., & Weis J. G. (1981). *Measuring delinquency.* Beverley Hills, CA: Sage.

Hirschi, T. (2004). Self-control and crime. In R. Baumeister & K. Vohs (Eds), *Handbook of self-regulation: Research, theory and applications.* New York: Guilford.

Hirschi, T. (1969). *Causes of delinquency.* Berkeley: University of California Press.

Hirschi, T. & Gottfredson, M. R. (2003). Punishment of children from the point of view of control theory." In C. Britt & M. Gottfredson (Eds), *Control theories of crime and delinquency*. New Brunswick: Transaction.

Hirschi, T. & Gottfredson, M. (1995). Control theory and the life-course perspective. *Studies of Crime and Crime Prevention*, 4, 131–142.

Hirschi, T. & Gottfredson, M. (1994). *The generality of deviance*. New Brunswick: Transaction.

Hirschi, T. & Gottfredson, M. (1983). Age and the explanation of crime. *American Journal of Sociology*, 89, 552–584.

Hirschi, T. & Selvin, H. (1967). *Delinquency research*. New York: The Free Press.

Hirtenlehner, H. & Kunz, F. (2017). Can self-control theory explain offending in late adulthood? Evidence from Germany. *Journal of Criminal Justice*, 48, 37–47.

Junger, M., Stroebe, W., & van der Laan, A. (2001). Delinquency, health behaviour and health. *British Journal of Health Psychology*, 6(2), 103–120.

Junger, M. & Tremblay, R. (1999). Self-control, accidents, and crime. *Criminal Justice and Behavior*, 26(4), 485–501.

Junger, M., van der Heijden, P., & Keane C. (2001). Interrelated harms: Examining the associations between victimization, accidents, and criminal behavior. *International Journal of Injury Control & Safety Promotion*, 8, 13–28.

Keane, C., Maxim, P., & Teevan, J. (1993). Drinking and driving, self control, and gender: Testing the general theory of crime. *Journal of Research in Crime and Delinquency*, 30, 30–46.

Kobayashi, E., Vazsonyi, A., Chen, P., & Sharp, S. (2010). A culturally nuanced test of Gottfredson and Hirschi's "general theory": Dimensionality and generalizability in Japan and in the U.S. *International Criminal Justice Review*, 20, 112–131.

Laub, J. & Sampson, R. J. (2003). *Shared beginnings, divergent lives*. Cambridge, MA: Harvard University Press.

Lanier, M. & Henry, S. (2004). *Essential Criminology*. Boulder, CO: Westview Press.

LeBlanc, M. & Girard, S. (1997). The generality of deviance: Replication over two decades with a Canadian sample of adjudicated boys. *Canadian Journal of Criminology*, 34, 171–183.

Loeber, R. & Dishion, T. (1983). Early predictors of male delinquency: A review. *Psychological Bulletin*, 94, 68–99.

Loeber, R. & Stouthamer-Loeber, M. (1986). Family factors as correlates and predictors of juvenile conduct problems and delinquency. In M. Tonry & N. Morris (Eds), *Crime and Justice: An Annual Review of Research*. Chicago: University of Chicago Press.

Macmillan, R. (2008). Review of key issues in criminal career research. *Contemporary Sociology*, 37(2), 159–160.

Marcus, B. (2004). Self-control in the general theory of crime: Theoretical implications of a measurement problem. *Theoretical Criminology*, 8(1), 33–55.

Marcus, B. (2003). An empirical examination of the construct validity of two alternative self-control measures. *Educational and Psychological Measurement*, 63(4), 674–706.

Maxfield, M. & Widom, C. (1996). The cycle of violence revisited 6 years later. *Archives of Pediatrics and Adolescent Medicine*, 150, 390–395.

McCord, W. & J. McCord. (1959). *Origins of crime*. New York: Columbia University Press.

Mischel, W., Shoda, Y., & Peake, P. (1988). The nature of adolescent competencies predicted by preschool delay of gratification. *Journal of Personality and Social Psychology*, 54, 687–696.

Moffitt, T. E., Arseneault, L., Belsky, D., Dickson, N., Hancox, R. J., Harrington, H., … & Sears, M. R. (2011). A gradient of childhood self-control predicts health, wealth, and public safety. *Proceedings of the National Academy of Sciences*, 108(7), 2693–2698.

Moffitt, T. E., Poulton, R., & Caspi, A. (2013). Lifelong impact of early self-control. *American Scientist*, 101, 352–359.

Olds, D., Pettitt, L. M., Robinson, J., Henderson, C., Eckenrode, J., Kitzman,

H., ... & Powers, J. (1998). Reducing risks for antisocial behavior with a program of prenatal and early childhood home visitation. *Journal of Community Psychology*, 26(1), 65–83.

Osgood, D. L., Johnston, P. O'Malley, & Bachman, J. (1988). The generality of deviance in late adolescence and early adulthood. *American Sociological Review*, 53, 81–93.

Perrone, D, Sullivan, C., Pratt, T., & Margaryan, S. (2004). Parental efficacy, self-control, and delinquency: A test of a general theory of crime on a nationally representative sample of youth. *International Journal of Offender Therapy and Comparative Criminology*, 48, 298–312.

Piquero, A., Farrington, D., Welsh, B., Tremblay, R., & Jennings, W. (2009). Effects of early family/parent training programs on antisocial behavior and delinquency. *Journal of Experimental Criminology*, 5, 83–120.

Piquero, A., Jennings, R., Diamons, G., & Farrington, D. (2016). A meta-analysis update on the effects of early family/parent training programs on antisocial behavior and delinquency. *Journal of Experimental Criminology*, 12(2), 229–248.

Piquero, A., Jennings, W., & Farrington, D. (2010). On the malleability of self-control: Theoretical and policy implications regarding a general theory of crime. *Justice Quarterly*, 27, 803–34.

Pratt, T. & Cullen, F. (2000). The empirical status of Gottfredson and Hirschi's general theory of crime: A meta-analysis. *Criminology*, 38, 931–964.

Ribeaud, D. & Eisner, M. (2010). Risk factors for aggression in preadolescence. *European Journal of Criminology*, 7(6), 460–498.

Robbins, L. (1966). *Deviant children grown up*. Baltimore: Williams and Wilkins.

Sampson, R. & Laub, J. (1995). *Crime in the Making: Pathways and turning points through life*. Cambridge, MA: Harvard University Press.

Schulz. S. (2006). *Beyond self-control: Analysis and critique of Gottfredson and Hirschi's general theory of crime*. Berlin: Duncker and Hirbult.

Sellers, C. (1999). Self-control and intimate violence: An examination of the scope and specification of the general theory of crime. *Criminology*, 37, 375–404.

Skardhamar, T. (2009). Reconsidering the theory of adolescent-limited and life-course persistent anti-social behaviour. *British Journal of Criminology*, 49, 863–878.

Tangney, J. P., Baumeister, R. F., & Boone, A. L. (2004). High self-control predicts good adjustment, less pathology, better grades, and interpersonal success. *Journal of Personality*, 72(2), 271–324.

Tittle, C. R., Ward, D. A., & Grasmick, H. G. (2003). Gender, age, and crime/deviance: A challenge to self-control theory. *Journal of Research in Crime and Delinquency*, 40(4), 426–453.

Tittle, C. R., Ward, D. A., & Grasmick, H. G. (2004). Capacity for self-control and individuals' interest in exercising self-control. *Journal of Quantitative Criminology*, 20(2), 143–172.

Unnever, J. D. & Cornell, D. G. (2003). Bullying, self-control, and ADHD. *Journal of Interpersonal Violence*, 18(2), 129–147.

Vazsonyi, A. & Belliston, L. (2007). The family, low self-control and deviance. *Criminal Justice and Behavior*, 34(4), 505–530.

Vazsonyi, A. T., Mikuska, J., & Kelley, E. (2017). It's time: A meta-analysis on the self-control deviance link. *Journal of Criminal Justice*, 48, 48–63.

Vazsonyi, A. T., Pickering, L. E., Junger, M., & Hessing, D. (2001). An empirical test of a general theory of crime: A four-nation comparative study of self-control and the prediction of deviance. *Journal of Research in Crime and Delinquency*, 38(2), 91–131.

Vazsonyi, A. T., Wittekind, J. E. C., Belliston, L. M., & Van Loh, T. D. (2004). Extending the General Theory of Crime to "The East": Low self-control in Japanese late adolescents. *Journal of Quantitative Criminology*, 20(3), 189–216.

Vold, G., Bernard, T., & Snipes, J. (2002). *Theoretical Criminology.* 5th Edition. Oxford: Oxford University Press.

West, D. & Farrington, D. P. (1973). *Who becomes delinquent?* London: Heineman.

Wolfgang, M., Figlio, R., & Sellin, T. 1972. *Delinquency in a Birth Cohort.* Chicago: University of Chicago Press.

Wright, J. & Cullen, F. (2001). Parental efficacy and delinquency behavior: Do control and support matter? *Criminology*, 39, 677–706.

Zhang, L., Welte, J., & Wieczorek, W. (2002). Underlying common factors of adolescent problem behaviors. *Criminal Justice and Behavior*, 29, 161–182.

18 Peers and Aggression: From Description to Prevention

Frank Vitaro, Mara Brendgen, and Michel Boivin

Introduction

"Deviant peer affiliation (DPA) is one of the strongest predictors of adolescent problem behavior." This sentence is the opening statement of virtually all empirical papers and review chapters examining the role of DPA in regard to the development of adolescent problem behavior, including aggression. Yet, the empirical evidence on which this statement rests comes mostly from one-child-per-family correlational studies, which are notoriously vulnerable to omitted third variables, including genetic influences. As shown by behavioral (i.e., quantitative) genetic studies, most aspects of human development such as aggression, as well as many environmental factors, including DPA, are subject to genetic influences (Moffitt, 2005b). Ignoring this evidence may contribute to a biased view of the role of DPA.

Here, we (1) present evidence derived from longitudinal one-child-per-family studies linking DPA to children's and adolescents' aggressive behavior; (2) examine the role of DPA in the context of genetically controlled studies, particularly twin studies, to see whether the evidence concords with longitudinal one-child-per-family studies; and (3) draw a number of implications for prevention and for future research.

The chapter is focused on aggressive behavior, distinguishing whenever possible between different *forms* (i.e., physical vs. social aggression) or different *functions* (i.e., reactive vs. proactive aggression). With respect to *form*, physical aggression typically refers to behaviors such as hitting and fighting, whereas social aggression typically refers to behaviors such as socially excluding, maliciously gossiping, and withdrawing support. *Function* is often inferred from assumed intent. Proactive aggression is calculated aggression aimed at achieving a personal goal, and is not generally motivated by anger. In contrast, reactive aggression is impulsive and driven by some form of arousal (e.g., anger) associated with a factual or imagined threatening or unpleasant stimulus, with the implicit goal of harming its author or rebuffing the insult (for more details, see Vitaro & Brendgen, 2012). However, studies addressing broader measures of antisocial behaviors, externalizing problems, conduct disorders, or delinquency were also considered when relevant, because these global measures often include several aggression- or violence-related items.

The Role of DPA According to Longitudinal One-Child-per-Family Studies

Although generally rejected by conventional peers, many aggressive children and adolescents have friends, and most of them participate in cliques (Boivin & Vitaro, 1995; Cairns, Perrin, & Cairns, 1985). Importantly, however, aggressive youth affiliate with friends and clique members that are similar to themselves with respect to aggression (Cairns, Xie, & Leung, 1998; Hektner, August, & Realmuto, 2000). This tendency for aggressive children to associate with other aggressive peers is already present during the preschool years (Estell, Cairns, Farmer, & Cairns, 2002; Snyder et al., 2005). In consequence, the lingering question over the past five decades has been whether these affiliations matter.

Consequences of Affiliating with Aggressive-Antisocial Friends/Peers

Despite some notable exceptions (Gottfredson & Hirschi, 1990), most researchers who have documented the association between DPA and increases in aggressive-antisocial behavior using a longitudinal one-child-per-family design have concluded that DPA is an important source of influence (see reviews by Boivin, Vitaro, & Poulin, 2005; Dishion & Tipsord, 2011; Prinstein & Giletta, 2016; Veenstra & Dijkstra, 2011). The only point of disagreement between scholars is whether this influence is unconditional (i.e., independent of participants characteristics) or conditional (i.e., dependent on participants' characteristics).

Theoretical models with respect to the role of DPA. Those who posit that deviant friends exert an unconditional influence on children's or adolescents' aggressive behavior, independent of participants' characteristics, endorse the *Causal model*. The Causal model has also been referred to as the Social Facilitation, Peer Influence, Cultural Deviance, Differential Association, or Socialization model, depending on whether one reads the psychological, sociological, or criminological literature (Elliott, Huizinga, & Ageton, 1985; Johnson, Marcos, & Bahr, 1987; Sutherland, 1947). According to this model, both behaviors and attitudes favorable to aggression can be learned from association with deviant friends, a position that is congruent with social learning principles. Two versions of the Causal model are possible. According to one version, deviant peers are a necessary and sufficient starting point for aggressive behaviors to emerge, evolve, or remain stable. In this version, deviant peers have a main effect on behavior. In the other version of the Causal model, affiliation with deviant peers is viewed as a mediator of the link between exposure to contexts such as coercive families (Kim, Hetherington, & Reiss, 1999), neighborhood disadvantage (Brody et al., 2001), or involvement with the criminal justice system (Johnson, Simons, & Conger, 2004) and an increase in antisocial behavior. In both cases, the effects of DPA are unconditional for all exposed participants.

There is strong evidence in support of the Causal model from studies using a one-child-per-family design. More specifically, DPA has been found to predict aggressive and antisocial behavior after controlling for the child's aggressive behavior as well as related social experiences such as peer rejection and parent coercion (Patterson, Capaldi, & Bank, 1991; Thomas, Bierman, & Conduct Problems Prevention Research Group, 2006; Vitaro, Pedersen, & Brendgen, 2007). As already mentioned, this evidence not only applies to adolescents but also to children. To illustrate, Snyder et al. (2005) reported that association with deviant peers in kindergarten predicted growth in overt conduct problems (e.g., aggressiveness) as well as covert conduct problems (e.g., lying, stealing) on the playground and in the classroom during the following two years. Moreover, there is experimental evidence in support of the Causal model. For example, Leve and Chamberlain (2005) showed that aggregating delinquent adolescents in group care centers increased both their involvement with delinquent peers and their delinquent behaviors over the course of one year in comparison to a foster care alternative treatment.

In contrast to the Causal model, the *Conditional model* (also called the Enhancement or the Social Interactional model; Dishion, 1990; Lacourse, Nagin, Tremblay, Vitaro, & Claes, 2003) posits an interaction between personal attributes and friends'/peers' deviancy in predicting later antisocial or aggressive behaviors. Hence, the link between DPA and aggression could be conditioned by personal or socio-environmental attributes (i.e., DPA as the moderated variable) or, alternatively, the link between personal or socio-environmental attributes and aggression could be conditioned by DPA (i.e., DPA as the moderator).

There is evidence from one-child-per-family studies that DPA could play a moderating role. For example, affiliation with aggressive peers has been found to exacerbate the likelihood that low self-regulation leads to later delinquent behavior (Gardner, Dishion, & Connell, 2008). However, the number of studies that examined the DPA-as-moderator version of the Conditional model is scarce compared to the ample evidence in support of the view that peers are influential but not equally across participants (i.e., the DPA-as-moderated variable version of the Conditional model). The most common moderators of the link between DPA and increase or maintenance of aggressive behaviors revolve around *personal characteristics*. More specifically, child and adolescent behavior profile has been shown to play a moderating role, although it is not yet clear whether peer influence is strongest for the most aggressive-antisocial individuals (Mrug & Windle, 2009; Warren, Schoppelrey, Moberg, & McDonald, 2005) or the moderately aggressive-antisocial (Vitaro, Tremblay, Kerr, Pagani, & Bukowski, 1997). In turn, positive attitudes towards deviant norms or high levels of hostile attributional biases have been found to exacerbate adolescents' susceptibility to negative peer influence (Molano, Jones, Brown, & Aber, 2013; Vitaro, Brendgen, & Tremblay, 2000). This may also be the case for high social anxiety and for low self-regulation (Gardner et al., 2008). Finally, susceptibility to peer influence, which may be measured directly through self-reports (Steinberg & Monahan, 2007) or through performance tasks (Allen, Porter, & McFarland, 2006; Prinstein, Brechwald, & Cohen, 2011) may also play a moderating role.

Other personal characteristics such as sex can also moderate the effect of DPA, although findings are equivocal (see Müller & Minger, 2013). In some studies, both girls' and boys' antisocial behavior has been shown to be influenced by deviant peers (Laird, Jordan, Dodge, Pettit, & Bates, 2001; Urberg, Degirmencioglu, & Pilgrim, 1997). However, as suggested by Hartup (2005), girls may exert more influence over girls than over boys with respect to some forms of aggressive behavior that are normative for girls (i.e., relational aggression), whereas boys may influence other boys more than girls with respect to the use of aggressive behaviors that are more normative for boys (i.e., physical aggression). Age can also play an important role in determining the consequences of affiliation with or exposure to deviant peers. The popular view is that susceptibility to peer influence tends to peak in early to middle adolescence (Müller & Minger, 2013). However, as detailed later, there is contradictory evidence about the interaction between DPA and age. Biological changes, such as early physical maturation, can also exacerbate the link between exposure to deviant friends and later antisocial behavior, in addition to showing a main effect (Fergusson, Vitaro, Wanner, & Brendgen, 2007).

At the socio-family level, insecure attachment to parents has been reported to moderate (i.e., exacerbate) the link between exposure to deviant friends and participants' antisocial behaviors (Vitaro et al., 2000). Parental practices have also been found to play a moderating role. For example, Galambos, Barker, and Almeida (2003) found that parents' behavioral control (i.e., regulation of the child's behavior through firm and consistent discipline) mitigated the link between exposure to deviant friends and increases in externalizing problems during early adolescence. Conversely, Mrug and Windle (2009) found that harsh and inconsistent parenting exacerbated the link between peer deviancy and an increase in externalizing behaviors (i.e., delinquency and substance use) during early adolescence. In addition to parental practices, low SES, high socio-family adversity, and parents' attitudes towards violence (i.e., support for fighting vs. support for nonviolence) have also been shown to increase physical aggression as well as moderate the socialization of physical aggression by the peer group (Farrell, Henry, Mays, & Schoeny, 2011; Farrington & West, 1993).

At the group level, child/adolescent social status has been found to play a moderating role. Studies that examined whether acceptance by conventional peers or popularity moderated the link between deviant friend involvement and delinquency found contradictory results. Using a peer-acceptance measure (i.e., a preference-based measure derived from positive and negative nomination) collected during pre-adolescence, Fergusson et al. (2007) found no interaction between social acceptance and exposure to deviant friends in predicting aggressive behavior. In contrast, Allen, Porter, McFarland, Marsh, and McElhaney (2005) and Haynie (2001) found that individuals' popularity (i.e., a reputation-based measure) exacerbated the link between affiliation with deviant friends and increased delinquency and drug use during adolescence. To complicate things further, Ellis and Zarbatany (2007) found that that individuals' high centrality in the peer group (established using a social cognitive map procedure) magnified peer socialization of relational aggression and deviant behavior but not physical aggression. To explain these results, it has been suggested that some deviant behaviors (i.e., drug use, truancy), as well as relational aggression, become more accepted during adolescence and that popular adolescents are thus more likely to endorse such behaviors than others (Allen et al., 2005). However, violent behavior does not seem to be part of the behaviors that gain popularity with age, which, in addition to sample age and type of popularity measures used, may help explain the contradictory findings. Finally, self-perceived low peer acceptance has been found to exacerbate the influence of deviant peers on delinquent behaviors (i.e., weapon carrying and physical fighting) (Prinstein, Boergers, & Spirito, 2001).

At the group level, peers' social status has also been found to play a moderating role. In line with social learning theory, Cohen and Prinstein (2006) found that average-status adolescents conformed more to peers' aggression, both in terms of attitudes and actual behaviors, when the peers appeared to be high in social status. The moderating role of best friend's social status within the peer group was also confirmed in another study (Nijhof, Scholte, Overbeek, & Engels, 2010). However, the direction of the moderating effect depended on the type of behavior and whether the associations between friend's behavior and participants' behavior were examined cross-sectionally or longitudinally.

Finally, at the dyad level, features of friendship such as mutuality have also been found to play a moderating role. For example, Nijhof et al. (2010) found that having a reciprocal friend who committed property offenses increased adolescents' risk of committing similar offenses, whereas adolescents with a unilaterally nominated friend showed a decreased risk over time. Reciprocity implies that participants nominate each other as best friends, whereas unilaterality implies that one participant nominates another as best friend while the other does not reciprocate. However, there is also evidence to the contrary. For example, Adams, Bukowski, and Bagwell (2005) reported more changes in a child's level of aggression when the relationship with an aggressive friend was non-mutual than when it was mutual.

Given that most mutual friends are initially more similar than desired unilateral friends, it is not totally surprising that unilateral friends may have more "influence" than reciprocal friends.

To summarize, a number of correlational studies support the Conditional model by showing that deviant peers exert influence, but that this influence is conditional on participants' and peers' personal, familial, and social characteristics. Results from experimental studies also indicate that some participants are more affected by exposure to deviant peers than others. For instance, Prinstein et al. (2011) showed that changes in adolescents' responses before and after exposure to a "chat room" experiment (i.e., reflecting peer influence susceptibility) moderated the association between best friends' baseline deviant behavior and adolescents' own deviant behavior 18 months later.

Mechanisms that Might Help Explain the Influence of Deviant Friends/Peers

If we assume that DPA actually plays an influential role in accordance with the Causal or the Conditional model, we need to understand the mechanisms through which deviant peer influence operates. Four possible mechanisms have been proposed.

Differential reinforcement through deviancy training. Positive verbal reinforcement by peers for deviant behaviors may be an important factor explaining peer influence. This process, labeled "deviancy training" by Dishion and his colleagues (Dishion, Spracklen, Andrews, & Patterson, 1996), has received substantial empirical support. Specifically, deviant peers tend to reinforce (through laughter or positive nonverbal feedback) rule-breaking talk or deviant acts while ignoring or punishing normative behaviors. In turn, this differential reinforcement of deviant behaviors has been found to result in an increase in youngsters' subsequent delinquent behavior and substance use (Dishion, Burraston, & Poulin, 2001; Poulin, Dishion, & Burraston, 2001). Snyder et al. (2005) has reported that deviancy training already occurs among kindergarten children. Specifically, engaging in deviant talk and imitative play of deviant behaviors with same-gender peers predicted an increase in overt and covert conduct problems on the playground, at school, and at home.

The degree of (dis)organization of adolescents' interactions (i.e., entropy) can also play a role in moderating the impact of deviancy training. In the social relationship context, entropy is a measure of the degree of disorganization and lack of consistency in the series of interactions between two or more individuals. A high entropy score represents a disorganized, unfocused, and unpredictable pattern of interactions, whereas a low entropy score reflects the opposite pattern. Dishion, Nelson, Winter, and Bullock (2004) reported that, by age 14, antisocial dyads with well-organized interactions (i.e., low entropy) but high levels of deviant talk were most likely to manifest antisocial behaviors by early adulthood even after controlling for current and past delinquency. In other words, exclusive focus on rule-breaking behaviors exacerbated the risk for continued antisociality.

Coercion and conflict among friends. Aggressive children have been found to be bossier with their friends and more frequently involved in coercive and conflictual exchanges than nonaggressive children (Deptula & Cohen, 2004; Dishion, Andrews, & Crosby, 1995). It is possible that this pattern of negative interactions among aggressive friends directly influences their problem behaviors through a coercive interactional process similar to the one identified by Patterson and colleagues in regard to parent-child interactions (Patterson, Littman, & Bricker, 1967). In line with this notion, some studies showed that conflict with a best friend or victimization by a best friend predicted an increase in children's aggression (Kupersmidt, Burchinal, & Patterson, 1995) or mediated the effect of best friends' aggressiveness on children's aggression (Vitaro et al., 2011). Analyses at the micro-social level similar to those used by Dishion and his collaborators to uncover the process of deviancy training are needed to confirm this coercive process.

Peer pressure to conform to norm-breaking behavior. There is evidence that pressure to conform to norm-breaking behaviors may serve as a mechanism for deviancy training in the friendships or cliques of aggressive children. For example, Bagwell and Coie (2004) reported that 10-year-old aggressive boys and their friends manifested more enticement for rule violations in situations that provided opportunities for rule-breaking behavior than nonaggressive boys and their friends. As expected, aggressive boys and their friends also engaged in more rule-breaking behavior than did nonaggressive boys and their friends. Interestingly, however, nonaggressive dyads also engaged in what Bagwell and Coie (2004) called "temptation talk" (i.e., exploration of potential rule violations), but they seldom escalated from temptation talk to actual norm-breaking behaviors. As suggested by

Bagwell and Coie (2004), temptation talk is a salient developmental process within friendships during late childhood and early adolescence, as it serves as a way for children to explore limits for behavior (i.e., norms) within the peer group. Temptation talk is not coercive, but the resulting peer enticements may provide the needed push for action in dyads where the children are prone to antisocial behaviors.

Modeling. Modeling of rule-breaking or aggressive behaviors may also partly explain how deviant peers support the maintenance or escalation of aggressive-antisocial acts (Cohen & Prinstein, 2006). Modeling need not be direct, however. As suggested by Jussim and Osgood (1989), group norms that are favorable to deviant behavior may be sufficient to encourage some youth to display behaviors compatible with these perceived norms. The indirect modeling effect resulting from perceived group norms is facilitated when members of the group are positively reinforced for displaying behaviors that are in line with these norms.

The Role of Deviant Peers/Friends According to Genetically Informed/Controlled Studies

Both the Causal and the Conditional model posit an active, likely causal, role for DPA. However, these models have been tested mostly using one-child-per-family designs. This is particularly true when friends are the independent factor, since it is not possible to experimentally manipulate friends' identity or characteristics. As already indicated, one-child-per-family designs are notoriously vulnerable to omitted third variables, including genetic influences. Not taking genetic influences into account may seriously bias the role of DPA.

It is well established from behavioral genetic studies that between 40 and 60% of the variance of aggressive behavior is influenced by genetic factors; the remaining variation is influenced by non-shared and, to a much lesser degree, by shared environmental factors (Harris, 1995; Moffitt, 2005a; Rhee & Waldman, 2002; Tuvblad & Baker, 2011; Viding, Larsson, & Jones, 2008). Several behavioral genetic studies have also found significant genetic influences on youngsters' propensity to affiliate with antisocial or aggressive peers (Baker & Daniels, 1990; Beaver, DeLisi, Wright, & Vaughn, 2009; Beaver et al., 2009; Button et al., 2007; Cleveland, Wiebe, & Rowe, 2005; Kendler, Jacobson, Myers, & Eaves, 2008; Manke, McGuire, Reiss, Hetherington, & Plomin, 1995; Rose, 2002; Rowe & Osgood, 1984; Tarantino et al., 2014). In these studies, between 20 and 40% of the variance in DPA is explained by genetic factors. Moreover, there is evidence from behavioral genetic studies that the role played by genetic factors in explaining friends' aggression/antisociality steadily increases from middle childhood to late adolescence. Specifically, Kendler and his colleagues (Kendler et al., 2007) found that genetic effects on friends' aggressive and general antisocial behavior (measured as the proportion of respondents' friends who engaged in specific aggressive or antisocial behaviors) increased substantially and steadily across five age periods: 8–11, 12–14, 15–17, 18–21, and 22–25. Prospective genetically informed studies concur with this view. To illustrate, van Lier and colleagues used data from the Quebec Newborn Twin Study (QNTS) to show that twins' genetic makeup explained only a small portion of their friends' aggression, with the remaining variance entirely explained by non-shared environmental effects. A similar lack of genetic effects on friends' aggression was also found in a follow-up study with the QNTS sample in grade 1 (Brendgen et al., 2008). Using the same sample and similar measures – but in contrast to previous results at younger ages – genetic influences on friends' aggression were found at ages 10 and 13 (Vitaro et al., 2016). In sum, friends' aggression seems to be partly driven by one's genetic makeup during adolescence but not yet during childhood, when it is a more or less random event, possibly resulting from proximity or other nonpersonal factors.

Such a phenomenon, where environmental experiences such as DPA are influenced by individuals' genetic disposition for certain traits or behaviors, is called *gene–environment correlation*, or *rGE*. Three types of rGE have been described (Plomin, DeFries, & Loehlin, 1977): (1) *passive* rGE (children and parents share genes that put the child at risk for aggression and predispose the parents to select environments where exposure to deviant peers is more likely); (2) *active* rGE (also called *selective*; e.g., when children with a genetic risk for aggression seek out and actively select friends that match their behavioral profile); and (3) *evocative* rGE (also called *reactive*; e.g., when children with a genetic risk for aggression attract deviant peers or repulse nondeviant peers).

Testing the Role of DPA While Accounting for rGE

The findings of genetic influence on friends' aggression during adolescence suggest that the role of DPA may have been overestimated in the past and may not hold once rGE is taken into account. This question was addressed in twin studies that explored the role of friends' aggression or antisocial behavior, while controlling for possible rGE through the use of the MZ-difference method. Since MZ twins share 100% of their genes (and the same family environment when raised together), the MZ-difference method affords a unique opportunity to examine associations between variables such as individuals' own and their friends' aggression, while controlling for family-wide (including genetic) influences on these variables. This is achieved by correlating within-pair differences in friends' aggression with later within-pair differences in twins' aggression, while controlling for baseline within-pair differences in aggression and within-pair differences in other types of relevant non-shared environmental experiences (see Vitaro, Brendgen, & Arseneault, 2009 for a full description of the method).

Studies that used the MZ-difference method with early or mid-adolescent samples found that within-pair differences in friends' aggression or antisocial behavior were unrelated to changes in within-pair differences in twins' aggressive or antisocial behavior (Beaver, 2008; Farrington, 1995; Feinberg & Shapiro, 2003; Hou et al., 2013; Vitaro et al., 2016). In contrast, Vitaro et al. (2011) found that within-pair differences in friends' aggression at age 6 predicted an increase in within-pair differences in twins' physical aggression from age 6 to 7, while controlling for possible confounders such as within-pair differences in peer rejection and coercive parenting. The tentative conclusion based on these studies is that friends' aggression contributes to the development of aggressive behavior in childhood, possibly because there are no rGE processes involved yet, but not in adolescence once rGE processes are active and controlled for analytically. In other words, the Causal model does not seem to apply to adolescents, but maybe the Conditional model does.

Testing the Role of DPA While Considering G x E

Even if DPA does not exert a main effect during adolescence once rGE is controlled for, it may nevertheless exert its influence on aggression in an interactive fashion, as proposed by the DPA-as-moderator version of the Conditional model. In the context of genetically informed studies, this would be observed when an individual's genetic liability is expressed differently depending on a given environment (i.e., DPA). Such a moderation effect refers to a mechanism known as a gene–environment interaction (G x E). G x E may arise through two types of processes (Brendgen, 2012): (1) peer experiences may exacerbate the expression of a genetic liability for aggression according to a *diathesis-stress model*; in this case, a liability for aggressive behavior would be expressed only, or more so, when children affiliate with peers who are aggressive. This process is also known as a contextual triggering process or a facilitation process (Shanahan & Hofer, 2005); (2) in contrast, the *bio-ecological model* (also known as a social control process; Bronfenbrenner & Ceci, 1994; Rutter, Moffitt, & Caspi, 2006; Shanahan & Hofer, 2005) describes patterns whereby inter-individual differences in genetic risk for aggression only explain inter-individual differences in aggressive behavior in the absence of risky environments such as aggressive peers. However, when environmental risk is high (i.e., a strong concentration of aggressive peers), even individuals without a genetic risk may resort to aggression. So far, support for a moderating role of aggressive friends regarding genetic influences on physical aggression is in line with the diathesis-stress model. For example, a study using the QNTS twin sample found that 6-year-old children were most likely to display high levels of aggression if they were at high genetic risk for such behavior *and* were also exposed to highly aggressive friends (van Lier, Wanner, & Vitaro, 2007). A follow-up study conducted with data collected in grade 1 (Brendgen et al., 2008) revealed that this G x E may only hold for the link between friends' and children's physical aggression, but not for social aggression.

Studies examining whether DPA interacts with genetic dispositions in predicting aggression during adolescence are rare. However, there is evidence of G x E in reference to related constructs such as substance use. For example, Harden, Hill, Turkheimer, and Emery (2008) found that adolescents with a stronger genetic propensity for substance use (i.e., drinking and smoking) were more likely than others to have substance-using friends (reflecting rGE). Moreover, adolescents with a higher genetic liability drank and smoked even more if their friends did as well (reflecting G x E). Using data from the same sample, Guo, Elder, Cai, and Hamilton (2009) reported a similar G x E specifically with respect to friends' and adolescents' own alcohol use. So far, all evidence from genetically informed studies uniformly suggests that DPA exerts its influence on aggressive/antisocial behavior not so much directly, but rather in an interactive fashion by facilitating the expression of a pre-existing personal disposition for these behaviors. These results are in line with the Conditional model. Moreover, this interactive effect seems to occur both during childhood and during adolescence, although a main effect of DPA is also possible during childhood (in accordance to the Causal model). As a conditional or unconditional source of influence or as a conditioner of individuals' genetic liability towards aggression, DPA represents an important target for preventive interventions because it has important consequences in all cases.

The Role of Peers in the Context of Prevention Programs

Preventing DPA

The best way to prevent DPA from exerting a main or a moderating effect is to prevent its occurrence by targeting relevant and modifiable risk factors such as early aggression, peer rejection, and parental monitoring. For example, by improving socio-cognitive skills and parenting through a two-year prevention program, it was possible to reduce disruptive boys' tendency to affiliate with each other, leading to fewer delinquent and criminal behaviors than in the control group (Vitaro, Barker, Brendgen, & Tremblay, 2012; Vitaro, Brendgen, & Tremblay, 2001). The program, known as the Montreal Experimental Longitudinal prevention program, included a home-based parent-training component and a school-based social-cognitive skills training component. Notably, the social-cognitive component was delivered at school in a small group format that included one or two target boys and three or four prosocial peers.

Early Risers, a multi-component prevention program for aggressive children, is another example of a multi-component prevention program that manipulates children's behavior, parental discipline, and children's peer relationships, all known risk factors for DPA. More specifically, Early Risers includes a child social skills group training program, a parent education and skills-training program, a teacher behavior-management program, and a student mentoring program focused on academic learning. The program also included a "buddy system," in which aggressive children are paired with a nonaggressive peer for various activities during a six-week summer camp. Using a RTC design, it was shown that participation in the Early Risers program significantly improved the quality of aggressive children's peer relations: they were more positively perceived by their peers, chose friends with lower aggression, and reported better-quality friendships (August, Egan, Realmuto, & Hektner, 2003). An extended version of Early Risers spanning over three intensive program years plus two booster program years significantly reduced symptoms of conduct disorder, oppositional defiant disorder, and major depressive disorder in participants by mid-adolescence compared to controls (August, Bloomquist, Realmuto, & Hektner, 2007). These effects were mediated by increased social skills and parental discipline effectiveness by the end of the three intensive program years (i.e., in grade 3) (Hektner, August, Bloomquist, Lee, & Klimes-Dougan, 2014).

Finally, in two randomized trials, Chamberlain and her colleagues showed that by training foster parents to prevent at-risk adolescents from interacting with deviant peers through close monitoring, violent delinquency could be reduced significantly (Chamberlain & Reid, 1998; Eddy, Whaley, & Chamberlain, 2004).

Capitalizing on Nonaggressive Peers

Unfortunately, it is not always possible to prevent at-risk children and adolescents from affiliating with each other. For this reason, other authors used conventional/nonaggressive peers to try to counteract the (conditional or unconditional) effects of DPA. To illustrate, Feldman (1992) randomly assigned delinquent and nondelinquent adolescent boys to one of three types of peer groups for a 24-session intervention program: (1) a peer group including only delinquent boys; (2) a peer group including only nondelinquent boys; or (3) a peer group including one or two delinquent boys but a majority of nondelinquent boys (i.e., the mixed group). In addition, group composition was crossed with two other experimentally manipulated factors: (1) group leaders' experience (experienced, inexperienced) and (2) type of intervention program (traditional social work, behavioral, minimal sensitization-control). Delinquent participants in the mixed group became less antisocial (according to self-ratings) compared to the delinquent boys in the all-delinquent groups, especially when led by experienced group leaders and exposed to the behavioral version of the program. Notably, the nondelinquent boys in the mixed groups did not seem adversely affected by their exposure to a few delinquent peers. Although compelling regarding the causal role of peers, these results are more suggestive than conclusive because a number of other outcomes, including self-reported aggression, were not in favor of the mixed group.

Mathys, Hyde, Shaw, and Born (2013) used a similar design to examine the effect of group composition on adolescents' deviancy training. Delinquent and nondelinquent adolescents aged 15 to 18 were randomly assigned to one of three types of groups: (1) all-delinquent groups; (2) all nondelinquent groups; or (3) mixed groups. However, contrary to Feldman (1992), who used large groups of 10 to 15 participants and a ratio of one delinquent participant to eight nondelinquent participants in the mixed group, Mathys et al. used a small group format of three to four participants per group and a ratio of 1:1 in the mixed group. Interactions among group members were videotaped during three sessions and topics of discussion and group reactions were coded. As expected, level of deviant talk and group reinforcement were lower in the mixed groups than in the all-delinquent groups. Together, these experimental studies demonstrate the power of the peer group in altering individuals' behavior. This power could be harvested in naturalistic settings through exposure of aggressive children to groups that manifest unfavorable norms towards aggression.

The Power of Group Norms

Two types of norms have been discussed that may influence an individual's behavior. *Descriptive norms* refer to how most group members behave. They are typically operationalized based on the overall prevalence (i.e., the mean level) of a behavior in a given group. In contrast, *injunctive norms* refer to what group members are expected to do, irrespective of the prevalence of this behavior, and are operationalized based on the group's level of approval or disapproval of the behavior. Some studies found that descriptive norms in the clique context (i.e., clique's average level of disruptiveness) plays an additive role with respect to an increase in participants' antisocial behavior, independent of best friends' level of disruptiveness (Witvliet, van Lier, Brendgen, Koot, & Vitaro, 2010). Other studies found that both descriptive and injunctive norms at the classroom or the school level predict changes in participants' aggression or condition its stability over time (e.g., Henry et al., 2000; Mercer, McMillen, & DeRosier, 2009; Müller, Hofmann, Fleischli, & Studer, 2015; Rodkin, Farmer, Pearl, & Van Acker, 2006; Thomas, Bierman, Powers, & Conduct Problems Prevention Research Group, 2011). Descriptive peer group norms in reference to relational aggression specifically predicted changes in dating violence during adolescence (Ellis, Chung-Hall, & Dumas, 2013). However, according to one study investigating the unique effects of descriptive versus injunctive norms on aggressive antisocial behavior, it is not so much the descriptive peer group norms but rather the injunctive norms that predict children's aggressive behavior or moderate the temporal stability of such behavior (Henry et al., 2000).

Genetically informed studies confirmed the power of injunctive norms by showing that they moderate the expression of a child's genetic disposition for aggression (i.e., another example of a G x E process). Brendgen, Girard, Vitaro, Dionne, and Boivin (2013) found that favorable injunctive norms in their grade 1 classroom fostered the expression of individuals' genetic liability for physical aggression. In a follow-up study using the same sample when children were 10 years old, Vitaro et al. (2015) also found that injunctive classroom norms moderated the expression of individuals' genetic liability for antisocial behavior (i.e., a composite of aggressive and nonaggressive antisocial behaviors). This G x E was not in line with a diathesis-stress process, however, but rather with a suppression effect. Specifically, genetic influences played a strong role in explaining interindividual differences in antisocial behavior when peer group norms were highly unfavorable toward such behavior. In contrast, the explanatory effect of genetic factors was much weaker when peer group norms were highly favorable toward such behavior.

The above results suggest that behavioral norms in children's peer group could be used for prevention or intervention purposes, provided they can be changed. Group norms may be changed by universal programs that target the whole classroom or the whole school. It is not possible to review each program in detail, but such programs exist and they have produced positive findings. Examples include the PATHS Curriculum to teach young children personal and interpersonal abilities (Greenberg, Kusche, Cook, & Quamma, 1995), the Good Behavior Game to manage classroom behavior problems through the use of group contingencies (Petras et al., 2008), or anti-bullying campaigns that establish anti-bullying policies at the school or the district level, raise public awareness about bullying and define roles and responsibilities for teachers, students, and parents (Olweus, 1994; Salmivalli, Kärnä, & Poskiparta, 2011).

If injunctive norms cannot be changed, they can still be put to good use by exposing aggressive children to peer groups where norms are "naturally" unfavorable to aggression. This strategy is another way to harvest the power of nondeviant peers. This strategy, however, needs to be complemented by other strategies to prevent rejection of aggressive children by normative peers, which could otherwise itself foster an increase in aggression.

Improving Resistance Skills and Friendship Quality

Despite all efforts, it is not always possible to avoid or deflect DPA and it is not always possible to expose at-risk children to normative peers. In that case, it may nonetheless be feasible to improve children's and adolescents' resistance skills to deviant peer influence. This can be achieved by specifically training resistance skills in a way similar to what is done in substance use prevention programs (Botvin, Griffin, & Nichols, 2006; Donaldson, Graham, Piccinin, & Hansen, 1995). It may also not always be possible – or even desirable – to prevent or break up friendships with aggressive peers. Although aggressive friends may exert negative influence on both externalizing and internalizing problems, partly because friendships among aggressive children are usually poor in quality (Marcus, 1996; Poulin, Dishion, & Haas, 1999), it is worth mentioning that friendlessness is also related to internalizing problems (Brendgen, Vitaro, & Bukowski, 2000a). It may prove worthwhile instead to improve the quality of friendships among aggressive children. First, evidence in support of this strategy comes from correlational studies showing that good-quality friendships predict a decrease in children's aggression, even for children who affiliate with aggressive peers (Engle, McElwain, & Lasky, 2011; Salvas et al., 2014; Salvas et al., 2011). The second line of evidence comes from an experimental study that aimed to improve the quality of the relationship between aggressive children and their friends. The findings indicate that the dyadic friendship quality intervention decreased children's physical aggression by improving the quality of one friendship feature, namely, conflict resolution (Salvas, Vitaro, Brendgen, & Cantin, 2016).

Conclusion

Findings from one-child-per-family studies and experimental studies support the notion of an unconditional or a conditional effect of DPA. Twin studies also support the notion of an unconditional effect of DPA, but during childhood only when rGE is not yet in place. Twin studies also support the notion of DPA as a moderator of an individual's genetic liability towards aggression. In sum, the bulk of the evidence supports the Conditional model, with DPA either as the moderated factor or the moderator. Despite our focus on deviant friends and their possible adverse effects, it is important to remember that having friends and being part of a peer group can have a very positive impact on children's social and emotional development (Bukowski, Newcomb, & Hartup, 1996; Sullivan, 1953). Again, this effect may operate either through main effects or by moderating individuals' genetic dispositions in a positive way. Youngsters with deviant friends, however, risk being deprived of these important benefits and, in addition, risk the aggravation of their externalizing problems. Continued research on the predictors and consequences of DPA, as well as on the underlying mechanisms and the best strategies for preventing or reducing its impact is essential if we want all youngsters to enjoy the positive sides of peer relations.

References

Adams, R. E., Bukowski, W. M., & Bagwell, C. (2005). Stability of aggression during early adolescence as moderated by reciprocated friendship status and friend's aggression. *International Journal of Behavioral Development*, 29(2), 139–145.

Allen, J. P., Porter, M. R., & McFarland, F. C. (2006). Leaders and followers in adolescent close friendships: Susceptibility to peer influence as a predictor of risky behavior, friendship instability, and depression. *Development and Psychopathology*, 18(1), 155–172.

Allen, J. P., Porter, M. R., McFarland, F. C., Marsh, P., & McElhaney, K. B. (2005). The two faces of adolescents' success with peers: Adolescent popularity, social adaptation, and deviant behavior. *Child Development*, 76(3), 747–760.

August, G. J., Bloomquist, M. L., Realmuto, G. M., & Hektner, J. M. (2007). The Early Risers "Skills for Success" program: A targeted intervention for preventing conduct problems and substance abuse in aggressive elementary school children. In P. Tolan, J. Szapocznik & S. Sambrano (Eds), *Preventing youth substance abuse: Science-based programs for children and adolescents* (pp. 137–158). Washington, DC: American Psychological Association.

August, G. J., Egan, E. A., Realmuto, G. M., & Hektner, J. M. (2003). Four years of the early risers early-age-targeted preventive intervention: Effects on aggressive children's peer relations. *Behavior Therapy*, 34, 453–470.

Bagwell, C. L. & Coie, J. D. (2004). The best friendships of aggressive boys: Relationship quality, conflict management, and rule-breaking behavior. *Journal of Experimental Child Psychology*, 88, 5–24.

Baker, L. A. & Daniels, D. (1990). Nonshared environmental-influences and personality-differences in adult twins. *Journal of Personality and Social Psychology*, 58(1), 103–110.

Beaver, K. M. (2008). Nonshared environmental influences on adolescent delinquent involvement and adult criminal behavior. *Criminology*, 46(2), 341–369.

Beaver, K. M., DeLisi, M., Wright, J. P., & Vaughn, M. G. (2009). Gene-environment interplay and delinquent involvement evidence of direct, indirect, and interactive effects. *Journal of Adolescent Research*, 24(2), 147–168.

Beaver, K. M., Schutt, J. E., Boutwell, B. B., Ratchford, M., Roberts, K., & Barnes, J. C. (2009). Genetic and environmental influences on levels of self-control and delinquent peer affiliation. *Criminal Justice and Behavior*, 36(1), 41–60.

Boivin, M. & Vitaro, F. (1995). The impact of peer relationships on aggression in childhood: Inhibition through coercion or promotion through peer support. In J. McCord (ed.), *Coercion and punishment in long-term perspectives* (pp. 183–197). New York: Cambridge University Press.

Boivin, M., Vitaro, F., & Poulin, F. (2005). Peer relationships and the development of aggressive behavior in early childhood. In R. E. Tremblay, W. W. Hartup & J. Archer (Eds), *Developmental origins of aggression* (pp. 376–397). New York: Guilford Press.

Botvin, G. J., Griffin, K. W., & Nichols, T. D. (2006). Preventing youth violence and delinquency through a universal school-based prevention approach. *Prevention Science*, 7(4), 403–408.

Brendgen, M. (2012). Genetics and peer relations: A review. *Journal of Research on Adolescence*, 22(3), 419–437.

Brendgen, M., Boivin, M., Vitaro, F., Bukowski, W. M., Dionne, G., Tremblay, R. E., & Pérusse, D. (2008). Linkages between children's and their friends' social and physical aggression: Evidence for a gene-environment interaction. *Child Development*, 79(1), 13–29.

Brendgen, M., Girard, A., Vitaro, F., Dionne, G., & Boivin, M. (2013). Do peer group norms moderate the expression of genetic risk for aggression? *Journal of Criminal Justice,* 41(5), 324–330.

Brendgen, M., Vitaro, F., & Bukowski, W. M. (2000a). Deviant friends and early adolescents' emotional and behavioral adjustment. *Journal of Research on Adolescence,* 10(2), 173–189.

Brody, G. H., Ge, X., Conger, R. D., Gibbons, F. X., Murry, V. M., Gerrard, M., & Simons, R. L. (2001). The influence of neighborhood disadvantage, collective socialization, and parenting on African American children's affiliation with deviant peers. *Child Development,* 72(4), 1231–1246.

Bronfenbrenner, U. & Ceci, S. J. (1994). Nature-nurture reconceptualized in developmental perspective – A bioecological model. *Psychological Review,* 101(4), 568–586.

Bukowski, W. M., Newcomb, A. F., & Hartup, W. W. (1996). *The company they keep: Friendship in childhood and adolescence.* Cambridge: Cambridge University Press.

Button, T. M. M., Corley, R. P., Rhee, S. H., Hewitt, J. K., Young, S. E., & Stallings, M. C. (2007). Delinquent peer affiliation and conduct problems: A twin study. *Journal of Abnormal Psychology,* 116(3), 554–564.

Cairns, R., Xie, H., & Leung, M. (1998). The popularity of friendship and the neglect of social networks: Toward a new balance. In W. M. Bukowski & A. H. Cillessen (Eds), *Sociometry then and now: Building on six decades of measuring children's experiences with the paper group: No. 80. New directions for child development* (pp. 5–24). San Francisco, CA: Jossey-Bass.

Cairns, R. B., Perrin, J. E., & Cairns, B. D. (1985). Social structure and social cognition in early adolescence: Affiliative patterns. *Journal of Early Adolescence,* 5, 339–355.

Chamberlain, P. & Reid, J. B. (1998). Comparison of two community alternative to incarceration for chronic juvenile offenders. *Journal of Consulting and Clinical Psychology,* 66, 624–633.

Cleveland, H. H., Wiebe, R. P., & Rowe, D. C. (2005). Sources of exposure to smoking and drinking friends among adolescents: A behavioral-genetic evaluation. *Journal of Genetic Psychology,* 166(2), 153–169.

Cohen, G. L. & Prinstein, M. J. (2006). Peer contagion of aggression and health risk behavior among adolescent males: An experimental investigation of effects on public conduct and private attitudes. *Child Development,* 77(4), 967–983.

Deptula, D. P. & Cohen, R. (2004). Aggressive, rejected, and delinquent children and adolescents: A comparison of their friendships. *Aggression and Violent Behavior,* 9, 75–104.

Dishion, T. J. (1990). Peer context of troublesome behavior in children and adolescents. In P. Leone (Ed.), *Understanding troubled and troublesome youth* (pp. 128–153). Beverly Hills, CA: Sage.

Dishion, T. J., Andrews, D. W., & Crosby, L. (1995). Antisocial boys and their friends in early adolescence: Relationship characteristics, quality, and interactional processes. *Child Development,* 66(1), 139–151.

Dishion, T. J., Burraston, B., & Poulin, F. (2001). Peer group dynamics associated with iatrogenic effects in group interventions with high-risk young adolescents. In C. Erdley & D. W. Nangle (Eds), *New directions in child development: The role of friendship in psychological adjustment* (pp. 79–92). San Francisco, CA: Jossey-Bass.

Dishion, T. J., Nelson, S. E., Winter, C. E., & Bullock, B. M. (2004). Adolescent friendship as a dynamic system: Entropy and deviance in the etiology and course of male antisocial behavior. *Journal of Abnormal Child Psychology,* 32(6), 651–663.

Dishion, T. J., Spracklen, K. M., Andrews, D. W., & Patterson, G. R. (1996). Deviancy training in male adolescent friendships. *Behavior Therapy,* 27, 373–390.

Dishion, T. J. & Tipsord, J. M. (2011). Peer Contagion in Child and Adolescent Social and Emotional Development. *Annual Review of Psychology,* 62, 189–214.

Donaldson, S. I., Graham, J. W., Piccinin, A. M., & Hansen, W. B. (1995). Resistance-skills training and onset of alcohol use: Evidence for beneficial and potentially harmful effects in public schools and in private Catholic schools. *Health Psychology*, 14(4), 291–300.

Eddy, J. M., Whaley, R. B., & Chamberlain, P. (2004). The prevention of violent behavior by chronic and serious male juvenile offenders: A 2-year follow-up of a randomized clinical trial. *Journal of Emotional and Behavioral Disorders*, 12(1), 2–8.

Elliott, D. S., Huizinga, D., & Ageton, S. S. (1985). *Explaining delinquency and drug use*. Beverly Hills, CA: Sage.

Ellis, W. E., Chung-Hall, J., & Dumas, T. M. (2013). The role of peer group aggression in predicting adolescent dating violence and relationship quality. *Journal of Youth and Adolescence*, 42(4), 487–499.

Ellis, W. E. & Zarbatany, L. (2007). Peer group status as a moderator of group influence on children's deviant, aggressive, and prosocial behavior. *Child Development*, 78(4), 1240–1254.

Engle, J. M., McElwain, N. L., & Lasky, N. (2011). Presence and quality of kindergarten children's friendships: Concurrent and longitudinal associations with child adjustment in the early school years. *Infant and Child Development*, 20(4), 365–386.

Estell, D. B., Cairns, R. B., Farmer, T. W., & Cairns, B. D. (2002). Aggression in inner-city early elementary classroom: Individual and peer-group configurations. *Merrill-Palmer Quarterly*, 48(1), 52–76.

Farrell, A. D., Henry, D. B., Mays, S. A., & Schoeny, M. E. (2011). Parents as moderators of the impact of school norms and peer influences on aggression in middle school students. [Article]. *Child Development*, 82(1), 146–161.

Farrington, D. P. (1995). The Twelfth Jack Tizard Memorial Lecture: The development of offending and antisocial behaviour from childhood: Key findings from the Cambridge Study in Delinquent Development. *Journal of Child Psychology and Psychiatry and Allied Disciplines*, 36(6), 929–964.

Farrington, D. P. & West, D. J. (1993). Criminal, penal and life histories of chronic offenders: Risk and protective factors and early identification. *Criminal Behavior and Mental Health*, 3, 492–523.

Feinberg, A. B. & Shapiro, E. S. (2003). Accuracy of teacher judgments in predicting oral reading fluency. *School Psychology Quarterly*, 18(1), 52–65.

Feldman, R. A. (1992). The St. Louis experiment: Effective treatment of antisocial youths in prosocial peer groups. In J. McCord & R. E. Tremblay (Eds), *Preventing Antisocial Behavior: Interventions from Birth to Adolescents* (pp. 233–252). New York: Guilford Press.

Fergusson, D. M., Vitaro, F., Wanner, B., & Brendgen, M. (2007). Protective and compensatory factors mitigating the influence of deviant friends on delinquent behaviours during early adolescence. *Journal of Adolescence*, 30(1), 33–50.

Galambos, N. L., Barker, E. T., & Almeida, D. M. (2003). Parents do matter: Trajectories of change in externalizing and internalizing problems in early adolescence. *Child Development*, 74, 578–594.

Gardner, T. W., Dishion, T. J., & Connell, A. M. (2008). Adolescent self-regulation as resilience: Resistance to antisocial behavior within the deviant peer context. *Journal of Abnormal Child Psychology*, 36(2), 273–284.

Gottfredson, M. R. & Hirschi, T. (1990). *A general theory of crime*. Stanford, CA: Stanford University Press.

Greenberg, M. T., Kusche, C. A., Cook, E. T., & Quamma, J. P. (1995). Promoting emotional competence in school-aged children: The effects of the paths curriculum. *Development and Psychopathology*, 7(1), 117–136.

Guo, G., Elder, G. H., Cai, T. J., & Hamilton, N. (2009). Gene-environment interactions: Peers' alcohol use moderates genetic contribution to adolescent drinking behavior. *Social Science Research*, 38(1), 213–224.

Harden, K. P., Hill, J. E., Turkheimer, E., & Emery, R. E. (2008). Gene-environment correlation and interaction in peer effects on adolescent alcohol and tobacco use. *Behavior Genetics*, 38(4), 339–347.

Harris, J. R. (1995). Where is the child's environment: A group socialization theory of development. *Psychological Review*, 102(3), 458–489.

Hartup, W. W. (2005). Peer interaction: What causes what? *Journal of Abnormal Child Psychology*, 33(3), 387–394.

Haynie, D. L. (2001). Delinquent peers revisited: Does network structure matter? *American Journal of Sociology*, 106(4), 1013–1057.

Hektner, J. M., August, G. J., Bloomquist, M. L., Lee, S., & Klimes-Dougan, B. (2014). A 10-Year Randomized Controlled Trial of the Early Risers Conduct Problems Preventive Intervention: Effects on Externalizing and Internalizing in Late High School. *Journal of Consulting and Clinical Psychology*, 82(2), 355–360.

Hektner, J. M., August, G. J., & Realmuto, G. M. (2000). Patterns and temporal changes in peer affiliation among aggressive and nonaggressive children participating in a summer school program. *Journal of Clinical Child Psychology*, 29(4), 603–614.

Henry, D., Guerra, N., Huesmann, R., Tolan, P., VanAcker, R., & Eron, L. (2000). Normative influences on aggression in urban elementary school classrooms. *American Journal of Community Psychology*, 28(1), 59–81.

Hou, J. Q., Chen, Z. Y., Natsuaki, M. N., Li, X. Y., Yang, X. D., Zhang, J., & Zhang, J. X. (2013). A longitudinal investigation of the associations among parenting, deviant peer affiliation, and externalizing behaviors: A monozygotic twin differences design. *Twin Research and Human Genetics*, 16(3), 698–706.

Johnson, L. M., Simons, R. L., & Conger, R. D. (2004). Criminal justice system involvement and continuity of youth crime: A longitudinal analysis. *Youth & Society*, 36, 3–29.

Johnson, R. E., Marcos, A. C., & Bahr, S. (1987). The role of peers in the complex etiology of drug use. *Criminology*, 323–340.

Jussim, L. & Osgood, D. W. (1989). Influence and similarity among friends: An integrative model applied to incarcerated adolescents. *Social Psychology Quarterly*, 52, 98–112.

Kendler, K. S., Jacobson, K., Myers, J. M., & Eaves, L. J. (2008). A genetically informative developmental study of the relationship between conduct disorder and peer deviance in males. *Psychological Medicine*, 38(7), 1001–1011.

Kendler, K. S., Jacobson, K. C., Gardner, C. O., Gillespie, N., Aggen, S. A., & Prescott, C. A. (2007). Creating a social world – A developmental twin study of peer-group deviance. *Archives of General Psychiatry*, 64(8), 958–965.

Kim, J. E., Hetherington, E. M., & Reiss, D. (1999). Associations among family relationships, antisocial peers, and adolescents' externalizing behaviors: Gender and family type differences. *Child Development*, 70, 1209–1230.

Kupersmidt, J. B., Burchinal, M., & Patterson, C. J. (1995). Developmental patterns of childhood peer relations as predictors of externalizing behavior problems. *Development and Psychopathology*, 7, 825–843.

Lacourse, É., Nagin, D., Tremblay, R. E., Vitaro, F., & Claes, M. (2003). Developmental trajectories of boys' delinquent group membership and facilitation of violent behaviors during adolescence. *Development and Psychopathology*, 15(1), 183–197.

Laird, R. D., Jordan, K. Y., Dodge, K. A., Pettit, G. S., & Bates, J. E. (2001). Peer rejection in childhood, involvement with antisocial peers in early adolescence, and the development of externalizing behavior problems. *Development and Psychopathology*, 13(2), 337–354.

Leve, L. D. & Chamberlain, P. (2005). Association with delinquent peers: Intervention effects for youth in the juvenile justice system. *Journal of Abnormal Child Psychology, 33*(3), 339–347.

Manke, B., McGuire, S., Reiss, D., Hetherington, E. M., & Plomin, R. (1995). Genetic contributions to adolescents extrafamilial social interactions: Teachers, best friends, and peers. *Social Development, 4*, 238–256.

Marcus, R. F. (1996). The friendships of delinquents. *Adolescence, 31*(121), 145–158.

Mathys, C., Hyde, L. W., Shaw, D. S., & Born, M. (2013). Deviancy and Normative Training Processes in Experimental Groups of Delinquent and Nondelinquent Male Adolescents. *Aggressive Behavior, 39*(1), 30–44.

Mercer, S. H., McMillen, J. S., & DeRosier, M. E. (2009). Predicting change in children's aggression and victimization using classroom-level descriptive norms of aggression and pro-social behavior. *Journal of School Psychology, 47*(4), 267–289.

Moffitt, T. E. (2005a). Genetic and environmental influences on antisocial behaviors: Evidence from behavioral-genetic research. In J. Hall (Ed.), *Advances in genetics* (Vol. 55, pp. 41–104). Amsterdam, The Netherlands: Elsevier Science Publishers.

Moffitt, T. E. (2005b). The new look of behavioral genetics in developmental psychopathology: Gene-environment interplay in antisocial behaviors. *Psychological Bulletin, 131*(4), 533–554.

Molano, A., Jones, S. M., Brown, J. L., & Aber, J. L. (2013). Selection and socialization of aggressive and prosocial behavior: The moderating role of social-cognitive processes. *Journal of Research on Adolescence, 23*(3), 424–436.

Mrug, S. & Windle, M. (2009). Bidirectional influences of violence exposure and adjustment in early adolescence: Externalizing behaviors and school connectedness. *Journal of Abnormal Child Psychology, 37*(5), 611–623.

Müller, C. & Minger, M. (2013). Which children and adolescents are most susceptible to peer influence? A systematic review regarding antisocial behavior. *Empirische Sonderpädagogik, 2*, 107–129.

Müller, C. M., Hofmann, V., Fleischli, J., & Studer, F. (2015). "Tell me what your classmates do and I will tell you what you are going to do?" The influence of classroom composition on the development of problem behavior in school. *Zeitschrift Fur Erziehungswissenschaft, 18*(3), 569–589.

Nijhof, K. S., Scholte, R. H. J., Overbeek, G., & Engels, R. C. M. E. (2010). Friends' and adolescents' delinquency: The moderating role of social status and reciprocity of friendships [Article]. *Criminal Justice and Behavior, 37*(3), 289–305.

Olweus, D. (1994). Bullying at school: Basic facts and effects of a school based intervention program. *Journal of Child Psychology and Psychiatry and Allied Disciplines, 35*(7), 1171–1190.

Patterson, G. R., Capaldi, D. M., & Bank, L. (1991). An early starter model for predicting delinquency. In D. J. Pepler & K. H. Rubin (Eds), *The development and treatment of childhood* (pp. 139–168). Hillsdale, NJ: Lawrence Erlbaum Associates.

Patterson, G. R., Littman, R. A., & Bricker, W. (1967). Assertive behavior in children: A step toward a theory of aggression. *Monographs of the Society for Research in Child Development, 32*, 1–43.

Petras, H., Kellam, S. G., Brown, C. H., Muthen, B. O., Ialongo, N. S., & Poduska, J. M. (2008). Developmental epidemiological courses leading to antisocial personality disorder and violent and criminal behavior: Effects by young adulthood of a universal preventive intervention in first- and second-grade classrooms. *Drug and Alcohol Dependence, 95*, S45–S59.

Plomin, R., DeFries, J. C., & Loehlin, J. C. (1977). Genotype-environment interaction and correlation in the analysis of human behavior. *Psychological Bulletin, 84*(2), 309–322.

Poulin, F., Dishion, T. J., & Burraston, B. (2001). 3-year iatrogenic effects associated with aggregating high-risk adolescents in cognitive-behavioral preventive interventions. *Applied Developmental Science*, 5, 214–224.

Poulin, F., Dishion, T. J., & Haas, E. (1999). The peer influence paradox: Friendship quality and deviancy training within male adolescent friendships. *Merrill-Palmer Quarterly*, 45, 42–61.

Prinstein, M. J., Boergers, J., & Spirito, A. (2001). Adolescents' and their friends' health-risk behavior: Factors that alter or add to peer influence. *Journal of Pediatric Psychology*, 26, 287–298.

Prinstein, M. J., Brechwald, W. A., & Cohen, G. L. (2011). Susceptibility to Peer Influence: Using a Performance-Based Measure to Identify Adolescent Males at Heightened Risk for Deviant Peer Socialization. *Developmental Psychology*, 47(4), 1167–1172.

Prinstein, M. J. & Giletta, M. (2016). Peer relations and developmental psychopathology. In D. Cicchetti (Ed.), *Developmental psychopathology* (3rd ed., vol. 1, pp. 527-579). Hoboken, NJ: Wiley.

Rhee, S. H. & Waldman, I. D. (2002). Genetic and environmental influences on antisocial behavior: A meta-analysis of twin and adoption studies. *Psychological Bulletin*, 128, 490–529.

Rodkin, P. C., Farmer, T. W., Pearl, R., & Van Acker, R. (2006). They're cool: Social status and peer group supports for aggressive boys and girls. *Social Development*, 15(2), 175–204.

Rose, R. J. (2002). How do adolescents select their friends? A behavior-genetic perspective. In L. Pulkkinen & A. Caspi (Eds), *Paths to successful development: Personality in the life course* (pp. 106–125). Cambridge: Cambridge University Press.

Rowe, D. C. & Osgood, D. W. (1984). Heredity and sociological theories of delinquency: A reconsideration. *American Sociological Review*, 49, 526–540.

Rutter, M., Moffitt, T. E., & Caspi, A. (2006). Gene-environment interplay and psychopathology: multiple varieties but real effects. *Journal of Child Psychology and Psychiatry*, 47(3–4), 226–261.

Salmivalli, C., Kärnä, A., & Poskiparta, E. (2011). Counteracting bullying in Finland: The KiVa program and its effects on different forms of being bullied. *International Journal of Behavioral Development*, 35(5), 405–411.

Salvas, M.-C., Vitaro, F., Brendgen, M., & Cantin, S. (2016). Prospective links between friendship and early physical aggression: Preliminary evidence supporting the role of friendship quality through a dyadic intervention. *Merrill-Palmer Quarterly*, 62(3), 285-305.

Salvas, M.-C., Vitaro, F., Brendgen, M., Dionne, G., Tremblay, R. E., & Boivin, M. (2014). Friendship conflict and the development of generalized physical aggression in the early school years: A genetically informed study of potential moderators. *Developmental Psychology*, 50(6), 1794–1807.

Salvas, M.-C., Vitaro, F., Brendgen, M., Lacourse, E., Boivin, M., & Tremblay, R. E. (2011). Interplay between friends' aggression and friendship quality in the development of child aggression during the early school years. *Social Development*, 20(4), 645–663.

Shanahan, M. J. & Hofer, S. M. (2005). Social context in gene-environment interactions: Retrospect and prospect. *Journals of Gerontology Series B-Psychological Sciences and Social Sciences*, 60 (Special Issue 1), 65–76.

Snyder, J., Schrepferman, L., Oeser, J., Patterson, G., Stoolmiller, M., Johnson, K., & Snyder, A. (2005). Deviancy training and association with deviant peers in young children: Occurrence and contribution to early-onset conduct problems. *Development and Psychopathology*, 17(2), 397–413.

Steinberg, L. & Monahan, K. C. (2007). Age differences in resistance to peer influence. *Developmental Psychology*, 43(6), 1531–1543.

Sullivan, H. S. (1953). *The interpersonal theory of psychiatry*. New York: Norton.

Sutherland, E. (1947). *Principles of criminology* (3rd edition). Philadelphia: Lippincott.

Tarantino, N., Tully, E. C., Garcia, S. E., South, S., Iacono, W. G., & McGue, M. (2014). Genetic and environmental influences on affiliation with deviant peers during adolescence and early adulthood. *Developmental Psychology*, 50(3), 663–673.

Thomas, D. E., Bierman, K. L., & Conduct Problems Prevention Research Group. (2006). The impact of classroom aggression on the development of aggressive behavior problems in children. *Development and Psychopathology*, 18(2), 471–487.

Thomas, D. E., Bierman, K. L., Powers, C. J., & Conduct Problems Prevention Research Group. (2011). The Influence of Classroom Aggression and Classroom Climate on Aggressive-Disruptive Behavior. *Child Development*, 82(3), 751–757.

Tuvblad, C. & Baker, L. (2011). Human aggression across the lifespan: Genetic propensities and environmental moderators (ch. 8). In R. Huber, P. Brennan & D. Bannasch (Eds), *Advances in genetics: Aggression* (Vol. 75, pp. 171–214). Boston, MA: Elsevier Press.

Urberg, K. A., Degirmencioglu, S. M., & Pilgrim, C. (1997). Close friend and group influence on adolescent cigarette smoking and alcohol use. *Developmental Psychology*, 33(5), 834–844.

van Lier, P. A. C., Wanner, B., & Vitaro, F. (2007). Onset of antisocial behavior, affiliation with deviant friends, and childhood maladjustment: A test of the childhood- and adolescent-onset models. *Development and Psychopathology*, 19, 167–185.

Veenstra, R. & Dijkstra, J. K. (2011). Transformations in adolescent peer networks. In B. Laursen & W. A. Collins (Eds), *Relationship Pathways: From Adolescence to Young Adulthood* (pp. 135–154). Los Angeles, CA: Sage.

Viding, E., Larsson, H., & Jones, A. P. (2008). Quantitative genetic studies of antisocial behaviour. *Philosophical Transactions of the Royal Society B: Biological Sciences*, 363(1503), 2519–2527.

Vitaro, F., Barker, E. D., Brendgen, M., & Tremblay, R. E. (2012). Pathways explaining the reduction of adult criminal behaviour by a randomized preventive intervention for disruptive kindergarten children. *Journal of Child Psychology and Psychiatry*, 53(7), 748–756.

Vitaro, F. & Brendgen, M. (2012). Subtypes of aggressive behaviors: Etiologies, development, and consequences. In T. Bliesener, A. Beelmann & M. Stemmler (Eds), *Antisocial behavior and crime: Contributions of developmental and evaluation research to prevention and intervention* (pp. 17–38). Cambridge, MA: Hogrefe Publishing.

Vitaro, F., Brendgen, M., & Arseneault, L. (2009). The discordant MZ-twin method: One step closer to the holy grail of causality. *International Journal of Behavioral Development*, 33(4), 376–382.

Vitaro, F., Brendgen, M., Boivin, M., Cantin, S., Dionne, G., Tremblay, R. E., … & Pérusse, D. (2011). A monozygotic twin difference study of friends' aggression and children's adjustment problems. *Child Development*, 82(2), 617–632.

Vitaro, F., Brendgen, M., Girard, A., Boivin, M., Dionne, G., & Tremblay, R. E. (2015). The expression of genetic risk for aggressive and non-aggressive antisocial behavior is moderated by peer group norms. *Journal of Youth and Adolescence*, 44(7), 1379–1395.

Vitaro, F., Brendgen, M., Girard, A., Dionne, G., Tremblay, R. E., & Boivin, M. (2016). Links between friends' physical aggression and adolescents' physical aggression: What happens if gene-environment correlations are controlled? *International Journal of Behavioral Development*, 40(3), 234–242.

Vitaro, F., Brendgen, M., & Tremblay, R. E. (2000). Influence of deviant friends on delinquency: Searching for moderator variables. *Journal of Abnormal Child Psychology*, 28, 313–325.

Vitaro, F., Brendgen, M., & Tremblay, R. E. (2001). Preventive intervention: Assessing its effects on the trajectories of delinquency and testing for mediational processes. *Applied Developmental Science*, 5(4), 201–213.

Vitaro, F., Pedersen, S., & Brendgen, M. (2007). Children's disruptiveness, peer rejection, friends' deviancy, and delinquent behaviors: A process-oriented approach. *Development and Psychopathology*, 19(2), 433–453.

Vitaro, F., Tremblay, R. E., Kerr, M., Pagani, L. S., & Bukowski, W. M. (1997). Disruptiveness, friends' characteristics, and delinquency: A test of two competing models of development. *Child Development*, 68(4), 676–689.

Warren, K., Schoppelrey, S., Moberg, D. P., & McDonald, M. (2005). A model of contagion through competition in the aggressive behaviors of elementary school students. *Journal of Abnormal Child Psychology*, 33(3), 283–292.

Witvliet, M., van Lier, P. A. C., Brendgen, M., Koot, H., & Vitaro, F. (2010). Longitudinal associations between clique membership status and internalizing and externalizing problems during late childhood. *Journal of Clinical Child & Adolescent Psychology*, 39(5), 693–704.

19 Developmental Processes of Resilience and Risk for Aggression and Conduct Problems

J. J. Cutuli, Jorge M. Carvalho Pereira, Sarah C. Vrabic, and Janette E. Herbers

Introduction

Here, we present a resilience framework regarding factors typically associated with the manifestation of aggression and conduct problems. First, we describe resilience as the product of common developmental processes, conceptualized as the interaction and coaction of embedded, dynamic systems over time. We illustrate this framework with findings and theories on the development of aggression, violence, and conduct problems. We note factors and emphasize processes that differentiate children who are exposed to risk but manifest different outcomes. We highlight intervention studies that target key processes contributing to resilience, both as experimental evidence for basic developmental science as well as evidence of the value of resilience frameworks for promoting well-being for children and youth at risk of poor outcomes.

Defining and Inferring Resilience in Development: Fundamental Considerations

Resilience scientists look to explain and, ultimately, promote the phenomenon of positive adaptation in contexts of risk or threat. Resilience is generally *the capacity of a dynamic system to adapt successfully to disturbances, allowing that system to continue functioning and developing* (Masten, 2014; Masten & Obradović, 2006), though definitions can vary between and within disciplines (e.g., see Southwick, Bonanno, Masten, Panter-Brick, & Yehuda, 2014). In developmental science, resilience occurs when individuals show positive adaptation and competent development despite having experiences generally associated with negative outcomes among groups of people (Cutuli, Herbers, Masten, & Reed, in press; Masten, 2001).

Fundamentally, this definition requires that two criteria be met to infer resilience. The first criterion requires that the person show competent developmental outcomes. A common way of determining competence is according to *developmental tasks*, societal or cultural expectations for the behavior of individuals of different ages at a point in history (see Burt, Coatsworth, & Masten, 2016; Elder, 1998). Developmental tasks outline what is considered typical or generally expected by a particular society for its members based on their ages. These expectations can vary from culture to culture, or across different points in history, but many fundamental developmental tasks are shared across cultures. For example, most cultures expect infants and toddlers to form attachment relationships with their primary caregivers, learn to walk and to talk, and follow simple instructions. As children get older, these expectations change while both guiding socialization practices and reflecting their efficacy: children are generally expected to engage in interpersonal relationships of increasing intimacy and sophistication, to control their behavior and comply with rules for personal conduct with increasing success, and to accumulate knowledge and skills in preparation for adult contributions to society (Burt et al., 2016).

As markers of competence, developmental tasks provide benchmarks by which to judge whether development is proceeding as expected, and whether positive adaptation has occurred despite the presence of risk. However, developmental tasks are more than mere standards. They are not haphazard; they are usually preparatory. They often demarcate abilities that will assist individuals in meeting the next challenges of typical development while also supplying them with resources they can use to navigate successfully any new experiences of risk (Burt et al., 2016; Yates, Egeland, & Sroufe, 2003). In this way, those who have success in developmental tasks at one age are more likely to continue to demonstrate competence, and those who fail at one age are less likely to succeed later.

This is the case with respect to continuity within a particular domain of functioning (Sroufe, 1979), such as when a child shows good (or poor) self-regulation as a preschooler and is more likely to show good (or poor) self-regulation in middle childhood and adolescence (Blair, Raver, & Finegood, 2016). Competence or failure in a given domain can also influence later functioning in other domains. Referred to as *developmental cascades* (Masten & Cicchetti, 2010), success or failure in one area can have consequences for competence in other areas over subsequent developmental periods. For example, aggression and delinquency in middle childhood undermines academic competence in adolescence, which, in turn, contributes to problems with anxiety and depression in early adulthood (Masten et al., 2005). Negative consequences of failure cascade across domains with negative consequences for competence in different areas. In other words, failure can spread to different areas of individuals' lives over time.

The second component necessary to infer resilience is the presence of one or more risk factors. "Risk" refers to any characteristic, circumstance, or experience that is associated with increased likelihood of some negative outcome (Obradović, Shaffer, & Masten, 2012; Sameroff, Seifer, Barocas, Zax, & Greenspan, 1987). Risk factors are established in studies that compare functioning between groups of individuals with and without the factor being considered. Because many of these studies are correlational, it is not always clear if particular risk factors are causal in producing negative outcomes, or whether they are associated with some other causal process (Cutuli et al., in press). Furthermore, multiple risk factors tend to accumulate in people's lives over time. There are various approaches to representing different levels of risk between individuals in risk and resilience research. Many studies create a cumulative risk score by adding the number of risks present for each person (Obradović et al., 2012). More sophisticated statistical modeling techniques have contributed to methodological advances such as latent class analysis that considers profiles of risk and their relation to developmental outcomes (Lanza, Rhoades, Nix, & Greenberg, 2010). In any event, there must be one or more risks that threaten healthy functioning and force adaptation in order for resilience to be inferred.

The presence of risk factors implies that there is a potential for negative developmental processes that may interfere and result in failure, while higher scores on a cumulative risk index or a latent risk profile represent a higher probability of poor outcomes. However, the presence of protective or promotive factors implies the potential for positive adaptation and resilience (see Cutuli et al., in press; Luthar, 2006; Luthar, Cicchetti, & Becker, 2000). Sometimes also referred to as "assets" or "strengths," these factors represent resources or processes that encourage positive development and buffer the negative impacts of risk. Protective factors have a particularly salient positive effect in the context of risk, and might have less or no impact in cases where risk is low or absent. Meanwhile, promotive factors support positive development regardless of the level of risk present. While these positive factors can take many forms when considering certain risks or specific developmental outcomes, several emerge rather consistently across studies of resilience: average-or-better cognitive functioning, including cognitive aspects of self-regulation, and having a positive relationship with at least one competent adult, often a parent (see Luthar, 2006; Masten, 2014; Masten & Cicchetti, 2016). These factors can take on special importance in contexts of risk, assisting individuals to avoid the negative consequences of adversity through positive adaptation, resulting in developmental competence (Masten & Cicchetti, 2016).

Despite having an often powerful effect on development, it is worth noting that most protective and promotive factors are not superhuman, rare, or even uncommon. Rather, these are ordinary features present in most people's lives that are responsible for fostering resilience when threats arise (Masten, 2001). Like risk, protective factors can occur at all levels of the individual and her context (Cicchetti & Blender, 2006; Cutuli et al., in press; Masten & Cicchetti, 2016). They are a feature of typical development, and past age-salient developmental tasks often prepare the individual with these resources.

Risk, adaptation, competence, and failure occur in the context of development. The above definition of resilience draws on conceptualizations of development as occurring through the functioning of multiply embedded systems that are dynamic and transact over time (Bronfenbrenner, 1979; Gottlieb, 1991; Sroufe, 1997; Zelazo, 2013). Children comprise physiological and psychological systems embedded in broader psychosocial systems, like family, school, peer networks, and others, which, in turn, are embedded in broader systems, such as cultures and similarly expansive ecologies. The functioning of each system is influenced by how the system has become organized (characteristics of the system's components), by characteristics and factors that can be attributed to other systems. A young child with poor conduct, for example, may evoke a response when he attends school for the first time. If high-quality, the school may respond to the child's behavior with effective limit-setting and behavior management through a coordinated response of teachers and administrators. In turn, the child may respond with better self-control at school that, over time, increases self-regulation abilities employed in other contexts (Blair et al., 2016). Conversely, a poorly coordinated or otherwise inappropriate school response would not have the same positive effect or could influence the student's developmental trajectory more negatively, continuing or worsening conduct and compounding problems over time (e.g., peer rejection and academic failure).

Risk and Resilience for Aggression and Conduct Problems

Conduct problems and externalizing symptoms refer to relatively persistent behaviors that include aggression, delinquency, and rule-breaking (e.g., see Dodge & Pettit, 2003). Much is known about different manifestations of aggression and conduct problems, including life-course-persistent vs. adolescent-limited pathways (Moffitt, 1993, 2006), reactive vs. proactive aggression (Crick & Dodge, 1996; Raine et al., 2006), sex differences and manifestations of relational aggression (Crick & Grotpeter, 1995; Murray-Close, Nelson, Ostrov, Casas, & Crick, 2016), and trajectories towards violence vs. nonviolent offending (see Bushman et al., 2016; Shaw & Taraban, 2016). We approach the literature by conceptualizing aggression and externalizing problems broadly and in relation to processes of risk and resilience. Numerous mechanisms, frameworks, and developmental models of conduct problems have been proposed to account for their manifestation and persistence across childhood and adolescence. Beyond likely genetic and early temperament factors, discussed below, differences in a number of sociodemographic factors are predictive. Work investigating negative neighborhood characteristics, especially rates of poverty, violence, and other forms of deprivation, tend to find a positive relation with higher levels of aggression and other forms of conduct problems for children and youth across multiple indicators (Assink et al., 2015; Dodge & Pettit, 2003; Labella & Masten, 2016). Multiple mechanisms have been proposed to help explain why this relation might exist, including an inability to participate in prosocial means of self-support and advancement due to structural social inequalities, cultural, or other beliefs that either encourage or discourage violence and delinquency, a higher likelihood of exposure to aggressive or delinquent peers, fewer community resources like quality schools or opportunities for recreation, higher rates of maltreatment or other severe potentially traumatic events, lasting alterations of the individual stress-response system due to chronic or acute stress exposure, and higher rates of deep poverty (Leff et al., 2014; McMahon, Wells, & Kotler, 2006; Van Goozen, Fairchild, Snoek, & Harold, 2007).

An exhaustive review of the theories, models, and wealth of empirical findings on the development of aggression and conduct problems is well beyond the scope of this chapter. Rather, we focus on some key principles of a resilience perspective in understanding the complex processes of risk that contribute to different presentations in development, providing illustrative examples from the vast empirical literature. Readers are referred to integrative models of the development of conduct problems, such as Dodge and Pettit's biopsychosocial account (Dodge & Pettit, 2003). Consistent with a developmental account and a resilience framework, this model attempts to integrate factors and processes at different levels of analysis, noting risks that can interfere with normative developmental processes, contributing to conduct problems. In addition, we highlight the protective and promotive factors that predict good conduct despite the presence of key risks. Meanwhile, we consider how risks and protective processes are interrelated across time, often transacting and cascading to enhance the likelihood of positive adaptation, competence, and resilience, or maladaptation, aggression, and compounded failures across multiple domains in development (Masten & Cicchetti, 2010).

Risks and Protective Factors in the Development of Aggression and Other Conduct Problems

Genetic, Prenatal, and Temperamental Factors

Scientists from diverse fields have long recognized that a variety of risk factors at multiple levels of analysis contribute to aggression and conduct problems in children and youth (Dodge & Pettit, 2003; Shaw & Taraban, 2016). A number of genetic factors and early-occurring temperamental characteristics have been associated with increased risk. Undeniably, male sex is associated with higher rates of aggression, though many nongenetic factors also correlate with sex and gender (Martel, 2013; Tiet, Wasserman, Loeber, McReynolds, & Miller, 2001). More tellingly, heritability estimates suggest a moderate-but-consistent shared genetic effect for aggression, delinquency, and related features like inattention and impulsivity (Haberstick, Schmitz, Young, & Hewitt, 2005; Salvatore & Dick, 2016). Meanwhile, studies of children adopted at birth show a relation between biological parents' antisocial behavior and child externalizing problems (Ge et al., 1996; Hyde et al., 2016). More-nascent approaches that involve consideration of candidate genes and gene–environment interplay continue to produce inconsistent findings (see Holz et al., 2016; Salvatore & Dick, 2016; Samek et al., 2016).

Prenatal factors also appear to contribute to later problems with aggression and poor conduct, likely through effects on developing physiology related to the stress response, self-regulation, and cognitive functioning. Prenatal exposure to teratogens such as lead, alcohol, nicotine, or a variety of illicit substances have been associated with higher rates of aggression and conduct problems (see Dodge & Pettit, 2003), though a considerable degree of these associations may be better attributed to other shared factors (Jaffee, Strait, & Odgers, 2012). Psychosocial stress experienced by the mother during pregnancy may also contribute. Hormones such as cortisol are already high during pregnancy. Cortisol is associated with the physiological stress response as well as other functions. Maternal cortisol can partially transcend the placental barrier, exposing the fetus to a fractional level of maternal glucocorticoids (Talge, Neal, & Glover, 2007). Cortisol during the prenatal period is necessary for typical development, neurocognitive or otherwise, though exposure to atypical levels of prenatal cortisol (e.g., associated with maternal stress) may contribute to differences in child reactivity in early life with implications for aggression and conduct problems (Labella & Masten, 2016; Talge et al., 2007).

Some characteristics of early-occurring temperament signal risk. Persistent difficulties with emotion regulation marked by hyperarousal have been linked to greater likelihood of aggression and other reactive conduct problems. Conversely, underarousal regarding negative emotions and low empathy, particularly when evident as part of a callous and unemotional interpersonal style, has been linked with a higher probability of severe conduct problems marked by psychopathy (Frick, Blair, & Castellanos, 2013; Frick & Morris, 2004). Meanwhile, prospective evidence suggests high levels of oppositionality, poor emotion regulation, and parenting rejection in toddlerhood differentiate violent vs. nonviolent offenders among low-income boys (see Shaw & Taraban, 2016). These early-occurring differences are likely the product of complex developmental processes involving genetic contributions, prenatal factors, and the child's early psychosocial context.

Heritable and other early-occurring risks may not result in conduct problems when other positive factors occur in individuals' lives. For example, Hyde and colleagues (Hyde et al., 2016) followed a cohort of young children adopted at birth. Those whose biological mothers showed severe antisocial behaviors were more likely to evidence callous-unemotional behaviors. However, higher levels of positive parenting marked by positive reinforcement moderated this relationship, buffering the heritable risk and reducing the likelihood of callous-unemotional behaviors. Other work, described below, similarly offers evidence of promotive and protective developmental processes buffering against risks for conduct problems.

Self-Regulation Throughout Childhood and Adolescence

Impulsivity and problems with dysregulated affect and behavior have been linked robustly with differences in aggression and poor conduct (Barker, Oliver, & Maughan, 2010; Beauchaine, Hinshaw, & Pang, 2010; Merikangas et al., 2010; Ollendick, Jarrett, Grills-Taquechel, Hovey, & Wolff, 2008; Rothbart & Bates, 2006; Schoemaker, Mulder, Deković, & Matthys, 2013). Relationships are found between aggression and some forms of physiological reactivity thought to be implicated with impulsivity and affect dysregulation (e.g., see Lorber, 2004). The construct of self-regulation is often considered broadly to encompass the ability of an individual to modulate their own behavior, and mechanisms through which they do this. Self-regulation involves a variety of related constructs like effortful control and executive functioning that span affective and cognitive sciences. Self-regulation develops throughout childhood and adolescence, with particularly rapid advances in early childhood, and appears to be influenced by factors at multiple levels of analysis, including the quality of caregiving and other relationships, genetic factors, and developmental history (Blair & Raver, 2012; Evans & Kim, 2013; McClelland, John Geldhof, Cameron, & Wanless, 2015; Montroy, Bowles, Skibbe, McClelland, & Morrison, 2016).

While many developmental models of risk for aggression implicate processes that compromise self-regulation along the way, the science of resilience consistently has recognized that good self-regulation can protect against negative effects of many different risks and adversities (Luthar, 2006; Masten & Cicchetti, 2016). Findings from a variety of populations at risk for externalizing problems indicate that those who show resilience are more likely to demonstrate good self-regulation, including samples experiencing an array of sociodemographic risks including poverty, maltreatment, and homelessness (Buckner,

Mezzacappa, & Beardslee, 2003; Cicchetti & Rogosch, 2009; Lengua, 2002; Masten et al., 2012; Obradović, 2010).

Parenting and the Parent-Child Relationship

The family system makes up the primary context of childhood development. Most notably, characteristics of parenting behavior and the parent-child relationship have implications for the development of conduct problems (see Labella & Masten, 2016). Harsh, inconsistent caregiving predicts poor conduct. Patterson (Patterson, 1982) explicated a developmental sequence involving coercive processes between parents and young children leading to aggression and poor conduct. These processes, in turn, contribute to other risks that perpetuate and elaborate on maladaptive patterns. Coercion occurs in interactions when the parent makes a demand of the child, the child responds with aversive behavior, such as an act of aggression or temper tantrum, and then the parent relents and rescinds the request in response to the child's behavior, which consequently ceases. This interaction serves to reinforce not only the child's inappropriate response to the parent's directive, but also the parent's decision to concede limits since dropping the request resulted in a secession of the child's aversive behavior. Similar processes can present in adolescence, as parental attempts at monitoring or limit setting, for example, are met with aggression, ignoring, or avoiding, leading to the parent disengaging. Over time, this pattern can dominate the child's approach to limits and authority, resulting in emotional overreaction, aggression, avoidance, and other coercive behaviors.

Harsh physical discipline is a risk factor for aggression and conduct problems, especially when parental warmth is low (Gershoff, Lansford, Sexton, Davis-Kean, & Sameroff, 2012; Taylor, Manganello, Lee, & Rice, 2010). Extreme forms of harsh discipline, or physical abuse, constitute a stronger risk, as does exposure to domestic violence (Dishion & Patterson, 2016; Wolfe, Crooks, Lee, McIntyre-Smith, & Jaffe, 2003). Explanations of this link can involve social learning accounts where violence is modeled, guiding the child's social responding towards aggression (Bandura, 1997). Other mechanisms suggest a "spillover" effect wherein exposures to violence impact caregiver functioning, which, in turn, increase the likelihood of adversity. In addition, findings from developmental social neuroscience and trauma literatures suggest that intense activation of stress response systems can contribute to lasting dysregulation of those systems in a way consistent with aggression and other externalizing presentations, especially if the stress is chronic (Bruce, Gunnar, Pears, & Fisher, 2013; Eiland & Romeo, 2013; Evans & Kim, 2013; Kim et al., 2013; Thompson, 2014). These explanations converge to provide a plausible account of mechanisms from harsh physical discipline to aggression and other conduct problems in development.

A number of studies have questioned the unique causal role of negative parenting practices on conduct problems (e.g., see Jaffee et al., 2012), testing whether and how parent and child behavior might influence each other over time in a way more consistent with accounts of transactions between dynamic systems. For example, Chang and Shaw (2016) report that parental negative control in tandem with child negative emotionality at 18 months predicts child disruptive behavior at 24 months, but more negative emotionality in children predicted less parental control over time. This is consistent with a coercion effect wherein parents become less likely to enforce limits when anticipating strong emotional responses from their children. Considering adolescents, Ge and colleagues (1996) found that adopted adolescents' conduct problems were related to birth parents' antisocial personality or substance use diagnoses, presumably through shared genetic influences. In addition, biological parents' psychiatric status influenced the quality of adopted parents' parenting behavior indirectly through the adolescents' antisocial and hostile behavior. These findings echo the conclusions of other behavior genetic designs that note considerable heritability in antisocial behavior (see Burt, 2009). Yet, other studies have confirmed that parent-child conflict and negative parenting practices contribute to increases in adolescent conduct problems longitudinally (Burt, McGue, Krueger, & Iacono, 2007; Klahr, McGue, Iacono, & Burt, 2011). Shared genetic effects appear important, but do not wholly account for the role of harsh, hostile, and inconsistent parenting in the development and maintenance of conduct problems.

Parenting behaviors and parent-child relationships marked by warmth, structure, and responsiveness are associated with lower levels of aggression and conduct problems (Boeldt et al., 2012; McFadyen-Ketchum, Bates, Dodge, & Pettit, 1996; McKee et al., 2007). Undoubtedly, some of this effect can be attributed to the relatively low rates of negative parenting practices among parents who engage in more positive behaviors; parents who impose structure and set consistent limits are less likely to perpetuate coercive family processes (e.g., Brumley & Jaffee, 2016). However, positive parenting structures developing capacities, such as child self-regulation and executive functioning (Herbers et al., 2011), and appears to be particularly beneficial when a variety of other risks are also present. For example, Herbers and colleagues (Herbers, Cutuli, Monn, Narayan, & Masten, 2014; Herbers, Cutuli, Supkoff, Narayan, & Masten, 2014) observed parent-child interactions among early school-aged children who were experiencing family homelessness to examine their effects. Parent-behaviors that were marked by warmth, positive control, and nondirective responsiveness were generally associated with better child executive functioning (including behavioral control), which, in turn, was related to lower externalizing symptoms and better peer acceptance later in school. Furthermore, homeless families differ in the level of other risks and adversities in their lives, where a greater number of adverse life events incrementally predicts higher average emotional and behavioral problems. Positive parenting moderated this association, where parents who showed higher levels of positive parenting more effectively buffered their children from higher levels of risk. These findings exemplify a robust conclusion in the resilience literature considering a variety of different risk factors: competent, positive parenting is a salient protective factor for many different developmental outcomes (Luthar, 2006; Masten & Cicchetti, 2016).

Peer Factors

Characteristics of child and youth peer networks predict differences in aggression and conduct problems. Children and youth who have aggressive peers are more likely to show aggression (Molano, Jones, Brown, & Aber, 2013; Rulison, Gest, &

Loken, 2013). Similarly, older children and youth who associate with delinquent peers are more likely to have conduct problems, while those with more competent peers in their networks appear protected from risks for poor conduct (e.g., see Gifford-Smith, Dodge, Dishion, & McCord, 2005).

Children demonstrating early conduct problems face risk for peer rejection in the transition to school because of poor social skills and aggressive behavior (e.g., see Patterson, DeBaryshe, & Ramsey, 1989; Patterson & Stoolmiller, 1991), a process that constitutes a developmental cascade (see Masten & Cicchetti, 2010). Consequently, peer-rejected children are more likely to affiliate with less competent peers, affiliating instead with children who show aggression and poor conduct. In this way, social rejection from peers also contributes to increased risk for aggression and conduct problems. Peers represent a context for further development of social skills, cognitive skills, and shared moral values. Consequently, peer networks that contain children and youth with poor social skills lack the capacity for competent socialization. Instead, these networks can represent training grounds that encourage and reinforce the continued development of aggression, delinquency, and other conduct problems (Patterson, 1993).

Related to peer functioning as well as other social contexts, biases in social information processing (SIP) contribute to aggression and other forms of poor conduct. Aggression and poor conduct, in turn, contribute to peer rejection and subsequent reinforcement of biased SIP to perpetuate conduct problems and maladjustment. In brief, Dodge and others (Crick & Dodge, 1994; Dodge, 1986, 2006) have outlined a process by which individuals take in information about an event or situation, make attributions about others' motives or goals, generate and evaluate possible responses, and then enact a particular response. Children and youth with aggression problems are more likely to show particular biases with respect to SIP (e.g., hypervigilance to hostile cues; formulating aggressive responses and believing they will be most effective), and children with pervasive SIP biases are at the highest risk (Dodge et al., 2015). Relevant to peer contexts, children with SIP biases are simultaneously more likely to experience peer rejection and to show aggression. Over time, aggression predicts increases in peer rejection while peer rejection reinforces and increases SIP biases (Lansford, Malone, Dodge, Pettit, & Bates, 2010). Children who initially show aggression are thereby less likely to have positive peer relationships that challenge biased SIP, discourage aggression, and encourage prosocial behavior. This sequence constitutes a developmental cascade as dynamic systems transact over time, compounding failure. Additional work has expanded consideration to other dynamic systems, such as linking neighborhood deprivation to biases in aggressive response generation (Galán, Shaw, Dishion, & Wilson, 2016).

School Factors

Just as with peers, children on pathways that involve aggression and other conduct problems are also more likely to have problems at school with respect to academics and the teacher-child relationship. These problems, in turn, also represent risk for worse conduct as well as other poor outcomes in the areas of internalizing problems, such as depression and anxiety, worse achievement, and lower academic attainment (Cutuli, Chaplin, Gillham, Reivich, & Seligman, 2006; Portilla, Ballard, Adler, Boyce, & Obradović, 2014; Zimmermann, Schütte, Taskinen, & Köller, 2013). This constitutes another possible developmental cascade contributing to conduct problems while threatening competence in other domains.

The teacher-student relationship represents a context that can exacerbate student conduct problems. Relationships marked by conflict can contribute to steeper increases in externalizing symptoms in the elementary school years, while those marked by higher levels of warmth, closeness, and support are generally associated with lower conduct problems and higher educational engagement, achievement, and peer functioning at school (O'Connor, Dearing, & Collins, 2011; Silver, Measelle, Armstrong, & Essex, 2005; Skalická, Belsky, Stenseng, & Wichstrøm, 2015). However, student conduct problems are related to more negative ratings of teacher-student relationship quality, and a diverse literature suggests that a host of other factors influence student- and teacher-ratings of relationship quality, such as differences in race, school-level poverty, feelings of safety and school violence, and others (e.g., Hamre & Pianta, 2001; Hughes, Bullock, & Coplan, 2014; Ly & Zhou, 2016).

Programs to Promote Resilience

Resilience science is necessarily applied at its core, interested in translating knowledge into action regarding how risk interferes with development and how promotive and protective factors bring about positive adaptation nonetheless. The above discussions provide examples of some of the important processes of risk and protection in the manifestation of aggression and other forms of conduct problems. Below we discuss a few examples of programs that translate this information in different ways to "make good" on the applied promise of resilience science: to increase the number of children who show resilience. When demonstrating positive effects through rigorous designs (e.g., randomized-control trials), these programs also provide experimental evidence of the processes of resilience in developmental pathways away from conduct problems. More importantly, they demonstrate that at least some protective or promotive factors are malleable and thus can be encouraged among those at risk.

Promoting Self-Regulation

Self-regulation has been targeted by intervention programs as a key protective factor against many sources of risk for conduct problems. A number of preschool curricula have demonstrated positive effects through direct intervention with children on the growth of self-regulation skills with implications for promoting good conduct (Barnett et al., 2008; Diamond, Barnett, Thomas, & Munro, 2007; but see also Wilson & Farran, 2012). These curricula, and some other specific contextual interventions, have their effect through structuring children's experiences in many ways that encourage the development of self-regulation skills (Diamond & Lee, 2011). Meanwhile, computerized attempts at increasing self-regulation through gains in executive functioning, so-called "brain training" programs, have produced inconsistent results that, in sum, do not support their efficacy in the general population (Simons et al., 2016). Increasing cognitive control through bolstering metacognitive abilities, like executive functions, requires a contextual approach.

An alternative tactic is to explicitly teach emotion regulation skills and challenge biased cognitions. The Penn Resiliency Program is a school-based intervention delivered in a series of afterschool sessions with early adolescents. Originally designed to prevent depression, the content draws on cognitive-behavioral principles to build emotion regulation skills, including identifying the links between beliefs and emotions, challenging inaccurate cognitions and biased social information processing, social skills training, and relaxation techniques. While the program's effects on preventing depression are well documented (Brunwasser, Gillham, & Kim, 2009; Cutuli et al., 2006), it also appears to be effective in reducing parent-reported externalizing symptoms across adolescence compared to a randomly assigned no-intervention control group (Cutuli et al., 2013).

Social Skills and School-Based Social-Emotional Learning Programs

Peer and school-based interventions for conduct problems commonly involve teacher training for behavior management techniques, programs, or curricula to boost student social-emotional development (e.g., self-regulation and/or social skills training). A host of school-based programs, curricula, and practices exist to directly support healthy social-emotional development with students, many specifically targeting aggression or other conduct problems as outcomes through supporting the development of self-regulation skills, social skills with peers, and/or problem solving techniques. A comprehensive review of these is beyond the scope of this chapter, but we refer interested readers to any of a number of reviews in the literature (Greenberg et al., 2003; Leff, Power, Manz, Costigan, & Nabors, 2001; Leff, Waasdorp, & Crick, 2010; McLeod et al., 2016).

Teacher training approaches look to impart effective means of setting and maintaining limits, usually while acknowledging the importance of a warm, positive teacher-child relationship. For example, the Incredible Years Teacher Classroom Management program emphasizes teacher behavior management and proactive teaching with children who show poor conduct in the classroom (Webster-Stratton, Reinke, Herman, & Newcomer, 2011). Teachers also learn how to encourage student self-regulation and social skills. In addition, the program involves teacher skill development in promoting positive relationships with students and increasing collaboration with parents. Randomized trials support the program's efficacy in improving classroom environments, improving relationships with parents, reducing student aggression and conduct problems, and increasing student cooperation, social skills, and self-regulation (Raver et al., 2008; Webster-Stratton & Reid, 2004; Webster-Stratton et al., 2011). In this way, teachers become better equipped to promote positive adaptation among students at-risk for conduct problems. The Incredible Years Teacher Classroom Management program positions teachers to more effectively promote resilience in the school setting through classroom management and teacher-child relationships, while also helping to coordinate and encourage promotive and protective factors in other dynamic systems, namely at home and in peer relationships.

Parenting and Multi-component Programs

Not surprisingly, many programs seek to promote resilience by targeting parenting and family functioning. The Fast Track program is a multi-component intervention that looks to compensate for the risks associated with conduct problems in development. The intervention included school-level components to manage behavior and promote social-emotional functioning, child social skills training, and peer components to promote and protect healthy peer relationships, parent behavior management skills training, and additional academic supports in the form of tutoring. The program was delivered across grades 1 to 10 and tested in a large-scale, multi-site, cluster-randomized trial with longitudinal follow-up.

The Fast Track program appeared to have the clearest positive effects on family and child functioning in the earliest years of the study. Families in the intervention condition showed lower levels of harsh discipline in early elementary school, and increases in warmth after first grade (Conduct Problems Prevention Research Group, 1999, 2002). Children at the highest levels of initial risk for conduct problems at the start of the study showed the clearest reduction in conduct problems through high school (Conduct Problems Prevention Research Group, 2011). Intervention-related differences in parenting partially accounted for intervention effects on lower conduct problems later in elementary school (Conduct Problems Prevention Research Group, 2002). More specifically, early reductions in harsh discipline were related to lower levels of conduct disorder symptoms in middle school. Meanwhile, increases in parenting warmth in elementary school were linked to lower levels of callous-unemotional traits in middle school (Pasalich, Witkiewitz, McMahon, Pinderhughes, & Conduct Problems Prevention Research Group, 2016). These indirect effects underscore the value of both removing sources of risk (harsh discipline) while adding promotive factors (warmth) to encourage positive adaptation and resilience.

In contrast to the above intensive approach, the early-childhood version of the Family Check Up is a relatively less intensive program in which families engage in an assessment and motivational interviewing to tailor the program to parent strengths and weaknesses. Families "check up" with the program annually. If indicated, families also complete an adapted curriculum developed to encourage effective parent behavior management strategies and discourage coercive family processes. This intervention appears effective when implemented with families with a toddler at risk for aggression and conduct problems based on the presence of sociodemographic or caregiving-related risk factors or early behavioral problems. Children in families receiving the program were less likely to display conduct problems or showed slower growth in conduct problems over time (Dishion et al., 2014; Dishion et al., 2008; Gardner, Shaw, Dishion, Burton, & Supplee, 2007; Shaw, Dishion, Supplee, Gardner, & Arnds, 2006; Shaw & Taraban, 2016). The exact mechanism(s) through which the Family Check Up program promotes resilience is somewhat unclear. Longitudinal program effects seem to be mediated by increases in positive parenting (Dishion et al., 2008) and self-control (Chang, Shaw, Shelleby, Dishion, & Wilson, 2016). Meanwhile, the Family

Check Up program also has positive longitudinal effects on other factors that are likely to promote or protect positive adaptation, including academic achievement (Brennan et al., 2013), effortful control (Chang et al., 2016), service use and treatment among the highest-risk children (Leijten et al., 2015), and caregivers' social support and relationship satisfaction (McEachern et al., 2013). Consistent with a dynamic systems account of resilience, Family Check Up effectively incorporates assessment of family strengths and risks to bolster varied promotive and protective systems for development. These systems not only prevent problems, but encourage healthy development and a strengthening of other systems that aid in subsequent positive adaptation. This constitutes a kind of positive developmental cascade wherein strengths and success in developmental tasks likely beget additional assets (Masten & Cicchetti, 2010).

Conclusion

Considering the development of aggression and conduct problems with a resilience framework encourages attention to potent risks as well as strengths. What matters are not only those factors that predict problems, but also the factors that explain how many individuals at risk for difficulties show healthy, competent outcomes. This information is useful because efforts to intervene with children and youth at risk for aggression and conduct problems cannot feasibly prevent or remove all threats that can occur across levels of genes, physiological functioning, temperament, relationships, and broader ecological systems. In many cases it may be more feasible to build and bolster the promotive and protective factors that can mitigate these threats. Translational and intervention research has demonstrated the promise of applying resilience concepts to prevent or redirect maladaptive developmental trajectories related to aggression. The most effective interventions are those that appreciate individuals within their contexts, addressing both risks and strengths that can generalize and foster more competent development.

References

Assink, M., van der Put, C. E., Hoeve, M., de Vries, S. L., Stams, G. J. J., & Oort, F. J. (2015). Risk factors for persistent delinquent behavior among juveniles: a meta-analytic review. *Clinical Psychology Review*, 42, 47–61.

Bandura, A. (1997). *Self-efficacy: The exercise of control*. New York: W. H. Freeman.

Barker, E. D., Oliver, B. R., & Maughan, B. (2010). Co-occurring problems of early onset persistent, childhood limited, and adolescent onset conduct problem youth. *Journal of Child Psychology and Psychiatry*, 51(11), 1217–1226.

Barnett, W. S., Jung, K., Yarosz, D. J., Thomas, J., Hornbeck, A., Stechuk, R., & Burns, S. (2008). Educational effects of the Tools of the Mind curriculum: A randomized trial. *Early Childhood Research Quarterly*, 23(3), 299–313.

Beauchaine, T. P., Hinshaw, S. P., & Pang, K. L. (2010). Comorbidity of attention-deficit/hyperactivity disorder and early-onset conduct disorder: Biological, environmental, and developmental mechanisms. *Clinical Psychology: Science and Practice*, 17(4), 327–336.

Blair, C. & Raver, C. C. (2012). Individual development and evolution: Experiential canalization of self-regulation. *Developmental Psychology*, 48(3), 647–657.

Blair, C., Raver, C. C., & Finegood, E. D. (2016). Self-Regulation and Developmental Psychopathology: Experiential Canalization of Brain and Behavior. In D. Cicchetti (Ed.), *Developmental Psychopathology* (Vol. 2). Hoboken, NJ: John Wiley & Sons.

Boeldt, D. L., Rhee, S. H., DiLalla, L. F., Mullineaux, P. Y., Schulz-Heik, R. J., Corley, R. P., ... & Hewitt, J. K. (2012). The association between positive parenting and externalizing behaviour. *Infant and Child Development*, 21(1), 85–106.

Brennan, L. M., Shelleby, E. C., Shaw, D. S., Gardner, F., Dishion, T. J., & Wilson, M. (2013). Indirect effects of the family check-up on school-age academic achievement through improvements in parenting in early childhood. *Journal of Educational Psychology*, 105(3), 762.

Bronfenbrenner, U. (1979). *The Ecology of Human Development: Experiments by Nature and Design*. Cambridge, MA: Harvard University Press.

Bruce, J., Gunnar, M. R., Pears, K. C., & Fisher, P. A. (2013). Early adverse care, stress neurobiology, and prevention science: Lessons learned. *Prevention Science*, 14(3), 247–256.

Brumley, L. D. & Jaffee, S. R. (2016). Defining and distinguishing promotive and protective effects for childhood externalizing psychopathology: a systematic review. *Social Psychiatry and Psychiatric Epidemiology*, 51(6), 803–815.

Brunwasser, S. M., Gillham, J. E., & Kim, E. S. (2009). A meta-analytic review of the Penn Resiliency Program's effect on depressive symptoms. *Journal of Consulting and Clinical Psychology*, 77(6), 1042.

Buckner, J. C., Mezzacappa, E., & Beardslee, W. R. (2003). Characteristics of resilient youths living in poverty: The role of self-regulatory processes. *Development and Psychopathology*, 15(1), 139–162.

Burt, K. B., Coatsworth, J. D., & Masten, A. S. (2016). Competence and Psychopathology in Development. In D. Cicchetti (Ed.), *Developmental Psychopathology* (3rd ed). Hoboken, NJ: John Wiley & Sons.

Burt, S. A. (2009). Rethinking environmental contributions to child and adolescent psychopathology: A meta-analysis of shared environmental influences. *Psychological Bulletin*, 135(4), 608.

Burt, S. A., McGue, M., Krueger, R. F., & Iacono, W. G. (2007). Environmental contributions to adolescent delinquency: A fresh look at the shared environment. *Journal of Abnormal Child Psychology*, 35(5), 787–800.

Bushman, B. J., Newman, K., Calvert, S. L., Downey, G., Dredze, M., Gottfredson, M., ... & Neill, D. B. (2016). Youth violence: What we know and what we need to know. *American Psychologist*, 71(1), 17.

Chang, H. & Shaw, D. S. (2016). The Emergence of Parent–Child Coercive Processes in Toddlerhood. *Child Psychiatry & Human Development*, 47(2), 226–235.

Chang, H., Shaw, D. S., Shelleby, E. C., Dishion, T. J., & Wilson, M. N. (2016). The Long-Term Effectiveness of the Family Check-up on Peer Preference: Parent-Child Interaction and Child Effortful Control as Sequential Mediators. *Journal of Abnormal Child Psychology*, 1–13.

Cicchetti, D. & Blender, J. A. (2006). A multiple-levels-of-analysis perspective on resilience: Implications for the developing brain, neural plasticity, and preventive interventions. *Annals of the New York Academy of Science*, 1094, 248–258.

Cicchetti, D. & Rogosch, F. A. (2009). Adaptive coping under conditions of extreme stress: Multilevel influences on the determinants of resilience in maltreated children. *New Directions in Child and Adolescent Development*, 124, 47–59.

Conduct Problems Prevention Research Group. (1999). Initial impact of the Fast Track prevention trial for conduct problems: I. The high-risk sample. *Journal of Consulting and Clinical Psychology*, 67(5), 631.

Conduct Problems Prevention Research Group. (2002). Using the Fast Track randomized prevention trial to test the early-starter model of the development of serious conduct problems. *Development and Psychopathology*, 14(4), 925.

Conduct Problems Prevention Research Group. (2011). The effects of the Fast Track preventive intervention on the development of conduct disorder across childhood. *Child Development*, 82(1), 331.

Crick, N. R. & Dodge, K. A. (1994). A review and reformulation of social information-processing mechanisms in children's social adjustment. *Psychological Bulletin*, 115(1), 74.

Crick, N. R. & Dodge, K. A. (1996). Social information-processing mechanisms in reactive and proactive aggression. *Child Development*, 67(3), 993–1002.

Crick, N. R. & Grotpeter, J. K. (1995). Relational aggression, gender, and social-psychological adjustment. *Child Development*, 710–722.

Cutuli, J. J., Chaplin, T. M., Gillham, J. E., Reivich, K. J., & Seligman, M. E. (2006). Preventing Co-Occurring Depression Symptoms in Adolescents with Conduct Problems. *Annals of the New York Academy of Sciences*, 1094(1), 282–286.

Cutuli, J. J., Gillham, J. E., Chaplin, T. M., Reivich, K. J., Seligman, M. E., Gallop, R. J., ... & Freres, D. R. (2013). Preventing adolescents' externalizing and internalizing symptoms: Effects of the Penn Resiliency Program. *International Journal of Emotional Education*, 5(2), 67.

Cutuli, J. J., Herbers, J. E., Masten, A. S., & Reed, M. G. J. (in press). Resilience in Development *Handbook of Positive Psychology* (3rd ed.). New York: Oxford University Press.

Diamond, A., Barnett, W. S., Thomas, J., & Munro, S. (2007). Preschool program improves cognitive control. *Science*, 318(5855), 1387–1388.

Diamond, A. & Lee, K. (2011). Interventions shown to aid executive function development in children 4–12 years old. *Science*, 333(6045), 959–964. doi: 10.1126/science.1204529.

Dishion, T. J., Brennan, L. M., Shaw, D. S., McEachern, A. D., Wilson, M. N., & Jo, B. (2014). Prevention of problem behavior through annual family check-ups in early childhood: intervention effects from home to early elementary school. *Journal of Abnormal Child Psychology*, 42(3), 343–354.

Dishion, T. J. & Patterson, G. R. (2016). The development and ecology of antisocial behavior: Linking etiology, prevention, and treatment. In D. Cicchetti (Ed.), *Developmental Psychopathology* (3rd ed., pp. 647–478). Hoboken, NJ: John Wiley & Sons.

Dishion, T. J., Shaw, D., Connell, A., Gardner, F., Weaver, C., & Wilson, M. (2008). The family check-up With high-risk indigent families: Preventing problem behavior by increasing parents' positive behavior support in early childhood. *Child Development*, 79(5), 1395–1414.

Dodge, K. A. (1986). A social information processing model of social competence in children. In M. Perlmutter (Ed.), *Cognitive Perspectives on Children's Social and Behavioral Development: The Minnesota Symposia on Child Psychology*, Volume 18 (pp. 77–126). New Jersey: Lawrence Erlbaum Associates.

Dodge, K. A. (2006). Translational science in action: Hostile attributional style and the development of aggressive behavior problems. *Development and Psychopathology*, 18(03), 791–814.

Dodge, K. A., Bierman, K. L., Coie, J. D., Greenberg, M. T., Lochman, J. E., McMahon, R. J., & Pinderhughes, E. E. (2015). Impact of Early Intervention on Psychopathology, Crime, and Well-being at Age 25. *The American Journal of Psychiatry*, 172(1), 59–70.

Dodge, K. A. & Pettit, G. S. (2003). A biopsychosocial model of the development of chronic conduct problems in adolescence. *Developmental Psychology*, 39(2), 349.

Eiland, L. & Romeo, R. D. (2013). Stress and the developing adolescent brain. *Neuroscience*, 249, 162–171.

Elder, G. H. (1998). The life course as developmental theory. *Child Development*, 69, 1–12.

Evans, G. W. & Kim, P. (2013). Childhood poverty, chronic stress, self-regulation, and coping. *Child Development Perspectives*, 7(1), 43–48.

Frick, P. J., Blair, R. J., & Castellanos, F. X. (2013). Callous-unemotional traits and developmental pathways to the disruptive behavior disorders. In P. H. Tolan and B. L. Leventhal (Eds), *Disruptive Behavior Disorders* (pp. 69–102). New York: Springer.

Frick, P. J. & Morris, A. S. (2004). Temperament and developmental pathways to conduct problems. *Journal of Clinical Child and Adolescent Psychology*, 33(1), 54–68.

Galán, C. A., Shaw, D. S., Dishion, T. J., & Wilson, M. N. (2016). Neighborhood deprivation during early childhood and conduct problems in middle childhood: mediation by aggressive response generation. *Journal of Abnormal Child Psychology*, 1–12.

Gardner, F., Shaw, D. S., Dishion, T. J., Burton, J., & Supplee, L. (2007). Randomized prevention trial for early conduct problems: Effects on proactive parenting and links to toddler disruptive behavior. *Journal of Family Psychology*, 21(3), 398.

Ge, X., Conger, R. D., Cadoret, R. J., Neiderhiser, J. M., Yates, W., Troughton, E., & Stewart, M. A. (1996). The developmental interface between nature and nurture: a mutual influence model of child antisocial behavior and parent behaviors. *Developmental Psychology*, 32(4), 574.

Gershoff, E. T., Lansford, J. E., Sexton, H. R., Davis-Kean, P., & Sameroff, A. J. (2012). Longitudinal links between spanking and children's externalizing behaviors in a national sample of White, Black, Hispanic, and Asian American families. *Child Development*, 83(3), 838–843.

Gifford-Smith, M., Dodge, K. A., Dishion, T. J., & McCord, J. (2005). Peer influence in children and adolescents: Crossing the bridge from developmental to intervention science. *Journal of Abnormal Child Psychology*, 33(3), 255–265.

Gottlieb, G. (1991). Experiential canalization of behavioral development: Theory. *Developmental Psychology*, 27(1), 4–13.

Greenberg, M. T., Weissberg, R. P., O'Brien, M. U., Zins, J. E., Fredericks, L., Resnik, H., & Elias, M. J. (2003). Enhancing school-based prevention and youth development through coordinated social, emotional, and academic learning. *American Psychologist*, 58(6–7), 466.

Haberstick, B. C., Schmitz, S., Young, S. E., & Hewitt, J. K. (2005). Contributions of genes and environments to stability and change in externalizing and internalizing problems during elementary and middle school. *Behavior Genetics*, 35(4), 381–396.

Hamre, B. K. & Pianta, R. C. (2001). Early teacher–child relationships and the trajectory of children's school outcomes through eighth grade. *Child Development*, 72(2), 625–638.

Herbers, J. E., Cutuli, J. J., Lafavor, T. L., Vrieze, D., Leibel, C., Obradovic, J., & Masten, A. S. (2011). Direct and indirect effects of parenting on academic functioning of young homeless children. *Early Education and Development*, 22(1), 77–104.

Herbers, J. E., Cutuli, J. J., Monn, A. R., Narayan, A. J., & Masten, A. S. (2014). Trauma, Adversity, and Parent-Child Relationships Among Young Children Experiencing Homelessness. *Journal of Abnormal Child Psychology*, 42(7), 1167–1174.

Herbers, J. E., Cutuli, J. J., Supkoff, L. M., Narayan, A. J., & Masten, A. S. (2014). Parenting and Coregulation: Adaptive systems for competence in children experiencing homelessness. *American Journal of Orthopsychiatry*, 84(4), 420–430.

Holz, N. E., Zohsel, K., Laucht, M., Banaschewski, T., Hohmann, S., & Brandeis, D. (2016). Gene x environment interactions in conduct disorder: Implications for future treatments. *Neuroscience & Biobehavioral Reviews*.

Hughes, K., Bullock, A., & Coplan, R. J. (2014). A person-centred analysis of teacher–child relationships in early childhood. *British Journal of Educational Psychology*, 84(2), 253–267.

Hyde, L. W., Waller, R., Trentacosta, C. J., Shaw, D. S., Neiderhiser, J. M., Ganiban, J. M., ... & Leve, L. D. (2016). Heritable and Nonheritable Pathways to Early Callous-Unemotional Behaviors. *American Journal of Psychiatry*.

Jaffee, S. R., Strait, L. B., & Odgers, C. L. (2012). From correlates to causes: can quasi-experimental studies and statistical innovations bring us closer to identifying the causes of antisocial behavior? *Psychological Bulletin*, 138(2), 272.

Kim, P., Evans, G. W., Angstadt, M., Ho, S. S., Sripada, C. S., Swain, J. E., ... & Phan, K. L. (2013). Effects of childhood poverty and chronic stress on emotion regulatory brain function in adulthood. *Proceedings of the National Academy of Sciences*, 110(46), 18442–18447.

Klahr, A. M., McGue, M., Iacono, W. G., & Burt, S. A. (2011). The association between parent–child conflict and adolescent conduct problems over time: Results from a longitudinal adoption study. *Journal of Abnormal Psychology*, 120(1), 46–57.

Labella, M. H., & Masten, A. S. (2016). Family Influences on Aggression and Violence. *Aggression and Violence: A Social Psychological Perspective*.

Lansford, J. E., Malone, P. S., Dodge, K. A., Pettit, G. S., & Bates, J. E. (2010). Developmental cascades of peer rejection, social information processing biases, and aggression during middle childhood. *Development and Psychopathology*, 22(03), 593–602.

Lanza, S. T., Rhoades, B. L., Nix, R. L., & Greenberg, M. T. (2010). Modeling the interplay of multilevel risk factors for future academic and behavior problems: A person-centered approach. *Development and Psychopathology*, 22(2), 313–335.

Leff, S. S., Baker, C. N., Waasdorp, T. E., Vaughn, N. A., Bevans, K. B., Thomas, N. A., ... & Monopoli, W. J. (2014). Social cognitions, distress, and leadership self-efficacy: Associations with aggression for high-risk minority youth. *Development and Psychopathology*, 26(03), 759–772.

Leff, S. S., Power, T. J., Manz, P. H., Costigan, T. E., & Nabors, L. A. (2001). School-based aggression prevention program for young children: Current status and implications for violence prevention. *School Psychology Review*, 30(3), 344.

Leff, S. S., Waasdorp, T. E., & Crick, N. R. (2010). A review of existing relational aggression programs: Strengths, limitations, and future directions. *School Psychology Review*, 39(4), 508.

Leijten, P., Shaw, D. S., Gardner, F., Wilson, M. N., Matthys, W., & Dishion, T. J. (2015). The Family Check-Up and service use in high-risk families of young children: A prevention strategy with a bridge to community-based treatment. *Prevention Science*, 16(3), 397–406.

Lengua, L. J. (2002). The Contribution of Emotionality and Self-Regulation to the Understanding of Children's Response to Multiple Risk. *Child Development*, 73(1), 144–161.

Lorber, M. F. (2004). Psychophysiology of aggression, psychopathy, and conduct problems: a meta-analysis. *Psychological Bulletin*, 130(4), 531.

Luthar, S. S. (2006). Resilience in development: A synthesis of research across five decades. In D. Cicchetti & D. J. Cohen (Eds), *Developmental Psychopathology: Volume 3. Risk, disorder, and adaptation* (2nd ed., pp. 739–795). Hoboken, NJ: John Wiley & Sons.

Luthar, S. S., Cicchetti, D., & Becker, B. (2000). The construct of resilience: A critical evaluation and guidelines for future work. *Child Development*, 71(3), 543–562.

Ly, J. & Zhou, Q. (2016). Bidirectional associations between teacher–child relationship quality and Chinese American immigrant children's behavior problems. *Journal of Clinical Child & Adolescent Psychology*, 1–13.

Martel, M. M. (2013). Sexual selection and sex differences in the prevalence of childhood externalizing and adolescent internalizing disorders. *Psychological Bulletin*, 139(6), 1221.

Masten, A. S. (2001). Ordinary magic: Resilience processes in development. *American Psychologist*, 56(3), 227–238.

Masten, A. S. (2014). *Ordinary Magic: Resilience in development*. New York: The Guilford Press.

Masten, A. S. & Cicchetti, D. (2010). Editorial: Developmental cascades. *Development and Psychopathology*, 22, 491–495.

Masten, A. S. & Cicchetti, D. (2016). Resilience in Development: Progress and Transformation. In D. Cicchetti (Ed.), *Developmental Psychopathology* (3rd ed.) (Vol IV, pp. 271–333). Hoboken, NJ: John Wiley & Sons.

Masten, A. S., Herbers, J. E., Desjardins, C. D., Cutuli, J. J., McCormick, C. M., Sapienza, J. K., ... & Zelazo, P. D. (2012). Executive function skills and school success in young children experiencing homelessness. *Educational Researcher*, 41(9), 375–384.

Masten, A. S. & Obradović, J. (2006). Competence and resilience in development. *Annals of the New York Academy of Sciences*, 1094(1), 13–27.

Masten, A. S., Roisman, G. I., Long, J. D., Burt, K. B., Obradović, J., Riley, J., ... & Tellegen, A. (2005). Developmental cascades: Linking academic achievement and externalizing and internalizing symptoms over 20 years. *Developmental Psychology*, 43, 733–746.

McClelland, M. M., John Geldhof, G., Cameron, C. E., & Wanless, S. B. (2015). Development and Self-Regulation. *Handbook of child psychology and developmental science*.

McEachern, A. D., Fosco, G. M., Dishion, T. J., Shaw, D. S., Wilson, M. N., & Gardner, F. (2013). Collateral benefits of the family checkup in early childhood: Primary caregivers' social support and relationship satisfaction. *Journal of Family Psychology*, 27(2), 271.

McFadyen-Ketchum, S. A., Bates, J. E., Dodge, K. A., & Pettit, G. S. (1996). Patterns of change in early childhood aggressive-disruptive behavior: Gender differences in predictions from early coercive and affectionate mother-child interactions. *Child Development*, 2417–2433.

McKee, L., Roland, E., Coffelt, N., Olson, A. L., Forehand, R., Massari, C., ... & Zens, M. S. (2007). Harsh discipline and child problem behaviors: the roles of positive parenting and gender. *Journal of Family Violence*, 22(4), 187–196.

McLeod, B. D., Sutherland, K. S., Martinez, R. G., Conroy, M. A., Snyder, P. A., & Southam-Gerow, M. A. (2016). Identifying common practice elements to improve social, emotional, and behavioral outcomes of young children in early childhood classrooms. *Prevention Science*, 1–10.

McMahon, R. J., Wells, K. C., & Kotler, J. S. (2006). Conduct problems. *Treatment of childhood disorders*, 3, 137–268.

Merikangas, K. R., He, J.-p., Burstein, M., Swanson, S. A., Avenevoli, S., Cui, L., ... & Swendsen, J. (2010). Lifetime prevalence of mental disorders in US adolescents: results from the National Comorbidity Survey Replication–Adolescent Supplement (NCS-A). *Journal of the American Academy of Child & Adolescent Psychiatry*, 49(10), 980–989.

Moffitt, T. E. (1993). Adolescence-limited and life-course-persistent antisocial behavior: A developmental taxonomy. *Psychological Review*, 100(4), 674–701.

Moffitt, T. E. (2006). Life-course-persistent versus adolescence-limited behavior. In D. Cicchetti & D. J. Cohen (Eds), *Developmental psychopathology, Volume 3: Risk, disorder, and adaptation. (2nd edition)*. Hoboken, NJ: John Wiley and Sons.

Molano, A., Jones, S. M., Brown, J. L., & Aber, J. L. (2013). Selection and Socialization of Aggressive and Prosocial Behavior: The Moderating Role of Social-Cognitive Processes. *Journal of Research on Adolescence*, 23(3), 424–436.

Montroy, J. J., Bowles, R. P., Skibbe, L. E., McClelland, M. M., & Morrison, F. J. (2016). The development of self-regulation across early childhood. *Developmental Psychology*, 52(11), 1744–1762.

Murray-Close, D., Nelson, D. A., Ostrov, J. M., Casas, J. F., & Crick, N. R. (2016). Relational aggression: A developmental psychopathology perspective. In D. Cicchetti (Ed.), *Developmental psychopathology: Risk, resilience, and intervention* (pp. 660–722). Hoboken, NJ: John Wiley & Sons Inc.

O'Connor, E. E., Dearing, E., & Collins, B. A. (2011). Teacher-child relationship and behavior problem trajectories in elementary school. *American Educational Research Journal*, 48(1), 120–162.

Obradović, J. (2010). Effortful control and adaptive functioning of homeless children: Variable-focused and person-focused analyses. *Journal of Applied Developmental Psychology*, 31, 109–117.

Obradović, J., Shaffer, A., & Masten, A. S. (2012). Adversity and risk in developmental psychopathology: Progress and future directions. In L. C. Mayes & M. Lewis (eds), *The Cambridge Handbook of Environment in Human Development* (pp. 35–57). New York: Cambridge University Press.

Ollendick, T. H., Jarrett, M. A., Grills-Taquechel, A. E., Hovey, L. D., & Wolff, J. C. (2008). Comorbidity as a predictor and moderator of treatment outcome in youth with anxiety, affective, attention deficit/hyperactivity disorder, and oppositional/conduct disorders. *Clinical Psychology Review*, 28(8), 1447–1471.

Pasalich, D. S., Witkiewitz, K., McMahon, R. J., Pinderhughes, E. E., & Conduct Problems Prevention Research Group. (2016). Indirect effects of the fast track intervention on conduct disorder symptoms and callous-unemotional traits: distinct pathways involving discipline and warmth. *Journal of Abnormal Child Psychology*, 44(3), 587–597.

Patterson, G. R. (1982). *Social Interactional Approach: Coercive Family Process* (Vol. 3). Eugene, OR: Castalia.

Patterson, G. R. (1993). Orderly change in a stable world: The antisocial trait as a chimera. *Journal of Consulting and Clinical Psychology*, 61(6), 911–919.

Patterson, G. R., DeBaryshe, B. D., & Ramsey, R. (1989). A developmental perspective on antisocial behavior. *American Psychologist*, 44(2), 329–335.

Patterson, G. R. & Stoolmiller, M. (1991). Replications of a dual failure model for boys' depressed mood. *Journal of Consulting and Clinical Psychology*, 59(4), 491.

Portilla, X. A., Ballard, P. J., Adler, N. E., Boyce, W. T., & Obradović, J. (2014). An integrative view of school functioning: Transactions between self-regulation, school engagement, and teacher–child relationship quality. *Child Development*, 85(5), 1915–1931.

Raine, A., Dodge, K. A., Loeber, R., Gatzke-Kopp, L., Lynam, D., Reynolds, C., ... & Liu, J. (2006). The reactive–proactive aggression questionnaire: Differential correlates of reactive and proactive aggression in adolescent boys. *Aggressive Behavior*, 32(2), 159–171.

Raver, C. C., Jones, S. M., Li-Grining, C. P., Metzger, M., Champion, K. M., & Sardin, L. (2008). Improving preschool classroom processes: Preliminary findings from a randomized trial implemented in Head Start settings. *Early Childhood Research Quarterly*, 23(1), 10–26.

Rothbart, M. & Bates, J. (2006). Temperament. In W. Damon, R. Lerner, & N. Eisenberg (eds), *Handbook of child psychology. Social, emotional, and personality development* (Vol. 3, pp. 99–166). New York: Wiley.

Rulison, K. L., Gest, S. D., & Loken, E. (2013). Dynamic social networks and physical aggression: The moderating role of gender and social status among peers. *Journal of Research on Adolescence*, 23(3), 437–449.

Salvatore, J. E., & Dick, D. M. (2016). Genetic influences on conduct disorder. *Neuroscience & Biobehavioral Reviews*.

Samek, D. R., Bailey, J., Hill, K. G., Wilson, S., Lee, S., Keyes, M. A., ... & Winters, K. C. (2016). A Test-Replicate Approach to Candidate Gene Research on Addiction and Externalizing Disorders: A Collaboration Across Five Longitudinal Studies. *Behavior Genetics*, 46(5), 608–626.

Sameroff, A. J., Seifer, R., Barocas, R., Zax, M., & Greenspan, S. (1987). Intelligence quotient scores of 4-year-old children: social-environmental risk factors. *Pediatrics*, 79(3), 343–350.

Schoemaker, K., Mulder, H., Deković, M., & Matthys, W. (2013). Executive functions in preschool children with externalizing behavior problems: A meta-analysis. *Journal of Abnormal Child Psychology*, 41(3), 457–471.

Shaw, D. S., Dishion, T. J., Supplee, L., Gardner, F., & Arnds, K. (2006). Randomized trial of a family-centered approach to the prevention of early conduct problems: 2-year effects of the family check-up in early childhood. *Journal of Consulting and Clinical Psychology*, 74(1), 1.

Shaw, D. S. & Taraban, L. E. (2016). New Directions and Challenges in Preventing Conduct Problems in Early Childhood. *Child Development Perspectives*.

Silver, R. B., Measelle, J. R., Armstrong, J. M., & Essex, M. J. (2005). Trajectories of classroom externalizing behavior: Contributions of child characteristics, family characteristics, and the teacher–child relationship during the school transition. *Journal of School Psychology*, 43(1), 39–60.

Simons, D. J., Boot, W. R., Charness, N., Gathercole, S. E., Chabris, C. F., Hambrick, D. Z., & Stine-Morrow, E. A. (2016). Do "brain-training" programs work? *Psychological Science in the Public Interest*, 17(3), 103–186.

Skalická, V., Belsky, J., Stenseng, F., & Wichstrøm, L. (2015). Reciprocal Relations Between Student–Teacher Relationship and Children's Behavioral Problems: Moderation by Child-Care Group Size. *Child Development*, 86(5), 1557–1570.

Southwick, S. M., Bonanno, G. A., Masten, A. S., Panter-Brick, C., & Yehuda, R. (2014). Resilience definitions, theory, and challenges: interdisciplinary perspectives. *European Journal of Psychotraumatology*, 5.

Sroufe, L. A. (1979). The coherence of individual development: Early care, attachment, and subsequent developmental issues. *American Psychologist*, 34(10), 834.

Sroufe, L. A. (1997). Psychopathology as an outcome of development. *Development and Psychopathology*, 9, 251–268.

Talge, N. M., Neal, C., & Glover, V. (2007). Antenatal maternal stress and long-term effects on child neurodevelopment: how and why? *Journal of Child Psychology and Psychiatry*, 48(3-4), 245–261.

Taylor, C. A., Manganello, J. A., Lee, S. J., & Rice, J. C. (2010). Mothers' spanking of 3-year-old children and subsequent risk of children's aggressive behavior. *Pediatrics*, 125(5), e1057–e1065.

Thompson, R. A. (2014). Stress and child development. *The Future of Children*, 24(1), 41–59.

Tiet, Q. Q., Wasserman, G. A., Loeber, R., McReynolds, L. S., & Miller, L. S. (2001). Developmental and sex differences in types of conduct problems. *Journal of Child and Family Studies*, 10(2), 181–197.

Van Goozen, S. H., Fairchild, G., Snoek, H., & Harold, G. T. (2007). The evidence for a neurobiological model of childhood antisocial behavior. *Psychological Bulletin*, 133(1), 149.

Webster-Stratton, C. & Reid, M. J. (2004). Strengthening social and emotional competence in young children – The foundation for early school readiness and success: Incredible years classroom social skills and problem-solving curriculum. *Infants & Young Children*, 17(2), 96–113.

Webster-Stratton, C., Reinke, W. M., Herman, K. C., & Newcomer, L. L. (2011). The incredible years teacher classroom management training: the methods and principles that support fidelity of training delivery. *School Psychology Review*, 40(4), 509.

Wilson, S. J. & Farran, D. C. (2012). Experimental Evaluation of the Tools of the Mind Preschool Curriculum. *Society for Research on Educational Effectiveness*.

Wolfe, D. A., Crooks, C. V., Lee, V., McIntyre-Smith, A., & Jaffe, P. G. (2003). The effects of children's exposure to domestic violence: A meta-analysis and critique. *Clinical*

Child and Family Psychology Review, 6(3), 171–187.

Yates, T. M., Egeland, B., & Sroufe, L. A. (2003). Rethinking resilience: A developmental process perspective. In S. S. Luthar (Ed.), *Resilience and vulnerability: Adaptation in the context of childhood adversities* (pp. 243–266). New York: Cambridge University Press.

Zelazo, P. D. (2013). Developmental Psychology: A New Synthesis. *The Oxford Handbook of Developmental Psychology, Vol. 1: Body and Mind*, 1, 3.

Zimmermann, F., Schütte, K., Taskinen, P., & Köller, O. (2013). Reciprocal effects between adolescent externalizing problems and measures of achievement. *Journal of Educational Psychology*, 105(3), 747.

20 Child Abuse and Neglect

Tamara Del Vecchio, Richard E. Heyman,
Amy M. Smith Slep, and Heather M. Foran

Introduction

Child maltreatment comprises both abuse (i.e., acts of commission) and neglect (i.e., acts of omission). Abuse is often categorized as physical, emotional or psychological, or sexual. Neglect ranges from extreme deprivation to failures to ensure adequate education and medical care. For over 50 years, child maltreatment has been recognized as a serious threat to children's well-being (Kempe, 1962), with deleterious impacts documented on children's neurological, emotional, cognitive, behavioral, psychological, and interpersonal outcomes (Cichetti, 2016). Yet, as will be discussed in this chapter, there is no universally accepted definition of what constitutes maltreatment. This is no trivial matter, as research across the translational spectrum – on prevalence, etiology, intervention, and dissemination – depends on the capacity to reliably and validly define and measure the target of interest (in this case, child physical, emotional, and sexual abuse and child neglect).

Here, we will review prevalence rates and impacts of child maltreatment and discuss issues regarding the definitions of child maltreatment. Then we will cover theoretical underpinnings and intervention efforts.

International prevalence estimates suggest maltreatment is far from rare. A review of child physical abuse (CPA) estimates in high-income countries found one-year prevalence rates of 4–16% (Gilbert et al., 2009). However, in other countries, such as Romania, India, and the Republic of Korea, rates of child physical abuse occur at alarmingly high rates, with one-third to one-half of all children experiencing physical abuse (Krug, Dahlberg, Mercy, Zwi, & Lozano, 2002). A review of 55 studies worldwide found a range of prevalence rates of 8–31% for female victims of child sexual abuse (CSA) and 3–17% for male victims of CSA (Barth, Bermetz, Heim, Trelle, & Tonia, 2013). Childhood prevalence of neglect is estimated at 6.5–19.2% in European and North American samples (Stoltenborgh, Bakermans-Kranenburg, Alink, & IJzendoorn, 2015). There is a high rate of co-occurrence among the maltreatment types, with 35–66% of victims of child maltreatment experiencing more than one type of maltreatment (e.g., Turner, Finkelhor, & Ormrod, 2010). However, the rank order of maltreatment types varies by country; for example, in Canada and the USA, neglect is most common (Trocmé, Tourigny, MacLaurin, & Fallon, 2003), whereas in Australia, emotional abuse is the most prevalent (Hatty & Hatty, 2001).

There have been notable declines in child maltreatment since the 1990s. The fourth US National Incidence Study of

Child Abuse and Neglect (NIS-4) results indicated a 26% decline in the frequency of child maltreatment, compared with rates reported in NIS-3 when child maltreatment peaked (Sedlak et al., 2010). These declines may be attributable to several shifts, including US federal maltreatment prevention and intervention initiatives (both in communities and the criminal justice system), and increased use of psychological and psychiatric services by parents who otherwise might have maltreated (Jones & Finkelhor, 2003).

Impacts of Child Maltreatment

Child maltreatment is consistently found to negatively impact mental health in childhood, and this risk continues into adulthood. Specifically, victimized children are more likely to be diagnosed with conduct disorders, attention deficit hyperactivity disorders, and depression, and have academic problems during childhood and adolescence (e.g., Teisl & Cicchetti, 2008). In adulthood, maltreatment is associated with substance abuse, depression, PTSD, antisocial personality disorder, and suicidal behaviors (e.g., Jonson-Reid, Kohl, & Drake, 2012; Norman et al., 2012). In addition, there is strong longitudinal evidence that severe neglect of young children can lead to a wide range of developmental problems, including emotional regulation problems, cognitive difficulties, and altered neurological development (e.g., Beckett et al., 2006). A variety of physical health problems have also been associated with child maltreatment, including high rates of type II diabetes, obesity, and cardiovascular disease, although a meta-analysis also revealed that magnitude of the effect is far from being established (Norman et al., 2012). Expectedly, child maltreatment is a significant cause of child homicide and unintentional death throughout the world (Krug, Dahlberg, Mercy, Zwi, & Lozano, 2002).

The effects of child maltreatment are considerably broader than the mental health and social outcomes noted above. More recently, researchers have identified persistent neurological changes in those who experienced child maltreatment. This biological entrenchment of maltreatment (Jaffe & Christian, 2014) is evidenced by several structural and functional differences in the brain. Studies reviewed by Danese and McEwen (2012) found that child maltreatment is associated with smaller prefrontal cortex and hippocampus, poorer executive functions, and greater activation of the hypothalamic-pituitary-adrenal (HPA) axis. In addition, psychiatric patients who were maltreated have a smaller corpus callosum when compared to healthy controls (by 17%) and other psychiatric patients who were not maltreated (11%). Furthermore, it appears that neglect, compared with other forms of maltreatment, plays the biggest role in reduced corpus callosum area (15–18% difference; Teicher et al., 2004).

Defining Child Maltreatment

The most systematically developed maltreatment criteria were created, field-tested, and disseminated in an initial series of studies. (See Heyman and Slep, in press, for a detailed summary of the 15-year research program.) Maltreatment criteria sets required (a) at least one signature act of that form of maltreatment (or, in the case of neglect, an act or omission) and (b) a clinically significant impact or a more than reasonable potential for a clinically significant impact. Given the intensely personal violation involved with sexual abuse and the brighter line drawn legally and culturally around any act of coercive, nonconsensual, or parent-child sexual contact, only a qualifying act was required (that is, harm or potential for harm was presumed).

The first two studies in developing the child maltreatment criteria addressed content validity of existing criteria, based on input from family maltreatment experts and field clinicians (Heyman & Slep, 2006, Studies 1 & 2). Based on the results of these two studies, criteria were iteratively fine-tuned to improve clarity, clinical utility, and agreement with master reviewers during an initial field trial with over 300 cases (Heyman & Slep, 2006, Study 3). Next, a semi-structured interview was developed to mirror the diagnostic criteria (similar to the Structured Interview for DSM; SCID; First, Spitzer, Gibbon, & Williams, 1997). Several alterations were made to the decision process to improve information and objective evaluation of each criterion, including the introduction of a computerized decision tree to allow decision makers to consider each criterion separately and take them to the next relevant criterion if warranted (see Heyman & Slep, 2006, Study 4). This approach led to very high reliability between master reviewers' and in-the-field decisions (92% agreement; kappa = 0.84). To further examine reliability under real-world conditions, 41 Air Force sites across the world participated in a randomized dissemination trial (Heyman & Slep, 2009). Decision making was similarly excellent (> 90% agreement with master reviewers). Based on these findings, the AF (and then the entire US military) adopted these criteria, policies, and procedures.

Recent and Ongoing Developments: DSM-5, ICD-11, and Field Testing

The *Diagnostic and Statistical Manual of Mental Disorders* (DSM-5; APA, 2013) used highly abridged versions of the Heyman and Slep (2006) criteria for its child physical abuse and child neglect criteria. The untested abridgement of these criteria whose strengths lay largely in its field-tested explicated language raises questions about their capacity to support high levels of reliability and validity (Heyman and Slep, in press). In contrast, the World Health Organization (2016) is currently considering physical abuse and neglect criteria for the *International Classification of Diseases* 11th edition (ICD-11) that hew closely to the Heyman and Slep (2006) criteria. For child, emotional/psychological and sexual abuse, both DSM-5 and ICD-11 closely follow Heyman and Slep's field-tested criteria.

Three field tests are of note. First, the WHO's proposed ICD-11 criteria are currently undergoing a programmatic series of field tests. In 2016, this included a study using experimentally manipulated vignettes to compare the use of ICD-10 and ICD-11 criteria (by hundreds of clinicians throughout the world) on diagnostic validity, reliability, and clinical utility (see Evans et al., 2015). Second, the US Army has commissioned a large-scale replication and extension of the AF research at the ten largest Army installations, comprising thousands of cases. Of note, the Army study will replicate whether the criteria reduce recidivism (Snarr et al., 2011) via re-offense brought to the maltreatment investigation agency. Finally, the Alaska Office of Children's Services, with support from their State Attorney General's office and input from Drs Heyman and Slep, incorporated the field-tested child maltreatment criteria into the state policies and practices in 2015. Plans are currently being developed to study the implementation. Given that the criteria have had little application thus far in civilian family protective services, Alaska's evidence-based approach can serve as a model for other jurisdictions.

The Intergenerational Transmission of Violence: Do Children Exposed to Family Violence Grow Up to Abuse their Children or their Intimate Partners?

The intergenerational transmission of violence is one of the most widely studied phenomena in family violence. The global question of "Does childhood exposure to violence lead to adulthood violence?" becomes much more complicated when one has to specify the type of adulthood violence, not to mention the gender of the child, whether the exposure was CM or exposure to intimate partner violence (IPV) or both, the genders of the parental IPV victim(s) and perpetrator(s), the severity of CM and/or IPV and later violence, and the child's developmental stage, to name only a few other factors. When one considers the number of permutations possible, it is no wonder that the answer to "Does childhood exposure to violence lead to adulthood violence?" has often been obscured by a tangle of inconsistent findings and methodological pitfalls (see Stith et al., 2009; Widom, 1989).

Heyman & Malik (2014) reviewed the evidence for myriad forms of intergenerational transmission of maltreatment. Here we summarize the conclusions for each form of maltreatment.

- *Does child maltreatment victimization lead to child maltreatment perpetration in adulthood?* Intergenerational transmission of child physical abuse occurs about one-third of the time. Thus, it appears likely that physical abuse victimization in childhood increases risk of physical abuse perpetration in adulthood substantially, but that the majority of abused children *do not* grow up to abuse as parents.
- *Does child maltreatment lead to IPV in adulthood?* Parent-child physical violence victimization appears to be weakly associated with adult physical IPV perpetration and victimization, although studies did not control for other co-occurring factors (e.g., non-IPV noxious family environmental factors, genetics, poverty, intergenerational alcohol abuse). The effects of other forms of maltreatment are unclear.
- *Does child exposure to parental IPV lead to CM perpetration in adulthood?* Being exposed to parental physical IPV as a child may be weakly related to perpetrating CM as an adult.
- *Does child exposure to parental IPV lead to IPV in adulthood?* Being exposed to parental physical IPV as a child may considerably increase the risk of IPV perpetration as an adult (and, to a much lower extent, IPV victimization). However, firm conclusions are difficult to draw because studies do not control for other noxious behaviors in the home (e.g., parent-child physical violence, interparental relationship discord, interparental emotional abuse, all of which co-occur at high rates of interparental physical IPV).

- *Does child victimization and exposure to parental IPV lead to family violence perpetration (IPV perpetration and child maltreatment in adulthood)?* Exposure to both parent-child physical violence and interparental IPV may considerably increase risk for women to maltreat their children and partners when they become adults. The results for men are more mixed. However, dual childhood exposure increased risk for adult physical IPV victimization for both women and men.
- *Does child victimization and/or exposure to parental IPV lead to violent criminal behavior?* Maltreated children are more likely to be arrested overall and for violent crimes, both as juveniles and as adults. The evidence for exposure to parental IPV is much more mixed (see also Smith & Ireland, 2009). The research on multiple exposure implies each has at least an additive impact on risk, as does prolonged vs. limited exposure of a single form (Smith & Ireland, 2009). Still, it's important to emphasize that "violence begets violence" occurs in the minority of cases (nearly 80% of those maltreated were never arrested for a violent crime).

Theoretical Conceptualizations of Child Maltreatment

Behavioral Theories

Two behavioral theories have been particularly prominent in the conceptualization of child maltreatment: coercion theory (Reid, Patterson, & Snyder, 2002) and social learning theory (e.g., Bandura, 1977, 1986). Coercion theory suggests positive and negative reinforcement that occur in dyadic conflict result in a learned pattern of aggressive escalation. A parent and child in a conflict escalate with increasingly aversive behaviors, until one person capitulates. The person who "wins" is negatively reinforced for escalating through the removal of the aversive conflict behavior and often positively reinforced through the attainment of a reward, such as gaining compliance. The person who "loses" is negatively reinforced via the other's cessation of aversive behavior. Physically abusive behavior patterns can occur as a result of the escalation process that crests with aggressive discipline and is reinforced due to its variable effectiveness at "winning." Through this process, abusive parents and their children may develop dysfunctional patterns for parent-child interactions that encourage conflict and aggression and the escalation of that aggression to injurious forms of discipline.

Social learning theory (e.g., Bandura, 1977, 1986), an extension of behavioral theory, posits that behavioral change occurs through vicarious reinforcement. In their oft-cited study on imitative learning of aggressive behavior, Bandura, Ross, and Ross (1961) demonstrated that observational learning of aggressive behaviors bypasses the need for learning of aggression through directly experienced consequences. Modeling as a mechanism for learning of aggressive behavior is well established (see Huesmann, 1997; Mineka & Hamida, 1998 for reviews). As discussed previously, the intergenerational transmission hypothesis asserts that children grow up to repeat what they experienced and saw as children with their own children. Social learning is most often presumed as a primary mechanism for the intergenerational transmission of child maltreatment.

Cognitive Theories

Social information processing models of abusive behavior emphasize the role of cognitive processes, such as schemas, attributions, and appraisals, as predictors of abusive parenting (Azar, Reitz, & Goslin, 2008). Parenting schemas, or mental scripts, develop from past experiences, and represent people's views of themselves as parents, the parenting role in general, and expectations for children. New information, such as a specific instance of child behavior, is then filtered through these schemas resulting in selective attention to schema-consistent cues in parent-child interactions. Once activated, schemas can influence simultaneous cognitive, affective, and behavioral responses. Contingent, responsive parenting requires the use of flexible schemas that are modified through trial-and-error learning, thus allowing for responding based on the needs of the particular situation (Azar & Weinzierl, 2005). In contrast, abusive parents rely on schemas that are rigid and negative affect-laden (Milner, 2000).

Within the social information processing framework, parents' negative attributions and evaluations of child behavior and positive outcome expectancies for abusive behavior are thought to contribute to abusive responding (Milner, 1993, 2000). Abusive parents are more likely to endorse negative attributions for child behavior and appraise child behavior more negatively (Bauer & Twentyman, 1985; Chilamkurti & Milner, 1993). For example, in one of the few studies to incorporate observational measures of child behavior, Reid et al. (2002) found that even though abusive parents reported significantly more aggression and hyperactivity than non-abusive parents, independent observers did not identify differences in the mean rate of aversive behavior or severity of conduct problems. Sexual abuse perpetrators overestimate children's sexual development and are more likely to misinterpret children's behaviors as sexual advances (Ward & Keenan, 1999). Parents at-risk for abuse may evidence positive outcome expectancies for abusive behavior; high-risk mothers perceive the use of power-assertive discipline by others as more appropriate than their counterparts (Chilamkurti & Milner, 1993). In addition, sexual abuse perpetrators are more likely to rationalize their behaviors and report that children benefit from the sexual behavior or actively sought out sexual contact (Stermac & Segal, 1989).

Stress/Coping and Anger Models

The roles of stress and anger in etiological models of child maltreatment have garnered considerable attention in the literature. The number of stressful life events is associated with child physical (Coohey & Braun, 1997; Dopke & Milner, 2000; Mash, Johnston, & Kovitz, 1983; Rodriguez & Green, 1997; Stith et al., 2009) and sexual abuse (Pianta, Egeland, & Erikson, 1989); abusive and high-risk parents report more stressful life events and more parenting stress than non-abusive parents. However, stress may not be a *sufficient* condition for child maltreatment perpetration. In a prospective study of low-income mothers, Egeland, Breitenbucher, and Rosenberg (1980) found that a majority of the stressed mothers in their sample did not abuse their children. Moreover, among stressed mothers, abusive mothers reported more aggression and defensiveness, and less seeking of support in reaction to the stress than mothers who did not abuse their children. Pianta (1984) argues that abusive parents have poor coping skills and are more likely to cope in negative ways, such as drinking and hostility, resulting in an increased risk for child-directed violence. Moreover, physically abusive and neglecting parents show deficits in problem-solving skills related to child-rearing and child care (Azar, Robinson, Hekimian, & Twentyman, 1984; Dawson, de Armas, McGrath, & Kelly, 1986). Thus, abusive parenting may reflect deficits in coping and the ability to determine and select effective solutions to child-rearing problems.

Anger is associated with child abuse risk and abusive status (Ammerman, 1990; Dopke & Milner, 2000; Rodriguez & Green, 1997). Abusive parents report feeling more angry or annoyed in response to children's behavior in general, and specifically with regard to social or moral transgressions, than non-abusive parents (Bauer & Twentyman, 1985; Dopke & Milner, 2000; Trickett & Kuczynski, 1986). A meta-analytic review by Stith et al. (2009), examining 155 studies, found that parent anger consistently predicted both child physical abuse and neglect. Moreover, abusive mothers evidence increased sensitivity to child negative affect (Frodi & Lamb, 1980; Milner, Halsey, & Fultz, 1995). Angry emotional responses to children may result in an overwhelming flood of negative emotions and selection of over-learned, schema-consistent, dysfunctional parenting techniques (Gottman, Katz, & Hooven, 1996).

Psychopathology Model

The psychopathological model of child maltreatment focuses on the perpetrator's mental health as an etiological factor. Although several disorders have been implicated as predictors of child physical abuse and neglect perpetration, two disorders have consistently evidenced associations with perpetration: depression (Stith et al., 2009) and substance abuse (Kelleher, Chaffin, Hollenberg, & Fischer, 1994).

Using wave II data from the National Institute for Mental Health's Epidemiologic Catchment Area survey, Chaffin, Kelleher, and Hollenberg (1996) found that depression predicted physical abuse and neglect univariately. However, the strength of the relation between depression and neglect fell to nonsignificant levels when controlling for substance use and demographic variables. Substance use predicted the onset of child physical abuse and neglect, even when controlling for depression, demographic variables, and social support (Chaffin et al., 1996; Kelleher et al., 1994). However, depression and substance use are neither necessary nor specific to cause child abuse perpetration.

Sociological Risk Model

Indicators of "high-risk" family environments, such as early motherhood, socioeconomic status, and a low level of education, influence the capacity to parent and have been implicated in the etiology of child physical abuse and neglect. Although parenting age is associated with a number of risk factors, including low level of education, higher levels of stress, less social support, and coercive discipline practices (Stith et al., 2009), young mothers are at only a slightly increased risk for physical abuse behaviors and neglect (Stith et al., 2009). The relation between parent age and child neglect and sexual abuse is unclear, with several studies indicating no effect (Stith et al., 2009). Moreover, mothers' age may have a skewed relation with child maltreatment, that is, a higher risk during adolescence (Brown, Cohen, Johnson, & Salzinger, 1998) that tapers by early adulthood (Belsky, Hancox, Sligo, & Poulton, 2012). The combination of age and SES might be a particularly powerful predictor of child maltreatment. According to Lee & Goerge, (1999), teen mothers who live in high-poverty areas are 17 times more likely to be indicated in cases of neglect than older mothers who live in low-poverty areas.

The association between demographic factors (such as SES or age) and maltreatment status may be indirect, mediated by other factors associated with the demographics. For example, poverty is correlated with educational level, single-parent status, low social support, and psychopathology, and each is associated with child maltreatment status (Berlin, Appleyard, & Dodge, 2011; Chaffin et al., 1996; Kelleher et al., 1994; Sherrod, O'Connor, Vietze, & Altemeier, 1984). Although variables indexing social disadvantage, such as poverty and a low level of education, are associated with abuse perpetration (Stith et al., 2009), child maltreatment is not exclusively a lower SES condition. In addition, in contrast to physical abuse and neglect, income and educational level are not related to child sexual abuse (Finkelhor & Baron, 1986; Putnam, 2003).

Ecological Model

Perhaps the most widely accepted etiological model of child maltreatment is a multidimensional integration of diverse factors operating at more proximal and more distal levels of influence. Based on Bronfenbrenner's perspective (1979), the ecological model of child maltreatment suggests that the environment influences parents at multiple levels of the ecological system (Belsky, 1980). The systems represent levels of influence from the most proximal (i.e., ontogenic – psychopathology, family-of-origin influences) to the most distal (i.e., cultural norms).

The empirical literature has identified risk and protective factors that exist at all levels of the ecology (see Stith et al., 2009 for a meta-analysis and Wojda et al., 2017 for multilevel analytic studies). Ecological models suggest that more proximal factors, such as parental psychopathology, have the most direct effect on maltreatment, and that the effects of more distal factors are often mediated through their impact on more proximal factors. In contrast, protective factors buffer against the effects of the risk factors, and can compensate for other, even proximal, risk factors, resulting in more successful outcomes (Cicchetti, 2004). Thus, it is not only the number of risk factors at each level of the ecology that determines the likelihood of child maltreatment, but also the balance among the factors; if risk factors outweigh protective factors, the risk for child maltreatment is increased. However, there is little data to suggest which risk factors are most important, how risk factors interact to increase overall risk, or whether it is the accumulation of risk factors that is most predictive.

Neurobiological Models

Childhood maltreatment victimization has the potential to fundamentally change the way in which children respond to the environment at the neurological and physiological levels (Repetti, Taylor, & Seeman, 2002). Child maltreatment impacts the structure and function of multiple brain regions including the prefrontal cortex (Danese & McEwen, 2012) and corpus callosum (Teicher et al., 2004). Child maltreatment also has negative effects on the hypothalamic-pituitary-adrenocortical system (HPA) and is associated with long-term cortisol elevations and short-term variations, i.e., elevated afternoon levels of cortisol (Perry, Pollard, Blakley, Baker, & Vigilante, 1995). The impact of these changes on neurobiological function include poorer executive functions and greater activation of the stress-response system; and these changes can have cumulative, long-term, adverse effects on victims of child maltreatment, including predisposing to child maltreatment perpetration in adulthood. However, perpetration risk is not solely reliant on neurobiological factors and likely better reflects a complex interaction between these predispositions and other environmental risk factors.

Attachment Theory

Attachment theory focuses on the primacy of the caregiver-caretaker relationship in establishing people's internal working models of themselves and their relationships with others. These internal models are first formed via interactions with the primary caregiver but are updated in later development via relationships with important others (e.g., romantic partners). Development of a secure attachment, one in which children view themselves as worthy and their caregiver trustworthy, is contingent upon consistent and responsive caregiving (Wolff & Ijzendoorn, 1997). Thus, the inconsistent and insensitive parenting typical of maltreating parents, places their children at an increased risk for insecure attachment (for review see Cyr, Euser, Bakermans-Kranenburg, & Ijzendoorn, 2010). There are several negative sequelae of insecure attachment, most notably peer and romantic relationship problems (Hesse & Main, 2006) and insensitive parent behavior (van Ijzendoorn, 1995). Moreover, disorganized/insecure attachment is disproportionally represented in maltreating parenting, suggesting that, for some, long-term risks for childhood victimization include maltreating their own children in adulthood (Adshead & Bluglass, 2005; Reijman et al., 2017), indicating poor attachment as a contributing factor to the intergenerational transfer of perpetration.

Empirically Supported Interventions

Several prevention and intervention programs have been found to be effective in reducing child maltreatment risk or the consequences of child maltreatment. Although the focus varies somewhat across interventions and depends on the age of the child for which the intervention was designed, all of the interventions that have been effective at reducing maltreatment risk focus on the parent-child relationship and/or parenting skills (i.e., teach parents deliver more consistent consequences for negative child behaviors, more positive reinforcement for positive child behaviors, and less hostility and criticism).

Two of the most extensively evaluated programs, Triple-P Positive Parenting Program and Parent-Child Interaction Therapy (PCIT), target parenting skills and have strong evidence for reducing maltreatment risk. Triple-P Positive Parenting Program (e.g., Sanders, 2012), when fully implemented, includes several intensities or doses of intervention, from information to light-touch consultations that can be provided in child care or primary care settings, to more intensive workshops and individualized treatment. This program is extensively evaluated in several countries and meta-analyses of randomized controlled trials (RCTs) document its effectiveness (e.g., Nowak & Heinrichs, 2008). PCIT was originally designed for children age 2 to 7 with externalizing behaviors and can be delivered by a family therapist or other mental health provider (Eyberg & Robinson, 1982; Schuhmann, Foote, Eyberg, Boggs, & Algina, 1998). A distinctive feature of PCIT is that the therapist observes the parent interact with the child through a one-way mirror and coaches the parent through a "bug-in-the-ear" device until the parent achieves pre-set criterion levels of a series of parenting skills. PCIT has been evaluated in several RCTs, including studies of parents who were maltreating (e.g., Chaffin et al., 2004). A less intensive option, Systematic Training for Effective Parenting (STEP) is a psychoeducational group parenting intervention that has been found to reduce child abuse potential in several samples of abusive parents (Fennell & Fishel, 1998; Huebner, 2002).

The Nurse-Family Partnership was designed as a secondary prevention effort that aimed to improve child and maternal outcomes through targeting low-income, first-time mothers and their infants. The program involves home visits before and after the birth of the child by a nurse or paraprofessional to provide support and education for a range of topics including child safety, nutrition, alcohol use, and the parent-child relationship. The Nurse-Family Partnership has strong evidence of its preventive impacts; it has been shown to be effective in reducing risk for child maltreatment even at long-term follow-ups (e.g., 15 years later; Olds et al., 1997) and three RCTs support its efficacy when implemented with fidelity (Olds, Henderson, Chamberlin, & Tatelbaum. 1986; Olds et al., 2002; Olds et al., 2004).

Several programs are also available to improve family functioning and positive parenting among adolescents and their parents in families at risk for maltreatment (Santisteban et al., 1997, 2003). For example, brief strategic family therapy has been shown to lead to improvements in family functioning as reported by parents and adolescents who received the program (Cohen's $d = 0.58$ for parent report, 0.42 for adolescent report). Further, these improvements were maintained one year later, and brief strategic family therapy outperformed individual psychodynamic child therapy and a recreation control condition at the follow-up.

In addition to, or instead of, interventions that target parenting, there are also several effective programs for helping children who have been maltreated. For example, "Alternatives for families: A Cognitive-Behavioral approach" (AF: CBT; Kolko, Iselin, & Gully, 2011; Kolko & Swenson, 2002) was developed for families with children between the ages of 5 and 17 who are at risk for abuse or have a history of abuse. For older children and adolescents, individual Trauma Focused Cognitive Behavior Therapy (TF-CBT; Cohen, Mannarino, & Deblinger; 2006) is another option to help trauma-related symptoms such as depression and anger. Cognitive Behavioral approaches for addressing trauma symptoms in children are also empirically supported (Kim, Noh, & Kim, 2016).

Thus, there are several efficacious prevention and treatment options that appear to reduce risk for child maltreatment or ameliorate sequelae of abuse. Further, these interventions vary in the training and background of the providers and the intensity of the intervention. Some could be easily imbedded into primary care settings, while others could be easily incorporated into a family therapist's practice. The potential benefit for children and families is tremendous if efficacious interventions can be successfully embedded throughout more of the health and mental care settings that families already use. This public health approach has the promise of reaching a broad spectrum of families, providing families with a variety of dosages to best meet their needs.

However, as we have suggested, families experiencing maltreatment can present with a variety of risk factors that may differ among families. Treatment research has begun to incorporate adaptive interventions, which offer treatment professionals options in intervention type or dosage in response to their clients' needs and progress in treatment (Almirall & Chronis-Tuscano, 2016), in contrast to a traditional one-for-all treatment approach. Adaptive approaches to treatment rely on a series of decision rules to determine whether treatment should be altered based on clients' presentation. Many good professionals likely already adapt treatments in response to families' progress; however, empirical guidance is lacking. Although adaptive interventions have been explored in response to other concerns (Almirall et al., 2016; Pelham et al., 2016), the extent to which maltreated children and their families would benefit more from this individualized design is not yet known.

References

Adshead, G. & Bluglass, K. (2005). Attachment representations in mothers with abnormal illness behaviour by proxy. *The British Journal of Psychiatry*, 187, 328–333.

Almirall, D. & Chronis-Tuscano, A. (2016) Adaptive interventions in child and adolescent mental health. *Journal of Clinical Child & Adolescent Psychology*, 45, 383–395.

Almirall, D., DiStefano, C., Chang, Y. C., Shire, S., Kaiser, A., Lu, X., ... & Kasari, C. (2016). Longitudinal effects of adaptive interventions with a speech-generating device in minimally verbal children with ASD. *Journal of Clinical Child & Adolescent Psychology*, 45, 442–456.

American Psychiatric Association. (2013). *Diagnostic and statistical manual of mental disorders (DSM-5)*. Washington, DC: American Psychiatric Publishing.

Ammerman, R. T. (1990). Etiological models of child maltreatment: A behavioral perspective. *Behavior Modification*, 14, 230–254.

Azar, S. T. & Weinzierl, K. M. (2005). Child maltreatment and childhood injury research: A cognitive behavioral approach. *Journal of Pediatric Psychology*, 30, 598–614.

Azar, S. T., Reitz, E. B., & Goslin, M. C. (2008). Mothering: Thinking is part of the job description: Application of cognitive views to understanding maladaptive parenting and doing intervention and prevention work. *Journal of Applied Developmental Psychology*, 29, 295–304.

Azar, S. T., Robinson, D. R., Hekimian, E., & Twentyman, C. T. (1984). Unrealistic expectations and problem-solving ability in maltreating and comparison mothers. *Journal of Consulting and Clinical Psychology*, 52, 687–691.

Bandura, A. (1977) Self-efficacy: Toward a unifying theory of behavioral change. *Psychological Review*, 84, 191–215.

Bandura, A. (1986) *Social Foundations of Thought and Action: A Social-Cognitive View*. Englewood Cliffs, NJ: Prentice-Hall.

Bandura, A., Ross, D., & Ross, S. A. (1961). Transmission of aggression through imitation of aggressive models, *Journal of*

Abnormal and Social Psychology, 63, 575–582.
Barth, J., Bermetz, L., Heim, E., Trelle, S., & Tonia, T. (2013). The current prevalence of child sexual abuse worldwide: a systematic review and meta-analysis. *International Journal of Public Health*, 58, 469–483.
Bauer, W. D. & Twentyman, C. T. (1985). Abusing, neglectful, and comparison mothers' responses to child-related and non-child-related stressors. *Journal of Consulting and Clinical Psychology*, 53, 335–343.
Beckett, C., Maughan, B., Rutter, M., Castle, J., Colvert, E., Groothues, C., ... & Sonuga-Barke, E. J. (2006). Do the effects of early severe deprivation on cognition persist into early adolescence? Findings from the English and Romanian adoptees study. *Child Development*, 77, 696–711.
Belsky, J. (1980). Child maltreatment: An ecological integration. *American Psychologist*, 35, 320–335.
Belsky, J., Hancox, R. J., Sligo, J., & Poulton, R. (2012). Does being an older parent attenuate the intergenerational transmission of parenting? *Developmental Psychology*, 48, 1570–1574.
Berlin, L. J., Appleyard, K., & Dodge, K. A. (2011). Intergenerational continuity in child maltreatment: Mediating mechanisms and implications for prevention. *Child Development*, 82, 162–176.
Bronfenbrenner, U. (1979). *The ecology of human development: Experiments by nature and design*. Cambridge, MA: Harvard University Press.
Brown, J., Cohen, P. J. G., Johnson, J. G., & Salzinger, S. (1998). A longitudinal analysis of risk factors for child maltreatment: Findings of a 17-year prospective study of officially recorded and self-reported child abuse and neglect. *Child Abuse & Neglect*, 22, 1065–1078.
Chaffin, M., Kelleher, K., & Hollenberg, J. (1996). Onset of physical abuse and neglect: Psychiatric, substance abuse, and social risk factors from prospective community data. *Child Abuse & Neglect*, 20, 191–203.
Chaffin, M., Silovsky, J. F., Funderburk, B., Valle, L. A., Brestan, E. V., Balachova, T., ... & Bonner, B. L. (2004). Parent-child interaction therapy with physically abusive parents: efficacy for reducing future abuse reports. *Journal of Consulting and Clinical Psychology*, 72, 500–510.
Chilamkurti, C. & Milner, J. S. (1993). Perceptions and evaluations of child transgressions and disciplinary techniques in high- and low-risk mothers and their children. *Child Development*, 64, 1801–1814.
Cicchetti, D. (2004). An odyssey of discovery: Lessons learned through three decades of research on child maltreatment. *American Psychologist*, 59, 731–741.
Cicchetti, D. (2016). Socioemotional, personality, and biological development: Illustrations from a multilevel developmental psychopathology perspective on child maltreatment. *Annual Review of Psychology*, 67, 187–211.
Cohen, J. A., Mannarino, A. P., & Deblinger, E. (2006). *Treating trauma and traumatic grief in children and adolescents*. New York: Guilford Press.
Coohey, C. & Braun, N. (1997). Toward an integrated framework for understanding child physical abuse. *Child Abuse & Neglect*, 21, 1081–1094.
Cyr, C., Euser, E. M., Bakermans-Kranenburg, M. J., & Van Ijzendoorn, M. H. (2010). Attachment security and disorganization in maltreating and high-risk families: A series of meta-analyses. *Development and Psychopathology*, 22, 87–108.
Danese, A. & McEwen, B. S. (2012). Adverse childhood experiences, allostasis, allostatic load, and age-related disease. *Physiology & Behavior*, 106, 29–39.
Dawson, B., de Armas, A., McGrath, M. L., & Kelly, J. A. (1986). Cognitive problem-solving training to improve the child-care judgment of child neglectful parents. *Journal of Family Violence*, 1, 209–226.

Dopke, C. A. & Milner, J. S. (2000). Impact of child noncompliance on stress appraisals, attributions, and disciplinary choices in mothers at high and low risk for child physical abuse. *Child Abuse & Neglect*, 24, 493–504.

Egeland, B., Breitenbucher, M. C., & Rosenberg, M. S. (1980). Prospective study of the significance of life stress in the etiology in child abuse. *Journal of Consulting and Clinical Psychology*, 48, 195–205.

Evans, S. C., Roberts, M. C., Keeley, J. W., Blossom, J. B., Amaro, C. M., Garcia, A. M., ... & Reed, G. M. (2015). Vignette methodologies for studying clinicians' decision-making: Validity, utility, and application in ICD-11 field studies. *International Journal of Clinical and Health Psychology*, 15, 160–170.

Eyberg, S. M. & Robinson, E. A. (1982). Parent-child interaction training: Effects on family functioning. *Journal of Clinical Child & Adolescent Psychology*, 11, 130–137.

Fennell, D. C. & Fishel, A. H. (1998). Parent education: An evaluation of STEP on abusive parents' perceptions and abuse potential. *Journal of Child and Adolescent Psychiatric Nursing*, 11, 107–120.

Finkelhor, D. & Baron, L. (1986). Risk factors for child sexual abuse. *Journal of Interpersonal Violence*, 1, 43–71.

First, M. B., Gibbon, M., Spitzer, R. L., & Williams, J. B. W. (1997). *Structured clinical interview for DSM-IV axis I disorders – Clinician version*. Washington, DC: American Psychiatric Association.

Frodi, A. M. & Lamb, M. E. (1980). Child abusers' responses to infant smiles and cries. *Child Development*, 51, 238–241.

Gilbert, R., Widom, C. S., Browne, K., Fergusson, D., Webb, E., & Janson, S. (2009). Burden and consequences of child maltreatment in high-income countries. *The Lancet*, 373, 68–81.

Gottman, J. M., Katz, L., & Hooven, C. (1996). Parental meta-emotion philosophy and the emotional life of families: Theoretical models and preliminary data. *Journal of Family Psychology*, 10, 243–268.

Hatty, S. E. & Hatty, J. (2001). Australia. In B. Schwartz-Kenney, M. Epstein, & M. McCauley (Eds), *Child Abuse: A Global View* (pp. 1–16). Westport, CT: Greenwood Publishing Group.

Hesse, E. & Main, M. (2006). Frightened, threatening, and dissociative parental behavior in low-risk samples: Description, discussion, and interpretations. *Development and Psychopathology*, 18, 309–343. doi: 10.10170S0954579406060172.

Heyman, R. E., & Malik, J. (2014). Intergenerational transmission of violence. In D. L. Chadwick, A. P. Giardino, & R. Alexander (Eds), *Child Maltreatment* (4th ed., Vol. 3, pp. 145–160). St. Louis: STM Learning, Inc.

Heyman, R. E. & Slep, A. M. S. (2006). Creating and field-testing diagnostic criteria for partner and child maltreatment. *Journal of Family Psychology*, 20, 397–408.

Heyman, R. E. & Slep, A. M. S. (2009). Reliability of family maltreatment diagnostic criteria: 41 site dissemination field trial. *Journal of Family Psychology*, 23, 905–910.

Heyman, R. E. & Slep, A. M. S. (in press). Relational diagnoses and beyond. In B. Friese (Ed.), *APA handbook of contemporary family psychology*. Washington, DC: American Psychological Association Press.

Huebner, C. E. (2002). Evaluation of a clinic-based parent education program to reduce the risk of infant and toddler maltreatment. *Public Health Nursing*, 19, 377–389.

Huesmann, L. R. (1997). Observational learning of violent behavior: Social and biosocial processes. In A. Raine, P. A. Brennan, et al. (Eds), *Biosocial bases of violence* (pp. 69–88). New York: Plenum Press.

Jaffe, S. R. & Christian, C. W. (2014). The biological embedding of child abuse and neglect. *Social Policy Report*, 28.

Jones, L. M. & Finkelhor, D. (2003). Putting together evidence on declining trends in sexual abuse: A complex puzzle. *Child Abuse & Neglect*, 27, 133–135.

Jonson-Reid, M., Kohl, P. L., & Drake, B. (2012). Child and adult outcomes of chronic child maltreatment. *Pediatrics*, 129, 839–845.

Kelleher, K., Chaffin, M., Hollenberg, J., & Fischer, E. (1994). Alcohol and drug disorders among physically abusive and neglectful parents in a community-based sample. *American Journal of Public Health*, 84, 1586–1590.

Kempe, C. H. Silverman, F. N., Steele, B. F., Droegemuller, W., & Silver, H. K. (1962). The battered child syndrome. *Journal of the American Medical Association*, 181, 17–24.

Kim, S., Noh, D., & Kim, H. (2016). A summary of selective experimental research on psychosocial interventions for sexually abused children, *Journal of Child Sexual Abuse*, 25, 597–617.

Kolko, D. J., Iselin, A. M. R., & Gully, K. J. (2011). Evaluation of the sustainability and clinical outcome of Alternatives for Families: A Cognitive-Behavioral Therapy (AF-CBT) in a child protection center. *Child Abuse & Neglect*, 35, 105–116.

Kolko, D. & Swenson, C. C. (2002). *Assessing and treating physically abused children and their families: A cognitive-behavioral approach*. Thousand Oaks, CA: Sage Publications.

Krug, E. G., Dahlberg, L. L., Mercy, J. A., Zwi, A. B., & Lozano, R. (Eds) (2002). *World report on violence and health*. Geneva: World Health Organization.

Lee, B. J. & Goerge, R. M. (1999). Poverty, early childbearing, and child maltreatment: A multinomial analysis. *Children and Youth Services Review*, 21, 755–780.

Mash, E. J., Johnston, C., & Kovitz, K. (1983). A comparison of the mother–child interactions of physically abused and non-abused children during play and task situations. *Journal of Clinical Child Psychology*, 12, 337–346.

Milner, J. S. (1993). Social information processing and physical child abuse. *Clinical Psychology Review*, 13, 275–294.

Milner, J. S. (2000). Social information processing and child physical abuse: Theory and research. In D. J. Hersen (Ed.), *Nebraska symposium on motivation (Vol. 45). Motivation and child maltreatment* (pp. 39–84). Lincoln, NE: University of Nebraska.

Milner, J. S., Halsey, L. B., & Fultz, J. (1995). Empathic responsiveness and affective reactivity to infant stimuli in high and low-risk for physical child abuse mothers. *Child Abuse & Neglect*, 19, 767–780.

Mineka, S. & Hamida, S. (1998). Observational and nonconscious learning. In W. O'Donohue (Ed.), *Learning and behavior therapy* (pp. 421–439). Needham Heights, MA: Allyn and Bacon.

Norman, R. E., Byambaa, M., De, R., Butchart, A., Scott, J., & Vos, T. (2012). The long-term health consequences of child physical abuse, emotional abuse, and neglect: A systematic review and meta-analysis. *PLoS Med*, 9, e1001349.

Nowak, C. & Heinrichs, N. (2008). A comprehensive meta-analysis of Triple P-Positive Parenting Program using hierarchical linear modeling: Effectiveness and moderating variables. *Clinical Child and Family Psychology Review*, 11, 114–144.

Olds, D. L., Eckenrode, J., Henderson, C. R., Kitzman, H., Powers, J., Cole, R., ... & Luckey, D. (1997). Long-term effects of home visitation on maternal life course and child abuse and neglect: Fifteen-year follow-up of a randomized trial. *JAMA*, 278, 637–643.

Olds, D. L., Henderson, C. R., Chamberlin, R., & Tatelbaum, R. (1986). Preventing child abuse and neglect: A randomized trial of nurse home visitation. *Pediatrics*, 78, 65–79.

Olds, D. L., Robinson, J., O'Brien, R., Luckey, D. W., Pettitt, L. M., Henderson, C. R., ... & Talmi, A. (2002). Home visiting by paraprofessionals and by nurses: a randomized, controlled trial. *Pediatrics*, 110, 486–496.

Olds, D. L., Robinson, J., Pettitt, L., Luckey, D. W., Holmberg, J., Ng, R. K., ... & Henderson, C. R. (2004). Effects of home visits by paraprofessionals and by nurses: Age 4 follow-up results of a randomized trial. *Pediatrics*, 114, 1560–1568.

Pelham, W. E., Fabiano, G. A., Waxmonsky, J. G., Greiner, A. R., Gnagy, E. M., Pelham, W. E., ... & Karch, K. (2016). Treatment sequencing for childhood ADHD: A multiple-randomization study of adaptive medication and behavioral interventions. *Journal of Clinical Child & Adolescent Psychology*, 45, 396–415.

Perry, B., Pollard, R., Blakley, T., Baker, W., & Vigilante, D. (1995). Childhood trauma, the neurobiology of adaptation, and "use-dependent" development of the brain: How "states" become "traits." *Infant Mental Health Journal*, 16, 271–291.

Pianta, B. (1984). Antecedents of child abuse. *School Psychology International*, 5, 151–160.

Pianta, R., Egeland, B., & Erikson, M. F. (1989). The antecedents of maltreatment: Results of the Mother-Child Interaction Research Project. In D. Cicchetti & V. Carlson (Eds), *Child maltreatment: Theory and research on the causes and consequences of child abuse and neglect* (pp. 203–253). New York: Cambridge University Press.

Putnam, F. W. (2003). Ten-year research update review: Child sexual abuse. *Journal of the American Academy of Child and Adolescent Psychiatry*, 42, 269–278.

Reid, J., Patterson, G. R., & Snyder, J. (Eds) (2002). *Antisocial behavior in children and adolescents*. Washington, DC: American Psychological Association.

Reijman, S., Alink, L. R., Compier-De Block, L. H., Werner, C. D., Maras, A., Rijnberk, C., ... & Bakermans-Kranenburg, M. J. (2017). Attachment representations and autonomic regulation in maltreating and nonmaltreating mothers. *Development and Psychopathology*, 29, 1075–1087.

Repetti, R. L., Taylor, S. E., & Seeman, T. E. (2002). Risky families: family social environments and the mental and physical health of offspring. *Psychological Bulletin*, 128, 330–366.

Rodriguez, C. M. & Green, A. J. (1997). Parenting stress and anger expression as predictors of child abuse potential. *Child Abuse & Neglect*, 21, 367–377.

Sanders, M. R. (2012). Development, evaluation, and multinational dissemination of the Triple P-Positive Parenting Program. *Annual Review of Clinical Psychology*, 8, 345–379.

Santisteban, D. A., Coatsworth, J. D., Perez-Vidal, A., Kurtines, W. M., Schwartz, S. J., LaPerriere, A., & Szapocznik, J. (2003). Efficacy of brief strategic family therapy in modifying Hispanic adolescent behavior problems and substance use. *Journal of Family Psychology*, 17, 121–133.

Santisteban, D. A., Coatsworth, J. D., Perez-Vidal, A., Mitrani, V., Jean-Gilles, M., & Szapocnik, J. (1997). Brief structural/strategic family therapy with African American and Hispanic high-risk youth. *Journal of Community Psychology*, 25, 453–471.

Schuhmann, E. M., Foote, R. C., Eyberg, S. M., Boggs, S. R., & Algina, J. (1998). Efficacy of parent-child interaction therapy: Interim report of a randomized trial with short-term maintenance. *Journal of clinical child psychology*, 27, 34–45.

Schumacher, J. A., Slep, A. M. S., & Heyman, R. E. (2001). Risk factors for child neglect. *Aggression and Violent Behavior*, 6, 231–254.

Sedlak, A. J. & Broadhurst, D. D. (1996). Third National Incidence Study of Child Abuse and Neglect: Final report. Washington, DC: US Department of Health and Human Services, Administration for Children and Families, National Center on Child Abuse and Neglect.

Sedlak, A. J., Mettenburg, J., Basena, M., Petta, I., McPherson, K., Greene, A., & Li, S. (2010). *Fourth national incidence study of child abuse and neglect (NIS-4): Report to Congress*. Washington, DC: US Department of Health and Human Services, Administration for Children and Families.

Sherrod, K. B., O'Connor, S., Vietze, P. M., & Altemeier, W. A. (1984). Child health and maltreatment. *Child Development*, 55, 1174–1183.

Smith, C. A. & Ireland, T. O. (2009). Family violence and delinquency. In M. D. Krohn, A. J. Lizotte, & G. P. Hall (Eds), *Handbook on crime and deviance* (pp. 493–523). New York: Springer.

Snarr, J. D., Heyman, R. E., Slep, A. M. S., Malik, J., & USAF Family Advocacy Program. (2011). Preventive impacts of reliable family maltreatment criteria. *Journal of Consulting and Clinical Psychology* 79, 826–833.

Stermac, L. E. & Segal, Z. V. (1989). Adult sexual contact with children. An examination of cognitive factors. *Behavioural Therapy*, 20, 573–584.

Stith, S. M., Liu, T., Davies, C., Boykin, E. L., Alder, M. C., Harris, J. M., ... & Dees, J. E. M. E. G. (2009). Risk factors in child maltreatment: A meta-analytic review of the literature. *Aggression and Violent Behavior* 14, 13–29.

Stoltenborgh, M., Bakermans-Kranenburg, M. J., Alink, L. R., & IJzendoorn, M. H. (2015). The prevalence of child maltreatment across the globe: Review of a series of meta-analyses. *Child Abuse Review*, 24, 37–50.

Teicher, M. H., Dumont, N. L., Ho, Y., Vaituzis, C., GIedd, J. N., & Andersen, S. L. (2004). Childhood neglect is associated with reduced corpus callosum area. *Biological Psychiatry*, 56, 80–85.

Teisl, M. & Cicchetti, D. (2008). Physical abuse, cognitive and emotional processes, and aggressive/disruptive behavior problems. *Social Development*, 17, 1–23.

Trickett, P. K. & Kuczynski, L. (1986). Children's misbehaviors and parental discipline strategies in abusive and nonabusive families. *Development Psychology*, 22, 115–123.

Trocmé, N. M., Tourigny, M., MacLaurin, B., & Fallon, B. (2003). Major findings from the Canadian incidence study of reported child abuse and neglect. *Child Abuse & Neglect*, 27, 1427–1439.

Turner, H. A., Finkelhor, D., & Ormrod, R. (2010). Poly-victimization in a national sample of children and youth. *American Journal of Preventive Medicine*, 38, 323–330.

van Ijzendoorn, M. H. (1995). Adult attachment representations, parental responsiveness, and infant attachment: A meta-analysis on the predictive validity of the Adult Attachment Interview. *Psychological Bulletin*, 117, 387–403.

Ward, T. & Keenan, T. (1999). Child molesters' implicit theories. *Journal of Interpersonal Violence*, 14, 821–838.

Widom, C. (1989) Does violence beget violence? A critical examination of the literature. *Psychological Bulletin*, 106, 3–28.

Wojda, A. K., Heyman, R. E., Slep, A. M. S., Foran, H. M., Snarr, J. D., & US Air Force Mental Health Division. (2017). Family violence, suicidality, and substance abuse in active duty military families: An ecological perspective. *Military Behavioral Health*, 5, 300–312.

Wolff, M. S. & Ijzendoorn, M. H. (1997). Sensitivity and attachment: A meta-analysis on parental antecedents of infant attachment. *Child Development*, 68, 571–591.

World Health Organization. (2016). *ICD-11 Beta Draft (Joint Linearization for Mortality and Morbidity Statistics). 24 Factors influencing health status and contact with health services.* Retrieved from https://icd.who.int/dev11/l-m/en. Accessed December 7, 2017.

21 The Role of Gender in Violent and Aggressive Behaviors

Jamie M. Ostrov and Kristin J. Perry

Introduction

A gender-balanced study of aggressive behavior has focused on two primary forms of aggression (i.e., physical and relational) within the psychological sciences literature. Even since the first edition of this chapter and volume (Crick, Ostrov, & Kawabata, 2007), there has been increasing attention and study on the role of relational aggression across development. Relational aggression meets the overall definition of aggression as behaviors intended to hurt, harm, or injure another person (Dodge, Coie, & Lynam, 2006) but the aggressor uses damage to relationships, or the threat of damage to relationships as the means of harm (Crick et al., 2007). Physical aggression is typically defined as the use of physical force, or the threat of physical force, to hurt, harm, or injure another person (Dodge et al., 2006). Both forms of aggression are believed to be part of a larger superordinate externalizing behavior construct (Tackett, Daoud, De Bolle, & Burt, 2013) and share some characteristics but are unique with regard to developmental antecedents, course, and outcomes. In this chapter, we also address the role of gender in violent behavior. We acknowledge the challenges in defining violence, but we consider violence to be an extreme or severe form of aggression likely resulting in serious injury or even death (Farrington, 2007; Tolan, 2007).

Here, we provide a review of the role of gender in violent and aggressive behaviors with a particular focus on these two forms of aggression (i.e., physical and relational) and the following: (1) developmental theory for the study of gender and aggression/violence, (2) recent findings on the role of gender and subtypes of aggression/violence, (3) limitations of the existing literature and directions for future work, (4) prevention and intervention efforts, (5) policy implications, and (6) overall conclusions. Importantly, the focus on the present chapter is on the role of gender and, as such, we limit our review of prior theory and recent findings to issues that are most relevant for understanding the role of gender in the development of aggressive and violent behavior. Readers interested in a general review of relational and physical aggression are directed to a recent comprehensive chapter (Murray-Close, Nelson, Ostrov, Casas, & Crick, 2016).

Theory

Research on trajectories of aggression and violence in youths has often been conducted within the broader constructs of conduct disorder, which is characterized by social rule violations and violating the rights of others, and antisocial behavior (Zahn-Waxler, Shirtcliff, & Marceau, 2008). Two key trajectories of conduct disorder in youth have been identified: a childhood and adolescent onset track (Moffitt, 1993; Moffitt & Caspi, 2001; Zahn-Waxler et al., 2008). On the childhood-onset track, where children meet criteria for the disorder prior to age 10, there are substantially more boys than girls, but this disparity between genders decreases on the adolescent-onset trajectory, where children begin exhibiting problems in adolescence (Fontaine, Carbonneau, Vitaro, Barker, & Tremblay, 2009; Moffitt & Caspi, 2001; Zahn-Waxler et al., 2008). Similarly, a study conducted by the NICHD Early Child Care Research Network (ECCRN), found that boys were more likely than females to be on a high-aggression trajectory, characterized by a high stable level of aggression from toddlerhood into middle childhood (NICHD ECCRN, 2004). However, prior to early childhood, girls and boys may not differ in their rates of behavior problems (e.g., Keenan & Shaw, 1997). This research suggests that transitional periods seem to be particularly salient for gender differences in aggression. In early childhood, girls but not boys experience a decrease in behavior problems such as physical aggression, which leads to a low prevalence of girls displaying physical aggression in middle childhood, whereas in adolescence, the rate of girls' conduct problems increases proportionally to boys.

Several theories have been proposed hypothesizing why substantially more boys than girls display physical aggression and other conduct problems in early and middle childhood. Girls may have certain biological, cognitive, and social advantages compared to boys (Keenan & Shaw, 1997). For example, girls physically mature faster and have better social and language skills than boys during these developmental periods (Crick & Zahn-Waxler, 2003). Keenan and Shaw (1997) proposed that girls, who may have been high on externalizing behavior in toddlerhood, adapt their behavior to a more internalizing form due to pressure from socialization agents. A second approach posits that researchers may not have accurately addressed these behaviors in girls. Thus, there may not be a difference in the prevalence of these behaviors among girls and boys but a qualitative gender difference, where the form of behavior and the manner in which children exhibit this behavior may be unique for boys and girls (Crick & Zahn-Waxler, 2003). In childhood, boys are much more likely to exhibit criteria of conduct disorder such as physical aggression, whereas girls who do have conduct disorder are more likely to exhibit criteria such as conflicts with authority (Zahn-Waxler et al., 2008). Additionally, research on relational and indirect aggression has established that girls in early and middle childhood exhibit aggression, and this aggression is more likely to be relational than physical in form (Crick & Zahn-Waxler, 2003; Ostrov, Kamper, Hart, Godleski, & Blakely-McClure, 2014). Furthermore, relational aggression contributes to psychosocial problems over and above physical aggression and other externalizing problems (Crick, Ostrov, & Werner, 2006).

Within childhood, gender may also play a role in a child's processing of cognitions, which contributes to the child's level of aggressive and violent behavior. The social information-processing model of children's social adjustment (SIP; Crick & Dodge, 1994) proposes that children have a "database" of past experiences, such as schemas, scripts, and memories, which help facilitate their social interactions through six steps: encoding of cues, interpretation of cues, clarification of goals, response access of construction, response decision, and behavioral enactment. This process may be moderated by gender, where gender schemas are impacted by socialization agents, which contribute to the child's self and gender identity, thus influencing availability of cues and social knowledge (Ostrov & Godleski, 2010). In step six of the SIP, the child considers whether their aggressive act was gender-consistent where gender-inconsistent acts lead to negative responses and, thus, decrease the likelihood of the act in the future (Ostrov & Godleski, 2010). For girls, socialization and negative responses from peers may be salient in reducing behaviors such as physical aggression. In toddlerhood, there is no difference in physical aggression for boys and girls, but boys exhibit more physical aggression in early childhood and beyond (Crick & Zahn-Waxler, 2003). At the end of toddlerhood and the beginning of early childhood, the various socialization agents may impact the gender schemas of girls, resulting in them incorporating gender-appropriate behavior into their schemas, and peers may begin to exhibit more negative reactions to girls' physical aggression compared to boys' physical aggression (Ostrov & Godleski, 2010). This feedback may result in girls beginning to favor relational aggression over physical aggression and, therefore, may be responsible for gender differences between boys' and girls' physical aggression in early childhood. In support of this theory, researchers have found that non-normative forms of aggression in middle childhood (i.e., physical/verbal aggression for girls and relational aggression for boys) are predictive of worse adjustment outcomes (Crick, 1997). Additionally, girls view physical aggression more negatively than boys, possibly because girls have different expectations of the peer group (for a review see Smith, Rose, and Schwartz-Mette, 2010). These studies suggest that children who ignore or disregard the feedback from peers and continue to violate aggression norms may experience more severe outcomes and display higher levels of aggression.

Girls may be protected from the childhood-onset track due to advanced development, physical aggression as a nonnormative behavior (which is then discouraged by various socialization agents and peer responses), and gender schemas that are inconsistent with physical aggression. However, from childhood to adolescence, more girls begin to engage in antisocial and aggressive behavior compared to boys (Fontaine et al., 2009; Silverthorn & Frick, 1999). In childhood, boys with conduct disorder are more likely to exhibit physically aggressive and nonaggressive behavior, but in adolescence, girls and boys exhibit an equivalent level of nonaggressive behavior, but boys still exhibit more physically aggressive behavior (Fontaine et al., 2009; Silverthorn & Frick, 1999). There is evidence that girls who enter puberty early are more likely to exhibit relational aggression and possibly delinquency, whereas boys who enter puberty early are more at risk for conduct problems (Susman et al., 2007; Zahn-Waxler et al., 2006; Zahn-Waxler et al., 2008). Lastly, longitudinal work has presented some evidence that with the transition to adolescence, girls but not boys experience an increase in relational aggression (for a review see Murray-Close et al., 2016). This effect may be present because, in adolescence, youth begin to engage in romantic relationships, which may become another outlet for girls to engage in relational aggression (Murray-Close et al., 2016).

By adolescence, rates of physical aggression have already substantially decreased, but more serious acts of violence, such as gang violence or sexual violence, which are often included in assessments of antisocial behavior (Johnson, Giordano, Manning, & Longmore, 2015; Moffitt, 1993), peak and then begin to decrease into emerging adulthood (Loeber & Hay, 1997). A longitudinal study that followed youth from the age of 13 to 28 found that female antisocial behavior peaked at 13 with a decreasing linear trend to age 28 (Johnson et al., 2015). Male antisocial behavior peaked around age 17, with a resulting decreasing linear trend to age 28 (Johnson et al., 2015). Throughout adolescence and emerging adulthood, males were more likely to exhibit antisocial behavior than females (Johnson et al., 2015). Emerging adulthood offers a unique opportunity for individuals to engage in violence with their partners, as there is generally more freedom at this age than at prior ages. This unique setting offers more opportunities for violence with some researchers suggesting that, within relationships, females are just as violent, if not more violent, than males. In one study of college students, researchers found that not only were women more likely to use verbal aggression in a relationship, they were also more likely to display any kind of physical violence, including severe physical violence, than men in a relationship (Magdol et al., 1997). A recent paper found similar findings, with females reporting more psychological and physical dating abuse perpetration in adolescence, but males reporting more sexual dating abuse perpetration (Ybarra, Espelage, Langhinrichsen-Rohling, & Korchmaros, 2016). Additionally, Johnson and colleagues (2015) found that there was no difference in physical intimate partner violence (IPV) perpetration from ages 13 to 16 for males and females, but, by age 17, females were more likely to be physical IPV perpetrators than males, with a peak around age 20. From ages 13 to 28, males were more likely to exhibit antisocial behavior than physical IPV, but females showed the opposite effect, where they were more likely to exhibit antisocial behavior than physical IPV up until age 16, where physical IPV perpetration became more common than antisocial behavior (Johnson et al., 2015). It should be noted that although women may be more physically violent than men in a relationship, men who are physically violent in a relationship are more deviant than females who are physically violent in a relationship, and the consequences of male violence within the relationship may be more severe (Magdol et al., 1997). Additionally, in emerging adulthood, researchers have found that females are more likely to engage in relational aggression in a romantic relationship compared to males (Goldstein, 2011; Murray-Close, Ostrov, Nelson, Crick, & Coccaro, 2010). This research suggests that although males continue to display more traditional types of antisocial behavior, such as physical aggression and violence, in most contexts compared to females, females may display more aggression in the romantic context, where they are more relationally aggressive, verbally aggressive, and physically aggressive than males.

Are there Gender Differences for the Forms of Aggression and Violence?

Crick and Grotpeter (1995) initially postulated that boys and girls have different social goals, which influence their use of aggression subtypes. That is, girls show a preference for dyadic interpersonal relationships and thus their social goal is the promotion of intimacy within close relationships. Crick and Grotpeter (1995) theorized that girls would use relational aggression as their preferred means of harming others because it was the most effective strategy for disrupting what girls value. Similarly, boys were predicted to engage in more physical aggression than other forms of aggression due to social goals that valued social dominance and hierarchy. The field spent a great deal of effort to examine between-group gender differences for physical and relational aggression and, despite some notable evidence for significant effects, and potential moderators like measurement type, developmental period, and culture, the evidence from meta-analytic studies to date suggests that there are only small and trivial differences for relational aggression with girls and boys engaging in similar levels of the behavior (Card, Stucky, Sawalani, & Little, 2008). However, boys are often found to engage in more physical aggression relative to girls. These findings are not that meaningful from a developmental perspective. Consistent with the integrated gender-linked model of aggression subtypes (Ostrov & Godleski, 2010), relational aggression is predicted to be the most common or modal form of aggression among young girls and relational aggression is predicted to be more developmentally salient in the prediction of adjustment outcomes for girls relative to boys. Similarly, for boys, physical aggression was theorized to be the modal form of aggression and developmental trajectories were hypothesized to be moderated by gender. These and other predictions from the model have been supported in recent years (Ettekal & Ladd, 2015; Spieker et al., 2012). For example, we found evidence for within-gender differences such that girls were more relationally aggressive than they were physically aggressive during early childhood (Ostrov et al., 2014).

We underscore the importance of examining for potential gender moderation, as there is clear evidence that gender moderates links between aggression subtypes and adjustment outcomes. For example, we have found that observations of relational aggression predict future teacher-reported peer rejection for girls; however, observations of physical aggression predict future teacher-reported peer rejection for boys (Crick et al., 2006). Similar gender moderation findings have emerged in middle childhood such that relational aggression was more strongly associated with blunted physiological reactivity for relational stressors among girls than boys (Murray-Close et al., 2014). We have also documented these effects in adolescence using the NICHD Study of Early Child Care and Youth Development and found that teacher-reported relational aggression in grade 5 was associated with decreases in academic self-concept at age 15 but only for girls and not for adolescent boys (Blakely-McClure & Ostrov, 2016). In addition, there are documented intercept (i.e., initial levels in the study) and slope (i.e., rate of change) differences in the rates of relational aggression for girls and boys during middle childhood/

adolescence (Murray-Close, Ostrov, & Crick, 2007; Spieker et al., 2012). Finally, a failure to include relational aggression into assessments of aggression has resulted in an under-identification of aggressive girls in prior studies (Crick & Grotpeter, 1995; Henington, Hughes, Cavell, & Thompson, 1998). For example, in a longitudinal study of relational and physical aggression during early childhood, Crick and colleagues indicated that without the assessment of relational aggression, between 36 and 50% of the highly aggressive girls at each of the four time points would not have been identified (Crick et al., 2006).

Several scholars have noted that the gender of the victim is an important consideration when understanding aggression subtypes and aggressive interactions among peers. During early and middle childhood gender segregation patterns emerge and often become entrenched and thus it is not too surprising that girls are more relationally aggressive to female peers than are boys (Ostrov, 2006; Ostrov & Keating, 2004). Moreover, focal boys are more relationally aggressive to male peers relative to focal girls (Ostrov, 2006). In addition, we often find that boys are more physically aggressive to male peers compared to focal girls (Ostrov, 2006). Pellegrini and Roseth (2006) argued that the gender of the target distinction is important given the probability that girls and boys may interpret relational aggression differently depending on whether the aggressor is a girl or boy (Pellegrini & Roseth, 2006). Additional explanations for this pattern of interaction has been in keeping with sexual selection theory and posits that individuals direct aggression toward same-sex individuals (across development) to secure limited resources (Pellegrini & Roseth, 2006).

How Do Children Learn About Gender-Linked Forms of Aggression?

Socialization agents are theorized to be a key factor in the social learning or modeling of relational aggression among children (Ostrov & Godleski, 2010). These socializing influences include: family relationships (parents, older siblings), peers, and the media (Ostrov & Godleski, 2010). These various agents have been well studied and findings support the notion that children often display behavior that matches what they have witnessed or experienced. First, psychological control (i.e., guilt induction, love withdrawal) has been shown to be a salient parenting strategy that may foster relationally aggressive behavior in children (see Kawabata, Alink, Tseng, van Ijzendoorn, & Crick, 2011) and early adolescents (Gaertner et al., 2010), but these effects are often qualified by the gender constellation of the parent-child dyad. That is, in a sample of Chinese preschoolers, psychological control by fathers was associated with relational aggression in girls, but psychological control was not associated with relational aggression in boys (Nelson, Hart, Yang, Olsen, & Jin, 2006); which is similar to a finding in a US sample during middle childhood (Nelson & Crick, 2002). Second, siblings are also an important socializing agent for the development of relational aggression (e.g., Ostrov, Crick, & Stauffacher, 2006). For example, a recent study demonstrated that maternal psychological control was associated with both psychological control and relational aggression within sibling relationships during adolescence (Campione-Barr, Lindell, Greer, & Rose, 2014). Third, peers are another important source of modeling.

In a young sample, we found that children that were relationally victimized by their peers at school showed an increase in only relational aggression across the academic year; whereas, children that were physically victimized by their peers showed an increase in only physical aggression during the year (Ostrov, 2010). These findings suggest learning from prior victimization experiences and point to the important social learning mechanisms likely involved in the development of both forms of aggression. Finally, media exposure to educational content or character development programs that likely depict some relationally aggressive conflict has been shown to lead to increases in relational aggression within an academic year and even two years later (Ostrov, Gentile, & Mullins, 2013). Collectively, these findings underscore the importance of understanding how children are exposed to and reinforced by aggressive models and socializing influences within the environment.

What Is the Role of Gender in Bullying Subtypes?

Bullying is a subset of aggressive behavior that includes power imbalance and usually repetition (Gladden, Vivolo-Kantor, Hamburger, & Lumpkin, 2014). Thus, all bullying is aggression but not all aggression is bullying (Leff et al., 2010; Ostrov & Kamper, 2015; Rodkin, Espelage, & Hanish, 2015). Aggression among equal-status peers (i.e., friends within a horizontal or egalitarian power structure) would be classified as general aggression and not bullying. Bullying may manifest in several ways, including via physical or relational means (Gladden et al., 2014; Hong & Espelage, 2012). A recent study examined the overlap in verbal, relational, physical, and electronic forms of bullying and demonstrated that the greatest risk for social-emotional problems (i.e., internalizing and externalizing symptomatology) was associated with individuals that experienced multiple forms of bullying (Bradshaw, Waasdorp, & Johnson, 2015). In addition, girls were more likely to experience relational victimization, whereas boys were more likely to experience physical victimization in bullying contexts (Bradshaw et al., 2015). These findings mirror prior research demonstrating that co-occurring victimization is associated with worse outcomes relative to being the victim of a single subtype of aggression (Prinstein, Boergers, & Vernberg, 2001). Importantly, similar to the study of relational and physical aggression, the study of bullying subtypes should take into consideration gender.

What Is the Role of Gender in Violence?

Other scholars have previously commented on the role of gender in violence (see Bennett, Farrington, & Huesmann, 2005; Tolan, 2007) and have concluded that males demonstrate a disproportionately higher rate of serious physical violence offending relative to females. In fact, a recent longitudinal analysis of 4,300 adolescents living in the city of Edinburgh, Scotland demonstrated that boys had odds of 3.00 to 4.60 (depending on the model) times greater than girls of displaying violent behavior (McAra & McVie, 2016). There have been numerous explanations and theoretical models (see Theory section, above) generated to address this gender difference and clearly multiple risk and protective factors are involved (e.g., Andershed, Gibson, & Andershed, 2016), but one of the more promising avenues with clear clinical implications is the potential for gender differences in social cognitive factors that impact the likelihood of violence perpetration. These factors include various constructs and models but are in keeping with the aforementioned SIP model (Crick and Dodge, 1994) and subsequent revisions to this model (Arsenio & Lemerise, 2004; Lemerise & Arsenio, 2000). That is, offenders typically lack empathy, perspective taking skills, interpersonal cognitive problem-solving skills, and related prosocial capacities (Bennett et al., 2005). It is conceivable that males and females differ on several dimensions that likely impact their social cognitive competence, which in turn places males at greater risk (see Bennett et al., 2005). The processes and mechanisms are likely complex and some of the patterns may work similarly for boys and girls even if the overall rates of violence are significantly different. For example, a prior study of adolescents and their teachers found that a low level of exposure to community violence was associated with increased likelihood of aggression at school and was mediated by biased social-cognitive indicators, and these SIP factors operated similarly for girls and boys (Bradshaw, Rodgers, Ghandour, & Garbarino, 2009). In addition to these SIP processes, gender stereotypes including the notion that violence is more tolerated among male peer groups and used to obtain and maintain dominance and status likely influence the gendered nature of violence offending (Long & Pellegrini, 2003; McAra & McVie, 2016), which is consistent with the integrated gender-linked model of aggression subtypes (Ostrov & Godleski, 2010). Interestingly, interactions with contextual factors may impact rates of violence perpetration, as demonstrated by the aforementioned study in Scotland, which reported that the odds of being a violent offender increase for girls from lower-socio-economic status backgrounds (McAra & McVie, 2016).

Limitations of Existing Literature and Future Directions

The existing literature on the role of gender and aggression/violence is limited in several key ways. First, greater attention is needed on the role of culture and potential differences in the manifestation and meaning of different types of aggression in various cultures. We advocate for an emic or culturally specific approach in future research so that assumptions are not made about the universal nature of aggressive behavior especially with regard to the role of gender. For example, French and colleagues (2002) conducted interviews with adolescent boys and girls in the USA and Indonesia that allowed for the respondents to spontaneously discuss relationally aggressive behaviors and provided greater confidence in the validity of this construct in a non-Western culture (French, Jansen, & Pidada, 2002). At a minimum, back-translation procedures and an examination of cross-cultural measurement invariance are needed to support the validity of our aggression constructs before using them in new cultures (e.g., Kawabata, Crick, & Hamaguchi, 2010). A full discussion of the ways in which developmental psychopathology investigators may take into consideration culture is beyond the scope of this chapter and other scholars have articulated a clear and needed roadmap (e.g., Causadias, 2013).

Second, greater emphasis should be placed on understanding gender-linked patterns of aggression and victimization across multiple relationship systems. For example, Espelage and colleagues (2012) found that homophobic name-calling was more frequent among male adolescents and relational victimization was more common among female participants (Espelage, Low, & De La Rue, 2012). In addition, adolescents that experience polyvictimization (i.e., experiencing multiple types of aggression or violence) or relational victimization were more likely to witness domestic violence and report past childhood maltreatment (Espelage et al., 2012). Future work should continue to examine how gender may enhance our understanding of the antecedents, course, and outcomes associated with forms of aggression and victimization.

Third, rather than focusing on convenience samples and typically developing samples, more research is needed in various contexts and with at-risk populations. From a developmental psychopathology perspective, our understanding of aggression and violence would be enhanced by conducting research with both typical and atypical populations (Cicchetti & Toth, 2009). For example, inclusion of a detained sample of adolescents greatly enhanced understanding of links between personality pathology like psychopathy and proactive functions of relational aggression among girls (Marsee & Frick, 2007). Relatedly, despite efforts to promote the understanding of relational aggression we must not neglect the study of boys and physical aggression, which is the modal form of aggression among males during childhood and adolescence (Card et al., 2008). In fact, boys that engage in high levels of relational aggression may be at particular risk, given that they are often violating norms and social goals consistent with their gender (Crick, 1997).

Fourth, long-term longitudinal studies that cut across multiple developmental periods are needed in order to truly understand how increased sanctions for physical aggression/violence coupled with changing gender boundaries impact the use and manifestation of aggression subtypes across development, but especially as children transition into adolescence. For example, romantic relationships become a new context for displaying relational aggression (Ellis, Crooks, & Wolfe, 2009; Pellegrini & Long, 2003) and may influence hostile interactions later in development (e.g., emerging adulthood) where men have reported higher levels of relational aggression relative to women (Bailey & Ostrov, 2008). These long-term prospective studies should acknowledge the role of other socializing agents beyond peers and other contexts beyond schools (e.g., workplace, neighborhood, online), which require our collective attention to better understand, predict, and control aggression (e.g., Sandstrom & Cillessen, 2010).

Finally, although there are notable exceptions (e.g., Thornton, Graham-Kevan, & Archer, 2013), given that girls are often excluded from recent studies of violent offending or gender is only used as a control variable in models predicting physical violence (e.g., Hemphill, Heerde, & Scholes-Balog, 2016; Reingle, Jennings, Lynne-Landsman, Cottler, & Maldonado-Molina, 2013), we suggest that the field continue to more directly address the role of gender and violence across development. Furthermore, we echo a recent call for more efforts to examine gender-specific protective factors or predictors of resilient pathways in the presence of cumulative risk for violence (Ttofi, Farrington, Piquero, & DeLisi, 2016).

Prevention and Intervention

The course, trajectories, and mechanisms in the development of aggression and violence vary by gender and, as such, interventions and preventions targeting these behaviors should consider the role of gender (Hipwell & Loeber, 2006). Historically, many intervention and prevention efforts targeting aggression or disruptive behavior focused on males or did not assess gender differences and, therefore, some interventions may not be generalizable to females (Hipwell & Loeber, 2006). Past research that has considered the effects of interventions by gender have generally found no gender differences or an intervention effect for males but not females. For example, a paper that reviewed the effects of both a family-centered and a classroom-based intervention found that boys in either intervention in grades 1 to 3 were more likely to switch from a high-aggressive/disruptive class at the time of the intervention to a low-aggressive/disruptive class in adolescence, compared to boys in the control group (Petras, Masyn, & Ialongo, 2011). There was no effect for females (Petras et al., 2011). From studies such as these, researchers may conclude that when there is a gender difference in intervention efficacy, aggression interventions are not effective for females. However, there is evidence for gender-specific risks and consequences for aggressive and/or delinquent girls, such as a greater risk that they will be excluded from their peer group due to their aggressive behavior and a greater likelihood that they will engage in peer and romantic relationships with older and deviant peers compared to their male counterparts (Hipwell & Loeber, 2006). Therefore, researchers should consider adding gender-specific content to their interventions.

One way researchers have begun including gender-specific content in interventions for aggressive behavior is by addressing relational aggression, in addition to physical aggression, within their interventions (see Leff, Waasdorp, & Crick, 2010). In early childhood, the Early Childhood Friendship Project (ECFP), targets relational and physical aggression and bullying at the classroom level, by promoting positive peer social skills through puppet shows that offer social, emotional, and problem-solving skills training, and discourage aggression (Ostrov, Godleski, Kamper-DeMarco, Blakely-McClure, & Celenza, 2015). Classrooms were randomly assigned to an intervention or control condition and results indicated that there were two intervention effects that were moderated by gender (Ostrov et al., 2015). Girls experienced a decrease in physical and relational victimization if they were in the intervention condition and an increase in physical and relational victimization if they were in the control condition (Ostrov et al., 2015). There was no effect of the intervention for boys on peer victimization although there were overall significant reductions in relational bullying, which was not moderated by gender (Ostrov et al., 2015). Additionally, in middle childhood, Preventing Relational Aggression in Schools Everyday (PRAISE) is a prevention program that was designed to reduce relational aggression and increase prosocial behavior through social-cognitive training, building empathy, and teaching perspective-taking skills for adolescents in urban schools (Leff et al., 2010). Results suggest that girls in classrooms randomly assigned to the PRAISE intervention had lower levels of relational aggression post-intervention compared to girls in classrooms randomly assigned to the control condition (Leff et al., 2010). There were no intervention effects for boys (Leff et al., 2010). Leff and colleagues (2010) theorized that for PRAISE to be effective for boys, skills might need to be taught in the context of competitive sports. Researchers implementing intervention and prevention programs for aggression have begun to recognize the importance of gender, but there is still a long way to go, with several papers not addressing potential gender effects at all (for a review of interventions for girls, see Hipwell & Loeber, 2006). Future intervention and prevention programs targeting aggression should include content that benefits aggressive girls.

Policy Implications

The CDC's uniform definition of bullying recognizes multiple forms of bullying, including relational bullying (Gladden et al., 2014), but this full definition was designed for research and public health surveillance systems and to our knowledge has not yet been fully adopted or incorporated into existing policy to reduce bullying in schools. A recent literature review and analysis of relational aggression within school settings suggests the importance of considering the implications of research on relational aggression for educational policy and concludes that much greater emphasis needs to be given to supporting the efficacy and replication efforts for existing relational aggression intervention programs (Dailey, Frey, & Walker, 2015). The intervention and prevention efforts specifically designed for relational aggression are promising (Dailey et al., 2015; Leff et al., 2010), but much more work is needed to guide key stakeholders on any potential changes to existing policy on aggression or bullying (see Hanish, Bradshaw, Espelage, Rodkin, Swearer, & Horne 2013). To this end, we echo Leadbeater's (2010) call for more university-community partnerships to facilitate collaborations, which are needed to effect long and continuous rates of improvement and to support the dissemination of empirically supported programs for children's aggressive behavior.

Conclusion

Aggression scholars have made a number of key advances and progress since the first edition of this volume, but we continue to echo calls for more long-term prospective longitudinal studies on physical and relational aggression with special attention to the role of gender in the onset, course, and outcomes associated with these behaviors. Moreover, recognizing that relationships are fundamental developmental contexts (Hartup & Laursen, 1991), we suggest that future research carefully examine lawful connections between multiple close relationship systems and aggression in various contexts (e.g., home, neighborhood, school, after-school activities, residential camps, detention centers, clinics, and the workplace) and cultures. As our societal or cultural notions of gender and masculine and feminine stereotypes continue to evolve we anticipate that many of the gender differences reported in this chapter may also continue to change. Therefore, the extant literature and our current findings are relative and cohort effects are not only possible but should be expected. As such, in our future developmental studies, we should continue to investigate for these important differences across time and place. In summary, we are excited by the continued interest in examining aggression subtypes and the role of gender in aggression and violent behavior and we look forward to continued advances within the field.

Acknowledgments

Preparation of this manuscript was supported by a grant from the National Science Foundation (BCS-1450777) to the first author. We acknowledge the late Dr. Nicki R. Crick and Dr. Yoshito Kawabata (now at University of Guam), who were authors of a related chapter in the first edition of this volume and who influenced our thinking on several topics within this chapter. We thank the UB Social Development Lab members for comments on a prior draft and special thanks to Hannah Holmlund for her assistance in the preparation of this chapter. We are also grateful to the directors, teachers, parents, and children that participated in the research described in this chapter.

References

Andershed, A.-K., Gibson, C. L., & Andershed, H. (2016). The role of cumulative risk and protection for violent offending. *Journal of Criminal Justice*, 45, 78–84.

Arsenio, W. F. & Lemerise, E. A. (2004). Aggression and moral development: Integrating social information processing and moral domain models. *Child Development*, 75, 987–1002.

Bailey, C. A. & Ostrov, J. M. (2008). Differentiating forms and functions of aggression in emerging adults: Associations with hostile attribution biases and normative beliefs. *Journal of Youth and Adolescence*, 37, 713–722.

Bennett, S., Farrington, D. P., & Huesmann, L. R. (2005). Explaining gender differences in crime and violence: The importance of social cognitive skills. *Aggression and Violence Behavior*, 10, 263–288.

Blakely-McClure, S. J. & Ostrov, J. M. (2016). Relational aggression, victimization and self concept: Testing pathways from middle childhood to adolescence. *Journal of Youth and Adolescence*, 45, 376–390.

Bradshaw, C. P., Rodgers, C. R. R., Ghandour, L. A., & Garbarino, J. (2009). Social-cognitive mediators of the association between community violence exposure and aggressive behavior. *School Psychology Quarterly*, 23, 199–210.

Bradshaw, C. P., Waasdorp, T. E., & Johnson, S. L. (2015). Overlapping verbal, relational, physical, and electronic forms of bullying in adolescence: Influence of school context. *Journal of Clinical Child and Adolescent Psychology*, 44, 494–508.

Campione-Barr, N., Lindell, A. K., Greer, K. B., & Rose, A. J. (2014). Relational aggression and psychological control in the sibling relationship: Mediators of the association between maternal psychological control and adolescents' emotional adjustment. *Development and Psychopathology*, 26, 749–758.

Card, N. A., Stucky, B. D., Sawalani, G. M., & Little, T. D. (2008). Direct and indirect aggression during childhood and adolescence: A meta-analytic review of gender differences, intercorrelations, and relations to maladjustment. *Child Development*, 79, 1185–1229.

Causadias, J. M. (2013). A roadmap for the integration of culture into developmental psychopathology. *Development and Psychopathology*, 25, 1375–1398.

Cicchetti, D. & Toth, S. L. (2009). The past achievements and future promises of developmental psychopathology: The coming of age of a discipline. *Journal of Child Psychology and Psychiatry*, 50, 16–25.

Crick, N. R. (1997). Engagement in gender normative versus nonnormative forms of aggression: Links to social–psychological adjustment. *Developmental Psychology*, 33, 610–617.

Crick, N. R. & Dodge, K. A. (1994). A review and reformulation of social information-processing mechanisms in children's social adjustment. *Psychological Bulletin*, 115, 74–101.

Crick, N. R. & Grotpeter, J. K. (1995). Relational aggression, gender, and social-psychological adjustment. *Child Development*, 66, 710–722.

Crick, N. R., Ostrov, J. M., & Kawabata, Y. (2007). Relational aggression and gender: An overview. In D. J. Flannery, A. T. Vazsonyi, & I. D. Waldman (Eds), *The Cambridge handbook of violent behavior and aggression* (pp. 245–259). New York: Cambridge University.

Crick, N. R., Ostrov, J. M., & Werner, N. E. (2006). A longitudinal study of relational aggression, physical aggression, and children's social-psychological adjustment. *Journal of Abnormal Child Psychology*, 34, 131–142.

Crick, N. R. & Zahn-Waxler, C. (2003). The development of psychopathology in females and males: Current progress and future challenges. *Development and Psychopathology*, 15, 719–742.

Dailey, A. L., Frey, A. J., & Walker, H. M. (2015). Relational aggression in school settings: Definition, development, strategies, and implications. *Children & Schools*, 37, 79–88.

Dodge, K. A., Coie, J. D., & Lynam, D. (2006). Aggression and antisocial behavior in youth. In W. Damon (series ed.) & N. Eisenberg (vol. ed.), *Handbook of child psychology: Vol. 3. Social, emotional, and personality development* (6th ed., pp. 719–788). Hoboken, NJ: Wiley.

Ellis, W. E., Crooks, C. V., & Wolfe, D. A. (2009). Relational aggression in peer and dating relationships: Links to psychological and behavioral adjustment. *Social Development*, 18, 253–269.

Espelage, D. L., Low, S., & De La Rue, L. (2012). Relations between peer victimization subtypes, family violence, and psychological outcomes during early adolescence. *Psychology of Violence*, 2, 313–324.

Ettekal, I. & Ladd, G. W. (2015). Costs and benefits of children's physical and relational aggression trajectories on peer rejection, acceptance, and friendships: Variations by aggression subtypes, gender, and age. *Developmental Psychology*, 51, 1756–1770.

Farrington, D. P. (2007). Origins of violent behavior over the life span. In D. J. Flannery, A. T. Vazsonyi, & I. D. Waldman (Eds), *The Cambridge handbook of violent behavior and aggression* (pp. 19–48). New York: Cambridge University.

Fontaine, N., Carbonneau, R., Vitaro, F., Barker, E. D., & Tremblay, R. E. (2009). Research review: A critical review of studies on the developmental trajectories of antisocial behavior in females. *Journal of Child Psychology and Psychiatry*, 50, 363–385.

French, D. C., Jansen, E. A., & Pidada, S. (2002). United States and Indonesian children's and adolescents' reports of relational aggression by disliked peers. *Child Development*, 73, 1143–1150.

Gaertner, A. E., Rathert, J. L., Fite, P. J., Vitulano, M., Wynn, P. T., & Harber, J. (2010). Sources of parental knowledge as moderators of the relation between parental psychological control and relational aggression. *Journal of Child and Family Studies*, 19, 607–616.

Gladden, R.M., Vivolo-Kantor, A.M., Hamburger, M.E., & Lumpkin, C.D. (2014). *Bullying surveillance among youths: Uniform definitions for public health and recommended data elements, version 1.0.* Atlanta,

GA: National Center for Injury Prevention and Control, Centers for Disease Control and Prevention and US Department of Education.

Goldstein, S. E. (2011). Relational aggression in young adults' friendships and romantic relationships. *Personal Relationships*, 18, 645–656.

Hanish, L. D., Bradshaw, C. P., Espelage, D. L., Rodkin, P. C., Swearer, S. M., & Horne, A. (2013). Looking toward the future of bullying research: Recommendations for research and funding priorities. *Journal of School Violence*, 12, 283–295.

Hartup, W. W. & Laursen, B. (1991). Relationships as developmental contexts. In R. Cohen & A. W. Siegel (Eds), *Context and development*. (pp. 253–279). Hillsdale, NJ: Erlbaum.

Hemphill, S. A., Heerde, J. A., & Scholes-Balog, K. E. (2016). Risk factors and risk-based protective factors for violent offending: A study of young Victorians. *Journal of Criminal Justice*, 45, 94–100.

Henington, C., Hughes, J. N., Cavell, T. A., & Thompson, B. (1998). The role of relational aggression in identifying aggressive boys and girls. *Journal of School Psychology*, 36, 457–477.

Hipwell, A. E. & Loeber, R. (2006). Do we know which interventions are effective for disruptive and delinquent girls? *Clinical Child and Family Psychology Review*, 9, 221–255.

Hong, J. S. & Espelage, D. L. (2012). A review of research on bullying and peer victimization in school: An ecological system analysis. *Aggression and Violent Behavior*, 17, 311–322.

Johnson, W. L., Giordano, P. C., Manning, W. D., & Longmore, M. A. (2015). The age–IPV curve: Changes in the perpetration of intimate partner violence during adolescence and young adulthood. *Journal of Youth and Adolescence*, 44, 708–726.

Kawabata, Y., Alink, L. R. A., Tseng, W-L., van IJzendoorn, M. H., & Crick, N. R. (2011). Maternal and paternal parenting styles associated with relational aggression in children and adolescents: A conceptual analysis and meta-analytic review. *Developmental Review*, 31, 240–278.

Kawabata, Y., Crick, N. R., & Hamaguchi, Y. (2010). The role of culture in relational aggression: Associations with social-psychological adjustment problems in Japanese and US school-aged children. *International Journal of Behavioral Development*, 34, 354–362.

Keenan, K. & Shaw, D. (1997). Developmental and social influences on young girls' early problem behavior. *Psychological Bulletin*, 121, 95–113.

Leadbeater, B. (2010). Can we see it? Can we stop it? Lessons learned from community-university collaborations about relational aggression. *School Psychology Review*, 39, 588–593.

Leff, S. S., Waasdorp, T. E., & Crick, N. R. (2010). A review of existing relational aggression programs: Strengths, limitations, and future directions. *School Psychology Review*, 39, 508–535.

Leff, S. S., Waasdorp, T. E., Paskewich, B., Gullan, R. L., Jawad, A. F., MacEvoy, J. P., ... & Power, T. J. (2010). The preventing relational aggression in schools everyday program: A preliminary evaluation of acceptability and impact. *School Psychology Review*, 39, 569–587.

Lemerise, E. A. & Arsenio, W. F. (2000). An integrated model of emotion processes and cognition in social information processing. *Child Development*, 71, 107–118.

Loeber, R. & Hay, D. (1997). Key issues in the development of aggression and violence from childhood to early adulthood. *Annual Review of Psychology*, 48, 371–410.

Long, J. D. & Pellegrini, A. D. (2003). Studying change in dominance and bullying with mixed models. *School Psychology Review*, 32, 401–417.

Magdol, L., Moffitt, T. E., Caspi, A., Newman, D. L., Fagan, J., & Silva, P. A. (1997).

Gender differences in partner violence in a birth cohort of 21-year-olds: Bridging the gap between clinical and epidemiological approaches. *Journal of Consulting and Clinical Psychology, 65,* 68–78.

Marsee, M. A. & Frick, P. J. (2007). Exploring the cognitive and emotional correlates to proactive and reactive aggression in a sample of detained girls. *Journal of Abnormal Child Psychology, 35,* 969–981.

McAra, L. & McVie, S. (2016). Understanding youth violence: The mediating effects of gender, poverty and vulnerability. *Journal of Criminal Justice, 45,* 71–77.

Moffitt, T. E. (1993). Adolescence-limited and life-course-persistent antisocial behavior: A developmental taxonomy. *Psychological Review, 100,* 674–701.

Moffitt, T. E. & Caspi, A. (2001). Childhood predictors differentiate life-course persistent and adolescence-limited antisocial pathways among males and females. *Development and Psychopathology, 13,* 355–375.

Murray-Close, D., Crick, N. R., Tseng, W. L., Lafko, N., Burrows, C., Pitula, C., & Ralston, P. (2014). Autonomic reactivity to stress and physical and relational aggression: The moderating roles of victimization, type of task, and child gender. *Development & Psychopathology, 26,* 589–603.

Murray-Close, D., Nelson, D. A., Ostrov, J. M., Casas, J. F., & Crick, N. R. (2016). Relational aggression: A developmental psychopathology perspective. In D. Cicchetti (Ed.), *Developmental Psychopathology* (3rd ed., pp. 660–722). New York: Wiley Publications.

Murray-Close, D., Ostrov, J. M., & Crick, N. R. (2007). A short-term longitudinal study of growth of relational aggression during middle childhood: Associations with gender, friendship intimacy, and internalizing problems. *Development and Psychopathology, 19,* 187–203.

Murray-Close, D., Ostrov, J. M., Nelson, D. A., Crick, N. R., & Coccaro, E. F. (2010). Proactive, reactive, and romantic relational aggression in adulthood: Measurement, predictive validity, gender differences, and association with intermittent explosive disorder. *Journal of Psychiatric Research, 44,* 393–404.

Nelson, D. A. & Crick, N. R. (2002). Parental psychological control: Implications for childhood physical and relational aggression. In B. K. Barber (Ed.), *Intrusive parenting: How psychological control affects children and adolescents.* (pp. 161–189). Washington, DC: American Psychological Association.

Nelson, D. A., Hart, C. H., Yang, C., Olsen, J. A., & Jin, S. (2006). Aversive parenting in China: Associations with child physical and relational aggression. *Child Development, 77,* 554–572.

NICHD Early Child Care and Research Network. (2004). Trajectories of physical aggression from toddlerhood to middle childhood: III. Person-centered trajectories of physical aggression. *Monographs of the Society for Research in Child Development, 69*(4), 41–49.

Ostrov, J. M. (2006). Deception and subtypes of aggression during early childhood. *Journal of Experimental Child Psychology, 93,* 322–336.

Ostrov, J. M. (2010). Prospective associations between peer victimization and aggression. *Child Development, 81,* 1670–1677.

Ostrov, J. M., Crick, N. R., & Stauffacher, K. (2006). Relational aggression in sibling and peer relationships during early childhood. *Journal of Applied Developmental Psychology, 27,* 241–253.

Ostrov, J. M., Gentile, D. A., & Mullins, A. D. (2013). Evaluating the effect of educational media exposure on aggression in early childhood. *Journal of Applied Developmental Psychology, 34,* 38–44.

Ostrov, J. M. & Godleski, S. A. (2010). Toward an integrated gender-linked model of aggression subtypes in early and middle childhood. *Psychological Review, 117,* 233–242.

Ostrov, J. M., Godleski, S. A., Kamper, K. E., Blakely-McClure, S. J., & Celenza L. (2015). Replication and extension of the early childhood friendship project: Effects on physical and relational bullying. *School Psychology Review*, 44, 445–463.

Ostrov, J. M. & Kamper, K. E. (2015). Future directions for research on the development of relational and physical peer victimization. *Journal of Clinical Child and Adolescent Psychology*, 44, 509–519.

Ostrov, J. M., Kamper, K. E., Hart, E. J., Godleski, S. A., & Blakely-McClure, S. J. (2014). A gender-balanced approach to the study of peer victimization and aggression subtypes in early childhood. *Development and Psychopathology*, 26, 575–587.

Ostrov, J. M. & Keating, C. F. (2004). Gender differences in preschool aggression during free play and structured interactions: An observational study. *Social Development*, 13, 255–277.

Pellegrini, A. D. & Long, J. D. (2003). A sexual selection theory longitudinal analysis of sexual segregation and integration in early adolescence. *Journal of Experimental Child Psychology*, 85, 257–278.

Pellegrini, A. D. & Roseth, C. J. (2006). Relational aggression and relationships in preschoolers: A discussion of methods, gender differences, and function. *Journal of Applied Developmental Psychology*, 27, 269–276.

Petras, H., Masyn, K., & Ialongo, N. (2011). The developmental impact of two first grade preventive interventions on aggressive/disruptive behavior in childhood and adolescence: An application of latent transition growth mixture modeling. *Prevention Science*, 12, 300–313.

Prinstein, M. J., Boergers, J., & Vernberg, E. M. (2001). Overt and relational aggression in adolescents: Social-psychological adjustment of aggressors and victims. *Journal of Clinical Child Psychology*, 30, 479–491.

Reingle, J. M., Jennings, W. G., Lynne-Landsman, S. D., Cottler, L. B., & Maldonado-Molina, M. M. (2013). Toward an understanding of risk and protective factors for violence among adolescent boys and men: A longitudinal analysis. *Journal of Adolescent Health*, 52, 493–498.

Rodkin, P. C., Espelage, D., & Hanish, L. D. (2015). A relational framework for understanding bullying: Developmental antecedents and outcomes. *American Psychologist*, 70, 311–321.

Sandstrom, M. J. & Cillessen, A. H. N. (2010). Life after high school: Adjustment of popular teens in emerging adulthood. *Merrill-Palmer Quarterly*, 56, 474–499.

Silverthorn, P. & Frick, P. J. (1999). Developmental pathways to antisocial behavior: The delayed-onset pathway in girls. *Development and Psychopathology*, 11, 101–126.

Smith, R. L., Rose, A. J., & Schwartz-Mette, R. A. (2010). Relational and overt aggression in childhood and adolescence: Clarifying mean-level gender differences and associations with peer acceptance. *Social Development*, 19, 243–269.

Spieker, S. J., Campbell, S. B., Vandergrift, N., Pierce, K. M., Cauffman, E., Susman, E. J., & Roisman, G. I. (2012). Relational aggression in middle childhood: Predictors and adolescent outcomes. *Social Development*, 21, 354–375.

Susman, E. J., Dockray, S., Schiefelbein, V. L., Herwehe, S., Heaton, J. A., & Dorn, L. D. (2007). Morningness/eveningness, morning-to-afternoon cortisol ratio, and antisocial behavior problems during puberty. *Developmental Psychology*, 43, 811–822.

Tackett, J. L., Daoud, S. L. S. B., De Bolle, M., & Burt, S. A. (2013). Is relational aggression part of the externalizing spectrum? A bifactor model of youth antisocial behavior. *Aggressive Behavior*, 39, 149–159.

Thornton, A. J. V., Graham-Kevan, N., & Archer, J. (2013). Development and confirmatory factor analysis of the non-violent and violent offending behavior scale (NVOBS). *Aggressive Behavior*, 39, 171–181.

Tolan, P. H. (2007). Understanding violence. In D. J. Flannery, A. T. Vazsonyi, & I. D. Waldman (Eds), *The Cambridge Handbook of Violent Behavior and Aggression* (pp. 5–18). New York: Cambridge University.

Ttofi, M. M., Farrington, D. P., Piquero, A. R., & DeLisi, M. (2016). Protective factors against youth offending and violence: Results from prospective longitudinal studies. *Journal of Criminal Justice*, 45, 1–3.

Ybarra, M. L., Espelage, D. L., Langhinrichsen-Rohling, J., Korchmaros, J. D., & Boyd, D. (2016). Lifetime prevalence rates and overlap of physical, psychological, and sexual dating abuse perpetration and victimization in a national sample of youth. *Archives of Sexual Behavior*, 45, 1083–1099.

Zahn-Waxler, C., Crick, N. R., Shirtcliff, E. A., & Woods, K. E. (2006). The origins and development of psychopathology in females and males. In D. Cicchetti, & D. J. Cohen (Eds), *Developmental psychopathology, Vol 1: Theory and method* (2nd ed., pp. 76–138). Hoboken, NJ: John Wiley & Sons.

Zahn-Waxler, C., Shirtcliff, E. A., & Marceau, K. (2008). Disorders of childhood and adolescence: Gender and psychopathology. *Annual Review of Clinical Psychology*, 4, 275–303.

22 Lessons Learned: Serial Sex Offenders Identified from Backlogged Sexual Assault Kits (SAKs)

Rachel Lovell, Daniel J. Flannery, and Misty Luminais

Introduction

Hundreds of thousands of untested rape kits, also known as sexual assault kits (SAKs), have languished in evidence storage facilities across the United States. This backlog denies justice to victims and allows rapists the opportunity to continue to harm others. Here, we provide an overview of the issues related to backlogged SAKs and present pilot data from one local initiative in Cuyahoga County, Ohio with a particular focus on what we are learning about serial sexual offenders. We conclude with a discussion of the utility of testing backlogged SAKs and implications for future research, practice, and policy.

A rape kit is a set of items used by medical professionals for collecting and preserving evidence from victims of sexual assault for investigation and prosecution. SAK examinations are usually administered in a hospital, take about four to six hours to complete, and involve medical professionals photographing, swabbing, and examining the victim's entire body for evidence (Campbell, Shaw, & Fehler-Cabral, 2015; RAINN, 2016a; The National Center for Victims of Crime, 2016). For sexual assaults, unlike other types of crime, the victim's body is treated as a crime scene (Johnson, Peterson, Sommers, & Baskin, 2012), but just because evidence was preserved does not necessarily mean that evidence was tested. While there are distinctions made based on whether a SAK has been submitted or is waiting to be tested (NIJ, 2015), the term "backlogged" is often used to refer to any unsubmitted and/or untested SAK regardless of how long the SAK has remained unsubmitted or untested (Pinchevsky, 2016).

The existence of such a large number of backlogged SAKs is problematic for a number of reasons. By not testing the SAK, the victim is often denied a speedy judicial resolution and, potentially, justice (Strom & Hickman, 2010). By comparison, testing SAKs, especially those long held on the shelf, sends a supportive message to victims (End the Backlog, 2016; Spohn, 2016). Not submitting a SAK for DNA testing also represents a missed opportunity to identify an unknown offender, confirm the identify of a known offender, connect an offender to previously unsolved crimes, possibly exonerate an innocent suspect, and populate the federal DNA database (the Combined DNA Index System, CODIS) (Campbell, Pierce, Sharma, Feeney, & Fehler-Cabral, 2016b; End the Backlog, 2016; Lovrich et al., 2004; Spohn, 2016). The existence of so many backlogged SAKs has highlighted the systemic problem of gender bias in the criminal justice system's response to sexual assault (Bettinger-Lopez, 2016; Department of Justice, 2016). These are all issues that can be addressed via the testing, investigation, and prosecution of backlogged SAKs.

The Scope of the Problem

Conservatively, hundreds of thousands of SAKs across the country are estimated to be in police evidence storage facilities waiting to be submitted to a crime lab for DNA analysis or have been submitted to labs but have not yet been tested (End the Backlog, 2016; National Institute of Justice, 2015; Reilly, 2015; Strom & Hickman, 2010). In the early 2000s, New York City and Los Angeles identified and tested almost 17,000 (Bettinger-Lopez, 2016) and 12,669 previously unsubmitted kits, respectively (Human Rights Watch, 2011; Peterson, Johnson, Herz, Graziano, & Oehler, 2012). Other jurisdictions followed – including Houston, Texas; Wayne County, Michigan (Detroit); Memphis, Tennessee; and Cuyahoga County, Ohio (Cleveland) – by inventorying and submitting their backlogged kits. The results were staggering – over 6,600 in Houston, 10,000 in Wayne County, over 12,000 in Memphis, and nearly 5,000 in Cuyahoga County.

According to the Accountability Project,[1] an attempt to uncover the number of backlogged SAKs in police custody in 48 cities across the country, more than 37,000 unsubmitted SAKs have already been identified in only 12 of the 48 cities (End the Backlog, 2016). This effort has led to an increase in jurisdictions that have begun the process of inventorying and testing their unsubmitted SAKs (Findell, 2016; Plackett, 2015; Poe, 2016; WTVQ Web Desk, 2016). The federal government has also increased the availability of funds to address the backlog, including the Debbie Smith Act of 2004, the Sexual Assault Forensic Evidence Reporting (SAFER) Act (2013), the National Institute of Justice's action-research grants to address unsubmitted SAKs, and, most recently, the Sexual Assault Kit Initiative (SAKI) (2015 and 2016) (Bettinger-Lopez, 2016; Bureau of Justice Affairs, 2016; Bureau of Justice Assistance, 2015). State legislatures are also responding to the issue of unsubmitted SAKs. Several states, including Arkansas, Iowa, Louisiana, and Minnesota, are requiring law enforcement to inventory their backlogged SAKs, and a mandatory "test-all" approach (also known as the "forklift" approach) is now being implemented in several states, including Ohio, Connecticut, Illinois, Michigan, and Texas.

However, not all jurisdictions believe that kits should be tested, and of those who are testing, they are not necessarily submitting all kits for DNA analysis (Munday, 2016; The Associated Press, 2016; *Voice of San Diego*, 2016). Even with legislative mandates requiring the submission of SAKs and successes in Houston, Wayne County, Cuyahoga County, and others, some jurisdictions can be reluctant

---

1 The Accountability Project is directed by the Joyful Heart Foundation, a nonprofit started by *Law and Order SVU* actress Mariska Hargitay that helps victims of sexual assault, domestic violence, and child abuse through advocacy, education, and healing programs.

to submit their SAKs or follow up on hits (Cocke, 2016; Stein, 2016; *Voice of San Diego*, 2016). For jurisdictions that have made a great deal of progress in implementing systemic change, constant vigilance is required to ensure that no new backlog develops. Houston, for example, recently found (and subsequently submitted) a "new" backlog – 333 SAKs that had been on property room shelves for more than 30 days without being submitted (Rogalski, 2016).

What Created the Backlog?

The large number of backlogged SAKs exists for several reasons. First, many SAKs pre-date modern DNA forensic analysis, which only became widely available in the late 1990s (National Institute of Justice, 2016; Ritter, 2016). In fact, if SAKs were tested at the time of collection, as compared to now, they would have had much less success at returning hits/matches in CODIS (Combined DNA Index System) because the technology for testing DNA has vastly improved in recent years. It has also taken years for CODIS to populate with profiles, so only in the past few years has CODIS had enough DNA profiles to matriculate in a higher percentage of matches or "hits" (Calandro, Reeder, & Cormier, 2005; Johnson et al., 2012; National Institute of Justice, 2016; Ritter, 2016; US Department of Justice, 2014).

Second, when DNA testing became available, it was too expensive for jurisdictions to be able to test the SAKs. Even when DNA testing was conducted, only certain SAKs were prioritized for testing (Dickson, 2014; Luminais, Lovell, & Flannery, forthcoming). Until recently, in most jurisdictions the decision to submit or not and which kits to submit was primarily the responsibly of the investigating officer (Campbell, Feeney, Fehler-Cabral, Shaw, & Horsford, 2015; Luminais et al., forthcoming; Pratt, Gaffney, Lovrich, & Johnson, 2006; Ritter, 2011) rather than a prosecutor or following an existing policy in the criminal justice system.

Research in Wayne County, Michigan (Detroit) has identified additional reasons for the large number of backlogged SAKs: victim-blaming behaviors and beliefs; the lack of written policies and protocols for submitting SAKs for DNA testing; budget cuts that resulted in a reduction in the number of sexual assault investigators and crime lab personnel; inefficient DNA testing methods and/or equipment; and high turnover in police leadership (Campbell et al., 2016). Campbell et al.'s (2016) findings concerning bias in investigators' evaluations of victims' credibility support earlier studies, including those in Los Angeles (Peterson et al., 2012) and Washington, DC (Human Rights Watch, 2013), among others (Jan, 2004; Ritter, 2016). Additional contributing factors to the backlog include strained relationships between police and prosecutors, lack of training (Bettinger-Lopez, 2016), SAKs being viewed as a prosecutorial rather than an investigative tool (Pratt et al., 2006; Ritter, 2016), concerns about the timeliness of the testing, closing cases before testing can be submitted (Strom & Hickman, 2016), lack of community-based advocacy services (Ritter 2016), outdated record keeping (Nelson, 2013; Ritter, 2016), and no centralized storage location for SAKs (Human Rights Watch, 2009).

While recent efforts have highlighted the importance of DNA analysis, testing is just the very first step in the process of seeking justice for victims of sexual assault, holding offenders accountable, and making communities safer. After testing is completed, jurisdictions must continue to maintain political buy-in and secure extensive resources to investigate and prosecute the cases resulting from the testing of the backlogged SAKs (Lovell, Butcher, & Flannery, 2016; Singer, Lovell, Flannery, and Butcher, 2016). To prevent future backlogs, jurisdictions testing their unsubmitted SAKs must grapple with engendering and maintaining systemic change to be more victim-centered and trauma-informed (Joyful Heart Foundation, 2016; Spohn, 2016). In the past, victims of sexual assault were often not treated in a victim-centered, trauma-informed manner by individuals in the criminal justice system or by the criminal justice system itself (Campbell, Feeney, et al., 2015; Lovell, Flannery, Overman, & Walker, 2016).

Below we describe some of the early key findings from Cuyahoga County, Ohio that implemented a forklift approach to testing its nearly 5,000 backlogged SAKs dating from 1993 through 2009, with a focus on the large number of serial sex offenders identified. To understand more about these serial sex offenders, we present data that compares criminal histories and offending patterns for serial and nonserial sex offenders. We then discuss reasons why Cuyahoga County has found such a large number of serial sex offenders in its backlogged SAKs. Last, we provide recommendations of how the findings on serial sex offenders can be used to inform policy and guide jurisdictions and researchers attempting to address the issue of unsubmitted SAKs.

Previous Research on Serial Sex Offenders

Much of the literature on serial sex offenders focuses on the characteristics of offenders, victim selection and typology, and the utility of understanding offending patterns (*modus operandi*) for criminal justice purposes. More recently, there has been a focus on differentiating serial sex offenders (defined variously by different authors) from nonserial sex offenders. Some studies find several differences in offending patterns, such as nonserial sex offenders being more likely to threaten the victim (Park, Schlesinger, Pinizzotto, & Davis, 2008), to engage in hitting or kicking (Park et al., 2008), and to force the victim to participate via kissing or sexual comments (Corovic, Christianson, & Bergman, 2012; Park et al., 2008). Serial sex offenders tend to display more forensic awareness or be more criminally sophisticated (Corovic et al., 2012; de Heer, 2016; Park et al., 2008). Serial sex offenders have also been shown to share some common traits, including having been sexually abused as children, displaying social deviance, and being impulsive (Abbey, Wegner, Pierce, & Jacques-Tiura, 2012; Balteri & Andrade, 2008; Burgess, Hazelwood, Rokous, Hartman, & Burgess, 1988; Hazelwood & Warren, 1989).

There exists some disagreement regarding how common serial sex offending is and its relation to other types of offending. Lisak and Miller (2002) traced undetected serial sex offenders' involvement with other types of violent crime through surveying commuter college students and found that serial sex offenders were more likely to engage in domestic violence, child abuse, battery, or child sexual abuse – 10 times more often than nonsexual offenders and 3.5 times more than nonserial sex offenders. Additionally, two-thirds of their sample of men who ever sexually assaulted did so more than once, suggesting that serial sex offending is more common than traditionally believed. Conversely, Swartout et al. (2015) examined repeat sexual offending among adolescent and college-aged men and found serial offending to be uncommon, but their study focused on whether subjects reoffended across multiple years and sampled a more constricted age range. These divergent findings can be tied to differences in how serial offending is defined, the methods by which it is identified, and differences in the population of offenders being studied.

With regards to the use of bodily force and injury in sexual assaults, Stevens' (1997) study of serial sex offender self-reports emphasized that their use of violence is selective and used sparingly. Warren et al. (1999) tried to identify rapists who tended to escalate their level of violence to life-threatening levels and found the strongest predictors were being Caucasian, having a longer duration for the first sexual assault, and the use of profanity during the sexual assault. They suggested sexual assaults with these characteristics should be given investigative priority.

One of the confounding findings in the literature is the relationship of sexual offenders to their victims. Hazelwood & Warren (1989) state that most victims are strangers to the offender, but many assaults occur in the offender's residence. In other studies, researchers limit themselves to studying stranger sexual assaults to avoid any "cross-relational confusion" (Slater, Woodhams, & Hamilton-Giachritsis, 2014), suggesting that non-stranger sexual assault is an entirely different phenomenon. These relationships have important implications for the way the police and prosecutors handle cases. Non-strangers (in reported cases) are less likely to be interviewed by the police, have their case referred for prosecution, or, if there is sufficient evidence for investigation and prosecution, to receive a prison sentence (Lisak & Miller, 2002; RAINN, 2016b).

With the widespread adoption of CODIS, some suggest that SAKs from stranger sexual assaults be given priority, as they may identify an unknown offender while testing known offenders primarily serves as confirmatory evidence (Strom & Hickman, 2016). Others argue that stranger sexual assaults should not be given priority over non-stranger sexual assaults because there is recent evidence that they are equally likely to return CODIS hits (Campbell et al., 2016). Research coming out of Wayne County's unsubmitted SAKs points to the utility of testing *all* SAKs, including those outside the statute of limitations, as these kits help populate the CODIS database and can link more recent crimes, including sexual assault, to crimes that cannot be pursued legally due to the statute of limitations (Campbell, Pierce, Sharma, Feeney & Fehler-Cabral, 2016a).

Data and Methodology

Data Sources

We were given access to the SAK case files by the Cuyahoga County, Ohio SAK Task Force (Task Force) via an electronic management platform organized so that documents necessary for prosecution are uploaded as PDFs into case files. Essentially, the platform functions as an electronic file drawer with some searchable data or fields, but mostly is PDF-driven and, therefore, not searchable. From the Task Force case files, the research team coded initial police reports, investigative reports (current reports conducted by Task Force investigators), lab reports from the Ohio Bureau of Criminal Investigation, and criminal histories of the victim and offender (if named).[2] From these files, we created a database of SAK cases, discussed in detail below.

Sampling

In these pilot data, the sampling unit was a sexual assault. Our population was a random sample of completed sexual assault investigations that either: (1) resulted in prosecution (i.e., indictment) or (2) were not indicted due to insufficient evidence (as of August 2015). We did not pool the cases when sampling but instead randomly selected both cases that resulted in prosecution and cases that were closed due to insufficient evidence. Thus, our sample distribution of cases was equal to the population distribution – 76% (n = 185) of the cases resulted in indictment and 24% (n = 58) were closed due to insufficient evidence. We focused on these cases because they represented those that could have been prosecuted. We began with a list of 342 SAKs that resulted in prosecution and 92 SAKs that were not pursued due to insufficient evidence. From this list, we coded a random sample of 243 sexual assaults.

Our sample consisted of sexual assaults that occurred between March 1993 and May 2014; however, the majority of the assaults we coded (74.1%) occurred between 1993 and 1997, which reflects the initial statute of limitation prioritization of cases. While the Task Force's focus is on unsubmitted SAKs from Cuyahoga County from 1993 through 2009, in some instances, if an offender is linked to a case from 2010 to the present, the Task Force, when applicable, will incorporate the current sexual assault investigation and prosecution with the unsubmitted SAK investigation and prosecution. This explains why our sample includes sexual assaults after 2009. Additionally, our pilot sample consists disproportionally of stranger sexual assaults.

Criminal History

Since criminal history is not at the sexual assault level but the individual level (offenders could be linked to more than one sexual assault), data on criminal histories were coded at the individual level and linked to SAKs via a unique identifier. For criminal history, we coded felony-level arrests prior and subsequent to the sexual assault connected to the SAK for Uniform Crime Report (UCR) offenses – murder (including manslaughter), sexual assault (i.e., forcible rape), assault (felony level), robbery, burglary, larceny/theft, motor vehicle theft, and arson – plus felony-level drug offenses and domestic violence (which are often misdemeanor offenses). We coded based upon arrest and not conviction because what a person is convicted of is often not reflective of the offense they allegedly committed (this is especially the case

---

[2] While many victims and victim advocates prefer the term "survivor" when referring to a person who has been a victim of sexual violence, in this paper we use the term "victim" as this is nomenclature used by the criminal justice system to refer to the complainant in the sexually based offense.

with sexually based and domestic violence offenses) (Spohn & Tellis, 2012). Coding at arrest instead of conviction also provides a more accurate glimpse into how often the offenders have criminal justice involvement.

Since the unit of analysis in this study was a sexual assault, offenders with more than one sexual assault (e.g., serial sex offenders) are represented more than once with respect to their criminal history in our sample.[3] We had criminal histories only for known offenders, meaning that they were already in CODIS, were connected to other SAKs, and/or were named offenders in initial police reports, with the majority of the known offenders being identified via CODIS. Thus, offenders with a DNA profile in CODIS are those who are more likely to have contact with the criminal justice system, which disproportionally includes more marginalized groups (such as people of color, the economically disadvantaged, etc.). Offenders without a DNA profile in CODIS are likely different (in some currently unknown way) from known offenders. Additionally, the more extensive subsequent criminal histories of offenders should also be interpreted as partially a function of time – approximately 15 to 20 years to offend.

Serial Sex Offenders

In this research a serial sex offender was defined as anyone associated with more than one linked SAK ("kit-to-kit") or a SAK and at least one arrest for a sexual offense(s) in his criminal history ("kit plus criminal history"). SAKs could be linked via DNA from the other unsubmitted SAKs or linked via an investigation as part of the unsubmitted SAK initiative in Cuyahoga County. A nonserial sex offender was defined as being linked to only one SAK and having no other arrests for rape in his criminal history (i.e., only one sexual assault that we know of). Of course, nonserial sex offenders might have committed additional sexual assaults.

In the analyses described below we conducted 2 x 2 chi-square tests of independence, where serial and nonserial sex offender status was a dummy variable and the presence or absence of an offense descriptor variable was also dummy coded (e.g., burglary, outdoors/outside, stranger, kidnapped, etc.). Results are presented in the tables below. We limit our discussion to statistically significant differences.

Consensus Coding of Cases

Two researchers coded SAK case files. For the first 50 sexual assaults, the researchers coded as a team – by each reviewing case files at the same time in the same room on their own computers and then coming to a consensus on how to code the variables. Then, one coder reexamined the other coder's case files. When a disagreement in the coding was found, the coders then came to a consensus. If agreement could not be reached among the coders, then the project director was consulted as to how to code.

---

3 We also analyzed differences in criminal history for serial and nonserial sex offenders in aggregate, for which serial sex offenders were only represented once in the analysis (results not shown). In the aggregation, the unit of analysis is the offender and not the sexual assault. A prior offense is, thus, operationalized to be prior to the first sexual assault and a subsequent offense is operationalized to be subsequent to the first sexual assault. Findings from the aggregation showed slightly higher percentages for all criminal offenses for serial sex offenders but the substantive findings remain the same whether or not serial sex offenders were aggregated. Thus, the data we present here more accurately capture whether an offense was prior to or subsequent to the sexual assault associated with the SAK.

Thus, the pilot data presented here represent codes that were identified by at least two, and some cases three, iterative, consensus-driven coding stages – making a final inter-rater reliability coefficient unnecessary.

Results

One of the most striking findings from analyzing data from the unsubmitted SAKs in Cuyahoga County is the large number of serial sex offenders. Of the 243 sexual assaults coded, 124 (51.0%) were connected to serial sex offenders. This figure should not be interpreted to say that more than half of all offenders in the unsubmitted SAKs are serial sex offenders. Rather, serial sex offenders are disproportionally represented in these data relative to their proportion of all unsubmitted SAKs due to the Task Force's prioritization of serial sex offenders for prosecution. Nonetheless, the number of serial sex offenders that have been linked to incidents, either by DNA and/or via an investigation, and their patterns of offending have been surprising to all involved in the initiative. Below, we detail some of these findings by comparing serial sex offenders to nonserial sex offenders including when, how, where, and against whom they offend as well as differences in criminal histories.

Offender Demographics

All offenders in our sample were male and had an average age of 29 at the time of the offense (range: 14–56), with 6.2% being minors (under the age of 18) at the time of offense (n = 15). Serial sex offenders were on average slightly older ($M = 30$) than nonserial sex offenders ($M = 27$), although this difference was not significant. The majority of offenders in our sample were African American/Black – 86.8%, 11.5% were Caucasian/White, and 1.6% were Hispanic/Latino. Serial sex offenders did not significantly differ from nonserial offenders by race.

Offender Criminal Histories

For offenses committed prior to the associated SAK, serial sex offenders had more extensive criminal histories compared to nonserial sex offenders. Serial sex offenders had, on average, almost twice as many felony offenses compared to nonserial sex offenders, 1.53 vs. 0.75 (Table 22.1). However, subsequent to the associated SAK sexual assault, serial and nonserial sex offenders did not differ from each other in the mean number of offenses (Table 22.1).

Table 22.1 also shows that 16.2% of serial offenders had a prior arrest for sexual assault and 57.7% had a subsequent arrest for a sexual assault. Serial sex offenders had a higher percentage of prior arrests for felony assault, larceny/theft, and motor vehicle theft compared to nonserial sex offenders. However, for subsequent offenses, serial and nonserial sex offenders did not differ for any of the listed offenses. Also of note are the similar frequencies for serial and nonserial sex offenders for domestic violence arrests both prior and subsequent to the associated SAK sexual assault, as previous literature has found that serial sex offenders are more likely to have domestic violence offenses (Lisak & Miller, 2002).

Difference in Modus Operandi ("MO") between Serial and Nonserial Sex Offenders

We examined *modus operandi* to assess whether serial and nonserial sex offenders differed in their offending patterns. As

Table 22.1 *Criminal History of Offenders Prior and Subsequent to the Associated SAK Sexual Assault by Type of Offense*

Type of Offense	Prior Serial Percent (n = 111)	Prior Nonserial Percent (n = 55)	Subsequent Serial Percent (n = 111)	Subsequent Nonserial Percent (n = 55)
Murder	4.5	—	4.5	3.6
Sexual assault	16.2	—	57.7	—
Felony assault	23.4***	5.5	32.4	45.5
Robbery	14.4	10.9	29.7	25.5
Burglary	19.8	14.5	22.5	20.0
Larceny/theft	22.5*	9.1	16.2	14.5
Motor vehicle theft	15.3**	1.8	9.0	16.4
Arson	—	—	2.7	—
Felony drug	26.1	20.0	39.6	45.5
Domestic violence	10.8	12.7	27.3	34.5
At least one offense	70.3*	50.9	86.4	78.2
Mean number of offenses	1.53***	0.75	2.40	2.05

Note: A total of 113 unique offenders corresponding to 166 sexual assaults. Criminal histories were only available for known offenders.

***$p < 0.001$, **$p < 0.01$, *$p < 0.05$.

illustrated by Table 22.2, 52.9% of sexual assaults committed by serial sex offenders were committed in open areas (which includes in a vehicle or outdoors/outside) compared to 31.0% for nonserial sex offenders. Sexual assaults committed by serial sex offenders were more frequently committed in a vehicle compared to nonserial sex offenders (32.2% vs. 16.8%). Conversely, sexual assaults committed by nonserial sex offenders were more frequently committed in the offender's residence compared to serial sex offenders (20.4% vs. 7.4%).

Table 22.2 also illustrates that serial sex offenders were more frequently strangers (67.8%) to their victims compared to nonserial sex offenders (45.8%) – with stranger sexual assaults representing 56.8% of all sexual assaults in our sample. This figure should not be interpreted to say that more than half of all sexual assaults in the unsubmitted SAKs are stranger sexual assaults, as serial sex offenders are more commonly associated with stranger sexual assaults in our data and the Task Force prioritized serial sex offenders for prosecution. We defined a recent acquaintance as someone the victim had just met (at a bar, party, on the street, etc.), whereas a casual acquaintance was defined as someone the victim knew something about ("around the neighborhood") but did not know very well. Nonserial sex offenders were more frequently current intimate partners/dating compared to serial sex offenders (13.1% vs. 8%).

Despite the high number of sexual assaults by strangers, victims were

Table 22.2 *Locations Where Sexual Assaults Occurred and Relationship of Victim and Offender for Serial vs. Nonserial Sex Offenders*

	Serial Sex Offenders	Nonserial Sex Offenders
	Percent	Percent
Type of Location		
In a vehicle	32.2**	16.8
Outdoors/outside	20.7	14.2
Garage	4.1	0.9
Victim's residence	21.5	23.0
Offender's residence	7.4**	20.4
Third-Party residence	9.9	18.6
Unknown	2.4	5.0
All other	4.1	6.2
Total	100.0	100.0
N	121	113
Type of Relationship		
Stranger	67.8**	45.8
Casual acquaintance	13.2	17.8
Recent acquaintance	5.0	10.3
Former intimate partner/dating	4.1	5.6
Current intimate partner/dating	0.8***	13.1
Friend/not romantic	3.3	1.9
Relationship unknown	5.8	5.6
All other	2.4*	10.1
Total	100.0	100.0
N	121	107

Note: Percentages based on nonmissing data

***$p < 0.001$, **$p < 0.01$, *$p < 0.05$.

frequently able to provide some type of identifying information about the offenders to the police at the time, according to the police reports (e.g., first and last name, a partial name/nickname, pointed out to police, or license plate number), in 44.8% of sexual assaults. Victims were able to provide police with at least some identifying information about the offender in 39.0% of the sexual assaults for serial offenders and in 50.8% of the sexual assaults for nonserial sex offenders.

Offenders differed with respect to some aspects of their MOs. Serial sex offenders less frequently committed sexual assaults with others (i.e., gang sexual assaults) – 12.1% of the sexual assaults involving serial sex offenders had more than one male involved in the assault vs. 22.7% for nonserial sex offenders. Table 22.3 illustrates that sexual assaults committed by serial sex offenders more frequently involved a weapon (41.0%) (e.g., primarily a firearm or a knife, respectively) than sexual assaults committed by nonserial sex offenders (19.8%). Table 22.3 also shows that sexual assaults committed by serial sex offenders more frequently

Table 22.3 *Type of Control and Bodily Force Used in the Sexual Assault for Serial and Nonserial Sex Offenders*

	Serial Sex Offenders	Nonserial Sex Offenders
	Percent	Percent
Type of Control Used*		
Kidnapped	44.3	35.1
Verbally threatened	32.0*	19.8
Physically threatened	24.6*	11.7
Restrained	47.5	53.2
Threatened with weapon	41.0***	19.8
N	122	111
Type of Bodily Force Used*		
Used any type of bodily force	73.3	73.4
Dragged	6.7	8.3
Punched/slapped	14.2**	28.4
Pushed	27.5	29.4
Strangled	6.7	8.3
Held down	25.0	33.9
Injured victim to complete sexual assault	7.4**	18.9
N	121	107

Note: Offenders could employ more than one type of control and bodily force; percentages based on nonmissing data.

***p < 0.001, **p < 0.01, *p < 0.05.

involved verbal threatening (32.0% vs. 19.8%) and physical threatening (24.6% vs. 11.7%) compared to nonserial sex offenders. Physical threats were defined as a threat of injury. Verbal threats were defined as those that entailed abusive language but did not specifically mention a threat to physically harm. A physical threat was also counted as a verbal threat. A threat with a weapon was also counted as a physical threat.

However, sexual assaults committed by serial sex offenders less frequently involved injuring the victim in order to complete the attack (in other words, "instrumental" and not gratuitous injury). While all sexual assaults injure victims, from the victim's account of the assault we specifically coded for the presence of injuries to the victim that occurred as part of the attack (e.g., how the offender was able to "get the upper hand"). Table 22.3 details the type of bodily force used (defined as force used over and above the assault) by serial and nonserial sex offenders in the sexual assaults. While overall serial and nonserial sex offenders used bodily force with equal frequency (73.3% vs. 73.4%), nonserial sex offenders more frequently used certain types of bodily force, most notably punching/slapping (28.4% vs. 14.2%).

Typical MO for Serial Sex Offenders

We were interested in exploring the extent to which serial sex offenders consistently used the same MO in multiple sexual assaults. To explore, we examined serial sex offenders with more than one linked SAK that we had coded (in other words, the "kit-to-kit" serial sex offenders), as this gave us access to the details of the multiple assaults. Our database included 30 of these serial sex offenders who committed 85 sexual assaults, with the average number of sexual assaults for these serial offenders being 2.83 (range: 2–6).

We examined the age span for these serial offenders and found that the mean number of years between their first and last sexual assault was 4.76 years (range: 0–19). However, 35% are within a year or less. The offender with the most number of sexual assaults that we coded (n = 6) was age 47 at the first and age 56 at the last sexual assault. Another offender was young when committing both of the sexual assaults we coded – 15 and 16. Considering the truncated time period for most of the sexual assaults (e.g., 1993–1997), these findings suggest that our data are, perhaps, only capturing a portion of their serial offending.

We also examined whether these 30 serial sex offenders committed the 85 offenses in similar locations – categorized as being (1) indoors (i.e., house or hotel), (2) outdoors (i.e., outside or in a vehicle), or (3) in a building (i.e., garage, university, commercial building). More than half (57.1%) of these 30 serial sex offenders committed all of their offenses in the same type of location; 14.2% committed the offense in the same types of location the majority of the time (e.g., more than 50% of the time); and 28.6% committed half of their offenses in the same type of location (e.g., 50% of the time). For the serial sex offenders who committed the most number of assaults (4+ sexual assaults, n = 7), out of the 32 assaults, 30 were outdoors.

Serial sex offenders did not appear to be as consistent with their use or threat of a weapon during the offense ("consistent" is defined as a weapon being used in all of their assaults) – 56.7% inconsistently had a weapon, 16.7% consistently had a weapon, and 26.7% consistently did not have a weapon in the assault. Serial sex offenders were relatively consistent with their use of bodily force – 50.0% consistently did not use bodily force against the victims, 16.7% consistently used bodily force, while 33.3% inconsistently used bodily force.

Relationship Crossover

According to the SAK Task Force, they observed anecdotally numerous instances where serial sex offenders sexually assaulted both strangers and non-strangers – relationship crossover. To empirically measure this, we assessed the relationship status for serial sex offenders where we had coded more than one of their sexual assaults (e.g., for the 30 offenders). We examined two types of relationships, stranger vs. non-stranger, where stranger was defined as an individual who was completely unknown to the victim – the most conservative definition of stranger. Our findings indicate that for the 30 serial sex offenders, 50% only assaulted strangers, 33.3% assaulted strangers and non-strangers, and 16.7% only assaulted non-strangers. Thus, in a third of the cases serial sex offenders assaulted both strangers and non-strangers.

Conclusion

Our findings show that serial sex offending is much more common than what was previously thought, potentially changing the way sexual assaults should be investigated and the way we view sexual assault, offenders, and victims. The overwhelming majority of both serial and nonserial sex offenders in our sample had felony-level criminal histories. Serial sex offenders had more extensive and violent criminal histories compared to nonserial sex offenders for offenses committed prior to the associated SAK.

Serial sex offenders more frequently assaulted in open areas (i.e., in a vehicle, outdoors) and were also more frequently strangers to their victims. Additionally, sexual assaults committed by serial sex offenders more frequently involved verbal and physical threats and threats with a weapon. However, sexual assaults committed by serial offenders less frequently involved the victims being punched/slapped and gratuitous injury. In other words, threatening with a weapon more frequently forced "acquiescence" from the victim and therefore less frequently resulted in the victim being injured above and beyond injury of the sexual assault.

Our findings suggest that serial offenders do not have a consistent offending profile. Serial sex offenders with more than one unsubmitted SAK more consistently assaulted in the same type of location and inflicted bodily force in the assault. However, they were less consistent with their use or threat of a weapon in the assault and with the type of relationship they had with the victim.

Limitations

When interpreting these findings, it is important to note that these data only represent unsubmitted SAKs with closed investigations that resulted in prosecution or were closed due to insufficient evidence – with a disproportionate number of serial sexual offenders and SAKs that occurred between 1993 and 1997. Our findings cannot be generalized to the entire population of sexual assaults or sexual assault victims in Cuyahoga County. Additionally, it should be noted that these data are derived from official documentation (e.g., initial police reports, investigative reports, lab reports, criminal histories). We could only code information that was contained in a case file. We did not interview victims nor did we employ participant observation of investigations or prosecutions.

Discussion and Future Directions

While serial sex offenders are disproportionately represented in our sample relative to their proportion of all offenders in the unsubmitted SAKs in Cuyahoga County, our findings illustrate that serial sex offending is common. This finding is likely a function of: (1) the use of DNA and CODIS being able to link at a much earlier stage in the process – at the time the victim reported and had a SAK collected – for a large number of sexual assaults (those with unsubmitted SAKs) and (2) serial sex offender being defined as more than one linked SAK or a SAK and an arrest for rape.

Most of what is known about serial sex offenders is based on offenders who have been convicted of multiple sexual assaults or offenders who self-report multiple assaults. In the former, convicted serial sex offenders represent a very small and skewed proportion of all sexual offenders. Research has consistently illustrated that convictions for sexual assault are much more likely to be the exception rather than the rule (RAINN, 2016b). Additionally, self-reported multiple offending has the inherent issue of relying on the offender to disclose and self-define more than one of their sexual acts as nonconsensual. Our data, on the other hand, is derived from a much larger sample of sexual assaults with unsubmitted SAKs. Moreover, we were able to expand our definition of serial to include an arrest and not conviction for sexual assault, as convictions are less common and often the convicting offense does not accurately reflect the offense that was reportedly committed (e.g., pleading to assault instead of sexual battery) (Spohn & Tellis, 2012).

Our findings also suggest that it is very likely that a sexual offender has either previously sexually assaulted or will offend again in the future. Investigating each sexual assault as possibly being perpetrated by a serial sex offender has the potential to reduce the number of sexual assaults if the focus of the investigation is more on the offender than on a single incident or merely the perceived credibility of the victim. Serial sex offenders have traditionally been investigated according to the consistency of the MO (e.g., who they assault, where they assault, how they assault). Our findings suggest that MOs (while definitely important to track for investigative purposes, especially when DNA is present) are not a consistently reliable link across assaults. Instead, there appears to be merit in shifting the focus of the sexual assault investigation from the victim to the offender, to reexamining every previously reported assault (including but not limited to sexual assaults) allegedly perpetrated by the offender, whether or not it fits the typical MO. In other words, fully examining sexual offenders when they come to the attention of law enforcement is likely one of the most important ways to investigate unsolved sexual assaults and reduce the number of future offenses. The findings also speak to the need to more fully examine sexual offenders' criminal history and mental health as these factors likely contribute to sexual offending, especially violent serial offending.

These findings also speak to how powerful DNA testing can be. Testing all SAKs not only populates the CODIS database for possible future matches; it also can link crimes across space and time – crimes that likely would never have been linked. Of course, a DNA match is only the first step in the process. Cases with a DNA match must still be thoroughly investigated. This SAK initiative illustrates that when all SAKs are tested and cases are thoroughly investigated and prosecuted, there is potential to greatly reduce the number of future offenses across the country.

These data provide a unique opportunity to begin to examine how serial sex offenders compare to nonserial sex offenders. Findings from this pilot data only scratch the surface. Additional research can help us gain a more nuanced understanding of serial sex offending. Our findings indicate that while serial sex offenders are different from nonserial sex offenders, they might also be quite different from each other – in other words, there exist different types of serial sex offenders. As this project matures we hope to investigate in greater detail topics such as the different types of serial sex offenders and nonserial sex offenders, what factors or combination of factors most influence the amount of force and injury inflicted on the victim, offender mobility, relationships between the victim and offender, and the social networks of offenders and victims.

One of the promising avenues for research in serial sexual assault, particularly when combined with the testing of SAKs, is that of criminal linkage or profiling. Traditional profiling is limited because samples are drawn from solved crimes, but to be useful it must be able to be applied to unsolved crimes; using DNA to link crimes, even unsolved ones, allows for the refinement of crime scene behavior assessments (Woodhams & Labuschagne, 2012). Linking cases through MOs has strong prosecutorial utility and may be useful in prioritizing cases (Deslauriers-Varin & Beauregard, 2013; Sorochinski, 2015). Another branch of profiling is geographic profiling (Canter & Larkin, 1993; Meaney, 2004; Strangeland, 2005), where an offender's spatial patterns are used to predict the areas where he may offend again. Future research should visualize offenses tied by DNA so we do not have to rely on solved crimes to examine geographic profiles. Above all else, we must ensure that our research and evaluation of SAK investigations and prosecutions are trauma-informed, victim-centered, and contribute to changing practice and policy for how we address sexual assaults in the future.

References

Abbey, A., Wegner, R., Pierce, J., & Jacques-Tiura, A. J. (2012). Patterns of Sexual Aggression in a Community Sample of Young Men: Risk Factors Associated with Persistence, Desistance, and Initiation over a 1-Year Interval. *Psychology of Violence*, 2(1), 1–15.

Balteri, D. & Andrade, A. G. (2008). Comparing Serial and Nonserial Sexual Offenders: Alcohol and Street Drug Consumption, Impulsiveness and History of Sexual Abuse. *Revista Brasileira De Psiquiatira*, 30(1), 25–31.

Bettinger-Lopez, C. (2016). The Sexual Assault Kit Initiative: An Important Step Toward Ending the Rape Kit Backlog. March 15, 2016. Retrieved December 5, 2017 from https://obamawhitehouse.archives.gov/blog/2016/03/15/sexual-assault-kit-initiative-important-step-toward-ending-rape-kit-backlog.

Bureau of Justice Affairs. (2016). National Sexual Assault Kit Initiative (SAKI) FY 2016 Competitive Grant Announcement. Washington, DC: US Department of Justice – Office of Justice Programs.

Bureau of Justice Assistance. (2015). National Sexual Assault Kit Initiative (SAKI) FY 2015 Competitive Grant Announcement. Washington, DC: US Department of Justice – Bureau of Justice Programs.

Burgess, A. W., Hazelwood, R. R., Rokous, F. E., Hartman, C. R., & Burgess, A. G. (1988). Serial Rapists and Their Victims: Reenactment and Repetition. *Annals of the New York Academy of Sciences*, 528, 277–295.

Calandro, L., Reeder, D. J., & Cormier, K. (2005,). Evolution of DNA for Crime Solving – A Judicial and Legislative History. *Forensic Magazine*. January 6, 2005. Retrieved September 28, 2016 from www.forensicmag.com/article/2005/01/evolution-dna-evidence-crime-solving-judicial-and-legislative-history.

Campbell, R., Feeney, H., Fehler-Cabral, G., Shaw, J., & Horsford, S. (2015). The National Problem of Untested Sexual Assault Kits (SAKs): Scope, Causes, and Future Directions for Research, Policy, and Practice. *Trauma, Violence, & Abuse*, 18(4), 363–376. 1524838015622436.

Campbell, R., Pierce, S. J., Sharma, D. B., Feeney, H., & Fedlor-Cabral, G. (2016a). Developing Empirically Informed Policies for Sexual Assault Kit DNA Testing: Is It

Too Late to Test Kits Beyond the Statute of Limitations? *Criminal Justice Policy Review*, 1–25. doi: 10.1177/0887403416638507.

Campbell, R., Pierce, S. J., Sharma, D. B., Feeney, H., & Fehler-Cabral, G. (2016b). Should Rape Kit Testing Be Prioritized by Victim-Offender Relationship? Empirical Comparison of Forensic Testing Outcomes for Stranger and Nonstranger Sexual Assaults. *Criminology & Public Policy*, 15(2), 555–583.

Campbell, R., Shaw, J., & Fehler-Cabral, G. (2015). Shelving Justice: The Discovery of Thousands of Untested Rape Kits in Detroit. *City & Community*, 14(2), 151–166.

Canter, D. & Larkin, P. (1993). The Environmental Range of Serial Rapists. *The Journal of Environmental Psychology*, 13(1), 63–69.

Cocke, S. (2016). Police Miss Deadline on Rape Kits. *Honolulu Star Advertiser.* September 19, 2016. Retrieved September 28, 2016 from www.staradvertiser.com/2016/09/19/hawaii-news/police-miss-deadline-on-rape-kits/.

Corovic, J., Christianson, S. Å., & Bergman, L. R. (2012). From Crime Scene Actions in Stranger Rape to Prediction of Rapist Type: Single-Victim or Serial Rapist? *Behavioral Sciences & the Law*, 30(6), 764–781.

de Heer, B. (2016). A Snapshot of Serial Rape. *Journal of Interpersonal Violence*, 31(4), 598–619.

Department of Justice. (2016). Identifying and Preventing Gender Bias in Law Enforcement Response to Sexual Assault and Domestic Violence. Washington, DC: Department of Justice.

Deslauriers-Varin, N. & Beauregard, E. (2013). Investigating Offending Consistency of Geographic and Environmental Factors Among Serial Sex Offenders: A Comparison of Multiple Analytical Strategies. *Criminal Justice and Behavior*, 40(2), 156–179.

Dickson, C. (2014). How the US Ended Up with 400,000 Untested Rape Kits. Retrieved September 23, 2016 from www.thedailybeast.com/articles/2014/09/23/how-the-u-s-ended-up-with-400-000-untested-rape-kits.html.

End the Backlog. (2016). Accountability Project. Retrieved September 28, 2016 from http://endthebacklog.org/backlog-where-it/accountability-project.

Findell, E. (2016). Austin Police Pledge to Find Money to Clear Up Rape Kit Backlog. *myStatesman*. September 12, 2016. Retrieved September 28, 2016 from www.mystatesman.com/news/news/local-govt-politics/austin-police-pledge-to-find-money-to-clear-up-rap/nsW6Z/.

Hazelwood, R. R. & Warren, J. (1989). *The Serial Rapist: His Characteristics and Victims (Conclusion)*. Law Enforcement Bulletin.

Human Rights Watch. (2009). Testing Justice: The Rape Kit Backlog in Los Angeles City and County. New York: Human Rights Watch.

Human Rights Watch. (2011). The City of Los Angeles Eliminates Historical Rape Kit Backlog. April 29, 2011. Retrieved September 28, 2016 from www.hrw.org/news/2011/04/29/city-los-angeles-eliminates-historical-rape-kit-backlog.

Human Rights Watch. (2013). Capitol Offense: Police Mishandling of Sexual Assault Cases in the District of Columbia. Chicago: Human Rights Watch.

Jan, J. (2004). Beyond Belief?: Police, Rape and Women's Credibility. *Criminal Justice: International Journal of Policy & Practice*, 4(1), 29–59.

Johnson, D., Peterson, J., Sommers, I., & Baskin, D. (2012). Use of Forensic Science in Investigating Crimes of Sexual Violence: Contrasting Its Theoretical Potential with Empirical Realities. *Violence Against Women*, 18(2), 193–222.

Joyful Heart Foundation. (2016). Navigating Notification: A Guide to Re-engaging Sexual Assault Survivors Affected by the Untested Rape Kit Backlog: Joyful Heart Foundation.

Lisak, D. & Miller, P. (2002). Repeat Rape and Multiple Offending Among Undetected Rapists. *Violence and Victims*, 17(1), 73–84.

Lovell, R., Butcher, F., & Flannery, D. (2016). Analysis of Cuyahoga County's Procedures for Alleviating the Backlog of Sexual Assault Kits. Cleveland, OH: Begun Center for Violence Prevention Research and Education at the Jack, Joseph and Morton Mandel School of Applied Social Sciences at Case Western Reserve University.

Lovell, R., Flannery, D., Overman, L., & Walker, T. (2016). What Happened with the Sexual Assaults Reports? Then vs. Now. Cleveland, OH: Begun Center for Violence Prevention Research and Education at the Jack, Joseph and Morton Mandel School of Applied Social Sciences at Case Western Reserve University.

Lovrich, N. P., Pratt, T. C., Gaffney, M. J., Johnson, C. L., Asplen, C. H., Hurst, L. H., & Schellberg, T. M. (2004). National Forensic DNA Study Report, Final Report. Pullman, WA: U.S. Department of Justice.

Luminais, M., Lovell, R., & Flannery, D. (forthcoming). How the Backlog Happened: Cuyahoga County Sexual Assault Kit Task Force Members' Understanding. Cleveland, OH: Begun Center for Violence Prevention Research and Education at the Jack, Joseph and Morton Mandel School of Applied Social Sciences at Case Western Reserve University.

Meaney, R. (2004). Commuters and Mauraders: An Examination of the Spatial Behaviour of Serial Criminals. *Journal of Investigative Psychology and Offender Profiling*, 1(2), 121–137.

Munday, D. (2016). Sex-Crime Evidence Ignored? Several Hundred Charleston-Area Kits Remain Untested. *The Post and Courier*. August 20, 2016. Retrieved September 28, 2016 from www.postandcourier.com/20160820/160829993/sex-crime-evidence-ignored-several-hundred-charleston-area-kits-remain-untested.

National Institute of Justice. (2015). Sexual Assault Kits: Using Science to Find Solutions. Washington, DC: National Institute of Justice.

National Institute of Justice. (2016). Untested Evidence in Sexual Assault Cases. Retrieved September 28, 2016 from www.nij.gov/topics/law-enforcement/investigations/sexual-assault/Pages/untested-sexual-assault.aspx#understanding.

Nelson, M. S. (2013). Analysis of Untested Sexual Assault Kits in New Orleans. Washington, DC: National Institute of Justice.

Park, J., Schlesinger, L. B., Pinizzotto, A. J., & Davis, E. F. (2008). Serial and Single-Victim Rapists: Differences in Crime-Scene Violence, Interpersonal Involvement, and Criminal Sophistication. *Behavioral Sciences & the Law*, 26(2), 227–237.

Peterson, J., Johnson, D., Herz, D., Graziano, L., & Oehler, T. (2012). Sexual Assault Kit Backlog Study: National Institute of Justice.

Pinchevsky, G. M. (2016). Criminal Justice Considerations for Unsubmitted and Untested Sexual Assault Kits: A Review of the Literature and Suggestions for Moving Forward. *Criminal Justice Policy Review*, 1–21. doi: 10.1177/0887403416662899.

Plackett, B. (2015). Federal Scientists Are Helping Police Catch Up with Rape Forensics. *Inside Science*. February 10, 2015. Retrieved September 28, 2016 from www.insidescience.org/news/federal-scientists-are-helping-police-catch-rape-forensics.

Poe, R. (2016). Smith to Lead City's Sexual Assault Kit Task Force. *The Commercial Appeal*. February 2, 2016. Retrieved September 28, 2016 from www.commercialappeal.com/news/government/city/smith-to-lead-citys-sexual-assault-kit-task-force-2acced50-e003-5bf5-e053-0100007f3b24-367370461.html.

Pratt, T. C., Gaffney, M. J., Lovrich, N. P., & Johnson, C. L. (2006). This Isn't CSI: Estimating the National Backlog of Forensic DNA Cases and the Barriers Associated With Case Processing. *Criminal Justice Policy Review*, 17(1), 32–47.

RAINN. (2016a). What is a Rape Kit? Retrieved September 28, 2016 from www.rainn.org/articles/rape-kit.

RAINN (2016b). The Criminal Justice System: Statistics. Retrieved November 3, 2016 from www.rainn.org/statistics/criminal-justice-system.

Reilly, S. (2015). Tens of Thousands of Rape Kits Go Untested Across USA. Retrieved September 28, 2016 from www.usatoday.com/story/news/2015/07/16/untested-rape-kits-evidence-across-usa/29902199/.

Ritter, N. (2011). The Road Ahead: Unanalyzed Evidence in Sexual Assault Cases. Washington, DC National Institute of Justice.

Ritter, N. (2016). Down the Road: Testing Evidence in Sexual Assaults. Washington, DC: National Institute of Justice.

Rogalski, J. (2016). City's Rape Kit Backlog Creeping Back Up. *KHOU.com*. April 4, 2016. Retrieved September 28, 2016 from www.khou.com/news/investigations/citys-rape-kit-backlog-creeping-back/119672065.

Slater, C., Woodhams, J., & Hamilton-Giachritsis, C. (2014). Can Serial Rapists be Distinguished from One-off Rapists? *Behavioral Sciences & the Law*, 32, 220–239.

Sorochinski, M. (2015). Assumptions Underlying Behavioral Linkage Revisited: A Multidimensional Approach to Ascertaining Individual Differentiation and Consistency in Serial Rape. PhD, New York: City University of New York.

Spohn, C. (2016). Untested Sexual Assault Kits. *Criminology & Public Policy*, 15(2), 551–554.

Spohn, C. & Tellis, K. (2012). The Criminal Justice System's Response to Sexual Violence. *Violence Against Women*, 18(2), 169–192.

Stein, R. (2016). Police: Backlog Testing of Rape Kits Yields Few Matches. *Amarillo Globe-News*. March 17, 2016. Retrieved September 30, 2016 from http://amarillo.com/news/crime-and-courts/2016-03-17/police-rape-kit-testing-yields-few-results-matches#.

Stevens, D. J. (1997). Violence and Serial Rape. *Journal of Police and Criminal Psychology*, 12(1), 39–47.

Strangeland, P. (2005). Catching a Serial Rapist: Hits and Misses in Criminal Profiling. *Police Practice & Research*, 6(5), 453–469.

Strom, K. J. & Hickman, M. J. (2010). Unanalyzed evidence in law-enforcement agencies. *Criminology & Public Policy*, 9(2), 381–404.

Strom, K. J. & Hickman, M. J. (2016). Untested Sexual Assault Kits: Searching for an Empirical Foundation to Guide Forensic Case Processing Decisions. *Criminology & Public Policy*, 15(2), 593–601.

Swartout, K. M., Koss, M. P., White, J. W., Thompson, M. P., et al. (2015) Trajectory Analysis of the Campus Serial Rapist Assumption. *JAMA Pediatrics*, 169(12), 1148–1154.

The Associated Press. (2016). Rape Kit System Unneccessary Since Most Accusations False, Idaho Sheriff Says. *The Oregonian*. March 17, 2016. Retrieved September 28, 2016 from www.oregonlive.com/pacific-northwest-news/index.ssf/2016/03/rape_kit_system_unnecessary_si.html.

The National Center for Victims of Crime. (2016). Sexual Assault Kit Testing: What Victims Need to Know. Retrieved September 28, 2016, from http://victimsofcrime.org/docs/default-source/dna-resource-center-documents/dna-sak-victim-brofinal.pdf?sfvrsn=2.

US Department of Justice. (2014). Advancing Justice through DNA Technology: Using DNA to Solve Crimes. US Department of Justice. September 9, 2014. Retrieved September 28, 2016 from www.justice.gov/ag/advancing-justice-through-dna-technology-using-dna-solve-crimes.

Voice of San Diego (2016). San Diego PD Doubles Down on Decision to Leave Some

Rape Kits Untested. *PublicCEO.* September 12, 2016. Retrieved September 28, 2016 from www.publicceo.com/2016/09/san-diego-pd-doubles-down-on-decision-to-leave-some-rape-kits-untested/.

Warren, J., Reboussin, R., Hazelwood, R. R., Gibbs, N. A., Trumbetta, S. L., & Cummings, A. (1999). Crime Scene Analysis and the Escalation of Violence in Serial Rape. *Forensic Science International*, 100(1–2), 37–56.

Woodhams, J. & Labuschagne, G. (2012). A Test of Case Linkage Principles with Solved and Unsolved Serial Rapes. *Journal of Police and Criminal Psychology*, 27(1), 85–98.

WTVQ Web Desk (2016). AG Beshar Holds Safe Summit to Address Sexual Assault Kit Backlog. Retrieved September 28, 2016 from www.wtvq.com/2016/09/14/ag-beshear-holds-safe-summit-address-sexual-assault-kit-backlogs/.

23 Research on Social Structure and Cross-National Homicide Rates

Meghan L. Rogers and William Alex Pridemore

> It seems to me what is called for is an exquisite balance between two conflicting needs: the most skeptical scrutiny of all hypotheses that are served up to us and at the same time a great openness to new ideas.
>
> – Carl Sagan

Introduction

This chapter addresses research on social structure and cross-national homicide rates. Interpersonal violence is an incredibly disruptive force, and security from it is a fundamental necessity for the health of individuals, families, and communities. Nations vary widely in their homicide rates, which likely reflects something important about the underlying nature of the state, culture, and social structure. This makes the study of the population-level causes of cross-national variation in homicide rates a worthwhile pursuit. There is a long history of such research. Our goal is not to summarize that literature, as other recent publications have done that (Nivette, 2011; Trent & Pridemore, 2011). Instead, we examine what we believe to be important elements of the past, present, and potential future of this research area.

In our consideration of the past we revisit what we think we know from the body of research on social structure and cross-national homicide rates. We explore what many scholars believe are stylized facts but in reality either have little empirical support or have recently been called into question. This includes widely held beliefs about the impact of the size of a nation's youthful population on its homicide rate, the association between inequality and cross-national homicide rates, and the presence of similar decades-long supranational trends in homicide rates throughout the world or in specific regions or types of nations.

Our present discussion addresses recent research developments on social structure and violence cross-nationally. This includes theoretical considerations of the roles of poverty and social protection. It also includes Pridemore's (2007, 2016) Criminological Transition Model, which attempts to explain how development and social change influence not only the rate, but the nature of interpersonal violence, such as the characteristics of victims, offenders, and events. We also describe innovations in data and methods used to study the association between social structure and cross-national homicide rates. This includes increasing data availability that allows scholars to more carefully operationalize theoretical concepts, as well as the application of techniques like model selection and panel modeling to cross-national homicide research.

In our discussion of future research, we present a challenge to cross-national homicide scholars. With some notable exceptions, this research area remained relatively stale for decades, with limited theoretical or empirical progress. Few old theories were discarded, few genuine ideas were tested, and scholars rarely took advantage of new data sources or applied improved methodological techniques. In this section we ask scholars to consider potential structural causes of variation in cross-national homicide rates beyond the usual structural covariates tested for decades, to expand beyond social structure to more carefully consider the influence of cultural characteristics, and to exploit nontraditional data sources that could help provide better insight into why nations vary so substantially in their rates of interpersonal violence.

The Past: Not-so-Stylized Facts

It doesn't matter how beautiful your theory is. It doesn't matter how smart you are. It doesn't matter what your name is. If it disagrees with experiment it's wrong.
– Richard Feynman

While the cross-national literature on social structure and homicide has yielded largely inconsistent results, over time a few ideas came to be accepted as stylized facts. In recent years, however, even these stylized facts have come under suspicion, at least in certain circumstances, which may force us to us to reconsider long and strongly held beliefs. This is not a critique of the research that produced these results but instead a natural progression of the accumulation of knowledge provided by the application of the scientific method to this phenomenon.

The Size of the Young Population and Cross-National Homicide Rates

One of the few stylized facts in this research area is that national homicide rates are sensitive to the size of a nation's youthful population, so that there is a strong positive association between "percent-young" and homicide rates. There is nearly universal belief of the presence of this association, there has been substantial theorizing about this effect, most cross-national studies contain a measure of percent-young, and nearly all reviewers of cross-national homicide studies will request a variable be included to control for percent-young's effect. The problem is there is overwhelming empirical evidence against such an association.

There are two general arguments for an association between percent-young and national homicide rates: composition and context. The first is not a structural but a compositional effect. The compositional hypothesis holds that young people, especially males, are at greater risk of violent offending and victimization and thus have the highest age-specific homicide rates. Therefore, the greater the size of the young population the higher a nation's homicide rate. While focusing on individual-level explanations for this phenomenon, Hirschi and Gottfredson (1983, p. 554) stated clearly the age-crime association is "invariant across social and cultural conditions." The precise reason for greater risk among the young is debated. For example, this compositional hypothesis is often connected to a routine activities framework (Cohen & Felson, 1979): nations with a higher proportion of the population at risk for offending and victimization have greater availability of offenders and potential targets (Bennett,

1991; Fiala & LaFree, 1988; Gartner, 1990). No matter the explanation, there is widespread agreement that the size of the young population is related both to within- and between-nation variation in homicide rates (Chilton & Spielberger, 1971; Gartner & Parker, 1990; Greenberg, 1977, 1985; Pampel & Williamson, 2001).

The contextual hypothesis argues a large birth cohort creates competition for scarce resources and thus higher rates of interpersonal violence, especially among young men (Easterlin, 1987). There are no direct tests of this hypothesis, though it is sometimes used as a point of speculative departure when attempting to explain why a measure of the size of the young population might be associated with cross-national homicide rates or should be included as a control when testing other explanations (South & Messner, 2000).

There are two serious problems with the stylized fact of an impact on cross-national homicide rates of the size of the young population. The first problem is that these hypotheses assume young people have the highest age-specific homicide rates. This assumption does not hold. Rogers (2014) found that, relative to rates among other age groups, age-specific homicide victimization rates for 15- to 24-year-olds are not consistently the highest across nations or within nations over time. Similarly, many studies of specific nations – Finland (Lehti & Kivivuori, 2012; Liem et al., 2012), Lithuania (Andresen, 2012), Sweden (Granath, 2012; Liem et al., 2012), Ukraine, Belarus, and Russia (Lysova, Shchitov, & Pridemore, 2012; Pridemore, 2003), and several Eastern and Central European nations (Stamatel, 2009) – found age-specific homicide rates were not highest among those between the ages of 15 and 24.

The second serious problem with this stylized fact is the overwhelming lack of empirical evidence supporting this association. In reviewing about three-dozen published studies, Rogers and Pridemore (2016a) found only 13% of all coefficients estimating an association between percent-young and cross-national homicide rates found the expected positive association. The authors' own systematic analyses (Rogers & Pridemore, 2016a, 2016b), which went much further in interrogating this relationship than prior studies, led them to conclude: (1) there was no evidence of an effect of percent-young on total, age-specific, or sex-specific cross-national homicide rates; (2) percent-young does not account for variance in homicide rates between nations; (3) the use of model selection techniques result in a best-fitting model that does not include percent-young; and thus (4) inclusion of percent-young actually impairs the performance of models of cross-national homicide rates.

These findings mean one of the most widely held beliefs about cross-national rates – that they are highest among and thus sensitive to the size of the young population – is inconsistent with dozens of empirical observations over a span of decades. Such instability of a supposedly stylized fact presents a threat to what we think we know about social structure and cross-national homicide rates.

Economic Inequality and Cross-National Homicide Rates

A second stylized fact is the very strongly held belief that nations with higher levels of economic inequality possess higher homicide rates. Two general hypotheses lead to the expectation of an inequality-homicide association. According to the first explanation, preferred mainly by economists, the greater the disparity between rich and poor in a nation – which is viewed as a measure of the gap between gains from crime and opportunity costs (Becker, 1968; Fajnzylber, Lederman, & Loayza, 2002; Kelly, 2000) – the tighter the labor market and the greater the competition for scarce resources. This competition is expected to create aggression, and given belief of the existence of higher homicide rates among the young this explanation is almost always tied closely to how young men are affected by these conditions. The second hypothesis, preferred mainly by criminologists, is that low-income individuals experience unequal distribution of resources, perceive this inequity as unjust, become increasingly dissatisfied by these inequitable circumstances, and eventually lash out due to pent-up frustration. This is an individual-level explanation of a population-level association, but it is the most common justification for expecting an inequality-homicide association.

This stylized fact about economic inequality is grounded more strongly in empirical findings than the stylized fact about the size of the young population. In many studies over many years scholars consistently found a positive association between income inequality and national homicide rates. This led LaFree (1999, p. 141), in his review of this literature, to conclude that a "positive association between economic inequality and homicide rates is among the most consistent findings in the cross-national literature." As suggested by the title of Wilkinson's (2004, p. 1) article, "Why is violence more common where inequality is greater?" he went substantially further, arguing "the most well-established environmental determinant of levels of violence is the scale of income differences between rich and poor."

Yet for decades there was something important missing from cross-national studies of inequality and homicide: poverty. This was problematic because there are theoretical reasons to expect an association between poverty and national homicide rates, and in countless studies of social structure and homicide in the USA, measures of inequality and of poverty are correlated, inequality is confounded with poverty, the impact of inequality on homicide is inconsistent when poverty is included in the model (Messner & Rosenfeld, 1999), and poverty is the most consistent predictor of area homicide rates (Pratt & Cullen, 2005; Pridemore, 2002; Sampson & Lauritsen, 1994). When scholars began including poverty in models of cross-national homicide rates, (1) poverty was consistently significantly associated with homicide and (2) the inequality-homicide association disappeared or became unstable (Paré & Felson, 2014; Pridemore, 2008, 2011; Rogers & Pridemore, 2013). This included two studies (Pridemore, 2008, 2011) that used data directly from prior analyses that had found an inequality-homicide association.

A key element of the frustration-aggression explanation of the inequality-homicide association is perceived inequality: low-income residents experience inequity, perceive this distribution of resources to be unfair, become frustrated with the unjust conditions, and act aggressively due to pent-up frustration. Tests of this explanation use the Gini coefficient to measure inequality. This measure of the overall income distribution, however, is not a valid operationalization of the theoretical concept of perceived inequality, which means this hypothesis has not actually been tested by prior studies. In a recent analysis, Rogers and Pridemore (2016c) used items from the World Values Survey and the International Social Survey Programme to measure population-level perceived inequality by nation. Their findings revealed no support for an association between perceived inequality and national homicide rates.

That national levels of inequality are positively associated with national homicide rates is a widely and very strongly held belief, is sometimes tied to political ideology, and sometimes evokes a fervent response when challenged. Unlike the young-homicide association discussed above, the inequality-homicide association was long supported by several studies. However, recent research that addresses a fundamental limitation of earlier analyses provides empirical evidence this second stylized fact about cross-national homicide rates, one about which some scholars have made very strong causal statements (Fajnzylber, Lederman, & Loayza, 2002; Wilkinson, 2004), is not as stable as previously thought.

Supranational Homicide Rate Trends

There is a general belief among cross-national homicide researchers of a global trend in homicide rates, that many nations experience the same homicide rate pattern over time. Earlier tests of this notion almost exclusively utilized graphical comparisons (Tonry, 2014), concluding there was a global homicide trend since mean-centered trends appeared to be the same. Tests of this idea utilizing more rigorous analyses, however, called into question the conclusion of a global trend. For instance, LaFree and colleagues (2015) explored LaFree's (2005) "elite" nation hypothesis. They found support for a trend among highly developed Western nations but found no global trend. Rogers and Pridemore (2016d) tested for multiple supranational trends, including global, regional, and sub-regional (i.e., European regions) trends, and trends among types of nations based on wealth and on level of development. The authors found no global homicide trend. They observed the strongest trends in Eastern European nations, which cuts against the narrative offered by earlier scholars arguing for a nearly identical trend in Western European nations. When these more rigorous methods are utilized the evidence does not favor a global trend or strong trends in Western Europe (LaFree et al., 2015; Rogers & Pridemore, 2016d).

Although supranational homicide rate trends worldwide or in all Western European nations may not have reached the level of stylized fact, the existence of these trends is believed by many and some scholars make strong statements about them. Again, the evidence suggests a more tempered approach.

The Present: Recent Developments

Theory

Poverty and social protection. One emerging finding from current cross-national homicide research is a significant positive association between poverty and homicide victimization rates (Paré & Felson, 2014; Pridemore, 2008, 2011; Rogers & Pridemore, 2013, 2016e; see also Messner, Raffalovich, & Sutton, 2011). Despite the consistent finding, what remains elusive is a strong theoretical explanation that accounts for this cross-national association. While researchers proposed a wide array of explanations, many of these (1) are constructed to explain the poverty-violence association at much lower levels like neighborhoods (Sampson & Groves, 1989) and (2) provide very different and sometimes competing hypotheses. Thus, the presence of an empirical poverty-homicide association in no way provides a definitive explanation of why there is an association.

One potential partial explanation for the poverty-homicide association is the role of social protection, which could have both direct and indirect effects. Social protection can be measured as monetary and in-kind benefits provided by government and nongovernment organizations to citizens, such as subsidized housing, old-age pensions, subsidized childcare, food stamps, and unemployment or underemployment benefits. Rogers and Pridemore (2013) found direct effects of social protection on national homicide rates. They also found a moderating effect, such that the poverty-homicide association was weaker in nations that provided greater social protection. There are many theoretical reasons why social protection might influence national violence rates. Currie (1997) argued that social protection insulates citizens from economic changes in nations where a market economy has hardened culture. Rogers and Pridemore (2013) proposed that social protection might limit the effects on violence rates of the antecedents of social disorganization. The operant mechanisms suggested by Currie and by Rogers and Pridemore, however, have yet to be tested. For example, testing Currie's hypothesis would require the classification of nations into market versus nonmarket economies and exploring over time the effect of social protection on homicide rates. Testing the social disorganization hypothesis would require multilevel modeling using neighborhood data from several nations. Thus, while the consistent findings of effects of both poverty and social protection on cross-national homicide rates are compelling, especially since poverty is the most consistent predictor of small-area homicide rates in the United States, explaining how these associations operate requires further careful theoretical development.

The Criminological Transition Model. Pridemore's (2007, 2016) Criminological Transition Model (CTM) proposes that social change alters the structure and nature of human relationships in ways that have implications for the nature of crime. While other criminological theories of change focused on how societal development influences the *crime rate*, CTM focuses on how development creates shifts in social relations that influence the *character of crime*, especially offenders, victims, and events.

Prior theories of this type concentrated mainly on development's impact on crime rate trends. For example, according to Durkheim (1897/1979, 1900/1957), during revolutionary rapid change social values are unable to keep pace with the swift transformation, which leads to norm confusion, social deregulation, and thus higher crime rates. During periods of evolutionary development, on the other hand, social norms gradually shift from privileging the collective to respect for the individual, which leads to long-term declining homicide rates. Another example is the work of Elias (1939/2000), who argued that centuries-long changes in how individuals perceived and responded to the social world led them to internalize restraints on their behavior, resulting in declining violence rates. A third example is Cohen and Felson (1979), who theorized that changes in the structure of daily routine activity in the United States following World War II – driven by factors like increasing disposable incomes and more leisure time spent away from the protections of the home and family – meant more opportunities for crime and thus higher predatory crime rates. Each of these theories certainly considered changing social relations, but the main interest in them has been how this affects crime rates as opposed to how it influences the nature of crime. Pridemore's CTM addresses the latter.

The Criminological Transition Model borrows generally from the Demographic Transition Model (DTM), which also describes how development and social change lead to shifts in foundational societal characteristics. The DTM reveals how moving from a pre-industrial to industrial economy results in declining birth and death rates, creating changes in population size and age structure. When paired with concomitant development in technology, health care and sanitation, the economy, and law, the demographic transition also usually is accompanied by outcomes like greater mobility, smaller family size, later age at first marriage and first birth, and increasing life expectancy. While there is variation in how societies experience this process and while the precise mechanisms responsible for these outcomes are debated, there is overwhelming evidence for the existence of a demographic transition.

The aim of the Criminological Transition Model is to describe the impact on the nature of crime of the changing structure and character of social relations resulting from societal development.

Central to the model, the characteristics of offenders, victims, and events are likely sensitive to societal development and to changes stemming from demographic transition. At this stage in theory construction the CTM has focused mainly on the attributes of violent crime. On average, offenders may become younger as adolescence is extended (e.g., higher proportion graduating high school and attending college, declining military service) and the proportion that are women may increase as they are exposed to a broader range of experiences beyond traditional gender roles. For victims, the proportion of female to male victims could change, and sex-, age-, and ethnic-specific victimization rate ratios could shift, in part due to changes in offender characteristics given the victim-offender overlap. For events, changes in the nature of social relations could lead to systematic changes in the proportion of incidents with particular motives (e.g., argument-relative to acquisitive-related) as societies develop from pre-industrial, to industrial, to post-industrial economies; in weapon use and the primary means of assault; in the proportion of events with multiple offenders; in the rural-urban ratio of events; and in the proportion of events occurring in specific locations (e.g., in the home, in public, at work). Similarly, technological advances could: (1) result in an increasing rate and proportion of all events that are property crimes relative to violent crimes; (2) create greater opportunities for identity theft, fraud, and related cybercrimes; (3) increase the proportion of crimes committed by strangers and thus increase the average distance of the victim-offender relationship; (4) reduce the opportunity for crime-seeking or requiring cash because of the movement toward cashless societies via expansion of electronic payment systems; and (5) reduce rates of certain crime types due to greater surveillance capabilities and the omnipresence of smart phones that may reduce victimization risk in multiple ways. Although all these potential changes have implications for crime rates, especially for certain crime types, the focus of the Criminological Transition Model is on how societal development can create systematic changes in the nature of crime.

There is substantial evidence that some characteristics of homicide offenders, victims, and events change over time. Age is one clear example. Criminologists accept without question that adolescents and young adults have the highest age-specific homicide offending and victimization rates. Yet this is a recent phenomenon in the United States and is uncommon in the rest of the world. It was not until the late 1980s that the 15–24-year-old age-specific homicide victimization rate surpassed that of 25–34-year-olds (Zahn & McCall, 1999, Figure 2.3, p. 14), and the proportion of all homicide victims that were between the ages of 15 and 29 was about 80% higher in Chicago in 2000 than it was in 1900 (Gruenewald & Pridemore, 2009). And as we saw earlier, the 15–24-year-old homicide victimization rate is not usually the highest across nations or in individual nations over time (Rogers & Pridemore, 2016a). Mean offender age also appears to decline over time. Monkkonen (1999) found the peak homicide offending age among the young now present in the U.S. was much different in the nineteenth century, when age-specific homicide rates were relatively flat among those in their early 20s and above. Chervyakov et al. (2002) also showed a decline in the mean age of those convicted of homicide in Russia following the collapse of the Soviet Union.

Thacher (2004) found changes in the demographic composition of the richest and poorest income quintiles – the proportion of the population that was young, of working status, of marital status, living in cities – were partially responsible for the increasing gap in victimization rates between the rich and the poor in the United States over time. Further, in the United States there appears to be an increasing distance in the mean victim-offender relationship over time (Zahn & McCall, 1999). In addition, data from Chicago in 1900 and 2000 revealed changes in circumstance, with an increase in profit-motivated and a decrease in argument-related homicides (Gruenewald & Pridemore, 2009). Pridemore (2007) found a similar increase in profit-motivated homicides in Russia after the fall of the Soviet Union. There is also evidence that higher homicide rates in urban relative to rural areas has not always been the norm in large nations like the United States (compare New York City homicide rates in Monkkonen, 1995 to national rates in Eckberg, 1995) and Russia (Chervyakov et al., 2002).

All these systematic changes to the traits of homicide offenders, victims, and events suggest the nature of crime covaries with the character of social relations as societies develop. This requires an explanatory framework with the goals of the Criminological Transition Model, just as the Demographic Transition Model describes how development leads to changes in birth and death rates and other demographic features of nations.

Data

Each year data on homicide and on its potential structural-level explanations become increasingly available. Many data sources have gone untapped, and we will discuss a few of these toward the end of this chapter. These data can allow scholars to better measure theoretical concepts and thus to test more carefully explanations for variation in cross-national homicide rates. We briefly discuss here recent examples of how more and better data provided cross-national homicide researchers opportunities to better test the existing theories of perceived income inequality and of Institutional Anomie Theory's institutional imbalance hypothesis.

As we described above, one explanation of an inequality-homicide association is rooted in perceived inequality. Prior studies measured economic inequality via the Gini coefficient or something similar, which gauges the distribution of income and not perceived inequality, and thus did not appropriately operationalize this key theoretical concept. There is strong evidence from other fields that perceived income inequality does not necessarily closely align with an unequal income distribution and that it does not have the same effects on outcomes as measures like the Gini coefficient. For instance, when exploring the role of income inequality in the level of happiness in nations (Clark & D'Ambrosio, 2014; Ferreri-i-Carbonell & Ramos, 2013; Macunovich, 2011), researchers observed that nations with high objective income inequality (as measured by the Gini coefficient) still reported high levels of happiness, while nations with high perceived income inequality had lower levels of reported happiness and often had lower levels of objective income inequality.

Rogers and Pridemore (2016c) utilized data from the World Values Survey (WVS) and the International Social Survey Programme: Social Inequality IV (2012) and confirmatory factor analysis to create multiple population-level measures of perceived income inequality. The authors found no correlation between their measures of perceived income inequality and the Gini coefficient, and only the conceptually weakest of their measures of perceived income inequality had a significant association with homicide victimization across nations. Overall, they found little support for the perceived inequality hypothesis, but they did find a difference in population-level-perceived inequality and the Gini coefficient, which has important implications for prior conclusions about the inequality-homicide association.

Messner and Rosenfeld (2007) proposed that the strength of the economic institution relative to other institutions can create institutional imbalance and thus anomic conditions within society, which results in higher crime rates. Prior cross-national tests of Institutional Anomie theory, however, focused on the absolute strength of the economic institution or explored interaction effects of the economy with only one or two other societal institutions. By utilizing the WVS, Rogers and Pridemore (2016f) were able to better test Messner and Rosenfeld's (2007) relative institutional imbalance argument. The authors measured respondents' institutional preference by using WVS questions about the economy, family, education, religion, and polity. After creating latent variables for the strength of each institution the authors created a ratio of institutional preference for the pairing of the economy with each of the other institutions. Using these operationalizations that more closely align with Messner and Rosenfeld's key theoretical construct and that more directly measure citizens' beliefs, Rogers and Pridemore (2016f) found no support for the institutional imbalance hypothesis.

Methods

Model selection. Model selection techniques are an important tool but underutilized by criminologists. These techniques have an undeserved negative reputation for being a method of searching for significant associations. However, when utilized correctly and in an ethical manner these methods are valuable for developing and testing theory. Cross-national criminology often is variable-driven and relies on a handful of underdeveloped hypotheses culled from explanations at other levels of analysis (e.g., neighborhoods) that do not carefully consider how national-level characteristics are associated with homicide rates. By using model selection techniques like Mallow's C_p, the PRESS statistic, and Sequential ANOVAs, and fully exploring all statistics related to the model (e.g., F-statistics and mean square error) it is possible to understand the impact of each variable on the overall model. Using these techniques, Rogers and Pridemore (2016a, 2016b) found that by including both a measure of economic health and of percent-young, criminologists were overfitting models of cross-national homicide and increasing the error in estimation. Their results showed that percent-young does little to aid the model even though it is a common covariate in cross-national homicide research and many believe it to be related to homicide rates. In a forthcoming study, Rogers and Pridemore (2016g) utilized model selection techniques (Mallow's C_p and PRESS) to test four criminological theories. These techniques not only aided in narrowing down variables purported to have an association with homicide rates across nations but also allowed for stronger prediction of homicide trends.

Hypothesis testing. The goal of all research is to help create a better understanding of the world around us and to build enough knowledge to allow for causal statements. Despite decades of studies, cross-national homicide research is still in the early stages of building a foundational base. To aid in strengthening this knowledge base, criminologists should consider using both cross-sectional and pooled cross-sectional panel analyses. The two methods of statistical estimation provide unique insights into the relationship between predictor variables and outcome variables. A cross-sectional approach provides a snapshot of the association between X and homicide rates at any given time. Panel techniques allow one to test if changes in X are associated with changes in Y over time. Panel models allow for the exploration of time lapses and the ability to control for national differences not captured in the model (i.e., nation-fixed effects). However, annual data are often unavailable for a large sample of nations across time and therefore researchers should be cognizant of the limitations of the statistical estimation techniques and subsequent conclusions.

More rigorous reporting of model specification should be provided in studies of cross-national homicide. For instance, reporting post hoc power analysis should be required for models with small samples that utilize cross-sectional analyses. A small sample size does not automatically disqualify a model. If the variables in the model account for a significant portion of the variance in the outcome, a small sample model will have significant power to strengthen any of the null conclusions drawn (Cohen, 1988). In addition, for panel models researchers should justify why they use first differences and fixed vs. random effects, and to test for autocorrelation and other relevant diagnostic statistics. Panel models can be easily manipulated so that any variable of interest can be forced to be significantly associated with an outcome. Sometimes even a slight change in model specification can change conclusions. With this knowledge, criminologists should not only provide information about diagnostic statistics but also provide the data and/or the statistical output provided by their program of choice (for instance in a STATA log file). One example of this for a small but growing number of cross-national homicide studies is found here: https://sites.google.com/site/homicidedata/home/home. On this webpage, we provide the output, and often the code, for all of our analyses in our published works. Therefore, readers of our articles can access and easily replicate everything we report in our published articles.

The Future

Beyond the Usual Suspects

Most hypotheses for why some nations have higher homicide rates than others focus on three explanations: modernization, the economy, and demographic characteristics (Lynch & Pridemore, 2011; Nivette, 2011; Trent & Pridemore, 2011). Criminologists have largely ignored potential explanations from other disciplines and have been slow to innovate and to update and test their own explanations of cross-national homicide rates.

Political legitimacy. Political legitimacy is the right of the government to rule, as perceived by citizens (Gilley, 2006). Within political science there is a debate about how to operationalize political legitimacy (Beetham, 1991; Gilley, 2006; O'Kane, 1993). Given the complexity of this theoretical concept one conclusion is that a multidimensional operationalization is necessary (Gilley, 2006; Nivette & Eisner, 2013). One of the strongest measures to date is Gilley's (2006) operationalization, which takes into account legality, justification, and consent. Legality refers to alignment of laws, rules, and customs with citizens' views. Justification is citizens' agreement with the moral reasoning provided by the state for why it has the power to govern via creating and enforcing laws. Consent is actions by citizens that reveal their acceptance of the authority their government has over them.

To explain an increase in crime rates in the United States over several decades following World War II, LaFree (1998) wrote about the decline in the USA of the legitimacy of political, economic, and family institutions. Cross-national homicide researchers largely ignored LaFree's (1998) arguments, but his general ideas are supported by research in related disciplines exploring the role of legitimacy in other negative outcomes (Gilley, 2006). Two notable exceptions were Nivette and Eisner (2013) and Chamlin and Cochran (2006).

Nivette and Eisner (2013) considered the theoretical mechanism through which political legitimacy may be associated with homicide victimization across nations. They tested both the direct effect of political legitimacy and the moderating effect of legitimacy on the association between income inequality and homicide rates. The authors discussed three possible mechanisms for political legitimacy's effect: social control, self-help, and inequality. The social control argument centers on citizens' willingness to allow the government to control their behavior. Citizens are more likely to be open to control if the government is perceived as legitimate. The self-help argument states that if the government is seen as illegitimate, citizens are more likely to utilize violence to correct a perceived wrongdoing instead of relying on the police or other government agencies. Finally, the social contract would be broken if the government does not ensure economic inequality is limited. The authors only tested for a direct association between political legitimacy and homicide and for the moderating effect of political legitimacy on income inequality's association with homicide, and their results showed only a significant direct negative association between political legitimacy and homicide victimization.

Chamlin and Cochran's (2006) exploration of political legitimacy, economic inequality, and homicide suggested that the ability of political legitimacy to moderate the association between economic inequality and homicide victimization may be complicated by another factor: modernity. The authors observed a significant positive interaction between perceived illegitimacy and modernity for homicide victimization rates. Thus, the criminogenic effects of political illegitimacy and economic inequality may be limited only to modern societies. The associations observed by both Chamlin and Cochran (2006) and Nivette and Eisner (2013) provided enough evidence for the continued exploration of political legitimacy in cross-national homicide research.

One noticeable omission from both Nivette and Eisner (2013) and Chamlin and Cochran (2006) was the role political legitimacy might play in a formal test of Institutional Anomie Theory (IAT). IAT (Messner & Rosenfeld, 2007) proposes that certain cultural characteristics result in imbalances in the influences of societal institutions, and these imbalances create variation in homicide rates. Based on the discussion of legitimacy by Nivette and Eisner (2013) and Gilley (2006) it could be argued institutional imbalances lead to a reduction in political legitimacy. In these instances, citizens will no longer support the state's right to govern them because the state is overly influenced by values that privilege the economic institution. If citizens are not situated in their roles in society (based both on their obligations and relationships) societal institutions will be less able to control their behavior (LaFree, 1998; Roth, 2009). If the economic institution dominates citizens' lives it weakens the influence of other institutions. Citizens are then not obligated to these other institutions and are more likely to experience a breakdown in relationships. Messner and Rosenfeld (2007) argued a similar idea when discussing how the economy crowds out the characteristics of other institutions – such as time spent tending to family or social governance – and comes to dominate noneconomic actions (e.g., education) by turning them into transactions with a means to an end (e.g., obtaining a high-paying job instead of well-rounded knowledge). Therefore, beyond political legitimacy's potential direct or moderating effects on homicide victimization it could have implications for testing IAT.

Culture. Cultural characteristics are often ignored as population-level explanations of the cross-national variation in homicide rates (Stamatel, 2016). This is likely the result of the difficulty of trying to quantify culture. It is much easier to quantify traits like immigration, age structure, and the health of the economy than the prevailing culture and values maintained within a nation. Exploring cultural explanations for cross-national differences in homicide rates is a promising area for future research and is becoming easier to do with available data.

Quantifying cultural characteristics has already been done in other fields, and among them the work of Hofstede (1998, 2001) seems a promising avenue for criminological research. Hofstede (1998) originally measured four dimensions of culture and then expanded to six. The original four dimensions were power distance (PDI), individualism vs. collectivism (IDV), masculinity vs. femininity (MAS), and uncertainty avoidance (UAI). The additional dimensions are long- vs. short-term orientation (LTO) and indulgence versus restraint (IND).

The PDI measures the legitimacy of power, reflecting how the less powerful view the power distribution within a nation. The higher a score on this index, the more accepting the less powerful are of the nation's power distribution. Criminologists could use this to measure the political legitimacy arguments discussed above. The IDV index measures the cohesiveness of a nation. Low scores on this index reflect a nation where individuals focus on themselves and their family. High scores reflect more collective values and indicate a more cohesive society where there is the expectation of looking after each other. This measure would lend itself to exploring the role of altruism vs. egocentrism, and to testing many of Durkheim's and other theorists' arguments regarding social cohesion. The MAS index measures a "masculine" versus "feminine" society. A more masculine society is one that is achievement-oriented, assertive, and views material rewards as necessary for success. The opposite end of the index is a feminine society characterized by more cooperation, modesty, and care for the quality of life of all of society. Among others, this could be used to operationalize aspects of Messner and Rosenfeld's (2007) "American Dream" or Currie's (1997) hard culture in market societies.

The UAI index measures the ability of society to deal with uncertainty. Nations that score high on the UAI are more rigid and intolerant of unorthodox behavior. Lower scores on the UAI represent a more open society with greater tolerance for behavior outside the norms. This measure would lend itself to testing some of the arguments found within Durkheim's discussion of the collective conscience. The LTO index reflects cultural values that are based on a deep historical tradition or a more modern approach. Lower scores indicate that more time-honored traditions and norms are prominent within the culture, while nations with higher scores have a more modern approach and are accepting of and even encourage societal change instead of viewing it with suspicion. Finally, the IND index measures if a society is epicurean or more restrained. The lower the score on this index the more a society is open to enjoying life through pursuing gratification. The higher the score, the more likely the nation is to suppress gratification and have more strictly regulated societal norms.

Scholars of cross-national homicide rates could employ a latent variable structure using various data sources to generate alternative measures of culture. Such sources could include the Worlds Value Survey, European Barometer, or any survey that provides citizens from several nations a chance to express their own values and their views about their country. Whether a scholar utilizes existing measures or generates their own, one clear observation is that there is a need to explore the role of cultural differences in generating homicide rates. Previous research simply allowed culture to be captured in fixed effects for nations, while new ideas and data provide an important opportunity to better understand why violence varies across nations. One example was Stamatel (2006), who provided insight into how culture can help understand why Eastern European nations have similar trends in homicide victimization, presenting strong evidence that between-nation heterogeneity in crime could be accounted for by cultural differences.

A Whole New World of Data

A wealth of untapped data sources could help further our understanding of cross-national violence rates. We briefly describe here several sources we think contain promising information.

The International Labour Organization (ILO) (2016) provides information for approximately 187 nations on population, labor force, employment, time-related underemployment, public sector employment, unemployment, persons outside the labor force, working time, earnings and employment-related income, labor costs, consumer prices, occupational injuries, labor inspection, strikes and lockouts, the working poor, and the informal sector and informal employment. For example, as part of the working poor data, information is available for many nations regarding the number of working-age individuals with incomes below the nationally defined poverty line (based on real disposable income). The data are further disaggregated by those who are employed, unemployed, and outside the labor force.

The World Health Organization's (2015) Health Behavior in School-Aged Children (2005/2006) provides substantial information on habits of school-aged children in 43 nations (the USA, Canada, and European nations). There is a user-friendly online portal with information on alcohol use, bullying, cannabis use, fighting, sexual behavior, tobacco use, and family (e.g., mother/father live in the home, stepparents, living in foster home, number of siblings, computers in the household, going to bed hungry, SES). The data can be disaggregated from nations to national region/municipality, school number, and class number.

The World Values Survey (2014) (WVS) provides considerable information for criminologists wishing to measure perceptions of individuals embedded within nations. The WVS has multiple waves of data ranging from 1981 to 2014 for a wide array of nations. There is also an online tool available to researchers not comfortable working with the raw data (World Values Survey, 2016). The online tool allows researchers to choose from 62 nations, most all of the survey questions in the WVS, allows for a map of responses using pictograms, and even a time-series breakdown of answers to the questions for the survey questions. For researchers more comfortable working with large data sets, the raw data can be downloaded for each individual wave of the WVS and a longitudinal file is available. The WVS also often includes the European Values

Survey (EVS) for European nations. In the raw data file, a variable provides the ability to know the exact source of information (WVS vs. EVS).

The International Crime Victims Survey (ICVS) provides data on criminal victimizations. Included are both personal and household crimes (over the past five years from the date of the survey or in the last year), along with an array of socioeconomic information. Additional information is gathered from the respondent regarding the most recent victimization incident, characteristics of the perpetrator, location, and weapon presence. Since it was first fielded in 1989, the ICVS has been administered on five other occasions: 1992, 1996, 2000, 2003/ 2004, and 2010 (see van Dijk, 2008). The ICVS targets 2000 respondents within each nation from a sampling frame of households, though in some nations the target samples are not reached. Where landline telephones are widely used the ICVS employs random-digit dialing of home phone numbers stratified by local area. National samples are comprised of 2000 respondents who are generally interviewed by telephone (van Dijk 2008, p. 321–339; van Kestern, 2007; van Kesteren, Mayhew, & Nieuwbeerta, 2000). In nations where landline telephones are not sufficiently available to the population a multistage stratified sampling method is used to select target households mainly from the nation's capital or main city for purposes of efficiency. In these circumstances the survey is administered to respondents via face-to-face interviews. Surveys are conducted with one household respondent age 16+. Sampled respondents are administered a comprehensive questionnaire translated into the languages of participating countries.

The International Social Survey Programme (2012) conducts international surveys exploring various rotating themes dating back to 1985. These themes include the role of the government (1985, 1990, 1996, 2006, 2016), social networks (1986, 2001, and scheduled for 2017), social inequality (1987, 1992, 2009, and scheduled for 2019), family and changing gender roles (1988, 1994, 2002, 2012), work orientation (1989, 1997, 2005, 2015), religion (1991, 1998, 2008, and scheduled for 2018), environment (1993, 2000, 2010), national identity (1995, 2003, 2013), citizenship (2004, 2014), and health (2011). For most nations, the ISSP interviews individuals age 18 and older, though the age range of respondents can vary across nations. The sample is obtained utilizing different methods in each nation. In some nations a partly simple random sample and in others a partly multistage stratified sample is utilized. Interview mode also varies by nation, including CAPI face-to-face interviews, paper surveys, and mail surveys. The survey is translated and conducted in the respondent's native language. The sample of nations generally increases over time and can vary by topic. The data in the surveys can be utilized to measure a multitude of variables that may lend themselves to accounting for cross-national variation in violent crime rates.

Conclusion

Interpersonal violence is a serious threat to the health and stability of individuals and communities. That national homicide rates vary so widely throughout the world suggests they are in part a reflection of population-level characteristics, including elements of social structure, national culture, and the ability of governments to protect their citizens. Cross-national homicide research allows us to assess theories attempting to explain this variation and potentially to discover techniques of harm reduction.

The application of the scientific method to cross-national homicide research means we must be at the same time both conservative and progressive. We must rigorously test old and new hypotheses and discard those that analyses do not support, no matter how nice the story they tell. We must also be skeptical of what we think we know, including what many believe to be stylized facts. In the face of that conservative approach, however, we must also be progressive. We must apply the criminological imagination to the evidence and be creative in our attempts to explain variation in national homicide rates and in our use of data and method to test these explanations.

In this chapter we highlighted what we hope are some of the key elements of the past, present, and future of cross-national homicide research. We challenged stylized facts, described some current explanations and methods, and suggested what we hope are a few fruitful pathways for future research on the population-level causes of national homicide rates. Social structure and homicide are complex phenomena, and we must recognize that we are still in the early stages of understanding how they are related. After many years of largely horizontal movement in this research area, however, we are encouraged by the increasing interest in the topic, the alternative explanations that move beyond the usual suspects, the thoughtful use of data to operationalize theoretical concepts, and the application of more rigorous methods. Interpersonal violence is a destructive force and a nation's homicide rate tells us something fundamental about its institutions and organization, which makes the association between social structure on cross-national homicide rates deserving of careful and continued scholarly attention.

References

Andresen, M. A. (2012). Homicide in Lithuania. In M. C. A. Liem & W. A. Pridemore (Eds), *Handbook of European Homicide Research*. New York: Springer, pp 437–449.

Becker, G. S. (1968). Crime and punishment: An economic approach. *Journal of Political Economy*, 76, 169–217.

Beetham, D. (1991). *The Legitimation of Power*. London: MacMillan.

Bennett, R. R. (1991). Development and crime: A cross-national, time-series analysis of competing models. *Sociological Quarterly*, 32, 343–363.

Bjerregaard, B. & Cochran, J. K. (2008). A cross-national test of institutional anomie theory: Do the strength of other social institutions mediate or moderate the effects of the economy on the rate of crime? *Western Criminology Review*, 9, 31–48.

Chamlin, M. B. & Cochran, J. K. (2006). Economic inequality, legitimacy, and cross-national homicide rates. *Homicide Studies*, 10, 231–252.

Chervyakov, V. V., Shkolnikov, V. M., Pridemore, W. A., & McKee, M. (2002). The changing nature of murder in Russia. *Social Science & Medicine*, 55, 1713–1724.

Chilton, R. & Spielberger, A. (1971). Is delinquency increasing? Age structure and the crime rate. *Social Forces*, 49, 487–493.

Clark, A. E. & D'Ambrosio, C. (2014). *Attitudes to income inequality: Experimental and survey evidence*. The Institute for the Study of Labor Working Paper Series, IZA DP No. 8136.

Cohen, J. (1988). *Statistical Power Analysis for Behavioral Sciences* (2nd ed.). Hillsdale, NY: Lawrence Erlebaum.

Cohen, L. E. & Felson, M. (1979). Social change and crime rate trends: A routine activity approach. *American Sociological Review*, 44, 588–608.

Currie, E. (1997). Market, crime and community: Toward a mid-range theory of post-industrial violence. *Theoretical Criminology*, 1, 147–172.

Durkheim, E. (1897/1979). *Suicide: A study in sociology*. Translated by John A. Spaulding and George Simpson. New York: Free Press.

Durkheim, E. (1900/1957). *Professional ethics and civic morals*. Translated by Cornelia Brookfield. New York: Routledge.

Easterlin, R. A. (1987). *Birth and fortune: The impact of numbers on personal welfare*. Chicago, IL: University of Chicago Press.

Eckberg, D. L. (1995). Estimates of early twentieth-century U.S. homicide rates: An econometric forecasting approach. *Demography*, 32, 1–16.

Elias, N. (1939/2000). *The civilizing process: Sociogenetic and psychogenetic investigations*. Oxford: Blackwell Publishing.

Fajnzylber, P., Lederman, D., & Loayza, N. (2002) Inequality and violent crime. *Journal of Law and Economics*, 45, 1–40.

Ferrer-i-Carbonell, A. & Ramos, X. (2013). Inequality and happiness. *Journal of Economic Surveys*, 28, 1016–1027.

Fiala, R. & LaFree, G. (1988). Cross-national determinants of child homicides. *American Sociological Review*, 53, 432–445.

Gartner, R. (1990). The victims of homicide: A temporal and cross-national comparison. *American Sociological Review*, 55, 92–106.

Gartner, R. & Parker, R. N. (1990). Cross-national evidence on homicide and the age structure of the population. *Social Forces*, 69, 351–371.

Gilley, B. (2006). The meaning and measure of state legitimacy: Results for 72 countries. *European Journal of Political Research*, 45, 499–525.

Granath, S. (2012). Homicide in Sweden. In M. C. A. Liem & W. A. Pridemore (Eds), *Handbook of European Homicide Research: Patterns, Explanations, and Country Studies*. New York: Springer, pp 405–414.

Greenberg, D. F. (1977). Delinquency and the age structure of society. *Contemporary Crisis*, 1, 189–223.

Greenberg, D. F. (1985). Age, crime, and social explanation. *American Journal of Sociology*, 91, 1–21.

Gruenewald, J. & Pridemore, W. A. (2009). Stability and change in homicide victim, offender, and event characteristics in Chicago between 1900 and 2000. *Homicide Studies*, 13, 355–384.

Hirschi, T. & Gottfredson, M. R. (1983). Age and the explanation of crime. *American Journal of Sociology*, 89, 552–584.

Hofstede, G. H. (1998). Attitudes, values, and organizational culture: Disentangling the concepts. *Organization Studies*, 19, 477–493.

Hofstede, G. H. (2001). *Culture's consequences: Comparing values, behaviors, institutions and organization across nations*. Thousand Oaks, CA: Sage.

International Labour Organization. (2016). Statistics and database. Retrieved July 1, 2016 from www.ilo.org/global/statistics-and-databases/lang--en/index.htm.

International Social Survey Programme. (2012). Social Inequality IV. Retrieved November 2, 2015 from http://zacat.gesis.org/webview/index.jsp?v=2&submode=abstract&study=http%3A%2F%2F193.175.238.79%3A80%2Fobj%2FfStudy%2FZA5400&mode=documentation&top=yes.

Kelly, M. (2000). Inequality and crime. *Review of Economics and Statistics*, 82, 530–539.

LaFree, G. (1999). A summary and review of cross-national comparative studies of homicide. In M. D. Smith & M. A. Zahn (Eds), *Homicide: A Sourcebook of Social Research* (pp. 125–145). Thousand Oaks, CA: Sage.

LaFree, G. (1998). *Losing legitimacy: Street crime and the decline of social institutions in America*. Oxford: Westview Press.

LaFree, G. (2005). Evidence for elite convergence in cross-national homicide victimization trends, 1956 to 2000. *The Sociological Quarterly*, 46, 191–211.

LaFree, G., Curtis, K., & McDowall, D. (2015). How effective are our "better angels"? Assessing country-level declines in homicide since 1950. *European Journal of Criminology*, 12, 482–504.

Lehti, M. & Kivivuori, J. (2012). Homicide in Finland. In M. C. A. Liem & W. A. Pridemore (Eds), *Handbook of European Homicide Research*. New York: Springer, pp 391–404.

Liem, M., Ganpat, S., Granath, S., Hagstedt, J., Kivivuori, J., Lehti, M., & Nieuwbeerta, P. (2012). Homicide in Finland, the Netherlands, and Sweden: First Findings From the European Homicide Monitor. *Homicide Studies*, 17, 75–95.

Lynch, J. P. & Pridemore, W. A. (2011). Crime in the international perspective. In J. Q. Wilson & J. Petersilia, *Crime and Public Policy* (2nd ed., pp. 5–52). New York: Oxford University Press.

Lysova, A. V., Shchitov, N. G., & Pridemore, W. A. (2012). Homicide in Russia, Ukraine, and Belarus. In M. C. A. Liem & W. A. Pridemore (Eds), *Handbook of European Homicide Research*. New York: Springer, pp 451–469.

Macunovich, D. J. (2011). *A note on inequality aversion across countries, using two new measures*. The Institute for the Study of Labor Working Paper Series, IZA DP No. 5734.

Messner, S. F., Raffalovich, L. E., & Sutton, G. M. (2011). NIH Public Access, 48, 1–22.

Messner, S. F. & Rosenfeld, R. (2007). *Crime and the American Dream*. Belmont, CA: Wadsworth.

Messner, S. F. & Rosenfeld, R. (1999). Social structure and homicide: Theory and research. In M. D. Smith & M. A. Zahn (Eds), *Homicide: A sourcebook of social research* (pp. 27–41). Thousand Oaks, CA: Sage.

Monkkonen, E. H. (1999). New York City offender ages: How variable over time? *Homicide Studies*, 3, 256–270.

Monkkonen, E. H. (1995). New York City homicides: A research note. *Social Science History*, 19, 201–214.

Nivette, A. E. (2011). Cross-National Predictors of Crime: A Meta-Analysis. *Homicide Studies*, 15, 103–131.

Nivette, A. E. & Eisner, M. (2013). Do legitimate polities have fewer homicides? A cross-national analysis. *Homicide Studies*, 17, 3–26.

O'Kane, R. H. T. (1993). Against legitimacy. *Political Studies*, 41, 471–487.

Pampel, F. C. & Williamson, J. B. (2001). Age patterns of suicide and homicide mortality rates in high-income nations. *Social Forces*, 80, 251–282.

Paré, P. P. & Felson, R. (2014). Income inequality, poverty and crime across nations. *British Journal of Sociology*, 65, 434–458.

Pratt T. C. & Cullen, F. T. (2005). Assessing macro-level predictors and theories of crime: A meta-analysis. *Crime and Justice: A Review of Research*, 32, 373–450.

Pridemore, W. A. (2002). What we know about social structure and homicide: A review of the theoretical and empirical literature. *Violence & Victims*, 17, 127–156.

Pridemore, W. A. (2003). Demographic, temporal, and spatial patterns of homicide rates in Russia. *European Sociological Review*, 19, 41–59.

Pridemore, W. A. (2007). Change and stability in the characteristics of homicide victims, offenders, and incidents during rapid social change. *British Journal of Criminology*, 47, 331–345.

Pridemore, W. A. (2008). Cross-national empirical literature on social structure and homicide: A first test of the poverty – homicide thesis. *Criminology*, 46, 133–154.

Pridemore, W. A. (2011). Poverty matters: A reassessment of the inequality-homicide relationship in cross-national studies. *British Journal of Criminology*, 51, 739–772.

Pridemore, W. A. (2016). *The Criminological Transition Model: A new theory of how societal evolution influences the nature of crime*. Presentation at the annual meeting of the

American Society of Criminology. New Orleans, LA.

Rogers, M. L. (2014). A descriptive and graphical analysis of the (lack of) association between age and homicide cross-nationally. *International Criminal Justice Review*, 24, 235–253.

Rogers, M. L. & Pridemore, W. A. (2013). The effect of poverty and social protection on national homicide rates: Direct and moderating effects. *Social Science Research*, 42, 584–595.

Rogers, M. L. & Pridemore, W. A. (2016a). A Comprehensive Evaluation of the Association between Percent Young and Cross-National Homicide Rates. *British Journal of Criminology*.

Rogers, M. L. & Pridemore, W. A. (2016b). The (Null) Effects of Percent Young on 15 to 24 Age-Specific and Male- and Female-Specific Cross-National Homicide Rates. *Homicide Studies*, 20, 257–292.

Rogers, M. L. & Pridemore, W. A. (2016c). *Perceived income inequality*. Manuscript in preparation.

Rogers, M. L. & Pridemore, W. A. (2016d). *Do national homicide rates follow supranational trends?* Manuscript submitted for publication.

Rogers, M. L. & Pridemore, W. A. (2016e). *How does social protection influence cross-national homicide rates in developed nations?* Manuscript submitted for publication.

Rogers, M. L. & Pridemore, W. A. (2016f). *Not just another test of IAT: Accessing relative institutional imbalance*. Manuscript submitted for publication.

Rogers, M. L. & Pridemore, W. A. (2016g). *The utility of model selection in testing criminological theory across nations*. Manuscript in preparation.

Roth, R. (2009). *American Homicide*. Cambridge, MA: Harvard University Press.

Sampson, R. J. & Groves, W. B. (1989). Community structure and crime: Testing social-disorganization theory. *The American Journal of Sociology*, 94, 774–802.

Sampson, R. J. & Lauritsen, J. L. (1994). Violent victimization and offending: Individual-, situational-, and community-level risk factors. In A. J. Reiss & J. A. Roth (Eds), *Understanding and Preventing Violence. Volume 2: Social Influences* (pp. 1–114). Washington, DC: National Academy Press.

South, S. J. & Messner, S. F. (2000). Crime and demography: Multiple linkages, reciprocal relations. *Annual Review of Sociology*, 26, 83–106.

Stamatel, J. P. (2006). Incorporating socio-historical context into quantitative cross-national criminology. *International Journal of Comparative and Applied Criminal Justice*, 30, 177-207.

Stamatel, J. P. (2009). Correlates of national-level homicide variation in post-communist East-Central Europe. *Social Forces*, 87, 1423–1448.

Stamatel, J. P. (2016). Democratic cultural values as predictors of cross-national homicide variation in Europe. *Homicide Studies: An Interdisciplinary & International Journal*, 20(3), 239–256..

Thacher, D. (2004). The rich get richer and the poor get robbed: Inequality in US criminal victimization, 1974–2000. *Journal of Quantitative Criminology*, 20, 89–116.

Tonry, M. (2014). Why crime rates are falling throughout the western world. *Crime and Justice: A Review of Research*, 43, 1–63.

Trent, C. L. S. & Pridemore, W. A. (2011). A review of the cross-national empirical literature on social structure and homicide. In M. C. A. Liem & W. A. Pridemore (Eds), *Handbook of European Homicide Research: Patterns, Explanations, and Country Studies*. New York: Springer.

van Dijk, J. (2008). *The world of crime: Breaking the silence on problems of security, justice and development across the world*. Thousand Oaks, CA: Sage Publications.

van Kesteren, J. (2007). *Integrated database from the International Crime Victim Survey (ICVS) 1989–2005, codebook and data*. Tiburg: INTERVICT.

van Kesteren, J., Mayhew, P., & Nieuwbeerta, P. (2000). *Criminal Victimization in*

Seventeen Industrialized Countries. The Netherlands: Justice Wetenschappelijk Onderzoeken Documentaciecentrum.

Wilkinson, R. (2004). Why is violence more common where inequality is greater? *Annals of the New York Academy of Sciences*, 1036, 1–12.

World Health Organization (2015). Health Behaviour in School-Aged Children. Retrieved July 1, 2016 from http://hbsc-nesstar.nsd.no/webview/index.jsp?v=2&submode=abstract&study=http%3A%2F%2F129.177.90.126%3A80%2Fobj%2FfStudy%2FHBSC2006OAed1.0&mode=documentation&top=yes.

World Values Survey (2014). Data and Documentation. Retrieved October 24, 2014 from http://www.worldvaluessurvey.org/WVSContents.jsp.

World Values Survey (2016). Online Data Analysis. Retrieved August 1, 2016 from http://www.worldvaluessurvey.org/WVSOnline.jsp.

Zahn, M. A. & McCall, P. L. (1999). Trends and patterns of homicide in the 20th-century United States. In M. D. Smith & M. A. Zahn (Eds), *Homicide: A sourcebook of social research* (pp. 9–23). Thousand Oaks, CA: Sage Publications.

24 Preventing Violent Crimes by Reducing Wrongful Convictions

Brian Forst and C. Ronald Huff

Introduction

Violent crime continues to pose a challenge in the United States. Although homicide and violent crime rates have been dropping for decades, especially after the 1991 peak in violent crimes associated with the crack cocaine epidemic, they are still too high, especially when compared with the rates of other Western nations. In fact, the violent crime rate in the United States has recently been at the lowest level since 1970 (Federal Bureau of Investigation, 2015; Congressional Research Service, 2015). A total of 1,165,383 violent crimes (murder and non-negligent homicides, rapes, robberies, and aggravated assaults) were reported by law enforcement agencies in 2014, which reflected a 0.2% decline from 2013 (Federal Bureau of Investigation, 2015). Recently, some major cities have seen an increase in violent crime, especially homicides (Lichtblau & Davey, 2016), while other cities have seen continued declines. What is clear is that violent crime and related public safety concerns continue to rank among the most important public policy issues in the nation. Violent crime involves the interaction of a number of contributing factors, and the prevention of violent crime will require careful analysis of those factors.

In public discussions about the factors that contribute to violent crime, little attention has been paid to wrongful conviction as a contributing factor. While the public and policy-makers have become increasingly aware of the problem of wrongful conviction and are frequently informed about cases in which DNA analyses have revealed the convictions of even more innocent persons, wrongful convictions have rarely been conceptualized as a factor contributing to violent crimes in America. But false positives, also known as Type I errors (the arrests and convictions of innocent persons), and false negatives, also known as Type II errors or errors of impunity (Forst, 2004) (the failure to arrest and convict culpable offenders), are inversely related statistically. In the vast majority of cases in which an innocent person is convicted, the actual offender typically remains free to commit more offenses, including violent crimes. And so, while failure to detect, apprehend, and convict those who commit crimes occurs far more often than do wrongful convictions, the conviction of an innocent person usually represents two simultaneous errors – taking away the innocent person's freedom and allowing the actual perpetrator to remain free. Both types of errors endanger public safety and undermine the public's confidence in the criminal justice system. We have been concerned about these errors and their implications for our criminal justice system for many years (Huff, Rattner, & Sagarin, 1986, 1996; Forst, 2004, 2011).

The Costs of Miscarriages of Justice

Wrongful convictions impose avoidable costs on three groups of people: wrongfully convicted defendants and their families and close friends, victims of crimes committed by culpable offenders who have not been convicted, and the incalculable but real costs to the community associated with the loss of criminal justice legitimacy following wrongful convictions, including the reduced willingness of the public to cooperate with criminal justice officials to reduce crimes. The first and third of these may be the most substantial, but the second category – the costs of wrongful convictions on victims of crimes subsequently committed by offenders not convicted because of the wrongful conviction – are likely to be substantial nonetheless.

Let us consider the costs of crimes committed by freed, culpable offenders on the community. Crime imposes two kinds of costs on the community: those that fall directly on victims and those associated more broadly with public and private expenditures for interventions to prevent and respond to crime. The crime costs include the losses and damages to property, costs associated with injury or death (medical costs, costs of pain and suffering), and lost income. Most of these costs are borne by the victim, often over a lifetime, due to lost income.

But much is borne by the community at large – including insurance coverage of property losses and medical costs; productivity losses borne by employers and the community; victim service agency costs; and increased fear of crime in the community. The costs of prevention and response include public expenditures for the criminal justice system and outlays for security personnel; costs borne by private citizens and commercial establishments for hardware and software in security systems (locks, hardened targets, protected parking facilities, cameras, movement sensors, alarms, etc.); costs incurred by dependents of incarcerated offenders and by witnesses whose time is taken up with police interviews and court obligations; and costs associated with community crime prevention activities.

All these costs conceivably could be much smaller if the police did more to leverage their small numbers – about one sworn officer per 500 citizens overall – by enlisting the community as partners in crime prevention and control, the fundamental idea behind community policing. Wrongful convictions only add to the costs of crime by undermining police legitimacy. Citizens aware of wrongful convictions, often from direct experience, are not likely to be easily persuaded to cooperate more with criminal justice officials to reduce crime.

Estimating the Magnitude of Wrongful Convictions and Exonerations

How often does wrongful conviction occur? How many wrongful convictions are there in the United States? The short answer is that it is impossible to know the answers to these questions with certainty. In a very real sense, we don't know until we know – that is, we don't know that someone was wrongfully convicted unless and until we have solid evidence of that error. So if one were asked how many innocent people are in prison today, the honest answer is that we do not know for sure. The challenge of estimating the actual number of wrongful convictions is even more difficult than the challenge of estimating how much crime there is, since in the latter case we have developed alternate measures such as the Uniform Crime Reports and victimization surveys to discover how many citizens have been victimized by crimes. But no official governmental database keeps track of all the wrongful convictions in the United States, and a survey asking inmates how many were wrongfully convicted would quickly be dismissed, of course, as unreliable. And so this poses a formidable estimation challenge. However, even though we cannot know the answers with certainty, we can make reasonable *estimates* of both the magnitude and the frequency of these errors.

The nation's most comprehensive database on wrongful convictions, the National Registry of Exonerations (NRE), has documented 1,851 DNA and non-DNA-based exonerations (cases in which a person was wrongly convicted of a crime and later cleared of all the charges based on new evidence of innocence) for crimes that have occurred since 1989 (National Registry of Exonerations, 2016a). In addition, using DNA analysis only, the Innocence Project (2016a) has documented 342 exonerations since 1992. These two databases have provided invaluable information to researchers and others seeking to understand the factors contributing to such miscarriages of justice, as well as how often they occur. The NRE is the more comprehensive database, since it includes both DNA-based and non-DNA-based exonerations, while the Innocence Project's data are derived solely from cases in which the current "gold standard" of proof (DNA) was used to confirm innocence.

The Innocence Project has been involved in more than half of all DNA exonerations to date (Innocence Project, 2016b). Its database concentrates heavily on the minority of crimes (less than 10%) in which biological evidence was available for testing. Those crimes are disproportionately crimes of violence. DNA testing offers a dual advantage when it comes to ensuring justice and protecting public safety. If the DNA analysis excludes a suspect, defendant, or inmate as the actual perpetrator of the crime, the DNA taken from the victim and/or crime scene can also be used to try to determine who actually did commit the crime, through searching existing databases for a match. In fact, of the first 342 DNA-based exonerations, DNA evidence was used to identify 147 actual perpetrators. So in 43% of those DNA exonerations, we subsequently found out who committed those crimes. How many crimes did they commit? The Innocence Project reported that those 147 actual perpetrators were subsequently convicted of *146 additional violent crimes*, including 77 sexual assaults, 34 murders, and 35 other violent crimes while innocent individuals sat in prison for years, serving time for crimes they did not commit (Innocence Project, 2016a). These are bound to be grossly conservative estimates, since the number of crimes they actually committed is surely much higher than the number for which they were convicted.

We know that only a small sample of such injustices ever get discovered, and those cases are not representative of all wrongful conviction cases. An early attempt to estimate how often wrongful convictions occur was based on a survey that elicited the opinions of a conservative sample of law enforcement officials, judges, prosecutors, and some public defenders in Ohio, as well as all state attorneys general (Huff, Rattner, & Sagarin, 1986). That estimate, based on their collective opinions, was that about 0.5% of all felony convictions were wrongful convictions at the time. However, that survey was undertaken just before DNA began to be used in criminal cases in the United States, which began in the mid-1980s, and it took some time before old cases could be reexamined and wrongful convictions could be discovered and publicized, thus beginning to change perceptions of the error rate. More contemporary estimates of the error rate tend to be higher. Samuel Gross, a leading scholar on wrongful convictions, has estimated that between 1% and 5% of serious felony convictions in the USA are erroneous and notes that:

> If as few as 1% of serious felony convictions are erroneous, that means that perhaps 10,000–20,000 or more of the nearly 2.3 million inmates in American prisons and jails ... are innocent, and thousands of new innocent defendants are locked up each year. If the rate is higher, those numbers will go up (Gross, 2013, p. 57).

Gross et al. (2014) have also noted the relatively high rate of exoneration among those sentenced to death. He and his colleagues, using survival analysis, estimated that if all death-sentenced defendants remained under sentence of death indefinitely, at least 4.1% would be exonerated. They concluded that this is a conservative estimate of the proportion of false conviction among death sentences in the United States (Gross et al., 2014).

Using existing databases from the Innocence Project and the National Registry of Exonerations, we can make some informed estimates concerning the magnitude of wrongful convictions in violent crime cases and what implications those wrongful convictions might have for the victimization of citizens by the actual perpetrators of those crimes, who remained free for varying periods of time. Recall that the Innocence Project has documented 147 actual perpetrators who were not initially brought to justice due to the convictions of the wrong persons. Those 147 individuals were known subsequently to have committed 146 additional violent crimes for which they were convicted, or about one violent crime per offender. It is very likely that the number of violent crimes committed by these individuals exceeds the number for which they were convicted. Next, we can revisit the NRE's database, where we find that, of the 1,851 exonerations, 1,125 cases clearly involved violent crimes, as follows: 742 murders, 287 sexual assaults, and 96 robberies. Extrapolating from the Innocence Project's data to the more inclusive and comprehensive NRE data, we can infer that if each of the actual perpetrators committed only one additional violent crime, that group alone would have accounted for more than 1,000 additional violent crimes (some with multiple victims) committed by those actual perpetrators who were not brought to justice earlier.

But we know that this is only the "tip of the iceberg" when it comes to wrongful convictions, as noted by Gross (2013) and Gross et al. (2014). So it is important to think about this estimation problem in another way, as well. We know that the police made 498,666 arrests for violent crime in 2014 (Federal Bureau of

Investigation, 2015). Some of those arrests did not lead to convictions, but according to the Bureau of Justice Statistics (2016) we know that "Among felony defendants whose cases were adjudicated within the one-year tracking period (89% of cases), 68% were convicted." Based on the 498,666 arrests for violent crime in 2014, and assuming a conviction rate of ~ 68%, that would yield about 339,093 convictions in that year alone. Next, if we apply even the *lowest* error estimate of 1% based on Gross's research, that would result in 3,391 wrongful convictions for violent crimes in 2014 alone. Applying the midpoint estimate of 3% would translate to an estimated 10,173 cases of wrongful conviction in violent crimes in that year. Based on the Innocence Project's findings (one additional violent crime per actual perpetrator), that would mean that one year's cohort of about 3,000 to 10,000 wrongful convictions for violent crimes could involve actual perpetrators who might subsequently commit 3,000 to 10,000 additional violent crimes (one each) while the wrong persons were incarcerated. That possibility is magnified by the facts that (1) the estimate is only for *one cohort* of offenders based on one year's worth of data (2014) and (2) the estimate does not include the 57% of DNA exonerations reported by the Innocence Project for which no actual perpetrators were identified.

A unique and valuable study (Baumgartner et al., 2014) provides us with an opportunity to see how the problem of wrongful conviction led to subsequent victimizations by true perpetrators in the state of North Carolina during the time between the date of the original crime and the date when they were arrested. The authors referred to this as a period of "wrongful liberty." Using the National Registry of Exonerations database and supplementing it with some wrongful convictions that had occurred prior to 1989 (the earliest cases included in the NRE database), the researchers analyzed 36 exonerations. They then identified nine true perpetrators who had not been brought to justice in those cases. In one case, the true perpetrator was arrested at the same time as the exoneree, which left eight cases with known perpetrators in their sample. Following up on the criminal histories of those eight perpetrators, they discovered that subsequent crimes were committed in six of those eight cases. Those six individuals were arrested and convicted of 99 subsequent crimes, including 35 felonies and 16 crimes of violence. The researchers noted, however, that "Since we lack complete information for the criminal records of some true perpetrators and about the identities of true perpetrators in several cases, these are very conservative estimates" (Baumgartner et al., 2014, p. 8). The 36 exonerees had collectively served nearly 400 years in prison for crimes they did not commit.

Therefore, although it is not possible to say with precision exactly how many (or what percentage of) wrongful convictions occur each year in cases involving violent crimes, we can make some informed estimates based on several existing databases, and those estimates suggest that we could reduce violent crimes in the United States by reducing the number of wrongful convictions in cases involving violent crimes and improving our ability to identify, convict, and incarcerate the true perpetrators of those crimes.

How do these wrongful convictions occur? What factors contribute to these errors? According to an analysis of the first 1600 exonerations reported by the

National Registry of Exonerations, official misconduct was the second leading factor that contributed to those wrongful convictions, following the leading factor – cases involving perjury or false accusations (National Registry of Exonerations, 2016c). The Registry defines official misconduct as follows: "Police, prosecutors, or other government officials significantly abused their authority or the judicial process in a manner that contributed to the exoneree's conviction" (National Registry of Exonerations, 2016d). Official misconduct was a contributing factor in 45% of those 1600 wrongful convictions, including 60% of the homicides; 30% of the robberies; 23% of sexual assaults; and 44% of other violent crimes. Since the great majority of this official misconduct involved police and prosecutors, the following discussion will focus on those errors and how they might be reduced.

Opportunities in Policing to Reduce Wrongful Convictions

To assess the extent of wrongful convictions and their effects on crime, we begin with law enforcement, since policing is the initial stage of the formal criminal justice process. Errors associated with the police have many origins. The police rely on information from a variety of sources, each of which may be seriously flawed. They often base arrest decisions on information provided by witnesses and informants of questionable credibility, and occasionally on misleading evidence at or near a crime scene. Their skills in identifying errors in these various sources of information, to seek out more pertinent evidence, and in using common-sense logic to validate their inferences vary from officer to officer and, because of organizational differences, from department to department.

As for individual cases, wrongful convictions typically begin with a call for service: an automated or manual alarm signal, a 911 call, or an in-person summons to the police. What the responding officers and investigators do, or fail to do, and how well they do it can have a profound impact on the ability of the police to solve crimes and reduce erroneous detentions and arrests. In responding, the police can misidentify suspects, often soon after arriving at a destination. Whether, and when, to designate a person officially as a suspect varies from department to department depending on the availability of resources, written and unwritten procedures, and a host of other factors; there is no single standard under the law. The responding officer typically files a report naming any and all suspects.

Wrongful convictions may be especially common for high-visibility unsolved cases, when the police are under greater pressure to find a pool of candidate suspects and solve the crime. Suspects are sometimes identified using modus operandi (MO) files and unreliable offender descriptions. Among a pool of initial suspects, one person typically emerges as the leading suspect, but a *leading* suspect does not automatically qualify as a *likely* suspect. The designation of "suspect" or "person of interest" can impose costs on the persons so named and is likely to impose other costs as well, most notably a tendency to expend resources on the wrong person while the true offender flies under the radar. The FBI's erroneous identification of Richard Jewell as the prime suspect in the fatal bombing at the 1996 Olympic Games in Atlanta is a prominent example when the police are under extraordinary pressure to solve a case (Ostrow, 2000). Other examples are the investigations of Wen Ho Lee and, following the extraordinary anthrax murders of 2001, Steven Hatfill as well – but the FBI's eagerness to report progress in each of these cases proved costly to their reputation. High-visibility cases call not only for good judgment in the identification of suspects, but for discretion in deciding what information to give to the media.

Policing errors that give rise to wrongful convictions range from fairly innocuous to grievous. Some of the errors are random and unavoidable; others are both systematic and systemic, associated with accountability systems that excessively encourage crime clearances and arrests, or characterized by various combinations of police frustrations, racism, and ethnic hatred. The systemic errors play out in a variety of aspects of policing: investigative and forensic failures; tunnel vision; interrogation practices leading to false confessions; and the improper use of informants and snitches.

One of the most frequent errors contributing to false convictions is mistaken witness identification (Donigan & Fisher, 1980; Huff, Sagarin, & Rattner, 1996; Scheck, Neufeld, & Dwyer, 2001). Two factors are especially common in cases involving mistaken witness identification: victims and witnesses not getting a good look at the offender in the first place, and police having a strong interest in solving the crime, often because it is serious or involves an offender in whom the police have developed a stake in arresting and convicting (Huff et al., 1996). Time is another factor: witnesses' memories of events tend to decay over time (Baddeley, Thompson, & Buchanan, 1975). Fear that overwhelms the senses is yet another factor: research findings to date give us reasons not to accept every witness claim of having been so frightened that the offender's face is accurately etched forever on the witness's memory (Huff et al., 1996).

Police lineups can be useful for confirming the accuracy of a witness's identity of an offender, but they can also introduce error when the witness either identifies a wrong person as the offender (either by chance or because the police bias the procedure) or fails to identify the actual offender standing in line. Defense counsel, especially those appointed by the court, cannot always be counted on to challenge improper lineup procedures at trial.

The police have been known to produce other sorts of testimonial evidence leading to wrongful convictions, including the improper use of informants; false accusations by people with an animus against an innocent person; the "jailhouse snitch"; and police inducements of false confessions, in violation of the Fifth Amendment protection against self-incrimination (Huff et al., 1996; Scheck et al., 2001). The police are responsible for minimizing the prospects for all such errors, but excessive zeal to solve crimes and incompetence have been found occasionally to get in the way (Connors et al., 1996; Scheck et al., 2001).

Several recommendations have been advanced to reduce law enforcement errors, including improved procedures for recruiting and screening and for training new officers (at formal police academies, in periodic retraining, and in on-the-job training programs; improved systems of accountability; improved systems for promoting officers and recruiting effective leaders; lab accreditation; and federal oversight). Recommendations to improve each of these aspects of police organization and management have been advanced by authorities ranging from public organizations, such as the National Academy of Sciences and the National Science Foundation, to private non-profit organizations, such as the Police Foundation, the Police Executive Research Forum, the International Association of Chiefs of Police, and the National Sheriffs Association (National Research Council, 2015; Willis, 2013).

One of us has proposed another reform: The police should focus not just on incriminating information, but should be no less interested in exculpatory information for an identified suspect. If the police focus excessively on catching criminals and too little on minimizing errors of false arrest, they risk losing credibility in the community and may end up less able to control crime than if they find a balance that minimizes the total social costs of false arrests and failures to arrest culpable offenders. Such a balance would serve the interests of justice and enhance police legitimacy as well (Forst, 2004, 2011).

Rank-and-file police officers are often less than enthusiastic about such reforms. Many have been profoundly frustrated by facing life-endangering risks with little appreciation and plenty of criticism. As for police frustrations and ethnic hatreds, it would help immensely for the police and politicians alike to acknowledge and confront a polarizing media and political climate that has legitimized these deep enmities. For example, the police are likely to find more members of the general public willing to sign on to the Police Lives Matter movement when they see more police genuinely supporting Black Lives Matter sentiments in the community.

Of particular interest to our inquiry, studies of police malpractices and the reforms recommended have not asked this basic question: Do some of the known sources of wrongful convictions lead to more crimes in the community than others? It is likely that some wrongful arrests and convictions have ended investigations that would have otherwise led to the arrest and conviction of the actual offender. It is equally likely that other wrongful arrests and convictions changed little, since the police would have ended the investigation in those cases anyway because resources were limited and other matters were perceived to be more pressing. It is virtually impossible to determine the actual prevalence of each of these prospects.

Of this we can be clear: The most serious type of police error that has contributed to crime is the killing of innocent persons – as we have witnessed in Ferguson, Missouri, Baltimore, Maryland, and elsewhere over the past few years. These cases do not produce wrongful convictions or allow culpable offenders to go free, but they are extreme forms of police miscarriages of justice that have enraged minority communities and set off deadly rounds of tit-for-tat killings of police in Dallas, Minneapolis, Baton Rouge, and elsewhere in 2016. They have also undermined police legitimacy and eroded important gains made under the community policing movement of the 1980s and 1990s (Chan, 2016). It may be no coincidence that the widespread attention given to these grievous acts has been followed by an uptick in crime in several urban areas in 2015 and 2016 after a significant and fairly steady decline in every category of crime over the previous 25 years (Davey & Smith, 2015).

The broadening gap between the police and minority communities strikes us as one of the great challenges to urban policing in the twenty-first century. A return to the principles of community policing set forth by Robert Peel in 1829 (Stewart, 2013) and about 150 years later by Herman Goldstein and others (Goldstein, 1977; Greene, 2000) could do much to improve policing generally and, more particularly, to reduce wrongful convictions and crime.

Opportunities in Prosecution to Reduce Wrongful Convictions

In the US criminal justice system, the prosecutor is arguably the single most powerful figure, yet the one who occupies the least visible role in the entire system. The prosecutor wields extensive authority in deciding whether to order an arrest; whom to charge or not charge with crimes; what crimes to charge them with; what evidence must be disclosed to the defense; whether or not to propose a plea agreement and, if so, what terms should be in that proposal; and what sentencing recommendations to make to the judge. In addition, the prosecutor can decide to drop charges at any time in the interest of justice. The prosecutor's duty, under our system, is to pursue justice, not just win convictions. This duty is affirmed by the American Bar Association's (ABA) *Standards for Criminal Justice* (1993a): "The duty of the prosecutor is to seek justice, not merely to convict"; by its *Model Rules of Professional Conduct* (American Bar Association, 1993b): "A prosecutor has the responsibility of a minister of justice and not simply of an advocate"; and by the *National Prosecution Standards* adopted by the National District Attorneys Association (2009): "The primary responsibility of a prosecutor is to seek justice, which can only be achieved by the representation and presentation of the truth."[1]

Also, when new evidence suggests innocence, the pursuit of truth is an absolute obligation. According to the *Model Rules of Professional Conduct*, Rule 3.8 (Special Responsibilities of a Prosecutor), when a prosecutor knows of "new, credible and material evidence creating a reasonable likelihood that a convicted defendant did not commit an offense of which the defendant was convicted," the prosecutor has an obligation to investigate, and if there is "clear and convincing evidence establishing that a defendant in the prosecutor's jurisdiction was convicted of an offense that the defendant did not commit, the prosecutor shall seek to remedy the conviction" (American Bar Association, 1993b).

The reality, however, is that some prosecutors violate these ethical norms in ways that help convict the innocent while allowing the guilty to remain free to commit crimes, some of which are violent. Some have even done so in multiple cases, representing a group that we might call "rogue prosecutors" or even "recidivist prosecutors," since their repeated ethical violations stand in such stark contrast with the ethical values of the profession.

---

1 An obvious antidote to the prosecutor's extraordinary power is to raise the standards of proof at every stage in the process. Obvious solutions, however, are not always prudent. Under a large variety of assumptions, it has been found that raising evidentiary standards to an extent that produces a 10% reduction in the conviction rate from current margins approximately doubles the number of true offenders set free per innocent person convicted and increases the total error rate by about 10% (Forst, 2004, p. 64). This would be a particularly counterproductive way to reduce crime.

The Innocence Project (2016b) lists the following types of prosecutorial misconduct that are often involved in cases resulting in wrongful conviction and exoneration:

- withholding exculpatory evidence from defense
- deliberately mishandling, mistreating, or destroying evidence
- allowing witnesses they know, or should know, are not truthful to testify
- pressuring defense witnesses not to testify
- relying on fraudulent forensic experts or evidence known to be fraudulent
- making misleading arguments that overstate the probative value of testimony

Space limitations preclude a discussion of all of these types of prosecutorial misconduct, but it is important to examine two of them in closer detail: *Brady* violations and the improper use of confidential informants, or "snitches."

Brady Violations

One of the most frequent types of prosecutorial misconduct in these miscarriages of justice involves "*Brady* violations." The US Supreme Court, in *Brady v. Maryland* (1963), ruled that "the suppression by the prosecution of evidence favorable to an accused upon request violates due process where the evidence is material either to guilt or punishment, irrespective of the good faith or bad faith of the prosecution." However, and despite the fact that this is an affirmative and mandatory obligation, violations of *Brady* have become increasingly apparent in cases of wrongful conviction, prompting Chief Judge Alex Kozinski of the Ninth Circuit Court of Appeals to state:

There is an epidemic of *Brady* violations abroad in the land. Only judges can put a stop to it … A robust and vigorously enforced *Brady* rule is imperative because all the incentives prosecutors confront encourage them not to discover or disclose exculpatory evidence. Due to the nature of a *Brady* violation, it's highly unlikely wrongdoing will ever come to light in the first place. This creates a serious moral hazard for those prosecutors who are more interested in winning a conviction than serving justice (*United States v. Olsen*, 2013).

In the most comprehensive study of prosecutorial misconduct in the Nation's largest state, California, researchers analyzed 4,000 publicly available cases in which prosecutorial misconduct was alleged to have occurred. Upon review, courts found that such misconduct had indeed occurred in 707 of those cases. However, they ruled that, in 548 cases, the prosecutorial error was "harmless" and that the defendant had received a fair trial. Shockingly, only six disciplinary actions against prosecutors were reported (Ridolfi & Possley, 2010). And despite their violations of professional ethics, the names of such prosecutors are often redacted from reports.

Prosecutors who commit these violations often substitute a "win at all costs" philosophy in place of their duty to seek justice, not just convictions. With such extensive discretionary authority, some prosecutors fall victim to Lord Acton's (1887) well-known warning: "Power tends to corrupt, and absolute power corrupts absolutely." But another critical dynamic is often at work – tunnel vision, which is a normal human occurrence, but one that can and does often result in identifying the wrong suspect and prematurely closing leads to the actual perpetrator. In an excellent paper on tunnel vision as it relates to wrongful conviction, Findley and Scott (2006) discuss two major cognitive components of tunnel vision: *confirmation bias* (the tendency to seek or interpret evidence in ways that support existing beliefs, expectations, or hypotheses) and *belief perseverance* or *belief persistence* (the tendency to resist changing our beliefs, even when faced with new evidence that is inconsistent with our initial beliefs). We see tunnel vision at work not only in the police and prosecutorial errors that help convict the wrong person but even following a DNA-based exoneration, when some prosecutors continue to insist that the exonerated person is, nonetheless, guilty. Recall that the Innocence Project reports that in 43% of DNA exonerations, the DNA was used to identify the actual perpetrator. Yet some prosecutors are so unwilling to acknowledge their error that they fail to request that the DNA be used to try and identify the actual perpetrator.

Unreliable "Snitch" Testimony

The misuse of confidential informants, or "snitches," has been an important factor in the United States and has been among the leading contributors to wrongful convictions in capital cases. One of the major types of prosecutorial misconduct has involved "jailhouse snitches" who testify against the defendants or suspects in return for favorable considerations in their own cases. Some have been used by prosecutors repeatedly. As one of us has pointed out elsewhere:

> (I)t is, at the very least, ironic that these same people, when they were coming before the court as defendants in their own cases, would never have been believed by the prosecutors, but now that they say they can help convict someone else, they are suddenly transformed into credible witnesses (Huff, 2016).

Some of these prosecutorial abuses have led to scandals involving "snitch testimony" in a number of jails and in the well-known case of Thomas Sophonow, a Canadian who was implicated by three jailhouse informants as the man responsible for a homicide. Upon examination of that case, it became clear that prosecutorial misconduct included undisclosed incentives for informant testimony, the use of an informant with a prior conviction for perjury, and obvious signs of unreliable testimony. The inquiry in that case led to important reforms that included limits on the use of such informant testimony, and the report stated, in part:

> Jailhouse informants comprise the most deceitful and deceptive group of witnesses known to frequent the courts ... They must be recognized as a very great danger to our trial system (Manitoba Justice, 2001).

What can be done to reduce these prosecutorial abuses? It is essential that reforms begin with a critical examination of the organizational culture in prosecutors' offices. That culture must emphasize the ethical duty of prosecutors to seek justice, not just convictions. Incentives and recognitions must be structured in such a way as to emphasize the importance of being a "minister of justice." That begins with leadership at the top. Consistent with a minister-of-justice model is the value of transparency. Toward that end, all states should follow the example of those states that have already adopted the "full file" or "open file" discovery model, in which the prosecutor's full file is open to the defense, as well. Why not adopt this approach if one's goal is to seek the truth? While not a total safeguard against prosecutorial misconduct by keeping important information out of the files, it would be an important step forward. It would also be helpful to utilize role-playing techniques, as some prosecutors' offices already do, prior to seeking indictments and convictions in major cases in which one assigned role is to challenge the evidence and argue against indictment or conviction. This technique can be very useful in resisting the common problems of groupthink and tunnel vision.

Finally, reforms should include a reassessment of the virtual immunity and absence of sanctions that currently characterizes prosecutorial misconduct leading to wrongful convictions. Immunity from sanctions should not attach in those cases where prosecutors have *knowingly* withheld potentially exculpatory evidence. Why should they be immune from sanctions in such cases? And why, when such unethical behavior has helped put innocent defendants in prison, should the prosecutors' names be redacted from investigative reports? How does that further the objective of deterrence in such cases? Or of transparency and prosecutorial legitimacy? Finally, meaningful sanctions for prosecutorial misconduct will also depend heavily on improved vigilance and willingness to take action by the disciplinary committees of state and local bar associations. Attorneys in the United States enjoy a monopoly since no one can practice law without a license, and, in return for that monopoly, their associations must take more responsibility for protecting the integrity of their profession. Cases of intentional misconduct by prosecutors, if proven, should result in disbarment and, when appropriate, criminal or civil penalties.

Conclusion

Wrongful convictions harm society in several ways. First and foremost, they are a gross injustice to the wrongfully convicted who, along with their families, bear the brunt of the harm. They harm the community as well by allowing the true perpetrators to go free and commit further crimes, including many violent crimes. And they undermine the legitimacy of the criminal justice system, even when they go undetected, reducing the public's willingness to cooperate with the criminal justice system. This chapter has provided a rough estimate of the number of violent crimes committed each year by actual perpetrators due to wrongful convictions.

One overarching need emerges from this analysis: the considerable social costs of wrongful convictions cries out for a stronger set of incentives for police and prosecutors to reduce the rate of wrongful convictions and the crimes that occur as a result. By reducing wrongful convictions, respect for the criminal justice system can be enhanced and violent crimes can be prevented by ensuring that the actual perpetrators do not remain free to continue inflicting harm on the community.

Further work is needed to refine our estimates of the number of actual offenders who escape due to wrongful convictions. Questions remain at the initial stages of the process, beginning with awareness that a crime was committed, continuing on to crimes known but not reported to the police, the decision of police to arrest, decisions of prosecutors to accept and process cases, jury decisions, and judicial decisions to review convictions when evidence emerges of a wrongful conviction. How each of the known sources of error – witness misidentification, police misconduct, forensic error, prosecutor misconduct, perjury, and so on – plays out at each of these stages remains a largely unresolved issue.

We can't answer all these questions, but we can at least frame the inquiry by identifying the essential ingredients and using informed judgment to decide where to focus, recognizing the flaws in the temptation to look for the keys under the DNA lamppost because the light is better there. This won't solve the vexing issues involved, but it can help make us usefully humble in dealing with this very serious, but complex, problem.

References

Acton, J. E. E. D. (Lord Acton) (1887). Letter to Bishop Mandell Creighton. April 5, 1887. Retrieved August 5, 2016 from oll.libertyfund.org/index.php?option=com_content&task=view&id=1407&Itemid=283.

American Bar Association (1983a). *Standards for Criminal Justice*. Prosecution Function, 2d Def. Function § 3-1.2(b) and (c).

American Bar Association (1983b). *The Model Rules of Professional Conduct*, §3.8.

Baddeley, A. D., Thompson, N., & Buchanan, M. (1975). Word length and the structure of memory. *Journal of Verbal Learning and Verbal Behaviour*, 1, 575–589.

Baumgartner, F., Grigg, A., Ramirez, R., Rose, K., & Lucy, J. S. (2014). The mayhem of wrongful liberty: Documenting the crimes of true perpetrators in cases of wrongful incarceration." Unpublished paper presented at the Innocence Network Conference, Portland, OR, April 11.

Bureau of Justice Statistics (2016). What is the probability of conviction for felony defendants? Retrieved July 24, 2016 from www.bjs.gov/index.cfm?ty=qa&iid=403.

Center for Prosecutor Integrity (2013a). An epidemic of prosecutor misconduct. Retrieved August 4, 2016 from www.prosecutorintegrity.org/wp-content/uploads/EpidemicofProsecutorMisconduct.pdf.

Center for Prosecutor Integrity (2013b). Most Americans doubt fairness of criminal justice system. June 11, 2013.

Chan, S. (2016). Shootings in Dallas, Minnesota and Baton Rouge: What we know. *New York Times*. July 8, 2016. Retrieved July 24, 2016 from www.nytimes.com/2016/07/09/us/dallas-attacks-what-we-know-baton-rouge-minnesota.html.

Congressional Research Service (2015). Is Violent Crime in the United States Increasing? Washington, DC: Congressional Research Service, October 29, 2015. Retrieved July 24, 2016 from www.fas.org/sgp/crs/misc/R44259.pdf.

Davey, M. & Smith, M. (2015). Murder Rates Rising Sharply in Many U.S. Cities. *New York Times*. August 31, 2015. Retrieved July 24, 2016 from www.nytimes.com/2015/09/01/us/murder-rates-rising-sharply-in-many-us-cities.html.

Donigan, R. L. & Fisher, E. C. (1980). *The Evidence Handbook* (4th ed.). Evanston, IL: Traffic Institute, Northwestern University.

Federal Bureau of Investigation (2015). Crime in the United States: 2014. Washington, DC: Federal Bureau of Investigation. Retrieved July 24, 2016 from https://ucr.fbi.gov/crime-in-the-u.s/2014/crime-in-the-u.s.-2014.

Findley, K. & Scott, M. S. (2006). The multiple dimensions of tunnel vision in criminal cases. *Wisconsin Law Review*, 2, 291–397.

Forst, B. (2004). *Errors of Justice*. New York: Cambridge University Press.

Forst, B. (2011). Managing miscarriages of justice from victimization to reintegration. *Albany Law Review*, 74(3), 1209–1275

Goldstein, H. (1977). *Policing in a Free Society*. New York: Harper-Collins.

Greene, J. R. (2000). *Community Policing in America: Changing the Nature, Structure, and Function of the Police. Volume 3: Policies, Processes, and Decisions of the Criminal Justice System*. Washington, DC: National Criminal Justice Reference Service.

Gross, S. R. (2013). How many false convictions are there? How many exonerations are there? In C. R. Huff & M. Killias (Eds), *Wrongful Convictions and Miscarriages of Justice: Causes and Remedies in North American and European Criminal Justice Systems* (pp. 45–59). New York: Routledge.

Gross, S. R., O'Brien, B., Hu, C., & Kennedy, E. H. (2014). Rate of false conviction of criminal defendants who are sentenced to death. *Proceedings of the National Academy of Sciences*, 111 (20): 7230–7235.

Huff, C. R. (2016). Wrongful convictions: Psychological and criminal justice system contributors. In A. Kapardis & D. P. Farrington (Eds), *The Psychology of Crime, Policing and Courts*. New York: Routledge.

Huff, C. R., Rattner, A., & Sagarin, E. (1986). Guilty until proved innocent: Wrongful conviction and public policy. *Crime & Delinquency*, 32, 518–544.

Huff, C. R., Rattner, A., & Sagarin, E. (1996). *Convicted but Innocent: Wrongful conviction and public policy*. Thousand Oaks, CA: Sage.

Innocence Project (2016a). DNA Exonerations in the United States. Retrieved July 22, 2016 from www.innocenceproject.org/dna-exonerations-in-the-united-states/.

Innocence Project (2016b). Government Misconduct. Retrieved August 5, 2016 from www.innocenceproject.org/causes/government-misconduct/.

James, N. (2015). Is violent crime in the United States increasing? Washington, DC: Congressional Research Service, October 29.

Lichtblau, E. & Davey, M. (2016). Homicide rates jump in many major US cities, new data shows. *New York Times*. May 13, 2016. Retrieved July 22, 2016 from www.nytimes.com/2016/05/14/us/murder-rates-cities-fbi.html.

Manitoba Justice (2001). *The Inquiry Regarding Thomas Sophonow*. Retrieved August 11, 2016 from http://digitalcollection.gov.mb.ca/awweb/pdfopener?smd=1&did=12713&md=1.

National District Attorneys Association (2009). *National Prosecution Standards* (3rd ed.), Amended 2009, Section 1–1.1.

National Registry of Exonerations (2016a). Home page. Retrieved July 22, 2016 from www.law.umich.edu/special/exoneration/Pages/about.aspx.

National Registry of Exonerations (2016b). Resources: Interactive Data Display. Retrieved July 22, 2016 from www.law.umich.edu/special/exoneration/Pages/Exonerations-in-the-United-States-Map.aspx.

National Registry of Exonerations (2016c). The first 1600 exonerations. Retrieved August 5, 2016 from www.law.umich.edu/special/exoneration/Documents/1600_Exonerations.pdf.

National Registry of Exonerations (2016d). Glossary and Criteria for Exoneration. Retrieved August 5, 2016 from www.law.umich.edu/special/exoneration/Pages/glossary.aspx.

National Research Council (2015). *Identifying the Culprit: Assessing Eyewitness Identification*. Washington, DC: National Academy of Sciences Committee on Scientific Approaches to Understanding and Maximizing the Validity and Reliability of Eyewitness Identification in Law Enforcement and the Courts. Retrieved July 25, 2016 from http://sites.nationalacademies.org/PGA/stl/Eyewitness_ID/index.htm.

Ostrow, R. J. (2000). Richard Jewell Case Study. Columbia University. Retrieved July 25, 2016 from www.columbia.edu/itc/journalism/j6075/edit/readings/jewell.html.

Purdy, M. (2001). The Making of a Suspect: The Case of Wen Ho Lee. *New York Times*. February 4, 2001. Retrieved August 16, 2016 from www.nytimes.com/2001/02/04/us/the-making-of-a-suspect-the-case-of-wen-ho-lee.html.

Ridolfi, K. M. & Possley, M. (2010). *Preventable error: A report of prosecutorial misconduct in California 1997–2009*. Santa Clara, CA: Northern California Innocence Project, Santa Clara University School of Law.

Scheck, B., Neufeld, P., & Dwyer, J. (2001). *Actual innocence: When justice goes wrong and how to make it right*. New York: New American Library/Penguin.

Stewart, J. (2013). *Peel's Principles of Law Enforcement*. Marron Institute of Urban Management, New York University. Retrieved August 16, 2016 from http://marroninstitute.nyu.edu/content/blog/peels-principles-of-law-enforcement.

Willis, J. (2013). *Improving Police: What's Craft Got to Do With It?* Washington, DC: Police Foundation.

Cases

Brady v. Maryland, 373 U.S. 83 (1963).

United States v. Olsen, 2013 WL 6487376 (9th Cir. 2013). Dissent by Chief Judge Alex Kozinski.

25 Strain Theory and Violent Behavior

Robert Agnew and Byongook Moon

Introduction

Strain theories state that certain strains or stressors increase the likelihood of violence. These strains upset individuals, creating pressure for corrective action. Some individuals may respond in a violent manner, with violence being used to reduce the strain being experienced and/or obtain revenge against the source of the strain or related targets. For example, individuals may rob someone to get the money they desperately need or assault the person who has been harassing them. Whether individuals cope with strains through violence depends on their ability to engage in legal and violent coping, the costs of violence for them, and their disposition for violence. Violence is defined as the actual, attempted, or threatened use of physical force for the purpose of inflicting unwanted physical or nonphysical harm on another person(s).

These are several versions of strain theory, the most recent and comprehensive being Agnew's general strain theory (Agnew, 1992, 2006). General strain theory (GST) draws heavily on prior strain theories (e.g., Berkowitz, 1989; Cloward & Ohlin, 1960; Cohen, 1955; Elliott, Ageton, & Canter, 1979; Greenberg, 1977; Merton, 1938), as well as on the stress, justice, and emotions literatures. This article focuses on GST, examining (1) the types of strains most likely to lead to violence; (2) why certain strains lead to violence; (3) why some individuals are more likely than others to respond to strains with violence; and (4) how group differences in violence can be explained, including age, gender, class, and race/ethnic differences.

The Types of Strains Most Likely to Lead to Violence

Strains refer to events and conditions that are disliked by the individual. There are three major types of strains. First, individuals may lose something they value; for example, their money or property may be stolen, a close friend or family member may die, or a romantic partner may break up with them. Second, individuals may be treated in an aversive or negative manner by others; for example, they may be sexually abused by family members or insulted by peers. Third, individuals may be unable to achieve their goals through legal channels; for example, they may be unable to obtain the money, status, or autonomy they want. Although GST focuses on the individual's personal experiences with strains, certain "vicarious" and "anticipated" strains may also contribute to violence (Agnew, 2002; Lin, Cochran, & Mieckowski, 2011). Vicarious strains refer to strains experienced by others around the individual, like family members and close friends. Anticipated strains refer to the individual's expectation that his or her current strains will continue or that new strains will be experienced.

Many hundreds of specific strains fall into the three major categories of strains listed by GST. GST, however, states that only certain of these strains increase the likelihood of violence (Agnew, 2001). In particular, a strain is most likely to lead to violence when the following occur:

A. The strain is seen as severe or high in magnitude. Strains are more likely to be seen as severe when they are high in degree (e.g., much money is lost, there is much physical injury); they are frequent, recent, of long duration, and expected to continue; and they threaten the core needs, goals, values, activities, and/or identities of the individual.
B. The strain is seen as unjust. Strains are more likely to be seen as unjust when they involve the voluntary and intentional violation of a relevant justice norm.
C. The strain is associated with low social control. That is, the strain does *not* involve close supervision by conventional others, such as parents and teachers; close ties to conventional others; a strong investment in conventional institutions, such as school and work; or the acceptance of conventional beliefs and values. This is the case, for example, with parental rejection. Children who are rejected by their parents generally have weak ties to their parents and are poorly supervised by them. However, this is not the case with that type of strain experienced by professionals who work long hours. This strain is associated with a strong investment in conventional institutions and the acceptance of conventional values.
D. The strain creates some pressure or incentive for violent coping. Certain strains are more easily resolved through violence and/or less easily resolved through nonviolent channels than are other strains. For example, that type of strain involving a desperate need for money is more easily resolved through violence than is that type involving the inability to achieve educational success. Also, certain strains involve exposure to others who model violence, reinforce violence, or teach beliefs favorable to violence. For example, individuals who experience child abuse are exposed to violent models.

Drawing on these characteristics, Agnew (2001) lists several specific strains that should have a relatively strong effect on violence. These strains include parental rejection; parental supervision that is erratic, excessive, and/or harsh; child abuse and neglect; negative secondary school experiences, including poor relations with teachers; abusive peer relations, including insults, ridicule, threats, attempts to coerce, and physical assaults; work in the secondary labor market (poorly paid jobs with unpleasant working conditions); chronic unemployment; marital problems, including frequent conflicts and verbal and physical abuse; criminal victimization; homelessness; experiences with race-/ethnic- and gender-based discrimination; and the inability to achieve certain goals – such as money and masculine status – through legal channels. Data suggest that these strains do increase the likelihood of crime and violence. In fact, certain of these strains – like criminal victimization – are the most important causes of criminal behaviors (e.g., Agnew, 1990, 1992,

2001, 2002, 2006; Agnew & Brezina, 1997; Agnew & White, 1992; Aseltine, Gore, & Gordon, 2000; Baron, 2004; Colvin, 2000; Eitle, 2002; Eitle & Turner, 2002; Hagan & McCarthy, 1997; Hay & Evans, 2006; Kort-Butler, 2010; Manasse & Ganem, 2009; Moon, Blurton, & McCluskey, 2008; Moon & Morash, 2013; Ousey, Wilcox, & Schreck, 2015; Simons, Chen, Stewart, & Brody, 2003).

Those strains which should have a relatively weak effect on violence include those which are not likely to be seen as unjust, such as strains that are the result of reasonable accident, natural causes, or the victim's own behavior; for example, strains are part of many stressful life event scales, such as accidents, serious illness, and family members leaving home for school. Still other strains should have a relatively weak effect on violence because they are associated with high social control or little pressure/incentive for violence. Such strains include the burdens associated with the care of conventional others, like children and sick/disabled spouses (except for family violence); the excessive demands associated with conventional pursuits that provide rewards like high pay and prestige; unpopularity with peers, especially criminal peers; isolation from unsupervised peer activities; and the failure to achieve goals such as educational and occupational success (which imply some commitment to conventional values).

Why Certain Strains Increase the Likelihood of Violence

Certain strains increase the likelihood of violence because they reduce the individual's ability to cope in a legal manner, reduce the perceived costs of violence, and create a disposition for violence. This section first describes how the experience of these strains may lead to a particular incident of violence or a series of related incidents, then describes how the chronic or repeated experience of these strains may create a general predisposition or willingness to engage in violence if provoked or tempted.

Particular incidents of violence. The high magnitude of those strains conducive to violence reduces the ability of individuals to cope in a legal manner. It is generally more difficult to legally cope with large rather than small strains. For example, it is more difficult to legally obtain a large rather than small amount of money. Likewise, it is more difficult to ignore repeated abuse than a single, minor slight.

The unjust nature of those strains conducive to violence contributes to anger. This anger, in turn, increases the likelihood of violence. Anger reduces the ability to cope in a legal manner, making it more difficult for the individual to reason with others. Anger also reduces the individual's awareness of and concern for the costs of crime (individuals are "consumed with rage"). Further, anger creates a disposition for violence, fostering the belief that violence is justified (to "right a wrong") and creating a desire for revenge. Empirical studies of GST indicate that strains substantially increase the likelihood that individuals will become angry, which in turn leads to crime, including violent crime (Hay & Evans, 2006; Jang, 2007; Jang & Johnson, 2003; Mazerolle, Piquero, & Capowich, 2003, Moon et al., 2009). The larger literature on anger is also compatible with these findings (e.g., Averill, 1982).

Strains conducive to violence may also temporarily reduce the individual's level of social control. For example, juveniles who are harshly punished by parents may come to dislike their parents for a brief period, or adults who are treated poorly at work may temporarily reduce their commitment to work. Finally, these strains may temporarily foster the social learning of crime. In particular, certain of these strains – like abuse and criminal victimization – involve exposure to others who model violence. Such exposure may lead individuals to (temporarily) conclude that violence is an appropriate or desirable coping mechanism.

A predisposition for violence. Chronic or repeated exposure to strains may create a predisposition for violence. Chronic or repeated strains reduce the ability of individuals to cope in a legal manner, since they tend to exhaust the individual's coping resources and social supports. Chronic or repeated strains may also foster negative emotional traits, like trait anger. Emotional traits are distinct from emotional states, with traits referring to the tendency to experience particular emotions. Someone high in trait anger, for example, tends to get angry a lot. They are upset by a broader range of factors than others and experience more intense anger when upset (Mazerolle, Piquero, & Capowich, 2003). Chronic strains may lead to trait anger partly because they reduce the individual's ability to legally cope, so that new strains are more likely to overwhelm the individual and elicit strong emotional reactions. Several studies indicate that individuals who experience more strains are higher in trait anger, and that such anger partly explains the effect of strains on violence (e.g., Agnew, 1985; Aseltine, Gore, & Gordon, 2000; Brezina, 1998; Mazerolle & Piquero, 1998; Moon et al., 2009).

Related to the above, chronic strains may foster personality traits conducive to crime, like low constraint and negative emotionality (Agnew, Brezina, Wright, & Cullen, 2002). Individuals subject to harsh, erratic treatment from parents, teachers, peers, and others may fail to develop self-restraint. In particular, data suggest that individuals develop self-restraint partly as a result of being consistently sanctioned in an appropriate manner when they misbehave (Colvin, 2000; Hay, 2003). Chronic mistreatment by others may also foster certain of the other traits that comprise low constraint and negative emotionality, including a tendency to attribute strains to the malicious behavior of others, little concern for the feelings or rights of others, and an antagonistic interactional style. These traits, in turn, reduce the ability to cope in a legal manner, reduce the awareness of and concern for the costs of violence, and create a predisposition for violence.

Further, chronic strains may reduce the individual's level of social control. Many of the above strains involve negative treatment by conventional others. This includes abuse and harsh discipline by parents; demeaning treatment by teachers; conflict with spouses; unemployment; and work in poorly paid, unpleasant jobs. Such strains may reduce the individual's emotional bond to conventional others. They may also reduce the individual's investment in conventional society, including the individual's commitment to school and work (see Bao, Haas, Chen, & Pi, 2012). In addition, they may reduce the extent to which the individual is supervised and sanctioned by others, since they may cause the individual to avoid or retreat from conventional others. These effects, in turn, may reduce the individual's acceptance of conventional values since the individual's ties to those who teach such values are weakened. Certain studies support these arguments, with data suggesting that chronic or repeated experiences with strains contribute to reductions in social control (Elliott, Huizinga, & Ageton, 1985; Hoffmann & Miller, 1998; Paternoster & Mazerolle, 1994).

In addition, chronic strains may foster the social learning of violence. In particular, the victims of chronic strains are more likely than others to associate with violent peers who model violence, reinforce violence, and teach beliefs favorable to violence. Those experiencing chronic strains often view violent peers as a solution to their strains. For example, individuals who cannot achieve status through conventional channels may join violent groups like gangs because the gang makes them feel important and respected (see Cohen, 1955). Likewise, individuals who cannot achieve their monetary goals through conventional channels may join violent groups in an effort to better achieve such goals (e.g., through robbery, drug-selling). Interviews with gang members support this argument, and quantitative studies indicate that juveniles experiencing more strains are more likely to join violent groups like gangs and delinquent peer groups (Agnew, 2005a; Bao et al., 2012; Eitle, Gunkel, & Van Gundy, 2004; Paternoster & Mazerolle, 1994).

Finally, chronic strains may directly foster the belief that violence is a desirable, justifiable, or excusable response to strains. Individuals experiencing chronic strains may believe that they have few legal options for dealing with such strains and that they are being unjustly treated by others. Further, their ties to conventional others and institutions may be weakened as a consequence of their strains. Such individuals may come to adopt beliefs favorable to violence. For example, Anderson (1994) states that many of the residents of poor, inner-city communities respond to the regular assaults on their status and physical safety by adopting the "code of the street," which justifies violent responses to even minor shows of disrespect.

Why Some Individuals Are More Likely to Respond to Strains with Violence

While certain strains increase the likelihood of violence, most individuals do not respond to these strains with violence. Juveniles who are subject to peer abuse, for example, may ignore such abuse, redefine such abuse in a way that minimizes its negative impact, reason with the abusers in an effort to get them to stop, or notify the authorities. GST, therefore, lists those individual and environmental characteristics that increase the likelihood that strained individuals will engage in violence (Agnew, 1992, 2006). These characteristics influence the ability to engage in legal and violent coping, the costs of violence, and the individual's disposition for violence.

Individuals are said to be most likely to cope with strains through violence if the following occur:

A. They have limited skills and resources for legal coping. Among other things, they are low in intelligence, have personality traits like low constraint and negative emotionality (are quick to anger and disposed to aggressive responses), have poor social and problem-solving skills, are low in self-efficacy (believe they lack the ability to cope in a legal manner), and have low socio-economic status.

B. They have abundant skills and resources for violent coping. Among other things, they have personality traits conducive to violence, like low constraint and negative emotionality. They are of large size, are physically strong, and possess fighting skills. They have ready access to a gun, and they are high in "violent self-efficacy" (believe they have the ability to successfully engage in violence).

C. They have low levels of conventional social support. That is, others, such as parents, teachers, and employers, are unlikely to provide them with assistance in coping with strains, including information, material assistance, emotional support, and direct assistance.

D. They are low in social control. In particular, they are not closely supervised by others and are not consistently sanctioned for violence; they have weak ties to conventional others; they have little investment in conventional institutions; and they do not believe that violence is wrong. Those low in social control are more likely to perceive the costs of violence as low.

E. They associate with violent others. These others are more likely to model violence, reinforce violence, and teach beliefs favorable to violence, thereby influencing the individual's disposition for violence. Others may also provide the individual with assistance in carrying out violent acts, thereby influencing their ability to engage in violence. Further, others may lower the perceived costs of violence, because they are seen engaging successfully in violence and there is strength in numbers.

F. They have beliefs favorable to violence. Although few individuals unconditionally approve of violence, some do believe that violence is desirable, justifiable, or excusable in certain situations. For example, they believe that violence is a justifiable response to a wide range of provocations, including what many would regard as mild insults.

G. They are in situations where the costs of violence are low and the benefits are high. The situational costs of violence are partly a function of the perceived ability of the target to resist violence and the likelihood that others will come to the aid of the target. In this area, Felson (1996) has found that small people seldom attack big people. The benefits of violence include the reduction of strain, as well as social approval from others, including audience members.

There has been some research on the extent to which certain of these factors influence or condition the effect of strains on crime, including violence. This research has produced mixed results (e.g., Agnew et al., 2002; Agnew & White, 1992; Aseltine, Gore, & Gordon, 2000; Baron, 2004, 2009; Botchkovar, Tittle, & Antonaccio, 2009; Mazerolle & Maahs, 2000; Moon et al., 2009; Paternoster & Mazerolle, 1994). For example, some studies suggest that strains are more likely to lead to crime and violence among those who associate with delinquent peers, while other studies do not. These mixed results may reflect the fact that it is difficult to detect conditioning effects using the survey research methods that criminologists commonly employ (McClelland & Judd, 1993). They may also reflect the fact that researchers rarely consider the individual's overall standing on the above factors; rather, they usually focus on one factor, with other factors controlled. Agnew (2013) argues that individuals must possess several of the above factors before the likelihood of violent coping becomes high (Mazerolle & Maahs, 2000).

Using GST to Explain Group Differences in Violence

Rates of criminal violence are higher among males, adolescents and young adults, lower-class individuals, the residents of economically deprived communities, and the members of certain race and ethnic groups, such as African-Americans (Agnew, 2005a). GST helps explain such differences by arguing that the members of these groups are more likely to experience strains conducive to violence and to cope with these strains through violence. GST can also help explain patterns of violent offending over the life-course, including that "life-course-persistent" pattern in which individuals commit relatively high rates of violence over much of their lives.

Gender differences in violence. Data suggest that females are as likely as or more likely than males to experience strains or stressors. At the same time, there is reason to believe that males are more likely to experience many of those strains conducive to violence, including harsh discipline by parents, abusive peer relations, criminal victimization, and the inability to achieve their monetary and masculine status goals (Agnew, 2006; Broidy & Agnew, 1997; Moon & Morash, 2014; Morash & Moon, 2007). Many of the strains more often experienced by females are not conducive to most forms of violence. This is particularly true of the burdens associated with caring for others, like children and sick or disabled spouses. These burdens tie females to the home, impose time-consuming obligations on them, and increase the costs of violence because violence may jeopardize their ability to care for others. These burdens, however, may be conducive to family violence, an area where gender differences in offending are relatively small. At the same time, it is important to note that females are more likely to experience certain strains conducive to violence, like sexual abuse and gender discrimination (Chesney-Lind, 1989; Eitle, 2002; Moon & Morash, 2014). Also, the number of females experiencing monetary strain has increased dramatically in recent decades, due largely to an increase in the number of female-headed households. Sexual abuse by family members is a major source of serious female crime, with females often running away to escape from such abuse and engaging in a range of crimes to survive on the street. The increase in monetary strain has been used to explain the fact that females have come to commit a larger share of most crimes in recent years (Heimer, 2000). GST, however, argues that, overall, males are more likely to experiences those strains conducive to violence and this partly explains their higher rates of violence.

GST also states that males are more likely than females to cope with strains through violence, although the data are somewhat mixed in this area (e.g., Broidy & Agnew, 1997; Hoffman & Su, 1997; Mazerolle, 1998; Moon & Morash, 2014; Piquero & Sealock, 2004). There are several possible reasons why males may be more prone to violent coping. Males are more likely to experience moral outrage in response to strains, with such outrage being conducive to other-directed violence. While females are as likely as males to get angry when they experience strains, the anger of females is more often accompanied by depression, guilt, anxiety, and shame. It is said that females more often blame themselves when experiencing strains, view their anger as inappropriate, and worry about hurting others and jeopardizing relationships. Males, however, are quicker to blame others for their strains, are less concerned about hurting others, and often view anger as an affirmation of their masculinity.

Gender differences in coping skills and resources may also explain why males may be more likely to engage in violent coping (Broidy & Agnew, 1997; Moffitt et al., 2001; Steffensmeier & Allan, 1996). Among other things, males are more likely to be lower in constraint and higher in negative emotionality, lower in certain types of conventional social support, and larger and physically stronger than females. Further, males are lower in certain types of social control than females. In particular, males are less well supervised by parents, more weakly tied to school, and less likely to believe that violence is wrong. Finally, males are more likely to associate with violent others and hold beliefs favorable to violence.

Age differences in violence. Age, along with gender, is the strongest socio-demographic correlate of violence, with the rates of violence among adolescents and very young adults exceeding those of other age groups. GST argues that part of the reason for this is that adolescents/young adults are more likely to experience strains conducive to violence (Agnew, 1997). Such individuals, in particular, are no longer closely protected by parents, but they have not yet formed families of their own or developed careers. Further, they interact with a larger, more diverse group of people, including many people they do not know well. This reflects the fact that they frequently attend large, diverse schools and have more active social lives. These factors increase the likelihood that they will be in situations where the risk of negative treatment is high; for example, they are more likely to spend time with peers in unstructured, unsupervised activities (Osgood, Wilson, O'Malley, Bachman, & Johnston, 1996).

In addition, adolescents and young adults come to develop a strong desire for goals such as money, status, and autonomy from others, reflecting their biological maturity and changed social circumstances. But they often have trouble achieving such goals through legal channels. For example, teachers and others often treat them in a demeaning manner and their legal sources of income are limited, so they experience increased levels of goal blockage. Limited data provide some support for these arguments, suggesting that several types of strain are more common among adolescents and young adults, including criminal victimization (Agnew, 1997, 2003).

Unfortunately, adolescents/young adults are also more likely than children and adults to cope with the strains they experience in a violent manner. Unlike children, they cannot rely on parents to cope on their behalf or provide extensive social support. Unlike adults, they are often deficient in social and problem-solving skills and in coping resources like power and money. Adolescents/young adults, however, are at the peak of their physical condition, increasing their ability to engage in violent coping. They are also lower in several types of social control than children and/ or adults, including supervision, ties to conventional others, investment in conventional activities, and beliefs condemning crime. Finally, adolescents/young adults are much more likely to associate with violent others and hold beliefs favorable to violence. Adolescents and young adults, then, experience more strains conducive to violence and are more likely to cope with such strains through violence.

Class differences in violence. GST argues that lower-class individuals have higher rates of violence partly because they are more likely to experiences strains like family problems, including harsh discipline and abuse; school problems; peer abuse; criminal victimization; homelessness; chronic unemployment; work in unpleasant jobs; and difficulty achieving monetary and status goals. In addition, lower-class individuals are more likely to cope with strains in a violent manner. They lack certain legal coping skills and resources, most notably money. They are lower in many types of social control, such as their investment in conventional institutions. They are more likely to associate with violent others, partly because they more often live in communities where such others are common. Finally, they are more likely to hold beliefs favorable to violence (see Agnew, 2005b).

Community differences in violence. Rates of violence are much higher in some communities than others, with the highest rates in very poor communities with high rates of mobility and family disruption. Part of the reason for these high rates has to do with the characteristics of the people who live in these communities, but there is some reason to believe that the nature of the community itself exerts an independent effect on levels of violence.

Residence in a deprived community contributes to several strains conducive to violence. In particular, data suggest that even after individual characteristics are taken into account, the residents of deprived communities have more trouble achieving their monetary and status goals. Among other things, the residents of deprived communities have less access to stable, well-paying jobs, which tend to be located outside the community, and to individuals with job connections. There are also fewer individuals in the community to teach and model those skills and attitudes necessary for successful job performance. The residents of such communities are also more likely to experience other strains, including family problems, such as abuse and harsh discipline; school problems; chronic unemployment; work in unpleasant jobs; peer abuse; criminal victimization; homelessness; and discrimination (Agnew, 1999, 2005a, 2006; Brezina, Piquero, & Mazerolle, 2001; Hay, Fortson, Hollist, Altheimer, & Schaible, 2006; Hoffmann, 2003; Warner & Fowler, 2003).

The residents of deprived communities are also more likely to respond to strains with violence. The residents of such communities are not only less able to legally cope as individuals, but are also less able to cope as a community. That is, they are less able to unite with one another to solve community problems. High levels of poverty, family disruption, and mobility impede efforts at collective problem-solving. In addition, levels of social control are lower in such communities, with residents being less likely to socialize young people in a conventional manner and intervene when violence occurs. Further, criminal groups are more common in such communities, and community residents – particularly young males – are more likely to develop values conducive to violence (Agnew, 1999, 2005a, 2006; Warner & Fowler, 2003).

Race/ethnic differences in violence. Certain race and ethnic groups, such as African-Americans and Latinos, have higher rates of violence than other groups (Hawkins, 2003). A substantial part of the reason for this is that the members of these groups are more likely to experience stressful events (Eitle & Turner, 2003) as they are poor and live in high-poverty communities (although most African-Americans and Hispanics are not poor). Poor African-Americans, in particular, are several times more likely to live in high-poverty communities than poor whites. As a consequence, African-Americans are more likely to experience strains conducive to violence and react to these strains with violence for reasons just indicated. In addition, African-Americans are subject to a range of discriminatory treatment by school officials, police, and others that results in additional strains beyond those associated with economic level. Further, African-Americans may be more likely to attribute the strains they experience to unjust treatment (Kaufman, Rebellon, Thaxton, & Agnew, 2008).

Patterns of violence over the life-course. Finally, GST can explain patterns of violence over the life-course, including the "life-course-persistent" pattern, in which individuals tend to commit relatively high rates of violence over much of their lives (Agnew, 1997, 2003, 2006; Moffitt, 1993). While life-course-persistent offenders make up a small portion of the population, they account for a large share of all violence, including a majority of serious violence.

GST argues that individuals engage in high rates of violence over their lives partly because they are more likely to experience strains conducive to violence and react to them with violence. This may occur because they develop the traits of low constraint and negative emotionality early in life. Individuals with these traits tend to provoke negative reactions from others. For example, they are more likely to antagonize parents, who may reject them or respond in a harsh manner. In addition, such individuals are more likely to select themselves into aversive environments, where they are treated in a negative manner by others. For example, they are more likely to be rejected by conventional peers and associate with delinquent peers, end up in unpleasant jobs, and be unmarried or involved in "bad" marriages. Further, such individuals are more likely to interpret events and conditions in a negative manner. That is, they are more easily upset than others and quicker to blame their strains on the malicious behavior of others. The more frequent strains experienced by these individuals directly contributes to high levels of crime and violence (Hoffmann & Cerbone, 1999). Such strains also help maintain the traits of low constraint and negative emotionality, as indicated earlier. Finally, such individuals are more likely to cope with strains in a violent manner (Agnew et al., 2002; Walsh, 2000).

Some individuals may also engage in high levels of violence over their lives because they are members of the urban underclass; that is, they are very poor individuals living in poor communities. As indicated above, such individuals are more likely to experience a range of strains conducive to violence and they are more likely to cope with these strains through violence. The violence of these individuals, in turn, has consequences that increase the likelihood of further violence over the life-course. Such violence, in particular, is likely to provoke negative treatment from others, thereby contributing to further strain. In addition, such violence reduces the likelihood of escape from the underclass, with violence impeding school performance and reducing prospects for decent work (De Li, 1999; Tanner, Davies, & O'Grady, 1999).

Conclusion

GST is based on a simple idea: if you treat people badly, they may respond with violence. GST, however, elaborates on this idea in several ways. In particular, GST describes those types of negative treatment most likely to increase violence, why such treatment increases violence, the characteristics of individuals most likely to engage in violent coping, and the effect of group characteristics on the experience of and reaction to strains. GST is compatible with other theories of violence, including bio-psychological, control, and social learning theories. Most notably, variables from these theories help explain why certain types of strain are more conducive to violence and why certain individuals are more likely to engage in violent coping. Further, the variables from these theories may mutually influence one another (e.g., personality traits like low constraint and negative emotionality contribute to strains, while strains contribute to these traits). Nevertheless, GST is distinct from these theories, with GST focusing on the effect of disliked events and conditions on violence and explaining this effect partly through negative emotions like anger.

References

Agnew, R. (1985). A revised strain theory of delinquency. *Social Forces*, 64, 151–167.

Agnew, R. (1990). The origins of delinquent events: An examination of offender accounts. *Journal of Research in Crime and Delinquency*, 27, 267–294.

Agnew, R. (1992). Foundation for a general strain theory of crime and delinquency. *Criminology*, 30, 47–87.

Agnew, R. (1997). Stability and change in crime over the life course: A strain theory explanation. In T. P. Thornberry (Ed.), *Developmental theories of crime and delinquency, Advances in criminological theory, Volume 7*, (pp. 101–132). New Brunswick, NJ: Transaction.

Agnew, R. (1999). A general strain theory of community differences in crime rates. *Journal of Research in Crime and Delinquency*, 36, 123–155.

Agnew, R. (2001). Building on the foundation of general strain theory: Specifying the types of strain most likely to lead to crime and delinquency. *Journal of Research in Crime and Delinquency*, 38, 319–361.

Agnew, R. (2002). Experienced, vicarious, and anticipated strain: An exploratory study focusing on physical victimization and delinquency. *Justice Quarterly*, 19, 603–632.

Agnew, R. (2003). An integrated theory of the adolescent peak in offending. *Youth & Society*, 34, 263–299

Agnew, R. (2005a). *Juvenile delinquency: Causes and control*. Los Angeles: Roxbury.

Agnew, R. (2005b). *Why do criminals offend? A general theory of crime and delinquency*. Los Angeles: Roxbury.

Agnew, R. (2006). *Pressured into crime: An overview of general strain theory*. Los Angeles: Roxbury.

Agnew, R. (2013). When criminal coping is likely: An extension of general strain theory. *Deviant Behavior*, 34, 653–670.

Agnew, R. & Brezina, T. (1997). Relational problems with peers, gender, and delinquency. *Youth & Society*, 29, 84–111.

Agnew, R., Brezina, T., Wright, J. P., & Cullen, F. T. (2002). Strain, personality traits, and delinquency: Extending general strain theory. *Criminology*, 40, 43–72.

Agnew, R. & White, H. R. (1992). An empirical test of general strain theory. *Criminology*, 30, 475–499.

Anderson, E. (1994). The code of the streets. *Atlantic Monthly*, 273 (May), 81–94.

Aseltine, R. H., Jr., Gore, S., & Gordon, J. (2000). Life stress, anger and anxiety, and delinquency: An empirical test of general strain theory. *Journal of Health and Social Behavior*, 41, 256–275.

Averill, J. R. (1982). *Anger and aggression: An essay on emotion*. New York: Springer-Verlag.

Bao, W. N., Haas, A., Chen, X., & Pi, Y. (2012). Repeated strains, social control, social learning, and delinquency: Testing an integrated model of general strain theory in China. *Youth & Society*, 46, 402–424.

Baron, S. W. (2004). General strain, street youth and crime: A test of Agnew's revised theory. *Criminology*, 42, 457–483.

Baron, S. W. (2009). Street youths' violent responses to violent personal, vicarious, and anticipated strain. *Journal of Criminal Justice*, 37, 442–451.

Berkowitz, L. (1989). The frustration-aggression hypothesis: An examination and reformulation. *American Psychologist*, 45, 494–503.

Botchkovar, E. V., Tittle, C. R., & Antonaccio, O. (2009). General strain theory: Additional evidence using cross-cultural data. *Criminology*, 47, 131–176.

Brezina, T. (1998). Adolescent maltreatment and delinquency: The question of intervening processes. *Journal of Research in Crime and Delinquency*, 35, 71–99.

Brezina, T., Piquero, A. R., & Mazerolle, P. (2001). Student anger and aggressive behavior in school: An initial test of Agnew's macro-level strain theory. *Journal of Research in Crime and Delinquency*, 38, 362–386.

Broidy, L. & Agnew, R. (1997). Gender and crime: A general strain theory perspective. *Journal of Research in Crime and Delinquency*, 34, 275–306.

Chesney-Lind, M. (1989). Girls' crime and woman's place: Toward a feminist model of female delinquency. *Crime and Delinquency*, 35, 5–29.

Cloward, R. & Ohlin, L. (1960). *Delinquency and opportunity*. Glencoe, IL: Free Press.

Cohen, A. K. (1955). *Delinquent boys*. Glencoe, IL: Free Press.

Colvin, M. (2000). *Crime & coercion*. New York: St. Martin's Press.

De Li, S. (1999). Legal sanctions and youths' status achievement: A longitudinal study. *Justice Quarterly*, 16, 377–401.

Eitle, D. J. (2002). Exploring a source of deviance-producing strain for females: Perceived discrimination and general strain theory. *Journal of Criminal Justice*, 30, 429–442.

Elliott, D., Ageton, S. & Canter, R. (1979). An integrated theoretical perspective on delinquent behavior. *Journal of Research in Crime and Delinquency*, 16, 3–27.

Eitle, D., Gunkel, S., & Van Gundy, K. (2004). Cumulative exposure to stressful life events and male gang membership. *Journal of Criminal Justice*, 32, 95–111.

Elliott, D., Huizinga, D., & Ageton, S. S. (1985). *Explaining delinquency and drug use*. Beverly Hills, CA: Sage.

Eitle, D. & Turner, R. J. (2002). Exposure to community violence and young adult crime: The effects of witnessing violence, traumatic victimization, and other stressful life events. *Journal of Research in Crime and Delinquency*, 39, 214–237.

Eitle, D. & Turner, R. J. (2003). Stress exposure, race, and young adult male crime. *The Sociological Quarterly*, 44, 243–269.

Felson, R. (1996). Big people hit little people: Sex differences in physical power and interpersonal violence. *Criminology*, 34, 433–452.

Greenberg, D. F. (1977). Delinquency and the age structure of society. *Contemporary Crises*, 1, 189–223.

Hagan, J. & McCarthy, B. (1997). *Mean streets*. Cambridge: Cambridge University Press.

Hawkins, D.F. (2003). *Violent Crime: Assessing Race and Ethnic Differences*. Cambridge: Cambridge University Press.

Hay, C. (2003). Family strain, gender, and delinquency. *Sociological Perspectives*, 46, 107–136.

Hay, C. & Evans, M. M. (2006). Violent victimization and involvement in delinquency: Examining predictions from general strain theory. *Journal of Criminal Justice*, 34, 261–274.

Hay, C., Fortson, E. N., Hollist, D. R., Altheimer, I., & Schaible, L. M. (2006). The impact of community disadvantage on the relationship between the family and juvenile crime. *Journal of Research in Crime and Delinquency*, 43, 326–356.

Heimer, K. (2000). Changes in the gender gap in crime and women's economic marginalization. In G. LaFree (Ed.), *The Nature of crime: Continuity and change, Criminal justice 2000, Volume 1* (pp. 427–483). Washington, DC: National Institute of Justice.

Hoffmann, J. P. & Cerbone, F. G. (1999). Stressful life events and delinquency escalation in early adolescence. *Criminology*, 37, 343–374.

Hoffman, J. P. & Su. S. S. (1997). The conditional effects of stress on delinquency and drug use: A strain theory assessment of sex differences. *Journal of Research in Crime and Delinquency*, 34, 46–78.

Hoffmann, J. (2003). A contextual analysis of differential association, social control, and strain theories of delinquency. *Social Forces*, 81, 753–786.

Jang, S. J. (2007). Gender differences in strain, negative emotions, and coping behaviors: A general strain theory approach. *Justice Quarterly*, 24, 523–553.

Jang, S. J. & Johnson, B. R. (2003). Strain, negative emotions, and deviant coping among African Americans: A test of general strain theory. *Journal of Quantitative Criminology*, 19, 79–105.

Kaufman, J. M., Revbellon, C. J., Thaxton, S., & Agnew, R. (2008). A general strain theory of racial differences in criminal offending. *The Australian and New Zealand Journal of Criminology*, 41, 421–437.

Kort-Butler, L. A. (2010). Experienced and vicarious victimization: Do social support and self-esteem prevent delinquent responses? *Journal of Criminal Justice*, 38, 496–505.

Lin, W. H., Cochran, J. K., & Mieczkowski, T. (2011). Direct and vicarious violent victimization and juvenile delinquency: An application of general strain theory. *Sociological Inquiry*, 81, 195–222.

Mazerolle, P. & Piquero, A. (1998). Linking exposure to strain with anger: An investigation of deviant adaptations. *Journal of Criminal Justice*, 26, 195–211.

Mazerolle, P. (1998). Gender, general strain, and delinquency: An empirical examination. *Justice Quarterly*, 15, 65–91.

Manasse, M. E. & Ganem, N. M. (2009). Victimization as a cause of delinquency: The role of depression and gender. *Journal of Criminal Justice*, 37, 371–378.

Mazerolle, P. & Maahs, J. (2000). General strain and delinquency: An alternative examination of conditioning influences. *Justice Quarterly*, 17, 323–343.

Mazerolle, P., Piquero, A. R., & Capowich, G. F. (2003). Examining the links between strain, situational and dispositional anger, and crime. *Youth & Society*, 35, 131–157.

McClelland, G. H. & Judd, C. M. (1993). Statistical difficulties of detecting interactions and moderator effects. *Psychological Bulletin*, 114, 376–390.

Merton, R. K. (1938). Social structure and anomie. *American Sociological Review*, 3, 672–682.

Moffitt, T. E. (1993). Adolescence-limited and life-course persistent antisocial behavior: A developmental taxonomy. *Psychological Review*, 100, 674–701.

Moffitt, T. E., Caspi, A., Rutter, M., & Silva, P. A. (2001). *Sex Differences in Antisocial Behaviour*. Cambridge: Cambridge University Press.

Moon, B., Blurton, D., & McCluskey, J. D. (2008). General strain theory and delinquency focusing on the influences of key strain characteristics on delinquency. *Crime & Delinquency*, 54, 582–613.

Moon, B. & Morash, M. (2013). General strain theory as a basis for the design of school interventions. *Crime & Delinquency*, 59, 886–909.

Moon, B. & Morash, M. (2014). Gender and general strain theory: A comparison of strains, mediating, and moderating effects explaining three types of delinquency. *Youth & Society*, Published online January 16. doi: 10.1177/0886260513516863.

Moon, B., Morash, M., McCluskey, C. P., & Hwang, H. W. (2009). A comprehensive test of general strain theory key strains, situational-and trait-based negative emotions, conditioning factors, and delinquency. *Journal of Research in Crime and Delinquency*, 46, 182–212.

Paternoster, R. & Mazerolle, P. (1994). General Strain Theory and delinquency: A replication and extension. *Journal of Research in Crime and Delinquency*, 31, 235–263.

Osgood, D. W., Wilson, J. K., O'Malley, P. M., Bachman, J. G., & Johnston, L. D. (1996). Routine activities and individual deviant behavior. *American Sociological Review*, 61, 635–655.

Ousey, G. C., Wilcox, P., & Schreck, C. J. (2015). Violent victimization, confluence of risks and the nature of criminal behavior: Testing main and interactive effects from Agnew's extension of General Strain Theory. *Journal of Criminal Justice*, 43, 164–173.

Piquero, N. L. & Sealock, M. D. (2004). Gender and general strain theory: A preliminary test of Broidy and Agnew's gender/GST hypotheses. *Justice Quarterly*, 21, 125–158.

Simmons, R. L., Chen, Y., Stewart, E. A., & Brody, G. H. (2003). Incidents of discrimination and risk for delinquency: A longitudinal test of strain theory with an African American sample. *Justice Quarterly*, 20, 827–854.

Steffensmeier, D., & Allan, E. (1996). Gender and crime: Toward a gendered theory of female offending. *Annual Review of Sociology*, 22, 459–487.

Tanner, J., Davies, S., & O' Grady, B. (1999). Whatever happened to yesterday's rebels? Longitudinal effects of youth delinquency on education and unemployment. *Social Problems*, 46, 250–274.

Warner, B. D. & Fowler, S. K. (2003). Strain and violence: Testing a general strain theory model of community violence. *Journal of Criminal Justice*, 31, 511–521.

Walsh, A. (2000). Behavior genetics and anomie/strain theory. *Criminology*, 38, 1075–1108.

26 On Cumulative Childhood Traumatic Exposure and Violence/Aggression: The Implications of Adverse Childhood Experiences (ACE)

Michael T. Baglivio

> Treat people as if they were what they ought to be and you help them to become what they are capable of being.
> –Johan Wolfgang von Goethe

Introduction

Childhood maltreatment remains a significant social problem, as evidenced by 3.4 million referrals, involving 6.3 million children, received by Child Protective Services in the USA alone in 2012 (US Department of Health and Human Services, 2013). The negative repercussions of childhood maltreatment on health, education, and later-life outcomes, including crime and delinquency, are well documented (Widom, 1989a, 1989b; Godinet, Li, & Berg, 2014). This chapter briefly outlines those findings, but furthermore places focus on the effects of cumulative childhood traumatic exposures, as measured specifically through the Adverse Childhood Experiences (ACE) score, on violence, aggression, and criminal behavior. As such, the ACE concept and ACE score are briefly described. Prevalence differences in ACE exposures of delinquents in comparison to general population samples are reviewed, as are negative dose-response health repercussions of heightened ACE exposure. A brief overview of the empirical link between maltreatment and several individual traumatic exposure indicators on crime and delinquency is highlighted, before examining the relationship between the ACE composite score and antisocial behavior, delinquency, and violence. Limitations to the ACE score are discussed, culminating with conclusions and policy implications for juvenile justice and child welfare systems and communities.

Theoretical Framework

A theoretical framework by which childhood maltreatment and traumatic exposure may be related to future delinquency, crime, and violence is Moffitt's developmental taxonomy (1993). One major contribution of Moffitt's position is the existence of two primary offending groups: adolescent-limited, and life-course-persistent (LCP) offenders. Most relevant to the current discussion is LCP offending where the "pathological" backgrounds of this typology are marked by neurocognitive deficits, behavioral problems during childhood, and inadequate parenting (Moffitt, 2006; Moffitt & Caspi, 2001). LCP offenders are distinguished, furthermore, by this ~5% of the population's early onset of delinquency, and disproportionate contribution to crime (Henwood, Chou, & Browne, 2015; Vaughn, DeLisi, Gunter, Fu, Beaver, Perron, & Howard, 2011; Vaughn, DeLisi, Salas-Wright, & Maynard, 2014; Wolfgang, Figlio, & Sellin, 1972). Critical, however, is the notion that neurological deficits (a hallmark of LCPs) must interact with adverse environments for LCP offending to materialize. Learning deficits and developmental exceptionalities may be *necessary*, but are not *sufficient* to initiate the risk; they must be juxtaposed with adverse rearing environments (Moffitt 1993; Tibbetts & Piquero 1999). Several scholars have noted the transactional relationship wherein poorly regulated child behaviors are often met with maltreatment-oriented parental behavior, which then, in turn, further disrupts neurological functioning (Duke, Pettingell, McMorris, & Borowsky, 2010; Granic & Lamey 2002; Granic & Patterson 2006; Lynch & Cicchetti 1998). It is the implications of childhood traumatic exposure on antisocial behavior, including serious and violent offending, that are reviewed below.

The ACE Study

The US Centers for Disease Control and Prevention (CDC) and the San Diego Department of Preventive Medicine at Kaiser Permanente (an integrated managed care consortium) collaborated on two waves of data collection (1995–1997) during which 17,421 well-educated, middle-class patients retrospectively completed a questionnaire regarding their adverse childhood experiences (ACE). The research sought to determine the rates of childhood trauma in the USA, and its relation to adult health. The survey, the Adverse Childhood Experiences Questionnaire, asked about ten specific abuse, neglect, and household dysfunction experiences prior to the patient's 18th birthday.[1] Specifically, the ten ACE indicators include emotional abuse, physical abuse, sexual abuse, emotional neglect, physical neglect, violent treatment toward mother, household substance abuse, household mental illness, parental separation or divorce, and having an incarcerated household member (CDC, 2015). Each indicator is dichotomous, indicating whether the individual has the exposure history or not (irrespective of the frequency or severity of occurrences). The exposures are summed for an ACE score composite ranging from 0 (no exposures) to 10 (exposed to each of the ten ACE indicators). The ACE score was first described and used in 1998 with the publication of the seminal "Relationship of childhood abuse and household dysfunction to many of the leading causes of death in adults: The Adverse Childhood Experiences (ACE) study" (Felitti et al., 1998).

Analyses have revealed that ACE indicators are common, highly interrelated, and exert a powerful cumulative effect on human development (Anda, Butchart, Felitti, & Brown, 2010; Baglivio & Epps, 2015; Dong et al., 2004; Scott et al., 2013) The interrelatedness of ACEs are such that exposures occur non-randomly, and the cumulative dose-response

---

[1] It should be noted that the original wave 1 study examined seven ACE indicators. The three additional indicators of emotional neglect, physical neglect, and parental separation/divorce were analyzed for the second period of data collection.

relationship between higher ACE scores and a host of negative life events (detailed below) necessitates examining ACEs as a collective composite (the ACE score), as opposed to inquiries examining unique effects of indicators individually (Baglivio, Epps, Swartz, Huq, Sheer, & Hardt, 2014; Dong et al., 2004; Finkelhor, Ormrod, & Turner, 2007). For over 8,500 men and women from the original ACE study, the odds of having at least one other of the nine remaining ACEs were 2 to 17.7 times higher for individuals with a given ACE exposure than those without that exposure (Dong et al., 2004). Among juvenile offenders, the odds of having another ACE exposure given one exposure were on average 2.3 times, and up to 1286 times, those of a youth without that exposure (Baglivio & Epps, 2015). Such findings have led to conclusions that an ACE exposure should not be assumed to be an isolated event and that both the negative short- and long-term influences of ACEs on health and behavior are cumulative, graded relationships (Dong et al., 2004; see also Anda et al., 1999; Dietz et al., 1999; Dong, Dube, Felitti, Giles, & Anda, 2003; Dube, Anda, Felitti, Chapman, Williamson, & Giles, 2001). The use of the composite ACE score as a measure of the cumulative effect of traumatic stress exposure during early childhood and adolescence is consistent with understanding of the effects of traumatic stress on neurodevelopment (Anda et al., 2010; Anda et al., 2006).

Health, Neurological, and Behavioral Repercussions, and Epidemiology

Deleterious repercussions of high ACE scores are well documented in the medical literature, beginning with the original ACE Study by Felitti and colleagues (1998). Higher ACE scores have been shown to increase the odds of developing many of the leading causes of death, including ischemic heart disease, cancer, chronic lung disease, morbid obesity, skeletal fractures, and liver disease (Felitti, 1998; see also Anda et al., 2006; Chartier, Walker, & Naimark, 2010; Flaherty et al., 2013). The odds of suffering such negative health outcomes are up to 12 times higher for individuals experiencing four or more ACEs (Felitti et al., 1998). Among the original ACE study participants, those reporting six or more ACEs died nearly 20 years earlier on average than those with zero ACEs (Brown et al., 2009). Additionally, high ACE scores and cumulative traumatic exposure has been identified with the near-term negative consequence of chromosomal damage (Shalev et al., 2013) and functional changes to the developing brain (Anda et al., 2010; Cicchetti, 2013; Danese & McEwan, 2012; Teicher et al., 2003). Childhood maltreatment victimization during critical developmental periods as well as chronic stress disrupt neurological development and effectuate neurobiological deficits (Painter & Scannapieco, 2013; Twardosz & Lutzker, 2010). This can lead to long-lasting biological and cognitive functioning changes (Lanius, Vermetten & Pain, 2011; Mills et al., 2010). Cumulative traumatic exposure is implicated in changes to the development of the prefrontal cortex and neurological pathways between the prefrontal cortex and the amygdala, which negatively impact essential self-regulatory behavioral and emotional responses (Anda et al., 2006; Bremner, 2003). Critical neurotransmitter systems necessary for affect regulation and social attachment are affected by maltreatment (Bennett et al., 2002; Caldji et al., 2000; Heim, Shugart, Craighead, & Nemeroff, 2010). Chronic stress exposure leads to a heightened neural state triggering excretion of adrenal steroids, which, when prolonged, produces an allostatic load that can result in permanent chemical elevations and negative physiological and behavioral responses (Cicchetti & Toth, 2005). Such self-regulation deficits are linked to internalized aggression (substance use, self-mutilation, suicide), and externalizing behaviors (delinquency and interpersonal violence; Evans-Chase, 2014; Perry & Pollard, 1998). Additionally, allostatic load may lead to volatile, extreme responses to even benign stimuli and interpretations of the actions and intents of others as hostile. These findings suggest childhood traumatic exposures facilitate the adoption of high-risk behaviors as coping strategies (Larkin, Felitti, & Anda, 2014). Mounting evidence suggests certain genotypes can moderate sensitivity to adverse trauma (Caspi et al., 2002), meaning individuals differ in responses to similar traumatic exposures.

While ACE prevalence among the original ACE study participants and within general populations were shocking revelations at first presentation, ACE exposures of offenders have since been demonstrated substantially higher (Baglivio, Epps, et al., 2014; Cannon, Davis, Hsi, & Bochte, 2016; Evans-Chase, 2014; Grevstad, 2010). Offender-based ACE studies mimic prior work showing heightened traumatic experiences and mental health problems in juvenile justice-involved youth (Dierkhising Ko, Woods-Jaeger, Briggs, Lee, & Pynoos, 2013), who evidence greater likelihood of multiple types of exposures (Abram, Teplin, Charles, Longworth, McClelland, & Dulcan, 2004).

In an unpublished examination of juvenile offenders, Tacoma Urban Network and Peirce County Juvenile Court were the first to use risk assessment items to create measures of ACE prevalence, finding juvenile offenders had approximately three times more ACEs than the original ACE study's privately insured, well-educated adults (Grevstad, 2010). Offenders with higher ACE scores had more substance abuse, self-harm behavior, and school-related problems. The first published account of ACE scores of juvenile offenders extrapolated the ten ACE indicators from a juvenile justice risk/needs assessment (Baglivio, Epps, et al., 2014). Authors demonstrated a sample of over 64,000 juvenile offenders were 13 times less likely to report zero (0) ACEs, and four times more likely to report four or more ACEs (50% compared to 13%) than Felitti and Anda's Kaiser-Permanente-insured adults. Furthermore, Baglivio and colleagues showed prevalence rates for each ACE indicator were similar for males and females, with the exception of sexual abuse, where the female rate was 4.4 times higher. Though indicators had similar prevalence individually, only 1.8% of the females reported no ACEs compared to 3.1% of the males, while 27.4% of the males and 45.1% of the females reported five or more ACEs. Similar rates of exposure by gender to each of 19 different trauma types were found in prior studies of justice-involved adolescents, yet, again, females evidenced higher rates of sexual abuse and sexual assault (Dierkhising et al., 2013; see also Cauffman, Feldman, Waterman, & Steiner, 1998). Among a sample of 151 adult male offenders, 48.3% reported four or more ACEs, in comparison to only 12.5% for the non-offender normative sample (Reavis et al., 2013).

A recent analysis of 220 juvenile justice youth placed in residential programs in New Mexico used the CDC's Behavioral Risk Factor Surveillance System (BRFSS) and diagnostic psychosocial evaluations to assess ACE exposures (Cannon et al., 2016). They illustrated that ACE exposures increase the deeper adolescent offenders penetrate the justice system. Deep-end residential youth evidenced higher ACE scores on average than the original ACE study adults, but also higher than those reported for juvenile offenders in Florida. Eighty-six percent of the New Mexico residential youth reported four or more ACEs, compared to 50% of Florida juvenile offenders (Cannon et al., 2016).

Widom (2014) cautioned that any relationship between child abuse and neglect with subsequent outcomes, such as delinquency/crime, is confounded by socioeconomic status, as maltreatment is concentrated in disadvantaged areas (Coulton, Crampton, Irwin, Spilsbury, & Korbin, 2007). Few studies have examined the multilevel effects of neighborhood context on childhood maltreatment, as most used aggregate *rates* of maltreatment rather than individual-level measures (Freisthler, Merritt, & LaScala, 2006). A rare exception analyzed of over 59,000 juvenile offenders on community supervision (Baglivio, Wolff, Epps, & Nelson, 2015). Concentrated disadvantage and affluence both affected ACE exposure, with higher ACEs among disadvantaged youth, net of controls for demographic, family support, and parental employment. The affluence-ACE relationship was more robust than that for disadvantage, indicating a protective effect for youth residing in affluent areas. The implications are that the economic reality of the neighborhood in which a juvenile offender resides affects the extent of childhood maltreatment likely experienced.

ACEs and Antisocial Behavior, Aggression, and Violence

There is a long tradition of examining the childhood abuse and neglect relationship with antisocial behavior. Seminal work, pioneered by Widom's (1989a) "Cycle of Violence," had long established a link between prior substantiated child abuse and neglect and delinquency. Smith and Thornberry's (1995) longitudinal analysis found that childhood maltreatment significantly increased the chances of both official and self-reported delinquency, increasing the risk of being arrested, frequency of arrests, and more serious and violent forms of delinquency. Involvement in the child welfare system due to parental maltreatment and foster care placement made unique contributions to the risk for delinquency among over 90,000 officially delinquent youth and an equal number of comparison youth (Barrett, Katsiyannis, Zhang, & Zhang, 2014). Youth with substantiated maltreatment allegations have an earlier age of delinquency onset (Barrett et al., 2014; Dannerbeck & Yan, 2011; Halemba & Siegel, 2011; Rivera & Widom, 1990), were 38% more likely to commit violent crimes (Widom, 1989b), and have more total arrests and were more likely to be incarcerated in adulthood (English, Widom, & Brandford, 2001; Fagan, 2005; Mersky & Topitzes, 2010), than youth without such allegations. Physically abused youth evidence more violent offenses than non-abused youth, controlling for socioeconomic status (Lasford et al., 2007). A seminal study showed exposure to trauma and abuse during childhood increased the odds of juvenile violent behavior by more than 200% (Maxfield & Widom, 1996). Exposure to physical abuse and other maltreatment leads to higher rates of self-reported total offending, property offending, and violent offending, net of controls for prior delinquency (Teague, Mazerolle, Legosz, & Sanderson, 2008). Observed associations between childhood maltreatment and adult criminality transcend racial and ethnic subgroups (English et al., 2001; Maxfield & Widom, 1996). Implications of trauma and abuse are further evident within juvenile justice residential facilities among serious and violent youth. A recent examination of all 3,382 juvenile offenders sentenced under the Texas Determinate Sentencing Act (juvenile/adult blended sentence) demonstrates that "compared to youth who experience low levels of traumatic experiences, high-trauma youths accumulate more total incidents of misconduct" while incarcerated, "display more suicidal activity," and "engage in more sexual misconduct" (Trulson, Haerle, Caudill, & DeLisi, 2016, p. 74).

Prior work indicated that males in particular who have experienced maltreatment are prone to violent behavior and delinquency (Chen, Propp, deLara, & Corvo, 2011; Mass, Herrenkohol, & Sousa, 2008; Yu-Ling Chui, Ryan, & Herz, 2011). Contradictory studies demonstrated a greater proportion of maltreated females committed violent offenses as juveniles or adults than non-maltreated females, while finding no differences for males (Herrera & McCloskey, 2001; Widom & Maxfield, 2001). Teague and colleagues (2008) found no gender differences in the heightened risk for violent offending among physically abused youth examining 480 male and female offenders. Analyzing a sample of over 1,500 economically disadvantaged minorities from birth through age 24 sought to uncover the pathways by which childhood maltreatment may influence delinquency and adult offending differentially for males and females (Topitzes, Mersky, & Reynolds, 2011). While childhood maltreatment was predictive of male delinquency only, it was significantly related to both male and female adult offending. Externalizing behavior during childhood, low school commitment, and impaired emotional regulation and peer social skills increased the risk of adult offending among maltreated males, while criminogenic family-related processes (such as low parental involvement and expectations) were more influential for adult offending among maltreated females.

Though socially acceptable and commonplace in current US society, parental divorce/separation shows moderate effect size associations with delinquency, as differences between those exposed to parental divorce and those from intact families have remained consistent over time (Amato, 2001; D'Onofrio et al., 2005); an effect that is not mediated by common genes (Burt, Barnes, McGue, & Iacono, 2008). Witnessing domestic violence as a child contributes to later maladaptive and antisocial behavior, both internalizing and externalizing (Evans, Davies, & DiLillo, 2008; Herrera & McCloskey, 2001; Moylan et al., 2010). Likewise, parental incarceration has a demonstrated association with antisocial behaviors up to age 32; an effect that holds upon considering other types of separation, and childhood risk factors (Geller, Garfinkely, Cooper, & Mincey, 2009; Murray & Farrington, 2005, 2008; Parke & Clarke-Stewart, 2002).

Implications for maltreatment on delinquency appear cumulative, as youth who experience multiple forms of maltreatment are at the greatest risk of violence and delinquency (Bender 2010; Crooks, Scott, Wolfe, Chiodo, & Killip, 2007; Currie & Tekin 2006; Mersky & Reynolds 2007). While these individual indicators of abuse, neglect, and childhood trauma have been linked to later maladaptive behavior and delinquency, empirical examinations of the ACE score composite of cumulative traumatic exposure have proliferated in recent years. It is these examinations to which we now turn.

Cumulative traumatic exposure, as measured by ACE scores, in addition to its long-term detrimental health implications, has been linked to more proximal negative outcomes with respect to antisocial behavior, aggression, and violence. In comparison to those reporting no ACE exposures, adults with six ACEs were found to be 2.5 times more likely to smoke cigarettes, and 46 times more likely to be intravenous drug users, while those with four or more ACEs were five times more likely to self-report alcoholism (Reavis, Looman, Franco, & Rojas, 2013). ACEs account for a 20–70% increased likelihood of mid-adolescence initiation of alcohol use (Dube et al., 2006). Among students from grades 7 to 12, those witnessing domestic violence, having a physical abuse history, and sexual abuse were up to three times more likely to have early alcohol-use initiation (Hamburger, Leeb, & Swahn, 2008). Higher ACE scores increase the odds of sexual risky behaviors, such as teenage pregnancy (Hillis, Anda, Dube, Felitti, Marchbanks, & Marks, 2004), 50 or more sexual partners, and intercourse prior to the age of 15 (Hillis, Anda, Felitti, & Marchbanks, 2001). Learning and behavior problems and obesity were found higher among high-risk urban pediatric patients with higher ACE scores (Burke, Hellman, Scott, Weems, & Carrion, 2011). Higher cumulative ACE scores among 1500 randomly sampled 18–70-year-old individuals (stratified by socioeconomic disadvantage) increased the odds of poor educational outcomes, unemployment, recent inpatient hospital care, involvement in violence, and having spent at least one night in jail in the last 12 months (Bellis, Lowey, Leckenby, Hughes, & Harrison, 2013). Among the 1500 adults, those with four or more ACEs were significantly more likely to have both punched, and been punched by, someone within the last year, and were eight times more likely to have spent at least one night in jail (Bellis et al., 2013). Examining six distinct ACE exposures among over 130,000 students, Duke and colleagues found each additional type of reported ACE increased the risk of violence perpetration by 35–144% among 136,549 students in grades 6, 9, and 12 (Duke, Pettingell, McMorris, & Borowsky, 2010). Notably, these results included both interpersonal violence (including delinquency, carrying a weapon, fighting, bullying, and dating violence) and self-directed violence (attempted suicide, self-mutilation). Among the female students, risk of violence perpetration was increased 1.7- to 5-fold by exposure to any ACE, while violence perpetration for males increased 1.7- to 44-fold by any ACE (Duke et al., 2010). A dose-response relationship had been found between ACE score and a history of suicide attempts in a prior analysis where those with four or more ACEs had a 1220% historical increase in attempted suicide (Felitti, 2002; Dube, Anda, Felitti, Chapman, et al., 2001). Examining over 64,000 juvenile offenders, Baglivio and colleagues found low-risk-to-reoffend youth (as assessed using a validated risk/needs tool) were 35.6 times more likely than high-risk youth to report zero ACE exposures, while high-risk youth were more likely to report three or more exposures (22% of the variance in risk to-reoffend category was explained by the ACE score; Baglivio, Epps, et al., 2014).

Hypothesizing ACEs distinguish between memberships in offending prevalence trajectory groups, the juvenile offending careers of 64,439 Florida offenders were examined (Baglivio, Wolff, Piquero, & Epps, 2015). Guided in part by Moffitt's taxonomy and their own research finding heighted ACE exposure among higher-risk youth (Baglivio, Epps, et al., 2014), Semi-Parametric Group-Based Modeling (SPGM) identified five latent trajectories of offending prevalence among the offenders from age 7 to 17. Increased ACE exposure distinguished membership in the early-onset, chronic offending trajectory, net of demographic, individual, familial, and personal history risks. Notably, the inclusion of mental health and substance abuse risks did not eliminate the significance of the ACE effect. The early-onset, persistent offending group represented 7% of the offenders, in keeping with Moffitt (1993), and research on the severe 5%, and serious, violent, chronic (SVC) offenders (Baglivio, Jackowski, Greenwald, & Howell, 2014; Vaughn et al., 2011; Vaughn et al., 2014). These youth averaged 17.8 arrests each as juveniles, and evidenced an average ACE score of 3.34, with 30% experiencing more than five ACEs. In contrast, only 10% of the late-onset group reported exposure to five or more ACEs. The odds of early-onset group membership were 345% greater for youth who suffered more than five types of traumatic childhood experiences. The authors concluded indication of the "robust and salient effect of adverse childhood experiences for distinguishing each delinquent trajectory group from one another, with the prevalence of adverse childhood experiences being associated with earlier onset and continued criminal justice involvement throughout adolescence" (Baglivio, Wolff, Piquero, & Epps, 2015, p. 237).

While the studies reviewed thus far had indicated an ACE-delinquency link, as had been established for official childhood maltreatment, none had used ACEs to predict recidivism. The effects of ACE exposure on subsequent offending were examined among ~28,000 juvenile offenders completing community-based supervision (Wolff, Baglivio, & Piquero, 2015). Cox regressions demonstrated increased exposure to multiple trauma types (higher ACE scores) increased the risk of, and led to a shorter time to, recidivism. Offenders with higher ACE scores not only reoffend at higher rates, but also they did so faster than those with lower ACE exposures (Wolff et al., 2015). Importantly, the effects of ACE on recidivism were consistent for both male and female offenders, and for Black and White youth (though the effects became nonsignificant for Hispanic youth with inclusion of all independent controls). Examining the timing of recidivism is integral, as traditional dichotomous analysis of the likelihood of recidivism may fail to assign proper weight to individual factors that affect the timing of that event (Schmidt & Witte, 1989).

The ability of ACEs to predict serious, violent, and chronic (SVC) offending was examined among juvenile offenders in Florida (Fox, Perez, Cass, Baglivio, & Epps, 2015). Prospective identification of SVC offenders has dramatic policy implications as less than 10% of all juvenile offenders commit over 50% of all serious and violent juvenile crime (Piquero, 2011). A recurring finding in SVC work has been the heightened exposure to trauma, neglect, and maltreatment among SVC offenders in comparison to less serious or non-offenders (Fox, Piquero, & Jennings, 2014; Loeber & Farrington, 2000). The Fox et al. (2015) sample included 10,714 SVC offenders and 11,861 juveniles whose only arrest prior to age 18 was a single non-violent felony (labeled "one and done"). Each additional ACE exposure increased the risk of a juvenile becoming an SVC offender vs. a "one-and-done" offender by 35 times, controlling for prominent individual risk factors. Additionally, SVC offenders had a significantly higher proportion of exposure to each of the nine ACE indictors examined.

As ACEs had now been directly linked to increased odds of recidivism and SVC offending among juvenile offenders, efforts to examine potential moderators of the ACE effect on future crime were pertinent for investigation. Craig and colleagues (2016) examined whether social bonds moderate the ACE-recidivism relationship, controlling for sex, age, race/ethnicity, socioeconomic status, impulsivity, and peer associations among over 28,000 juvenile offenders completing community-based services (such as probation). Social bonds were measured as an index of four items assessing attachment to conventional others: positive adult non-family relationships; prosocial ties to the community; prosocial peers; whether the youth felt close to prosocial parents/caretakers. Stronger social bonds lowered the risk of re-offending, while each additional ACE increased the odds of recidivism by 9%. However, social bonds did not reduce the toxic effects on crime of ACE exposures.

Weaker bonded youth did evidence significantly higher ACE scores. Few gender differences in how ACEs and social bonds predict rearrests were found. In sum, ACEs increased a juvenile's odds of recidivism regardless of their strength of attachment to conventional others.

A further attempt to untangle the pathways by which ACEs affect recidivism considered a direct ACE→ recidivism pathway and an indirect ACE→ negative emotionality→ recidivism pathway (Wolff & Baglivio, 2016). Negative emotionality, a temperament construct, encompasses the extent to which situations and others are interpreted as potentially hostile, and the ease to which emotional reactions to situations are aroused (Clarke, 2005; Rothbart & Bates, 2006). Higher negative emotionality entails enhanced emotional arousal and a more hostile interpretation of others. Prior work indicates negative emotionality to be a general risk factor and predictive of externalizing problem behavior (Clark, Watson, & Mineka, 1994; Eisenberg et al., 1996; Eisenberg, Fabes, et al., 2000; Lengua, West, & Sandler, 1998; Rothbart & Bates, 1998). Additionally, negative emotionality coalesces with the understanding of the neurological implications of chronic stress exposure. Hypothesizing offenders who had suffered more traumatic exposures would be more likely to suffer from frustration, hostility, and difficulty expressing themselves (negative emotionality), Wolff and Baglivio (2017) measured negative emotionality using an index of tolerance for frustration, hostile interpretation of the actions of others, dealing with emotions, and anxiety/depression. Structural equation models indicated ACEs have both a direct and an indirect effect on recidivism. Nearly half of the total effect of ACEs operated through negative emotionality, where higher ACEs positively predicted negative emotionality, which positively predicted recidivism. It is essential that research continues to examine *how* ACEs effect antisocial behavior and violence in addition to simply whether or not they do.

ACEs and Sexual Offenders

Higher rates of child maltreatment and family dysfunction and higher ACE scores among sexual offenders in comparison to the general population have been found (Jespersen, Lalumière, & Seto, 2009; Levenson, Willis, & Prescott, 2014a, 2014b; Reavis, Looman, Franco, & Rojas, 2013; Wijkman, Bijleveld, & Hendriks, 2010). Among male juvenile sexual offenders, 95% reported at least one traumatic exposure, with nearly half experiencing both physical and sexual abuse (McMackin, Leisen, Cusack, LaFratta, & Litwin, 2002). Less than 16% of sex offenders in one study endorsed no ACE indicator, while almost half reported four or more ACEs (Levenson et al., 2014b). A history of child sexual abuse victimization is one particular ACE indicator endorsed disproportionately by sex offenders in comparison to non-sex offenders (Jespersen et al., 2009). Additionally, childhood sexual abuse among sex offenders has been correlated with younger victims and pedophilic interests (Nunes, Hermann, Reness, Malcom, & Lavoie, 2013).

Limited prior work has examined ACEs and the reoffending patterns of sexual offenders. One notable exception examined sexual and non-sexual re-offending among 740 sexual offenders surveyed in outpatient and civil commitment treatment programs across the USA (Levenson & Socia, 2015).

Higher ACE scores were positively associated across sexual and non-sexual recidivism outcomes, indicative of the effects of childhood traumatic experiences on a plethora of antisocial behavior and criminal continuity. Additionally, Levenson and Socia (2015) found higher ACE scores among rapists with adult victims than those victimizing minors only. The strongest ACE indicators in the prediction of sexual offense arrest frequency were childhood sexual abuse, emotional neglect, and domestic violence, while stronger predictors of non-sexual arrest were identified as household substance abuse, divorce/separation, and incarceration history of a family member. Conclusions suggest that abuse and neglect are more predictive of sexual offending while household dysfunction predicts criminal offending more generally. An additional study comparing sex offenders to child abusers and domestic violence offenders found sex offenders more likely to report exposure to four or more ACE in comparison to child abusers, and domestic violence offenders more likely to report no ACEs than sex offenders (Reavis et al., 2013). Sexual abuse victimization was the only ACE which significantly differed from adult sexual offenders and non-sex offenders, with sexual offenders more likely to report that victimization. Prior work had shown that boys who were sexually abused were 45 times more likely to engage in dating violence in comparison to males who were not (Duke et al., 2009).

Limitations to the ACE Score

Perhaps the strongest limitation levied against the ACE concept is the binary nature of each indicator, which takes no account of the frequency, duration, or severity of exposures (Nofzinger & Kurtz, 2005; Smith & Thornberry, 1995). For example, history of sexual abuse is counted as one exposure regardless of whether the abuse was one occurrence or daily abuse over a period of years with progressive severity. Concerns have been noted over exclusion of additional exposures such as peer rejection, witnessing violence outside of the family, low socioeconomic status, and low academic achievement (Finkelhor, Shattuck, Turner, & Hamby, 2012).

Further, questions arise concerning whether the effects of self-reported abuse, neglect, and traumatic exposures differ from official child welfare responses to such claims, and whether substantiated maltreatment differs from unsubstantiated cases. A concern of using official childhood maltreatment measures, however, is differences in definition, recognition, and reporting; observed differences may be differences in reporting and not in maltreatment behavior (Coulton et al., 2007). Prior work has shown youth with substantiated maltreatment evidence delinquency rates 47% greater than youth without at least one substantiated allegation (Ryan & Testa, 2005). No differences in reoccurrence of maltreatment rates or school performance outcomes were found in one study following cases for 4.5 years, though unsubstantiated cases had lower risk of delinquency than substantiated cases (Drake, Johnson-Reid, Way, & Chung, 2003). Youth with substantiated reports of maltreatment evidenced 2.2 times the relative risk of arrest than unsubstantiated cases among 38,000 Los Angeles youth (Chiu, Ryan, & Herz, 2011). Using structural equation modeling, a study of 12,955 serious and violent youth completing juvenile residential programs examined the direct effects of ACEs on recidivism, and their indirect effects through child welfare involvement (Baglivio et al., 2015). Crossover youth (both dually involved youth currently in the juvenile justice systems with a history of child welfare involvement, and youth dually adjudicated with open juvenile justice and child welfare cases concurrently) were compared with juvenile justice youth having no history of child welfare involvement. ACEs failed to exert a direct effect on 12-month rearrest, but did exert a significant indirect effect through child welfare involvement, which was itself associated with recidivism. Higher ACE scores increased the odds of child welfare placement across sex and race/ethnicity subgroups. Furthermore, recent child welfare involvement during the last five years but closed prior to the juvenile justice placement was more detrimental than concurrent child welfare and juvenile justice involvement, suggesting that the timing of system exposures matters. These findings were in contrast to prior work, which found crossover youth in Washington State with open substantiated neglect cases had higher recidivism rates than those with closed cases or those with no child welfare history (Ryan, Williams, & Courtney, 2013). Questions remain as to whether increased recidivism is due to multi-agency open cases, or the proximity of the dependency placement to the delinquency placement. Future studies should address the timing of ACE exposures, and the timing of child welfare and juvenile justice system placements. This would better uncover the implications of infant maltreatment from early and late adolescence maltreatment. Continued attendance to differences in antisocial and violent behavior between self-reported traumatic exposure, such as the ACE score, and official maltreatment is needed.

Additional limitations of the ACE score include the retrospective recall involved in asking about childhood abuse (see Dube et al., 2004). Examinations of adolescents arguably suffer less from relying on long-term retrospective recall, as the traumatic exposures were more proximal. There is some possibility of selection effects where those who find themselves in negative situations may be more likely to externally attribute blame and/or recall negative childhoods.

The limitations of the ACE score, arguably, are also its strengths. The possibility of a ten-item self-report screening significantly correlated with negative health outcomes, including early death, as well as antisocial behavior, crime, and violence seems invaluable. While more sophisticated or item-weighted assessments or administration by licensed clinicians may be favorable from a predictive validity standpoint, the cost-effectiveness and ease of administration of an ACE questionnaire may trump those concerns in many instances.

Policy Implications, Prevention Efforts, and Intervention

Childhood adversity has been referred to as a public health issue (Anda et al., 2010), with direct and indirect costs making child maltreatment among the most costly in the USA (Putnam, 2006). As others have noted, US social policy has historically resorted to offender punishment and child welfare system placement in response to child maltreatment, rather than primary prevention strategies (Levenson & Socia, 2015). In contrast, ACE scores could be used as an early screening tool by pediatricians, school personnel, juvenile justice and child welfare workers, and other practitioners to identify risk factors for offending and violence before a child is ever, or more deeply, involved in the justice system. Trauma-informed care curricula in universities (such as medical schools, and psychology and education-related degree tracts), and training in child welfare and juvenile justice systems encompassing a universal precaution approach, as well as policies for avoidance of re-traumatization for youth in custody settings is paramount (Miller & Najavits, 2012). The CDC has called for prioritizing prevention and early intervention programs to benefit youth residing in disadvantaged environments, consistent with studies finding juvenile offenders residing in areas of concentrated disadvantage having higher ACE scores (Baglivio, Wolff, Epps, & Nelson, 2015). These socioeconomic conditions unduly affect minority youth, who are disproportionately represented in both the juvenile justice and child welfare systems, which makes ACE prevention an integral disproportionate minority contact (DMC) and reducing ethnic disparities (RED) strategy. Strategies could include leveraging structural and contextual resources to improve both health and justice system outcomes for the "truly disadvantaged" through comprehensive ACE prevention policies. While the ACE score is an aggregation of abuse/trauma types, communities will be disproportionately plagued by some ACE types over others. Targeted prevention will be instrumental to curbing localized ACE exposures, but requires community ACE assessment efforts. Prominent prevention program targets include high school dropout and teen pregnancy prevention, and job skills/life skills intervention and prevention, both in schools and as accessible community resources. Prevention services like the celebrated Nurse–Family Partnership may help curb the intergenerational transfer of childhood maltreatment, as may early-family/child training programs (Piquero, Farrington, Welsh, Tremblay, & Jennings, 2009).

Additional localized efforts include the potential for legislation, such as the recently passed ACE reduction law in Washington State, which recognizes ACE as "powerful common determinant of a child's ability to be successful at work, to avoid behavioral and chronic physical health conditions, and to build healthy relationships" (SHB 1965, C32, L11, E2, Sec. 1, 2011). Furthermore, localized efforts include enhancing data-sharing between child welfare and juvenile justice agencies, coordinated case management, joint supervision, and dual-jurisdictional court systems with one judge/one family calendaring (Baglivio, Wolff, Piquero, Bilchik, et al., 2016). Along this vein of data sharing, one vendor of risk/needs assessment software has incorporated an ACE indicator and overall ACE score into its automated software reports, meaning case workers and probation officers of all juvenile offenders assessed are provided those scores. Inclusion of ACE information has forced the learning and understanding of ACE among these staff as they now must address and explain ACEs to youth, parents, and the court.

Beyond primary and secondary prevention, intervention efforts should examine which treatments and services, and at what dosages, best attenuate the effects of ACE on delinquency and violence. Intervention for those with multiple exposures should target self-regulatory skills, using cognitive behavioral framework to reinforce "stop and think" and to teach individuals to weigh consequences of behavioral options. These interventions may be most effective targeted during late adolescence or early adulthood (Evans-Chase, 2014). Additional work should examine protective factors, such as a support network for the family, school engagement, or optimism for the future, which may mitigate the effects of ACEs on re-arrest and criminal continuity. Additional efforts to promote resilience and youth and family engagement are clearly warranted (Dierkhising et al., 2013).

The composite ACE score has proven itself a useful metric for capturing cumulative traumatic exposures, with demonstrated relationships to multidisciplinary outcomes across hundreds of published studies. While in its infancy with respect to associations with and predictive ability of criminal behavior and violence, ACE scores are a productive avenue of exploration. Individuals with multiple exposures to maltreatment and childhood traumatic events have been demonstrated to be at increased odds of delinquency and committing violent acts, regardless of whether adults, students, or subtypes of offenders have been the subjects of inquiry. Heightened ACE exposure is found among the most serious, violent, and chronic offenders, with early onset of antisocial behavior indicative of ACEs' effects on criminal continuity. Findings regarding the deleterious effects of ACEs are growing rapidly. Cause for optimism is that most ACEs are entirely preventable. Physical and emotional neglect and abuse, sexual abuse, and domestic violence are preventable. Resources can be leveraged for social programs to attenuate the effects of parental separation, household substance abuse, mental illness, and parental incarceration. Unfortunately for youth with high ACEs, "instead of being raised by their parents, most were lowered by them" (Trulson et al., 2016, p. 168). This chapter began with an epigraph of treating people as they ought to become for them to actualize their full potential; however, it elucidates the devastating effects of trauma, neglect, debasement, and degradation on exactly what they may become.

References

Abram, K. M., Teplin, L. A., Charles, D. R., Longworth, S. L., McClelland, G. M., & Dulcan, M. K. (2004). Posttraumatic stress disorder and trauma in youth in juvenile detention. *Archives of general psychiatry*, 61, 403–410.

Amato, P. R. (2001). Children of divorce in the 1990's: An update of the Amato and Keith (1991) meta-analysis. *Journal of Family Psychology*, 15, 355–370.

Anda, R. F., Butchart, A., Felitti, V. J., & Brown, D. W. (2010). Building a framework for global surveillance of the public health implications of Adverse Childhood Experiences. *American Journal of Preventive Medicine*, 39, 93–98.

Anda, R. F., Croft, J. B., Felitti, V. J., Nordenberg, D., Giles, W. H., Williamson, D. F., & Giovino, G. A. (1999). Adverse childhood experiences and smoking during adolescence and adulthood. *Journal of the American Medical Association*, 282, 1652–1658.

Anda, R. F., Felitti, V. J., Bremner, J. D., Walker, J. D., Whitfield, C., Perry, B. D., Dube, S. R., & Giles, W. H. (2006). The enduring effects of abuse and related adverse experiences in childhood: A convergence of evidence from neurobiology and epidemiology. *European Archives of Psychiatry and Clinical Neuroscience*, 256, 174–186.

Baglivio, M. T. & Epps, N. (2015). The interrelatedness of Adverse Childhood Experiences among high-risk juvenile offenders. *Youth Violence and Juvenile Justice*. doi: 10.1177/1541204014566286.

Baglivio, M. T., Epps, N., Swartz, K., Huq, M. S., Sheer, A., & Hardt, N. S. (2014). The prevalence of Adverse Childhood Experiences (ACE) in the lives of juvenile offenders. *Journal of Juvenile Justice*, 3, 1–23.

Baglivio, M. T., Jackowski, K., Greenwald, M. A., & Howell, J. C. (2014). Serious, violent, and chronic juvenile offenders: A statewide analysis of prevalence and prediction of subsequent recidivism using risk and protective factors. *Criminology & Public Policy*, 13, 83–116.

Baglivio, M. T., Wolff, K. T., Epps, N., & Nelson, R. (2015). Predicting Adverse Childhood Experiences: The importance of neighborhood context in youth trauma among delinquent youth. *Crime & Delinquency*, 1–23. doi: 10.1177/0011128715570628.

Baglivio, M. T., Wolff, K. T., Piquero, A. R., Bilchik, S. Jackowski, K., Greenwald, M. A., & Epps, N. (2016). Maltreatment, child welfare, and recidivism in a sample of deep-end crossover youth. *Journal of Youth and Adolescence*, 45, 625–654.

Baglivio, M. T., Wolff, K. T., Piquero, A. R., & Epps, N. (2015). The relationship between Adverse Childhood Experiences (ACE) and juvenile offending trajectories in a juvenile offender sample. *Journal of Criminal Justice*, 43, 229–241.

Barrett, D. E., Katsiyannis, A., Zhang, D., & Zhang, D. (2014). Delinquency and recidivism, A multicohort, matched-control study of the role of early adverse experiences, mental health problems, and disabilities. *Journal of Emotional and Behavioral Disorders*, 22, 3–15.

Bellis, M. A., Lowey, H., Leckenby, N., Hughes, K., & Harrison, D. (2013). Adverse childhood experiences: Retrospective study to determine their impact on adult health behaviors and health outcomes in a UK population. *Journal of Public Health*, 36, 81–91.

Bender, K. (2010). Why do some maltreated youth become juvenile offenders? A call for further investigation and adaption of youth services. *Children and Youth Services Review, 32,* 466–473.

Bennett, A. J., Lesch, K. P., Heils, A., Long, J. C., Lorenz, J. G., Shoaf, S. E., Champoux, M., Suomi, S. J., Linnoila, M. V., & Higley, J. D. (2002). Early experience and serotonin transporter gene variation interact to influence primate CNS function. *Molecular Psychiatry, 7,* 118–122.

Bremner, D. (2003). Long-term effects of childhood abuse on brain and neurobiology. *Child and Adolescent Psychiatric Clinics of North America, 12,* 271–292.

Brown, D. W., Anda, R. F., Tiemeier, H., Felitti, V. J., Edwards, V. J., Croft, J. B., & Giles, W. H. (2009). Adverse childhood experiences and the risk of premature mortality. *American Journal of Preventive Medicine, 37,* 389–396.

Burke, N. J., Hellman, J. L., Scott, B. G., Weems, C. F., & Carrion, V. G. (2011). The impact of adverse childhood experiences on an urban pediatric population. *Child Abuse and Neglect, 35,* 408–413.

Burt, A. S., Barnes, A. R., McGue, M., & Iacono, W. G. (2008). Parental divorce and adolescent delinquency: Ruling out the impact of common genes. *Developmental Psychology, 44,* 1668–1677.

Caldji, C., Francis, D., Sharma, S., Plotsky, P. M., & Meaney, M. J. (2000). The effects of early rearing environment on the development of GABA and the central benzodiazepine receptor levels and novelty induced fearfulness in the rat. *Neuropsychopharmacology, 22,* 219–229.

Cannon, Y., Davis, G., Hsi, A., & Bochte, A. (2016). *Adverse childhood experiences in the New Mexico juvenile justice population.* Albuquerque, NM: New Mexico Sentencing Commission.

Caspi, A., McClay, J., Moffitt, T. E., Mill, J., Martin, J., Craig, I. W., Taylor, A., & Poulton, R. (2002). Role of genotype in the Cycle of Violence in maltreated children. *Science, 297,* 851–854.

Cauffman, E., Feldman, S., Waterman, J., & Steiner, H. (1998). Posttraumatic stress disorder among female juvenile offenders. *Journal of the American Academy of Child and Adolescent Psychiatry, 37,* 1209–1216.

Centers for Disease Control and Prevention. (d). Injury prevention and control: Adverse childhood experiences (ACE) study. Retrieved March 20, 2016 from www.cdc.gov/violenceprevention/acestudy/.

Chartier, M. J., Walker, J. R., & Naimark, B. (2010). Separate and cumulative effects of adverse childhood experiences in predicting adult health and heath care utilization. *Child Abuse and Neglect, 34,* 454–464.

Chen, W. Y., Propp, J., deLara, E., & Corvo, K. (2011). Child neglect and its association with subsequent juvenile drug and alcohol offense. *Child & Adolescent Social Work Journal, 28,* 273–290.

Chiu, Y., Ryan, J. P., & Herz, D. C. (2011). Allegations of maltreatment and delinquency: Does risk of juvenile arrest vary substantiation status? *Children and Youth Services Review, 33,* 855–860.

Cicchetti, D. (2013). Annual research review: Resilient functioning in maltreated children – past, present, and future perspectives. *Journal of Child Psychology and Psychiatry, 54,* 402–422.

Cicchetti, D. & Toth, S. L. (2005). Child maltreatment. *Annual Review of Clinical Psychology, 1,* 409–438.

Clark, L. A. (2005). Temperament as a unifying basis for personality and psychopathology. *Journal of Abnormal Psychology, 114,* 505–521.

Clark, L. A., Watson, D., & Mineka, S. (1994). Temperament, personality, and the mood and anxiety disorders. *Journal of Abnormal Psychology, 103,* 103–116.

Coulton, C. J., Crampton, D. S., Irwin, M., Spilsbury, J. C., & Korbin, J. E. (2007). How neighborhoods influence child maltreatment: A review of the literature and alternative pathways. *Child Abuse & Neglect, 31,* 1117–1142.

Craig, J. M., Baglivio, M. T., Wolff, K. T., Piquero, A. R., & Epps, N. (2016). Do social bonds buffer the impact of adverse childhood experiences on reoffending? *Youth Violence and Juvenile Justice*, 1–18. doi: 10.1177/1541204016630033.

Crooks, C. V., Scott, K. L., Wolfe, D. A., Chiodo, D., & Killip, S. (2007). Understanding the link between childhood maltreatment and violent delinquency: What do schools have to add? *Child Maltreatment*, 12, 269–280.

Currie, J. & Tekin, E. (2006). *Does child abuse cause crime?* IZA discussion papers, No. 2063.

Dannerbeck, A. & Yan, J. (2011). Missouri's crossover youth: Examining the relationship between maltreatment history and their risk of violence. *Journal of Juvenile Justice*, 1, 78–97.

Danese, A. & McEwen, B. S. (2012). Adverse childhood experiences, allostasis, allostatic load, and age-related disease. *Physiology and Behavior*, 106, 29–39.

Dierkhising, C. B., Ko, S. J., Woods-Jaeger, B., Briggs, E. C., Lee, R., & Pynoos, R. S. (2013). Trauma histories among justice-involved youth: Findings from the National Child Traumatic Stress Network. *European Journal of Psychotraumatology*, 4, doi: 10.3402/ejpt.v4i0.20274.

Dietz, P. M., Spitz, A. M., Anda, R. F., Williamson, D. F., McMahon, P. M., Santelli, J. S., Nordenberg, D. F., Felitti, V. J., & Kendrick, J. S. (1999). Unintended pregnancy among adult women exposed to abuse or household dysfunction during their childhood. *Journal of the American Medical Association*, 282, 1359–1364.

Dong, M., Anda, R. F., Felitti, V. J., Dube, S. R., Williamson, D. F., Thompson, T. J., Loo, C. M., & Giles, W. H. (2004). The interrelatedness of multiple forms of childhood abuse, neglect, and household dysfunction. *Child Abuse and Neglect*, 28, 771–784.

Dong, M., Dube, S. R., Felitti, V. J., Giles, W. H., & Anda, R. F. (2003). Adverse childhood experiences and self-reported liver disease: New insights into the causal pathway. *Archives of Internal Medicine*, 163, 1949–1956.

D'Onofrio, B. M., Turkheimer, E., Emery, R. E., Slutske, W. S., Heath, A. C., Madden, P. A., & Martin, N. G. (2005). A genetically informed study of marital instability and its association with offspring psychopathology. *Journal of Abnormal Psychology*, 114, 570–586.

Drake, B., Jonson-Reid, M., Way, I., & Chung, S. (2003). Substantiation and recidivism. *Children Maltreatment*, 8, 248–260.

Dube, S. R., Anda, R. F., Felitti, V. J., Chapman, D. P., Williamson, D. F., & Giles, W. H. (2001). Childhood abuse, household dysfunction and the risk of attempted suicide throughout the life span: Findings from the Adverse Childhood Experiences Study. *Journal of the American Medical Association*, 286, 3089–3096.

Dube, S. R., Miller, J. W., Brown, D. W., Giles, W. H., Felitti, V. J., Dong, M., & Anda, R. F. (2006). Adverse childhood experiences and the association with ever using alcohol and initiating alcohol use during adolescence. *Journal of Adolescent Health*, 38, 444.e1–444.e10.

Duke, N. N., Pettingell, S. L., McMorris, B. J., & Borowsky, I. W. (2010). Adolescent violence perpetration: Associations with multiple types of adverse childhood experiences. *Pediatrics*, 125, 778–786.

Eisenberg, N., Fabes, R. A., Guthrie, I. K., Murphy, B. C., Maszk, P., Holmgren, R., & Suh, K. (1996). The relations of regulation and emotionality to problem behavior in elementary school children. *Development and Psychopathology*, 8, 141–162.

Eisenberg, N., Fabes, R. A., Guthrie, I. K., & Reiser, M. (2000). Dispositional emotionality and regulation: Their role in predicting quality of social functioning. *Journal of Personality and Social Psychology*, 78, 136–157.

English, D., Widom, C., & Brandford, C. (2001). *Childhood victimization and delinquency, adult criminality, and violent criminal behavior: A replication and extension* (NCJ 192291). Washington, DC: National Institute of Justice.

Evans-Chase, M. (2014). Addressing trauma and psychosocial development in juvenile justice-involved youth: A synthesis of the developmental neuroscience, juvenile justice and trauma literature. *Laws*, 3, 744–758.

Evans, S. E., Davies, C., & DiLillo, D. (2008). Exposure to domestic violence: A meta-analysis of child and adolescent outcomes. *Aggression and Violent Behavior*, 13, 131–140.

Fagan, A. A. (2005). The relationship between adolescent physical abuse and criminal offending: Support for an enduring and generalized cycle of violence. *Journal of Family Violence*, 20, 279–290.

Felitti, V. J. (2002). The relationship between adverse childhood experiences and adult health: Turning gold into lead. *The Permanente Journal*, 6, 44–47.

Felitti, V. J., Anda, R. F., Nordenberg, D., Williamson, D. F., Spitz, A. M., Edwards, V., Koss, M. P., & Marks, J. S. (1998). Relationship of childhood abuse and dysfunction to many of the leading causes of death in adults: The Adverse Childhood Experiences (ACE) study. *American Journal of Preventive Medicine*, 14, 245–258.

Finkelhor, D., Ormrod, R., & Turner, H. A. (2007). Polyvictimization and trauma in a national longitudinal cohort. *Development and Psychopathology*, 19, 149–166.

Finkelhor, D., Shattuck, A., Turner, H., A. & Hamby, S. (2012). Improving the adverse childhood experiences study scale. *JAMA Pediatrics*, 167, 70–75.

Flaherty, E. G., Thompson, R., Dubowitz, H., Harvey, E. M., English, D. J., Proctor, L. J., & Runyan, D. K. (2013). Adverse childhood experiences and child health in early adolescence. *JAMA Pediatrics*, 167, 622–629.

Fox, B. H., Perez, N., Cass, E., Baglivio, M. T., & Epps, N. (2015). Trauma changes everything: Examining the relationship between adverse childhood experiences and serious, violent and chronic juvenile offenders. *Child Abuse & Neglect*, 46, 163–173.

Fox, B. H., Piquero, A. R., & Jennings, W. (2014). Serious, chronic, and violent offenders. In W. Church & D. Springer (Eds), *Juvenile justice sourcebook: Past, present and future* (pp. 554–579). New York: Oxford University Press.

Freisthler, B., Merritt, D. H., & LaScala, E. A. (2006). Understanding the ecology of child maltreatment: A review of the literature and directions for future research. *Child Maltreatment*, 11, 263–280.

Geller, A., Garfinkel, I., Cooper, C. E., & Mincy, R. B. (2009). Parental incarceration and child well-being: Implications for urban families. *Social Science Quarterly*, 1, 1186–1202.

Godinet, M. T., Li, F., & Berg, T. (2014). Early childhood maltreatment and trajectories of behavioral problems: Exploring gender and racial differences. *Child Abuse and Neglect*, 38, 544–556.

Granic, I. & Lamey, A. V. (2002). Combining dynamic systems and multivariate analyses to compare the mother–child interactions of externalizing subtypes. *Journal of Abnormal Child Psychology*, 30, 265–283.

Granic, I. & Patterson, G. R. (2006). Toward a comprehensive model of antisocial development: A dynamic systems approach. *Psychological Review*, 113, 101–131.

Grevstad, J. A. (2010). *Adverse childhood experiences and juvenile justice*. PowerPoint delivered to Washington State Family Policy Council, June 8, 2010.

Halemba, G. & Siegel, G. (2011). *Doorways to delinquency: Multisystem involvement of delinquent youth in King County* (Seattle, WA). Pittsburgh: National Center for Juvenile Justice.

Hamburger, M. E., Leeb, R. T., & Swahn, M. H. (2008). Childhood maltreatment and early alcohol use among high risk adolescents. *Journal of Studies on Alcohol and Drugs*, 69, 291–295.

Heim, C., Shugart, M., Craighead, W. E., & Nemeroff, C. B. (2010). Neurobiological and psychiatric consequences of child abuse and neglect. *Developmental Psychobiology*, 52, 671–690.

Henwood, K. S., Chou, S., & Browne, K. D. (2015). A systematic review and meta-analysis on the effectiveness of CBT informed anger management. *Aggression and Violent Behavior*, 25(Part B), 280–292.

Herrera, V. M. & McCloskey, L. A. (2001). Gender differences in the risk for delinquency among youth exposed to family violence. *Child Abuse and Neglect*, 25, 1037–1051.

Hillis, S. D., Anda, R. F., Dube, S. R., Felitti, V. J., Marchbanks, P. A., & Marks, J. S. (2004). The association between adverse childhood experiences and adolescent pregnancy, long-term psychosocial consequences, and fetal death. *Pediatrics*, 2, 320–327.

Hillis, S. D., Anda, R. F., Felitti, V. J., & Marchbanks, P. A. (2001). Adverse childhood experiences and sexual risk behaviors in women: A retrospective cohort study. *Family Planning Perspective*, 5, 206–211.

Jespersen, A. F., Lalumière, M. L., & Seto, M. C., (2009). Sexual abuse history among adult sex offenders and non-sex offenders: A meta-analysis. *Child Abuse & Neglect*, 33, 179–192.

Lanius, R., Vermetten, E., & Pain, C. (2011). *The impact of early life trauma on health and disease: The hidden epidemic.* New York: Cambridge University Press.

Larkin, H., Felitti, V. J., & Anda, R. F. (2014). Social work and adverse childhood experiences research: Implications for practice and health policy. *Social Work in Public Health*, 29, 1–16.

Lasford, J. E., Miller-Johnson, S., Berlin, L. J., Dodge, K. A., Bates, J. E., & Pettit, G. S. (2007). Early physical abuse and later violent delinquency: A prospective longitudinal study. *Child Maltreatment*, 12, 233–245.

Lengua, L. J., West, S. G., & Sandler, I. N. (1998). Temperament as a predictor of symptomatology in children: Addressing contamination of measures. *Child Development*, 69, 164–181.

Levenson, J. S. & Socia, K. M. (2015). Adverse childhood experiences and arrest patterns in a sample of sexual offenders. *Journal of Interpersonal Violence*, 1–29. doi: 10.1177/08862605155751.

Levenson, J. S., Willis, G., & Prescott, D. (2014a). Adverse childhood experiences in the lives of female sex offenders. *Sexual Abuse: A Journal of Research and Treatment*, 27, 258–283.

Levenson, J. S., Willis, G., & Prescott, D. (2014b). Adverse childhood experiences in the lives of male sex offenders and implications for trauma-informed care. *Sexual Abuse: A Journal of Research and Treatment*. doi:10.1177/1079063214535819.

Loeber, R. & Farrington, D. P. (2000). Young children who commit crime: Epidemiology, developmental origins, risk factors, early interventions, and policy implications. *Development and Psychopathology*, 12, 737–762.

Lynch, M. & Cicchetti, D. (1998). An ecological transactional analysis of children and contexts: The longitudinal interplay among child maltreatment, community violence, and children's symptomology. *Developmental Psychopathology*, 10, 235–257.

Mass, C., Herrenkohl, T. I., & Sousa, C. (2008). Review of research on child maltreatment and violence in youth. *Trauma, Violence, & Abuse*, 9, 56–67.

Maxfield, M. G. & Widom, C. S. (1996). The cycle of violence: Revisited six years later. *Archives of Pediatric Adolescent Medicine*, 150, 390–395.

McMackin, R. A., Leisen, M. B., Cusack, J. F., LaFratta, J., & Litwin, P. (2002). The relationship of trauma exposure to sex offending behavior among male juvenile offenders. *Journal of Child Sexual Abuse*, 11, 25–40.

Mersky, J. P. & Reynolds, A. J. (2007). Child maltreatment and violent delinquency: Disentangling main effects and subgroup effects. *Child Maltreatment*, 12, 246–258.

Mersky, J. P. & Topitzes, J. (2010). Comparing early adult outcomes of maltreated and non-maltreated children: A prospective longitudinal investigation. *Children and Youth Services Review*, 36, 22–29.

Miller, N. A. & Najavits, L. M. (2012). Creating trauma-informed correctional care: A balance of goals and environment. *European Journal of Psychotraumatology,* 3, 1–8. doi: 10.3402/ejpt.v3i0.17246.

Mills, R., Alati, R., O'Callaghan, M., Najman, J., Williams, G., Bor, W., et al. (2010). Child abuse and neglect and cognitive functioning at 14 years of age: Findings from a birth cohort. *Pediatrics,* 127, 4–10.

Moffitt, T. E. (1993). Adolescent-limited and life-course persistent antisocial behavior: A developmental taxonomy. *Psychological Review,* 100, 674–701.

Moffitt, T. E. (2006). Life-course persistent versus adolescent-limited antisocial behavior. In D. Cicchetti & D. J. Cohen (Eds), *Developmental psychopathology: Risk, disorder, and adaptation* (pp. 570–598). New York: Wiley.

Moffitt, T. E. & Caspi, A. (2001). Childhood predictors differentiate life-course persistent and adolescence-limited antisocial pathways among males and females. *Development and Psychopathology,* 13, 255–375.

Moylan, C. A., Herrenkohl, T. I., Sousa, C., Tajima, E. A., Herrenkohl, R. C. & Russo, M. J. (2010). The effects of child abuse exposure to domestic violence on adolescent internalizing and externalizing behavior problems. *Journal of Family Violence,* 25, 53–63.

Murray, J. & Farrington, D. P. (2005). Parental imprisonment: Effects on boys' antisocial behavior and delinquency through the life-course. *Journal of Child Psychology and Psychiatry,* 46, 1269–1278.

Murray, J. & Farrington, D. P. (2008). Parental imprisonment: Long-lasting effects on boys' internalizing problems through the life course. *Development and Psychopathology,* 20, 273–290.

Nofziger, S. & Kurtz, D. (2005). Violent lives: A lifestyle model linking exposure to violence to juvenile violent offending. *Journal of Research in Crime and Delinquency,* 42, 3–26.

Nunes, K. L., Hermann, C. A., Renee Malcom, J., & Lavoie, K. (2013). Childhood sexual victimization, pedophilic interest, and sexual recidivism. *Child Abuse & Neglect,* 37, 703–711.

Painter, K. & Scannapieco, M. (2013). Child maltreatment: The neurobiological aspects of posttraumatic stress disorder. *Journal of Evidence-Based Social Work,* 10, 276–284.

Parke, R. & Clarke-Stewart, K. (2002). *Effects of parental incarceration on young children.* Washington, DC: US Department of Health and Human Services.

Perry, B. D. & Pollard, R. (1998). Homeostasis, stress, trauma, and adaption: A neurodevelopmental view of childhood trauma. *Child and Adolescent Psychiatric Clinics of North America,* 7, 33–51.

Piquero, A. R. (2011). James Joyce, Alice in Wonderland, the Rolling Stones, and criminal careers. *Journal of Youth and Adolescence,* 40, 761–775.

Piquero, A. R., Farrington, D. P., Welsh, B. C., Tremblay, R. E., & Jennings, W. G. (2009). Effects of early family/parent training programs on antisocial behavior and delinquency: A systematic review. *Journal of Experimental Criminology,* 5, 83–120.

Putnam, F. W. (2006). The impact of trauma on child development. *Juvenile and Family Court Journal,* 57, 1–11.

Reavis, J., Looman, J., Franco, K., & Rojas, B. (2013). Adverse childhood experiences and adult criminality: How long must we live before we possess our own lives? *The Permanente Journal,* 17, 44–48.

Rivera, B. & Widom, C. S. (1990). Childhood victimization and violent offending. *Violence and Victims,* 5, 19–35.

Rothbart, M. K. & Bates, J. E. (1998). Temperament. In W. Damon & N. Eisenberg (Eds), *Handbook of Child Psychology: Vol. 3. Social, emotional, and personality development* (pp. 105–176). New York: Wiley.

Rothbart, M. K. & Bates, J. E. (2006). Temperament. In N. Eisenberg, W. Damon, & R. Lerner (Eds), *Handbook of Child Psychology: Vol. 3. Social, emotional, and personality development* (6th ed., pp. 99–167). Hoboken, NJ: John Wiley.

Ryan, J. P. & Testa, M. F. (2005). Child maltreatment and juvenile delinquency: Investigating the role of placement and placement instability. *Children and Youth Services Review*, 27, 227–249.

Ryan, J. P., Williams, A. B., & Courtney, M. E. (2013). Adolescent neglect, juvenile delinquency and the risk of recidivism. *Journal of Youth and Adolescence*, 42, 454–465.

Schmidt, P. & Witte, A. D. (1989). Predicting criminal recidivism using "split population" survival time models. *Journal of Econometrics*, 40, 141–159.

Scott, B. G., Burke, N. J., Weems, C. F., Hellman, J. L., & Carrion, V. G. (2013). The interrelation of Adverse Childhood Experiences within an at-risk pediatric sample. *Journal of Child & Adolescent Trauma*, 6, 217–229.

Shalev, I., Moffitt, T., Sugden, K., Williams, B., Houts, R. M., Danese, A., Mill, J., Arseneault, & Caspi A. (2013). Exposure to violence during childhood is associated with telomere erosion from 5 to 10 years of age: A longitudinal study. *Molecular Psychiatry*, 18, 576–581.

Smith, C. & Thornberry, T. P. (1995). The relationship between childhood maltreatment and adolescent involvement in delinquency. *Criminology*, 33, 451–477.

Teague, R., Mazerolle, P., Legosz, M., & Sanderson, J. (2008). Linking childhood exposure to physical abuse and adult offending: Examining mediating factors and gendered relationships. *Justice Quarterly*, 25, 313–348.

Teicher, M. H., Andersen, S. L., Polcari, A., Anderson, C. M., Navalta, C. P., & Kim, D. M. (2003). The neurobiological consequences of early stress and childhood maltreatment. *Neuroscience & Biobehavioral Reviews*, 27(1–2), 33–44.

Tibbetts, S. G. & Piquero, A. R. (1999). The influence of gender, low birth weight, and disadvantaged environment in predicting early onset offending: A test of Moffitt's interactional hypothesis. *Criminology*, 37, 843–878.

Topitzes, J., Mersky, J. P., & Reynolds, A. J. (2011). Child maltreatment and offending behavior: Gender-specific effects and pathways. *Criminal Justice and Behavior*, 38, 492–510.

Trulson, C. R., Haerle, D. R., Caudill, J. W., & DeLisi, M. (2016). *Lost causes: Blended sentencing, second chances, and the Texas Youth Commission*. Austin, TX: University of Texas Press.

Twardosz, S. & Lutzker, J. R. (2010). Child maltreatment and the developing brain: A review of neuroscience perspectives. *Aggression and Violent Behavior*, 15, 59–68.

US Department of Health and Human Services, Administration for Children and Families, Administration on Children, Youth and Families, Children's Bureau. (2013). *Child maltreatment 2012*. Retrieved March 20, 2016 from www.acf.hhs.gov/programs/cb/research-data-technology/statistics-research/child-maltreatment.

Vaughn, M. G., DeLisi, M., Gunter, T., Fu, Q., Beaver, K. M., Perron, B. E., & Howard, M. O. (2011). The severe 5%: A latent class analysis of the externalizing spectrum in the United States. *Journal of Criminal Justice*, 39, 75–80.

Vaughn, M. G., DeLisi, M., Salas-Wright, C., & Maynard, B. R. (2014). Examining violence and externalizing behavior among youth in the United States: Is there a severe 5%? *Youth Violence and Juvenile Justice*, 12, 3–21.

Widom, C. S. (1989a). The cycle of violence. *Science*, 244(4901), 160–166.

Widom, C. S. (1989b). Child abuse, neglect, and adult behavior: Research design and findings on criminality, violence, and child abuse. *American Journal of Orthopsychiatry*, 59, 355–367.

Widom, C. S. (2014). The 2013 Sutherland Address: Varieties of violent behavior. *Criminology*, 52, 313–344.

Widom, C. S. & Maxfield, M. G. (2001). *An update on the "cycle of violence."* Washington, DC: National Institute of Justice, US Department of Justice.

Wijkman, M., Bijleveld, C., & Hendriks, J. (2010). Women don't do such things!

Characteristics of female sex offenders and offender types. *Sexual Abuse: A Journal of Research and Treatment*, 22, 135–156.

Wolff, K. T. & Baglivio, M. T. (2017). Adverse childhood experiences, negative emotionality, and pathways to juvenile recidivism. *Crime & Delinquency*, 1–27. 63(12), 1495–1521.

Wolff, K. T., Baglivio, M. T., & Piquero, A. R. (2015). The relationship between adverse childhood experiences and recidivism in a sample of juvenile offenders in community-based treatment. *International Journal of Offender Therapy and Comparative Criminology*, 1–33. doi: 10.1177/0306624X15613992.

Wolfgang, M. E., Figlio, R. M., & Sellin, T. (1972). Delinquency in a birth cohort. Chicago: University of Chicago Press.

Yu-Ling Chiu, Y. L., Ryan, J. P., & Herz, D. C. (2011). Allegations of maltreatment and delinquency: Does risk of juvenile arrest vary substantiation status? *Children and Youth Services Review*, 33, 855–860.

PART IV

Contextual Factors for Violence and Aggression

27 Youth Gangs and Violent Behavior

Victor Mora and Scott H. Decker

Introduction

Gangs and violence have become interchangeable terms in the past decade. The dramatic increase in youth homicide in the early 1990s led several commentators to conclude that gangs could be implicated in that increase. Indeed, when the term "gangs" is mentioned in the media or among public audiences, the context typically includes a violent event. However, this relationship between youth gangs and violent behavior is far more complex than it might appear. Although the focus in gang violence is often on homicide and gangs are disproportionately involved in homicide compared to other groups, there is more to gang violence than homicide – much more.

Here, we review what is known about youth gangs and violent behavior. We begin by considering the definitions of gang violence, a key to understanding the problem. The first section of the chapter pays particular attention to the differentiation between gang and nongang violence, noting the salience of who does the defining of such incidents, as well as the impact of such definitions for problem identification and for interventions. The next section of the chapter is devoted to a consideration of gang homicide. Here we present data from both national surveys of law enforcement and the Uniform Crime Reports. This discussion leads naturally to the next section of the chapter: instrumentalities associated with gang violence. Here we consider the role that guns and drugs specifically play in gang violence. We then assess what is known about gang violence from the perspective of the medical setting. This is followed by a review of theories of youth gang violence, specifically the role of structural and social process variables, and next by a section on prison gangs. We then move to an examination of the nature of gang violence in non-American settings in order to isolate the factors that are common and unique to the US context. We conclude this chapter with a set of observations about the future of gang violence.

Definition

The key to understanding youth gangs and violent behavior lies in an appreciation of the difficulty of defining the problem. Like many topics in the study of violence, the definitional issues are complicated and engender many debates. The study of gangs has been replete with dilemmas about definition since Thrasher's seminal work in 1927. One of the key methodological issues in the study of gangs has been whether the unit of analysis is the gang, the gang member, or the act (crime) committed by the gang member or members. As Short (1985, 1989) has ably demonstrated, the unit of analysis issue has important implications for what is learned about gangs.

In analyzing youth gangs and violent behavior, the key issue is whether an act of violence was that of a youth gang. The issue sounds simpler than it is, and, surprisingly, there is no consensus on what the definition of a gang crime is or should be. At the federal level, the FBI (1999) has offered a sweeping definition of a gang:

> The Federal Bureau of Investigation defines a Violent Street Gang/Drug Enterprise As: A criminal enterprise having an organizational structure, acting as a continuing criminal conspiracy, which employs violence and any other criminal activity to sustain the enterprise. From the FBI's perspective a gang is a group of individuals involved in continuing criminal activity. A gang DOES NOT have to have similar clothing (colors), tattoos, hand signs, initiation rituals, or even have a specific name such as Crips or Bloods.

This definition focuses heavily on the organizational aspects of the gang and is inconsistent with what most local law enforcement agencies and researchers understand about gangs.

Local law enforcement agencies define gangs and gang crimes differently. Their definitions fall roughly into two groups. The first approach defines a gang crime based on the participation of a gang member in the act, either as a victim or an offender. This is the definition used by the city of Los Angeles and many other cities in Southern California. This is a broad and inclusive definition that depends only on the ability of an officer or investigator to determine whether a victim or offender is a documented gang member. Other cities, such as Chicago, use a much more restrictive definition, relying instead on the motive for an offense. These definitions are referred to as "motive-based" definitions. Thus, an offense that may involve a gang member, both as victim and offender, may only be classified as gang-related if the motive has something to do with the intentions or desires of the gang or furthers its interests. Such acts often include battles over gang turf, retaliation against rival gangs or gang members, or crimes committed to generate economic gain for the gang.

The use of a motive-based definition requires considerably more information and investigation than the use of a member-based definition of gang crime. There are other consequences to the choice of definition of gang crime as well. Klein and Maxson (Klein, Maxson, & Cunningham, 1991; Maxson & Klein, 1990, 1996) have examined homicides in Los Angeles using both the Los Angeles gang member definition and the Chicago gang motive definition. Their findings are instructive. The member-based definition yields nearly twice as many gang-related homicides as the narrower gang motive definition. This finding underscores the dramatic difference that definition makes in the study of gang violence. Equally important, however was the finding that, regardless of the definition that was used, the substantive characteristics of each group of homicides did not differ. Thus they found that the demographic characteristics of the individuals involved (race, age, and gender) and the situational characteristics (guns, location, victim offender relationship) of the events for motive and member-based definitions were the same. In terms of measuring gang membership, self-nomination has proven to be a robust measure that is capable of differentiating gang and non-gang youth (Esbensen, Winfree, He, & Taylor, 2001). Decker and colleagues also determined that self-nomination was valid when measuring an individual's disengagement from the gang (Decker, Pyrooz, Moule, & Sweeten, 2014).

Homicide

There are several sources of data to assess the magnitude of gang homicide, though all of them have some basis in police reports. It is important to note that, because there is no national source of gang crime reporting, the picture regarding gang crime and violence must be constructed by compiling a variety of sources. Maxson (1999) credits Walter Miller (1982) with the first attempt to bring data on gang homicide together in a single source. Based on a limited sample of nine gang cities, his work demonstrated that gang homicides represented a significant part of the homicide problem in these cities. A number of other researchers (Curry, Ball, & Decker, 1996; Maxson, Gordon, & Klein, 1985) have also surveyed cities to determine the number of gang homicides and gang members reported by law enforcement. This task was formalized by the National Youth Gang Center (NYGC) beginning in 1995. Their work builds on the foundation provided by Curry and Maxson, who serve as consultants to the NYGC in its annual survey of law enforcement.

The Office of Juvenile Justice and Delinquency Prevention (OJJDP) funds the National Youth Gang Center. Looking across these studies of gang homicide, several patterns are evident. First, the *pattern* of gang homicide appears similar to that for youth homicide in the United States, experiencing a dramatic increase in the early 1990s and leveling off by the end of the 1990s. Despite this pattern, the overall *level* of gang homicide is considerably higher than for other subcategories of homicide, including domestics and robbery, reinforcing the consistent finding that gang membership is a significant risk factor for involvement in violence, both as a perpetrator and a victim (Decker & Van Winkle, 1996; Thornberry et al., 2002). Juveniles are also more likely to carry and fire a gun than older offenders and their gun behavior is largely influenced by gang membership (Watkins, Huebner, & Decker, 2008). Finally, the individual and situational *characteristics* of gang homicides are distinctive from those of homicides in general. Gang homicides are far more likely to involve males, racial or ethnic group minority members, and guns, and to occur outside and with multiple participants than are other homicides. This distinctive character is the key thesis for this chapter.

The NYGC survey data on gang homicide begin with the year 1996, when 1,330 gang homicides were reported by cities with populations over 100,000 (Curry, Egley, & Howell, 2004). This figure declined steadily to its level of 1,082 in 1999 and 1,080 in 2000. However a dramatic increase was observed over the next three years, with the number of gang homicides increasing to 1,451 for 2003 (again, in cities with a population of over 100,000), the highest level recorded by the NYGC survey methodology. This is an increase of 34% over 1999, the nadir in the trend. It is important to note that this increase occurred during a time when national homicide levels were falling since their peaks in the early 1990s, making the increase in gang homicides more troubling and more significant and reinforcing the distinctive character of gang homicides.

Historically, Chicago and Los Angeles have stood out for their exceptionally high levels of gang violence, particularly gang homicide. To a large extent, changes in gang homicide figures for cities with a population of over 100,000 are driven by changes in gang homicide in Chicago and Los Angeles. In 2003, Los Angeles and Chicago accounted for 39% of all gang homicides reported nationally for cities with a population of over 100,000, and in 2002 they accounted for 53% of all gang homicides, the largest proportion in the eight years that the NYGC has counted gang homicides (Curry et al., 2004). However, the dramatic increase between 1999 and 2003 in gang homicides cannot be attributed wholly to Los Angeles and Chicago, as there was an increase in gang homicides in all other jurisdictions as well. In 2009, one-half of the homicides in Los Angeles and one-third of the homicides in Chicago were gang-related (Howell, Egley, Tita, & Griffiths, 2011). It is important to note, however, that one-quarter of the homicides in cities with populations of over 100,000 were gang-related as well (Howell et al., 2011).

Because of their prominent role in gang homicide, Los Angeles and Chicago have been the site of a considerable number of studies of gang homicide. Maxson (1999) provides a comparison in trends in gang homicides for these two cities that documents a dramatic increase in both the number of gang homicides and percent of all homicides represented by gang homicides since 1980. The last year in the time series for both cities, 1995, also represents the peak year for the proportion of all homicides classified as gang homicides in these two cities. Forty-five percent of all homicides in Los Angeles County could be classified as gang-related, whereas, in Chicago, roughly one-quarter of all homicides were classified as gang-related. These comparisons illustrate the magnitude of the gang problem for these municipal areas, as well as the impact of using ways of defining whether an offense is related to gang involvement. Tita and Abrahamse (2004) examined gang homicide in Los Angeles County for the period 1981–2001. They document small declines in the percent of all homicides represented by gang homicides since 1995, until the years 2000 and 2001, when the percentages jumped to 41 and 48%, respectively. In an interesting analysis, they calculate what the expected gang homicide rate should be based on the demographic characteristics of the population in Los Angeles County and contrast that with the State of California. Their results show that the state of California has about one-third the number of homicides that would be expected, but that Los Angeles County has more than twice that number when controlling for age and race characteristics of county residents. Tita and Abrahamse (2004, p. 15) also show that some forms of homicide, specifically homicides involving rape and non-gun felony homicides, have declined during the period of increasing gang homicides and that other forms of homicides, such as "arguments with a stranger, gun involved" have leveled off.

It is important to underscore that gang members are overrepresented both as offenders and victims in homicides. Gang members in large US cities have been reported to have homicide rates nearly 100 times higher than the national average (Decker & Pyrooz, 2010). It is also worth noting that communities with the highest concentration of gang members have the highest rates of gun assault (Huebner et al., 2014). Gang membership has been identified as a risk factor for violent victimization, a fact that in turn leads to a large volume of retaliatory violence. Indeed, an ethnographic study of gang members in St. Louis (Decker & Van Winkle, 1996) found that nearly one-quarter of the 99 members of the initial sample had been murdered within a three-year period following the conclusion of the study.

These results suggest that gangs represent something different when it comes to violence; that is, gangs make a dramatic difference in the level and nature of violence, particularly lethal violence. This chapter examines that distinctive character of gang violence, specifically considering the role of instrumentalities, social structure, and social processes.

Instrumentalities

This chapter has documented a number of correlates that distinguish gang from non-gang homicide, including a prior relationship between the victim and the offender, the occurrence of the event outdoors, the involvement of multiple suspects, and the presence of firearms and drugs.

Firearms

The disproportionate role of firearms in gang-related homicides and gang violence has been well documented in criminological research. In their 11-city study of arrestees, Decker, Pennell, and Caldwell (1996) found that self-reported gang members were more likely than other subgroups to report wanting, owning, using, and being victimized by firearms.

Others (Bjerregaard & Lizotte, 1995; Lizotte, Tesoriero, Thornberry, & Krohn, 1994) report that gun ownership remains one of the strongest correlates of gang membership and gang violence. For instance, Lizotte and colleagues (1994) report that youth who carry guns for protection are five times more likely to be in a gang than youth who own guns for sporting purposes. The accumulation of firearms becomes a power struggle between rival gangs (Blumstein, 1995; Watkins et al., 2008).

Youth who carry guns are also more attractive gang members for recruitment purposes, and gang members are more likely to carry guns outside their homes compared to other youth with similar backgrounds from comparable neighborhoods (Bjerregaard & Lizotte, 1995). Firearms are the weapon of choice among gang members, a preference for ownership that has increased over the course of the past four decades (Howell, 1998). This fact appears to be linked closely to the increased lethality of gang assaults (Block & Block, 1993). This fact appears to be linked closely to the high levels of violent death rates in gang-involved populations in ethnographic research (Decker & van Winkle, 1996) and in official data (Decker & Pyrooz, 2010). There may be a restriction to gun access based on age or prior criminal history, but gang members in Chicago are more likely to get guns from family, acquaintances, and fellow gang members rather than purchasing them from a licensed dealer or stealing them (Cook, Park, & Pollack, 2015).

Firearms are intimately linked to a particular and highly publicized form of gang violence: drive-by shootings. Firearms capable of firing multiple projectiles (typically semi-automatic pistols or rifles) are integral to the execution of such violent activities by gang members. In Los Angeles (Hutson, Anglin, & Eckstein, 1996) one estimate is that, during a five-year period, one-third of gang homicides occurred during a drive-by shooting. Drive-by shootings exemplify many features of gang violence as described by Sanders (1994). He characterizes gang life as one in which "the violent aspects of gang life are always there – either defensively or as an offensive option" (p. 146), a view echoed for St. Louis gang members, whose lives are characterized by "threat" from rival gangs, one's own gang, and the police (Decker & Van Winkle, 1996). In St. Louis, gang youth are six times more likely to get shot than their non-gang youth counterparts (Curry, Decker, & Egley, 2002). What makes the drive-by shooting the quintessential gang crime is that it is unpredictable, generates considerable fear among gang and non-gang members in communities, and creates intimidation among gang and community residents alike (Howell, 1998). These neighborhoods with high concentrations of gang members create a potentially volatile situation where members frequently interact with rival gang members, thus increasing the likelihood of gun violence (Huebner et al., 2014; Papachristos, Hureau, & Braga. 2013). Despite their large media exposure, drive-by shootings should be considered infrequent occurrences. In West Oakland, California, offenders were ten times more likely to walk up to a target and shoot than to use a vehicle for the shooting (Wilson & Riley, 2004). Similarly, an analysis of homicides in San Diego, California between 1999 and 2003 revealed that drive-by shootings accounted for nearly 10% of the total homicides (Wilson et al., 2004).

Drugs

The involvement of youth gang members in drug sales increased dramatically, coinciding with the widespread availability of crack cocaine in the late 1980s. This dramatic increase occurred at a time when the urban underclass also deepened in many large American cities. There is considerable overlap among drug use, drug trafficking, and involvement in violent crime among gang members. Howell and Decker (1999) document the considerable overlap between involvement in drug markets and the use of violence. Entire neighborhoods are divided into territories of competing gangs (Decker & van Winkle, 1996; Papachristos et al., 2013). Block and Block (1993) identify disputes over drug turf as being at the heart of a considerable amount of gang violence. Similarly, Klein et al. (1991) document the substantial involvement of gang members in drug sales. A host of ethnographic studies (Decker & Van Winkle, 1996; Hagedorn, 1998, 1994; Vigil, 1988) have documented that gang members are extensively involved in the sale of drugs. Drug use among gang members has also been reported in a host of studies (Decker & Van Winkle, 1994; Hagedorn, 1988; Howell & Decker, 1999). Despite this involvement, a causal relationship between gangs and drugs sales is not supported by the empirical literature.

There are two competing views about the role of gangs and gang members in street drug sales. The first view is that street gangs are well-organized and effective mechanisms for the distribution of illegal drugs and invest drug sales profits into their gang. An alternative explanation posits that gang and gang member drug sales are seldom well organized, with gang members operating independently of their gangs in drug sales.

Two issues that are critical to understanding the link between gangs and drugs and that have implications for gang violence are the organizational aspects of gangs and the nature of the street drug market. Skolnick (1990) and Sanchez-Jankowski (1991) describe gangs as formal-rational organizations with a leadership structure, roles, rules, common goals, and control over members. On the other hand, Klein et al. (1991), Klein and Maxson (1994), and Decker and Van Winkle (1994, 1996) all describe gangs as loosely confederated groups that lack much internal cohesion or formal characteristics of organization.

To control drug sales effectively, gangs must possess several characteristics. First, gangs must have an organizational structure, with a hierarchy of leaders, roles, and rules. Second, gangs must have group goals that are widely shared among members. Third, gangs must promote stronger allegiance to the larger organization than to subgroups within it. Finally, gangs must possess the means to control and discipline their members to produce compliance with group goals. Most gang members sell drugs, though the level at which they sell may not be increased by gang membership alone. It is clear that involvement in drug trafficking is a risk factor for becoming the victim or, for that matter, the perpetrator of violence. Despite that involvement, conflict between gangs accounts for more gang violence, including homicide, than does involvement in the drug trade. Involvement in the drug trade is different from drug use. Vigil (2007) explains that heavy drug and alcohol use as well as violence, crime, and territoriality are part of certain gang cultures. Recent ethnographies have shown that violence is often retaliatory in nature and is commonly a result of inter-gang conflict over honor and prestige. In London, the gang members that Densley (2013) interviewed recounted that violence was the most efficient way to promote in the gang. Violence was believed to be fundamental in protecting turf and gang business (Densley, 2013). In his work in Little Village, a predominantly Hispanic neighborhood community in Chicago, Vargas (2016) found that gang violence stemmed from disputes over honor and respect rather than drug trade disputes. Lauger (2012), in his work in Indianapolis, Indiana, noted that the members of the DFW Boyz (Down For Whatever) would use violence as a source of gaining legitimacy within the gang as well as respond to violence with greater violence to improve their status amongst other gangs. Klein and Maxson (1985; Klein, Maxson, & Cunningham, 1988, 1991; Maxson, 1995, 1998) have shown that the relationship between drug trafficking and gang homicide is not causal and generally not strong. This finding has been supported in research from Boston, St. Louis, and Chicago (Howell & Decker, 1999). That said, increased involvement in entrepreneurial activities (Coughlin & Venkatesh, 2003) appears to be related to increased involvement in violence, particularly in cities with more organized gangs.

Theories of Gang Violence

Theories of gang violence have either emphasized community-level explanations or approaches that emphasize the role of social processes. The former theories underscore the role of community structure and other social variables, including measures of community social control, in the generation of patterns and trends in homicide. Such explanations typically include measures of racial composition, concentrated poverty, gun availability, and the presence of drug markets and drug use in the neighborhood or city as the unit of analysis (Rosenfeld, Bray, & Egley, 1999). Such approaches often use spatial analysis (Blumstein, Cohen, Cork, Engberg, & Tita, 2002; Cohen & Tita, 1999). Explanations that emphasize collective behavior point to the role of social processes, such as contagion and retaliation, and depend more often on ethnographic or case study materials. The former approach emphasizes the spatial distribution of individual and neighborhood characteristics, whereas the latter highlights dynamic social processes.

Structural Explanations

Curry and Spergel (1988) examined homicide and gang delinquency among both Latinos and African-Americans in Chicago. They conclude that gang homicides have a significantly different ecological pattern than do non-gang homicides and conform to classic models of social disorganization and poverty. They argue that conceptualizing gang groups as a function of mobility patterns is a productive conceptual means of understanding gang homicides. Thus, in neighborhoods in the process of undergoing shifts in population composition, overall mobility, and economic change, social disorganization was likely to be found. This disorganization was subsequently linked to gang homicide and other forms of gang crime, particularly violence. This conclusion was reached by examining a host of structural variables, including race/ethnicity and poverty.

The strong spatial concentration of gang homicides in neighborhoods characterized by poverty and social change is a consistent theme throughout the literature (Block, 1991; Block & Block, 1993; Kennedy, Braga, & Piehl, 1998; Rosenfeld et al., 1999; Wilson, 1987). In Chicago, a chronic gang city, Block and Block (1993) found very strong spatial concentrations of gang homicide. They conclude that "the rate of street-gang motivated crime in the 2 most dangerous areas was 76 times that of the 2 safest" (p. 1). Gang rivalries were at the core of the primary motivation in most of the gang homicides recorded in this study. Blumstein et al. (2002) conducted national, cross-city, and within-city analyses of youth homicide from the late 1980s into the mid-1990s. They documented a process of structural diffusion of youth and gang violence across and within cities that involved the growth of street-level crack cocaine sales, which in turn produced a heightened need for firearms to protect the product, profit, and purveyors of this drug. The need for firearms protection for this illicit industry fueled an escalation of armed youth, many of whom were involved in gangs. Spatial concentrations of gang members also create an environment where individuals are more exposed to situations that are more prone to result in gun violence (Huebner et al., 2014).

The spatial concentration of gang violence has been documented in a number of other cities, particularly Boston (Kennedy et al., 1998). Findings from Boston for gang homicide correspond with those reported by Block for Chicago and by Maxson (1999) for Los Angeles. In Boston, Kennedy et al. (1998) report an especially strong spatial concentration among gang homicides and document that with an important sociogram depicting the conflict between gangs. Similarly, Tita, Riley, and Greenwood (2002) have documented the strong spatial concentration of gang violence in the South Central neighborhoods of Los Angeles and the role of intergang conflict. Such events disproportionately involve gun assaults, firearms, and drugs. This finding is similar to that reported by Rosenfeld, Bray, and Egley (1999) for St. Louis, as well as by Cohen and Tita (1999) and Cohen, Cork, Engberg, and Tita (1998).

Social Processes

Studies of violence have increasingly focused on the social processes involved in the generation of such violence (Loftin, 1984). This type of analysis is concerned with the dynamics of interactions that lead to initial and, perhaps more important, retaliatory acts of gang violence. This level of analysis is consistent with the middle-range explanation encouraged by Short (1985, 1989), who underscored the role of group process and social-psychological variables in the understanding of gangs and gang activities. In the context of understanding violence, such variables are particularly important, as much gang violence has a retaliatory character. Research[1] on gang violence often fails to find the initial incident that motivated a specific act of violence. Although protecting neighborhood turf, drug turf, or both (Block & Block, 1993; Decker & Van Winkle, 1996; Sanchez-Jankowski, 1991; Sanders, 1994) is associated with a large fraction of gang violence, this correlation does not shed light on the motivations for specific incidents of gang violence. Recently, such explanations have looked to patterns of interaction in an effort to better account for the underlying mechanisms involved in the escalation and decline of incidents of gang violence (Decker, Melde, & Pyrooz, 2013).

Decker (1996) identified collective behavior processes in gang violence among St. Louis gang members. He observed spikes in gang violence that were often quite dramatic in magnitude. Such spikes are not consistent with a "smooth" process of increase or decline. He argued for the role of "threat" in the explanation of gang homicides, especially the retaliatory character of many gang homicides. The emphasis on retaliation in such approaches is important, as it has been identified as a common feature in much gang violence. Such a view emanates from Short's (1989) emphasis on identifying the group aspects of gang violence, rather than isolating the individual characteristics of such acts. This approach better accounts for the observation that gang violence can escalate rapidly, as one event precipitates another. An assault could initiate a sequence of retaliatory violence that moves beyond an individual neighborhood and its original participants (Papachristos, 2009; Cohen & Tita, 1999; Decker, 1996).

Such an approach emphasizes the dynamic social processes that resemble collective behavior among informal groups and lead to retaliatory violence between gangs and gang members. Decker (1996) and Decker and Curry (2002) argue that such explanations are consistent with both the organizational and normative features of youth gangs. It is important to note in

---

[1] Because of the contagious and retaliatory nature of gang violence (Kirk & Papachistos, 2011; Zeoli, Pizarro, Grady, & Melde, 2012), it is difficult for researchers to identify the initial act of violence that mobilizes gang violence and subsequent gang attacks. This initial act does not need to be overt or substantial. It could be a rumor, a social slight, or misperception. One of these acts can set off a cycle of retaliations by participants who may not even be aware of the initial precipitating incident.

this context the role that offending plays in victimization, particularly for gang members (Pyrooz, Decker, & Moule 2014) where offending and victimization are linked in a series of inter-relationships.

Vigil (2004) provides an explanation for some of the social psychological processes by which individuals come to participate in "senseless" acts of gang violence. The characteristics of these acts are such that the participants often refer to them as "loco." Vigil argues that in the most marginalized communities – whether that marginalization is a product of economic, cultural, or racial and ethnic marginalization (or all three) – community and social norms lose their potency for the control of behavior. Many individuals in marginalized communities also may experience a series of personal tragedies, including the violent or premature death of a family member or loved one, and the accumulation of such experiences takes a psychological toll on these individuals (Pynoos & Nader, 1988). This is particularly true for individuals who have experienced such personal trauma and who are gang members, as the gang is an effective vehicle for encouraging and supporting involvement in extreme acts of seemingly senseless violence. Thus from the perspective of a marginalized individual living in a marginalized community who has suffered considerable personal trauma, the gang can be an effective mechanism for supporting violent aggression in what appear to be irrational ways.

Support for the "violence escalation hypothesis" can also be found in Klein and Maxson (1989, p. 219) and in Maxson (1999). Their research documents that gang violence can best be understood as a series of reciprocal actions between rival gangs, each of which draws another, often sharper reaction. This reciprocity is reflected in gang rivalries. Such rivalries can be the consequence of a number of factors (drug turf, neighborhood dominance, symbolic ascendance, etc.) that over time are sublimated to the more immediate need to dominate turf, a rival, or both. Klein and Maxson also report that gangs have weak internal structures and generate little cohesion among their members. As such, they are generally ineffective mechanisms for generating compliance among members, thus failing to control acts of violence.

Further support for the role of collective behavior as an explanation for gang homicide comes from the work of Pizzaro and McGloin (2004). They examined homicide incidents occurring over five years in Newark, New Jersey. Using the Los Angeles definition of gang homicide as "gang-related" they compared the explanatory power of social disorganization and escalation variables to assess the relative importance of each in the explanation of gang homicides. Consistent with much prior research on gang violence, they found that the use of firearms, the event taking place outside, the involvement of multiple suspects, and an acquaintance relationship between victims and offenders statistically distinguished gang from non-gang homicides. Measures of the escalation/social process hypothesis included a threat against the group (gang) or status of the group that led to retaliatory function. Their logistic regression models documented the superiority of measures of social process compared to structural variables in explaining the difference between gang and non-gang homicides. In St. Louis, Decker (1996) also concluded that gang violence produces more violence through a process of threat and contagion that reflects elements of collective behavior.

Theories emphasizing the social processes involved in gang violence typically underscore the lack of structural control in gangs (Decker & Curry, 2002), particularly the weak control that gangs have over their members, and the role that rivalries can play in leading to violence within and between gangs. In addition, these studies document the role that the transitory nature of gang membership plays in such rivalries, reinforcing the notion that gangs may not be organizations capable of controlling the behavior of their members. This process has been enhanced by the widespread availability of technology, particularly social media. As the "digital divide" (Moule, Pyrooz, & Decker, 2013) has shrunk and gang members more frequently engage in the use of social media to fan the flames of violence (Pyrooz, Decker, & Moule, 2014; Patton, Eschmann, & Butler 2013) there is a new medium for keeping conflicts alive. Social media also helps to spread violence to new groups and potentially involve new victims.

Prison Gang Violence

Imprisonment often follows involvement in violent acts by gang members. The increased use of zero-tolerance policies regarding firearms violence, the subsequent dramatic rise in imprisonment during the 1990s, and the proliferation of street gang violence resulted in a large number of gang members going to prison or juvenile detention and correctional facilities. One national estimate places the proportion of confined juveniles who claim gang membership at 40% (Parent, Leiter, Livens, Wentworth, & Stephen, 1994), and another placed the figure at 78% (Knox & Tromanhauser, 1991). The Sheley and Wright (1995) survey of inner-city high-school students and residents of juvenile correctional facilities concluded that just over two-thirds (68%) of residents were gang members. Adult gang members also constitute an important part of the prison population (Camp & Camp, 1985; Ralph & Marquart, 1991) with dramatic increases in the 1990s. Gang members populate all facets of incarceration in the United States. It is estimated that gang members comprise roughly 13% of jail populations (Ruddell, Decker, & Egley, 2006), 12–17% of state prison populations (Griffin & Hepburn, 2006; Kreinert & Fleisher, 2001, and 9% of the federal prison population (Gaes et al., 2002).

Prison gangs are more structured than street gangs and have much stronger leadership (Pyrooz, Decker, & Fleisher, 2011). The rank-and-file membership often has several gradations, making prison gangs look much like organized crime groups. Research on street gangs shows that where profits are at stake, violence is often the outcome. Inside prisons, the same pattern appears, as prison gangs are heavily involved in prison violence (Ingraham & Wellford, 1987). Camp and Camp (1985) noted that prison gang members comprised 3% of the prison population, but caused 50% or more of the prison violence. In prison, gangs can have a virtual monopoly on drug sales and other gang-related services, such as gambling and prostitution (Fleisher, 1989), which often leads to competition between gangs for illegal markets (Fong, Vogel, & Buentello, 1992).

Prison also appears to compel many young men toward gang membership. Imprisonment may strengthen ties between gang members and their gangs, as gang affiliation is one of the few remaining sources of identification that may remain for incarcerated gang members. It also plays a role in maintaining the inmate code (Mitchell, Fahmy, Pyrooz, & Decker, 2017). Prison plays an increasingly important role in gang violence. As gang members become more involved in crime, their likelihood of going to prison increases. Street gangs may come to be directed by and influenced by prison gang culture. Going to prison also provides gang members with additional status when they return to the street.

Medical Settings

For males between the ages of 15 and 25 in the USA, violence is the second leading cause of death, but it is the leading cause of death for African American males between the ages of 15 and 25 (CDC, 2011). The volume of gang violence, particularly in Los Angeles, has had repercussions for the medical profession. Not surprisingly, a large number of the victims of gang violence require medical attention and end up in trauma facilities. This outcome has provided another opportunity to differentiate gang violence from other forms of violence.

Dealing with gunshot wounds is not new to the medical profession or to trauma centers. However, gunshot wounds caused by gang violence appear to be different both qualitatively and quantitatively from other gunshot wounds. A 29-month investigation of gang shootings in Los Angeles County (Song, Naude, Gilmore, & Bongard, 1996) revealed several important patterns in gang violence that help differentiate it from other forms of violence. Trauma registry records were used to identify the population, with links to law enforcement data regarding gang membership. Gang members were the victims in 272 of the 856 gunshot (32%) injuries during this time. Fifty-five of the gang victims were pediatric, and the rest were adults. The overwhelming majority of these gunshot victims (89%) were males, and less than 5% were classified as Whites. Trauma and injury severity scores were extremely high for this group, and 9% of the gunshot victims died of their wounds. Forty-three percent of the gunshot wound victims underwent emergency surgery, and interestingly the vast majority (86%) entered the hospital during hours when staffing was low, causing considerable stress to patient care. The financial toll of the gunshot wounds suffered by gang members was high as well. The cost of providing medical services to these 272 gang-related gunshot victims was just under $5 million ($4,828,828), and 55% of the victims had no third-party health insurance reimbursement. Ninety-one percent of these individuals suffered some form of disability. Together these data present some estimate of the toll placed on trauma centers by gang violence, at least in Los Angeles. Miller and Cohen (1997) contend that the toll of gun-related violence in the US will be significantly higher if psychological costs and the value of quality of life are included in the estimate.

Additional research on gang violence from a medical perspective also comes from Los Angeles. Hutson, Anglin, and Pratts (1994) examined drive-by shootings. Using police data, they examined the universe of victims in drive-by shootings involving someone under the age of 18 for the nature and extent of their injuries, as well as to establish prevalence estimates for such incidents. During calendar year 1991, 673 juveniles were shot at in drive-by shootings; of these, 63% had a gunshot wound, and 5% died from their injuries. These juveniles represent 38% of the total victims (1,548) in drive-by shootings in Los Angeles during 1991. Consistent with the work by Song et al., (1996), the vast majority of victims were either Black or Hispanic (97%, combined). Nearly three-quarters (71%) of the drive-by victims were gang members. The three most prevalent situational characteristics of gang shootings were the location (the inner city on public streets), time of day (night), and the type of firearm used (handguns in 71% of the cases). Hutson and his colleagues report that gang-related homicides among adolescents in Los Angeles represent over half (53%) of all adolescent murders, and between 1 and 2 children in 10 in Los Angeles have witnessed a homicide.

Hutson, Anglin, and Mallon (1992) found that drive-by shootings are not random and that many aspects of this form of youth gang violence are highly patterned. Specifically, the location (outside on inner-city streets), gender and race representations (Hispanic and African-American males), choice of weapon (handguns), and ages (highly concentrated among teenagers) are all consistent features across the majority of drive-by shootings. As such, they argue that interventions that are culturally specific and address specific risk factors are needed. In addition, they argue (Hutson et al., 1992) that such injuries can be prevented through effective use of public health strategies. A similar perspective has been endorsed by Hixon (1996), who argues for the use of screening questions in emergency rooms to assess the level of gang involvement and subsequent risk for violent victimization. Such information, from Hixon's perspective, can profitably be used for crafting emergency room interventions that involve counseling.

Gangs in Global Context

Until recently, the academic and policy focus on gangs has been almost exclusively on the United States. Indeed, the United States has the longest history of youth gangs, and violence among American youth gangs dwarfs the levels in other countries. But that focus has changed dramatically over the past decade. The Eurogang research network has identified gangs in 50 European cities and 16 European countries (Klein, Weerman, & Thornberry, 2006). Similarly, gangs and gang violence are present in each of the highly populated continents – North American, South America, Europe, Africa, and Asia (Decker & Pyrooz, 2010). These studies note the role that globalization, modernization, and immigration have played in the transmission of American cultural images and institutional practices around the world. Like in the USA, gang membership in Europe is closely tied to delinquency and peer factors (Haymoz, Maxson, & Killias, 2014) while life in the gang is also short-lived (Weerman, Lovegrove, & Thornberry, 2015). However, early studies indicate that although gangs in Europe (about which we know the most, with the best sources of information) resemble American youth gangs in many ways, they participate in violence at much lower levels (Decker, Van

Gemert, & Pyrooz, 2009) and are typically less organized (Pyrooz, Fox, Katz, & Decker, 2012).

Despite this difference, the migration of American gang styles and cultural symbols to Europe, South American, Asia, and Africa has grown dramatically in the past decade. Many studies of gangs in the international context have underscored the role of popular culture and the media in spreading and popularizing gangs and gang membership, though clearly the growth of immigrant groups in large cities can also be linked to these trends (Van Gemert & Decker, 2008). It is clear that the same sorts of youth culture and affiliational processes at work in the United States occur in many European contexts. However, we generally lack the same sort of police surveys in Europe that would serve to better document levels of street gang violence and make comparisons with the United States more appropriate.

Violence plays a central role in creating solidarity within American youth gangs. It appears that, in the European setting, ethnic identity can be substituted to a large extent for the role of violence. This is not to say, however, that gangs in Europe do not engage in violence. The work of Van Gemert and Fleisher (2005) in The Hague and Amsterdam underscores the instrumental role that violent thefts play in gang solidarity among Dutch gangs. However, recent research by Van Gemert, Roks, and Drogt (2016) notes that the Dutch Crips have begun to fade and only the original core members remain. A decline in membership, which necessitates a decline in gang violence, may be due in part to the lack of appeal of a gang identity that is based on American stereotypes to the new generation living in a liquid society (Van Gemert, Roks, & Drogt 2016). Lien (2005a, 2005b) documents the prevalence and role of violence by gangs comprised largely of ethnic minorities in Oslo. She reports that one gang member describes the gang as "hard men, like iron" (2005a, p. 35), and that fighting and robbery are more common among youth gangs than other Norwegian youth. In a comparison between gang violence in Brussels, Belgium and Caracas, Venezuela, researchers Vandenbogaerde and Van Hellemont (2016) found that violence was commonly driven by retaliation and fear of retaliation. Fighting is reported to be common among street gangs in Genoa, Italy (Gatti, Angelini, Marengo, Melchiorre, & Sasso, 2005), Russians of German descent in Germany (Weitekamp, Reich, & Kerner, 2005), and particularly among Russian youth gangs (Shashkin & Salagaev, 2005; Shashkin, Salagaev, Sherbakova, & Touryanskiy, 2005).

The emergence of youth gangs in Russia provides perhaps the closest parallels to the American situation, with the use of guns, armed robbery, and fighting being more common than in other European settings, particularly among gangs of older individuals. Distinguishing between adult and youth gangs in the Russian context is important. Although turf is not as important a source of rivalry among Russian gangs as in many American cities, it does play an important role in many gangs. In addition, masculinity plays a critical role in the generation and maintenance of gang violence. Groups of men with a history of fighting often evolve into gangs in the Russian context. Shashkin and his colleagues (2005) have documented extensive involvement in violence among Russian gangs, particularly in Moscow and Kazan. Indeed, their work has documented a particular form of gangs that has come to be known as "gangs of the Kazan type," which regularly engage in violence. They describe in detail the predatory activities of Russian youth gangs that are active in the Middle Volga region of Russia. The majority of illegal activity conducted by these groups is predatory – selling drugs, organizing small prostitution rings, and robbery. Shashkin et al. (2005) note the impact of several economic changes in Russia in creating a market for illegal goods and the consequent need for groups of young men to provide protection and enforcement for shop owners who dealt in those illegal goods. It is clear from these emerging descriptions of Russian gangs that the links between adult and youth gangs, the involvement in organized crime, and the penetration of organized crime into youth street gang culture provide a rapidly changing – and increasingly violent – context for Russian youth gangs. Recent research has noted that interest in street gangs has declined, which has led to a decrease in street fights amongst gang members, meanwhile racist skinhead groups have seemingly become more active across Russia (Safin, Salagaev, & Makarov, 2010; Shashkin, 2008).

What appears to set European gangs apart from American youth gangs with regards to violence, at least at this point in time, is their access to guns, extensive involvement in drug sales, and defense of turf. Levels of European youth gang violence are considerably lower than in the United States. Clearly, the absence of an established history of gangs, reduced access to guns, lower levels of overall violence, and lower social disparities between social classes are important aspects of the explanation for this reduced level of violence. However, there are signs of increasing street gang violence in Europe, particularly as immigration and globalization pressures increase.

Conclusion

To wrap up the discussion of gangs, it is important to address possible future concerns. As terrorism becomes more of a discussion point in the media, the question begins to shift towards gangs. Is it possible for gangs to become radicalized and be used as vehicles for terror? The short answer is: very unlikely. The major differences in organizational structure and beliefs are the major reasons why not (Decker & Pyrooz, 2010). The internet is also growing at a rapid pace. Is it possible for gangs to move to identity theft and online scams? This is also highly unlikely. Gang members are usually teenagers and use the internet for social media and for symbolic reasons rather than instrumental reasons (Pyrooz, Decker, & Moule, 2015). Finally, as marijuana becomes more socially and legally accepted, it will be interesting to see how gang members who deal drugs will respond. As legal marijuana begins to saturate the market, it is possible that violence will break out for limited profits or dealers will begin to push harder drugs.

This chapter has documented the involvement of youth gangs in violent behavior. Regardless of how a gang is defined and of how gang-related crime is defined, a large proportion of violence is related to gang activity. It appears that this pattern of involvement has increased since the turn of the twenty-first century. It is no longer possible to argue that the more extreme forms of gang violence are confined largely to the Los Angeles and Chicago areas, as cities across the country report a substantial part of their homicide problem as being related to gangs. Gang violence embodies several distinctive characteristics that make it distinguishable from other forms of violence. First, the participants in gang violence share in common a large number of demographic and situational characteristics. Males, inner-city residents, and Hispanics and African-Americans are disproportionately involved in gang violence, both as victims and as perpetrators. Firearms are used in gang violence more than in other types of violence, and there seems to be a preference for handguns in such violent crimes. Gang violence is most likely to take place out-of-doors, where it can be observed and felt by a large circle of individuals beyond the perpetrator and their intended victim. Gang violence, more than other forms of violence, is likely to involve multiple victims and multiple suspects. The research dedicated to females in gangs has also grown over the years. Females are enticed to join gangs for many of the same push and pull factors as males. The end of a gang career was also discussed. These careers typically do not last very long. Violence and fear of victimization become burdensome and the reasons for leaving often become the same reasons that made joining the gang appealing in the first place.

Although structural variables, such as concentrated economic and social disadvantage, are associated with the presence of gang violence, social processes also play an important role in such events. Because a large proportion of gang violence involves retaliation between individuals with an ongoing feud of some sort, understanding the processes that create and perpetuate gang violence is an important task. Much gang violence appears to have a contagious character, spreading from one neighborhood to another and outliving the initial source of the problem. These characteristics of gang violence have consequences for the increase and spread in prison gang violence. The links between street gangs and prison gangs are most important in this regard, with many incidents in prison linked to the street and many incidents of street violence linked to prison gangs. The role of prison gangs has especially important consequences for current re-entry initiatives. Involvement in prison gangs may thwart community reintegration and make transition to the community more difficult for such individuals. Gang violence has had increasingly important consequences for the medical profession, particularly those who work in trauma or emergency settings. In these settings the costs and volume of cases have become excessive in some jurisdictions. Finally, the problems of youth gangs and violent behavior are no longer confined to the United States. Youth gang violence, particularly in the form of assault and robbery, can be found throughout Western and Eastern Europe, and increasingly in Central and South America. The prospects for youth gangs becoming an entrenched part of global youth culture is enhanced by this spread of gangs. Youth gang violence – and the research of said violence – has become a global phenomenon. Gang activity has been found in every highly populated continent. As the research methodologies become more refined, the prevalence of gangs around the world will become clearer.

References

Bjerregaard, B. & Lizotte, L. (1995). Gun ownership and gang membership. *Journal of Criminal Law and Criminology*, 86, 37–58.

Block, C. R. (1991). Gang homicide in Chicago: Patterns over time, area of city, and type of victim. Presented to Midwestern Criminal Justice Association. Chicago, Illinois.

Block, C. & Block, R. (1993). Street gang crime in Chicago. Research in Brief. Washington, DC: National Institute of Justice.

Blumstein, A. (1995). Youth violence, guns, and the illicit-drug industry. *The Journal of Criminal Law and Criminology*, 86(1), 10–36.

Blumstein, A., Cohen, J., Cork, D., Engberg, J., & Tita, G. (2002). *Diffusion processes in homicide*. Washington, DC: National Institute of Justice.

Braga, A. A. (2008). Pulling levers focused deterrence strategies and the prevention of gun homicide. *Journal of Criminal Justice*, 36(4), 332–343.

Braga, A. A., Hureau, D. M., & Papachristos, A. V. (2014). Deterring gang-involved gun violence: measuring the impact of Boston's operation ceasefire on street gang behavior. *Journal of Quantitative Criminology*, 30(1), 113–139.

Camp, G. M. & Camp, C. G. (1985). *Prison gangs: Their extent, nature, and impact on prisons*. Washington, DC: US Government Printing Office.

Centers for Disease Control and Prevention. (2011). *Web-based injury statistics query and reporting system*. Retrieved March 30, 2017 from www.cdc.gov/injury/wisqars/.

Cohen, J., Cork, D., Engberg, J., & Tita, G. (1998). The role of drug markets and gangs in local homicide rates. *Journal of Homicide Studies*, 2, 241–262.

Cohen, J. & Tita, G. E. (1999). Spatial Diffusion in Homicide: An Exploratory Analysis. *Journal of Quantitative Criminology*, 15, 451–493.

Cook, P. J., Parker, S. T., & Pollack, H. A. (2015). Sources of guns to dangerous people: What we learn by asking them. *Preventive Medicine*, 79, 28–36.

Coughlin, B. C. & Venkatesh, S. A. (2003). The urban street gang after 1970. *Annual Review of Sociology*, 29, 41–64.

Covey, H. C. (2003). *Street gangs throughout the world*. Springfield, IL: Charles C. Thomas.

Curry, G. D., Ball, R. A., & Decker, S. H. (1996). Update on gang crime and law enforcement recordkeeping: Report of the 1994 NIJ extended national assessment survey of law enforcement anti-gang information resources. Washington, DC: US Department of Justice.

Curry, G. D., Decker, S. H., & Egley Jr, A. (2002). Gang involvement and delinquency in a middle school population. *Justice Quarterly*, 19(2), 275–292.

Curry, G. D., Egley, H., & Howell, J. C. (2004). *Youth gang homicide trends in the National Youth Gang Survey*. Paper Presented at the American Society of Criminology Meetings. Nashville, TN.

Curry, G. D. & Spergel, I. (1988). Gang homicide, delinquency, and community. *Criminology*, 26, 381–405.

Decker, S. H. (1996). Collective and normative features of gang violence. *Justice Quarterly*, 13(2), 243–264.

Decker, S. H. & Curry, G. D. (2002). Gangs, gang homicides and gang loyalty: Organized crimes or disorganized criminals? *Journal of Criminal Justice*, 30, 343–352.

Decker, S. H., Melde, C., & Pyrooz, D. C. (2013). What do we know about gangs and gang members and where do we go from here? *Justice Quarterly*, 30, 369–402.

Decker, S. H., Pennell, S. P., & Caldwell, A. (1996). *Arrestees and firearms*. National Institute of Justice. Washington, DC: National Institute of Justice.

Decker, S. H., & Pyrooz, D. C. (2010). Gang violence worldwide: Context, culture, and country. In *Small Arms Survey 2010: Gangs, groups, and guns* (pp. 128–155). Cambridge: Cambridge University Press.

Decker, S. H., Pyrooz, D. C., Moule, R. K., & Sweeten, G. (2014). Validating self-nomination in gang research: Assessing differences in gang embeddedness across non, current, and former gang members. *Journal of Quantitative Criminology*, 30(4), 577–598.

Decker, S. H., Van Gemert, F., & Pyrooz, D. C. (2009). Gangs, migration, and crime: The changing landscape in Europe and the USA. *Journal of International Migration and Integration*, 10(4), 393–408.

Decker, S. H. & Van Winkle, B. (1994). Slingin' dope: The role of gangs and gang members in drug sales. *Justice Quarterly*, 11, 583–684.

Decker, S. H. & Van Winkle, B. (1996). *Life in the gang; Family, friends and violence*. New York. Cambridge University Press.

Densley, J. (2013). *How gangs work: An ethnography of youth violence*. Basingstoke: Palgrave Macmillan.

Esbensen, F. A., Winfree, L. T., He, N., & Taylor, T. J. (2001). Youth gangs and definitional issues: When is a gang a gang, and why does it matter? *Crime & Delinquency*, 47(1), 105–130.

Federal Bureau of Investigation. (1999). *FBI gang alert*. Washington, DC: Author.

Fleisher, M. S. (1989). *Warehousing violence*. Newbury Park, CA: Sage.

Fong, R. S., Vogel, R. E., & Buentello, S. (1992). Prison gang dynamics: A look inside the Texas Department of Corrections. In P. J. Benekos & A. V. Merlo (Eds), *Corrections: Dilemmas and directions* (pp. 57–77). Cincinnati, OH: Anderson Publishing

Gaes, G. G., Wallace, S., Gilman, E., Klein-Saffran, J., & Suppa, S. (2002). The influence of prison gang affiliation on violence and other prison misconduct. *The Prison Journal*, 82(3), 359–385.

Gatti, U., Angelini, F., Marengo, G., Melchiorre, N., & Sasso, M. (2005). An old fashioned gang in Genoa. In S. Decker & F. Weerman (Eds), *European street gangs and troublesome youth groups* (pp. 63–102). Walnut Creek, CA: Alta Mira.

Griffin, M. L. & Hepburn, J. R. (2006). The effect of gang affiliation on violent misconduct among inmates during the early years of confinement. *Criminal Justice and Behavior*, 33(4), 419–466.

Hagedorn, J. M. (1988). *People and folks: Gangs, crime and the underclass in a Rust Belt city*. Chicago: Lakeview Press.

Hagedorn, J. M. (1994). Homeboys, dope fiends, legits and new jacks. *Criminology*, 32, 197–217.

Haymoz, S., Maxson, C., & Killias, M. (2014). Street gang participation in Europe: A comparison of correlates. *European Journal of Criminology*, 11(6), 659–681.

Hixon, A. L. (1999). Preventing street gang violence. *American Family Physician*, 125, 1–7.

Howell, J. C. (1998). *Youth gangs: An overview*. Washington, DC: US Department of Justice.

Howell, J. C. & Decker, S. H. (1999). *The youth gangs, drugs, and violence connection*. Washington, DC: US Department of Justice.

Howell, J. C., Egley, A., Jr., Tita, G. E., & Griffiths, E. (2011). *US gang problem trends and seriousness, 1996–2009*. Washington, DC: US Department of Justice.

Howell, J. C. & Lynch, J. P. (2000). *Youth gangs in schools*. Washington, DC: US Department of Justice.

Huebner, B. M., Martin, K., Pyrooz, D. C., Moule, R. K., & Decker, S. H. (2014). Dangerous places: Gang members and neighborhood levels of gun assault. *Justice Quarterly*, 30, 1–27.

Hutson, H. R., Anglin, D., & Eckstein, M. (1996). Drive-by shootings by violent street gangs in Los Angeles: A five-year review from 1989 to 1993. *Academic Emergency Medicine*, 3, 300–303.

Hutson, H. R., Anglin, D., & Mallon, W. (1992). Injuries and deaths from gang violence: They are preventable. *Annals of Emergency Medicine*, 21, 1234–1236.

Hutson, H. R., Anglin, D., & Pratts, M. J. (1994). Adolescents and children injured or killed in drive-by shootings in Los Angeles. *New England Journal of Medicine*, 330(5), 324–327.

Ingraham, B .L. & Wellford, C. F. (1987). The totality of conditions test in eighth-amendment litigation. In S. D. Gottfredson & S. McConville (Eds), *America's correctional crisis: Prison populations and public policy* (pp. 13–36). New York: Greenwood Press.

Kennedy, D. M., Braga, A. A., & Piehl, A. M. (1998). The (un)known universe: Mapping gangs and gang violence in Boston. In D. Weisburd & J. T. McEwen (Eds), *Crime mapping and crime prevention* (pp. 219–262). New York: Criminal Justice Press.

Kirk, D. S. & Papachristos, A. V. (2011). Cultural mechanisms and the persistence of neighborhood violence. *American Journal of Sociology*, 116(4), 1190–1233.

Klein, M. W., Weerman, F. M., & Thornberry, T. P. (2006). Street gang violence in Europe. *European Journal of Criminology*, 3(4), 413–437.

Klein, M. W., Kerner, H.-J., Maxson, C. L., & Weitekamp, E. G. M. (2001). *The eurogang paradox: Street gangs and youth groups in the U.S. and Europe*. Dordrecht: Kluwer.

Klein, M. W. & Maxson, C. L. (1989). Street gang violence. In N. A. Weiner & M.E. Wolfgang (Eds), *Violent crime, violent criminals* (pp. 198–234). Newbury Park, CA: Sage.

Klein, M. W. & Maxson, C. L. (1994). Gangs and Cocaine Trafficking. In D. MacKenzie and C. Uchida (Eds), *Drugs and the Criminal Justice System*. Newbury Park, CA: Sage Publications.

Klein, M. W., Maxson, C. L., & Cunningham, L. C. (1988). Gang involvement in cocaine rock trafficking. Unpublished report. Los Angeles, CA: Social Science Research Institute, University of Southern California.

Klein, M. W., Maxson, C. L., & Cunningham, L. C. (1991). Crack, street gangs, and violence. *Criminology*, 29(4), 623–650.

Knox, G. W. & Tromanhauser, E. D. (1991). Gangs and their control in adult correctional institutions. *Prison Journal*, 71, 15–22.

Krienert, J. L., & Fleisher, M. S. (2001). Gang membership as a proxy for social deficiencies: A study of Nebraska inmates. *Corrections Management Quarterly*, 5, 47–58.

Lauger, T. R. (2012). *Real gangstas: legitimacy, reputation, and violence in the intergang environment*. New Brunswick, NJ: Rutgers University Press.

Lien, I.-L. (2005a). Criminal gangs and their connections: Metaphors, definitions and structures. In S. Decker & F. Weerman (Eds), *European street gangs and troublesome youth groups* (pp. 35–62). Walnut Creek, CA: Alta Mira.

Lien, I.-L. (2005b). The role of crime acts in constituting the gang's mentality. In S. Decker & F. Weerman (Eds), *European street gangs and troublesome youth groups* (pp. 137–164). Walnut Creek, CA: Alta Mira.

Lizotte, A., Tesoriero, J. M., Thornberry, T. P., & Krohn, M. D. (1994). Patterns of adolescent firearms ownership and use. *Justice Quarterly*, 11, 51–73.

Loftin, C. (1984). Assaultive violence as contagious process. *Bulletin of the New York Academy of Medicine*, 62, 550–555.

Maxson, C. L. (1998). Gang homicide: A review and extentsion of the literature. In M. D. Smith and M. A. Zahn (Eds), *Homicide Studies: A sourcebook of social research* (pp. 197–220). Newbury Park, CA : Sage

Maxson, C. L. (1999). Gang homicide: A review and extension of the literature. In D. Smith & M. A. Zahn (Eds), *Homicide: A sourcebook of social research* (pp. 239–236). Newbury Park, CA: Sage.

Maxson, C. L. (2002). Play groups no longer: Urban street gangs in the Los Angeles region. In M. J. Dear (Ed.), *From Chicago to L.A.: Making sense of theory* (pp. 235–266). Thousand Oaks, CA: Sage.

Maxson, C. L. & Klein, M. W. (1990). Street Gang Violence: Twice as Great, or Half as Great. In C. R. Huff (Ed.), *Gangs in America* (p. 71–100). Newbury Park, CA.

Maxson, C. L. & Klein, M. W. (1996). Defining gang homicide: An updated look at member and motive approaches. In C. R. Huff (Ed.), *Gangs in America* (2nd ed.). Newbury Park, CA: Sage Publications.

Maxson, C. L., Gordon, M. A., & Klein, M. W. (1985). Differences between Gang an Nongang Homicides. *Criminology*, 23, 209–222.

Maxson, C. L., Whitlock, M. L., & Klein, M. W. (1998). Vulnerability to street gang membership: Implications for practice. *Social Service Review*, 72(1), 70–91.

Miller, W. B. (1982). *Crime by youth gangs and groups in the United States*. Washington,

DC: Office of Juvenile Justice and Delinquency Prevention. US Department of Justice.

Miller, T. R. & Cohen, M. A. (1997). Costs of gunshot and cut/stab wounds in the United States, with some Canadian comparisons. *Accident Analysis & Prevention*, 29(3), 329–341.

Mitchell, M. M., Fahmy, C., Pyrooz, D. C., & Decker, S. H. (2016). Criminal Crews, Codes, and Contexts: Differences and Similarities across the Code of the Street, Convict Code, Street Gangs, and Prison Gangs. *Deviant Behavior*, 38(10), 1197–1222.

Morenoff, J. D., Sampson, R. J., & Raudenbush, S. W. (2001). Neighborhood inequality, collective efficacy, and the spatial dynamics of urban violence. *Criminology*, 39(3), 517–558.

Moule, R. K., Jr., Pyrooz, D. C., & Decker, S. H. 2013. From 'What the f#@% is a Facebook?' to 'Who doesn't use Facebook?' The role of criminal lifestyles in the adoption and use of the Internet. *Social Science Research*, 42: 1411–1421.

Office of Juvenile Justice and Delinquency Prevention. (1996). *Victims of gang violence: A new frontier in victim services.* Washington, DC: Author.

Papachristos, A. V. (2009). Murder by Structure: Dominance Relations and the Social Structure of Gang Homicide. *American Journal of Sociology*, 115(1), 74–128.

Papachristos, A. V., Hureau, D. M., & Braga, A. (2013). The corner and the crew: The Influence of geography and social networks on gang violence. *American Sociological Review*, 78(3) 417–447.

Parent, D., Leiter, V., Livens, L., Wentworth, D., & Stephen, K. (1994). *Conditions of confinement: Juvenile detention and corrections facilities.* Washington, DC: US Department of Justice.

Patton, D. U., Eschmann, R. D., & Butler, D. A. (2013). Internet banging: New trends in social media, gang violence, masculinity and hip hop. *Computers in Human Behavior* 29: A54–A59.

Pizzaro, J. M. & McGloin, J. M. (2004). Explaining gang homicides in Newark: Collective behavior or social disorganization? Paper presented at the 2004 Meeting of the American Society of Criminology, Nashville, TN.

Pynoos, R. S. & Nader, K. (1988). Psychological first aid and treatment approach to children exposed to community violence: Research implications. *Journal of Traumatic Stress*, 1, 445–473.

Pyrooz, D., Decker, S., & Fleisher, M. (2011). From the street to the prison, from the prison to the street: Understanding and responding to prison gangs. *Journal of Aggression, Conflict and Peace Research*, 3(1), 12–24.

Pyrooz, D. C., Decker, S. H., & Moule, R. K. (2014). The Contribution of Gang Membership to the Victim-Offender Overlap. *Journal of Research in Crime and Delinquency*, 51(3), 315–348.

Pyrooz, D. C., Fox, A. M., Katz, C. M., & Decker, S. H. (2012). Gang organization, offending, and victimization: A cross-national analysis. In F. A. Esbensen, & C. L. Maxson (Eds), *Youth gangs in international perspective: Results from the Eurogang program of research* (pp. 85–105). New York: Springer.

Pyrooz, D. C., Moule, R. K., & Decker, S. H. (2015). Criminal and routine activities in online settings: Gangs, offenders, and the Internet. *Justice Quarterly*, 32(3), 471–499.

Ralph, P. H. & Marquart, J. W. (1991). Gang violence in Texas prisons. *Prison Journal*, 71, 38–49.

Rosenfeld, R. B., Bray, T., & Egley, H. (1999). Facilitating violence: A comparison of gang-motivated, gang-affiliated, and non-gang youth homicides. *Journal of Quantitative Criminology*, 15, 495–516.

Ruddell, R., Decker, S. H., & Egley, A. (2006). Gang Interventions in Jails a National Analysis. *Criminal Justice Review*, 31(1), 33–46.

Safin, R. R., Salagaev, A. L., & Makarov, A. S. (2010). Violent youth groups in the Tatarstan Republic of Russia. *Grupės ir aplinkos*, (2), 175–182.

Sanchez-Jankowski, M. (1991). *Islands in the Street*. Berkeley, CA: University of California Press.

Sanders, W. B. (1994). *Gangbangs and drivebys: Grounded culture and juvenile gang violence*. New York: Aldine.

Shashkin, A. (2008). Origins and development of racist skinheads in Moscow. In F. Van Gemert, D. Peterson, & I.-L. Lien (Eds), *Street gangs, migration and ethnicity* (p. 97–114). Cullompton: Willan Publishing.

Shashkin, A. & Salagaev, A. (2005). Violence and victimisation on the street: Power struggle and masculine hierarchies in Russia. In T. Hoikkala & L. Suurpaa (Eds), *Masculinities and Violence in Youth Microcultures* (pp. 11–45). Helsinki: Finnish Youth Research Network.

Shashkin, A., Salagaev, A., Sherbakova, I., & Touryanskiy, E. (2005). Contemporary Russian gangs: History, membership and crime involvement. In. S. Decker & F. Weerman (Eds), *European street gangs and troublesome youth groups* (pp. 209–240). Walnut Creek, CA: Alta Mira.

Sheley, J. F. & Wright, J. D. (1995). *In the line of fire: Youth, guns and violence in urban America*. New York: Aldine de Gruyter.

Short, J. F., Jr. (1985). The level of explanation problem in criminology. In R. F. Meier (Ed.), *Theoretical models in criminology* (pp. 51–72). Beverly Hills, CA: Sage.

Short, J. F., Jr. (1989). Exploring integration of theoretical levels of explanation: Notes on gang delinquency. In A. E. Liska, M. Krohn, & S. F. Messner (Eds), *Theoretical integration in the study of deviance and crime* (pp. 243–259). Albany, NY: SUNY Press.

Skarbek, D. (2011). Governance and prison gangs. *American Political Science Review*, 105(4), 702–716.

Skolnick, J. (1990). The social structure of street drug dealing. *American Journal of Police*, 9, 1–41.

Song, D. H., Naude, G. P., Gilmore, D. A., & Bongard, F. (1996). Gang warfare: The medical repercussions. *Journal of Trauma, Injury, Infection and Critical Care*, 40(5), 810–815.

Thornberry, T. P. & Burch, J. H. II. (1997). *Gang members and delinquent behavior*. Washington, DC: US Department of Justice.

Thornberry, T., Krohn, M. D., Lizotte, A. J., Smith, C. A., & Tobin, K. (2002). *Gangs in developmental perspective: The origins and consequences of gang membership*. New York: Cambridge University Press.

Thrasher, F. (1927). *The gang*. Chicago: University of Chicago Press.

Tita, G. & Abrahamse, A. (2004). *Gang homicide in LA, 1981–2001 Perspectives on violence prevention*. Sacramento, CA: California Attorney General's Office.

Tita, G., Riley, J., & Greenwood, P. (2002). From Boston to Boyle Heights: The process and prospects of a "pulling levers" strategy in a Los Angeles barrio. In S. Decker (Ed.), *Policing gangs and youth violence* (pp. 102–130). Belmont, CA: Wadsworth.

Van Gemert, F. & Fleisher, M. (2005). In the grip of the group: Ethnography of a Moroccan street gang in the Netherlands. In S. Decker & F. Weerman (Eds), *European street gangs and troublesome youth groups* (pp. 11–34). Walnut Creek, CA: Alta Mira.

Vigil, J. D. (1988). *Barrio gangs: Street life and identity in Southern California*. Austin, TX: University of Texas Press.

Vigil, J. D. (2003). Urban violence and street gangs. *Annual Review of Anthropology*, 32, 225–242.

Vigil, J. D. (2004). The gang subculture and locura: Variations in acts and actors. In R. Martinez, Jr. (Ed.), *Beyond racial dichotomies of violence: Immigrants, ethnicity, and race*. New York: Routledge.

Watkins, A. M., Huebner, B. M., & Decker, S. H. (2008). Patterns of Gun acquisition, carrying, and use among juvenile and adult arrestees: Evidence from a high-crime city. *Justice Quarterly*, 25(4), 674–700.

Weerman, F. M., Lovegrove, P. J., & Thornberry, T. (2015). Gang membership transitions and its consequences: Exploring changes related to joining and leaving gangs in two countries. *European Journal of Criminology*, 12 (1), 70–91.

Weitekamp, E., Reich, K., & Kerner, H.-J. (2005). Why do young male Russians of German descent (Aussiedlers) tend to join or form gangs where violence plays a major role? In S. Decker & F. Weerman (Eds), *European street gangs and troublesome youth groups* (pp. 103–136). Walnut Creek, CA: Alta Mira.

Wilson, W. J. (1987). *The truly disadvantage: The inner city, the underclass and public policy*. Chicago: University of Chicago Press.

Wilson, J., Hiromoto, S., Fain, T., Tita, G., & Riley, R. (2004). *Homicide in San Diego: A Case Study Analysis*. Santa Monica, CA: RAND.

Wilson, J. & Riley, K. (2004). *Violence in East and West Oakland: Description and Intervention*. Rand Public Safety and Justice Working Paper. Santa Monica, CA: RAND.

Vandenbogaerde, E. & Van Hellemont, E. (2016). Fear and retaliation: Gang violence in Brussels and Caracas. In C. L. Maxson, & Esbensen, F. A. (Eds), *Gang transitions and transformations in the international context* (pp. 51–63). Switzerland: Springer.

Van Gemert, F. & Decker, S. H. (2008) Migrant groups and gang activity: A contrast between Europe and the USA. In F. Van Gemert, D. Peterson, & I.-L. Lien (Eds), *Street gangs migration and ethnicity* (p. 15–30). Cullompton: Willan Publishing.

Van Gemert, F., Roks, R., & Drogt, M. (2016). Dutch Crips run dry in liquid society. In C. L. Maxson, & Esbensen, F. A. (Eds), *Gang transitions and transformations in the international context* (pp. 157–172). Switzerland: Springer.

Vargas, R. (2016). *Wounded City: Violent Turf Wars in a Chicago Barrio*. Oxford: Oxford University Press.

Vigil, J. D. (2007). *The projects: Gang and non-gang families in East Los Angeles*. Austin, TX: University of Texas Press.

Zeoli, A. M., Pizarro, J. M., Grady, S. C., & Melde, C. (2014). Homicide as infectious disease: Using public health methods to investigate the diffusion of homicide. *Justice Quarterly*, 31(3), 609–632.

28 Social Networks and Violence

Mark S. Fleisher and Christopher C. McCarty

Introduction

In 1979, J. Clyde Mitchell, a pioneer of network analysis, wrote that the "idea of the social network is becoming increasingly popular among both social anthropologists and sociologists as one way of understanding behavior, particularly in larger scale complex (less structured) societies" (p. 279). In February, 2017, a Google Scholar search of the term "social network" identified 3.4 million publications (Erickson, 1997; Watts, 2004). Over the decades, social network analysis has been integrated into major scholarly disciplines, including sociology, political science, anthropology, organizational science, medical science, and mental health. In this chapter, we review social network theory and concepts, and social network research methods, including ego-network (personal) analysis and socio-centric (whole) network analysis. We describe methods of network data collection and empirical measures derived by social network analysis, which offer a basis for rich description and nuanced interpretations of behavior. We also describe applications of social network analysis in public health, such as mortality, obesity, disease transmission, and addiction, and in violence intervention policy.

Social Networks: Concepts and Theory

Human communities share a common social feature: people (actors) are to linked to one another through relational ties in complex webs of personal social interactions whose actors include casual acquaintances, family, friends, and innumerable others. Network actors can be groups, organizations, locations, and countries. Countries and corporations are linked in networks of trading relationships on a global scale.

Actors connected by relational ties form a social network. Relational ties are an inherent property of the linkage between actors, such as friendship, kinship, lender, and borrower, and boss and employee. Social network analysis assumes that: 1) actors and social ties are inter-related; 2) social ties have functions, offering, for instance, social, and economic support among actors; 3) patterns of behavior formed by recurring social interaction create social structure; and 4) social structure influences, for example, the flow of information within social networks (Wasserman & Faust, 1994).

Social network theorists assume that 1) individuals' behavior is affected by the structure of social networks linking them; 2) individuals' behavior cannot be adequately explained by examining only personal attributes of individuals, such as sex and age; and 3) explanations of behavior must consider structural patterns of specific types linking social ties (Wellman & Berkowitz, 1988). Two core features of social networks, the nature of the social ties among nodes and the patterns these ties create across nodes, have been applied to account for individuals' quality of life, including physical and mental health, mortality, disease transmission, criminal behavior, smoking initiation and cessation, and alcohol use (Berkman & Glass, 2000; Smith & Christokis, 2008).

Social theory calls for analytic approaches that specify the social mechanisms, which can explain what people do and what influences their behavior (Hedstrom & Swedbert, 1998). An early theory of social mechanisms, Granovetter's (1978) theory of collective behavior explicates social forces acting on individuals (ego) as they make decisions about whether to participate in activities. Granovetter argues that egos' decision is influenced, in part, by the presence or absence of other actors (alters) participating in these activities. A decision to participate depends on egos' consideration of their place within a group's observed social structure within which egos wish to engage. That means that egos' decision considers their relationship with alters in the group, alters' relationship to egos, and the nature of social ties between egos and alters. Egos determine if they have friends in the group, the proportion of friends to non-friends, and values shared between egos and group alters.

Granovetter's theory conceptualizes key measures in contemporary social network analysis. These measures are, for example, structural variables measured on pairs of actors, such as friends, and compositional variables measured on actors, such as gender and race. Relational ties are the bonding mechanism binding together nodes (actors and alters). Granovetter's concept of social mechanisms recognizes social processes or social structures through which social changes occur (Gross, 2009).

Construction of Social Networks

Social networks are composed of ties between and among nodes. Social dyads are ties linking two actors. A dyad is the simplest form of a network. Research has shown that the nature of dyadic interactions can have positive health benefits, that married people have lower mortality rates than unmarried persons (Hu & Goldman, 1990), and that non-spousal dyadic social relationships, too, can have positive health benefits (Granovetter, 1973).

Dyadic relations are core building blocks of social networks. There are four functional ties in dyadic social interactions. Borgatti, Mehra, Brass, and Labianca (2009) identify these types of ties: similarities, social relations, interactions, and flows. Similar ties link actors in the same place and time and with attributes, such as sex, attitudes, and values. Social relations refer to the nature of social ties, such as kinship and friendship. Interactional ties describe actors' interactions, such as people we talk to, people we ask advice from, and people who come to our aid or we befriend. Flows are ties indicating action, speed of information flowing among corporate departments, and sharing resources along a network. Americans' knowledge of what happens in US politics depends on their personal network and the flow of information to them from sources of information. Television channels direct the flow of information. CNN and Fox News offer different political perspectives and interpretations of the performance of the federal officials.

In addition to dyads, other units of analysis include: triads, groups, and subgroups. A triad is a subset of three actors and the relational ties among them. Analysis of triads, groups, and subgroups illustrate the functional capacities of relational ties. In a triad, nodes [i, j, & k] represent actors. If [i] likes [j] and [j] likes [k] then [i] will like [k]. The flow of friendship among these nodes illustrates the property of transitivity, in this case, the flow of friendship between actors, which functions as a principle in balance theory (Wasserman & Foust, 1994).

Triads, a set of three actors and ties among them, and subgroups and groups are units of social network analysis. A finite set of actors and ties among them comprise a group. Organizations are social groups with stable patterns of interaction, and can be studied with a network approach (Klerks, 2001; Sparrow, 1991). Organizations geared toward product production and distribution require formal patterns of interaction denoted by organizational charts, which identify nodes and functional ties among nodes that guide informational flow. Dyads and triads and combinations of these affect efficiency critical to manufacturing and delivering products.

Tichy, Tushman, and Fombrun (1979) and Lazega and Duijn (1997) illustrate an organizational context of social networks concepts. Organizations monitor the intensity of relations between individuals, reciprocity in collaborations, and multiplexity (viz.: multifunctional ties, or social role overlap, linking collaborating individuals who are friends and siblings). Organizations' structural characteristics play a critical role in the production and distribution of information. Corporations are mindful of outside entities. Openness measures the number of actual external links as a proportion of all possible external links. Reachability measures the actual number of ties linking egos to alters. Networks with too many nodes slow information flow. Networks with too few nodes can lose information.

Network Types and Measures

Social network analysis relies on measurements of networks – measuring the size, structure, and composition. Data are collected on multiple levels of analysis (see Marsden, 1990). Data on a sample of individuals in subgroups or groups form ego-centric (personal) networks. Data on closed populations form socio-centric networks.

Ego-centric analysis examines attributes' effects on relationships (McCarty, 2002). Characteristics among ego-centric network members include, for example, gender, age, place of residence, closeness of friendship, and frequency of contact. Socio-centric analysis focuses on the overall social structure of a population, such as occupational groups. Socio-centric networks are formed out of the aggregate of ties among all members of groups, such as a school classroom or an office. Burt's (1997; also see Krackhardt, 1999) study of social capital in organizational contexts shows that personal characteristics of company employees interact with their positions in the corporate hierarchy and influence operations and information flow.

A characteristic of personal networks is homophily (McPherson, Smith-Lovin & Cook, 2001). The expression "birds of a feather flock together" captures the core principle of homophily. A social network is homophilous if people in ego networks share similarities, such as level of education, experience working at similar jobs, and sharing political ideas. People with similar attributes have more contact with one another than do dissimilar people.

Actors in homophilous networks concentrate and form social groups. In the 2017 US presidential election, homophilous groups influenced the election's outcome. Republican voters were White, male, over age 65, rural residents, without a college education vs. Democractic voters, who were urban residents, young (under age 29), female, with a college education (Tyson & Maniam, 2016). Fleisher (2002) found that, among gang members, behaviors such as possession of weapons, willingness to participate in drug crime, and hiding one another from police are more likely to occur between best friends (affective tie) and neighbors (residential ties), even if they were members of different gangs.

Fleisher (2002) elicited personal network data from young women who said they were gang members and were willing to discuss their friendship networks. Friends' names, family members' names, and acquaintances' names were collected in structured interviews from 74 gang women in a neighborhood known locally as the North End, in Champaign, IL. Interviews began with a cohort of eight informants and then proceeded to friends of each informant. Personal networks varied widely in number (Campbell, 1991; Killworth, Johnsen, Bernard, Shelley, & McCarty, 1990; McCarty, Bernard, Killworth, Shelley, & Johnsen, 1997). Analysis showed geographically expansive networks, which included more than 500 male and female gang members distinguished as egos' friends, close friends, and best friends. Active gang members hung out with friends frequently, spending many hours together per week. They had larger personal networks than inactive gang members, who spent few days and hours together per week. Network size and composition were significant in women's adaptations to life in a poor neighborhood. More friends each young woman had, the more alters she could call upon for social, emotional, and instrumental support. These women shared meals and babysitting and sought emotional support from one another (Fleisher, 2015a).

These young women's personal networks were homophilous on personal and family characteristics. Their mothers, grandmothers, and aunties, and more distant ancestors going back generations, had been residents of the North End since the 1930s. The young women in this neighborhood remained there and became the next generation of stable residents (Bojanowski & Corten, 2014). They and their mothers and other female relatives had shared friends and support networks their entire adult lives. These extended friendship and kinship networks crisscrossed the neighborhood and were homophilous on numerous attributes: few had education beyond high school; few had paying jobs outside the neighborhood; they resided close to one another; and there were descendants of migrants who moved north from southern states in the Great Migration (Tolney, 2003) and arrived in Champaign by the 1930s.

A longitudinal study of a homophilous social support network over ten years found that different types of problems women faced led to variations in support networks (Suitor & Keeton, 1997; Wellman, Wong, Tindal, & Nazer, 1997). Analysis of the North End's women's friendship networks had similar findings among women who were homophilous on race, education, employment, and residence. Friends realigned based on fewer variables, such as adolescent women with babies vs. those without babies. These homophilous networks changed composition and structure again when teenage women became pregnant and then again when young mothers formed their own households, independent on their natal family relatives (Fleisher & Krienert, 2004).

Learning that members of homophilous networks share values, attitudes, and beliefs raises a theoretical query: what is the role of network structure vs. cultural affiliation on network members' behavior? Do network members act similarly as a sole function of network homophily or does cultural affiliation of network members influence their behavior? What has greater influence on behavior, the role of social interaction or group culture? Mische (2008) studied Brazilian youth activists and documented the emergence of varying styles of political communication and multiple roles in political activities. That finding illustrates the fusion of social structure, language, and relational ties (Mutzel, 2009).

Socio-centric network analysis studies the structural characteristics of socially defined groups. This type of analysis uses the concept of mode. Mode refers to the number of sets of actors on which occur structural measures. A one-mode socio-matrix displays social proximity on dyadic relationships, such as degree of friendship and frequency of contact (McCarty, 2002).

One-mode matrices are the basis for matrix-based analyses, which identify structural measures, such as density and centrality of actors comprising the whole group. McCarty (2002) argues and has demonstrated that measures on attributes, such as tie strength, are useful in personal network analysis and can be valuable in socio-centric structural measures on personal network data. McCarty defines six structural measures: density, degree centrality, closeness centrality, betweenness centrality, cliques, and components. Density measures the percentage of ties between actors as a percentage of all possible ties.

Degree centrality measures network activity, a measure of direct ties among actors: actors who have a high number of ties to other actors have higher centrality than actors who have fewer ties to other actors. Degree centrality heightens actors' visibility in the network. Actors who have a high number of ties have high degree centrality; actors who can reach a high number of alters have high out-degree centrality. Actors who receive a high number of ties are prominent. A high number of nondirectional ties increase an actor's prominence (Zemljic & Hlebec, 2004).

In the world of professional basketball, Cleveland Cavaliers' LeBron James is well known worldwide. He has high prestige, high indegree centrality, and receives ties from far-reaching places. At a conference in Antalya, located on Turkey's south central coast, Fleisher participated on a panel discussion of best-practices of delinquency programs. Introduced by the panel's chair as a professor at university in Cleveland, Ohio, an audience member, a young Turkish man who had never visited the United States, immediately stood up and asked him a question: who is the world's best basketball player, Kobe or LeBron?

Closeness centrality focuses on paths from an actor to other actors. Each network actor is not reachable by a single direct tie to all other actors. An actor has high closeness centrality if an actor can be reached by shortest path, the fewer ties, to many other actors. Betweenness centrality extends the concept of closeness centrality in measuring the number of paths that connect actors. If an actor has high betweenness centrality, that actor lies on many paths between other actors. An actor with high betweenness centrality controls the flow of information. A clique in a personal network refers to a set of alters, each of whom has a direct tie to all others in the set. Actors are directly tied to one another. Cliques are subgroups within a population.

In Fleisher's (2002) study of young women, most belonged to one of three gangs prominent on the North End. Membership was highest among Vice Lords, which had more than 100 self-proclaimed members. The number of Vice Lords was determined by counting the Vice Lords in the personal networks of the 74 young women in the study. Years of firsthand observation showed that Vice Lords as a group never gathered. Analysis showed that the group was parsed first by residential areas, second by housing types, and third by cliques of close and best friends.

Social Networks and Gangs

There are many definitions of the term gang, referring to street or youth gangs. A gang definition builds on the concept of a group. Gang researchers have used a standard gang definition, a group of three or more people who commit crime, or some variation of that definition, for decades. (Curry, 2015; Klein, 1997). In an appeal of a criminal case (*Lanzetta v. New Jersey*, 306 US 451), the United States Supreme Court (1929) rejected the standard gang definition stating it was too ambiguous, too vague, and that people come together in groups of three or more with no intention of committing crime.

Sierra-Arevalo and Papachristos (2015) wrote that "[g]angs are more than a collection of individuals. Gangs are a group in the true sense of the word ... [these] operate at the supra-individual or collective level" (p. 164). They attribute gang group activities to cohesion among group members. Cohesion, then, enhances gang members' willingness to sustain their gang membership and commit crime. Social processes effecting cohesion, the researchers argue, explain gang behavior, but they don't specify measures of cohesion. In this conceptualization a gang group is: (1) a multiplex, cohesive group and, (2) upon membership, confers upon new gang members multiple types of relations, creating a sense of one-for-all, all-for-one.

Fleisher (2005) offers an alternative perspective on the conventional nature of a gang group, which infers that gang affiliation automatically confers multiplex relations upon members. Wasserman and Faust (1994, p. 19) specify measures of cohesion. Acquiring multiplex ties in groups depends on the closeness of friendship among group members; frequency of spending time together; amount of time group members spend together; and willingness of group members to engage in crime, such as drug-dealing. Fleisher (2005) describes behavior that identifies overt behavioral indicators of cohesive ties between individuals: willingness to hide a gang member sought by the police; willingness to lend a gang member a firearm; and willingness to lend money, or drugs, which can be sold to specific individuals.

Centrality measures on each gang group in the study area had a high frequency of ties out of their gang to others gangs (out-degree), and a high frequency of ties reaching into each gang from other gangs (in-degree) (Fleisher, 2002, p. 164–165). Gang members had non-gang friends in their neighborhood and other residential area in the community. They categorized non-gang and gang friends by location, such as non-gang school friends. Bolden's (2014) social network research has shown that membership in one gang does preclude ties to members of other gangs. Gangs as social groups and gang affiliation requires a closer examination.

Fleisher and McCarty (2004) analyzed centrality data elicited in Fleisher's (2002) social network ethnographic study of women in gangs in Champaign, IL. They sought to test participation observation data on perceived centrality of gang women, collected in an ethnographic study from 1996–2000 (Fleisher, 2015), against an empirical analysis of structurally important gang women, using data gathered in a study of gang women's ego-networks from 2000–2002. Fleisher's ethnographic observations led to an assumption that five women out of 74 informants were the most central actors in the neighborhood and were most active in local social and instrumental support networks. These five were the most visible women on the street. They appeared to have a wide array of gang and non-gang friends and helped one another on household responsibilities, including babysitting and shopping, hung out together chatting and doing one another's hair on weekends, and shared food and baby clothes.

Centrality analysis showed that Fleisher's ethnographic observation missed underlying structural patterns (Fleisher, 2006). Among the 74 informants, 15 had the highest measures on betweenness centrality. In-degree on these 15 women ranged from 43 to 6. Out-degree ranged from 25 to 3. In eight cases, there was a strong imbalance between in-degree and out-degree, resulting in a negative ratio of out/in-degree. The woman with an in-degree of 43 had an out-degree of 11, resulting in in-/out-degree imbalance of −11. Analysis identified a woman with betweenness measure of 22, 11 out-degree, and 19 in-degree as the structurally most important woman. This woman was not highly visible on the street, did not hang out like her friends did, but had the strong influence on peers in social and instrumental support networks.

This finding offered insight into research on gang leadership and crime, which, in the absence of structural measures, makes claims about leadership (shot callers) and the role hardcore vs. marginal gang members (Curry & Spergel, 1988), who are prominent and influential. Actors with high in-degree and out-degree have high prestige and, in theory, a high level of influence. Fleisher and McCarty's (2004) research indicates that gang members with high in-degree centrality are not necessarily more influential in promoting or preventing crime (cf. Burk, Vorst, Kerr, & Stattin, 2012). High centrality actors have greater access to more resources and less need to commit crime, such as drug dealing, burglary, and fencing stolen property. On the other hand, these actors have access to more gang members and can influence and instigate crime, while not participating directly in crime.

Structural analysis and studies of social process are not equivalent. Observations of social process in ethnographic research and structural analysis can be complementary. In gang research this distinction of multi-methods can be important: gang leaders, youth most active in crime, or youth who are most violent, might not be the most structurally central members of a youth gang network (Fleisher, 2002, 2005, 2006; Fleisher & Papachristos, 2010). Leaders can just as easily spring up on the network's structural margin, depending on personal traits of potential leaders and structural properties of the total network.

To date, we don't know of published structural measures for common labels indicating structural positions of gang members, such as core, regular, peripheral members, and wannabes. Intra-gang group assumptions of structural positions of social role players have been conceptualized as a hierarchy; for instance, a set of nested circles with the core members in the inner-most circle, regular members around the core, peripheral members around the regular, and wannabes at the margin. Hierarchical sketches appear too, with core members at the top or in the center with regular members below them and wannabes located at the bottom or alongside others. Conventional, law-enforcement gang terminology (Skolnick, 1990) creates a false portrayal of the structural nature of a gang group. Short and Strodtbeck (1963) and Vigil (1988) offer nuanced interpretations of gang social process, leadership, and inter-personal influence.

Fleisher (2015b) claims that adolescent social groups and youth gangs are, in fact, built out of the same youthful social building blocks, but gang adolescents' attributes are distinctly different from non-gang adolescents'. Adolescents who claim gang affiliation are episodically and literally homeless youth; abused and abandoned youth; youth suffering mental illness and personality disorders; addictions to multiple drugs; and youth plagued by feeling of alienation and loneliness, which can alter perceptions of social relationships (Cacioppo, Cacioppo, & Capitanio, 2015). Adolescents engulfed by feelings of loneliness can find themselves among peers whom they sought to quell feelings of loneliness, but later found these peers increased their risk of injury. Seen at a distance, a youth social group that fits popular images of neighborhood drug gangs can be recast as a social group of alienated youth who were injured by adult caretakers and neglected by social services, selling drugs to buy food and clothes (Fleisher, 1998).

Social Network Analysis: Applications in Public Health Research

Applications of social network concepts, theory, and methods have appeared in wide range of social sciences (Luke & Harris, 2007; Valente & Pitts, 2017) as a way of framing social issues in terms of research questions that can be answered with social network analysis. Espelage, Wasserman, and Fleisher (2007) present a cross-section of social network concepts, theory, methods, and analysis with examples of applications in studies of gang violence and school violence and bullying.

Social network analysis has been used to study aging, social isolation, mortality, obesity, HIV, gangs, domestic and intimate partner violence, community social support networks, crime and criminal intelligence, psychiatric disorders, addiction, violence in school, and terrorism and national security. In this final section, we review several examples illustrating social network analysis value in the investigation of complex social problems. Van der Hulst (2009) offers a systematic pedagogical overview of social network analysis and its applications.

Peer influence in adolescents' personal networks has been well documented (Valente & Pitts, 2003). Barman-Adhikari, Rice, Winetrobe, and Petering (2015) studied homeless adolescents' drug use and drug users' structural position within a homeless group of more than 100 adolescents. Their study sought to understand drug use as a function of structural position in a large network. Structural position measures closeness among youth; in this instance, centrality of drug users either associates them socially closer to or more distant from drug users. They found, within the network of homeless youth, an association of structural positions by subgroups of adolescents using different drugs. They also report the cultural and psychological variables influencing drug use. Confounding a clear association of structural position with types of drugs used are complexities of the socio-psychological injuries of these homeless youth as victims of parental abuse, neglect, and adolescents' behavioral dysfunction.

Long-term ethnographic research (Fleisher, 1998) among a racially and ethnically mixed co-ed youth gang has shown that within a large gang group of adolescents spending long hours together day-to-day, users of particular drugs, those who only use marijuana vs. more potent drugs – such as cigarettes dipped into formaldehyde, dried and smoked – sort themselves into subgroups by drug preference. First-hand observation over a long period can compensate for reporting bias in collecting social network data, reporting too much or too little drug use in self-reports, particularly among chronic drug users whose memories are fuzzy.

Christakis and Fowler's (2007) longitudinal study analyzed an interconnected network of 12,067 obese persons. These researchers learned that biological and behavioral traits are bound within network structural characteristics and that obesity spreads through social ties. Researchers knew that in spite of the stigma attached to obesity, weight gain was a voluntary choice. In terms of network influence, weight gain by some people can influence weight gain by others, resulting in homophilous networks of obese people who shared a similar attitude of tolerance toward weight gain and obesity. Same-sex friends and siblings of obese people had more influence on one another than did opposite-sex friends and siblings. Researchers concluded that obesity spreads in social networks and can, in part, account for an obesity epidemic.

Cacioppo et al.'s (2015) study of the effects on morbidity and mortality of social isolation (viz. diminished personal networks) can perhaps be applied to obesity. Obese people's personal networks shrink, leaving them isolated and lonely. If obesity leads to less contact with non-obese health friends and relatives, then bio-chemical consequences of social isolation in addition to obesity might increase mortality. Vogt, Mullooly, Ernst, Pope, and Hollis's (1992) study of heart disease, cancer, and strokes found that increased social participation among patients led to a more effective recovery.

Violence is contagious. Mechanisms of violence contagion were investigated by Papachristos, Wildeman, and Roberto (2015), who applied social network analysis to non-fatal gunshot victimization in personal networks based on six years of gunshot victimization and arrest data in Chicago. Social contagion refers to "the extent to which one's probability of victimization is related to direct and indirect exposure to gunshot victims in one's social network" (p. 140). These researchers used an affiliation analysis, a two-mode analysis using a set of actors (individuals arrested) and a set of events (nonfatal gunshot incidents). In affiliation analysis, actors are linked by affiliation to events and events are linked by affiliation to actors. Actors linked events and events linked actors.

Violent incident arrest records were used to generate co-offending networks. A co-offending network refers to a network composed of two or more individuals (actors) who were arrested for involvement in the same crime (events). Among 418,032 individual offenders reported in police incident reports, 41% of gunshot incidents lead to the arrest of two or more people; 35% of all arrest events had more than one offender. The analysis had significant findings: 1) less than 6% of Chicago's population were involved in nonfatal shootings; 2) 89% of victims were contained in a single network of 107,740 individuals; 3) the probability of victimization was strongly associated with sharing network affiliation with a victim of a nonfatal shooing. If a person's social network is saturated with gunshot victims, the probability increases that that person will be a gunshot victim. If a person has friends who have been gunshot victims, that person is more likely to become a gunshot victim. This research had significance for gun violence intervention policy: wide-scale policies based on race and ethnicity are less likely to have an effect on gun violence reduction than policies that focus on risky behavior.

Conclusion

Social network analysis offers social researchers another set of theoretical, conceptual, and analytic tools. Social network analysis requires practice proposing research questions that can be answered more thoroughly with an analysis of personal and whole networks. To our collective chagrin, the complexities of human behavior in Western, industrialized countries and in non-Western, non-literate cultures are rarely transparent. What we know depends on what questions we ask. Social network analysis gives us another way to ask research questions, a way of thinking about human behavior, and a better understanding of social complexities, such as a high rate of gun violence in a major American city. We can count fatal and nonfatal victimizations and locate shootings in one or another neighborhood. That alone is insufficient in developing violence intervention policy mindful of the behavior complexities hidden in social networks. Social network analysis offers a method that leads to another way of understanding the nature of interpersonal violence. How we know what we know takes on an entirely new dimension when we conceptualize and measure human behavior through the lens of social network analysis. Social network research can be integrated into and designed to complement survey research, increase the value of small-scale qualitative research by gathering quantifiable social network data, and built into long-term ethnographic fieldwork, adding a longitudinal dimension to cross-sectional field research.

References

Barman-Adhikari, A., Rice, E., Winetrobe, H., & Petering, R. (2015). Social network correlates of methamphetamine, heroin, and cocaine use in a sociometric network of homeless youth. *Journal of the Society of Social Work and Research*, 6(3), 433–457.

Berkman, L. F. & Glass, T. (2000). Social integration, social networks, social support, and health. *Social Epidemiology*, 1, 137–173.

Bernard, H. D., Johnsen, E. C., Killworth, P. D., McCarty, C. & Shelley, G. A., & Robinson, S. (1990). Comparing four different methods for measuring personal social networks. *Social Networks*, 12, 179–215.

Bolden, C. L. (2014). Friendly foes: Hybrid gangs or social networking. *Group Processes & Intergroup Relations*, 17(6), 730–749.

Bojanowski, M. & Corten, R. (2014). Measuring segregation in social networks. *Social Networks*, 39, 14–32.

Borgatti, S. P., Jones, C., & Everett, M. G. (1998). Network measures of social capital. *Connections*, 21(2), 27–36.

Borgatti, S. P., Mehra, A., Brass, D., & Labianca, G. (2009). Network analysis in the social sciences. *Science*, 323, 892–895.

Burk, W. J., Vorst, H. V. D., Kerr, M., & Stattin, H. (2012). Alcohol use and friendship dynamics: selection and socialization in early-, middle-, and late-adolescent peer networks. *Journal of Studies on Alcohol and Drugs*, 73, 89–98.

Burt, R. (1997). A note on social capital and network content. *Social Networks* 19, 355–373.

Cacioppo, J. T., Cacioppo, S., Capitanio, J. P., & Cole, S. W. (2015). The neuroendocrinology of social isolation. *Annual Review of Psychology*, 66, 733–767.

Campbell, K. E. (1991). Name generators in surveys of personal networks. *Social Networks*, 13, 203–221.

Carrington, J. S., Scott, J., & Wasserman, S. (Eds) (2005). *Models and Methods in Social Network Analysis*. Cambridge: Cambridge University Press.

Christakis, N. A. & Fowler, J. H. (2007). The spread of obesity in a large social network over 32 years. *New England Journal of Medicine*, 357, 370–379.

Clifton, A., Pilkonis, P. A., & McCarty, C. (2007). Social networks in borderline personality disorder. *Journal of Personality Disorders*, 21(4), 434–441.

Curry, D. G. (2015). The logic of defining gangs revisited. In S. H. Decker & D. C. Pyrooz (Eds), *The Handbook of Gangs* (pp. 7–27). Malden, MA: Wiley & Sons.

Erickson, B. H. (1997). Social networks and history: a review essay. *Historical Methods*, 30(3), 149–157.

Espelage, D., Wasserman, S., & Fleisher, M. S. (2007). Social networks and violent behavior. In Flannery, D. J., Vazsonyi, A., & Waldman, I. (Eds), *Cambridge Handbook of Violent Behavior* (pp. 450–464). New York: Cambridge University Press.

Everett, M. G. (1990). A testing example for positional analysis techniques. *Social Networks*, 12, 253–260.

Everett, M. G. & Borgatti, S. P. (1999). The centrality of groups and classes. *The Journal of Mathematical Sociology*, 23(3), 181–201.

Everett, M. G. & Borgatti, S. P. (2005). Ego network betweenness. *Social Networks*, 27(1), 31–38.

Ferligoj, A. & Hlebec, V. (1999). Evaluation of social network measurement instruments. *Social Networks*, 21, 111–130.

Feld, S. L. (1997). Structural embeddedness and stability of interpersonal relations. *Social Networks*, 19, 91–95.

Fleisher, M. S. (2002). *Women and Gangs: A Field Research Study*. Washington, DC: Department of Justice, Office of

Juvenile Justice and Delinquency Prevention. Retrieved April 24, 2017 from www.ncjrs.gov/pdffiles1/nij/198317.pdf.

Fleisher, M. S. (2005). The application of social network analysis to field research: Different methods creating complementary perspectives. *Journal of Contemporary Criminal Justice*, 21(5), 120–134.

Fleisher, M. S. (2006). Degree centrality and youth gangs as an ecological adaptation. In Short, J. & Hughes, L. (Eds), *Studying Youth Gangs* (pp. 85–98). Walnut Creek, CA: AltaMira Press.

Fleisher, M. S. (2015a). *Living Black: Social Life in an African American Neighborhood.* Madison: University of Wisconsin Press.

Fleisher, M. S. (2015b). Gang and drugs: connections, divergence, and culture. In S. H. Decker & D.C. Pyrooz (Eds), *The handbook of gangs* (pp. 193–207). Malden, MA: Wiley & Sons.

Fleisher, M. S. & Krienert, J. L. (2004). Life-course events, social networks, and the emergence of violence among female gang members. *Journal of Community Psychology*, 32(5), 607–622.

Fleisher, M. S. & McCarty, C., (2004). Structural Holes: *Macher* or *Nebbish*: the structural position of important people. International Sunbelt Social Network Conference, Slovenia, May 2004.

Fleisher, M. S. & Papachristos, A. V. (2010). Social Network Analysis and Ethnography: Complementary Tools to Understand the Complexities of Real-life Behavior. *International Network of Social Network Analysts Conference*, Riva del Garda, Italy, July.

Freeman, L. C. (1978). Centrality in social networks conceptual clarification. *Social Networks*, 1(3), 215–239.

Freeman, L. C. (2008). Going the wrong way on a one-way street: centrality in physics and biology. *Journal of Social Structure*, 9(2), 1–15.

Granovetter, M. S. (1973). The strength of weak ties. *American Journal of Sociology*, 78(6), 1360–1380.

Granovetter, M. S. (1978). Threshold models of collective behavior. *The American Journal of Sociology*, 83(6), 1420–1443

Gross, N. (2009). A pragmatist theory of social mechanisms. *American Sociological Review*, 74, 358–379.

Hedstrom, P. & Swedberg, R. (1998). *Social Mechanisms: An Approach to Social Theory.* Cambridge: Cambridge University Press.

Hlebec, V. & Ferligoj, A. (2001). Respondent mood and the instability of survey network measurements. *Social Networks*, 23(2), 125–140.

Hu, Y. & Goldman, N. (1990). Mortality differentials by marital status: an international comparison. *Demography*, 27(2), 233–250.

Huang, G. & Tausig, M. (1990). Network range in personal networks. *Social Networks*, 12, 261–268.

Killworth, P. D., Johnsen, E. C., & Bernard, H. R., Shelley, G. A., & McCarty, C. (1990). Estimating the size of personal networks. *Social Networks,* 12, 289–312.

Klerks, P. (2001). The network paradigm applied to criminal organisations [sic]: Theoretical nitpicking or a relevant doctrine for investigators? Recent developments in the Netherlands. *Connections*, 24(3), 53–65.

Klein, M. W. (1997). *The American Street Gang: Its Nature, Prevalence, and Control.* Oxford: Oxford University Press.

Kogovsek, T. & Ferligoj, A. (2005). Effects of reliability on validity of ego-centered network measurements. *Social Networks*, 27, 205–229.

Krackhardt, D. (1999). The ties that torture: Simmelian tie analysis in organizations. *Research in the Sociology of Organizations*, 16, 183–210.

Krackhardt, D. & Kilduff, M. (2002). Structure, culture and Simmelian ties in entrepreneurial firms. *Social Networks*, 24, 279–290.

Kriegel, L. S., Hsu, H. T., & Wenzel, S. L. (2015). Personal networks: A hypothesized mediator in the association between incarceration and HIV risk behaviors among women with histories of homelessness. *Journal of the*

Society for Social Work and Research, 6(3), 407–432.

Lanzetta v. New Jersey, 306 U.S. 451 (1939).

Lazega, E. & van Duijn, M. (1997). Position in formal structure, personal characteristics and choices of advisors in a law firm: a logistic regression model for dyadic network data. *Social Networks*, 19, 375–397.

Lofors, J. & Sundquist, K. (2007). Low-linking social capital as a predictor of mental disorders: a cohort study of 4.5 million Swedes. *Social Science & Medicine*, 64, 21–34.

Luke, D. A. & Harris, J. K. (2007). Network analysis in public health: history, methods, and applications. *Annual Review of Public Health*, 28, 69–93.

Lusher, D., Robins, G., & Kremer, P. (2010). The application of social network analysis to team sports. *Measurement in physical education and exercise science*, 14(4), 211–224.

Marsden, P. V. (1990). Network data and measurement. *Annual Review of Sociology*, 16, 435–463.

McCarty, C. (2002). Measuring Structure in Personal Networks. *Journal of Social Structure*, 3(1), 20.

McCarty, C., H. R. Bernard, Killworth, P. D., Shelley, G. A., & Johnsen, E. C. (1997). Eliciting representative samples of personal networks. *Social Networks*, 19, 303–323.

McPherson, M., Smith-Lovin, L., & Cook, J. M. (2001). Birds of a feather: homophily in social networks. *Annual Review of Sociology*, 27, 415–444.

Mische, A. (2008) *Partisan Publics: Communication and Contention across Brazilian Youth Activist Networks*. Princeton, NJ: Princeton University Press.

Mitchell, J. C. (1974). Social networks. *Annual Review of Anthropology*, 3, 279–299.

Morgan, D. L., Neal, M. B., & Carder, P. (1997). The stability of core and peripheral networks over time. *Social Networks*, 19(1), 9–25.

Mutzel, S. (2009). Networks as culturally constituted processes: a comparison of relational sociology and actor-network theory. *Current Sociology*, 57(6), 871–887.

Papachristos, A. V. (2006). Social network analysis and gang research: theory and methods. In Short, J. & Hughes, L. (Eds), *Studying Youth Gangs* (pp. 99–116). Walnut Creek, CA: AltaMira Press.

Papachristos, A. V., Wildeman, C., & Roberto, E. (2015). Tragic, but not random: the social contagion of nonfatal gunshot injuries. *Social Science & Medicine*, 125, 139–150.

Orth-Gomer. L. & Johnson, J. V. (1987). Social network interaction and mortality: a six year follow-up study of a random sample of the Swedish population. *Journal of Chronic Diseases*, 40(10), 949–957.

Rice, E. & Yoshioka-Maxwell, A. (2015). Social network analysis as a toolkit for the science of social work. *Journal of the Society of Social Work and Research*, 6(3), 369–383.

Robins, G., Pattison, P., & Woolcock, J. (2004). Missing data in networks: exponential random graph (p*) models for networks with non-respondents. *Social Networks*, 26, 257–283.

Ruan, D., Freeman, L. C., Dai, X., Pan, Y., & Zhang, W. (1997). On the changing structure of social networks in urban China. *Social Networks*, 19(1), 75–89.

Short, J. F. & Strodtbeck, F. L. (1965). *Group Process and Gang Delinquency*. Chicago: University of Chicago Press.

Shye, D., Mullooly, J. P., Freeborn, D. K., & Pope, C. R. (1995). Gender differences in the relationship between social network support and mortality: a longitudinal study of an elderly cohort. *Social Science & Medicine*, 41(7), 935–947.

Sierra-Arevalo, M., & Papachristos, A. V. (2015). Social network analysis and gangs. In S. H. Decker and D. C. Pyrooz (Eds), *The Handbook of Gangs* (pp. 157–177). Malden, MA: Wiley & Sons.

Skolnick, J. H. (1990). *Gang organization and migration: drugs, gangs, and law enforcement*. Office of the Attorney General, California Department of Justice.

Smith, K. P. & Christakis, N. A. (2008). Social networks and Heath. *Annual Review of Sociology*, 34, 405–429.

Sparrow, M. K. (1991). The application of network analysis to criminal intelligence: an assessment of the prospects. *Social Networks* 13, 251–274.

Suitor, J. & Keeton, S. (1997). Once a friend, always a friend? Effects of homophily on women's support networks across a decade. *Social Networks*, 13, 51–62.

Suitor, J. J., Wellman, B., & Morgan, D. L. (1997). It's about time: how, why, and when networks change. *Social Networks*, 19, 17.

Tichy, N. M., Tushman, M. L., & Fombrun, C. (1979). Social network analysis for organizations. *Academy of Management Review*, 4(4), 507–519.

Tolnay, S. E. (2003). The African American "Great Migration" and beyond. *Annual Review of Sociology*, 29, 209–232.

Tyson, A. & Maniam, S. (2016). Behind Trump's victory: divisions by race, gender, education. *Pew Research Center*. Retrieved February 9, 2017 from ww.pewresearch.org/fact-tank/2016/11/09/behind-trumps-victory-divisions-by-race-gender-education.

Uzzi, B., (1997). Social structure and competition in interfirm networks: the paradox of embeddedness. *Administrative Science Quarterly*, 42(1), 35–67.

Valente, T. W. (2003). Social network influences on adolescent substance use: an introduction. *Connections*, 25(2), 11–16.

Valente, T. W. & Pitts, S. R. (2017). An appraisal of social network theory and analysis as applied to public health: challenges and opportunities. *Annual Review of Public Health*, 38(4), 1–4, p. 16.

Van der Hulst, R. C. (2009). Introduction to social network analysis as an investigative tool. *Trends in Organized Crime*, 12, 101–121.

Vigil, J. D. (1988). Group process and street identity: adolescent Chicano gang members. *Ethos*, 16(4), 412–445.

Vogt, T. M., Mullooly, J. P., Ernst, D., Pope, C. R., & Hollis, J. F.. (1992). Social networks as predictors of ischemic heart disease, cancer, stroke and hypertension: incidence, survival and mortality. *Journal of Clinical Epidemiology*, 45(6), 659–666.

Ward, M. D., Stovel, K., & Sacks, A. (2011). Network analysis and political science. *Annual Review of Political Science*, 14, 243–264.

Wasserman, S. & Faust, K. (1994). *Social Network Analysis*. Cambridge: Cambridge University Press.

Watts, D. J. (2004). The "new" science of networks. *Annual Review of Sociology*, 30, 243–70.

Wellman, B. & Berkowitz, S. D. (1988). *Social Structures: A Network Approach* (Vol. 2). Cambridge: Cambridge University Press.

Wellman, B., Wong, R. Y., Tindal, D., & Nazer, N. (1997). A decade of network change: turnover, persistence and stability in personal communities. *Social Networks*, 19, 27–50.

Zemljic, B. & Hlebec, V. (2005). Reliability of measures of centrality and prominence. *Social Networks*, 27, 73–88.

29 The Contagion of Violence

L. Rowell Huesmann

Introduction

Sudden acts of individual violence have long fascinated the public far out of proportion to the damage they cause. Whether it is "Lizzie Bordon taking an ax and giving her husband 40 whacks," Leopold and Loeb kidnapping and murdering a child for no apparent reason, Charles Manson and cronies killing Hollywood celebrities, Dillon Klebold and Eric Harris murdering classmates in Columbine High School, Norwegian Anders Breivik shooting 69 youth on an island, or Colorado's James Holmes shooting a score of people in a movie theater, the attention of the public becomes riveted on these events. We seek to understand what seems inexplicable, we seek to find the underlying cause that made these perpetrators do what they did, and we try to differentiate these perpetrators from the others around us who look no different on the surface.

In these environments there are many villains that are easy to blame, and usually they all receive some blame without any evidence to support the claim – poor parenting, defective genes, bad friends, easy availability of guns, and most recently media violence. Some people believe that the only reason some of these causes (e.g., gun availability and media violence) are blamed is that they are easy targets that deflect attention from the individual and from other more complex causes that society does not want to address. They may be easy targets, but that does not mean they are incorrect targets. Regardless, scholars studying violent behavior have the responsibility of critically addressing all possible causes in a dispassionate manner. Such scientific critical evaluation must involve two important linked components: 1) a theory that illuminates a psychological process by which the hypothesized cause produces the effect on violent behavior and 2) a body of empirical evidence that supports the theory. Here, I am arguing that we can archieve a better understanding of violent behavior by adopting this theoretical perspective that violence is a contagious disease. After I explicate the theory, I will provide of number of illustrations of situations where violence has been contagious and that illuminate the psychological processes that make it contagious.

Violence Is a Contagious Disease

Certainly, one of the best established findings in the psychological literature on aggressive and violent behavior is that violence begets violence. People "catch" the violence bug from being exposed to other people who are violent. This contagion of violence appears to be a universal phenomenon. The contagion of violence occurs within families. Violence between partners increases the risk of violence directed at children and increases the risk of the children behaving violently themselves. Having one violent individual in a family makes it more likely there will be others. It is true within peer-groups. Violence by some peers increases the risk of violence by other peers. Violence by peers directed outward not only stimulates violence by others that is directed outward, but stimulates violence between peers within the group. It is true in neighborhoods and communities. Violent communities and neighborhoods breed violence in those who join the community or neighborhood. Introducing violence into a community increases the risk of greater violence throughout the community. It even appears to be true within nations and cultures. And it is true across generations. Children catch it from their parents, and parents can catch it from their children.

Thus, violence has the spread characteristic of a highly contagious disease. It is not only spread from the perpetrators of violence to the victims, it is spread to the onlookers and observers of violence. It is not surprising that violent victimization leads to violent retaliation within and between families, peer groups, schools, communities, ethnic groups, cultures, and countries. What may be more surprising to some is that simply the observation of violence also leads to increased violence within and between all these groups. Violence can even be spread to far-away people who observe violence at a distance. The boundaries of time and space that apply to most biological contagions do not apply to the contagion of violence.

Why is violent behavior so contagious and how does it spread? What psychological processes are involved? How could the spread be halted? Severe violent behavior, like most social behaviors, is almost always the product of predisposing individual differences and precipitating situational factors (Huesmann, 1998). The theme of this essay is that one important environmental experience that contributes both to predisposing a person to behave more violently in the long run and to precipitating violent behavior in the short run is exposure to other violent people. Psychological theories that have emerged over the past few decades now explain the short-term precipitating effects of exposure to violence on violent behavior mostly in terms of priming, mimicry, and excitation transfer. Priming is the neurological process through which seeing violence produces a spreading activation in the neurons of the brain that activates all sorts of ideas related to violence – making violence more likely. Mimicry of violence in the short run occurs because human beings, from a very young age, have a wired in tendency to mimic whatever they see. Excitation transfer means that, when someone provokes us, we feel angrier if we have recently been aroused and made angry by something we observed, such as violence.

The long-term predisposing effects of observing violence, however, involve more complex processes of observational learning of cognitions and of emotional desensitization. Obviously, being victimized always also includes observing violence – part of the mind of the child who is being spanked or the youth who is being beaten up is observing the interaction while another part is suffering from the interaction. Although the emotional reactions to victimization may be more intense and immediate, observation alone also produces both intense emotional

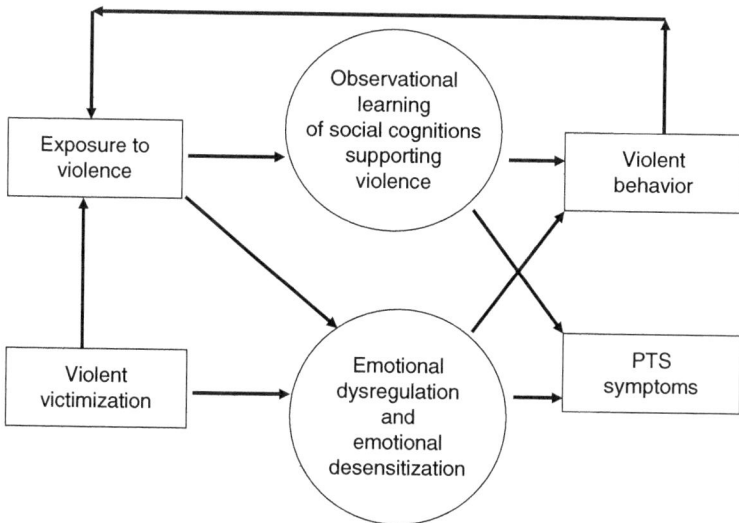

Figure 29.1 *The cycle of contagion of violence. (Source: Huesmann [2012].)*

and intense cognitive reactions that can have long-term effects on a person's mental health (e.g., post-traumatic-stress symptoms) and behavior problems (e.g., violent behavior). The consequence is a vicious circle or downward spiral of a person observing violent behavior and behaving violently, which instigates violent behavior in another, which increases the person's exposure to violence, and so on, as diagramed in Figure 29.1.

Although the underlying tenets of the current theories explaining how exposure to violence infects the observer with a propensity toward violent behavior were formulated decades ago (see Bandura, 1973; Bandura, Ross, & Ross, 1961, 1963a, b, c; Berkowitz, 1962; Eron, Walder, & Lefkowitz, 1971), researchers from a variety of disciplines, primarily psychology, communication, and sociology, have developed, tested, and refined ever-better theoretical models accounting for the consequences of exposure to violence. The generally accepted theories that have evolved not only explain why exposure to violence increases aggressive and violent behavior but also suggest numerous factors that might exacerbate or mitigate the effect. These models (e.g., Anderson & Bushman, 2001; Dodge, 1986, 1993; Huesmann, 1982, 1986, 1988, 1997, 1998) generally fall under the rubric of social-cognitive information-processing models. Such models focus on how people perceive, think, learn, and come to behave in particular ways as a result of interactions with their social world, a world that includes observation of and participation in real social interactions (e.g., with parents and peers), as well as fictional social interactions (e.g., with various forms of media). These models explain how – within the overall structure of multiple predisposing individual-difference factors interacting with multiple precipitating situational factors to instigate violent behavior – observation of violence plays a role on both sides of the equation. It plays a role as something that

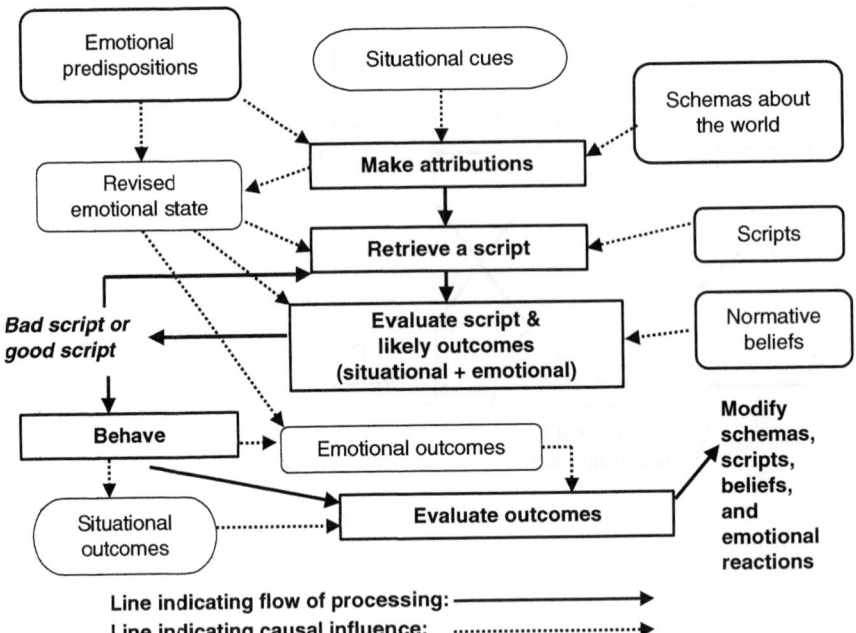

Figure 29.2 *The information-processing social-cognitive model for social problem-solving. The rounded boxes in bold represent enduring cognitive and emotional predispositions that differ across individuals. Flow of information processing is indicated by solid arrows, and causal influences are indicated by dotted arrows.*
(Source: adapted from Huesmann [1998].)

predisposes individuals in the long run to be more likely to behave violently, and it plays a role as something that precipitates violent behavior in the short run.

The Social-Cognitive Information-Processing Model

Over the past three decades at least three similar information-processing models have been proposed to explain the psychological processing underlying social information processing (e.g., Anderson & Bushman, 2001; Dodge, 1986, 1993; Huesmann, 1982, 1986, 1988, 1997, 1998). Although these models differ in their details, all view the social problem-solving process as one in which situational factors are evaluated, social scripts are retrieved, and these scripts are evaluated until one is selected to guide behavior. The latest revision of Huesmann's model is displayed in Figure 29.2 and is used below to describe the psychological processes through which exposure to violence exerts both short-term and long-term effects.

The model describes the information flow and decision processes that occur when an individual is faced with any social decision. The processes begin with evaluation of the social situation and end with the decision to behave in a certain way and then with the post-hoc self-evaluation of the consequences of behaving that way. The solid lines connecting the bold descriptions of processes in Figure 29.2 represent the flow of information, whereas the dotted lines represent the causal influences of one factor on another.

Four social-cognitive/emotional factors play important roles in individual differences in social problem-solving according to this model: *social scripts, world schemas, normative beliefs, and emotional predispositions.*

Central to the model is the concept that social behavior is controlled to a great extent by social scripts. Scripts are sets of "production rules" representing sequences of expected behaviors and responses, and they describe how to deal with a variety of situations, including conflict (Abelson, 1981; Anderson & Huesmann, 2003; Huesmann, 1988, 1998; Huesmann & Miller, 1994). Scripts are stored in a person's memory and are used as guides for behavior and social problem-solving. A script incorporates both procedural and declarative knowledge and suggests what events are to happen in the environment, how the person should behave in response to these events, and what the likely outcome of those behaviors would be. It is presumed that while scripts are first being established they influence the child's behavior through "controlled" mental processes (Schneider & Shriffrin, 1977; Shriffrin & Schneider, 1977), but these processes become "automatic" as the child matures. Correspondingly, scripts that persist in a child's repertoire, as they are rehearsed, enacted, and generate consequences, become increasingly more resistant to modification and change. A more violent person is generally a person whose repertoire of social scripts emphasizes violence.

World schemas are a second kind of cognition assumed to influence behaviors. Such schemas are the database that the individual employs to evaluate environmental cues and make attributions about others' intentions. These attributions in turn will influence the search for a script for behaving. An individual who believes the world is a mean place is more likely to make hostile attributions about others' intent and consequently more likely to retrieve a more aggressive script (Dodge et al., 2016).

Normative beliefs are a third kind of cognitive schema hypothesized to play a central role in regulating aggressive behavior. Normative beliefs are cognitions about the appropriateness of aggressive behavior (Huesmann & Guerra, 1997). They are related to perceived social norms, but are different in that they concern what's "right for you." Normative beliefs are used to interpret others' behaviors, to guide the search for social scripts, and to filter out inappropriate scripts and behaviors. An individual who believes it is wrong for them to hit a female is likely to reject retrieved scripts that involving hitting females.

Finally, individual differences in emotional predispositions involve a variety of emotion-related tendencies, including a person's overall level of arousal, a person's propensity to become angered, a person's ability to regulate and control his or her emotions, and the associations between situations and emotions that an individual holds. In a social problem-solving situation a person's initial emotional state is modified by the situation and the person's attributions about the situation. The exact relation between propensities toward violence and emotional predispositions depends on the kind of aggressive and violent behavior (e.g., proactive or reactive). Those quick to anger and poor at regulating their emotions are more likely to retrieve violent scripts, behave impulsively, and thus behave reactively violently (Caprara et al., 1985; Eisenberg et al., 1994; Strellau, 1982; Zajonc et al., 1989). Those who are under-aroused and do not experience intense emotions should not be particularly likely to retrieve violent scripts, but, if such a script meets the goals of the situation, they would also not be likely to reject it because of the negative emotional outcomes it might have. Whereas normal individuals may reject many scripts when they imagine the negative emotional consequences of the script during the script evaluation phase, under-aroused individuals are less likely to feel any negative emotions during the evaluation phase. Thus, the characteristically under-aroused individual is more likely to behave violently (Raine, 1997).

In any given social setting, therefore, the characteristics of the situation interact with these four individual-difference factors to determine how the individual behaves. Imagine a teenage male suddenly discovering his girlfriend holding hands with another male. He makes attributions about what is happening on the basis of his current emotional state and his schemas about the world. Perhaps these lead to hostile attributions. His anger increases, and he is more likely to access a violent script for how to behave. If his repertoire of scripts is heavily loaded with aggressive scripts, accessing one becomes even more likely. He retrieves a script to hit his girlfriend. He evaluates the likely outcomes of the script and filters it through his normative beliefs. Does he feel any negative emotions as he imagines hitting the girl? Does he expect any negative consequences? Is hitting the girl consistent with his normative beliefs about what is OK for him to do? If all these tests are passed, he hits the girl. Finally, he may modify his schemas, scripts, normative beliefs, or emotional predispositions on the basis of the actual outcomes.

Short-Term Effects of Exposure to Violence

This model allows for three ways in which the exposure to violence can increase the risk of violent behavior in the observer in the short run: 1) the observed violent scene primes the retrieval of social scripts for violence that the observer has previously acquired; 2) the observer imitates immediately (mimics) what he or she has just seen to solve a social problem; or 3) the observer becomes angered and/or aroused by the violence he or she sees and that arousal increases the risk of behaving violently to a provocation afterwards because of the existing arousal makes the emotions stimulated by the provocation seem stronger. This is called excitation transfer (Bryant & Zillmann, 1979; Geen & O'Neal, 1969).

Priming of Violent Scripts and Schemas

Neuroscientists and cognitive psychologists have discovered that the human mind often acts as an associative network in which ideas are partially activated (primed) by associated stimuli in the environment (Fiske & Taylor, 1984). An encounter with some event or stimulus can prime, or activate, related concepts and ideas in a person's memory even without the person being aware of this influence (Bargh & Pietromonaco, 1982). For example, exposure to violent scenes may activate a complex set of associations that are related to aggressive ideas or emotions, thereby temporarily increasing the accessibility of aggressive thoughts, feelings, and scripts (including aggressive action tendencies). In other words, aggressive primes or cues make aggressive schemas more easily available for use in processing other incoming information, creating a temporary interpretational filter that biases subsequent perceptions. If these aggressive schemas are primed while certain events – such as ambiguous provocation – occur, the new events are more likely to be interpreted as involving aggression, thereby increasing the likelihood of an aggressive response. Priming effects related to aggression have been empirically demonstrated both for cues usually associated with violence, such as weapons (Anderson, Benjamin, & Bartholow, 1998; Bartholow, Anderson, Benjamin, & Carnagey, 2005; Berkowitz & LePage, 1967; Carlson, Marcus-Newhall, & Miller, 1990), and for initially neutral cues that have been observed repeatedly to be connected to violence, such as the color of a room in which violence is repeatedly observed (Leyens & Fraczek, 1983).

Priming effects are often seen as purely short-term influences. But, of course, the aggressive script or schema being primed may have been acquired long before the exposure to violence that primes its activation. In addition, research by cognitive and social-cognitive scientists has shown that repeated priming of certain scripts or schemas eventually makes them chronically accessible. Frequently primed aggression-related thoughts, emotions, and behavioral scripts become automatically and chronically accessible. That is, they become part of the normal internal state of the individual, thereby increasing the likelihood that any social encounter will be interpreted in an aggression-biased way, and therefore increasing the likelihood of aggressive encounters throughout the individual's life (e.g., Anderson & Huesmann, 2003).

Mimicry of Violent Scenes

In recent years indisputable evidence has accumulated that human and primate young have an innate tendency to mimic whomever they observe (Meltzoff, 2005; Meltzoff & Moore, 1977). They imitate expressions in early infancy and imitate behaviors by the time they can walk. Aggressive behaviors are no different from other observable motor behavior in this regard. Thus, the hitting, grabbing, pushing behaviors that young children see in the family, in the neighborhood, or in the mass media are often immediately mimicked unless the child has been taught not to mimic them (Bandura, 1977; Bandura, Ross, & Ross, 1961, 1963a, 1963b, 1963c). Furthermore, there is good reason to believe that the automatic imitation of expressions on others' faces also leads to the automatic activation of the emotion that the other was experiencing, as expressions are innately linked to emotions (Prinz, 2005; Strack et al., 1988).

Emotional Arousal and Excitation Transfer

Observing violence is highly emotionally arousing (e.g., disturbing) for most people. That is, it increases heart rate, the skin's conductance of electricity, and other physiological indicators of arousal. There is evidence that this arousal can increase aggression in three different ways. First, the arousal that violence produces is experienced as unpleasant by most people. As such it can increase aggression inclinations just like any other unpleasant stimuli (e.g., loud noises, hot temperatures, foul odors, frustrations, provocations; Berkowitz, 1983). This would be particularly true if the arousal stimulated by the violence is "angry arousal." Second, arousal, regardless of the reason for it, can reach such a peak that performance on complex tasks declines, inhibition of inappropriate responses is diminished, and dominant scripts tend to be displayed in social problem-solving. High arousal seems to energize or strengthen whatever an individual's dominant action tendency happens to be at the time. Third, if a person is provoked or otherwise instigated to aggress right after being aroused by something they see, heightened aggression can result (e.g., Bryant & Zilmann, 1979; Geen & O'Neal, 1969). This process is called "excitation transfer." Thus, a person who is aroused by seeing violence may feel greater anger from a subsequent provocation afterwards. As a result, their propensity to behave aggressively in response to that annoyance would be increased. Thus, people tend to react more violently to provocations immediately after being exposed to violence that produces an emotional reaction in the observer. This kind of effect, called "excitation transfer," is usually short-lived, perhaps lasting only minutes.

The frequently observed short-term effects of arousal have led theorists to posit that some individual differences in the propensity to behave aggressively are related to individual differences in the propensity to become highly aroused and experience negative affect. Berkowitz (1993), Caprara (Caprara et al., 1985), Eisenberg (Eisenberg et al., 1994), and Strelau (1982), among others, have suggested that individuals who are "quick to anger," "often in bad moods," and have difficulty "controlling their emotions" are more at risk for behaving aggressively. Implied but unsaid in a lot of this discussion has been the point that such individuals are more at risk particularly for hostile, emotional, reactive aggression, rather than for instrumental, proactive aggression. Significant empirical evidence has also accumulated that supports this individual-difference perspective on high reactivity or arousability (Berkowitz, 1993).

Individual-difference research has also revealed, however, what might at first seem to be a paradoxical finding about reactivity or arousability. Substantial evidence now exists that those males who are characteristically *lower* in baseline arousal are *more likely* to behave aggressively and antisocially over a period of time. For example, Raine and colleagues (Raine, Reynolds, Venables, & Mednick, 1997; Raine, Venables, & Williams, 1990) found in a longitudinal study of males from age 15 to 29 that those who at 15 had lower baseline heart rates, lower baseline skin conductance, and lower baseline EEG activation were significantly more likely to be arrested for a crime in the next 14 years. The psychological concept of psychopathy includes, as a major element, low reactivity (Hare, 1965, 1978), and psychopathy and low reactivity (particularly low electrodermal reactivity to aversive stimuli) have been shown to relate significantly to antisocial and aggressive behavior (Fowles, 1993; Lykken, 1995) though not particularly to violent behavior.

This result is not really paradoxical. In fact, three different theoretical explanations have been offered to explain why low reactivity might be related to antisocial and aggressive behavior. Perhaps the most widely cited have been the "poor conditioning" theories that have argued that low reactivity or arousability makes conditioning difficult and therefore makes appropriate socialization less likely (Eysenck, 1997). Another alternative has been the sensation-seeking theory that holds that individuals who are characteristically below their optimal level of arousal engage in antisocial and aggressive behavior for the "thrills" in order to raise their arousal level to a more "pleasant" place (Zuckermann, 1979). Still a third theoretical explanation is provided by the social-cognitive information-processing model described above. According to this model an individual's evaluation of a potential social script includes an evaluation of the emotions that are likely to result. Will it be an unpleasant experience or a pleasant experience? If a person experiences negative affect and arousal when thinking about the script and its outcome, its use will be inhibited. Consequently, those individuals who experience *less* "anxious arousal" at thoughts of aggression are *more* likely to use aggressive scripts to solve social problems.

This third theory (Huesmann & Kirwil, 2007; Huesmann et al., 2016) differs from the other two in that it suggests that aggressive behavior is related not only to low reactivity or arousability in general but also specifically to low negative emotional reactivity to thinking about aggression. General lower baseline arousal, according to this theory, is related to more aggression because lower baseline arousal translates into lower anxious arousal in response to thoughts of violence. However, individuals with average or even above-average baseline arousal who also experience lower anxious arousal to thoughts of aggression would also display more aggressive behavior according to this theory. This social information-processing theory also neatly explains how increased tendencies to become angered can result from repeated exposures to highly provoking scenes. The emotional reaction produced by attributions about the scene in the initial phase of information processing becomes associated with social and contextual cues present in the scene through classical conditioning. Subsequently the cues prime the reactions and probably the attributions as well, thereby making violence more likely.

Long-Term Socializing Effects of Exposure to Violence

In addition to the short-term precipitating effects that exposure to violence has on violent behavior, exposure to violence also has long-term socializing effects that predispose those exposed to violence to be more at risk of behaving violently for a long time. These socialization processes alter the four enduring individual differences that affect social behavior according to the model in Figure 29.1: (1) world schemas, (2) social scripts, (3) normative beliefs, and (4) emotional predispositions. Of course, any of these individual differences can be altered through the enactive learning processes (classical and operant conditioning) by which people learn on the basis of experience. However, repeated exposure to violence changes these individual differences through two other complex learning processes: (1) the observational learning of cognitions (world schemas, scripts, and normative beliefs) that make violent behavior more likely and (2) learned changes in emotional predispositions relevant to violence.

Observational Learning from Exposure to Violence

Humans begin imitating other humans at a very early age, and the observation of others' behaviors is the likely source of many of a young child's motor and social skills (Bandura, 1977; Meltzoff & Moore, 1977). The innate neurophysiological processes that make imitation automatic facilitate the incorporation of simple social scripts into the child's repertoire of scripts at a very young age. Social interactions then hone these behaviors that children first acquire through observation of others, but observational learning remains a powerful mechanism for the acquisition of new social behaviors throughout childhood and maturity. As a child grows older, more complex scripts are acquired. Then, the acquired scripts become more abstract, and beliefs and attitudes are acquired from inferences made about observed social behaviors (Huesmann & Guerra, 1997; Guerra, Huesmann, & Spindler, 2003). Theoretically, children can be expected to learn from whomever they observe – parents, siblings, peers, or media characters. Much of this learning takes place without intention to learn and without an awareness that learning has occurred.

According to observational-learning theory, the likelihood that an individual will acquire an observed social script is increased when the model performing the script is similar to or attractive to the viewer, the viewer identifies with the model, the context is realistic, and the viewed behavior is followed by rewarding consequences (Bandura, 1977). The reinforcements a person receives when imitating a behavior are largely responsible for whether the behavior persists. For example, youngsters might be rewarded or punished by people in their social environment (parents, teachers, peers) for the actions they exhibit, or they might vicariously experience the rewards or punishments other persons obtain when these others imitate the portrayed behavior. Through imitation and reinforcement, children develop habitual modes of behavior (e.g., Bandura, 1977; Huesmann, 1997).

Having the use of an aggressive script reinforced by the environment is not the only way an aggressive script can become more firmly encoded in a youth's brain. For example, if a child fantasizes about using an aggressive script that the child has acquired from observing others, the script will become more firmly encoded and more likely to be used in the future. Fantasy is a form of mental rehearsal (e.g., imagining this kind of behavior), and social scripts – just like other cognitions – will become more firmly encoded in the brain with rehearsal. Fantasizing about using aggressive scripts can even start a vicious circle of fantasizing, behaving, and fantasizing. Finally, through inferences children are likely to make from repeated observations, children also develop beliefs about the world in general (e.g., is it hostile or benign) and about what kind of behavior is acceptable.

Encoding scripts in memory through observational learning could be a conscious act, but more often it is an automatic mental process. Recent theoretical and empirical work (e.g., Bargh & Chartrand, 1999; Neuman & Strack, 2000) suggests that some types of imitative behaviors are very automatic, nonconscious, and likely to be short-lived. It has been demonstrated that movements of human and robotic stimuli as well as their schematic visual presentations elicit automatic imitation in observers (Press, Bird, Flach, & Heyes, 2005; Fadiga, Craighero, & Olivier, 2005).

Similarly, observational learning of complex scripts and schemas (e.g., beliefs, attitudes, and other types of knowledge that guide perception, interpretation, and understanding) can also occur outside of awareness, even with no immediate imitation of behaviors. Theoretically, it should not matter much for the long-term consequences of observation of violent behavior whether or not the child is aware of its influence. Repeated observation of aggressive behavior should increase the likelihood that children will incorporate aggressive scripts into their repertoires of social scripts, particularly if their own use of those scripts is followed by reinforcement.

Changes in Emotions Associated with Violence and Provocation

In the earlier material on short-term effects, we discussed the role that heightened arousal from observing violence can play in increasing aggression in the short run through *excitation transfer* that makes a subsequent provocation seem more severe. Increased arousal and particularly increased negative affect increase the risk for aggression. However, emotional arousal has a much more complex relation in the long run. As discussed above, individuals who have characteristically lower propensities to be aroused and, in particular, to experience less negative affect when exposed to violence, seem to be more at risk to behave violently. However, these individual differences in the propensity to be aroused in the long run seem to change with repeated exposures to violence. In particular, repeated exposures to violence seem to lessen the negative effect that the individual experiences when exposed to violence again. As a group these effects have come to be known in the literature as *desensitization effects*.

Emotional Desensitization to Violence

Emotional desensitization is the name given to the habituation process through which repeated exposures to violence hypothetically cause a reduction in the observer's emotional reactions to violence. Desensitization to violence is seen as a natural, very subtle, and unconscious process, which occurs as an effect of repeated exposure to violent stimuli and results from the habituation learning process. Habituation of neurophysiological responses over time is a well-established psychological phenomenon (see McSweeney & Swindell, 2002). Repeated presentation of the same stimulus usually results in smaller and smaller neurophysiological responses to that stimulus. Systematic desensitization procedures, based on this neurophysiological process, are highly successful in the treatment of strong unpleasant feelings typical of phobias (e.g., Bandura & Adams, 1977; Wolpe, 1958, 1982) and other anxiety or fear disorders (e.g., Pantalon & Motta, 1998). For example, systematically exposing someone with a snake phobia to snakes (initially under conditions designed to minimize anxiety and later under more anxiety-producing conditions) reduces the original anxiety reactions to such an extent that the person is no longer snake-phobic. One feature of modern systematic desensitization treatments is to have the phobic person observe other people (live or filmed) successfully interacting with the feared stimulus (Bandura, Grusec, & Menlove, 1967; Bandura & Menlove, 1968). However, the term "desensitization" has been employed in so many different ways that the exact meaning of any particular usage can be quite unclear.

In our usage emotional desensitization to violence is understood as a decrease in both the physiological markers of the emotional arousal normally associated with fight/flight mobilization (e.g., decreases of electric skin conductance, heart rate, and blood pressure) and a change in the cognitive interpretations of that arousal. The reactivity becomes gradually smaller with repeated exposures. This means that the organism is building up an emotional tolerance to violence in general or at least to an observed kind of violence. When this process being considered is a single response to a repeating single stimulus, the term "emotional habituation" is usually used. But when the process being considered is the emotional response to a repeating complex set of stimuli over a long run and in a broader context, the term "emotional desensitization" becomes more appropriate. Emotional desensitization thus refers to the joint processes of habituation of many characteristics of a complex stimulus that normally elicit strong emotional reactions.

In summary, we suggest that the label *emotional desensitization to violence* should be reserved to refer to a reduction in distress-related physiological reactivity to observations or thoughts of violence (Carnagey, Bushman, & Anderson, 2005; Krahe et al., 2011). Emotional desensitization occurs when people who are exposed to a lot of violence no longer respond with as much unpleasant physiological arousal as they did initially. Because the unpleasant physiological arousal and negative emotional reactions normally associated with violence have an inhibitory influence on thinking about violence, condoning violence, or behaving violently, emotional desensitization – the diminution of the unpleasant arousal – can result in a heightened likelihood of violent thoughts and behaviors.

Empirical Evidence of the Long-Term Contagion of Violence

Having presented the underlying theory that explains the various psychological processes that explain why exposure to violence should increase violent behavior in the short run and in the long run, let me now review of some of the empirical evidence supporting the theory that habitual exposure to violence infects people with violence. As many fine recent reviews and meta-analyses have covered the empirical evidence for short-term laboratory effects in great detail (Anderson et al., 2003; Anderson & Bushman, 2001; Paik & Comstock, 1994; Savage, 2004), and as one can generally not assess serious physically violent behavior in the laboratory, I will only review a few key longitudinal field studies that show how exposure to various types of violence infects the observer with an increased propensity to engage in serious physical violence and even criminal violence. In other words the risk of such serious violent behavior is increased by exposure to violence. Again as with any contagious disease, not all who are exposed to an infecting agent will catch the disease. Some will be more susceptible, and some will be less susceptible. It is also important to note again that I define violent behavior as serious physical aggression intended to harm someone and that does harm someone. Such aggression might fit into a category of criminal behavior or it might not, and, if it did fit into a category it might be reflected in criminal statistics or it might not. However, for testing a theory that violence is contagious, that is a mute point.

Infection by War Violence: The Palestine-Israeli Exposure to Violence Study

Probably no children in the world are exposed to more violence on a day-in and day-out basis than those who live in regions of war and ethnic violence. They are regularly exposed to scenes of extreme human violence at rates that would be hard to find even in American's most violent ghettos. My research team has recently collected three years of data on children in one such region – Palestine (West Bank and Gaza) and Israel (Israeli Jewish and Arab communities) (Huesmann et al., under review, 2018). We interviewed 600 Palestinian, 450 Arab Israeli, and 450 Jewish Israeli children and their parents individually three times at one-year intervals from 2007 to 2010. At the start of the interviews the children were age 8, 11, or 14. Each year we asked the children and their parents to report on how much violence they had been exposed to in the past year. For example, we asked, "How often have you seen right in front of you Palestinian (or Israeli for Israeli children) buildings or buses or other property destroyed by Israelis (or Palestinians for Israeli children)." We asked many questions of this type including about "seeing a family member die," "seeing friends die," "seeing them injured," "seeing them held hostage or tortured," etc. The rates of observation in person were very high – for example, 55% of Palestinian children had seen a friend die due to the Israelis, 43% had seen someone tortured or held hostage, and 63% had seen someone crying because someone they knew had died. The rates of seeing such things rose to over 90% for the past year when observing in the mass media was included. The rates for Israeli Jewish children were about half as much and for Israeli Arab children half as much again, but even among them about one out of every 20 children had seen someone killed or be seriously injured in front of them in the past year.

These rates are appallingly high. The question is does such exposure to such violence infect the children with an increased propensity to behave violently and aggressively at their peers who have not attacked them as our theory of contagion of violence hypothesizes. The answer, we discovered, is clearly yes. The violence spreads like a contagious disease among them. For example, as shown in Figure 29.3 below, kids who fall in the top 25% on the amount of war violence they have seen in years 1 and 2 are about 40% more likely to punch or beat a peer in year 3, 12 times more likely to choke a peer, and twice as likely to knife or threaten to knife a peer than kids who fall in the lowest 25% on violence exposure. If we create a composite aggressive-acts-at-peers score (see Huesmann et al., 2016b for details) that includes not only self-reports of these very violent acts, which were only frequent for older children, but also self-reports of less violent aggressive acts frequent with younger children (such as "pushing or shoving other kids") and parent reports of all kinds of aggressive and violent acts (such as "gets in many fights" or "threatens people"), we get a much larger sample size and find a very strong relation between exposure to ethnic-political violence in years 1 and 2 and aggressive behavior in year 3, $r = 0.46$ ($N = 1233$, $p < 0.0001$).

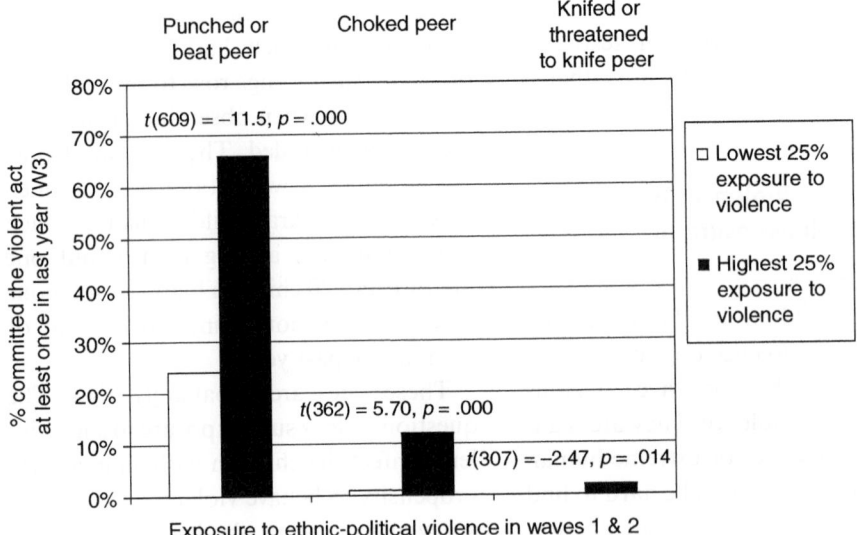

Figure 29.3 *Exposure to war violence predicts subsequent increased risk of violent behavior against peers (Huesmann, Dubow, Boxer, et al., 2016).*

These youth have not been victimized by their peers; yet they attack their peers. These results cannot be explained by demographic differences, age differences, or gender differences. Differences in exposure to violence account for more of the individual differences in aggression than any other single factor. Also, because we collected the data over three years, we could do the analyses in Figure 29.4 (from Huesmann et al., 2016b) that show that the effect of earlier exposure on later aggression is significantly greater than the effect of earlier aggression on later exposure.

As Figure 29.4 shows, exposure to violence stimulates later increases in violent behavior significantly more than behaving violently leads to more exposure to war violence. The standardized effect size from exposure to war violence in year 1 on violent behavior directed at peers in year 3 is over three times greater than the effect of violent behavior in year 1 on exposure to war violence in year 3.

Why do these youth seem to catch the disease of violent behavior from exposure to ethnic-political violence? A boy who has grown up observing more ethnic-political violence around him almost every day will believe that the world is a more hostile place than do other boys and will be biased toward making hostile attributions about those who annoy him. He will also have encoded a larger and more accessible repertoire of aggressive scripts over time while observing violence. This will then make it more likely that he will rehearse the aggressive scripts through fantasizing. His hostile attributions about peers coupled with his readily accessible repertoire of aggressive scripts then make it more likely that he will behave aggressively and violently toward peers. Additionally, from his exposures to violence, he will be more likely to have acquired normative beliefs that such aggressive and violent behavior is appropriate. Finally, his repeated exposures to violence will have blunted

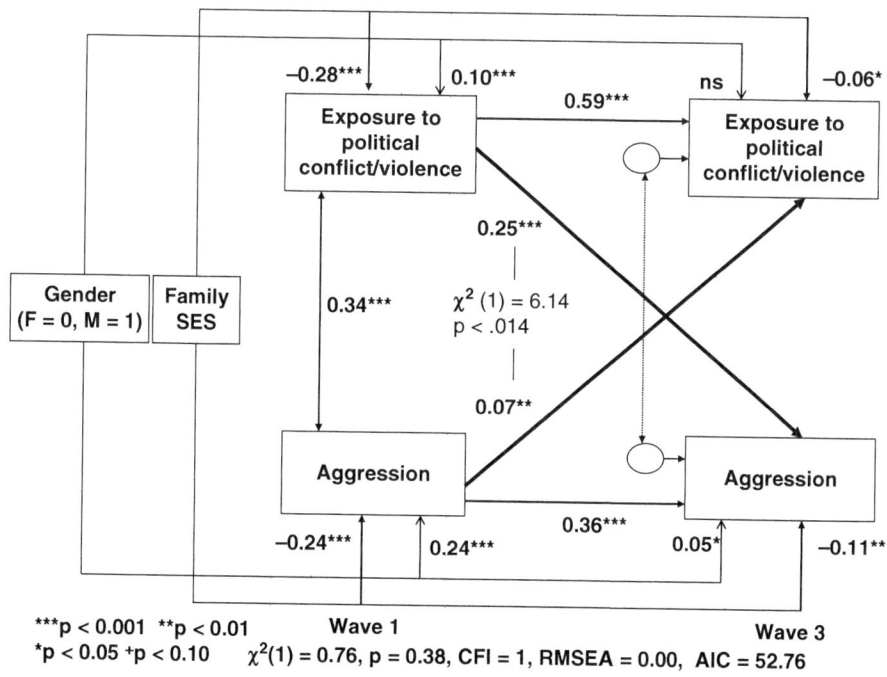

Figure 29.4 Cross-lagged structural modeling analyses showing that it is more plausible that exposure to war violence stimulates subsequent violent behavior than vice-versa (Huesmann, Dubow, Boxer, et al., 2016).

the negative emotional responses (anxiety and fear) that humans normally experience when they see violence or think about violence that might inhibit such behavior. Thus, the more a youth is exposed to war violence, the more certainly he or she will be infected with violence and behave violently toward others, even though the others may have no connection to the war violence. These mediating processes are evident in our samples of Palestinian and Israeli youth, as illustrated in Figure 29.5 from Huesmann et al., 2016b.

The numbers in this diagram provide confirmation of the validity of this mediation model. The youth who have been exposed to more ethnic conflict/violence in year 1 fantasized more about behaving aggressively in year 2 (that is, they rehearse aggressive scripts more), held stronger beliefs that aggressive behavior at others is OK in year 2, and showed higher levels of emotional distress in year 2. Each of these effects in turn stimulated them to behave more aggressively at their peers in year 3.

Infection by Neighborhood Violence: The Metropolitan Area Child Study

A very similar technique was used by Guerra, Huesmann, and Spindler (2003) to demonstrate a longitudinal effect of exposure to neighborhood violence on later serious aggressive behavior in children. As we said earlier in this chapter, the theory for how exposure to violence infects youth with the propensity to behave aggressively does not distinguish between whether the violence is observed in the streets outside

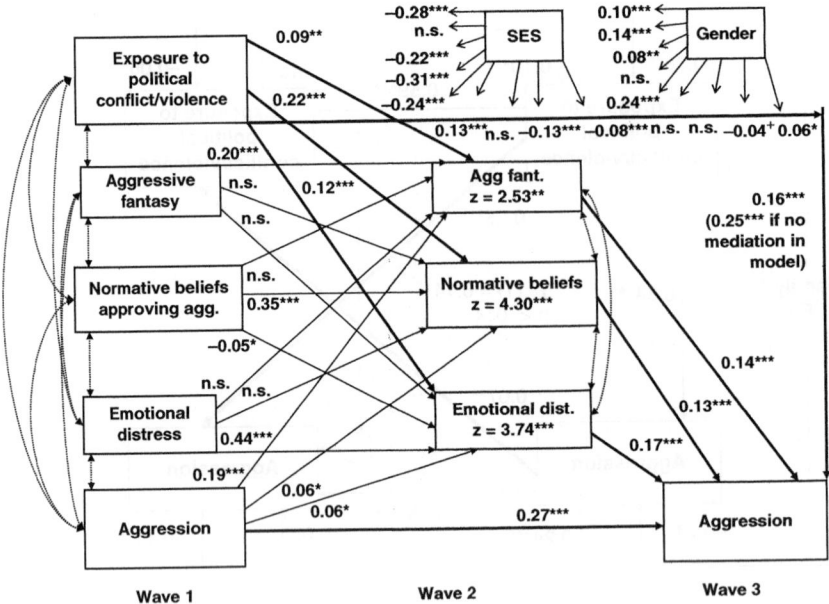

Figure 29.5 *Longitudinal structural model showing that the effect of exposure to war violence on subsequent violent behavior is partially mediated by rehearsal of aggressive scripts, adoption of normative beliefs supporting aggression, and emotional dysregulation (Huesmann, Dubow, Boxer, et al., 2016).*

a child's house or on the TV. In this particular study I and my colleagues (Len Eron, Nancy Guerra, David Henry, Pat Tolan, and Rick VanAcker) examined over 4000 6–11-year-old youth growing up in very high-risk neighborhoods in the Chicago metropolitan area. We interviewed and tested them, their peers, and their parents at one year intervals over 6 years. We computed an exposure to violence score for each one by asking them and their parents about their exposure to neighborhood violence with items from Attar, Guerra, and Tolan's (1994) neighborhood violence scale, e.g., "Have you seen someone beaten, shot, or really hurt by someone? Have you seen or been around people shooting guns?" We computed a violent behavior score for each one on the basis of how many times they were nominated by their school peers and teachers on questions like, "Who is always getting into fights and hitting others?" We also assessed their normative beliefs approving of aggression each year (Huesmann & Guerra, 1997).

We found that their exposure to neighborhood violence was significantly correlated with their current violent behavior in both grade 2 ($r = 0.18$, $p < 0.001$, $N = 1485$) and grade 6 ($r = 0.18$, $N = 679$, $p < 0.001$). More importantly, using a hierarchical linear growth curve model, we found that the youth's violent behavior in each year was significantly predicted by their exposure to neighborhood violence in the prior year ($\beta = 0.10$, $p < 0.001$) even controlling for the youth's prior violent behavior, as shown in Figure 29.6 (Guerra, Huesmann, & Spindler, 2003).

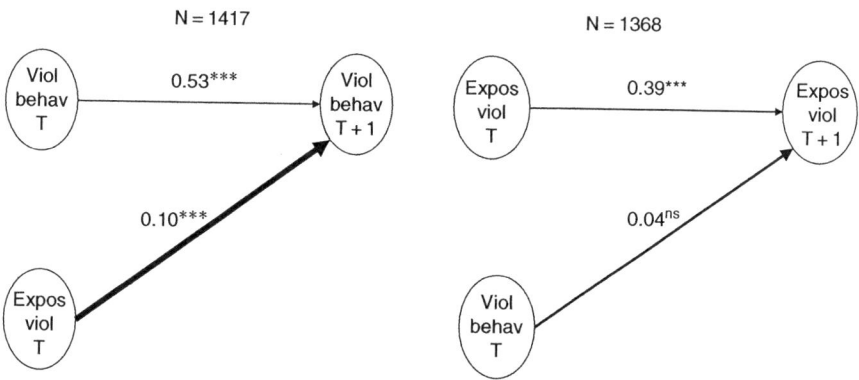

Figure 29.6 *HLM 3-level (Time, Person, School) growth curve longitudinal model showing that exposure to neighborhood violence in one year significantly increases the risk of the exposed behaving more violently in the next year while behaving violently in one year does not increase the risk of exposure to neighborhood violence in the next year (Huesmann, Guerra, & Spindler, 2003).*

The β = 0.10 effect from exposure to violence in one year to behaving aggressively in the next year was significant and 2.5 times stronger than the non-significant effect of aggressive behavior on exposure to neighborhood violence in the next year. This result makes it much more plausible that the major reason for the correlation between a youth's exposure to neighborhood violence and their subsequent own violent behavior is that the exposure to violence infects the youth with the propensity to behave violently rather than that youths' violent behaviors are causing them to be exposed to more neighborhood violence.

Finally, as with exposure to war violence, we were able to demonstrate in this study (see Huesmann, Guerra, & Spindler, 2003) that one of the infection's proximal effects was to increase the youths' beliefs about the normativeness of aggression, which in turn increased the propensity of the youth to behave aggressively and violently.

Infection by Television Violence

Between 1977 and 1995 Huesmann and colleagues completed a longitudinal study in which childhood habitual exposure to TV violence was related to serious physical aggression and criminal violence in young adulthood (Huesmann et al., 2003). Among the sample of 329 males and females from the Chicago area, the researchers found significant correlations between repeated exposures to television violence over two years when a child was either 6 or 9 years old and serious physical aggression 15 years later for both men ($r = 0.19$, $n = 153$, $p < 0.01$) and women ($r = 0.15$, $n = 176$, $p < 0.01$). Serious violent behavior was assessed by having each participant and someone who knew the participant well rate them on how often they perpetrated three groups of violent behaviors: shoot or threaten to shoot someone with a gun; stab or threaten to stab someone with a knife; choke, punch, or beat another adult; or slap or kick another adult. Exposure to TV violence in childhood was assessed by having the children tell us their favorite programs from Nielsen's top 80 programs for children and tell us how often they watched each program. Then the programs were rated for violence by highly reliable independent

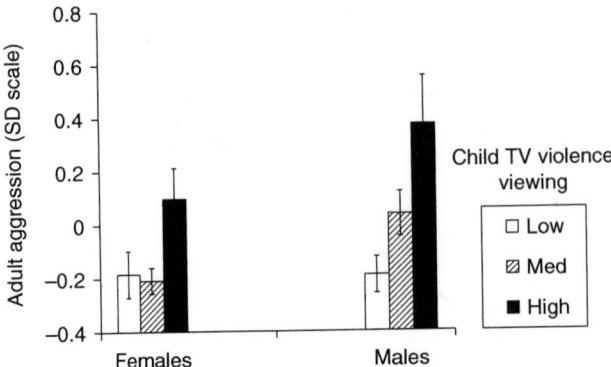

Figure 29.7 *Results from 15-year longitudinal study (Huesmann, Moise, Podolski, & Eron, 2003) showing that children age 6 to 9 who are in the upper 25% on habitually watching TV violence behave, on average, significantly more aggressively and violently 15 years later as young adults.*

raters; so we could compute a total exposure to violence score. In addition to the 15-year correlations, we found that highest violence exposure group in childhood (the top 25%), committed significantly more acts of physical aggression and violence, such as "pushing, grabbing, or shoving their spouses" (42% vs. 22% in the case of males) or "shoving, punching, beating or choking" someone who had made them angry (17% vs. 4% in the case of females). The males in the high childhood violence exposure group were also much more likely to be convicted of a crime in Illinois by the time they were 25 (10.7% vs. 3.1%, $p < 0.03$), while the females in the high-TV violence exposure group self-reported the commission of more crimes than did the females in the low-TV violence exposure group (48.6% vs. 29.5%, $p < 0.01$). When we computed a composite adult aggression score from both the subject's self-reports, their scores on a standardized test of aggressiveness, and a close friend's reports of their aggressive acts, we found very strong 15-year relations for both men and women. As Figure 29.7 shows, the 25% of both males and females who were exposed to the most childhood TV violence scored about 0.3 to 0.5 standard deviations higher on adult aggression.

Like we showed above for infections from war violence or infections from neighborhood violence, structural modeling analyses (see Figure 29.8) demonstrated habitual exposure to TV violence during childhood predicted significantly higher levels of total aggressive behavior 15 years later, while childhood aggressive behavior had only a weak predictive effect on the amount of TV violence a youth would watch 15 years later. This result again suggests that it is more plausible that exposure to violence is infecting youth with the propensity to behave more aggressively than that aggressive behavior is stimulating more exposure to violence. This pattern of longitudinal results did not change and remained significant even when we controlled statistically for parents' education, child-rearing behaviors, aggression, and many other factors, including the children's academic achievement.

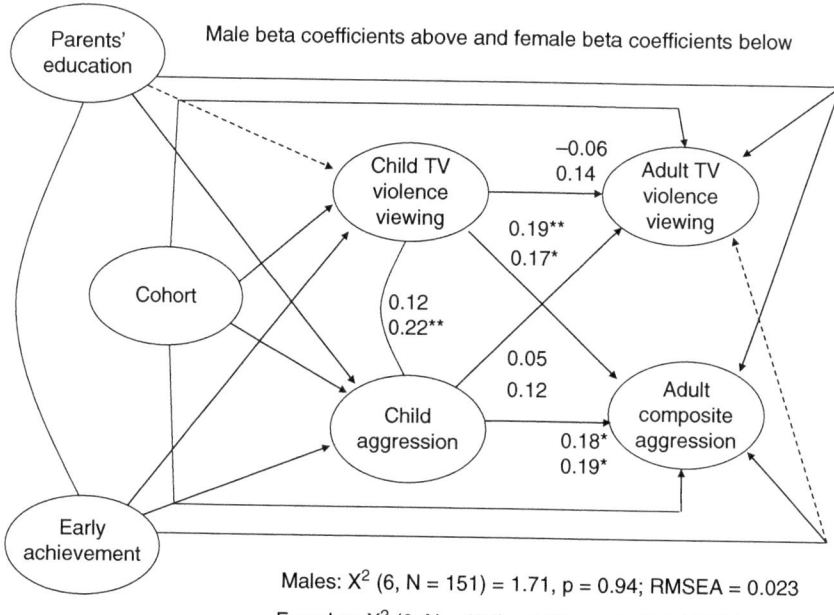

Figure 29.8 *Cross-lagged longitudinal structural equation model from Huesmann, Moise, Podolski, & Eron (2003) showing that it is more plausible that exposure to TV violence stimulates subsequent aggressive and violent behavior than that aggressive and violent behavior stimulates increased violence viewing.*

Also, similarly, to the studies reported above on exposure to war violence and exposure to neighborhood violence, the infection with violent behavior form exposure to TV violence seemed to be mediated by changes in social cognitions – in particular normative beliefs. As reported by Huesmann (2016) and shown in Figure 29.9, for both males and females normative beliefs approving of aggression acted as a significant mediator of the effect of early TV violence viewing on young adult aggressive and violent behavior.

Infection from Media Violence that Leads to Criminally Violent Behavior

The ideal field research to examine early causes of criminally violent behavior is a prospective longitudinal study of a representative sample of the population like the ones reviewed above. The theory of contagion of violence certainly suggests that exposure to criminal violence in the mass media should increase the risk that the observer would be infected with social cognitions that promote criminally violent behavior, and the Huesmann et al. (2003) 15-year prospective study described above does show this contagion for a very small sample size. Given the small rates of criminal violence, it is difficult to do such prospective studies of criminal violence with much larger sample sizes. However, one way to achieve a more substantial sample size and more robust results would be to assess childhood exposure to media violence retrospectively in a high-risk population with a high incidence of criminal violence. Huesmann et al. (under review, 2018)

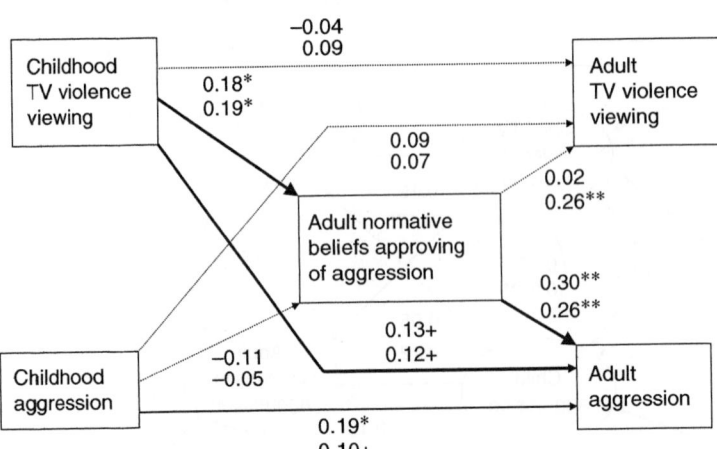

Figure 29.9 Longitudinal structural equation model showing that increases in normative beliefs supporting aggression partially mediate the longitudinal effects of TV violence on aggressive and violent behavior (Huesmann, 2016).

conducted two such studies – one with adjudicated delinquents and high-risk high school students, and the other with imprisoned young adults.

The Michigan High-Risk Adolescent Study

In this study, as reported previously (Boxer et al., 2009; Huesmann et al., under review, 2018), we interviewed 820 adolescents, with sampling divided about evenly between a population of adolescents attending high schools (n = 430) in rural, suburban, and urban moderate-risk communities in Michigan (M age = 16.83 years, SD = 0.71; 45.9% racial/ethnic minority; 51.6% female) and a higher-risk population of adolescents (n = 390) who were adjudicated delinquents detained in county and state juvenile justice facilities in Michigan (M age = 15.55 years, SD = 1.53; 45.1% racial/ethnic minority; 26.4% female).

We conducted extensive one-on-one interviews of the participants, their parents/guardians (of 812 youth), and teachers/institutional-staff (of 706 youth) who dealt with them. Specifically, we collected cross-informant assessments of the youths' violent behavior (e.g., "slapping or kicking others, punching or beating others, choking others, or cutting or shooting others or threatening to do it, shooting others or threatening to do it") and an array of expected risk factors for violent behavior. From the youth we collected information on their childhood media violence exposure using a guided recall procedure in which we asked participants to think back to when they were in grade 2 or 3. After they answered some general questions that required them to think

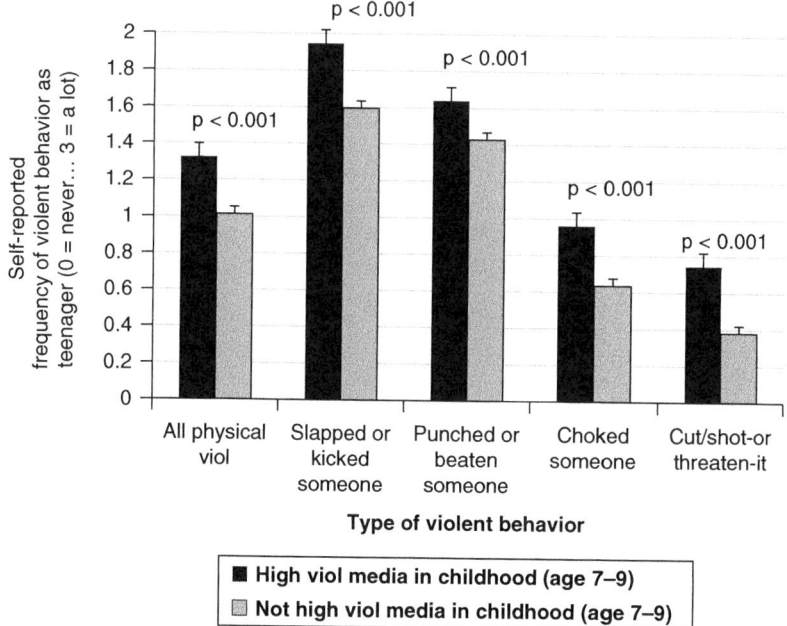

Figure 29.10 *The frequency of serious violent behavior by "high-risk" teenagers as a function of their self-reported exposure to TV, film, and video game violence when children (Huesmann et al., under review, 2018).*

back about what was happening in their lives at that time, we asked them to tell us what their three favorite TV programs were (if they watched TV), what their three favorite video games were (if they played video games), and what their three favorite movies were that they saw in theaters or on TV. All the TV programs, video games, and movies named were rated reliably on a common scale for violent content by a cadre of undergraduate raters who were required to be familiar with any title they rated. A score was then computed for the "violence of each participant's favorite childhood media" by computing the average of the violence ratings of all the titles each participant named.

We found, as reported in Huesmann et al. (under review, 2018) that this exposure to media violence score was correlated very significantly ($r = 0.26$, $p < 0.001$) with the average cross-informant scores on physical violence. To illustrate the dimensions of this relation, in Figure 29.10 we examined the mean differences in the various types of self-reported violent behavior of those teenagers who were in the highest quartile on childhood media violence compared to the rest of the teenagers. One can see from the figure that indeed the children in the highest 25% on childhood media violence scored significantly higher on every type of teenage violent behavior we assessed than children who had been in the lower 75%.

To test whether these relations could be explained by gender or other personal factors, we computed two multiple regressions predicting youths' self-reported and teacher-reported teenage violent behavior from the overall violence of

Table 29.1 *Predicting Serious Physically Violent Behavior in Teenagers from the Violence in their Favorite Media (TV Programs, Films, and Video Games) When they Were Age 7 to 9, Controlling for Other Factors*

Predictor	Standardized Effect on Self-reported Violent Behavior of Teenager β	Significance	Standardized Effect on Teacher-reported Violent Behavior of Teenager β	Significance
Sex (0 = female, 1 = male)	0.05	t = 1.24, n.s.	−0.05	t = 0.99, n.s.
Violence of favorite media in childhood (age 7–9)	**0.17*****	t = 4.20, p < 0.001	**0.14****	t = 2.46, p = 0.014
Intellectual/ academic skills	0.04	t = 1.16, n. s.	−0.10*	t = 2.29, p = 0.023
Parents' income level	−0.14***	t = 3.65, p < .001	−0.03	t = 0.78, n.s.
Exposure of child to neighborhood violence	0.30***	t = 8.17, p < .001	0.23***	t = 5.39, p < 0.001
	R^2 = 0.181 (n = 675)	F (5,670) = 29.5, p < 0.001	R^2 = 0.092 (n = 582)	F (5,577) = 11.7, p < 0.001

Notes: *p < 0.05, **p < 0.01, ***p < 0.001.

their favorite media in childhood with the covariates of sex, age, parental income, teenager's academic performance, and the neighborhood violence to which they were exposed during childhood in the equation. The results are shown in Table 29.1 from Huesmann et al. (under review, 2018). One can see that the significant effect of media violence exposure in childhood on teenage violent behavior (β = 0.17, p < 0.001) remains when these other factors are covaried out. This analysis also shows, as our theory of contagion would predict, that exposure to neighborhood violence and exposure to media violence have independent contagious effects (for neighborhood violence, b = 0.30, p < 0.001) in infecting the youth with violent behavior.

The Indiana Adult Prisoner Study

The participants for this study (Huesmann et al., under review, 2018) were 149 prisoners in an Indiana state prison for males and 184 prisoners in an Indiana state prison for females (F = 55.3%). Of the 333 prisoners

Table 29.2 *Predicting Whether Young Adult Prisoners are Imprisoned for Violent or Non-violent Crimes from their Self-reports of Violence in their Favorite Childhood Media (TV Programs, Films, and Video Games), Controlling for Other Factors*

Predictor (Self Reports)	Odds Ratio	Significance
Sex (0 = female, 1 = male)	**1.88**	$p < 0.035$
Ave. violence of favorite media in childhood (age 7–9) (0 = no visible violence … 4 = high visible violence)	**2.04**	$p < 0.001$
Prisoner's educational achievement (1 = "< = grade 6"… 10 = "graduated from college")	1.05	n. s.
Prisoners' exposure to neighborhood viol. in childhood (0 = none … 4 = all types listed)	**1.24**	$P < 0.045$

who participated, we were able to determine whether they were imprisoned for a violent crime or a non-violent crime for 321 of them. We found that 158 were imprisoned for a violent crime (F = 39.9%) and 163 were imprisoned for a non-violent crime (F = 68.1%). Some of the examples of the convictions of the prisoners placed in the violent category were homicide (46 cases), assault or battery (24 cases), rape or sexual assault (13 cases), and robbery (31 cases). Some of the examples of the convictions for the prisoners placed in the non-violent category were burglary (25 cases), forgery and fraud (27 cases), and dealing or possessing drugs (47 cases).

All the prisoners were interviewed by trained staff on measures mostly identical to those used in the above study with adolescents and using procedures mostly identical to those used with the incarcerated delinquents. However, instead of asking them to report the frequency of their violent behaviors when they were a teenager, we asked them to report on their frequency of each type of violent behavior in the year before they were imprisoned. The coding of answers, data processing, and analyses procedures are reported in Huesmann et al. (under review, 2018).

For this sample of prisoners we found that childhood exposure to media violence was correlated with every type of violent behavior we assessed and in particular with "cutting or shooting someone or threatening to do it" ($r = 0.23$, $p < 0.001$). We also computed a logistic regression predicting whether the participant was imprisoned for a violent or non-violent crime from the overall violence of their favorite media in childhood with the covariates of sex, marital status, their educational achievement, and the neighborhood violence they were exposed to during childhood as covariates in the equation. The results are shown in Table 29.2. One can see that amount of exposure to media violence in childhood significantly predicts whether the prisoner has been convicted of a violent or non-violent crime. As expected, exposure to neighborhood violence when a child again seems to increase the youths' infection with violence independently of the youths' exposure to media violence.

The Columbia County Longitudinal Study

Given the independent contagion effects of exposure to media violence and exposure to neighborhood violence in the above studies, we decided to examine whether multiple exposures to violence would have a substantial cumulative effect in infecting a youth more certainly with the violence disease and whether the same social cognitive mediators we had been studying could account for being infected from multiple exposures and sources. Fortunately, we already possessed a data set that would allow an examination of this question.

The Columbia County Longitudinal Study (Eron et al., 1971; 1972; Huesmann et al., 1984; 2009) is known as one of the earliest studies to show that exposure to TV violence increased a 8-year-old boy's risk for behaving aggressively ten years later when he was 18. The researchers also assessed the participants exposure to peer and family violence. Because the 748 initial participants in the study were intensively tested and interviewed (and had their parents interviewed) when they were 8 and then were re-interviewed and tested at age 18–19, at age 30, and at age 48, the study provides unique information on the long-term effects of exposure to multiple sources of violence, the contagion of such violence, and what mediates the contagion.

For the 535 participants on whom we had data both from ages 8 to 18 and ages 48 to 49, we found a highly significant correlation of $r = 0.20$ ($p < 0.001$) from total exposure of peer, family, and media violence at ages 8 and 18 to risk for violent and aggressive behavior 30 to 40 years later at age 48 to 49 (Huesmann et al., 2009). We measured aggressive and violent behavior at age 48 to 49 with a combination of self-reports serious physical violence as described in the other studies above, milder physical and verbal aggression, and scores on scales F49 of the MMPI that is known to assess antisocial behaviors. Even more interesting from the perspective of theorizing about the process of contagion of violence is that this correlation over 30 to 40 years appeared mostly due to the exposure to violence infecting the participant with normative beliefs supporting aggression and violence and infecting them with aggressive and violent scripts that they then revealed by rehearsing them (see Figure 29.11).

These longitudinal studies provide good evidence that the regular observation of violence in childhood infects youth with deviant social cognitions and emotional reactions that manifest themselves by promoting serious aggressive behavior later in life. Furthermore, these studies contradict the theory that the correlation between exposure to violence and actual violent behavior is due to more violent people exposing themselves to more violence in various domains (war violence, neighborhood violence, peer violence, media violence). The long-term effect can be explained theoretically by changes in social cognitions and emotions that are engendered by exposure to violence and then persist for a long time, and existing longitudinal studies now proved some evidence in support of this. However, the amount of evidence demonstrating

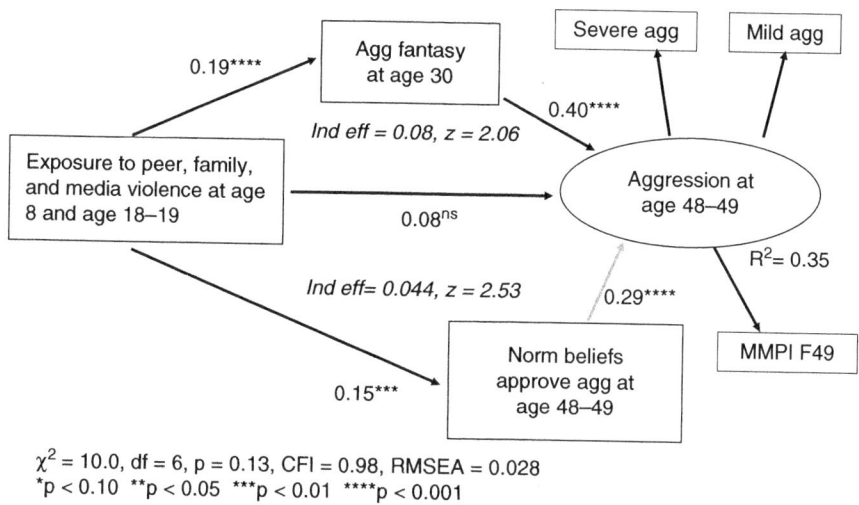

Figure 29.11 *A structural equation model using data from the Columbia County Longitudinal Study showing that those youth who were exposed to more peer, family, and TV violence from ages 8 to 19 were significantly more likely to behave violently and aggressively 30 years later and that the effect was mostly mediated by their fantasy rehearsal of aggressive scripts by their normative beliefs approving of aggression (Huesmann et al., 2009).*

that such cognitive changes or emotional changes do indeed mediate the effect is still limited.

Moderators of the Long-Term Effects of Exposure to Violence

Not every child who is exposed to violence will behave noticeably more violently or aggressively, even if they are affected to some extent. Most children are highly resilient, and it requires a convergence of many bad things to make them seriously "bad." The observation of violence is just one factor among many predisposing and precipitating factors that combine to influence aggressive and violent behavior. These factors do not simply combine additively. They combine interactively. The most important moderating factors have been discussed in detail in several recent reviews (Anderson et al., 2003; Bushman & Huesmann, 2002; Huesmann & Kirwil, 2007), and we only summarize a few of their conclusions here. For example, identification with the aggressive perpetrator is a very important moderator of the effects, as are the extent to which the violence (1) seems true to life, (2) is portrayed as justified, and (3) is perceived as rewarded. At the person level, the most aggressive behaviors will come from exposing already aggressive individuals to more violence, though exposure affects even nonaggressive individuals. Children experience more lasting effects than adults. Although children with lower IQs and lower SES are both exposed to more violence and behave more aggressively, exposure seems to affect children on all levels of these factors. Finally, the effects seem to be less for children whose parents co-view with the child and discuss with the child what they are seeing (i.e., engage in parental mediation; Nathanson, 1999).

Conclusion

Violence is a contagious disease. Psychological theories that have emerged over the past few decades now explain the short-term precipitating effects of exposure to violence mostly in terms of priming, simple imitation, and excitation transfer. However, the long-term predisposing effects involve more complex processes of observational learning of social cognitions and of emotional desensitization to violence. When a youth is exposed to the violence disease sufficiently, the disease changes the youth's social cognitions and emotional reactions. The infected youth then often retains these changes for a long time and manifests the disease externally with its primary symptom – violent and aggressive behavior.

What social cognitions and emotional reactions are altered by the infection? All social behavior is guided by encoded scripts (programs for behavior) that we all have acquired as we grew up. When confronted with a social problem, youths first make attributions about what is going on in the situation and then retrieve from their minds whatever social scripts are most easily recalled and seem most relevant. These generally are scripts that are most strongly primed by the social situation and have been most strongly learned from past experiences. Thus, a boy who has grown up observing violence around him almost every day (whether war violence, neighborhood violence, gang violence, school violence, or family violence) will believe that the world is a hostile place and will be biased toward making hostile attributions about those who annoy him. Such attributions and the repertoire of aggressive scripts the boy will have encoded over time will then make it more likely that he will use an aggressive social script for dealing with such a person. Additionally, he will be more likely to view behaving in such an aggressive manner as normative and acceptable. Equally importantly, repeated exposures to violence will blunt the negative emotional responses (anxiety and fear) that humans normally experience when they see violence or think about violence. These internal psychological changes that the infection produces can last for a long time, and, while they last, the risk of the person behaving violently and aggressively will be heightened.

References

Abelson, R. P. (1981). Psychological status of the script concept. *American Psychologist*, 36, 715–729.

Anderson, C. A., Benjamin, A. J., & Bartholow, B. D. (1998). Does the gun pull the trigger? Automatic priming effects of weapon pictures and weapon names. *Psychological Science*, 9, 308–314.

Anderson, C. A., Berkowitz, L., Donnerstein, E., Huesmann, L. R., Johnson, J., Linz, D., et al. (2003). The influence of media violence on youth. *Psychological Science in the Public Interest*, 4(3), 81–110.

Anderson, C. A. & Bushman, B. J. (2001). Effects of violent video games on aggressive behavior, aggressive cognition, aggressive affect, physiological arousal, and prosocial behavior: A meta-analytic review of the scientific literature. *Psychological Science*, 12, 353–359.

Anderson, C. A. & Huesmann, L. R. (2003). Human aggression: A social-cognitive view. In M. A. Hogg & J. Cooper (Eds), *Handbook of social psychology* (pp. 296–323). London: Sage.

Attar, B. K., Guerra, N. G., & Tolan, P. H. (1994). Neighborhood disadvantage, stressful life events, and adjustment in urban elementary school children. *Journal of Clinical Child Psychology*, 23(4), 391–400.

Bandura, A. (1973). *Aggression: A social learning theory analysis*. Englewood Cliffs, NJ: Prentice Hall.

Bandura, A. (1977). *Social learning theory*. Englewood Cliffs, NJ: Prentice Hall.

Bandura, A. & Adams, N.E. (1977). Analysis of self-efficacy theory of behavioral change. *Cognitive Therapy and Research*, 1, 287–310.

Bandura, A., Grusec, J. E., & Menlove, F. L. (1967). Vicarious extinction of avoidance behavior. *Journal of Personality and Social Psychology*, 5, 16–23.

Bandura, A. & Menlove, F. L. (1968). Factors determining vicarious extinction of avoidance behavior through symbolic modeling. *Journal of Personality and Social Psychology*, 8, 99–108.

Bandura, A., Ross, D., & Ross, S. A. (1961). Transmission of aggression through imitation of aggressive models. *Journal of Abnormal and Social Psychology*, 63, 575–582.

Bandura, A., Ross, D., & Ross, S. A. (1963a). Imitation of film-mediated aggressive models. *Journal of Abnormal and Social Psychology*, 66, 3–11.

Bandura, A., Ross, D., & Ross, S. A. (1963b). A comparative test of the status envy, social power, and secondary reinforcement theories of identificatory learning. *Journal of Abnormal and Social Psychology*, 67, 527–534.

Bandura, A., Ross, D., & Ross, S. A. (1963c). Vicarious reinforcement and imitative learning. *Journal of Abnormal and Social Psychology*, 67, 601–607.

Bargh, J. A., & Chartrand, T. L. (1999). The unbearable automaticity of being. *American Psychologist*, 54, 462–479.

Bargh, J. A. & Pietromonaco, P. (1982). Automatic information processing and social perception: The influence of trait information presented outside of conscious awareness on impression formation. *Journal of Personality and Social Psychology*, 43, 437–449.

Bartholow, B. D., Anderson, C. A., & Carnagey, N. L. (2005). Interactive effects of life experience and situational cues on aggression: The weapons priming effect in hunters and nonhunters. *Journal of Experimental Social Psychology*, 41(1), 48–60.

Berkowitz, L. (1962). *Aggression: A social psychological analysis*. New York: McGraw-Hill.

Berkowitz, L. (1983). Aversively stimulated aggression: Some parallels and differences in research with animals and humans. *American Psychologist*, 38, 1135–1144.

Berkowitz, L. (1993). *Aggression: Its causes, consequences, and control*. New York: McGraw-Hill.

Berkowitz, L. & LePage, A. (1967). Weapons as aggression-eliciting stimuli. *Journal of Personality and Social Psychology*, 7, 202–207.

Boxer, P., Huesmann, L. R., Bushman, B., O'Brien, M., & Moceri, D. (2009). The role of violent media preference in cumulative developmental risk for violence and general aggression. *Journal of Youth and Adolescence*, 38(3), 417–428.

Bryant, J. & Zillmann, D. (1979). Effect of intensification of annoyance through unrelated residual excitation on substantially delayed hostile behavior. *Journal of Experimental Social Psychology*, 15, 470–480.

Bushman, B. J. & Huesmann, L. R. (2001). Effects of televised violence on aggression. In D. G. Singer & J. L. Singer (Eds), *Handbook of children and the media* (pp. 223–254). Thousand Oaks, CA: Sage.

Carlson, M., Marcus-Newhall, A., & Miller, N. (1990). Effects of situational aggression cues: A quantitative review. *Journal of Personality and Social Psychology*, 58, 622–633.

Carnagey, N. L., Bushman, B. J. & Anderson, C. A. (2005). *Video game violence desensitizes players to real world violence*. Manuscript submitted for publication.

Dodge, K. A. (1986). A social information processing model of social competence in children. In M. Perlmutter (Ed.), *The Minnesota symposium on child psychology* (Vol. 18, pp. 77–125). Hillsdale, NJ: Erlbaum.

Dodge, K. A. (1993). Social-cognitive mechanisms in the development of conduct disorder and depression. *Annual Review of Psychology*, 44, 559–584.

Dodge, K. A., Malone, P. S., Lansford, J. E., Sorbring, E., Skinner, A. T., Tapanya, S., Tirado, L. M. U., Zelli, A., Alampay, L. P., Al-Hassan, S. M., Bacchini, D., Bombi, A. S., Bornstein, M. H., Chang, L., Deater-Deckard, K., Di Giunta, L., Oburu, P., & Pastorelli, C. (2015). Hostile attributional bias and aggressive behavior in global context. *Proceedings of the National Academy of Sciences*, 112(30), 9310–9315.

Dubow, E. F., Huesmann, L. R., & Boxer, P. (2009). A Social-Cognitive-Ecological Framework for Understanding the Impact of Exposure to Persistent Ethnic-Political Violence on Children's Psychosocial Adjustment. *Clinical Child and Family Psychology Review*, 12(2), 113–126.

Ekman, P. (1992). Are there basic emotions? *Psychological Review*, 99, 550–553.

Eron, L. D., Huesmann, L. R., Lefkowitz, M. M., & Walder, L. O. (1972). Does television violence cause aggression? *American Psychologist*, 27, 253–263.

Eron, L. D., Walder, L. O., & Lefkowitz, M. M. (1971). *The learning of aggression in children*. Boston: Little, Brown.

Eysenck, H. J. (1997). Personality and the biosocial model of anti-social and criminal behaviour. In A. Raine, D. P. Farrington, P. O. Brennen, & S. A. Mednick (Eds), *The biosocial basis of violence* (pp. 21–37). New York: Plenum Press.

Fiske, S. T. & Taylor, S.E. (1984). *Social cognition*. Reading, MA: Addison-Wesley.

Fowles, D. (1993). Electrodermal activity and antisocial behavior: Empirical findings and theoretical issues. In J.-C. Roy, W. Boucsein, D. Fowles, & J. Gruzelier (Eds), *Progress in electrodermal research* (pp. 223–237). London: Plenum Press.

Geen, R. G. & O'Neal, E. C. (1969). Activation of cue-elicited aggression by general arousal. *Journal of Personality and Social Psychology*, 11, 289–292.

Guerra, N. G., Huesmann, L. R., & Spindler, A. J. (2003). Community violence exposure, social cognition, and aggression among urban elementary-school children. *Child Development*, 74(5), 1507–1522.

Hare, R. D. (1965). A conflict and learning theory analysis of psychopathic behavior. *Journal of Research in Crime and Delinquency*, 12–19.

Hare, R. D. (1978). Electrodermal and cardiovascular correlates of psychopathy. In R. D. Hare & D. Schalling (Eds), *Psychopathic behavior: Approaches to research* (pp. 107–144). New York: John Wiley & Sons.

Huesmann, L. R. (1986). Psychological processes promoting the relation between exposure to media violence and aggressive behavior by the viewer. *Journal of Social Issues*, 42(3), 125–139.

Huesmann, L. R. (1988). An information processing model for the development of aggression. *Aggressive Behavior*, 14, 13–24.

Huesmann, L. R. (1997). Observational learning of violent behavior: Social and biosocial processes. In A. Raine, D. P. Farrington, P. O. Brennen, & S. A. Mednick (Eds), *The biosocial basis of violence* (pp. 69–88). New York: Plenum Press.

Huesmann, L. R. (1998). The role of social information processing and cognitive schema in the acquisition and maintenance of habitual aggressive behavior. In R. G. Geen & E. Donnerstein (Eds), *Human aggression: Theories, research, and implications for social policy* (pp. 73–109). New York: Academic Press.

Huesmann, L. R. (2012). The Contagion of Violence: The extent, the processes, and the outcomes. In D. M. Patel & R. M. Taylor (Eds), *The Social and Economic Costs of Violence* (pp. 63–83), Forum on Global

Violence Prevention, Institute of Medicine, National Academy of Sciences, Washington, DC: The National Academies Press.

Huesmann, L. R. (2016). The role of normative beliefs in mediating the long-term effects of exposure to media violence on aggression. Presented at meetings of the *International Society for Research on Aggression*, July 2016, Sydney, Australia.

Huesmann, L. R., Boxer, P., Moceri, D., Bushman, B. J., Johnson, T. J., O'Brien, M., & Hamburger, M. (under review, 2018). The Relation of Violent and Criminal Behavior in Adolescents and Young Adults to Childhood Habitual Exposure to Media Violence. *Aggressive Behavior.*

Huesmann, L. R., Dubow, E. F., & Boxer, P. (2009). Social Cognitive Mediators of the Relation between Exposure to Violence during Childhood and Adolescence and Adulthood Aggression: Findings from the Columbia County Longitudinal Study. In E. F. Dubow (Chair), Social cognitive mediators for developmental effects of exposure to violence. Presented at the biennial meeting of the *Society for the Study of Human Development*, October, 2009, Ann Arbor, MI.

Huesmann, L. R., Dubow, E. F., Boxer, P., Landau, S. F., Gvirsman, S. D., & Shikaki, K. (2016). Children's exposure to violent political conflict stimulates aggression at peers by increasing emotional distress, aggressive script rehearsal, and normative beliefs favoring aggression, *Development and Psychopathology*. doi: 10.1017/S0954579416001115, 11/21/16, 1–12.

Huesmann, L. R., Dubow, E. F., Boxer, P., & Shikaki, K. (July 2016). Consequences of Exposure to War Violence: Discriminating Those with Heightened Risk for Aggression from Those with Heightened Risk for PTS Symptoms. Presented at meetings of the *International Society for Research on Aggression*, Sydney, Australia.

Huesmann, L. R., Moise, J., Podolski, C. P., & Eron, L. D. (2003). Longitudinal relations between childhood exposure to media violence and adult aggression and violence: 1977–1992. *Developmental Psychology*, 39(2), 201–221.

Huesmann, L. R. & Kirwil, L. (2007). Why observing violence increases the risk of violent behavior in the observer. In D. J. Flannery, A. T. Vazsonyi, & I. D. Waldman (Eds), *The Cambridge Handbook of Violent Behavior and Aggression* (pp. 545–570). Cambridge: Cambridge University Press.

Huesmann, L. R. & Miller, L. S. (1994). Long-term effects of repeated exposure to media violence in childhood. In L. R. Huesmann (Ed.), *Aggressive behavior: Current perspectives* (pp. 153–183). New York: Plenum Press.

Huesmann, L. R., Moise-Titus, J., Podolski, C. L., & Eron, L. (2003). Longitudinal relations between children's exposure to TV violence and their aggressive and violent behavior in young adulthood: 1977–1992. *Developmental Psychology*, 39, 201–221.

Krahe, B., Moeller, I., Huesmann, L. R., Kirwil, L., Felber, J., & Berger, A. (2011). Desensitization to media violence: Links with habitual media violence exposure, aggressive cognitions, and aggressive behavior. *Journal of Personality and Social Psychology*, 100(4), 630–646.

Leyens, J. P. & Fraczek, A. (1983). Aggression as an interpersonal phenomenon. In H. Tajfel (Ed.), *The social dimension* (Vol. 1, p. 192). Cambridge: Cambridge University Press.

Lykken, D. T. (1995). The antisocial personalities. Hillsdale, NJ: Erlbaum.

McSweeney, F. K. & Swindell, S. (2002). Common processes may contribute to extinction and habituation. *Journal of General Psychology*, 129(4), 364–400.

Meltzoff, A. N. (2005). Imitation and other minds: The "Like Me" hypothesis. In S. Hurley & N. Chater (Eds), *Perspectives on imitation: From mirror neurons to memes* (Vol. 2, pp. 55–78). Cambridge, MA: MIT Press.

Meltzoff, A. N. & Moore, K. M. (1977). Imitation of facial and manual gestures by human neonates. *Science*, 109, 77–78.

Nathanson, A. (1999). Identifying and explaining the relationship between parental mediation and children's aggression. *Communication Research*, 26(2), 124–143.

Neuman, R. & Strack, F. (2000). "Mood contagion": The automatic transfer of mood between persons. *Journal of Personality and Social Psychology*, 79, 211–223.

Paik, H. & Comstock, G. (1994). The effects of television violence on antisocial behavior: A meta-analysis. *Communication Research*, 21, 516–546.

Press, C., Bird, G., Flach, R., & Heyes, C. (2005). Robotic movements elicit automatic imitation. *Cognitive Brain Research*, 25, 632–640.

Pantalon, M. V. & Motta, R. W. (1998). Effectiveness of anxiety management training in the treatment of posttraumatic stress disorder: A preliminary report. *Journal of Behavior Therapy and Experimental Psychiatry*, 29, 21–29.

Prinz, J. J. (2005). Imitation and moral development. In S. Hurley & N. Chater (Eds), *Perspectives on imitation: From mirror neurons to memes* (Vol. 2, pp. 267–282). Cambridge, MA: MIT Press.

Raine, A., Reynolds, C., Venables, P. H., & Mednick, S. A. (1997). Biosocial bases of aggressive behavior in childhood. In A. Raine, D. P. Farrington, P. O. Brennen, & S. A. Mednick (Eds), *The biosocial basis of violence* (pp. 107–126). New York: Plenum Press.

Raine, A., Venables, P. H., & Williams, M. (1990). Relationships between CNS and ANS measures of arousal at age 15 and criminality at age 24. *Archives of General Psychiatry*, 47, 1003–1007.

Savage, J. (2004). Does viewing violent media really cause criminal violence? A methodological review. *Aggression and Violent Behavior*, 10, 99–128.

Schneider, W. & Shiffrin, R. M. (1977). Controlled and automatic human information processing: I. Detection, search, and attention. *Psychological Review*, 84, 1-66.

Shiffrin, R. M. & Schneider, W. (1977). Controlled and automatic human information processing: II. Perceptual learning, automatic attending, and general theory.

Strack, F., Martin, L., & Stepper, S. (1988). Inhibiting and facilitating conditions of the human smile: A nonobtrusive test of the facial feedback hypothesis. *Journal of Personality and Social Psychology*, 54(5), 768–777.

Strelau, J. (1982). Biologically determined dimensions of personality or temperament? *Personality and Individual Differences*, 3, 355–360.

Wolpe, J. (1958). *Psychotherapy by reciprocal inhibition*. Stanford, CA: Stanford University Press.

Zajonc, R. B., Murphy, S. T., & Inglehart, M. (1989). Feeling and facial efference: Implications of vascular theory of emotions. *Psychological Review*, 96, 395–416.

Zuckermann, M. (1979). *Sensation seeking: Beyond the optimal level of arousal*. Hillsdale, NJ: Erlbaum.

30 School Violence

Gary D. Gottfredson and Denise C. Gottfredson

Introduction

The public is naturally concerned for the safety of children attending school. Gallup polls show the percentage of parents fearing for their children's safety in school increased from 24% in 1977 to 55% in April 1999 immediately following the Columbine High School shootings, and decreased to 21% by 2005 (Jones, 2005). Dramatic instances of shooting violence involving multiple fatalities in Columbine, Santana High, Paducah, Red Lake, Newtown, and elsewhere have periodically heightened this concern. With these exceptions, parents' concerns about safety have been relatively level, ranging from 25% to 28% in recent years (Auter, 2016). Data indicate, however, that while schools are often the venue for a great deal of incivility, they are only rarely the locus of extreme violence. Calculations based on data presented by Zhang, Musu-Gillette, and Oudekevik (2016) imply that between the 1992–1993 and 2012–2013 school years, 493 school-associated violent deaths have occurred in the United States, and the median annual incidence of school-associated violent deaths for this interval was 22. During this period, 1.3% of homicides of persons aged 5 to 19 years occurred at school.

Estimates of the extent of a wider range of violence and disorder in schools come from reports from several sources, including student victimization surveys, student self-reports of their own violent behavior, teacher surveys, and principal reports. These sources provide disparate estimates.

In a 2014 national household survey of nonfatal victimization of 12–18-year-olds (National Crime Victimization Survey; Zhang, Musu-Gillette, & Oudekerk, 2016), 58% of victimizations took place in school and 36% of all *serious* violent victimizations (e.g., those including rape, sexual assault, robbery, or aggravated assault) occurred in school or on the way to and from school. About 59% of violent victimizations reported in this household survey (defined as those crimes included in serious violent victimization plus simple assault) occurred in school. Rates of theft and violent victimization of 12–18-year-olds in recent years are far below those observed in the 1990s.

Less serious forms of crime have been relatively common in and around schools for at least the past 30 years. Considering *all* forms of crime measured in the NCVS for 2015, more crime victimization occurs in school than out of school. In all, 58% of crimes against students aged 12 to 18 occurred at school or on the way to and from school despite youths spending less time in school than elsewhere. Young people aged 15 to 19 spent 24% of their time in educational activities and related travel in the 2015 American Time Use Survey (Bureau of Labor Statistics, n. d.). The percentage of serious violent victimizations in school or on the way to school in the 2014 data was 36%.

School-based self-report studies of victimization in schools (G. Gottfredson & Gottfredson, 1985; G. Gottfredson, Gottfredson, Czeh, Cantor, Cross, & Hantman, 2000) have typically found that although serious victimization in schools is rare, minor victimizations and indignities are common in schools. In the more recent survey, 18% of secondary students reported having been threatened with a beating in school, 13% reported having been attacked in school, and 5% threatened with a knife or gun. Schools are by no means havens against crimes. On the contrary, when all criminal victimizations, rather than only the most serious, are considered, youths are at elevated risk for victimization when they are in school or on the way to and from school.

School Characteristics and School Violence: Evidence from Survey Research

Research implies that certain school characteristics are robustly related to school disorder. Different forms of school disorder including rates of violence are related (Gottfredson et al., 2000). Schools experiencing high levels of theft from teachers, for example, are also likely to experience high levels of student attacks. In an early examination of the effects of school characteristics on rates of victimization in schools (G. Gottfredson & Gottfredson, 1985), we analyzed the National Institute of Education's (1978) Safe School Study data for a national sample of over 600 US secondary schools. In this sample, community and school demographic characteristics explained 54% and 44% of the variance in teacher victimization rates for middle/junior and senior high schools, respectively. Specifically, community poverty and disorganization (including racial composition and socioeconomic status), urban (vs. rural) location, community crime, and total school enrollment (junior high schools only) were significantly related to teacher victimization rates.

Racial heterogeneity and compositional characteristics, including mean student grade level and the percentage male students, also predicted the level of student but not teacher victimization. We also found that malleable school characteristics accounted for an additional 12% and 18% of variance in teacher victimization net of community and school demographic characteristics in middle/junior and senior high schools, respectively. Several potentially manipulable school characteristics were associated with high rates of teacher victimization net of statistical controls. Specifically, schools in which teachers teach a large number of students, schools with few teaching resources, schools with low levels of cooperation between teachers and administrators, schools in which teachers have punitive attitudes, schools in which the rules are not perceived by students as fair and firmly enforced, and schools in which students had low levels of belief in conventional rules and laws governing behavior experienced higher levels of teacher victimization.

Results from other school-level studies of school organization and climate dimensions and student misbehavior have been mixed. Galloway, Martin, and Wilcox

(1985) and Hellman and Beaton (1986) found no evidence for school effects on student absenteeism or suspension once community characteristics were controlled. In these studies, the school characteristics examined were limited to features of the school building (e.g., age of building) and aspects of formal school organization commonly found in archival records. Welsh, Stokes, and Greene (2000) found "school culture" to reduce disciplinary incidents in a study of 43 Philadelphia middle schools, but "school culture" was measured using archival measures of student absence and dropout – indicators commonly used as dependent measures in other studies. In a study that used more appropriate measures of school social organization and included more schools, Ostroff (1992) showed that teacher satisfaction and commitment predict student drop-out, attendance, and disciplinary problems.

In a more recent study of hypotheses about school-level predictors of school violence in a nationally representative sample of 254 secondary schools (G. Gottfredson, Gottfredson, Payne, & Gottfredson, 2005), we found that measures of school climate explained substantial variance in teacher victimization, student self-reported delinquency, and student victimization, controlling for the effects of community characteristics and school student composition. Schools with better discipline management (students perceived greater fairness and clarity of rules) had less delinquent behavior and less student victimization, although discipline management did not influence teacher victimization. Schools with more positive psycho-social climates had less teacher victimization, but climate did not influence student victimization or delinquent behavior. Using the same sample, Payne, Gottfredson, and Gottfredson (2003) found that communally organized schools experience less disorder, and that the relation between communal school organization and school disorder is partially mediated by student bonding.

Several studies have estimated school effects while controlling for individual-level processes. Felson, Liska, South, & McNulty (1994) examined the effects of normative school values regarding violence on individual interpersonal violence, theft and vandalism, and school delinquency. They found that school norms about violence predicted individual involvement in all three forms of delinquent behavior. The authors concluded that normative values characterizing a school provide additional social control beyond the social control due to individually held values. Similarly, Brezina, Piquero, and Mazerolle (2001), studying a male high school sample, found that school average approval of aggression, but not school-average anger, predicted individual-level aggressive behavior. They also found that students in larger schools experienced less aggression than students in smaller schools.

Bryk and colleagues (Bryk & Driscoll, 1988; see also chapter 11 in Bryk, Lee, & Holland, 1993) examined a subset of schools from the national High School and Beyond study to explore the effects of school sense of community on student learning and behavior. Their study separated the effects of school composition (e.g., the average academic and social class background of the students, minority concentration, and ethnic and social class heterogeneity) from the effects of individual-level demographic characteristics. According to their model, larger school size increased behavioral problems (absenteeism, class-cutting, classroom disorder, and dropping out). Communal organization reduced problem behaviors controlling for school composition, size, parental cooperation, and student selectivity. In addition, communal organization mediated the effects of composition and school size. The authors interpret their results to imply that school composition and size influence problem behavior indirectly via communal organization.

Lee and Croninger (1996) conducted a multi-level study of perceptions of safety among high school students using data from 5,486 students in 377 schools. They found that 17% of the variability in individual perceptions of safety lies between schools, about 29% of this between-school variance is accounted for by student-level demographics, and school-level variables explain an additional 42% of the between-school variance. The compositional characteristics of the school (percentage minority and average school SES) explained the most variance in student-characteristic-adjusted school average perceptions of safety, followed by positive student-teacher relations. In their models, school size and urban location did not predict perceptions of safety.

Other studies have also used hierarchical modeling to examine school climate effects on school disorder as measured by student reports of fighting and being punished in school. Using a sample from 11 schools from a single urban district, Welsh, Greene, and Jenkins (1999) found that individual student characteristics (including school effort, rewards, positive peer associations, involvement, belief in rules, as well as demographic characteristics) accounted for 16% of the variance in school disorder, school and community characteristics accounted for an additional 4.1–4.5%, but, among the community and school climate measures, only community poverty significantly predicted the level of school disorder. Stewart (2003) also predicted school misbehavior as measured by school punishments and fighting from school characteristics in a large national sample of 10,578 students from 528 schools. Stewart's measures of school climate were based on administrator and student reports of school social problems, and teacher and student reports of school cohesion. Stewart found that although larger schools in urban areas experienced more disorder, the other school characteristics did not explain a significant amount of variation in student misbehavior.

Wilcox and Clayton (2001) found that weapon-carrying was explained by school-level as well as individual-level factors in a multi-level examination of a sample of 21 schools, although the school-level variables explained far less of the variance in weapon-carrying than did the individual-level factors. School-level SES was the only contextual variable to effect weapon carrying in their analysis. The SES effect was mediated by "school capital" (a scale based on mean levels of protective factors for students in the school) and "school deficits" (a scale based on mean levels of risk factors for students in the school). Some multi-level studies have demonstrated that characteristics of the school environment also moderate the influence of individual-level risk factors on problem behavior outcomes. For example, using data from the same national sample of 254 secondary schools discussed earlier, Payne (2008) found that the student-level school bonding has less of an effect on delinquency in schools that were more communally organized.

Recent large-scale studies of schools in Virginia have shed additional light on school climate and another form of violent behavior: bullying. Eliot et al. (2010)

studied student perceptions of support and student willingness to seek help for bullying and threats of violence in a sample of 7,318 grade 9 students from 291 high schools. Hierarchical linear modeling indicated that students who perceived their teachers and other school staff to be supportive were more likely to endorse positive attitudes toward seeking help for bullying and threats of violence. A different analysis of these same data showed that teacher support, as well as firm and consistent discipline management, are related to lower levels of bullying and other forms of victimization (Gregory et al., 2010).

In short, prior studies have examined a wide array of measures of school characteristics to predict a variety of measures of problem behavior, but heterogeneity across studies, sample variability, and flawed measures make them difficult to summarize. Nevertheless, these studies have documented several clusters of school characteristics that appear robustly related to school disorder. Many, but not all, studies have shown that community characteristics and school characteristics that are largely outside of the control of individual schools account for much of the between-school variance in disorder. These school and community characteristics include racial heterogeneity, size of school, auspices (public vs. private), urban location, community poverty and disorganization, residential crowding, community crime, and characteristics of the students in the school including their percentage male, and average student age. The level of prior problem behavior of students attending a school also influences the level of disorder experienced in the school.

Research has also shown that school characteristics that can potentially be manipulated predict the level of school disorder beyond the influences of difficult-to-manipulate determinants. Schools that establish and maintain rules, effectively communicate clear expectations for behavior, consistently enforce rules, and provide rewards for rule compliance and punishments for rule infractions experience lower levels of victimization (G. Gottfredson & Gottfredson, 1985; G. Gottfredson et al., 2005; Gregory et al., 2010). Schools with lower levels of crime are also characterized by more positive psycho-social climates (Bryk & Driscoll, 1988; Eliot et al., 2010): A sense of community – a network of caring adults who interact regularly with the students and who share norms and expectations about their students – seems to produce lower levels of problem behavior. Payne et al. (2003) and Payne (2008) also documented a relationship between communal school organization and school disorder. Felson et al. (1994) and Brezina et al. (2001) showed that the school normative beliefs influence violence or aggressive behavior. Lee and Croninger (1996) demonstrated that positive student-teacher relations are associated with lower levels of fear among students, and Ostroff (1992) showed that teacher satisfaction and commitment predict student drop-out, attendance, and disciplinary problems. These school effects have generally been small, and not all studies find effects of school manipulable features of school organization.

What Schools Can Do About Violence: Evidence from Intervention Research

This section shifts attention to research on interventions to reduce or prevent youth violence, including interpersonal aggression, bullying, and (for younger students) biting and throwing things at others. The aggressive acts of younger children have been shown to be precursors of later violent behavior (Tolan & Gorman-Smith, 1998). The section describes a range of school-based violence-prevention interventions that have been studied, including brief descriptions of the most effective approaches. The interventions fall into two classes: (a) interventions that manipulate school or classroom environment or practices and (b) interventions that influence characteristics of individuals. For example, an intervention that seeks to reduce violence by manipulating the fairness and clarity of school rules is an environmental intervention, and a program that seeks primarily to alter features of individual behaviors, beliefs, and attitudes is an individual intervention.

The dependent variables examined in research summarized here include measures of (a) youth violence or aggression, (b) associated outcomes, or (c) both. Associated outcomes include problem behaviors correlated with violence and aggression, including delinquent behavior, other problem behavior, and low self-control. Studies reporting outcome measures, which included items measuring violence or aggression combined with items measuring other forms of problem behavior, were classified as associated outcomes. If we were uncertain whether or not a study actually demonstrated effects on violence or aggression, we classified it as targeting associated outcomes.

Environmental Interventions

Environmental interventions manipulate school or classroom characteristics or practices. These interventions range from the use of metal detectors to screen entrants into schools for weapons to broad efforts to alter the ways schools organize themselves to signal desired behavior and respond to behavior. The following paragraphs characterize each category and provide illustrations of interventions that appear on the basis of the evidence to be effective in reducing aggression, violence, or related problem behavior when well implemented.

Security or surveillance procedures. Many schools employ approaches to preventing violence by attempting to limit access to schools by intruders or prevent weapons from coming into the schools. Kupchik and Monahan (2006) documented an increasing reliance on such school security measures. A recent survey of principals from a nationally representative sample of US public schools showed that during the 2013–2014 school year, most schools used numerous security and surveillance techniques. For example, 93% of schools employed strategies to control access to the school building, and 43% to school grounds. Security cameras were used in 75% of schools (Gray & Lewis, 2015). With the exception of survey research, there is little research on the effects of the use of metal detectors or other security procedures in schools. In a sample of high school students in New York City to compare the frequency of weapon-carrying in schools with and without metal detectors, Ginsberg and Loffredo (1993) found that students in schools with metal detectors were half as likely to carry a weapon to school as students in schools without metal detectors. More and better research is required to examine the effectiveness of these approaches to promoting school safety, particularly in view of the practical difficulties involved in putting many of these approaches into use on a consistent basis.

Police or school resource officers in schools. Beginning in the late 1990s, there was an increase in the deployment of police officers in schools. According to the School Survey on Crime and Safety, from 1999 to 2013 the percentage of students reporting the use of security staff, such as police officers, in their schools grew from 54% to 70% (Morgan et al., 2015). This increase in the use of police in schools has been fueled in large part through a program of funding made available through the US Department of Justice. Several studies of the effects of placing police officers in schools have been conducted, but none of these studies are sufficiently rigorous to guide policy. Two of the more rigorous studies suggest that there are both beneficial and unwanted effects of deploying police officers in schools. Na and Gottfredson (2011) studied a longitudinal sample including 475 schools and found that as schools increase their use of police, they record more crimes involving weapons and drugs and report a higher percentage of their non-serious violent crimes to law enforcement. Owens (2016) examined the effects of SROs on arrest rates by using exogenous variation in hiring SROs generated by federal grants from the Department of Justice's Community Oriented Policing Services (COPS). The results suggested that SROs improve school safety, but at the cost of increasing arrest rates, particularly for youth under the age of 15. In view of the cost of deploying uniformed officers in schools, better evidence should be developed about their usefulness in preventing violence.

Discipline management processes and procedures. School and discipline management interventions include decision making processes or authority structures to enhance the organizational capacity of the school to regulate the behavior of students. These interventions may involve collaboration among staff and sometimes parents, students, and community members to identify problems within the school, develop potential solutions, and design activities to improve the school.

One early example of such an intervention, Project PATHE (Gottfredson, 1986), altered the organization and management structures in seven secondary schools. School teams utilized a structured organizational development method (Program Development Evaluation; G. Gottfredson, 1984) to plan, initiate, and sustain needed changes. The intervention schools planned and implemented activities to increase the clarity of school rules, consistency of rule enforcement, and increase students' success experiences and feelings of belonging in the school. The students in the intervention schools reported less delinquent behavior and drug use and fewer punishments in school relative to the students in the comparison schools.

A more recent example of an approach to discipline management that incorporates behavioral principles into comprehensive systems that include school-wide discipline policies and practices as well as targeted behavioral interventions is *school-wide positive behavior support* (SWPBS; Sugai & Horner 2008), a school-wide approach emphasizing systemic and individual behavioral interventions to foster social and learning and prevent problem behavior. This widely promoted system uses a school-team approach to apply behavioral interventions at different levels of intensity for students at different levels of need. Universal interventions focus on clarity of school and classroom rules and consistency of enforcement, and on screening for more serious behavior disorders. Group-based behavioral interventions are employed with the 5–10% of youths who do not respond to the universal interventions. In addition, intensive, individualized behavioral interventions are employed to manage the behavior of the small segment of the population that is especially at risk. Dozens of studies have demonstrated that the behavioral interventions often used in the full SWPBS program for selective intervention with targeted children are efficacious for reducing problem behavior. Recent research testing the effects of the universal components of the program (that is, with no systematic manipulation of selective interventions for children displaying problem behavior) showed improvements in the organizational health in the participating elementary schools relative to randomized control schools (Bradshaw et al., 2009) as well as reductions in suspensions and improvements in academic performance in grade 5 (Bradshaw et al., 2010) relative to controls. Rigorous research that would test the effects of the full SWPBS program on a wider range of outcomes remains needed. Evaluations of a number of programs that alter school management or discipline management imply that this type of intervention can be effective for reducing problem behaviors.

Interventions to establish clear norms or expectations regarding "bullying" or other interpersonal aggression. These interventions make school-wide efforts to signal appropriate behavior through vehicles such as newsletters, posters, ceremonies during which students publicly declare their behavioral intentions, and displays of symbols or reminders of appropriate behavior. Two examples are the Bullying Prevention Program (Olweus, Limber, & Mihalic, 1999), and the Safe Dates Program (Foshee et al., 1996; Foshee et al., 1998).

Olweus's anti-bullying program targets students in elementary, middle, and high schools employing school-wide, classroom, and individual components. School-wide components include increased adult supervision at bullying "hot spots" and school-wide discussions of bullying. Classrooms develop and enforce rules against bullying. And individual children identified as bullies and victims are counseled. Olweus et al. (1999) summarized evidence that the program can lead to reductions in student bullying and victimization and declines in vandalism, fighting, and theft.

The Safe Dates Program aimed at changing norms for dating violence among adolescents. Within the school, intervention components include a theater production performed by peers; a ten-session curriculum addressing dating violence norms, gender stereotyping, and conflict management skills; and a poster contest. In the community, intervention components include services for adolescents experiencing abuse and training for community service providers. An evaluation of the program for students in grades 8 and 9 (Foshee et al., 1998) found that the students in intervention schools reported less psychological abuse and violence against dating partners than did students in control schools. Based largely on relatively rigorous evaluation of these two programs, D. Gottfredson et al. (2002) concluded that interventions to establish norms or expectations for behavior can be effective in preventing aggression and other problem behavior.

Classroom or instructional management. These interventions use practices intended to fully engage students in learning, improve achievement, and increase attachment to school. These practices are varied, differing in the extent to which they have a basis in research on instructional effectiveness. They range from well-studied cooperative learning techniques to less well defined "experiential learning" strategies. This heterogeneous category of interventions also includes classroom management strategies such as avoiding wasting instructional time in transitions between activities in the classroom, stablishing and enforcing classroom rules, applying rewards and punishments, and using external resources, including parent volunteers and police officers. Taken together, the studies reviewed by D. Gottfredson et al. (2002) suggest that classroom instructional and management strategies can reduce problem behavior, but when only studies with reasonable scientific rigor are examined the results are mixed. Although some reasonably rigorous studies have found significant positive effects on measures of anti-social behavior, violence, and aggression (Hawkins et al., 1991, 1999), the inconsistency of the findings across studies makes it impossible to draw firm conclusions about the category of interventions as a whole. The programs with the most positive effects tended to be of longer duration and to combine classroom and instructional management strategies with some other major ingredient (e.g., parent training or social skills instruction).

Reorganizing scheduling, classes, or grades. These interventions involve school reorganization to create smaller units, allow continuity in the interaction of students with teachers who know them well, create homogeneity or heterogeneity in student groupings, or provide flexibility in arrangements for instruction. These interventions may involve the school schedule (e.g., introduction of block scheduling) or the formation of grade-level "teams" or "houses."

Project STATUS (Gottfredson & Gottfredson, 1992) is an early example of this type of intervention. STATUS regrouped grade 7 and 8 students at elevated risk of problem behavior into extended two-hour daily classes to receive an integrated social studies and English program. Instruction included law-related curriculum and emphasized active student participation. The evaluation found positive effects on crime and drug use. The Gottfredson et al. (2002) meta-analytic review identified only two evaluations of programs that involved the reorganization of grades or classes which measured violence, aggression, or associated outcomes. Cook, Gottfredson, and Na (2010) also concluded there is insufficient evidence on the effectiveness of this category of interventions, but that this is a promising area for further inquiry.

Architectural arrangements. These arrangements include the use of features of school design that allow for the observation of activities in all parts of the school or particularly of entrances and hallways, the physical design of cafeterias and pathways for ingress and egress, arrangements to regulate the flow of persons throughout the school (e.g., separate stairwells for students in different grades or up-only and down-only stairways), or the construction of obstacles that prevent access to unoccupied portions of a school building. Schools differ considerably in these architectural arrangements, new buildings are sometimes constructed to allow invigilation of many parts of the school from a central office, and old buildings in urban areas of declining enrollment are sometimes altered to block off areas of excess capacity. Most school principals report arrangements to promote safety and orderliness in cafeterias, and two-thirds report using physical arrangements to regulate traffic flow within the building (G. Gottfredson & Gottfredson, 2001). Despite the widespread use of these architectural strategies, almost no systematic research on their effects on violence or school safety seems to have been conducted.

Interventions to Influence the Characteristics of Individuals

Interventions to influence characteristics of individual students may be directed at knowledge, skills, attitudes or beliefs, expectations, and so on. These may be universal interventions intended to reduce the risk of violence or problem behavior for all students in a school, selective interventions to reduce risk for individuals at elevated risk of violence or problem behavior, or indicated interventions to ameliorate problem behavior for individuals who are displaying it. The following paragraphs characterize each category and provide illustrations of interventions that appear on the basis of the evidence to be effective in reducing aggression, violence, or related problem behavior when well implemented.

Cognitive-behavioral social competency instruction. This category of instructional interventions seeks to develop students' skills in recognizing situations in which they are likely to get into trouble, controlling or managing their impulses, anticipating the consequences of their actions, accurately perceiving the feelings or intentions of others, coping with peer influence that may lead to trouble – hence the term "social competency" instruction. These interventions use cognitive-behavioral methods, so called because they use cognitive techniques such as explicitly teaching principles for self-regulation and recognizing antecedents of problem behavior, provide cues to help young people remember and apply the principles, use modeling to demonstrate the principles and associated behavior, involve goal setting, provide opportunities for rehearsal and practice of the behavior in social situations (role-playing), provide feedback on student performance, and promote self-monitoring and self-regulation. The instruction generally has roots in cognitive social learning theory (Bandura, 1986) and cognitive-behavioral intervention research more generally (Kaslow & Thompson, 1998; Kazdin & Weisz, 1998).

The PATHS curriculum is an example of a universal program that incorporates cognitive behavioral social competency instruction. It is designed to promote emotional and social competencies and reduce aggression and behavior problems in elementary school-aged children. The curriculum is designed to be taught to entire classrooms two or three times per week for a minimum of 20–30 minutes per day by regular teachers for the entire elementary school period. A randomized controlled trial involving 198 intervention and 180 control classrooms in 54 schools across four sites demonstrated that PATHS is effective for reducing problem behaviors. In this study, teacher ratings, socio-metric measures, and classroom observations converged in suggesting a positive effect of the curriculum on antisocial classroom behavior after one year of intervention (Conduct Problems Prevention Research Group, 1999b). Positive effects on teacher reports of child behavior were sustained at the end of grade 3 (Conduct Problems Prevention Research Group, 2010a).

In the same study, researchers implemented a wide array of components incorporating cognitive behavioral approaches to reduce problem behavior is a sample of high-risk children. FAST Track integrates five components to promote competence in the family, child, and school to prevent conduct problems and school failure, and to improve interpersonal relations. The program trains parents in family management, and it makes home visits to reinforce skills learned in the training and promote parental feelings of efficacy. Intervention components directed at the children include social skills coaching, tutoring, and a classroom instruction focusing on social competencies. Teachers are trained to employ specific classroom management strategies. The experimental evaluation described above showed that the FAST Track interventions had positive effects on child social cognitive skills and several measures of problem behavior, including aggression during the elementary school years (Conduct Problems Prevention Research Group, 1999b). Subsequent follow-ups of the high-risk treatment and control youths showed that by the end of high school, the rates of diagnosed conduct disorder for the program children who were at the highest risk initially were half as high as those for the control group (Conduct Problems Prevention Research Group, 2010a). Also, two arrest measures (severity-weighted frequency of juvenile arrests and onset of arrests) were lower for the intervention than the control children at the end of grade 12 (Conduct Problems Prevention Research Group, 2010b).

In summary, instructional programs that teach self-control or social competency skills using cognitive-behavioral or behavioral instructional methods are effective for reducing a range of problem behaviors, and they are most effective when targeted at youths who are at elevated risk for subsequent problem behavior (Cook, Gottfredson, & Na, 2010).

Other instructional interventions. Schools engage in a large number of other instructional interventions intended to prevent violence or problem behavior (G. Gottfredson & Gottfredson, 2001), but many of them do not meet the criteria for the cognitive-behavioral category. These other instructional programs depend more on traditional methods of instruction such as workbooks, lectures, and class discussion. These interventions may provide factual information, seek to increase student awareness of social influences to engage in misbehavior, teach about risky or potentially harmful behaviors or situations, or provide instruction on moral virtues and so forth. In contrast to cognitive-behavioral instructional interventions, two meta-analyses have concluded that these programs are ineffective for reducing youth violence, aggression, or other problem behavior (D. Gottfredson et al., 2002; Lipsey & Wilson, 1998), although a few specific studies have found positive effects.

Behavior modification or cognitive-behavioral interventions to change behavior directed at high-risk individuals or groups. Behavior modification interventions focus directly on changing behaviors by targeting specific behaviors to change, analyzing environmental antecedents and rewards for undesirable behavior, and applying contingent rewards for desired behavior or punishment for undesired behavior. Some behavioral interventions for delinquent individuals or groups of individuals at elevated risk of problem behavior also involve cognitions. These cognitive-behavioral extensions of behavioral interventions are based in part on a substantial body of research indicating that aggressive or delinquent children and youths tend to be impulsive, tend not to make self-attributions for negative personal outcomes, tend to have hostile attribution bias in interpreting ambiguous social cues, fail to consider alternative solutions to problems, and lack effective communication skills (Dodge, Bates, & Pettit, 1990).

The Good Behavior Game (GBG; Barrish, Saunders, & Wolf, 1969) is an example of a group-based behavior-management program for elementary-aged children. Small student teams are formed within each classroom, and the teams are rewarded for achieving behavioral standards. Because the team reward depends upon the behavior of each member of the team, peer pressure is used to promote desired behavior. Dolan et al. (1993) utilized a randomized control group design to assess the effectiveness of GBG in inner-city schools, and found that GBG males were rated by their peers (but not by their teachers) as significantly less aggressive at the end of first grade. For females, teacher ratings (but not peer ratings) of aggression were significantly lower for GBG students. D. Gottfredson et al. (2002) pooled data across sexes and raters, and found an overall significant effect of GBG on aggressive behavior in the Dolan et al. (1993) results.

The D. Gottfredson et al. (2002) meta-analytic review concluded that behavioral and cognitive-behavioral interventions can be effective for reducing youth violence, aggression, and problem behavior. A meta-analytic review by Lipsey and Wilson (1998) also found this type of intervention effective for youthful criminal offenders.

Counseling, social work, and other therapeutic interventions (other than behavioral or cognitive-behavioral). Counseling activities to prevent problem behavior or promote a safe school environment are almost as common in schools as are instructional programs (G. Gottfredson & Gottfredson, 2001), with 75% of schools employing some sort of counseling, social work, or therapeutic intervention. To merely say that an intervention involves "counseling" is to say very little, however. Counseling involving behavioral or cognitive-behavioral interventions would be classified in the previous category. Perhaps greater clarification about specific techniques and their effectiveness may at some point become available, but at present only the behavioral and cognitive-behavioral variety described earlier has been regularly found effective in reducing aggression or other problem behavior. At present, however, convincing evidence of the efficacy of garden-variety counseling is lacking, and at least one evaluation implies that harmful effects are possible (G. Gottfredson, 1987).

Mentoring, tutoring, and work-study interventions. These interventions usually involve one-on-one interaction with older, more experienced persons to provide advice or assistance. The older adult is generally not a professional counselor, and the interaction is generally not focused on the individuals' problem behavior. Positive effects on several outcomes, including self-reports of trouble with the police, were reported from a randomized efficacy study of one program providing school services to high school students (Hahn, Leavitt, & Aaron, 1994; Taggart, 1995). A recent systematic review (Tolan et al., 2013) of 46 studies of mentoring program effects on delinquency, aggression, drug use, and academic functioning found that mentoring for high-risk youth has a modest positive effect for delinquency and academic functioning, with trends suggesting similar benefits for aggression and drug use.

Recreation, community service, enrichment, and leisure activities without behavioral or cognitive-behavioral instructional components. These include wilderness challenge programs and "ropes" courses, drop-in recreation centers, after-school and week-end programs, dances, community service activities, and other activities often seen as having potential for keeping young people out of trouble. Two meta-analytic reviews (D. Gottfredson et al., 2002; Lipsey & Wilson, 1998) concluded that there is insufficient evidence to determine the effectiveness of these interventions on violence, aggression, or other problem behavior. Naturally, there is potential for recreational or after-school programs that incorporate well-implemented interventions of other kinds – such as cognitive-behavioral treatment or instruction – to prevent violence or other problem behaviors (see, for example, Gottfredson et al., 2004). Despite this possibility, there is little in the available evidence to lead to the expectation that the enrichment or recreational activities not supplemented by effective components will be helpful in preventing violence.

The Special Case of School Multi-victim Shootings

A number of multiple-victim shootings in schools have had a special place in focusing the public's attention on violence and safety in schools. A number of episodes that might be characterized as rampage violence are chronicled and analyzed in a National Research Council Report (Moore, Petrie, Braga, & McLaughlin, 2003). Perhaps the most egregious of such events was the 2012 fatal shooting at Sandy Hook Elementary School of 20 six- and seven-year-olds. These rampages are rare, making the identification of statistical regularities difficult. The result is that the examination of these incidents is a source of tentative hypotheses (at best) about the possible causes and remedies. Among the apparent regularities in these cases are perpetrators who in some sense felt aggrieved, these events evidently spiked in the late 1990s, these rampages are *not* characteristically inner-city phenomena, all involved boys and firearms, informal peer groups (differing in nature in urban from suburban or rural schools) may have in some way been related to the school experiences of the shooters, and adults in the schools and communities seem to have been mostly unaware of the grievances felt by the perpetrators.

The dramatic nature of these rampages naturally stimulates the impulse to identify either potential shooters or schools in which an incident is likely. But one feature of these events renders the effort to identify or predict essentially futile: These events are rare. Even if well-validated predictors were available – and they are not – the practical application of prediction devices would result mostly in classification errors. Identification of potential school shooters is thwarted by the low base rate for these events (Meehl & Rosen, 1955). In contrast, the prediction rates of violence and disorder in schools, and the search for interventions that will reduce violence and other problem behavior, are more tractable problems. Most of the survey and intervention research reviewed earlier in this chapter are directed at these problems. Much remains to be done, and the following section briefly suggests productive directions for research.

Future Directions

At present, a few intervention strategies have persuasive evidence of effectiveness. Many plausible strategies remain untested in sound research, and most of what schools currently do (G. Gottfredson & Gottfredson, 2001) to prevent violence and problem behavior is not only untested in research but also appears to be of low quality (D. Gottfredson & Gottfredson, 2002). The intervention approaches that have been well-evaluated tend to be focused on changing the characteristics of individuals and involve interventions that can be tested in small-scale research. Despite evidence from survey research that characteristics of school environments are related to a variety of measures of school disorder, environmentally focused interventions are unstudied or understudied: school security arrangements, school architecture, and school management, for example. Rigorous studies of environmental interventions are difficult and expensive to carry out, but examples of rigorous evaluations of organizational and environmental interventions to reduce youth violence can be found (e.g., Sherman & Berk's [1984] random assignment of alternative police practices and Wagenaar, Murray, & Toomey's [2000] random assignment of communities to community mobilization). Rigorous evaluations of a broader range of school violence prevention strategies are required.

The evaluations of these interventions should have stronger designs than characterizes most currently available research. More studies should use randomized experimental research designs. Furthermore, few studies of school-based or other youth violence prevention interventions measure long-term program effectiveness, and many studies of school programs addressing problem behavior fail to measure violent behavior directly. These limitations of outcome measurement leave ambiguity about the effectiveness of interventions in preventing violence. Finally, greater attention should be given in conducting and reporting school-based intervention research to the measurement of and reporting on strength of implementation. In the long run, this will be as important in learning about what works as are increasing the range of what is tested and the quality of outcome evaluation designs.

References

Anderson, M., Kaufman, J., Simon, T., Barrios, L., Paulozzi, L., Ryan, G., ... & the School-Associated Violent Deaths Study Group. (2001). School-associated violent deaths in the United States, 1994–1999. *Journal of the American Medical Association, 286,* 2695–2702.

Auter, Z. (2016, August 19). U.S. Parents' Fears for Child's Safety at School Unchanged. Retrieved January 3, 2017 from www.gallup.com/poll/194693/parents-fears-child-safety-school-unchanged.aspx.

Bandura, A. (1986). *Social foundations of thought and action*. Englewood Cliffs, NJ: Prentice Hall.

Barrish, H. H., Saunders, M., & Wolf, M. M. (1969). Good behavior game: Effects of individual contingencies for group consequences on disruptive behavior in a classroom. *Journal of Applied Behavior Analysis*, 2, 119–124.

Bradshaw, C. P., Koth, C. W., Thornton, L. A., & Leaf, P. J. (2009). Altering school climate through school-wide positive behavioral interventions and supports: Findings from a group-randomized effectiveness trial. *Prevention Science*, 10, 100–115.

Bradshaw, C. P., Mitchell, M. M., & Leaf, P. J. (2010). Examining the effects of school-wide positive behavioral interventions and Supports on student outcomes: Results from a randomized controlled effectiveness trial in elementary schools. *Journal of Positive Behavior Interventions*, 12, 133–148.

Brezina, T., Piquero, A. R., & Mazerolle, P. (2001). Student anger and aggressive behavior in school: An initial test of Agnew's macro-level strain theory. *Journal of Research in Crime and Delinquency*, 38, 362–386.

Bryk, A. S. & Driscoll, M. E. (1988). *The school as community: Theoretical foundations, contextual influences, and consequences for students and teachers*. Madison, WI: University of Wisconsin, National Center on Effective Secondary Schools.

Bryk, A. S., Lee, V. E., & Holland, P. B. (1993). *Catholic schools and the common good*. Cambridge, MA: Harvard University Press.

Bureau of Labor Statistics (n. d.). *American Time Use Survey*. Statistics produced January 4, 2017 using the tool at www.bls.gov/tus/database.htm.

Conduct Problems Prevention Research Group (1999a). Initial impact of the Fast Track prevention trial for conduct problems: I. The high risk sample. *Journal of Consulting and Clinical Psychology*, 67, 631–647.

Conduct Problems Prevention Research Group (1999b). Initial impact of the Fast Track prevention trial for conduct problems: II. Classroom effects. *Journal of Consulting and Clinical Psychology*, 67, 648–657.

Conduct Problems Prevention Research Group (2007). Fast Track randomized controlled trial to prevent externalizing psychiatric disorders: Findings from grades 3 to 9. *Journal of the American Academy of Child Adolescent Psychiatry*, 46, 1250–1262.

Conduct Problems Prevention Research Group. (2010a). The effects of a multiyear universal social–emotional learning program: The role of student and school characteristics. *Journal of Consulting and Clinical Psychology*, 78, 156–168.

Conduct Problems Prevention Research Group. (2010b). Fast track intervention effects on youth arrest and delinquency. *Journal of Experimental Criminology* 6, 131–157.

Cook, P. J., Gottfredson, D. C., & Na, C. (2010). School crime control and prevention. In M. Tonry (Ed.), *Crime and Justice: A Review of Research*. Chicago: The University of Chicago Press.

Dodge, K. A., Bates, J. E., & Pettit, G. S. (1990). Mechanisms in the cycle of violence. *Science*, 250, 1678–1683.

Dolan, L. J., Kellam, S. G., Brown, C. H., Werthamer-Larsson, L., Rebok, G. W., Mayer, L. S., … & Wheeler, L. (1993). The short-term impact of two classroom-based preventive interventions on aggressive and shy behaviors and poor achievement. *Journal of Applied Developmental Psychology*, 14, 317–345.

Eliot, M., Cornell, D., Gregory, A., & Fan, X. (2010). Supportive school climate and student willingness to seek help for bullying and threats of violence. *Journal of School Psychology*, 48, 533–553.

Felson, R. B., Liska, A. E., South, S. J., & McNulty, T. L. (1994). The subculture of violence and delinquency: Individual vs. school context effects. *Social Forces*, 73, 155–173.

Foshee, V. A., Bauman, K. E., Arriaga, X. B., Helms, R. W., Koch, G. G., & Linder, G. F. (1998). An evaluation of Safe Dates, an adolescent dating violence prevention program. *American Journal of Public Health*, 88, 45–50.

Foshee, V. A., Linder, G. F., Bauman, K. E., Langwick, S. A., Arriaga, X. B., Heath, J. L., ... & Bangdiwala, S. (1996). The safe dates project: Theoretical basis, evaluation design, and selected baseline findings. *American Journal of Preventive Medicine*, 12, 39–47.

Galloway, D., Martin, R., & Wilcox, B. (1985). Persistent absence from school and exclusion from school: The predictive power of school and community variables. *British Educational Research Journal*, 11, 51–61.

Ginsberg, C. & Loffredo, L. (1993). Violence-related attitudes and behaviors of high school students–New York City 1992. *Journal of School Health*, 63, 438–439.

Gottfredson, D. C. (1986). An empirical test of school-based environmental and individual interventions to reduce the risk of delinquent behavior. *Criminology*, 24, 705–731.

Gottfredson, D. C. & Gottfredson, G. D. (1992). Theory-guided investigation: Three field experiments. In J. McCord & R. Tremblay (Eds), *The prevention of antisocial behavior in children* (pp. 311–329). New York: Guilford Press.

Gottfredson, D. C. & Gottfredson, G. D. (2002). Quality of school-based prevention programs: Results from a national survey. *Journal of Research in Crime and Delinquency*, 39, 3–35.

Gottfredson, D.C. Weisman, S. A., Soulé, D. A., Womer, S. C., & Lu, S. (2004). Do after school programs reduce delinquency? *Prevention Science*, 5(4), 253–266.

Gottfredson, D. C., Wilson, D. B., & Najaka, S. S. (2002). School based crime prevention. In L. W. Sherman, D. P. Farrington, B. C. Welsh, & D. L. MacKenzie (Eds), *Evidence-based crime prevention* (pp. 56–164). London: Routledge.

Gottfredson, G. D. (1984). A theory ridden approach to program evaluation: A method for stimulating researcher implementer collaboration. *American Psychologist*, 39, 1101–1112.

Gottfredson, G. D. & Gottfredson, D. C. (1985). *Victimization in schools*. New York: Plenum.

Gottfredson, G. D. (1987). Peer group interventions to reduce the risk of delinquent behavior: A selective review and a new evaluation. *Criminology*, 25, 671–714.

Gottfredson, G. D. & Gottfredson, D. C. (2001). What schools do to prevent problem behavior and promote safe environments. *Journal of Educational and Psychological Consultation*, 12, 313–344.

Gottfredson, G. D. Gottfredson, D. C., Czeh, E. R., Cantor, D., Crosse, S. B., & Hantman, I. (2000). *National Study of Delinquency Prevention in Schools: Final report*. Ellicott City: Gottfredson Associates, Inc.

Gottfredson, G. D., Gottfredson, D. C., Payne, A. A., & Gottfredson, N. C. (2005). School climate predictors of school disorder: Results from the National Study of Delinquency Prevention in Schools. *Journal of Research in Crime and Delinquency*, 42, 412–444.

Gray, L. & Lewis, L. (2015). *Public School Safety and Discipline: 2013–14* (NCES 2015–051). US Department of Education. Washington, DC: National Center for Education Statistics. Retrieved January 3, 2017 from http://nces.ed.gov/pubsearch.

Gregory, A., Cornell, D., Fan, X., Sheras, P., & Shih, T. (2010). Authoritative school discipline: High school practices associated with lower student bullying and victimization. *Journal of Educational Psychology*, 102, 483–496.

Hahn, A., Leavitt, T., & Aaron, P. (1994). *Evaluation of the Quantum Opportunities Program (QOP): Did the program work?: A report on the post secondary outcomes and cost-effectiveness of the QOP Program*. Unpublished manuscript, Brandeis University, Waltham, MA.

Hawkins, J. D., Catalano, R. F., Kosterman, R., Abbott, R., & Hill, K. G. (1999). Preventing adolescent healthrisk behaviors by strengthening protection during childhood. *Archives of Pediatrics & Adolescent Medicine*, 153, 226–234.

Hawkins, J. D., Von Cleve, E., & Catalano, R. F. (1991). Reducing early childhood aggression: Results of a primary prevention program. *Journal of the American Academy of Child and Adolescent Psychiatry*, 30, 208–217.

Hellman, D. A. & Beaton, S. (1986). The pattern of violence in urban public schools: The influence of school and community. *Journal of Research in Crime and Delinquency*, 23, 102–127.

Jones, J. M. (2005, September 20). *Fear of children's safety at school remains low: Environment a big fear factor*. Retrieved October 31, 2005 from http://institution.gallup.com.proxy-um.researchport.umd.edu/content/default.aspx?ci=18694.

Kaslow, N. J. & Thompson, M. (1998). Applying the criteria for empirically supported treatments to studies of psychosocial interventions for child and adolescent depression. *Journal of Clinical Child Psychology*, 27, 146–155.

Kazdin, A. E. & Weisz, J. R. (1998). Identifying and developing empirically supported child and adolescent treatments. *Journal of Consulting and Clinical Psychology*, 66, 19–36.

Kupchik, A. & Monahan, T. (2006). The New American School: Preparation for post-industrial discipline. *British Journal of Sociology of Education*, 27(5), 617–631. doi: 10.1080/01425690600958816.

Lee, V. E. & Croninger, R. G. (1996). The social organization of safe high schools. In K. M. Borman, P. W. Cookson, Jr., & J. Z. Spade (Eds), *Implementing educational reform: Sociological perspectives on educational policy* (pp. 359–392). Norwood, NJ: Ablex Publishing Corporation.

Lipsey, M. W. & Wilson, D. B. (1998). Effective intervention for serious juvenile offenders. In R. Loeber & D. P. Farrington (Eds), *Serious and violent juvenile offenders: risk factors and successful intervention* (pp. 248–283). Thousand Oaks, CA: Sage.

Meehl, P. E. & Rosen, A. (1955). Antecedent probability and the efficiency of psychometric signs, patterns, or cutting scores. *Psychological Bulletin*, 52, 194–216.

Moore, M. H., Petrie, C. V., Braga, A. A., & McLaughlin, B. L. (Eds). (2003). *Deadly lessons: Understanding lethal school violence*. Washington, DC: National Academies Press.

Morgan, R. E., Musu-Gillette, L., Robers, S. & Zhang, A. (2015). *Indicators of school crime and safety: 2014*. (NCES 2015-072/NCJ 248036). National Center for Education Statistics, US Department of Education, and Bureau of Justice Statistics, Office of Justice Programs, US Department of Justice. Washington, DC.

Na, C. & Gottfredson, D. (2011). Police officers in schools: Effects on school crime and the processing of offending behaviors. *Justice Quarterly*, 30(4): 619–650.

National Institute of Education. (1978). *Violent schools–Safe schools: The Safe School Study report to Congress*. Washington, DC: Author.

National School Safety Center. (2005, April). *School Associated Violent Deaths*. Westlake Village, CA: Author. Retrieved October 31, 2005 from www.nssc1.org.

Olweus, D., Limber, S., & Mihalic, S. F. (1999). *Blueprints for violence prevention: Bullying prevention program*. Center for the Study and Prevention of Violence, Boulder, CO.

Ostroff, C. (1992). The relationship between satisfaction, attitudes, and performance: An organizational level analysis. *Journal of Applied Psychology*, 77, 963–974.

Owens, E. (2016). Testing the school-to-prison pipeline. *Journal of Policy Analysis and Management*, 1–38.

Payne, A. A., Gottfredson, D. C., & Gottfredson, G. D. (2003). Schools as communities: The relationships among communal school organization, student bonding, and school disorder. *Criminology*, 41, 749–778.

Payne, A. A. (2008). A multilevel model of the relationships among communal school disorder, student bonding, and delinquency. *Journal of Research in Crime and Delinquency*, 45(4), 429–455.

Sherman, L. W. & Berk, R. A. (1984). The specific deterrent effects of arrest for domestic assault. *American Sociological Review*, 49, 261–272.

Stewart, E. A. (2003). School social bonds, school climate, and school misbehavior: A multilevel analysis. *Justice Quarterly*, 20, 575–601.

Sugai, G. & Horner, R. H. (2008). What we know and need to know about preventing problem behavior in schools. *Exceptionality*, 16, 67–77.

Taggart, R. (1995). *Quantum Opportunity Program*. Philadelphia, PA: Opportunities Industrialization Centers of America.

Tolan, P. H. & Gorman-Smith, D. (1998). Development of serious and violent offending careers. In R. Loeber & D. P. Farrington (Eds), *Serious and violent juvenile offenders: Risk factors and successful interventions* (pp. 68–85). Thousand Oaks, CA: Sage.

Tolan, P., Henry, D., Schoeny, M., Bass, A., Lovegrove, P., & Nichols, E. (2013). Mentoring Interventions to Affect Juvenile Delinquency and Associated Problems: A Systematic Review. *Campbell Systematic Reviews* (2013), 10. doi: 10.4073/csr.2013.10.U.S.

Wagenaar, A. C., Murray, D. M., & Toomey, T. L. (2000). Communities mobilizing for change on alcohol (CMCA): Effects of a randomized trial on arrests and traffic crashes. *Addiction*, 95(2), 209–217.

Welsh, W. N., Greene, J. R., & Jenkins, P. H. (1999). School disorder: The influence of individual, institutional, and community factors. *Criminology*, 37, 73–116.

Welsh, W. N., Stokes, R., & Greene, J. R. (2000). A macro-level model of school disorder. *Journal of Research in Crime and Delinquency*, 37, 243–83.

Wilcox, P. & Clayton, R. R. (2001). A multilevel analysis of school-based weapon possession. *Justice Quarterly*, 18, 509–541.

Zhang, A., Musu-Gillette, L., & Oudekerk, B. A. (2016). *Indicators of school crime and safety: 2015* (NCES 2016–079/NCJ 249758). Washington, DC: National Center for Education Statistics, US Department of Education, and Bureau of Justice Statistics, Office of Justice Programs, US Department of Justice.

31 Violence and Culture in the United States

Mark Warr

Introduction

Americans are exposed to an unrelenting diet of images and messages about violence, messages that emanate from television, movies, newspapers, popular fiction, magazines, and other media. This state of affairs is no accident, nor is it an accurate reflection of the social world most Americans inhabit. Instead, it is the result of a confluence of forces – commercial, aesthetic, scientific, social psychological – that emerged during the social and technological turmoil of nineteenth- and twentieth-century America.

To be sure, violent events are intrinsically interesting events. As tense and sometimes dramatic episodes of human conflict, they raise profound questions about human motivation, the misfortune of innocents, the capacity of government to maintain order, and, ultimately, the presence of justice in human affairs. At an elemental level, they are also *frightening* events, and this feature, as we shall see later, is a key to understanding their peculiar force and appeal. Still, what is so disturbing about the United States is how disproportionately *depictions* of violence in the mass media outnumber actual *incidents* of violence. That disparity and its implications are two of the principal issues of this chapter.

The Mass Communication of Violence

The first truly mass medium to turn to crime for its subject matter was the newspaper. Crime stories have been a staple of many American newspapers since the early nineteenth-century "penny press." Capitalizing on rising literacy rates and technological improvements in mass printing, these largely working-class newspapers relied on police reports for an endless source of intrigue and scandal (Briggs & Burke, 2002) and were the forerunner of the "yellow journalism" that emerged later in the century (Surette, 1998). Even today, newspapers, which are read daily by about four out of ten Americans (down from seven out of ten in 1972; see National Opinion Research Center, 2004), selectively cull police reports for the most "newsworthy" (meaning violent) crimes, which, as it happens, are also the least frequent crimes (see below). A similar process operates in the production of television newscasts, although visual interest and certain other criteria come into play (Ericson, Baranek, & Chan, 1987).

However selective they might be, news accounts of crime in newspapers, radio, and television are ostensibly aimed at recounting real events. These accounts pale in number, however, when compared with dramatic depictions of violent crimes in movies, literature, and television. An entire genre of literature (mystery) continues to follow in the footsteps of Poe (its founder), Conan Doyle, and Christie, and occupies a sizable portion of most modern bookstores. Movies, which draw heavily from books, use violence to meet the perceived entertainment "needs" of audiences (including excitement and sadomasochism – see Jowett & Linton, 1989) and to maintain an advantage over their "free" but more closely regulated competitor, television. In fact, the advent of consumer television in the late 1940s nearly spelled the death of theatrical movies, not to mention radio. Thousands of theatres closed and the number of theatergoers dropped by almost half (Biagi, 1990). Today, along with more graphic violence and sex, movies rely on the star system, spectaculars, special effects, and other devices to draw audiences away from their television sets and into the theater (Jowett and Linton, 1989; Biagi, 1990). The decades-old rivalry between movies and television resembles the contemporary struggle for viewers between cable television and the major broadcast networks.

The Television Age

Television is the dominant medium of our age, having largely replaced the written-word culture that flourished in early America and that began to decline with the introduction of telegraphy and photography (Postman, 1986). Fully 96% of Americans report that they average at least one hour of television viewing per day, with most watching a good deal more (National Opinion Research Center, 2004).

After experimenting with Broadway fare and live dramas, early television turned, ironically, to movies as a source of content, and networks bought up the holdings of major movie studios like Warner Brothers and Twentieth Century-Fox (Biagi, 1990). Along with comedies, soap operas, quiz and talk shows, dramas like *Dragnet* (1951), *Perry Mason* (1957), and *The Untouchables* (1959) established niches for police, courtroom, private-detective, and other crime-theme shows that eventually blossomed into the seemingly ubiquitous and comparatively graphic fare of today.

Based on an historical analysis of network programming, Surette (1998, p. 36) has concluded that "the proportion of television time devoted to crime and violence makes crime the largest single subject matter on television." In its promotional material for the 2004/2005 television season, for example, *CBS* emphasized its "Crimetime Saturday" line-up (despite the fact that crime shows also appear in prime time every other night of the week).

Obsession with Violence

Why such a preoccupation with crime and violence in the mass media? In addition to their dramatic value and intrinsic human interest, stories of crime – real or fictional – speak to citizens' sense of personal safety, and social psychological research suggests that "fear appeals increase attention. People are more likely to pay attention to messages that relate to their well-being" or that of "persons for whom they are responsible" (Heath & Bryant, 2000, p. 182). This phenomenon helps to explain not only the ubiquity of violence in news and entertainment, but the prevalence of fear appeals in commercial advertising. Tacit or explicit threat messages are used to sell everything from life insurance to automobile options (remote ignitions, flat-less tires) to cellular phones (stay in contact at all times!) to airline travel insurance (terrorism) because people will often pause to pay attention to messages that "alert" them to risks and how they can be avoided.

Surette (1998, p. 25) has argued that "portrayals of crime also allow audiences voyeuristic glimpses of rare and bizarre acts – often coupled with lofty discussions of justice, morality, and society." Producers and writers of crime dramas claim access to "insider" information about the "secret" world of crime, information that, whatever its veracity, they offer to share with the viewer:

> Crime has been attractive to the entertainment media precisely because it is the preeminent backstage behavior. By nature and necessity, most crime is private, secretive, and hidden, surreptitiously committed and studiously concealed. To the degree that entertainment involves escapism and novelty, the backstage nature of crime inherently increases its entertainment value and popularity (Surette, 1998, p. 25).

No abundance of messages about violence, of course, can affect the public if they do not receive or pay attention to those messages. Yet it is clear that most do both. In a study of residents of Chicago, Philadelphia, and San Francisco, Skogan and Maxfield (1981, p. 128) found that "more than three-quarters of the residents of these cities reported hearing about a crime story on television or reading about one in the newspapers on the previous day," and the authors describe their respondents as "hooked on the media" (1980, p. 140). When asked where they get their information about crime, members of the general public overwhelmingly cite the mass media (Roberts & Stalans, 1997; Graber, 1980; Skogan & Maxfield, 1981).

Mass media messages about violence clearly penetrate the information haze to reach the public, and that brings us again to a point raised earlier. Because violent crimes are statistically rare events, even in the United States (O'Brien, 1995), citizens are far more likely to hear about, read about, or watch violent events than to experience them. This fact has two immediate implications. First, the social consequences of violence cannot be understood by focusing exclusively on victims of violence. Without discounting the plight of victims, one must look beyond those who are directly victimized to those who suffer forms of "indirect victimization" (Conklin, 1975), the most pervasive of which is fear of crime. Second, media portrayals of violence are important not merely because they are ubiquitous, but because they are the only foundation (save for personal conversations about crime – see Skogan & Maxfield, 1981) on which most Americans can form their beliefs about violence. As we will see later, that foundation is unreliable.

Fear of Crime in the United States

The most widely and carefully studied social consequence of violence in the United States has been public fear of crime. Some four decades ago, the President's Commission on Law Enforcement and Administration of Justice (1967, p. 3) offered this brief but trenchant observation: "The most damaging of the effects of violent crime is fear, and that fear must not be belittled." That statement prefigured a fundamental shift in the way that criminologists think about crime, drawing attention away from the causes of crime and criminal victimization toward an examination of indirect victims. The wisdom of this approach was quickly borne out by survey research demonstrating that fear of crime in the United States was far more common than actual victimization (often by orders of magnitude) and that Americans respond to this fear via a variety of precautionary behaviors so widespread and habitual that they form a defining element of American culture (Warr, 1994). We shall return to those reactions shortly, after first exploring the nature of fear of crime.

The Nature of Fear

Fear is an emotion, a feeling of alarm or dread caused by an awareness or expectation of danger (Sluckin, 1979). This affective state is ordinarily (though not invariably) associated with certain physiological changes, including increased heart rate, rapid breathing, sweating, decreased salivation, and increased galvanic skin response (Thomson, 1979; Mayes, 1979).

Fear may be aroused by an immediate danger, as when an individual is confronted by an armed attacker or is threatened verbally with harm. This type of intense, immediate experience appears to be what some have in mind when they speak of fear of crime. As sentient and symbolic beings, however, humans have the ability to anticipate or contemplate events that lie in the future or are not immediately apparent. Hence people may experience fear merely in anticipation of possible threats or in reaction to environmental cues (e.g., darkness, litter, graffiti, loud voices) that seem to imply danger. Psychologists commonly use the terms fear and anxiety to differentiate reactions to immediate threats (fear) from reactions to future or past events (anxiety). Thus, an individual would fear an approaching assailant, but grow anxious when thinking about walking home late at night. This kind of clarity has not been consistently maintained in research on fear of crime, but it appears that most research has been designed to capture anxiety rather than fear of victimization.

By its very nature, the notion of fear seems to imply a deleterious emotional or psychological condition. Unlike love, pleasure, or happiness, fear is not a state that people ordinarily pursue. To assume that fear is therefore dysfunctional for an organism, however, is sorely inaccurate. Fear, in fact, is an essential survival mechanism. Without fear, prey animals would walk amid predators, and humans would stroll across busy freeways, knowingly eat toxic substances, or leave their infants unprotected. From an evolutionary point of view, organisms that lacked fear would be unlikely to live long enough to reproduce (Russell, 1979; Mayes, 1979). Fear, then, is not intrinsically bad. It is when fear is out of proportion to objective risk that it becomes dysfunctional for an organism or a society.

Survey Research on Fear of Crime

A bewildering variety of questions have been employed by investigators over the years to measure fear of crime (see Ferraro, 1995; Ferraro & LaGrange, 1987; DuBow et al., 1979). Much of this diversity stems from variation in the context stipulated in survey questions. Some ask about fear during the day; others, at night. Some pertain to fear at home, others outside the dwelling. Still others ask respondents about their fear when alone, or with others.

One item, however, has become something of a *de facto* standard for measuring fear of crime: "Is there anywhere near where you live – that is, within a mile – where you would be afraid to walk alone at night?" The item has become conventional not because it was chosen by social scientists but because it has been used by both the Gallup Organization and the National Opinion Research Center to measure fear since the 1960s. During the past three decades, approximately 40–50% of Americans surveyed each year have responded affirmatively to this question (Maguire & Pastore, 2001; Warr, 1995).

The Gallup/NORC item has been criticized (e.g., Ferraro, 1995) on many grounds: it is hypothetical (how afraid *would* you be), is limited to nighttime, does not mention crime, and only crudely measures intensity. In fairness, the measured prevalence of fear obtained with this item is not radically different from that measured in other national surveys (Warr, 1995) and the routine use of the item facilitates longitudinal comparisons of fear, if only in relative terms.

There is a more fundamental issue raised by questions of this kind, however. More than 20 years ago, Warr and Stafford (1983) asked residents of Seattle to report their everyday fear, not of "crime" in general, but of a variety of specific offenses ranging from violent crimes like homicide, rape, and robbery to various property and public order offenses. The rank order of offenses that emerged from their analysis remains surprising to many even today. Murder, for instance, fell low on the list of fears, whereas residential burglary out-ranked all other offenses on fear. Warr and Stafford showed that these findings were not anomalous or even counterintuitive. Fear, they demonstrated, is not determined solely by the perceived seriousness of offenses. Instead, the degree of fear attached to crimes is a multiplicative function of the perceived seriousness and the perceived risk (i.e., the subjective likelihood) of the offenses. In order to generate strong fear, an offense must be perceived to be both serious *and* likely to occur. Residential burglary, the most feared crime in the United States, holds that title because it is viewed as relatively serious and rather likely. Murder, on the other hand, is perceived to be very serious but very unlikely to occur.

Since the publication of Warr and Stafford's research, scattered offense-specific data on fear have been gathered (Warr, 1995; Ferraro, 1995; Haghighi & Sorenson, 1996). These data generally corroborate the hierarchy of fear observed by Warr and Stafford insofar as they use comparable offenses, but fear continues to be monitored primarily through generalized, omnibus measures of the sort used by Gallup and NORC. Such measures are not without value as an overall assessment of fear, but they offer an imperfect picture of fear.

Fear and Situational Cues to Danger

By their nature, surveys are better suited to measuring anxiety about crime rather than fear, strictly defined. In everyday life, fear of crime (in the strict sense) is likely to occur as people navigate their environment away from home – walking to school, or the grocery store, or a doctor's appointment, or traveling to work – and encounter signs of danger in their environment.

What exactly are these signs of danger? Using a factorial survey design, Warr (1990) identified several cues to danger that affect people in public places. One particularly potent cue is *darkness;* by its very nature, darkness obscures potential threats that may lurk in the vicinity. Another cue to danger (and not merely to humans – see Russell, 1979) is *novelty;* novel (unfamiliar) environments are more frightening than familiar ones. Still another cue is the *presence of bystanders or companions.* The presence of other people in the immediate vicinity ordinarily acts to alleviate the fear that individuals would otherwise feel if alone. This calming effect does not operate, however, if those "others" are themselves perceived to be dangerous persons. Warr (1990) found that young males are frightening to many individuals, and few cues are more alarming to the public than *a group* of young males.

In additional to these cues, a number of investigators have considered various "signs of incivility" that can provoke fear (Ferraro, 1995). These include physical features of neighborhoods like graffiti, broken windows, trash and litter, stripped cars, or abandoned buildings, and social cues such as beggars or homeless persons, raucous groups of young people, drug sellers and users, and prostitutes. Empirical evidence regarding the potency of such cues in producing fear is generally supportive (LaGrange, Ferraro, & Supancic, 1992), although it is largely indirect, and investigators rarely control for objective crime rates when examining the impact of incivilities.

Who Is Afraid?

One of the most distinctive features of fear of crime is that it is not uniformly distributed in the population. One of the largest differences is that between men and women. Women are more than twice as likely as men, for example, to report that they would be afraid to walk alone at night near their home (Maguire & Pastore, 2001).

At first glance, this pattern might seem to reflect the actual probability of victimization. That is, women might be more afraid than men simply because they are more likely to be victims of crime. In fact, exactly the opposite is true. Although they have the greatest fear, females are actually at substantially lower risk of victimization for most crimes than are males (Stafford & Galle, 1984).

How, then, can one explain the greater fear of women? One reason seems to be that women exhibit greater *sensitivity to risk.* That is, when exposed to the same risk of victimization, women are more afraid than men. Why? Apparently, women perceive crime in a way that differs significantly from men. Specifically, among most women, crimes are subjectively linked together in a way that is not true for men. For example, a substantial correlation exists between fear of burglary and fear of murder among women, suggesting that for women, murder is viewed as a likely outcome of burglary. Among men, however, the correlation is much lower, implying that the two crimes are not cognitively linked. In much the same way, a strong correlation exists between fear of "being approached by a beggar" and fear of robbery among women, but not men. These sorts of subjective linkages between different types of crimes (termed "perceptually contemporaneous offenses" by Warr, 1984) appear more frequently and more strongly among women than among men. The result is that many situations that appear relatively innocuous to men are likely to be viewed as more dangerous by women because of the offenses they portend (Warr, 1984).

One offense that looms large for women and for which they are *not* at lower risk, of course, is rape. According to one study of fear of rape (Warr, 1985; see also Ferraro,

1996), (1) rape is feared more than any other crime among young women, (2) rape is viewed as approximately equal in seriousness to murder by women, (3) the highest sensitivity displayed by any age or sex group to any crime is that of young women to rape, (4) fear of rape is closely associated with a variety of other offenses for which rape is a logical (though not necessary) outcome (for example, burglary, robbery, receiving an obscene phone call) or precursor (for example, homicide), and (5) fear of rape is strongly associated with certain lifestyle precautions (not going out alone, for example). Clearly, then, rape is central to the fears of many women.

Gender differences aside, fear of crime is often thought to be strongest among the elderly. There is in fact some evidence for this position, but age differences in fear occur only for some offenses and are generally not as large as sex differences in fear. Moreover, where age differences in fear do exist, fear is often strongest among middle-aged persons (i.e., those aged about 50–65) rather than among the truly elderly (Warr, 1984; Ferraro, 1995; LaGrange & Ferraro, 1989). The association between fear and age, then, is not as simple or straightforward as it is sometimes depicted.

Altruistic Fear

When individuals face an ostensibly dangerous environment, they may naturally fear for their own personal safety. At the same time, they may also fear for *other* persons (e.g., children, spouses, friends) whose safety they value. It is important, therefore, to distinguish *personal* fear (fear for oneself) from *altruistic* fear (fear for others).

The prevalence and power of altruistic fear are illustrated by the enormous public reaction that often attends crimes committed against children (for example, the cases of Polly Klaas and JonBenét Ramsey). Such reactions surely reflect not only distress for the victim but parents' profound concern for the safety of their own children. Using data from a survey of Texas residents, Warr and Ellison (2000) found that, within family households, altruistic fear is in fact more common and frequently more intense than personal fear. Husbands were more likely to worry about their wives than *vice versa* (especially at younger ages) and often exhibited greater concern for their wives than for themselves. Unlike personal fear, which is more common among women, men were highly susceptible to altruistic fear, both for their wives and for their children. And unlike personal fear, altruistic fear generally declined through the life-course. In fact, it appeared from these data that most individuals follow a life-course trajectory in which altruistic fear slowly gives way to personal fear as the dominant reaction to the threat of crime.

Another finding of Warr and Ellison was a pronounced and unmistakable concern directed toward one population group: young women. Why? The most likely explanation is that parents and husbands of young women are often acutely afraid for the safety of those women because they are potential victims of sexual assault. The analysis also indicated that what at first glance appear to be reactions to personal fear – installing home security devices, purchasing or carrying a weapon, participating in community crime watch programs – are often more strongly correlated with altruistic fear than with personal fear. These findings underscore the need to differentiate personal fear from altruistic fear in research on fear of crime.

Fear and the Mass Media

Do depictions of crime and violence in the mass media affect public fear of crime in the United States? To address that question, it is instructive to consider first how crime is depicted in the news media. The mass media, as we saw earlier, are a powerful amplifying mechanism with respect to crime; information known only to a few can within hours or days become known to thousands or millions. But the information promulgated through the media is not a full accounting of crime, nor even a representative sampling of crime events. On the contrary, a number of forms of distortion in news coverage of crime have been documented and these distortions tend to exaggerate the frequency and the seriousness of crime.

In the real world, for example, crimes occur in inverse proportion to their seriousness; the more serious the crime, the more rarely it occurs. Thus, in the USA, burglaries occur by the millions, robberies by the hundreds of thousands, and homicides by the thousands. In news coverage of crime, however, the emphasis is on "newsworthiness," and a key element of newsworthiness is seriousness; the more serious a crime, the more likely it is to be reported. By using seriousness as a criterion, then, the media are most likely to report precisely those crimes that are least likely to occur to individuals (Surette, 1998; Skogan & Maxfield, 1981; Sherizen, 1978; Sheley & Ashkins, 1981; Roshier, 1973).

This mirror image of crime means that the media place extraordinary emphasis on violent crime. Skogan and Maxfield (1981) reported that homicides and attempted homicides constituted one-half of all newspaper crime stories in the cities they examined, even though homicides are only a minute fraction of all criminal offenses. Furthermore, the number of homicide stories reported in city newspapers did not closely match the actual homicide rates of the cities examined, suggesting that the amount of space devoted to crime has more to do with the "newshole" allocated to crime by editors than with the true crime rate. Much like homicides, child abductions – though rarer still – can dominate the news for days at a time because, as newscasters understand, they speak to the primal fears of parents (Warr & Ellison, 2000).

News coverage of crime has been criticized on other grounds as well, including the practice of using crime news as "filler" when other news is slow, the use of crime news to attract larger audiences ("If it bleeds, it leads"), and a tendency to report trends in crime using numbers rather than rates, thereby ignoring changes in population (Graber, 1980; Warr, 1980, 1995; Surette, 1998).

How do these forms of media distortion affect the public, if at all? The evidence on this question is indirect and limited, but it is highly suggestive. In the early 1980s, Warr (1980; see also Bordley, 1982) presented evidence that the objective and perceived incidence of offenses are related by a power function ($y = aX^b$). That is, people tend to systematically overestimate the frequency of rare offenses while underestimating the frequency of common ones. Public perceptions, to be sure, were remarkably accurate as to the relative frequencies of different crimes (people recognize that homicide is less common than burglary, for example), but considerably less accurate as to absolute frequencies.

As it happens, Warr's findings are corroborated by a small but persuasive body of research in cognitive psychology

(Lichtenstein et al., 1978; Slovic, Fischoff, & Lichtenstein, 1979, 1982) indicating that individuals tend to significantly exaggerate the risk of rare lethal events (that is, causes of death like tornadoes, homicide, floods, fire, accidents, or botulism) while underestimating the risk of common lethal events (e.g., deaths due to heart disease, diabetes, or cancer). Slovic, Fischoff, and Lichtenstein (1982) attribute this tendency to a common error of judgment arising from the *availability heuristic* (Tversky & Kahneman, 1982), or the tendency to judge the frequency of events by the ease with which they can be recalled or imagined.

But why would members of the public readily imagine or recollect what are actually rare causes of death? Slovic et al. cite evidence from Combs and Slovic (1979) showing that public perceptions of the frequency of various causes of death closely match the frequency with which those causes are reported in newspapers. Newspaper accounts, in turn, are glaringly at odds with reality:

> [M]any of the statistically frequent causes of death (e.g., diabetes, emphysema, various forms of cancer) were rarely reported by either paper during the period under study. In addition, violent, often catastrophic, events such as tornadoes, fires, drownings, homicides, motor vehicle accidents, and all accidents were reported much more frequently than less dramatic causes of death having similar (or even greater) statistical frequencies. For example, diseases take about 16 times as many lives as accidents, but there were more than 3 times as many articles about accidents, noting almost 7 times as many deaths. Among the more frequent events, homicides were the most heavily reported category in proportion to actual frequency. Although diseases claim almost 100 times as many lives as do homicides, there were about 3 times as many articles about homicides as about disease deaths. Furthermore, homicide articles tended to be more than twice as long as articles reporting disease and accident deaths (Slovic, Fischoff, & Lichtenstein, 1982, p. 468).

These investigators do not insist on a causal connection between media reports and public perceptions, but they suggest that the pattern of errors in the two is much too similar to be coincidental.

In the end, the fact that the media present a distorted image of crime is no guarantee that the public believes or heeds what is sees, hears, and reads. Nevertheless, the evidence concerning public perceptions of crime and media distortion of crime news is strikingly corroborative, and it is difficult to believe that the media have little or no effect on perceptions, especially when the public cites the media as their primary source of information on crime, and spends so much time attuned to them.

In the end, the causal influence of media crime coverage cannot be established without simultaneous measurements of (1) media content, (2) public exposure to that content, and (3) the post-exposure effects of media communications. Such research is difficult to conduct in natural settings because of the enormous quantity and variety of media and interpersonal messages on crime to which the public is exposed (e.g., Graber, 1980). Still, the weight of existing evidence points toward a substantial media impact on public perceptions of crime.

The Consequences of Fear

What makes fear of crime so egregious as a social problem is the depth and breadth of its consequences for our society. Over the years, investigators have identified a large number of behavioral precautions that are associated with fear of crime. These range from relatively trivial and nearly universal behaviors (e.g., turning on lights and locking doors when leaving the home) to more personally and socially consequential actions (staying home at night, or not going out alone) (Skogan & Maxfield, 1981; Warr, 1994, 2000).

According to survey data, the single most common reaction to fear of crime in the United States is *spatial avoidance,* or staying away from places that are perceived to be dangerous (Warr, 1994). In surveys of Seattle and Dallas residents, for example, Warr found that 63% and 77% of respondents, respectively, reported that they "avoided certain places in the city." More recently, 56% of respondents in a national Gallup survey answered affirmatively when asked whether they "avoid going to certain places or neighborhoods you might otherwise want to go" because of "concern over crime" (Maguire & Pastore, 2001). Along with spatial avoidance, fear of crime seems to affect the routes that people take, the forms of transportation they employ, and the times they choose to leave their residence (DuBow, 1979; Warr, 1994). Not surprisingly, some precautionary behaviors are much more common among women than among men. Whereas 42% of women in a Seattle survey reported that they avoided going out alone, for example, only 8% of men reported the same precaution. And whereas 40% of women reported that they avoided going out at night, only 9% of men said the same (Warr, 1985).

Taken together, precautions like these suggest that the ecology of American cities is influenced to a significant degree by fear of crime, including patterns of commerce, road use, leisure activities, tourism, and social interaction. Virtually all American cities have places or areas – parks, neighborhoods, beaches, parking garages – that are perceived to be dangerous places by residents, and it does not require a trained eye to discern the consequences of such a reputation. Retail businesses that are located in putatively dangerous areas, for instance, are likely to suffer a shortage of customers, and reputedly dangerous neighborhoods are likely to find themselves socially isolated (Conklin, 1975; Skogan, 1990).

Contemporary social commentators often assert that fear of crime has torn the very fabric of our society, making us afraid of one another as we go about our everyday business, and rupturing the common trust that binds together communities. There may be some truth to this argument, but it is important to bear in mind that fear of crime also brings citizens *together*. As the sociologist Emile Durkheim noted long ago, crime integrates communities by drawing them together in the face of danger. Today, millions of Americans participate in community crime watch programs, cooperative police-community associations, "bring back the night" rallies and marches, and other forms of communal solidarity. Whether these two countervailing social forces – fear and community activism – ultimately cancel one another out is difficult to say, but fear is surely an integrative as well as a disintegrative force.

Conclusion

Crime and violence are integral elements of American culture. They pervade our news, our entertainment, and, at least vicariously, our lives. At the same time that they fear for their safety, however, many Americans remain fascinated by violent crime and romanticize criminals like Bonnie and Clyde, John Dillinger, the outlaws of the Old West (Jesse James, Butch Cassidy), or the gangsters of Prohibition (Al Capone). To others, criminals symbolize one of our most cherished values – rugged individualism – and thereby hold a rightful place in the iconography of American culture (see Surette, 1998).

The intense preoccupation of the mass media with crime and violence, on the other hand, is difficult to interpret as anything other than mercenary, and there are few signs of social responsibility among those who fill our television and movie screens and the racks at the local bookstore. The immense capacity of the media to deliver information and convey meaning could be used beneficially, of course, to provide citizens with objective information on crime risks and protective strategies, but that is unlikely to happen. Even government efforts to rein in violent content in movies and other entertainment media (such as video games) encounter obstacles like "ratings creep," or produce strangely incongruous results, as when television networks advertise the "v-chip" to block the very content they are continually promoting, or use the "viewer discretion advised" caution as an enticement rather than as a genuine warning.

For their part, most citizens have little scientific foundation for their beliefs about crime and violence. In their daily lives, they are constantly confronted with information from sources that may not appreciate nor care about the accuracy of that information and who may use violence to win votes, entertain, sell, advertise, or exploit. In the end, most citizens are left to reason as best they can about the risks of victimization. Because the consequences of victimization can be catastrophic for themselves and those they love, many are likely to err on the side of caution, worrying about and guarding against violence more than is necessary or defensible. The result is an unfortunate and needless constriction of freedom – the land of the free as the gated community.

Such a state of affairs would not be tolerated if the risk in question were, say, a communicable disease. The public would demand information on the associated risks, and public officials and government agencies would scramble to investigate and communicate any pertinent information. Yet violence is not like some virulent disease whose risks and epidemiology are poorly understood. The risks associated with most violent criminal offenses are understood with a degree of certitude that would startle many casual observers, and such information was developed largely at public expense.

In an ideal world, the risks of violence would be communicated to the general public in a thoughtful, dispassionate, and scientifically defensible manner, in much the same way that public campaigns about smoking and heart disease have been successfully conducted (National Research Council, 1989). Information could be disseminated through public schools, police departments (via public information officers), and through the mass media themselves (for example, as public service announcements). In recent years an entirely new field known as risk communication has emerged in the sciences, one concerned with the problems, methods, and efficacy of communicating risk to the general public (National Research Council, 1989). This field has largely concentrated on new technological risks (recombinant DNA, nuclear power, pesticides, toxic waste disposal), medical/health risks (smoking, seat belts, cholesterol, alcohol, cancer) and both natural and man-made disasters (hurricanes, floods, aircraft crashes, lightening, tornadoes, earthquakes), but the lessons of the field are directly applicable to violence. Many Americans might be surprised to learn, for example, that they are more likely to be a victim of suicide than of homicide, that automobiles kill more individuals than all violent crime, or that, as a group, children face greater danger from their parents than from strangers.

For the moment, however, it appears that violence is simply too entertaining and too lucrative to demystify, and Americans seem content to continue "amusing ourselves to death" (Postman, 1986). In an age with few standards of public morality, where celebrities and felons are often the same people, the glorification, commercialization, and normalization of violence proceed without serious opposition or public uproar. But they are not without consequence.

References

Amos, T. & Kahneman, D. (1982). Availability: A heuristic for judging frequency and probability. In D. Kahneman, P. Slovic, & A. Tversky (Eds), *Judgment under uncertainty: Heuristics and biases* (pp. 163–178). Cambridge: Cambridge University Press.

Biagi, S. (1990). *Media impact: An introduction to mass media*. Belmont, CA: Wadsworth.

Bordley, R. F. (1982). Public perceptions of crime: A derivation of Warr's power function from the Bayesian odds relations. *Social Forces*, 61, 134–143.

Briggs, A. & Burke, P. (2002). *A social history of the media: From Gutenberg to the internet*. Malden, MA: Blackwell.

Combs, B. & Slovic, P. (1979). Newspaper coverage of causes of death. *Journalism Quarterly*, 56, 837–843.

Conklin, J. (1975). *The impact of crime*. New York: Macmillan.

DuBow, F., McCabe, E., & Kaplan, G. (1979). *Reactions to crime: A critical review of the literature*. Washington, DC: US Government Printing Office.

Ericson, R. V., Baranek, P. M., & Chan, J. B. L. (1987). *Visualizing deviance: A study of news organization*. Toronto: University of Toronto Press.

Ferraro, K. F. (1995). *Fear of crime: Interpreting victimization risk*. Albany, NY: State University of New York Press.

Ferraro, K. F. (1996). Women's fear of victimization: Shadow of sexual assault? *Social Forces*, 75, 667–690.

Ferraro, K. F. & LaGrange, R. (1987). The measurement of fear of crime. *Sociological Inquiry*, 57, 70–101.

Graber, D. A. (1980). *Crime news and the public*. New York: Praeger.

Haghighi, B. & Sorensen, J. (1996). America's fear of crime. In T. J. Flanagan & D. R. Longmire (Eds), *Americans view crime and justice: A national public opinion survey* (pp. 16–30). Thousand Oaks, CA: Sage Publications.

Heath, R. L. & Bryant, J. (2000). *Human communication theory and research* (2nd ed.). Mahwah, NJ: Erlbaum.

Jowett, G. & Linton, J. M. (1989). *Movies as mass communication* (2nd ed.). Newbury Park, CA: Sage.

LaGrange, R. L. & Ferraro, K. F. (1987). The elderly's fear of crime: A critical examination of the research. *Research on Aging*, 9, 372–391.

LaGrange, R. L. & Ferraro, K. F. (1989). Assessing age and gender differences in perceived risk and fear of crime. *Criminology*, 27, 697–719.

LaGrange, R. L., Ferraro, K. F. & Supancic, M. (1992). Perceived risk and fear of crime: Role of social and physical incivilities. *Journal of Research in Crime and Delinquency*, 29, 311–334.

Lichtenstein, S., Slovic, P., Fischoff, B., Layman, M., & Combs, B. (1978). Judged frequency of lethal events. *Journal of Experimental Psychology*, 4, 551–578.

Maguire, K. & Pastore, A. L. (2001). *Sourcebook of criminal justice statistics 2000*. US Department of Justice. Bureau of Justice Statistics. Washington, DC: US Government Printing Office.

Mayes, A. (1979). The physiology of fear and anxiety. In W. Sluckin (Ed.), *Fear in Animals and Man* (pp. 24–55). New York: Van Nostrand Reinhold.

National Opinion Research Center. (2004). *General social survey codebook*. Retrieved July 13, 2004 from http://webapp.icpsr.umich.edu/GSS/.

National Research Council, Committee on Risk Perception and Communication. (1989). *Improving risk communication*. Washington, DC: National Academy Press.

O'Brien, R. M. (1995). Crime and victimization data. In J. Sheley (Ed.), *Criminology: A contemporary handbook* (2nd ed., pp. 57–80). New York: Wadsworth.

Postman, N. (1986). *Amusing ourselves to death: Public discourse in the age of show business*. New York: Viking Penguin.

President's Commission on Law Enforcement and Administration of Justice. (1967). *The challenge of crime in a free society*. Washington, DC: US Government Printing Office.

Roberts, J. V. & Stalans, L. J. (1997). *Public opinion, crime, and criminal justice*. Boulder, CO: Westview Press.

Roshier, B. (1973). The selection of crime news by the press. In S. Cohen, & J. Young (Eds), *The manufacture of news* (pp. 28–39). Beverly Hills: Sage.

Russell, P. A. (1979). Fear-evoking stimuli. In W. Sluckin (Ed.), *Fear in animals and man* (pp. 86–124). New York: Van Nostrand Reinhold.

Sheley, J. S. & Ashkins, C. D. (1981). Crime, crime news, and crime views. *Public Opinion Quarterly*, 45, 492–506.

Sherizen, S. (1978). Social creation of crime news: All the news fitted to print. In C. Winick (Ed.), *Deviance and mass media* (pp. 203–224). Beverly Hills, CA: Sage.

Skogan, W. G. (1990). *Disorder and decline: Crime and the spiral of decay in American neighborhoods*. New York: Free Press.

Skogan, W. G. & Maxfield, M. G. (1981). *Coping with crime: Individual and neighborhood reactions*. Beverly Hills, CA: Sage Publications.

Slovic, P., Fischoff, B., & Lichtenstein, S. (1979). Rating the risks. *Environment*, 21, 14–20, 36–39.

Slovic, P., Fischoff, B., & Lichtenstein, S. (1980). Facts and fears: Understanding perceived risk. In R. C. Schwing, & W. A. Albers, Jr. (Eds), *Societal risk assessment: How safe is safe enough?* (pp. 181–214). New York: Plenum.

Slovic, P., Fischoff, B., & Lichtenstein, S. (1982). Facts versus fears: Understanding perceived risk. In D. Kahneman, P. Slovic, & A. Tversky (Eds), *Judgment under uncertainty: Heuristics and biases* (pp. 463–492). Cambridge: Cambridge University Press.

Sluckin, W. (1979). *Fear in animals and man*. New York: Van Nostrand Reinhold.

Stafford, M. C. & Galle, O. R. (1984). Victimization rates, exposure to risk, and fear of crime. *Criminology*, 22, 173–185.

Surette, R. (1998). *Media, crime, and criminal justice: Images and realities* (2nd ed.). Belmont, CA: Wadsworth.

Thomson, R. (1979). The concept of fear. In W. Sluckin (Ed.), *Fear in animals and man* (pp. 1–23). New York: Van Nostrand Reinhold.

Tversky, A. & Kahneman, D. (1982). Availability: A heuristic for judging frequency and probability. In D. Kahneman, P. Slovic, & A. Tversky (Eds), *Judgment under uncertainty; Heuristics and biases* (pp. 163–178). Cambridge: Cambridge University Press.

Warr, M. (1980). The accuracy of public beliefs about crime. *Social Forces*, 59, 456–470.

Warr, M. (1984). Fear of victimization: Why are women and the elderly more afraid? *Social Science Quarterly*, 65, 681–702.

Warr, M. (1985). Fear of rape among urban women. *Social Problems*, 32, 238–250.

Warr, M. (1990). Dangerous situations: Social context and fear of victimization. *Social Forces*, 68, 891–907.

Warr, M. (1994). Public perceptions and reactions to violent offending and victimization. In A. J. Reiss, Jr. & J. A. Roth (Eds), *Understanding and preventing violence. Consequences and Control* (Vol. 4, pp. 1–66). Washington, DC: National Academy Press.

Warr, M. (1995). Public perceptions of crime and punishment. In J. F. Sheley (Ed.), *Criminology: A contemporary handbook* (2nd ed., pp. 15–30). New York: Wadsworth.

Warr, M. (1995). Poll trends: Public opinion on crime and punishment. *Public Opinion Quarterly*, 59, 296–310.

Warr, M. (2000). Fear of crime in the United States: Avenues for research and policy. In D. Duffee (Ed.), *Criminal justice 2000. Measurement and analysis of crime and justice* (Vol. 4, pp. 451–489). Washington, DC: US Department of Justice. National Institute of Justice.

Warr, M. & Ellison, C. G. (2000). Rethinking social reactions to crime: Personal and altruistic fear in family households. *American Journal of Sociology*, 108, 551–578.

Warr, M. & Stafford, M. C. (1983). Fear of victimization: A look at the proximate causes. *Social Forces*, 61, 1033–1043.

32 Violence Prevention in a Global Context: Progress and Priorities for Moving Forward

Linda L. Dahlberg, Alexander Butchart, and Christopher Mikton

Introduction

More than 1.4 million people worldwide die each year as a result of interpersonal, self-directed, and collective violence, accounting for 2.5% of global mortality (WHO, 2012). Deaths, however, represent only a fraction of the worldwide burden of violence. Tens of thousands of people each day come to the attention of medical authorities to receive some form of emergency medical, medico-legal, or other care as a result of violence (WHO, 2014a). Nonfatal violence among young men and against children and women is also highly prevalent in countries throughout the world. Recent estimates based on nationally representative survey data from 96 countries indicate that 1 billion children globally – over half of all children aged 2 to 17 – have experienced physical, sexual, or emotional violence in the past 12 months alone (Hillis, Mercy, Amobi, & Kress, 2016). A growing body of evidence shows that violence contributes to lifelong ill health and premature mortality through the adoption of harmful alcohol use, tobacco use, and physical inactivity, and impacts on the brain, cardiovascular, immune, and other biological systems (Bellis et al., 2014; Felitti et al., 1998; Moffitt et al., 2009; Norman et al., 2012; Shonkoff & Phillips, 2000). Violence also places a heavy strain on local and national economies, with some estimates suggesting the global costs might be as high as 11% of the world's gross domestic product when factoring in homicide, violent crime, child abuse, intimate partner violence, and sexual violence (Fearon & Hoeffer, 2014).

Violence has long been considered a problem for the criminal justice system and has been included in resolutions by the United Nations dating back to 1986 (e.g., the 1986 Seville Statement on Violence; the 1989 Convention on the Rights of the Child; the 1993 Declaration on the Elimination of Violence against Women; WHO, 2014a). It was placed on the international public health agenda in 1996 when the World Health Assembly (WHA) adopted resolution WHA49.25 declaring violence a leading worldwide public health problem. The WHA called upon Member States to give urgent consideration to the problem and requested the Director-General of the World Health Organization (WHO) to develop a science-based approach to understanding and preventing violence. WHO responded to the resolution in part with the *World report on violence and health (WRVH)* – the first comprehensive examination of violence as a preventable global public health problem

(Krug, Dahlberg, Mercy, Zwi, & Lozano, 2002). The WRVH became a catalyst for change helping to advance national and global policy discussions, prevention efforts at the country, regional, and global level, and improvements in the science of prevention (WHO, 2014a). Now, more than a decade since the WRVH was published, it is important to take stock of the progress made and determine the key priorities for moving violence prevention efforts forward in the next decade. Here, we aim (1) to describe the public health approach for defining and understanding the nature, context, and forms of violence, (2) to provide an overview of the global burden and impact of violence and progress made in preventing and responding to violence, and (3) to highlight recent efforts to move violence prevention efforts up on the global agenda and priorities for moving forward in the decade ahead.

Public Health Approach to Violence

By definition, public health is not about individual patients. Its focus is on dealing with diseases and with conditions and problems affecting the health of populations and aims to provide the maximum benefit for the largest number of people. The public health approach to violence prevention is multidisciplinary and emphasizes collective action (Mercy, Rosenberg, Powell, Broome, & Roper, 1993). Cooperative efforts from such diverse sectors as health, education, social services, justice, and policy are necessary to address the problem of violence and achieve sustainable reductions in violence. It complements criminal justice, human rights, and gender approaches to violence. Gender and human rights-based approaches, for instance, place an emphasis on universality, equality and nondiscrimination, indivisibility and interdependence of human rights, participation and inclusion, accountability, and rule of law (World Bank, 2013).

The public health approach to violence is based on the rigorous requirements of the scientific method (Mercy et al., 1993). In moving from problem to solution, it places an emphasis on systematically collecting data on the magnitude, characteristics, costs, and consequences of violence; conducting research to determine the factors that increase or buffer against the risk of violence; determining which interventions effectively prevent violence; and scaling up and ensuring the widespread adoption of effective interventions. Above all, it places an emphasis on prevention. Rather than simply accepting or reacting to violence, its starting point is the strong conviction that violent behavior and its consequences can be prevented.

Defining Violence

Any comprehensive framework for understanding violence should begin with a definition of violence so as to facilitate its scientific measurement. There are many possible ways to define violence, ranging from defining it narrowly as an intentional act of excessive or destructive force to defining it much more broadly as an act of violation of rights, typically of human rights (Bufacchi, 2005). The public health definition of violence falls somewhere in the middle of these two concepts. Public health defines violence as:

> The intentional use of physical force or power, threatened or actual, against oneself, another person, or against a group or

community, that either results in or has a high likelihood of resulting in injury, death, psychological harm, maldevelopment or deprivation (World Health Organization, 1996).

This definition encompasses interpersonal violence as well as suicidal behavior and other collective forms of violence such as armed conflict. It covers a wide range of acts, going beyond physical acts to include threats and intimidation and those acts that result from a power relationship. It also allows for the possible inclusion of structural and institutional violence. The definition includes a broad range of outcomes – including psychological harm, deprivation, and maldevelopment – recognizing that not all violence results in injury or death. Many forms of violence against women, children, and the elderly, for instance, can result in physical, psychological, and social problems that do not necessarily lead to injury or death. These consequences can be immediate, as well as latent, and can last for years after the initial victimization.

One of the more complex aspects of the definition is the matter of intentionality. The definition associates intentionality with the committing of the act itself, irrespective of the outcome it produces. Two important points about this have been noted (Dahlberg & Krug, 2002). First, even though violence is distinguished from unintended events that result in injuries, the presence of an "intent to use force" does not necessarily mean that there was an "intent to cause damage." Indeed, there may be a considerable disparity between intended behavior and intended consequence. A perpetrator may intentionally commit an act that, by objective standards, is judged to be dangerous and highly likely to result in adverse health effects, but the perpetrator may not perceive it as such. For example, a youth may be involved in a physical fight with another youth. The use of a fist against the head or the use of a weapon in the dispute certainly increases the risk of serious injury or death, though neither outcome may be intended.

A second point related to intentionality lies in the distinction between the intent to harm and the intent to "use violence." Violence, according to Walters & Park (1964), is culturally determined. Some people mean to harm others, but based on their cultural backgrounds and beliefs, do not perceive their acts as violent. The definition above, however, defines violence as it relates to health outcomes. Certain behaviors – such as hitting a spouse – may be regarded by some people as acceptable cultural practices, but are considered violent acts with important health implications.

Other aspects of violence, though not explicitly stated, are also included in the definition. For example, the definition implicitly includes all acts of violence, whether they are public or private; reactive (in response to previous events such as provocation) or proactive (instrumental for, or anticipating, more self-serving outcomes) (Dodge & Coie, 1987); criminal or noncriminal. Each of these aspects is important in understanding violence and in designing prevention programs.

Types and Contexts of Violence

There are many different types of violence and they occur in a variety of contexts. They are also linked to each other in important ways, often sharing similar risk and protective factors (Foshee et al., 2015; Hamby & Grych, 2013; Johannesen & Logiudice, 2013; Milaniak & Widom, 2015; Wilson et al., 2014). The typology in the WRVH represents the first attempt to capture the different types of violence as well as the nature of violent acts (Dahlberg & Krug, 2002). The typology first divides violence into three broad categories according to characteristics of those committing the violent act: self-directed violence, interpersonal violence, and collective violence. This initial categorization differentiates between violence a person inflicts upon himself or herself; violence inflicted by another individual or by a small group of individuals; and violence inflicted by larger groups such as nation states, organized political groups, militia groups, or terrorist organizations (see Figure 32.1).

These three broad categories are each divided further to reflect more specific types of violence. The typology also illustrates the nature of violent acts, which can be physical, sexual, psychological, or involving deprivation or neglect. The horizontal axis in Figure 32.1 shows who is affected, and the vertical describes how they are affected. For instance, violence against children committed by a parent can include physical, sexual, and psychological abuse, as well as neglect. Community violence can include physical assaults between young people, sexual assaults in the workplace, and neglect of older people in long-term care facilities. Political violence can include such acts as rape during armed conflicts and physical and psychological warfare.

The typology, while neither universally accepted nor perfect, provides a useful framework for understanding both the complex patterns of violence taking place around the world, as well as violence in the everyday lives of individuals, families, and communities. It captures the nature of violent acts, the relevance of setting, the relationship between perpetrator and victim, and – in the case of collective violence – possible motivations for the violence. One thing it does not do is give sufficient attention to the role of gender and, for that reason, some groups prefer conceptual frameworks that give greater visibility to population groups (e.g., violence against women; violence against children) (UN Women, 2016; Global Partnership to End Violence Against Children, 2016).

Understanding How and Why Violence Occurs

Public health draws upon various conceptual frameworks and models to describe violent events, to identify risk and protective factors associated with violence, and to suggest appropriate points of intervention (Powell, Mercy, Crosby, Dahlberg, & Simon, 1999). By virtue of its interdisciplinary nature, it also draws upon many theories of behavior, social processes, and social organization to understand and prevent violence. One model that is widely used by public health researchers to illustrate the multifaceted and interactive nature between the individual and contextual factors of violence is the social ecological model (see Figure 32.2). The model, itself, is not new and also has its limitations. First introduced in the late 1970s, the model was initially applied to child abuse (Bronfenbrenner, 1979; Garbarino & Crouter, 1978), and then to youth violence (Tolan & Guerra, 1994), intimate partner violence (Heise, 1998), and elder abuse (Schiamberg & Gans, 1999). The model is useful to the extent that it provides a conceptual framework for distinguishing the myriad of influences on violence while at the same time providing a framework for understanding how they might interact. It also helps to convey the importance of a multi-level response for prevention.

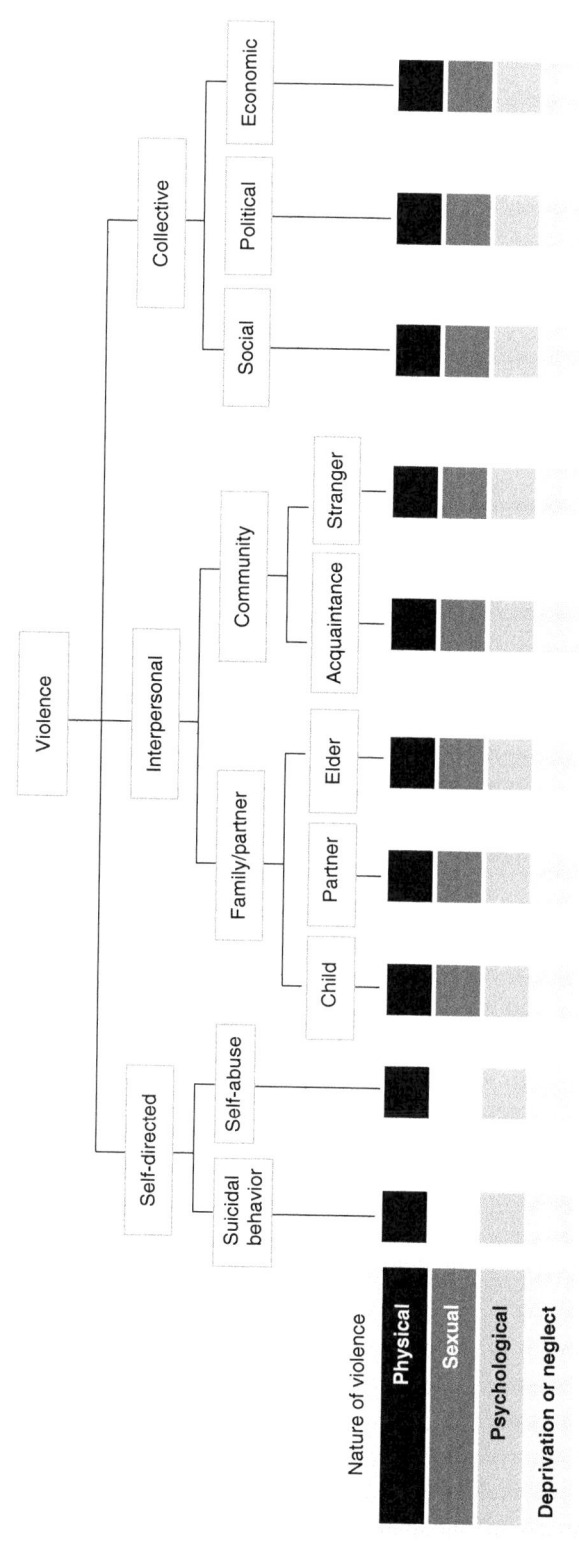

Figure 32.1 *Typology of violence.*
(Source: Dahlberg & Krug [2002].)

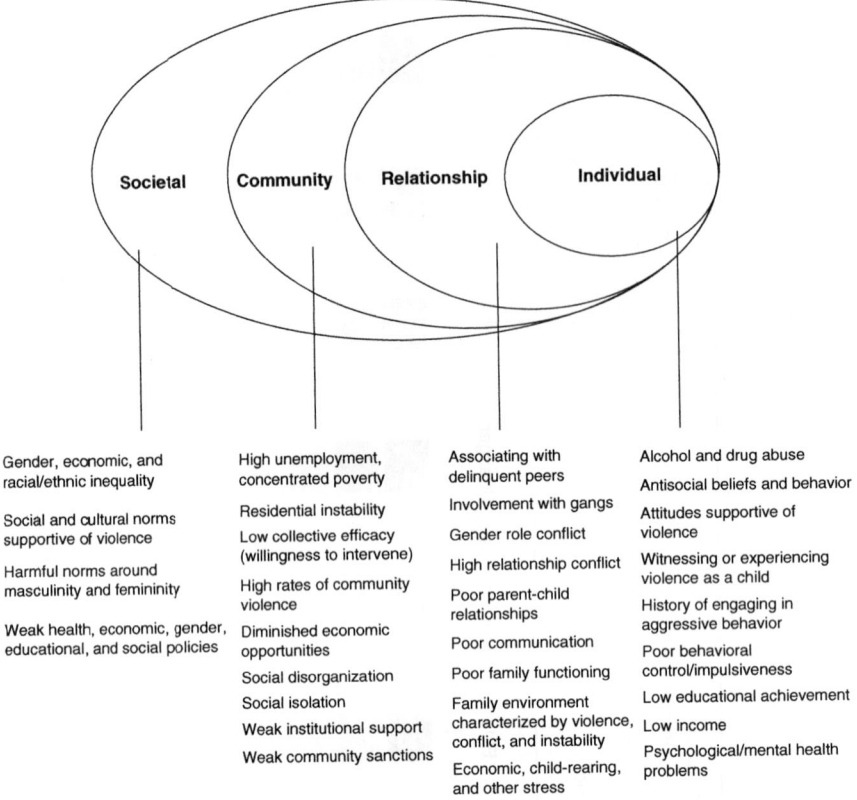

Figure 32.2 *Social ecological model. (Source: Dahlberg & Krug [2002].)*

The first level of the model seeks to identify the biological and personal history factors that influence how individuals behave and increase their likelihood of becoming a victim or perpetrator of violence. It includes biological and demographic factors, as well as factors such as poor behavioral control, low educational attainment, substance abuse, witnessing violence in the home or community, and prior history of aggression and abuse. The second level explores how proximal social relationships – for example, relations with peers, intimate partners and family members – increase the risk of being a victim or perpetrator of violence. Family environments characterized by disruption, conflict, poor cohesion, and communication, for instance, are associated with multiple forms of violence (Capaldi, Knoble, Shortt, & Kim, 2012; Meinck, Cluver, Boyes, & Mhlongo, 2015; Whitaker et al., 2008; WHO, 2015).

The third level examines the community contexts in which social relationships are embedded – such as schools, workplaces, and neighborhoods – and seeks to identify the characteristics of these settings that are associated with violence. Drug trafficking, high levels of residential mobility, and population density are examples of such characteristics. Areas of poverty or physical deterioration, where there are few institutional supports and widespread social isolation (for example, people not knowing their neighbors or having no involvement in the local community) are examples of other characteristics.

The fourth level of the social ecological model looks at the broad societal factors that help create a climate in which violence is encouraged or inhibited, including social and cultural norms supportive of violence and harmful gender norms around masculinity and femininity. Larger societal factors also include the health, education, economic, and social policies that maintain high levels of economic, gender, racial/ethnic, or social inequality between groups in society. Norms about violence, gender, and race/ethnicity, for instance, are often rooted in customs, institutional practices, and policies, impacting health and equitable access to goods, services, and opportunities.

Although the social ecological model is an explicitly multi-level model and methods to analyze the influence of factors at the different levels and the interactions between them are available, much of the risk factor research tends to focus on individual- or group-level factors (e.g., relationship) with less attention given to the interactions between factors at the different levels (Susser, 1998; Diez-Roux, 2000; Wemrell, Merlo, Mulinari, & Hornborg, 2016). Even as individual- or group-level factors, the relative importance of the different risk factors and the strength of their association with the outcome is not always clear nor is the causal status of the various risk factors (McDowell, 2008). Too often, the methods tend to focus on measuring associations of exposure and outcomes rather than understanding the causation of exposure and outcomes in the population (Pearce, 1996; McDowell, 2008; Wikström & Sampson, 2006). Related to the latter limitation, less attention is also given to how macro-level factors (e.g., structural drivers of inequalities) shape and determine health outcomes (Wemrell et al., 2016). Even though much more could be done to strengthen the research, the social ecological model has served a critical role in highlighting that violence is not the result of any single factor but the outcome of multiple influences interacting within and across different levels, ranging from the individual to the societal.

Besides helping to conceptualize the complex interactions between individual and contextual factors, the ecological model also suggests that in order to prevent violence it is necessary to address factors at all levels. This includes modifying individual behavior directly; modifying individual behavior by influencing close, interpersonal relationships and family environments; addressing the settings people move through – for example, schools, workplaces, and neighborhoods; and by making more societal, system-wide changes to improve, for example, educational or economic opportunities or change social and cultural norms.

In the sections that follow, we examine global progress in applying the public health approach to violence prevention beginning with progress made in understanding the burden of violence at the global, regional, and country level. From there we examine progress made in preventing and responding to violence, including progress made in building and strengthening the evidence for prevention strategies across the various levels of the social ecological model and the uptake of those strategies.

Taking Stock of Global Progress

Violence is a major contributor to premature death, disability, injury, and a host of other health and social consequences. The WRVH called upon countries to enhance their capacity for collecting data on violence (Krug et al., 2002). The full impact of violence and the burden it places on countries, however, remains unknown because countries are at different stages in the development of their data systems. There is also a great deal of variation in the completeness, quality, reliability, and usefulness of available information for both fatal and nonfatal violence.

Fatal Violence

Mortality data are the most widely collected and available of all sources of data on violence. The majority (88%) of these data come from police sources (WHO, 2014a). Nearly 60% of countries do not have usable data on homicide from civil or vital registration sources (WHO, 2014a). In order to produce comparable estimates of homicide across countries, the World Health Organization draws upon available data from both sources as well as data from surveys, censuses, and epidemiological studies to determine the global burden of homicide. Using methods for quantifying biases and correcting for underreporting and misclassification, the WHO produces model-based estimates to characterize the burden across regions and the world and by country income level (see WHO, 2014a for detailed description of estimation methods).

Like many other health problems in the world, violence is not distributed evenly among countries, regions, or sex and age groups. In 2012 (the latest year available for comparable estimates), there were an estimated 474,930 victims of homicide worldwide, which was equivalent to an age-adjusted rate of 6.7 per 100,000 population (Table 32.1). The homicide rate for high-income countries is about half the rate for low and middle-income countries (3.8 vs. 7.4 per 100,000). For low- and middle-income countries, the highest number (165,617) and rates of homicide are in the Americas, with an annual rate of 28.5 deaths per 100,000 population (accounting for nearly one-third of all homicides in the world), followed by the African region, with 98,081 homicides and a rate of 10.7 per 100,000 population. The two regions with the highest rates of homicide among high-income countries are the Americas and the Eastern Mediterranean region, each with an estimated annual rate of about 5 per 100,000. The region with the lowest estimated rate of homicide in the world, regardless of country income, is the Western Pacific region, which has an annual rate (2.0 per 100,000) that is three times lower than the global rate.

The regions differ not only in their rates of homicide but also in the weapons used in homicide. Approximately 75% of all homicides in the low- and middle-income countries of the Americas involve a firearm (Figure 32.3). Nearly half of all homicides in the low- and middle-income countries in the Eastern Mediterranean region also involve a firearm (47%). By contrast, the proportion of homicides committed with a firearm versus a sharp instrument (e.g., knife) or other method is more evenly distributed across low- and middle-income countries in the other regions. Firearms are also the predominant method used in homicide among the high-income countries

Table 32.1 *Estimated Age-adjusted Rates* of Homicide per 100,000 Population, by WHO Region and Country Income Status, 2012*

WHO Region	Low- and Middle-income Homicide Rate per 100,000	High-income Homicide Rate per 100,000	All Countries Number of Homicides	Homicide Rate per 100,000
African region	10.9	3.5	98,107	10.9
Region of the Americas	28.5	5.2	185,233	19.4
Eastern Mediterranean region	6.9	5.5	41,066	6.8
European region	3.8	3.8	34,469	3.8
South East Asia region	4.3		78,331	4.3
Western Pacific region	2.1	0.9	36,120	2
Total	7.4	3.8	474,930[a]	6.7

[a] Includes 1,604 homicides estimated for non-member states.
* Rates are standardized to the WHO World Standard Population.

Source: WHO (2012).

of the Americas, accounting for 73% of homicides. This stands in stark contrast to the other high-income countries where the percentage of homicides committed with a firearm (29%) is similar to the percentage committed with a sharp instrument (26%) and both are lower than other methods (44%). Thus, the differences in rates of homicide between the Americas and other regions reflect, in part, the lethality of the method used in homicide.

Almost everywhere, rates of homicide are higher among males than females (Table 32.2). Globally, males account for 82% of homicide victims, with an estimated homicide rate of 10.8 per 100,000 that is four times the estimated rate of 2.5 for females. Males age 15 to 29 have the highest homicide rate (18.2 per 100,000) of all age groups, followed closely by a rate of 15.7 among males age 30 to 44. Homicide rates among females are also highest in the 18–29 age group, relative to other age groups, with an estimated homicide rate of 3.2 per 100,000. For both males and females the lowest homicide rates are in the 5–14 age group.

Globally, homicide rates are decreasing. From 2000–2012, the rate decreased from 8.1 to 6.7 per 100,000 (Figure 32.4). Regionally, there were steep decreases in the European and African regions. Homicide rates in the European region more than halved, decreasing from 8.1 to 3.8 per 100,000, and rates in the African region showed a steady and substantial decrease, from 14.3 in the year 2000 to 10.8 in 2012. With the exception of the Americas,

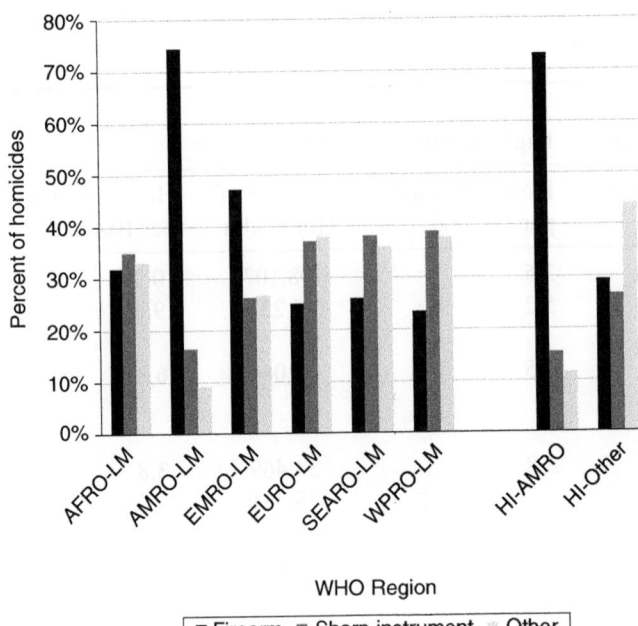

Figure 32.3 *Proportion of homicides by mechanism and WHO region, 2012. (Source: WHO [2012].)*

LM = Low- and middle-income countries.

HI-AMRO = High-income countries in the Americas region (Antigua and Barbuda, Bahamas, Barbados, Canada, Chile, Saint Kitts and Nevis, Trinidad and Tobago, Uruguay, and the United States of America).

HI-Other = High-income countries in regions other than the Americas.

Table 32.2 *Estimated Homicide Rate per 100,000 by Age Group and Sex, 2012*

	Homicide Rate per 100 000 Population		
Age Group (years)	Male	Female	Total
0–4	2.8	2.7	2.8
5–14	1.7	1.2	1.5
15–29	18.2	3.2	10.9
30–44	15.7	2.7	9.3
45–59	10.2	2.0	6.1
≥ 60	6.7	2.7	4.5
Total	10.8	2.5	6.7

Source: WHO (2012).

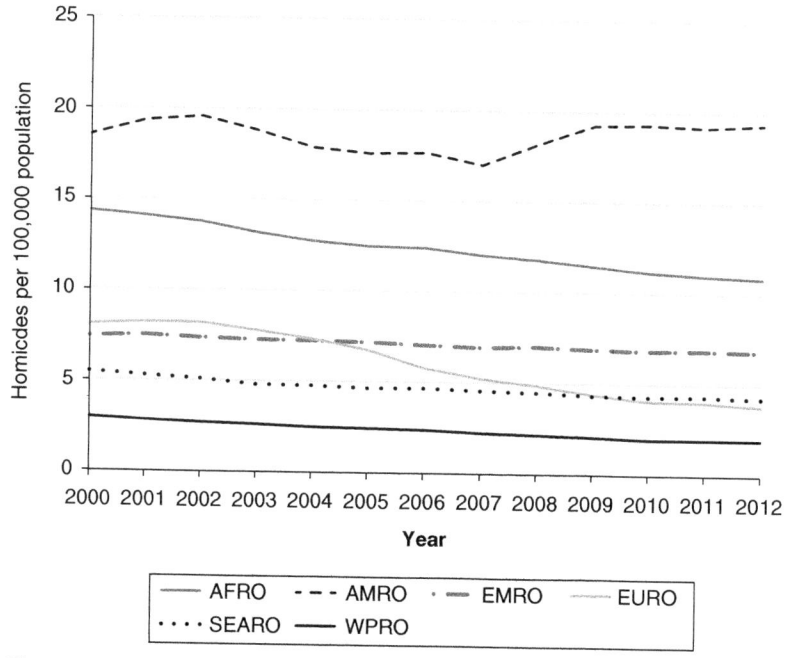

Figure 32.4 *Estimated age-adjusted homicide rates* by WHO region, 2000–2012. (Source: WHO [2012].)*
*Rates are standardized to the WHO World Standard Population.

homicide rates in the remaining regions – Eastern Mediterranean, South East Asian, and Western Pacific – also decreased. While rates in the Americas showed some decline from 2002 to 2007, this downward trend shifted upwards by 2012, increasing from 17.0 in 2007 to 19.3 in 2012.

There are nearly twice as many suicides as homicides globally. In 2012 (the latest year of available global burden data), there were an estimated 803,900 suicide deaths worldwide, which was equivalent to an age-adjusted rate of 11.4 per 100,000 population. Unlike homicide where the rate in high-income countries is much lower than the rate in low- and middle-income countries, the age-adjusted rate of suicide is higher in high-income countries relative to low- and middle-income countries (12.7 vs. 11.2 per 100,000), and the difference between the rates is not as large. There are also important regional differences in rates of suicide (Figure 32.5). For low- and middle-income countries, the highest rates of suicide are in the South East Asian and European regions (17.7 and 12.0 per 100,000 population). The lowest rates are in the Americas and in the Eastern Mediterranean region (6.1 and 6.4 per 100,000, respectively). It is also worth noting that rates of suicide in the South East Asian and European regions (17.7 and 12.0) are more than four times greater than the homicide rates in these regions (4.3 and 3.8 per 100,000, respectively). The opposite is true for the Americas, which has the lowest suicide rate in the world and a rate of homicide that is nearly five times greater than the rate of suicide (28.5 vs 6.1).

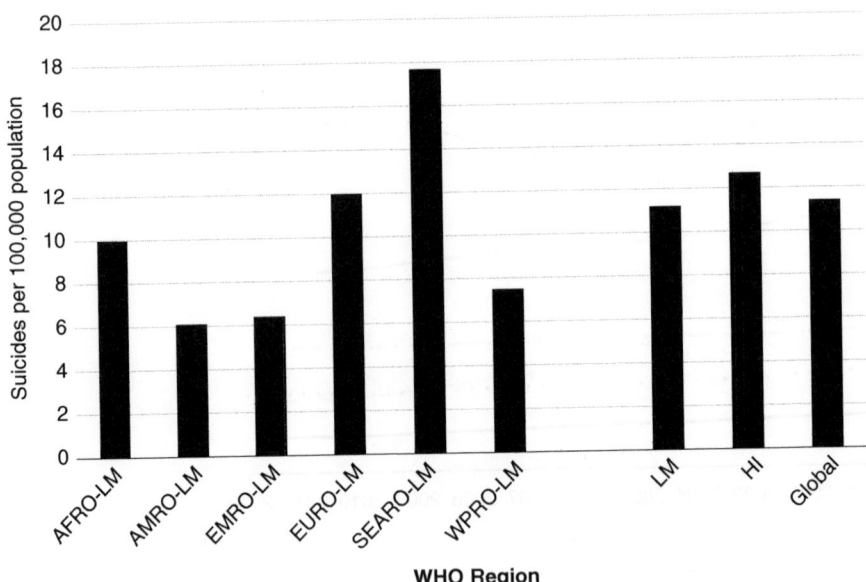

Figure 32.5 *Estimated age-adjusted suicide rates* by WHO region and country income status, 2012. (Source: WHO [2012].)*
LM = Low- and middle-income countries.
HI = High-income countries.
*Rates are standardized to the WHO World Standard Population.

Globally, the rate of suicide among males is nearly twice that of females (15.0 vs. 8.0 per 100,000). However, there are important differences between high-income and low- and middle-income countries in the ratio of male-to-female suicide rates. In high-income countries the rate ratio is 3.5, whereas in low- and middle-income countries it is 1.6, suggesting that the suicide rate is only about 57% higher in men than women in low- and middle-income countries (WHO, 2014b). In contrast to homicide, where rates are higher among the younger age groups, suicide rates increase with age and are highest among persons age 70 and older in most regions of the world, although there are regional differences in these patterns (WHO, 2014b). In low- and middle-income countries, for example, rates of suicide among young adults and elderly women are higher and rates of suicide among middle-aged men are lower relative to the rates for their counterparts in high-income countries (WHO, 2014b). Similar to homicide, suicide rates are decreasing globally. From 2000–2012 suicide rates fell 26% worldwide (WHO, 2014b). The only exception to this general pattern was in the low- and middle-income countries in the African region.

Nonfatal Violence

Nonfatal violence is much more common than fatal violence. Similar to mortality data, important gaps remain in understanding the true extent of nonfatal violence at country, regional, and global levels. However, important progress has

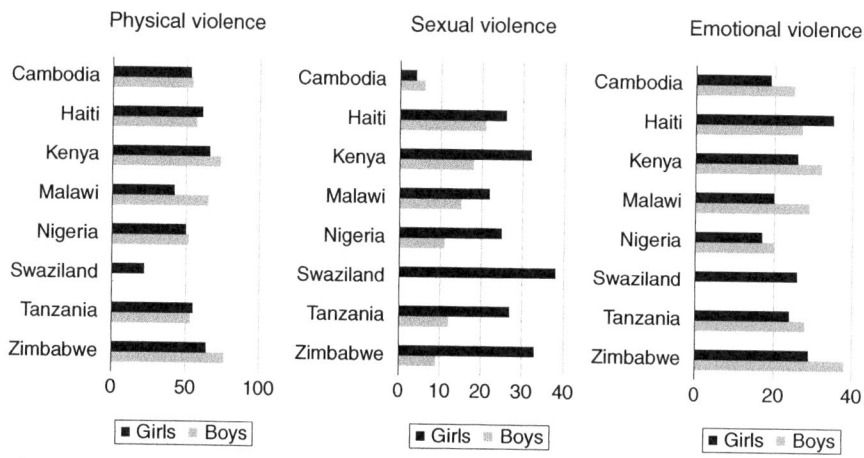

Figure 32.6 *Percentage of individuals age 18 to 24 who experienced physical, sexual, and emotional violence prior to age 18 – Violence Against Children Surveys. (Source: Centers for Disease Control and Prevention [2016a].)*

been made in the use of meta-analyses based on studies conducted around the world to derive global estimates of prevalence for child abuse and other forms of interpersonal violence, as well as in the systematic assessment of violence at the country level using nationally representative household and school surveys (Chiang et al., 2016; Devries et al., 2013; Hillis et al., 2016; Stoltenborgh, Bakermans-Kranenburg, Alink, & Ijzendoorn, 2015; WHO, 2013; Yon, Mikton, Gassoumis, & Wilder, 2016). Multi-country studies of violence against children, violence against women, and assessments of physical fighting and bullying among school-aged youth show considerable variation across countries and regions.

Estimates of the global prevalence of child abuse indicate that 25% of all adults report having been physically abused as children (Stoltenborgh, Bakermans-Kranenburg, van Ijzendoorn, & Alink, 2013), and that 1 in 5 women and 1 in 13 men report having been sexually abused as a child (Stoltenborgh, van Ijzendoorn,

Euser, & Bakermans-Kranenburg, 2011). For child physical, sexual, and emotional abuse, national household surveys of violence against children conducted in Asia, Latin America, and Africa reveal high rates of victimization. The Violence Against Children Surveys (VACS) systematically measure physical, sexual, and emotional violence experienced during childhood and in the 12 months prior to the survey among participants age 13 to 24 using a randomized cluster sample survey design (Chiang et al., 2016). The surveys are implemented under the leadership of country governments with participation from in-country partners and technical assistance from the US Centers for Disease Control and Prevention. Sixteen national surveys have been conducted to date (as of 2017); eight additional surveys are underway.

Findings from countries with available final data are shown in Figure 32.6 (CDC, 2016b). The high prevalence of physical violence (including being punched, kicked, whipped, beaten, intentionally burned or scalded, threatened, or attacked with a weapon) is evident across countries, with more than one-half of males in all countries surveyed indicating that they had experienced such violence in childhood, and in only two of the eight countries by fewer than half of the females. The prevalence of emotional violence was lower, ranging from 20–38% for males and 20–39% for females. In contrast to physical and emotional violence, which both tended to be slightly higher among males than females in most countries, the prevalence of sexual violence (including physically forced sex, pressured sex, unwanted attempted sex, and unwanted sexual touching) was higher in females than males. More than 1 in 4 females reported that they had experienced sexual violence prior to the age of 18, and in males, the prevalence was over 10% in five of the eight countries. Cambodia stands as an exception, where rates of sexual violence were lower for both females and males compared to the other countries.

Findings from the Global School-based Student Health Survey (GSHS), which is one of the few cross-nationally comparable sources of information on self-reported involvement in physical fighting and bullying, shows that these forms of violence are common among youth in countries around the world. Across all countries, nearly one in two males age 13 to 15 reported involvement in physical fighting during the past 12 months compared to 1 in 4 females (Table 32.3) (findings from the Global School-based Student Health Survey [www.who.int/chp/gshs/en/]). By country, the prevalence of physical fighting ranged from a low of 21% in Myanmar to a high of 73% in Samoa, and for females from a low of 8% in Myanmar to a high of 62% in Samoa. Sex differences were less pronounced for bullying, with a cross-country average of 42% for boys and 37% for girls. The highest reported prevalence of bullying was in Egypt, where 70% of both boys and girls reported having been bullied in the past month, and lowest in Morocco (17% boys and 21% girls). A cross-national study of trends in bullying victimization using data from the Health Behavior in School-Aged Children surveys found significant declines in both occasional and chronic bullying victimization from 2001–2010 for both boys and girls in one-third of the 33 countries studied, indicating at least some progress in this form of violence (Chester et al., 2015).

Findings from national surveys also reveal high rates of physical and sexual intimate partner violence against women. For instance, a multi-country study conducted in Bangladesh, Brazil, Ethiopia, Japan, Namibia, Peru, Samoa, Serbia and Montenegro, Thailand, and Tanzania found that the prevalence of physical and/or sexual violence by an intimate partner ranged from 15% in Japan to approximately 70% in Ethiopia and Peru, with most sites reporting rates of between 29% and 62% (Garcia-Moreno et al., 2005). Globally, the lifetime prevalence of physical and/or sexual intimate partner violence among all ever-partnered women is estimated to be 30% (WHO, 2013), with higher rates reported in the WHO African, Eastern Mediterranean, and South-East Asia regions (37%); similar rates in the region of the Americas (30%); and lower rates than the global average reported in the low- and middle-income countries of the European and the Western Pacific regions (25%), and across all high-income

Table 32.3 *Percentage of Youth Aged 13–15 Years Reporting Being Involved in a Physical Fight or Bullied, by Sex, Selected Countries (Various Years Between 2003 and 2013)*

Region	Physical Fighting (past 12 months) Male	Female	Bullying (past 30 days) Male	Female
Africa				
Benin	35%	27%	43%	41%
Botswana	54%	42%	53%	52%
Malawi	24%	21%	43%	47%
Swaziland	27%	14%	33%	31%
Americas				
Bolivia	45%	21%	32%	28%
Dominica	48%	30%	29%	26%
Honduras	36%	21%	32%	32%
Jamaica	61%	39%	40%	39%
Eastern Mediterranean				
Egypt	62%	29%	70%	70%
Iraq	50%	22%	32%	22%
Morocco	57%	26%	17%	21%
Qatar	63%	38%	49%	35%
South-East Asia				
Indonesia	48%	20%	55%	45%
Maldives	45%	17%	45%	39%
Myanmar	21%	8%	23%	16%
Thailand	47%	21%	32%	23%
Western Pacific				
Malaysia	45%	17%	45%	39%
Mongolia	63%	19%	37%	20%
Philippines	44%	32%	47%	48%
Samoa	73%	62%	79%	69%
All Regions (average)				
	47%	26%	42%	37%

Source: WHO (2015).

countries combined (23%) (WHO, 2013). Globally an estimated 7% of women have also experienced non-partner sexual violence over their lifetime, ranging from a high of 12% in the African region to a low of 5% in the South-East Asian region. However, owing to an absence of studies, the prevalence of non-partner sexual violence for the Eastern Mediterranean region has yet to be estimated (WHO, 2013).

With a rapidly aging population in countries around the world, there is an increasing number of older people that are vulnerable to abuse, neglect, and exploitation. Globally, an estimated 16%, or about 1 in 6 older adults aged 60 or older, experienced some form of abuse (physical, psychological, sexual, financial, or neglect) in the past year (Yon, Mikton, Gassoumis, & Wilbe, 2016). Given the approximate 2015 population estimate of 901 million people aged 60 and older worldwide, this rate amounts to 141 million victims of elder abuse annually. The most common form of abuse was psychological (12%), followed by financial abuse (7%), neglect (4%), physical abuse (3%), and sexual abuse (1%) (Yon et al., 2016). There are, however, serious regional gaps in the available data, with very few prevalence studies for South East Asia and none for Africa, regions that may have high rates of elder abuse based on the prevalence of violence in these regions for other population groups.

Impact of Violence

Ill health caused by violence forms a significant portion of the global burden of disease, and violence has been linked to many immediate and long-term health outcomes. Injuries are among the most immediate consequences of violence. They include broken teeth, bruises, burns, fractures, lacerations, ocular damage, internal injuries, and brain and spinal cord injuries. When severe, such injuries can result in disability, including amputations, brain damage and paralysis, and disfigurement (Mercy et al., 2017). The high frequency of violence-related injuries means they constitute a considerable burden on healthcare systems. For instance, in England and Wales, nearly 250,000 violence-related cases received treatment in a sample of 151 emergency departments over a four-year period (Sivarajasingam et al., 2016). In the USA, more than 1.5 million people are treated in emergency departments each year for injuries sustained in an assault (Centers for Disease Control and Prevention, 2016b).

Physical injuries due to violence are outweighed by a wide spectrum of behavioral, cognitive, mental health, sexual and reproductive health problems and social effects that arise from exposure to violence. Exposure to violence at an early age can impair brain and nervous system development and damage the circulatory, endocrine, immune, musculoskeletal, reproductive, and respiratory systems (Danese & McEwen, 2012; Hart & Rubia, 2012; Miller, Chen, & Parker, 2011; Suglia, Sapra, & Koenen, 2015; Twardosz & Lutzker, 2010). High-risk behaviors such as alcohol misuse, drug abuse, and smoking are more frequent among victims of violence, and these behaviors, in turn, increase the risk of cardiovascular disease, cancers, chronic lung disease, liver disease, and other noncommunicable diseases (Felitti et al., 1998; Moffitt et al., 2009; Norman et al., 2012). For instance, findings from a multi-country study in Eastern Europe found that young adults who had four or more adverse childhood experiences (such as child physical or sexual abuse), were ten times more likely to be problem drinkers and six times more likely to use illicit drugs than young adults without these experiences (Bellis et al., 2014). Furthermore, those who experienced adverse events in their childhood had a 2.4-times-increased risk of cancer, 5.8-times-increased risk of stroke and 49-fold increased risk of attempting suicide compared to those without adverse child experiences

(Bellis et al., 2014). Victims of violence are also at higher risk of depression, anxiety, post-traumatic-stress disorder, and suicidal behavior (Black, 2011; Bellis et al., 2014; Leeb, Lewis, & Zolotor, 2011; Andrews, Corry, Slade, Issakidis, & Swanton, 2004; WHO, 2013).

Violence against women and girls is an important risk factor for HIV, other sexually transmitted diseases, unwanted pregnancies, and other reproductive health problems. In some regions, women who have experienced partner violence are 1.5 times more likely to acquire HIV and 1.6 times more likely to have syphilis (WHO, 2013). Women who have experienced partner violence have a 16% greater chance of having a low-birth-weight baby and are over twice as likely to have an induced abortion (WHO, 2013).

The high prevalence and enduring consequences of violence mean that it has a substantial economic impact. This arises from both direct costs – such as those associated with providing medical treatment for the consequences – and indirect costs – such as lost earnings due to premature mortality or time away from work. In the USA, the total lifetime economic burden associated with new cases of child maltreatment occurring in one year was $124 billion in 2008 (Fang, Brown, Florence, & Mercy, 2012). In the East Asia and Pacific region it is estimated that the economic costs for some of the health consequences of child maltreatment (e.g., mental disorders, illicit drug use, smoking, problem drinking, self-harm) are equivalent to 1.4–2.5% of the region's annual GDP (Fang et al., 2015). In 2004, efforts to estimate the direct and indirect economic costs of all forms of interpersonal violence found these to account for 0.4% of gross domestic product (GDP) in Thailand, 1.2% of GDP in Brazil, and 4% of GDP in Jamaica (WHO, 2008).

Preventing and Responding to Violence

The WRVH called upon countries to address the burden and impact of violence and significant progress has been made both in the range of strategies being used to address the different forms of violence and in the evidence demonstrating preventive effects on violence outcomes or risk and protective factors for violence. Some of the more common strategies are shown in Table 32.4. These include parenting and early childhood development strategies designed to reduce child and adolescent behavior problems, improve parent-child interactions, increase positive parenting skills, and strengthen the foundation for positive academic, social, and other health outcomes across developmental periods. Systematic reviews of the evidence indicate that several parenting and early childhood development programs are effective in reducing child behavior problems, improving parental mental health, increasing positive parenting skills, reducing negative or harsh parenting, and reducing delinquency, co-occurring problem behaviors, and other risk factors for youth violence (Barlow, Simkiss, & Stewart-Brown, 2006; Bilukha et al., 2005; Burrus et al., 2012; Furlong et al., 2013; MacMillan et al., 2009; Piquero, Farrington, Welsh, Tremblay, & Jennings, 2009; Sandler, Schoenfelder, Wolchik, & MacKinnon, 2011; WHO, 2015). Much of the evidence for these programs comes from high-income countries (Hughes et al., 2014; WHO, 2015), although there is good evidence of these programs being flexible and effective across cultural

Table 32.4 *Examples of Violence Prevention Strategies*

Strategies to strengthen parenting and early childhood development	• Home visitation • Parenting and family-based programs • Preschool education with parental involvement
Strategies to strengthen skills to protect against violence	• Life skills/social development programs • Bullying prevention programs • Programs for developing safe and healthy intimate relationships • Sexual and reproductive health programs
Strategies to engage peers and caring adults in prevention	• Mentoring programs • Bystander and other peer norm approaches • Peer mediation • Gang prevention programs
Strategies to mitigate risk or harms of violence	• Therapeutic approaches • Screening and intervention (IPV, SV, EA, suicidal behavior)[a] • Gatekeeper training • Hospital-community programs (e.g., wraparound services and case management for assault-injured youth)
Strategies to change community-level risk factors	• Improvements to settings (schools, workplaces, residential institutions, neighborhoods) • Street outreach approaches • Alcohol policies to reduce harmful use • Community and problem-oriented policing • Housing policies
Strategies to change societal-level risk factors	• Cultural and social norm change approaches • Income and economic supports for women and families • Reducing access to lethal means • Legal remedies and judicial reforms • Reducing poverty and inequality (economic, gender, racial/ethnic)

Note: The programs, practices, and policies included in the table do not represent an exhaustive list, nor have they necessarily been evaluated and/or proved to be effective.

[a] Intimate partner violence (IPV), sexual violence (SV), child maltreatment (CM), elder abuse (EA).

groups and a growing body of evidence on their transportability across countries (Gardner, Montgomery, & Knerr, 2015; Knerr, Gardner, & Cluver, 2013; Ogden, Forgatch, Askeland, Patterson, & Bullock, 2005). Even so, findings from the Global Status Report on Violence Prevention indicate that between 35% and 38% of countries report that they are widely implementing these types of programs (Figure 32.7) and mostly in the Americas and European region (WHO, 2014a).

Strategies designed to strengthen skills that protect against violence and related

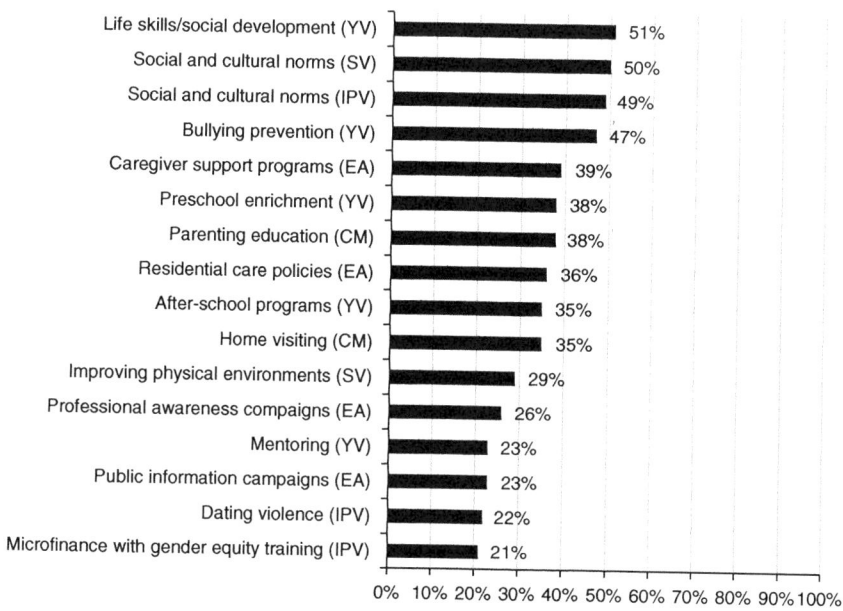

Figure 32.7 *Proportion of countries reporting implementation of violence prevention programs on a larger scale by type of program (n = 133 reporting countries). (Source: WHO [2014a].) Key: CM = child maltreatment; EA = elder abuse; IPV = intimate partner violence; SV = sexual violence; YV = youth violence. While each program is shown as relevant to a particular type of violence, some of the programs listed in the figure have shown preventive effects on several types of violence.*

risk factors (e.g., substance use, high-risk sexual behavior) focus on improving communication, problem-solving, conflict resolution and management, empathy, emotional regulation and impulse control, and fostering safe and healthy intimate relationships. Skills-based programs are one of the most commonly studied programs in both high-income and low- and middle-income countries (Hughes et al., 2014). They are also among the most widely implemented of prevention programs across countries to address youth violence (Figure 32.7). A systematic review of universal school-based programs found a 15% relative reduction in violence across school years and a 29% reduction in violence among students in secondary schools (Hahn et al., 2007). These types of programs have demonstrated reductions in peer violence, teen dating violence, sexual violence, and adolescent suicidal behavior (Foshee et al., 2004, 2014; Wolfe et al., 2003, 2009; Wasserman et al., 2014; Schilling, Aseltine, & James, 2016). Other systematic reviews have also documented significant impacts of these programs on aggression, delinquency, bullying perpetration and victimization, substance use, adolescent pregnancy, and sexually transmitted infections, including HIV (Botvin & Griffin, 2004; Chin et al., 2012; Matjasko et al., 2012; Ttofi & Farrington, 2011; Wilson & Lipsey, 2007).

Strategies to engage peers and caring adults in prevention vary depending on the nature of the program model (e.g., mentoring, bystander, and peer norm approaches). One common ingredient across program models is the desire to influence behavioral choices; reinforce positive norms about masculinity, gender, violence, and help-seeking; and reduce young people's involvement in violence, substance use, suicidal behavior, and high-risk sexual behavior. Mentoring programs, for instance, pair youth with a volunteer from the community. The goal of such programs is to connect youth with a caring, supportive role model who can identify growth opportunities and help the young person develop skills and achieve success across behavioral, social, and academic domains (DuBois & Karcher, 2014). Bystander approaches have been used to address bullying and other forms of youth violence and are also becoming an important approach for preventing teen dating and sexual violence (Basile et al., 2016; Coker et al., 2017; Coker et al., 2015; Polanin, Espelage, & Pigott, 2012; Salmivalli, 2014). Social norm change promoted by peers and influential adults (e.g., coaches, teachers) is an important component of these approaches. Peer norm approaches have also been used to prevent youth suicidal behavior by engaging peer leaders to promote adaptive behaviors, help-seeking, and connectedness to other peers and trusting adults.

Systematic reviews of mentoring programs show significant impacts on aggression, delinquency, substance use, and academic performance, and other social and emotional domains (DuBois, Portillo, Rhodes, Silverthorn, & Valentine, 2011; Tolan, Henry, Schoeny, Lovegrove, & Nichols, 2014). Findings from a meta-analysis of bystander education to prevent sexual assault on college campuses found moderate effects on both bystander efficacy and intentions to help others at risk as well as smaller but significant effects on self-reported bystander helping behaviors and rape-supportive attitudes (Katz & Moore, 2013). Evidence for secondary school populations shows significant reductions in both victimization and perpetration of sexual violence and teen dating violence (Coker et al., 2017). Peer norm approaches also show promise in increasing behaviors that are protective against adolescent suicide (Wyman et al., 2010). Other programs to engage peers – for example, those that use age mates to help resolve disputes (peer mediation) or attempt to redirect peer-group activities, or prevent associations with antisocial peers (gang prevention programs) have also been tried in many countries, although with limited evidence of effectiveness (WHO, 2015). Some have also led to iatrogenic effects (i.e., unintended consequences or increases in violent behavior; Dodge, Dishion, & Lansford, 2006).

Strategies to mitigate risk and the harms of violence include therapeutic approaches to lessen the trauma and health effects of violence exposures (e.g., depression, anxiety, post-traumatic stress disorder, and negative coping behaviors), as well as to prevent future victimization and perpetration (Lipsey, Landenberger, & Wilson, 2007; Litschge, Vaughn, & McCrea, 2010; Wethington et al., 2008). Other approaches include screening and intervention services for survivors of intimate partner violence, sexual violence, elder abuse, and suicidal behavior (e.g., victim-centered services such as crisis intervention, housing, medical and legal advocacy, access to community resources) (Bair-Merritt et al., 2014; Hegarty et al., 2013; Krug et al., 2002); gatekeeper training programs to prevent suicidal behavior (WHO, 2014b); and hospital-community programs to prevent future assaults and injury among youth (Cunningham et al., 2012; Purtle, Corbin, Rich, & Rich, 2015). Although evidence from high-income countries shows many of these intensive interventions and services to be effective in reducing the harms of violence exposures (Cary & McMillen, 2012; de Arellano et al., 2014; Wethington et al., 2008) and effective in preventing future victimization and perpetration (Cunningham et al., 2012, 2013; Lipsey et al., 2007; Litschge et al., 2010; Sawyer & Borduin, 2011; van der Stouwe, Asscher, Stams, Deković, & van der Laan, 2014; Wagner, Borduin, Sawyer, & Dopp, 2014), there has been less implementation and outcome evaluation of these approaches in low- and middle-income countries. Many therapeutic interventions (e.g., Trauma-Focused Cognitive Behavior Therapy, Multisystemic Therapy) require delivery by licensed and trained providers (which are in short supply in low- and middle-income countries) making them less feasible for implementation in less resourced settings (WHO, 2015). Comprehensive services to identify, refer, protect, and support survivors of interpersonal and self-directed violence are also lacking in many low- and middle-income countries (WHO, 2014a, 2014b).

Strategies to change community-level risk factors focus on modifying the characteristics of settings that increase the risk for violent behavior or create the conditions for violence to occur. These include efforts to improve the physical and social environments of school, workplace, and neighborhood settings – for example, through improved transport, lighting, green space and other urban upgrades, community engagement activities, and by managing the accessibility to buildings and public spaces. Other types of community-level interventions include those that focus on changing attitudes, beliefs, and behavior through public information campaigns; street outreach to mediate conflicts and change community norms around the acceptability of violence (e.g., Cure Violence; Butts, Roman, Bostwick, & Porter 2015); community and problem-oriented policing; as well as those that address the density and affordability of housing, and the pricing, hours/days of sale, and location and concentration of alcohol outlets.

Evidence for community-level strategies is growing in both high-income countries and in low- and middle-income countries. Improvements to the physical and social environment, for instance, are associated with reductions in robberies, violent crime, gun assaults, youth homicide, and neighborhood disorder (Bogar & Beyer, 2016; Branas et al., 2011; Cassidy, Inglis, Wiysonge, & Matzopoulos, 2014; Culyba et al., 2016; MacDonald, Golinelli, Stokes, & Blumenthal, 2010). Reductions in gun violence, homicide, and nonfatal assault-related injuries are associated with street outreach approaches (Butts et al., 2015) and alcohol-related policies such as pricing, limiting the days of sale, and limiting the clustering of outlets (Fitterer, Nelson, & Stockwell, 2015; Anderson, Chisholm, & Fuhr, 2009; Wagenaar, Tobler, & Komro, 2010). A systematic review of community policing, on the other hand, found positive effects on perceptions of disorder and overall satisfaction among residents, but limited effects on crime and fear of crime (Gill, Weisburd, Telep, Vitter, & Bennett, 2014). The evidence is also limited for public information campaigns, which have been widely used in countries around the world to dispel myths, raise awareness, and influence behavior change around partner violence, sexual violence, and elder abuse (Arango, Morton, Gennari, Kiplesund, & Ellsberg, 2014; Campbell & Manganello, 2006; Whitaker, Baker, & Arias, 2007; WHO, 2009, 2011). While these efforts can complement other preventive interventions and help to improve knowledge and awareness, they are less effective in changing behavior (WHO, 2009).

Societal strategies focus on the cultural, social, and economic factors related to violence – addressing such issues as access to lethal means, gender, racial/ethnic, economic, or educational inequality – and emphasize changes in legislation, institutional and other policies, and the larger social and cultural environment to reduce rates of violence. Examples of measures for reducing access to lethal means include waiting periods, rules on licensing and registration, safe storage practices, gun buy-back programs, and policing of the illegal possession and trafficking of guns. With suicide, addressing access to lethal means may also include fencing in high bridges, limiting access to roofs and high exteriors of tall buildings, automatic shut-off devices for motor vehicles, limiting access to pesticides and fertilizers, and measures to make analgesic and other drugs safer (e.g., packaging; monitoring access and use). Other societal measures may include legal and judicial remedies to criminalize abuse by intimate partners, to broaden the definition of rape, to criminalize the sexual abuse and exploitation of women and children, and to criminalize the harsh, physical punishment of children in various settings (Calkins, Jeglic, Beattey, Zeidman, & Perillo, 2014; Krug et al., 2002; WHO, 2014a). Also included are reforms to educational systems, policies to reduce poverty and inequality and improve support for families, as well as efforts to change social and cultural norms around issues of gender, racial and ethnic discrimination, and harmful traditional practices.

With respect to societal-level strategies, there is strong evidence that reducing access to lethal means is effective in reducing suicide (Cox et al., 2013; Pirkis et al., 2015). The evidence pertaining to firearm policies specifically, however, is more mixed. A recent systematic review of evidence from 130 studies across ten countries noted that reductions in firearm deaths were more strongly associated with the simultaneous implementation of multiple laws than single legislative measures (Santaella-Tenorio, Cerdá, Villaveces, & Galea, 2016). In terms of other legal and judicial remedies, the evidence points to laws banning the violent punishment of children by parents, teachers, and other caregivers. These types of laws are associated with reductions in the use of severe corporal punishment against children and attitudes supportive of the use of such punishment (Bussman, Ethal, & Schroth, 2011; Osterman, Bjorkqvist, & Wahlbeck, 2014; Zolotor & Puzia, 2010).

Even though social and cultural norm change strategies are among the most widely implemented strategies in countries to address intimate partner violence and sexual violence (Figure 32.7), few have been rigorously evaluated (Arango et al., 2014; Ellsberg et al., 2015; WHO, 2009, 2010). There is more evidence for efforts focused on improving women's economic and social empowerment, which is an important strategy to help address poverty in high-income as well as low- and middle-income countries (Arango et al., 2014; Ellsberg et al., 2015; Verma et al., 2008; Vyas & Watts, 2009). Systematic reviews of the evidence suggest that poverty reduction, women's economic empowerment, male and female access to secondary education, and reductions in inequality in education may have protective impacts on intimate partner violence and children's exposure to intimate partner violence (Vyas & Watts, 2009). Increasing family income through subsidies or cash transfers has also been shown to reduce child abuse and neglect (Cancian, Yang, & Slack, 2013).

Diffusion of Violence Prevention Strategies

Putting knowledge into practice is one of the most important functions of public health and also one of the more challenging endeavors. Even though the evidence base for the different strategies has increased substantially over time, many countries, regardless of their income level, are not implementing prevention strategies on a scale that is commensurate with the burden of violence (WHO, 2014a).

The importance of the transfer or diffusion of knowledge, science or evidence into practice (also referred to as implementation science, translational research, dissemination, and knowledge transfer and exchange) is gaining more attention in the field (Goodman et al., 1998; Graham et al., 2006; Mikton et al., 2011; Mitton, Adair, McKenzie, Patten, & Perry, 2007; Spoth et al., 2013; Wandersman et al., 2008). This is partly the result of the realization that generating sound knowledge of what works and how it works (*intervention research*) is only a first step. The complex processes and systems through which evidence-based interventions are adopted, implemented, and sustained on a large scale to achieve population impact is equally important and in need of scientific understanding (*implementation research*) (Mitton et al., 2007; Spoth et al., 2013; Wandersman et al., 2008).

A conclusion of reviews in this area is that there is limited empirical evidence about the effectiveness of the different models of diffusion (Mitton et al., 2007; Pentland et al., 2011). The models, however, point to a number of important factors to consider, including assessments of community readiness; assessments of existing legislation and policies; implementation drivers such as support and awareness among key stakeholders and support and commitment from decision-makers; and building infrastructure (e.g., material, human, and financial resources) and the capacity to support the delivery and systems-oriented scale-up of evidence-based interventions (Durlak, 2013; Mikton et al., 2011; Spoth et al., 2013; Pentland et al., 2011; Wandersman et al., 2008). Developing measures for implementation, monitoring, and tracking impact and plans for sustainability are also critical (Durlak, 2013; Wandersman et al., 2008).

There is some empirical evidence for capacity development and readiness models as well as data-driven prevention planning systems. These models have been successfully used in high-income countries – and in a handful of low- and middle-income countries – to help communities with this work (Almuneef et al., 2014; Center for the Study and Prevention of Violence, 2016; Florence, Shepherd, Brennen, & Simon, 2011; Kostadinov, Daniel, Stanley, Gancia, & Cargo, 2015; Mikton, 2012; Mikton et al., 2013; Spoth et al., 2015). The Community Readiness Model, for instance, defines nine stages of community readiness and provides an instrument to assess a community's level of readiness along with strategies for successful implementation related to each stage of readiness (Edwards, Jumper-Thurman, Plested, Oetting, & Swanson, 2000; Plested, Edwards, & Jumper-Thurman, 2006). The model has primarily been used in the USA for the prevention of alcohol abuse, intimate partner violence, child maltreatment, suicide, head injuries, obesity, and HIV/AIDS (Edwards et al., 2000; Kostadinov et al., 2015; Plested, Edwards, & Thurman, 2006, 2007; Silwa et al., 2011), although has also been used in Australia, Canada, India, and Liberia (Kostadinov et al., 2015; Silwa et al., 2011). Another model developed by WHO specifically for child maltreatment prevention (Readiness Assessment for the Prevention of Child Maltreatment – RAP-CM), aims to identify the conditions that need to be met within a country or community for the successful implementation of evidence-based child maltreatment programs on a large scale using a ten-dimensional model (Mikton, 2011; WHO, 2016a). This model has been used in Brazil, the Former Yoguslav Republic of Macedonia, Malaysia, Saudi Arabia, and South Africa (Al-Muneef et al., 2014; Mikton et al., 2012, 2013).

Communities that Care (CTC) and the Cardiff Violence Prevention Partnership model are examples of data-driven prevention planning models that have been rigorously evaluated and used to help communities address youth violence, substance abuse, and assault-related injuries (Center for the Study and Prevention of Violence, 2016; Boyle, Snelling, White, Ariel, & Ashelford, 2013; Florence, Shepherd, Brennen, & Simon, 2011; Florence, Shepherd, Brennan, & Simon, 2014). CTC, for example, engages and guides community stakeholders through a prevention planning process designed to address a community's profile of risk and protective factors with evidence-based programs. CTC also helps communities monitor implementation and track outcomes with a series of benchmarks and milestones to guide progress and make adjustments as indicated by the data (Center for the Study and Prevention of Violence, 2016). It is associated with reductions in rates of youth violence, crime, and alcohol and tobacco use (Center for the Study and Prevention of Violence, 2016). The Cardiff model is a collaborative model whereby anonymized information related to assaults from hospital emergency departments (e.g., location of the incident, time/day, weapon used, demographic, and other information) is combined with police data and shared routinely to inform violence prevention strategies. The model is associated with reductions in total and wound-related assaults (Florence et al., 2011), is cost-effective (Florence et al., 2014), and has also been validated (Boyle et al., 2013).

Moving Violence Prevention Up on the Global Agenda

Developments in the violence prevention field and the surrounding international policy context over the last four to five years have created new windows of opportunity to strengthen science-based approaches to understanding and preventing violence and reducing the global burden of violence. These developments include moving violence prevention up on the international agenda with its inclusion in the Sustainable Development Goals; a Global Plan of Action endorsed by the World Health Assembly; expanded partnerships and alignment of UN, US

Government, and other key partners around a core set of strategies to prevent violence against children; high-profile reports drawing attention to interpersonal and self-directed violence; and the first benchmarks upon which to track global progress in preventing violence in countries around the world.

A key development in the international policy context is inclusion in the Sustainable Development Goals (SDG) of targets that directly focus on violence, and others that address many underlying causes of violence (Sustainable Development Goals, 2016). The SDGs were adopted by the UN General Assembly in September 2015. Target 5.2 is to "eliminate all forms of violence against women and girls in the public and private spheres, including trafficking and sexual and other types of exploitation." Target 16.1 is to "significantly reduce all forms of violence and related deaths everywhere," and Target 16.2 is to "end abuse, exploitation, trafficking and all forms of violence against and torture of children." The SDGs also cover many important risk factors for multiple forms of violence, such as poverty reduction, social protection, gender equality, mental health, drug and alcohol abuse, and early childhood development. With these SDG targets, violence prevention decision-makers are now in a stronger position to give greater attention to violence prevention and also to consider a "violence prevention in all policies" approach that foregrounds prevention through SDG-based strategies that address many of the underlying causes of violence.

Within the health sector, adoption by the May 2016 World Health Assembly of Resolution 69.5, endorsing the first ever WHO Global Plan of Action to strengthen the role of the health system in addressing violence, provides a powerful new incentive for increased health sector involvement in preventing and responding to violence (World Health Assembly, 2016). The plan's three sections cover violence against women and girls, violence against children, and all forms of interpersonal violence. Each section describes evidence-based actions that can be taken by Member States, national and international partners, and the WHO secretariat. The plan covers the period 2016–2030, and is keyed to the SDGs. World Health Assembly resolutions are adopted following consensus by the nearly 200 Member States, and this resolution provides a tool by which advocates and decision-makers can leverage increased health sector participation in preventing and responding to violence.

With the goal of assisting countries in achieving SDG Target 16.2, the Global Partnership to End Violence Against Children was launched in 2016 (www.end-violence.org). The Partnership supports those working to prevent and respond to violence against children (0–18 years of age) within and across government sectors such as education, health, justice, and social welfare. It also includes other stakeholders such as the UN and World Bank, other development agencies, as well as nongovernmental organizations, faith-based organizations, the private sector, foundations, and researchers. By harnessing the expertise and reach of partners in prevention, the Partnership supports national- and local-level work to implement and scale up strategies that effectively prevent violence, monitor their effectiveness, and expand the evidence base.

Central to the Partnership's work is a multi-agency technical package, INSPIRE: Seven Strategies for Ending

Violence Against Children (WHO, 2016b). The package represents a select group of strategies based on the best available evidence to help countries and communities intensify their focus on the prevention programs and services with the greatest potential to reduce violence against children. The alignment of multiple UN and US Government agencies around a core set of strategies represents an unprecedented opportunity to support the widespread adoption of these strategies at the country level.

Other issues have also gained more widespread attention in the last few years. The problem of suicide and the importance of bringing greater public health resources to bear on its prevention were highlighted in the first ever world report on suicide – *Preventing Suicide: A Global Imperative*, published in 2014 (WHO, 2014b). The report raises awareness of the public health significance of suicide; presents the latest data on suicide; identifies evidence-based approaches to suicide prevention that can be adapted to different settings; and in recognizing the close links between suicide and several forms of interpersonal violence, encourages strategic, collaborative actions to have the greatest impact.

The global violence prevention field has been described as having developed in three phases: a formative phase that ran from the mid-1970s to the late 1990s; a normative phase extending from the late 1990s to around 2010, and from 2011 onwards an operational phase consistent with the most recent developments described here (Butchart & Mikton, 2015). In line with this, the next big advances in global violence prevention will in all likelihood entail a stronger emphasis on implementing evidence-based prevention programming and policy at the national and local levels, coupled with a new drive to better measure the nature, reach, and quality of evidence-based policies and programs at national and local levels.

Toward this end, the WHO, the United Nations Development Programme, and the United Nations Office on Drugs and Crime published the *Global status report on violence prevention 2014* (WHO, 2014a). The report represents a systematic assessment of country progress in implementing the recommendations of the WRVH, including the extent to which countries are collecting data on fatal and nonfatal violence to inform prevention; whether national plans are in place to address violence; the current status of program, policy, and legislative measures to prevent violence at the country level; and the availability of healthcare, social, and legal services for victims of violence. The findings represent a set of indicators and a baseline measure to track future progress within countries and globally. In this regard, the report brings violence prevention in line with other issues such as alcohol and health, climate change, mental health, road safety, tobacco, and tuberculosis, where similar systematic assessments of efforts have led to substantial investment, worldwide preventive attention, and action at all levels (Mikton, Butchart, Dahlberg, & Krug, 2016).

Conclusion

As this chapter has shown, the field of violence prevention has made great progress over the last few decades. Studies of violence at the country level are increasing as are outcome evaluation studies of what works to prevent it. Violence prevention is increasingly part of the global agenda alongside other important public health problems. The opportunity for violence prevention stakeholders to join forces and step up their activities and investments to a level commensurate with the burden of the problem has never been greater (Butchart, Mikton, & Krug, 2014).

Disclaimer

The findings and conclusions in this manuscript are those of the authors and do not necessarily represent the official position of the US Centers for Disease Control and Prevention or the views, decisions, or policies of the World Health Organization or the University of the West of England.

References

Almuneef, M., Qayad, M., Noor, I. K., Al-Eissa, M. A., Albuhairan, F. S., Inam, S., & Mikton, C. (2014). Multidimensional model to assess the readiness of Saudi Arabia to implement evidence based child maltreatment prevention programs at a large scale. *Child Abuse & Neglect*, 38(3), 527–532.

Anderson, P., Chisholm, D., & Fuhr, D. C. (2009). Effectiveness and cost-effectiveness of policies and programs to reduce the harm caused by alcohol. *The Lancet*, 373, 2234–2246.

Andrews, G. J., Corry, J., Slade, T., Issakidis, C., & Swanton, H. (2004). Child sexual abuse. In M. Ezzati, A. D. Lopez, A. Rodgers, & C. J. L. Murray (Eds), *Comparative Quantification of Health Risks: Global and Regional Burden of Disease Attributable to Selected Major Risk Factors* (Vol. 1, pp. 1851–1940). Geneva: World Health Organization.

Arango, D. J., Morton, M., Gennari, F., Kiplesund, S., & Ellsberg, M. (2014). *Interventions to Prevent or Reduce Violence Against Women and Girls: A Systematic Review of Reviews*. Washington, DC: Women's Voice, Agency and Participation Research Series, World Bank.

Bair-Merritt, M. H., Lewis-O'Connor, A., Goel, S., Amato, P., Ismailji, T., Jelley, M., ... & Cronholm, P. (2014). Primary care–based interventions for intimate partner violence: a systematic review. *American Journal of Preventive Medicine*, 46(2), 188–194.

Barlow, J., Simkiss, D., & Stewart-Brown, S. (2006). Interventions to prevent or ameliorate child physical abuse and neglect: findings from a systematic review of reviews. *Journal of Children's Services*, 1(3), 6–28.

Basile, K. C., DeGue, S., Jones, K., Freire, K., Dills, J., Smith, S. G., & Raiford, J. L. (2016). *STOP SV: A Technical Package to Prevent Sexual Violence*. Atlanta, GA: National Center for Injury Prevention and Control, Centers for Disease Control and Prevention.

Bellis, M. A., Hughes, K., Leckenby, N., Jones, L., Baban, A., Kachaeva, M., ... & Terzic, N. (2014). Adverse childhood experiences and associations with health-harming behaviors in young adults: surveys in the European Region. *Bulletin of the World Health Organization*, 92, 641–655B.

Bilukha, O., Hahn, R. A., Crosby, A., Fullilove, M. T., Liberman, A., Moscicki, E., ... & Task Force on Community Preventive Services (2005). The effectiveness of early childhood home visitation in preventing violence: a systematic review. *American Journal of Preventive Medicine*, 28 (2 Suppl. 1), 11–39.

Black, M. C. (2011). Intimate partner violence and adverse health consequences: implications for clinicians. *American Journal of Lifestyle Medicine*, 5(5), 428–439.

Bogar, S. & Beyer, K. M. (2016). Green space, violence, and crime: a systematic review. *Trauma, Violence, & Abuse*, 17(2), 160–171.

Botvin, G. J. & Griffin, K. W. (2004). Life Skills Training: empirical findings and future directions. *The Journal of Primary Prevention*, 25(2), 211–232.

Boyle, A. A., Snelling, K., White, L., Ariel, B., & Ashelford, L. (2013). External validation of the Cardiff model of information sharing to reduce community violence: natural experiment. *Emergency Medicine Journal*, 30, 1020–1023.

Branas, C. C., Cheney, R. A., MacDonald, J. M., Tam, V. W., Jackson, T. D., & Ten Have, T. R. (2011). A difference-in-difference analysis of health, safety, and greening vacant urban space. *American Journal of Epidemiology*, 174(11), 1296–1306.

Bronfenbrenner, V. (1979). *The ecology of human development: experiments by nature and design.* Cambridge, MA: Harvard University Press.

Bufacchi, V. (2005). Two concepts of violence. *Political Studies Review*, 3(2), 193–204.

Burrus, B., Leeks, K. D., Sipe, T. A., Dolina, S., Soler, R. E., Elder, R. W., … & Community Preventive Services Task Force. (2012). Person-to-person interventions targeted to parents and other caregivers to improve adolescent health: a community guide systematic review. *American Journal of Preventive Medicine*, 42(3), 316–326.

Bussman, K., Erthal, C., & Schroth, A. (2011). Effects of banning corporal punishment in Europe – A five nation comparison. In J. E. Durrant & A. B. Smith (Eds), *Global Pathways to Abolishing Physical Punishment* (pp. 299–322). New York: Routledge.

Butchart, A. & Mikton, C. (2015). The history and role of international agencies in violence prevention. In P. D. Donnelly & C. L. Ward (Eds), *The Oxford Textbook of Violence Prevention: Epidemiology, Evidence and Policy* (pp. 309–313), Oxford: Oxford University Press.

Butchart, A., Mikton, C., & Krug, E. (2014). Governments must do more to address interpersonal violence. *The Lancet*, 384(20/27), 2183–2185.

Butts, J. A., Roman, C. G., Bostwick, L., & Porter J. R. (2015). Cure Violence: a public health model to reduce gun violence. *Annual Review of Public Health*, 36, 39–53.

Calkins, C., Jeglic, E., Beattey, R. A., Zeidman, S., & Perillo, A. D. (2014). Sexual violence legislation: a review of case law and empirical research. *Psychology, Public Policy, and Law*, 20(4), 443–462.

Campbell, J. C. & Manganello, J. (2006). Changing public attitudes as a prevention strategy to reduce intimate partner violence. *Journal of Aggression, Maltreatment & Trauma*, 13(3–4), 13–39.

Cancian, M., Yang, M., & Slack, K. S. (2013). The effect of additional child support income on the risk of child maltreatment. *Social Service Review*, 87(3), 417–437.

Capaldi, D. M., Knoble, N. B., Shortt, J. W., & Kim, H. K. (2012). A systematic review of risk factors for intimate partner violence. *Partner Abuse*, 3(2), 231–280.

Cary, C. E. & McMillen, J. C. (2012). The data behind the dissemination: a systematic review of trauma-focused cognitive behavioral therapy for use with children and youth. *Children and Youth Services Review*, 34, 748–757.

Cassidy, T., Inglis, G., Wiysonge, C., & Matzopoulos, R. (2014). A systematic review of the effects of poverty deconcentration and urban upgrading on youth violence. *Health & Place*, 14(26), 78–87.

Centers for Disease Control and Prevention. (2016a). Violence Against Children Surveys (VACS) fact sheet and country reports. Retrieved August, 2016 from www.cdc.gov/violenceprevention/vacs/publications.html.

Centers for Disease Control and Prevention. (2016b). *Web-based Injury Statistics Query and Reporting System – WISQARS.* Retrieved August, 2016 from www.cdc.gov/injury/wisqars/index.html.

Center for the Study and Prevention of Violence. (2016). *Communities that Care. Blueprints for Violence Prevention.* Boulder, CO: University of Colorado Boulder, Institute of Behavioral Science, Center for the Study and Prevention of Violence. Retrieved June, 2016 from www.blueprintsprograms.com/factsheet/communities-that-care..

Chester, K. L., Callaghan, M., Cosma, A., Donnelly, P., Craig, W., Walsh, S., & Molcho,

M. (2015). Cross-national time trends in bullying victimization in 33 countries among children age 11, 13 and 15 from 2002–2010. *The European Journal of Public Health*, 25(2), 61–64.

Chiang, L. F., Kress, H., Sumner, S. A., Gleckel, J., Kawemama, P., & Gordon, R. N. (2016). Violence Against Children Surveys (VACS): towards a global surveillance system. *Injury Prevention*, 22(Suppl 1), i17–i22.

Chin, H., Sipe, T., Beeker, C., Elder, R., Mercer, S., Wethington, H., ... & the Community Preventive Services Task Force. (2012). The effectiveness of comprehensive risk reduction and abstinence education interventions to prevent or reduce the risk of adolescent pregnancy, HIV and STIs: two systematic reviews and meta-analyses. *American Journal of Preventive Medicine*, 42(3), 272–294.

Coker, A. L., Bush, H. M., Cook-Craig, P. G., DeGue, S. A., Clear, E. R., Brancato, C. J., Fisher, B. S., & Recktenwald, E. A. (2017). RCT testing bystander effectiveness to reduce violence. *American Journal of Preventive Medicine*, 52(5), 566–578.

Coker, A. L., Fisher, B. S., Bush, H. M., Swan, S. C., Williams, C. M., Clear, E. R., & DeGue, S. (2015). Evaluation of the Green Dot bystander intervention to reduce interpersonal violence among college students across three campuses. *Violence Against Women*, 12, 1507–1527.

Cox, G. R., Owens, C., Robinson, J., Nicholas, A., Lockley, A., Williamson, M., ... & Pirkis, J. (2013). Interventions to reduce suicides at suicide hotspots: a systematic review. *BMC Public Health*, 13(1), 1–12.

Culyba, A. J., Jacoby, S. F., Richmond, T. S., Fein, J. A., Hohl, B. C., & Branas, C. C. (2016). Modifiable neighborhood features associated with adolescent homicide. *JAMA Pediatrics*, 170(5), 473–480.

Cunningham, R. M., Chermack, S. T., Zimmerman, M. A., Shope, J. T., Bingham, C. R., Blow, F. C., & Walton, M. A. (2012). Brief motivational interviewing intervention for peer violence and alcohol use in teens: one-year follow-up. *Pediatrics*, 129(6), 1083–1090.

Cunningham, R. M., Whiteside, L. K., Chermack, S. T., Zimmerman, M. A., Shope, J. T., Raymond Bingham, C., ... & Walton, M. A. (2013). Dating violence: outcomes following a brief motivational interviewing intervention among at-risk adolescents in an urban emergency department. *Academic Emergency Medicine*, 20(6), 562–569.

Dahlberg, L. L. & Krug, E. G. (2002). Violence – a global public health problem. In: E. G. Krug, L. L. Dahlberg, J. A. Mercy, A. B. Zwi, & R. Lozano (Eds), *World Report on Violence and Health* (pp. 1–21). Geneva, Switzerland: World Health Organization.

Danese, A. & McEwen, B. S. (2012). Adverse childhood experiences, allostasis, allostatic load, and age-related disease. *Physiology & Behavior*, 106(1), 29–39.

de Arellano, M. A., R. Lyman, D. R., Jobe-Shields, L., George, P., Dougherty, R. H., Daniels, A. S., ... & Delphin-Rittmon, M. E. (2014). Trauma-focused cognitive behavioral therapy: assessing the evidence. *Psychiatric Services*, 65(5), 591–602.

Devries, K. M., Mak, J. Y., García-Moreno, C., Petzold, M., Child, J. C., Falder, G., ... & Watts, C. H. (2013). The global prevalence of intimate partner violence against women. *Science*, 340(6140), 1527–1528.

Diez-Roux, A. V. (2000). Multilevel analysis in public health research. *Annual Review of Public Health*, 21(1), 171–192.

Dodge, K. A. & Coie, J. D. (1987). Social information processing factors in reactive and proactive aggression in children's peer groups. *Journal of Personality and Social Psychology*, 53, 1146–1158.

Dodge, K., Dishion, T., & Lansford, J. (Eds) (2006). *Deviant Peer Influences in Programs for Youth: Problems and Solutions*. New York: The Gilford Press.

DuBois, D. L. & Karcher, M. J. (Eds) (2014). *Handbook of Youth Mentoring. Second edition*. Thousand Oaks, CA. Sage Publications.

DuBois, D. L., Portillo, N., Rhodes, J. E., Silverthorn, N., & Valentine, C. (2011). How effective are mentoring programs for youth? a systematic assessment of the evidence. *Psychological Science in the Public Interest*, 312(2), 57–91.

Durlak, J. (2013). *The importance of quality implementation for research, practice and policy*. Office of the Assistant Secretary for Planning and Evaluation, US Department of Health and Human Services, Research Brief, 2/1/2013. Retrieved June, 2016 from https://aspe.hhs.gov/basic-report/importance-quality-implementation-research-practice-and-policy.

Edwards, R. W., Jumper-Thurman, P., Plested, B., Oetting, E. R., & Swanson, L. (2000). Community readiness: research to practice. *Journal of Community Psychology*, 28(3), 291–307.

Ellsberg, M., Arango, D. J., Morton, M., Gennari, F., Kiplesund, S., Contreras, M., & Watts, C. (2015). Prevention of violence against women and girls: what does the evidence say? *The Lancet*, 385(9977), 1555–1566.

Fang, X., Brown, D. S., Florence, C. S., & Mercy, J. A. (2012). The economic burden of child maltreatment in the United States and implications for prevention. *Child Abuse & Neglect*, 36, 156–165.

Fang, X., Fry, D., Brown, D., Mercy, J., Dunne, M., Butchart, A., ... & Swales, D. (2015). The burden of child maltreatment in the East Asia and Western Pacific region. *Child Abuse and Neglect*, 42, 146–162.

Felitti, V. J., Anda, R. F., Nordenberg, D., Williamson, D. F., Spitz, A. M., Edwards, V., ... & Marks, J. S. (1998). Relationship of childhood abuse and household dysfunction to many of the leading causes of death in adults. The Adverse Childhood Experiences (ACE) Study. *American Journal of Preventive Medicine*, 14(4), 245–258.

Fearon, J. & Hoeffler, A. (2014). *Post-2015 Consensus: Conflict and Violence Assessment*. Copenhagen: Copenhagen Consensus Centre.

Fitterer, J. L., Nelson, T. A., & Stockwell, T. (2015). A review of existing studies reporting the negative effects of alcohol access and positive effects of alcohol control policies on interpersonal violence. *Frontiers in Public Health*, 3(253), 1–11.

Florence, C., Shepherd, J., Brennan, I., & Simon, T. (2014). An economic evaluation of anonymized information sharing in a partnership between health services, police and local government for preventing violence-related injury. *Injury Prevention*, 20(2), 108–114.

Florence, C., Shepherd, J., Brennan, I., & Simon, T. (2011). Effectiveness of anonymised information sharing and use in health service, police, and local government partnership for preventing violence related injury: experimental study and time series analysis. *British Medical Journal*, 342, 1–9.

Foshee, V. A., Bauman, K. E., Ennett, S. T., Linder, G. F., Benefield, T., & Suchindran, C. (2004). Assessing the long-term effects of the Safe Dates program and a booster in preventing and reducing adolescent dating violence victimization and perpetration. *American Journal of Public Health*, 94(4), 619–624.

Foshee, V. A., McNaughton Reyes, L., Tharp, A. T., Chang, L. Y., Ennett, S. T., Simon, T. R., ... & Suchindran, C. (2015). Shared longitudinal predictors of physical peer and dating violence. *Journal of Adolescent Health*, 56(1), 106–112.

Foshee, V. A., Reyes, L. M., Agnew-Brune, C. B., Simon, T. R., Vagi, K. J., Lee, R. D., & Suchindran, C. (2014). The effects of the evidence-based Safe Dates dating abuse prevention program on other youth violence outcomes. *Prevention Science*, 15(6), 907–916.

Furlong, M., McGilloway, S., Bywater, T., Hutchings, J., Smith, S. M., & Donnelly, M. (2013). Cochrane review: behavioral and cognitive-behavioral group-based parenting programs for early-onset conduct problems in children aged 3 to 12 years. *Evidence-Based*

Child Health: A Cochrane Review Journal, 8(2), 318–692.

Garbarino, J. & Crouter, A. (1978). Defining the community context for parent-child relations: the correlates of child maltreatment. Child Development, 49(3), 604–616.

Garcia-Moreno, C., Jansen, H., Watts, C., Ellsberg, M., Heise, L., & Country Research Teams. (2005). WHO Multi-Country Study on Women's Health and Domestic Violence Against Women. Geneva, World Health Organization.

Gardner, F., Montgomery, P., & Knerr, W. (2015). Transporting evidence-based parenting programs for child problem behavior (age 3–10) between countries: systematic review and meta-analysis. Journal of Clinical Child & Adolescent Psychology, 53, 1–14.

Gill, C., Weisburd, D., Telep, C. W., Vitter, Z., & Bennett, T. (2014). Community-oriented policing to reduce crime, disorder and fear and increase satisfaction and legitimacy among citizens: a systematic review. Journal of Experimental Criminology, 10(4), 399–428.

Global Partnership to End Violence Against Children. (2016). Retrieved June, 2016 from www.end-violence.org.

Goodman, R. M., Speers, M. A., McLeroy, K., Fawcett, S., Kegler, M., Parker, E., ... & Wallerstein, N. (1998). Identifying and defining the dimensions of community capacity to provide a basis for measurement. Health Education & Behavior, 25(3), 258–278.

Graham, I. D., Logan, J., Harrison, M. B., Straus, S. E., Tetroe, J., Caswell, W., & Robinson, N. (2006). Lost in knowledge translation: time for a map? Journal of Continuing Education in the Health Professions, 26(1), 13–24.

Hamby, S. & Grych, J. (2013). The Web of Violence: Exploring Connections Among Different Forms of Interpersonal Violence and Abuse. New York: Springer Briefs in Sociology.

Hahn, R., Fuqua-Whitley, D., Wethington, H., Lowy, J., Crosby, A., Fullilove, M., Johnson, R., Liberman, A., Moscicki, E., Price, L., Snyder, S., Tuma, F., Cory, S., Stone, G., Mukhopadhaya, K., Chattopadhyay, S., Dahlberg, L., & Task Force on Community Preventive Services (2007). Effectiveness of universal school-based programs to prevent violent and aggressive behavior: A systematic review. American Journal of Preventive Medicine, 33(2), S114–S129.

Hart, H. & Rubia, K. (2012). Neuroimaging of child abuse: a critical review. Frontiers in Human Neuroscience, 6, 52.

Hegarty, K., O'Doherty, L., Taft, A., Chondros, P., Brown, S., Valpied, J., Astbury, J., Taket, A., Gold, L., Feder, G. & Gunn, J. (2013). Screening and counselling in the primary care setting for women who have experienced intimate partner violence (WEAVE): a cluster randomized controlled trial. The Lancet, 382(9888), 249–258.

Heise, L. (1998). Violence against women: An integrated, ecological framework. Violence Against Women, 4(3), 262–290.

Hillis, S., Mercy, J., Amobi, A., & Kress, H. (2016). Global prevalence of past-year violence against children: a systematic review and minimum estimates. Pediatrics, 137(3), 1–13.

Hughes, K., Bellis, M. A., Hardcastle, K. A., Butchart, A., Dahlberg, L. L., Mercy, J. A., & Mikton, C. (2014). Global development and diffusion of outcome evaluation research for interpersonal and self-directed violence prevention from 2007–2013: a systematic review. Aggression and Violent Behavior, 19(6), 655–662.

Johannesen, M. & LoGiudice, D. (2013). Elder abuse: a systematic review of risk factors in community-dwelling elders. Age and Ageing, 42(3), 292–298.

Kostadinov, I., Daniel, M., Stanley, L., Gancia, A., & Cargo, M. (2015). A systematic review of community readiness tool applications: implications for reporting. International Journal of Environmental Research in Public Health, 12(4), 3453–3468.

Katz, J. & Moore, J. (2013). Bystander education training for campus sexual assault prevention: an initial meta-analysis. *Violence and Victims*, 28(6), 1054–1067.

Knerr, W., Gardner, F., & Cluver, L. (2013). Improving positive parenting skills and reducing harsh and abusive parenting in low- and middle-income countries: a systematic review. *Prevention Science*, 14(4), 352–363.

Krug, E. G., Dahlberg, L. L., Mercy, J. A., Zwi, A. B., & Lozano R. (Eds) 2002. *World Report on Violence and Health*. Geneva, Switzerland: World Health Organization.

Leeb, T. R., Lewis, T., & Zolotor, A. J. (2011). A review of physical and mental health consequences of child abuse and neglect and implications for practice. *American Journal of Lifestyle Medicine*, 5(5), 454–468.

Lipsey, M., Landenberger, N. A., & Wilson, S. J. (2007). Effects of cognitive-behavioral programs for criminal offenders: a systematic review. *Campbell Systematic Reviews*, 3(6).

Litschge, C. M., Vaughn, M. G., & McCrea, C. (2010). The empirical status of treatments for children and youth with conduct problems: an overview of meta-analytic studies. *Research on Social Work Practice*, 20(1), 21–35.

MacMillan, H. L., Wathen, C. N., Barlow, J., Fergusson, D. M., Leventhal, J. M., & Taussig, H. N. (2009). Interventions to prevent child maltreatment and associated impairment. *The Lancet*, 373(9659), 250–266.

Matjasko, J. L., Vivolo-Kantor, A. M., Massetti, G. M., Holland, K. M., Holt, M. K., & Cruz, J. D. (2012). A systematic meta-review of evaluations of youth violence prevention programs: common and divergent findings from 25 years of meta-analyses and systematic reviews. *Aggression and Violent Behavior*, 17(6), 540–552.

MacDonald, J., Golinelli, D., Stokes, R. J., & Bluthenthal, R. (2010). The effect of business improvement districts on the incidence of violent crimes. *Injury Prevention*, 16(5), 327–332.

McDowell, I. (2008). From risk factors to explanation in public health. *Journal of Public Health*, 30(3), 219–223.

Meinck, F., Cluver, L. D., Boyes, M. E., & Mhlongo, E. L. (2015). Risk and protective factors for physical and sexual abuse of children and adolescents in Africa: a review and implications for practice. *Trauma, Violence, & Abuse*, 16(1), 81–107.

Mercy, J. A., Rosenberg, M. L., Powell, K. E., Broome, C. V., & Roper, W. L. (1993). Public health policy for preventing violence. *Health Affairs*, 12(4), 7–29.

Mercy, J. A., Hillis, S. D., Butchart, A., Bellis, M. A., Ward, C. L., Fang, X., & Rosenberg, M. (2017). Interpersonal violence: global impact and paths to prevention. In Mock, C. N., Nugent, R., Kobusingye, O., & Smith, K. R. (Eds), *Injury Prevention and Environmental Health. Disease Control Priorities*, Third Edition (Vol. 7, pp. 71–96). Washington, DC: The World Bank Group.

Mikton, C. (2012). Technical report on the assessment of readiness to implement evidence-based child maltreatment prevention programmes of Brazil, the Former Yugoslav Republic of Macedonia, Malaysia, Saudi Arabia, and South Africa. Geneva: World Health Organization.

Mikton, C., Butchart, A., Dahlberg, L. L., & Krug, E. (2016). Global status report on violence prevention. *American Journal of Preventive Medicine*, 50(5), 652–659.

Mikton, C., Mehra, R., Butchart, A., Addiss, D., Almuneef, M., Cardia, N., ... & Raleva, M. (2011). A mulitdimensional model for child maltreatment prevention readiness in low- and middle-income countries. *Journal of Community Psychology*, 39(7), 826–843.

Mikton, C., Power, M., Raleva, M., Makoae, M., Al Eissa, M., Cheah, I., ... & Almuneef, M. (2013). The assessment of the readiness of five countries to implement child maltreatment prevention programs on a large scale. *Child Abuse & Neglect*, 37(12), 1237–1251.

Milaniak, I. & Widom, C. S. (2015). Does child abuse and neglect increase risk for perpetration of violence inside and outside the home? *Psychology of Violence*, 5(3), 246–255.

Miller, G. E., Chen, E., & Parker, K. J. (2011). Psychological stress in childhood and susceptibility to the chronic diseases of aging: moving toward a model of behavioral and biological mechanisms. *Psychological Bulletin*, 137(6), 959–997.

Mitton, C., Adair, C. E., McKenzie, E., Patten, S. B., & Perry, B. W. (2007). Knowledge transfer and exchange: review and synthesis of the literature. *Milbank Quarterly*, 85(4), 729–768.

Danese, A., Moffitt, T. E., Harrington, H., Milne, B. J., Polanczyk, G., Pariante, C. M., Poulton, R., & Caspi, A. (2009). Adverse childhood experiences and adult risk factors for age-related disease: depression, inflammation, and clustering of metabolic risk markers. *Archives of Pediatric and Adolescent Medicine*, 163(12), 1135–1143.

Norman, R. E., Byambaa, M., De, R., Butchart, A., Scott, J., & Vos, T. (2012). The long-term health consequences of child physical abuse, emotional abuse and neglect: a systematic review and meta-analysis. *PLoS Medicine*, 9(11), 42–44.

Ogden, T., Forgatch, M., Askeland, E., Patterson, G., & Bullock, B. (2005). Implementation of parent management training at the national level: the case of Norway. *Journal of Social Work Practice*, 19(3), 317–329.

Osterman, K., Bjorkqvist, K., & Wahlbeck, K. (2014). Twenty eight years after the complete ban on physical punishment of children in Finland: trends and psychosocial concomitants. *Aggressive Behavior*, 40(6), 568–581.

Pearce, N. (1996). Traditional epidemiology, modern epidemiology, and public health. *American Journal of Public Health*, 86(5), 678–683.

Pentland, D., Forsyth, K., Maciver, D., Walsh, M., Murray, R., Irvine, L., & Sikora, S. (2011). Key characteristics of knowledge transfer and exchange in healthcare: integrative literature review. *Journal of Advanced Nursing*, 67(7), 1408–1425.

Piquero A. R., Farrington, D. P., Welsh, B. C., Tremblay, R., & Jennings, W. G. (2009). Effects of family/parent training programs on antisocial behavior and delinquency. *Journal of Experimental Criminology*, 5(2), 83–120.

Pirkis, J., Too, L. S., Spittal, M. J., Krysinska, K., Robinson, J., & Cheung, Y. T. D. (2015). Interventions to reduce suicides at suicide hotspots: a systematic review and meta-analysis. *The Lancet Psychiatry*, 2(11), 994–1001.

Plested, B. A., Edwards, R. W., & Jumper-Thurman, P. (2006). *Community Readiness: A Handbook for Successful Change*. Fort Collins, CO: Tri-Ethnic Center for Prevention Research.

Plested, B. A., Edwards, R. W., & Jumper-Thurman, P. (2007). Disparities in community readiness for HIV/AIDS prevention. *Substance Use & Misuse*, 42(4), 729–739.

Polanin, J. R., Espelage, D. L., & Pigott, T. D. (2012). A meta-analysis of school-based bullying prevention programs' effects on bystander intervention behavior. *School Psychology Review*, 41(1), 47–65.

Powell, K. E., Mercy, J. A., Crosby, A. E., Dahlberg, L. L., & Simon, T. R. (1999). Public health models of violence and violence prevention. In: L. R. Kurtz (Ed.), *Encyclopedia of Violence, Peace, and Conflict* (pp. 175–187). San Diego, CA: Academic Press.

Purtle, J., Corbin, T. J., Rich, L. J., & Rich, J. A. (2015). Hospitals as a locus for violence intervention. In P. D. Donnelly & C. L. Ward (Eds), *Oxford Textbook of Violence Prevention: Epidemiology, Evidence, and Policy* (pp. 231–238). Oxford: Oxford University Press.

Salmivalli, C. (2014). Participant roles in bullying: how can peer bystanders be utilized in interventions? *Theory Into Practice*, 53(4), 286–292.

Sandler, I., Schoenfelder, E., Wolchik, S., & MacKinnon, D. (2011). Long-term impact of prevention programs to promote effective parenting: lasting effects but uncertain processes. *Annual Review of Psychology*, 62, 299–329.

Santaella-Tenorio, J., Cerdá, M., Villaveces, A., & Galea, S. (2016). What do we know about the association between firearm legislation and firearm-related injuries? *Epidemiologic Reviews*, 38(1), 140–157.

Sawyer, A. M. & Borduin, C. M. (2011). Effects of Multisystemic Therapy through midlife: a 21.9-year follow-up to a randomized clinical trial with serious and violent juvenile offenders. *Journal of Consulting and Clinical Psychology*, 79(5), 643–652.

Schiamberg, L. B. & Gans, D. (1999). An ecological framework for contextual risk factors in elder abuse by adult children. *Journal of Elder Abuse and Neglect*, 11(1), 79–103.

Schilling, E. A., Aseltine, R. H., Jr. & James, A. (2016). The SOS Suicide Prevention Program: further evidence of efficacy and effectiveness. *Prevention Science*, 17(2), 157–166.

Shonkoff, J. P, & Phillips, D. A. (Eds) (2000). *From Neurons to Neighborhoods: The Science of Early Childhood Development*. National Research Council and Institute of Medicine. Washington, DC: National Academy Press.

Sivarajasingam, V., Page, N., Wells, J., Morgan, P., Matthews, K., Moore, S., & Shepherd, J. (2016). Trends in violence in England and Wales 2010–2014. *Journal of Epidemiology and Community Health*, 70(6), 616–621.

Sliwa, S., Goldberg, J. P., Clark, V., Junot, B., Nahar, E., Nelson, M. E., ... & Hyatt, R. R. (2011). Using the Community Readiness Model to select communities for a community-wide obesity prevention intervention. *Prevention of Chronic Disease*, 8(6), A150.

Spoth, R., Rohrbach, L. A., Greenberg, M., Leaf, P., Brown, C. H., Fagan, A., ... & Society for Prevention Research Type 2 Translational Task Force Members and Contributing Authors (2013). Addressing core challenges for the next generation of type 2 translation research and systems: the translation science to population impact (TSci Impact) framework. *Prevention Science*, 14(4), 319–351.

Spoth, R. L., Trudeau, L. S., Redmond, C. R., Shin, C., Greenberg, M. T., Feinberg, M. E., & Hyun, G. (2015). PROSPER partnership delivery system: effects on adolescent conduct problem behavior outcomes through 6.5 years past baseline. *Journal of Adolescence*, 45, 44–55.

Stoltenborgh, M., Bakermans-Kranenburg, M. J., Alink, L. R., & Ijzendoorn, M. H. (2015). The prevalence of child maltreatment across the globe: review of a series of meta-analyses. *Child Abuse Review*, 24(1), 37–50.

Stoltenborgh, M., Bakermans-Kranenburg, M. J., van Ijzendoorn, M. H., & Alink, L. R. A. (2013). Cultural-geographical differences in the occurrence of child physical abuse? A meta-analysis of global prevalence. *International Journal of Psychology*, 48(2), 81–94.

Stoltenborgh, M., van Ijzendoorn, M. H., Euser, E. M., & Bakermans-Kranenburg, M. J. (2011). A global perspective on child sexual abuse: meta-analysis of prevalence around the world. *Child Maltreatment*, 16(2), 79–101.

Suglia, S. F., Sapra, K. J., & Koenen, K. C. (2015). Violence and cardiovascular health: a systematic review. *American Journal of Preventive Medicine*, 48(2), 205–212.

Susser, M. (1998). Does risk factor epidemiology put epidemiology at risk? Peering into the future. *Journal of Epidemiology and Community Health*, 52(10), 608–611.

Sustainable Development Goals. (2016). Sustainable Development Knowledge Platform. Retrieved August, 2016 from https://sustainabledevelopment.un.org/.

Tolan, P. H. & Guerra, N. G. (1994). *What works in reducing adolescent violence: a empirical review of the field* (pp. 1–94). Boulder, CO: The Center for the Study and Prevention of Violence, Institute for Behavioral Sciences, University of Colorado.

Tolan, P. H., Henry, D. B., Schoeny, M. S., Lovegrove, P., & Nichols, E. (2014). Mentoring programs to affect delinquency and associated outcomes of youth at risk: a comprehensive meta-analytic review.

Ttofi, M. M. & Farrington, D. P. (2011). Effectiveness of school-based programs to reduce bullying: a systematic and meta-analytic review. *Journal of Experimental Criminology*, 7(1), 27–56.

Twardosz, S. & Lutzker, J. R. (2010). Child maltreatment and the developing brain: a review of neuroscience perspectives. *Aggression and Violent Behavior*, 15(1), 59–68.

UNWomen (2016). Retrieved June, 2016 from www.unwomen.org/en/what-we-do/ending-violence-against-women.

van der Stouwe, T., Asscher, J. J., Stams, G. J., Deković, M., & van der Laan, P. H. (2014). The effectiveness of Multisystemic Therapy (MST): a meta-analysis. *Clinical Psychology Review*, 34(6), 468–481.

Verma, R., Pulerwitz, J., Mahendra, V., Khandekar, S., Singh, A., Das, S., ... & Barker, G. (2008). *Promoting gender equity as a strategy to reduce HIV risk and gender-based violence among young men in India*. Washington, DC: Population Council.

Vyas, S. & Watts C. (2009). How does economic empowerment affect women's risk of intimate partner violence in low- and middle-income countries? A systematic review of published evidence. *Journal of International Development*, 21(5), 577–602.

Wagenaar, A. C., Tobler, A. L., & Komro, K. A. (2010). Effects of alcohol tax and price policies on morbidity and mortality: a systematic review. *American Journal of Public Health*, 100(11), 2270–2278.

Wagner, D. V., Borduin, C. M., Sawyer, A. M., & Dopp, A. R. (2014). Long-term prevention of criminality in siblings of serious and violent juvenile offenders: a 25-year follow-up to a randomized clinical trial of Multisystemic Therapy. *Journal of Consulting and Clinical Psychology*, 82(3), 492–499.

Walters, R. H. & Parke, R. D. (1964). Social motivation, dependency, and susceptibility to social influence. In L. Berkowitz (Ed.), *Advances in Experimental Social Psychology* (Vol. 1, pp. 231–276). New York: Academic Press.

Wandersman, A, Duffy, J., Flaspohler, P., Noonan, R., Lubell, K., Stillman, L., ... & Saul, J. (2008). Bridging the gap between prevention research and practice: the interactive systems framework for dissemination and implementation. *American Journal of Community Psychology*, 41(3–4), 171–81.

Wasserman, D., Hoven, C. W., Wasserman, C., Wall, M., Eisenberg, R., Hadlaczky, G., et al. (2014). School-based suicide prevention programs: The SEYLE cluster-randomized, controlled trial. *The Lancet*, 385(9977), 1536–1544.

Wemrell, M., Merlo, J., Mulinari, S., & Hornborg, A. C. (2016). Contemporary epidemiology: a review of critical discussions within the discipline and a call for further dialogue with social theory. *Sociology Compass*, 10(2), 153–171.

Wethington, H. R., Hahn, R. A., Fuqua-Whitley, D. S., Sipe, T. A., Crosby, A. E., Johnson, R. L., ... & Task Force on Community Preventive Services. (2008). The effectiveness of interventions to reduce psychological harm from traumatic events among children and adolescents: a systematic review. *American Journal of Preventive Medicine*, 35(3), 287–313.

Whitaker, D. J., Baker, C. K., & Arias, I. (2007). Interventions to prevent intimate partner violence. In: L. Doll, S. Bonzo, D. Sleet, J. Mercy, & E. Hass (Eds), *Handbook of Injury and Violence Prevention* (pp. 183–201), New York: Springer.

Whitaker, D. J., Le, B., Karl, H. R., Baker, C. K., McMahon, P. M., Ryan, G., ... & Rice, D. D. (2008). Risk factors for the perpetration of child sexual abuse: a review and meta-analysis. *Child Abuse & Neglect*, 32(5), 529–548.

Wikström, P. O. H., & Sampson, R. J. (Eds) (2006). *The Explanation of Crime: Context, Mechanisms and Development*. Cambridge: Cambridge University Press.

Wilson, N., Tsao, B., Hertz, M., Davis, R., & Klevens J. (2014). *Connecting the Dots: An Overview of the Links Among Multiple Forms of Violence*. National Center for Injury Prevention and Control, Centers for Disease Control and Prevention (Atlanta, GA) and Prevention Institute, Oakland CA.

Wilson, S. J. & Lipsey, M. W. (2007). School-based interventions for aggressive and disruptive behavior: update of a meta-analysis. *American Journal of Preventive Medicine*, 33(2), S130–S143.

Wolfe, D. A., Wekerle, C., Scott, K., Straatman, A. L., Grasley, C., & Reitzel-Jaffe, D. (2003). Dating violence prevention with at-risk youth: a controlled outcome evaluation. *Journal of Consulting and Clinical Psychology*, 71(2), 279–291.

Wolfe, D. A., Crooks, C., Jaffe, P., Chiodo, D., Hughes, R., Ellis, W., ... & Donner, A. (2009). A school-based program to prevent adolescent dating violence: a cluster randomized trial. *Archives of Pediatrics & Adolescent Medicine*, 163(8), 692–699.

World Bank. (2013). *A Study of Gender and Human Rights-Based Approaches in Development*. Retrieved June, 2016 from http://siteresources.worldbank.org/PROJECTS/Resources/40940-1331068268558/Report_of_Gender_and_HumanRightsApproaches.pdf.

World Health Assembly. (2016). *Resolution 69.5. WHO global plan of action on strengthening the role of the health system within a national multisectoral response to address interpersonal violence, in particular against women and girls, and against children*. Geneva: World Health Assembly. Retrieved August, 2016 from http://apps.who.int/gb/e/e_wha69.html.

World Health Organization. (1996). *Violence: A Public Health Priority*. WHO Global Consultation on Violence and Health (Document WHO/EHA/SPI.POA.2). Geneva, Switzerland: World Health Organization.

World Health Organization. (2008). *Manual for Estimating the Economic Costs of Injuries Due to Interpersonal and Self-Directed Violence*. Geneva: World Health Organization.

World Health Organization. (2009). *Violence Prevention: The Evidence*. Geneva: World Health Organization.

World Health Organization. (2010). *Preventing Intimate Partner and Sexual Violence Against Women: Taking Action and Generating Evidence*. Geneva: World Health Organization.

World Health Organization. (2011). *European Report on Preventing Elder Maltreatment*. Rome, Regional Office for Europe, World Health Organization.

World Health Organization. (2012). *Global, Regional and Country-Level Cause-Specific Mortality Estimates,* WHO Global Burden of Disease Statistics. Geneva: World Health Organization.

World Health Organization. (2013). *Global and Regional Estimates of Violence Against Women: Prevalence and Health Effects of Intimate Partner Violence and Non-Partner Sexual Violence*. Geneva: World Health Organization.

World Health Organization. (2014a). *Global Status Report on Violence Prevention 2014*. Geneva, World Health Organization, United Nations Development Programme, and United Nations Office on Drugs and Crime.

World Health Organization (2014b). *Preventing Suicide: A Global Imperative*. Geneva: World Health Organization.

World Health Organization. (2015). *Preventing Youth Violence: An Overview of the Evidence*. Geneva, World Health Organization.

World Health Organization. (2016a). *Readiness Assessment for the Prevention of Child Maltreatment (RAP-CM)*. Retrieved August, 2016 from http://www.who.int/violence_injury_prevention/violence/child/cmp_readiness/en/.

World Health Organization. (2016b). *INSPIRE: Seven Strategies For Ending*

Violence Against Children. Geneva: World Health Organization.

Wyman, P. A., Brown, C. H., LoMurray, M., Schmeelk-Cone, K., Petrova, M., Yu, Q., ... & Wang, W. (2010). An outcome evaluation of the Sources of Strength suicide prevention program delivered by adolescent peer leaders in high schools. *American Journal of Public Health*, 100(9), 1653–1661.

Yon, Y., Mikton, C. R, Gassoumis, Z. D., & Wilber, K. H. (2016). Elder abuse prevalence: a systematic review and meta-analysis. Submitted to *The Lancet*, July 2016.

Zolotor, A. J. & Puzia, M. E. (2010). Bans against corporal punishment: a systematic review of the laws, changes in attitudes and behaviors. *Child Abuse Review*, 19(4), 229–247.

33 Terrorism as a Form of Violence

Kevin R. Carriere, Georgia Garney, and Fathali M. Moghaddam

"Gilles Bouleau: The state of emergency is said to end on July the 26th. Can you confirm this information?

François Hollande: Yes ... I want to be very clear with the French people, we can not extend the state of emergency eternally! That would make no sense. That would mean we are no longer a Republic with a rule of law that applies in all circumstances." July 14, 2016. (Hollande, 2016b).

"In these circumstances, we must show an absolute vigilance and demonstrate our determination. Many measures have already been taken. Our legal weapons have been largely strengthened. But we must, since this is summer, once again increase our level of protection ... Finally, I have decided that the state of emergency that was supposed to end on July the 26th will be extended for 3 months. A draft law will be submitted to the Parliament by the end of next week." François Hollande, July 14, 2016 (Hollande, 2016a).

Introduction

On July 14, 2016, French President François Hollande sat in front of reporters and spoke about the current state of France (this event serves a purpose similar to the US President's annual "State of the Nation" address). Hollande reported on various issues – including the direction of the country, his choice of using a €10,000-a-month hairdresser, and the state of emergency in France. The entire country of France had been under this state of emergency since November 2015, when terrorist attacks in Paris took the lives of 130 people. The use of states of emergency in France is relatively rare. France has only called six states of emergency between 1955 and 2015, and only two of those have been within the French nation (Algeria and New Caledonia being the other four) (Laurent, 2015). In comparison, the USA has called 53 states of emergency between 1976 and 2014, with 30 active states of emergency not related to disasters of floods, tornadoes, or hurricanes (Korte, 2014).

The state of emergency grants the French government the authority to search any home at any time. The government can place any individual under house arrest, requiring them to check in with police regarding their location three times a day, and only leave their house under police escort. It provides authority to disband groups, close privately owned venues such as bars and theaters, and restrict access to any webpage (Loi n°2015-1501, 2016). The state of emergency was set to end after two weeks, but the French Senate voted 336 to 0 (with 12 abstentions) to extend the state of emergency for an additional three months in November (Severson, 2015), February (Loi n°2016–162, 2016), and again in May (Loi n°2016–62, 2016). France also expanded the power of their own Surveillance law (Loi n°2015–912, 2015) (comparable with the US Patriot Act) to give extreme surveillance power to their police officers in addition to intelligence agencies. The law allows wire-tapping, prohibits visiting terrorist websites for nonacademic purposes, and gives the government the authority to access all citizens' emails and browsing histories (Loi n°2016–731, 2016; Breeden, 2016).

Critics have condemned the French government's state of emergency implementation and its use of these "additional powers" as violations of human rights. In the first 14 days following the attacks, French authorities had searched over 1,600 premises and arrested 211 individuals (RFI, 2015) and by February these numbers had doubled (Human Rights Watch, 2016). Yet, while these numbers continued to increase, Amnesty International noted that only four cases of terrorism-related investigations were ever opened (Amnesty International, 2016). Those citizens who get placed under house arrest all have very similar, and strikingly sad, stories. For example, this is the story of Ayub:

> "Ayub," a Muslim who has been in France as a refugee for 10 years and lives with his wife and four children, said police raided his home on November 20, 2015, and placed him under house arrest on grounds of being a "radical" and collecting money to fund jihad in Syria, which he categorically denies.
> Ayub has a prosthetic leg and said that going to his local police station three times a day requires more physical exertion than his normal routine and results in serious physical pain. The order also forbids him from leaving the small town near Orleans where he lives and from leaving his home between 8 p.m. and 6 a.m. …
> Ayub takes extra medication to relieve the pain, causing abdominal bleeding for which he was admitted to the hospital. He also said that the walking had created chafing, also resulting in pain and discomfort. "I'm tired morally and physically and depressed because of this house arrest" (Human Rights Watch, 2016, p. 4–5).

By February 2016, citizens across the nation began to protest this continued state of emergency (De Roffignac, Pennetier, & Trompiz, 2016). In response, the French government began prohibiting certain individuals from engaging in protests and limiting their movement while protests were ongoing (Cross, 2016).

And yet, only a few hours after the interview, the state of emergency that Hollande had promised to end was actually extended. France had just suffered another horrific terrorist attack. In the town of Nice, a truck drove through a crowd gathered to celebrate Bastille Day, causing 77 casualties. As the world watched the news of the latest terrorist attack in disbelief, President Hollande spoke of extending of the state of emergency. In eight months, the policy had only led to the prosecution of four individuals for ties to terrorism after 3,200 searches (Amnesty International, 2016) and clearly failed to prevent another attack. Yet, President Hollande spoke of "increasing the level of protection" and "strengthening their legal weapons" in light of this tragedy. In the face of terror, France's leadership promised to increase restrictions of human rights – of movement, association, and speech – against their own people.

Violence from terrorism extends far beyond the thousands of lives lost at the hands of terrorists. Relative to the number of people annually killed in car crashes and by suicide (about 30,000 and 40,000 in the USA, respectively), the number of people killed in terrorist attacks each year in the USA is small, with only 36 deaths on US soil between 2004 and 2013 (LaFree, Dugan, & Miller, 2015). Although terrorism results in relatively small number of deaths, the devastation caused by terrorist attacks is profound in other ways – particularly in societies that are relatively open and democratic. Terrorist attacks change both our cognitions and actions. For example, prejudice and hate crimes increase after terrorist attacks. People also change their behavior to avoid future attacks, but sometimes with counterintuitive consequences. For example, more Americans travelled by car following September 11, dramatically increasing motor vehicle mortality and injury rates (Blalock, Kadiyali, & Simon, 2007). Most importantly, terrorist attacks lead to new government restrictions on civil liberties and basic freedoms.

In this chapter we shed new light on both terrorism and violence by examining the relationship between them. We begin by briefly exploring terrorism from a psychological perspective. Next, we examine varieties of violence first discussed by Galtung (1969), and seek to extend this typology through society's psychological reactions to terrorism. We end by arguing that the greatest threat posed by terrorism arises from our willingness to restrict basic freedoms and put aside democratic values for the sake of the goal of achieving stronger security.

Defining Terrorism

Terrorism is "politically motivated violence, perpetrated by individuals, groups, or state-sponsored agents, intended to instill feelings of terror and helplessness in a population in order to influence decision-making and to change behavior" (Moghaddam, 2005, p. 161).

According to this definition, terrorism has several components. First, terrorism is politically motivated violence. Terrorism is not a random act – such as a building collapsing due to structural deficiencies – but a violent action targeted to influence governmental policy. The target of terrorism may be a singular government – the attacks on abortion clinics by Reverend Michael Bray in the USA were committed in order to defend "unborn foetuses" against the US government that denied them protection (Juergensmeyer, 2000). Or the target may be multiple, "Western" governments – frequently cited as targets in attacks by Al Qaida and the Islamic State. Terrorism seeks policy change through various forms of violence, which we define as behavior intended to harm others or the self.

Terrorism comes in many forms, such as so-called "lone wolf" terrorists, who carry out terrorist acts as independent individuals. An example of a lone wolf terrorist is Theodore Kaczynski, better known across the USA as the "Unabomber." He used mail-bombing tactics across a period of 15 years with a demand to have his political manifesto published (Nacos, 2007). The strength of a lone wolf terrorist is that they are relatively harder to track – lacking the group membership, infrastructure, and breadth of more advanced organizations such as ISIS, Al Qaida, and Boko Haram. Their digital and manual "footprints" are harder to detect. They are able to operate out of their homes and garages, not attracting as much attention as larger criminal groups. While their isolation is a strength in regards to avoiding detection, it comes as a weakness when considering the reach and scope of their destruction. Their choice to work alone requires expertise in many areas – weapon design, planning, and execution, to name a few. The lack of division of labor for his or her plan restricts the complexity of a lone wolf terrorist attack.

Unlike a lone wolf, terrorists working in small groups or large organizations have specialized roles, such as networkers, cell managers, fund-raisers, sources of inspiration, technical experts, "fodder" (expendable cell members), local agitators and guides, and strategists (Moghaddam, 2006). These groups are able to create mass-mediated fear (Breckenridge & Zimbardo, 2006) through inciting a perception of vulnerability in the targeted population. The prevalence of terrorist threats is augmented because larger groups are able to create "cells" across the globe, operating in smaller hierarchies, and are capable of carrying out illicit activity on their own.

While many terrorist groups are funded through participation in crime, some groups find financial support through state-level entities as well. The Liberation Tigers of Tamil Eelam were funded in large part by the Indian government (Byman & Kreps, 2010) and research has shown that state-sponsored terrorist groups are more damaging and deadly than non-state-sponsored groups (Byman, 2005). State-sponsored terrorism should not be downplayed. State-sponsored terrorism attempts to hide under the cover of "freedom fighters." We disagree with the notion that one person's freedom fighter is another person's terrorist. The actions of a terrorist are clear and extend beyond the actions and means of an individual peacefully striving for social change. The number of participants, the support they receive, and the number of individuals harmed is not relevant when deciding what is terrorism. Accepting the idea that freedom fighters and terrorists are the same can risk allowing state-sponsored terrorism to continue unquestioned (c.f. Moghaddam, 2006).

The motives of a terrorist can widely vary. While some terrorists attack for religious motives – and research shows these groups are the most deadly (Hoffman, 1998) – others are motivated by political or national goals. The Irish Republican Army (IRA) used terrorism to push for Irish independence. The Earth Liberation Front, one of the leading domestic terrorist groups in the USA, attempts to change government policies through physical attacks. For example, members of the Earth Liberation Front set fire to a ski resort in Colorado in 1998, causing between $12,000,000 and $18,000,000 in damages, to push their environmental agenda (Leader & Probst, 2003). Along with the Animal Liberation Front, the Earth Liberation Front has been responsible for an estimated $43 million worth of damages between 1996 and 2002.

Current Research on Terrorism

In the previous section, we defined terrorism and noted variations in the targets of terrorism, types of terrorism, and motives of terrorists. In addition to exploring these differences, current research has attempted to better understand the cultural and contextual cues that a terrorist experiences on a daily basis, and what moves an individual from being a functional member of society to becoming a terrorist (Doosje, Moghaddam, Kruglanski, de Wolf, Mann, & Feddes, 2016; Moghaddam, 2006). This radicalization process of "citizen to terrorist" stems in part from perceptions of deprivation and unfair treatment. These psychological factors are key in predicting terrorism, and are in some contexts far more important than material conditions – research has found little to no correlation between economic factors and terrorism (Abadie, 2006). Famously, Osama bin Laden was a millionaire when he orchestrated the attacks of September 11 (Halliday, 2005).

While economic conditions do not influence the quantity of attackers, they do seem to influence at least the educational quality of attackers. In areas of high unemployment, terrorists are able to recruit better-educated suicide bombers, who are able to select more important bombing targets (Benmelech, Berrebi, & Klor, 2012). In some cases, recruits quickly escalate from coming to see the world in categorical "we are good – they are bad" terms, to becoming completely absorbed within a new terrorist group that accepts them, but from which they have little chance to escape (Moghaddam, 2005). Seeing the world from the terrorist's psychological point of view can assist us in understanding both why they enter a terrorist organization and why they find it so difficult to leave.

There is some debate about the impact of terrorism. Compared to wars without terrorism, wars that involve terrorist acts (such as attacking civilians to influence a wider audience, suicide bombings, or coercion) last longer. Compared to movements that do not involve terrorism, movements involving terrorism face greater resistance to their political objectives from governments (Fortna, 2015; Abrahms, 2012). The definition of "political objectives" is complex, but one of the major political objectives of terrorism is to damage democratic societies. Terrorist violence has increasingly targeted Western democracies (Lafree, Dugan, & Miller, 2015). In this chapter, we argue that direct acts of terrorist violence have resulted in democratic societies restricting their own freedoms and in this way weakening themselves.

Terrorism and Violence

In the previous section, we noted the rise in terrorism in democratic societies. The relationship between terrorism and violence is complex, because different types of violence are integral to this relationship. Terrorists are individually and collectively motivated by claims based primarily on structural violence: that national and international institutions have been designed to harm their group. Sometimes, this claim is based on institutions legitimizing direct violence against the terrorists. For example, Islamic terrorists have been motivated by the claim that international organizations, such as the United Nations (UN) and the North Atlantic Treaty Organization (NATO), legitimized (structural violence) the 2003 US-led invasion of Iraq, which resulted in the killing and displacement of millions of Muslims (direct violence).

Structural violence was also a motivating factor for Anders Behring Breivik, a radical Norwegian nationalist who detonated a bomb in Oslo, killing eight people, before shooting and killing 69 young participants at a summer camp on July 22, 2011. In his manifesto *2083: A European Declaration of Independence*, released hours before his deadly attack, Breivik made clear that the official laws and institutions of Norway and the European Union had inflicted harm (structural violence) on Christian, White, European culture, by failing to prevent an "Islamic invasion." Likewise, the attacks on the 1996 Olympics in Atlanta and the 2013 Boston Marathon were not targeted at sports or marathon races, but at the government and communities that "failed" the (terrorist) Eric Robert Rudolph, the Tsarnaev brothers, and their families (Spaaij & Hamm, 2015).

There is a clear pattern of terrorists with different ideologies feeling threatened by structural violence, particularly because of what they see to be unjust national and international authorities, acting on the basis of unjust laws. For example, on April 19, 1995, the white American terrorists Timothy McVeigh and Terry Nichols carried out a bomb attack against a federal government building in downtown Oklahoma City, killing 168 people and seriously injuring hundreds more. These attackers were part of a wave of "Patriotic" and "Christian" extremists, who see their own actions as "defensive" in the face of government "over-reach" and a "New World Order" prejudiced against their group (Durham, 1996). In response to perceived structural violence, terrorists attempt to inflict maximum psychological violence. They do this mainly by inflicting direct violence, in attacks involving bombings, shootings, knife attacks, and the like. The concept of terrorist violence is further examined below.

Etymology of Violence

The meaning of violence can vary across cultural contexts, and there are different systems of classifying types of violence. One influential system provides three different views on violence. The first view is known as the "wide view." From this "wide" view, violence can be typified by more than just physical aggression, but also instances of social injustice (Coady, 1986). In a wide view of violence, any direct or indirect harm to an individual or group is considered violent if it infringes on personal rights or freedom. The second type of definition is the "restricted view." This narrower definition seeks only to define direct physical injury (Coady, 1986). The third type of definition is known as "legitimist." This subset focuses on the legality of the use of violence by different actors as the foundation for what can be defined as violence (Coady, 1986). The legitimist definition of violence is considered the most narrow, as it is focused purely on whether or not the use of violence complies with legal norms. In this sense, force when used by an authority is legal and expected, whereas violence is seen as illegal and negative.

Recently there has been increasing interest in how cultures *experience and perceive* violence. This is a psychological understanding of violence, compared to the more philosophical and criminological conception of violence. In particular, Galtung's tripartite model of violence (Galtung, 1969, 1990) has had wide influence in the realms of both research and practice. Galtung's model incorporates the "wide view" of violence, while at the same time focusing attention on the contextual and culture characteristics that drive, promote, and enable violence.

Galtung's Typology of Violence

Any understanding of terrorism must address the types of violence *experienced* by people beyond just the traditional conception of physical or direct violence.

Galtung argues that violence is the phenomenon by which the actual *experiences* of a particular individual are suboptimal as compared to the potential realizations of a given situation or experience (Galtung, 1969). These discrepancies between actual and potential were proposed through a triangular model of violence. In this model, violence experienced by the people in a society can be viewed as direct, structural, or cultural.

Direct Violence

One of the primary forms of violence tackled by conflict resolution practitioners is that of direct violence, or when the means of realization of these potentials are not only withheld, but also flat-out destroyed (Galtung, 1969). Direct violence is therefore violence during which an actor physically harms another individual, similar to the narrow view of violence. Direct violence can be exemplified by sub-state violence perpetrated by guerrilla organizations and revolutionary movements, as well as forms of violence performed and encouraged by state-level actors. Instances of direct violence are frequently featured in the almost-daily cover stories of major media and news sources.

Individual terrorists and terrorist organizations have utilized direct violence as a means of achieving their political goals. Acts of violence used by terrorists range from bombings, to assaults, to assassinations, to hostage-taking. In recent years, terrorists have frequently used direct violence against populations across almost all of the continents. Midway through 2016 alone, more than 30 major terrorist attacks had occurred on five continents, with fatalities totaling to almost 2,000 (Dorell, 2016). The Global Terrorism Database has demonstrated that since the 1980s, fatalities and injuries related to terrorism has almost quadrupled, with the largest increase in fatalities occurring post-2010 (LaFree, Dugan, & Miller, 2015). Below we present a brief list of direct terrorist violence that took place in the first six months of 2016.

A Timeline of Direct Violence in the First Half of 2016

January 11, 2016: Iraq experienced a series of brutal attacks across three cities including Baghdad, Muqdadiyah, and Sharaban. In these attacks, over 132 people were killed or injured in bombings claimed by the Islamic State (Kalin, 2016).

February 11, 2016: over 70 people were killed in a double suicide bombing at a Nigerian Internally Displaced Person camp in the Borno state. The attack, claimed by Boko Haram, was perpetrated by two young girls. A third girl was arrested; fortunately she had refused to detonate her own suicide vest (Al-amin & Searcey, 2016).

February 17, 2016: A bombing in Ankara, Turkey, left at least 28 people dead and an additional 61 injured following the detonation of a car bomb. This instance of terrorism was primarily aimed at a number of passing military buses, yet civilians were also among the casualties (Bacon, 2016).

March 8, 2016: a slew of stabbings occurred throughout Tel Aviv, Israel, as a young Palestinian man attacked bystanders, injuring 12 and killing 1. The attacker was a member of the Palestinian organization Hamas. This attack led to significant media coverage as the violence coincided with a state visit by the US Vice President, Joe Biden (Hadid, 2016).

March 22, 2016: Global violence continued as Brussels experienced a double attack in the bombing of the Zaventem airport and a metro stop in the city center (Wagner & Chappell, 2016). This attack left 32 people dead and 340 injured. The Maelbeek metro station bombing occurred in close proximity to United Nations, European Union, and European Commission offices.

June 12, 2016: A mass shooting occurred at Pulse Nightclub in Orlando, Florida. Considered the worst shooting attack on US soil, the massacre left 50 people dead and an additional 53 wounded (Alvarez & Pérez-Peña, 2016).

June 29, 2016: An attack in Istanbul at Ataturk Airport killed 41 people and wounded another 239. The attackers were nationals of the Caucasus region and claimed allegiance to the Islamic State (Karimi, Almasy, & Tuysuz, 2016).

July 1, 2016: An attack by gunmen in the diplomatic neighborhood of Dhaka, Bangladesh, led to the death of 28 restaurant-goers following a 12-hour standoff (Kumar & Moinuddin, 2016).

July 3, 2016: A suicide bombing in the Karada neighborhood of Baghdad, Iraq, killed over 200 people. The Islamic State claimed responsibility for the attack, which targeted a Shia neighborhood at the end of Ramadan (Tawfeeq, Sterling, Ap, & Alkhshali, 2016).

July 14, 2016: A truck driven into a celebrating crowd on Bastille Day in Nice, France killed 84 people. The truck was driven for over one mile along the Nice coastline. The Islamic State claimed responsibility for the attack (Birnbaum, Branigin, & Kaplan, 2016).

July 23, 2016: A manhunt occurred throughout the German city of Munich following the deadly shooting of nine people at a shopping center. The German attack is considered a "lone-wolf" terrorist incident (Callimachi, Eddy, & Jacobs, 2016).

July 23, 2016: the Islamic State claimed responsibility for a dual bombing in a Shi'ite Hazara-minority neighborhood in Kabul, Afghanistan. The attacks killed at least 80 people while injuring an additional 230. This was one of the most deadly attacks in Kabul since the 2001 US invasion (Harooni, 2016).

As this timeline demonstrates, direct violence perpetrated by terrorist organizations is not limited to a single country, continent, ethnic group, or organization. Direct violence has become an almost-daily occurrence across the globe as a tool to manipulate public opinion and political decisions.

Structural Violence

In addition to direct physical assault, violence can be inherent to societal structures. Structural violence can be measured by examining theoretically preventable losses that are attributed to power and resource differences (Weigert, 2008). In its essence, structural violence is primarily expressed through laws and institutions that perpetuate formal violence and unnecessary loss of life.

One of the main complexities of structural violence is its latent nature, making it far more difficult to combat and bring to an end. A single person being sexually assaulted is direct violence, but the continued existence and silence around human trafficking, commonly run by terrorist organizations, is structural violence. This silent form of violence victimizes the powerless and minimizes their agency. Structural violence appears everywhere, in the form of gender inequalities, racial prejudice, and economic injustices.

Structural violence is not as easily recognized as direct violence, but the effects of structural violence are potentially even more detrimental to society. The existence of Apartheid limited the movement, political participation, and general quality of life for millions of South Africans. The economic, psychological, and social damage done to the Black majority in South Africa was overwhelming and can still be felt today. The Jim Crow laws within the Southern USA provide another example of structural violence, which resulted in terrible injustices against African-Americans. Terrorists justify many of their motivations on claims of structural violence – the "West" brought and supported conflict to the Middle East (for example, through the 2003 US-led invasion of Iraq), which justifies their response of direct violence.

Cultural Violence

In addition to direct and structural violence, Galtung (1990) points to the importance of cultural violence, defined as the specific cultural aspects that can encourage direct or structural violence by normalizing exploitation and discrimination against others. The cultural components of a society, such as religion, beliefs, and art can be used to justify both structural and direct violence (Galtung, 1990). For example, in the case of structural violence, when a culture endorses belief in high social mobility – the ability to move in and out of social classes – the members of that culture are likely to be more accepting of discrimination and inequality (Kaufman, 2014). This occurs not only in the context of social mobility, but also economic mobility. Individuals who are led to believe there is economic mobility in their society are more willing to accept income inequality (Shariff, Wiwad, & Aknin, 2016). Belief in mobility (social or economic) allows individuals to divert the blame of inequality away from the culture and onto the victims, who are seen as "lazy" and "not trying hard enough." This diffusion of responsibility can lead to further violent action on the "lazy" victims.

Cultural violence at its heart primes individuals to believe in a normative system that justifies violence. It may be a politician reporting that any worker can rise to riches with hard effort. It may be the extremist readings of religious texts (which can also be interpreted to support peaceful actions) or the belief that "our society is justified to use violence to fight injustices against us by others." The media's glorification of violence allows sections of society to be comfortable with violent behavior and supportive of war, drugs, and other illicit activity. Or, it could be the priming of nationalism and the unification of in-groups against other out-groups. Palestinian citizens were more likely to support increases in violence against the Jewish people when they were primed to think of their own group (Pyszczynski et al., 2012). Thinking about our own group, compared to thinking about the global community, can lead us to be defensive, nervous, and scared. Cultural violence that evokes fear can have drastic consequences; we elaborate on this in the next section.

The Broader Violence of Terrorism

Galtung's tripartite model has helped researchers move towards a deeper understanding of violence and its structural and cultural roots. We argue that violence from terrorism is better understood using Galtung's model, but that it is also useful to give more importance to psychological experiences. In particular, we examine forms of psychological violence, defined as experiences and reactions of victims of terrorist attacks that directly or indirectly cause further damage in democratic societies.

Psychological Violence

The violence of terrorism has widespread impact at the psychological level, and we argue this is particularly important for democracies (Jaspal, Carriere, & Moghaddam, 2016). It is the goal of terrorists to incite fear, sow discord, and create moral panic (Walsh, 2016), and they do this through psychological violence, which is associated with all three types of violence outlined above. At the center of all types of violence are the subjective experiences and understandings of societies and individuals.

The damage of a terrorist attack is not limited to those physically injured or killed by the attack. On September 11, 2001, when the planes crashed into the World Trade Center, almost 3,000 were immediately killed. However, economists estimate that the number of deaths and injuries resulting from people switching from air to road transportation dwarfs the number directly resulting from the September 11 attacks (Blalock, Kadiyali, & Simon, 2007). As more individuals drove cars out of fear of terrorist attacks on aircrafts, more individuals died at the car wheel.

Psychological violence is dependent on the perceptions of both collectives and individuals and their understanding of group membership. Prior to September 11, many people did not fear or perceive themselves to be threatened by the risk of a terrorist attack. There was a lack of *threat salience* or *perceived threat*. Perceived threats can lead to collective action (van Zomeren, Postmes, & Spears, 2008) through enhanced group memberships and reminders of social identity. Citizens of Turkey who more strongly identified as Kurdish perceived higher threats from the Turkish majority and were more willing to take collective action to improve Kurdish well-being. The same trend was evident with respect to the behavior of the majority group (Turks) toward the minority (Kurds) (Çakal, Hewstone, Güler, & Heath, 2016). A related study found that the higher the perceived (not actual) size of an out-group minority, the more the majority saw the minority as a threat and supported exclusionary policies such as limiting economic, political, and human rights (Semyonov, Raijman, Yom Tov, & Schmidt, 2004). In US politics and media, the Syrian refugee crisis has caused quite a stir, even though the actual number of Syrian refugees the USA is accepting is extremely low (around 10,000 Syrian refugees have entered the USA, compared to over a million entering Germany). This high level of concern is probably because of the exaggerated perceived size of the Syrian refugee group entering the USA Instead of focusing on the refugees as "new Americans," politicians frame their identity as "non-American" and "potential terrorist," leading citizens to fear.

Researchers study "fear of terrorism" by asking questions such as "To what extent do you fear a future terrorist attack" or "To what extent do you fear a member of your family becoming a victim of terrorism" (for example, such questions were used by Fischer, Haslam, & Smith,

2010; Welch, 2016). Female citizens of the United Kingdom primed to think of their national identity reported higher perceived terrorist threat in response to images that threatened the nation compared to images that threatened their gender identity. Those who were primed to think of themselves in relation to their gender reported higher levels of terrorist threat when viewing images of Taliban misogyny compared to images of the London bombings (Fischer, Haslam, & Smith, 2010).

Experimental evidence shows that support for restrictions and exclusionary policies increases in response to terrorism. When individuals are led to believe there is a high probability of terrorist attacks, they support harsher punishments against petty crime (Fischer, Greitemeyer, Kastenmüller, Frey, & Oßwald, 2007). Related studies showed that fear of a loved one becoming a victim of a terrorist attack was positively associated with support for harsh methods to punish terrorism, including torture, wire-tapping, and withholding of rights (Huddy, Feldman, & Weber, 2007; Welch, 2016). Extreme examples of this process are found in Rwanda, where a culture of fear and threat from the Tutsi population built up for years before the Rwanda genocide took place (McDoom, 2012).

At the same time, fear of terrorism can lead to consequences that are unexpectedly positive. Individuals who are higher in terrorist threat have increased contact with their families (Goodwin, Willson, & Gaines, 2005), bringing society closer together. This unification after or leading up to a threat has important practical consequences, such as the significant increase in blood donations following a disaster (Glynn et al., 2003). Finally, some research has shown promise in reducing feelings of threat. Those who can understand why the perpetrators of a terrorist plot committed the crime report lower perceived terrorist threat (Fischer, Postmes, Koeppl, Conway, & Fredriksson, 2011). While the media can prime us to fear an out-group, knowledge and understanding can, under certain conditions, reduce that fear.

Of course, while terrorist threats can have some positive consequences, the negative consequences are far greater. In dealing with the September 11 attacks, Americans rallied together as "a nation." While this unifies us, it also can lead us to become inward-looking, adopt "us-vs.-them," overly simplistic rhetoric, and overestimate future attacks. Perceived threat from terrorism can divide us and lead us to reduce the freedoms of others in the name of security. In the following section, we further explore this threat to democratic values.

Intra-cultural Violence

Our argument is that in terrorist attacks, psychological and other forms of violence can surpass damage from direct physical violence. For example, the fear of being attacked has limited our freedoms and moved more power and resources out of the hands of ordinary citizens and into the hands of the government. This fear has changed the normative systems of the Western world, resulting in a weakening of our democratic values and principles. This is the most devastating violence that terrorism brings – shifting and promoting authoritarian values and systems in place of democracy.

Intra-cultural Violence: US Case Study

While the militarization of police departments in the USA has been increasing since the 1970s (in part because of a "war on drugs"), the increased presence and visibility of paramilitary police units has been attributed to the newfound "War on Terrorism," allowing a normalization and formalization of armed forces (Muzzatti, 2005). These units are being deployed at alarming rates – a 2,000% increase in deployments from 1986 to 1996 (Balko, 2013) and 90% of cities larger than 50,000 citizens having their own dedicated SWAT team (Kraska & Cubellis, 1997). Critics claim this new militarized state (Kraska & Cubellis, 1997; Kraska, 2007) is a serious challenge for democratic values in the face of terrorism, causing larger acceptance of a surveillance state. Recent estimates put SWAT teams being deployed at rates of 100 homes per day (Balko, 2013). As revealed by Edward Snowden and others, the National Security Agency (NSA) has been illegally collecting large amounts of data on US citizens, as well as the citizens of other nations around the globe (Greenwald, 2014) through wire-tapping, amassing emails, and more.

Through the leaks of Edward Snowden, the public has learned about some of the rights that have been trampled in the name of national security. The US government has granted itself the right to search any home without notice, wiretap onto any phone call, and monitor email messages, even for doctor-patient, attorney-client, or husband-wife relations (Whitehead & Aden, 2002). It seems that some Americans, at least, are willing to be spied on by their own government as a result of the risk of being the victims of an attack that is 50 times less likely than being struck by lightning (Silver, 2010). Unfortunately, we have learned that such "close government surveillance" does not always prevent terrorist attacks. The FBI reported that they were watching the 2016 Orlando nightclub shooter and the 2013 Boston Marathon bombers, yet the FBI and security services were still not able to prevent these terrible acts of violence. Even though government authorities have carried out extensive surveillance, it seems clear that the efficacy of these policies is questionable.

Increased government surveillance can lead to a weakening of American democracy by damaging relations between the community and the government. An example is what happened in Irvine, California, in 2010. A local mosque was so concerned with the disruptive actions of a man attending the mosque that they reported him to the FBI, only to discover that the man was an FBI informant. The informant reported he had been trained to entrap Muslims into making false statements (Markon, 2010). The trust of minorities has been further shaken by political races, in which recent presidential candidates are considering policies to deport all individuals of certain backgrounds and beliefs. Instead of moving towards a more open, accepting, actualized democracy, there is a possibility that we are moving further towards the other side of the spectrum – towards authoritarianism (Moghaddam, 2013).

Support is greater among right-wing authoritarians for greater restrictions on freedoms and stronger aggression against outgroups, and terrorism only further increases this support. In the lead-up to the invasion of Iraq, right-wing authoritarianism was predictive of support for the war, as well as the belief that Saddam Hussein was supporting terrorism (Crowson, Debacker, & Thoma, 2006). The populist anti-foreigner sentiment was also reflected by British exit from the European Union, and the rise of politicians such as Donald Trump in the USA, Norbert Hofer in Austria, and the DDP in Denmark. Conservatism in the USA has also been related to support for revenge against attackers and a willingness to restrict the civil liberties of visitors and citizens (Breckenridge & Moghaddam, 2012), and these unequal treatments were applied even when controlling for one's level of support for human rights (Abrams, Houston, Van de Vyer, & Vasiljevic, 2015). The effect of being constantly exposed to terrorist attacks in Israel over the past 20 years has led to deterioration in political tolerance (Getsmansky & Zeitzoff, 2014; Peffley, Hutchison, & Shamir, 2015).

Intra-cultural Violence: France Case Study

The limitations of freedoms in response to terrorism extend beyond the USA We see similar policies taking shape in Europe as well. In France, the Islamic population has reached well over six million, with 9.1% of French citizens reporting to be Muslim (Muslims in Europe, 2005). However, within this group, only about 1,500 to 2,000 individuals report that they wear the full veiled *burqa* (Wires, 2010). Even with such a low percentage of individuals reporting to wear the full *burqa,* in 2004, French law banned primary school students from wearing the veil (loi n°2004–228, 2004), and, in 2010, banned all concealments of the face in public (loi °2010-1192, 2010). Obviously, the target of this law was the Islamic *burqa.*

This negative targeting of Muslims can also be seen within the attitudes of the French population. In 2005, 78% of the French population said they were in favor of the banning of the veil (Morin & Horowitz, 2010), and by the time the law was passed in 2010, this number had increased to 82% (PEW Global, 2010). In 2005, twice the number of French citizens had an unfavorable view of Islam as compared to Judaism and Christianity, and this percentile increased from 34 to 38 unfavorable in just three years (PEW Global, 2008).

French Muslims have found little favor in either the government or public's eyes. A study conducted by the Open Society Foundation found that out of 32 Muslim veiled women, "thirty women stated that they had suffered some form of verbal abuse from members of the public, with 19 women out of 30 experiencing abuse 'often' or 'every time they left their house'" (Open Society Foundations, 2011, p. 19) as well as a few cases of physical abuse as well. This is not the first time the veil ban has been at the center of conflict. There have been peaceful protests (Chrisafis, 2011) as well as violent protests (Vinocur & John, 2013) against the new law, during which buildings have been set on fire and rocks have been thrown.

From the perspective of many people in Western countries, "veiled Muslim women are seen as oppressed, backward, illiterate ... in need of liberation" (Rosenbaum, 2013, p. 214) and the veil represents an "intolerable symbol of control over female sexuality" (Mullally, 2011, p. 35), oversimplifying a complex relationship between clothing, individuals, and identity (Klaus & Kassel, 2005). The role, functions, and consequences of the veil have been the center of heated debate. For certain individuals, the veil functions more than just a religious symbol. For example, it can be used as a form of resistance to Western domination, a way to visually withdraw from the public space, be flirtatious through not showing a lot, bring benefits in a society concerned about indecency and nudity, a way to be fashionable, and more (Rasmussen, 2013). Critics contend that by not considering the alternative meanings behind the veil, France has ignored the agency of the women who choose to wear the veil and removed their freedom of expression. According to John Dalhuisen of Amnesty International,

> A complete ban on the covering of the face would violate the rights to freedom of expression and religion of those women who wear the *burqa* or the *niqab* as an expression of their identity or beliefs (Amnesty International, 2010).

By banning the *hijab* in all public spaces, the French Government has banned all individuals who wear the *hijab* from entering the public space, restricting their freedom of movement under the guise of "security." This attempt to control the clothing worn by women is extremist and misguided, just as the dictatorial governments of Iran, Saudi Arabia, and other Muslim dictatorships are extremist and misguided to ban women from entering the public space without the veil. Women in all countries should be free to choose their own clothing, not be forced by governments to either wear or not wear the veil through legislation.

Conclusion

When we examine the violence resulting from terrorism, it is easy to get lost in the numbers of casualties and the horrific images repeatedly broadcasted by media outlets. Terrorism is so unexpected, so sudden, and so damaging that it increases our fears, magnifies our distrust, and forces us to face our own mortality. Yet, instead of facing these threats as we face other serious risks that are far more likely to kill – such as drink-driving, heart disease, and suicide – we resort to reducing the freedoms of entire populations, increasing divisions within our societies, and weakening our democracies. In the name of security, we allow mass surveillance through the Patriot Act and the NSA. But government agencies sometimes also go beyond what is legal, to carry out unwarranted searches and seizures, house arrests, and torture. When we change the fundamental values of who we are as psychological citizens engaging in the globalized world, we have given the terrorists exactly what they wanted. For the greatest impact of terrorism is not always in the initial terrorist action, but in the governmental reaction.

Acknowledgments

The authors would like to thank Constance de Saint Laurent for her translations of the speeches of President François Hollande.

References

Abadie, A. (2006). Poverty, Political Freedom, and the Roots of Terrorism. *American Economic Review*, 96(2), 50–56.

Abrahms, M. (2012). The Political Effectiveness of Terrorism Revisited. *Comparative Political Studies*, 45(3), 366–393.

Abrams, D., Houston, D. M., Vyver, J. V., & Vasiljevic, M. (2015). Equality hypocrisy, inconsistency, and prejudice: The unequal application of the universal human right to equality. Peace and Conflict: *Journal of Peace Psychology*, 21(1), 28–46.

Al-amin, U. S. & Searcey, D. (2016). Young Bombers Kill 58 at Nigerian Camp for

Those Fleeing Boko Haram. February 10, 2016. Retrieved August 1, 2016 from www.nytimes.com/2016/02/11/world/africa/suicide-bomber-girls-kill-58-in-nigerian-refugee-camp.html.

Alvarez, L. & Pérez-Peña, R. (2016). Orlando Gunman Attacks Gay Nightclub, Leaving 50 Dead. *New York Times*. June 12, 2016. Retrieved August 1, 2016 fromwww.nytimes.com/2016/06/13/us/orlando-nightclub-shooting.html?_r=0.

Amnesty International. (2010). *France: Votes to ban full-face veils* (press release). July 13, 2010. Retrieved August 1, 2016 from www.amnestyusa.org/news/press-releases/france-votes-to-ban-full-face-veils.

Amnesty International. (2016). *Upturned lives the disproportionate impact of france's state of emergency*. London, UK: Amnesty International Publications.

Bacon, J. (2016). Death Toll Rises to 28 in Turkish Car Bomb Blast. February 17, 2016. Retrieved August 1, 2016 from www.usatoday.com/story/news/world/2016/02/17/ankara-turkey-eplosion/80502062/.

Balko, R. (2013). *Rise of the warrior cop: The militarization of America's police forces*. New York: PublicAffairs.

Benmelech, E., Berrebi, C., & Klor, E. F. (2012). Economic Conditions and the Quality of Suicide Terrorism. *The Journal of Politics*, 74(1), 113–128.

Birnbaum, M., Branigin, W., & Kaplan, S. (2016). Truck Rams Bastille Day Crowd in Nice, France, Killing at least 84. July 15, 2016. Retrieved August 1, 2016 from www.washingtonpost.com/world/europe/truck-rams-bastille-day-crowd-in-southern-france/2016/07/14/18772ce6-4a0d-11e6-bdb9-701687974517_story.html.

Blalock, G., Kadiyali, V., & Simon, D. (2007). The Impact of Post-9/11 Airport Security Measures on the Demand for Air Travel. *The Journal of Law and Economics*, 50(4), 731–755.

Breckenridge, J. N. & Moghaddam, F. M. (2012). Globalization and a Conservative Dilemma: Economic Openness and Retributive Policies. *Journal of Social Issues*, 68(3), 559–570.

Breckenridge, J. N. & Zimbardo, P. G. (2006). The Strategy of Terrorism and the Psychology of Mass-Mediated Fear. In B. Bongar, L. M. Brown, L. E. Beutler, J. N. Breckenridge, & P. G. Zimbardo (Eds), *Psychology of Terrorism* (pp. 116–133). Oxford: Oxford University Press.

Breeden, A. (2016). French Authorities Given Broader Powers to Fight Terrorism. May 25, 2016. Retrieved August 1, 2016 from www.nytimes.com/2016/05/26/world/europe/france-terrorism-laws.html.

Byman, D. & Kreps, S. E. (2010). Agents of Destruction? Applying Principal-Agent Analysis to State-Sponsored Terrorism. *International Studies Perspectives*, 11(1), 1–18.

Byman, D. (2005). *Deadly connections: States that sponsor terrorism*. Cambridge: Cambridge University Press.

Çakal, H., Hewstone, M., Güler, M., & Heath, A. (2016). Predicting Support for Collective Action in the Conflict between Turks and Kurds: Perceived Threat as a Mediator of Intergroup Contact and Social Identity. *Group Processes & Intergroup Relations*, 19(6), 732–752.

Callimachi, R., Eddy, M., & Jacobs, A. (2016). Gunman in Munich Kills 9, Then Himself, the Police Say. July 22, 2016. Retrieved August 1, 2016 from www.nytimes.com/2016/07/23/world/europe/munich-mall.html.

Chrisafis, A. (2011). Muslim women protest on first day of France's face veil ban. April 11, 2011. Retrieved August 1, 2016 from www.theguardian.com/world/2011/apr/11/france-bans-burqa-and-niqab.

Coady, C. A. (1986). The Idea of Violence. *Journal of Applied Philosophy*, 3(1), 3–19.

Cross, T. (2016). France's state of emergency used to ban activists from labour law protests. May 16, 2016. Retrieved August 1, 2016 from http://en.rfi.fr/france/20160516-frances-state-emergency-used-ban-activists-labour-law-protests.

Crowson, H. M., Debacker, T. K., & Thoma, S. J. (2006). The Role of Authoritarianism, Perceived Threat, and Need for Closure or Structure in Predicting Post-9/11 Attitudes and Beliefs. *The Journal of Social Psychology*, 146(6), 733–750.

De Roffignac, H., Pennetier, M., & Trompiz, G. (2016). French protesters call for end to state of emergency. January 31, 2016. Retrieved August 1, 2016 from www.reuters.com/article/france-attacks-emergency-protests-idUSKCN0V9048.

Doosje, B., Moghaddam, F. M., Kruglanski, A. W., de Wolf, A., Mann, L., & Feddes, A. R. (2016). Terrorism, radicalization, and de-radicalization. (2016). *Current Opinion in Psychology*, 11, 79–84.

Dorell, O. (2016). 2016 already marred by nearly daily terror attacks. July 15, 2016. Retrieved August 1, 2016 from www.usatoday.com/story/news/world/2016/06/29/major-terrorist-attacks-year/86492692/.

Durham, M. (1996). Preparing for armageddon: Citizen militias, the patriot movement and the Oklahoma city bombing. *Terrorism and Political Violence*, 8(1), 65–79.

Fischer, P., Greitemeyer, T., Kastenmüller, A., Frey, D., & Oßwald, S. (2007). Terror salience and punishment: Does terror salience induce threat to social order? *Journal of Experimental Social Psychology*, 43(6), 964–971.

Fischer, P., Haslam, S. A., & Smith, L. (2010). "If you wrong us, shall we not revenge?" Social identity salience moderates support for retaliation in response to collective threat. *Group Dynamics: Theory, Research, and Practice*, 14(2), 143–150.

Fischer, P., Postmes, T., Koeppl, J., Conway, L., & Fredriksson, T. (2011). The Meaning of Collective Terrorist Threat: Understanding the Subjective Causes of Terrorism Reduces Its Negative Psychological Impact. *Journal of Interpersonal Violence*, 26(7), 1432–1445. doi: 10.1177/0886260510369137.

Fortna, V. P. (2015). Do Terrorists Win? Rebels' Use of Terrorism and Civil War Outcomes. *International Organization*, 69(03), 519–556.

Galtung, J. (1969). Violence, peace, and peace research. *Journal of Peace Research*, 6(3), 167–191.

Galtung, J. (1990). Cultural violence. *Journal of Peace Research*, 27(3), 291–305.

Glynn, S. A., Busch, M. P., Schreiber, G. B., Murphy, E. L., Wright, D. J., Tu, Y., & Kleinman, S. H. (2003). Effect of a National Disaster on Blood Supply and Safety. *The Journal of the American Medical Association*, 289(17), 2246–2253.

Goodwin, R., Willson, M., & Stanley, G. (2005). Terror threat perception and its consequences in contemporary Britain. *British Journal of Psychology*, 96(4), 389–406.

Greenwald, G. (2014). *No place to hide: Edward Snowden, the NSA, and the U.S. surveillance state*. New York: Metropolitan Books.

Hadid, D. (2016). American graduate student killed in stabbing rampage near Tel Aviv. Retrieved August 1, 2016 from https://www.nytimes.com/2016/03/09/world/middleeast/jaffa-israel-stabbing-attacks.html.

Halliday, F. (2005). *100 myths about the Middle East*. Berkeley, CA: University of California Press.

Harooni, M. (2016). Anger, mourning in Afghanistan after Kabul suicide attack. Retrieved August 1, 2016 from https://www.reuters.com/article/us-afghanistan-blast/anger-mourning-in-afghanistan-after-kabul-suicide-attack-idUSKCN1040E4.

Hoffman, B. (1998). *Inside terrorism*. New York: Columbia University Press.

Hollande, F. (2016a). *Déclaration à la suite des événements de Nice*. July 14, 2016. Speech presented at Déclaration à la suite des événements de Nice in France, Paris.

Hollande, F. (2016b). TV Interview with President François Hollande (Interview by G. Bouleau & D. Pujadas, Transcript). July 14, 2016. In *Entretien télévisé du 14 juillet*. Paris: Elysee.

Huddy, L., Feldman, S., & Weber, C. (2007). The Political Consequences of Perceived Threat and Felt Insecurity. *The ANNALS of the American Academy of Political and Social Science*, 614(1), 131–153.

Human Rights Watch. (2016). France: Abuses Under State of Emergency. February 3, 2016. Retrieved August 1, 2016 from www.hrw.org/news/2016/02/03/france-abuses-under-state-emergency.

Jaspal, R., Carriere, K. R., & Moghaddam, F. M. (2016). Bridging macro-, meso-, and microprocesses in social psychology. In J. Valsiner, G. Marsico, N. Chaudhary, T. Satō, & M. V. Dazzani (Eds), *Psychology as the science of human being: The Yokohama Manifesto* (Vol. 13, Annals of Theoretical Psychology, pp. 265–276). Cham, Switzerland: Springer.

Juergensmeyer, M. (2000). *Terror in the mind of God: The global rise of religious violence*. Berkeley, CA: University of California Press.

Kalin, S. (2016). At least 51 killed in attacks in Iraqi capital, eastern town. January 11, 2016. Retrieved August 1, 2016 from www.reuters.com/article/us-mideast-crisis-iraq-violence-idUSKCN0UP1R420160111.

Karimi, F., Almasy, S., & Tuysuz, G. (2016). ISIS leadership helped plan Istanbul attack, source says. June 20, 2016. Retrieved August 1, 2016 from www.cnn.com/2016/06/30/europe/turkey-istanbul-ataturk-airport-attack/.

Kaufman, A. (2014). Thinking Beyond Direct Violence. *International Journal of Middle East Studies*, 46(2), 441–444.

Klaus, E. & Kassel, S. (2005). The veil as a means of legitimization: An analysis of the interconnectedness of gender, media and war. *Journalism*, 6(3), 335–355.

Korte, G. (2014). Special report: America's perpetual state of emergency. October 23, 2014. Retrieved August 1, 2016 from www.usatoday.com/story/news/politics/2014/10/22/president-obama-states-of-emergency/16851775/.

Kraska, P. B. & Cubellis, L. J. (1997). Militarizing Mayberry and beyond: Making sense of American paramilitary policing. *Justice Quarterly*, 14(4), 607–629.

Kraska, P. B. (2007). Militarization and Policing – Its Relevance to 21st Century Police. *Policing*, 1(4), 501–513.

Kumar, N. & Moinuddin, A. K. (2016). Police End Siege in Bangladeshi Capital's Diplomatic Zone. July 1, 2016. Retrieved August 1, 2016 from http://time.com/4391961/bangladesh-capital-dhaka-hostages-diplomatic-zone/.

LaFree, G., Dugan, L., & Miller, E. (2015). *Putting terrorism in context: Lessons from the global terrorism database*. London: Routledge.

Laurent, O. (2015). Here's the Last Time France Declared a State of Emergency. November 13, 2015. Retrieved August 1, 2016 from http://time.com/4112625/france-state-of-emergency/.

Leader, S. H. & Probst, P. (2003). The Earth Liberation Front And Environmental Terrorism. *Terrorism and Political Violence*, 15(4), 37–58.

Loi n° 2004–228. (2004). Encadrant, en application du principe de laïcité, le port de signes ou de tenues manifestant une appartenance religieuse dans les écoles, collèges et lycées publics. March 15, 2004.

Loi n° 2010-1192. (2010). Loi interdisant la dissimulation du visage dans l'espace public. September 14, 2010.

Loi n° 2015–912. (2015). Relative au renseignement. July 24, 2015.

Loi n° 2015-1501. (2015). Prorogeant l'application de la loi n° 55–385 du 3 avril 1955 relative à l'état d'urgence et renforçant l'efficacité de ses dispositions (Loi n'appelant pas de décret d'application). November 20, 2015.

Loi n° 2016–162. (2016). Prorogeant l'application de la loi n° 55–385 du 3 avril 1955 relative à l'état d'urgence. February 19, 2016.

Loi n° 2016–629. (2016). Prorogeant l'application de la loi n° 55–385 du 3 avril 1955 relative à l'état d'urgence. May 20, 2016.

Loi n° 2016–731. (2016). renforçant la lutte contre le crime organisé, le terrorisme et leur financement, et améliorant l'efficacité et les garanties de la procédure pénale. June 3, 2016.

Markon, J. (2010). Mosque infiltration feeds Muslims' distrust of FBI. *Washington*

Post. December 5, 2010. Retrieved August 1, 2016 from www.washingtonpost.com/wp-dyn/content/article/2010/12/04/AR2010120403720.html.

McDoom, O. S. (2012). The Psychology of Threat in Intergroup Conflict: Emotions, Rationality, and Opportunity in the Rwandan Genocide. *International Security*, 37(2), 119–155.

Moghaddam, F. M. (2005). The Staircase to Terrorism: A Psychological Exploration. *American Psychologist*, 60(2), 161–169.

Moghaddam, F. M. (2006). *From the terrorists' point of view: What they experience and why they come to destroy*. Westport, CT: Praeger Security International.

Moghaddam, F. M. (2013). *The psychology of dictatorship*. Washington, DC: American Psychological Association.

Morin, R. & Horowitz, J. M. (2010). Europeans Debate the Scarf and the Veil. April 1, 2010. Retrieved from www.pewglobal.org/2006/11/20/europeans-debate-the-scarf-and-the-veil/.

Mullally, S. (2011). Civic Integration, Migrant Women and the Veil: At the Limits of Rights? *The Modern Law Review*, 74(1), 27–56.

Muslims in Europe: Country Guide. (2005). December 23, 2005. Retrieved August 1, 2016 from http://news.bbc.co.uk/2/hi/europe/4385768.stm.

Muzzatti, S. L. (2005). The Police, the Public, and the Post-Liberal Politics of Fear: Paramilitary Policing Post-9/11. In J. F. Hodgson & C. Orban (Eds), *Blue Culture and the Public: Paramilitary Policing Post-September 11th* (pp. 107–127). Monsey, NY: Criminal Justice Press.

Nacos, B. L. (2007). *Mass-mediated Terrorism: The central role of the media in terrorism and counterterrorism*. New York: Rowman & Littlefield.

Open Society Foundations. (2011). *Unveiling the truth: Why 32 Muslim Women Wear the Full-face Veil in France*. New York: Open Society Foundations.

Peffley, M., Hutchison, M. L., & Shamir, M. (2015). The Impact of Persistent Terrorism on Political Tolerance: Israel, 1980 to 2011. *American Political Science Review*, 109(4), 817–832.

PEW Global. (2008). Chapter 1. Views of Religious Groups. September 17, 2008. Retrieved June 1, 2016 from www.pewglobal.org/2008/09/17/chapter-1-views-of-religious-groups/.

PEW Global. (2010). Widespread Support For Banning Full Islamic Veil in Western Europe. July 8, 2010. Retrieved June 1, 2016 from www.pewglobal.org/2010/07/08/widespread-support-for-banning-full-islamic-veil-in-western-europe/.

Pyszczynski, T., Motyl, M., Vail, K. E., Hirschberger, G., Arndt, J., & Kesebir, P. (2012). Drawing attention to global climate change decreases support for war. *Peace and Conflict: Journal of Peace Psychology*, 18(4), 354–368.

Rasmussen, S. J. (2013). Re-casting the veil: Situated meanings of covering. *Culture & Psychology*, 19(2), 237–258.

RFI. (2015). France to opt out of European human rights convention because of Paris attacks. November 27, 2015. Retrieved June 1, 2016 from http://en.rfi.fr/europe/20151127-france-opt-out-european-human-rights-convention-because-paris-attacks.

Rosenbaum, P. J. (2013). The role of projective identification in constructing the "Other": Why do Westerners want to "liberate" Muslim women? *Culture & Psychology*, 19(2), 213–224.

Semyonov, M., Raijman, R., Tov, A. Y., & Schmidt, P. (2004). Population size, perceived threat, and exclusion: A multiple-indicators analysis of attitudes toward foreigners in Germany. *Social Science Research*, 33(4), 681–701.

Severson, D. (2015). *France's Extended State of Emergency: What New Powers Did the Government Get?* (Publication). November 22, 2015. Retrieved June 1, 2016 from www.lawfareblog.com/frances-extended-state-emergency-what-new-powers-did-government-get.

Shariff, A. F., Wiwad, D., & Aknin, L. B. (2016). Income Mobility Breeds Tolerance for Income Inequality: Cross-National and Experimental Evidence. *Perspectives on Psychological Science*, 11(3), 373–380.

Silver, N. (2010). Crunching the numbers. *Wall Street Journal*. January 8, 2010. Retrieved June 1, 2016 from www.wsj.com/articles/SB10001424052748703481004574646963713065116.

Spaaij, R. & Hamm, M. S. (2015). Endgame? Sports Events as Symbolic Targets in Lone Wolf Terrorism. *Studies in Conflict & Terrorism*, 38(12), 1022–1037.

Tawfeeq, M., Sterling, J., Ap, T., & Alkhshali, H. (2016). Bombing that killed more than 200 deadliest attack in Baghdad in years. July 4, 2016. Retrieved August 1, 2016 from www.cnn.com/2016/07/04/middleeast/baghdad-car-bombs/.

Van Zomeren, M., Postmes, T., & Spears, R. (2008). Towards an integrative social identity model of collective action: A quantitative research synthesis of three socio-psychological processes. *Psychological Bulletin*, 134(4), 504–535.

Vinocur, N. & John, M. (2013). Paris Riots: France Defends Veil Ban And Conduct Of Police During Violent Protests. June 22, 2013. Retrieved August 1, 2016 from www.huffingtonpost.com/2013/07/22/paris-riots-france-defends-veil-ban_n_3633692.html.

Wagner, L. & Chappell, B. (2016). Terrorist Bombings Strike Brussels: What We Know. March 22, 2016. Retrieved August 1, 2016 from www.npr.org/sections/thetwo-way/2016/03/22/471391497/what-we-know-terrorist-bombing-at-brussels-airport.

Walsh, J. P. (2016). Moral panics by design: The case of terrorism. *Current Sociology*, 1, 1–20.

Weigert, K. M. (2008). Structural Violence. In G. Fink (Ed.), *Stress of war, conflict and disaster* (pp. 126–133). Amsterdam: Academic Press.

Welch, K. (2016). Middle Eastern Terrorist Stereotypes and Anti-Terror Policy Support: The Effect of Perceived Minority Threat. *Race and Justice*, 6(2), 117–145.

Whitehead, J. W. & Aden, S. H. (2002). Forfeiting "Enduring Freedom" for "Homeland Security": A Constitutional Analysis of the USA Patriot Act and the Justice Department's Anti Terrorism Initiatives. *American University Law Review*, 51(6), 1081–1133.

Wires, N. (2010). French "burqa" ban passes last legal hurdle. October 7, 2010. Retrieved August 1, 2016 from www.france24.com/en/20101007-french-burqa-ban-passes-last-legal-hurdle-constitutional-council-veil.

34 Psychopharmacology of Violence

Jan Volavka and Leslie Citrome

Introduction

Many mental disorders are associated with elevated risk of violent behavior. This includes psychoses, disruptive, impulse-control, and conduct disorders, as well as substance use disorders. Many of these mental disorders are frequently observed to occur simultaneously, in various combinations, in individual patients. This is clinically diagnosed as comorbidity of separate disorders according to DSM-5, although there are shared genetic risks for major psychiatric disorders, substance abuse, and violent crime.

Most individuals with mental disorders are not violent, and persons with mental disorders are more likely to be the victims than the perpetrators of violent crimes. However, the evidence supporting the elevated risk of violence in such persons is robust. Much of the evidence was generated in studies of schizophrenia. A meta-analysis (Fazel, Gulati, Linsell, Geddes, & Grann, 2009) showed a two-fold increase of violence risk in schizophrenia without substance abuse comorbidity, and a nine-fold increase with that comorbidity. This latter increase must be seen in the context of the risk of substance abuse, which is approximately four times higher in persons with schizophrenia than in the general population.

In summary, violence in the mentally ill is a serious problem whose management is vitally important. Psychopharmacological treatment, in conjunction with psychosocial interventions, is the key management tool. The purpose of this chapter is to update and expand our previous reviews of this topic (Citrome & Volavka, 2014; Volavka, 2014) with particular focus on violence in psychoses.

Agitation, Aggression, Violence, and Hostility: Definitions and Measurement Methods

Agitation is characterized by excessive motor and/or verbal activity. It can escalate into aggressive behavior, and in its severe form represents a medical emergency requiring immediate treatment. Several rating scales have been developed for the quantitative assessment of agitation. These include the Behavioral Activity Rating Scale (BARS; Swift et al., 2002) and the Positive and Negative Syndrome Scale (PANSS) Excited Component (PEC). The PEC consists of the five PANSS (Kay et al., 1989) items that reflect excitement and agitation (Montoya et al., 2011).

Aggression is overt action, by humans or animals, intended to harm. Human aggression can be assessed quantitatively with rating scales such as The Overt Aggression Scale (OAS; Yudofsky et al., 1986) and its modification (Modified Overt Aggression Scale [MOAS; Kay et al., 1989; Kay et al., 1988]). These scales separately assess verbal aggression, physical aggression against objects, against self, and against others.

Aggressive behavior can be classified into subtypes. A widely used classification defines two subtypes: impulsive or premeditated aggression. Aggressive behavior in psychoses can have characteristics of impulsiveness or premeditation, and may be related to psychotic symptoms. Violence is defined as physical aggression among humans. The terms violence and aggression are sometimes used interchangeably. Violence perpetrated by psychiatric patients in the community can be assessed by the MacArthur Community Violence Interview (Steadman et al., 1998).

Hostility denotes unfriendly attitudes manifested by overt irritability, anger, resentment, or verbal aggression. The usual tool to assess hostility is the "hostility" item in the PANSS, rated from 1 (absent) to 7 (extreme). The principal clinical importance of hostility is its close association with violence. This association is highly statistically significant (Swanson et al., 2006). The association has led to a widespread use of hostility as a proxy measure of violence. Hostility is also associated with nonadherence to medication (Lindenmayer et al., 2009) and treatment discontinuation (Volavka et al., 2016).

Psychopharmacological Treatment of Agitation and Acute Violence

Agitation can be associated with a number of different mental disorders and requires rapid intervention in order to avoid escalation to aggression or violence (Zeller & Citrome, 2016). In addition to verbal de-escalation techniques (Richmond et al., 2012), psychopharmacological interventions are usually employed (Wilson et al., 2012). Ruling out somatic causes for an altered mental status is imperative in order to avoid missing life-threatening illness (Nordstrom et al., 2012).

Regulatory authorities have approved several different medications for the indication of agitation associated with schizophrenia and/or bipolar mania. These include rapid-acting intramuscular preparations of three different second-generation antipsychotics, ziprasidone 10–20 mg (Pfizer, 2016), olanzapine 10 mg (Eli Lilly, 2016), and aripiprazole 9.75 mg (Otsuka, 2016), as well as an inhaled preparation of a first-generation antipsychotic, loxapine 10 mg (Galen, 2017). The effect sizes for response, as measured by a 40% decrease on the PEC or equivalent at two hours after administration, are roughly equivalent among these choices, as well as when compared with haloperidol 6.5–7.5 mg or lorazepam 2 mg (Citrome, 2007, 2012). A substantial advantage to using the second-generation antipsychotics, as well as inhaled loxapine, is the relatively low rate of acute dystonic reactions or akathisia compared to what can be observed when using haloperidol.

Inhaled loxapine can result in a rapid decrease in agitation, with an effect superior to that observed with placebo as early as ten minutes post-administration. In the United States, concerns over pulmonary safety has restricted the use of inhaled loxapine in hospitals; patients need to be prescreened for the presence of pulmonary disease, as well as monitored for signs and symptoms of bronchospasm for one hour post-dose administration, as per a Food and Drug Administration-mandated Risk Evaluation and Mitigation Strategy (Citrome, 2013). An additional non-injectable alternative is sublingual asenapine 10 mg, where efficacy for agitation was evidenced in a single-site placebo-controlled study demonstrating an effect size comparable to that of injectable antipsychotics (Pratts et al., 2014). However, asenapine has not been specifically approved for this indication and its use would be "off-label." Nonetheless, noninvasive formulations, although requiring cooperation from patients, have the potential to improve overall patient experience, thereby improving future cooperation between patients and healthcare providers. Inhaled loxapine and sublingual asenapine represent reasonably rapid-acting options, in contrast to regular tablets and capsules of other antipsychotics where the time required to reach peak plasma concentrations is longer (Zeller & Citrome, 2016).

Antipsychotics are generally preferred over benzodiazepines in agitated persons with schizophrenia or bipolar mania, principally because antipsychotics address the patient's underlying psychopathology. However, if the initial dose does not control the agitation, the addition of a benzodiazepine is recommended over an increased dose of the same antipsychotic or addition of a second antipsychotic (Wilson et al., 2012). In the case of acute withdrawal from alcohol or benzodiazepines the preferred medication intervention is a benzodiazepine, of which lorazepam can be effectively administered orally or intramuscularly. Midazolam, another fast-acting benzodiazepine, has also been used in the emergency setting, and can be administered intranasally (Zedie, Amory, Wagner, & O'Hara, 1996). The main caveat regarding the use of lorazepam or midazolam is that they are used for sedation and have no antipsychotic effects; these agents will not be expected to ameliorate hallucinations or delusions, and will not treat the underlying psychosis that may be engendering the agitation.

Long-Term Treatment of Violence in Psychoses

Antipsychotics

Long-term treatment of violence in schizophrenia relies primarily on atypical antipsychotics. The next section provides an overview of randomized trials using various medications.

Clozapine is an effective drug to reduce aggression and hostility in schizophrenia. These effects were first demonstrated in numerous uncontrolled studies (Comai et al., 2012; Volavka, 2002; Volavka, Swanson, & Citrome, 2012) and confirmed in randomized controlled trials, which showed clozapine's superior efficacy in comparison with haloperidol against aggression (Krakowski et al., 2006; Volavka et al., 2004) and against hostility (Citrome et al., 2001). Clozapine showed superior antiaggressive effects in comparison with olanzapine in one randomized study (Krakowski et al., 2006), but no differences in efficacy between clozapine, risperidone, and olanzapine in another randomized study (Volavka et al., 2004). None or incomplete response to clozapine was observed during the dose escalation period, before the fully effective dose level was achieved.

Clozapine's antiaggressive effects in randomized studies were (statistically) independent of other positive symptoms of schizophrenia, as well as of its sedative effects, and in that sense they were specific. Finally, a large multinational observational study of schizophrenia patients (n = 7655) has demonstrated clozapine *inferiority* in reducing aggression in comparison with olanzapine and risperidone (the relative lack of effectiveness of clozapine may be specific to this study population and may be due in part to selection bias) (Bitter et al., 2005).

Thus, the preponderance of available evidence indicates that clozapine's effectiveness against aggression and hostility in schizophrenia is superior to other antipsychotics. This superiority is perhaps most pronounced in treatment-resistant schizophrenia (Frogley, Taylor, Dickens, & Picchioni, 2012), which is the indication for which it had been initially approved. Additional controlled studies with large numbers of various types of schizophrenia patients comparing clozapine with other antipsychotics are needed.

The main risk of clozapine is agranulocytosis, developing in approximately 1% of patients. The danger of agranulocytosis necessitates regular blood sampling to monitor white cell counts. This is a reason why some patients refuse clozapine treatment or discontinue it. Other adverse effects of clozapine include weight gain, metabolic abnormalities, seizures, and myocarditis. Thus, clozapine treatment is burdened with a risk of dangerous adverse effects, which may be one of the reasons why it is underutilized. In clinical decisions, the risks of adverse effects should be weighed against the risks of undertreated aggression. It should be noted that a large epidemiological study has demonstrated that clozapine treatment is associated with a lower mortality than any other antipsychotic (Tiihonen et al., 2009). Overall, clozapine is considered the treatment of choice for persistent aggression and hostility in schizophrenia and schizoaffective patients.

Olanzapine has demonstrated superior efficacy in comparison with typical antipsychotics against aggression (Krakowski et al., 2006) and hostility (Volavka et al., 2014; Volavka et al., 2011) in randomized studies. Comparisons with other second-generation (atypical) antipsychotics (except for clozapine) showed no significant differences from olanzapine's efficacy against aggression (Swanson et al., 2008a), but olanzapine was superior in efficacy against hostility for both first-episode patients with schizophrenia (Volavka et al., 2011) and those with more chronic illness (Volavka et al., 2014).

Olanzapine use is associated with weight gain and metabolic changes (Citrome, Holt, Walker, & Hoffmann, 2011); the risk of these adverse effects requires monitoring. Overall, olanzapine can be considered a second-choice treatment of persistent aggressive behavior in schizophrenia or schizoaffective disorder, suitable for patients who will not or cannot be treated with clozapine.

Risperidone was superior to placebo in reducing hostility in a randomized study (Czobor, Volavka, & Meibach, 1995), but inconsistent results were observed using other study designs enrolling more refractory patients (Beck et al., 1997; Buckley et al., 1997). Overall, risperidone efficacy against aggression was statistically indistinguishable from other atypicals tested in randomized studies.

Ziprasidone effect against hostility was superior to that of haloperidol only in the first week of a six-week, open-label study (Citrome et al., 2006), and its efficacy against aggression was indistinguishable from perphenazine, risperidone, olanzapine, and quetiapine in a randomized trial (Swanson et al., 2008a).

In the same trial, quetiapine efficacy against aggression was indistinguishable from that of risperidone, olanzapine, or ziprasidone, but inferior to that of perphenazine (Swanson et al., 2008). Comparisons in terms of efficacy against aggression or hostility with placebo were implemented in post-hoc analyses of randomized studies of aripiprazole, cariprazine, lurasidone, and quetiapine. Each of these analyses demonstrated superiority over placebo. In summary, atypical antipsychotics are effective against hostility and aggression in schizophrenia. The most effective among them is clozapine, followed by olanzapine.

Other Medications

Various medications have been employed to augment antiaggressive effects of antipsychotics, or as monotherapy. Adrenergic beta-blockers such as propranolol (Whitman, Maier, & Eichelman, 1987) and pindolol (Caspi et al., 2001) have shown promising results, but their adverse effects on blood pressure and pulse rate has limited their use. Anticonvulsants, particularly valproate, have been used in efforts to reduce aggressive behavior in psychoses and personality disorders, but a small randomized trial of risperidone alone compared with risperidone plus valproate showed no effect of valproate augmentation on hostility (Citrome et al., 2007), although a post-hoc analysis from a four-week randomized controlled trial demonstrated a signal for efficacy, particularly at the start of treatment when valproate was added to risperidone or olanzapine (Citrome et al., 2004). A Cochrane review of antiaggressive effects of four anticonvulsants did not result in any firm conclusions regarding the effectiveness of these compounds (Huband, Ferriter, Nathan, & Jones, 2010).

Limitations of Long-Term Psychopharmacological Treatment of Hostility and Aggression

Clozapine may be the most effective treatment of aggression and hostility in schizophrenia currently available, and yet many patients, perhaps as many as 50%, fail to respond to it. Some of those nonresponders whose aggressive behavior continues in spite of clozapine treatment are those with a history of conduct disorder and/or current comorbid antisocial personality disorder (Swanson et al., 2008b; Volavka, 2014). Assaults driven by an antisocial (psychopathic) personality factor have been detected in a prospective observational study of schizophrenia and schizoaffective inpatients (Nolan et al., 2003). In such patients, psychosis is apparently not the direct cause of hostility and aggression.

There are many other potential reasons for a failure to respond to psychopharmacological treatment. One of them is treatment nonadherence, which is well known to elevate the risk of aggressive behavior and relapse in schizophrenia (Alia-Klein, O'Rourke, Goldstein, & Malaspina, 2007; Volavka & Citrome, 2011). The link between hostility and nonadherence is discussed above in the section on Definitions. Long-acting injectable formulations of second-generation antipsychotics may be helpful in this regard (Citrome, 2013; Citrome et al., 2016).

Given the limitations of psychopharmacology, it is not surprising that standard psychiatric treatment programs relying only on pharmacological approaches have limited success in reducing recidivistic violent and criminal behaviors. Successful treatment must include a component dealing with comorbidities, particularly substance use and personality disorders. Various cognitive behavioral treatment programs were developed for recidivistic violent and criminal patients (Cullen et al., 2012; Haddock et al., 2009; Yates et al., 2010).

Conclusion

Several effective options exist for the acute treatment of agitation associated with psychoses, with intramuscular formulations of ziprasidone, olanzapine, and aripiprazole approved by regulatory authorities for this purpose. These agents have advantages over haloperidol in terms of avoiding acute dystonia or akathisia. Non-injectable alternatives include inhaled loxapine (also approved for this indication) and the off-label use of sublingual asenapine. Benzodiazepines also have a role in the acute management of agitation, particularly in instances of withdrawal from alcohol. Clozapine is the most effective long-term treatment for aggression and violence, followed by olanzapine and then other second-generation antipsychotics. However, the value of these treatments is somewhat limited by adverse effects, and particularly by our poor understanding of the causation of hostility and aggression.

Future directions should combine treatment studies with molecular genetic and epigenetic investigations, family history of mental illness and criminal and violent behavior, data on early trauma and adult victimization, history of conduct disorder, and careful personality assessment. Such interdisciplinary research will have the greatest chance of success if conducted in the framework of large longitudinal prospective cohort studies.

References

Alia-Klein, N., O'Rourke, T., Goldstein, R., & Malaspina, D. (2007). Insight into illness and adherence to psychotropic medications are separately associated with violence severity in a forensic sample. *Aggressive Behavior,* 33, 86–96.

Beck, N., Greenfield, S., Gotham, H., Menditto, A., Stuve, P., & Hemme, C. (1997). Risperidone in the management of violent, treatment-resistant schizophrenics hospitalized in a maximum security forensic facility. *Journal of the American Academy of Psychiatry and the Law,* 25, 461–468.

Bitter, I., Czobor, P., Dossenbach, M., & Volavka, J. (2005). Effectiveness of clozapine, olanzapine, quetiapine, risperidone, and haloperidol monotherapy in reducing hostile and aggressive behavior in outpatients treated for schizophrenia: a prospective naturalistic study (IC-SOHO). *European Psychiatry,* 20, 403–408.

Buckley, P., Ibrahim, Z., Singer, B., Orr, B., Donenwirth, K., & Brar, P. (1997). Aggression and schizophrenia: efficacy of risperidone. *Journal of the American Academy of Psychiatry and Law,* 25, 173–181.

Caspi, N., Modai, I., Barak, P., Waisbourd, A., Zbarsky, H., Hirschmann, S., & Ritsner, M. (2001). Pindolol augmentation in aggressive schizophrenic patients: a double-blind crossover randomized study. *International Clinical Psychopharmacology,* 97, 111–115.

Citrome, L. (2007). Comparison of intramuscular ziprasidone, olanzapine, or aripiprazole for agitation: a quantitative review of efficacy and safety. *Journal of Clinical Psychiatry,* 68, 1876–1885.

Citrome, L. (2012). Inhaled loxapine for agitation revisited: focus on effect sizes from 2 Phase III randomised controlled trials in persons with schizophrenia or bipolar disorder. *International Journal of Clinical Practice*, 66, 318–325.

Citrome, L. (2013). Addressing the need for rapid treatment of agitation in schizophrenia and bipolar disorder: focus on inhaled loxapine as an alternative to injectable agents. *Therapeutic and Clinical Risk Management*, 9, 235–245.

Citrome, L. (2013). New second-generation long-acting injectable antipsychotics for the treatment of schizophrenia. *Expert Reviews in Neurotherapy*, 13, 767–783.

Citrome, L., Casey, D., Daniel, D., Wozniak, P., Kochan, L., & Tracy, K. (2004). Adjunctive divalproex and hostility among patients with schizophrenia receiving olanzapine or risperidone. *Psychiatric Services*, 55, 290–294.

Citrome, L., Du, Y., Risinger, R., Stankovic, S., Claxton, A., Zummo, ... & Ehrich, W. (2016). Effect of aripiprazole lauroxil on agitation and hostility in patients with schizophrenia. *International Clinical Psychopharmacology*, 31, 69–75.

Citrome, L., Holt, R., Walker, D., & Hoffmann, V. (2011). Weight gain and changes in metabolic variables following olanzapine treatment in schizophrenia and bipolar disorder. *Clinical Drug Investigation*, 31, 455–482.

Citrome, L., Shope, C., Nolan, K., Czobor, P., & Volavka, J. (2007). Risperidone alone versus risperidone plus valproate in the treatment of patients with schizophrenia and hostility. *International Clinical Psychopharmacology*, 22, 356–362.

Citrome, L. & Volavka, J. (2014). The psychopharmacology of violence: making sensible decisions. *CNS Spectrums*, 19, 411–418.

Citrome, L., Volavka, J., Czobor, P., Brook, S., Loebel, A., & Mandel, F. (2006). Efficacy of ziprasidone against hostility in schizophrenia: Post hoc analysis of randomized, open-label study data. *Journal of Clinical Psychiatry*, 67, 638–642.

Citrome, L., Volavka, J., Czobor, P., Sheitman, B., Lindenmayer, J., McEvoy, J., ... & Lieberman, J. (2001). Effects of clozapine, olanzapine, risperidone, and haloperidol on hostility in treatment-resistant patients with schizophrenia and schizoaffective disorder. *Psychiatric Services*, 52, 1510–1514.

Comai, S., Tau, M., Pavlovic, Z., & Gobbi, G. (2012). The Psychopharmacology of Aggressive Behavior: A Translational Approach: Part 2: Clinical Studies Using Atypical Antipsychotics, Anticonvulsants, and Lithium. *Journal of Clinical Psychopharmacology*, 32, 83–94.

Cullen, A., Clarke, A., Kuipers, E., Hodgins, S., Dean, K., & Fahy, T. (2012). A multisite randomized trial of a cognitive skills program for male mentally disordered offenders: Violence and antisocial behavior outcomes. *Psychological Medicine*, 42, 557–569.

Czobor, P., Volavka, J., & Meibach, R. (1995). Effect of risperidone on hostility in schizophrenia. *Journal of Clinical Psychopharmacology*, 15, 243–249.

Eli Lilly and Company. (2015). Zyprexa Prescribing Information. Retrieved June 14, 2016 from pi.lilly.com/us/zyprexa-pi.pdf.

Fazel, S., Gulati, G., Linsell, L., Geddes, J., & Grann, M. (2009). Schizophrenia and violence: systematic review and meta-analysis. *PLoS Medicine*, 6, e1000120.

Frogley, C., Taylor, D., Dickens, G., & Picchioni, M. (2012). A systematic review of the evidence of clozapine's anti-aggressive effects. *International Journal of Neuropsychopharmacol*, 15, 1351–1371.

Galen US Inc. (2017). Adasuve Prescribing Information. Retrieved December 6, 2017 from www.adasuve.com/PDF/AdasuvePI.pdf.

Haddock, G., Barrowclough, C., Shaw, J., Dunn, G., Novaco, R., & Tarrier, N. (2009). Cognitive-behavioural therapy v. social activity therapy for people with psychosis and a history of violence: randomised controlled trial. *British Journal of Psychiatry*, 194, 152–157.

Huband, N., Ferriter, M., Nathan, R., & Jones, H. (2010). Antiepileptics for aggression and associated impulsivity. *Cochrane Database of Systematic Reviews*, 2, No. CD003499. doi: 10.1002/14651858.CD003499.pub3.

Kay, S., Opler, L., & Lindenmayer, J. (1989). The Positive and Negative Syndrome Scale (PANSS): rationale and standardisation. *British Journal of Psychiatry*, 155, 59–65.

Kay, S., Wolkenfeld, F., & Murrill, L. (1988). Profiles of aggression among psychiatric patients. I. Nature and prevalence. *Journal of Nervous and Mental Disease*, 176, 539–546.

Knoedler, D. (1989). The Modified Overt Aggression Scale. *American Journal of Psychiatry*, 146, 1081–1082.

Krakowski, M., Czobor, P., Citrome, L., Bark, N., & Cooper, T. (2006). Atypical antipsychotic agents in the treatment of violent patients with schizophrenia and schizoaffective disorder. *Archives of General Psychiatry*, 63, 622–629.

Lindenmayer, J., Liu-Seifert, H., Kulkarni, P., Kinon, B., Stauffer, V., Edwards, S., ... & Volavka, J. (2009). Medication nonadherence and treatment outcome in patients with schizophrenia or schizoaffective disorder with suboptimal prior response. *Journal of Clinical Psychiatry*, 70, 990–996.

Montoya, A., Valladares, A., Lizan, L., San, L., Escobar, R., & Paz, S. (2011). Validation of the Excited Component of the Positive and Negative Syndrome Scale (PANSS-EC) in a naturalistic sample of 278 patients with acute psychosis and agitation in a psychiatric emergency room. *Health Quality of Life Outcomes*, 9, 18.

Nolan, K., Czobor, P., Roy, B., Platt, M., Shope, C., Citrome, L., & Volavka, J. (2003). Characteristics of assaultive behavior among psychiatric inpatients. *Psychiatric Services*, 54, 1012–1016.

Nordstrom, K., Zun, L., Wilson, M., Ng, A., Bregman, B., & Anderson, E. (2012). Medical evaluation and triage of the agitated patient: consensus statement of the American Association for Emergency Psychiatry Project Beta Medical Evaluation Workgroup. *West Journal of Emergency Medicine*, 13, 3–10.

Otsuka Pharmaceutical Company. (2016). Abilify Prescribing Information. Retrieved June 14, 2016 from www.otsuka-us.com/media/images/AbilifyPI_538.pdf.

Pfizer Inc. (2015). Geodon prescribing information. Retrieved June 14, 2016 from http://labeling.pfizer.com/ShowLabeling.aspx?format=PDF&id=584.

Pratts, M., Citrome, L., Grant, W., Leso, L., & Opler, L. (2014). A single-dose, randomized, double-blind, placebo-controlled trial of sublingual asenapine for acute agitation. *Acta Psychiatrica Scandinavica*, 130, 61–68.

Richmond, J. S., Berlin, J. S., Fishkind, A. B., Holloman, G. H., Jr., Zeller, S. L., Wilson, M. P., Rifai, M. A., Ng, A. T. (2012). Verbal De-escalation of the Agitated Patient: Consensus Statement of the American Association for Emergency Psychiatry Project BETA De-escalation Workgroup. *The Western Journal of Emergency Medicine*, 13, 17–25.

Steadman, F., Mulvey, E., Monahan, J., Robbins, P., Appelbaum, P., Grisso, T., ... & Silver, E. (1998). Violence by people discharged from acute psychiatric inpatient facilities and by others in the same neighborhoods. *Archives of General Psychiatry*, 55, 393–401.

Swanson, J., Swartz, M., Van Dorn, R., Elbogen, E., Wagner, H., Rosenheck, R., ... & Lieberman, J. (2006). A national study of violent behavior in persons with schizophrenia. *Archives of General Psychiatry*, 63, 490–499.

Swanson, J., Swartz, M., Van Dorn, R., Volavka, J., Monahan, J., Stroup, T., ... & Lieberman, J. (2008a). Comparison of antipsychotic medication effects on reducing violence in people with schizophrenia. *British Journal of Psychiatry*, 193, 37–43.

Swanson, J., Van Dorn, R., Swartz, M., Smith, A., Elbogen, E., & Monahan, J. (2008b). Alternative pathways to violence in persons with schizophrenia: the role of childhood antisocial behavior problems. *Law & Human Behavior*, 32, 228–240.

Swift, R., Harrigan, E., Cappelleri, J., Kramer, D., & Chandler, L. (2002). Validation of the behavioural activity rating scale (BARS): a novel measure of activity in agitated patients. *Journal of Psychiatric Research*, 36, 87–95.

Tiihonen, T., Lonnqvist, J., Wahlbeck, K., Klaukka, T., Niskanen, L., Tanskanen, A., & Haukka, J. (2009). 11-year follow-up of mortality in patients with schizophrenia: a population-based cohort study (FIN11 study). *The Lancet*, 374, 620–627.

Volavka, J. (2002). *Neurobiology of violence*. Washington, DC: American Psychiatric Publishing.

Volavka, J. (2014). Comorbid personality disorders and violent behavior in psychotic patients. *Psychiatric Quarterly*, 85, 65–78.

Volavka, J. & Citrome, L. (2011). Pathways to aggression in schizophrenia affect results of treatment. *Schizophrenia Bulletin*, 37, 921–929.

Volavka, J., Czobor, P., Citrome, L., & Van Dorn, R. (2014). Effectiveness of antipsychotic drugs against hostility in patients with schizophrenia in the Clinical Antipsychotic Trials of Intervention Effectiveness (CATIE) study. *CNS Spectrums*, 19, 374–381.

Volavka, J., Czobor, P., Derks, E., Bitter, I., Libiger, J., Kahn, R., & Fleischhacker, W. (2011). Efficacy of antipsychotic drugs against hostility in the European First-Episode Schizophrenia Trial (EUFEST). *Journal of Clinical Psychiatry*, 72, 955–961.

Volavka, J., Czobor, P., Nolan, K., Sheitman, B., Lindenmayer, J., Citrome, L., ... & Lieberman, A. (2004). Overt aggression and psychotic symptoms in patients with schizophrenia treated with clozapine, olanzapine, risperidone, or haloperidol. *Journal of Clinical Psychopharmacology*, 24, 225–228.

Volavka, J., Swanson, J., & Citrome, L. (2012). Understanding and managing violence in Schizophrenia. In J. A. Lieberman & R. M. Murray (Eds), *Comprehensive Care of Schizophrenia: A Textbook of Clinical Management* (pp. 262–290). New York: Oxford University Press.

Volavka, J., Van Dorn, R., Citrome, L., Kahn, R., Fleischhacker, W., & Czobor, P. (2016). Hostility in schizophrenia: An integrated analysis of the combined Clinical Antipsychotic Trials of Intervention Effectiveness (CATIE) and the European First Episode Schizophrenia Trial (EUFEST) studies. *European Psychiatry*, 31, 13–19.

Whitman, J., Maier, G., & Eichelman, B. (1987). Beta-adrenergic blockers for aggressive behavior in schizophrenia. *American Journal of Psychiatry*, 144, 538–539.

Wilson, M., Pepper, D., Currier, G., Holloman, Jr., G., & Feifel, D. (2012). The psychopharmacology of agitation: consensus statement of the American Association for Emergency Psychiatry Project Beta Psychopharmacology Workgroup. *Western Journal of Emergency Medicine*, 13, 26–34.

Yates, K., Kunz, M., Khan, A., Volavka, J., & Rabinowitz, S. (2010). Psychiatric patients with histories of aggression and crime five years after discharge from a cognitive-behavioral program. *Journal of Forensic Psychiatry & Psychology*, 21, 167–188.

Yudofsky, S., Silver, J., Jackson, W., Endicott, J., & Williams, D. (1986). The Overt Aggression Scale for the objective rating of verbal and physical aggression. *American Journal of Psychiatry*, 143, 35–39.

Zedie, N., Amory, D., Wagner, B., & O'Hara, D. (1996). Comparison of intranasal midazolam and sufentanil premedication in pediatric outpatients. *Clinical Pharmacology Therapy*, 59, 341–348.

Zeller, S. & Citrome, L. (2016). Managing agitation associated with Schizophrenia and Bipolar Disorder in the emergency setting. *Western Journal of Emergency Medicine*, 17, 165–172.

35 Individual, Family, Neighborhood, and Regional Poverty/Socioeconomic Status and Exposure to Violence in the Lives of Children and Adolescents: Considering the Global North and South

Holly Foster and Jeanne Brooks-Gunn

Introduction

Extant reviews of children's exposure to violence are essential in underscoring the importance of understanding multiple influences, in addition to SES and poverty, which constitute the array of risk factors for children's exposure to violence, including the 2014 report on child maltreatment by the Institute of Medicine and National Research Council (Black, Heyman, & Smith-Slep 2001; Buka et al., 2001; Garbarino & Bradshaw, 2003; Gershoff, 2002). Empirical studies that incorporate multiple covariates in addition to poverty/SES are essential in isolating the former's effects, sometimes revealing no net risk influences of economic factors (e.g., on the outcome of spanking at age 3) (e.g., MacKenzie, Nicklas, Waldfogel, & Brooks-Gunn, 2012). However, few systematic reviews exist of associations and implications of poverty/SES and ETV in children's lives. We build on the two reviews (e.g., Drake & Jonson-Reid 2014; Foster, Brooks-Gunn, & Martin, 2007) that focus on the role of poverty/SES in relation to children's ETV given multiple forms of violence in children's lives, as well as the need to make sense of findings around economic factors using multiple indicators, levels of analyses, and social contexts. In particular, we further add to research on child maltreatment (Drake & Jonson-Reid, 2014) by incorporating research on poverty/SES in relation to community and war violence in children's lives. We also build on our earlier review by taking a more global perspective on these associations by incorporating research in the Global South, specifically from the continent of Africa. While poverty and SES are most often found to be risk factors for children's violence exposure, we conclude with the need to consider access to education as a protective factor that can foster resilience among children, youth, and young adults particularly in developing regions, including areas of the Global South.

Poverty and socioeconomic disadvantages in the neighborhood and family environments are associated with children's behavioral and emotional problems (Brooks-Gunn & Duncan, 1997; Brooks-Gunn, Duncan, & Aber, 1997; Brooks-Gunn, Duncan, Klebanov, & Sealand, 1993; Duncan & Brooks-Gunn, 1997; Duncan, Yeung, Brooks-Gunn, & Smith, 1998; Evans, 2004; Leventhal & Brooks-Gunn, 2000; McLeod & Shanahan, 1993). Poverty and socioeconomic status (SES) are also associated with exposure to violence (ETV) in the lives of children and youth, which in turn has pervasive short- and long-term effects on children's behavior problems and well-being (Buka, Stichick, Birdthistle, & Earls, 2001; Foster & Brooks-Gunn, 2009, 2015; Hagan & Foster, 2001; Lynch & Cicchetti, 1998; Margolin & Gordis, 2000; Osofsky, 1999; Overstreet, 2000). Although poverty has been systematically reviewed in relation to violent behaviors (e.g., Crutchfield & Wadsworth, 2003), less in-depth attention has generally been given to the association between exposure to violence and SES/poverty.

Attention to the Global South is especially pressing as Meink, Cluver, and Boyes (2015) recently observe that relatively few studies look at risk and protective factors for child abuse in low-income contexts compared to the more thorough investigation of the topic in high-income countries. This also holds for risk and protective factors for children's exposure to violence more broadly. We therefore hone in on empirical studies that have further assessed correlations or patterns between childhood abuse, community violence, war violence, and poverty/ socio-economic status in countries in Africa.

A recent review on substance use further explains the importance of understanding poverty additionally in the Global South: "(i)n Africa, in general, the problem of poverty is compounded by political instability and social unrest, manifesting in the forms of wars, refugee problems, inter and intra-ethnic strife and forced immigration arising from poor economic conditions" (Odejide, 2006). In South Africa, for example, poverty is found to be widespread in a highly unequal societal context (Richter & Dawes, 2008). Richter & Dawes (2008) chronicle that in South Africa about 11 million children live in households in which less than $1 per day is spent on their well-being; 71% of children live in households in which no adult is employed; 17% live in households with a single room; 18% don't have access to tap water; and 15% of children go hungry sometimes. The context and type of poverty experiences therefore differ globally. Furthermore, regions in the Global South including Africa have exposure to war violence not seen in Global North (Benjet, 2010). We argue in the contemporary context that there is a need to better understand how SES and poverty are associated with children's exposure to violence more globally, which we begin to address.

Stress Process Model of Poverty/SES and ETV Among Children and Adolescents

Drake and Jonson-Reid (2014) review some theories that have been used to understand poverty/SES associations with child maltreatment, noting that most tend to emphasize individual and family factors with some extending to neighborhood influences moving toward developmental/ecological perspectives. We have applied a general stress process model of children's exposure to violence applied in both the Global North and South contexts (Foster & Brooks-Gunn, 2009; 2015; Pearlin et al., 1981). We revisit that model here by highlighting in more depth the roles of poverty and SES. In our review, this model most centrally includes a role of poverty/SES as a structural correlate or risk factor for violence exposure as indicated in Figure 35.1 (path a) and the degree to which these associations are supported by type of violence, measure of poverty/SES, and global context. Moreover, indicators of poverty/SES over the life-course, including children's access to education, are also considered as potential mediators and moderators (path c, e, and d, respectively) of the influences of exposure to violence on mental health problems. In this way, we consider the role of poverty/SES not only as a risk factor, but also in different forms as a potential source of resilience or protective factor in children's and adolescents lives. Furthermore, following a stress process model for emotional and behavioral problems for children and adolescents, Figure 35.1 also includes a direct effect hypothesized between poverty/SES and child emotional and behavioral problems (path f) as well as an indirect effect hypothesized to work through the mediating variable of exposure to violence (paths a and b). The anticipated effects of SES/poverty on mental health problems are rooted in social structural perspectives on stress exposure, where those in more disadvantaged social locations should have higher levels of exposure to violence (Aneshensel, 1992; McLeod & Kaiser, 2004, p. 637; Mirowsky & Ross, 2003; Pearlin, 1989; Turner, Wheaton, & Lloyd, 1995). The causal pathway from SES to ETV is also consistent with ecological perspectives on child maltreatment and social disorganization perspectives on violence in criminology (Garbarino & Sherman, 1980; Sampson, 1997; Sampson, Raudenbush, & Earls, 1997). In keeping with these theoretical directions, higher levels of violence exposures are hypothesized to in turn increase children's emotional and behavioral problems (path b). The stress process model is an integrative model that considers how SES/poverty affects exposure to violence and its consequences for children by taking into account multiple factors in an overall process.

In the following sections, we review estimates of exposure to three types of violence in the lives of children and youth: parent-to-child physical maltreatment, community violence exposure, and war violence. We then consider the range of indices available to measure individual, family, and community poverty/SES in the Global North and South, where for the former we focus on the USA and Canada and for the latter we focus on countries in Africa. In subsequent sections, we consider the evidence across studies for associations between individual, family, neighborhood, and regional poverty/SES and each of the three types of ETV. We examine in each section whether relationships are similar or different when comparing across areas in the Global North and South.

Estimates of Children's Exposure to Violence

The Developmental Victimization Survey (DVS) conducted most recently in 2014 is a US national study obtained through random-digit dialing and includes children (age 0–17) and their parents (Finkelhor, Turner, Shattuck, & Hamby, 2015). This study provides survey-based prevalence national estimates for the three types of violence featured in our

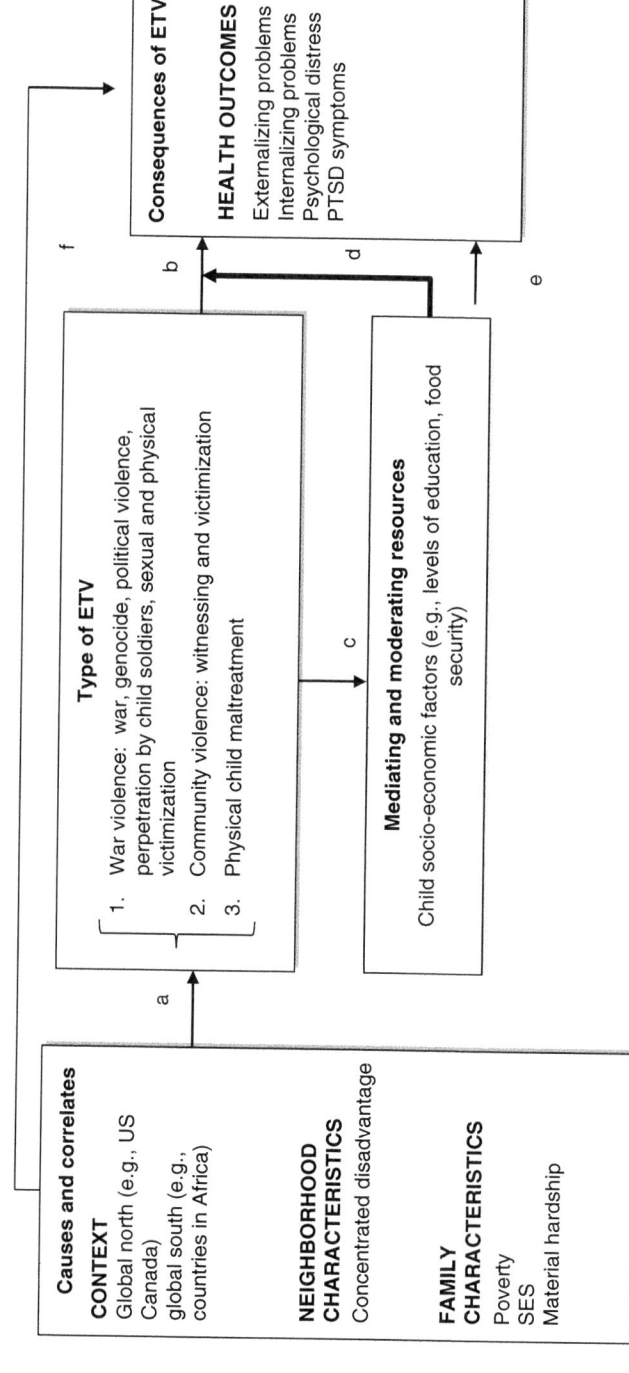

Figure 35.1 *Stress process model of poverty/SES and exposure to violence (ETV) among children and adolescents.*

review: physical child abuse, children's exposure to community violence, and exposure to war violence. Using the Juvenile Victimization Questionnaire, this study found 5% of children have been physically abused in the past year and 9.8% have been physically abused over their lifetime. Physical child abuse in this study measured whether an adult in a child's life hit, beat, kicked, or physically abused the child in any way and excluded spanking (Finkelhor et al., 2015). This respondent reported information augments information of official substantiated cases of child maltreatment in the United States (which includes child neglect and physical and sexual abuse), yielding an estimate that 1 in every 8 children has experienced a substantiated case of child maltreatment (Wildeman et al., 2014). The article notes most of these occurrences are of child neglect. The prevalence in one year (2011) is 0.9% of US children experiencing substantiated abuse and neglect, but it is important to look at the cumulative prevalence from birth to 18, at 12.5% (Wildeman et al., 2014).

Survey based data also yields estimates on children's exposure to community violence. Using the instrument in the Development Victimization Survey, one item asked about witnessing assaults in the community (indirect victimization) (i.e., "child saw someone (nonfamily) attacked or hit") (Finkelhor et al., 2015), which yielded prevalence estimates of 18.4% in the past year and 27.7% over children's lifetimes. Direct victimization was measured through a number of items and included an assessment of any physical assault toward the child (excluding threats, physical intimidation, relational aggression, and internet harassment), yielding past-year prevalence estimates for any physical assault of 37.3% and a lifetime estimate of 51.4%. War violence was measured through an item where children and caregivers were asked about having been "in the middle of a war where (he/she/you) could hear real fighting with guns or bombs?" Only 1.4% of children had been exposed to war violence in their lifetimes, and 0.4% in the past year (Finkelhor et al., 2015).

Other broad community studies in the Global North of parent-to-child physical aggression (PCPA) yield somewhat higher estimates than the recent national data above (5–10%), depending on the items included in the measure. The Project for Human Development in Chicago Neighborhoods (PHDCN) included items from the Conflict Tactics Scales (Straus, 1979) indicating approximately 69.9% of children age 3 to 15 had experienced minor PCPA (which includes being slapped/spanked or pushed/grabbed/shoved, or having had their parent throw something at them); 32% had experienced severe PCPA (includes hit/tried to hit with object, beaten up, kicked/bit/hit with fist, or burned/scalded); and 5.5% had experienced very severe PCPA (same as severe PCPA, but excludes hit/tried to hit with object; Molnar, Buka, Brennan, Holton, & Earls, 2003, p. 90). Further gauging abuse prevalence levels, retrospective estimates from a large community survey in an Eastern Canadian province of children followed from age 4–16 to 21–35 years indicates 31% experienced childhood physical abuse (before age 16) using a modified version of the Childhood Experiences of Violence Questionnaire (MacMillan, Tanaka, Duku, Vaillancourt, & Boyle, 2013). This measure includes three composite items measuring (1) being slapped, hit or spanked; (2) being pushed, grabbed, shoved, or having something thrown at them; and (3) being kicked, bitten, punched, choked, burnt, or physically attacked. However, the Canadian study indicates a lower proportion than the PHDCN sample experienced severe physical abuse (i.e., occurred at higher frequencies) indicated by 19.9% of the sample.

Further complexity by age is revealed in research focused on spanking. Although spanking is not equivalent to abuse, higher frequencies of spanking may signal an elevated risk of child maltreatment and studies are therefore included in this review (Brooks-Gunn et al., 2013). Using the longitudinal birth cohort data from the Fragile Families and Child Well-Being Study, analyses reveal that at about 12 months of age, 17.6–36.4% of mothers report spanking children (MacKenzie, Nicklas, Brooks-Gunn, & Waldfogel, 2011). However, the same study shows estimates are lower but still notable for high-frequency spanking, ranging from 3 to 8.8% of mothers. At age 3, 12.6% mothers report higher-frequency spanking (two or more times per week) and 5.5% report higher-frequency spanking when children are age 5 (MacKenzie, Nicklas, Waldfogel, & Brooks-Gunn, 2013). Yet, the latter study also shows that physical punishment remains quite common in the USA, with 44.4% of mothers reporting lower-frequency spanking when children are age 3 and 46.6% of mothers report this at age 5. The reports from fathers show similar patterns, although at slightly lower levels, with 7.3% of fathers reporting high-frequency spanking when children are age 3, while 33% report lower-frequency spanking. When children are age 5, 3% of fathers report higher-frequency spanking and 30.2% report lower-frequency spanking. Subsequent analyses with this cohort of children at age 9 show that the risk of physical aggression toward them decreases from age 5 to 9 (Schnieder et al., 2017). Furthermore, in comparing estimates across studies, higher-frequency spanking may be in keeping with estimates of more severe forms of abuse (e.g., Molnar et al., 2003), and lower-frequency spanking would be in line with estimates of more minor parent-to-child physical aggression in similar research. The estimates together show physical punishment is a regular occurrence in the lives of children.

Finally, while the US national data indicate that 18–30% have witnessed community violence (Finkelhor et al., 2015), an analysis of a subset of youth from the PHDCN (age 9 to 24) using a broad range of items indicated that considerable percentages of youth witness community violence over their lifetimes, ranging from 88% seeing someone hit to 23% seeing a person killed (Selner-O'Hagan et al., 1998, p. 218). Direct victimization in the same study ranged from 68% having been hit to 5% having been shot over their lifetimes. Furthermore, estimates from a recent longitudinal birth cohort study in Connecticut based on parent responses to a survey further provides data on very young children, indicating that 8.5% of 1–3-year-olds (n = 1788) are exposed to violence in the community (Briggs-Gowan, Ford, Fraleigh, McCarthy, & Carter, 2010. The most common form of community violence exposure among young children is having "seen someone hit, push, kick a family member."

The above estimates indicate that exposure to violence is a significant problem in childhood in the United States. Minor aggression is the most common form of child physical maltreatment (up to 70% in research inclusive of children of multiple ages, and indicating higher levels of spanking around age 3 and 5 compared to age 1). Lower but still notable estimates are found in research on more severe forms of aggression toward children, with 32% of children experiencing severe, and 5% very severe, forms of parent-to-child aggression (Molnar et al., 2003). Other research with national survey data similarly shows that up to 10% of children experience severe physical abuse (Finkelhor et al., 2015). Furthermore, estimates of officially substantiated cases of child maltreatment tend to be lower than those obtained from respondent-reported survey studies (Wildeman et al., 2014), where both yield valuable information. Across the different forms of violence considered in this review, the estimates suggest that community violence exposure tends to be more common than the more severe forms of child maltreatment, and exposure to war violence is extremely rare in the USA.

Global South: Regions in Africa

Comparisons around child maltreatment between the Global North and South are facilitated by a recent world-wide meta-analysis synthesizing studies using the Childhood Trauma Questionnaire (CTQ). This review analyzed studies across continents, finding similar mean levels of child maltreatment between studies using this questionnaire from North America (CTQ mean value estimate of 44.23) and Africa (CTQ mean value estimate 43.50) (Viola et al., 2016). However, estimates from Africa also vary considerably and some show some high prevalence levels. Another comprehensive review of child and adolescent maltreatment in various countries in Africa indicates levels of physical abuse (i.e., involving physical harm) in the home ranging from 7.6% to 45% (Meinck, Cluver, Boyes, & Mhlongo, 2015). This range is higher than the 5% estimate found nationally in US data (Finkelhor et al., 2015) and both overlap and exceed some of the estimates of experiencing severe physical child maltreatment in other US studies above (around 30%).

Further recent data from a household-based community sample in two provinces in South Africa supports the higher end of this estimate range, where the lifetime prevalence of self-reported physical abuse experiences in the lives of 10–17-year-olds (n = 3515) was 56.3% (Meink, Cluver, Boyes, & Loening-Voysey, 2016). Another article with these data (Meink et al., 2015) show baseline estimates of frequent physical abuse at 17% for boys and 19.1% for girls, but by follow-up (a year later) frequent physical abuse was considerably higher, at 44.5% for boys and 55.5% for girls (a non-significant difference by gender within each time point). The location of the abuse in these estimates is more encompassing, however, where a study with these data on where the abuse occurred indicates that it is most often experienced in the home followed by the school, and was engaged in by caregivers and teachers (Meink et al., 2016). Regarding abuse at school, the South African Schools Act of 1996 outlawed physical punishment in schools (Breen, Daniels, & Tomlinson, 2015); however, the former quantitative empirical study shows it still occurs. Qualitative research conducted directly with a small sample of young children (age 8 to 12) in South Africa further reveals that corporal punishment is an everyday experience for them either at home or at school (Breen et al., 2015).

While general population surveys are important for gauging prevalence levels, those including special groups are also highly informative. Orphans constitute one such special group of children in Africa, linked to regional adversities. In Sub-Saharan Africa there are an estimated 15 million orphaned children due to the AIDS epidemic (Collishaw, Gardner, Aber, & Cluver, 2016; United Nations Children's Fund, 2013) and approximately 56 million orphans total (Morantz et al., 2013; United Nations Children's Fund, 2010). Accordingly, there has been a line of research inquiry on whether levels of physical abuse are higher among orphans compared to non-orphans on the continent yielding mixed conclusions. A review of the qualitative literature finds physical abuse is prevalent among orphans (Morantz et al., 2013); however, a meta-analytic review of the quantitative literature found no significant difference in the prevalence of physical abuse between orphans and non-orphans (Nichols et al., 2014). However, the latter study cautions that the available studies were limited in number, and varied in definitions of physical abuse. A recent study in Cape Town, South Africa found orphans are more exposed to community violence victimization than non-orphans, but the two groups were similar in exposure to a combined measure of physical and emotional abuse (Collishaw et al., 2016).

While the national US data (Finkelhor et al., 2015) show many children and youth are exposed to community violence in the Global North with varying estimates given above, studies in Africa also show high levels of children's exposure to community violence. Our recent review of studies in four countries in Africa found witnessing violence in the community was very common, with estimates ranging from 58.1% seeing someone attacked with a weapon in the neighborhood (South Africa) (Shields et al., 2009) to 86.7% seeing someone beaten up or mugged (Gambia, West Africa) (O'Donnell et al., 2011; Foster & Brooks-Gunn, 2015). In a recent study of 16–18-year-old adolescents in four low-socio-economic-status suburbs in Johannesburg, South Africa, the prevalence of indirect or witnessing community violence was high, at 67% (Otwombe et al., 2015). Direct victimization estimates are also high, with 48.4% of youth in Gambia reporting that they themselves have been beaten up or mugged (O'Donnell et al., 2011) and 68.4% of young adolescents in South Africa reported being a victim of violence (Ward et al., 2007; Foster & Brooks-Gunn, 2015). Direct community victimization was still notable in a recent study of older adolescents, also in South Africa, at 28% (Otwombe et al., 2015). One study uses the same measure in a sample from the United States and South Africa (Shields, Nadasen, & Pierce, 2013). This study found higher mean levels of witnessing violence and direct victimization in the neighborhood in the sample in South Africa, however, the study finds higher levels of psychological distress in the US sample. Noting the difficulties often involved in comparing prevalence estimates of community violence internationally, Shields et al. (2013) also note the murder rate in South Africa is 34.1/100,000 (2009–2010) compared to 5 per 100,000 in 2009 in the USA.

Finally, regarding exposure to community violence in special sub-groups in the African context, another important group of at-risk youth includes refugees. A recent study compared levels of community violence exposure between refugee youth compared to non-refugee youth in grades 10 and 11 in Gambia (West Africa). This study found significantly higher mean levels of both community witnessing and direct victimization among refugee youth comparted to non-refugee youth (O'Donnell & Roberts, 2015).

Exposure to war violence is unequivocally higher among children in Africa than North America. This can be seen with respect to national data in the US estimating low levels of exposure to war violence among children and youth in the USA (at just over 1%) (Finkelhor et al., 2015), where our review of studies in four countries in Africa indicate children's and adolescent's exposure to dead bodies and seeing someone killed at between 32.5 and 40.3% (Foster & Brooks-Gunn, 2015; Kaminer et al., 2013; Martin et al., 2013; Shields et al., 2013). Information from a subsample from the PHDCN study in Chicago also yields a direct estimate of seeing a dead body at 36% in children's lifetimes and 24% in the past year (Selner O'Hagan et al., 1998). Exposure to war violence in Africa encompasses many forms of exposure in that context, is indexed through extensive checklists (Foster & Brooks-Gunn, 2015). A general community survey in Rwanda (Central, Eastern Africa) provides broad epidemiological estimates of prevalence of exposure to war-violence using the Wartime Violence Checklist (Neugebauer et al., 2009). Results from this study of 8–19-year-olds show the scope of war exposures, with 34.3% reporting bereavement (e.g., death of mother, father, and siblings) 96.1% reporting being victim of threat of violence, 93.5% witnessing violence against people, 27.1% witnessing rape or sexual mutilation, and 14.2% reporting hiding under corpses (Neugebauer et al., 2009).

Furthermore, a study of a special subgroup in the African context finds 90% of former child soldiers in Sierra Leone have witnessed war-related violence more broadly (e.g., massacres, raids on villages) (Betancourt et al., 2010).

A comparative study concludes that there are similar levels of child maltreatment across studies in Africa and the USA (Viola et al., 2016). Studies show physical abuse is experienced by between about 8–45% of children (e.g., Meink et al., 2015), and up to 56% of 10–17-year-olds. As was found in the USA, exposure to community violence is more common among children than is child maltreatment. Estimates in Africa given above range from 58.1 to 86.7%. However, children in countries in Africa are further exposed to war violence in ways that children in the USA are not. Estimates differ depending on the specific type of war violence exposure involved and range from 14–96% (e.g., Neugebauer et al., 2009), with special groups of children (e.g., former child soldiers) showing very high levels of war violence exposure (e.g., over 90%) (e.g., Betancourt et al., 2010).

Measurement of SES/Poverty

In the Global North, various measures of socioeconomic disadvantage in children's lives range from those indexing separate dimensions of resource deprivation, including total family or household income, parental education, parental unemployment, and welfare receipt, up to more composite indices involving combinations of education, occupational prestige, and income. Income-based measures range from continuous dollar amounts through indicators of poverty status and income-to-needs ratios. Family poverty status is measured using poverty thresholds that take household size into account and are adjusted each year for cost of living using the consumer price index. Categorical measures of poverty status for any given year may be derived from use of the poverty thresholds, in which families with incomes above the threshold are considered "not poor," whereas those below the threshold are considered "poor" (Brooks-Gunn, Duncan, & Maritato, 1997, p. 3).

Income-to-needs or income-to-poverty ratios are size-adjusted measures of family income that are obtained by dividing total household income by the official US poverty threshold corresponding to the size of the given household (Duncan et al., 1998, p. 412; US Census Bureau, 2005). Income-to-needs ratios may also be used to form categorical measures distinguishing among income groups. More finely grained distinctions are possible through this form of measurement in which, for example, ratios of less than 1 may be used to distinguish those living in poverty (income-to-needs ratios of 0.5 to 1.0) from those in deep poverty (income-to-needs ratios of 0.5 or less). Income-to-needs ratios greater than 1 may be used to distinguish among those living in near-poverty (income-to-needs ratios of 1.0 to 1.5), low-income (income-to-needs ratios of 1.5 to 2.0), middle-income (income-to-needs ratios of 2.0 to 3.0), as well as in affluent families (income-to-needs ratios of 3.0 or higher; Brooks-Gunn, Duncan, & Rebello Britto, 1999). Measures involving income have also been used to capture dynamics in family economic status over time (e.g., Duncan & Moscow, 1997). These measures include information on poverty dynamics gained by examining children's duration of exposure, distinguishing children living in persistent poverty conditions from those experiencing transitory poverty (McLeod & Shanahan, 1993), and the timing of exposure to poverty in the child's life (Duncan et al., 1998). Finally, similar measures are used in Canada where family income classified below Statistics Canada's low income cut-offs (taking into account family size and area of residence) are used to determine family poverty status (MacMillan et al., 2013).

An inclusive definition of SES measures includes those indexing the "relative position of an individual or family on a hierarchical social structure, based on their access to or control over wealth, prestige, and power" (Willms, 2002, p. 71). Other measures of SES status use composite indices involving occupational prestige scales, parental education, and household income (e.g., Hauser & Warren, 1997). Some of the research on children's exposure to violence uses the Hollingshead two-factor index, a composite measure of SES based on education and occupation of parents (e.g., Dodge, Pettit, & Bates, 1994; O'Keefe & Sela-Amit, 1997).

Furthermore, measures of SES status have also been formed for neighborhood contexts, consistent with ecological perspectives on child development (Bronfenbrenner, 1986; Earls & Carlson, 2001; Garbarino, 1977; Leventhal & Brooks-Gunn, 2000). Neighborhood-level measures of SES of geographical areas include continuous factor-analyzed scores based on census data, as well as categorical indices classifying neighborhoods as poor (e.g., the proportion of families in a census tract with incomes under $10,000 or another meaningful level) and affluent (the fraction of families in a census tract with incomes over $30,000 or another meaningful level; Brooks-Gunn et al., 1993; Duncan & Aber, 1997). A measure of neighborhood-concentrated disadvantage may also be formed by taking neighborhood poverty into account, along with other geographic factors highly associated with neighborhood poverty. For example, a scale of neighborhood concentrated disadvantage was formed from 1990 Census data and was used in analyses with the Project for Human Development in Chicago neighborhoods study involving poverty, public assistance, percent of female-headed families, percent unemployed, the density of children (younger than 18), and the percentage of Black residents (Sampson et al., 1997). Research on children's ETV, including parent-to-child maltreatment, has also incorporated concentrated disadvantage at the neighborhood level into analyses (Molnar et al., 2003).

Finally, moving from neighborhoods to even higher-level macro measures of economic insecurity is a recent direction in research in the United States on spanking and abuse toward children, including traumatic brain injuries (Drake & Jonson-Reid, 2014). Some of these studies with the Fragile Families and Child Well-Being data include measures of economic hardship during the Great Recession (2007–2010). This period covers the economic downturn in the United States, as measured by the national Consumer Sentiment Index keyed to the date of interview of respondents, city unemployment rates, and home foreclosure rates (Brooks-Gunn, Schneider, & Waldfogel 2013; Schneider, Waldfogel, & Brooks-Gunn, 2017). Inclusion of macro-level conditions in children's violence, net of family socio-economic factors, helps to sort out the influence of a range of economic conditions. Therefore, predictors of children's exposure to violence in the Global North has been further expanded beyond neighborhood factors by also including macro-level economic factors.

Global South: Regions in Africa

Giving insight into globally sensitive understandings of poverty, Akande (2000) observes that "poverty means different things in different societies" (p. 64). In our review of literature on children's exposure to violence in African countries, several studies yield clear insight into measuring poverty in South Africa and Rwanda in particular. In South Africa, poverty is linked to the apartheid political landscape and especially the experiences of Black children in that context (Akande, 2000). While income per se is important for child well-being in South Africa, a comprehensive understanding of poverty goes beyond income. In fact, the poverty level in South Africa is defined as the "need to spend more than two thirds of the household income on food" (Akande, 2000, p. 64). In keeping with this approach, a study in South Africa measured household poverty using two items from the South African National Food Consumption Survey regarding days per week without sufficient food (Meink, Cluver, Boyes, & Ndhlovu, 2015). Extreme poverty in that study was measured through an indicator of three or more days without access to sufficient food. The same study also gauged household deprivation using an indicator of going to bed hungry more than three nights per week, and looked at household employment of at least one person as a potentially protective factor in relation to child abuse.

Several studies used composite indices to comprehensively measure poverty in countries in Africa. In South Africa, a recent study of children's violence exposure measured poverty using an index of access to eight of the highest socially perceived necessities for children in that context (Meink, Cluver, & Boyes, 2015). These include: enough clothes to remain warm and dry, soap to wash every day, three meals per day, a visit to the doctor and medicines when needed, school uniform, money for school fees, and more than one pair of shoes. Items were scored with a 1 to indicate no access to the item and 0 otherwise, and a total score was derived totaling the degree of children's lack of access to these necessities. Higher scores therefore indicated more poverty where 10–17-year-old boys and girls showed similar levels (mean levels of 2.61 and 2.74, respectively). A similar comprehensive approach was used in Rwanda in a study of genocide survivors, former prisoners, and their adolescents and children (n = 188 parent-child pairs) (Rieder & Elbert, 2013). That study used a composite measure of economic status to index poverty involving ratings of possessions (e.g., house, agriculture), any monthly monetary income, and the capacity to satisfy the family's needs and facts on typical nutrition (e.g., number of meals, with or without added proteins). The index therefore included income, but more broadly took into account food-related concerns and types of possessions available to the household. Therefore, researchers use various measures to index poverty in Africa including household income, access to basic necessities, and indices of food insecurity.

Many of the studies on exposure to community violence in countries in Africa focus on impoverished samples and tend to not collect additional measures of family socio-economic-status or poverty. However, Otwombe et al. (2015), in a study of exposure to various forms of violence among adolescents (age 16–18) in four low-socio-economic–status suburbs of Johannesburg, South Africa, also included a measure of parent/guardian education (i.e., primary school, up to secondary school, and post-school training). Another study that includes information on exposure to violence among refugee and non-refugee children in Gambia also included a measure of parental education (e.g., father or mother had received no education) (O'Donnell & Roberts, 2015). Finally, indicating some of the problems with gathering information on family poverty and SES in studies of exposure to violence, a study of students in secondary schools in Cape Town, South Africa (n = 787, average age = 16.37) found that 89.9% of the sample did not know family income and a related measure of SES (e.g., parental job information) was also poorly measured (Fincham, Altes, Stein, & Seedat, 2009).

Studies of war violence often take place in highly disadvantaged contexts. At least one study of childhood survivors (i.e., with orphaned heads of households) of the Rwandan genocide also measured respondent poverty status using their degree of lack of access to resources including: things you can't do because you lack the means, sometimes lack food, problems getting food, no water in your home, no permanent job, no electricity in your home, typically eating less than two meals a day, unemployed, and being a cultivator/farmer (Ng, Ahishakiye, Miller, & Meyerowitz, 2015). This same study also included a measure of respondent education (i.e., a seven-level item ranging from less than primary school (1) to graduate school (7)), which yielded insight into SES as a source of resilience among genocide survivors as covered in the last section of this chapter. The modal category among orphaned heads of households in the Rwandan study was having completed secondary school (33.33% of the sample). Another study of children and exposure to war violence in Rwanda also included a measure of respondent education (e.g., Neugebauer et al., 2009). Generally, however, finer-grained contextual measures of poverty in smaller geographic areas (e.g., neighborhood SES or concentrated disadvantage in neighborhoods) are lacking in studies of community violence, in contrast to approaches in the Global North. Also, studies of war violence in countries in Africa take place in the broad context of generally very highly impoverished conditions.

SES/Poverty and ETV Associations

In keeping with Figure 35.1, we review in this section the evidence for path a, linking levels of poverty/socio-economic status to exposure to our three focal forms of violence exposure in children's lives: physical abuse and physical aggression toward children, witnessing of and/or victimization by violence in the community, and war violence. We include information around this association most often being one of risk in the Global North and South contexts. We then conclude the chapter with a section on the potential of SES, most often through education, as a pathway to resilience for violence exposed children (paths c and e).

Parent-to-Child Maltreatment

Reviews of poverty and child maltreatment as measured by official data tend to indicate a consistent positive risk association between these two variables (Gelles, 1992). Most recently, a review concludes that "poor children are overrepresented among maltreated children at a ratio of 3:1 or higher" (Drake & Jonson Reid 2014, p. 133). Furthermore, these authors report associations between low SES and child maltreatment tend to be strongest for neglect (ratio of 7:1) and weaker but still notable for child physical and sexual abuse (ratio of 3:1). However, interpretations are not always straightforward as more disadvantaged families may be monitored more easily by social control agents, for example, through contacts with public agencies. For example, labeling biases are likely at play in associations found between poverty and child abuse in official data (Gelles, 1992, p. 258). Yet, Drake and Jonson-Reid's review also addresses this issue and concludes that although some bias exists, the observed ratio between low SES/poverty and child maltreatment still holds and is therefore evidence of a robust association. Furthermore, self-reported survey data also indicate associations between family and community economic disadvantages and child maltreatment. However, the consistency of the patterns depend on the measurement of child maltreatment used and several other modifiers considered below.

Family SES/Poverty

Economic deprivation indicated by income-based poverty measures is associated with various indicators of child maltreatment in survey data. Studies of harsh parenting practices clarify these associations with poverty. Although family poverty is associated with harsher parenting as measured by the number of times the parent spanked the child (age 4 to 8), these effects are further distinguished by the duration of poverty exposure (McLeod & Shanahan, 1993). Persistent poverty over time is negatively associated with the number of times the child was spanked, whereas an indicator of the family being currently poor was positively associated with the number of times spanked. These findings indicate that parenting is taxed by *recent* poverty in particular (McLeod & Shanahan, 1993). Second, an analysis of the antecedents of physical punishment in a sample of low-birthweight infants found that household income effects on very young children (age 3) differed by the child's gender (Smith & Brooks-Gunn, 1997). Males in poor and near-poor households were more likely than those in affluent families to be at an elevated risk for maternal hitting and maternal self-reported use of more than one physical punishment per week. In contrast, female children in all household income levels were not at an elevated risk of harsh maternal punishment (Smith & Brooks-Gunn, 1997).

Another set of studies found associations between a range of child maltreatment outcomes and family poverty and socioeconomic disadvantages. Comparisons of the percentage of youth ever victimized across five types of violence in a national survey of 2,000 10-to-16-year-olds in the USA finds that two of these types of violence varied significantly with family income levels (Finkelhor & Dziuba-Leatherman, 1994, p. 417). A higher percentage of victimized youth were found among families with very low incomes (< $20,000) compared to those in households with incomes above this amount for both family assault and genital violence. The family assault item includes perpetration by siblings and/or caregivers, and the genital violence item includes any occurrence. These findings therefore indicate a variation in family assault against children by SES, but it is not clear whether the patterns specifically pertain to violence by parents as perpetrators against their children or to violence from another source instead (e.g., siblings or related adults).

A more recent national study by Finkelhor and colleagues (2005) of children age 2 to 17 further examined a broad range of violence exposures among youth in association with household income and race/ethnicity. Physical abuse, sexual assault by a known adult, and child neglect were *not* associated with household income in this study. However, youth in families with incomes of $20,000 or lower had higher rates of psychological and emotional abuse than did youth in families with higher incomes (Finkelhor et al., 2005). A national study of 12–17-year-olds shows more complex patterning of SES with different forms of violence exposure, contingent on race/ethnicity (Crouch, Hanson, Saunders, Kilpatrick, & Resnick, 2000). The lifetime prevalence of physically abusive punishment by a parent or someone in charge of the child was found to have an inverse relationship by household income for White youth, but not for African-American or Hispanic youth (Crouch et al., 2000, p. 633).

Another group of studies focus on child maltreatment specifically, rather than a range of violence exposures. Two of these studies use national survey data, conducted in 1979 and 1985, respectively, finding that families with poverty-level income or below reported higher percentages of *severe and very severe* physical violence (measured by the Conflict Tactics Scales or CTS [Straus, 1979]) against children than did families with higher incomes (Gelles,

1992, p. 264). The poverty-child maltreatment association varied by the type of violence (severe vs. overall) and was stronger among younger children, those living with younger parents, and in single-parent families (Gelles, 1992).

Further research shows consistency in poverty/SES-maltreatment associations when the severity of violence is considered. For example, maternal education ranks among the strongest risk factors for infant homicide: less than or equal to 11 years of maternal education increases the relative risk of infant homicide (during the first year of life) by eight times in the United States (Overpeck, Brenner, Trumble, Trifiletti, & Berendes, 1998). In bivariate analyses, higher levels of maternal education are also protective against inflicted traumatic brain injury in children during the first two years of life (Keenan et al., 2003). Results from a large cohort study of infants born in 1996 in Florida found that higher risks of substantiated cases of infant maltreatment (age 0 to 3) were associated with lower maternal education (Wu et al., 2004. However, more research is necessary on parental education as a comprehensive review of risk factors for child abuse found mixed patterns regarding the association between parent education and parent-to-child physical aggression (Black, Heyman, & Smith Slep, 2001; Molnar et al., 2003).

Furthermore, regarding socio-economic status more broadly measured using indicators of income and occupational class together or alone also showed mixed patterns where some studies indicate lower SES was associated with physical abuse of children, while other studies did not support this association (Black et al., 2001). In sum, the literature shows conflicting findings regarding associations between poverty/SES and child abuse, while some studies show greater levels of socioeconomic disadvantage are associated with higher levels of child maltreatment (both in self-report data and official data). However, associations also vary by the type of maltreatment considered and is modified by the age and gender of children, among other factors revealing complexities in this connection.

A recent review by Conrad-Hiebner & Scanlon (2015) of literature on economic conditions more broadly (i.e., income, socio-economic status, welfare receipt, unemployment, and material hardship) and child physical abuse similarly also concludes mixed support for these associations. Regarding family household conditions, that review concludes the strongest relationships appear for child maltreatment and income, unemployment, cumulative hardships and housing hardship. Moderate associations were observed between child physical abuse and food insecurity, and weaker associations reviewed with health insurance and utility shutoffs (p. 61).

Finally, there is some evidence of racial and ethnic contingencies in the link between family SES/poverty and spanking, where this association is strongest among non-Hispanic Whites, and not significant among African Americans or Hispanics (MacKenzie, Nicklas, Brooks-Gunn, & Waldfogel, 2011). This study using a measure of spanking suggests that in addition to research on general trends, sub-group contingencies should therefore be examined in understanding connections between SES/poverty and forms of child maltreatment.

Neighborhood SES/Poverty

Although family economic disadvantages are associated with child maltreatment, fewer studies have examined neighborhood

SES. An article links low neighborhood SES to situations conducive to children's firearms injuries and deaths through risky firearms storage practices in the household (e.g., keeping the gun loaded; Vacha & McLaughlin, 2004). Criminological research indicates that the presence of firearms increases the likelihood of a crime being completed (Wintemute, 2000, p. 47). Therefore the situational factor of the accessibility of firearms in lower-income communities may also increase the potential *lethality* to children of exposure to violence in and beyond the household.

The review on economic conditions and child maltreatment by Conrad-Hiebner and Scanlon (2015) concludes there are associations (moderate) pertaining to neighborhood effects, although the studies reviewed tend to more often include rates of child maltreatment. We further include two multileveled studies that are consistent with ecological perspectives on child maltreatment in linking neighborhood SES to child maltreatment. One of these studies examined the child maltreatment potential of caregivers with a child under age 18 in the home, which is a measure of risk for maltreatment, rather than actual acts of maltreatment. This study found that 5% of the variance in this outcome was attributable to between-neighborhood variation, whereas 2% of the variance in actual physical abuse was due to between-neighborhood variance (Coulton, Korbin, & Su, 1999). Molnar et al. (2003) also partitioned the variance in parent-to-child physical aggression (PCPA; as measured by the CTS) reported at Wave 1 of the Project for Human Development in Chicago Neighborhoods and similarly found that 2% of the variance in PCPA was due to between-neighborhood variation. These findings concur with ecological perspectives by indicating that neighborhood-level factors are associated with child maltreatment at the individual level of analysis.

More detailed analyses of neighborhood effects on child maltreatment specify how neighborhoods affect children's PCPA. Hierarchical linear models indicate that concentrated neighborhood disadvantage increases PCPA, net of children's age and gender (Molnar et al., 2003). This association is fully mediated when family factors are added to the model. Net of individual and neighborhood characteristics, robust effects are found for higher family SES on decreasing PCPA, whereas parental unemployment increases PCPA (Molnar et al., 2003).

Another multileveled study found cross-level interactions between family risk and protective factors and neighborhood characteristics. The study showed that violence in the family of origin was a weaker predictor of child maltreatment in more impoverished areas and that parental educational attainment was only protective against child maltreatment under neighborhood conditions of low childcare burden (Coulton et al., 1999). Although only marginally significant, these findings are nonetheless suggestive of future research directions addressing how family and neighborhood factors combine to affect child maltreatment and children's exposure to violence more generally (e.g., Sheidow, Gorman-Smith, Tolan, & Henry, 2001). Together, the findings on child maltreatment in the Global North tend to be consistent with stress process perspectives, as per Figure 35.1, by which poverty/low SES in the family and communities leads to financial strains, and elevates more severe forms of child maltreatment, which in turn elevates children's behavior problems.

Moving from neighborhood effects to macro-level conditions more broadly considered, there are mixed findings on the role of economic factors. For example, in their review, Drake and Jonson-Reid (2014) find that studies using hospital-based data do not yield firm conclusions on the role of the Great Recession. However, research with a longitudinal birth cohort of families with children finds positive associations between the Consumer Sentiment Index (coded to indicate a decline in consumer confidence during the Great Recession) and higher-frequency spanking net of multiple control variables as well as the lagged dependent variable (Brooks-Gunn, Schneider, & Waldfogel 2013). Additional research on the influence of the Great Recession shows that, by age 9, both the unemployment rate and a worse Consumer Sentiment Index increased high-frequency physical aggression toward children, but these factors do not increase supervisory neglect (Schneider et al., 2017).

Global South: Regions in Africa

Meink and colleagues (2015) conducted a comprehensive review of a range of risk and protective factors for physical and sexual child abuse in Africa, inclusive of family socio-economic indicators. They highlight why a focused review is necessary of risk and protective factors in Africa in that child maltreatment takes place in that context alongside war, exposure to poverty, high levels of HIV, and sociocultural variations in family structures and attitudes. Regarding the focus of the current chapter on poverty and SES in particular, they found in quantitative studies that household poverty indexed by different measures is associated with physical child abuse in Africa, but there are mixed findings regarding parental education. The literature shows inconsistent patterns where some indicate higher education is associated with child abuse, and others indicate lower maternal education is a risk factor. Another review article using only qualitative studies in sub-Saharan Africa, focused on the child abuse and neglect experiences of orphans. In 9 of the 15 such studies reviewed, poverty was found to be present as a contributory factor (Morantz et al., 2013).

Another empirical study is supportive of a positive association in a study in Rwanda of 188 parent-child pairs inclusive of parents (e.g., genocide survivors and prisoners) and their descendants (i.e., who were born after 1994 and were between the ages of 13 and 15, or were adolescent or child survivors of the genocide from age 19 to 31). Specifically, family economic status (i.e., indexed by a composite measure of income, possessions, and nutrition) was negatively correlated with childhood trauma using a broad composite measure of physical, emotional, sexual abuse, and physical and emotional neglect measured by the Childhood Trauma Questionnaire (Rieder & Elbert, 2013). More family economic resources are therefore protective against child violence in post-genocide Rwanda, a context more broadly characterized by poverty and starvation prior to the genocide, but further involving widowed and female-headed households afterward (Rieder & Elbert, 2013). Furthermore, a study in South Africa in deprived areas with 13–19-year-olds also supports that another indicator of poverty, that of going to bed hungry, is associated in a multivariate model of a combined measure of child physical and emotional abuse (Meink et al., 2015).

Meink, Cluver, and Boyes (2015), with a prospective longitudinal sample of youth (age 10 to 17) in South Africa, provide new insight into pathways through which risks in the form of family illness works through poverty (i.e., measured by access to perceived necessities) to affect physical child abuse. Their sample included children and youth living in AIDS-ill households, other parental illness households, as well as healthy households. The findings establish that poverty is associated with child physical and emotional abuse in both types of illness-related households compared to healthy households. This study is particularly important for understanding how contextual risks in Africa, such as the AIDS epidemic, work through poverty to affect child abuse. By identifying poverty status as a mediator, this study suggests an opportunity for prevention and intervention.

Children's Exposure to Community Violence

The salience of family and community poverty/SES as risk factors in the Global North for exposure to violence is most consistent in the context of community violence. In this section, we examine the associations between SES and children's exposure to violence in the community, including their witnessing and direct victimization, as found in empirical studies and recent comprehensive reviews (Buka et al., 2001; Sheidow et al., 2001). SES tends to be measured at the familial level of analysis in extant research on children's exposure to violence, but several studies include community SES. These findings point to the pervasiveness and severity of community violence exposure predominantly in the lives of disadvantaged adolescents.

Family SES/Poverty

Results from a recent national survey of children (age 2 to 17) and their parents showed inverse associations between family income and rates of community violence exposure (Finkelhor et al., 2005). Children and youth with lower household incomes had higher levels of direct physical victimization than those with higher family incomes (e.g., assault with a weapon and multiple perpetrator assault). Children and youth residing in households with lower incomes also had higher rates of witnessing or indirect exposure to community violence – in the forms of witnessing assault with a weapon, exposure to shooting, bombs, and riots, and having someone close murdered – than those with higher incomes (Finkelhor et al., 2005, p. 16). The exception to the inverse association between income and ETV in this national study was for being victimized by bullying, in which youth living in families with higher incomes (i.e., > $50,000) reported higher levels than youth with lower SES. Together, these findings indicate that youth living in families with lower incomes are at risk of more severe types of violence exposures and higher levels of overall violence exposure, including both direct and indirect exposure in their communities.

Fewer studies have examined younger children's exposure to community violence than among adolescents, but a study with a large northeastern community sample of very young children (age 1 to 3), found that parent-reported community violence exposure was related to poverty (Briggs-Gowan et al., 2010). Poor children (based on household size, income, and receipt of public assistance) were more likely to be exposed to three forms of witnessing community violence (e.g., seen violence in neighborhood, seen someone use a weapon or threaten to hurt a family member, seen someone hit, push, or kick a family member). This study found a bivariate odds ratio between witnessing community ETV and poverty at 3.7 ($p < 0.001$); therefore, poor children have almost four times the odds of non-poor children of being exposed to community violence at very young ages.

Prior studies on community ETV in the lives of children and youth involved highly disadvantaged samples that further indicated inverse associations between SES and community ETV. Richters and Martinez (1993) found that, among younger children (age 6 to 10) in a highly disadvantaged sample (i.e., one-quarter received public assistance and the majority of parents had not completed high school), there was a trend in the findings toward decreased parental education and the type of violence exposure. Decreased parental education was associated with ETV involving a person familiar to the child, but not to ETV involving a stranger. A second study involved a sample of highly disadvantaged youth with 2,000 students in grades 6, 8, and 10, of whom approximately half received a free lunch (Schwab-Stone et al., 1995). This study found that receipt of a school lunch was significantly associated with more frequent exposure to *severe* violence as measured by the self-reported frequency of having seen someone shot or stabbed in the past year.

However, other studies with broader samples find mixed effects of SES on children's exposure to violence. Multivariate analyses of a sample of adolescents drawn from a range of schools (i.e., inner-city and other schools) in Los Angeles County found no significant associations between parental education and adolescent victimization in the community (Malik et al., 1997). In contrast, multivariate analyses with national data indicate an inverse effect of family SES, using the Hollingshead scale based on parental occupation and education, in which higher family SES was protective and was associated with lower adolescent physical victimization risk between the ages of 13 and 17 (Macmillan & Hagan, 2004, p. 142). Analyses of a Los Angeles sample of approximately 1,000 high school students showed a similar pattern in descriptive results, in which higher levels of ETV were found at lower levels of SES, also using the Hollingshead scale (O'Keefe & Sela-Amit, 1997). However, in the latter study, the initial descriptive pattern did not hold in multivariate analyses in that SES was no longer a significant predictor of ETV. This study further found that race/ethnicity effects held net of SES: Blacks, Latinos, and Asians were more exposed to violence than Whites (O'Keefe & Sela-Amit, 1997).

Another set of studies on family SES and community ETV found that the inverse association was further modified by the adolescent's race/ethnicity. A study of a national probability sample of over 3,000 adolescents (age 12 to 17) examined their direct violent victimization (physical and sexual) and their indirect exposure, including witnessing violence (Crouch et al., 2000). This study further supported the patterns found in other studies in that lower household income was associated with higher levels of witnessing violence and exposure to physical and sexual assault. However, when race/ethnicity of adolescents was taken into account, more complex patterns emerged. The inverse association between lower income and higher witnessing of violence held among White youth, but this pattern was not supported among African American and Hispanic youth (Crouch et al., 2000). Furthermore, within each SES level, race/ethnicity differentiated risk for ETV, in which minority youth had consistently higher risks of exposure to violence than White youth. These findings again suggest the importance of attending to other aspects of the social contexts in which youth live to better differentiate risk for violence exposure, as has been noted in other work on violence (Sampson & Wilson, 1995). Further research on associations between family SES and exposure to community violence is needed on ethnically and socioeconomically diverse samples as well as on younger children in addition to studies of adolescents.

Neighborhood SES/Poverty

One of the early studies of exposure to violence among adolescents (aged 11 to 24) compared levels among youth who attended medical clinics across two locales (Gladstein, Rusonis, & Heald, 1992). One of the clinics was situated in an inner-city environment comprised of predominantly African American youth, and the other involved predominantly White adolescents in a resort community. Comparisons between youth in the two locales were conducted in which community location was used to index the respondent's SES. The comparative results clearly indicated that more youth in lower SES circumstances had been victims, or had witnessed violence, or knew the victim of the violence personally. Types of violent victimization that were higher among low-SES youth included very severe violent acts, in which the respondent was robbed with a weapon, assaulted with a weapon, raped without a weapon, shot, knifed, or had their life threatened. Differences between the samples were also found on indirect exposure to the more severe items in terms of incidents in which they had known the victim personally, with the exception of no group differences in robbery or assault without a weapon. However, statistically significant differences were shown for higher levels of witnessing violence among low-SES youth on all types of violence (Gladstein et al., 1992). These results support the consistent pattern shown in other studies of more severe violence exposure in disadvantaged samples.

More recent literature incorporates contextual neighborhood conditions, including community SES, in examining children's violence exposure risks (Sampson, 1997). In their review of the literature on children's exposure to community violence, Buka and colleagues (2001) found evidence across at least six studies that ETV was highest among those in poorer communities (p. 301). Their review further indicates that differences in the type or severity of violence exposure varied across neighborhood contexts, with more severe exposure occurring in urban rather than suburban areas (Buka et al., 2001, p. 302; Fitzpatrick & Boldizar, 1993). Results from the Project for Human Development in Chicago Neighborhoods indicate that the severity of violence exposure among youth (age 9 to 24) varies with neighborhood conditions (Selner-O'Hagan et al., 1998). Past-year exposure to violence was greater in high- and medium-crime neighborhoods than in low-crime neighborhoods (Selner-O'Hagan et al., 1998).

Global South: Regions in Africa

Several studies in Africa provide descriptive information on family poverty/SES and patterns of community violence exposure. However, that information is often embedded in research focused more broadly on investigating the effects of community ETV on mental health outcomes. For example, in a study of the relationship between violence exposure and symptoms of post-traumatic stress, Seedat, Nyami, Njenga, Vythlingum, & Stein (2004) provided some comparative descriptive statistics on a South African sample and a Kenyan sample of youth (average ages of 15.9 and 15.6, respectively). These samples were comprised of school students selected in Cape Town (South Africa) and Nairobi (Kenya) that were representative of the ethnic and socio-economic makeup of the population in each city. Available family SES information in the study was limited to the percentage of parental unemployment, and a measure of tap water availability in the home or community was also included. Although descriptive patterns show higher levels of parental unemployment among both fathers and mothers in South Africa than in Kenya, the differences were not statistically significant. The Kenyan sample further showed a higher prevalence of community violence exposure, with 69% indicating witnessing violence in the street, neighborhood, or school compared to 58% in South Africa, which was a significant difference. Yet, despite lower levels of community ETV, South African youth reported higher levels of PTSD symptoms than Kenyan youth. The study's tables allow for some further comparison of the percentages of children and youth regarding witnessing and direct community victimization by parental educational level. The patterns are not clear for either form of violence exposure, where percentages were often similar across educational categories. However, results for the measure of the family source of water shows that those with tap water in the home were slightly more likely to see an act of violence in the community, but those with community tap water were more likely to experience direct victimization. Yet, in multivariate results, socio-economic factors did not emerge as significant predictors of community violence exposure. More studies of adolescent's violence exposure are needed to more definitively understand SES-community ETV associations in countries in Africa.

Another study also included information on parental education in research on community and other ETV among a highly disadvantaged sample in South Africa (Otwombe et al., 2015). That study of involved 16–18-year-olds in four low socio-economic suburbs in Johannesberg. Again, patterns were unclear regarding parental education levels in relation to two items measuring community violence exposure. Percentages were presented by the gender of participants and tended to show similarities over parental education level in witnessing violence. A slightly stronger gradient of a reduction of exposure for females was seen as parental education increased. This gradient was also seen for females in terms of direct community victimization but patterns were not so clear for male adolescents.

Further descriptive information is provided by two other studies. Although the studies did not test the relationship between SES and ETV directly, there was some suggestive further research directions suggested by sample characteristics.

In comparing AIDS-orphans to non-orphans, the former have higher levels of violent victimization and are more likely to be food-insecure (Collishaw et al., 2016). However, a direct test of that association is needed for more definitive conclusions. Furthermore, a surprising pattern emerged in considering refugee children in Gambia (West Africa). This group showed higher parental education levels than a comparative sample of adolescents attending school in Gambia; however, refugee children nonetheless had significantly higher levels of community witnessing violence and direct victimization (O'Donnell & Roberts, 2015). The latter pattern begins to highlight the complexities of understanding family SES-ETV associations in areas of political instability and upheaval. Together, the reviewed studies are suggestive about some mixed roles of family SES in relation to community violence exposure, but additional research is needed. Furthermore, studies on community violence in Africa most often pertain to adolescents and studies with younger children are required.

Children's Exposure to War Violence

In a review of childhood adversities in low-income countries, a review observes how many youth in these areas are exposed to war-related violence, including events like witnessing someone being killed or beaten, and witnessing rape or sexual mutilation (Benjet, 2010). An epidemiological study from Rwanda is included among the studies reviewed on war violence (Benjet, 2010; Neugebauer et al., 2009), however the review cautions about the difficulties of conducting research in conflict zones, which may limit conclusions about SES-ETV associations. Furthermore, broad epidemiological studies are essential for providing prevalence estimates, but some include indices of adolescent education but not family SES more broadly (e.g., Neugebauer et al., 2009).

Studies from more select samples do, however, yield some initial information on family socio-economic status in relation to war violence. In a study of adults who were double-orphans at the time of the Rwanda genocide (1994) (age 13.81 in 1994) involved with an orphan-serving organization in Rwanda, Ng and colleagues (2015) find material hardship (e.g., lack of access to resources including food and water) was positively correlated ($r = 0.41$, $p < 0.01$) with retrospective reports of greater exposure to genocidal violence (e.g., up to 41 events including being threatened with death, seeing someone killed, massacres, being raped, and seeing people being raped). Therefore, this study provides some evidence that poverty has a positive association with war violence, in addition to broader country SES conditions. However, most studies of children's exposure to war violence in African countries do not include additional measures of family poverty/SES (Foster & Brooks-Gunn, 2015). As Ng and colleagues discuss, there are considerable secondary adversities connected to war conditions, including the destruction of a society's economy and infrastructure, poverty, and the destruction of homes and livelihoods. Thus, there is often an implied inter-relatedness and correspondence of impoverished family economic situations to broader and overwhelming structural strains in war conditions. Yet, gathering explicit measures of poverty/family SES when possible may be additionally beneficial to measuring both variation and similarity in family situations and furthering empirical research in this area.

Further noting the interrelatedness of poverty with war violence, Borba et al. (2016) conducted a study with key informants who had experience working with youth in Liberia about perceptions in post-civil-war Liberia (where the war occurred between 1989–2004). In assessing the major traumatic events that key informants perceived as having a detrimental emotional impact on children and youth, conflict and war stress were rated most highly, followed by poverty. Again, these top concerns indicate a co-occurrence and overlap in these societal conditions in postwar contexts. Furthermore, when asked about functional limitations facing adolescents and young adults in Liberia, the key informants indicated concerns around access to income and living expenses suggesting socio-economic problems endure in war-affected regions (Borba et al., 2016). Again, direct research with children and youth themselves on the connections between poverty/SES in war and postwar conditions would be further beneficial.

Toward Resilience Against Violence Exposure in the Global South

Studies have pursued the role of protective factors leading to resilience among children and adolescents exposed to community violence in the Global North (e.g., see Jain, Buka, Subramanian, & Molnar, 2012). Meink et al. (2015) make a compelling case, however, that we need to explore both risk and protective factors in the African context moving beyond the findings from the Global North. Inroads have been made in identifying some factors that protect children and youth from community and war violence in regions in Africa (e.g., see reviews by Betancourt & Khan, 2008; Foster & Brooks-Gunn, 2015). However, in addition to these directions, we suggest a more focused look is additionally needed at *economic resources*. Our chapter has highlighted the role of poverty and SES as risk factors for violence exposure in the Global North and South. We now consider how education is emerging as a source of protection against violence exposure in the Global South for young people.

In this endeavor, we are guided by our stress process model (Figure 35.1, paths c and e) where education and SES are considered as mediating or explanatory factors and may further moderate or buffer (path d) the associations between exposure to violence and mental health problems. Studies support how violence exposure during the life-course compromises educational attainments in the Global North (Macmillan, 2001; Macmillan & Hagan, 2004): However, it is important to recognize how education may further work in relation to war and other violence exposure in the Global South.

The results of a study of orphaned heads of household in Rwanda following the 1994 genocide (n = 61) is particularly instructive. This research found that educational attainment among these youth mediated the effect of genocide violence exposure on post-traumatic stress disorder symptoms (Ng et al., 2015). While genocide violence exposure directly increased PTSD symptoms, it was also found to have an indirect effect on PTSD by decreasing youth's educational attainment. Decreased educational attainment was in turn associated with more PTSD symptoms. An implication of this study is that access to education is a key pathway through which war violence exposure works over the long term in the postwar context. Furthermore, a life-course-dynamic view of education is necessary, as seen in other research on poverty assessed over time (e.g., Brooks-Gunn & Duncan, 1997; Duncan et al., 1998; McLeod & Shanahan, 1993). For example, Neugebauer et al. (2009) in Rwanda found one's own education at the time of the genocide was not protective on PTSD in the short term, however the research by Ng and colleagues shows how over the long term, educational trajectories may be a mechanism through which resilience may be promoted.

Further identifying what qualities about education may be important, some insight is provided through a study of youth in Malawi (southeast Africa) and South Africa of children in various HIV-status families (i.e., HIV-positive, HIV-affected, and HIV-free). Findings indicate physical violence in the home decreases school progress, but not school enrollment nor school attendance (Sherr et al., 2016). Therefore, multiple measures of educational progress as well as attainments may be particularly important to understanding resilience following violence exposure in the Global South.

Studies of violence exposure among children and adolescents may also benefit from including multiple indicators of economic resources. For example, in a study of resilience (i.e., operationalized as the absence of mental health problems) of children and adolescents (age 10 to 19) in Cape Town (South Africa), a positive bivariate association was found with food security (Collishaw et al., 2016). Future work on protective factors against violence exposure in Africa may build on this research with multivariate models regarding whether food security, or other measures of SES, mediate ETV effects on mental health outcomes as per the pathways summarized in Figure 35.1.

Conclusion

This chapter found that children in more socio-economically disadvantaged households and community circumstances are often at risk for elevated levels of exposure to violence concerning physical abuse, community violence, and war violence in the Global North and the Global South. However, there is some variation in the consistency of associations between poverty/SES and specific forms of violence in children's lives. In the Global North, there is particularly consistent evidence for family poverty/low SES and exposure to community violence. In the Global South and North there is suggestive but mixed evidence that family poverty is associated with child physical abuse. In the Global South, there is additional evidence that impoverished community circumstances are intertwined with children's exposure to war violence. Therefore, poverty and low SES constitute risk factors for children and youth's exposure to violence in both contexts. However, special attention is needed to the various forms of violence exposure encountered in each setting as well as the most appropriate indicators of poverty and low SES. This includes measures of poverty and low SES across levels of analysis, as research in the Global North is now finding connections between macro-economic indicators of the Great Recession and physical aggression toward children, net of family factors

(Brooks-Gunn et al., 2013; Schneider et al., 2017).

Furthermore, based on a recent theoretical direction advanced in criminology by Robert Agnew (2012), research is beginning to theorize how climate change, including "extreme weather events," may exacerbate the association between poverty/SES and violence, which can be further extended to children's exposure to violence. Extending Agnew's insights about increasing inequality and developing contexts (2012, p. 29), we now see that the Global South faces conditions of famine and drought (Gettleman, 2017) that begins to highlight the role of contextual stressors (or "exposure to threats resulting from membership in social units" [Wheaton et al., 2013, p. 307]) (e.g., countries or regions) that we need to add to the model in Figure 35.1. However, this region also has fewer economic resources to mitigate this relationship. The Global North faces other extreme weather conditions that may be related to climate change, including the recent floods in Houston (Bogost, 2017). Yet, the Global North has more economic resources to mitigate these effects. Therefore, the association between SES/poverty and children's exposure to violence may depend on global context: in the Global South this association may be particularly exacerbated relative to the Global North due to contextual stressors and lower resources to cope with them. Therefore, climate change is not included in Figure 35.1 but we hope future research will include extreme weather events, including droughts and cyclones, through the exacerbation of links between poverty, violence, and youth outcomes. Furthermore, contextual stressors may even constitute forms of "historical traumas" (i.e., "community-specific trauma") (Evans-Campbell, Lincoln, & Takeuchi 2007, p. 173) and this distinction may further aid in understanding children's violence exposure globally.

Also, by including research from the Global South in this chapter, there is some suggestion that, where SES is concerned, there are even more complexities in relationships than are represented in Figure 35.1. For example, war violence can create family SES problems, which in turn may engender family violence (Reider & Elbert, 2013). That points to potential interventive efforts around improving family socio-economic conditions to prevent family violence. Other interventions in the context of war violence exposure concern the role of investing in and promoting child educational attainments and achievements in post-conflict settings. Betancourt and colleagues (2013) provide a review of promising directions regarding education along these lines for former child soldiers as well as participation in the labor force. More research is needed on the types of socio-economic resources that may offset violence exposure effects on children and adolescents in Africa, which would add to efforts to chronicle resilience resources in war-torn regions.

Furthermore, while international comparisons are challenging and require care with respect to measurement and sampling, it is essential to take a global view in understanding children's exposure to violence as high levels are encountered in both contexts. A global view reveals some qualitative differences concerning additional forms of exposure to war violence in low-income countries, as well as heightened risks around violence exposures in vulnerable sub-populations in Africa (e.g., orphans, child soldiers, those living in HIV-affected families). Research on socio-economic status in the Global North and

South must also include attention to race and ethnicity as per contextual conditions (e.g., Black children growing up in Apartheid-era South Africa). This is also necessary in the American context given ample evidence of the disproportionate location of African-Americans and other minorities in highly disadvantaged contexts and with longer duration of exposure to impoverished conditions (Benson et al., 2000; Brooks-Gunn et al., 1997). Research on spanking, for example, shows connections with low socio-economic status among non-Hispanic Whites, but not African-Americans or Hispanics, again suggesting the need for further attention to race and ethnicity in these associations (MacKenzie et al., 2011).

Another important area of future research guided by ecological-transactional perspectives on child maltreatment would involve examining interconnections among forms and levels of violence exposure (Lynch & Cicchetti, 1998; Margolin & Gordis, 2004). For example, research testing the ecological-transactional model indicates that residence in a community with higher levels of violence (i.e., exosystem) is positively associated with physical abuse in children in families (i.e., microsystem; Lynch & Cicchetti, 1998, p. 245). A further systematic investigation of interconnections among risk of exposure to different forms of violence in different contexts (e.g., community violence and child abuse, or war violence and child abuse) is needed to better understand the etiology of children's exposure to violence and would further advance the stress process conceptualization in Figure 35.1. One particularly salient research direction involves examining how children in disadvantaged families and neighborhoods may be at risk for multiple ETV exposures at any one point in time, as well as cumulatively over their life-course, further elaborating theoretical research on cumulative disadvantage and research on poly-victimization (Finkelhor, Omrod, & Turner, 2007; Lynch & Cicchetti, 1998; Margolin & Gordis, 2000; 2004; Rutter, 1989; Sampson & Laub, 1993).

While a detailed and focused review of poverty/SES and ETV associations is necessary as a knowledge baseline, further research on this topic would involve more complex models with a fuller consideration of mediating and moderating factors as well as the inclusion of sexual abuse. Furthermore, some studies found poverty/SES and ETV associations were further modified by race/ethnicity and gender. Investigation of the conditions under which poverty/SES is connected to ETV would better inform its prevention and intervention. In most of the studies reviewed on children's exposure to violence, poverty/SES was often measured at only one time point and this area needs further exploration in terms of the dynamics of poverty exposure, including its duration and timing. Exploring the dynamics of poverty and socio-economic resources in children's lives is especially pressing for understanding risk and resilience in regions exposed to war and its aftermath. This review finds both similarities in low-SES/poverty influences on some types of children's exposure to violence across contexts (e.g., community violence, child maltreatment), but also points to key differences including the qualitative form of violence exposure children experience (e.g., war violence) revealed by including literature from areas of the Global South. Future research may consider how "poly-victimization," or multiple co-occurring violence exposures (Finkelhor et al., 2007) is similar and different across countries in the Global North and South. Finally, research is necessary on children facing multiple forms of risk in their lives, including poverty/low SES in their families, communities, and countries.

Acknowledgments

We gratefully acknowledge the support provided for this research by the National Institute of Child Health and Human Development (Grant #R01 HD049796-01), the MacArthur Foundation, and the Marx Family Foundation. A version of this chapter was presented at the American Society of Criminology Annual Meetings in Philadelphia, PA in November 2017. We thank audience members for their feedback.

References

Agnew, R. (2012). Dire Forecast: A theoretical model of the impact of climate change on crime. *Journal of Theoretical Criminology*, 16, 21–42.

Akande, A. (2000). Effects of exposure to violence and poverty on young children: The Southern African context. *Early Child Development and Care*, 163, 61–78.

Aneshensel, C. S. (1992). Social stress: Theory and research. *Annual Review of Sociology*, 18, 15–38.

Benjet, C. (2010). Childhood adversities of populations living in low-income countries: Prevalence, characteristics, and mental health consequences. *Current Opinion in Psychiatry*, 23, 356–362.

Benson, M. L., Fox, G. L., DeMaris, A., & Van Wyck, J. (2000). Violence in families: The intersection of race, poverty, and community context. In G. L. Fox & M. L. Benson (Eds), *Families, crime, and criminal justice* (pp. 91–109). New York: JAI Press.

Bergman, L. (1992). Dating violence among high school students. *Social Work*, 37, 21–27.

Betancourt, T. S. & Khan, K. T. (2008). The mental health of children affected by armed conflict: Protective processes and pathways to resilience. *International Review of Psychiatry*, 20, 317–328.

Betancourt, T. S., Borisova, I. I., Williams, T. P., Brennan, R. T., Whitfield, T. H., de la Soudiere, M., ... & Gilman, S. E. (2010). Sierra Leone's former child soldiers: A follow-up study of psychosocial adjustment and community reintegration. *Child Development*, 81, 1077–1095.

Betancourt, T. S., Borisova, I., Williams, T. P., Meyers-Ohki, S.E., Rubin-Smith, J. E., Annan, J., & Kohrt, B. A. (2013). Research review: Psychosocial adjustment and mental health in former child soldiers – a systemic review of the literature and recommendations for future research. *Journal of Child Psychology & Psychiatry*, 54, 17–36.

Black, D. A., Heyman, R. E., & Smith Slep, A. M. (2001). Risk factors for child physical abuse. *Aggression and Violent Behavior*, 6, 121–188.

Bogost, I. (2017). Houston's Flood is a Design Problem. *The Atlantic*, www.theatlantic.com/technology/archive/2017/08/why-cities-flood/538251/.

Borba, C. P. C., Ng, L. C., Stevenson, A., Vesga Lopez, O., Harris, B. L., Parnarouskis, L., ... & Henderson, D. C. (2016). A mental health needs assessment of children and adolescents in post-conflict Liberia: Results from a quantitative key-informant survey. *International Journal of Culture and Mental Health*, 9, 56–70.

Breen, A., Daniels, K., & Tomlinson, M. (2015). Children's experiences of corporal punishment: A qualitative study in an urban township of South Africa. *Child Abuse & Neglect*, 48, 131–139.

Briggs-Gowan, M., Ford, J. D., Fraleigh, J. D., McCarthy, K., & Carter, A. S. (2010).

Prevalence of exposure to potentially traumatic events in a healthy birth cohort of very young children in the Northeastern United States. *Journal of Traumatic Stress*, 23, 725–733.

Bronfenbrenner, U. (1986). Ecology of the family as a context for human development: Research perspectives. *Developmental Psychology*, 22, 723–742.

Brooks-Gunn, J. & Duncan, G. J. (1997). The effects of poverty on children. *Future of Children*, 7(2), 55–71.

Brooks-Gunn, J., Duncan, G., & Aber, J. L. (Eds) (1997). *Neighborhood poverty: Context and consequences for children* (Vol. 1). New York: Russell Sage Foundation.

Brooks-Gunn, J., Duncan, G. J., Klebanov, P. K., & Sealand, N. (1993). Do neighborhoods influence child and adolescent development? *American Journal of Sociology*, 99, 353–395.

Brooks-Gunn, J., Duncan, G. J., & Maritato, N. (1997). Poor families, poor outcomes: The well-being of children and youth. In G. J. Duncan & J. Brooks-Gunn (Eds), *Consequences of growing up poor* (pp. 1–17). New York; Russell Sage Foundation.

Brooks-Gunn, J., Duncan, G. J., & Rebello Britto, P. (1999). Are socioeconomic gradients for children similar to those for adults? Achievement and health of children in the United States. In D. P. Keating & C. Hertzman (Eds), *Developmental health and the wealth of nations: Social, biological, and educational dynamics* (pp. 94–124). New York: Guilford Press.

Brooks-Gunn, J., Schneider, W., & Waldfogel, J. (2013). The Great Recession and risk for child maltreatment. *Child Abuse & Neglect*, 10, 721–890.

Buka, S. L., Stichick, T. L., Birdthistle, I., & Earls, F. (2001). Youth exposure to violence: Prevalence, risks, and consequences. *American Journal of Orthopsychiatry*, 71, 298–310.

Cicchetti, D. & Lynch, M. (1993). Toward an ecological/transactional model of community violence and child maltreatment: Consequences for children's development. *Psychiatry*, 56, 96–118.

Collishaw, S., Gardner, F., Aber, J. L., & Cluver, L. (2016). Predictors of mental health resilience in children who have been parentally bereaved by AIDS in Urban South Africa. *Journal of Abnormal Child Psychology*, 44, 719–730.

Conrad-Hiebner, A. & Scanlon, E. (2015). The economic conditions of child physical abuse: A call for national research, policy and practice agenda. *Families in Society: The Journal of Contemporary Social Services*, 96, 59–66.

Coulton, C. J., Korbin, J. E., & Su, M. (1999). Neighborhoods and child maltreatment: A multi-level study. *Child Abuse and Neglect*, 23, 1019–1040.

Crouch, J. L., Hanson, R. F., Saunders, B. E., Kilpatrick, D. G., & Resnick, H. S. (2000). Income, race/ethnicity, and exposure to violence in youth: Results from the National Survey of Adolescents. *Journal of Community Psychology*, 28, 625–641.

Crutchfield, R. D. & Wadsworth, T. (2003). Poverty and violence. In W. Heitmeyer & J. Hagan (Eds), *International handbook of violence research* (pp. 67–82). Dordrecht, The Netherlands: Kluwer Academic.

Dodge, K. A., Pettit, G. S., & Bates, J. E. (1994). Socialization mediators of the relation between socioeconomic status and child conduct problems. *Child Development*, 65, 649–665.

Drake, B. & Jonson-Reid, M. (2014). Poverty and child maltreatment. In J. E. Korbin and R. D. Krugman (Eds), *Handbook of Child Maltreatment, Child Maltreatment* (Vol. 2, pp. 131–148). New York: Springer.

Duncan, G. J. & Aber, J. L. (1997). Neighborhood models and measures. In J. Brooks-Gunn, G. J. Duncan & J. L. Aber (Eds), *Neighborhood poverty. Volume I: Context and consequences for children* (pp. 62–78). New York: Russell Sage Foundation.

Duncan, G. J. & Brooks-Gunn, J. (1997). *Consequences of growing up poor*. New York: Russell Sage Foundation.

Duncan, G. J. & Moscow, L. (1997). Longitudinal indicators of children's poverty and dependence. In R. M. Hauser, B. V. Brown, & W. R. Prosser (Eds), *Indicators of children's well-being* (pp. 258–278). New York: Russell Sage Foundation.

Duncan, G. J., Yeung, W. J., Brooks-Gunn, J., & Smith, J. R. (1998). How much does childhood poverty affect the life chances of children? *American Sociological Review*, 63, 406–423.

Earls, F. & M. Carlson. (2001). The social ecology of child health and well-being. *Annual Review of Public Health*, 22, 143–166.

Evans, G. W. (2004). The environment of childhood poverty. *American Psychologist*, 59, 77–92.

Evans-Campbell, T., Lincoln, K. D., & Takeuchi, D. T. (2007). Race and mental health: past debates, new opportunities. In Avison, W. R., McLeod, J. D., & Pescosolido, B. A. (Eds), *Mental Health, Social Mirror* (pp. 169–189). New York: Springer.

Fincham, D. S., Altes, L. K., Stein, D. J., & Seedat, S. (2009). Posttraumatic stress disorder symptoms in adolescents: Risk factors versus resilience moderation. *Comprehensive Psychiatry*, 50, 193–199.

Finkelhor, D., & Dziuba-Leatherman, J. (1994). Children as victims of violence: A national survey. *Pediatrics*, 94, 413–420.

Finkelhor, D., Ormrod, R., Turner, H., & Hamby, S. (2005). The Victimization of Children and Youth: A Comprehensive, National Survey. *Child Maltreatment*, 10, 5–25.

Finkelhor, D., Omrod, R. K., & Turner, H. A. (2007). Poly-victimization: A neglected component of child victimization. *Child Abuse & Neglect*, 31, 7–26.

Finkelhor, D., Turner, H., Shattuck, A., & Hamby, S. L. (2015). Prevalence of childhood exposure to violence, crime and abuse: Results from the National Survey of Children's Exposure to Violence. *JAMA Pediatrics* 169: 746–754.

Finkelhor, D., Turner, H., Shattuck, A., & Hamby, S. L. (2015) JAMA Pediatrics Supplementary Online Content Appendix 1. 2013 Juvenile Victimization Questionnaire Used in NatSCEV 2014. Retrieved November 3, 2016 from http://jamanetwork.com/journals/jamapediatrics/fullarticle/2344705.

Fitzpatrick, K. M. & Boldizar, J. P. (1993). The prevalence and consequences of exposure to violence among African American youth. *Journal of the American Academy of Adolescent Psychiatry*, 32, 424–430.

Foster, H. & Brooks-Gunn, J. (2009). Toward a stress process model of children's exposure to physical family and community violence. *Clinical Child and Family Psychology Review*, 12, 71–94.

Foster, H. & Brooks-Gunn, J. (2015). Children's exposure to community and war violence and mental health in four African countries. *Social Science & Medicine*, 146, 292–299.

Foster, H., Brooks-Gunn, J., & Martin, A. (2007). Poverty/ socio-economic status and exposure to violence in the lives of children and adolescents. In D. Flannery, A. T. Vazsonyi, & I. D. Waldman (Eds), *Cambridge Handbook of Violent Behavior* (pp. 664–687). Cambridge: Cambridge University Press.

Garbarino, J. (1977). The human ecology of child maltreatment: A conceptual model for research. *Journal of Marriage and the Family*, 39, 721–735.

Garbarino, J. & C. Bradshaw. (2003). Violence against children. In W. Heitmeyer & J. Hagan (Eds), *International handbook of violence research* (pp. 719–735). Dordrecht, The Netherlands: Kluwer Academic.

Garbarino, J. & Sherman, D. (1980). High-risk neighborhoods and high-risk families: The human ecology of child maltreatment. *Child Development*, 51, 188–198.

Gelles, R. J. (1992). Poverty and violence toward children. *American Behavioral Scientist*, 35, 258–274.

Gershoff, E. T. (2002). Corporal punishment by parents and associated child behaviors and experiences: A meta-analytic and theoretical review. *Psychological Bulletin*, 128, 539–579.

Gettleman, J. (2017). Drought and War Heighten Threat Not Just 1 famine but 4. *New York Times*, www.nytimes.com/2017/03/27/world/africa/famine-somalia-nigeria-south-sudan-yemen-water.html.

Gladstein, J., Rusonis, E. J. S., & Heald, F. P. (1992). A comparison of inner-city and upper-middle class youths' exposure to violence. *Journal of Adolescent Health*, 13, 275–280.

Hagan, J. & Foster, H. (2001). Youth violence and the end of adolescence. *American Sociological Review*, 66, 874–899.

Institute of Medicine (IOM) and National Research Council (NRC). (2014). *New directions in child abuse and neglect research*. Washington, DC: The National Academies Press.

Jain, S., Buka, S. L., Subramanian, S. V., & Molnar, B. E. (2012). Protective factors for youth exposed to violence: Role of developmental assets in building emotional resilience. *Youth Violence and Juvenile Justice*, 10, 107–129.

Kaminer, D., Hardy, A., Heath, K., Mosdell, J., & Bawa, U. (2013). Gender patterns in the contribution of different types of violence to posttraumatic stress among South African urban youth. *Child Abuse & Neglect*, 37, 320–330.

Keenan, H. T., Runyan, D. K., Marshall, S. W., Nocera, M. A., Merten, D. F., & Sinal, S. H. (2003). A population-based study of inflicted traumatic brain injury in young children. *Journal of the American Medical Association*, 290, 621–626.

Leventhal, T. & Brooks-Gunn, J. (2000). The neighborhoods they live in: The effects of neighborhood residence on child and adolescent outcomes. *Psychological Bulletin*, 126, 309–337.

Lynch, M. & Cicchetti, D. (1998). An ecological-transactional analysis of children and contexts: The longitudinal interplay among child maltreatment, community violence, and children's symptomatology. *Development and Psychopathology*, 10, 235–257.

MacKenzie, M. J., Nicklas, E., Brooks-Gunn, J., & Waldfogel, J. (2011). Who spanks children and toddlers? Evidence from the Fragile Families and Child Well-Being Study. *Child and Youth Services Review*, 33, 1364–1373.

MacKenzie, M. J., Nicklas, E., Waldfogel, J., & Brooks-Gunn, J. (2012). Corporal punishment and child behavioral and cognitive outcomes through 5 years of age: Evidence from a contemporary urban birth cohort study. *Infant and Child Development*, 21, 3–33.

MacKenzie, M. J., Nicklas, E., Waldfogel, J., & Brooks-Gunn, J. (2013). Spanking and child development across the first decade of life. *Pediatrics*, 132, e1118–e1125.

MacMillan, H., Tanaka, M., Duku, E., Vaillancourt, T., & Boyle M. H. (2013). Child physical and sexual abuse in a community sample of young adults: Results from the Ontario Child Health Study. *Child Abuse & Neglect*, 37, 14–21.

MacMillan, R. (2001). Violence and the life course: The consequences of victimization for personal and social development. *Annual Review of Sociology*, 27, 1–22.

MacMillan, R. & Hagan, J. (2004). Violence in the transition to adulthood: Adolescent victimization, education, and socioeconomic attainment in later life. *Journal of Research on Adolescence*, 14, 127–158.

Malik, S., Sorenson, S. B., & Aneshensel, C. S. (1997). Community and Dating Violence Among Adolescents: Perpetration and Victimization. *Journal of Adolescent Health*, 21, 291–302.

Margolin, G. & Gordis, E. B. (2000). The effects of family and community violence on children. *Annual Review of Psychology*, 51, 445–479.

Margolin, G. & Gordis, E. B. (2004). Children's exposure to violence in the family and community. *Current Directions in Psychological Science*, 13, 152–155.

Martin, L., Revington, N., & Seedat, S. (2013). The 39-item Child Exposure to Community Violence (CECV) scale: Exploratory factor analysis and relationship to PTSD symptomatology in trauma-exposed children and adolescents. *International Journal of Behavioral Medicine*, 20, 599–608.

McLeod, J. D. & Kaiser, K. (2004). Childhood emotional and behavioral problems and educational attainment. *American Sociological Review*, 69, 636–658.

McLeod, J. D. & Shanahan, M. J. (1993). Poverty, parenting, and children's mental health. *American Sociological Review*, 58, 351–366.

Meink, F., Cluver, L. D., & Boyes, M. E. (2015). Household illness, poverty and physical and emotional abuse victimization: findings from South Africa's first prospective cohort study. *BMC Public Health*, 15, 444. doi: 10.1186/s12899-015-1792-4.

Meink, F., Cluver, L. D., Boyes, M. E., & Loening-Voysey, H. (2016). Physical, emotional, and sexual adolescent abuse victimization in South Africa: prevalence, incidence, perpetrators and locations. *Journal of Epidemiology and Community Health*, 70, 910–916.

Meinck F, Cluver L. D., Boyes, M. E., & Mhlongo, E. L. (2015). Risk and protective factors for physical and sexual abuse of children and adolescents in Africa: a review and implications for practice. *Trauma, Violence & Abuse*, 16, 81–107.

Meinck, F., Cluver, L., Boyes, M. E., & Ndhlovu, L. (2015). Risk and protective factors for physical and emotional abuse victimisation amongst vulnerable children in South Africa. *Child Abuse Review*, 24, 182–197.

Mirowsky, J., & Ross, C. E. (2003). *Social causes of psychological distress* (2nd ed.). New York: Aldine De Gruyter.

Molnar, B. E., Buka, S. L., Brennan, R. T., Holton, J. K., & Earls, F. (2003). A multilevel study of neighborhoods and parent-to-child physical aggression: Results from the Project for Human Development in Chicago neighborhoods. *Child Maltreatment*, 8, 84–97.

Morantz, G., Cole, D., Vreeman, R., Ayaya, S., Ayuku, D., & Braitstein, P. (2013). Child abuse and neglect among orphaned children and youth living in extended families in sub-Saharan Africa: What have we learned from qualitative inquiry? *Vulnerable Children and Youth Studies*, 8, 338–352.

Neugebauer, R., Fisher, P. W., Turner, J. B., Yamabe, S., Sarsfield, J. A., & Stehling-Ariza, T. (2009). Post-traumatic stress reactions among Rwandan children and adolescents in the early aftermath of genocide. *International Journal of Epidemiology*, 38, 1033–1045.

Nichols, J., Embleton, L., Mwangi, A., Morantz, G., Vreeman, R., Ayaya, S., … & Braistein, P. (2014). Physical and sexual abuse in orphaned compared to non-orphaned children in sub-Saharan Africa: A systematic review and meta-analysis. *Child Abuse & Neglect*, 38, 304–316.

Ng, L. C., Ahishakiye, N., Miller, D. E., & Meyerowitz, B. E. (2015). Life after genocide: mental health, education, and social support among orphaned survivors. *International Perspectives in Psychology: Research, Practice, Consultation*, 4, 83–97.

Odejide, A. O. (2006). Status of Drug Use/Abuse in Africa: A Review. *International Journal of Mental Health Addiction*, 4, 87–102.

O'Donnell, D. A., Roberts, W. C., & Schwab-Stone, M. E. (2011). Community violence exposure and post-traumatic stress reactions among Gambian youth: The moderating role of positive school climate. *Social Psychiatry and Psychiatric Epidemiology*, 46, 59–67.

O'Donnell, D. A. & Roberts, W. C. (2015). Experiences of violence, perceptions of neighborhood, and psychosocial adjustment among West African Refugee youth. *International Perspectives in Psychology: Research, Practice, Consultation*, 4, 1–18.

O'Keefe, M. & Sela-Amit, M. (1997). An examination of the effects of race/ethnicity and social class on adolescents' exposure to violence. *Journal of Social Services Research*, 22, 53–71.

Osofsky, J. D. (1999). The impact of violence on children. *Future of Children*, 9(3), 33–49.

Otwombe, K. N., Dietrich, J., Sikkema, K. J., Coetzee, J., Hopkins, K. L., Laher, F., & Gray, G. E. (2015). Exposure to and experiences of violence among adolescents in lower socio-economic groups in Johannesburg, South Africa. *BMC Public Health*, 15, 450. doi: 10.1186/s12899-015-1780-8.

Overpeck, M. D., Brenner, R. A., Trumble, A. C., Trifiletti, L. B., & Berendes, H. W. (1998). Risk factors for infant homicide in the United States. *New England Journal of Medicine*, 339, 1211–1216.

Overstreet, S. (2000). Exposure to community violence: Defining the problem and understanding the consequences. *Journal of Child and Family Studies*, 9, 7–25.

Pearlin, L. I. (1989). The sociological study of stress. *Journal of Health and Social Behavior*, 30, 241–256.

Pearlin, L. I., Leiberman, M. A., Menaghan, E. G., & Mullan, J. T. (1981). The stress process. *Journal of Health and Social Behavior*, 22, 337–356.

Reider, H. & Elbert, T. (2013). The relationship between organized violence, family violence and mental health: findings from a community-based survey in Muhanga, Southern Rwanda. *European Journal of Psychotraumatology*, 4, 21329. doi: 10.3402/ejpt.v4i0.21329.

Richter, L. M. & Dawes, A. R. L. (2008). Child abuse in South Africa: Rights and wrongs. *Child Abuse Review*, 17, 79–93.

Richters, J. & Martinez, P. (1993). The NIMH community violence project: Children as victims of and witnesses to violence. *Psychiatry*, 56, 7–21.

Rutter, M. (1989). Pathways from childhood to adult life. *Journal of Child Psychology and Psychiatry*, 30, 23–51.

Sampson, R. J. (1997). The embeddedness of child and adolescent development: A community-level perspective on urban violence. In J. McCord (Ed.), *Violence in childhood in the inner city* (pp. 31–77). New York: Cambridge University Press.

Sampson, R. J. & Laub, J. H. 1993. *Crime in the making: Pathways and turning points through life*. Cambridge, MA: Harvard University Press.

Sampson, R. J., Raudenbush, S. W., & Earls, F. (1997). Neighborhoods and violent crime: A multilevel study of collective efficacy. *Science*, 277, 918–924.

Sampson, R. J. & Wilson, W. J. (1995). Toward a theory of race, crime, and urban inequality. In J. Hagan & R. Peterson (Eds), *Crime and inequality* (pp. 37–56). Stanford, CA: Stanford University Press.

Schneider, W., Waldfogel, J., & Brooks-Gunn, J. (2017). The Great Recession and risk for child abuse and neglect. *Children and Youth Services Review*, 72, 71–81.

Schwab-Stone, M. D., Ayers, T. S., Kasprow, W., Voyce, C., Barone, C., Shriver, T., et al. (1995). No safe haven: A study of violence exposure in an urban community. *Journal of the American Academy of Child and Adolescent Psychiatry*, 34, 1343–1352.

Seedat, S., Nyami, F., Njenga, F., Vythlingum, B., & Stein, D. J. (2004). Trauma exposure and post-traumatic stress symptoms in urban African schools. Survey in Cape Town and Nairobi. *The British Journal of Psychiatry*, 184, 169–175.

Selner-O'Hagan, M. B., Kindlon, D. J., Buka, S. L., Raudenbush, S. W., & Earls, F. J. (1998). Assessing exposure to violence in urban youth. *Journal of Child Psychology and Psychiatry*, 39, 215–224.

Sheidow, A. J., Gorman-Smith, D., Tolan, P. H., & Henry, D. B. (2001). Family and community characteristics: Risk factors for violence exposure in inner-city youth. *Journal of Community Psychology*, 29, 345–360.

Sherr, L., Hensels, I. S., Skeen, S., Tomlinson, M., Roberts, K. J., & Macedo, A. (2016).

Exposure to violence predicts poor educational outcomes in young children in South Africa and Malawi. *International Health*, 8, 36–43.

Shields, N. S., Nadasen, K., & Pierce, L. (2009). Posttraumatic stress symptoms as a mediating factor on the effects of exposure to community violence among children in Cape Town, South Africa. *Journal of Interpersonal Violence*, 24, 1192–1208.

Shields, N., Nadasen, K., & Pierce, L. (2013). Community violence and psychological distress in South African and U.S. Children. *International Perspectives in Psychology: Research, Practice, Consultation*, 2, 286–300.

Smith, J. R. & Brooks-Gunn, J. (1997). Correlates and consequences of harsh discipline for young children. *Archives of Pediatrics & Adolescent Medicine*, 151, 777–786.

Straus, M. A. (1979). Measuring intrafamily conflict and violence: The Conflict Tactics (CT) Scales. *Journal of Marriage and the Family*, 41, 75–88.

Turner, R. J., Wheaton, B., & Lloyd, D. A. (1995). The epidemiology of social stress. *American Sociological Review*, 60, 104–125.

United Nations Children's Fund. (2010). Children and AIDS: Fifth stocktaking report, 2010. New York: UNICEF.

United Nations Children's Fund. (2013). Towards an AIDS-Free Generation – Children and AIDS: Sixth Stocktaking Report, 2013. New York: UNICEF.

US Census Bureau. (2005). How the Census Bureau measures poverty. Retrieved April 29, 2005 from www.census.gov/hhes/poverty/povdef.html.

Vacha, E. F. & McLaughlin, T. F. (2004). Risky firearms behavior in low-income families of elementary school children: The impact of poverty, fear of crime, and crime victimization in keeping and storing firearms. *Journal of Family Violence*, 19, 175–184.

Viola, T. W., Salum, G. A., Kluwe-Schiavon, B., Sanvicente-Viera, B., Levandowski, M. L., & Grassi-Oliveira, R. (2016). The influence of geographical and economic factors in estimates of childhood abuse and neglect using the Childhood Trauma Questionnaire: A worldwide meta-regression analysis. *Child Abuse & Neglect*, 51, 1–11.

Ward, C. L., Martin, E., Theron, C., & Distiller, G. B. (2007). Factors affecting resilience in children exposed to violence. *South African Journal of Psychology*, 37, 165–187.

Wheaton, B., Young, M., Montazer, S., & Stuart-Lahman, K. (2013). Social stress in the twenty-first century. In Aneshensel, C. S., Phelan, J. C., & Bierman, A. (Eds), *Handbook of the Sociology of Mental Health*, Second Edition (pp. 299–323). New York: Springer.

Wildeman, C., Emanuel, N., Leventhal, J. M., Putnam-Hornstein, E., Waldfogel, J., & Lee, H. (2014). The prevalence of confirmed maltreatment among US children, 2004 to 2011. *JAMA Pediatrics*, 168, 706–713.

Willms, J. D. (2002). Socioeconomic gradients for childhood vulnerability. In J. D. Willms (Ed.), *Vulnerable children: Findings from Canada's National Longitudinal Survey of Children and Youth* (pp. 71–102). Edmonton, Alberta: University of Alberta Press.

Wintemute, G. (2000). Guns and gun violence. In A. Blumstein & J. Wallman (Eds), *The crime drop in America* (pp. 45–96). Cambridge: Cambridge University Press.

Wu, S. S., Ma, C. X., Carter, R. L., Ariet, M., Feaver, E. A., Resnick, M. B., & Roth, J. (2003). Risk factors for infant maltreatment: A population-based study. *Child Abuse & Neglect*, 28, 1253–1264.

36 Firearms and Violence

Brandon Turchan and Anthony A. Braga

Introduction

Firearms are versatile tools that are used for a wide range of legitimate purposes, including hunting, sports, and self-protection. For many Americans, guns are an integral and essential part of their identity. According to recent estimates by the Congressional Research Service, there are more than 300 million firearms in the United States (Krouse, 2012). The total number of guns in the United States equates to roughly one firearm per person, but only 35–38% of households report owning a gun (Hepburn et al., 2007; Smith, 2001). Only a small fraction of privately owned firearms are ever involved in crime or unlawful violence (Kleck, 1991). Nevertheless, gun violence remains a persistent problem in the United States of America. In 2014, there were 9,652 gun-involved homicide victims[1] and an additional 60,470 nonfatal assaultive gunshot injuries in the USA (National Center for Injury Prevention and Control, 2016). Tragic mass shootings in Newtown, Connecticut; Orlando, Florida; and elsewhere underscore the great harm that can be generated by firearms misused by those who should not have them.

Firearm violence not only exacts social and monetary tolls on victims and their families, but it also generates economic burdens on society at large. Estimates of the average medical cost associated with treating a gunshot injury range from $10,000 to $17,000 per instance (Cook et al., 1999; Morrison et al., 2015). The accumulation of these direct costs, as well as indirect, are sizable. After considering the expenses related to lost work productivity, medical care, mental health care, emergency transportation, police, criminal justice organizations, processing insurance claims, employer costs, and quality of life, the Pacific Institute of Research and Evaluation estimated gunshot injuries in 2010 alone cost the United States upwards of $174 billion (Miller, 2013).

Here, we provide a concise overview of the available scientific evidence on firearms and violence. We begin by reviewing recent trends in US gun violence and presenting the basic characteristics of gun violence victims and offenders. Since most firearms violence is concentrated in cities, we then describe the underlying dynamics associated with persistent urban gun violence. We then examine the influence of firearms and their availability on the lethality of violent events, and describe the pathways through which high-risk individuals illegally acquire guns. Finally, the available evaluation evidence on the prospects of

---

[1] http://www.ojjdp.gov/ojstatbb/ezashr/ (accessed August 11, 2016).

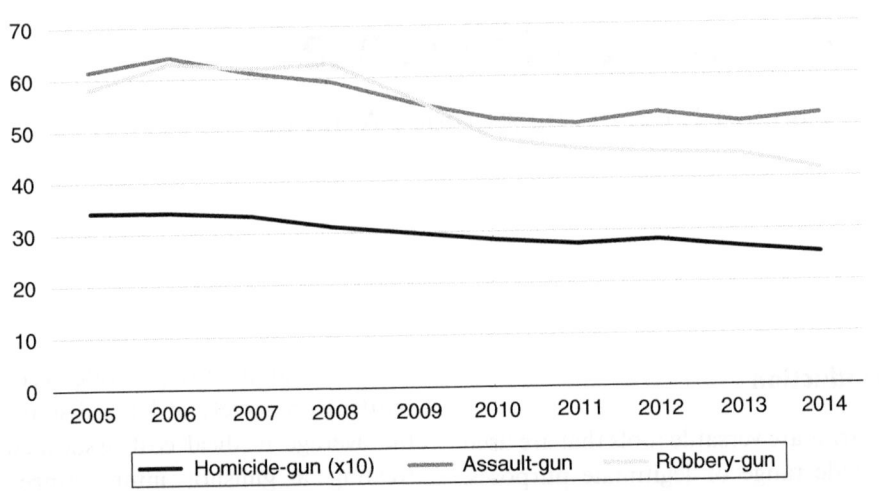

Figure 36.1 *Annual gun-involved crime per 100,000 people, 2005 to 2014 (FBI, 2015).*

controlling gun violence through different kinds of policy interventions is considered.

Prevalence, Recent Trends, and Basic Characteristics

After large declines over the course of the mid-1990s and early 2000s, gun violence in the United States has continued to decrease over the past decade. According to the US Federal Bureau of Investigation (FBI) Uniform Crime Reports (UCR), gun homicide victimization rates decreased by 24% from 3.4 per 100,000 people in 2005 to 2.6 per 100,000 people in 2014.[2] Both gun-involved robbery and gun-involved aggravated assault trends followed similar downward trajectories during this time period. Gun-involved robbery victimization rates declined more than 28%, from 58.0 per 100,000 residents in 2005 to 41.6 per 100,000 residents in 2014. Rates of gun-involved aggravated assault victimization rates declined 15% from 61.5 per 100,000 residents to 52.3 per 100,000 people over this same ten-year span.[3] Further, in contrast to gun-involved homicide and gun-involved robbery, which experienced a relatively consistent decline from 2005 to 2014, gun-involved aggravated assault rates have leveled off over the last five years (see Figure 36.1).

While 2014 gun homicide victimization rates represented a 51-year low in gun homicide rate trends, the United States is well known for having an extraordinarily high percentage and rate of firearm homicides relative to other industrialized nations (Zimring & Hawkins, 1997). The United States also has the unenviable distinction of experiencing more gun homicides each year than all other high-income countries in the Organisation for Economic Co-operation and Development (OECD) combined (Richardson & Hemenway, 2011). In terms of reference points, the number of United States residents killed by guns

---

[2] https://ucr.fbi.gov/crime-in-the-u.s/2014/crime-in-the-u.s.-2014/offenses-known-to-law-enforcement/expanded-homicide (accessed June 4, 2016).
[3] https://ucr.fbi.gov/crime-in-the-u.s/2014/crime-in-the-u.s.-2014/tables/table-19 (accessed June 4, 2016).

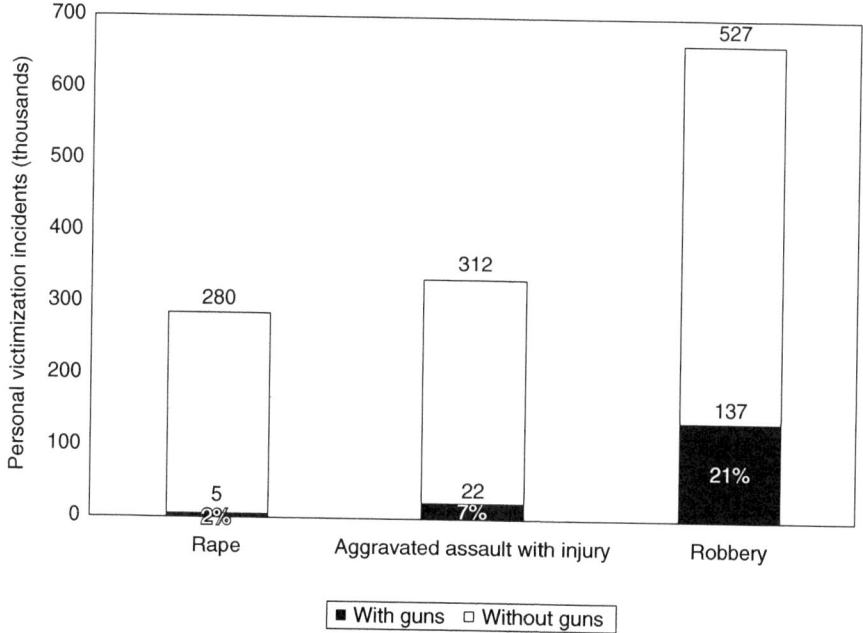

Figure 36.2 *Personal crimes of violence, 2014 (Bureau of Justice Statistics, 2016).*

each year is equivalent to the total number of American deaths during the Korean War and the US homicide rate is about 50% lower than the yearly highway fatality rate (Cook, Braga, & Moore, 2011).

Firearms are the most frequently used weapons in killings as about two-thirds of all US homicides involve guns. In 2014, according to the FBI UCR, handguns were used in 69% of gun homicides.[4] It is important to note that only about one in six gun assault victims suffers a fatal wound and many more gun violence victims do not suffer any gun injuries (Cook, 1985). Indeed, many violent crimes are completed without firearms despite the purported tactical advantage of using guns to gain victim compliance via threats. According to the 2014 National Crime Victimization Survey (NCVS), 21% of robberies (roughly 137,000 of 527,000 total robberies) were committed with a gun. By comparison, much smaller portion of rapes and aggravated assaults with injury involved guns: only 2% of the estimated 280,000 rapes and nearly 7% of the estimated 312,000 aggravated assaults with injury involved guns (see Figure 36.2).

When measured as a homicide problem, the available data reveals that gun violence tends to concentrate in particular gender, race, and age groups. Data from the FBI's 2014 Supplementary Homicide Reports (SHR) shows males account for the vast majority of gun homicide victims (83%).[5] While Black residents represented slightly less than 13% of the US population

---

[4] https://ucr.fbi.gov/crime-in-the-u.s/2014/crime-in-the-u.s.-2014/offenses-known-to-law-enforcement/expanded-homicide (accessed June 4, 2016).
[5] http://www.ojjdp.gov/ojstatbb/ezashr/ (accessed August 11, 2016).

in 2014,[6] some 59% of gun homicide victims were Black while only 39% were White. Youth tend to be over-represented among gun homicide victims. Juveniles (age 17 and younger) account for a relatively small portion of total gun homicide victimizations, at over 6%, whereas young adults (age 18 to 24) represent 29% of victimizations; in sum, more than 57% of gun homicide victims are under 30 years old.[7] Young Black males face tragically high risks of violent gun victimization. In 2014, among 15–24-year-olds, Black males experienced a gun homicide victimization rate of 83.9 per 100,000 persons while White males experienced a gun homicide victimization rate of only 4.7 per 100,000 persons.[8] When comparing these two rates, Black males were victims of gun homicide at approximately 18 times the rate of White males in the same age group.

The demographic composition of gun homicide offenders largely mirrors the demographics of gun homicide victims. SHR data on 7,731 known gun-involved homicide offenders in 2014 reveal that 91% were male and nearly 61% were Black (compared to over 35% White).[9] Also, Black males accounted for the largest race-gender offending group. Over 56% of known gun-involved homicide offenders were Black males, while 32% were white males. Black females and White females each represented approximately 4% of all known gun homicide offenders.

There is a large body of research evidence that indicates having a prior criminal history is another risk factor for individual involvement in serious gun violence. Many adult and youth killers are not "law abiding" but rather have a history of criminal behavior. Wolfgang (1958) was among the first to document the concentration of homicide victimization and perpetration among individuals with a criminal record; a pattern that holds when applied specifically to gun crime. For instance, a recent study of individuals arrested for illegal gun possession and violent gun offenses in 2014 by the Boston Police Department found that 80% of the adult arrestees had prior criminal records (Braga & Cook, 2016). What is more, illegal gun possessors were as involved in crime as those who were arrested for gun violence – murder, robbery, and assault.

Although gun violence in rural areas is a concern (see Morrison et al., 2015), research has primarily focused on urban environments where gun violence rates are nearly ten times greater than suburban, metropolitan, and non-metropolitan counties (Nance et al., 2002). Large cities (those with 100,000 residents or more) account for approximately 60% of all gun homicides (Cooper & Smith, 2011). Prevalence, however, is not the only distinguishing feature between rural and urban gun violence. While handguns accounted for more than half of gun deaths in both types of settings, Dresang (2001) found the percentage of gun deaths involving shotguns and rifles was significantly higher in rural areas compared to urban areas.

---

6 https://factfinder.census.gov/faces/tableservices/jsf/pages/productview.xhtml?pid=ACS_14_5YR_DP05&src=pt (accessed August 16, 2016).
7 https://ucr.fbi.gov/crime-in-the-u.s/2014/crime-in-the-u.s.-2014/offenses-known-to-law-enforcement/expanded-homicide (accessed June 4, 2016).
8 http://www.ojjdp.gov/ojstatbb/ezashr/ (accessed August 11, 2016).
9 http://www.ojjdp.gov/ojstatbb/ezashr/ (accessed August 11, 2016).

The Nature of Urban Gun Violence

Disproportionate violent gun victimization and offending rates among young Black males is connected to specific neighborhood characteristics and dynamics within cities (Branas et al., 2009; Huebner et al., 2016). Urban policy-makers, practitioners, and scholars have long considered the variations in neighborhood characteristics that lead to high rates of violence in particular urban communities. Empirical evidence suggests that the capacity of neighborhood residents to achieve a common set of goals and exert control over youth and public spaces, termed "collective efficacy," is a protective factor against serious violence (Sampson, Raudenbush, & Earls, 1997). Concentrated disadvantage in urban neighborhoods undermines local collective efficacy and gravely limits the ability of residents to address serious violent crime problems. Drawing on this line of neighborhood effects research, Wiebe and colleagues (2016) found nonfatal gunshot victimization was lower in areas with higher levels of neighbor connectedness. Unfortunately, due to a long history of exclusion from economic and social opportunities, residents of disadvantaged urban neighborhoods are primarily minorities and often Black (Sampson & Wilson, 1995).

Research has also documented that gun violence is highly concentrated at very small places within neighborhoods. In Minneapolis, 64% of the city's shootings were linked to only 8% of all city blocks, and 36% of shootings occurred in less than 3% of all city blocks (Koper, Egge, & Lum, 2015). In Boston, a longitudinal analysis found that 74% of serious gun assault incidents were generated by only 5% of street block faces and intersections in the city between 1980 and 2008 (Braga, Papachristos, & Hureau, 2010). The most active 60 street block faces and intersections in Boston experienced more than 1,000 shootings during the study period. Gun violence hot spots were more likely to be found within disadvantaged, minority Boston neighborhoods; and, these small places were often characterized by the presence of gang turf and illegal drug markets.

Beyond these geographic concentrations, urban gun violence has also been noted to be highly clustered among criminally active individuals participating in high-risk social networks. For instance, in 2006, only 1% of Boston's population between the ages of 14 and 24 were members of street gangs involved in gun violence; however, gang-related disputes generated more than two-thirds of gun homicides and gang members were involved as offenders, victims, or both in nearly 70% of nonfatal shootings (Braga, Hureau, & Winship, 2008). In a recent study of one disadvantaged Boston community, roughly 85% of all gunshot victims were in a single co-offending network of gang members, drug dealers, and others representing less than 5% of the community's population (Papachristos, Braga, & Hureau, 2012). Furthermore, the increased risk of violence among gang members may spread to non-gang members with whom they associate. An analysis of fatal and nonfatal shootings in a co-offending network in Newark, New Jersey found that social closeness to a gang member was strongly associated with a higher risk of gun victimization, re-iterating the importance of network connections for risk of gun violence (Papachristos et al., 2015).

The Influence of Firearm Possession and Use on Serious Violence

Beyond the influence of criminal associations and neighborhood context on gun violence, it is important to consider whether the type of weapon used influences the lethality of violent events. If the weapon type deployed in violent events determines whether a victim lives or dies, then restricting access to firearms by violent individuals would reduce gun homicides. However, guns also potentially provide would-be victims with the ability to escape serious injury and death by deterring potential attackers.

The instrumentality hypothesis posits firearm use increases the lethality of violent events (Zimring, 1968). Compared to other weapons, such as knives or blunt objects, guns are substantially more lethal. This suggests that robberies and assaults committed with guns are more likely to result in the victim's death. Indeed, Cook (1987) found gun-involved robberies were three and ten times more likely to end in a fatality than robberies involving knives or other weapons, respectively. For assaults that result in an injury, gun assaults are more likely to result in the death of the victim when compared to non-gun assaults (Kleck & McElrath, 1991). To some observers, however, the lethality of the event is determined by the intent of the attacker and the choice of weapon is determined by their desire to inflict a deadly wound (Wolfgang, 1958; Wright, Rossi, & Daly, 1983). Essentially, even if a gun was not available, it is argued that determined killers would still find a way to inflict deadly harm on their victims.

Professor Frank Zimring's (1968, 1972) studies of wounds inflicted in gun and knife assaults, however, demonstrate considerable overlap between fatal and nonfatal attacks, suggesting that the difference between life and death is just a matter of chance (see also Cook, 1987). This suggests that the difference between a gun homicide and a nonfatal shooting event is contingent on several uncontrollable factors – the aim of the shooter, the distance to the target, a rapid call to the police, the response time of medical assistance, whether the bullet hits a vital organ, and so on. In essence, death is a probabilistic outcome of violent crime. His studies suggest that firearms increase the probability of death in violent events, as do technological features, such as the caliber of the firearms deployed.

Other research studies examine whether the availability of firearms influences community levels of gun violence and individual victimization. The prevalence of gun ownership differs widely among communities in the United States (Kleck, 1991; Cook & Ludwig, 1996), but no official data systems in the United States track gun ownership rates across jurisdictions. The best available proxy measure for gun prevalence over time at regional and state levels is the fraction of suicides that involve a firearm (FSS) (Azrael, Cook, & Miller, 2004). Several studies report a strong positive correlation between the FSS proxy and homicide rates across counties (Cook & Ludwig, 2002; Miller, Azrael, & Hemenway, 2002). Unfortunately, these cross-sectional studies suffer from some well-known methodological limitations such as an inability to control for systematic differences over time in gun-rich jurisdictions (e.g., Mississippi) relative to jurisdictions with few guns (e.g., Massachusetts) (Cook et al., 2011). The best available panel-data evidence suggests that more guns lead to more homicides, which is driven entirely by a relationship between gun prevalence and homicides committed with firearms; there is little association of gun prevalence with non-gun homicides or other types of crimes (Duggan, 2001). However, the prevalence of gun ownership has no discernible effect on the overall volume of violent crime (Cook et al., 2011).

A series of case-control studies suggest that the presence of guns in the home make owners and their family members less safe (see Kellerman et al., 1993). A recent review of these studies concluded that a gun in the home is far more likely to end up being used to kill a member of the household (including suicide) than to kill or injure an intruder (Hemenway, 2004). However, these studies have been critiqued for possibly not controlling all relevant variables and risk factors (see National Research Council, 2005). Moreover, these studies have not considered whether homeowners may have deployed their firearms to repel or scare off potential intruders. A fairer comparison would consider possible self-defense benefits as well as any observable harms associated with household gun ownership.

Defensive Gun Use and Right-to-Carry Laws

While gun misuse by criminals generates considerable harm, firearms also provide some crime victims with the means of escaping serious injury or property loss. Indeed, self-protection is an important reason offered by citizens and criminals alike when acquiring firearms, especially handguns (Kellerman & Cook, 1999). How often gun owners repel would-be offenders is far from definitive, however.

The National Self-Defense Survey estimated there were some 2.5 million defensive gun uses (DGUs) per year in the United States (Kleck & Gertz, 1995). Other studies yield much smaller annual DGU estimates. Administered by the US Census Bureau, the NCVS is generally considered the "gold standard" in crime survey research. Annual DGU estimates using NCVS data have included 65,000 (McDowall & Wiersema, 1994), 108,000 (Cook, Ludwig, & Hemenway, 1997), and 116,000 (McDowall, Loftin, & Presser, 2000).

The 1994 National Study of Private Ownership of Firearms (Cook & Ludwig, 1996) used the same DGU measurement approach developed by Kleck and Gertz (1995). Broadly consistent with the National Self-Defense Survey, Cook and colleagues (1997) estimated some 1.5 million DGUs per year. Through extrapolation of results from their survey, they estimated 132,000 perpetrators were shot (fatally or nonfatally) by armed citizens who discharged their weapon in self-defense. The authors concluded this estimate was unrealistically high. The estimate obtained was nearly equivalent to the number of all firearm fatalities or emergency room admissions for nonfatal gunshot wounds that year, the majority of which were due to criminal victimization, suicide, or accident (Cook et al., 1997).

Cook and Ludwig (1998) demonstrated there is a large positive bias when estimating DGU from survey data. They found 45 respondents in the National Study of Private Ownership of Firearms reported a DGU in the past year; but projecting results from this sample over the whole US population corresponds to an estimated 3.1 million DGUs annually. When disaggregated by crime type, survey results suggested 322,000 rapes, 462,000 aggravated assaults, and 527,000 robberies involved DGU by the victim. Incorporating data from the NCVS, Cook and Ludwig (1998) noted that these results suggest that every rape or attempted rape involved DGU. The National Research Council's (2005) Committee to Improve Research Information and Data on Firearms concluded the striking differences in estimated DGU prevalence suggest that existing surveys were measuring different concepts and recommended the establishment of a research program to address these measurement issues.

Another important line of research examining firearm use by the public to defend against crime considers whether law-abiding citizens should be permitted to carry concealed guns in public. Investigations into the relationship between legal concealed gun carrying and crime has primarily focused on state-level policy and right-to-carry (RTC) laws. In states with RTC laws, authorities must issue concealed carry permits to law-abiding individuals who apply and meet an established minimum eligibility criteria. As of 2016, only eight states and the District of Columbia have laws that give licensing authorities complete discretion over whether to issue concealed carry permits to individuals.[10]

Early research studies found that RTC laws were unrelated to violent crime rates (see Kleck & Patterson, 1993; McDowall, Loftin, & Wiersema, 1995). However, two well-publicized empirical studies by Lott and Mustard (1997) and Lott (2000) suggested that significant reductions in violent crime followed the enactment of state RTC laws. While some subsequent replication studies found mixed support for Lott and Mustard's conclusion (e.g., Olson & Maltz, 2001; Plassmann & Tideman, 2001), a number of studies using the same dataset found the passage of RTC laws were unrelated to violent crime rates or actually increased violent crime rates (e.g., Ayres & Donohue, 2003; Black & Nagin, 1998). The National Research Council (2005) attempted to replicate Lott's findings using a revised dataset and successfully reproduced similar results with the exception for the direction of the relationship for aggravated assault. However, the Council report outlined a number of methodological concerns that undermined the validity of Lott's findings including missing data, omitted variable bias, model misspecification, and inappropriate computation of standard errors. Finally, a series of sensitivity tests performed by the Council to address the methodological shortcomings further confirmed the fragility of the Lott (2000) and Lott and Mustard (1997) results and, as such, undermined the case that the passage of RTC laws reduced violent crime.

The Illegal Supply of Guns to Criminals

Some of the most influential work establishing how high-risk possessors obtain guns draws upon now-dated survey research on incarcerated felons, juveniles in secure facilities, and high school students (Wright & Rossi, 1994; Sheley & Wright, 1995). In their survey of more than 1,800 incarcerated felons, Wright and Rossi (1994) found that illegal gun acquisition was typically an "off the

---

10 https://www.nraila.org/gun-laws/ (accessed August 20, 2016).

books" process, with more than 80% of documented handgun transactions made by informal arrangements with friends, family, and "various black market outlets." The authors also found that more than 50% of those surveyed had stolen a gun in the past – mostly as a crime of opportunity – and estimated that between 40% and 70% of all guns described in their survey were stolen.

Others studies have confirmed that theft does seem to play an important role in the supply of illegal guns, with current estimates suggesting some 250,000 guns are stolen in the USA per year (Langton, 2012). However, as will be discussed further below, prohibited possessors seem to acquire firearms from a diversity of sources including illegal diversions of firearms from legal commerce. A well-recognized limitation to the Wright and Rossi (1994) and Sheley and Wright (1995) studies is that the surveys could not precisely determine if theft itself was the proximate cause of a gun's move into the "illegal" market or if theft occurred within the "criminal" domain after a gun was already illegally diverted from legal commerce (Kennedy, Piehl, & Braga, 1996). While theft may play a greater role at an earlier stage of moving guns from the licit to the illicit sector, more contemporary surveys of prison and jail populations suggest that theft plays a much more modest role in the direct supply of crime guns than previously thought. Illegal transfers from largely unregulated secondary firearms market sources seem to be a key source of firearms for prohibited persons.

A recent analysis of data drawn from the 2004 Survey of Inmates in State Correctional Facilities (SISCF), the 2004 Survey of Inmates in Federal Correctional Facilities (SIFCF), and the 2002 Survey of Inmates in Local Jails (SILJ) suggests that very few illegal gun users directly acquire their guns through theft. Among male respondents age 18 to 40 who were in the first two years of their prison term and admitted in the survey interview they had a gun at the time of crime Cook, Parker, and Pollock (2015) found that only 4% reported directly stealing their most recent crime gun. Cook and colleagues (2015) also found that only 10% of recently incarcerated state prison inmates who carried a gun indicated they purchased that gun from a licensed dealer (gun store or pawnbroker). Most of the transactions, roughly 70%, were with social connections (friends and family) or with "street" sources (fences, drug dealers, illicit gun brokers, and gangs).

Other research suggests that prohibited possessors circumvent lax laws and regulations governing legal firearms commerce to acquire guns. Much of this evidence comes from analyses of Bureau of Alcohol, Tobacco, Firearms, and Explosives (ATF) firearm trace data and firearms trafficking investigations that indicate some percentage of the guns used in crime were recently diverted from legal firearms commerce (ATF 1997, 2000, 2002; Braga et al., 2012; Cook & Braga, 2001; Pierce et al., 2004). Among the main findings of these research studies are: (1) New guns are recovered disproportionately in crime (Cook & Braga, 2001; Pierce et al., 2004; Zimring, 1976). (2) Some licensed firearm retailers (Federal Firearms Licensees or FFLs) are disproportionately frequent sources of crime guns; these retailers are linked to more guns traced by ATF than would be expected from their overall volume of gun sales (there could be many reasons for these patterns, see Wintemute, Cook, & Wright, 2005). (3) Under test conditions, significant proportions of licensed retailers and private-party gun sellers will knowingly participate in illegal gun sales (Sorenson & Vittes, 2003; Wintemute, 2010). (4) On average, about one-third of guns used in crime in any community are acquired in that community, another third come from elsewhere in the same state, and a third are imported from other states (ATF, 1997, 2002; Cook & Braga, 2001). (5) There are longstanding interstate trafficking routes for crime guns, typically from states with weaker gun regulations to states with stronger ones. The best-known of these is the Interstate 95 "Iron Pipeline" from the Southeast to the Middle Atlantic and New England states (Cook & Braga, 2001; Pierce et al., 2004).

While survey research highlights the importance of theft and secondary market acquisitions in supplying adult criminals and juveniles with guns, these studies also complement analyses of firearm trace and investigation data in suggesting a fairly substantial role, either direct or indirect, for retail outlet sales in supplying criminals with guns. For instance, Wright and Rossi (1994) reported that 21% of male prisoners had acquired their most recent handgun from a licensed dealer. Sheley and Wright (1995) found that 32% of juvenile inmates had asked someone, typically a friend or family member, to straw purchase a gun for them in a gun shop, pawnshop, or other retail outlet. Survey studies also find that "street" and "black market" sources are important, sources that may well include traffickers who are buying from retail outlets and selling on the street (Cook et al., 2015).

Reducing Gun Violence

Cook and colleagues (2011) classified gun-control measures into three categories: those that are intended to reduce overall gun ownership; those that are intended to keep guns away from particularly dangerous people; and those that are intended to influence choices about how guns are used and to what effect. The available research suggests that these three approaches have some merit. In this section, we borrow this same analytic framework to highlight the effectiveness and vulnerabilities of varying kinds of gun violence reduction strategies.

Raising Prices and Reducing Gun Availability

Following basic economic theory, the goal of these strategies is to make guns too expensive to be obtained by high-risk individuals. By reducing the available supply of guns, prices will increase and fewer consumers will be able to acquire them. In turn, violent individuals will be less likely to own or acquire a firearm, will be more likely to use less-lethal weapons, and gun violence will be reduced. However, given the large number of firearms in private hands in the United States, critics of this approach argue it would be futile to try to reduce the availability of guns to determined criminals (see Wright, 1995).

Gun violence reduction initiatives aimed at increasing price and reducing availability typically rely on government action at the national, state, or local levels. Gun bans and legislation that enact restrictive licensing requirements have not had clear impacts on gun violence (Cook & Ludwig, 2006). Efforts to raise the price of guns have been made through the imposition of safety requirements on gun manufacturers (Cook, 1981), including "child-proofing," protections against accidental discharge, trigger locks, and loaded chamber indicators (Teret & Wintemute, 1993). By adding minimum safety requirements, manufacturers incur more costs, which are then passed along to the consumer in the form of higher prices (Cook et al., 2011).

Gun buybacks, amnesties, and exchange programs have wide appeal for communities impacted by gun violence for understandable reasons (Braga & Wintemute, 2013). The theoretical premise of gun buybacks is that these programs will reduce the number of firearms available to criminals, mentally ill persons, and other high-risk individuals who may harm themselves or others with a gun. Moreover, these programs arguably empower participants and supporters to take an active role in the fight against gun violence and, as a result, believe that they are making a difference in their communities.

Early studies in the United States identified shortcomings limiting gun buybacks' potential effectiveness (Romero, Wintemute, & Vernick, 1998; Kuhn et al., 2002). Buybacks disproportionately recovered firearms that were old, broken, of low caliber and ammunition capacity, and differing from the firearms most frequently used in crime. Moreover, many of the individuals who turned in firearms tended to be middle-aged gun owners and not older adolescents and young adults, who are at highest risk for involvement in criminal activity.

The typical gun buyback program yields less than 1,000 guns (National Research Council, 2005). Relative to the existing stock of some 300 million firearms in civilian hands, the small scale of these programs also makes it difficult to generate the desired effects on the availability of guns to criminals and others who should not have them. As such, it is not surprising that impact evaluations have failed to find any link between gun buyback programs and subsequent decreases in gun violence. The National Research Council (2005) Committee to Improve Research Information and Data on Firearms concluded that the theory underlying gun buyback programs is flawed and the empirical evidence demonstrates the ineffectiveness of these programs.

Outside the United States, there have been a small number of very large-scale gun buybacks in response to high-profile mass murders with firearms. After a lone gunman killed 35 people in Tasmania in 1996, for example, the Australian government prohibited particular kinds of long guns and provided funds to buy back all such firearms in private hands. Some 640,000 firearms, representing about 20% of the estimated civilian stock of firearms, were bought by the government at an average price of $350 per long gun (Leigh & Neill, 2010). The most comprehensive long-term evaluation of the Australian gun buyback found the program led to substantial decreases in gun suicide and gun homicide rates (Leigh & Neill, 2010). Importantly, the states with the highest numbers of firearms bought back experienced the largest decreases in gun deaths. The evaluation concluded that, by withdrawing firearms from the civilian stock on such a large scale, Australia had saved itself 200 gunshot deaths and $500 million (in US dollars) in costs each year.

Restricting Access to Guns

One broad class of gun-control policy instruments are those designed to influence who has access to different kinds of firearms (Cook et al., 2011; Braga, Kennedy, & Tita, 2002). In essence, these "supply-side" interventions seek to reduce gun crimes by keeping guns out of the wrong hands without denying access to legitimate owners or infringing on legitimate uses of guns (Braga & Cook, 2016). Indeed, many killers do not have felony convictions prior to committing their crimes and, as such, would not be prohibited from possessing firearms (Cook, Ludwig, & Braga, 2005). Some states extend federal gun prohibitions to other high-risk populations, such as violent misdemeanants (Wintemute et al., 2001), and others choose to limit the concealed carrying of firearms by law-abiding citizens (Moody & Marvell, 2008).

The enactment of the Brady Handgun Violence Prevention Act in 1994 established the National Instant Criminal Background Check System (NICS), which is used to perform background checks on individuals seeking to purchase a handgun from a FFL. The available evidence reveals that the Brady Act has prevented a large number of prohibited persons from buying handguns at licensed dealers. Between 1994 and 1998, Brady background checks resulted in about 320,000 requests for purchase being denied, with 220,000 of the rejections due to prior felony convictions or pending indictments (Bureau of Justice Statistics, 1999). Other would-be handgun purchasers may have been discouraged from trying, knowing that their purchase would have been denied as a result of the background check.

Research has also shown enacting legislation that restricts access to guns for select high-risk populations may reduce gun violence. Laws prohibiting individuals convicted of a violent misdemeanor from purchasing guns have been shown to reduce their involvement in gun-related crime (Wintemute et al., 2001). Prohibitions on purchasing handguns for individuals under domestic violence restraining orders have been related to significantly reduced rates of gun and non-gun intimate partner homicide (Vigdor & Mercy, 2006; Zeoli & Webster, 2010).

Successful attempts to screen high-risk individuals from acquiring guns can, unfortunately, be undermined by illegal diversions of firearms from varying sources such as corrupt FFLs, straw purchases, and unregulated transfers in secondary firearms markets. While crime guns are stolen from legal owners, the available scientific evidence reviewed above suggests that a noteworthy portion of crime guns are illegally diverted from legal commerce. Supply-side interventions designed to shut down illegal gun market operations could be promising in limiting criminal access to firearms. A key element of supply-side interventions involves the investigation, apprehension, and prosecution of illegal gun traffickers and others who illegally divert guns to criminals.

Despite multiple illegal sources of firearms for criminals, ethnographic research suggests that illegal gun markets may not work very well in particular urban environments. Cook et al. (2007) found evidence of considerable frictions in the underground market for guns in Chicago. These frictions were due primarily to the fact that the underground gun market was both illegal and "thin" – the number of buyers, sellers, and total transactions was small, and relevant information on reliable sources of guns were scarce. The research further found that Chicago street gangs helped to overcome these market frictions, but the gangs' economic interests caused gang leaders to limit supply primarily to gang members, and even then transactions were usually loans or rentals with strings attached. Thin underground gun markets may be particularly vulnerable to focused gun market disruption strategies.

A growing body of evaluation evidence suggests that enforcement and regulatory interventions focused on retail sales practices can generate subsequent reductions in new guns recovered in crime. In Detroit and Chicago, the number of guns recovered within a year of first retail sale from someone other than the original purchaser was sharply reduced after undercover police stings and lawsuits targeted scofflaw retail dealers (Webster et al., 2006). In Boston, a gun market disruption strategy focused on the illegal diversion of new handguns from retail outlets in Massachusetts, southern states along Interstate 95, and elsewhere resulted in a significant reduction in the percentage of new handguns recovered in crime by the Boston Police Department (Braga & Pierce, 2005). In Milwaukee, the number of guns recovered within a year of first retail sale from someone other than the original purchaser dramatically decreased after voluntary changes in the sales practices of a gun dealer received negative publicity for leading the United States in selling the most guns recovered by police in crime (Webster, Vernick, & Bulzacchelli, 2006). In Chicago, an analysis of recovered crime handguns found that the 1994 implementation of the Brady Handgun Violence Prevention Act was associated with a marked decrease in crime handguns imported from other states (Cook & Braga, 2001).

Controlling Gun Use

This third category of gun control strategies focuses on limiting unsafe and criminal use of guns (Cook et al., 2011). One subset of interventions attempt to regulate firearm design and limit the production of certain types of guns. For instance, federal firearms law greatly restricts the sale of sawed-off shotguns and fully automatic machine guns (Teret et al., 1998). Research testing the effectiveness of bans on specific kinds of guns suggest mixed impacts on gun violence. The 1994 assault rifle ban limited offender access to assault rifles in the short-term due to heightened price, but the substantial increase in assault rifle production that occurred prior to the law's enactment resulted in an abundance of supply and an eventual price drop, making the weapons more accessible on the illegal market (Koper & Roth, 2002). However, Webster, Vernick, and Hepburn (2002) found Maryland's banning of "Saturday night specials," a low-end and relatively cheap handgun conducive to engaging in crime, resulted in a 7–11% reduction in gun-involved homicide when the impact of the law was modeled as delayed or gradual.

Relative to other gun control policies, sentencing-enhancement provisions for the use of a gun in crime has the clear advantage of not interfering with legitimate uses of guns. While there is no consensus on the efficacy of sentencing enhancements, one study of violent crime trends in a specific jurisdiction suggests that the adoption of such provisions can reduce gun homicide (McDowall, Loftin, & Wiersema, 1992). However, in their analysis, Marvell and Moody (1995) find that such policies have no discernible effect.

Law enforcement can play a critical role in controlling criminal use of guns. Research shows focusing efforts at high-risk places and on high-risk persons are effective law enforcement strategies for reducing gun violence. Place-based interventions concentrate police resources on high-crime areas, or "hot spots"

(Braga, Papachristos, & Hureau, 2014). The Kansas City Gun Project examined the gun violence prevention effects of proactive patrol and intensive enforcement of firearms laws via safety frisks during traffic stops, plain view searches and seizures, and searches incident to arrests on other charges (Sherman & Rogan, 1995). The quasi-experimental evaluation revealed that proactive patrols focused on firearm recoveries resulted in a statistically significant 65% increase in gun seizures and a statistically significant 49% decrease in gun crimes in the target beat area; gun seizures and gun crimes in the comparison beat area did not significantly change (Sherman & Rogan, 1995). An assessment of potential displacement found none of the contiguous beats showed significant increases in gun crime and two of the contiguous beats reported significant decreases in gun crimes. Broadly similar gun reduction impacts of police gun patrols have been noted in evaluations in Indianapolis (McGarrell et al., 2001) and Pittsburgh (Cohen & Ludwig, 2003).

The "focused deterrence" framework, which is often referred to as "pulling-levers policing" (Kennedy, 1997), has been found to be effective in controlling serious urban gun violence (Braga & Weisburd, 2012). Pioneered in Boston as a problem-oriented policing project to halt serious gang violence during the 1990s (Braga et al., 2001), the focused deterrence framework has been applied in many US cities through federally sponsored violence prevention programs such as the Strategic Alternatives to Community Safety Initiative and Project Safe Neighborhoods (PSN) (Dalton, 2002). Focused deterrence strategies honor core deterrence ideas, such as increasing risks faced by offenders, while finding new and creative ways of deploying traditional and nontraditional law enforcement tools to do so, such as communicating incentives and disincentives directly to targeted offenders (Kennedy, 1997).

In its simplest form, the focused deterrence approach consists of selecting a particular crime problem, such as gang homicide; convening an interagency working group of law enforcement, social service, and community-based practitioners; conducting research to identify key offenders, groups, and behavior patterns; framing a response to offenders and groups of offenders that uses a varied menu of sanctions ("pulling levers") to stop them from continuing their violent behavior; focusing social services and community resources on targeted offenders and groups to match law enforcement prevention efforts; and directly and repeatedly communicating with offenders to make them understand why they are receiving this special attention (Kennedy, 1997). A systematic review of ten rigorous program evaluations concluded that focused deterrence strategies were associated with significant reductions in targeted crime problems, particularly gang-involved gun homicide (Braga & Weisburd, 2012).

Beyond assessing any measurable gun violence reduction impacts, policymakers and program implementers need to know more about community reaction to increased levels of police enforcement action. Since these programs were centered on offenders immediately engaged in violence and engaged community members and social service providers to halt continued gun offending, focused deterrence approaches have been described as a more desirable alternative to less-customized aggressive policing strategies (Butterfield, 1999). Indeed, some observers question the fairness and intrusiveness of aggressive law enforcement approaches and caution that street searches, especially of young men and minorities, look like police harassment (Moore, 1980; Kleck, 1991). At the same time, the results of the Kansas City and Indianapolis projects suggest that residents of communities suffering from high rates of gun violence welcome intensive police efforts against guns (Shaw, 1995; McGarrell et al., 2001). The police managers involved in these projects secured community support before and during the interventions through a series of meetings with community members, and stressed to their officers that they needed to treat citizens with respect and explain to citizens why they were stopped.

Conclusion

Thousands of US citizens are killed by gunfire each year and hundreds of thousands more are threatened or injured in robberies and assaults. While some would-be attackers seem to be dissuaded by armed citizens, the use of firearms in violent crimes increases the likelihood of fatal injuries sustained by victims. The burden of gun violence in urban areas is particularly high. Gun violence is highly concentrated in a small number of places in disadvantaged urban neighborhoods and among high-risk individuals involved in or connected to criminal networks. Prohibited persons, such as previously convicted felons, acquire guns through a diverse set of illicit pathways, including theft, sales by scofflaw dealers, straw purchasers, and unregulated secondary-market transfers.

Developing and implementing government programs to make guns less readily available, especially to those inclined toward violence, deserve a high priority in the quest to save lives and reduce the burden of crime on our society. The American public seems willing to make investments and pass new gun laws to reduce the harms associated with gun violence. A nationally representative survey reported that 76% of respondents expressed a willingness to pay an additional $50 annually to reduce gun violence victimization by 30%, and 64% reported they would contribute an additional $200 per year for the same gun violence reduction (Cook & Ludwig, 2002). While broad characterizations of "gun control" produce strict partisan divides, bipartisan political support is generally found for specific gun-related proposals. For instance, a recent Pew Research Center (2015) survey found that a majority of respondents from both Republican and Democratic parties supported three specific gun control proposals: background checks for gun shows and private sales, laws to prevent the mentally ill from buying guns, and the establishment of a federal database to track gun sales. Unfortunately, too many US politicians are unduly influenced by special-interest gun rights groups such as the National Rifle Association.

The available evidence suggests that some forms of gun control and certain strategic law enforcement interventions may indeed reduce firearm violence. However, as Cook et al. (2011) observe, the debate over gun control is not only concerned with factual issues. There are important value conflicts as well, conflicts concerning the proper relationship between the individual, the community, and the state. Even a definitive study finding that a gun-control measure saves lives would not persuade someone who believes in an absolute individual right to keep and bear arms.

The US Supreme Court has weighed in on this matter, finding that the Second Amendment to the Constitution does provide an individual right to keep a handgun in the home for self-defense (*District of Columbia v. Heller*).[11] Nevertheless, we believe that the harms and social costs associated with gun violence requires active exploration and experimentation with alternative gun-control initiatives to develop more effective interventions than those we now rely upon.

References

Ayres, I. & Donohue, J. J. III (2003). Shooting down the more guns, less crime hypothesis. *Stanford Law Review*, 55(4), 1193–1314.

Azrael, D., Cook, P. J. & Miller, M. (2004). State and local prevalence of firearms ownership measurement, structure, and trends. *Journal of Quantitative Criminology*, 20(1), 43–62.

Black, D. & Nagin, D. (1998). Do "right to carry" laws reduce violent crime? *Journal of Legal Studies*, 27(1), 209–219.

Braga, A. A. & Cook, P. J. (2016). The criminal records of gun offenders. *Georgetown Journal of Law and Public Policy*, 14(1).

Braga, A. A., Hureau, D., & Winship, C. (2008). Losing faith? Police, black churches, and the resurgence of youth violence in Boston. *Ohio State Journal of Criminal Law*, 6(1), 141–172.

Braga, A. A., Kennedy, D. M., & Tita, G. (2002). New approaches to the strategic prevention of gang and group-involved violence. In C. R. Huff (Ed.), *Gangs in America* (3rd edn., pp. 271–286). Thousand Oaks, CA: Sage Publications.

Braga, A. A., Kennedy, D. M., Waring, E. J., & Piehl, A. M. (2001). Problem-oriented policing, deterrence, and youth violence: An evaluation of Boston's Operation Ceasefire. *Journal of Research in Crime and Delinquency*, 38(3), 195–225.

Braga, A. A., Papachristos, A. V., & Hureau, D. M. (2010). The concentration and stability of gun violence at micro places in Boston, 1980–2008. *Journal of Quantitative Criminology*, 26(1), 33–53.

Braga, A. A., Papachristos, A. V., & Hureau, D. M. (2014). The effects of hot spots policing on crime: An updated systematic review and meta-analysis. *Justice Quarterly*, 31(4), 633–663.

Braga, A. A. & Pierce, G. L. (2005). Disrupting illegal firearms markets in Boston: The effects of Operation Ceasefire on the supply of new handguns to criminals. *Criminology and Public Policy*, 4, 717–748.

Braga, A. A. & Weisburd, D. (2012). The effects of focused deterrence strategies on crime: A systematic review and meta-analysis of the empirical evidence. *Journal of Research in Crime and Delinquency*, 49(3), 323–358.

Braga, A. A. & Wintemute, G. J. (2013). Improving the potential effectiveness of gun buyback programs. *American Journal of Preventive Medicine*, 45(5), 668–671.

Braga, A. A., Wintemute, G. J., Pierce, G. L., Cook, P. J., & Ridgeway, G. (2012). Interpreting the empirical evidence on illegal gun market dynamics. *Journal of Urban Health*, 89(5), 779–793.

Branas, C. C., Richmond, T. S., Culhane, D. P., Ten Have, T. R., & Wiebe, D. J. (2009). Investigating the link between gun possession and gun assault. *American Journal of Public Health*, 99(11), 2034–2040.

Bureau of Alcohol, Tobacco, and Firearms (ATF). (1997). *Crime gun trace analysis reports: The illegal youth firearms market in 17 communities*. Washington, DC: US Department of Treasury.

Bureau of Alcohol, Tobacco, and Firearms (ATF). (2000). *Following the gun: Enforcing federal laws against firearms traffickers*.

---

11 *District of Columbia v. Heller*, 554 U.S. 570 (2008).

Washington, DC: US Department of Treasury.

Bureau of Alcohol, Tobacco, and Firearms (ATF). (2002). *Crime gun trace reports (2000): National report.* Washington, DC: US Department of Treasury.

Bureau of Justice Statistics. (1999). *Presale handgun checks, the Brady interim period, 1994–1998.* Washington, DC: Bureau of Justice Statistics, US Department of Justice.

Bureau of Justice Statistics. (2016). NCVS victimization analysis tool (NVAT). Washington, DC: US Department of Justice, Office of Justice Programs. Retrieved June 4, 2016 from www.bjs.gov/index.cfm?ty=nvat.

Butterfield, F. (1999). Citizens as allies: Rethinking the strong arm of the law. *The New York Times.* April 4, 1999.

Cohen, J. & Ludwig, J. (2003). Policing crime guns. In J. Ludwig & P. J. Cook (Eds), *Evaluating gun policy: Effects on crime and violence* (pp. 217–250). Washington, DC: Brookings Institution Press.

Cook, P. J. (1981). The effect of gun availability on violent crime patterns. *Annals of the American Academy of Political and Social Science,* 455(1), 63–79.

Cook, P. J. (1985). The case of the missing victims: Gunshot woundings in the National Crime Survey. *Journal of Quantitative Criminology,* 1(1), 91–102.

Cook, P. J. (1987). Robbery violence. *Journal of Criminal Law and Criminology,* 78(2), 357–376.

Cook, P. J. & Braga, A. A. (2001). Comprehensive firearms tracing: Strategic and investigative uses of new data on firearms markets. *Arizona Law Review,* 43(2), 277–309.

Cook, P. J., Braga, A. A., & Moore, M. H. (2011). Gun control. In J. Q. Wilson & J. Petersilia (Eds), *Crime and public policy* (pp. 257–292). New York: Oxford University Press.

Cook, P. J., Lawrence, B. A., Ludwig, J., & Miller, T. R. (1999). The medical costs of gunshot injuries in the United States. *Journal of the American Medical Association,* 281(5), 447–454.

Cook, P. J. & Ludwig, J. (1996). *Guns in America: Results of a comprehensive national survey on firearms ownership and use.* Washington, DC: Police Foundation.

Cook, P. J. & Ludwig, J. (1998). Defensive gun uses: New evidence from a national survey. *Journal of Quantitative Criminology,* 14(2), 111–131.

Cook, P. J. & Ludwig, J. (2002). The costs of gun violence against children. *The Future of Children,* 12(2), 86–99.

Cook, P. J. & Ludwig, J. (2006). Aiming for evidence-based gun policy. *Journal of Policy Analysis and Management,* 25(3), 691–735.

Cook, P. J., Ludwig, J., & Braga, A. A. (2005). Criminal records of homicide offenders. *Journal of the American Medical Association,* 294(5), 598–601.

Cook, P. J., Ludwig, J., & Hemenway, D. (1997). The gun debate's new mythical number: How many defensive uses per year? *Journal of Policy Analysis,* 16(3), 463–469.

Cook, P. J., Ludwig, J., Venkatesh, S., & Braga, A. A. (2007). Underground gun markets. *The Economic Journal,* 117(524), F558–F588.

Cook, P. J., Parker, S. T., & Pollack, H. A. (2015). Sources of guns to dangerous people: What we learn by asking them. *Preventive Medicine,* 79, 28–36.

Cooper, A. & Smith, E. L. (2011). *Homicide trends in the United States, 1980–2008: Annual rates for 2009 and 2010.* Washington, DC: US Department of Justice, Bureau of Justice Statistics.

Dalton, E. (2002). Targeted crime reduction efforts in ten communities: Lessons for the Project Safe Neighborhoods Initiative. *U.S. Attorney's Bulletin,* 50(1), 16–25.

Dresang, L. T. (2001). Gun deaths in rural and urban settings: Recommendations for prevention. *Journal of the American Board of Family Medicine,* 14(2), 107–115.

Duggan, M. (2001). More guns, more crime. *Journal of Political Economy,* 109(5), 1086–1114.

FBI. (2015). UCR *Publications: Crime in the United States*. Washington, DC: US Department of Justice, Federal Bureau of Investigations. Retrieved June 4, 2016 from https://ucr.fbi.gov/ucr-publications.

Hemenway, D. (2004). *Private guns, public health*. Ann Arbor, MI: University of Michigan Press.

Hepburn, L., Miller, M., Azrael, D., & Hemenway, D. (2007). The US gun stock: Results from the 2004 National Firearms Survey. *Injury Prevention*, 13(1), 15–19.

Huebner, B. M., Martin, K., Moule, Jr., R. K., Pyrooz, D., & Decker, S. H. (2016). Dangerous places: Gang members and neighborhood levels of gun assault. *Justice Quarterly*, 33(5), 836–862.

Kellermann, A. L. & Cook, P. J. (1999). Armed and dangerous: Guns in American homes. In M. A. Bellesiles (Ed.), *Lethal imagination: Violence and brutality in American history* (pp. 425–440). New York: New York University Press.

Kellermann, A. L., Rivara, F. P., Rushforth, N. B., Banton, J. G., Reay, D. T., Francisco, J. T., … & Somes, G. (1993). Gun ownership as a risk factor for homicide in the home. *New England Journal of Medicine*, 329, 1084–1091. doi: 10.1056/NEJM199310073291506.

Kennedy, D. M. (1997). Pulling levers: Chronic offenders, high-crime settings, and a theory of prevention. *Valparaiso University Law Review*, 31(2), 449–484.

Kennedy, D. M., Piehl, A. M., & Braga, A. A. (1996). Youth violence in Boston: Gun markets, serious youth offenders, and a use-reduction strategy. *Law and Contemporary Problems*, 59(1), 147–196.

Kleck, G. (1991). *Point blank: Guns and violence in America*. New York: Aldine de Gruyter.

Kleck, G. & Gertz, M. (1995). Armed resistance to crime: The prevalence and nature of self-defense with a gun. *Journal of Criminal Law and Criminology*, 86(1), 150–187.

Kleck, G. & McElrath, K. (1991). The effects of weaponry on human violence. *Social Forces*, 69(3), 669–692.

Kleck, G. & Patterson, E. B. (1993). The impact of gun control and gun ownership levels on violence rates. *Journal of Quantitative Criminology*, 9(3), 249–288.

Koper, C. S., Egge, S. J. & Lum, C. (2015). Institutionalizing place-based approaches: Opening 'cases' on gun crime hot spots. *Policing*, 9(3), 242–254.

Koper, C. S. & Roth, J. A. (2002). The impact of the 1994 Federal Assault Weapons Ban on gun markets: An assessment of short-term primary and secondary market effects. *Journal of Quantitative Criminology*, 18(3), 239–266.

Krouse, W. J. (2012). *Gun control legislation*. Washington, DC: Congressional Research Service.

Kuhn, E. M., Nie, C. L., O'Brien, M. E., Withers, R. L., Wintemute, G. J., & Hargarten, S. W. (2002). Missing the target: A comparison of buyback and fatality related guns. *Injury Prevention*, 8(2), 143–146.

Langton, L. (2012). *Firearms stolen during household burglaries and other property crimes, 2005–2010*. Washington, DC: US Department of Justice, Bureau of Justice Statistics.

Leigh, A. & Neill, C. (2010). Do gun buybacks save lives? Evidence from panel data. *American Law and Economics Review*, 12(2), 462–508.

Lott, J. (2000). *More guns, less crime* (2nd edn.). Chicago: University of Chicago Press.

Lott, J. R. & Mustard, D. B. (1997). Crime, deterrence, and right-to-carry concealed handguns. *Journal of Legal Studies*, 26(1), 1–68.

Marvell, T. B. & Moody, C. E. (1995). The impact of enhanced prison terms for felonies committed with guns. *Criminology*, 33(2), 247–281.

McDowall, D., Loftin, C., & Presser, S. (2000). Measuring civilian defensive firearm use: A methodological experiment. *Journal of Quantitative Criminology*, 16(2), 1–19.

McDowall, D., Loftin, C., & Wiersema, B. (1992). A comparative study of the preventive effects of mandatory sentencing laws for gun crimes. *Journal of Criminal Law and Criminology*, 83(2), 378–394.

McDowall, D., Loftin, C., & Wiersema, B. (1995). Easing concealed firearms laws: Effects on homicide in three states. *The Journal of Criminal Law and Criminology*, 86(1), 193–206.

McDowall, D. & Wiersema, B. (1994). The incidence of defensive firearm use by US crime victims, 1987 through 1990. *American Journal of Public Health*, 84(12), 1982–1984.

McGarrell, E. F., Chermak, S., Weiss, A., & Wilson, J. (2001). Reducing firearms violence through directed police patrol. *Criminology and Public Policy*, 1(1), 119–148.

Miller, M., Azrael, D., & Hemenway, D. (2002). Rates of household firearm ownership and homicide across US regions and states, 1988–1997. *American Journal of Public Health*, 92(12), 1988–1993.

Miller, T. R. (2013). *The cost of gun violence*. Calverton, MD: Pacific Institute of Research and Evaluation.

Moody, C. E. & Marvell, T. B. (2008). The debate on shall-issue laws. *Econ Journal Watch*, 5(3), 269–293.

Moore, M. H. (1980). The police and weapons offenses. *Annals of the American Academy of Political and Social Science*, 452(1), 22–32.

Morrison, C., Gross, B., Horst, M., Bupp, K., Rittenhouse, K., Harnish, C., ... & Rogers, F. B. (2015). Under fire: Gun violence is not just an urban problem. *Journal of Surgical Research*, 199(1), 190–196.

Nance, M. L., Denysenko, L., Durbin, D. R., Branas, C. C., Stafford, P. W., & Schwab, W. (2002). The rural-urban continuum: Variability in statewide serious firearm injuries in children and adolescents. *Archives of Pediatrics and Adolescent Medicine*, 156(8), 781–785.

National Center for Injury Prevention and Control. (2016). *20 leading causes of nonfatal violence-related injury, United States: 2014, all races, both sexes, disposition: All cases*. Washington, DC: NCIPC.

National Research Council. (2005). *Firearms and violence: A critical review*. Committee to Improve Research Information and Data on Firearms. Washington, DC: The National Academies Press.

Olson, D. E. & Maltz, M. D. (2001). Right-to-carry concealed weapon laws and homicide in large U.S. counties. *Journal of Law and Economics*, 44(2), 747–770.

Papachristos, A. V., Braga, A. A., & Hureau, D. (2012). Social networks and the risk of gunshot injury. *Journal of Urban Health*, 89(6), 992–1003.

Papachristos, A. V., Braga, A. A., Piza, E., & Grossman, L. S. (2015). The company you keep? The spillover effects of gang membership on individual gunshot victimization in a co-offending network. *Criminology*, 53(4), 624–649.

Pew Research Center. (2015). *Continued bipartisan support for expanded background checks on gun sales, more polarized views on the NRA's influence*. Washington, DC: Pew Research Center.

Pierce, G. L., Braga, A. A., Hyatt, R. R., & Koper, C. S. (2004). The characteristics and dynamics of illegal firearms markets: Implications for a supply-side enforcement strategy. *Justice Quarterly*, 21(2), 391–422.

Plassmann, F. & Tideman, T. N. (2001). Does the right to carry concealed handguns deter countable crimes? *Journal of Law and Economics*, 44(2), 771–798.

Richardson, E. G. & Hemenway, D. (2011). Homicide, suicide, and unintentional firearm fatality: Comparing the United States with other high-income countries, 2003. *Journal of Trauma and Acute Care Surgery*, 70(1), 238–234.

Romero, M., Wintemute, G., & Vernick, J. (1998). Characteristics of a gun exchange program, and an assessment of potential benefits. *Injury Prevention*, 4(3), 206–210.

Sampson, R. J., Raudenbush, S. W., & Earls, F. (1997). Neighborhoods and violent crime: A multilevel study of collective efficacy. *Science*, 277(5328), 918–924.

Sampson, R. J. & Wilson, W. J. (1995). Toward a theory of race, crime, and urban inequality. In J. Hagan & R. Peterson (Eds), *Crime and inequality* (pp. 37–56). Stanford, CA: Stanford University Press.

Shaw, J. W. (1995). Community policing against guns: Public opinion of the Kansas City gun experiment. *Justice Quarterly*, 12(4), 695–710.

Sheley, J. F. & Wright, J. D. (1995). *In the line of fire: Youth, guns, and violence in urban America*. New York: Aldine de Gruyter.

Sherman, L. W. & Rogan, D. P. (1995). Effects of gun seizures on gun violence: "Hot spots" patrol in Kansas City. *Justice Quarterly*, 12(4), 673–693.

Smith, T. W. (2001). *2001 National gun policy survey of the National Opinion Research Center: Research findings*. Chicago: National Opinion Research Center, University of Chicago.

Sorenson, S. B. & Vittes, K. A. (2003). Buying a handgun for someone else: Firearm retailer willingness to sell. *Injury Prevention*, 9(2), 147–150.

Teret, S. P., DeFrancesco, S., Hargarten, S. W., & Robinson, K. (1998). Making guns safer. *Issues in Science and Technology*, 14(4), 37–40.

Teret, S. P. & Wintemute, G. J. (1993). Policies to prevent firearm injuries. *Health Affairs*, 12(4), 96–108.

Vigdor, E. R. & Mercy, J. A. (2006). Do laws restricting access to firearms by domestic violence offenders prevent intimate partner homicide? *Evaluation Review*, 30(3), 313–346. doi: 10.1177/0193841X06287307.

Webster, D. W., Bulzacchelli, M. T., Zeoli, A. M., & Vernick, J. S. (2006). Effects of undercover police stings of gun dealers on the supply of new guns to criminals. *Injury Prevention*, 12(4), 225–230.

Webster, D. W., Vernick, J. S., & Bulzacchelli, M. T. (2006). Effects of a gun dealer's change in sales practices on the supply of guns to criminals. *Journal of Urban Health*, 83(5), 778–787.

Webster, D. W., Vernick, J. S., & Hepburn, L. M. (2002). Effects of Maryland's law banning "Saturday Night Special" handguns on homicides. *American Journal of Epidemiology*, 155(5), 406–412.

Wiebe, D. J., Richmond, T. S., Guo, W., Allison, P. D., Hollander, J. E., Nance, M. L., & Branas, C. C. (2016). Mapping activity patterns to quantify risk of violent assault in urban environments. *Epidemiology*, 27(1), 32–41.

Wintemute, G. J. (2010). Firearm retailers' willingness to participate in an illegal gun purchase. *Journal of Urban Health*, 87(5), 865–878.

Wintemute, G. J., Cook, P. J., & Wright, M. A. (2005). Risk factors among handgun retailers for frequent and disproportionate sales of guns used in violent and firearm related crimes. *Injury Prevention*, 11(6), 357–363.

Wintemute, G. J., Wright, M. A., Drake, C. M., & Beaumont, J. J. (2001). Subsequent criminal activity among violent misdemeanants who seek to purchase handguns: Risk factors and effectiveness of denying handgun purchase. *Journal of the American Medical Association*, 285(8), 1019–1026.

Wolfgang, M. (1958). *Patterns in criminal homicide*. Philadelphia, PA: University of Pennsylvania Press.

Wright, J. D. (1995). Ten essential observations on guns in America. *Society*, March/April, 63–68.

Wright, J. D. & Rossi, P. H. (1994). *Armed and considered dangerous: A survey of felons and their firearms* (2nd edn.). New York: Aldine de Gruyter.

Wright, J. D., Rossi, P. H., & Daly, K. (1983). *Under the gun: Weapons, crime, and violence in America*. New York: Aldine de Gruyter.

Zeoli, A. M. & Webster, D. W. (2010). Effects of domestic violence policies, alcohol taxes and police staffing levels on intimate partner homicide in large US cities. *Injury Prevention*, 16(2), 90–95.

Zimring, F. E. (1968). Is gun control likely to reduce violent killings? *University of Chicago Law Review*, 35(4), 21–37.

Zimring, F. E. (1972). The medium is the message: Firearm caliber as a determinant of death from assault. *Journal of Legal Studies*, 35, 21–37.

Zimring, F. E. (1976). Street crime and new guns: Some implications for firearms control. *Journal of Criminal Justice*, 4(2), 95–107.

Zimring, F. E. & Hawkins, G. (1997). *Crime is not the problem: Lethal violence in the United States*. New York: Oxford University Press.

PART V

Looking Toward the Future

37 The Interrelationship of Self-Control and Violent Behavior: Pathways and Policies

Brie Diamond, Jennifer R. Gonzalez, Wesley Jennings, and Alex R. Piquero

Introduction

Low self-control represents one of the premiere correlates of crime and its influence on a range of maladaptive outcomes is well documented in the literature (Pratt & Cullen, 2000). The leading theory of self-control, Gottfredson & Hirschi's (1990) General Theory of Crime, has dominated criminological literature and generated important insights into violence and aggression, alongside virtually all criminal and maladaptive behaviors. Moving beyond the theory's representation of self-control to one supported by multidisciplinary findings allows us to elaborate upon the link between self-control and aggressive behavior in the cycle of violence. This chapter will begin by describing the tenets of the general theory of crime and the neurological nature of self-control. Next, it will define the relationship between self-control and violent and aggressive behavior. Finally, this chapter will conclude with a discussion about interventions to improve self-control at various stages of the life-course.

The General Theory of Crime

Gottfredson & Hirschi (1990) view low self-control as the key correlate in a wide range of criminal and analogous behaviors – from violence and property crime to smoking and promiscuous sex and even excessive television watching. They define low self-control as the "coming together" of several individual characteristics: impulsivity, affinity for risks and simple tasks, a tendency for lack of planning, and a general disregard for the well-being of others. As according to this paradigm, individuals with low self-control are drawn to aggressive and violent behaviors because such acts are largely impetuous, dangerous, simple to execute, and are predicated upon their lack of concern for the other person's health and wellness.

The theorists are clear in arguing that self-control is the principle correlate of crime. Many of the other explanations for violence likely covered in this volume concerning education, neighborhoods, peers, etc., are, per the theorists, spurious relationships that are explained by the influence of self-control on both violence and these other "causal" factors (Hay & Meldrum, 2016; Hay, Meldrum, & Piquero, 2013). While other key correlates, especially those related to social learning and strain theory, are of key importance to the prediction of criminal behavior, the association between low self-control and crime has been firmly established (Pratt & Cullen, 2000).

The theory purports that self-control is established early in life, by mid-childhood, largely to the credit of an individual's parents. Gottfredson and Hirschi (1990) view the caregiver's ability to monitor, recognize, and punish antisocial behavior as the key to fostering self-control in a child. Current research in criminology, however, often fails to support this proposition concerning the importance of parenting practices to the formation of self-control (Wright & Beaver, 2005; Wright, Beaver, DeLisi, & Vaughn, 2008; Nofziger, 2008). In fact, numerous studies show that self-control is primarily an inherited trait passed down from parent to child (Boisvert, Wright, Knopik, & Vaske, 2012; Connolly & Beaver, 2014; Wright et al., 2008) and that when such heredity is controlled for parenting practices exhibit little to no influence on a child's level of self-control (Wright et al., 2008).

Likewise, the stability of self-control beyond childhood has often been scrutinized. The theorists take the viewpoint that beyond childhood it is increasingly improbable that relative changes in self-control would occur. Gottfredson and Hirschi (1990) consider low self-control to span one's life-course, though the manifestations may change with age. A person with low-self control will be kicking and biting in early childhood, stealing and smoking in adolescence, and failing to keep jobs or marriages intact in adulthood. While the focus may change with age, low-self control remains a constant trait across the individual's entire life (Hirschi & Gottfredson, 1994).

However, employing a variety of methods, several studies provide considerable evidence that relative losses and gains in self-control can and do occur – at least for some individuals – across the life-course (Burt, Sweeten, & Simons, 2014; Diamond, 2016; Diamond, Morris, & Piquero, 2017; Hay & Forrest 2006; Higgins, Jennings, Tewskbury, & Gibson, 2009; Jennings, Higgins, Akers, Khey, & Dobrow, 2013; Ray, Jones, Loughran, & Jennings, 2013; Turner & Piquero, 2002). Importantly, underlying constructs of self-control follow different patterns of stability with impulsivity stabilizing for most in childhood and risk-seeking behavior increasing during adolescence (Burt et al., 2014; Diamond, 2016; Steinberg, Albert, Cauffman, Banich, Graham, & Woolard, 2008). While these findings must be tempered by methodological idiosyncrasies limiting the ability to discern relative stability (Barnes et al., 2017), the idea that self-control is bereft of intervention defies the literature. To understand how self-control forms over time, it is imperative to examine the neurological basis of this construct.

Neurological Development of Self-Control

Despite Gottfredson and Hirschi's contentions, self-control is most aptly considered a neurological phenomenon (DeLisi, 2015). The clusters of behavior outlined by Gottfredson and Hirschi – impulsivity, poor decision making, lack of consideration of others, poor emotional control – are all managed by an area of the prefrontal cortex called the orbitofrontal cortex. The prefrontal cortex of the brain is the decision making center and this area is responsible for compiling sensory input to execute planned responses. As such, self-control appears to be an *executive function*: defined as efforts to plan and execute adaptive behavior in response to one's environment (Beaver, Wright, & DeLisi, 2007; Monahan, Steinberg, & Piquero, 2015).

Importantly, it is more than possible that self-control is also influenced by heritable factors. Various genetic polymorphisms affecting neurotransmission have been implicated in self-control deficits. Certain alleles of dopamine, norepinephrine, and serotonin-related genes have been associated with the expression of low self-control (Hirata, Zai, Nowrouzi, Beitchman, & Kennedy, 2013; Kochanska, Philibert, & Barry, 2009; Smith, Sheikh, Dyson, Olino, Laptook, Durbin, et al., 2012). In addition, these genetic risk factors often interact with negative environments to produce these effects on self-control. Specific genes have also been shown to predict low self-control when coupled with other risk factors such as delinquent peers or neuropsychological deficits (Beaver, DeLisi, Vaughn, & Wright, 2010; Beaver, Ratchford, & Ferguson, 2009).

These deficits result in various behavioral manifestations of low self-control. These individuals act impulsively, have trouble sustaining attention on any certain task; they fail to consider the full impact of their choices on themselves and others and they have difficulty controlling their emotions – especially negative emotions related to anger (see Piquero, Langton, & Gomez-Smith, 2004). These characteristics of low self-control, for many individuals, lead to the exhibition of various forms of antisocial behavior from conduct disorder to violent crime (Moffitt & Caspi, 2001; Piquero, MacDonald, Dobrin, Daigle, & Cullen, 2005). Importantly, these outcomes of low self-control emerge early in childhood (Vaughn, DeLisi, Beaver, & Wright, 2009) and extend well into the life-course (Moffitt, Arsenault, Belsky, Dickson, Hancox, Harrington, et al., 2011).

Despite these inconsistencies between the theoretical and practical understanding of the nature of self-control, the construct itself is strongly linked to a wide variety of criminal and maladaptive behavior (Pratt & Cullen, 2000). While self-control does not do well at predicting corporate crimes (Simpson & Piquero, 2002), it is a robust predictor of nearly every crime type, for every demographic, across various cultures (Burton, Evans, Cullen, Olivares, & Dunaway, 1999; Miller, Jennings, Alvarez-Rivera & Lanza-Kaduce, 2009; Pratt & Cullen, 2000; Tittle, Ward, & Grasmick, 2003; Vazsonyi, Clifford Wittekind, Belliston, & Van Loh, 2004; Vazsonyi, Pickering, Junger, & Hessing, 2001). Given the strong evidence concerning the relationship between self-control and various adverse behaviors, this theoretical construct uniquely contributes to our understanding of the cycle of violence and aggression – as self-control can be viewed as both an outcome and a cause of such behavior.

Self-Control and the Cycle of Violence

Violence and the Formation of Self-Control

While self-control is strongly linked to heritable factors, it is also related to experiences of violence and neglect – especially in childhood. Severe child abuse has been linked to decreased orbitofrontal cortex volume and these deficits may be more profound depending on the age of onset and the duration of the abuse (De Bellis et al., 1999; Thomaes, Dorrepaal,

Draijer, de Ruiter, van Balkom, Smit, & Veltman, 2010). Deficits in the orbitofrontal cortex are in turn linked to low-self-control manifestations such as emotional dysregulation, impulsivity, and poor decision making (Bechara, Damasio, & Damasio, 2000; van der Kolk & Fisler, 1994). Further, hostile or aggressive parenting has been shown to combine with genetic risk to increase the likelihood of low self-control (Sheese, Rothbart, Voelker, & Posner, 2012; Smith et al., 2012).

The importance of social context extends beyond the household to implicate the community or neighborhood experience in the development of self-control as well (Burt, Simons, & Simons, 2006; Pratt, Turner, & Piquero, 2004; Raver, 2004; Turner, Piquero, & Pratt, 2005; cf. Gibson, Sullivan, Jones, & Piquero, 2010). Growing up in a community marked by violence has been shown to increase the risk of exhibiting low self-control and associating with violent peers. In addition, disadvantaged schools in these areas may exert their own influence on an individual's self-control by not providing children and adolescents with the requisite educational experience.

A recent line of research has attempted to relate trends in violence across the Western world to generational changes in self-control. Pinker (2011) documented that levels of violence, including homicide, have steadily declined across recorded civilization. Child abuse, deaths from war, homicide, and violent crime declines, for example, have occurred across all Western countries and have done so while markers of civility – literacy and civil rights, among others – have evidenced an increase in society. Eisner (2001, 2014) expands upon this finding to relate homicide declines to social efforts to bolster self-control or to lower the need for self-control. He shows that decreases in the European homicide rates are correlated with such historical trends as the temperance movement of the Victorian age, the expansion of literacy, and the hedonistic moral climate of the mid- to late 1900s. He argues that, while causality is precluded from these analyses, broad social changes that require politeness, personal responsibility, and refraining from earthly indulgence may have fostered self-control in the general populace while efforts to reduce exposure to alcohol and sexual indulgence served to reduce the need for self-control in an opportunistic sense.

Self-Control and the Formation of Violence

Experiences of maltreatment early in life compound with genetic predispositions to significantly increase an individual's risk of violent and impulsive behaviors (Caspi, McClay, Moffitt, Mill, Martin, Craig, et al., 2002). In turn, deficits in executive functions seem to elicit aggression and impulsive violence (Davidson, Putnam, & Larson, 2000; Seguin, Nagin, Assaad, & Tremblay, 2004; Seguin, Pihl, Harden, Tremblay, & Boulerice, 1995). Those exhibiting low self-control are routinely shown to respond aggressively to provocation and the likelihood of these responses increases with more demands on self-control (DeWall, Baumeister, Stillman, Gailliot, 2007). Finally, low self-control is a strong predictor of a variety of violent and aggressive behavior (Piquero et al., 2005) including intimate partner violence (Finkel, DeWall, Slotter, Oaten, & Foshen, 2009; Sellers, 1999), bullying (Archer & Southall, 2009; Unnever & Cornell, 2003), workplace aggression

(Douglas & Martinko, 2001), and cyberbullying (Vazsonyi, Machackova, Sevcikova, Smahel, & Cerna, 2012).

Policy Recommendations to Improve Self-Control

To the credit of Gottfredson and Hirschi, self-control does seem to be more malleable early in life, to manifest differently across the life-course and, thus, require different interventions according to age. As such, this section will describe several of the programs and policies that have been shown to reduce violence and aggression by increasing an individual's self-control. These interventions are commonly broken down into primary prevention (prenatal and childhood), adolescent interventions with youth exhibiting self-control deficits (secondary prevention), and adults ensnared in the criminal justice system due to violence and aggression (tertiary prevention).

Primary (Childhood) Prevention

Ideally, prevention would occur before the pathways for low self-control have ever been established. Mothers' prenatal decisions, such as smoking (McGloin, Pratt, & Piquero, 2006, and child abuse and neglect (Avakame, 1998; Chapple, Tyler, & Bersani, 2005) have been shown to negatively impact children's self-control. Nurse home visitation programs have been arguably the most effective at addressing these issues and improving outcomes for mothers and children alike (Olds et al., 1997, 1998; Olds, Henderson, Chamberlin, & Tatelbaum, 1986). These programs with low-SES mothers provide prenatal nutrition and parenting training early in pregnancy and extending through the infant's second birthday. Children born to these mothers exhibit significantly fewer instances of child abuse and were significantly less likely to exhibit behavioral problems in school or involvement in the justice system during late adolescence.

Further, programs aimed at bolstering self-control in early childhood have been shown to increase self-control and also reduce violence, aggression, and other behavioral problems well into adolescence (Piquero, Farrington, Welsh, Tremblay, & Jennings, 2009; Piquero, Jennings, Farrington, Diamond, & Reingle Gonzalez, 2016). These programs typically focus on emotional communication and social problem solving skills, all of which involve self-control (Tremblay et al., 1991). For example, the PATHS (Promoting Alternative THinking Strategies) school-based program for elementary-aged youth teaches self-control, problem resolution, and emotional awareness in a classroom setting. Evaluations of these programs show that participating youth are rated as having higher self-control and are rated as less aggressive by their peers (Conduct Problems Prevention Research Group, 1999a). Combining this approach with parent training and home visits has also been shown to decrease aggressive behavior even up to three years after the program (Bierman et al., 2008; Conduct Problems Prevention Research Group, 1999b). Importantly, this training appears to reduce aggression indirectly through its effects on self-control (Riggs, Greenberg, Kusche, & Pentz, 2006).

Secondary (Adolescent) Prevention

Some of the most effective interventions introduced during the adolescent years tend to invoke a wraparound approach involving the families, schools, and/or community organizations of youth exhibiting behavioral problems. One key approach, Multisystemic Therapy, has been shown to reduce aggression and arrest for violent crimes in serious juvenile offenders by implementing multiple interventions that bolster self-control, such as social skills training, conflict resolution, and cognitive behavioral therapy (Borduin et al., 1995; Henggeler, Melton, & Smith, 1992; Schaeffer & Borduin, 2005).

Cognitive behavioral therapy (CBT) is perhaps one of the most effective means of sustaining reductions in violence and aggression among adolescents and adults. CBT seeks to disrupt maladaptive thinking patterns in order to elicit behavior change. It does this by assisting the individual in identifying problematic beliefs or thoughts that occur prior to engaging in violent or otherwise antisocial behavior. CBT trains individuals to acknowledge, challenge, and change these thoughts in order to condition prosocial behavior. These treatment programs often include anger management strategies and social skills training, which act directly on self-control capabilities. It has been shown to be highly effective in reducing violence and aggression in late childhood and adolescent populations (Kendall & Braswell, 1982; Landenberger & Lipsey, 2005; Lipsey, 1992).

Evidence suggests that the success of CBT lies in its ability to alter the functional abnormalities in the brain. Key to the influence of self-control, these therapies have been shown to reduce abnormalities in the prefrontal cortex and basal ganglia, which have both been implicated in self-control (Brody et al., 2001; Martin et al., 2001; Vaske, Galyean, & Cullen, 2011). It seems that the sustained success of CBT programs may largely stem from their ability to address these cognitive deficits.

Tertiary (Adult) Prevention

Interventions on self-control are arguably less effective among adults exhibiting violent and other problem behavior than those at earlier stages of the life-course, but cognitive-based interventions may reduce violence by about 7–9% (Jolliffe & Farrington, 2009). CBT has been shown to reduce violence and aggression with adult populations, including domestic violence and assault (Landenberger & Lipsey, 2005; Wilson, Bouffard, & Mackenzie, 2005).

Gottfredson and Hirschi argue that low self-control is difficult to change in adulthood and, therefore, the most effective strategy for deterring violence and aggression in these individuals is to reduce their opportunities for such behavior. Primarily, this means the selective incapacitation of chronically violent offenders. Historically, accurately predicting these populations has been poor (Auerhahn, 1999); however, assessment tools such as the LSI-R have become increasingly adept at accurately determining violent, chronic offending with some studies reporting predictive accuracy exceeding 70% (Gendreau, Little, & Goggin, 1996; Hanson, 2005; Liu, Yang, Ramsey, Li, & Coid, 2011; Williams, 2012; Williams & Grant, 2006).

Conclusion

Within the field of criminology, there may be no theory that has occupied the theoretical, empirical, and policy imagination to such great lengths as Gottfredson and Hirschi's (1990) general theory of crime. As a general theory, with primary emphasis on how low self-control impacts a range of antisocial and negative behaviors throughout the life-course, the theorists put forth a relatively clear and simple theory of crime that places the onus on those not partial to general theories of crime in supporting the need for more complicated frameworks that point to different groups of offenders, different correlates of crime, and different explanations across crime type.

In this chapter, we reviewed the evidence with respect to the correlates of self-control – including highlighting the importance genetic influences on the development of self-control, how self-control is implicated in aggression and violence, and how self-control may be modifiable in childhood, adolescence, and to a lesser extent adulthood. Although we find that the field has recognized the importance of self-control on such issues, there remain several gaps in the knowledge base that require attention. Below, we highlight a few of these.

First, because of criminology's preoccupation with street crime, much less is known about the effect of self-control on alternative forms of aggression and violence that are not necessarily captured by police arrest data. For example, both emotional and physical workplace bullying appear to be an important area of research within the self-control context. This is heightened as well about the importance of self-control as a characteristic that is implicated in educational and employment success. Individuals in positions of power within the workplace surely have evidenced some modicum of self-control to attain such a position. Yet, those same people may also exhibit low self-control, situationally, by making others in the workplace (and likely subservient to them) do things that they may not want to do. Cataloging such effects offers one important avenue of research.

A second strand of research would focus on understanding the contexts in which poor self-control may increase the likelihood of violence occurring. For example, not all persons with low self-control will consistently react with violence in a given situation – they just have a higher risk of doing so. What is it, then, about the context and/or opportunity structure that moderates how low self-control leads to violence? Is it some sort of chemical imbalance? Is it a provocation? Is it the influence of peers in a given situation? We believe that outlining the contexts under which low self-control leads to more violence is an exciting but largely untapped area of research.

Last, although several evidence-based programs have been found to improve an individual's self-control, and in turn also lead to reductions in delinquency and crime, too few studies have considered whether these programs operate in the same manner for serious and especially violent offenders. Knowledge on that front is important as ensuing research may lead to conclusions that may alter program details and/or delivery.

References

Archer, J. & Southall, N. (2009). Does cost-benefit analysis or self-control predict involvement in bullying behavior by male prisoners? *Aggressive Behavior*, 35, 31–40.

Auerhahn, K. (1999). Selective incapacitation and the problem of prediction. *Criminology*, 37(4), 703–734.

Avakame, E. F. (1998). Intergenerational transmission of violence, self-control, and conjugal violence: A comparative analysis of physical violence and psychological aggression. *Violence and Victims*, 13(3), 301–316.

Barnes, J. C., El Sayed, S., TenEyck, M., Nedelec, J. L., Connolly, E. J., Schwartz, J. A., ... & Anderson, N.E. (2017). Estimating relative stability in developmental research: A critique of modern approaches and a novel method. *Journal of Quantitative Criminology*, 33(2), 319–346.

Beaver, K. M., Delisi, M., Vaughn, M. G., & Wright, J. P. (2010). The intersection of genes and neuropsychological deficits in the prediction of adolescent delinquency and self-control. *International Journal of Offender Therapy and Comparative Criminology*, 54, 22–42.

Beaver, K. M., Ratchford, M., & Ferguson, C. J. (2009). Evidence of genetic and environmental effects on the development of low self-control. *Criminal Justice and Behavior*, 36, 1148–1162.

Beaver, K. M., Wright, J. P., & DeLisi, M. (2007). Self-control as an executive function: Reformulating Gottfredson & Hirschi's parental socialization thesis. *Criminal Justice and Behavior*, 34(10), 1345–1361.

Bechara, A., Damasio, H., & Damasio, A. R. (2000). Emotion, decision making and the orbitofrontal cortex. *Cerebral Cortex*, 10, 295–307.

Bierman, K. L., Domitrovich, C. E., Nix, R. L., Gest, S. D., Welsh, J. A., Greenberg, M. T., ... & Gill, S. (2008). Promoting academic and social-emotional school readiness: The Head Start REDI Program. *Child Development*, 79, 1802–1817.

Boisvert, D., Wright, J. P., Knopik, V., & Vaske, J. (2012). Genetic and environmental overlap between self-control and delinquency. *Journal of Quantitative Criminology*, 28, 477–507.

Borduin, C. M., Mann, B. J., Cone, L. T., Henggeler, S. W., Fucci, B. R., Blaske, D. M., & Williams, R. A. (1995). Multisystemic treatment of serious juvenile offenders: Long-term prevention of criminality and violence. *Journal of Consulting and Clinical Psychology*, 63(4), 569–578.

Brody, A. L., Saxena, S., Stoessel, P., Gillies, L. A., Fairbanks, L. A., Alborzian, S., ... & Baxter, L. R. (2001). Regional brain metabolic changes in patients with major depression treated with either paroxetine or interpersonal therapy. *Archives of General Psychiatry*, 631–640.

Burt, C. H., Simons, R. L., & Simons, L. G. (2006). A longitudinal test of the effects of parenting and the stability of self-control: Negative evidence for the general theory of crime. *Criminology*, 44, 353–396.

Burt, C. H., Sweeten, G., & Simons, R. L. (2014). Self-control through emerging adulthood: Instability, multidimensionality, and criminological significance. *Criminology* 52(3), 450–487.

Burton, V. S., Evans, T. D., Cullen, F., Olivares, K. M., & Dunaway, R. G. (1999). Age, self-control, and adults' offending behaviors: A research note assessing a general theory of crime. *Journal of Criminal Justice*, 27, 45–54.

Caspi, A., McClay, J., Moffitt, T. E., Mill, J., Martin, J., Craig, I. W., ... & Poulton, R. (2002). Role of genotype in the cycle of violence in maltreated children. *Science*, 297, 851–854.

Chapple, C. L., Tyler, K. A., & Bersani, B. E. (2005). Child neglect and adolescent violence: Examining the effects of self-control and peer rejection. *Violence and Victims*, 20(1), 39–53.

Conduct Problems Prevention Research Group. (1999a). Initial impact of the Fast Track prevention trial for conduct problems: I. The high-risk sample. *Journal of Consulting and Clinical Psychology*, 67(5), 631–647.

Conduct Problems Prevention Research Group. (1999b). Initial impact of the Fast Track prevention trial for conduct problems: II. Classroom effects. *Journal of Consulting and Clinical Psychology*, 67(5), 648–657.

Connolly, E. J. & Beaver, K. M. (2014). Examining the genetic and environmental influences on self-control and delinquency: Results from a genetically informative analysis of sibling pairs. *Journal of Interpersonal Violence*, 29(4), 707–735.

Davidson, R. J., Putnam, K. M., & Larson, C. L. (2000). Dysfunction in the neural circuitry of emotion regulation – A possible prelude to violence. *Science*, 289, 591–594.

De Bellis, M. D., Keshavan, M. S., Clark, D. B., Casey, B. J., Giedd, J. N., Boring, A. M., ... & Ryan, N. D. (1999). Developmental traumatology Part II: Brain Development. *Biological Psychiatry*, 45, 1271–1284.

DeLisi, M. (2015). Low self-control is a brain-based disorder. In K. M. Beaver, J. C. Barnes, & B. B. Boutwell (Eds), *The Nurture Versus Biosocial Debate in Criminology* (pp. 172–182). Thousand Oaks, CA: Sage.

DeWall, C. N., Baumeister, R. F., Stillman, T. F., & Gailliot, M. T. (2007). Violence restrained: Effects of self-regulation and its depletion on aggression. *Journal of Experimental Social Psychology*, 43, 62–76.

Diamond, B. (2016). Assessing the determinants and stability of self-control into adulthood. *Criminal Justice and Behavior*, 43(7), 951–968.

Diamond, B., Morris, R. G., & Piquero, A. R. (2017). Stability in the underlying constructs of self-control. *Crime & Delinquency*, 63(3), 235–266.

Douglas, S. C. & Martinko, M. J. (2001). Exploring the role of individual differences in the prediction of workplace aggression. *Journal of Applied Psychology*, 86(4), 547–559.

Eisner, M. (2001). Modernization, self-control and lethal violence: The long-term dynamics of European homicide rates in theoretical perspective. *British Journal of Criminology*, 41, 618–638.

Eisner, M. (2014). From swords to words: Does macro-level change in self-control predict long-term variation in levels of homicide? *Crime & Justice*, 43(1), 65–134.

Finkel, E. J., DeWall, C. N., Slotter, E. B., Oaten, M., & Foshee, V. A. (2009). Self-regulatory failure and intimate partner violence perpetration. *Journal of Personality and Social Psychology*, 97, 483–499.

Gendreau, P., Little, T., & Goggin, C. (1996). A meta-analysis of the predictors of adult offender recidivism: What works! *Criminology*, 34,(4), 575–608.

Gibson, C. L., Sullivan, C. J., Jones, S., & Piquero, A. R. (2010). "Does it take a village?" Assessing neighborhood influences on children's self-control. *Journal of Research in Crime & Delinquency*, 47(1), 31–62.

Gottfredson, M. & Hirschi. T. (1990). *The general theory of crime*. Stanford, CA: Stanford University Press.

Hanson, R. K. (2005). Twenty years of progress in violence risk assessment. *Journal of Interpersonal Violence*, 20(2), 212–217.

Hay, C. & Forrest, W. (2006). The development of self-control: Examining self control theory's stability thesis. *Criminology*, 44, 739–774.

Hay, C. & Meldrum, R. C. (2016). *Self-control and crime over the life course*. Thousand Oaks, CA: Sage Publications.

Hay, C., Meldrum, R. C., & Piquero, A. R. (2013). Negative cases in the nexus between self-control, social bonds, and delinquency. *Youth Violence and Juvenile Justice*, 11(1), 3–25.

Henggeler, S. W., Melton, G. B., & Smith, L. A. (1992). Family preservation using multisystemic therapy: An effective alternative to incarcerating serious juvenile offenders. *Journal of Consulting and Clinical Psychology*, 60(6), 953–961.

Higgins, G., Jennings, W. G., Tewksbury, R., & Gibson, C. L. (2009). Exploring the link between self-control and violent victimization trajectories in adolescents. *Criminal Justice & Behavior*, 36, 1070–1084.

Hirata, Y., Zai, C. C., Nowrouzi, B., Beitchman, J. H., & Kennedy, J. L. (2013). Study of the catechol-o-methyltransferase (COMT) gene with high aggression in children. *Aggressive Behavior*, 39, 45–51.

Hirschi, T. & Gottfredson, M. R. (1994). *The generality of deviance*. New Brunswick, NJ: Transaction Publishers.

Jennings, W. G., Higgins, G. E., Akers, R. L., Khey, D. N., & Dobrow, J. (2013). Examining the influence of delinquent peer association on the stability of self-control in late childhood and early adolescence: Toward an integrated theoretical model. *Deviant Behavior*, 34, 407–422.

Jolliffe, D. & Farrington, D. P. (2009). Effectiveness of interventions with adult male violent offenders. Report prepared for The Swedish National Council for Crime Prevention. Stockholm: Swedish Council for Crime Prevention, Information and Publications.

Kendall, P. C. & Braswell, L. (1982). Cognitive-behavioral self-control therapy for children: A components analysis. *Journal of Consulting and Clinical Psychology*, 50(5), 672–689.

Kochanska, G., Murray, K. T., & Harlan, E. T. (2000). Effortful control in early childhood: Continuity and change, antecedents, and implications for social development. *Developmental Psychology*, 36, 220–232.

Kochanska, G., Philibert, R. A., & Barry, R. A. (2009). Interplay of genes and early mother-child relationship in the development of self-regulation from toddler to preschool age. *Journal of Child Psychology and Psychiatry*, 50(11), 1331–1338.

Landenberger, N. A. & Lipsey, M. W. (2005). The positive effects of cognitive-behavioral programs for offenders: A meta-analysis of factors associated with effective treatment. *Journal of Experimental Criminology*, 1, 451–476.

Lipsey, M. (1992). The effect of treatment on juvenile delinquents: Results from meta analysis. In F. Losel, D. Bender, & T. Bliesener (Eds), *Psychology and law: International perspectives*, pp. 131–143.

Liu, Y. Y., Yang, M., Ramsay, M., Li, X. S., & Coid, J. W. (2011). A comparison of logistic regression, classification and regression tree, and neural network models in predicting violent re-offending. *Journal of Quantitative Criminology*, 27, 547–573.

Martin, S. D., Martin, E., Rai, S. S., Richardson, M. A., Royall, R., & Eng, C. (2001). Brian blood flow changes in depressed patients treated with interpersonal psychotherapy or venlafaxine hydrochloride. *Archives of General Psychiatry*, 58, 641–648.

McGloin, J. M., Pratt, T. C., & Piquero, A. R. (2006). A life-course analysis of the criminogenic effects of maternal cigarette smoking during pregnancy: A research note on the mediating impact of neuropsychological deficits. *Journal of Research in Crime and Delinquency*, 43(4), 412–426.

Miller, H. V., Jennings, W. G., Alvarez-Rivera, L. L., Lanza-Kaduce, L. (2009). Self-control, attachment, and deviance among Hispanic adolescents. *Journal of Criminal Justice*, 37, 77–84.

Moffitt, T. E., Arsenault, L., Belsky, D., Dickson, N., Hancox, R. J., Harrington, H., ... & Caspi, A. (2011). A gradient of childhood self-control predicts health, wealth, and public safety. *Proceedings of the National Academy of Sciences of the United States of America*, 108(7), 2693–2698.

Moffitt, T. E. & Caspi, A. (2001). Childhood predictors differentiate life-course persistent and adolescence-limited antisocial pathways among males and females. *Development & Psychopathology*, 13(2), 355–375.

Monahan, K., Steinberg, L., & Piquero A. R. (2015). Juvenile Justice Policy and Practice: A Developmental Perspective. In M. Tonry (Ed.), *Crime and Justice: A Review of Research* (Vol. 44, pp. 577–619). Chicago: University of Chicago Press.

Nofziger, S. (2008). The "cause" of low self-control: The influence of maternal self-control. *Journal of Research in Crime and Delinquency*, 45(2), 191–224.

Olds, D. L., Eckenrode, J., Henderson, C. R., Kitzman, H., Powers, J., Cole, R., Sidora, K., Morris, P., Pettitt, L., & Luckey, D. (1997). Long-term effects of home visitation on maternal life course and child abuse and neglect. *The Journal of the American Medical Association*, 278(8), 637–643.

Olds, D. L., Henderson, C. R., Cole, R., Eckenrode, J., Kitzman, H., Luckey, D., Pettitt, L., Sidora, K., Morris, P., & Powers, J. (1998). Long-term effects of nurse home visitation on children's criminal and antisocial behavior: 15-year follow-up of a randomized controlled trial. *The Journal of the American Medical Association*, 280(14), 1238–1244.

Olds, D. L., Henderson, C. R., Tatelbaum, R., & Chamberlin, R. (1986). Improving the delivery of prenatal care and outcomes of pregnancy: A randomized trial of nurse home visitation. *Pediatrics*, 77(1), 16–28.

Pinker, S. (2011). *The better angels of our nature*. New York: Viking.

Piquero, A. R., Farrington, D. P., Welsh, B. C., Tremblay, R., & Jennings, W. G. (2009). Effects of early family/parent training programs on antisocial behavior and delinquency. *Journal of Experimental Criminology*, 5, 83–120.

Piquero, A. R., Jennings, W. G., Farrington, D. P., Diamond, B., & Reingle Gonzalez, J. M. (2016). A meta-analysis update on the effectiveness of early self-control improvement programs to improve self-control and reduce delinquency. *Journal of Experimental Criminology*, 12(2), 249–264.

Piquero, A., Langton, L., & Gomez-Smith, Z. (2004). Discerning unfairness where others may not: Low self-control and perceiving sanctions as unfair. *Criminology*, 42, 699–734.

Piquero, A. R., MacDonald, J., Dobrin, A., Daigle, L. E., & Cullen, F. T. (2005). Self-control, violent offending, and homicide victimization: Assessing the general theory of crime. *Journal of Quantitative Criminology*, 21(1), 55–71.

Pratt, T. C. & Cullen, F. T. (2000). The empirical status of Gottfredson and Hirschi's general theory of crime: A meta-analysis. *Criminology*, 38(3), 931–964.

Pratt, T. C., Turner, M. G., & Piquero, A. R. (2004). Parental socialization and community context: A longitudinal analysis of the structural sources of low self-control. *Journal of Research in Crime and Delinquency*, 41(3), 219–243.

Raver, C. C. (2004). Placing emotional self-regulation in sociocultural and socioeconomic contexts. *Child Development*, 75(2), 346–353.

Ray, J. V., Jones, S., Loughran, T. A., & Jennings, W. G. (2013). Testing the stability of self-control: Identifying unique developmental patterns and associated risk factors. *Criminal Justice and Behavior*, 40, 588–607.

Riggs, N. R., Greenberg, M. T., Kusche, C. A., & Pentz, M. A. (2006). The meditational role of neurocognition in the behavioral outcomes of a social-emotional prevention program in elementary school students: Effects of the PATHS curriculum. *Prevention Science*, 7(1), 91–102.

Schaeffer, C. M. & Borduin, C. M. (2005). Long-term follow-up to a randomized clinical trial of multisystemic therapy with serious and violent juvenile offenders. *Journal of Consulting and Clinical Psychology*, 73(3), 445–453.

Seguin, J. R., Nagin, D., Assaad, J. M., & Tremblay, R. E. (2004). Cognitive-neuropsychological function in chronic physical aggression and hyperactivity. *Journal of Abnormal Psychology*, 113, 603–613.

Seguin, J. R., Pihl, R. O., Harden, P. W., Tremblay, R. E., Boulerice, B. (1995). Cognitive and neuropsychological characteristics of physically aggressive boys. *Journal of Abnormal Psychology*, 104, 614–624.

Sellers, C. S. (1999). Self-control and intimate violence: An examination of the scope and specification of the general theory of crime. *Criminology*, 37(2), 375–404.

Sheese, B. E., Rothbart, M. K., Voelker, P. M., & Posner, M. I. (2012). The dopamine receptor D4 gene 7-repeat allele interacts with parenting quality to predict effortful control in four year old children. *Child Development Research*. doi:10.1155/2012/863242.

Simpson, S. & Piquero, N. L. (2002). Low self-control, organizational theory and corporate crime. *Law and Society Review*, 36(3), 509–548.

Smith, H. J., Sheikh, H. I., Dyson, M. W., Olino, T. M., Laptook, R. S., Durbin, C. E., ... & Klein, D. N. (2012). Parenting and child DRD4 genotype interact to predict children's early emerging effortful control. *Child Development*, 83(6), 1932–1944.

Steinberg, L., Albert, D., Cauffman, E., Banich, M., Graham, S., & Woolard, J. (2008). Age differences in sensation seeking and impulsivity as indexed by behavior and self-report: Evidence for a dual systems model. *Developmental Psychology*, 44(6), 1764–1778.

Thomaes, K., Dorrepaal, E., Draijer, N., de Ruiter, M. B., van Balkom, A. J., Smit, J. H., Veltman, D. J. (2010). Reduced anterior cingulate and orbitofrontal volumes in child abuse-related complex PTSD. *Journal of Clinical Psychiatry*, 71(12), 1636–1644.

Tittle, C. R., Ward, D. A., & Grasmick, H. G. (2003). Gender, age, and crime/deviance: A challenge to self-control theory. *Journal of Research in Crime and Delinquency*, 40, 333–365.

Tremblay, R. E., Loeber, R., Gagnon, C., Charlebois, P., Larivee, S., & LeBlanc, M. (1991). Disruptive boys with stable and unstable fighting behavior patterns during junior elementary school. *Journal of Abnormal Child Psychology*, 19(3), 285–300.

Turner, M. G. & Piquero, A. R. (2002). The stability of self-control. *Journal of Criminal Justice*, 30, 457–471.

Turner, M. G., Piquero, A. R., & Pratt, T. C. (2005). The school context as a source of self-control. *Journal of Criminal Justice*, 33(4), 327–339.

Unnever, J. D. & Cornell, D. G. (2003). Bullying, self-control, and ADHD. *Journal of Interpersonal Violence*, 18(2), 129–147.

Van der Kolk, B. A., & Fisler, R. E. (1994). Childhood abuse and neglect and loss of self-regulation. *Bulletin of the Menninger Clinic*, 58(2), 145–168.

Vaske, J., Galyean, K., & Cullen, F. T. (2011). Toward a biosocial theory of offender rehabilitation: Why does cognitive behavioral therapy work? *Journal of Criminal Justice*, 39, 90–102.

Vaughn, M. G., DeLisi, M., Beaver, K. M., & Wright, J. P. (2009). Identifying latent classes of behavioral risk based on early childhood manifestations of self-control. *Youth Violence and Juvenile Justice*, 7, 16–31.

Vazsonyi, A. T., Clifford Wittekind, J. E., Belliston, L. M., & Van Loh, T. D. (2004). Extending the general theory of crime to "the East": Low self-control in Japanese late adolescents. *Journal of Quantitative Criminology*, 20, 189–216.

Vazsonyi, A. T., Machackova, H., Sevcikova, A., Smahel, D., & Cerna, A. (2012). Cyberbullying in context: Direct and indirect effects by low self-control across 25 European countries. *European Journal of Developmental Psychology*, 9(2), 210–227.

Vazsonyi, A. T., Pickering, L. E., Junger, M., Hessing, D. (2001). An empirical test of a general theory of crime: A four-nation comparative study of self-control and the prediction of deviance. *Journal of Research in Crime & Delinquency*, 38(2), 91–131.

Walsh, A., Taylor, C. Y., & Yun, I. (2015). The role of intelligence and temperament in interpreting the SES-crime relationship. In K. M. Beaver, J. C. Barnes, & B. B. Boutwell (Eds), *The Nurture Versus Biosocial Debate in Criminology*, (pp. 91–108). Thousand Oaks, CA: Sage.

Williams, K. R. (2012). Family violence risk assessment: A predictive cross-validation study of the domestic violence screening instrument-revised (DVSI-R). *Law & Human Behavior*, 36(2), 120–129.

Williams, K. R. & Grant, S. R. (2006). Empirically examining the risk of intimate partner violence: The domestic violence screening instrument. *Public Health Reports*, 121(4), 400–408.

Wilson, D. B., Bouffard, L. A., & Mackenzie, D. L. (2005). A quantitative review of structured, group-oriented, cognitive behavioral programs for offenders. *Criminal Justice and Behavior*, 32(2), 172–204.

Wright, J. P. & Beaver, K. M. (2005). Do parents matter in creating self-control in their children? A genetically informed test of Gottfredson and Hirschi's low self-control. *Criminology*, 43(4), 1169–1202.

Wright, J., Beaver, K., DeLisi, M., & Vaughn, M. (2008). Evidence of negligible parenting influences on self-control, delinquent peers, and delinquency in a sample of twins. *Justice Quarterly*, 25(3), 544–569.

Woodworth, M. & Porter, S. (2002). In cold blood: Characteristics of criminal homicides as a function of psychopathy. *Journal of Abnormal Psychology*, 111(3), 436–445.

38 The New Frontier: Leveraging Innovative Technologies to Prevent Bullying

Catherine P. Bradshaw, Lindsey M. O'Brennan, Tracy E. Waasdorp, Elise Pas, Julia Blumenstyk, Danielle Bartolo, and Stephen S. Leff

Bullying is broadly defined as intentional and repeated acts of aggression that occur through direct verbal (e.g., threatening, name calling), direct physical (e.g., hitting, kicking), and indirect (e.g., spreading rumors, influencing relationships, cyberbullying) forms; it also typically occurs in situations in which there is a power or status difference (Olweus, 1993). Despite some recent evidence that rates of bullying may be stabilizing, or even declining slightly (Musu-Gillette, Zhang, Wang, Zhang, & Oudekerk, 2017; Waasdorp, Pas, Zablotsky, & Bradshaw, 2017), bullying continues to be one of the most common forms of aggression and victimization experienced by school-aged children (Nansel et al., 2001; Spriggs et al., 2007). There is increasing awareness of the multitude of problems associated with bullying among youth (National Academies of Sciences, Engineering, and Medicine, 2016). In fact, all 50 states have now passed legislation regarding some form of bullying-related policy, many of which recommend the use of "evidence-based" prevention programs (Heilbrun & Cornell, 2017).

A wide range of programs and approaches have been developed with the goal of preventing bullying. Some of these programs are aimed at individuals, whereas others are more focused on classrooms or entire schools. In fact, the vast majority of bullying prevention programs have focused on schools, with relatively limited attention to other contexts, like community, family, peer context, or online environment (National Academies of Science, Engineering, and Medicine, 2016. Furthermore, most of the programs developed and rigorously tested have been universal, rather than targeted to higher-risk youth or those already involved in bullying (Bradshaw, 2015). Although many of these programs have demonstrated significant effects on bullying perpetration and victimization, the effect sizes tend to be rather modest, suggesting there is considerable room for embedding novel and innovative approaches to bullying prevention programming. There appears to be an emerging trend in the field for the inclusion of more technological tools and activities, which in part may be more engaging for youth and the adults delivering these programs. However, relatively few studies have focused specifically on the potential utility of these activities and programmatic elements, either tested alone or in combination with other program elements. Yet there is growing interest in these approaches and the potential they may afford with regard to bullying prevention.

The current chapter is focused on bullying prevention approaches and programs that leverage technology, including online platforms for collecting data on bullying and school climate, online gaming, virtual reality, statistical approaches, and social media. We focus on a few examples of these types of innovative technologies and the potential role they may play in helping to tailor, augment, or adapt bullying prevention programming and related activities. Although not intended to be exhaustive or comprehensive, it is our hope that this chapter will prompt increased use of and research on innovative approaches to bullying prevention.

Tailoring Prevention Programming Through the Use of Bullying-Related Data

A core recommended element of many traditional, school-wide bullying prevention approaches has been the use of some type of data on bullying to identify potential hot spots where bullying occurs, or the types of bullying youth are engaging in. A broader but relevant construct to measure is school climate, as high levels of bullying and peer victimization can reinforce social norms related to aggressive behavior and potentially alter the school climate (O'Brennan & Bradshaw, 2017). Interventions should aim to reduce the prevalence of bullying in schools by increasing adult supervision in structured settings, and particularly in unstructured school settings, where bullying often occurs (Leff, Costigan, & Power, 2004). School staff also need training and professional development to help enhance their ability to detect and effectively intervene in bullying situations (Bradshaw, Waasdorp, O'Brennan, & Gulemetova, 2013). For instance, a study by Bradshaw, Sawyer, and O'Brennan (2007) found that over half of the students surveyed perceived that school staff were not doing enough to prevent bullying, a belief that was particularly common among students frequently involved in bullying. Furthermore, there are often great discrepancies between the way in which adults and youth perceive issues like bullying and school climate (Bradshaw, Sawyer, & O'Brennan, 2009). Thus, it may be advantageous for school staff to review data from students and other staff on bullying, so that they may better understand areas of discrepancies and agreement with youth perceptions, and respond accordingly (O'Brennan & Bradshaw, 2017).

For example, the Olweus Bullying Prevention Program (Olweus et al., 2007) includes the collection of data, typically anonymous self-report data on various forms of bullying, characteristics of bullying (who is involved, where it occurs), and attitudes related to bullying. Through the support of a trained coach, school leadership teams learn to leverage these data to make decisions on program implementation. Similarly, other school-wide programs, such as Positive Behavioral Interventions and Supports (i.e., PBIS; Sugai & Horner, 2006), aim to alter school norms regarding student behavior and promote positive behavioral expectations, by leveraging data collected on discipline problems and/or school climate. Specifically, certain data collection programs, like the School-Wide Information System (SWIS), have been created with the goal of facilitating data-based decision making related to behavior problems, including bullying (Irvin et al., 2004). These data systems not only help schools collect data, but they also have the advantage of built-in visual display technologies and enable users to conduct analyses of the data via a user-friendly platform.

Online data systems have been created to collect data more specifically on school climate and bullying and are used across the country. One example is the Maryland Safe and Supportive Schools (MDS3) Survey System (Bradshaw et al., 2014), which facilitates analyses, provides visual displays of data, generates a variety of data reports, and supports decision making related to school climate and bullying. A number of tools have been created within the MDS3 Survey System that help schools identify particular areas of need, and specific evidence-based programs that can be used to address those particular concerns. Such online data collection programs facilitate data-based decision making through ease of use and interpretation of those data, and are developed to support PBIS implementation, and can be particularly helpful for addressing bullying. They can also be used to identify when schools may need to consider adopting selective and indicated preventive interventions to address the needs of youth more directly involved in bullying and already exhibiting some of the mental health and behavioral concerns associated with bullying (for a review, see Bradshaw, 2015; National Academies of Science, Engineering, and Medicine, 2016). Recent studies of the MDS3 data system have shown that its use, particularly when used in conjunction with coaching, is associated with improvements in climate and reductions in discipline problems, including bullying (Bradshaw et al., 2014; Waasdorp, Pas et al., 2017). An integrated version of PBIS and bullying prevention has recently been developed (Ross & Horner, 2009), which links classroom-based lessons and activities focused on bullying prevention with the school-wide PBIS program. Specifically, PBIS schools that identify bullying as a significant concern within their data can opt to also implement classroom-based lessons and activities focused on bullying prevention that complement and extend their school-wide behavioral expectations (see www.pbis.org/school/bully-prevention).

Another way in which data can be used to tailor a bullying prevention program at an individual or group level is through the use of social network analyses. For example, a recent line of research by Paluck and colleagues has investigated the powerful influences of popular youth on a range of bullying prevention-related factors, like school climate and peer conflict (Paluck, 2011). One such study collected peer nomination data on students with the goal of identifying popular, and therefore influential, youth who may be particularly well-suited to lead bullying prevention programs and school climate promoting activities (Paluck & Shepherd, 2012). Some experimental studies by this team suggest that these approaches can have a significant impact on a range of bullying-related outcomes. Taken together, this line of research highlights the potential ways in which innovative statistical technologies like social network analysis may be particularly helpful in identifying nonaggressive youth who are highly influential; these youth may be important individuals to not only lead groups, but also help facilitate a change in the social norms within schools, which in turn reduce bullying, or increase active bystander behavior.

Mixed-Reality Simulators to Build Teacher Skills in Bullying Prevention

As mentioned earlier, one of the main challenges to addressing bullying in schools is that teachers struggle to detect bullying and rarely implement effective strategies to respond to bullying when it is detected (Bradshaw, Sawyer, & O'Brennan, 2007; Demaray, Malecki, Secord, & Lyell, 2013). Focus groups conducted with 17 students and 16 teachers reflected how addressing bullying in classrooms is complicated for teachers; both students and teachers shared that teachers feel they lack the time needed to address bullying issues, but also lack knowledge on how best to respond. Gaps in the relationships between teachers and students were also highlighted by both groups. For example, students indicated that when teachers do not respond or respond ineffectively, they perceive that teachers do not care about them; however, teachers indicated they would like to intervene but due to time constraints and lacking efficacy, they cannot address all bullying situations (Waasdorp, Debnam, Pas, & Bradshaw, 2017). Addressing bullying in schools requires teacher skill development as well as making clear to teachers how bullying affects their students socially and emotionally, as well as academically. Simulated guided practice experiences can provide opportunities that may not otherwise be available in the classroom, but they also permit individualization to teacher needs.

TeachLivE (TLE) is one example of a simulation technology that allows for an immersive, mixed-reality (i.e., part-real, part-synthetic) experience, where the teacher interfaces with five computer-generated, animated middle school-aged student *avatars*, who react to the human teacher with the guidance of a live actor (Dieker et al., 2008; http://teachlive.org/). TeachLivE is not scripted, rather it leverages true-to-life experience, virtually enacted by trained actors; it is also modifiable, allowing for virtual students to be programmed as needed (e.g., ensuring the occurrence of bullying behaviors in the virtual classroom; Dieker et al., 2014). Research on TLE indicates that teachers quickly became comfortable interacting with the avatars (Dieker et al., 2014; Elford, Carter, & Aronin, 2013; Pas et al., 2016) and there are promising findings regarding teachers' acquisition and use of new classroom management skills following practice in the simulator (Pas et al., 2016).

An ongoing pilot study of this technology used within the context of coaching supports teachers' use of this mixed-reality simulator to practice the skills of detecting, responding, and preventing bullying in their classrooms. Specifically, portable equipment is used to make the simulation available to teachers within their school buildings and teachers come to three separate sessions, in pairs with a peer teacher, for practice. Within each session, teachers watch one another as a means for additional exposure and growth. During the first session, the teachers take turns practicing a targeted strategy, while the other observes and makes note of each instance of bullying or aggressive behavior observed. In a debrief, the coach not only provides feedback about the frequency and quality of their strategy use, but provides feedback to the teachers regarding whether they detected all student aggressive or bullying behaviors. This allows teachers to identify whether detection is of concern for them, and can be tailored to facilitate additional practice on detection. In the next session, as teachers have reached mastery in detection, they practice responding to bullying. Teachers are taught to: (1) immediately stop the behavior and encourage coping strategies, (2) maintain a calm and firm voice, (3) label the behavior as bullying and characterize it has harmful or unacceptable, (4) indicate that they want to help/discuss this situation with the bully and the victim separately outside of class time, and (5) continue their instruction while implementing prevention strategies to avoid further issues. Teachers are also taught how to express empathy to victims. Following their practice of this response sequence, teachers practise prevention strategies, so the final response step can be adequately implemented. Specifically, teachers practise to increase their monitoring of the classroom, to state clear behavioral expectations for interactions with peers, and use specific praise when students follow the stated expectations. A benefit of these mixed-reality simulators is that teachers can learn skills without exposing real students to the harms of unsuccessful attempts at using new skills (Dieker, Hynes, Stapleton, & Hughes, 2007; Dieker et al., 2014). Furthermore, it can be especially helpful to use simulation experiences for guided practice with harmful behaviors such as bullying. Stimulator programs can also be effective tools when used within the context of teacher coaching that allows for tailoring professional development as they offer opportunities for the coach to provide direct, observational feedback to teachers about their use of intervention techniques.

Multimedia, Interactive, and Online Games for Youth

The integration of online gaming and video-based activities into anti-bullying programs is an emerging and promising trend in the prevention field. A meta-analysis of bullying prevention programs conducted by Farrington and Ttofi (2009; also see Ttofi & Farrington, 2011) indicated that out of the 44 evaluations they reviewed, 21 included some type of video but just three (i.e., studies of the Finnish KiVa Anti-Bullying Program [Salmivalli et al., 2004; 2005], an anti-bullying program tested in the Netherlands by Fekkes et al. [2006], and Evers et al.'s [2007] Build Respect, Stop Bullying™ Program tested in the USA) included some type of virtual reality computer game. Their review indicated that the inclusion of a video component (typically as a part of a multi-component program) was among the strongest of the 20 components examined across studies with regard to impacts on victimization (Farrington & Ttofi, 2009).

As noted above, the KiVa Anti-Bullying Program is one such multicomponent bullying prevention program that includes universal social-emotional skill development activities as well as anti-bullying videos and videogames to teach the harms associated with bullying, and how to respond when youth encounter bullying behavior. The program was created for youth age 6 to 16. KiVa includes a set of developmentally appropriate activities for adults to facilitate with youth to help prevent bullying before it occurs, and to respond effectively and responsibly when it does occur. KiVa provides youth and adults opportunities to practice responding prosocially to bullying situations. It leverages decades of work on other skill-focused programs that highlight the importance of providing opportunities to practice engaging in certain behaviors, such as conflict resolution or managing difficult social situations.

Originally developed in Finland, KiVa has been more recently adapted for implementation in other countries, like Italy, the United Kingdom, and the Netherlands. The program has been rigorously tested in Finland through a series of randomized trials as well as some scale-up studies. These studies have consistently demonstrated significant impacts on both bullying and victimization, as well as other favorable outcomes, such as school climate (Kärnä et al., 2013; Kärnä et al., 2011; Nocentini & Menesini, 2016; Williford, Noland, Little, Kärnä, & Salmivalli, 2012).

Another example of an anti-bullying videogame is the stand-alone online bullying prevention program called StandUp (Timmons-Mitchell, Levesque, Harris, Flannery, & Falcone, 2016). This three-session online program is based on the transtheoretical model of behavior change and the Teen Choices: A Program for Healthy, Nonviolent Relationships, a three-session computer-tailored intervention for teenage dating violence prevention (Levesque, Johnson, & Prochaska, 2017). StandUp delivers content focused on six core areas related to healthy relationship skills, including understanding and respecting other people's feelings and needs; using calm, nonviolent ways to deal with disagreements; respecting the boundaries of others; communicating feelings; making decisions in social situations; and effective bullying bystander behavior. A recent pilot of StandUp with approximately 100 high schoolers demonstrated significant or marginally significant effects on perpetrating and experiencing emotional and physical bullying and bystander behavior (Timmons-Mitchell et al., 2016)

A third example of the use of related technology is the recently developed interactive 3D bullying prevention multimedia show called Free2B (Leff, Waasdorp, & Winston, 2017). Free2B was developed through an innovative partnership between Violence Prevention Initiative researchers at the Children's Hospital of Philadelphia and multimedia experts from Life Changing Experiences for students in grades 6 to 8. Free2B was developed to be a feasible and sustainable alternative to existing bullying prevention programs. It combines empirically supported bullying prevention strategies with the latest technological advances to engage youth in a fun and interactive technologically sophisticated experience. Utilizing community-based participatory research, researchers sought feedback from a local youth advisory group in multiple locations across the country and world regarding components of the show, which is delivered to schools as a cinematic experience in the auditorium. The Free2B show consists of: (a) an engaging 3D movie that highlights the harmful impact of bullying (e.g., physical, relational, and cyber) and the role that positive bystanders can play in helping to promote a safe school climate; (b) video testimonials in which youth share their experiences about bullying and victimization in an effort to inspire students to take a stand against bullying; and (c) an interactive quiz show in which youth answer questions and learn about bullying using a hand-held device. The overall goal of Free2B is to motivate youth to prevent bullying and promote positive bystander behaviors.

The development team recently conducted a series of pilot studies of Free2B; the most recent pilot included 714 students in grades 7 and 8 from five Philadelphia-area public schools that were diverse in location (urban and suburban) and student SES (Leff et al., 2016; Leff et al., 2017). Students completed approximately ten questions using handhelds immediately before and after Free2B in order to assess changes in attitudes and knowledge, feasibility, and favorability. Results showed that the majority of students found the show to be highly acceptable, important, and fun. Additionally, results suggested significant changes in problem-solving knowledge, increased sympathy, and improved confidence in helping in bullying situations.

Although preliminary, these findings suggest that Free2B is an innovative and systematic approach to catalyze bullying prevention programming. The team intends to conduct a larger study of Free2B to further examine the effectiveness and to determine if the effects are translated into behavior changes by students and school personnel, which in turn decreases bullying over time. The data collected from the Free2B show is also being utilized to provide tailored school action plans based upon the data collected pre-, post-, and during the show using handheld remote devices.

Social Media Campaigns

As teenagers adopt smartphones, they have a variety of methods for communication and sharing at their disposal. Texting is an especially important mode of communication for teens as recent research shows 90% of teens with phones exchange texts, and a typical teen sends and receives 30 texts per day (Pew Research Center, 2015). However, their attention is often divided across a variety of platforms at any given time, engaging with a variety of social media platforms. Facebook remains the most commonly used social media site among American youth age 13 to 17, with 71% of all teens using the site, even as half of teens use Instagram and 40% use Snapchat (Pew Research Center, 2015). In texts and on social media, the use of emojis is increasingly abundant. Used as shorthand for expressing thoughts and feelings, emojis amplify happy messages and pacify harsh ones, often "lightening" the mood. Thus, anti-bullying social media campaigns could harness the "language" teens are using online as a way for youth to take a stand against bullying and show support for someone who is being bullied.

In 2015, the Ad Council, the leading producer of public service ads in the USA, brought together a coalition of nonprofit, corporate, technology, and media partners to address bullying through the "I Am A Witness" social media campaign. The campaign aimed to stop bullying by activating the "silent majority" of teens (age 11 to 15) who witness it each day, transforming them from passive bystanders into an empowered and active collective who will speak up online against bullying and encourage their friends and peers to do the same. Too often, they do not do anything to stop it – whether it is because they are unsure what to do, or because they fear being victimized. By creating a collective of witnesses, not bystanders, the goal is to reduce the isolation to make them "feel bigger," thereby helping them to "flex their collective strength," giving them the confidence to act, and empowering them with ways to act. This led to the development of the "Witness" emoji, which aims to empower youth to take a stand against bullying and show their support to their others being bullied.

Created pro-bono by Goodby Silverstein & Partners, this digital-focused campaign is designed to reach and inspire teens through digital, mobile, and social media. Key to this campaign is a free downloadable "eye" emoji available on every iPhone with iOS 9.1 and, later, on Android devices running Marshmallow. The emoji, which can be downloaded using onto the phone's keyboard, is shaped like a speech bubble with an eye in the center. Teens are encouraged to use the eye emoji when they witness bullying online either through text messaging, group messaging, social media websites and apps (e.g., Facebook, Instagram, Snapchat), and other online platforms. Users are also encouraged to use the campaign's hashtag, #iamawitness, to further show their support online. The campaign website (http://iwitnessbullying.org/) provides additional information on how to access the emoji, as well as resources that arm teens with the confidence to act to stop bullying behavior.

The campaign was informed by multiple rounds of qualitative and quantitative research to understand key attitudes and beliefs about bullying, and to ensure that the creative concepts resonated with the target audience. For example, working with Play Collective, qualitative research was conducted with in-person friendship pairs to learn about key attitudes and beliefs about bullying, in addition to getting reactions to the campaign concept. Teens (age 11–15) thought the campaign could provide a useful resource, and the emoji was well received. Although the campaign uses the term "witness," this is intended to promote an active, rather than a passive, response to such events by providing specific actions that the youth are intended to take. By providing youth with a low barrier way to intervene in an online bullying situation using their social and digital language, I Am A Witness intended to boost youth's confidence to act in real-time to stop bullying behavior and provide tangible emotional support for victims. By transforming youth from passive bystanders into a united, empowered collective that will speak up against bullying, the campaign provides a value exchange by giving children and teens who do not know what to do – but who want to do something – an easy, digital way to take a stand.

Consumer research indicated that all campaign materials should outline specific steps teens could take to stop or prevent bullying, and that the messaging should emphasize the role and meaning of the emoji in combating bullying and highlight how teens can use it in a variety of contexts. Furthermore, qualitative usability testing was conducted on the emoji keyboard to determine how teens (age 13–16) perceive and react to the idea. The participating youth welcomed the keyboard as a solution, and the purpose of the campaign resonated and was clearly understood. The youth also were more motivated to use the keyboard when a friend/peer was the one being bullied, and reported that a greater variety of emoji would help them find the "right" emoji for the situation at hand.

In addition to the emoji, social media influencers, including YouTube creators and Snapchat celebrities, were tapped to amplify the campaign message. Other platform-specific activations on Facebook,

Instagram, Twitter, musical.ly, live.ly, Whisper, We Heart It, After School, and Wishbone/Slingshot, among others, have also been initiated to further extend the campaign's reach and impact. Given the digital and social focus of this campaign, social media monitoring and analytics are integral to the campaign's evaluation. The I Am A Witness campaign has driven significant engagement. Between the launch in October 2015 through January 2017, there were 864K website sessions, 88.9K+ public online mentions, and 191K total emoji/stickers shared from the custom downloadable keyboard and via partner integrations and activations. A unique lesson to take away from this example is its wide-scale dissemination and outreach to the universe of media outlets. The public service announcements were disseminated to more than 33,000 of media outlets in the United States with countless pathways into homes – through broadcast, digital, mobile, and alternative media partners. This multilayered media outreach strategy maximizes national and local support from traditional, digital, mobile, social, and alternative media partners to deliver premier media placements.

Conclusions and Future Directions

Despite increased attention to the issue of bullying in the prevention literature and educational policies, the prevention models and approaches that have received the most empirical attention and broadest dissemination have largely used traditional "low-tech" approaches. Yet there is an increasing trend in bullying prevention programming, like other youth-focused efforts, to include more technology – be it technologically facilitated data collection and decision-support processes to social media campaigns with emojis. Such efforts have the potential to be more engaging for youth, and provide more opportunity for further interactions with the content and bullying prevention process. These approaches may also increase the reach and dissemination of prevention programming, and have the added benefit of standardized delivery of the relevant or core program content. Further, their technological foundation allows for the collection of data, for program evaluation, that would otherwise not be present. Such engagement strategies may in fact yield a more meaningful and memorable experience for youth and the adults who help disseminate these approaches.

Despite the growing enthusiasm regarding the use of these types of approach, additional research is needed to determine whether these approaches have a significant effect, either as a stand-alone program or activity, or perhaps as a complement to other more traditional approaches. Although the preliminary findings from these pilot studies of tech-focused approaches and others, like those tested as part of multicomponent programs (see Farrington & Ttofi, 2009), are promising, we caution that there needs to be more testing to ensure that the interventions and technologies are being used as intended, and more importantly, are having the intended effect. Bearing these issues in mind, it is exciting to see increased use of technology and this level of innovation to benefit and advance the field of bullying prevention, particularly when applying the basic foundations (i.e., raising awareness and knowledge, teaching skills, allowing for the practice and use of new skills) that the field has established as necessary for preventing bullying.

Acknowledgments

We would like to thank Hannah Blatt and Allison Greenwald from the Ad Council for their assistance with the preparation of elements of this chapter. Funding for some of the projects summarized in this report come from National Institute of Justice to the lead author.

References

Ad Council. (2016). I Am A Witness Campaign. Retrieved November 12, 2017 from http://iwitnessbullying.org/.

Bradshaw, C. P. (2015). Translating research to practice in bullying prevention. *American Psychologist*, 70 (4), 322–332.

Bradshaw, C. P., Debnam, K. J., Lindstrom Johnson, S., Pas, E., Hershfeldt, P., Alexander, A., ... & Leaf, P. J. (2014). Maryland's evolving system of social, emotional, and behavioral interventions in public schools: The Maryland Safe and Supportive Schools Project. *Adolescent Psychiatry*, 4(3), 194–206.

Bradshaw, C. P., Sawyer, A. L., & O'Brennan, L. M. (2007). Bullying and peer victimization at school: Perceptual differences between students and school staff. *School Psychology Review*, 36(3), 361–382.

Bradshaw, C. P., Sawyer, A. L., & O'Brennan, L. M. (2009). A social disorganization perspective on bullying-related attitudes and behaviors: The influence of school context. *American Journal of Community Psychology*, 43, 204–220.

Bradshaw, C. P., Waasdorp, T. E., O'Brennan, L., & Gulemetova, M. (2013). Teachers' and education support professionals' perspectives on bullying and prevention: Findings from a National Education Association (NEA) survey. *School Psychology Review*, 42, 280–297.

Demaray, M. K., Malecki, C. K., Secord, S. M., & Lyell, K. M. (2013). Agreement among students', teachers', and parents' perceptions of victimization by bullying. *Children and Youth Services Review*, 35(12), 2091–2100.

Dieker, L., Hynes, M., Stapleton, C., & Hughes, C. (2007). Virtual classrooms: STAR simulator building virtual environments for teacher training in effective classroom management. *New Learning Technology SALT*, 4, 1–22.

Dieker, L. A., Hynes, M. C., Hughes, C. E., & Smith, E. (2008). Implications of mixed reality and simulation technologies on special education and teacher preparation. *Focus on Exceptional Children*, 40(6), 1–20.

Dieker, L. A., Rodriguez, J. A., Lignugaris/Kraft, B., Hynes, M. C., & Hughes, C. E. (2014). The potential of simulated environments in teacher education: Current and future possibilities. *Teacher Education and Special Education: The Journal of the Teacher Education Division of the Council for Exceptional Children*, 37(1), 21–33.

Elford, M., Carter, R. A., Jr., & Aronin, S. (2013). Virtual reality check: Teachers use bug-in-ear coaching to practice feedback techniques with student avatars. *Journal of Staff Development*, 34(1), 40–43.

Evers, K. E., Prochaska, J. O., Van Marter, D. F., Johnson, J. L., & Prochaska, J. M. (2007). Transtheoretical-based bullying prevention effectiveness trials in middle schools and high schools. *Educational Research*, 49, 397–414.

Farrington, D. P. & Ttofi, M. M. (2009). *School-based programs to reduce bullying and victimization*. Oslo, Norway: Campbell Systematic Reviews. doi: 6, 10.4073/csr.2009.6.

Fekkes, M., Pijpers, F. I. M., & Verloove-Vanhorick, S. P. (2006). Effects of antibullying school program on bullying and health complaints. *Archives of Pediatrics and Adolescent Medicine*, 160, 638–644.

Heilbrun, A. & Cornell, D. (2017). Policies related to the prevention of bullying. In C. P. Bradshaw (Ed.), *Handbook on Bullying Prevention: A Life Course Perspective* (pp. 241–250). New York: National Association of Social Workers Press.

Irvin, L. K., Tobin, T. J., Sprague, J. R., Sugai, G., & Vincent, C. G. (2004). Validity of office discipline referral measures as indices of school-wide behavioral status and effects of school-wide behavioral interventions. *Journal of Positive Behavior Interventions, 6,* 131–147.

Kärnä, A., Voeten, M., Little, T., Alanen, E., Poskiparta, E., & Salmivalli, C. (2013). Effectiveness of the KiVa antibullying program: Grades 1–3 and 7–9. *Journal of Educational Psychology, 105,* 535–551.

Kärnä, A., Voeten, M., Little, T., Poskiparta, E., Kaljonen, A., & Salmivalli, C. (2011). A large-scale evaluation of the KiVa antibullying program. *Child Development, 82,* 311–330.

Leff, S. S., Costigan, T. E., Power, T. J. (2004). Using participatory-action research to develop a playground-based prevention program. *Journal of School Psychology, 42,* 3–21.

Leff, S. S., Waasdorp, T. E., Paskewich, B., & Winston, F. (2016). *Free2B: Bridging the Gap Betweem Theory, Practice, and Innovation in Bullying Prevention Programming*. Poster presentation at the Mid-Atlantic Regional Education Research, Policy, and Practice Conference, May 2016, Philadelphia, PA.

Leff, S. S., Waasdorp, T. E., & Winston, F. (2017). *The Free2B Multi-Media Bullying Prevention Experience: Initial Evaluation of Feasibility and Efficacy*. Paper presentation at the Annual Meeting of the Pediatric Academic Societies, May 2017.

Levesque, D. A., Johnson, J. L., & Prochaska, J. M. (2017). Teen Choices, an online stage-based program for healthy, nonviolent relationships: Development and feasibility trial. *Journal of School Violence,* 16(4), 376–385.

Musu-Gillette, L., Zhang, A., Wang, K., Zhang, J., & Oudekerk, B. A. (2017). *Indicators of School Crime and Safety: 2016* (NCES 2017-064/NCJ 250650). National Center for Education Statistics, US Department of Education, and Bureau of Justice Statistics, Office of Justice Programs, US Department of Justice. Washington, DC.

Nansel, T. R., Overpeck, M., Pilla, R. S., Ruan, W. J., Simons-Morton, B., & Scheidt, P. (2001). Bullying behaviors among US youth: Prevalence and associations with psychosocial adjustment. *JAMA,* 285(16), 2094–2100.

National Academies of Sciences, Engineering, and Medicine. (2016). *Preventing Bullying Through Science, Policy, and Practice*. Washington, DC: National Academies Press. doi: 10.17226/23482.

Nocentini, A. & Menesini, E. (2016). KiVa anti-bullying program in Italy: Evidence of effectiveness in a randomized control trial. *Prevention Science, 17,* 1012–1023.

O'Brennan, L. & Bradshaw, C. P. (2017). The transactional association between school climate and bullying. In C. P. Bradshaw (Ed.), *Handbook on Bullying Prevention: A Life Course Perspective* (pp. 165–176). New York: National Association of Social Workers Press.

Olweus, D. (1993). *Bullying at school*. Oxford: Blackwell.

Olweus, D., Limber, S. P., Flerx, V. C., Mullin, N., Riese, J. & Snyder, M. (2007). *Olweus Bullying Prevention Program: Schoolwide guide*. Center City, MN: Hazelden.

Paluck, E. L. (2011). Peer pressure against prejudice: A high school field experiment examining social network change. *Journal of Experimental Social Psychology, 47,* 350–358.

Paluck, E. L. & Shepherd, H. (2012). The salience of social referents: A field experiment on collective norms and harassment behavior in a school social network. *Journal of Personality and Social Psychology, 103,* 899–915.

Pas, E.T., Johnson, S. R., Larson, K., Brandenburg, L., Church, R., & Bradshaw, C. P. (2016). Reducing behavior problems among students with an ASD: A pilot study of coaching teachers in a mixed-reality setting. *Journal of Autism and Developmental Disorders, 46,* 3640–3652. doi: 10.1007/s10803-016-2898-y.

Pew Research Center. (2015). *Teens, Social Media & Technology Overview*. Retrieved November 12, 2017 from: www.pewinternet.org/2015/04/09/teens-social-media-technology-2015/.

Timmons-Mitchell, J., Levesque, D. A., Harris, L. A., Flannery, D. J., & Falcone, T. (2016). Pilot test of StandUp, an online school-based bullying prevention program. *Children & Schools*, 38, 71–79.

Ross, S. W. & Horner, R. H. (2009). Bully prevention in Positive Behavior Support. *Journal of Applied Behavior Analysis*, 42, 747–759.

Salmivalli, C., Kaukiainen, A., Voeten, M., & Sinisammal, M. (2004). Targeting the group as a whole: The Finnish anti-bullying intervention. In P. K. Smith, D. Pepler, & K. Rigby (Eds), *Bullying in schools: How successful can interventions be?* (pp. 251–275). Cambridge: Cambridge University Press.

Salmivalli, C., Kaukiainen, A., Voeten, M. (2005). Anti-bullying intervention: Implementation and outcome. *British Journal of Educational Psychology*, 75, 465–487.

Spriggs, A. L., Iannotti, R. J., Nansel, T. R., & Haynie, D. L. (2007). Adolescent bullying involvement and perceived family, peer and school relations: Commonalities and differences across race/ethnicity. *Journal of Adolescent Health*, 41, 283–293.

Sugai, G. & Horner, R. (2006). A promising approach for expanding and sustaining school-wide positive behavior support. *School Psychology Review*, 35, 245–259.

Timmons-Mitchell, J., Levesque, D. A., Harris, L. A., Flannery, D. J., & Falcone, T. (2016). Pilot Test of StandUp, an Online School-Based Bullying Prevention Program. *Children and Schools*, 38, 71–79.

Ttofi, M. M. & Farrington, D. P. (2011). Effectiveness of school-based programs to reduce bullying: A systematic and meta-analytic review. *Journal of Experimental Criminology*, 7, 27–56.

Waasdorp, T. E., Debnam, K. J., Pas, E. T., & Bradshaw, C. P. (2017,). *Teacher and Student Perceptions of Bullying in the Classroom: Identifying Effective Strategies for Teacher Intervention*. Paper presented at Annual Meeting of the Society for Prevention Research, June 2017, Washington, DC.

Waasdorp, T. E., Pas, E., Zablotsky, B., & Bradshaw, C. P. (2017). Ten-year trends in bullying and related attitudes among 4th-12th graders. *Pediatrics*, 139(6), e20162615.

Williford, A., Noland, B., Little, T., Kärnä, A., & Salmivalli, C. (2012). Effects of the KiVa Antibullying Program on adolescents' perception of peers, depression, and anxiety. *Journal of Abnormal Child Psychology*, 40, 289–300.

39 Neural Substrates of Youth and Adult Antisocial Behavior

Rebecca Waller, Hailey L. Dotterer, Laura Murray, and Luke W. Hyde

Introduction

Antisocial behavior (AB) refers to a diverse range of behaviors, including violence, rule-breaking, and substance use, which are harmful and costly to individuals, communities, and society. Beyond criminal outcomes, AB is associated with a range of poor mental and physical health problems, including suicide and depression (Odgers et al., 2008). Neuroimaging research aims to identify neural correlates of AB to improve understanding of etiology of AB and inform the creation of effective and personalized treatments. Behavioral research has established that individuals with AB exhibit a range of impairments, such as socioemotional processing deficits, emotion regulation problems, reward-dominant behavior, and impulsivity (Blair, Leibenluft, & Pine, 2014; Hyde, Shaw, & Hariri, 2013) that have, in turn, guided the targets of neuroimaging research.

Here, we focus first on fMRI studies that have identified brain regions implicated in adult and youth AB related to behavioral deficits in socioemotional processing, abnormal learning and motivated behavior, and low inhibitory/cognitive control (Figure 39.1). Second, we outline research examining structural differences in specific regions implicated in AB. Third, we examine evidence suggesting differences in the connections between brain regions implicated in AB through studies of functional connectivity and the white-matter tracts that connect regions. Finally, we end by highlighting emerging research and future directions, including examining intrinsic connectivity networks of the brain, neuroprediction of AB, and incorporating the study of genetic and environmental risk factors into neural models of AB development.

Functional Neuroimaging Studies

Socioemotional Processing

AB has been associated with impairments in socioemotional processing, including poor recognition of emotional faces and low empathic concern (Marsh & Blair, 2008), as well as fearlessness and decreased physiological responses to affectively laden and startle tasks (Raine, 2002). Given the role of the amygdala and broader limbic system in emotional learning and fear responsivity, these behavioral impairments implicate deficits in the limbic system as an important etiological factor in AB (Kiehl, 2006).

Amygdala. Consistent with this hypothesis, multiple fMRI studies have linked AB to differences in amygdala reactivity, particularly reactivity to emotional faces.

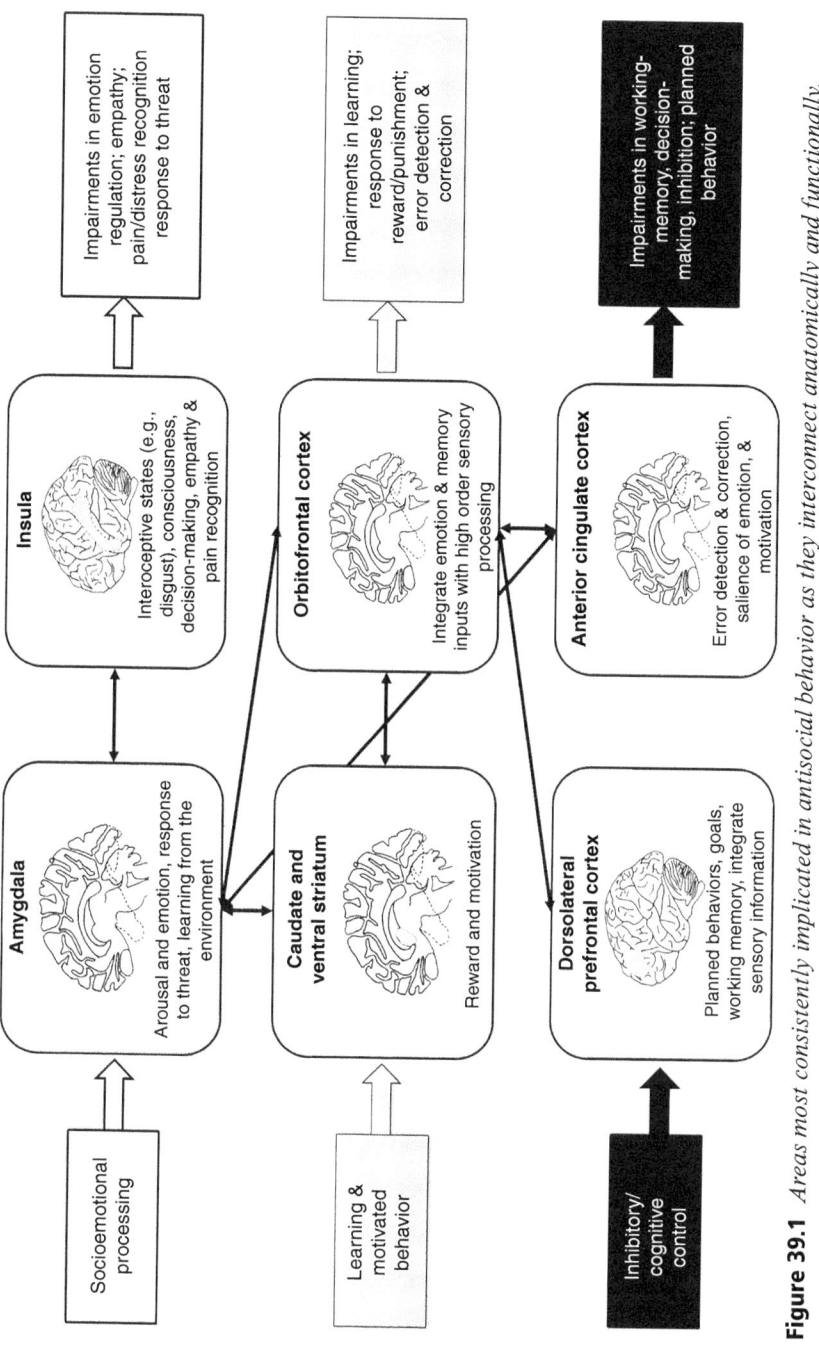

Figure 39.1 *Areas most consistently implicated in antisocial behavior as they interconnect anatomically and functionally, presented in relation to deficits in affective processing, contingency processing, and inhibitory/cognitive control that characterize highly aggressive and violent individuals. Note that many of these neural regions are implicated in multiple types of behaviors (e.g., the OFC and ACC are also important for socioemotional behaviors, beyond their additional roles in learning and inhibition; Blair et al., 2014; Hyde et al., 2013).*

However, the direction of associations has been mixed, with some studies reporting greater amygdala reactivity and others reporting reduced reactivity to emotional stimuli. This pattern of findings has been explained by the presence or absence of psychopathic or callous-unemotional (CU) traits. CU traits in children and the affective and interpersonal components of psychopathy in adults tap a lack of empathy, reduced interpersonal affect, and lack of guilt (Frick, Ray, Thornton, & Kahn, 2014; Hare & Neumann, 2008). Several prominent theories posit that AB has a divergent neuroetiology, particularly with regard to amygdala reactivity to interpersonal emotion, which is contingent on levels of CU or psychopathic traits. Specifically, antisocial individuals who are low on CU and psychopathic traits are posited to show exaggerated amygdala reactivity to emotion, particularly interpersonal threat (i.e., angry facial expressions), which leads to reactively motivated aggression in the context of emotional dysregulation. In contrast, a small group of individuals high on CU and psychopathic traits are thought to have diminished amygdala reactivity to emotional stimuli, particularly social signals of distress (i.e., fearful faces with a directed eye gaze), which leads to more proactively motivated aggression and deficits in empathy (Blair et al., 2014; Hyde et al., 2013).

Research has generally supported this distinction. For example, Viding and colleagues (2012) found that among youth with diagnosable AB, those with high CU traits had lower amygdala reactivity to fearful faces, whereas those with AB but without CU traits had greater amygdala reactivity to fearful faces when compared to healthy controls. Similarly, in a sample of community adults, Hyde and colleagues (2014) found that the variance unique to AB mapped onto high negative emotionality and greater amygdala reactivity to emotional faces, whereas variance unique to psychopathic traits mapped onto lower negative emotionality and lower amygdala reactivity (Hyde, Byrd, Votruba-Drzal, Hariri, & Manuck, 2014). Moreover, a similar study in youth found these same divergent relationships between amygdala reactivity and AB and CU traits explained the higher proactive aggression in youth high on AB and CU traits (Lozier, Cardinale, VanMeter, & Marsh, 2014). These findings are consistent with other studies of youth. For example, antisocial youth with high CU traits have been shown to exhibit amygdala hyporesponsivity, particularly to fearful faces, in several studies when compared to youth low on AB and CU traits (Harenski, Harenski, & Kiehl, 2014; Jones, Laurens, Herba, Gareth, & Viding, 2009; Marsh et al., 2008). In contrast, more generally antisocial youth (presumably with low CU traits) have shown greater amygdala reactivity to emotional stimuli (Decety, Michalska, Akitsuki, & Lahey, 2009; Herpertz et al., 2008). Similarly, among adults, decreased amygdala activity has been reported during affective processing tasks among criminal psychopaths, including tasks contrasting emotional to neutral phrases (Kiehl et al., 2001), viewing sad and fearful facial expressions (Decety, Skelly, Yoder, & Kiehl, 2014), and emotional face-matching (Contreras-Rodríguez et al., 2014). Moreover, studies that focused on reactive forms of adult AB have found greater amygdala reactivity to negative emotional stimuli in those with impulsive aggression (e.g., Coccaro, McCloskey, Fitzgerald, & Phan, 2007). Studies from community samples suggest these divergent relationships between amygdala reactivity and AB vs. psychopathic traits generalize to normative dimensions of AB and psychopathy (Carré, Hyde, Neumann, Viding, & Hariri, 2013; Hyde et al., 2014).

Thus, these studies suggest that those high on AB are generally emotionally dysregulated in their behavior due to amygdala sensitivity to emotion, whereas those with CU or psychopathic traits engage in proactive aggression due to their diminished amygdala and affective reactivity to signals of fear in others. Although this literature broadly supports a divergent pattern of amygdala reactivity related to the level of CU traits in AB, two studies of large samples have failed to find that CU traits are uniquely related to amygdala reactivity (Hyde et al., 2016; Passamonti et al., 2010), with some question as to whether CU traits-amygdala reactivity correlations actually reflect AB severity, rather than CU traits per se.

Orbitofrontal cortex (OFC). The orbitofrontal cortex (OFC) has also been implicated in AB because of its role in socioemotional processing, including integration and representation of affective information (Kringelbach, 2005). In particular, the amygdala is thought to transmit reinforcement information associated with emotional stimuli to the OFC, which represents this information. Crucially, disruptions to OFC representation of affective stimuli are thought to impair empathic or sensitive responses to the distress or fear of others seen in individuals high on AB (Blair, 2007), and more broadly may stem from disruptions in the role of the OFC in inhibitory control (Damasio, Grabowski, Frank, Galaburda, & Damasio, 1994). In support of this theory, studies of criminal psychopaths have found reduced OFC activation while participants viewed aversive cues (Decety, Chen, Harenski, & Kiehl, 2013), emotional facial expressions (Decety et al., 2014), and during an emotional memory task (Kiehl et al., 2001). Reduced OFC activity to angry facial expressions has also been found in patients with intermittent explosive disorder (Coccaro et al., 2007), suggesting that deficits in OFC function may not be specific to psychopathy, but rather broadly to AB across affective contexts.

Anterior cingulate cortex (ACC). The anterior cingulate cortex is also relevant to socioemotional processing in AB, as it shows strong functional and structural connectivity with the amygdala and OFC, and plays a role in processing emotional states (Devinsky, Morrell, & Vogt, 1995). In particular, dorsal portions of the ACC are thought to act on the representation of affective information from the amygdala via connections to the OFC, and translate this information into responses (Blair, 2007). The poor moral decision making and reduced responsivity to fear or distress of others seen in individuals high on AB have been theorized to reflect disrupted ACC processing (Blair, 2007). In support of this theory, studies of antisocial youth have reported decreased activation of the ACC during tasks assessing the processing of negative pictures (Sterzer, Stadler, Krebs, Kleinschmidt, & Poustka, 2005) and emotional words (Kalnin et al., 2011). Decreased ACC activation has also been found among adult antisocial groups (see Rilling et al., 2007 for an exception), particularly among criminal psychopaths during tasks assessing empathy (Meffert, Gazzola, den Boer, Bartels, & Keysers,

2013), emotionally salient scenes (Müller et al., 2003), and painful facial expressions (Decety et al., 2013).

Caudate and ventral striatum. The caudate and ventral striatum, while primarily involved in learning, are also relevant to understanding socioemotional processing deficits in AB. In particular, individuals with AB and psychopathic/CU traits are hypothesized to show reduced recruitment of regions that guide behavioral choices based on expected value information (Blair, 2013). For example, youth with AB showed decreased caudate activation during vignettes portraying interpersonal interactions (Sharp, Burton, & Ha, 2011). In adult forensic samples, studies have reported reduced functioning of the ventral striatum during an affective memory task involving negative-valence stimuli (Kiehl et al., 2001) and reduced functioning of the caudate during a moral judgment task (Yoder, Harenski, Kiehl, & Decety, 2015). Reduced reactivity in the caudate and ventral striatum to emotionally salient stimuli may lead to failures in evaluating or predicting the potential for negative outcomes following behavior, increasing the likelihood that individuals will choose aggressive or harmful actions, and risk for AB.

Insula. Studies have begun to investigate the role of the insula in AB, given work implicating the insula in empathy and integrating sensory information (Naqvi & Bechara, 2009), making the insula relevant for understanding the empathy and socioemotional processing deficits seen in individuals high on AB. For example, a study of children high on AB found that conduct problems and CU traits were related to lower insula activity when viewing harmful behaviors directed to others (Michalska, Zeffiro, & Decety, 2015) and boys high on AB showed reduced insula activity to animations eliciting affective vs. cognitive theory of mind (Sebastian et al., 2012). Finally, a study of adult psychopathic offenders found reduced insula activation during an emotional processing task relative to healthy controls (Meffert et al., 2013). These findings suggest that some of the behavioral deficits among individuals high on AB arise because of impairments processing of emotionally salient cues by the insula that should signify empathy.

Several neural regions of interest have been identified that may contribute to deficits in socioemotional behaviors implicated in AB, including difficulty recognizing others' emotions, responding to others with empathy, regulating affective responses, and generating appropriate fearful or affective responses, particularly in response to interpersonal interactions. Much work has focused on the role of amygdala reactivity in AB with mounting data suggesting that AB is generally related to greater amygdala reactivity to interpersonal affect, whereas AB in the context of high CU traits or psychopathy is related to relatively reduced amygdala reactivity, particularly to interpersonal signals of distress or fear. A broader limbic network has also been implicated in which the reductions in OFC responding may lead to difficulty integrating and generating affective responses and inhibiting emotion dysregulation, and impaired ACC activity impairs the processing of emotional difficulties of others, leading to reduced empathic concern.

Learning and Motivated Behavior

Although a large body of studies has focused on socioemotional processing in AB, studies have also examined the neural bases of learning, response to reward and punishment, and other deficits in responding to changing contingencies seen in AB. These neuroimaging studies are motivated by the reward-dominant behavior seen in AB, with particular deficits seen in reversal learning, inhibiting a rewarded response in the face of potential punishment, reduced arousal to cues of punishment, and impulsivity (Byrd, Loeber, & Pardini, 2014). In particular, studies suggest that individuals high on AB differ in their response to reward and punishment paradigms in brain regions associated with learning, motivated behavior, and error monitoring (Blair et al., 2006; Byrd et al., 2014).

Amygdala. In addition to socioemotional processing, the amygdala is relevant for understanding AB because of its role in learning and classical (fear) conditioning (Baxter & Murray, 2002). Across studies of youth and adults, AB is characterized by reduced amygdala reactivity during processing of punishment cues, particularly among those high on CU or psychopathic traits. For example, decreased amygdala activation was reported among psychopathic criminal offenders during aversive classical conditioning compared to controls (Birbaumer et al., 2005; Veit et al., 2002) and among a healthy sample in response to unfair monetary offers (Osumi et al., 2012). Finally, youth high on AB and callous-unemotional traits showed decreased amygdala activity during reward feedback (Cohn et al., 2015). Consistent with long-standing theories of AB, these findings suggest that amygdala processes involved in learning, particularly classical conditioning and punishment sensitivity, may disrupt the development of typical reward learning and responding (Blair et al., 2006). More recently, the differential activation model purported that severe AB and psychopathy arise from reduced reactivity, specifically in the basolateral region of the amygdala, which confers failures in representing the value of stimuli and disrupts unconditioned-conditioned stimulus associations (Moul, Killcross, & Dadds, 2012)

Prefrontal regions. Prefrontal regions of the brain, including the OFC/ventromedial prefrontal cortex (vmPFC) and dorsolateral prefrontal cortex (dlPFC) have also been examined in relation to contingency learning in AB due to their role in decision making, executive function, and working memory (Fuster, 2001). In particular, individuals high on AB show differences in inhibition, reward, and representing the expected value of outcomes, which implicates potential dysfunction in these prefrontal regions (Blair, 2013; Finger et al., 2011; White et al., 2013). In support of this notion, a meta-analysis of 31 functional imaging studies assessing cognitive processing tasks found that AB was associated with reduced functioning of the left dlPFC, which is associated with response perseveration and decision making (Yang & Raine, 2009). Youth high on AB have been shown to exhibit reduced OFC activity compared to healthy controls, during aversive conditioning tasks (Birbaumer et al., 2005), a continuous rewarded task that compared responsivity to receipt of reward versus non-reward (Rubia et al., 2009b), and decision-making tasks in the context of reward (Crowley et al., 2010), as well as reduced vmPFC activation during a passive avoidance decision-making task (White et al., 2013). Findings of reduced recruitment of prefrontal regions during reward, learning, and motivation tasks appear particularly pronounced among youth with AB and high CU traits (Finger et al., 2011).

Anterior cingulate cortex (ACC). Several studies have reported dysfunction in the ACC, which is involved with contingency learning, error detection, and monitoring of performance (Bush, Luu, & Posner, 2000). Decreased activation in the ACC has been observed in antisocial youth after both non-rewarded (Gatzke-Kopp et al., 2009) and rewarded trials (Crowley et al., 2010). Adult AB has also been linked to decreased ACC reactivity during tasks assessing social cooperation (Rilling et al., 2007), aversive conditioning (Birbaumer et al., 2005; Veit et al., 2002), and decision making (Prehn et al., 2013). The majority of studies thus suggest that AB is related to hyporeactivity of the ACC in processing changing contingencies and reinforcement information (although see Gregory et al., 2015 for an exception).

Caudate and ventral striatum. The ventral striatum (VS) is implicated in AB because of its role in learning, processing the motivational salience of stimuli, and reward-related behaviors (Berridge & Robinson, 2003). Moreover, activity in the VS has been consistently associated with behaviors seen in individuals high on AB, including heightened reward sensitivity and impulsivity (Buckholtz et al., 2010). Similarly, the caudate is thought to be important for understanding learning and motivated behavior deficits in AB because of its role in reward-prediction errors and the comparison of actual versus predicted reward (O'Doherty et al., 2004). Consistent with the notion that individuals with AB perseverate on previously rewarded behavior even in the face of changing reward contingencies, children with psychopathic traits demonstrated increased activity in the caudate when task-related errors were punished, whereas controls showed decreased activity (Finger et al., 2011). Similarly, youth with AB showed increased VS activity to both rewarded and non-rewarded trials, while control participants demonstrated increased VS activity to reward only and effectively shifted to increased ACC activity during non-rewarded trials (Gatzke-Kopp et al., 2009). Thus, in this study, it appeared that typically developing children showed expected activation (i.e., the VS) during reward, but then appropriately switched to activation in regions associated with error processing (i.e., the ACC) when contingencies changed, whereas the AB group continued to activate reward regions. Among adult samples, work with healthy participants has linked increased VS reactivity to higher impulsive-antisocial traits of psychopathy during reward anticipation (Buckholtz et al., 2010) and reward processing (Bjork, Chen, & Hommer, 2012). Interestingly, in an incarcerated sample, the increased VS response to rewards found among psychopathic inmates when compared to non-psychopathic inmates was found to be driven by reduced VS response to loss (Pujara, Motzkin, Newman, Kiehl, & Koenigs, 2014). In summary, these findings suggest that individuals high on AB show hypersensitivity of the VS to reward, and fail to respond appropriately to changing contingencies or punishment and loss, which may explain their propensity to maintain potentially rewarding but highly risky, harmful, or punishable behaviors (i.e., theft, interpersonal aggression, substance use).

Inhibitory/Cognitive Control

Finally, AB is associated with reduced inhibitory/cognitive control and deficits in executive function, an umbrella term that refers to the initiation, planning, and regulation of goal-directed behavior (Morgan & Lilienfeld, 2000). A meta-analysis of 39 studies of youth and adults across clinical and forensic samples found that AB was associated with poor executive functioning and cognitive control, with the largest effect sizes found in tasks assessing working memory, spatial working memory, and attention (Ogilvie, Stewart, Chan, & Shum, 2011). Additionally, behavioral research suggested that the deficits associated with psychopathy in particular may stem from a failure to reallocate attention to affective stimuli while engaged in other goal-directed behavior, such that the primary deficit in AB with high psychopathy may be more akin to an "attention bottleneck" rather than a specific deficit in affective processing (Baskin-Sommers, Curtin, & Newman, 2011).

Amygdala. Although amygdala-driven affective processing deficits have been a major focus of neuroimaging studies of AB, some researchers have argued that this view undervalues cognitive processes that modulate behaviors associated with AB and their shaping of amygdala reactivity (Baskin-Sommers et al., 2011; Newman, Curtin, Bertsch, & Baskin-Sommers, 2010). In support of this notion, recent studies suggest that the level of attentional load required by imaging tasks accounts for differences in findings for amygdala reactivity for individuals high on AB (Baskin-Sommers et al., 2011; White et al., 2012). For example, Larson and colleagues (2013) reported decreased amygdala activity in psychopathic offenders during an instructed fear task, but this deficit was only present when attention was engaged in an alternative goal-relevant task (Larson et al., 2013). Such research suggests that, despite the substantial body of work examining neural correlates of AB, it is unclear whether functional abnormalities in AB stem from specific amygdala deficits (i.e., bottom-up under-reactivity to affective cues), or brain regions that module amygdala reactivity (i.e., top-down attentional focus may lead to less attention to affective stimuli and thus less amygdala response). Other studies also suggest that other attention factors, such as the attention to the eye region during a socioemotional processing task (i.e., emotional faces), may also moderate amygdala effects, such that those high on AB may only have under-reactivity to emotional faces because they spend less time looking at the most simulating portion of the picture – the eyes (Dadds et al., 2012; Han, Alders, Greening, Neufeld, & Mitchell, 2011). Thus, more research is needed to identify the role of attention versus automatic emotional processing in AB.

OFC and dlPFC. The OFC and dlPFC play major roles in executive function and cognitive control tasks, particularly during tasks requiring planning, working memory, and cognitive flexibility (Fuster, 2001). Deficits in these neural regions could lead to impulsivity, which may include both inhibition of pre-potent responses and poor decision making, especially when there is a strong reward-driven component to behavior. To that end, impulsivity and reward learning behaviors may result in similar behaviors underpinned by distinct, though overlapping, neural networks. Thus, much of the literature on dysfunctional reward, learning, and motivation behavior in prefrontal regions is relevant when considering impairments in cognitive/inhibitory control seen in AB. In a study that isolated more specific components of executive function, Rubia and colleagues utilized a task tapping attention and inhibition, comparing youth with diagnosable AB versus ADHD. Both groups displayed reduced activation in the dlPFC (and activation in this area was correlated with level of AB), but the ADHD group showed disorder-specific decreases in activation in the ventral lateral PFC (Rubia et al., 2009a). This study is a good example of how to disentangle what may be underlying differences between individuals with pure ADHD versus AB by selecting specific behavioral deficits (e.g., attention/inhibition) and may help researchers to address findings from the ADHD literature and determine if such differences are specific to ADHD or to broader AB/externalizing problems (Hyde et al., 2013).

Anterior cingulate cortex (ACC). Given the central role of the ACC in error detection and avoidance learning, this region is also thought to contribute to the poor cognitive control seen in individuals high on AB. In support of this notion, adults high on AB exhibited reduced ACC activation during tasks tapping frustration (Pawliczek et al., 2013), working memory (Kumari et al., 2006), and during conflict- and error-related monitoring (Schiffer et al., 2014). Moreover, decreased activation in the ACC was observed among antisocial youth during attention tasks (Rubia et al., 2009a), suggesting that the ACC is disrupted in AB during both socioemotional (i.e., negative pictures and emotional words) and cognitive control tasks (i.e., error monitoring and attention).

In sum, AB appears to arise from dysfunction in brain areas linked to inhibition and reward, including the orbitofrontal cortex and vmPFC, as well as dysfunction in areas that process social emotion and threat, including the amygdala and cingulate cortex (Blair, 2001; see Figure 39.1). Functional MRI studies support these theories by demonstrating decreased prefrontal cortex functioning during reward-based and reinforcement learning tasks among adults and youth with AB (Finger et al., 2011; Yang & Raine, 2009). Abnormal amygdala reactivity to threatening stimuli has also been established as a neural marker of AB among adult and youth samples, though potentially in divergent direction based on level of CU traits. Together, these findings suggest that AB likely arises from dysfunction in a network of regions critical to emotion processing, reward, and learning (Kiehl et al., 2001).

Structural Neuroimaging Findings

Structural MRI studies assess the volume of cortical and subcortical structures. The majority of studies appear to implicate the same brain regions emphasized in the functional imaging literature. For example, a recent meta-analysis of 13 structural MRI studies found that youth with AB had significantly decreased gray matter volume in the left amygdala, right insula, left medial superior frontal gyrus (extending into the right ACC), and left fusiform gyrus (Rogers & De Brito, 2016). Structural abnormalities within adult AB have also been consistently found, with a meta-analysis of 12 studies demonstrating reduced gray matter volume in the right OFC, left dlPFC, and right ACC (Yang & Raine, 2009). Reduced gray matter volume among adults high on AB and/or psychopathic traits has also been reported for the amygdala (Pardini, Raine, Erickson, & Loeber, 2014) and hippocampus (Barkataki, Kumari, Das, Taylor, & Sharma, 2006).

Functional Connectivity

Given theories that AB arises from the interaction between key neural regions linked to inhibition and affect (e.g., the interaction between OFC and the amygdala), recent studies have begun to identify connectivity between regions during tasks and found that decreased functional connectivity between neural regions may be important in understanding AB. For example, decreased connectivity between the amygdala and OFC was found in youth with psychopathic traits during a moral judgment task (Marsh et al., 2011) and between the amygdala, ACC, and insula when observing harm directed to others (Yoder, Lahey, & Decety, 2016). Similarly, adult psychopaths had decreased functional connectivity between the amygdala and visual and prefrontal cortices during a face-matching task (Contreras-Rodríguez et al., 2014), and between the amygdala and OFC during a perspective-taking task (Decety et al., 2013). Based on these functional connectivity findings and the reciprocal connections between the OFC and amygdala (among many other limbic regions), it is likely that the balance between prefrontal regions and subcortical structures is important in the development of AB (Hyde et al., 2013). For example, subcortical regions may initiate activation to prefrontal regions, which "qualifies" the activation and either suppress or enhance it (Fuster, 2001). Thus, dysfunction in one region (e.g., OFC) could lead to dysfunction in another region (e.g., amygdala).

White Matter Tract Structural Connectivity

Impairments in the functioning or communication between regions may be the result of disrupted structural connectivity between these regions. Studies have begun to investigate abnormalities in the structural connectivity between brain regions implicated in AB using diffusion tension imaging (DTI), which assesses water diffusion as an index of the integrity of white matter structures. Based on findings of functional and structural imaging studies of AB, DTI studies have focused on the uncinate fasciculus (UF), a key white matter tract that connects the amygdala and prefrontal regions, particularly the OFC. However, the link between AB and altered UF white matter integrity has not been consistently replicated, with studies reporting decreased integrity, no differences, or even increased integrity among individuals high on AB relative to healthy controls (e.g., Motzkin, Newman, Kiehl, & Koenigs, 2011; Passamonti et al., 2012). Indeed, more recent studies have reported that AB is linked to abnormal integrity in other white matter tracts beyond the UF in both adult (Sundram et al., 2012) and youth samples (Haney-Caron, Caprihan, & Stevens, 2014). A review of this literature integrating ten adult studies suggests that AB and psychopathy are associated with reduced integrity of a wide range of white matter tracts, including the corpus callosum, cingulum, superior longitudinal fasciculus, and uncinate fasciculus (Waller, Dotterer, Murray, Maxwell, & Hyde, 2017). These findings contradict the notion that AB arises from a specific reduction to UF integrity, suggesting instead that AB reflects dysfunction in white matter tract connectivity across regions and hemispheres, consistent with behavioral characteristics associated with AB that encompass deficits in socioemotional, cognitive, attentional, and reward processing. Though a clear picture of widespread decreases in structural connectivity emerged for adult AB, among youth, the evidence from 12 studies was more mixed. In youth, the most consistent trend was *increased* integrity in a range of white matter tracts, but other studies reported decreased integrity or no difference in the integrity among identical tracts (Waller et al., 2016). These differences may be due to large age spans in the samples included in these studies, while white matter tracts are still undergoing significant developmental change. Thus, given the developmental trajectory of white matter across adolescence, longitudinal research is needed to identify how the development of these tracts leads to AB.

Future Directions

Since the first neuroimaging studies of AB emerged, the field has grown at a tremendous rate. Much of the initial fMRI studies focused on the role of the amygdala, but over time this literature has become increasingly nuanced and has begun to branch out into an investigation of other neural regions and tasks, along with a focus on connectivity. However, there are still multiple emerging areas more broadly in neuroimaging that may lead to new leads for understanding AB.

Structural and Functional Brain Networks

Adopting a network approach is useful for conceptualizing AB as the consequence of abnormalities in multiple brain areas. Indeed, while the majority of neuroimaging research has been driven by a focus on regionally specific neural correlates, emerging research is establishing how distributed networks of brain regions contribute to AB. In particular, AB appears to be underpinned by abnormal functioning in a wide range of highly interconnecting brain regions (see Figure 39.1). By investigating dysfunction with brain *networks* rather than individual regions alone, we may gain a better understanding of the neurobiological basis of AB. For example, the default model network (DMN) is a brain network that encompasses the medial temporal lobes, posterior cingulate cortex, medial prefrontal cortex, and angular gyrus. The DMN is typically more active under conditions of rest (i.e., mind-wandering, day-dreaming), but less active during cognitively demanding tasks (Raichle & Snyder, 2007). The DMN is critical to the construction of mental representations of the self and one's own and others' possible future actions, thoughts, and feelings, particularly theory of mind and morality judgments (Buckner, Andrews-Hanna, & Schacter, 2008), activities which appear impaired in those high on AB. Recent studies have shown that aberrant connectivity of DMN regions may be related to AB, including reduced DMN connectivity being linked to higher interpersonal and affective deficits of psychopathy among adult inmates (Philippi et al., 2015) and diagnosable AB among youth (Broulidakis et al., 2016). The finding of impaired DMN connectivity has been interpreted to suggest that difficulties in evaluating own or others' mental state hinders the ability to learn from punishment, show empathy, or evaluate choices, increasing risk for the harmful behaviors that characterize AB. However, many other psychiatric disorders have been linked to DMN dysfunction, including ADHD, autism, and schizophrenia (Broyd et al., 2009), such that any abnormalities may not be specific to AB. Thus, future studies are needed to isolate aberrant network functioning that is specific to AB, including connectivity *within* the DMN and connectivity *between* the DMN and other large-scale brain networks implicated in AB, including the cingulo-opercular and fronto-parietal networks, which act together in the integration of emotional and cognitive information to facilitate goal-orientated behavior (Menon, 2011).

Neuroprediction of AB

Despite the robustness with which functional and structural MRI studies have established dysfunction within paralimbic circuitry to be linked to AB, the vast majority of studies are cross-sectional. Thus, it is difficult to establish whether brain function or structure abnormalities are causally implicated in the development of AB, or arise as a consequence of AB. For example, AB often involves substance use, which may alter neural structure and function (Boulos et al., 2016; Squeglia, Jacobus, & Tapert, 2009). To address this question, prospective longitudinal and experimental study designs are needed to map potential "neuroprediction" in which brain structure or function might predict future changes in AB. For example, using a prospective design, Pardini and colleagues (2014) found that adult men with lower amygdala volumes were at increased risk for exhibiting future aggression, violence, and psychopathic traits, even after earlier levels of these variables were controlled for in models (Pardini et al., 2014). Further, Aharoni and colleagues (2013) found that reduced anterior cingulate activity during an impulse control task predicted re-arrest among adult offenders within four years of release (Aharoni et al., 2013). Finally, a recent review offered preliminary evidence that behavioral treatments for childhood AB are mediated through changes in neural functioning, although this experimental literature is very much in its infancy (Cornet, Kogel, Nijman, Raine, & Laan, 2015). These studies lay the foundation for future studies to use neurocognitive biomarkers of personality and behavior to identify groups at high risk for recidivism, violence, or aggression. Such approaches could have far-reaching impact on diagnosis and treatment protocols. At the same time, this literature will present complex ethical questions as it is evident that a host of sociocultural and personality factors influence trajectories of severe AB, and the relative influence of neural functional or structural abnormalities on risk for future violence or aggression needs significant further study that continues to be mindful of ethical and moral implications.

Multimodal Methods

Finally, research is needed that employs multimodal approaches that take into account other aspects of underlying biology (e.g., genes, hormones) as well as environmental context. In particular, studies are needed that examine the interaction between genes and environment as a predictor of neural differences associated with aggression and violence, while also integrating findings from animal models and other complimentary techniques, such as PET or imaging genetics (Bogdan, Hyde, & Hariri, 2012; Hyde, Bogdan, & Hariri, 2011). For example, the most consistent evidence for gene x environment (G x E) interaction pathways to AB have been found with a common variant in the promoter of the MAOA gene (which affects degradation of monoamines). Specifically, the low-activity allele of MAOA (MAOA-L) appears to be related to increased risk for AB among males, but only in the context of childhood adversity and typically more strongly in samples of boys/men (Byrd & Manuck, 2014). Additionally, genes affecting the dopamine (e.g., DRD4, DRD2) and serotonin (e.g., 5-HTTLPR) neurotransmitter systems appear to interact with environmental context (particularly parenting and prenatal risk) to predict youth AB (see Waller, Dotterer, & Hyde, 2015 for a review).

More recently, studies have begun to examine how some of these same genes and the various G x E interactions implicated in AB could affect neural functioning and, in turn, increase risk for AB (Waller et al., 2015). For example, a recent study established an imaging genetics pathway whereby men with a risky oxytocin receptor gene variant had relatively increased amygdala reactivity to angry facial expressions, which in turn was related to higher levels of AB (Waller et al., 2016). This study provides a useful example of how a multimodel imaging genetics approach can be used to provide empirical documentation for the basic premise that genetic variation indirectly influences behavioral outcomes, such as AB or psychopathy, by biasing the response of underlying neural circuitries (Hariri, Drabant, & Weinberger, 2006). To extend this work further, future studies are needed to test the conditional mechanisms through which genes and environment interact to affect neural structure and function, and resulting AB. Indeed, burgeoning research highlights that by adopting genes, experiences, and behaviors into an imaging G x E approach, we can better understand the complex development of AB (Hyde, Swartz, Waller, & Hariri, 2015).

At the same time, a major issue for future research seeking to establish imaging G x E interaction pathways to AB centers on development. The majority of studies to date have examined samples assessed in late adolescence or adulthood. However, many genetic variants relevant to AB (e.g., MAOA, 5-HTTLPR) are likely to have influences on neural functioning in utero or very early in development. Environmental experiences also likely differ in their impact on brain function and structure depending on developmental stage (Sroufe & Rutter, 1984) and whether environmental insult occurs during particular "sensitive periods" of development (Meaney, 2010). For example, in relation to imaging G x E interactions and the development of AB, harsh parenting may only moderate the effect of certain genotypes when harsh parenting is measured in early childhood and when AB is measured in adolescence. In contrast, interactions between genotype and deviant peer experiences or exposure to community violence may only relate to AB later in adolescence or into adulthood. Studies that test imaging G x E interactions longitudinally across multiple developmental periods are likely to help uncover these more complex interactions (Hyde, 2015).

Conclusion

The rapidly growing body of functional and structural neuroimaging literature examining AB is beginning to consistently implicate several brain areas, including the amygdala and OFC, as well as the insula, ACC, caudate, and dlPFC (Figure 39.1). Studies have broadly connected these specific brain areas to impairments seen among highly aggressive and violent individuals, including deficits in emotion processing, empathy, reward responsivity, and learning and attention, each of which appears to have somewhat distinct neural underpinnings (Figure 39.1). Differences in the functioning of the amygdala and related areas (e.g., OFC) among antisocial individuals are seen mostly during social and affective tasks, whereas dlPFC and other prefrontal areas appear to show functional differences in attention, learning, and inhibition tasks, implying possible subdomains of functioning to be explored in future studies. However, many fundamental questions remain, including whether psychopathic/CU traits or more general severity of AB are driving reported findings, with some suggestion that amygdala deficits may be specific to CU and psychopathic traits, whereas reward and impulsivity related neural deficits may be broadly related to AB and not moderated by level of CU traits (Blair et al., 2014). Additional questions center on whether there are specific brain areas that might be expected to show greater versus lesser response, and to which types of tasks, whether some affective deficits may actually be driven by attentional deficits, and whether fMRI can help to uncover any other distinct subgroups that vary in both behavior and neural functioning (e.g., whether reactive versus proactive aggression have different neural correlates). Further, in the study of AB, an understanding of one area will likely prove less informative than understanding how functioning is linked across regions. As the field evolves, studies are needed that combine task-related functional imaging with methods that assess resting-state and structural connectivity to fully characterize large-scale brain networks from childhood to adulthood that contribute to persistent and severe trajectories of AB. Moreover, these findings will need to be examined developmentally and linked to contexts and genes to understand the origins of AB-related neural reactivity.

References

Aharoni, E., Vincent, G. M., Harenski, C. L., Calhoun, V. D., Sinnott-Armstrong, W., Gazzaniga, M. S., & Kiehl, K. A. Neuroprediction of future rearrest. *Proceedings of the National Academy of Sciences*, 110, 6223–6228.

Barkataki, I., Kumari, V., Das, M., Taylor, P., & Sharma, T. (2006). Volumetric structural brain abnormalities in men with schizophrenia or antisocial personality disorder. *Behavioural Brain Research*, 169, 239–247.

Baskin-Sommers, A., Curtin, J., & Newman, J. (2011). Specifying the attentional selection that moderates the fearlessness of psychopathic offenders. *Psychological Science*, 2, 226–234.

Baxter, M. G., & Murray, E. A. (2002). The amygdala and reward. *Nature Reviews Neuroscience*, 3, 563–573.

Berridge, K. C. & Robinson, T. E. (2003). Parsing reward. *Trends in Neurosciences*, 26, 507–513.

Birbaumer, N., Veit, R., Lotze, M., Erb, M., Hermann, C., Grodd, W., & Flor, H. (2005). Deficient fear conditioning in psychopathy: a functional magnetic resonance imaging study. *Archives of General Psychiatry*, 62, 799–805.

Bjork, J. M., Chen, G., & Hommer, D. W. (2012). Psychopathic tendencies and mesolimbic recruitment by cues for instrumental and passively obtained rewards. *Biological Psychology*, 89, 408–415.

Blair, K. S., Newman, C., Mitchell, D. G., Richell, R. A., Leonard, A., Morton, J., & Blair, R. J. R. (2006). Differentiating among prefrontal substrates in psychopathy: neuropsychological test findings. *Neuropsychology*, 20, 153–165.

Blair, R. (2007). Dysfunctions of medial and lateral orbitofrontal cortex in psychopathy. *Annals of the New York Academy of Sciences*, 1121, 461–479.

Blair, R. J. R. (2001). Neurocognitive models of aggression, the antisocial personality disorders, and psychopathy. *Journal of Neurology, Neurosurgery & Psychiatry*, 71, 727–731.

Blair, R. J. R. (2013). The neurobiology of psychopathic traits in youths. *Nature Reviews Neuroscience*, 14, 786–799.

Blair, R. J. R., Leibenluft, E., & Pine, D. S. (2014). Conduct Disorder and Callous–Unemotional Traits in Youth. *New England Journal of Medicine*, 371, 2207–2216.

Bogdan, R., Hyde, L., & Hariri, A. (2012). A neurogenetics approach to understanding individual differences in brain, behavior, and risk for psychopathology. *Molecular Psychiatry*, 18, 288–299.

Boulos, P. K., Dalwani, M. S., Tanabe, J., Mikulich-Gilbertson, S. K., Banich, M. T., Crowley, T. J., & Sakai, J. T. (2016). Brain Cortical Thickness Differences in Adolescent Females with Substance Use Disorders. *PLoS ONE*, 11, e0152983.

Broulidakis, M. J., Fairchild, G., Sully, K., Blumensath, T., Darekar, A., & Sonuga-Barke, E. J. (2016). Reduced Default Mode Connectivity in Adolescents With Conduct Disorder. *Journal of the American Academy of Child & Adolescent Psychiatry*. doi: 10.1016/j.jaac.2016.1005.1021.

Broyd, S. J., Demanuele, C., Debener, S., Helps, S. K., James, C. J., & Sonuga-Barke, E. J. (2009). Default-mode brain dysfunction in mental disorders: a systematic review. *Neuroscience & Biobehavioral Reviews*, 33, 279–296.

Buckholtz, J. W., Treadway, M. T., Cowan, R. L., Woodward, N. D., Benning, S. D., Li, R., Ansari, M. S., Baldwin, R. M., Schwartzman, A. N., Shelby, E. S., & Smith, C. E. (2010). Mesolimbic dopamine reward system hypersensitivity in individuals with psychopathic traits. *Nature Neuroscience*, 13, 419–421.

Buckner, R. L., Andrews-Hanna, J. R., & Schacter, D. L. (2008). The Brain's default network. *Annals of the New York Academy of Sciences*, 1124, 1–38.

Bush, G., Luu, P., & Posner, M. I. (2000). Cognitive and emotional influences in anterior cingulate cortex. *Trends in Cognitive Sciences*, 4, 215–222.

Byrd, A. L., Loeber, R., & Pardini, D. A. (2014). Antisocial behavior, psychopathic features and abnormalities in reward and punishment processing in youth. *Clinical Child and Family Psychology Review*, 17, 125–156.

Byrd, A. L., & Manuck, S. B. (2014). MAOA, childhood maltreatment, and antisocial behavior: Meta-analysis of a gene-environment interaction. *Biological Psychiatry*, 75, 9–17.

Carré, J. M., Hyde, L. W., Neumann, C. S., Viding, E., & Hariri, A. R. (2013). The neural signatures of distinct psychopathic traits. *Social Neuroscience*, 8, 122–135.

Coccaro, E. F., McCloskey, M. S., Fitzgerald, D. A., & Phan, K. L. (2007). Amygdala and orbitofrontal reactivity to social threat in individuals with impulsive aggression. *Biological Psychiatry*, 62, 168–178.

Cohn, M. D., Veltman, D. J., Pape, L. E., van Lith, K., Vermeiren, R. R., van den Brink, W., Doreleijers, T. A., & Popma, A. (2015). Incentive processing in persistent disruptive behavior and psychopathic traits: a functional magnetic resonance imaging study in adolescents. *Biological Psychiatry*, 78, 615–624.

Contreras-Rodríguez, O., Pujol, J., Batalla, I., Harrison, B. J., Bosque, J., Ibern-Regàs, I., Hernández-Ribas, R., Soriano-Mas, C., Deus, J., López-Solà, M., & Pifarré, J. (2014). Disrupted neural processing of emotional faces in psychopathy. *Social Cognitive and Affective Neuroscience*, 9, 505–512.

Cornet, L. J., Kogel, C. H., Nijman, H. L., Raine, A., & Laan, P. H. (2015). Neurobiological changes after intervention in individuals with anti-social behaviour: A literature review. *Criminal Behaviour and Mental Health*, 25, 10–27.

Crowley, T. J., Dalwani, M. S., Mikulich-Gilbertson, S. K., Du, Y. P., Lejuez, C. W., Raymond, K. M., & Banich, M. T. (2010). Risky decisions and their consequences: neural processing by boys with antisocial substance disorder. *PLoS ONE*, 5, e12835.

Dadds, M. R., Allen, J. L., Oliver, B. R., Faulkner, N., Legge, K., Moul, C., Woolgar, M., & Scott, S. (2012). Love, eye contact and the developmental origins of empathy v. psychopathy. *The British Journal of Psychiatry*, 200, 191–196.

Damasio, H., Grabowski, T., Frank, R., Galaburda, A. M., & Damasio, A. R. (1994). The return of Phineas Gage: clues about the brain from the skull of a famous patient. *Science*, 264, 1102–1105.

Decety, J., Chen, C., Harenski, C., & Kiehl, K. A. (2013). An fMRI study of affective perspective taking in individuals with psychopathy: imagining another in pain does not evoke empathy. *Frontiers in Human Neuroscience*, 7, 1–12.

Decety, J., Michalska, K. J., Akitsuki, Y., & Lahey, B. B. (2009). Atypical empathic responses in adolescents with aggressive conduct disorder: a functional MRI investigation. *Biological Psychology*, 80, 203–211.

Decety, J., Skelly, L., Yoder, K. J., & Kiehl, K. A. (2014). Neural processing of dynamic emotional facial expressions in psychopaths. *Social Neuroscience*, 9, 36–49.

Devinsky, O., Morrell, M. J., & Vogt, B. A. (1995). Contributions of anterior cingulate cortex to behaviour. *Brain*, 118, 279–306.

Finger, E. C., Marsh, A. A., Blair, K. S., Reid, M. E., Sims, C., Ng, P., Pine, D. S., & Blair, R. J. R. (2011). Disrupted reinforcement signaling in the orbitofrontal cortex and caudate in youths with conduct disorder or oppositional defiant disorder and a high level of psychopathic traits. *American Journal of Psychiatry*, 168, 152–162.

Frick, P. J., Ray, J. V., Thornton, L. C., & Kahn, R. E. (2014). Can callous-unemotional traits enhance the understanding, diagnosis, and treatment of serious conduct problems in children and adolescents? A comprehensive review. *Psychological Bulletin*, 140, 1–40.

Fuster, J. (2001). The prefrontal cortex – an update: time is of the essence. *Neuron*, 30, 319–333.

Gatzke-Kopp, L. M., Beauchaine, T. P., Shannon, K. E., Chipman, J., Fleming, A. P., Crowell, S. E., Liang, O., Johnson, L. C., & Aylward, E. (2009). Neurological correlates of reward responding in adolescents with and without externalizing behavior disorders. *Journal of Abnormal Psychology*, 118, 203–213.

Gregory, S., Blair, R. J., Simmons, A., Kumari, V., Hodgins, S., & Blackwood, N. (2015). Punishment and psychopathy: a case-control functional MRI investigation of reinforcement learning in violent antisocial personality disordered men. *The Lancet Psychiatry*, 2, 153–160.

Han, T., Alders, G. L., Greening, S. G., Neufeld, R. W. J., & Mitchell, D. G. V. (2011). Do fearful eyes activate empathy-related brain regions in individuals with callous traits? *Social Cognitive and Affective Neuroscience*, 7(8), 958–968.

Haney-Caron, E., Caprihan, A., & Stevens, M. C. (2014). DTI-measured white matter abnormalities in adolescents with Conduct Disorder. *Journal of Psychiatric Research*, 48, 111–120.

Hare, R. D. & Neumann, C. S. (2008). Psychopathy as a clinical and empirical construct. *Annual Review of Clinical Psychology*, 4, 217–246.

Harenski, C. L., Harenski, K. A., & Kiehl, K. A. (2014). Neural processing of moral violations among incarcerated adolescents with psychopathic traits. *Developmental Cognitive Neuroscience*, 10, 181–189.

Hariri, A. R., Drabant, E. M., & Weinberger, D. R. (2006). Imaging genetics: perspectives from studies of genetically driven variation in serotonin function and corticolimbic affective processing. *Biological Psychiatry*, 59, 888–897.

Herpertz, S. C., Huebner, T., Marx, I., Vloet, T. D., Fink, G. R., Stoecker, T., Jon Shah, N., Konrad, K., & Herpertz-Dahlmann, B. (2008). Emotional processing in male adolescents with childhood-onset conduct disorder. *Journal of Child Psychology and Psychiatry*, 49, 781–791.

Hyde, L. W. (2015). Developmental psychopathology in an era of molecular genetics and neuroimaging: A developmental neurogenetics approach. *Development and Psychopathology*, 27, 587–613.

Hyde, L. W., Bogdan, R., & Hariri, A. R. (2011). Understanding risk for psychopathology through imaging gene-environment interactions. *Trends in Cognitive Sciences*, 15, 417–427.

Hyde, L. W., Byrd, A. L., Votruba-Drzal, E., Hariri, A. R., & Manuck, S. B. (2014). Amygdala reactivity and negative emotionality: divergent correlates of antisocial personality and psychopathy traits in a community sample. *Journal of Abnormal Psychology*, 123, 214–224.

Hyde, L. W., Shaw, D. S., & Hariri, A. R. (2013). Neuroscience, developmental psychopathology and youth antisocial behavior: Review, integration, and directions for research. *Developmental Review*, 33, 168–223.

Hyde, L. W., Swartz, J. R., Waller, R., & Hariri, A. R. (2015). Neurogenetics approaches to mapping pathways in developmental psychopathology. In D. Cicchetti (Ed.), *Developmental Psychopathology* (3rd ed., Vol. 2). Hoboken, NJ: Wiley.

Hyde, L. W., Shaw, D. S., Murray, L., Gard, A., Hariri, A. R., & Forbes, E. E. (2016). Dissecting the role of amygdala reactivity in antisocial behavior in a sample of young, low-income, urban men. *Clinical Psychological Science*, 4, 527–544.

Jones, A. P., Laurens, K. R., Herba, C. M., Gareth, J. B., & Viding, E. (2009). Amygdala hypoactivity to fearful faces in boys with conduct problems and callous-unemotional traits. *American Journal of Psychiatry*, 166, 95–102.

Kalnin, A. J., Edwards, C. R., Wang, Y., Kronenberger, W. G., Hummer, T. A., Mosier, K. M., Dunn, D. W., & Mathews, V. P. (2011). The interacting role of media violence exposure and aggressive–disruptive behavior in adolescent brain activation during an emotional Stroop task. *Psychiatry Research: Neuroimaging*, 192, 12–19.

Kiehl, K. A. (2006). A cognitive neuroscience perspective on psychopathy: evidence for paralimbic system dysfunction. *Psychiatry Research*, 142, 107–128.

Kiehl, K. A., Smith, A. M., Hare, R. D., Mendrek, A., Forster, B. B., Brink, J., & Liddle, P. F. (2001). Limbic abnormalities in affective processing by criminal psychopaths as revealed by functional magnetic resonance imaging. *Biological Psychiatry*, 50, 677–684.

Kringelbach, M. L. (2005). The human orbitofrontal cortex: linking reward to hedonic experience. *Nature Reviews Neuroscience*, 6, 691–702.

Kumari, V., Aasen, I., Taylor, P., Das, M., Barkataki, I., Goswami, S., O'Connell, P., Howlett, M., Williams, S. C., & Sharma, T. (2006). Neural dysfunction and violence in schizophrenia: an fMRI investigation. *Schizophrenia Research*, 84, 144–164.

Larson, C., Baskin-Sommers, A., Stout, D., Balderston, N., Curtin, J., Schultz, D., Kiehl, K. A., & Newman, J. P. (2013). The interplay of attention and emotion: top-down attention modulates amygdala activation in psychopathy. *Cognitive, Affective, & Behavioral Neuroscience*, 13, 757–770.

Lozier, L. M., Cardinale, E. M., VanMeter, J. W., & Marsh, A. A. (2014). Mediation of the relationship between callous-unemotional traits and proactive aggression by amygdala response to fear among children with conduct problems. *JAMA Psychiatry*, 71, 627–636.

Marsh, A. A., & Blair, R. J. R. (2008). Deficits in facial affect recognition among antisocial populations: a meta-analysis. *Neuroscience & Biobehavioral Reviews*, 32, 454–465.

Marsh, A. A., Finger, E. C., Fowler, K. A., Jurkowitz, I. T., Schechter, J. C., Henry, H. Y., Pine, D. S., & Blair, R. J. R. (2011). Reduced amygdala–orbitofrontal connectivity during moral judgments in youths with disruptive behavior disorders and psychopathic traits. *Psychiatry Research: Neuroimaging*, 194, 279–286.

Marsh, A. A., Finger, E. C., Mitchell, D. G. V., Reid, M. E., Sims, C., Kosson, D. S., Towbin, K. E., Leibenluft, E., Pine, D. S., & Blair, R. J. R. (2008). Reduced amygdala response to fearful expressions in children and adolescents with callous-unemotional traits and disruptive behavior disorders. *American Journal of Psychiatry*, 165, 712–720.

Meaney, M. J. (2010). Epigenetics and the biological definition of gene × environment interactions. *Child Development*, 81, 41–79.

Meffert, H., Gazzola, V., den Boer, J. A., Bartels, A. A., & Keysers, C. (2013). Reduced spontaneous but relatively normal deliberate vicarious representations in psychopathy. *Brain*, 136, 2550–2562.

Menon, V. (2011). Large-scale brain networks and psychopathology: a unifying triple network model. *Trends in Cognitive Sciences*, 15, 483–506.

Michalska, K. J., Zeffiro, T. A., & Decety, J. (2015). Brain response to viewing others being harmed in children with conduct disorder symptoms. *Journal of Child Psychology and Psychiatry*, 57, 510–519.

Morgan, A. B. & Lilienfeld, S. O. (2000). A meta-analytic review of the relation between antisocial behavior and neuropsychological measures of executive function. *Clinical Psychology Review*, 20, 113–136.

Motzkin, J. C., Newman, J. P., Kiehl, K. A., & Koenigs, M. (2011). Reduced prefrontal connectivity in psychopathy. *Journal of Neuroscience*, 31, 17348–17357.

Moul, C., Killcross, S., & Dadds, M. R. (2012). A model of differential amygdala activation in psychopathy. *Psychological Review*, 119, 789–806.

Müller, J. L., Sommer, M., Wagner, V., Lange, K., Taschler, H., Röder, C. H., Schuierer, G., Klein, H. E., & Hajak, G. (2003). Abnormalities in emotion processing within cortical and subcortical regions in criminal psychopaths: evidence from a functional magnetic resonance imaging study using pictures with emotional content. *Biological Psychiatry*, 54, 152–162.

Naqvi, N. H. & Bechara, A. (2009). The hidden island of addiction: the insula. *Trends in Neurosciences*, 32, 56–67.

Newman, J. P., Curtin, J. J., Bertsch, J. D., & Baskin-Sommers, A. R. (2010). Attention moderates the fearlessness of psychopathic offenders. *Biological Psychiatry*, 67, 66–70.

O'Doherty, J., Dayan, P., Schultz, J., Deichmann, R., Friston, K., & Dolan, R. J. (2004). Dissociable roles of ventral and dorsal striatum in instrumental conditioning. *Science*, 304, 452–454.

Odgers, C. L., Moffitt, T. E., Broadbent, J. M., Dickson, N., Hancox, R. J., Harrington, H., Poulton, R., Sears, M. R., Thomson, W. M., & Caspi, A. (2008). Female and male antisocial trajectories: From childhood origins to adult outcomes. *Development and Psychopathology*, 20, 673–716.

Ogilvie, J., Stewart, A., Chan, R., & Shum, D. (2011). Neuropsychological measures of executive function and antisocial behavior: A meta analysis. *Criminology*, 49, 1063–1107.

Osumi, T., Nakao, T., Kasuya, Y., Shinoda, J., Yamada, J., & Ohira, H. (2012). Amygdala dysfunction attenuates frustration-induced aggression in psychopathic individuals in a non-criminal population. *Journal of Affective Disorders*, 142, 331–338.

Pardini, D. A., Raine, A., Erickson, K., & Loeber, R. (2014). Lower amygdala volume in men is associated with childhood aggression, early psychopathic traits, and future violence. *Biological Psychiatry*, 75, 73–80.

Passamonti, L., Fairchild, G., Fornito, A., Goodyer, I. M., Nimmo-Smith, I., Hagan, C. C., & Calder, A. J. (2012). Abnormal anatomical connectivity between the amygdala and orbitofrontal cortex in conduct disorder. *PLoS ONE [Electronic Resource]*, 7, e48789.

Passamonti, L., Fairchild, G., Goodyer, I. M., Hurford, G., Hagan, C. C., Rowe, J. B., & Calder, A. J. (2010). Neural abnormalities in early-onset and adolescence-onset conduct disorder. *Archives of General Psychiatry*, 67, 729–738.

Pawliczek, C. M., Derntl, B., Kellermann, T., Gur, R. C., Schneider, F., & Habel, U. (2013). Anger under control: neural correlates of frustration as a function of trait aggression. *PLoS ONE*, 8, e78503.

Philippi, C. L., Pujara, M. S., Motzkin, J. C., Newman, J., Kiehl, K. A., & Koenigs, M. (2015). Altered resting-state functional connectivity in cortical networks in psychopathy. *The Journal of Neuroscience*, 35, 6068–6078.

Prehn, K., Schlagenhauf, F., Schulze, L., Berger, C., Vohs, K., Fleischer, M., Hauenstein, K., Keiper, P., Domes, G., & Herpertz, S. C. (2013). Neural correlates of risk taking in violent criminal offenders characterized by emotional hypo-and hyper-reactivity. *Social Neuroscience*, 8, 136–147.

Pujara, M., Motzkin, J. C., Newman, J. P., Kiehl, K. A., & Koenigs, M. (2014). Neural correlates of reward and loss sensitivity in psychopathy. *Social Cognitive and Affective Neuroscience*, 9, 794–801.

Raichle, M. E. & Snyder, A. Z. (2007). A default mode of brain function: a brief history of an evolving idea. *Neuroimage*, 37, 1083–1090.

Raine, A. (2002). Biosocial studies of antisocial and violent behavior in children and adults: A review. *Journal of Abnormal Child Psychology*, 30, 311–326.

Rilling, J. K., Glenn, A. L., Jairam, M. R., Pagnoni, G., Goldsmith, D. R., Elfenbein, H. A., & Lilienfeld, S. O. (2007). Neural correlates of social cooperation and non-cooperation as a function of psychopathy. *Biological Psychiatry*, 61, 1260–1271.

Rogers, J. C. & De Brito, S. A. (2016). Cortical and Subcortical Gray Matter Volume in Youths With Conduct Problems: A Meta-analysis. *JAMA Psychiatry*, 73, 64–72.

Rubia, K., Halari, R., Smith, A., Mohammad, M., Scott, S., & Brammer, M. (2009a). Shared and disorder specific prefrontal abnormalities in boys with pure attention deficit/hyperactivity disorder compared to boys with pure CD during interference inhibition and attention allocation. *Journal of Child Psychology and Psychiatry*, 50, 669–678.

Rubia, K., Smith, A. B., Halari, R., Matsukura, F., Mohammad, M., Taylor, E., & Brammer, M. J. (2009b). Disorder-specific dissociation of orbitofrontal dysfunction in boys with pure conduct disorder during reward and ventrolateral prefrontal dysfunction in boys with pure ADHD during sustained attention. *American Journal of Psychiatry*, 166, 83–94.

Schiffer, B., Pawliczek, C., Mu, B., Forsting, M., Gizewski, E., Leygraf, N., & Hodgins, S. (2014). Neural mechanisms underlying cognitive control of men with lifelong antisocial behavior. *Psychiatry Research: Neuroimaging*, 222, 43–51.

Sebastian, C. L., McCrory, E. J., Cecil, C. A., Lockwood, P. L., De Brito, S. A., Fontaine, N. M., & Viding, E. (2012). Neural responses to affective and cognitive theory of mind in children with conduct problems and varying levels of callous-unemotional traits. *Archives of General Psychiatry*, 69, 814–822.

Sharp, C., Burton, P. C., & Ha, C. (2011). "Better the devil you know": a preliminary study of the differential modulating effects of reputation on reward processing for boys with and without externalizing behavior problems. *European Child & Adolescent Psychiatry*, 20, 581–592.

Squeglia, L. M., Jacobus, J., & Tapert, S. F. (2009). The influence of substance use on adolescent brain development. *Clinical EEG and Neuroscience*, 40, 31–38.

Sroufe, L. A. & Rutter, M. (1984). The domain of developmental psychopathology. *Child Development*, 55, 17–29.

Sterzer, P., Stadler, C., Krebs, A., Kleinschmidt, A., & Poustka, F. (2005). Abnormal neural responses to emotional visual stimuli in adolescents with conduct disorder. *Biological Psychiatry*, 57, 7–15.

Sundram, F., Deeley, Q., Sarkar, S., Daly, E., Latham, R., Craig, M., Raczek, M., Fahy, T., Picchioni, M., Barker, G. J., & Murphy, D. G. (2012). White matter microstructural abnormalities in the frontal lobe of adults with antisocial personality disorder. *Cortex*, 48, 216–229.

Veit, R., Flor, H., Erb, M., Hermann, C., Lotze, M., Grodd, W., & Birbaumer, N. (2002). Brain circuits involved in emotional learning in antisocial behavior and social phobia in humans. *Neuroscience Letters*, 328, 233–236.

Viding, E., Sebastian, C. L., Dadds, M. R., Lockwood, P. L., Cecil, C. A., De Brito, S. A., & McCrory, E. J. (2012). Amygdala response to preattentive masked fear in children with conduct problems: the role of callous-unemotional traits. *American Journal of Psychiatry*, 160, 1109–1116.

Waller, R., Corral-Frías, N. S., Vannucci, B., Bogdan, R., Knodt, A. R., Hariri, A. R., & Hyde, L. W. (2016). An oxytocin receptor polymorphism predicts amygdala reactivity and antisocial behavior in men. *Social Cognitive and Affective Neuroscience*, 11, 1218–1226.

Waller, R., Dotterer, H. L., & Hyde, L. W. (2015). An imaging gene by environment interaction (IG×E) approach to understanding youth antisocial behavior. *Emerging Trends in the Social and Behavioral Sciences*: John Wiley & Sons, Inc.

Waller, R., Dotterer, H. L., Murray, L., Maxwell, A. M., & Hyde, L. W. (2017). White-matter tract abnormalities and antisocial behavior: A systematic review of diffusion tensor imaging studies across development. *Neuroimage: Clinical*, 14, 201–215.

White, S. F., Marsh, A. A., Fowler, K. A., Schechter, J. C., Adalio, C., Pope, K., Pine, D. S., & Blair, R. J. R. (2012). Reduced amygdala response in youths with disruptive behavior disorders and psychopathic traits: decreased emotional response versus increased top-down attention to non-emotional features. *American Journal of Psychiatry*, 169, 750–758.

White, S. F., Pope, K., Sinclair, S., Fowler, K. A., Brislin, S. J., Williams, W. C., Pine, D. S., & Blair, R. J. R. (2013). Disrupted expected value and prediction error signaling in youths with disruptive behavior disorders during a passive avoidance task. *American Journal of Psychiatry*, 170, 315–323.

Yang, Y. & Raine, A. (2009). Prefrontal structural and functional brain imaging findings in antisocial, violent, and psychopathic individuals: a meta-analysis. *Psychiatry Research: Neuroimaging*, 174, 81–88.

Yoder, K., Harenski, C., Kiehl, K., & Decety, J. (2015). Neural networks underlying implicit and explicit moral evaluations in psychopathy. *Translational Psychiatry*, 5, e625.

Yoder, K. J., Lahey, B. B., & Decety, J. (2016). Callous traits in children with and without conduct problems predict reduced connectivity when viewing harm to others. *Scientific Reports*, 6, 20216.

40 Research Designs and Methods for Evaluating and Refining Interventions for Youth Violence Prevention

Albert D. Farrell and Krista R. Mehari

Introduction

A major focus of violence prevention efforts has been on reducing rates of violence among young people. A national survey in 2011 found that 65% of school-aged children had been exposed to a violence prevention program, with 55% reporting that they had participated in a program in the past year (Finkelhor, Vanderminden, Turner, Shattuck, & Hamby, 2014). Unfortunately, this same survey concluded that less than 15% of the sample reported being exposed to a program that met the authors' standards for a "high quality program." Similar findings were reported by a 2014 national survey, which found that although 76% of elementary and middle schools and 84% of high schools required students to receive instruction on violence prevention, the mean hours of instruction was only 4.2 or less per year (School Health Policies and Practices Study, 2015). This suggests that the situation has not changed much since 2001, when the US Surgeon General concluded that "much of the money America spends on youth violence prevention is spent on ineffective – sometimes even harmful – programs and policies" (Office of the Surgeon General, 2001, p. 99).

The widespread implementation of violence prevention programs of limited or unknown effectiveness is not due to the unavailability of effective programs. Matjasko et al. (2012) reviewed 37 meta-analyses and 15 systematic reviews of the literature evaluating youth violence prevention programs. They found that most reviews concluded that youth violence prevention programs are capable of producing moderate effects on violence-related outcomes. There was, however, considerable variability in the strength of effects across target populations, types of prevention strategy, and reviews. Some interventions were found to produce weak or, in some cases, iatrogenic effects. Other reviewers (Fagan & Catalano, 2012) identified 17 interventions directed at youth under the age of 18 that produced significant reductions in physical or sexual violence in well-conducted evaluations. These represented a variety of school, family, and community interventions that produced small- to medium-sized effects on outcomes. The authors concluded that further work is needed to increase the number of effective interventions.

Although progress has been made in developing interventions to reduce youth violence, further work is needed to develop effective interventions suitable for widespread implementation. This effort will require the creative application of research designs and methods that are well suited to addressing objectives at different stages of an intervention's development. These include (a) establishing whether an intervention appears promising; (b) determining the efficacy of an intervention under ideal conditions; (c) evaluating the effectiveness of an intervention under routine conditions; (d) identifying factors that influence its effectiveness; and (f) determining how an intervention can be improved. In this chapter we provide an overview of research strategies that address each of these objectives.

Methodological Issues

Although there are numerous factors to consider when evaluating interventions, the key considerations are related to five broad criteria. These are recruiting a relevant sample, implementing a research design that provides an appropriate comparison group or counterfactual, determining the extent to which the intervention is successfully implemented, obtaining sound measures of key constructs, and conducting appropriate statistical analyses. How these are addressed will vary depending on the objectives of the evaluation (e.g., pilot testing a new intervention versus conducting an effectiveness trial).

Sample and Setting Recruitment

A key consideration in any study is ensuring the sample adequately represents the population of interest. This influences external validity or the extent to which the findings of a study can be generalized to other conditions – in this case, to other potential participants and settings. In particular, researchers must ensure that the sample and sampling unit are consistent with the focus of the intervention being evaluated. Much of the work on youth violence prevention has been guided by ecological systems theory (Bronfenbrenner, 1979), which states that individuals are influenced by multiple forces that include historical time and lived experience; their internal world; and interactions with family, peer, school, and neighborhood and community networks. This has led to interventions that focus not just on the individual, but also on larger units such as schools (Farrell, Meyer, Kung, & Sullivan, 2001) and communities (Matjasko et al., 2012). School-level interventions often focus on promoting changes in individual-level factors such as social-emotional skills and in the broader school environment (e.g., peer and school climate, school disciplinary practices). Community-level interventions focus on community factors such as providing positive opportunities for youth and building social capital. This means that researchers need to sample schools or communities and individuals within those units that represent the population of interest. The number of units at each level must also be large enough to ensure adequate statistical power. Gottfredson (2001) noted that a minimum of 44 schools may be required to achieve sufficient statistical power to detect intervention effects.

Research Design

One of the most critical issues in designing an outcome study is using a research design that provides a credible counterfactual. According to Rubin's (1974) potential outcomes framework, the treatment effect can be viewed as the difference between two potential outcomes: (a) the outcome individuals would experience if they received the treatment; and (b) the counterfactual, which represents the outcome they would experience if they did not. The fundamental problem of causal inference is that it is only possible to observe outcomes under one of these conditions for any given individual. Within this framework, the key to sound experimental design is obtaining a credible estimate of the counterfactual. The absence of outcomes for the counterfactual makes it difficult to attribute any observed changes (or lack of changes) in outcomes to the intervention rather than other influences. For example, decreases in students' aggression at a school where an intervention is implemented could be due to maturation, changes within the school (e.g., changes in disciplinary practices, a new principal) or the community (e.g., a new after-school program), or other factors unrelated to the intervention.

Designs use different methods to provide a counterfactual. Randomized trials are based on the assumption that individuals randomly assigned to the control condition represent surrogates for those assigned to the intervention condition such that their outcomes represent the outcomes individuals in the intervention condition would have experienced had they not received the intervention. Quasi-experimental designs use approaches other than random assignment to establish groups to serve as controls. These include matched control designs in which pretest data are used to demonstrate that participants in the intervention and control groups are similar on key variables (Shadish, Cook, & Campbell, 2002). Within-group analyses, such as interrupted time-series designs, use multiple pre-intervention observations to predict what would have happened if the intervention had not been implemented. This makes it possible to determine the extent to which the trajectory after initiating the intervention differs from what is predicted by the pre-intervention data. These designs can be expanded to provide between-group comparisons when data from comparison units (e.g., schools or communities) are also obtained (see Farrell, Henry, Bradshaw, & Reischl, 2016 for examples). Researchers have also adapted single case designs, such as multiple baseline designs, originally designed for studying individuals to examine changes within larger units, such as schools or communities (Biglan, Ary, & Wagenaar, 2000).

Assessment of Integrity of Implementation

Studies cannot provide a fair test of an intervention if it is not successfully implemented. Integrity of implementation represents the quality and fidelity of implementation. Integrity subsumes four broad constructs (Bumbarger, 2014). Dosage refers to how much of the intervention is delivered to participants. Engagement represents to the extent to which the individuals participate in and are sufficiently engaged by the intervention. Adherence is the degree to which key components of the intervention are implemented. Quality of delivery refers to how well, or how skillfully, the intervention is delivered. It is important that all four constructs of integrity fidelity are assessed, as it is possible for an intervention to have adherence, but low quality of implementation, dosage, or engagement. Without this information, it is difficult to determine whether a failure to find significant intervention effects is due to an ineffective intervention or a potentially effective intervention that was poorly implemented. Conversely, finding significant effects for a poorly implemented intervention raises questions about whether the intervention or some other factor was responsible for any observed effects. Differences in treatment integrity may also lead to differences in intervention effects across studies.

Measurement of Key Constructs

Researchers evaluating violence prevention programs must ensure that appropriate measures are used to assess key constructs. Ideally, outcome batteries should include primary outcome variables, measures of the intervening variables that represent proximal effects of the intervention, and measures of moderator variables that may influence intervention effects (Farrell et al., 2001). The need to assess primary outcomes such as reductions in rates of violence is obvious as these represent the ultimate goals of the intervention. However, it is also important to assess the intervening variables directly targeted by an intervention's theory of change. This makes it possible to test the intervention's logic model, which comprises action theory and conceptual theory. Action theory specifies the risk or protective factors targeted by the intervention (e.g., emotion regulation skills, school climate), whereas conceptual theory specifies the link between the intervening variables targeted by the intervention and the primary outcomes of interest (e.g., reductions in aggression) (Chen, 1990). Taken together, this information can be used to test the validity of the logic model and to guide efforts to improve an intervention's impact and efficiency. Assessing covariates, or possible confounding factors, helps establish the efficacy of the intervention by making it possible to control for other factors that could account for differences between intervention and control groups. Measures of potential moderators that could influence the impact of the intervention are also important to determine for whom the intervention works and under what conditions (Farrell, Henry, & Bettencourt, 2013).

Identifying appropriate measures can be challenging. Researchers have used a variety of approaches to assess youth violence (Dahlberg, Toal, Swahn, & Behrens, 2005). These have included adolescents' reports of their own behavior, peer nominations, peer ratings, ratings by teachers and parents, observational measures, and archival data, such as school disciplinary code violations and community surveillance data. Because each method suffers from some inherent source of bias, researchers often include measures from multiple sources. Regardless of their source, measures must meet minimum psychometric standards and be appropriate for the age and other characteristics of the specific target population (Farrell et al., 2001). Consideration must also be given to the timing of assessments. Studies that collect only pre and immediate post-intervention data do not provide a basis for determining the extent to which any observed effects are sustained or identifying sleeper effects that only emerge over time (Sklad, Diekstra, Ritter, Ben, & Gravesteijn, 2012).

Data Analyses

Researchers evaluating the impact of violence prevention programs need to conduct statistical analyses appropriate for their study's design. This includes consideration of the distribution properties of measures and the unit of analysis (e.g., nesting of individuals within schools or communities). Analyses should also be designed to provide a clear test of a study's hypotheses. Researchers need to move beyond simply stating whether intervention effects are significant by providing estimates of effect size. In recent years, there have been important advances in analytic methods that provide researchers with greater power to evaluate prevention effects (Brown et al., 2012). This includes alternatives to intent-to-treat analyses that provide a basis for examining intervention effects for those who fully participate in the intervention, propensity scores to identify appropriate control comparisons, and methods for reducing bias resulting from missing data.

Evaluating an Intervention's Promise

Evaluating a new intervention can present developers with a serious dilemma. Rigorous evaluations require considerable resources, often involving years of effort. Justifying such an effort requires evidence that an intervention has the potential to produce its desired effects. This, in turn, requires a fairly rigorous evaluation. Pilot studies are often a first step to evaluating an intervention's potential. Unfortunately, the limited resources typically available for pilot studies may lead to limitations that make it difficult to draw clear conclusions about an intervention's impact. Researchers may not be able to recruit a sufficiently large number of participants to provide adequate statistical power to detect effects. This is particularly true when interventions focus on schools or communities as the unit of analysis. The designs used in pilot studies may also be less than ideal. Pilot studies may lack a control group (e.g., Herman & Waterhouse, 2014), use quasi-experimental designs to compare outcomes in intervention and comparison schools (e.g., Farrell, Valois, Meyer, & Tidwell, 2003) or communities (e.g., Koper, Woods, & Isom, 2016), or rely on within-subject designs to compare cohorts within the same schools that differ in their exposure to the intervention (e.g., Olweus, 2005). Pilot studies may lack the resources to monitor, let alone assure, a high quality of implementation. Pilot studies may also collect limited data on outcomes, often relying on archival data or measures from a single source. Finally, they may assess only short-term effects. This precludes determining whether any initial effects are sustained over time, or if other effects emerge later.

Although pilot studies often fall short of larger-scale efficacy and effectiveness trials, there are strategies that can produce more interpretable findings. Pilot studies are often conducted in situations where it is not possible to use random assignment. Although it can be difficult to draw strong causal inferences from quasi-experimental studies, the collection of pretest data and use of carefully selected comparison groups can help rule out many alternative explanations (Shadish et al., 2002). Alternatives, such as time-series designs that require as few as two participating schools or communities, may be particularly well-suited to initial evaluations of interventions and can address many potential threats to internal and external validity (Biglan et al., 2000; Farrell et al., 2016). The collection of data on intervening variables targeted by the intervention may also have value in establishing its promise and guiding efforts to improve its impact (e.g., Bosworth, Espelage, & Du, 1998). In short, pilot studies can provide useful data on the feasibility of implementing an intervention, but may at times provide limited information for determining whether it has sufficient promise to justify the resources to pursue a more extensive evaluation. This may lead to abandoning potentially effective interventions or pursing interventions that ultimately prove to have limited value. The findings of pilot studies should thus not be considered definitive, but should be interpreted within the context of other information, including the strength of the intervention's logic model.

Collins, Murphy, Nair, and Strecher (2005) proposed an alternative approach for developing and evaluating prevention programs that involves more intensive evaluations of intervention components prior to conducting efficacy trials. Their multiphase optimization strategy (MOST) involves a component screening phase that uses randomized studies guided by theory to evaluate the performance of individual intervention components, and a refinement phase in which randomized studies are used to determine optimal dosage levels and combinations of components. Components include aspects of the intervention and processes for delivering the intervention. Both phases involve a series of carefully randomized experiments that are completed prior to efficacy trials. These determine the effectiveness of different combinations of intervention components. One challenge for applying this strategy to violence prevention is that intervention effects may take some time to emerge. In such cases, Collins et al. (2005) suggested that researchers focus on the impact on more proximal outcomes. They argued that whereas this approach requires a considerable investment of time during the intervention development stage, it can save resources by reducing the likelihood that larger-scale evaluations will be conducted on interventions that have limited impact (Collins et al., 2005). More systematic and intensive approaches to the early stages of intervention development could ultimately yield more effective prevention approaches.

Evaluating the Efficacy of an Intervention

Once the promise of an intervention has been established, the next stage typically involves an efficacy study. Efficacy studies are designed to minimize threats to internal validity, which represent factors other than the intervention that may be responsible for any observed changes (or lack of changes) in outcomes. This is reflected in their recruitment approach, research design, implementation monitoring, and measurement of outcomes. Efficacy studies are typically conducted in settings such as schools or communities that have a strong interest and commitment to participating in the evaluation. Efficacy studies may also use incentives to ensure adequate participation rates, and interventions may be implemented by highly trained project staff members who are monitored to ensure that the intervention is implemented with a high degree of integrity. Although these strategies enhance internal validity, they reduce external validity by evaluating an intervention under circumstances that are unlikely to reflect how it would ultimately be implemented. For example, school-based interventions are typically implemented by teachers or other school staff members without close monitoring. Similarly, interventions implemented outside of a research context may lack resources to provide transportation and are unlikely to pay family members to participate in a family intervention component. Indeed, it has been argued that most schools are not likely to have the resources or technical expertise to implement most available programs (Samples & Aber, 1998).

Increasing recognition of the need for more comprehensive intervention approaches has led to increasingly complex efficacy studies. Initial evaluations of school-based interventions often involved within-school designs in which classrooms were randomized to intervention and comparison conditions. The need to address broader environmental factors has led to larger-scale cluster-randomized trials in which entire schools (e.g., Espelage, Low, Polanin, & Brown, 2013; Henry, Farrell, & MVPP, 2004) or communities (e.g., Hawkins et al., 2008) are randomly assigned to conditions. Other research strategies include interrupted time-series designs and multiple baseline designs to evaluate community-level effects (for examples, see Farrell et al., 2016). Well-designed efficacy trials require careful monitoring to ensure that interventions are implemented with a high degree of integrity (e.g., Durlak, Weissberg, Dymnicki, Taylor, & Schellinger, 2011), and the inclusion of multiple measures of key outcomes and intervening variables targeted by the interventions. Although they may have limited external validity, the rationale for focusing on efficacy studies is that they provide a more rigorous test of an intervention's impact and its potential for producing positive effects.

Evaluating the Effectiveness of an Intervention

Effectiveness studies bridge the gap between efficacy studies and service provision by evaluating the impact of interventions under routine conditions in typical settings (Gottfredson et al., 2002). In so doing, they sacrifice some measure of internal validity in order to increase external validity. Evaluations of program effectiveness are less common than efficacy studies. This is unfortunate, as such efforts are critical to judging whether outcomes obtained in research settings can be obtained when programs are brought into the real world. Perhaps not surprisingly, school-based programs implemented by researchers for the purposes of demonstrating efficacy tend to have larger effect sizes than those implemented in routine practice (Wilson, Lipsey, & Derzon, 2003). In fact, Gottfredson and colleagues (2002) argued that there is hardly any evidence supporting the general effectiveness of delinquency prevention programs – including violence prevention programs. More recent meta-analyses and reviews suggest that violence prevention programs can have clinically and statistically significant effects (e.g., Centers for Disease and Prevention [CDC], 2007). For example, Durlak et al.'s (2011) meta-analysis found that classroom programs implemented by teachers had more significant effects on desired outcomes than those implemented by non-school personnel. Based on this they argued that such programs can be effective as part of routine practice.

A major difference between efficacy and effectiveness studies is the participants and settings where they are conducted. Efficacy studies are typically conducted in schools or communities that have agreed to submit to what is often a fairly involved research protocol that requires schools and parents to have considerable trust in the research team and a shared belief in the importance of participating in research. This may result in a sample of schools that are not representative of other schools. Effectiveness studies, in contrast, typically involve implementation of interventions for which there is some evidence of efficacy, use less intrusive protocols, use existing staff to implementing the intervention, and have limited resources for promoting participation.

The designs suitable for effectiveness studies are generally the same as those used for efficacy trials. These include randomized trials, quasi-experimental designs, interrupted time-series designs, and single-case designs. Evaluating the integrity of implementation is particularly critical in efficacy studies because of its strong relation to effectiveness. One of the standards for effectiveness studies endorsed by the Society for Prevention Research requires comparing the degree of treatment integrity in the effectiveness study to what is obtained in efficacy trials (Gottfredson et al., 2015). Although it is becoming more common for effectiveness studies to measure and report integrity, it may be difficult to compare the findings of these studies to efficacy studies because of differences in measures typically used. Integrity in effectiveness studies is often assessed by having program facilitators complete measures (e.g., Low, Smolkowski, & Cook, 2016), rather than by direct observation, as is often the case in efficacy trials. However, some efficacy studies have collected observational data using community members to assess multiple aspects of fidelity, including adherence, dosage, quality of delivery, and participant engagement (Fagan, Hanson, Hawkins, & Arthur, 2008). This simultaneously provides accountability through more objective reporting and is sustained by the community rather than researchers. Effectiveness studies should include measures of primary outcomes and of the intervening variables represented in the intervention's logic model. In addition, evaluations of interventions that target school- or community-level factors should assess systems-level changes (Durlak et al., 2007). Although many effectiveness studies have used surveys or archival data, some studies have used direct observations, such as of teacher proactive classroom management and student disruptive behaviors (e.g., Low et al., 2016). Such strategies are expensive in terms of resources but can provide compelling, objective evidence about clinically important changes in student behavior and classroom functioning.

In many respects, effectiveness studies, if properly conducted, provide the true test of an intervention's potential impact. Further work is needed to identify factors that may reduce the effectiveness of interventions when they are implemented outside of research settings. Such studies may be particularly challenging because of the time required to develop partnerships between researchers and community sites (Rohrbach, Grana, Sussman, & Valente, 2006). The discrepancy between the strength of findings in efficacy trials and effectiveness studies underscores the necessity of an iterative process to improve violence prevention programs. Effectiveness studies must be conducted in such a way that information is gathered on why the intervention may have limited effectiveness and how it can be improved to address those issues.

Identifying Factors that Moderate Intervention Effectiveness

The diverse array of factors that influence and maintain violent behavior makes it clear that no single program will be universally effective. Violence prevention programs will only be successful to the extent that they address the specific risk and protective factors relevant to a particular target population (Coie et al., 1993; Kellam, Koretz, & Moscicki, 1999). Progress in producing population-level reductions in youth violence will thus require providing decision makers with information to guide their selection of appropriate prevention programs and procedures that ensure their successful implementation. This requires developing a knowledge base that identifies factors related to participants, settings, and implementation that influence the degree to which various interventions produce the desired outcomes.

Participant and Setting Factors

Researchers evaluating the impact of youth violence prevention programs have found variability in outcomes across individuals and settings (Farrell et al., 2013). Such variability is not surprising, particularly for universal interventions that are implemented with all individuals in settings such as schools, classrooms, or neighborhoods. The development and maintenance of violence is determined by multiple factors within the individual and their broader environment, which may vary among individuals both within and across settings (Lipsey & Derzon, 1998). The effects of violence prevention programs may thus vary across individuals who differ in their degree of exposure to the specific factors targeted by the intervention and in other factors that may be maintaining their behavior. For this reason, the Standards of Evidence for identifying effective prevention programs adopted by the Society for Prevention Research (Flay et al., 2005) recommended that researchers conduct subgroup analyses on heterogeneous samples with respect to variables such as age, gender, race or ethnicity, and risk level. Identifying individual and setting characteristics that moderate the effects of specific violence prevention programs makes it possible to improve the effectiveness of prevention efforts by targeting them at the individuals who are most likely to benefit (Yale, Scott, Gross, & Gonzalez, 2003), and by informing efforts to develop interventions to address the needs of individuals who do not benefit from existing interventions.

Examining potential moderators of intervention effects has become increasingly common. Farrell et al. (2013) identified 68 studies that investigated factors that moderated outcomes in their review of subgroup effects of universal school-based violence prevention trials. The majority of studies examined individual-level variables, including demographic factors, initial levels of aggression, and risk factors. Their review revealed an inconsistent pattern of findings for demographic variables (e.g., gender, age, race or ethnicity, poverty status). More consistent support was found for stronger intervention effects for individuals with higher levels of initial aggression, though effects were not consistent across outcomes or waves. A smaller number of studies found support for classroom-level (i.e., level of aggression and norms supporting aggression) and school-level variables (i.e., school norms, principal leadership, school poverty rates). They found only two studies that examined the moderating effects of neighborhood poverty and crime rates on intervention effects.

Meta-analyses have also been used to determine participant and setting influences on intervention effects. Matjasko et al. (2012) summarized the findings of meta-analyses and systematic reviews that examined moderators of the effects of youth violence prevention programs. Their analysis revealed inconsistent findings across reviews that examined differences in effects across age, gender, race, parenting and family life stress, family poverty, and family structure. One of the complicating factors in interpreting the results of these meta-analyses is that they examined the effects of moderators across studies that evaluated different interventions. This does not address the possibility that potential moderators may not function the same way for different types of prevention programs implemented under different conditions. For example, one intervention strategy may produce stronger effects for male adolescents, whereas another may produce stronger effects for female adolescents. Findings may also vary as a function of the specific outcomes assessed and the timing of measures. These potential confounds may account for the apparent discrepancies across studies that are not evident from these reviews.

Implementation Factors

The most common factor that researchers have explored as a predictor of intervention effectiveness is adherance, or the extent to which an intervention is implemented as intended by its developers (Dusenbury, Brannigan, Falco, & Hansen, 2003). Meta-analyses of violence prevention studies have found that studies that noted implementation problems reported significantly lower effect sizes than those who did not (Durlak et al., 2011; Wilson et al., 2003). Despite the recent emphasis on assessing integrity, there is still a lack of knowledge about which aspects of implementation integrity are most closely related to outcomes. For example, Low et al. (2016) found that adherence by itself was not as important as engagement, perhaps because low engagement on the part of the teacher was associated with low generalization of skills by the students.

Research Designs

Because studies evaluating potential moderators are conducted within the context of outcome studies, they need to meet the same basic requirements in terms of the sample, design, selection of measures, and analysis. Researchers need to be particularly thoughtful in selecting an appropriate sample to examine potential moderator effects. Farrell et al. (2013) noted that prior studies have typically not provided a clear rationale for why intervention effects would vary across the specific factors they investigated. They urged researchers to rely on logic models to formulate specific *a priori* hypotheses regarding the individuals most likely to benefit from a given intervention, the contextual factors that would be expected to moderate outcomes, and the mechanisms responsible for variability in effects across individuals, families, schools, or communities. This suggests a more purposeful approach to sampling to provide a basis for testing these hypotheses rather than the more typical approach of conducting post-hoc analyses of a host of potential moderators.

Few studies have sampled a sufficiently large or diverse set of schools or communities to provide the depth and scope needed to examine the moderating effects of school and community characteristics (Farrell et al., 2013). For example, testing the extent to which intervention effects vary across communities could involve obtaining an adequate sample of communities that vary in their rates of poverty and crime. The resources required to complete such a study could, however, be beyond the scope of an individual study. An alternative would be to conduct separate replications of intervention studies across a diverse array of communities. This would require using similar designs and measures, and maintaining a consistent degree of intervention integrity to reduce potential confounds. Amassing a sufficient number of such studies could provide the basis for meta-analyses to compare the effects of interventions implemented in schools and communities that differ on important characteristics (e.g., Wilson et al., 2003). At present, however, few evaluations of specific interventions have been sufficiently replicated in diverse settings to provide a basis for meta-analyses. This has limited prior meta-analyses that examine moderator effects based on combining results across different interventions. This effort could be facilitated by more careful assessment and consistent reporting of individual-level characteristics and the characteristics of the school and community settings in which they are implemented.

Providing a credible counterfactual may be particularly challenging for studies examining moderators. Although participants can be randomized to intervention and control groups it is generally not possible to randomize them to different levels of many moderator variables (e.g., risk level, family structure). This results in multiple confounding factors at the individual and group levels. For example, studies examining the potential role of individual-level risk factors as a moderator of intervention effects need to control for gender differences in risk factors (e.g., Farrell et al., 2013). Studies examining the potential moderating role of community-level factors such as poverty and crime rates need to consider other factors associated with neighborhood disadvantage, location (e.g., urban versus rural setting), and implementation integrity that may also differ across settings. Such factors must also be considered in interpreting findings. For example, differences in intervention effects across two communities examined in the Metropolitan Area Child Study Research Group (2002) study were attributed to differences in community levels of poverty and crime. However, comparing results across only two communities makes it difficult to rule out other potential factors that may have influenced intervention effects. Individual and setting factors may also interact. For example, the experiences of minority youth may differ depending on the ethnic composition of their school (Mehari & Farrell, 2013). This issue may not be readily addressed by procedures such as matching, which may create samples that do not reflect the populations from which they are drawn (Kazdin, 2016). Researchers not finding evidence of moderation in carefully conducted studies with adequate statistical power may be able to reasonably conclude that effects were fairly robust. Those finding evidence of moderation, however, may find the results more difficult to interpret. This further underscores the need for researchers to carefully specify individual and community-level factors that may underlie any differential patterns of effects.

Similar issues must be addressed by studies examining the impact of intervention integrity on outcomes. Whereas studies have examined the relation between implementation factors and outcomes (Durlak et al., 2011; Dusenbury et al., 2003), implementation factors are based on observed variability rather than experimentally manipulated (e.g., random assignment to different levels of implementation quality). The degree to which such factors can be explored may be limited in that most studies attempt to maintain a consistently high quality of implementation. This restricted range may attenuate relations between implementation factors and outcomes. Relations between implementation factors and outcomes may also be difficult to interpret because of other factors that may influence integrity. For example, Mihalic and Irwin (2003) found that adherence was predicted by characteristics of the community, and the dosage and the continued implementation of the program over time were best predicted by characteristics of the program itself (e.g., complexity of the program, quality of materials, cost and time burden). Integrity may also differ across settings. For example, teachers working in under-resourced schools under pressure to improve standardized test scores may consider implementing all aspects of a prevention program a lower priority. Disruptive chaotic school environments may also make it difficult to achieve a high degree of implementation integrity. Understanding what affects integrity, and then adapting programs to improve feasibility and ease of implementation, is a vital and underemployed step in effectiveness research. At the very least, limited progress will be made without careful assessment of intervention integrity and reporting this information in articles.

Studies evaluating differences in intervention effects across participants and settings are also needed to inform efforts to tailor interventions to meet the needs of specific populations. Castro, Barrera, and Martinez (2004) noted the need for expanding current scientific models to include cultural variables and address cultural adaptation issues. They recommended controlled studies comparing culturally adapted versions of model prevention programs against the original versions. A key dilemma is striking the appropriate balance between implementing an intervention with integrity vs. tailoring it to make it more relevant to a particular population and context. There is a tension between program developers, who prioritize adherence, and program providers, who may adapt programs to improve feasibility and goodness-of-fit (Dusenbury et al., 2003). Although there is a large body of research indicating that greater adherence is associated with better outcomes (e.g., Gottfredson et al., 2002; Rohrbach et al., 2006; Wilson et al., 2003), there is also evidence that under certain circumstances modifications can improve outcomes (Dusenbury et al., 2003). Conceptualizing deliberate, local additions or modifications as adaptations, rather than lack of adherence, may help to advance the field by quantifying and assessing the effects of adaptations in a systematic way (e.g., Berkel, Mauricio, Schoenfelder, & Sandler, 2011). In their theoretical review of studies on adaptation and fidelity, Berkel et al. (2011) suggested that additive adaptations may increase effectiveness by increasing participant responsiveness. Low et al. (2016) argued that it is important to understand that adaptation and adherence, rather than existing in isolation, take place within the context of implementer engagement in the material. Rather than identifying adherence as a primary goal, they suggested that researchers identify behavior change as the primary goal. This may result in implementers using methods of promoting behavior change that are not strictly within the prevention program manual. However, there is a valid concern that adaptations or modifications may result in the deletion of active ingredients or in the addition of material that may have iatrogenic effects (Dusenbury et al., 2003). Thus, it is important that studies explore how and when modifications and adaptations improve outcomes (Dusenbury et al., 2003).

Determining How an Intervention Can Be Improved

Evaluating an Intervention's Logic Model

Assessing the validity of an intervention's logic model can provide important information to inform revisions to an intervention. Chen (1990) described three basic stages in evaluating logic models. Stage 1 involves specifying the intervention's logic model by identifying the intervening variables or causal mechanisms by which an intervention produces its effects on outcomes. Stage 2 requires collecting data on these intervening variables and the primary outcomes of interest. During stage 3, analyses are conducted to test the intervention's logic model. Its action theory is tested by determining the extent to which the intervention produces changes on the causal processes that are believed to be responsible for its effect. Its conceptual theory is tested by determining the extent to which changes on the causal mechanisms targeted by the intervention mediate its effects on the primary outcomes.

Evaluating an intervention's logic model can be extremely useful. It can guide revisions in cases where an intervention does not produce its desired effects. Finding weak support for the action theory, combined with support for the conceptual theory, indicates that the intervention is targeting the correct intervening variables but is not sufficient to produce changes in those variables. This may lead to considering modifications to the intervention (e.g., increasing dosage) or alternative strategies for addressing the intervening variables. Finding strong support for the action theory, but weak support for the conceptual theory, indicates that the intervention has been successful in altering the intervening variables, but changing the intervening variables is not having the desired effects on the primary outcome of interest (e.g., reducing aggression). This suggests that the intervention may not be targeting the most relevant risk factors for a specific population. Regardless of whether support is found for the action theory, the failure to find support for the conceptual theory indicates the need to reconsider the logic model, to identify more relevant intervening variables, and to develop strategies for altering them.

Evaluating the logic model can also provide useful information when an intervention produces its desired effects on primary outcomes, but support is not found for either the action theory or conceptual theory. This can raise questions about the extent to which the research design has adequately controlled for other threats to internal validity that may account for changes in the primary outcomes. Alternatively, it may suggest that the intervention has promise, but that further work is needed to better understand the mechanisms by which it produces its desired effects. Testing the logic model can be particularly useful in evaluating interventions with multiple components. Determining that an intervention component is producing minimal effects on an intervening variable that is supported by the conceptual model suggests that it may need to be revised or replaced by an alternative strategy. In contrast, finding that the intervening variable targeted by an intervention component is not supported in the conceptual model suggests that it could be removed without altering the impact of the intervention.

Evaluating an intervention's logic model may be conducted within the context of a pilot, efficacy, or effectiveness trial. Such efforts require consideration of several methodological issues, in addition to those previously described for each type of study. Patterns of risk and protective factors might differ across individuals within and across settings. The relevance and effectiveness of specific intervention strategies designed to address these factors may also differ across settings. Researchers must therefore ensure that there is a clear fit between the sample and the logic model (Farrell & Vulin-Reynolds, 2007). Valid measures of the proximal outcomes targeted by an intervention are needed to provide a complete test of an intervention's logic model. Finally, conducting tests of logic models involves conducting appropriate analyses designed to assess mediation effects (e.g., MacKinnon, 2008).

Studies examining an intervention's logic model may be particularly useful during its development stage. Baseline data on proximal outcomes can provide useful information about the relevance of the intervening variables (i.e., do participants show high levels of risk factors or low levels of protective factors targeted by the intervention?). Examining their correlations with primary outcomes can also provide a partial test of the intervention's conceptual theory. In many cases, interventions may not be expected to produce immediate effects on primary outcomes. Effects on proximal outcomes may be expected to emerge more quickly and may serve as leading indicators of an intervention's potential for producing changes on primary outcomes (e.g., Hawkins et al., 2008). In contrast, the failure to find effects on the intervening variables targeted by the intervention may help to identify components or aspects of the intervention that require modification or replacement. Such changes may best be completed before conducting a larger efficacy trial.

Incorporating measures of intervening variables into efficacy and effectiveness studies can provide strong tests of an intervention's action theory and conceptual theory. This can provide guidance for improving an intervention's efficacy. Efficacy studies that ensure that the intervention is implemented with a high degree of integrity are critical to ensuring an accurate evaluation of an intervention's logic model. In contrast, collecting data on intervention integrity within the context of an effectiveness study can determine the extent to which implementation factors influence an intervention's impact on intervening variables. Within the context of an effectiveness study, examining intervention effects on intervening variables may help identify specific intervention components that may not have been adequately implemented. Including measures of intervening variables in analyses examining moderator effects may also be extremely useful. Significant moderated effects in tests of the action theory may indicate that the intervention strategy varies in its ability to alter the intervening variables targeted by the intervention. For example, differential intervention effects on intervening variables across settings may suggest the need for cultural adaptations or identification of other salient risk factors that attenuate an intervention's effectiveness (e.g., peer climate, parental influences). Significant moderator effects in tests of the conceptual model may identify individuals or groups of individuals for whom the intervention is less relevant.

Obtaining Input from Participants and Other Stakeholders

Interventions can also be improved by obtaining input from program participants and other stakeholders on the relevance of an intervention and factors that could support or limit its relevance. For example, Farrell, Mehari, Mays, Sullivan, and Le (2015) conducted qualitative analyses of interviews with 141 middle school students who had participated in a school-based violence prevention program. They assessed participants' reactions to the intervention, the extent to which they used skills taught by the intervention, the degree to which they found them useful, and outcomes they experienced when they used the skills. Participants' responses suggested the need for more intensive efforts to ensure that participants master intervention skills and are able to use them correctly. They also raised concerns about the intervention's relevance. In a follow-up study, Farrell, Mehari, Kramer-Kuhn, Mays, and Sullivan (2015) analyzed participants' descriptions of factors that would influence their likelihood of using specific skills taught by the intervention. Their responses highlighted some of the challenges and successes adolescents experienced in their efforts to use the skills targeted by the intervention. These included individual-level factors such as values and beliefs about the use of aggression versus nonviolent methods of addressing problem situations, their perceptions of the relevance of a skill and its effectiveness in a given situation, and their capacity to use the skill. Participants also identified contextual factors including the school environment, peer influences, and concerns about their reputation that would influence their use of intervention skills. These findings led to recommendations for improving the intervention, including tailoring the content of the intervention to increase its relevance, addressing perceived barriers to using a skill, addressing beliefs and values that might prevent adolescents from using a specific skill, and addressing contextual factors such as peer influences and the school culture.

Understanding the experiences, beliefs, values, and goals of youth and other stakeholders, and involving them in the research process, can be of benefit at each stage of the process by providing a more holistic understanding of the problem and developing prevention strategies that are both aligned with the community's goals and values and feasible for the community to implement. For example, Ybarra, Prescott, and Espelage (2016) worked closely with youth via focus groups and a content advisory team to develop a bullying intervention program delivered through text-messaging. This provides an excellent example of researchers adapting methods to be responsive to the preferences of their participants. Community input must be sought in an iterative process, both to improve the effectiveness of interventions and to maintain their relevance as times change.

Conclusion

Although progress has been made in developing strategies with the potential to reduce youth violence, further work is needed to provide communities and policy-makers with the information needed to guide their selection of the most appropriate intervention to implement in a particular setting, and the necessary details to ensure that it will produce its desired effects. Addressing these needs will require an iterative process in interventions to go through successive cycles of being implemented, evaluated, and revised (Farrell et al., 2001). It is critical that interventions be informed by advances in basic research identifying the most relevant risk and protective factors associated with various forms of violence, and the most effective methods to address these factors for specific populations and settings (Coie et al., 1993). Improving the quality of violence prevention programs will also require improvements in the methodology used to evaluate them that move beyond simply determining whether an intervention produces change on major outcomes. In particular, there is a need for more sophisticated studies to establish optimum implementation methods (e.g., modes of delivery, dosage, characteristics of interventionists), establish the conditions necessary for producing change (e.g., school readiness, institutional support), determine the specific components that contribute to their effectiveness, and identify the individuals and settings where an intervention is most likely to produce an impact (Farrell & Camou, 2006).

Traditional research strategies that progress from pilot studies to efficacy studies to effectiveness trials may not be the optimum approach for developing interventions that will ultimately be used in the real world. Much might be gained from alternative strategies that address external validity from the outset (Rohrbach et al., 2006). Coffey and Horner (2012), for example, suggested prerequisites for sustaining interventions implemented in school settings. These include having an intervention that is contextually appropriate and that shares vision with the institution; establishing buy-in from stakeholders; and providing multiple levels of leadership, administrative support, and technical assistance. They also argued for an iterative approach, noting that continuous regeneration is a prerequisite for sustainability. The MOST approach advocated by Collins et al. (2005) illustrates the potential of another, less traditional approach that provides a rigorous evaluation of intervention components at the early stages of intervention development. This contrasts with the more typical approach in which small-scale pilots are conducted and followed by efficacy studies, with efforts to identify effective intervention components and delivery mechanisms coming much later in the process. Gottfredson et al. (2015) also recently argued for a less linear approach to intervention development that incorporates research on factors relevant to scale-up efforts through each phase of intervention development and evaluation.

At a more practical level, further work is needed to conduct cost-benefit analyses that assess the social, economic, and environmental impact of programs (Nicholls, Lawlor, Neitzert, & Goodspeed). One review of universal, school-based violence prevention programs noted that of all the studies reviewed, only one calculated and reported costs and benefits (Hahn et al., 2007). However, the results of that study provide a strong argument for investing in violence prevention efforts. More specifically, Aos, Lieb, Mayfield, Miller, and Pennucci (2004) estimated that the Seattle Social Development Project produced a $3 return on investment for $1 spent, with net savings per participant at around $9,800.

Although this chapter largely focused on school and community interventions and prevention programs, a variety of other approaches to violence prevention have been developed. Efforts to evaluate these strategies may pose unique challenges, but may also offer opportunities. A recent systematic review of media campaigns targeting youth violence indicated that few studies have assessed their impact on beliefs and attitudes, and only one examined changes in actual behavior (Cassidy, Bowman, McGrath, & Matzopoulos, 2016). Cassidy et al. (2016) discussed the possible benefits of media campaigns, but also cautioned against mass-implementation of strategies that are not founded on research. This is especially important given that some video messaging has been shown to have iatrogenic effects (e.g., Cassidy et al., 2016). Similarly, a variety of policies aimed at reducing violence at multiple systems levels have been implemented, from zero-tolerance policies in schools to state policies on bullying and firearm licensing and registration. Unfortunately, some iatrogenic effects of policy changes have been noted, such as the effect of zero-tolerance policies on the school-to-prison pipeline (Curtis, 2014). At present it is difficult to parse out which specific policies are effective, which are iatrogenic, and which are ineffective (Kaufman & Wiebe, 2015). Given the large scale at which policy change operates, it is vital that the results of such efforts be rigorously evaluated.

References

Aos, S., Lieb, R., Mayfield, J., Miller, M., & Pennucci, A. (2004). *Benefits and costs of prevention and early intervention programs for youth*. Olympia: Washington State Institute for Public Policy, 2004.

Berkel, C., Mauricio, A. M., Schoenfelder, E., & Sandler, I. N. (2011). Putting the pieces together: An integrated model of program implementation. *Prevention Science, 12*(1), 23–33.

Biglan, A., Ary, D., & Wagenaar, A. C. (2000). The value of interrupted time-series experiments for community intervention research. *Prevention Science, 1*(1), 31–49.

Bosworth, K., Espelage, D., & Du, T. (1998). A computer based violence prevention intervention for adolescents: Pilot study. *Adolescence, 33*, 785–795.

Bronfenbrenner, U. (1979). Contexts of child rearing: Problems and prospects. *American Psychologist, 34*(10), 844.

Brown, C. H., Kellam, S. G., Kaupert, S., Muthén, B. O., Wang, W., Muthén, L. K., ... & McManus, J. W. (2012). Partnerships for the design, conduct, and analysis of effectiveness, and implementation research: Experiences of the prevention science and methodology group. *Administration and Policy in Mental Health and Mental Health Services Research, 39*, 301–316.

Bumbarger, B. K. (2014). Understanding and promoting treatment integrity in prevention. In Hagermoser Sanetti, L. M. & Kratochwill, T. R. (Eds), *Treatment integrity: A foundation for evidence-based practice in applied psychology* (pp. 35–54). Washington, DC: American Psychological Association.

Cassidy, T., Bowman, B., McGrath, C., & Matzopoulos, R. (2016). Brief report on a systematic review of youth violence prevention through media campaigns: Does the limited yield of strong evidence imply methodological challenges or absence of effect? *Journal of Adolescence*, 52, 22–26.

Castro, F. G., Barrera, M., Jr., & Martinez C. R., Jr. (2004). The cultural adaptation of prevention interventions: Resolving tensions between fidelity and fit. *Prevention Science*, 5(1), 41–45.

Centers for Disease Control and Prevention. (2007). The effectiveness of universal school-based programs for the prevention of violent and aggressive behavior: A report on recommendations of the Task Force on Community Preventive Services. *Morbidity and Mortality Weekly Report*, 56(RR-7), 1–11.

Chen, H. T. (1990). *Theory-driven evaluations*. Newbury Park, CA: Sage.

Coffey, J. H. & Horner, R. H. (2012). The sustainability of schoolwide positive behavior interventions and supports. *Exceptional Children*, 78, 407–422.

Coie, J. D., Watt, N. F., West, S. G., Hawkins, J. D., Asarnow, J. R., Markman, H. J., … & Long, B. (1993). The science of prevention: A conceptual framework and some directions for a national research program. *American Psychologist*, 48(10), 1013–1020.

Collins, L. M., Murphy, S. A., Nair, V. N., & Strecher, V. J. (2005). A strategy for optimizing and evaluating behavioral interventions. *Annals of Behavioral Medicine*, 30, 65–73.

Curtis, A. (2014). Tracing the school-to-prison pipeline from zero-tolerance policies to juvenile justice dispositions. *Georgetown Law Journal*, 102(4), 1251–1278.

Dahlberg, L. L., Toal, S. B., Swahn, M., Behrens, C. B. (2005). *Measuring Violence-Related Attitudes, Behaviors, and Influences Among Youths: A Compendium of Assessment Tools* (2nd ed.). Atlanta, GA: Centers for Disease Control and Prevention.

Durlak, J. A., Taylor, R. D., Kawashima, K., Pachan, M. K., DuPre, E. P., Celio, C. I., … & Weissberg, R. P. (2007). Effects of positive youth development programs on school, family, and community systems. *American Journal of Community Psychology*, 39, 269–286.

Durlak, J. A., Weissberg, R. P., Dymnicki, A. B., Taylor, R. D., & Schellinger, K. B. (2011). The impact of enhancing students' social and emotional learning: A meta-analysis of school-based universal interventions. *Child Development*, 82, 405–432.

Dusenbury, L., Brannigan, R., Falco, M., & Hansen, W. B. (2003). A review of research on fidelity of implementation: Implications for drug abuse prevention in school settings. *Health Education*, 18, 237–256.

Espelage, D. L., Low, S., Polanin, J. R., & Brown, E. C. (2013). The impact of a middle-school program to reduce aggression, victimization, and sexual violence. *Journal of Adolescent Health*, 53, 180–186.

Fagan, A. A. & Catalano, R. F. (2012). What works in youth violence prevention: A review of the literature. *Research on Social Work Practice*, 23, 141–156.

Fagan, A. A., Hanson, K., Hawkins, J. D., & Arthur, M. W. (2008). Implementing effective community-based prevention programs in the Community Youth Development Study. *Youth Violence and Juvenile Justice*, 6, 256–278.

Farrell, A. D. & Camou, S. (2006). School-based interventions for youth violence prevention. In J. R. Lutzker (Ed.), *Preventing violence: Research and evidence-based intervention strategies* (pp. 125–145). Washington, DC: American Psychological Association.

Farrell, A. D., Henry, D. B., & Bettencourt, A. (2013). Methodological challenges examining subgroup differences: Examples from universal school-based youth violence prevention trials. *Prevention Science*, 14(2), 121–133.

Farrell, A. D., Henry, D., Bradshaw, C., & Reischl, T. (2016). Designs for evaluating the community-level impact of comprehensive prevention programs: Examples from the CDC centers of excellence in youth violence prevention. *Journal of Primary Prevention,* 37, 165–188.

Farrell, A. D., Mehari, K. R., Kramer-Kuhn, A. M., Mays, S. A., & Sullivan, T. N. (2015). A qualitative analysis of factors influencing middle school students' use of skills taught by a violence prevention curriculum. *Journal of School Psychology,* 53(3), 179–194.

Farrell, A. D., Mehari, K. R., Mays, S., Sullivan, T. N., & Le, A. T. (2015). Participants' perceptions of a violence prevention curriculum for middle school students: Was it relevant and useful? *Journal of Primary Prevention,* 36, 227–246.

Farrell, A. D., Meyer, A. L., Kung, E. M., & Sullivan, T. N. (2001). Development and evaluation of school-based violence prevention programs. *Journal of Clinical Child Psychology,* 30(2), 207–220.

Farrell, A. D., Valois, R. F., & Meyer, A. L. (2002). Evaluation of the RIPP-6 violence prevention program at a rural middle school. *American Journal of Health Education,* 33(3), 167–172.

Farrell, A. D., Valois, R. F., Meyer, A. L., & Tidwell, R. P. (2003). Impact of the RIPP violence prevention program on rural middle school students. *Journal of Primary Prevention,* 24(2), 143–167.

Farrell, A. D. & Vulin-Reynolds, M. (2007). Violent behavior and the science of prevention. In D. J. Flannery, A. T. Vazsonyi, & I. D. Waldman (Eds), *The Cambridge handbook of violent behavior and aggression* (pp. 767–786). New York: Cambridge University Press.

Finkelhor, D., Vanderminden, J., Turner, H., Shattuck, A., & Hamby, S. (2014). Youth exposure to violence prevention programs in a national sample. *Child Abuse & Neglect,* 38(4), 677–686.

Flay, B. R., Biglan, A., Boruch, R. F., Castro, F. G., Gottfredson, D., Kellam, S., ... & Ji, P. (2005). Standards of evidence: Criteria for efficacy, effectiveness and dissemination. *Prevention Science,* 6(3), 151–175.

Gottfredson, D. C. (2001). *Schools and delinquency.* New York: Cambridge University Press.

Gottfredson, D. C., Cook, T. D., Gardner, F. E., Gorman-Smith, D., Howe, G. W., Sandler, I. N., & Zafft, K. M. (2015). Standards of evidence for efficacy, effectiveness, and scale-up research in prevention science: Next generation. *Prevention Science,* 16(7), 893–926.

Gottfredson, G. D., Gottfredson, D. C., Czeh, E. R., Cantor, D., Crosse, S. B., & Hantman, I. (2002). *National Study of Delinquency Prevention in Schools: Summary.* Ellicott City, MD: Gottfredson Associates.

Hawkins, J. D., Brown, E. C., Oesterle, S., Arthur, M. W., Abbott, R. D., & Catalano, R. F. (2008). Early effects of Communities That Care on targeted risks and initiation of delinquent behavior and substance use. *Journal of Adolescent Health,* 43(1), 15–22.

Henry, D. B., Farrell, A. D., & MVPP. (2004). The study designed by a committee: Design of the Multisite Violence Prevention Project. *American Journal of Preventive Medicine,* 26(Suppl), 12–19.

Herman, J. W. & Waterhouse, J. K. (2014). A feasibility study to assess the effectiveness of Safe Dates for teen mothers. *Journal of Obstetric, Gynecologic & Neonatal Nursing,* 43, 695–709.

Kaufman, E. J. & Wiebe, D. J. (2015). State injury prevention policies and variation in death from injury. *Injury Prevention,* 22, 99–104.

Kazdin, A. E. (2016). *Research design in clinical psychology* (5th ed.). Boston, MA: Pearson.

Kellam, S. G., Koretz, D., & Mościcki, E. K. (1999). Core elements of developmental epidemiologically based prevention research. *American Journal of Community Psychology,* 27(4), 463–482.

Koper, C. S., Woods, D. J., & Isom, D. (2016). Evaluating a police-led community initiative to reduce gun violence in St. Louis. *Police Quarterly*, 19, 115–149.

Lipsey, M. W. & Derzon, J. H. (1998). Predictors of violent or serious delinquency in adolescence and early adulthood: a synthesis of longitudinal research. In R. Loeber & D. P. Farrington (Eds), *Serious & violent juvenile offenders: Risk factors and successful interventions* (pp. 86–105). Thousand Oaks, CA: Sage Publications, Inc.

Low, S., Smolkowski, K., & Cook, C. (2016). What constitutes high quality implementation of SEL programs? A latent class analysis of Second Step. *Prevention Research*. Advance online publication.

MacKinnon, D. P. (2008). *Introduction to statistical mediation analysis*. New York: Lawrence Erlbaum.

Matjasko, J. L., Vivolo-Kantor, A. M., Massetti, G. M., Holland, K. M., Holt, M. K., & Cruz, J. D. (2012). A systematic meta-review of evaluations of youth violence prevention programs: Common and divergent findings from 25 years of meta-analyses and systematic reviews. *Aggression and Violent Behavior*, 17(6), 540–552.

Mehari, K. R. & Farrell, A. D. (2013). The relation between peer victimization and adolescents' well-being: The moderating role of ethnicity within context. *Journal of Research on Adolescence*, 25(1), 118–134.

Mihalic, S. F. & Irwin, K. (2003). Blueprints for Violence prevention from research to real-world settings – factors influencing the successful replication of model programs. *Youth Violence and Juvenile Justice*, 1(4), 307–329.

Metropolitan Area Child Study Research Group (MACS). (2002). A cognitive-ecological approach to preventing aggression in urban settings: Initial outcomes for high risk children. *Journal of Consulting and Clinical Psychology*, 70, 179–194.

Nicholls, J., Lawlor, E., Neitzert, E., & Goodspeed, T. (2009). *A guide to Social Return on Investment*. Cabinet Office, Office of the Third Sector. Retrieved December 4, 2017 from http://b.3cdn.net/nefoundation/aff3779953c5b88d53_cpm6v3v71.pdf.

Office of the Surgeon General; National Center for Injury Prevention and Control; National Institute of Mental Health; Center for Mental Health Services. (2001). *Youth violence: A report of the Surgeon General*. Rockville, MD: Office of the Surgeon General.

Olweus, D. (2005). A useful evaluation design, and effects of the Olweus Bullying Prevention Program. *Psychology, Crime & Law*, 11(4), 389–402.

Rohrbach, L. A., Grana, R., Sussman, S., & Valente, T. W. (2006). Type II translation: Transporting prevention interventions from research to real-world settings. *Evaluation and the Health Professions*, 29, 302–333.

Rubin, D. (1974). Estimating causal effects of treatments in randomized and nonrandomized studies. *Journal of Educational Psychology*, 66, 688–701.

Samples, F. & Aber, L. (1998). Evaluations of school-based violence prevention programs. In D. Elliott, B. Hamburg, & K. Williams (Eds), *Violence in American schools* (pp. 217–252). New York: Cambridge University Press.

School Health Policies and Practices Study. (2015). Results from the School Health Policies and Practices Study 2014. U.S. Department of Health and Human Services & Centers for Disease Control and Prevention.

Shadish, W. R., Cook, T. D., & Campbell, D. T. (2002). *Experimental and quasi-experimental designs for generalized causal inference*. Boston, MA: Houghton, Mifflin and Company.

Sklad, M., Diekstra, R., Ritter, M. D., Ben, J., & Gravesteijn, C. (2012). Effectiveness of school-based universal social, emotional, and behavioral programs: Do they enhance students' development in the area of skill, behavior, and adjustment? *Psychology in the Schools*, 49(9), 892–909.

Wilson, S. J., Lipsey, M. W., & Derzon, J. H. (2003). The effects of school-based intervention programs on aggressive behavior: A meta-analysis. *Journal of Consulting and Clinical Psychology*, 71, 136–149.

Yale, M. E., Scott, K. G., Gross, M., & Gonzalez, A. (2003). Using developmental epidemiology to choose the target population for an intervention program in a high-risk neighborhood. *Journal of Clinical Child and Adolescent Psychology*, 32(2), 236–242.

Ybarra, M. L., Prescott, T. L., & Espelage, D. L. (2016). Stepwise development of a text messaging-based bullying prevention program for middle school students (BullyDown). *Journal of Medical Internet Research mHealth and uHealth*, 4(2), e60.

41 New Directions in Research on Violence: Bridging Science, Practice, and Policy

Alexander T. Vazsonyi, Daniel J. Flannery, and Matt DeLisi

Introduction

Usually, the final chapter in a handbook such as this one is an attempt to synthesize the assorted works on aggression and violence that appear herein. Across the incredible diversity of approaches to understanding aggression in all of its varied manifestations, editors look for unifying themes that tie the works together as they relate to theory, basic research, and applied prevention programs and criminal justice system interventions. There is nothing wrong with this traditional approach; however, we have opted for a different tack because, like the chapters in this handbook, the editors are quite diverse in terms of their research foci, teaching background, and practitioner and clinical experiences in responding to aggression and violence. Here, the editors offer their unique perspective on the current state and future of science, practice, and policy as they relate to aggression and violence based on the contributions to the handbook.

Alexander T. Vazsonyi

In a recent paper, Birmingham, Bub, and Vaughn (2017) tested a key developmental model designed to further elucidate the underlying processes in the development of self-regulation. More specifically, self-regulation, which was operationalized by delay of gratification, attention focusing, inhibitory control, impulsivity, and sustained attention – in so many ways, very characteristic of the multitude of approaches and conceptualizations that have emerged over the past decades in how to tap into self-regulatory or self-control capacities – was measured at the age of 54 months and the authors sought to understand the extent to which they could explain variability in this construct through three key mechanisms, namely an infant's attachment history between the ages of 15 and 36 months, maternal sensitivity assessed between the ages of 6 and 15 months, and the quality of the whole as assessed between the ages of 6 and 15 months, measured by the well-known HOME inventory, based on a sample of over 1,000 children who were part of the NICHD Study of Early Child Care and Youth Development (SECCYD). Their final model, which specified maternal sensitivity and home quality as direct predictors of self-regulation as well as indirect predictors, as mediated through attachment history, explained an astounding 57% of the variance in self-regulatory behaviors at the age of 4½, while controlling for a number of potentially competing explanatory constructs, including child sex, racial background, temperament, chronic working poverty status during childhood, as well as maternal education.

The importance of this work, though not directly linked to aggression and violence by Birmingham et al. (2017), lies in the fact that, based on a review of contributions to the current handbook, about half of all contributed chapters focused on the etiology, explanation, or treatment of aggressive and violent behaviors, make reference to or focus on constructs that are closely linked to self-regulatory or self-control capacity, or a lack thereof. These contributions focus on a very pervasive and persistent theme, not only in the handbook, which is composed of very diverse contributions ranging from influences by molecular genetics, via neural substrates, to a discussion of violence and aggression from a public health perspective in a global context, but also in the field more generally, namely the extent to which we can understand aggression and violence by considering deficits in self-regulatory skills, deficits in impulse control, deficits in self-control.

This insight is not entirely novel, as Moffitt et al. (2011) made a similar argument in which they suggest that self-control unites all social and behavioral sciences and that it is an umbrella construct that bridges different operationalizations and measurements from across disciplines. They make this argument in part because they found that different measures, including lack of control, impulse aggression, hyperactivity, lack of persistence, impulsivity, and inattention, which were assessed by parents, teachers, observers, as well as self-reports, were all positively and significantly correlated. Furthermore, they also found a number of different measures assessed at the age of 5, including liability, low frustration tolerance, lack of reserve, resistance, restlessness, impulsivity, requiring attention, fleeting attention, and lacking persistence, all to be part of what they term self-control. Based on their sample of about 1,000 children who were part of the Dunedin multidisciplinary health and development study, who have been followed for over 40 years at this time, the authors concluded that self-control assessed during the first decade of life was subsequently associated with early smoking, school dropout, and teen parenthood, and subsequently, and more importantly, with a whole host of indicators tapping most globally into adult health, wealth, and crime.

Moffitt, Poulton, and Caspi (2013) also concluded that these observed relationships were independent of intelligence status or socioeconomic status. Their policy recommendation, with a consideration of economic burden, mandates that society focuses on a one-two punch strategy that principally happens during early childhood, but also to some (and slightly lesser) extent during adolescence. Consistent with work by Birmingham and colleagues, childhood emerges as the key developmental period when parents (Agnew & Moon, this volume; Baglivio, this volume), educators (Cutuli, Pereira, Vrabic, & Herbers, this volume; Gottfredson & Gottfredson, this volume), mental health (Aebi & Steinhausen, this volume) and health professionals or society at large (Dahlberg, Butchart, & Mikton, this volume), can "still" positively influence children in their ability to self-regulate – their emotions, their cognitions, and, importantly, their behaviors (see Enjaian, Bell, Whitt, & DeWall, this volume; Huesmann, this volume; Waller, Dotterer, Murray, & Hyde, this volume). This is when lifelong trajectories

(Figueredo, Patch, Perez-Ramon, & Cruz, this volume) can be altered away from a host of deleterious adjustment outcomes. As illustrated in the contribution by Diamond, Gonzales, Jennings, and Piquero (this volume; see also Farrington, this volume), interventions can and do work even though, as children enter adolescence, most self-regulatory capacities are already formed (Farrington, this volume; Gottfredson, this volume; Gottfredson & Hirschi, 1990), and socialization or intervention efforts have limited, albeit still positive effects.

The evidence by Birmingham et al. (2017) also highlights that though many of children's self-regulatory skills are explained through socialization mechanisms (something that could be debated), much remains unexplained, something also supported by behavior genetic and other evidence focused on biology, traits, heritability, or neural substrates (Baglivio, this volume; Barnes & Tielbeek, this volume; Blonigen & Patrick, this volume; DeLisi, this volume; Hyatt, Sleep, Weiss, & Miller, this volume; McLernon, Feiger, & Schug, this volume; Seguin, Booij, Lillienfeld, this volume; Vailancourt, this volume; Vaughn, Salas-Wrigth, Reingle-Gonzales, this volume; Waller, Dotterer, Murray, & Hyde, this volume) on the variability of aggression and violence, where about half is due to heritability and half due to the environment (see DeLisi, this volume). What is clear from the evidence in work part of the volume and in work based on recent large-scale, longitudinal studies is that (1) self-regulatory or self-control capacity is key in understanding a substantial portion of the variability in the development of and manifestation of aggression or violent behaviors (as well as crime and deviance), both across developmental contexts as well as across the lifespan; (2) much variability in the development of this capacity is heritable (about half), the balance due to environmental influences; and (3) environmental influences or effects appear to be the most salient developmentally during the first decade of a child's life (Birmingham et al., 2017; Vazsonyi & Ksinan, in press), though some positive limited effects can also be found, and achieved through interventions and reinforcement mechanisms, during adolescence (see Cutuli et al., this volume; Gottfredson & Gottfredson, this volume; Diamond et al., this volume).

The accumulating evidence appears unexpectedly consistent with Gottfredson and Hirschi's (1990) original theoretical work on the etiology of crime and deviance – direct relevance for the understanding of aggression and violent behaviors, namely as simply manifestations of severe interpersonal norm-violations, of deviance – which is frequently misunderstood and misinterpreted, particularly related to the importance of non-environmental effects, the importance of early socialization by primary caregivers during the first decade of life, and the developmental course and influences of low self-control across the lifespan (Vazsonyi, Roberts, & Huang, 2015). In a recent re-analysis of the seminal Gluecks' data (Ksinan & Vazsonyi, 2017), which has provided the basis of informal social control theory and highlighted the importance of both employment and marriage, we found that self-regulatory capacity measured during late childhood/adolescence remains consistently associated with measures of norm-violations until the mid-30s, above and beyond employment and marriage, thus providing evidence of a high level of stability, not of self-control or self-regulation per se, but of the effects of it on measures of norm violations.

One contribution in the current handbook also focused in part on impulse or self-control, is the one by Pulkkinen; it is particularly noteworthy as it is the culmination and resulting insights (28 specific ones to be precise), following 50 years of work on the etiology and manifestations of aggression, based principally on two longitudinal studies. Very early in her work, Pulkkinen (this volume) worked to develop an explanatory framework for aggression that focused on what she termed a "two-dimensional impulse control model" – very similar to the "new" dual-systems model that was developed in part based on insights from neurobiology (Casey, Jones, & Hare, 2008; Casey & Caudle, 2013; see also Casey et al., 2011; Mischel et al., 2011 for evidence of the links between laboratory delay of gratification tasks and recent neurobiological evidence) – in which one dimension focused on the expression of impulsivity, while the second focused on cognitive control. Pulkkinen concludes her chapter with the following comment, 42 years following the development of the model:

> My view is that aggression is a vulnerability trait that causes risks for social and personality adjustment if it exceeds a critical threshold. Aggression primarily is a natural self-defensive reaction, but *human beings can learn to regulate self-defensive behavior and avoid the expression of aggression.* In unfortunate living conditions (sometimes also for neurological and temperament reasons), this learning process may remain poor or external pressures may become overwhelming, which may cause an excessive use of aggression for self-defense, and additionally for other purposes such as gaining power over other people (Pulkkinen, this volume, p. 27, italics added).

In addition to a number of parallels in terms of etiology of self-control per se, by Gottfredson and Hirschi, including learning to avoid acting out, acting out in the absence of external controls, and the general stability of one manifestation of poor "impulse control," Pulkkinen also concluded that developmental trajectories of very highly aggressive individuals remain high, albeit not precluding developmental or maturational declines (or aging out) over the life-course. This insight is also largely supported by the Gluecks' data, which includes evidence from 52 or the 1,000 original boys up to the age of 70 years (for additional evidence, see also Gottfredson, this volume). Of course, it is also consistent with the work by Moffitt, Caspi, and colleagues, based both on the Dunedin Study as well as the Environmental-Risk Longitudinal Twin Study, a British cohort study of 2,232 twin siblings. While the Dunedin sample provided in essence the same evidence, by documenting consistently poorer developmental outcomes (that declined in frequency over the life-course, simply as a maturational process) when tracking the "lowest" self-control quintile as compared to the full study sample, based on a subset of over 500 fraternal twin pairs, the E-risk study also showed that because self-control is in part learned and malleable, the project provided the unique opportunity to compare adjustment over time, based on different self-control scores, despite being raised in the same household. Substantial twin differences were found as early as age 12, on measures of antisocial behaviors, health risk behaviors, and measures of academic achievement.

Conclusion

Where does all this leave us? Is this simply obtuse theorizing with limited real-world applications? The accumulating evidence tells a different story. Diamond et al. (this volume) describe the efficacy of primary (childhood), secondary (adolescence), and tertiary (adult) rehabilitation efforts focused on self-control; Moffitt et al. (2013) conclude that a "one-two punch" strategy focused on self-control holds the greatest promise (see also Farrington, this volume) in addressing not only behavior problems, including aggression, violent behaviors, and crime, but, more broadly, a whole host of economic, health, and social indicators of success and well-being. They highlight Heckmann's (2006) economic analysis on interventions, which documents how as a society we focus on tertiary interventions, even though these show limited returns long-term or on a larger scale, in comparison to the returns from primary (and to some extent, secondary) ones. The problem, clearly, is one that we need and are overwhelmed with addressing present-day issues related to interpersonal violence, mostly perpetrated by adults; although this cannot be changed, based on the overwhelming evidence from decades of longitudinal research conducted on individuals from birth, and based on overwhelming economic evidence, we must turn to seriously, broadly, and comprehensively scaling up from small, local efforts targeting children and families, to implementing sweeping changes in how we try to prevent aggression and violence, until tertiary efforts inevitably become unimportant.

Daniel J. Flannery

My training is as a developmental and clinical-child psychologist. I have been director of a multi-disciplinary center for the prevention of violence since 1997 at two different institutions, one public and one private. When I first developed the center my faculty appointment was in a department of criminal justice studies and then as a faculty person in public health. Since 2011, the Center and my faculty appointment have been in a graduate school of social work (Flannery & Singer, 2014). Prior to 1997, I held an appointment first as an Assistant Professor in a school of family studies and then as Associate Professor in a medical school in a department of Psychiatry. Two things (among many) that I have come to realize over my career are that: (1) violence is a complicated public health problem; and (2) to effectively address violence, we need to invest in sustained approaches that incorporate a variety of disciplinary, systems, and levels perspectives. Let me expand on these two points, and then provide some examples of where I think research, practice, and policy are heading in the area of violence prevention.

A public health perspective on violence helps guide the narrative about what to do about this complicated social problem (Dahlberg, Butchart, & Mikton, 2018). To effectively address violence, we need to commit resources to prevention and intervention, and within the scope of intervention, we need to address those at risk for violence as well as those already involved with violence as perpetrators or those who have been victims of violence. A public health perspective does not require one to only focus on the most severe forms of violence. Recent research on bullying, for example, has shown that school-based prevention programs that are universal in scope but assume that all students are at risk for being perpetrators or victims of bullying can successfully reduce rates of bullying victimization and perpetration among elementary and middle school youth (Flannery, Todres, Bradshaw, et al., 2016; National Academies of Science,

Engineering, and Medicine, 2016). Research on bullying has also shown how we must address the issue over the long-term, as early victimization can lead to lifelong deleterious outcomes on mental health and well-being. A greater understanding of bullying has also shown how early experiences of victimization can lead to subsequent perpetration (bully victims), and also how bullying experiences may be related to more serious acts of violence such as school shootings, although the research on these rare events has yet to identify bullying as a consistent risk factor or motivator for perpetrators (Flannery, Modzeleski, & Kretschmar, 2013).

Outside of the realm of bullying specifically, researchers who have examined violent behavior along its vast continuum from most to least serious forms of violence have persistently demonstrated the value of prevention, early identification, and early intervention as key to effectively reducing violence (Sumner, Mercy, Dahlberg, Hillis, Klevens, & Houry, 2015). This theme is also illustrated in several chapters in this volume, including, for example, Baglivio (2018) and Cutuli, Pereira, Vrabic, and Herbers (2018).

Research on more extreme forms of violent behavior has also benefited from a public health approach. Research on homicides and firearm deaths has demonstrated the importance of understanding how the availability of firearms contributes to accidental deaths, increased risk for suicide, and rates of violent death from interpersonal and domestic disputes. Research reviewed in this volume addresses the role of firearms in violence victimization and perpetration. As several authors in this volume note, we also need to continue to investigate the comorbid roles of substance use, mental health, and personality factors such as poor impulse control and how they affect violence.

Most plans to address serious violence require a long-term commitment to a comprehensive approach that attempts to address violence at the individual, family, community, and system levels (Sumner et al., 2015). Cleveland, Ohio is one community that has developed such a plan as part of the US Department of Justice National Youth Forum Initiative. Several other cities are further along than Cleveland (Seattle, Boston), but the elements of Cleveland's IMPACT25 plan are similar to other cities: (1) a focus on the 15–25-year-old age group who consistently represent those with the highest rates of victimization and perpetration of violence, and for whom preventive and intervention services have been most lacking; (2) an approach that is multidisciplinary and spans multiple systems (e.g., justice, education, mental health) and levels (e.g., individual, family, neighborhood, community); (3) a strategy that strengthens and builds upon existing evidence-based programs and commits to implementing programs that have demonstrated effectiveness; and (4) an initiative that supports significant neighborhood-based community input and data-driven decision making.

One of the cornerstones of Cleveland's IMPACT25 plan, which is viewed as critical for an effective long-term approach to violence reduction, is a commitment to improving police-community relationships. This is an emerging topic of concern for communities across the country and should be a priority focus of researchers, practitioners, and policymakers addressing violence. Improving police-community relations is important from the community perspective particularly related to whether persons trust law enforcement, how individuals and officers act when they are interacting with each other, and how communities respond when incidents of misconduct by law enforcement occur or how they cooperate when acts of violence shake a community.

In many ways, police officers are now expected to take on the role of proactive first "social responders" and not merely as reactive enforcers of law and code (Bartholomew, Singer, Gonzalez, & Walker, 2013). This makes sense on a number of levels, but most importantly it reflects the reality that most interactions between police and the community involve non-arrest situations, and many calls for service to police involve quality-of-life issues or dealing with individuals who are under the influence of substances or have mental health issues. It has become increasingly important for law enforcement to be trained in how to effectively recognize and intervene in these situations so that interactions can be handled without resorting to the use of force or violence. It is also important for community members to recognize and respond to legitimate requests from law enforcement for information or assistance. In the trainings that we conduct with police officers on youth-focused policing we emphasize adolescent developmental issues, new research on brain development and trauma, and we employ vignettes of how to interact effectively with youth who may have experienced trauma, are depressed or suicidal, or who have developmental disorders such as autism. Some of the most compelling interactions we have with officers involve discussions about their own experiences with violence and trauma and how this can affect how they interact with young persons or with citizens with mental health issues.

The importance of police-community relations and the role of the justice system has played out recently in several different ways. First is the increased use of body cameras by police departments. The use of cameras has already been shown in limited studies to reduce the number of complaints by both officers and community members, and to reduce the number of use-of-force incidents (Ariel, Farrar, & Sutherland, 2015). Second, initiatives that involve collaboration between law enforcement and the faith community have provided restorative and procedural justice to persons with outstanding warrants for nonviolent felony and misdemeanor offenses. One such initiative, the Fugitive Safe Surrender program, has been implemented in faith-based locations in cities around the country since 2005 (Flannery, 2013). Originally developed in Cleveland, the FSS program has seen over 50,000 individuals with open warrants voluntarily surrender at places of worship in order to resolve their open warrants (although across the country nearly 1 in 5 persons to surrender do not have an open warrant that can be identified; Flannery & Kretschmar, 2012).

The FSS program has brought to light a number of important issues. First, the number of persons with open warrants in this country (or those who think they have an open warrant) probably runs into the millions (Bierie, 2014). Persons who voluntarily surrender at an FSS site most typically report that they are "tired of running" or that they want to take care of their warrant status because of family responsibilities or because they cannot obtain a valid driver's license or legitimate employment or education with an open warrant.

On average, persons had more than four open warrants that were over two years old. The most frequently endorsed reason persons reported that they had not previously addressed their warrant status was because they did not have money to pay a fine or post bond. This theme illustrates the fiscal pressure that the justice system places on persons who are arrested for misdemeanor violations or cited for traffic offenses, not just persons who are charged with violent felonies, which has significant implications for policy and practice related to violence prevention.

For example, programs like FSS illustrate how law enforcement (local and federal) and community partners can work together to prevent violence and provide opportunities for persons involved in the justice system to take care of their past transgressions and to obtain information about needed other support services. Second, it illustrates how frustrating and complicated the justice system can be to navigate, which is not only fiscally burdensome but pragmatically complex as well. Some persons just do not show up in court because they do not know where to go. Thousands of persons appeared at FSS sites because they were told they did not have to pay money to see a judge to hear their case, and because the entire justice system was present in one location. Programs like FSS have thus led to recent efforts at bail reform in the criminal justice system. The hours of waiting were worth it compared to the many days and weeks it might take for a person to navigate through an issue in the normal course of business.

Yet another theme emerged across the 35 or so cities where FSS formally has been implemented (though many other cities in the USA and Canada have held similar programs under a different name since 2005). It is the trust and communication factor in police-community relationships. Over the past several years we have begun asking participants questions about whether coming to FSS has changed their perceptions of law enforcement, particularly regarding trust, and 70% of persons report an improvement in their perceptions and trust of law enforcement. We have also asked them about the likelihood of talking to police when asked about a crime or if they had knowledge of a crime being committed. Just over half (51%) of persons surveyed reported that they would not talk to police knowing they had an open warrant, nor would they report a crime perpetrated against them by someone else knowing that they had an open warrant for another offense. Having their warrant status resolved especially by being able to voluntarily surrender at a neutral place of worship (i.e., the historical sanctity of the church) is a significant factor in giving persons a second chance (Flannery, 2013).

Another cornerstone of successful community-based violence prevention initiatives is a commitment to data-driven strategies. This is not just do collect data for the sake of collecting information on impacts and outcomes, but it is a commitment to gathering the right kinds of information on a regular basis to inform the community, practitioners, and policy-makers about the reality of the problem. Experiencing a single loss of life is unacceptable, but it is also important to gather information over time so a community knows whether trends in homicides are an increasing problem, consistent with previous trends, or actually an improvement compared to past years. Reviewing specific incidents of violent death that result from intentional injury can provide a great deal of information about the factors that may be driving changes in the occurrence of homicides. It may be that an increase in incidents is occurring in a particular neighborhood or around a particular group of dilapidated properties. An increase in homicides may be related to recent gang-involved shootings or may be retaliatory violence. Understanding trends, where resources (community and police) should be focused, and determining what is effective depends on the timely ongoing access to, analysis of, and dissemination of relevant information about violence perpetration, victimization, and related issues (e.g., firearm violence, intentional injury victimization, domestic violence).

If applied research is going to inform about effective violence prevention, we as researchers need to make a commitment to become embedded with our community partners. This is the only way to establish trusting relationships so that systems (e.g., law enforcement, hospitals, and schools) are willing to develop protocols in which sensitive, protected information about violence can be shared in a responsible manner. One such example locally is our participation with our county prosecutor's office on a U.S. Department of Justice-funded initiative to examine information gathered from the backlogged sexual assault kits. As embedded members of the team of investigators, police officers, prosecutors, and victim advocates, we are provided access to all information available on old sexual assaults where the kit is being retested for DNA evidence and investigators are re-opening cases that were not fully investigated in the past. We have access to past and current police reports, investigative reports, prosecutor data, DNA analyses, and victim interviews. As reflected in this volume (Lovell, Flannery, & Luminais, 2018) we have been working with our local prosecutor to identify patters and differences between serial and non-serial offenders, characteristics of stranger vs. non-stranger assaults, and to identify the factors associated with various case dispositions (e.g., successful prosecutions vs. case dismissed). The Sexual Assault Kit Initiative (SAKI) has provided valuable information from old cases about how the system and investigations of sexual assaults and the treatment of victims can be improved, not just from a law enforcement or criminal justice perspective, but how to best bring justice to victims of sexual violence.

The current volume brings some focus to emerging themes in the field of violence prevention. First is the dramatic increase in research on the brain, reflected in the substantial increase in this volume in the number of chapters devoted to related issues, including brain neurochemistry, in our understanding of the importance of the prefrontal cortex to self-regulation and impulse control related to the perpetration of aggression and violence, and how the brain is affected by violence victimization and trauma.

Increased use of social media has a significant impact on individual exposure to violence. Access to global information on a constant basis increases our immediate exposure to incidents of violence. Exposure is more immediate, intense, and constant than ever before. This can affect individual mental health (increased rates of anxiety or depression, feelings of insecurity) or overall perceptions that rare events (e.g., school shootings) are more common and prevalent. Constant exposure to daily and rare acts of violence can lead to a collective sense of despair, feelings that violence is all random and can happen anywhere (it can, but random violence is still the exception rather than the rule), and a sense that there is little that we can do to prevent, mitigate, or reduce violence in our homes, in our schools, in our neighborhoods, or in other parts of the world.

An increased focus on social networks as a way to understand violence via interpersonal relationships that contribute to cycles of victimization or perpetration is also an emerging area of research than can provide insight into a variety of violence-specific phenomena such as homicides, sexual assaults, firearm violence, or gang-related violence. Coupled with increasingly sophisticated strategies such as geo-mapping with social network analyses we can begin to understand better the overlap between interpersonal relationships and networks and patterns of crime or the location of dilapidated housing or drug activity.

Research on our understanding of aggression and violence has moved beyond discussions of whether violence is learned behavior, descriptive studies of trends in perpetration and victimization, and discourse about how to define behaviors on the continuum of aggressive and violent behaviour, to more sophisticated studies of brain neurochemistry, to attempts to examine the underlying processes and mechanisms (genetic, environmental, personality) related to aggressive and violent behavior, to longitudinal studies of individual risk and protective factors and studies of treatment modalities and intervention strategies that are being implemented to reduce or prevent violence. These are important advances that, to be successful, will necessarily need to integrate multi-disciplinary perspectives and strategies. Violence is not just an individual person's issue, and it is not just an issue of understanding the psychology of violence. Rather, violence is also a family issue, it is a community issue, it is a systemic issue, it can be a religious or political issue and it is definitely a global issue. If we are truly going to effectively prevent or reduce its prevalence and impact, as researchers, practitioners, or policymakers, we must come out of our offices and away from our intellectual and hypothetical conversations and jump into the real world, into our homes, neighborhoods and schools, and police cars and treatment agencies and prosecutor's offices and work with our partners who deal with violence every day in every way. Only then will we be able to say we tried our best to make sense of and make a different with, such a complicated social problem.

Matt DeLisi

Psychology and particularly psychiatry have been leading disciplines in demonstrating the ways that constructs from multiple disciplinary areas interconnect to produce all human behavior, including aberrant, externalizing, aggressive, violent, and criminal forms. While this handbook is formally a psychology volume, it is clear that the social sciences are now interdisciplinary and multidisciplinary in their perspective. Increasing numbers of psychologists employ neuroimaging and genetic data in their research designs and pair blood oxygenation level-dependent imaging in fMRI studies with specific tasks or measured genetic polymorphisms with environmental conditions to model how nature and nurture interact. Admittedly, the biosocial revolution has not fully been embraced by psychology (and certainly not in criminology for that matter), but even agnostic scholars have become somewhat conversant in understanding brain regions involved in emotional regulation (e.g., amygdala, insula, among others), learning and reward (e.g., caudate, ventral striatum, orbitofrontal cortex, among others), executive functioning (e.g., dorsolateral prefrontal cortex, anterior cingulate cortex, among others), and how impairments in the structure and function of these brain regions give rise to a host of problems, including impaired empathy, deficits in response to punishment, and broad deficits in self-regulation. Psychopathy, likely the most pernicious psychological condition in terms of its associations with aggression and violence, has a profound neurological basis (Glenn & Raine, 2014). Today, more than ever before, ADHD, traumatic brain injury, prenatal exposure to drugs and other teratogens, and the Phineas Gage case study are fully understood for their biological, psychological, and sociological implications.

Even agnostic scholars recognize that genes involved in neurotransmission, particularly less efficient variants of those genes (e.g., DAT1, DRD2, DRD4, SLC6A4, MAOA, COMT, and others), matter for understanding variance in mood, personality, and behavior. And especially when less-efficient variants of those genes are coupled with adverse environmental contexts, the result is disproportionately associated with maladaptive behaviors, aggression, crime, and violence. Molecular genetic association studies also shed light on which individuals will respond to interventions designed to reduce aggression and antisocial behavior. For example, in the Fast Track intervention, which aims to prevent externalizing behaviors among high-risk kindergarteners, the rs10482672 single-nucleotide polymorphism of the NR3C1 gene interacted with the intervention among White children. White children with this polymorphism that were in the control group evinced increased risk for conduct problems, whereas White children with this polymorphism in the intervention group displayed reduced risk for conduct problems (Albert et al., 2015). Among African-American children, intervention effects were not moderated by this gene. Substantively similar gene x intervention effects have been found in other interventions and using other genes (see Chhangur et al., 2016; Musci et al., 2014; Schlomer et al., 2015). Without question, many of the contributors to this volume will lead the way in articulating how genetic, neurological, and other types of data can inform programs designed to reduce aggression and its downstream social problems.

Beyond research and interventions, DNA has another important application. Hundreds of thousands of sexual assault or rape kits sit dormant in evidence storage facilities in the United States. The lack of attention to and processing of these sexual assault kits is an obvious affront to sexual assault victims, to due process, and to crime control. In this volume, Lovell et al. (2018) analyzed dormant or unsubmitted sexual assault kits and found that more than half were connected to serial sexual offenders whose criminal histories contained twice as many felony offenses compared to non-serial sexual offenders in the data. Among the serial sexual offenders, nearly 5% had previously been arrested for murder, more than 16% had previously been arrested for rape, and nearly one in four had previously been arrested for felony assault. After the case associated with their unsubmitted sexual assault kit, nearly 58% of serial sexual offenders were arrested for additional sexual assault and more than 86%

had at least one subsequent criminal offense. The data are comparably dire for non-serial sexual offenders. After the case that was associated with the unsubmitted sexual assault kits among non-serial sexual offenders, nearly 4% were arrested for murder, nearly 46% were arrested for felony assault, and more than 78% had at least one criminal offense. The effects of a single sexual victimization are catastrophic. These data provide a frightening glimpse into the repeat victimizations that many sexual offenders inflict.

In the United States, there is considerable variation in statutes that require the collection of DNA from criminal suspects. Some states require the collection of DNA for all felony arrestees, some states require it for a subset of serious felony crimes, some states require a warrant, and still other states have additional criteria for collection of biological data. In the aforementioned study, all discoveries stemmed from biological material incidental to the sexual assault. How many more crimes could be cleared, and how many more recidivistic and violent offenders could be stopped with greater attention to the power of DNA? The mere seconds it takes to perform a buccal swab can clear more cases than dozens of the most seasoned detectives. That attests to the powerful potential of a biosocial understanding of and control of aggression and violence.

References

Albert, D., Belsky, D. W., Crowley, D. M., Latendresse, S. J., Aliev, F., Riley, B., ... & Dodge, K. A. (2015). Can genetics predict response to complex behavioral interventions? Evidence from a genetic analysis of the Fast Track Randomized Control Trial. *Journal of Policy Analysis and Management*, 34(3), 497–518.

Ariel, B., Farrar, W. A., & Sutherland, A. J. (2015). The effect of police body-worn cameras on use of force and citizen's complaints against police: A randomized controlled trial. *Journal of Quantitative Criminology*, 31, 509–535.

Baglivio, M. (2018). On cumulative traumatic exposure and violence/aggression: The implications of adverse childhood experiences (ACE). In A. T. Vazsonyi, D. J. Flannery, & M DeLisi (Eds), *The Cambridge handbook of violent behavior and aggression, second edition*. New York: Cambridge University Press.

Bartholomew, J., Singer, M., Gonzalez, A., & Walker, M. (2013). Police assisted referrals: Empowering law enforcement to be first social responders. *Law Enforcement Executive Forum*, 13, 38–49.

Bierie, D. M., (2014). Fugitives in the United States. *Journal of Criminal Justice*, 42, 327–337.

Birmingham, R. S., Bub, K. L, & Vaughn, B. E. (2017). Parenting in infancy and self-regulation in preschool: an investigation of the role of attachment history. *Attachment and Human Development*, 19(2), 107–129.

Casey, B. J., Jones, R. M., & Hare, T. A. (2008). The adolescent brain. *Annals of the New York Academy of Sciences*, 1124, 111–126.

Casey, B., Somerville, L., Gotlib, I., Ayduk, O., Franklin, N., Askren, M., ... Shoda, Y. (2011). Behavioral and neural correlates of delay of gratification 40 years later. *Proceedings of the National Academy of Sciences of the United States of America*, 108(36), 14998–15003.

Casey, B. & Caudle, K. (2013). The Teenage Brain: Self Control. *Current Directions in Psychological Science*, 22(2), 82–87.

Chhangur, R. R., Weeland, J., Overbeek, G., Matthys, W., Castro, B., Giessen, D., & Belsky, J. (2016, in press). Genetic moderation of intervention efficacy: Dopaminergic genes, The Incredible Years, and externalizing behavior in children. *Child Development*.

Cutuli, J. J., Pereira, J., Vrabic, S. C., & Herbers, J. E. (2018). Developmental processes of resilience and risk for aggression and conduct problems. In A. T. Vazsonyi, D. J. Flannery, & M. DeLisi (Eds), *The Cambridge handbook of violent behavior and aggression, second edition*. New York: Cambridge University Press.

Dahlberg, L., Burchart, A., & Mikton, C. (2018). Violence prevention in a global context: Progress and priorities for moving forward. In A. T. Vazsonyi, D. J. Flannery, & M. DeLisi (Eds), *The Cambridge handbook of violent behavior and aggression, second edition*. New York: Cambridge University Press.

Flannery, D. J. (2013). *Wanted on Warrants: The Fugitive Safe Surrender Program*. Kent, OH: Kent State University Press.

Flannery, D. J. & Kretschmar, J. M. (2012). Fugitive Safe Surrender: Program description, initial findings, and policy implications. *Criminology & Public Policy*, 11, 437–459.

Flannery, D. J., Modzeleski, W., & Kretschmar, J. M. (2013). Violence and school shootings. *Current Psychiatry Reports*, 15, 331–338.

Flannery, D. J., Todres, J., Bradshaw, C. P., et al. (2016). Bullying prevention: A summary of the report of the National Academies of Sciences, Engineering, and Medicine: Committee on the Biological and Psychological Effects of Peer Victimization: Lessons for Bullying Prevention. *Prevention Science*, 17, 1044–1053.

Flannery, D. J. & Singer, M. (2014). The Begun Center for Violence Prevention, Research and Education at Case Western Reserve University. *Research on Social Work Practice*, 25, 278–285.

Glenn, A. L. & Raine, A. (2014). *Psychopathy: An introduction to biological findings and their implications*. New York: New York University Press.

Gottfredson, M. R. & Hirschi, T. (1990) *A General Theory of Crime*, Stanford, CA: Stanford University Press.

Heckman, J. J. 2006. Skill formation and the economics of investing in disadvantaged children. *Science*, 312, 1900–1902.

Ksinan, A. & Vazsonyi, A. T. (2017). Individual, family, and socio-structural precursors of deviance: Revisiting the Gluecks' Data. Unpublished manuscript.

Lovell, R., Flannery, D. J., & Luminais, M. (2018). Lessons learned: Serial sex offenders identified from backlogged sexual assault kits (SAKs). In A. T. Vazsonyi, D. J. Flannery, & M. DeLisi (Eds), *The Cambridge handbook of violent behavior and aggression, second edition*. New York: Cambridge University Press.

Mischel, W., Ayduk, O., Berman, M. G., Casey, B. J., Gotlib, I. H., Jonides, J., ... & Shoda, Y. (2011). "Willpower" over the life span: decomposing self-regulation. *Social Cognition and Affective Neuroscience*, 6(2), 252–256.

Moffitt, T. E., Arseneault, L., Belsky, D., Dickson, N., Hancox, R. J., Harrington, H., ... & Caspi, A. (2011) "A gradient of childhood self-control predicts health, wealth, and public safety." *Proceedings of the National Academy of Sciences of the United States of America*, 108, 2693–2698.

Moffitt, T. E., Poulton, R., & Caspi, A. (2013) "Lifelong impact of early self-control: Childhood self-discipline predicts adult quality of life," *American Scientist*, 101, 352–359.

Musci, R. J., Bradshaw, C. P., Maher, B., Uhl, G. R., Kellam, S. G., & Ialongo, N. S. (2014). Reducing aggression and impulsivity through school-based prevention programs: A gene by intervention interaction. *Prevention Science*, 15(6), 831–840.

National Academies of Sciences, Engineering, and Medicine. (2016). *Preventing Bullying Through Science, Policy, and Practice*. Washington, DC: The National Academies Press.

Schlomer, G. L., Cleveland, H. H., Vandenbergh, D. J., Feinberg, M. E., Neiderhiser, J. M., Greenberg, M. T., ... & Redmond, C. (2015). Developmental differences in early adolescent aggression: A gene × environment × intervention analysis. *Journal of Youth and Adolescence*, 44(3), 581–597.

Sumner, S., Mercy, J., Dahlberg, L., Hillis, S., Klevens, J., & Houry, D. (2015). Violence in the United States: Status, challenges and opportunities. *JAMA*, 314, 478–488. doi: 10.1001/jama.2015.8371.

Vazsonyi, A. T., Roberts, J., & Huang, L. (2015). Why focusing on nurture made and still makes sense: The biosocial development of self-control. In M. J. DeLisi & M. G. Vaughn (Eds), *Routledge International Handbook of Biosocial Criminology* (pp. 263–280). Routledge, Taylor & Francis Group.

Vazsonyi, A. T. & Ksinan, G. J. (in press). On the development of self-control and deviance from preschool to middle adolescence. *Journal of Criminal Justice.* doi: 10.1016/j.jcrimjus.2017.08.005.

Index

Accountability Project, 400
acquired sociopathy, 141
action theory, 759, 768, 769–770
Add Health, 166, 208
addiction. *See* substance use
addiction to aggression, 271
adrenergic beta-blockers, 649
Adverse Childhood Experiences score. *See also* child maltreatment
   affluence and, 471
   Behavioral Risk Factor Surveillance System, 471
   binary nature, 476–477
   concentrated disadvantage, 471, 478
   development of, 468–469
   gender differences, 470
   health correlations, 469–470, 473
   intervention programs, 479
   juvenile offending, 470–471, 473–474
      recidivism, 474, 475–476, 477
      serious, violent, and chronic offending, 474–475
   moderators
      negative emotionality, 475–476
      social bonds, 475
   neglect, 468, 471, 473, 475, 476, 477, 479
   prevention programs, 478–479
   questionnaire, 468, 478
   sex offenders, 476
   substantiated vs. unsubstantiated maltreatment, 477–478
   suicide, 473
   violence correlations, 473
affective and cognitive lability, 71, 75, 76
age differences
   age/crime curve, 303–305
   violence and, 460–461

aggression
   definition, 32, 260–261, 645–646
   dimensions of, 32–35
   proactive vs. reactive, 32, 225, 278, 280, 324, 534
Aggression Machine (PAM), 34–35
Aggression Questionnaire, 37, 38, 40
agitation, 645, 646–647
agreeableness, 222, 224, 225, 226, 227, 228, 230, 231, 244, 245, 250, 252
AIDS. *See* HIV
Al Qaida, 628
alcoholism. *See* substance use
alienation, 9, 245, 250–251, 255, 520
Alternatives for Families, 375
altruism, 69, 224, 430
   altruistic fear, 581
American Psychiatric Association. *See* Diagnostic and Statistical Manual of Mental Disorders
American Public Health Association, 216
American Time Use Survey, 558
Anderson, C. A., 221, 224, 225, 261, 264, 529, 530, 531, 533, 538, 551
Animal Liberation Front, 629
antagonistic social schema, 66, 67, 68, 70, 71, 72–75, 76
anticonvulsants, 649
antipsychotics, 647–649
antisocial personality disorder, 138
   acquired, 141
   adjusted odds ratio, 242
   comorbidity, 649
   executive function, 149
   genetics, 92, 197, 248
   neuroimaging, 108, 109, 110, 113, 115, 117
   psychopathy and, 138, 246, 248–249
   recidivism, 253

Antisocial Process Screening Device, 246
anxiety disorders, 286–287
Apartheid, 634, 664, 679
aripiprazole, 646, 649
armed forces normalized by War on
    Terrorism, 637
asenapine, 647
assortative mating, 12, 56
Atlanta Olympics attack, 631
attachment theory, 374
attention bottleneck, 743
attention deficit with hyperactivity disorder,
    146, 148
  behavioral interventions, 288–291
  comorbidity, 144
  genetics, 165, 167, 192
  head injury, 161
  impulsiveness, 11
  neuroimaging, 744
  as risk factor, 17
Australia, 697
automatic emotional processing, 743
autonomic arousal, 130, 152
Avon Longitudinal Study of Parents and
    Children, 165

Bates, J. E., 13, 39, 288, 326, 350, 352, 353,
    475, 568, 663
Bayout, Abdelmalek, 269
Behavioral Activity Rating Scale, 645
behavioral genetics, 787
  additive influence, 86
  broad-sense heritability, 86
  direct genetic effects, 167–168
  DNA structure, 189–191
  epigenetics, 99, 140
  epistatic influence, 86
  equal environments assumption, 87
  fourth law, 167
  gene–environment correlation, 163–164, 331
  gene–environment interaction, 332
  gene × environment studies, 164–168
  gene finding, 88–89, 189
    candidate gene studies, 89–91, 191–195
    genome-wide association, 91–98, 195–196
    MAOA gene, 90, 98, 167, 194–195, 197,
      207, 748
  child maltreatment, 164–165, 198
  delinquency, 166
  impulsivity, 267
  nutrition, 167
  social rejection, 266
  narrow-sense heritability, 86
  neuroimaging, 98–99
  variance decomposition, 84–88, 187–189
Behavioral Risk Factor Surveillance
    System, 471
behavioral skills training, 19
behavioral theory of violence, 308
benzodiazepines, 647
Biden, Joe, 632
Big Five personality model. *See* Five-Factor
    Model of personality
biosocial research, 786–788
  bioecological model, 332
  biological protective factors, 128–129
  biosocial mediation, 130–131
  diathesis-stress model, 162–163, 164,
    198, 332
  differential susceptibility, 129–130, 163,
    164, 198
  dual-risk model, 128, 129, 468
  environmental protective factors, 166–167
  prevention and treatment uses, 131,
    168–169, 198–200
    public health approach, 216–217
    substance use, 215–216
  social push model, 128, 198
bipolar disorder, 138, 151, 285–286, 646–647
Boko Haram, 628, 632
borderline personality disorder, 229, 242, 270
Boston Marathon attack, 631, 637
Brady Handgun Violence Prevention Act,
    698, 699
brain. *See* neuroimaging; neuropsychology;
    traumatic brain injury
Bray, Michael, 628
Breivik, Anders, 527, 630
Brendgen, M., 19, 178, 324, 325, 326, 327, 331,
    332, 333, 335, 336
Brief Ratings Inventory of Executive
    Function, 69
Bring Back the Night marches, 584
British Cohort Study, 14, 780

British National Survey of Health and
    Development, 13
brittle individuals, 45
brittle lifestyle, 45, 46
Broad Antisocial Behavior Consortium, 96
Build Respect, Stop Bullying Program, 728
bullying. *See also* school violence
    cyberbullying, 178, 715, 724
    definition, 392, 724
    Facebook, 730
    gender differences, 388, 392
    high- vs. low-status bullies, 175–176
    intervention technologies, 725
        data-driven tailoring, 725–727
        mixed-reality simulator for teachers,
            727–728
        multimedia, interactive, and online
            games, 728–730
        social media campaigns, 730–732
    perpetrator outcomes, 175
    power or status difference, 724
    relational, 175, 180
    school climate, 560–561
    victim outcomes
        cortisol dysregulation, 176–179
        epigenetic, 180–181
        inflammation, 179–180
    witnessing of, 730–732
Bullying Prevention Program, 564
Bushman, B. J., 221, 224, 225, 228, 242, 260,
    261, 263, 264, 268, 348, 529, 530,
    538, 551

California Achievement Test, 11
callous-unemotional traits, 138, 246, 247, 292,
    350, 356, 738, 741
Cambridge Study in Delinquent Development,
    4–5, 6, 7, 8, 10, 11, 12, 14, 15, 16,
    126, 129
Cambridge-Somerville Youth Study, 13
Canada, 663
Capaldi, D. M., 7, 15, 53, 56, 57, 58, 59,
    325, 594
Capone, Al, 585
Cardiff ADHD Genetic Study, 167
Cardiff Violence Prevention Partnership, 612
cariprazine, 649

cascade model, 70–71
Caspi, A., 8, 13, 22, 90, 159, 161, 164, 165,
    167, 181, 189, 192, 195, 197, 213, 222,
    244, 250, 266, 278, 292, 332, 383, 467,
    470, 649, 713, 714, 778, 780
Cassidy, Butch, 585
CBS, 576
Centers for Disease Control and
    Prevention, 601
Central Eight criminogenic needs, 254
Chicago Youth Development Study, 13
Child Development Project, 39
child maltreatment. *See also* Adverse
    Childhood Experiences score
    attachment theory, 374
    coercion theory, 370
    definition, 367–369
    divorce/separation, 472
    ecological model, 373
    gender differences, 472
    Global North, 666–670, 671–673
    Global South, 670–671, 674–676
        resilience factors, 676–677
    impacts of, 367
    intergenerational transmission of,
        369–370, 374
    interventions, 374–376
    neurobiological models, 373–374
    over-learned dysfunctional parenting
        techniques, 372
    parental incarceration, 472
    prevalence, 366–367, 601–602
        Global North, 656–660
        Global South, 660–662
    psychopathology model, 372
    social cognition models, 371
    social learning theory, 370
    sociological risk model, 372–373
    stress and anger models, 371–372
    stress process model, 655–656
        community violence, 671–675
        parental violence, 666–671
        resilience factors, 676–677
        war violence, 675–676
    witnessing domestic violence, 472, 473
Child Protective Services, 467
Childhood Trauma Questionnaire, 660, 670

Christchurch Health and Development Study, 14, 165
Cincinnati Lead Study, 162
Cleckley, Hervey, 246
clozapine, 647–648, 649
CNN, 515
coercion theory, 55, 370
cognitive behavioral therapy, 270, 650, 716
collective conscience, 430
Columbia County Longitudinal Study, 38, 39, 550
Columbia County Study, 13
Columbine shooting, 527, 557
communal solidarity, 584
Communities that Care, 612
Community Oriented Policing Services, 563
community policing, 439, 445–446, 609
Community Readiness Model, 611
comorbidity, 645, 649
compositional hypothesis, 419–420
concentrated disadvantage, 471, 478, 664, 666, 691
conceptual theory, 759, 768, 769–770
conduct disorder, 279, 282, 291–293
   comorbidity, 148–149, 288, 649
   gender, 383–384
   neuroimaging, 110 111
   risk factors, 289
Conflict Tactics Scales, 58, 658, 667
conscientiousness, 222, 223, 224, 225, 226, 227, 230, 231, 244, 245, 252
Consumer Sentiment Index, 664, 670
contagion of violence
   long-term
      emotional desensitization, 537–538
      media violence, 543–550
      moderating factors, 551
      neighborhood violence, 541–543
      observational learning, 536–537
      war/ethnic violence, 539–541
   short-term, 532–535
      emotional arousal, 533–535
      mimicry, 533
      priming, 532–533
   social-cognitive information-processing model, 530–532
control theory, 307–309
Convention on the Rights of the Child, 589
conviction rates, 5–6
Copenhagen Perinatal Project, 9
Crick, N. R., 58, 181, 260, 348, 353, 355, 382, 383, 384, 385, 386, 387, 389, 390, 391, 393
crime
   age/crime curve, 303–305
   career criminals, 161, 246, 304
   Central Eight criminogenic needs, 254
   childhood predictors, 303
      academic failure, 43
      aggression, 40–42
      low prosocial behavior, 43–44
      low self-control, 43
      multi-problem patterns, 44
      norm-breaking behavior, 43
      person-oriented approach, 42–45
   crime watch programs, 581, 584
   family predictors, 305–306
   newsworthiness, 582
   spontaneity of violence, 307
   unpredictability of individual violence, 307
   violent/nonviolent correlation, 7, 307
Criminological Transition Model, 423–425
culture of honor, 263–264, 267, 271
cumulative risk index, 347
Cure Violence program, 609
cystic fibrosis, 191

Dahlberg, L. L., 367, 590, 591, 592, 614, 759, 778, 781, 782
Dark Triad traits, 66, 76–78, 226, 228
   antagonistic social schema, 66, 67, 68, 70, 71, 72–75, 76
   executive function, 66–67, 71, 77
   measurement, 68–69, 70–71
   mutualistic social schema, 69, 70, 71, 75, 76
   Super-K factor, 70, 71–75, 76
data-driven intervention, 784–785
Debbie Smith Act, 400
Declaration on the Elimination of Violence against Women, 589
Demographic Transition Model, 424
depression
   academic failure, 346
   child maltreatment, 372, 375
   child/teacher relationship, 353
   cortisol, 177, 179

emotional regulation skills, 355
exposure to violence, 608
female, 460
internalizing and, 245
irritability, 279
low self-control and, 159
major, 284–285
negative emotionality index, 475
outcome of antisocial behavior, 736
psychopathy, 248
reduced by PATHS, 168
relational peer victimization, 180, 181
serotonin, 181
social media use, 785
victimized children, 367
victims of violence, 605
descriptive model of aggression, 32, 33
Developmental Victimization Survey, 656, 658
deviant peer affiliation
  Causal model, 325–326
  chronic strain, 457
  Conditional model, 326–328
  counteraction by group norms, 334–336
  counteraction by prosocial peers, 334
  dynamic developmental systems model, 55–56
  general strain theory, 458
  genetic factors, 330–333
  improving friendship quality, 336
  intimate partner violence and, 58–59
  mechanisms of
    coercion, 329
    low-entropy interaction, 329
    modeling, 330
    peer pressure, 329–330
    positive reinforcement, 328–329
  moderating factors
    age, 327
    gender, 326–327
    mutual friendship, 328
    parenting, 327
    personal characteristics, 326
    social status, 327–328
  prevention, 333–334
  as risk factor, 16–17
  training resistance to, 336
DFW Boyz, 497

Diagnostic and Statistical Manual of Mental Disorders, 138, 226, 243, 245, 249, 279
  antisocial personality disorder, 114, 149, 246
  child abuse, 368
  comorbidity, 645
  conduct disorder, 114, 292
  disruptive mood dysregulation disorder, 138, 151, 286
  intermittent explosive disorder, 117, 147
  obsessive-compulsive disorders, 287
  oppositional defiant disorder, 291
  Personality and Personality Disorders Workgroup, 251
  prenatal alcohol exposure, 281
  psychopathy, 138, 253
  substance abuse disorder, 282
  trait-based personality disorders, 225–226, 241–242, 243, 251–253, 255
dialectical behavioral therapy, 270
differential susceptibility, 129–130, 163, 164, 198
Dillinger, John, 585
Dishion, T., 303, 305, 325, 326, 328, 329, 336, 351, 353, 356, 608
disruptive mood dysregulation disorder, 151, 286
District of Columbia v. Heller, 702
Dodge, K. A., 13, 39, 224, 251, 262, 263, 288, 326, 348, 349, 352, 353, 373, 382, 383, 389, 529, 530, 531, 568, 591, 608, 663
dopamine
  antisocial personality disorder, 117
  delinquent peer association, 164
  environmental risk factors, 197
  genes, 92, 164, 165, 192–193, 195, 207, 208, 266, 748
  humans vs. primates, 89
  hyperactivity, 167
  MAO-A, 112, 194
  neuroimaging, 111, 118
  psychopathy, 117
  rat aggression, 89
  self-control, 713
  ventral tegmental area, 210
Dunedin Multidisciplinary Health and Development Study, 8, 13, 14, 159, 164, 167, 250, 778, 780
Durkheim, Emile, 423, 430, 584

Dutch Crips, 504
dynamic developmental systems model, 54–55,
     See also intimate partner violence
  deviant peer groups, 55–56
  family-of-origin, 55
  partner choices, 56

Early Childhood Friendship Project, 391
Early Childhood Longitudinal Study, 160, 161–162
Early Risers program, 333
Earth Liberation Front, 629
ecological model of child maltreatment, 373
elder abuse, 603–604
ENIGMA Consortium, 99
Environmental Risk Longitudinal Twin Study, 165
Environmental Risk Study, 167
epilepsy, 141, 280–281
Eurogang research network, 503
European Barometer, 431
executive function, 36, 107, 112, 141, 161, 209, 210
  antisocial personality disorder, 149
  Brief Ratings Inventory of Executive Function, 69
  child maltreatment, 367
  Dark Triad traits, 66–67, 71, 77
  neuropsychology, 143–145
  parenting effect on, 352
  psychopathy, 145
  self-control, 712
  sex offenders, 147
  substance use, 150
  therapy, 168
  training of, 354
Externalizing Spectrum Inventory, 245

Family Check Up, 356–357
Farrington, D. P., 3, 4, 5, 6, 7, 8, 11, 12, 13, 14, 15, 16, 17, 18, 19, 22, 126, 128, 129, 130, 175, 212, 303, 312, 313, 327, 331, 382, 388, 391, 472, 475, 479, 605, 607, 715, 716, 728, 732, 779, 781
Fast Track, 356
FAST Track, 567
fear and anxiety, 578, See also terrorism

fear conditioning, 115, 125, 126, 127, 129
Federal Bureau of Investigation
  gang violence, 492
  Supplementary Homicide Report, 689
  surveillance of terrorists, 637
  Uniform Crime Report, 187, 404, 440, 491, 688, 689
Fetal Alcohol Syndrome. See prenatal toxin exposure
Finkelhor, D., 366, 367, 373, 469, 477, 656, 658, 659, 660, 661, 662, 667, 671, 679, 756
firearms violence in USA
  defensive use, 693–694
  demographics, 689–690
  economic burden, 687
  gangs, 495–496, 691
  gun supply to criminals, 694–696
  Iron Pipeline, 696
  poverty and spatial concentration, 691
  prevalence, 688–689
  prior offenders, 690
  reduction of
    controlling gun use, 699–701
    reducing gun availability, 696–697
    restricting gun access, 697–699
  right-to-carry laws, 694
  rural, 690
  urban, 691
  weapon choice and lethality, 692–693
Five-Factor Model of personality, 221–222, 244
  aggression, 222–224, 229–230
  proactive vs. reactive, 224–225
  relational, 225
Fox News, 515
Fragile Families and Child Well-Being Study, 659, 664
France, 626–627, 638–639
Free2B, 729–730
frustration-aggression theory, 32
Fugitive Safe Surrender program, 783–784
functional magnetic resonance imaging, 106

GABA, 150, 192, 194
Gage, Phineas, 161
Gallup Organization, 579

Gambia, 661, 662, 665, 675
gender
  Adverse Childhood Experiences score, 470
  bullying, 388, 392, 602
  child maltreatment, 472
  conduct disorder
    differential rates, 382–383, 384–385
    protective factors for girls, 383–384
  deviant peer affiliation, 326–327
  fear of crime, 580–581, 584
  female educational careers, 44–45
  fighting, 602
  firearms violence, 689, 690
  general strain theory, 459–461
  homicide rates, 597
  intimate partner violence, 53–54, 57, 58, 385
  level of aggression, 37
  MAS index, 430
  masculine vs. feminine society, 430
  physical vs. relational aggression, 37–38, 326, 348, 383, 384, 385, 386, 388
  prevention and intervention programs, 391–392
  rating of aggression, 37, 39
  research
    convenience samples vs. at-risk-populations, 390
    cross-cultural study, 389–390
    longitudinal studies, 390
  resilience, 391
  social information-processing, 383–384, 389
  substance use, 282
  suicide rates, 600
  violence, 388–389
general aggression model, 261
general strain theory
  anticipated strains, 454
  community differences, 461
  deviant peer affiliation, 457, 458
  gender differences, 459–461
  incentive for violent coping, 454
  injustice, 454, 455
  life-course-persistent violence, 462–463
  low social control, 454, 455–457, 458
  predisposition for violence, 456
  race differences, 462
  severity of strain, 454, 455

  situational costs of violence, 458
  socioeconomic status, 461
  susceptibility to violent coping, 457–459
  types of strain, 453–455
    goal failure, 453
    loss, 453
    negative treatment, 453
  vicarious strains, 453
general theory of crime, 316–318
genetics. *See* behavioral genetics
Global Partnership to End Violence Against Children, 613–614
Global Plan of Action (WHO), 613
Global School-based Student Health Survey, 602
Global Status Report on Violence Prevention, 606, 614
Global Terrorism Database, 632
Good Behavior Game, 568
Gottfredson, M. R., 40, 43, 44, 160, 301, 302, 303, 304, 305, 306, 307, 308, 309, 310, 311, 312, 313, 314, 316, 317, 325, 419, 711, 712, 715, 716, 779, 780
Guerra, N. G., 531, 536, 541, 542, 543, 592
guilt emotions, 268

haloperidol, 646
Hamas, 632
Harris, Eric, 527
Health Behavior in School-Aged Children Surveys, 602
heart rate, 126–127
High School and Beyond Study, 559
HIV, 521, 605, 607, 612, 661, 670, 671, 675, 677, 678
Hofer, Norbert, 638
Hollande, François, 626, 627
Hollingshead scale, 672
Holmes, James, 527
homicide rates
  compositional hypothesis, 419–420
  contextual hypothesis, 420
  Criminological Transition Model, 423–425
  cultural differences, 429–431
  data sources, 431–432
  Demographic Transition Model, 424
  economic inequality, 420–422, 426

homicide rates (*cont.*)
    global prevalence, 596–599
    Institutional Anomie Theory, 426–427, 429
    political legitimacy, 428–429
    poverty, 421
        social protection, 422–423
    study methodology, 427–428
    supranational trends, 422
    young population size, 419–420
hormones, 266
hostile attribution bias, 262–263
hostility, 646
Huesmann, L. R., 13, 38, 260, 263, 370, 388, 528, 529, 530, 531, 533, 535, 536, 539, 540, 541, 542, 543, 545, 546, 547, 548, 549, 550, 551, 778
Huntington's disease, 191, 216
Hussein, Saddam, 637

I Am A Witness campaign, 730–732
I³ theory, 261–262
Imminent Risk Rating Scale, 69
IMPACT25 plan, 782
impulse control, 267–268
Incredible Years Teacher Classroom Management, 355
Indiana Adult Prisoner Study, 548–550
individualism vs. collectivism, 430
indulgence versus restraint, 430
Innocence Project, 440
INSPIRE: Seven Strategies for Ending Violence Against Children, 614
Institutional Anomie Theory, 426–427, 429
intergenerational transmission of antisocial behavior, 12, 369–370, 374
intermittent explosive disorder, 138, 147–148, 266
    neuroimaging, 109, 117
International Classification of Diseases, 138, 279, 282, 291, 292, 368
International Crime Victims Survey, 432
International Labour Organization, 431
International Social Survey Programme, 422, 426, 432
intimate partner violence. *See also* dynamic developmental systems model
    bi-directional, 53–54, 58
    firearms, 698

prevalence, 53, 602–603
    by gender, 385
risk factors, 56–57
    childhood intervention programs, 59, 60
    depression, 57
    deviant peer groups, 58–59
    family-of-origin, 58
    gender differences, 58
    relationship satisfaction, 59
    substance use, 59
young couple relationships, 54
intracultural violence, 636–639
Irish Republican Army, 629
Islamic State, 628, 632, 633
Ixtapaluca, 67

James, Jesse, 585
Jim Crow laws, 634
judicial sentencing, 269
juvenile offenders
    anxiety disorders, 286–287
    attention deficit with hyperactivity disorder, 288–291
    bipolar disorder, 285–286
    categorical psychiatric perspective, 278–279, 293
    conduct disorder, 279, 282, 288, 289, 291–293, 326, 327, 335, 345, 346, 350, 351, 353, 354, 366, 421, 422
    depression, 284–285
    disruptive mood dysregulation disorder, 286
    epilepsy, 280–281
    obsessive-compulsive disorder, 287
    oppositional defiant disorder, 291
    post-traumatic stress disorder, 287–288
    prenatal toxin exposure, 281
    schizophrenia, 283–284
    substance use, 282–283
    traumatic brain injury, 279–280
Juvenile Victimization Questionnaire, 658
Jyväskylä Longitudinal Study of Personality and Social Development (JYLS), 31, 34, 35, 36, 38, 39, 40, 43, 44, 45, 46

Kaczynski, Theodore, 628
Kansas City Gun Project, 700, 701
Karolinska Scales of Personality, 37, 38
Kenya, 674

Kindergarten Study (Pitkänen), 31, 34, 35
KiVa Anti-Bullying Program, 728–729
Klaas, Polly, 581
Klebold, Dillon, 527
Krueger, R. F., 165, 222, 226, 227, 241, 243, 244, 245, 247, 249, 250, 251, 252, 352

labeling and police bias, 216
lexical hypothesis, 221
Liberia, 676
life course of violence/aggression
   adolescence-limited, 6, 303–304
   childhood aggression, 263
      adult aggression and, 263
      adult crime and, 42, 43, 159, 303, 304–305
   continuity, 6–7, 35–40, 211–213
      homotypic and heterotypic, 40
   life-course-persistent, 6, 161, 462–463, 467–468
   neuropsychology, 139
   nonviolent offending correlation, 7, 306–307
   person-oriented approach, 42–45
   socioemotional development, 45–47
   substance use, 215, 282–283
   versatility vs. specialization, 7
life history theory, 65–66
   Dark Triad traits, 66, 76–78
      executive function, 66–67, 71, 77
      measurement, 68–69, 70–71
   "fast" vs. "slow" strategies, 65–66
Lilienfeld, S. O., 136, 143, 144, 145, 147, 148, 227, 246, 247, 265, 743
Linking the Interests of Families and Teachers Study, 53, 57, 58, 59, 60
LISREL model, 40
Loeber, R., 3, 4, 5, 6, 8, 11, 12, 13, 14, 17, 18, 19, 161, 175, 222, 263, 283, 303, 305, 349, 385, 391, 392, 475, 741, 744
lorazepam, 646, 647
loxapine, 646
LSI-R, 716
lurasidone, 649
Lynam, D. R., 11, 161, 167, 222, 224, 225, 227, 228, 229, 230, 244, 382

Machiavellianism, 228–229, 248
Maelbeek bombing, 633
Malawi, 677

Manson, Charles, 527
Maryland Safe and Supportive Schools (MDS3) Survey System, 726
MAS index, 430
masculinity versus femininity, 430
Mask of Sanity, 246
McVeigh, Timothy, 631
media violence, influence of, 264, *See also* USA and violence
midazolam, 647
Milwaukee longitudinal study of hyperactive and normal-activity children, 167
Minnesota Twin Family Study, 165
mistrust. *See* alienation
Mobley, Stephen, 269
Moffitt, T. E., 6, 8, 11, 13, 22, 99, 139, 142, 146, 159, 161, 164, 167, 209, 210, 212, 214, 222, 250, 278, 292, 301, 302, 303, 309, 313, 317, 318, 324, 330, 332, 383, 385, 460, 462, 467, 468, 474, 589, 604, 713, 714, 778, 780, 781
Montreal Longitudinal-Experimental Study, 19, 168, 333
Multidimensional Personality Questionnaire, 244, 245, 250
multidisciplinary collaboration, 231
multisystemic therapy, 21, 231, 288, 293, 609, 716
mutualistic social schema, 69, 70, 71, 75, 76

naltrexone, 271
narcissism, 227–228, 248, 265
National Crime Victimization Survey, 187, 557, 689, 693
National Instant Criminal Background Check System, 698
National Institute of Child Health and Human Development, 383, 386, 777
National Institute of Mental Health
   Epidemiologic Catchment Area survey, 372
   Research Domain Criteria, 138, 254
National Longitudinal Study of Adolescent to Adult Health, 166, 167
National Opinion Research Center, 579
National Registry of Exonerations, 440
National Research Council Committee to Improve Research Information and Data on Firearms, 694, 697

National Security Agency, 637
National Self-Defense Survey, 693
National Study of Private Ownership of Firearms, 693
National Youth Forum Initiative, 782
National Youth Gang Center, 493–494
negative emotionality
    adolescent executive function, 209
    Adverse Childhood Experiences score, 475–476
    amygdala reactivity, 738
    antisocial personality disorder, 117
    chronic strain, 456
    conducive to violence, 458
    exacerbates strain, 463
    frequent strain, 462
    gender differences, 460
    incapacity for legal coping with strain, 457
    infantile, 351, 462
    Multidimensional Personality Questionnaire, 244
    neuroticism, 230
    personality dimensions, 9
NEO Personality Inventory, 221, 226, 244
neuroimaging
    amygdala, 736–739, 741, 743
    behavioral genetics, 98–99
    brain networks, 746–747
    caudate and ventral striatum, 740, 742
    childhood interventions, 118
    cingulate cortex, 112–115, 739–740, 742, 744
    dorsolateral prefrontal cortex, 743–744
    frontal lobe, 107–112
    functional connectivity, 745
    insula, 740
    legal system, 118
    limbic system, 115–118
    medication, 118
    multimodal studies, 747–748
    murderers, 142
    orbitofrontal cortex, 739, 743–744
    prediction of anti-social behavior, 747
    prefrontal regions, 741
    white-matter tract connectivity, 745–746
neuropsychology, 266
    brain development risk factors, 139–140
    brain lesions, 140–141, 161, 162
    clinical syndromes, 138–139, 143–145

    antisocial personality disorder, 149
    conduct disorder, 148–149
    intermittent explosive disorder, 147–148, 266
    mood disorders, 151
    psychopathy, 145–146
    schizophrenia, 150–151
    substance use, 149–150, 209–211
    criminality and delinquency, 146–147
    infant deficits, 161–162
    longitudinal research, 139
    self-control, 712–713
    study of violent individuals, 141–143
    test methods, 136–137
neuroticism, 222, 224, 225, 230, 231, 244, 246, 250, 271
Newtown shooting, 557, 687
Nichols, Terry, 631
norepinephrine, 89, 266, 713
North Atlantic Treaty Organization, 630
Nurse-Family Partnership Program, 20–21, 375
nutrition, 20, 140, 152, 167, 375, 665, 670, 715

observational learning of aggression, 370, 536–537, 552
observational learning of violence, 528
obsessive-compulsive disorder, 287
Office of Juvenile Justice and Delinquency Prevention, 493
Oklahoma bombing, 631
olanzapine, 646, 647, 648, 649
Olweus Bullying Prevention Program, 725
oppositional defiant disorder, 291
Orebro Project, 6, 10
Oregon Social Learning Center, 53
Oregon Youth Study, 7, 14, 15, 53, 54, 56, 57, 59
Orlando shooting, 633, 637, 687
over-learned dysfunctional parenting techniques, 372
Overt Aggression Scale, 646

Paducah shooting, 557
Palestine-Israeli Exposure to Violence Study, 539–541
PAM. *See* Aggression Machine
PANSS Excited Component, 645, 646

paranoia, 242, 251, 284
Parent-Child Interaction Therapy, 374–375
parenting programs, 20–21
PATHS. *See* Promoting Alternative THinking Strategies Curriculum
Patrick, C. J., 227, 243, 245, 246, 247, 248, 249, 250, 254
Patriot Act, 627
Patterson, G. R., 7, 14, 15, 53, 55, 58, 59, 290, 325, 328, 329, 351, 353, 468
peers. *See* deviant peer affiliation
Penn Resiliency Program, 355
perceived hostility, 265
Perfect Storm Theory, 262
perphenazine, 649
Perry Preschool Program, 20
personality. *See also* borderline personality disorder; Dark Triad traits; Five-Factor Model of personality; Machiavellianism; narcissism; psychopathy; Three-Factor Model of personality
  callous-unemotional traits, 138, 246, 247, 292, 350, 356, 738, 741
  categorical "disorder" approach, 226–229, 241–243
  externalizing spectrum model, 244–246, 247–250
  lexical hypothesis, 221
  therapeutic intervention, 230–231
  trait-based structural approach, 225–226, 243–244
    DSM-5 Section III model, 251–253
    prevention and treatment implications, 253–254
    specific violence-promoting processes, 250–251
Pettit, G. S., 39, 288, 326, 348, 349, 352, 353, 568, 663
Philadelphia Collaborative Perinatal Project, 11, 130
pindolol, 649
Piquero, A. R., 4, 6, 7, 16, 18, 126, 162, 212, 306, 316, 391, 455, 456, 459, 461, 468, 474, 475, 479, 559, 605, 711, 712, 713, 714, 715, 779
Pittsburgh Youth Study, 5, 6, 8, 10, 11, 12, 13, 14, 15, 16, 17, 18, 126, 161

police
  community policing, 439, 445–446, 609, 782–784
  labeling and police bias, 666
  school violence, 563
  wrongful conviction, 443–446
positive affect from aggression, 268
Positive Behavioral Interventions and Supports, 725, 726
positive emotionality, 244
positivism, 312
positron emission tomography, 106
post-traumatic stress disorder, 177, 178, 179, 287–288, 676
poverty
  firearms violence in USA, 691
  homicide rates, 421, 422–423
  violence exposure in USA, 666–670
  youth gang violence, 498–499
power distance, 430
pregnancy
  birth complications, 137, 140
  drinking and smoking during, 20, 140
  nursing visits, 20
  parenting training during, 715
  prevention programs, 478
  psychosocial stress during, 349
  teenage, 14, 130, 302, 473, 517, 607
  unwanted, 605
prenatal toxin exposure, 162, 281, 349
preschool education, 19, 20
President's Commission on Law Enforcement and Administration of Justice, 577
Preventing Relational Aggression in Schools Everyday, 391
Preventing Suicide: A Global Imperative, 614
priming effects, 230, 261, 528, 532–533, 552, 634
proactive aggression. *See under* aggression
Project for Human Development in Chicago Neighborhoods, 658, 659, 662, 664, 669, 673
Project PATHE, 563
Project Safe Neighborhoods, 700
Project STATUS, 565

Promoting Alternative THinking Strategies
    (PATHS) Curriculum, 168, 335,
    566–567, 715
propranolol, 649
prosociality, 35, 37, 43–44, 198, 389
  bullying and, 175
  media influence, 264
  peer influence, 21, 163, 333, 334
  promoting, 231, 353, 391, 716, 729
  psychopathy, 138
  recidivism, 475
  social inequalities, 348
provocation, 37, 264–265
  ambiguous, 533
  culture of honor, 271
  excitation transfer, 528, 532, 534, 537
  executive function, 150
  general strain theory, 458
  narcissism, 228, 265
  overreaction to, 35, 224, 714
  prefrontal lesions, 141
  proactive response, 47
  reactive response, 278
  repeated exposure to, 535
pseudopsychopathy, 141
psychopathy, 197, 246–247, 350
  amygdala reactivity, 117, 738, 741, 743
  antisocial personality disorder and, 138,
    248–249
  attention bottleneck, 743
  automatic emotional processing, 743
  caudate and ventral striatum, 740, 742
  cingulate cortex, 113, 114, 739
  comorbidity, 649
  conduct disorder and, 292
  frontal regions, 107–108, 110
  functional neural connectivity, 114, 117, 745
  impaired integration theory, 146
  insula activation, 740
  limbic system, 115, 116
  low reactivity, 534
  Machiavellianism and, 229
  orbitofrontal cortex, 739
  personality traits, 226–227
  proactive and reactive aggression, 265
  Psychopathic Personality Inventory, 247
  Psychopathy Checklist, 246, 247, 249, 253
  response modulation theory, 145
  triarchic model, 247, 248
psychopharmacology. *See also individual drugs*
  agitation, 646–647
  long-term violence, 650
psychophysiology
  heart rate, 126–127
  skin conductance, 127–128
psychosis. *See* bipolar disorder;
    schizophrenia
public health approach, 590, 781–782
  biosocial research, 216–217
  burden of violence
    economic cost, 605
    mental health, 604–605
    physical injury, 604
    reproductive health, 605
    substance use, 604
  definition of violence, 590–591
  global agenda, 612–614
    child maltreatment, 613–614
    health sector, 613
    suicide, 614
    sustainable development, 613
  global prevalence of violence
    bullying, 602
    child maltreatment, 601–602
    elder abuse, 603–604
    fighting, 602
    homicide, 596–599
    intimate partner violence, 602–603
    sexual assault, 602–603
    suicide, 599–600
  prevention and intervention, 605–611
    community strategies, 609–610
    diffusion of, 611–612
    economic empowerment, 610–611
    engaging peers and caregivers, 607–608
    screening and therapy, 608–609
    societal strategies, 610
    strengthening skills and resilience,
      606–607
  social ecological model, 592–595
  typology of violence, 591–592

Quebec Newborn Twin Study, 330, 332
quetiapine, 649

Index

Raine, A., 87, 98, 107, 108, 109, 111, 118, 125, 126, 127, 128, 129, 130, 131, 142, 145, 150, 161, 193, 348, 532, 534, 787
Ramsey, JonBenet, 581
rape. *See* sexual assault kits; sexual offending
reactive aggression. *See under* aggression
Readiness Assessment for the Prevention of Child Maltreatment, 612
recidivism, 269–270
   Adverse Childhood Experiences score, 474, 475–476, 477
   antisocial personality disorder, 253
   attention deficit with hyperactivity disorder, 289
   childhood predictors, 303
   cognitive behavioral therapy, 650
   neuropsychology, 147
   oppositional defiant disorders, 291
   psychopathy, 107, 227, 249
   psychopharmacology, 650
   substance use, 283
Red Lake shooting, 557
relational aggression
   academic self-concept, 386
   adolescent dating violence, 335
   blunted physiological reactivity, 386
   definition, 382
   depression, 180, 181
   direct vs. indirect, 261
   Five-Factor Model, 225
   gender, 37–38, 326, 348, 383, 384, 385, 386, 387, 388, 390
   intervention, 391–392
   pain of, 260
   pathology and, 390
   peer socialization of, 327
   romantic relationships, 385, 390
   socialization of, 387–388
   under-identification of, 387
resilience
   definition, 345–348
   developmental cascades, 346, 353, 354
   developmental tasks, 345–346
   gender, 391
   parenting factors, 351–352, 356–357
   peer factors, 352–353
   promotion of, 354–357
   protective factors, 350
   risk factors, 346–347, 348
      early temperament, 349–350
      genetic, 349
      prenatal, 349
   school factors, 353–354, 355
   self-regulation, 350–351, 354–355
   social information processing, 353
restraint theory. *See* self-control theory
reward
   behavior modification, 568
   exposure to violence, 551
   externalizing spectrum model, 248
   material in masculine society, 430
   monetary ends of aggression, 224
   neurobiology of, 192, 208, 209, 210, 211, 266, 268, 740–742, 743, 744, 745, 749, 787
   psychopharmacology and, 271
   reward-dominant behavior, 736
   rule compliance and, 561, 565
   self-regulation, 267
   social scripts, 536
   substance use, 150
rhesus monkeys, 267
risk factors, 3, 7–8, 348, 595
   antisocial parents, 11–12
   cumulative risk index, 347
   family, 13–14, 15–16, 46, 160, 351
      broken families, 13–14, 15–16
      household size, 15
      physical punishment, 13, 17, 77, 351
      young mothers, 12–13
   gang membership, 495
   impulsiveness, 8–11
   low intelligence, 11
   peer delinquency, 16–17
   prenatal toxin exposure, 162, 281
   relationship status, 16
   risk mechanisms, 15–17
   risk-focused prevention, 18–21
   socioeconomic, 14–15, 46
   unemployment, 16
Risk-Need-Responsivity model, 254
risperidone, 647, 648, 649
Rochester Youth Development Study, 13
rule governance, 65, 71, 75–76
   Rule Governance Scale, 69

Rwanda, 662, 665, 675
  genocide, 636, 665, 670, 675, 676–677

sadism, 271
Safe Dates Program, 564
Safe School Study, 558
Sampson, R. J., 212, 313, 421, 423, 595, 656, 664, 673, 679, 691
Sandy Hook shooting, 569
Santana High shooting, 557
schizophrenia, 138, 150–151, 283–284, 645
  neuroimaging, 113, 115
  pharmacological treatment, 646–650
School Survey on Crime and Safety, 563
school violence. *See also* bullying
  contributory factors, 558–561
    class size, 558
    communal organization, 559
    demographics, 558, 560, 561
    large size, 560
    normative school values, 559
    rules and discipline, 558, 559, 560, 561
    school size, 560
    teacher attitudes, 561
  environmental interventions
    architectural arrangements, 565–566
    classroom management, 565
    communal organization, 560, 565
    normative school values, 564
    police presence, 563
    rules and discipline, 563–564
    security and surveillance, 562–563
  individual interventions
    behavior modification, 567–568
    cognitive behavioral, 566–567
    counseling, 568
    mentoring, 568–569
    recreational resources, 569
  multi-victim shootings, 569–570
  prevalence, 557–558
School-wide Information System, 725
School-wide Positive Behavior Support program, 563–564
Seattle Secondary Disability Study, 281
Seattle Social Development Project, 9, 13, 772
Séguin, J. R., 136, 137, 139, 142, 143, 144, 146, 148, 149

self-control theory, 309–310, 711–712, *See also* self-regulation
  cycle of violence, 713–715
  definition of violence, 307–309
  general theory of crime, 316–318
  genetic factors, 713
  neuropsychology, 712–713
  parenting intervention studies, 315–316
  prevention
    adolescent, 715–716
    adult, 716
    child, 715
  situational context, 717
  socialization, 310–313
  validity studies of, 313–315
  workplace bullying, 717
self-esteem, contingent, 265–266
self-regulation, 40, 159–160, 350–351, 777–781, *See also* self-control theory
  parenting effect on, 352
  socioemotional development and, 45–47, 301–302
September 11 attack, 635, 636
serotonin
  alcohol abuse, 208
  bullying, 180–181
  deficient inhibitory response process, 111–112
  effect of adverse exposures on, 140, 150
  fly aggression, 89
  genes, 92, 164, 192, 193–194, 207, 266, 748
  impulsivity, 267
  intermittent explosive disorder, 114
  MAO-A, 112, 194
  maternal attachment, 166
  monkey aggression, 89, 267
  neuroimaging, 106, 111, 118
  psychopathy, 197
  rat aggression, 89
  self-control, 713
Seville Statement on Violence, 589
Sexual Assault Forensic Evidence Reporting Act, 400
sexual assault kits. *See also* sexual offending
  backlog, 399
    adverse consequences, 399–400
    contributing factors, 401

expense of DNA analysis, 401
jurisdictions not victim-centered, 401–402
kits pre-dating DNA analysis, 401
regional reluctance to submit for testing, 401
scope of, 400
CODIS, 401, 403, 411, 412
criminal linkage, 413
Cuyahoga County study, 402
consensus coding, 405–406
criminal history of offenders, 404–405, 406, 412
data sources, 403–404
demographics, 406
limitations of, 411
sampling, 404
serial offender modus operandi, 410, 411, 412
serial offenders, coding of, 405
serial offenders, prevalence of, 406, 411, 412
serial vs. non-serial modus operandi, 406–409, 412–413
stranger vs. non-stranger, 407–408, 410
definition, 399
sexual offending. *See also* sexual assault kits
Adverse Childhood Experiences score, 476
CODIS, 401, 403, 405, 411, 412
criminal linkage, 413
low conviction rate, 411–412
prevalence, 602–603
serial vs. nonserial offenders, 402–403, 411, 412–413
criminal histories, 406
modus operandi, 406–410
offender demographics, 406
stranger vs. non-stranger, 403, 410
shame emotions, 268–269
single photon emission computerized tomography, 106
skin conductance, 127–128
Snowden, Edward, 637
social cohesion, 430
social ecological intervention, 215
social learning theory, 370
social networks, 786
definition, 513–514

gangs, 516–517, 518–520
measurement, 515–518
obesity, 521–522
structure, 514–515
substance use, 521
violence, 522
social rejection, 265, 266, 268
Social Science Genetic Association Consortium, 93
social-cognitive information-processing model
emotional predispositions, 531–532
normative beliefs, 531
scripts, 531
world schemas, 531
Society for Prevention Research, 763, 764
socioeconomic status. *See also* child maltreatment, stress process model
child exposure to violence
child maltreatment, 666–671
community violence, 671–675
ecological perspectives, 656
resilience to, 676–677
war violence, 675–676
continuity of aggression, 39
general strain theory, 461
measurement
Global North, 662–664
Global South, 664–666
risk factors and, 14–15
South Africa, 655, 660, 661, 664, 665, 670, 671, 674, 677
South African Schools Act, 660
StandUp, 729
Stop Now and Plan Program, 19
strain theory. *See* general strain theory
Strategic Alternatives to Community Safety Initiative, 700
stress process model of children's exposure to violence, 656
substance use, 41, 42, 149–150, 192, 282–283
addiction not single gene disorder, 207
adolescent onset, 213–215, 282
child maltreatment, 372
childhood precursors, 211–213
genetic factors, 206–209
neurobiology, 209–210
drugs/violence nexus, 210–211

substance use (*cont.*)
  prevention programs, 216
  public policy, 217
  rehabilitation, 283
  schizophrenia, 645
  social networks, 521
suicide, 604, 608
  Adverse Childhood Experiences score, 473
  firearms, 610, 692, 693, 697, 782
  global public health agenda, 614
  prevalence, 599–600
  prevention, 612
  suicide bombers, 630, 632, 633
Super-K factor, 70, 71–75, 76
Survey of Inmates in Federal Correctional Facilities, 695
Survey of Inmates in Local Jails, 695
Survey of Inmates in State Correctional Facilities, 695
Sustainable Development Goals, 612, 613
syphilis, 605
Syrian refugee crisis, 635
Systematic Training for Effective Parenting, 375

Taliban, 636
Tamil Tigers, 629
TeachLivE, 727–728
Teen Choices, 729
television violence, 576
terrorism
  cells, 629
  cultural violence, 634
  damage to democracy, 630, 636
    France, 626–627, 638–639
    USA, 636–638
  definition, 628
  direct violence, 632–633
  Islam, 627, 630, 631, 637, 638–639
  "lone wolves," 628–629
  motives, 629
  psychological violence, 635–636
  radicalization process, 629–630
  state-sponsored, 629
  structural violence, 630–631, 633–634
Three-Factor Model of personality, 223
Tracking Adolescents' Individual Lives Survey, 165

Trauma Affect Regulation: Guide for Education and Therapy, 288
Trauma Focused Cognitive Behavior Therapy, 288, 375, 609
traumatic brain injury, 279–280
Tremblay, R. E., 19, 43, 44, 137, 139, 140, 142, 143, 149, 168, 212, 227, 263, 291, 306, 314, 326, 333, 383, 479, 605, 714, 715
Trier Social Stress Test, 178
Triple-P Positive Parenting Program, 20–21, 374
Trump, Donald, 638
Tsarnaev family, 631

Unabomber, 628
uncertainty avoidance, 430
United Nations, 613, 614, 630
US National Incidence Study of Child Abuse and Neglect, 367
US National Longitudinal Study of Adolescent Health, 11
US National Youth Survey, 5, 6, 14
US Study of Early Child Care and Youth Development, 162
USA and violence. *See also* firearms violence in USA
  child exposure to community violence, 671–673
  child maltreatment, 656–660
  depiction/incident disparity, 575, 577
  fear of crime, 577–578, *See also* fear and anxiety
    age differences, 581
    altruistic vs. personal fear, 581
    availability heuristic, 583
    consequences, 583–584
    gender differences, 580–581, 584
    hierarchy of fear, 579
    media distortion, 582–583
    situational fear cues, 579–580
    survey research, 578–579
  mass representation
    books, 576
    cinema, 576
    news media, 575, 582–583
    television, 576
    voyeurism, 577
  measuring poverty, 662–664
  poverty and violence exposure, 666–670

Index

valproate, 649
Vice Lords, 518
violence
   definition, 260
      control theory perspective, 307–309
      direct violence, 632
      legitimist perspective, 631
      public health perspective, 590–591
      social injustice as violence, 631
   prevalence, 5–6, 52
      bullying, 602
      child maltreatment, 366–367, 601–602
      elder abuse, 603–604
      firearms, 688–689
      homicide, 596–599
      intimate partner, 53, 385, 602–603
      school, 557–558
      sexual assault, 603
      suicide, 599–600
      USA, 187, 438
      youth gang homicide, 493–495
Violence Against Children Surveys, 601
Vitaro, F., 19, 164, 165, 168, 178, 324, 325, 326, 327, 329, 331, 332, 333, 335, 336, 383
vulnerability trait, aggression as, 48

War on Terrorism, 637
Wartime Violence Checklist, 662
Widom, C. S., 288, 306, 311, 313, 369, 467, 471, 472, 591
Woodlawn project, 6, 11
World Bank, 613
World Health Assembly, 589, 612, 613
World Health Organization, 431, 589, 596, 602, 612, 614
World Report on Violence and Health, 589–590, 591–592, 596, 605, 614
World Values Survey, 422, 426, 431–432
wraparound youth intervention, 716
wrongful conviction
   costs of, 439
   death sentences, 441
   DNA evidence, 440, 441, 448
   false accusation, 443
   official misconduct, 443
   police failings, 443–446
      killing of innocent persons, 445
      mistaken witness identification, 444
      pressure to solve cases, 443–444
      reform proposals, 444–445
   prevalence, 439–442
   prosecutor failings, 446–449
      Brady violations, 447
      reform proposals, 448–449
      snitch testimony, 448
      tunnel vision, 447–448

youth gang violence. *See also* social networks
   definition, 491–493
   drugs, 496–497
   firearms, 495–496, 691
   homicide
      characteristics, 493
      prevalence, 493–495
   international comparison, 503–505
   medical treatment, 502–503
   poverty and spatial concentration, 498–499
   prison gangs, 501–502, 506
   retaliation and social processes, 499–501
   USA, 491–503
      Chicago, 492, 494, 495, 497, 498, 505
      Los Angeles, 492, 494, 496, 498, 499, 500, 502–503, 505
youth violence intervention research
   evaluation
      effectiveness, 762–763
      efficacy, 761–762
      initial promise, 760–761
   improving interventions
      logic model evaluation, 768–770
      stakeholder input, 770–771
   methodology
      counterfactuals, 757–758
      data analysis, 759–760
      implementation integrity, 758–759
      measurement, 759
      samples, 757
   moderators of effectiveness
      implementation, 765
      participants and settings, 764–765
      research design, 765–768

ziprasidone, 646, 648, 649